MW01697845

AMERICAN REPUBLIC

FIFTH EDITION

bju press

Greenville, South Carolina

American Republic
Fifth Edition

Writers
Kirsten-Leeann Alexander, MEd
Joseph Jarrell, MS, MA

Previous Edition Writers
Rachel Larson, PhD
Dennis Peterson, MS

Biblical Worldview
Brian Collins, PhD
Bryan Smith, PhD

Academic Integrity
Jeff Heath, EdD

Academic Oversight
Rachel Santopietro
Michael Winningham, MA

Editors
Joanna Lynch, MA
Ben Sinnamon, MA, MLIS

Consultants
Gregg Frazer, PhD
Elizabeth Olsen, MEd
L. Michelle Rosier
Mark Sidwell, PhD

Design Consultant
Elly Kalagayan

Cover Design
Michael Asire

Cover Art
Frank Ordaz

Book Design
Emily Heinz
Craig Oesterling
Dan VanLeeuwen

Project Coordinators
Dan Berger
Chris Daniels

Page Layout
Sarah Centers

Permissions
Sharon Belknap
Sylvia Gass
Sarah Gundlach
Elizabeth Walker

Illustration
Jim Brooks
Seb Camagajevac (Beehive Illustration)
Preston Gravely Jr.
Emily Heinz
Katy Labadorf
Cynthia Long
John Roberts
Lynda Slattery
Del Thompson
Dan VanLeeuwen

Digital Content Management
Peggy Hargis

Photograph credits begin on page 691.
Text acknowledgments appear on-page with text selections.
The text for this book is set in Adobe Minion Pro, Aleo by Alessio Laiso, Alfa Slab One by JM Solé, Montserrat by Julieta Ulanovsky, Oswald by Vernon Adams, and Roboto by Christian Robertson.

ISBN 978-1-62856-888-2

15 14 13 12 11 10 9 8 7 6 5 4 3 2

Contents

Unit 1: Settling a Wilderness

Unit 2: Establishing a Country

Unit 3: Spanning a Continent

Unit 4: Facing a Crisis

Unit 5: Expanding the Nation

Unit 6: Taking the Lead

Unit 7: Facing New Challenges

Features of the Book

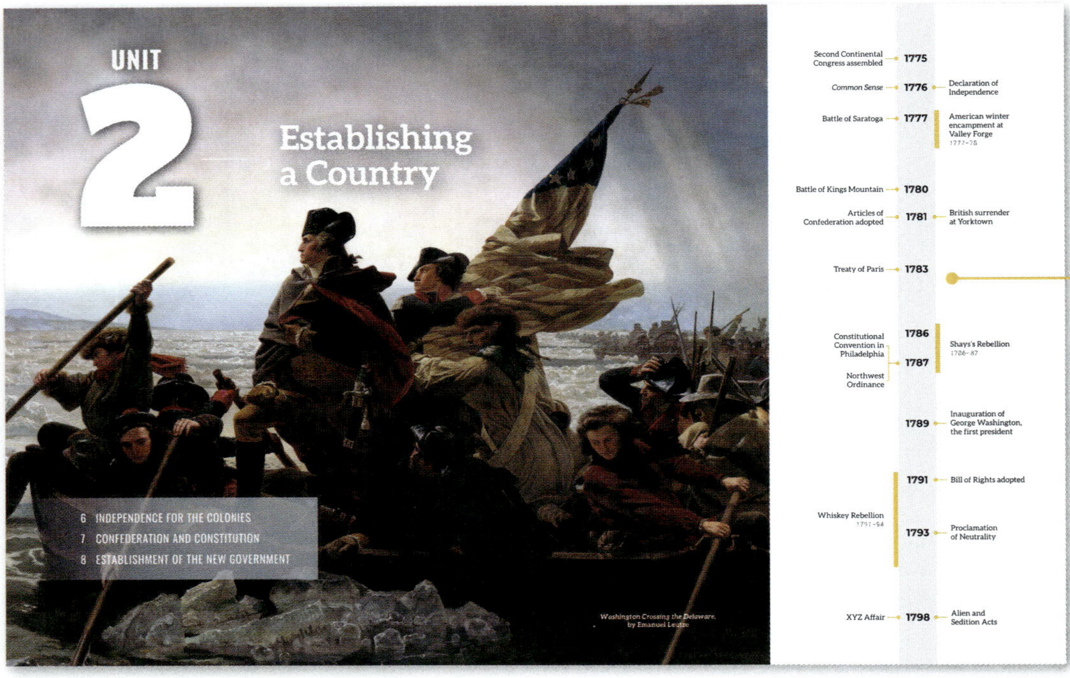

Unit openers offer a timeline of major events covered within the chapters of the unit.

Guiding questions also help prepare students to read the material more carefully.

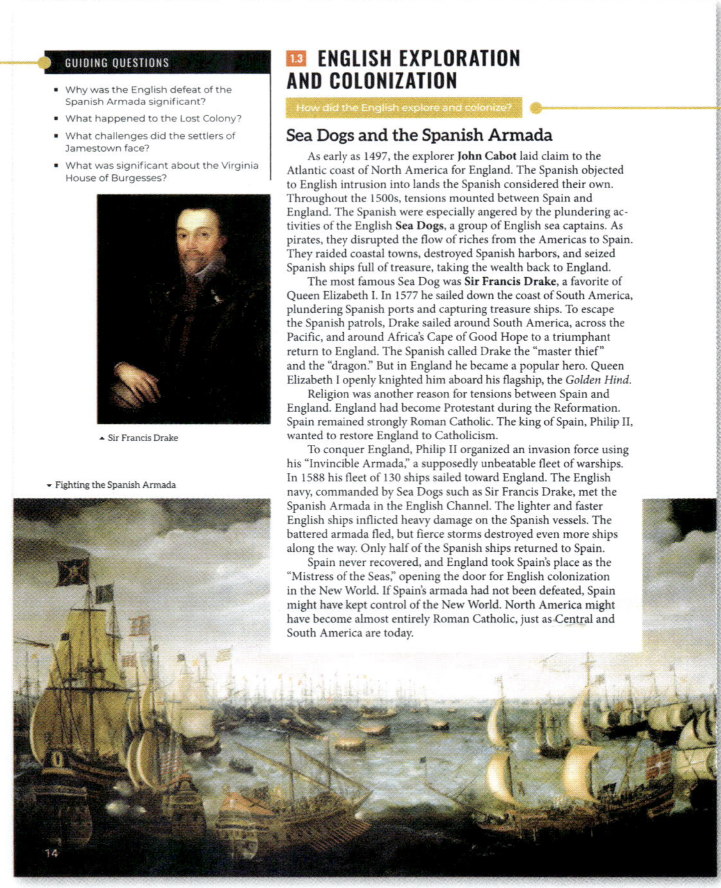

GUIDING QUESTIONS

- Why was the English defeat of the Spanish Armada significant?
- What happened to the Lost Colony?
- What challenges did the settlers of Jamestown face?
- What was significant about the Virginia House of Burgesses?

1.3 ENGLISH EXPLORATION AND COLONIZATION

How did the English explore and colonize?

Sea Dogs and the Spanish Armada

As early as 1497, the explorer **John Cabot** laid claim to the Atlantic coast of North America for England. The Spanish objected to English intrusion into lands the Spanish considered their own. Throughout the 1500s, tensions mounted between Spain and England. The Spanish were especially angered by the plundering activities of the English **Sea Dogs**, a group of English sea captains. As pirates, they disrupted the flow of riches from the Americas to Spain. They raided coastal towns, destroyed Spanish harbors, and seized Spanish ships full of treasure, taking the wealth back to England.

The most famous Sea Dog was **Sir Francis Drake**, a favorite of Queen Elizabeth I. In 1577 he sailed down the coast of South America, plundering Spanish ports and capturing treasure ships. To escape the Spanish patrols, Drake sailed around South America, across the Pacific, and around Africa's Cape of Good Hope to a triumphant return to England. The Spanish called Drake the "master thief" and the "dragon." But in England he became a popular hero. Queen Elizabeth I openly knighted him aboard his flagship, the *Golden Hind*.

Religion was another reason for tensions between Spain and England. England had become Protestant during the Reformation. Spain remained strongly Roman Catholic. The king of Spain, Philip II, wanted to restore England to Catholicism.

To conquer England, Philip II organized an invasion force using his "Invincible Armada," a supposedly unbeatable fleet of warships. In 1588 his fleet of 130 ships sailed toward England. The English navy, commanded by Sea Dogs such as Sir Francis Drake, met the Spanish Armada in the English Channel. The lighter and faster English ships inflicted heavy damage on the Spanish vessels. The battered armada fled, but fierce storms destroyed even more ships along the way. Only half of the Spanish ships returned to Spain.

Spain never recovered, and England took Spain's place as the "Mistress of the Seas," opening the door for English colonization in the New World. If Spain's armada had not been defeated, Spain might have kept control of the New World. North America might have become almost entirely Roman Catholic, just as Central and South America are today.

▲ Sir Francis Drake

▼ Fighting the Spanish Armada

14

An **essential question** is included for each section of each chapter to help students focus on the central idea presented.

Maps, charts, and diagrams help students visualize concepts and geographic locations.

Principles in the Constitution

The delegates included several vital principles in the Constitution. These principles affect the nature and operation of the US government, even today.

Written Law

Under the Constitution, leaders rule by written law. Government leaders cannot change their own powers according to their desires. The Constitution limits those powers, establishing what government may and may not do. Only an amendment can change the written law of the Constitution. Because amendments are somewhat difficult to enact, major changes in constitutional law are rare.

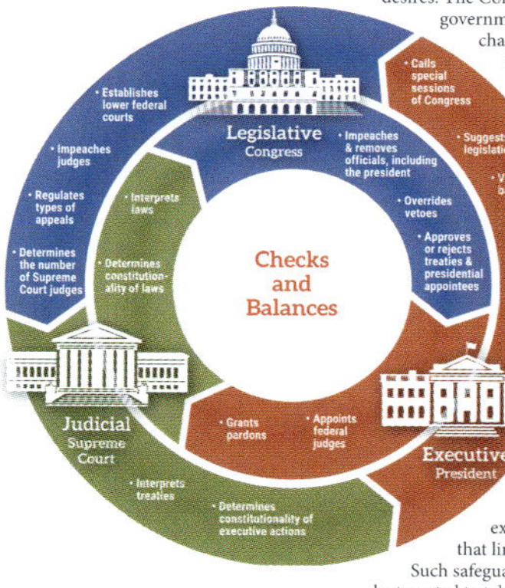

Separation of Powers

The Constitution divides the government's powers among three branches: the legislative, executive, and judicial branches. The delegates relied heavily on the ideas of the French philosopher Montesquieu in developing the idea of the **separation of powers**. This principle ensures that no branch has too much power. Congress, which is the legislative branch, makes the laws. The executive branch, led by the president, enforces the laws. And the courts of the judicial branch interpret the laws as they apply to specific cases.

Checks and Balances

A system of **checks and balances** keeps each of the three branches of government from exercising too much power. Each branch has powers that limit, or check, the powers of the other two branches. Such safeguards are useful because government leaders might be tempted to take additional powers. Checks keep the powers of each branch balanced with those of the other branches.

A Federal System

Under the Articles of Confederation, the states acted almost as independent nations. They reserved, or kept, most powers for themselves; Congress had only limited ones. At the Constitutional Convention, the delegates sought to strengthen the national government's power, but they did not intend to take all powers from the states. To accomplish this, the delegates established a **federal system** that divides the government's powers between the national government and the states.

The Constitution assigns duties and powers to the level of government best equipped to handle them. Neither level has total power. Under the Constitution, the national government has power over issues that are important to the whole nation, such as common defense. Many other powers, such as those relating to health, safety, elections, and punishment for crimes, are shared by the national and state governments.

a **BROADER USE** *of the term* **FEDERAL**

Though the term *federal* refers to dividing the powers of the country's government between the national government and the state governments, it can be used in a broader way. For example, we often call the national government in Washington, DC, the *federal government*. And we describe things that are related to the national government as "federal," such as federal employees, federal regulations, and federal agencies.

142

Terms in bold type draw attention to important facts, ideas, individuals, or definitions.

The death of Garfield made clear what many had been arguing—the civil service (government employee) system needed reform. **Chester A. Arthur**, Garfield's vice president, called upon Congress to make needed changes when he became the nation's leader.

In January 1883 Arthur signed the Pendleton Act. It provided for the elimination of much of the spoils system, where political offices were awarded based on loyalty to a political party or politician. Instead, appointment to many federal government jobs would now be given to those who passed civil service examinations. The **Civil Service Commission** would oversee this new system. Within a few years, about 12 percent of the federal offices were filled using these new procedures, and that number steadily continued to increase.

Cleveland, Harrison, and Cleveland Again

In the 1884 presidential election, Republicans bypassed Arthur and nominated James G. Blaine of Maine. Blaine's candidacy was hurt by allegations that he had been involved in scandals. Democrats nominated New York's former governor **Grover Cleveland**, noted for his honesty and for fighting corruption.

The 1884 election was a spirited, hard-fought event better remembered for its mudslinging than for any issues that were debated. Cleveland won a narrow victory. Had Blaine won the extremely close race in New York—he lost there by only a thousand votes of more than a million cast—he would have won the election. Cleveland's election was the first Democratic presidential victory in twenty-eight years.

The Democrats renominated the popular Cleveland in 1888. The Republicans nominated Indiana's **Benjamin Harrison**. He was the grandson of President William Henry Harrison, a fact the Republicans loudly proclaimed. Cleveland won more popular votes, but Harrison won more electoral votes and hence the presidential election.

The next presidential election, in 1892, was a rematch between Benjamin Harrison and Grover Cleveland. Former president Cleveland made a former president of Harrison by recapturing the White House with a clear victory. Cleveland is the only president to serve two nonconsecutive terms. He had been the twenty-second president, and in 1893 he became the twenty-fourth president.

Did you know?

Because Grover Cleveland was both the 22nd and 24th presidents, there is some confusion today. For example, although Ronald Reagan is listed as the 40th president, he was the 39th person to occupy the position.

Grover Cleveland 22 24

Born	March 18, 1837
Died	June 24, 1908
Home state	New York (born in New Jersey)
Wife	Frances Folsom
Church	Presbyterian
Occupation	lawyer
Party	Democrat
Years served as president	1885–89 and 1893–97
Terms	2 nonconsecutive
Vice presidents	1st—Thomas A. Hendricks 2nd—Adlai E. Stevenson

Benjamin Harrison 23

Born	August 20, 1833
Died	March 13, 1901
Home state	Indiana (born in Ohio)
Wives	1st—Caroline Scott 2nd—Mary Dimmick
Church	Presbyterian
Occupation	lawyer
Party	Republican
Years served as president	1889–93
Terms	1
Vice president	Levi P. Morton

371

Presidential profiles aid the introduction of each new president.

Did You Know boxes provide interesting, and sometimes unusual, information.

Section reviews help students remember what they have learned.

There were also innovations in aviation. For a while, Germany used zeppelins, large aircraft similar to blimps, to bomb Britain. But zeppelins moved slowly, so airplanes soon replaced them. Airplanes were first used to spy on the enemy. But they attacked enemy planes and bombed targets as well. Aerial battles between planes were called "dogfights." Pilots fired machine guns at each other. At first, firing forward was risky because they could destroy their own propellers. A new invention, the synchronized machine gun, timed the propeller rotation with the firing of the machine gun.

Fighter pilots who shot down five or more enemy planes became special heroes called "aces." Manfred von Richthofen, nicknamed the Red Baron, was Germany's top ace. He achieved 80 "kills." Other top aces included France's René Fonck (75 kills), Canada's Billy Bishop (72 kills), and Great Britain's Edward "Mick" Mannock (61 kills). When the United States entered the war, Eddie Rickenbacker became the most famous American ace. He finished the war with 26 kills. Rickenbacker, like other American aces, flew in the war three fewer years than pilots from many other countries.

Other modernized equipment was also used in the war. Trucks and automobiles aided in the transportation of military goods and personnel. Improved weapons for more effective fighting included rifles, cannons, grenades, and mines. The German navy made extensive use of submarines, which the Allies called **U-boats** (from *Unterseeboot*, German for "undersea boat," their term for a submarine). Other nations soon began constructing their own submarines.

the LAFAYETTE ESCADRILLE

Early in World War I, a group of American pilots petitioned the French government to create an all-American squadron in the French air force. Permission was granted, and in April 1916 the Escadrille Américaine, consisting of volunteer American pilots, was formed.

Since the United States was neutral at the time and the group's name implied that the United States was helping France, the squadron's name was changed to the Lafayette Escadrille. It honored the Marquis de Lafayette for his assistance to the United States during the War for Independence.

▾ A World War I German airplane (left) and a British one (top right). America's most famous pilot of the war, Eddie Rickenbacker (inset).

SECTION REVIEW 20.1

1. What were four major factors leading to the first world war?
2. What event sparked World War I?
3. What countries were part of the Central Powers?
4. What countries were part of the Allied Powers?
5. What three new weapons were first used during World War I?
6. Why do you think the use of poison gas is generally seen as an unacceptable method of warfare?

20.4 AMERICAN FORCES "OVER THERE"

How was America's military involved in World War I?

The chief function of the US Navy was to get troops and supplies safely to Europe. Congress provided funds for enlarging the navy even before the country entered the war. Later the navy was significantly expanded to accomplish its major tasks.

Doughboys

In World War I, the American army was called the **American Expeditionary Force (AEF)**. It was commanded by General **John J. Pershing**. Pershing worked closely with Marshal Ferdinand Foch, a Frenchman who served as supreme Allied commander.

After the US declaration of war in April 1917, American troops, often called **doughboys**, began arriving in Europe in late June. At first the numbers were small; for example, the first group numbered fewer than 15,000. More soldiers arrived in the fall. Because of required training (a minimum of three months) and other delays, most American combat troops did not reach Europe until the spring of 1918. About 2 million American soldiers arrived on the continent by the war's end in November 1918.

British and French soldiers were weary and discouraged from three years of war, so the arrival of Americans was a welcome relief. The British and the French wanted to place American doughboys in already existing armies and use them to replace British and French losses, but Pershing refused. Fearing that American morale would suffer, he insisted that the American troops fight as a separate force under the command of American officers. American units were then assigned their own areas of the battlefields to defend.

GUIDING QUESTION

- How did American forces help end World War I?

Did you know?

A 1917 song written by George M. Cohan entitled "Over There" became popular in the United States during the war. Its lyrics included, "Over there, over there . . . the Yanks [used to refer to all Americans] are coming . . . and we won't come back 'til it's over over there."

US soldier teaching two younger ones how to clean a rifle

BLACK AMERICAN SOLDIERS IN WORLD WAR I

Of the 4 million Americans who served in the war, about 350,000 were African Americans. Military units were segregated, and most blacks were assigned to support roles, such as cooks and laborers. However, some 40,000 were involved in combat.

One of the most distinguished African American units was the 369th Infantry, the "Harlem Hellfighters." The French government honored them with the prestigious Croix de Guerre (the war cross) in recognition of their bravery.

Private Henry Johnson, a member of the Harlem Hellfighters, was one of many who performed heroically in France. When on guard duty during the night of May 14, 1918, he fought Germans who had launched a night attack. He killed four enemy soldiers, wounded an estimated ten to twenty others, and rescued a fellow soldier. In the process, he received 21 wounds in hand-to-hand combat. Though his deeds were reported in the *New York World* and *The Saturday Evening Post* in 1918, it was decades after his 1929 death before he received the honors he deserved. Johnson was posthumously [after death] awarded the Purple Heart in 1996 and the Distinguished Service Cross in 2002. He eventually received America's highest and most prestigious military award—the Congressional Medal of Honor. President Barack Obama presented it in a ceremony at the White House on June 2, 2015.

African Americans in other units also received awards. For example, Corporal Freddie Stowers of the 371st Infantry received the Congressional Medal of Honor; President George H. W. Bush awarded it posthumously in 1991.

Feature boxes provide a deeper look at people, events, or concepts mentioned in the text.

The **chapter outline** lists the major topics that will be covered.

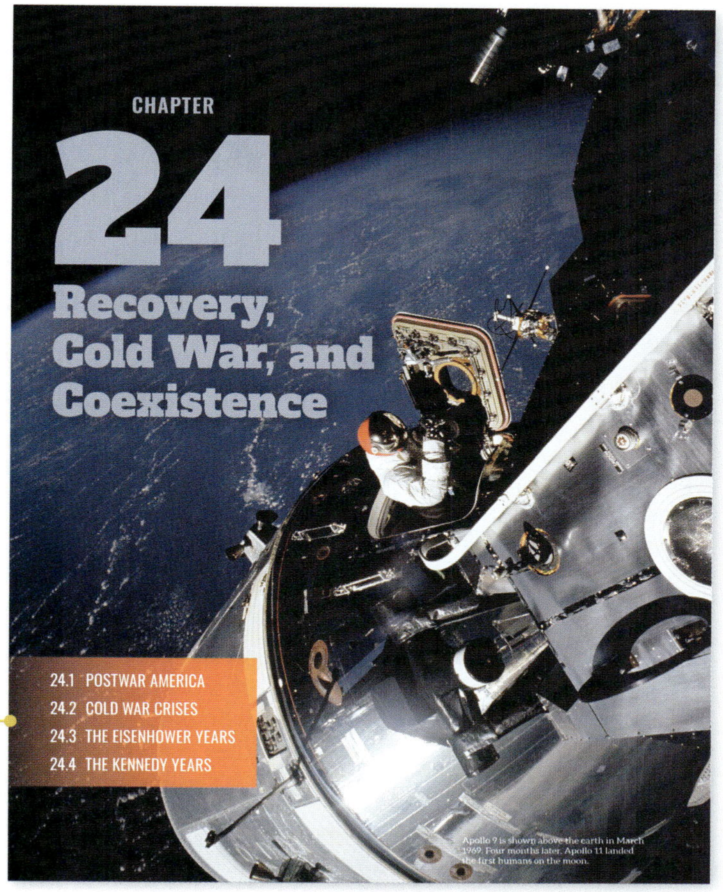
CHAPTER 24

Recovery, Cold War, and Coexistence

24.1 POSTWAR AMERICA
24.2 COLD WAR CRISES
24.3 THE EISENHOWER YEARS
24.4 THE KENNEDY YEARS

Apollo 9 is shown above the earth in March 1969. Four months later, Apollo 11 landed the first humans on the moon.

The **chapter review** asks students about terms, people, places, and concepts to help them think critically, improve understanding, and prepare for assessments.

Photographs, illustrations, and artwork assist students in "seeing" the sites, people, and events discussed in the text.

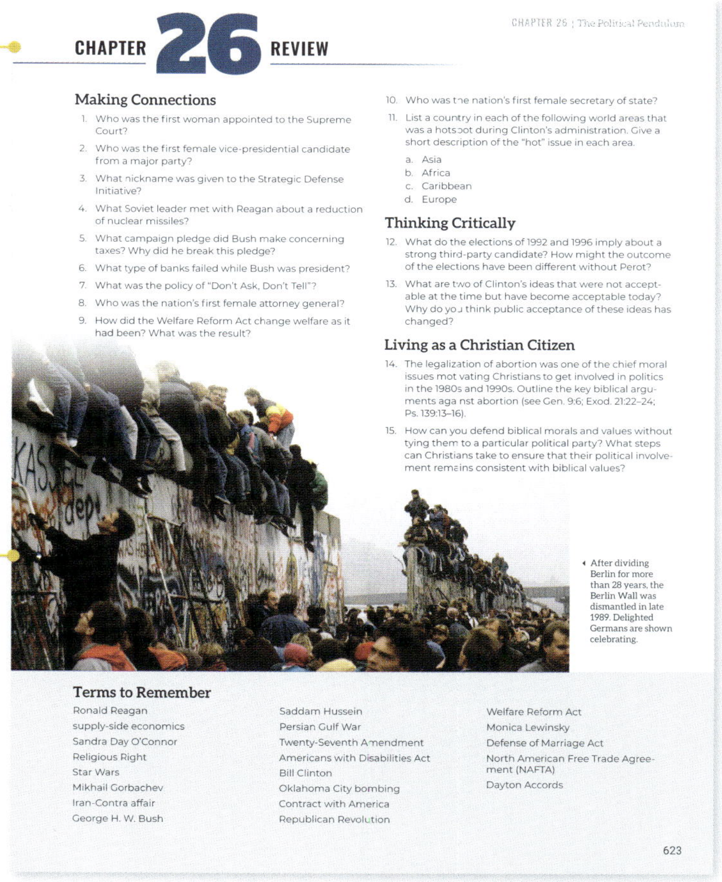
CHAPTER 26 REVIEW

CHAPTER 26 | The Political Pendulum

Making Connections

1. Who was the first woman appointed to the Supreme Court?
2. Who was the first female vice-presidential candidate from a major party?
3. What nickname was given to the Strategic Defense Initiative?
4. What Soviet leader met with Reagan about a reduction of nuclear missiles?
5. What campaign pledge did Bush make concerning taxes? Why did he break this pledge?
6. What type of banks failed while Bush was president?
7. What was the policy of "Don't Ask, Don't Tell"?
8. Who was the nation's first female attorney general?
9. How did the Welfare Reform Act change welfare as it had been? What was the result?
10. Who was the nation's first female secretary of state?
11. List a country in each of the following world areas that was a hotspot during Clinton's administration. Give a short description of the "hot" issue in each area.
   a. Asia
   b. Africa
   c. Caribbean
   d. Europe

Thinking Critically

12. What do the elections of 1992 and 1996 imply about a strong third-party candidate? How might the outcome of the elections have been different without Perot?
13. What are two of Clinton's ideas that were not acceptable at the time but have become acceptable today? Why do you think public acceptance of these ideas has changed?

Living as a Christian Citizen

14. The legalization of abortion was one of the chief moral issues motivating Christians to get involved in politics in the 1980s and 1990s. Outline the key biblical arguments against abortion (see Gen. 9:6; Exod. 21:22–24; Ps. 139:13–16).
15. How can you defend biblical morals and values without tying them to a particular political party? What steps can Christians take to ensure that their political involvement remains consistent with biblical values?

After dividing Berlin for more than 28 years, the Berlin Wall was dismantled in late 1989. Delighted Germans are shown celebrating.

Terms to Remember

Ronald Reagan
supply-side economics
Sandra Day O'Connor
Religious Right
Star Wars
Mikhail Gorbachev
Iran-Contra affair
George H. W. Bush
Saddam Hussein
Persian Gulf War
Twenty-Seventh Amendment
Americans with Disabilities Act
Bill Clinton
Oklahoma City bombing
Contract with America
Republican Revolution
Welfare Reform Act
Monica Lewinsky
Defense of Marriage Act
North American Free Trade Agreement (NAFTA)
Dayton Accords

623

GUIDING QUESTIONS

- What are four key American values?
- What role does justice play in government?
- Why should Christians study history?

Introduction

American Core Values

American Republic is designed to be more than a record of names, dates, and wars. It presents American history as the unfolding of several **core values**, the guiding ideas and beliefs that create a common culture and bind a people together. Americans tend to value such basic ideas as freedom, individualism, equality, and growth. In addition to focusing on these values, thankfulness is also presented throughout the book as an appropriate response to God's providence and goodness. Since American Christians should strive to glorify God and serve their country, Christians need to understand these core values and know how to apply them with the Word of God in mind.

Freedom

Freedom, also called liberty, is typically viewed as a condition in which people make their own choices without fear—as long as those choices do not harm anyone else. Americans value the freedom to worship as they wish, choose their own jobs, own whatever property they can afford, and play a role in government.

Is it good to be free? True freedom flourishes when people choose to love and obey God and to love and do good to others (Matt. 22:37–39). Freedom is not good when choices are made to disobey God or to harm others. The Bible values freedom (1 Cor. 7:21–23; Rom. 6:17–22) but also emphasizes that people must obey God and His Word as well as the authorities over them (Rom. 13:1–7; 1 Pet. 2:13–17; Heb. 13:17). A nation that refuses to submit to God will experience His judgment (Ps. 2:10–12; 9:17).

Problems arise when people argue that it is more important to be free than to be biblically good. A society that values freedom over goodness encourages people to do whatever they wish. If people choose to do wrong, they harm others. Such a society may question what is right and may even value the freedom to do wrong.

Individualism

Individualism is the belief that people have the right to be independent: taking care of themselves and taking responsibility for their own actions. Not all cultures prioritize this value—many favor the group over individual identity or rights.

God values people as individuals. He condemns and rewards them individually (Ezek. 18:20; Rom. 2:6–12), and He demands that governments do the same (Deut. 24:16). He praises those who stand against the wrongdoing of their community (Num. 13:25–33; 14:22–24; Gal. 2:11–14). Each person has a duty to work diligently and be good and wise stewards. (Prov. 27:23–24; 2 Thess. 3:10). Individualism should not be an excuse to act selfishly.

However, the Bible also recognizes the importance of living in community and depending on others (1 Cor. 12:20–27; Gal. 6:2). One job of the community is to care for the poor within it (Exod. 23:11; Deut. 15:7–11; James 2:15–17). God declared that it was not good for man to be alone (Gen. 2:18). He instituted families and churches as community groups. In eternity the saved will live together in community—in a city, the new Jerusalem. Of course, the most important dependence is upon God through Jesus Christ for salvation. Salvation cannot be achieved in one's own strength, though each person must individually choose this path.

Throughout much of their nation's history, Americans have taken pride in individualism. The story of America is the story of people and groups that have sought political, social, and religious independence. It is the story of explorers, pioneers, inventors, and entrepreneurs and the story of communities, churches, businesses, and volunteer organizations.

Equality

The Pledge of Allegiance says, "with liberty and justice for all." Equality is a social condition in which all people have the same rights and opportunities despite various conditions and situations of life.

The Declaration of Independence affirms: "We hold these truths to be self-evident, that all men are created equal." But Americans have often failed to embrace this value, many times failing to treat others as fellow image bearers of God. Some of the worst injustices in America's history have been the result of the failure to live by this value.

The Bible teaches that all people have equal value because they are made in God's image (Gen. 1:26–27). Even a king should not take a person's life or property unjustly (2 Sam. 11–12; 1 Kings 21). Yet the Bible also teaches the existence of various authority structures (Eph. 5:22–24; 6:1; 1 Pet. 2:13–17), which result in statuses or positions that are not equal. For example, while children and parents have equal value in the sight of God, children do not have equal authority with their parents. When people try to remove these authority structures, injustice often results.

Growth

Most Americans love growth, or the idea of expanding and advancing—gaining wealth, buying property, inventing new technology, and growing in knowledge and wisdom.

God gives this desire for growth. In the **Creation Mandate** of Genesis 1:28, He calls humans to exercise authority over His earth. This huge task can only be accomplished with growth in areas such as knowledge, technology, and culture.

The desire for growth appears in every period of American history. During the colonial period, Europeans left the security of home to find new opportunities to gain wealth and property and to spread Christianity. After Americans declared their independence from England, they continued looking across the continent to find more land and the opportunities it provided. American inventions and ingenuity have made the United States a leading manufacturer and trade partner in the world.

Because people are fallen, the desire for growth can easily develop into greed and selfishness. Some Americans have pursued growth unjustly by taking land from others or by mistreating those who worked for them. Even when growth is pursued correctly, people may become preoccupied with the things of this world rather than with the things of Christ.

Establishing Justice: A Biblical Purpose for Government

According to the Bible, establishing justice is a primary purpose of government (1 Kings 10:9; Ps. 72:1–2, 11–14; Prov. 29:14). In the Preamble to the Constitution, the Founding Fathers state their duty to establish justice when forming the government.

What is justice? People answer this question in various ways. There is a temptation to define justice without considering God's Word. Since people often disagree about what is right and wrong, modern philosophers have sought to define justice without making judgments about right and wrong. One popular view asserts that justice is achieved when the greatest happiness is reached for the most people. Another approach says that freedom of choice for everyone maximizes justice for everyone. But who decides the correct definition of happiness or freedom? Whose happiness? Whose freedom?

True justice is based on the fact that God created the world to work a certain way. Justice will conform to that order. For instance, the fact that all people bear the image of God forms the basis for the right to life (Gen. 1:26–27; 9:6) and for freedom from enslavement (Exod. 21:16). God made a world with such rights as to be paid for work, to protect property, and to prohibit theft (Lev. 19:13; Exod. 22:1–15). Because God created marriage between one man and one woman for life (Gen. 2:24; Matt. 19:4–9), it is just to protect this ideal of marriage.

The Christian and America

Historically, Americans have valued religion and held strong religious beliefs, most often some form of Christianity. But for some Americans today, freedom has come to mean independence from religion. This leads to **secularism**, the belief that religion has no place in government. Students of history should observe the positive effects of biblical Christianity on American culture both in the past and present. They should also notice the negative results of society's increasing disinterest in Christianity.

One reason to study America's history is to learn lessons for life. American history includes many wrongs and injustices. It also includes many good things for which Christians should thank God. Thankfulness to God in every circumstance is one of the key marks of a Christian (1 Thess. 5:18) and a second reason to study American history.

A third reason to study American history is to learn how to become a good citizen. Citizens play an important role in government in our republic. The history of the United States contributes greatly to the cultural identity of each American. Christians should guide their government toward pleasing God whenever they have the opportunity. Christians are to submit to government, good or bad (Rom. 13:1), except when obedience to God is at stake (Acts 5:29). Even then, Christians must be willing to suffer for doing right (Phil. 1:29; 1 Pet. 2:20–21).

Understanding the history of America—its values, its mistakes, and its successes—is an important part of becoming a better citizen.

INTRODUCTION REVIEW

Making Connections

1. What is true freedom?
2. Why are all people equal in value under God?
3. What is true justice based on?
4. List three reasons to study American history.

Thinking Critically

5. Should freedom be absolute or unlimited? Why?
6. How might growth be both good and bad?

Living as a Christian Citizen

7. How should conflicts between core values be resolved?
8. How might a Christian practice individuality and community at the same time?

Terms to Remember

core values

Creation Mandate

secularism

UNIT 1

Settling a Wilderness

Native American observes Henry Hudson's ship entering New York Harbor, 1609.

1492 — Columbus's arrival in the New World

1565 — City of St. Augustine, Florida, founded by the Spanish

1607 — Jamestown founded

1619 — House of Burgesses formed in Virginia

1620 — Pilgrims' arrival in the New World

1630 — Massachusetts Bay Colony formed

1636 — Harvard founded

1692 — Salem witch trials

1720

Great Awakening 1720–60

1733 — Georgia settled

1754

French and Indian War 1754–63

1765 — Stamp Act passed

1770 — Boston Massacre

1773 — Boston Tea Party

1774 — First Continental Congress

1775 — Battles of Lexington and Concord

CHAPTER

1 America, Europe, and Africa before 1620

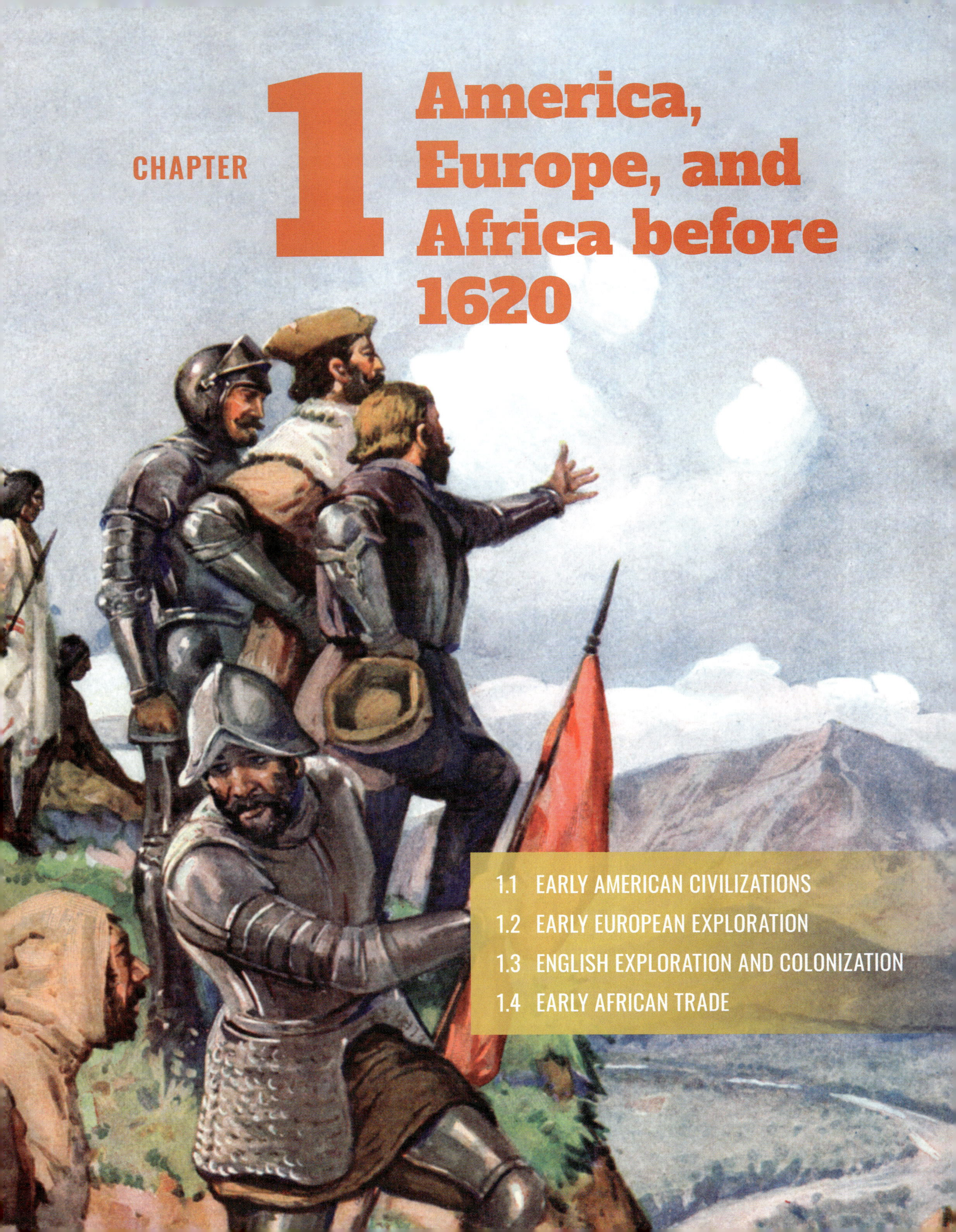

1.1 EARLY AMERICAN CIVILIZATIONS

1.2 EARLY EUROPEAN EXPLORATION

1.3 ENGLISH EXPLORATION AND COLONIZATION

1.4 EARLY AFRICAN TRADE

▲ Amazon rainforest, Brazil

◂ Jacques Cartier claims Canada for France.

▲ Mayan hieroglyphics

There is a land of mystery, a land of hieroglyphics and mummies. Above the mist rise pyramids and colossal statues carved from huge, imported boulders. Here the people worship the sun god and believe in the underworld. But this is not Egypt.

1.1 EARLY AMERICAN CIVILIZATIONS

What were the cultures of the Americas like before Europeans arrived?

GUIDING QUESTIONS

- What were the civilizations of Central and South America like before the arrival of Europeans?
- What were North American Indians like?
- What were the cultures and religions of Native American civilizations?

It is uncertain how and when the first people arrived in North and South America. After the confusing of languages at the tower of Babel in Genesis 11, people scattered across the earth. Perhaps they crossed a land bridge that linked Asia to Alaska. Perhaps they sailed across the waters or down the coast. Regardless of their route, they clearly lived in the Americas long before the Europeans came.

Spread out across North and South America, these indigenous (original or native) groups were divided into hundreds of clans, or tribes, each with its own language, lifestyle, and chief. Some were **nomadic**, constantly on the move in search of game (wild animals hunted for food) and wild plants. Other groups settled and raised crops. Tribes lived in different kinds of shelters, movable or permanent, depending on their way of life.

Civilizations of Central and South America

In Mesoamerica (present-day Mexico and Central America) and South America, several groups built large civilizations before Europeans arrived, living in cities and developing specialized skills. These groups constructed canals, stone pyramids, and elaborate road networks.

▾ Mayan temple in Mexico

▶ Olmec and ▶ Maya

The Olmec occupied southern Mexico centuries before Jesus was born. They grew crops such as maize (corn) and root vegetables such as cassava. They carved mammoth stone heads from basalt boulders brought down from the mountains. They also discovered practical uses for the rubber tree (Olmec means "rubber people"), such as crafting toys and balls. By about 400 BC, the Olmec started to lose influence and their civilization faded.

The Maya arrived in the tropical rainforests of what is now southern Mexico and Guatemala before 1000 BC. About AD 250 their golden age began. They built large cities with temples and step pyramids. The Olmec greatly influenced the Maya civilization. Each developed a system of writing similar to Egyptian hieroglyphics. The Olmec's and Maya's study of the sun, moon, and stars as well as advances in mathematics were used to create a 365-day calendar. The Maya discovered new concepts in math, such as the idea of zero; and created the Long Count Calendar, which did not end until 2012. The Maya worshiped many gods. They were known for human sacrifice, which they believed the gods required to satisfy their need for blood. Eventually, the Maya began to abandon their cities, and by AD 900 the civilization's influence had virtually disappeared. Though historians are uncertain why it disappeared, many theories, including drought, disease, warfare, and lack of usable water, are considered.

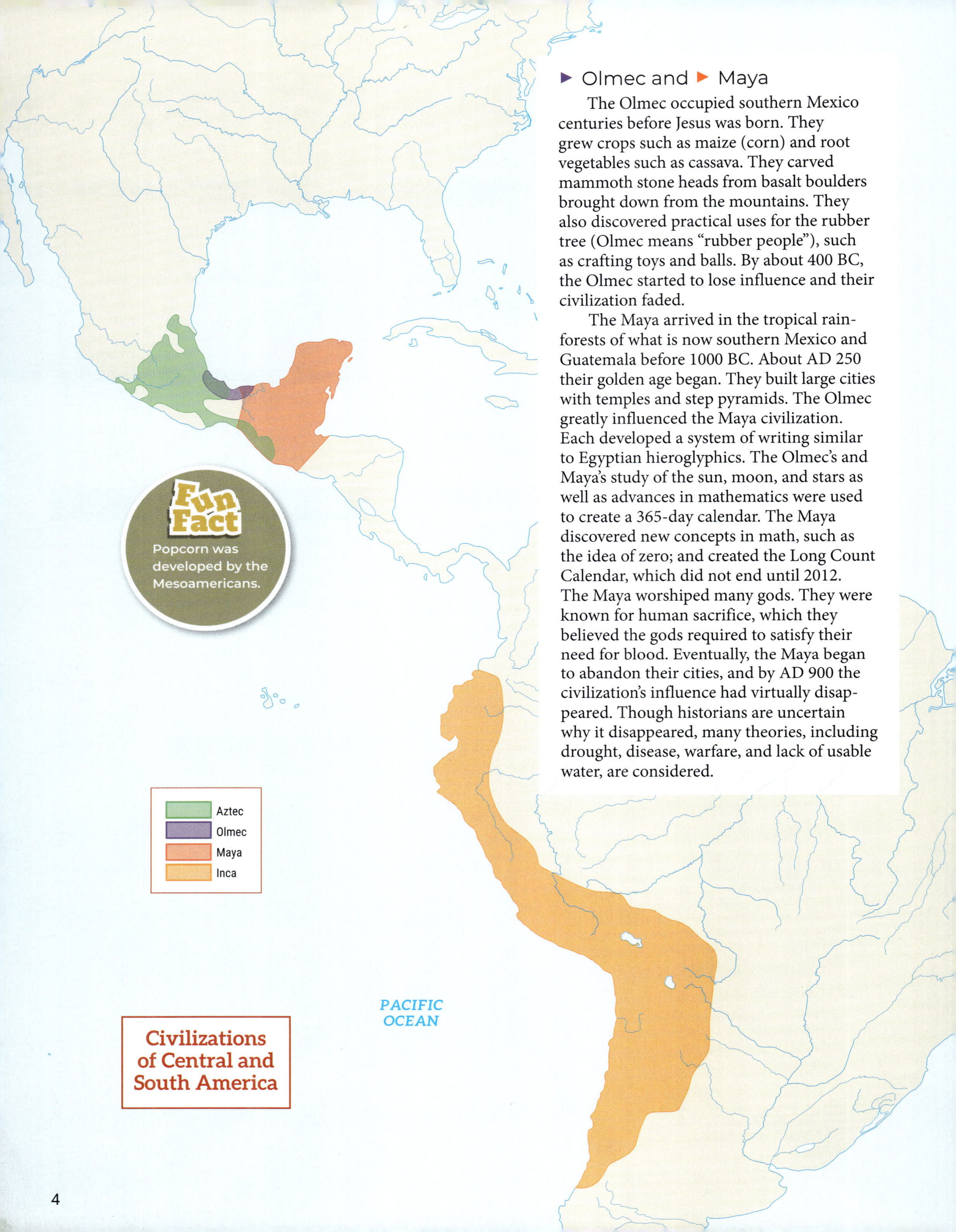

Fun Fact

Popcorn was developed by the Mesoamericans.

Aztec

The Aztec civilization in Mexico developed later than the Olmec and Maya civilizations. Founded in the AD 1200s, the Aztec civilization was a warrior empire. The Aztecs built a large city, Tenochtitlan, from drained swamp land. Today it is the site of Mexico City. The Aztecs used advanced methods of irrigation for agriculture. Their religion mimicked the human sacrifices of the Maya and frequently included the removal of the heart, often performed at the top of a pyramid built for that purpose.

The Aztec empire was still expanding under the leader Montezuma when it was overthrown by the Spanish **conquistadors** (conquerors). Through warfare and diseases for which the Aztecs had no immunity, the Aztec population shrank to roughly half between 1519 and 1521. Their great numbers of people and skill at fighting were no match for Spanish weapons.

Fun Fact

Chili, avocado, guacamole, and *coyote* are Aztec words.

Inca

The Incan empire extended in a long, narrow strip along the western side of South America. Existing during the same general time period as the Aztecs, the Inca built astounding architectural works in hard-to-reach places like the mountaintop ceremonial city of Machu Picchu. They built many other cities linked by a complex network of roads.

A decade after the fall of the Aztecs, this civilization was also devastated by the conquistadors. Francisco Pizarro, the cousin of Aztec conqueror Hernando Cortés, desired the famous Incan gold. He kidnapped the ruler and later executed him. Though the Inca fought back, Spanish weapons were again superior, and soon the Spanish took over the empire. Smallpox killed millions more in this diverse empire.

the ICE MAIDEN

In 1995, the best-preserved mummy in the world was discovered when the body of a twelve- or thirteen-year-old frozen girl tumbled down the side of a dormant volcano in Peru. She lived more than five hundred years ago, during the 1400s. Incan human sacrifice was somewhat different from that of the Maya and Aztecs. The chosen children were fattened with good food and drugged with coca leaves and corn alcohol. They were then taken atop a high mountain peak and left to freeze to death in order to please the gods, hopefully resulting in good harvests. The Ice Maiden is so well preserved that her hair has been used to discover what she ate.

▾ Machu Picchu

The People of North America

Unlike the natives to the south, the natives of North America did not form large civilizations. In the area that became the United States, most Indians lived in small villages in several main regions: the Northwest Coast, the Great Basin and Plateau, the Southwest, the Arctic and Subarctic, the Eastern Woodlands, the Southeast, and the Great Plains.

Did you know?

In reality, the "low man on the totem pole" was the most important of all!

▸ Northwest Coast

The Indians of the Pacific Northwest built sturdy houses from cedar in villages along the ocean, rivers, and streams. The waters supplied them with abundant food. They caught salmon from the streams and ate oysters and fish from the sea. From tall trees they carved **totem poles** that represented family history, local legends, and important events.

Fun Fact

Northwest Indians used the inside bark of cedar trees to make raincoats.

▸ Great Basin and ▸ Plateau

The Great Basin and Plateau Indians such as the Shoshone, Ute, and Nez Perce were nomadic hunter-gatherers who lived between the Rocky Mountains and the western coastal mountains. Over time many became similar to the Great Plains Indians, living in tepees and hunting bison. The climate in the Great Basin and Plateau was harsh, with land that could not be farmed, but the Indians survived by gathering wild nuts and berries, hunting for small animals, and fishing. These Indians made baskets and left behind petroglyphs, or rock drawings, that illustrate their lifestyle.

Did you know?

The animals referred to as *buffalo* in America are actually bison and live only in North America. True buffalo live in Africa and Asia.

▸ Southwest

In what is now Colorado, Utah, Arizona, and New Mexico, tribes called cliff dwellers constructed elaborate houses in the sides of cliffs. Southwestern Indians were expert architects and masons. Some tribes designed homes with many rooms, like those in apartment buildings, and made houses with adobe, a dried clay-and-straw mixture. Navajo often lived in hogans, houses made of logs and earth. Southwestern Indian tribes such as the Pueblo, Apache, Hopi, and Navajo farmed the desert, gathered wild plants, and hunted small animals. Southwestern tribes are well-known for their beautiful turquoise jewelry, pottery, and woven goods.

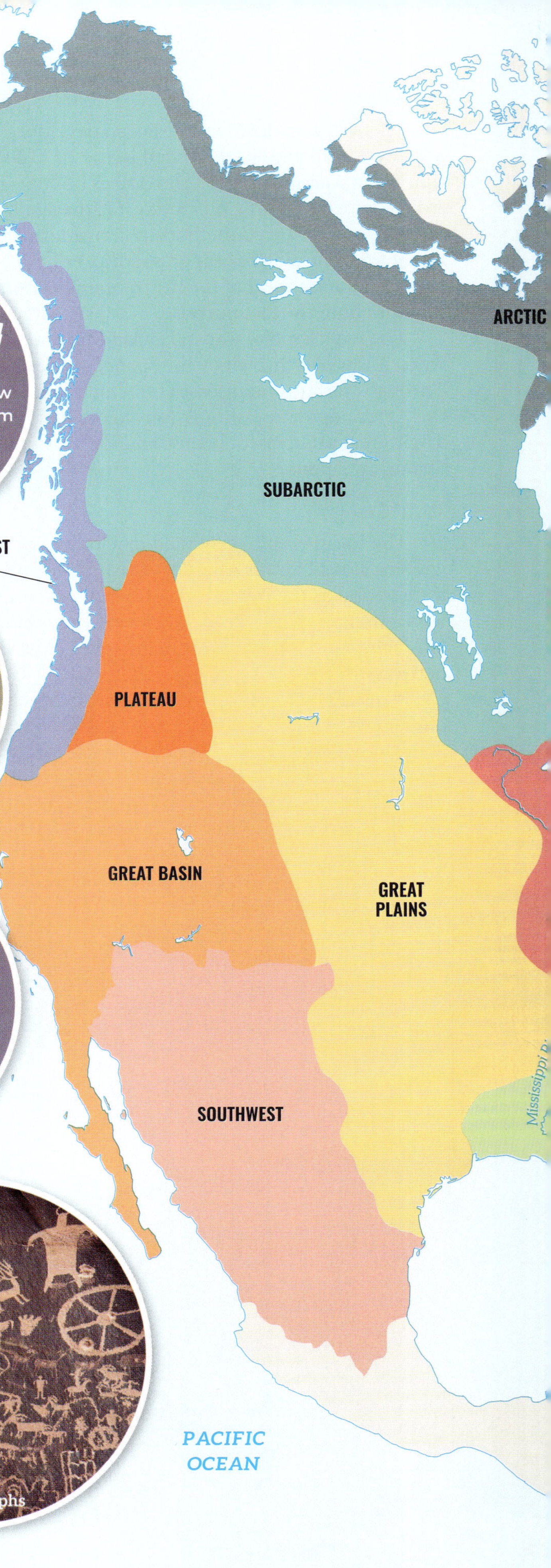

Petroglyphs

Caribou

Arctic and Subarctic

The Inuit settled the frigid regions of Canada, Alaska, and Greenland near the Arctic Circle. Adapting to the cold climate, they were skilled at using what was available. Snow and ice blocks were used to form igloos. Caribou (reindeer), whales, seals, and walruses were hunted for food and clothing, and whale oil was burned for light. Small boats and kayaks were also made from the skins of hunted animals.

Iroquois longhouse

Eastern Woodlands

The Woodland Indians lived in the East, from the Atlantic Ocean to the Mississippi River. In addition to hunting and fishing, tribes such as the Algonquian and Huron planted maize, squash, and tobacco. Because they had stable sources of food, they built permanent villages. Many lived in wigwams, which were dome shaped and covered with leaves, bark, or animal skins. Some tribes, such as the Iroquois, built longhouses—large, rectangular dwellings that housed extended families. The Iroquois were later responsible for forming a tribal alliance called the Iroquois League of Five Nations.

Burial mound in West Virginia

Southeast

In the Ohio Valley and in the Southeast lived the mound builders. Mounds were made of earth and could be used as tombs or for religious ceremonies. The Great Serpent Mound in Ohio is the largest earthworks mound in the world. The largest number of mounds in one place was located at Cahokia, where Missouri and Illinois now meet. In 1200 Cahokia was the largest pre-Columbian (before Columbus) city in North America, having a population larger than that of London in that same year. It existed from about 700 to 1400, although it began to decline after 1200. Once again, the reason for the decline of the civilization is unknown. The Southeast was also comprised of such tribes as the Cherokee, Seminole, and Creek.

Tepees

Great Plains

The Indians generally portrayed in older cowboy movies were the Great Plains Indians. They lived on the prairies between the Mississippi River and the Rocky Mountains, often in small villages along rivers and lakes. After horses were brought to the area, they became more nomadic. They lived in tepees, which were easy to transport, and roamed the grasslands to hunt the bison. The Sioux, Cheyenne, and Blackfoot tribes became powerful in the Plains.

Native American Culture and Religion

Because Europeans and their descendants frequently viewed the Native American peoples as "backward," not recognizing the God-given capabilities bestowed on all people as bearers of His image, in the past, Native American peoples were sometimes characterized as "savage." However, the natives of pre-Columbian America skillfully shaped their environments and developed their cultures, unknowingly fulfilling the command to fill and subdue the earth (Gen. 1:28). In Central America, great ruins of highly developed civilizations still stand. In the American Southwest, Native Americans built cliff dwellings and irrigation systems. Along the Atlantic coast, Indians burned the forests once or twice a year to clear the undergrowth, making hunting and travel easier. But some Native Americans overhunted, killing more animals than needed. Others used the slash-and-burn method to prepare land for crops, destroying many potentially useful trees. After depleting fields of nutrients, some simply moved to new locations.

Religions among the North American Indians were typically based on belief in the Great Spirit, leading naturally to **animism**, the belief that all natural objects, whether animate (living) or inanimate (nonliving), have souls. Indian priests and shamans (sorcerers) attempted to communicate with these spirits. Sometimes whole villages performed ceremonies to please the spirits in the hope of having a good harvest or a successful hunt. Angry spirits were thought to cause problems such as wars, diseases, or poor crops.

SECTION REVIEW 1.1

Throughout the book, shaded questions indicate critical thinking questions.

1. What are some leading theories on how people first came to the Americas?
2. How were the cultures of Mesoamerica similar to that of ancient Egypt?
3. How does human sacrifice violate God's Word?
4. Which regional groups of North American natives settled permanent villages and which were nomadic?
5. Define *animism*.
6. How were the religious ideas of Central and South American Indians different from those of North American Indians?

▾ Cliff dwellings in Colorado

1.2 EARLY EUROPEAN EXPLORATION

Where in the Americas did the Vikings, Spanish, and French explore?

GUIDING QUESTIONS

- Why did countries explore?
- Which groups explored and colonized the Americas?

No one knows when the Native Americans first saw a European. Columbus is generally regarded as the "discoverer" of America, but he was not the first European to see the Americas. There are many theories about who arrived first. Stories are told of Phoenician sailors who arrived centuries before the birth of Christ. There is also the legend of Madoc, a Welsh prince who founded a settlement among Indians during the Middle Ages. Tales of Welsh-speaking, blue-eyed Indians continued until the 1800s. Other stories tell of Irish monks who visited America over a thousand years ago. But these are only legends.

The Vikings

Evidence in eastern Canada indicates that the Vikings visited North America about AD 1000. The Vikings, or Norsemen, were seamen from northern Europe. They planted colonies in Iceland and Greenland. From Greenland, the Vikings sailed their ships westward to Canada. The best known Viking adventurer was **Leif Ericson**. Ericson found a new land to the west in present-day Newfoundland, Canada, and called it Vinland.

Other Vikings likely journeyed to America after Ericson. But other Europeans were unaware of their voyages. It was not until Columbus's "discovery" that a new era dawned for both Europe and the Americas.

Did you know?

One misconception, popularized by Washington Irving's romanticized biography of Columbus, was that Columbus was trying to prove that the earth was round. But from ancient times, educated people have always known this. Even so, Columbus's calculations were based on the world being smaller than it actually is.

The Spanish

Before the 1400s few Europeans ventured far out to sea because their ships could not handle the rough conditions away from the shore. This situation improved after the Portuguese adapted small fishing boats to long-distance travel by adding specially designed sails. These fast sailing ships were called *caravels*.

By the end of the 1400s, Europe was ready to explore the world. New instruments helped them navigate the seas. Much of the early exploration focused on finding new routes to the Indies (the Orient or the Far East) where spices were readily available. Europeans also wanted the silk, porcelain, gems, and precious metals available in the East. Since great profits could be made by obtaining these goods, merchants and monarchs were willing to search for new trade routes. While the Portuguese tried to find a way eastward around Africa, others thought the Orient could be reached by sailing west. This belief led to the exploration of the Western Hemisphere.

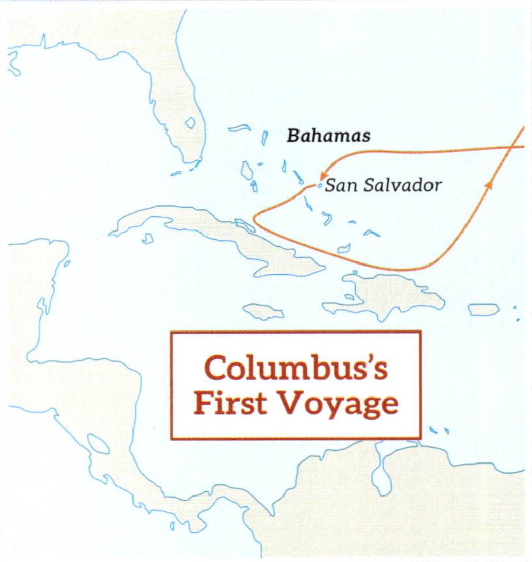

Columbus's Search for the Indies

The Italian sailor **Christopher Columbus** was convinced that by sailing west he could reach the rich lands of the Indies. Having no success in persuading the Portuguese to finance his voyage, Columbus turned to Spain for help, eventually securing the support of King Ferdinand and Queen Isabella.

In August of 1492 Columbus set sail on his historic voyage with three ships, the *Niña*, the *Pinta*, and the *Santa María*. The *Niña* and the *Pinta* were caravels. Columbus kept his crew on course until land was sighted on October 12, 1492. Christopher Columbus had arrived in the Bahamas, opening the door to what Europeans would call the "New World." He called the native people "Indians" because he believed he had found the East Indies. Later that day, he went ashore on the island he named San Salvador.

For years, the Indians had passed down stories of great spirits who would visit them from across the seas. When the Europeans came to America, many Indians believed that these spirits had arrived. They watched the newcomers approach on "floating islands." They were amazed at the Europeans' pale, hairy faces and dark, heavy clothes. And they marveled at the strangers' shiny trinkets and noisy weapons.

The Europeans were equally shocked at the Indians. They considered the Indians wild people because they wore little clothing and practiced pagan rituals and superstitions. Many Indians celebrated the newcomers, treating them as gods. The Europeans gave gifts and boldly displayed their guns. The two groups soon learned to trade with each other for items they wanted and needed.

Columbus gave religious names to the islands he discovered. He hoped that his arrival in the New World would spread Catholicism. But Columbus tried to spread his religion the wrong way. He mistreated the Indians and took some of them back as slaves to Spain, hoping they would be converted. He attempted to force Catholicism on people who had no knowledge of anything Christian.

Columbus returned to Spain with news of what he thought was the Indies. Other explorers began investigating the lands across the Atlantic. They soon realized that Columbus had not found the Far East. One of the first explorers to suggest this was an Italian merchant named **Amerigo Vespucci**. Vespucci realized that the coasts he explored did not match those of mapped Asian coasts. He claimed that the lands were a "new world." A German mapmaker included the new continent on a map and named it *America* after Amerigo.

▲ Christopher Columbus

Fun Fact

Europeans had no chocolate, sugar, corn, or potatoes before the discovery of the Americas.

Other Spanish Explorers

Spain's early explorations occurred primarily along the coasts of Central and South America. However, they eventually pushed inland, led by the conquistadors. Because the conquistadors found treasure in Central and South America, most of Spain's attention was focused on those lands. As early as 1519 the Spanish began to colonize what is now Mexico. However, a few conquistadors also tried to find wealth in North America, resulting in Spain's claim to territory in what is today Florida, Texas, and the Southwest.

The Spanish took unfamiliar plants, such as corn and potatoes, back to Europe. They brought animals, such as horses and cattle, to the Americas. They also established their language, customs, and Roman Catholic religion in the lands they claimed. Columbus's discovery produced some tragic results. The conquistadors often plundered wealth and mistreated natives, enslaving and killing many of them. Besides warfare and slavery, Indians quickly fell sick to foreign diseases carried on European ships. An incredible percentage of Indians died in epidemics of smallpox or measles, diseases to which they had never been exposed. By the time the English arrived more than one hundred years later, many Indian villages had completely disappeared.

After Spain's early explorations, other countries saw the advantages of making their own claims in the Americas. The resulting struggle for land helped shape the heritage of the United States.

In 1540 **Francisco Coronado** came from Mexico to the Southwest. He sought the legendary golden cities of Cíbola (cities of gold said to rival the wealth of the Aztecs). Although he never found golden cities, Coronado did discover the adobe villages of the Pueblo Indians. He was also the first European to see the Grand Canyon. He and his men explored as far north as present-day Kansas before turning back. The horses they had brought with them fascinated the Plains Indians, who later became skilled horsemen.

Hernando de Soto hoped to find riches in North American Indian settlements. Starting in Florida in 1539, de Soto traveled the Southeast until he discovered the Mississippi River.

In 1565 the Spanish founded the city of **St. Augustine**, Florida, the oldest permanent city settled by Europeans in the United States.

The first Spaniard to explore Florida was **Juan Ponce de León**. He arrived in 1513, searching for riches, among other things. He may have been the first European to see land that is now the United States.

The French

The French were also interested in the Americas. Because the Spanish had a strong hold on the Caribbean, France concentrated on exploring other parts of North America and hoped to find a water passage through the northern part of the continent to the Far East.

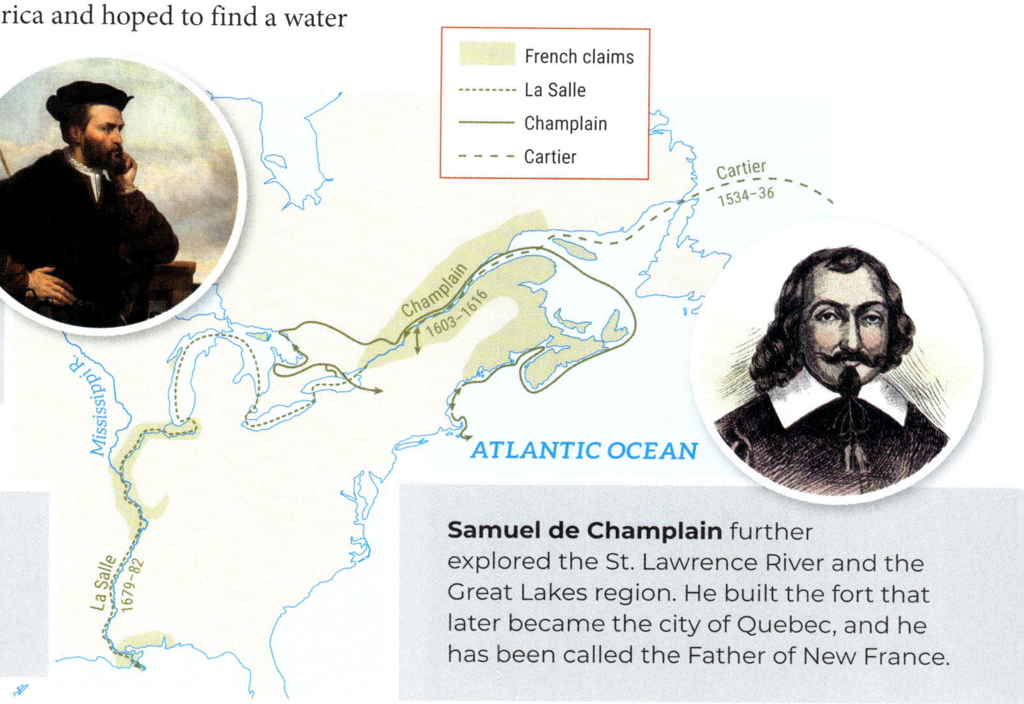

The French explorer **Jacques Cartier** was sailing in search of a waterway across the continent when he discovered the St. Lawrence River in 1534, leading France to claim a large section of North America.

Robert de La Salle claimed the Mississippi River for France.

Samuel de Champlain further explored the St. Lawrence River and the Great Lakes region. He built the fort that later became the city of Quebec, and he has been called the Father of New France.

France was slow to develop its claims in the region. The French were preoccupied with affairs in Europe and had not found gold or silver, as the Spanish had to the south. It was almost a century after the first French explorers laid claim to parts of North America that the French really began to extensively explore the land. Throughout the seventeenth century (1600s), the French settled along the St. Lawrence and Mississippi Rivers and around the Great Lakes. The lakes and rivers were like roads, opening the interior to French trade with the Indians. Trading clothing and tools, such as axes and pots, for the skins of foxes, moose, otters, and beavers became a rewarding business for the French. Rather than establishing well-organized towns, the French built military forts, missions, and trading posts at key places to protect French traders and trappers. These outposts—such as Quebec, Montreal, Detroit, and New Orleans—became centers of French culture and religion in the New World.

As there were few opportunities for quick riches, French colonies did not attract many settlers. The colonies were under the strict control of the French king and did not allow local government or self-rule. Furthermore, beginning in the mid-1600s, only Roman Catholics were allowed to settle in the French colonies. This excluded a skilled, industrious group of French Protestants called Huguenots, many of whom settled in English territory after fleeing France's religious persecution.

A few other countries, such as the Netherlands, sent explorers in hopes of gaining land and treasures. But most land was taken by the Spanish, French, and English. While the Spanish concentrated on mining riches and the French cornered the fur-trade market, the British took another approach to developing their claims in the Americas.

SECTION REVIEW 1.2

1. What Viking adventurer sailed west of Greenland? What did he name the land that he found?
2. What nation financed Columbus's voyages?
3. Why did Columbus call the people he met "Indians"?
4. What do you think about Columbus's method to spread Catholicism?
5. How did America get its name?
6. Name three Spanish explorers and the areas each explored.
7. What city, founded in 1565, is the oldest permanent European city in the United States?
8. Besides warfare and slavery, what great tragedy accompanied Spanish exploration?
9. Name three French explorers and the areas each explored.
10. What was the key industry in French lands in the Americas?
11. What changes could the French government have made that would have attracted more settlers to their colonies?

GUIDING QUESTIONS

- Why was the English defeat of the Spanish Armada significant?
- What happened to the Lost Colony?
- What challenges did the settlers of Jamestown face?
- What was significant about the Virginia House of Burgesses?

▲ Sir Francis Drake

1.3 ENGLISH EXPLORATION AND COLONIZATION

How did the English explore and colonize?

Sea Dogs and the Spanish Armada

As early as 1497, the explorer **John Cabot** laid claim to the Atlantic coast of North America for England. The Spanish objected to English intrusion into lands the Spanish considered their own. Throughout the 1500s, tensions mounted between Spain and England. The Spanish were especially angered by the plundering activities of the English **Sea Dogs**, a group of English sea captains. As pirates, they disrupted the flow of riches from the Americas to Spain. They raided coastal towns, destroyed Spanish harbors, and seized Spanish ships full of treasure, taking the wealth back to England.

The most famous Sea Dog was **Sir Francis Drake**, a favorite of Queen Elizabeth I. In 1577 he sailed down the coast of South America, plundering Spanish ports and capturing treasure ships. To escape the Spanish patrols, Drake sailed around South America, across the Pacific, and around Africa's Cape of Good Hope to a triumphant return to England. The Spanish called Drake the "master thief" and the "dragon." But in England he became a popular hero. Queen Elizabeth I openly knighted him aboard his flagship, the *Golden Hind*.

Religion was another reason for tensions between Spain and England. England had become Protestant during the Reformation. Spain remained strongly Roman Catholic. The king of Spain, Philip II, wanted to restore England to Catholicism.

To conquer England, Philip II organized an invasion force using his "Invincible Armada," a supposedly unbeatable fleet of warships. In 1588 his fleet of 130 ships sailed toward England. The English navy, commanded by Sea Dogs such as Sir Francis Drake, met the Spanish Armada in the English Channel. The lighter and faster English ships inflicted heavy damage on the Spanish vessels. The battered armada fled, but fierce storms destroyed even more ships along the way. Only half of the Spanish ships returned to Spain.

Spain never recovered, and England took Spain's place as the "Mistress of the Seas," opening the door for English colonization in the New World. If Spain's armada had not been defeated, Spain might have kept control of the New World. North America might have become almost entirely Roman Catholic, just as Central and South America are today.

▼ Fighting the Spanish Armada

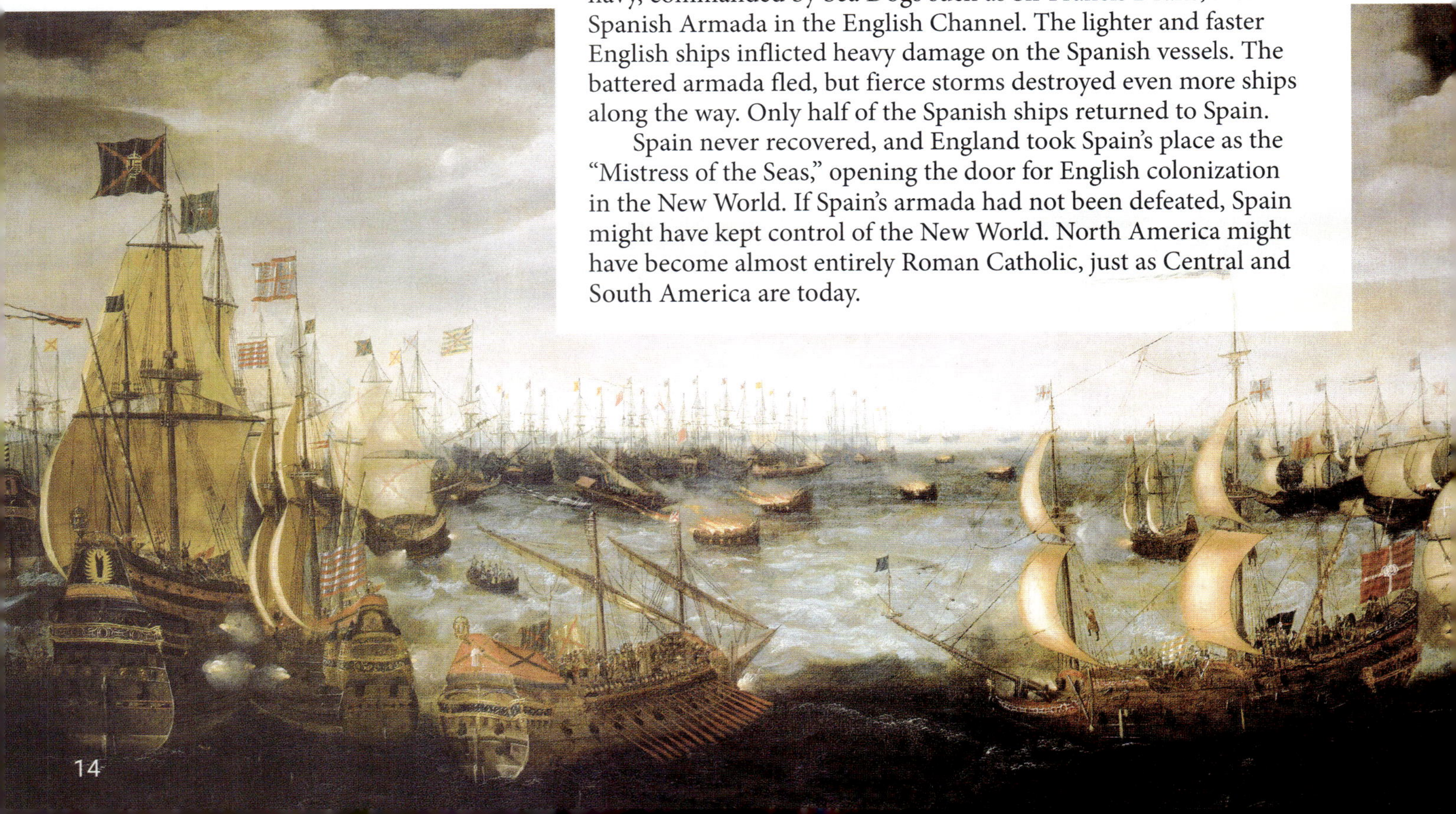

Reasons for Colonization

There were seven primary motives for the founding of colonies by the English.

LAND

For the common people of England, the most important reason to colonize was the chance to own land. England's population was rising rapidly. The vast majority of land was held by wealthy families, and tradition kept families from selling that land to anyone else. Unless Englishmen inherited land from relatives, they had little hope of owning their own property. Most farmers rented farmland or worked for a landholder. Explorers returned to Europe praising the beauty and bounty of America. There was plenty of land, which symbolized for many the opportunity of growth and improvement.

POLITICAL FREEDOM

Second, many of the English desired greater political freedom. The Magna Carta, signed by King John in 1215, limited the power of the English monarch (king or queen). It also guaranteed certain basic rights to the people. In the 1600s, however, kings tried to strengthen royal power. Many Englishmen went to America seeking freedom from this oppressive rule.

PERSONAL RICHES

Third, some people were motivated by the potential for personal riches. Investors paid the expenses of many colonists, hoping that raw materials from the colonies would return a healthy profit.

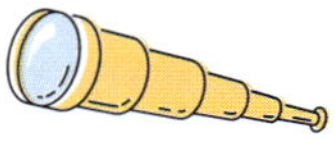

ADVENTURE

Fourth, a new world inspired dreams of adventure. Because little was known of these new lands, they were attractive. But the reality of hardships often ruined the excitement. Many settlers found plenty of adventure whether they wanted it or not.

ENGLISH DOMINATION

Fifth, England wanted to stop the advance of Spain and Catholicism. The king, as head of the Church of England, hoped that converting the Indians would prevent them from making alliances with Spain.

NATIONAL WEALTH

Sixth, establishing permanent colonies would provide raw materials and create new markets for England's goods. With this trade, England hoped to compete with Spain's great wealth.

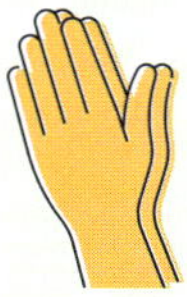

RELIGIOUS FREEDOM

Seventh, the reason for settlement that distinguished the English colonies from other European colonies was the desire for religious freedom. English monarchs established the Church of England, or the Anglican Church, as the official church. Everyone in England was required to attend and to pay the taxes supporting it. No other churches were allowed. Some Englishmen were dissatisfied because they did not agree with certain doctrines or practices, and a few were severely punished for their beliefs. Many believed that settlements in the Americas would be havens where they could escape persecution and worship God freely.

The Lost Colony

Although he did not journey to the New World himself, **Sir Walter Raleigh**, an English nobleman and another favorite of the queen, organized two colonizing expeditions to **Roanoke** Island. The first attempt, made in 1585, failed because of famine, Indian attacks, and poor leadership. After one year, the settlers returned home.

In 1587 Raleigh tried again. A man named John White was placed in charge of the new group. Shortly after the settlers landed, White returned to England for supplies. His return to America was delayed for three years because of conflicts and fighting with Spain. When he finally returned, the colony had disappeared. White's daughter and baby granddaughter were among the missing colonists. The baby, Virginia Dare, was the first English baby born in the New World. The only clue to the colony's disappearance was the word *Croatoan* carved in a tree. Some thought that the nearby Croatoan Indians had taken the people captive, but to this day no one knows what happened to the "Lost Colony" of Roanoke Island. While originally part of the territory of Virginia (named after the unmarried queen, Elizabeth I), today Roanoke Island is part of the Outer Banks of North Carolina.

Jamestown

The English finally established their first permanent colony in May 1607, when three small ships containing over one hundred men and boys sailed into present-day Chesapeake Bay, Virginia. These colonists had been sent by the Virginia Company, a group of London merchants. Seeking gold and silver and adventure, they sailed up the James River and selected a site near the coast to build a settlement. They named it **Jamestown** in honor of the new English ruler, James I, who had taken the throne when Queen Elizabeth died in 1603.

The **Powhatan Indians**, a group of Woodland Indians, inhabited the part of Virginia where the English had decided to settle. The Powhatan tribes lived in villages along rivers where they fished, hunted, and farmed. They owed allegiance to a chief, also called Powhatan. They brought food or trinkets in exchange for the chief's provision of protection for the tribes. Almost from the start, he viewed the often violent English colonists with suspicion.

Many of the English settlers were noblemen, or gentlemen, who considered themselves too good to work. They preferred to spend their time searching for gold. Those who labored to plant crops grew

▾ Reconstruction of Jamestown

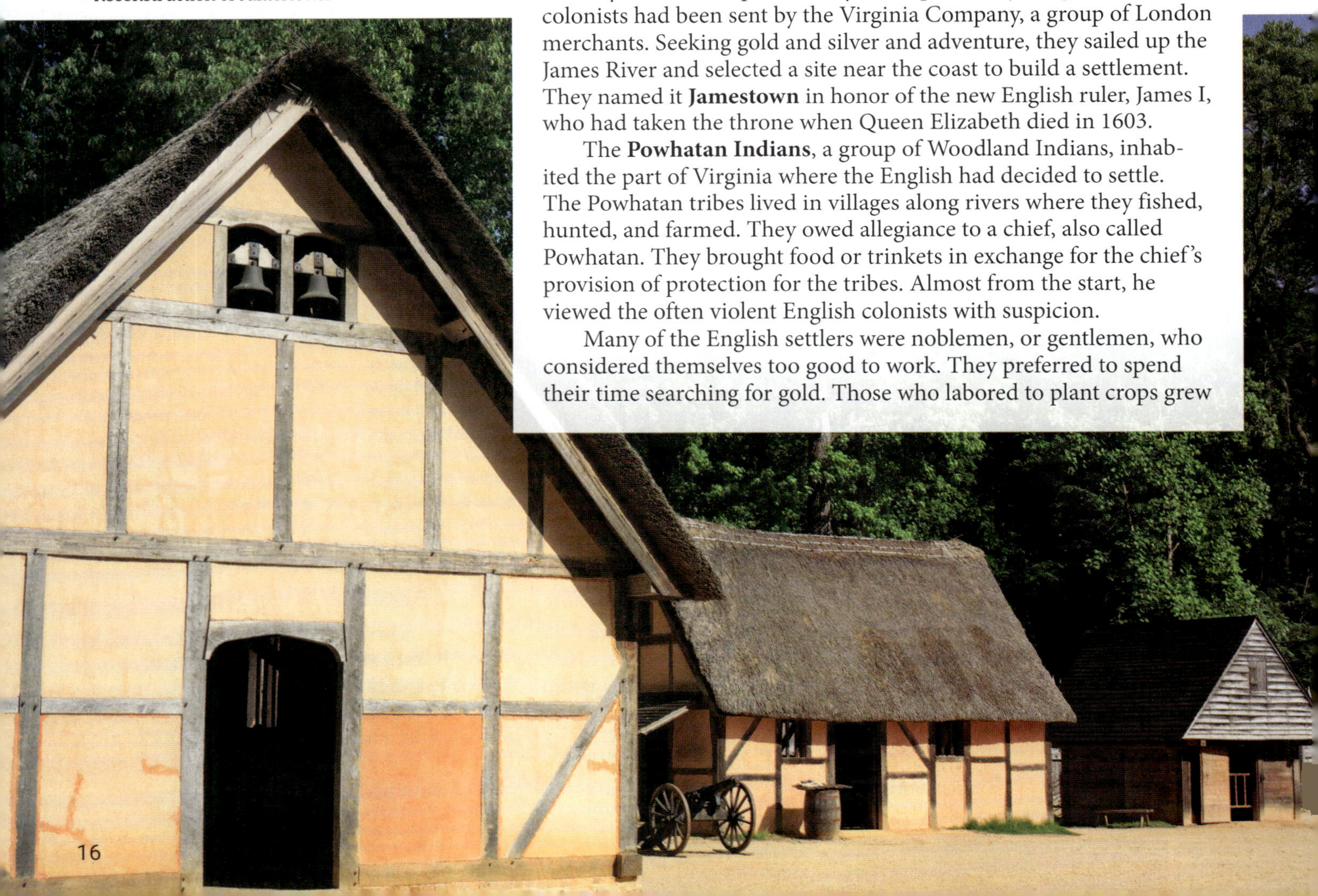

discouraged when their entire harvest was placed into a common storehouse for everyone. As a result, these men stopped working, and soon there was a shortage of food. Disease also took its toll. The drinking water was impure, and malaria-carrying mosquitoes bred in the swampy areas that surrounded Jamestown.

One man who helped Jamestown survive was **John Smith**, a rough soldier who demanded obedience. He declared that any man who did not work would not eat. He set the example, and soon everyone was busy planting, hunting, or building. Smith also initiated a relationship with the Indians, gaining food and advice. When Smith was injured in a gunpowder explosion and had to return to England, problems mounted again. There were Indian attacks, fires, and disease. But most devastating was a terrible famine that plagued the settlement during the winter of 1609–10. This period was called the "starving time" because so many died. The colonists ate anything they could find—horses, dogs, snakes, and mice; the most desperate even practiced cannibalism on those already dead. Of the 220–250 who lived in Jamestown at the beginning of the winter, only 60 were alive by the end.

In the spring of 1610, ships arrived from England with more men and supplies along with the new governor, Lord De La Warr. He encouraged many to stay in Jamestown rather than return to England. Soon the settlers learned to plant crops that could support the colony. Tobacco became a profitable cash crop. The first two women had come to the colony in 1608, and others came eleven years later. The colony grew as settlers married and began to raise families.

In 1619, the Virginia Company allowed the colonists to create the Virginia **House of Burgesses**, the first representative assembly in America. Burgesses (representatives of the people) gathered to pass laws for the good of the colony. In this way, Jamestown played a role in the beginning of the American republic.

▲ John Smith

Pocahontas

Pocahontas, the daughter of the Powhatan chief, was probably quite young when the English first arrived in Virginia. According to John Smith, Pocahontas saved his life when the Indians wanted to kill him. Although his story might not be entirely true, Pocahontas did help the colonists through difficult months, providing food and furs for trade.

In 1613, the English kidnapped Pocahontas and held her for ransom. The colonists hoped that Powhatan would swap several captive Englishmen for her. While in captivity, Pocahontas learned English, converted to Christianity, and changed her name to Rebecca. After she married tobacco planter John Rolfe in 1614, the English and the Indians enjoyed a period of peace.

In 1616 the Rolfes traveled to England. Rebecca was celebrated by the English and even met King James I. But she died of a sudden illness shortly before her return to Virginia and was buried in Gravesend, England.

SECTION REVIEW 1.3

1. Which explorer claimed the Atlantic coast of America for England?
2. How did the English and the Spanish differ in their opinions about the Sea Dogs?
3. What pirate circumnavigated the globe and became a knight?
4. What effect did the defeat of the Spanish Armada have on exploration?
5. What Englishman sponsored two colonizing attempts to the Lost Colony?
6. On what island was the Lost Colony located?
7. Answer the following questions about Jamestown:
   a. What group of Indians lived in the area?
   b. What man declared that any who would not work would not eat?
   c. What was the winter of 1609–10 called? Why?
   d. What Indian girl married a colonist and traveled to England?
8. What was the significance of the Virginia House of Burgesses?

GUIDING QUESTIONS

- How did Mansa Musa heighten trade in Western Africa?
- How did technology from the Middle East and China advance the Age of Exploration?
- How did Africans first come to the Americas?

Did you know?

The phrase "worth its weight in gold" was a reality in the western African empires, where a pound of gold would be traded for a pound of salt. Gold was so plentiful and salt so desired that their values often became equal. The word *salary* comes from *salt*.

1.4 EARLY AFRICAN TRADE

How did technology and trade lead to the arrival of Africans in the Americas?

Empires in Western Africa

Sailing to new lands greatly expanded with the inventions and technology of the Age of Exploration. The Portuguese pioneered this exploration by sailing down and eventually around the coast of Africa to India and beyond. These sailors found places with desirable items and established trade routes. As in South and Central America, certain people groups founded impressive civilizations with their God-given abilities. A few empires in western Africa had been trading items such as gold, salt, slaves, and ivory for centuries and had become immensely wealthy.

Ghana

The empire of Ghana (hundreds of miles north of the present-day country of Ghana in present-day Mali, Mauritania, and Senegal) possessed so much gold that even the animals were dressed with it. Building a trading post on the edge of the Sahara, the empire became immensely rich by taxing imports and exports (items coming into and going out of the empire). In addition to gold, Ghana built a thriving trade selling copper, salt, and slaves. The peak of its power occurred about AD 1000. Eventually, gold was found elsewhere, and the competition caused the empire of Ghana to decline. It was soon absorbed into the rising empire of Mali.

Mali

Most of the history of sub-Saharan Africa has been passed down orally rather than in written form. But the fame and wealth of Mansa Musa, considered the wealthiest man to ever live, was recorded by

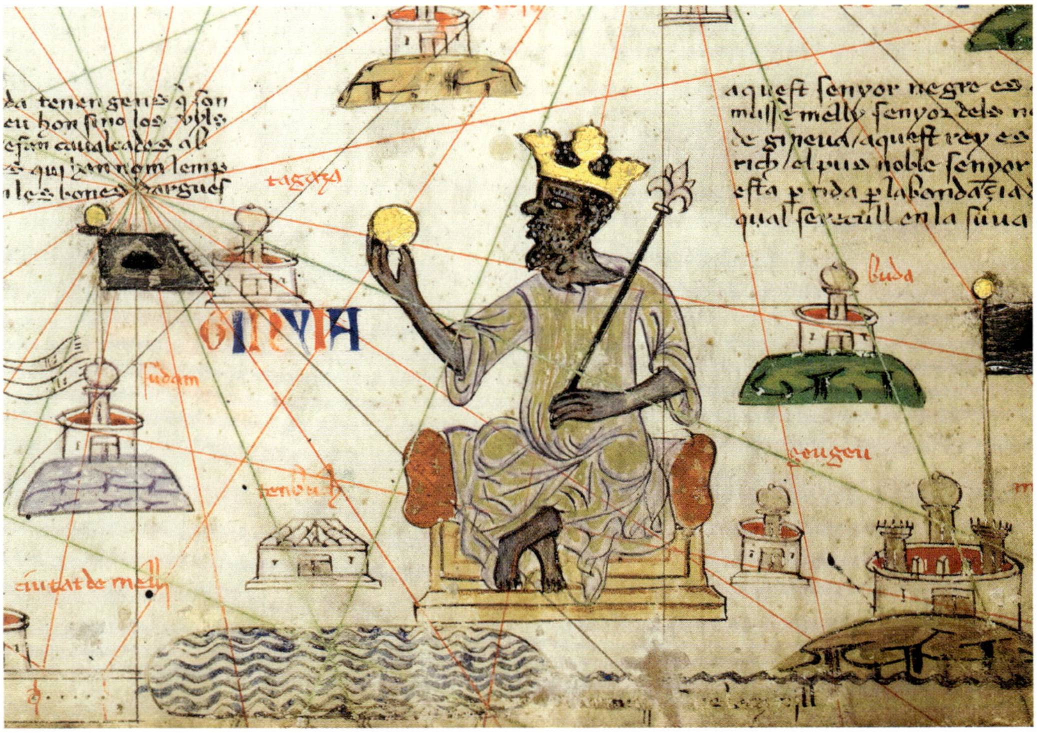

Map with Mansa Musa holding a gold coin

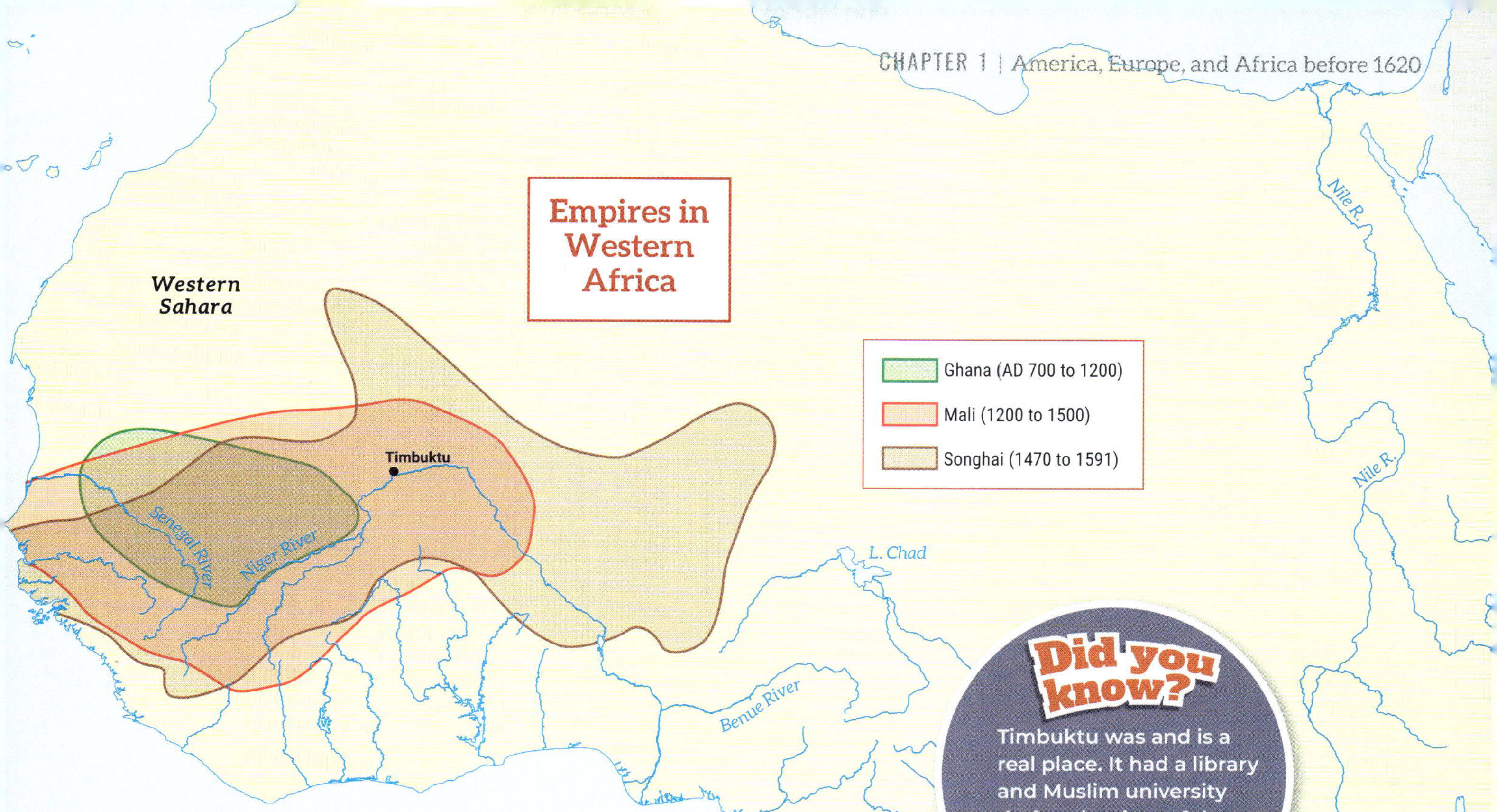

Did you know?

Timbuktu was and is a real place. It had a library and Muslim university during the time of the great western African empires.

multiple civilizations. He took a pilgrimage to Mecca in the early 1300s and spent vast amounts of money on his way, expending so much gold that he caused economic havoc in the areas he visited, particularly Egypt. With Mali's takeover of the two major trading cities of Timbuktu and Gao, Mali became larger than the empire of Ghana had been. Leaders of these western African lands converted to Islam, but the common people mostly continued their belief in animism, resulting in a mixed version of the Muslim religion.

Songhai

During the Age of Exploration in the 1400s and 1500s, the rulers of Gao (the Songhai) made their city independent and then expanded to take Mali's place. Songhai conquered the city of Timbuktu, which continued to grow and gain importance. Like Ghana and Mali earlier, Songhai became rich and large. In the late 1500s, Morocco, with its new Portuguese weapons, was able to overcome Songhai's well-trained javelin-throwing army.

The Portuguese found a thriving trade market in the Songhai Empire and eagerly joined in. They swapped their horses and weaponry for African goods and slaves. Slaves had long been used in Africa as gold and salt miners, soldiers, and even advisors. With the coming of the Europeans, the transAtlantic slave trade exploded and new slaves were captured by Africans to meet the demand. Pirates from the Barbary coast of northern Africa became involved in the new trade during the 1600s–1800s, kidnapping and selling not only other Africans, but anyone they could capture, including European sailors and coastal villagers.

▲ Astrolabe

▼ Chinese star chart

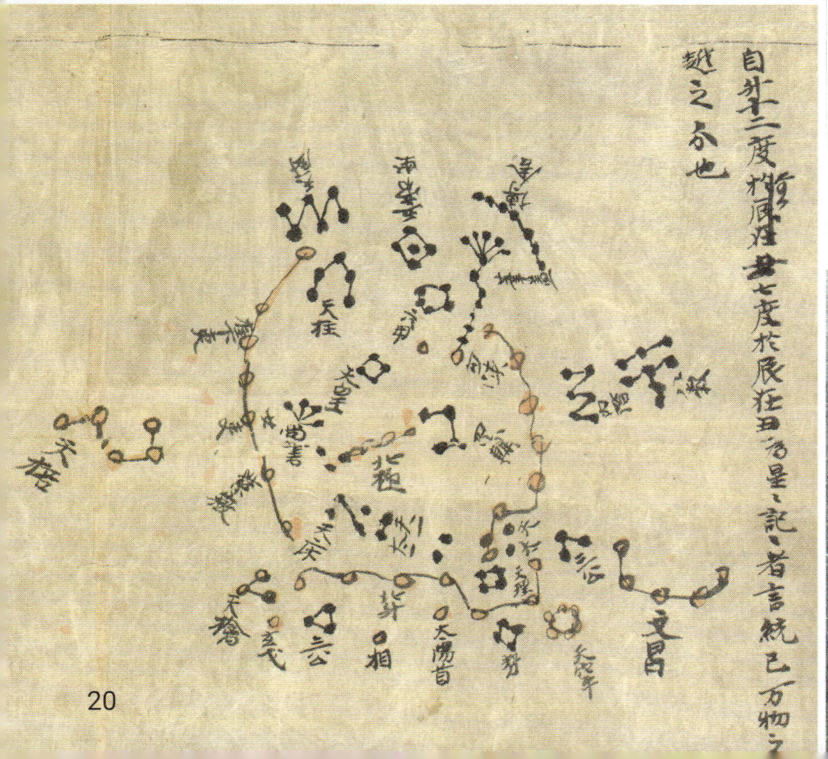

Advances in Technology

How did the age of exploration propel the meeting of multiple cultures in the first place? Without the travels of explorers, other lands would not have been discovered. Neither Europeans nor Africans would have landed so far from home. Inventions and innovations came from around the world, with the golden ages of two cultures leading the way.

Middle Eastern Contributions

Using their knowledge of the stars as well as their advanced mathematics, Middle Eastern Arabs designed and improved tools for exploration. One such improved tool was the astrolabe; it was able to tell direction and time by lining up horizons and star coordinates. This also made it possible to tell direction. It became invaluable to explorers seeking distant lands. Eventually, the astrolabe gave way to the sextant, also created by the Arabs. These tools were the cutting-edge technology of the day and continued to provide evidence that the world was round.

Chinese Contributions

China also developed many mathematical and scientific ideas. Its people used magnetic and, eventually, floating compasses. Their careful record of the stars resulted in the creation of accurate star charts, maps that could be used on clear nights. When these combined with knowledge from Islamic advisors and administrative assistants, China entered an age of sea exploration. The height of this age came with the voyages of Zheng He during the Ming dynasty. Sailing ever farther in his seven long journeys, Zheng He "discovered" India, Arabia, and much of the east coast of Africa, bringing back exotic animals such as giraffes as gifts for the emperor.

Each new technological advance helped aid exploration. Exploration enabled trade; and, unfortunately, trade enabled the expansion of slavery.

Africans in America

In 1619, the same year that the first large group of women arrived in Jamestown, a Dutch ship carrying about twenty Africans also landed in Virginia. These Africans appear to have been treated as indentured servants. This term, which will be discussed more fully in Chapter 4, refers to individuals who agreed to work for someone for a few years in exchange for being transported across the Atlantic Ocean. Afterward, the servant obtained his freedom. However, soon almost all Africans brought to America were brought as slaves, not as indentured servants. Slaves typically made the journey in chains under horrible conditions in what was called the "**Middle Passage**." The average slave cost about five times more than the money spent to bring an indentured servant to America, but the slave spent his life working for a master. If slaves had children, the children, too, became the "property" of their master. Although early English colonists wanted freedom for themselves, they did not always extend this freedom and equality to others.

The European and American demand for cheap labor created a market for slaves from West Africa. Most slaves came from the nations on Africa's western coast. They were typically captured in tribal raids and sold to traders for profit. This was particularly true during the time of the empire of Songhai and led to enormous profits for the slave traders who lived and worked there.

▾ Esteban

Esteban

In the early 1500s, a century before the arrival of Africans in Jamestown, another African roamed the South. Esteban was the Moroccan slave of a Spanish nobleman-turned-explorer who came from Spain to join a group of explorers in Cuba and Florida. Chased by Native Americans and forced to flee along the Gulf Coast, the group built crude escape boats that capsized near Galveston, Texas. Here the eighty survivors of the shipwreck were held in captivity by the natives, dying off until only four remained. These four escaped and wandered the Southwest. Esteban learned native languages easily and was able to adapt to the cultures of the native groups they encountered. After years of wandering, the group discovered other Spanish explorers who pointed them toward present-day Mexico City, one thousand miles away, which they successfully found.

After hearing of their exploits and of tales about the fabled cities of Cíbola, the governor of Mexico City asked the group to explore once more. The three Spaniards declined, but Esteban was sold to the governor, who sent him back to explore with a Catholic friar. Esteban usually journeyed ahead of the nervous friar and would leave or send wooden crosses of varying sizes to give an indication of the wealth he had found. At one point, he sent a cross the size of a man. But as the friar traveled closer, native guides informed him that Esteban had been killed. The friar did not dare continue and returned to Mexico City.

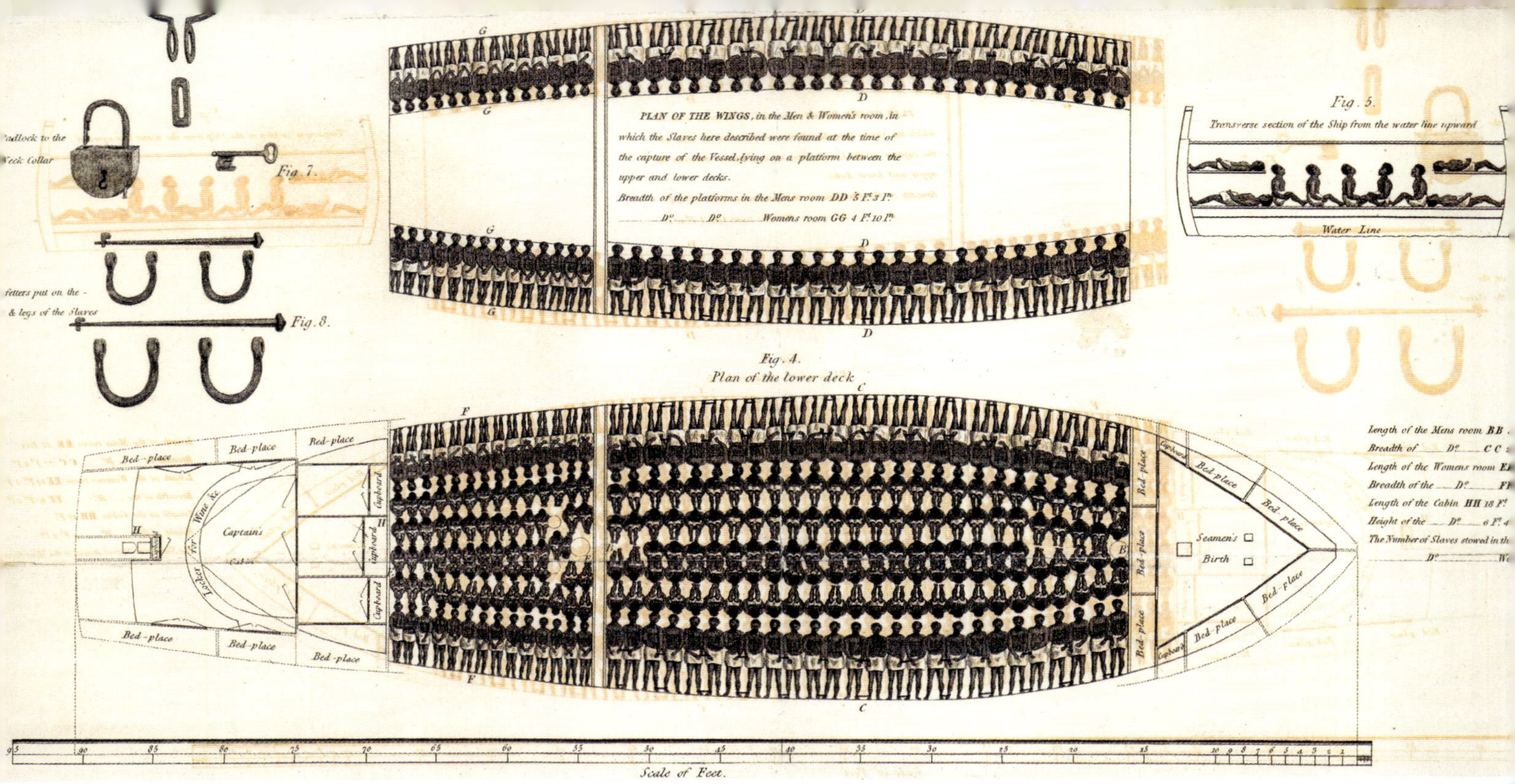

▲ Diagram of a slave ship

the MIDDLE PASSAGE

A horrific experience for slaves was crossing the Atlantic to the Americas. This crossing was called the "Middle Passage." (The first passage took the slave to the coast of Africa; the third passage involved the final sale to slave owners in the Americas.) Once aboard the slave ships, the Africans were trapped there for five weeks to four months. Since the slave traders wanted to make as much money as possible, they tried to place as many slaves on the ships as they could. The slaves were stacked on top of one another or chained side by side with no room to move. Since they were so close together, they had to lie in human waste and had little pure air to breathe. Disease spread quickly in this terrible environment, and many died. Some slaves who were ill or went insane were thrown overboard. Some killed themselves.

When the weather was good, the slaves were brought on deck for fresh air and exercise. If the weather was bad, the slaves were chained below. Typically twice a day the slaves were fed rice, cornmeal, or yams. They received about half a pint of water a day.

There were very few revolts aboard slave ships. The crews were armed, and any rebellion brought severe punishment. But some slaves rebelled in other ways. Some refused to eat so that they would die and thus damage the ship's "cargo."

When the slave ships arrived in the Americas, some slaves were turned away or forced to wait for fear that they carried disease. Traders took their "cargo" ashore in smaller boats after feeding the slaves well and improving their appearance with oils.

SECTION REVIEW 1.4

1. How did Mansa Musa's wealth affect other civilizations?
2. What items of trade did the West African empires produce?
3. What explorer's tool did the Arabs perfect?
4. How did the Chinese help extend navigation on the seas?
5. How did Middle Eastern and Chinese technologies contribute to the rise of exploration and the resulting trade which included slaves?
6. Who is considered the first African in America?
7. Why were Africans brought to the Americas?
8. How did the Middle Passage show the lack of humanity offered to the Africans as image-bearing humans?

CHAPTER 1 REVIEW

Making Connections

1. What four people groups created large civilizations in Central and South America before the arrival of Columbus?
2. What were the seven main Indian regions in North America?
3. For what were early explorers searching?
4. Create a chart with three columns labeled *Spanish*, *French*, and *English*. From the Terms to Remember below, place each explorer (except Ericson, Vespucci, and Smith) in the proper column.
5. Give two reasons why Spain was angry with England during the age of exploration.
6. What were seven motivations for English exploration? Which one made England different from other countries?
7. In what chronological order did the three large trading empires of West Africa exist?
8. The demand for cheap labor in the Americas created a market with West African civilizations for what item of trade?

Thinking Critically

9. How do ancient native civilizations show that all people reflect God's image? How did they fulfill the Creation Mandate?
10. How were English settlers different from those that came from France and Spain?
11. How might America have been different if England had not established a strong presence in America?

Living as a Christian Citizen

12. What are some acceptable, biblical ways to spread Christianity? How do these methods differ from those used by Europeans who came to the Americas?
13. How should Christians respond when they see a part of their culture that violates biblical principles?

Aztec knife with carved wooden handle, used for human sacrifice

Terms to Remember

nomadic
conquistadors
totem poles
animism
Leif Ericson
Christopher Columbus
Amerigo Vespucci
Francisco Coronado
Hernando de Soto
St. Augustine
Juan Ponce de León
Jacques Cartier
Robert de La Salle
Samuel de Champlain
John Cabot
Sea Dogs
Sir Francis Drake
Sir Walter Raleigh
Roanoke
Jamestown
Powhatan Indians
John Smith
Pocahontas
House of Burgesses
Middle Passage

CHAPTER 2

Settling the Thirteen Colonies

2.1 DIFFICULTIES OF COLONIZATION

2.2 THE NEW ENGLAND COLONIES

2.3 THE MIDDLE COLONIES

2.4 THE SOUTHERN COLONIES

Leaving home is difficult. The Englishmen who decided to leave their country must have felt a great fear of the unknown. They left behind family, friends, and familiar surroundings. They were entering a new land and meeting its native people. Yet these settlers proceeded with boldness. They transferred England's traditions, laws, and language to the colonies and built a new civilization that eventually became the United States of America.

GUIDING QUESTIONS

- What were the different types of colonies and how were they funded?
- What physical hardships did the colonists face?

2.1 DIFFICULTIES OF COLONIZATION

What were the difficulties of colonization?

Both the Spanish and the French dictated who could go to their colonies in America. The Spanish mainly sent noblemen, soldiers, slaves, and priests. The French permitted only Catholics into New France (Canada). In contrast, England allowed almost anyone to go to its North American colonies. This policy opened the region to most Englishmen, who had various reasons for starting a life in that new land.

Moving to an American colony in the 1600s and early 1700s was not easy. The men and women who decided to do so faced many challenges. They first had to find a way to pay for their voyage. They also had to survive the long and uncomfortable trip across the Atlantic. Although promoters billed America as a paradise on earth, settlers drawn by such promises soon found that the new land held many hardships. Once the settlers arrived, they faced a host of new problems, including hunger, sickness, and a lack of organized government.

Financial Support and Colonial Organization

Founding a new colony was expensive. It was not easy to raise the money needed for ships and supplies. Some men, like Sir Walter Raleigh who had organized the colonizing expeditions to Roanoke Island in the 1580s, risked their fortunes to settle colonies. Many earned little or no profit for their efforts. Such prospects made the wealthy reluctant to sponsor colonization.

To pay for colonies, English investors sometimes formed **joint-stock companies**. Jamestown was one colony funded by such a company. These businesses were the forerunners of our modern corporations. Groups of Englishmen pooled their money to form a company. They allowed others to invest by buying "shares of stock" at a certain price. Then the businessmen invested the shareholders' money in a colony, hoping that the colony would prosper and make a profit. This investing not only helped provide for the initial cost of the colony but also furnished money to maintain the settlement for a while. If the venture failed, each investor lost only the amount he had contributed. If the venture became profitable, the profits were split among the investors according to the number of shares each held.

The king gave each joint-stock company a charter for establishing its colonies. Each charter contained rules governing where a colony would be located and how it would be administered. A charter was the official permission for founding a colony. Colonies founded under these conditions were called **charter colonies**.

◂ The Pilgrims boarding the *Mayflower*

▾ Seal of the Virginia Company showing King James I

the VIRGINIA COMPANY

One of the best-known joint-stock companies was the Virginia Company. It was formed by a group of Englishmen who wanted to get raw materials, such as metals, minerals, dyes, and medicines, from America. One part of this company known as the London group financed Jamestown, the first permanent English settlement in North America.

▲ A charter for one of the earlier colonies, the Massachusetts Bay Colony

There were two other kinds of colonies. **Proprietary colonies** were those that the king gave to individuals or groups. The men who received these colonies from the king were called proprietors, and they could govern their colonies as they pleased. In other colonies called **royal colonies**, the king took direct control.

Physical Hardships

If a colonist survived the hazardous voyage to America, he faced more dangers in the new land. Food and shelter were the immediate needs. Colonists who lacked these often did not survive the long, cold winter months. For example, in Jamestown more than a third of the original colonists died from disease, hunger, or cold in the colony's first nine months. (As noted in Chapter 1, several years later during the "starving time," an even larger percentage of colonists died.) Such suffering was common in the early years of settlements.

Relations between the colonists and the Indians posed another problem. Although some Indians were friendly, it is understandable that many began opposing the settlers when the Europeans began taking their land. In 1622 an Indian attack killed more than three hundred settlers around Jamestown. By 1700 conflicts between Indians and settlers posed less of a threat in the more populated colonies; however, in the South and along the western frontier, clashes continued.

As a result of these challenges, the colonists learned to support themselves in a new land. They formed their own culture and strengthened their abilities, gradually developing into Americans.

Did you know?

Royal colonies were often called crown colonies.

SECTION REVIEW 2.1

1. How were the English colonies funded?
2. How did joint-stock companies make it easier to invest in exploration?
3. Describe the three types of English colonies in America.
4. What physical hardships did the early settlers encounter?

2.2 THE NEW ENGLAND COLONIES

How did religion affect the founding of the various New England colonies?

GUIDING QUESTIONS

- How were the Separatists and Puritans different?
- What circumstances surrounded the founding of the Plymouth Colony?
- How did the Plymouth Colony govern itself?
- How was the Massachusetts Bay Colony structured?
- Why were the colonies of Rhode Island, Connecticut, and New Hampshire created?

Massachusetts

Most settlers who arrived in New England were searching for religious freedom. Many English Christians were unhappy with the Church of England, or the **Anglican Church**. They believed the church did not worship according to the Bible. One group, called **Separatists**, chose to separate themselves completely from the church and hold their own worship services.

A second group became known as **Puritans**. These Christians hoped to purify the Anglican Church of various Roman Catholic practices and ceremonies. Many Puritans believed that a church congregation should govern itself. They also stressed the authority of Christ and the Scriptures over that of the church and its traditions.

Plymouth

Because it was illegal in England to worship apart from the Anglican Church, a group of Separatists in Scrooby, England, believed that they would be safer in another country. In 1607 they began moving to the Netherlands (also called Holland), where they could worship freely. After a few years, however, the congregation began to worry about new outside influences. Parents became concerned that their children would speak Dutch (the language of the Netherlands) and embrace the lower moral standards that were common in the area. They also worried about new religious groups developing around them.

These Separatists, who are known today as the **Pilgrims**, decided to go to the New World. There they could live as Englishmen but still have freedom to worship according to the Bible. They could also be used by God to spread the gospel to other parts of the world. Too poor to finance a voyage to America themselves, the Pilgrims arranged for financial support from a group of English businessmen. These investors would receive any profits the colony made in its first seven years. The Pilgrims received permission from the Virginia Company to settle in Virginia, just north of Jamestown.

In September 1620, the Pilgrims set sail from Plymouth, England, in a ship named the *Mayflower*. Also on the ship were other Englishmen who wanted to share in founding the new colony. Since these unfamiliar people were not part of their group, the Pilgrims called them Strangers. The two groups learned to get along because each had skills that the colony needed for survival.

After more than two stormy months at sea, the *Mayflower* arrived in America in early November. The storms had driven the ship off course, so its passengers were far north of their destination. Instead of being just north of Jamestown, they were off Cape Cod in what is today Massachusetts. The Pilgrim leaders were troubled; they had no authority to settle that far north. But with winter coming on and sickness beginning to spread throughout the passengers, there was no time to sail farther south.

▾ Plymouth Rock marks the spot where the *Mayflower* is said to have landed.

To maintain the peace in the new colony, the men wrote and signed an agreement known as the **Mayflower Compact**. This document established the first self-government in the New World. They elected one of their leaders, John Carver, to be their governor.

PRIMARY SOURCE: THE MAYFLOWER COMPACT

In the name of God, Amen. We, whose names are underwritten, the loyal subjects of our dread sovereign lord King James, by the grace of God, of Great Britain, France, and Ireland, king, defender of the Faith, &c. Having undertaken for the glory of God, and advancement of the Christian faith, and honour of our king and country, a voyage to plant the first colony in the northern parts of Virginia; do by these presents, solemnly and mutually, in the presence of God and one another, covenant and combine ourselves together into a civil body politick, for our better ordering and preservation, and furtherance of the ends aforesaid: And by virtue hereof do enact, constitute, and frame, such just and equal laws, ordinances, acts, constitutions, and officers, from time to time, as shall be thought most meet and convenient for the general good of the colony; unto which we promise all due submission and obedience. In witness whereof we have hereunto subscribed our names at Cape-Cod the eleventh of November, in the reign of our sovereign lord King James, of England, France, and Ireland, the eighteenth, and of Scotland, the fifty-fourth, Anno Domini; 1620.

▲ Signing the Mayflower Compact

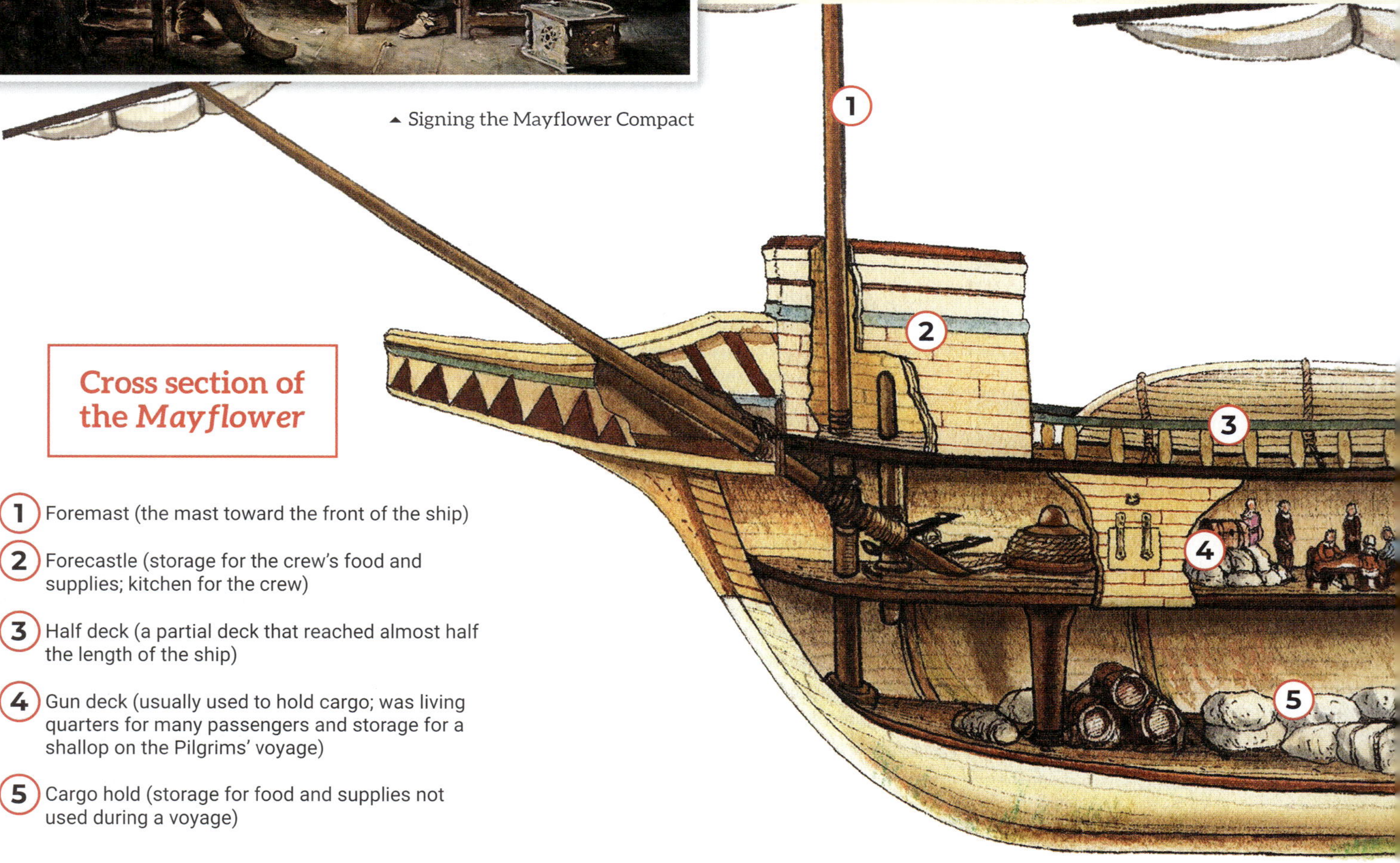

Cross section of the *Mayflower*

1. Foremast (the mast toward the front of the ship)
2. Forecastle (storage for the crew's food and supplies; kitchen for the crew)
3. Half deck (a partial deck that reached almost half the length of the ship)
4. Gun deck (usually used to hold cargo; was living quarters for many passengers and storage for a shallop on the Pilgrims' voyage)
5. Cargo hold (storage for food and supplies not used during a voyage)

After exploring parties investigated the surroundings, the Pilgrims selected a location and began to build their colony in December. They named it **Plymouth** after the port in England from which they had sailed. Like the settlers at Jamestown, the Plymouth settlers had a difficult first winter. Since they landed at Plymouth so late in the year, they had no time to plant crops. Weak, sick, and hungry, nearly half the colonists, including Governor Carver, died during the first winter.

When spring arrived matters began to improve. An Indian named Samoset arrived in the village and greeted the settlers in English. He had learned the language from coastal fishermen. Samoset told the settlers of another Indian named **Squanto**, who spoke even better English. Samoset also informed them that his chief, Massasoit, wished to meet with them. Massasoit concluded a peace agreement with the settlers and left Squanto with them. Squanto showed the settlers how to plant corn and squash. He also helped them develop trade with the neighboring Indians. To prepare for times when the Indians might not be so friendly, Miles Standish, one of the Strangers, trained the men to defend their colony.

▲ Squanto teaching Pilgrims how to grow corn

6 Mainmast (the principal mast that held the mainsail)

7 Upper deck (during calm weather, a place for passengers to find fresh air)

8 Steerage (storage for the whipstaff and tiller, which were both used for steering the ship)

9 Mizzenmast (the mast behind the mainmast)

10 Gunroom (storage for powder and shot for the ship's guns)

11 Cabins (living quarters for the rest of the ship's crew; may have housed up to thirty-six passengers on the Pilgrims' voyage)

12 Poop deck (living quarters for the ship's captain and high-ranking crew)

a time of THANKSGIVING

If you traveled back in time and joined the Pilgrims for their Thanksgiving feast, you probably would be surprised by the meal. In 1621, the Pilgrims did not prepare any ham, potatoes, or pumpkin pie. You might have seen a roasted turkey, but it would be only one of many meats prepared.

When the Indians arrived, they brought five deer to be eaten. The Pilgrims might also have eaten duck, goose, cod, bass, lobster, and eel. Instead of potatoes and corn, they probably had peas, beans, and carrots. The Pilgrims likely also ate nuts (such as walnuts or acorns) and plums. But without sugar, there were few dessert choices.

William Bradford became governor of Plymouth in 1621. His wise and godly leadership helped guide the Pilgrims through many difficulties in the early months as well as in the following years. Despite their hardships, they had much for which to be thankful at the end of their first year in Plymouth. Although many had died, those who survived had managed to ally with the Indians and provide themselves with food. After the harvesting of crops was completed, sometime between late September and mid-November 1621, the colonists observed a time of celebration and thanksgiving. Though the details about this event are few, we know that the Indians participated in the feasting and games that continued for three days.

By the mid-1620s the Plymouth Colony was doing well. The settlers' labor in farming and trade supplied their needs. Though they had faced numerous obstacles, they fared better than the early Jamestown settlers. Why? One reason was that the Pilgrims embraced hard work. Unlike some of the noblemen in Jamestown, no Plymouth settlers refused to work. Another reason was that entire families came aboard the *Mayflower*. Jamestown, on the other hand, had mostly men for its first twelve years. The presence of families in Plymouth forced the colonists to make the area livable for women and children. This situation civilized the colony more quickly. Adults toiled to provide not only for themselves but also for their children.

However, the most important reason for Plymouth's success was the Pilgrims' motivation. They came to the New World for the freedom to worship God according to His Word. They had devoted their lives to God, and they lived to be His servants. They wanted the new land to be their home, where they could serve and worship God. Many at Jamestown were not similarly dedicated and let their selfish desires hinder the colony's welfare.

Plymouth was never a large or rich colony. Neither was it a perfect colony. For example, it had several violent encounters with the Indians. After seventy years, Plymouth was absorbed by its larger neighbor, the Massachusetts Bay Colony. As a result, Plymouth did not become one of the individual colonies that formed the United States. However, the Pilgrims remain an important part of America's heritage because of the example they set. They sought religious freedom; they established a responsible self-government system; and they worked diligently, persevering through difficult times.

Massachusetts Bay

Puritan attempts to reform the Church of England from within met with little success. They soon tired of persecution and government corruption. Though most Puritans remained in England, several of their leaders decided to begin an experiment in America. They formed the **Massachusetts Bay Company** to establish a colony there. After receiving a charter from the king, the leaders of the Massachusetts Bay Company began recruiting settlers. The colonists chose **John Winthrop** as their first governor.

In June 1630 four ships carrying nearly five hundred settlers arrived in Massachusetts Bay. These settlers joined an earlier group that had built the town of Salem. Salem, founded for commercial purposes, was struggling when the Puritans arrived. Fortunately learning from others' mistakes, Winthrop had planned well and brought many supplies from England. As soon as a town filled the land allotted to it, the settlers formed another town. Soon, new towns and villages, such as Boston, Newtowne (later called Cambridge), Watertown, and Dorchester, were thriving. The Massachusetts Bay Colony grew rapidly during the 1630s as more than fifteen thousand new colonists arrived. As a result, this period in the colony's history was called the Great Migration.

For the most part, the Puritans who came to America were wealthier and better educated than the Pilgrims. Among the Puritans were merchants, craftsmen, doctors, and preachers. Because the Puritans believed that the Bible is the Word of God and stressed that God speaks to people through it, they valued education as a means of learning to read and obey Scripture. The Massachusetts Bay Colony had more college-educated settlers than any other colony. Yet most of the colonists were farmers who constantly struggled to provide for themselves and their families.

▾ John Winthrop

the PURITAN VISION

Like the Pilgrims, the Puritans came to America seeking religious freedom, and they wanted to make a good home for themselves and their children. To them, religious freedom included establishing an ideal community based on biblical principles. Before reaching America, Governor John Winthrop addressed the Puritans, and one of his points referenced Jesus' Sermon on the Mount in which Christ said that believers are the salt of the earth and the light of the world. Winthrop said that Massachusetts would be "a city upon a hill." In other words, the colony would be exposed for all to see and a model for other governments. Winthrop reminded his fellow Puritans to provide an example of godly behavior.

Puritans saw a clear connection between a nation's prosperity and its obedience to God. Winthrop believed that if the Puritans obeyed God, He would "make [them] a praise and glory" and an example to future generations. On the other hand, Winthrop thought that if they failed to keep God's commands, God would remove His hand of blessing.

Puritans recognized the importance of having government leaders who were Christians. They even said that the voters who elected the leaders should also be Christians. This meant only members of the church could legally vote.

Though the Puritans wanted a Christian government, they also practiced some separation of church and state. For example, they did not want the English monarch to meddle in religious matters, and they did not think that church courts in England should punish people with fines, as secular courts did. Furthermore, the Puritans had laws that prevented the government from interfering in church discipline. And although ministers could give advice to officials, ministers could not hold office or require officials to govern according to their advice.

The colony's charter gave the stockholders of the Massachusetts Bay Company full power to govern the colony. Thus the English government did not interfere during the colony's early years. Not everyone who settled in the Massachusetts Bay Colony was a Puritan. Eventually, Puritans were not even in the majority. Yet they established the government, built the churches, and opened the schools. Because they would be "a city upon a hill," church and state leaders worked closely together in promoting a godly society. Everyone was required to attend church—even non-Puritans. The state also imposed a strict standard of moral conduct on the community.

The colony's leaders wanted to preserve the distinctly Puritan beliefs of the colony. Because the Puritans came to America to form a society in which life and worship were governed by the Bible, they did not extend religious freedom to other religious groups, such as Quakers and Baptists, whose worship practices differed from what the Puritans considered biblical. Though at first only Puritan church members were given the right to vote, others were allowed to live in the community as long as they did not disrupt Puritan teaching or authority. By 1634 the colony was too large for all voters to participate effectively in every decision. The leaders decided that each town would elect two delegates to serve in a body known as the General Court. This representative group functioned much like the House of Burgesses in Virginia.

As the Massachusetts Bay Colony grew, some settlers left to establish new colonies. Some of them sought better farmland, where they could enjoy greater prosperity. Others wanted more religious liberty. People were not allowed to remain in Massachusetts if they disagreed with the way the colony was operated. To some it seemed strange that people who left England for religious liberty would deny that same liberty to others. But the Puritans did not think that liberty meant the freedom to do whatever one wished. They believed that true liberty was the freedom to live under the rule of Christ. They also believed that God made a covenant with Christian nations to establish churches according to Scripture. Puritans taught that those who believed differently were radicals. They feared that too much liberty would lead to false teachings and unbelief.

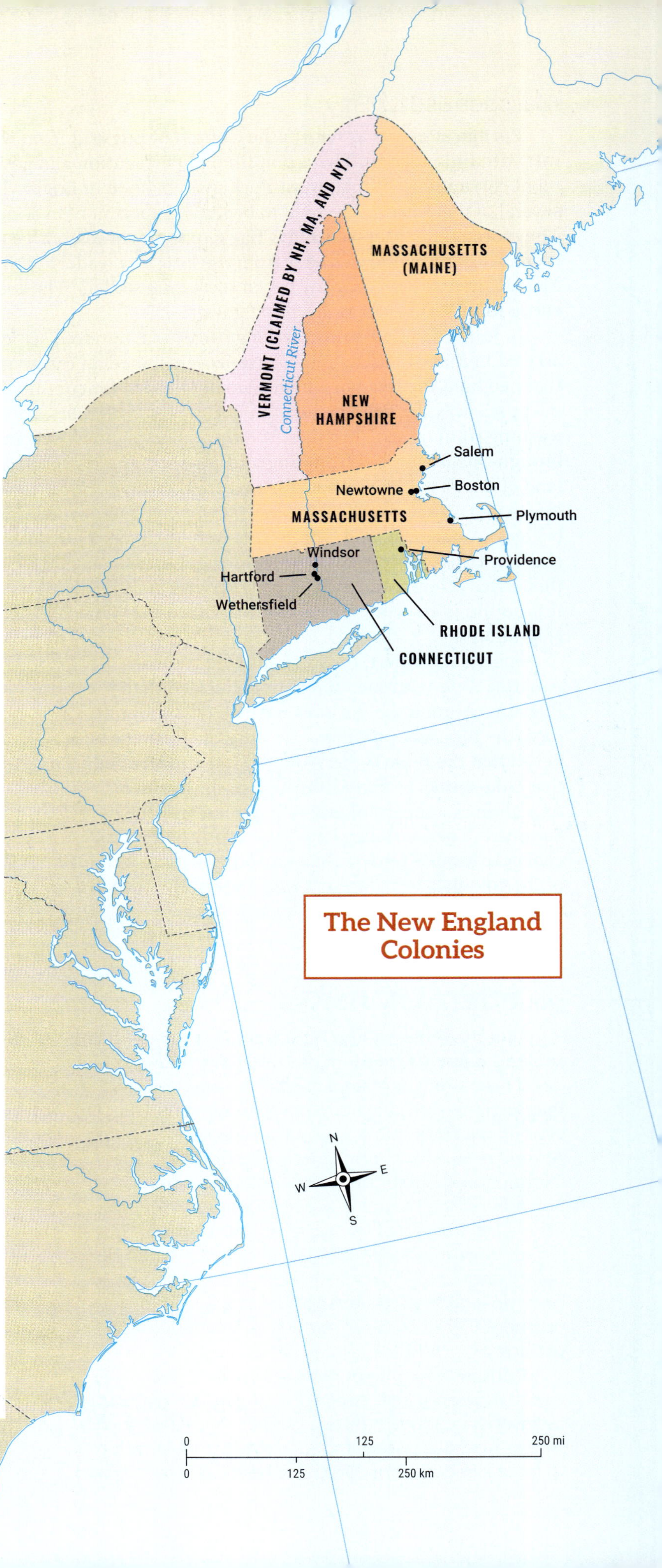

The New England Colonies

Rhode Island

▲ Roger Williams developed a friendly relationship with the Narragansett Indians, who sheltered him during his winter in exile.

Roger Williams arrived in Massachusetts in 1631. Though he had embraced Puritan ideas in England, his beliefs were soon more aligned with those of the Separatists. In America, he increasingly criticized a number of Puritan teachings, being one of the first to openly challenge the Puritan leaders. For example, he was convinced that worship could not be kept pure if unbelievers participated in any part of it; thus, he thought that unbelievers should not be permitted to listen to preaching in church and that families should not pray together if some of the children were unsaved.

Williams also disagreed with how the Puritans governed. He said that the government's only purpose was to protect people's bodies and goods from harm. He argued that rulers do not need to be Christians to do that. Though he believed government should enforce laws prohibiting theft, murder, adultery, and other immoral acts, he advocated complete separation of church and state (government). He said that people should be free to worship according to their consciences, whether they were Puritans, Quakers, or members of another religious group. Williams also stated that the king of England did not have the authority to give the colony its land; therefore, he said that the Puritans needed to buy it from the Indians.

To preserve the peace, the Puritans expelled Williams from Massachusetts but offered to let him stay through the winter if he would stop spreading his views while waiting for spring. But Williams continued to gather followers. Officials moved to arrest him and place him on a ship back to England; however, he was able to slip away and spent the winter with the Narragansett Indians.

In the spring Williams traveled south to Narragansett Bay, where he bought a tract of land from the Indians and founded a village. He named it Providence. By 1644 Parliament recognized four towns, including Providence, as the colony of Rhode Island. The colony devised a constitution (plan of government) guaranteeing that the government would have authority "only in civil [nonreligious] things." Williams's ideas gained popularity in the next hundred years, and some were eventually included in the Bill of Rights (the first ten amendments to the US Constitution).

Connecticut

Unlike the settlement of Rhode Island, the settlement of Connecticut did not arise from controversy. Settlers continued to arrive in Massachusetts Bay and soon overcrowded the colony. Several settlers decided to move to the fertile Connecticut River valley.

▲ Thomas Hooker with his group of Puritans

There they settled Windsor (1633) and Wethersfield (1635). In 1636, **Thomas Hooker,** a pastor in Newtowne, Massachusetts, received permission to move his congregation to Connecticut and there founded the town of Hartford.

In 1639 these newly settled villages merged to form the colony of Connecticut and named Hartford its capital. They adopted a plan of union called the **Fundamental Orders of Connecticut**; it was the first written constitution in America. For this reason, Connecticut's nickname is the Constitution State. According to the document, the government's authority lay in the consent of the people. For the most part, Connecticut's government copied that of Massachusetts. However, Connecticut did not make church membership a requirement for voting.

New Hampshire

Overcrowding in Massachusetts also led colonists to move north into New Hampshire and Maine. These areas were proprietary colonies for a while, but they were not very successful. As more Puritans migrated, Massachusetts extended its control over the new settlements. In 1679 several towns received their own royal charter. That charter made New Hampshire a separate colony. New Hampshire and the three other New England colonies (Massachusetts, Connecticut, and Rhode Island) later became four of the thirteen original states of the new nation.

Maine did not become a separate colony. It remained part of Massachusetts until 1820, when it became a state. Vermont, which is also located in New England, was never one of the thirteen English colonies, but in 1791 it became the fourteenth state in the new nation.

SECTION REVIEW 2.2

1. What is another name for the Church of England?
2. How did the Separatists and Puritans differ?
3. Which colony was settled by Separatists? What is another name for this group of settlers?
4. According to the Mayflower Compact, why did the Pilgrims come to America?
5. Name the two Native Americans who helped the Pilgrim settlers.
6. How did the Puritans influence the Massachusetts Bay Colony?
7. Do you agree with the Puritan handling of the conflict with Roger Williams? Why or why not?
8. Why were the following colonies founded?
    a. Rhode Island
    b. Connecticut and New Hampshire
9. Why is each of the following documents significant?
    a. The Mayflower Compact
    b. The Fundamental Orders of Connecticut

2.3 THE MIDDLE COLONIES

What were the roles of European countries and individuals in the founding of the middle colonies?

GUIDING QUESTIONS

- How were New York and New Jersey founded?
- How did the colonies of Pennsylvania and Delaware begin?

New England was settled primarily by the English, who shared a common heritage. Several of the middle colonies, however, were influenced first by other nations. The Dutch and the Swedes claimed parts of this region decades before the arrival of the first Englishmen. By the time England gained control, the middle colonies reflected a variety of cultures.

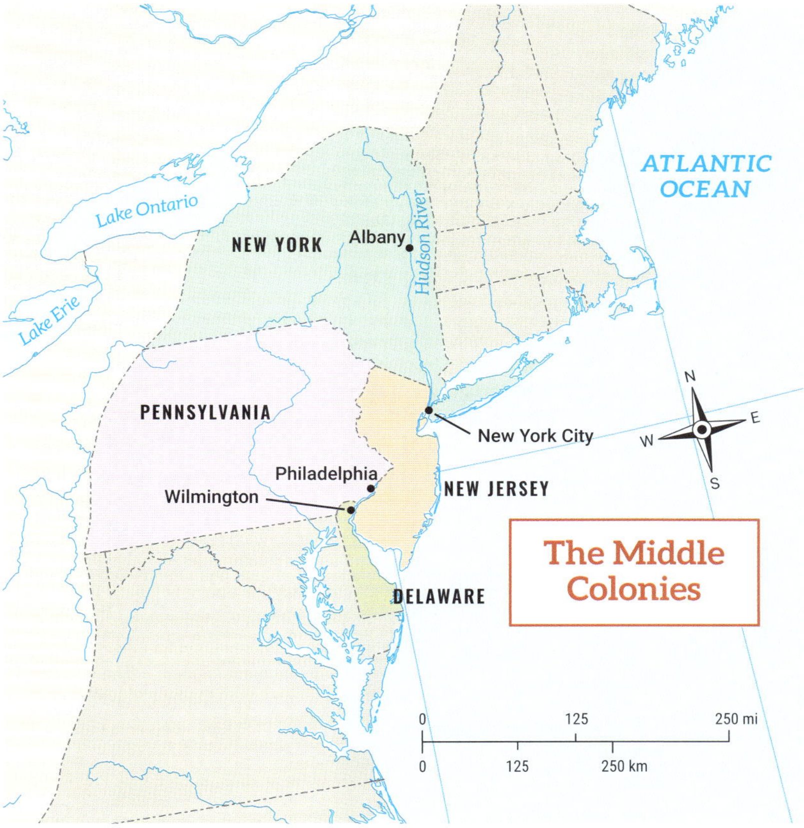

The Middle Colonies

New York

An Englishman named **Henry Hudson** explored for both England and the Netherlands. While sailing for the Netherlands in 1609, Hudson discovered the river that now bears his name. He sailed up the river to the present site of Albany, New York. His exploration gave the Dutch claim to the region, and they called it **New Netherland**. It eventually became the colony of New York.

Unlike many English settlers, the Dutch did not colonize for religious reasons. Instead, the Dutch colonists were a mercantile, or trading, group that concentrated on finding gold and, later, furs. The Dutch government decided which companies could explore and settle. Merchants organized these companies and hoped to profit from new settlements.

In 1624 a Dutch ship brought thirty families from the Netherlands to America. The settlers landed on Manhattan Island. Many others also settled up the Hudson River at Fort Orange, near the present site of Albany.

Two years later, a more permanent settlement began on Manhattan. The governor of the colony, Peter Minuit, "bought" the island from Indians with cloth and trinkets. There were problems with this "purchase." First, the Indian concept of ownership did not include fences or property deeds; land was often viewed as a common resource to be used by all. Second, the tribe that "sold" the land was not the tribe that controlled most of the island. Those Indians, therefore, must have thought it strange that Minuit paid them for something that they did not even own. Nevertheless, the town that grew there, later called New Amsterdam, became the capital of New Netherland. Today, the area is part of New York City.

MERCANTILISM

Throughout the 1600s and 1700s, most European nations were guided by an economic system known as **mercantilism**. According to this system, wealth was measured by the amount of gold and silver a nation possessed.

European nations tried to become self-sufficient. They disliked purchasing goods from rival countries because doing so drained their own supply of gold and silver while enriching their rivals. Most European nations sought to remedy this problem by establishing colonies and building empires.

The European countries that had established colonies viewed them as sources of raw materials for European industries and as markets (where goods from the mother countries could be sold). Selling goods in the colonies increased the mother countries' wealth and power. By regulating the colonies' economies—strictly controlling with whom the colonies could trade and taxing their trade activities—mother countries could reap large profits.

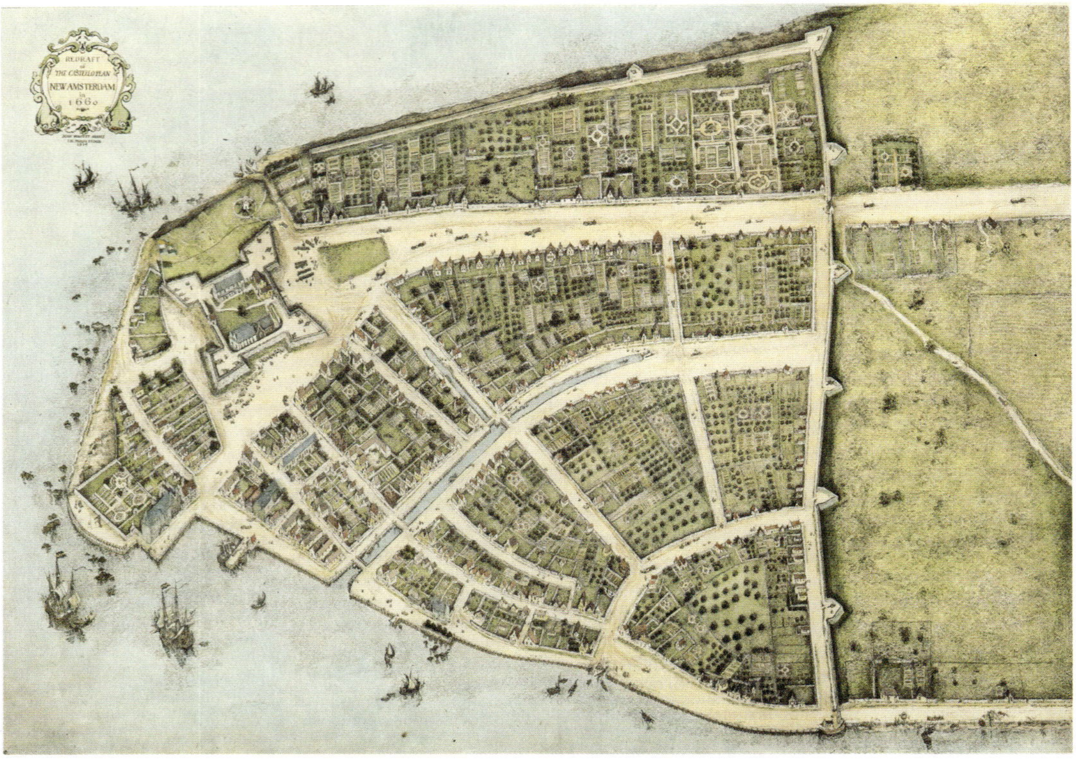

▲ The Castello Plan of 1660 is the earliest-known map of New Amsterdam (today Manhattan in New York City).

The Dutch promised large grants of land to anyone who could bring fifty settlers to the New World. Recipients of these large grants were called patroons. People who could not bring fifty settlers received as much land as they could farm themselves. Although many of the farmers were successful, the development of the new land did not bring as much profit as the Dutch investors hoped.

Peter Stuyvesant, New Netherland's best-known governor, wanted to adopt some of the laws of the English colonies in New England. For example, he favored requiring church attendance and enforcing moral laws. However, his superiors in the Netherlands were more interested in making New Amsterdam a major trading hub, and they blamed Stuyvesant for their financial disappointments in the colony. Soon the Netherlands began to neglect its unprofitable colony, sending few new colonists and offering little aid.

The Dutch settlements along the Hudson River made the English envious. New Amsterdam had one of the finest harbors on the Atlantic coast. Moreover, New Netherland stood between New England and colonies further south, thereby preventing England from controlling the entire Atlantic coast.

More than a century earlier, in 1497, John Cabot had claimed the Atlantic coast of North America for England, thus providing the basis for England to declare that it had a rightful claim to New Netherland. In 1664, King Charles II gave to his brother James, the Duke of York, a proprietary colony consisting of all the land that the Dutch had held. When the duke sent warships to capture the colony, the settlers in New Amsterdam saw the fleet and decided to surrender. They were dissatisfied with the Dutch government and were not prepared to defend themselves. Thus the Dutch colony passed peacefully into the hands of the English, who renamed it New York.

Did you know?

The Duke of York became King James II of England in 1685 and changed New York from a proprietary colony to a royal colony.

New Jersey

Shortly after the Dutch surrendered New Netherland to the English, the Duke of York gave the southern portion of his new territory to two of his friends, Sir George Carteret and Lord John Berkeley. The colony was named New Jersey in honor of the island of Jersey, located in the English Channel, where Carteret served as governor. To attract settlers, the two leaders offered cheap land, full religious liberty, and some self-government. Unrest plagued the colony for a time, and it was divided into East and West Jersey. It was later reunited as a royal colony under the direct rule of the English king.

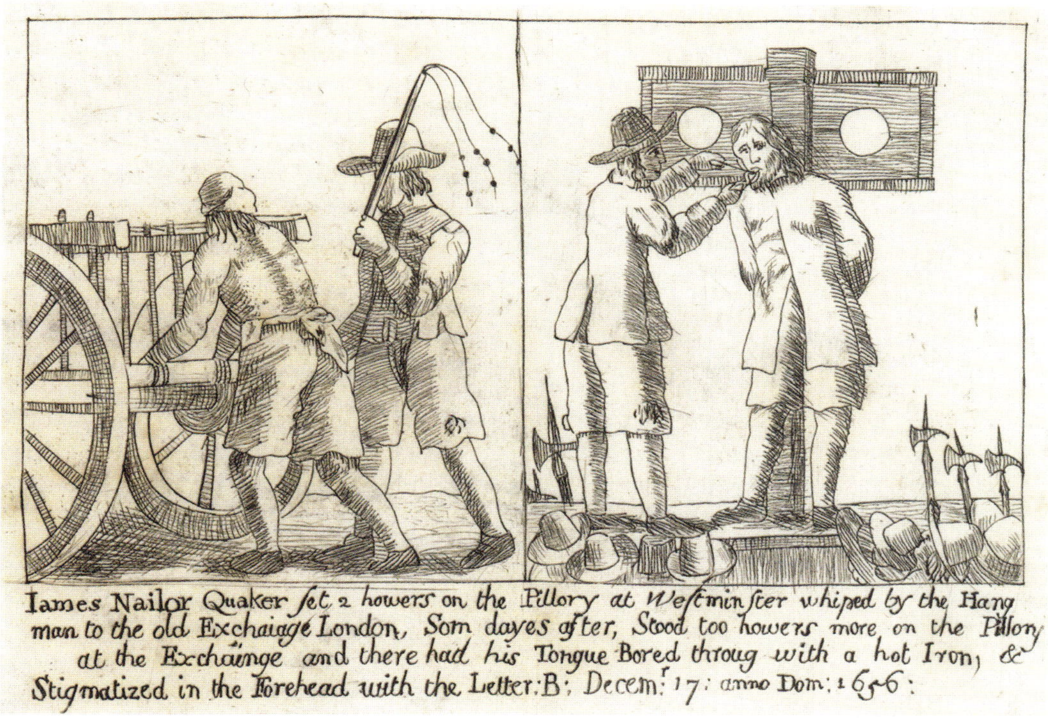

A 1656 drawing of Quaker punishments, showing whipping, stocks, and boring through a tongue with a hot iron

Pennsylvania

Pennsylvania, like Plymouth, was established because of persecution in England. The Society of Friends separated from the Church of England because they agreed with few of that church's accepted religious ceremonies. They were nicknamed the **Quakers** because they were said to "tremble at the word of the Lord." Trembling and shaking sometimes took place during their meetings.

Quakers viewed all people as equal, regardless of gender, ethnicity, or social status. Unfortunately, the Quakers did not think that every part of the person is affected by sin. Instead, they believed that people have an "inner light" that tells them God's will; therefore, Quakers emphasized following the "inner light" instead of emphasizing learning from the Scriptures. They also opposed war and refused to take oaths. Their beliefs made them unpopular both in England and in the American colonies.

One Quaker, **William Penn**, was a member of a wealthy English family. King Charles II owed Penn's father a large sum of money. The debt was to be paid to William Penn when his father died. In 1681 the king agreed to compensate Penn by giving him a large piece of land in America. Penn called it Sylvania, Latin for *woodland*. The king called it Penn's Sylvania. Although the land was Penn's by royal decree, he wisely bought the land from the Indians. He thereby made friends with them and avoided the attacks that plagued other colonies.

Penn hoped to use his proprietary colony to provide a haven for himself and his persecuted Quaker friends. He referred to his colony as a "Holy Experiment." His goal was to establish a colony ruled by "brotherly love," which would result in peace and prosperity. He established laws granting religious freedom to all who believed in one God. There was no established, or official, church in the colony that prevented people from worshiping God in their own way. This freedom attracted other persecuted religious groups from Europe.

William Penn

Many of them were from Germany; they called themselves Deutsch (Germans). The non-Germans referred to these people as the Pennsylvania Dutch. Unfortunately, this caused confusion when talking about the Pennsylvania Dutch, who were German, by making it sound like they were Dutch, the nationality of the Netherlands.

With many industrious people and more fertile land than that of New England, Pennsylvania became the most prosperous colony in North America. By 1776 its capital, Philadelphia—"the city of brotherly love"—was the largest city in America. Approximately 40,000 residents lived there at the time.

Delaware

This region was settled by the Swedes in the 1630s. Their colony, known as New Sweden, later passed to the Dutch and eventually to the English. By the 1680s William Penn controlled it. He later gave the area the right to form its own legislature, and it became a separate colony in 1704. However, it continued to have the same governor as Pennsylvania until 1776.

SECTION REVIEW 2.3

1. Who explored for both England and the Netherlands?
2. What is the current name of New Netherland? New Amsterdam?
3. Who was given the Dutch lands in America by his brother, the king of England? What was his title?
4. How might mercantilism be both good and bad?
5. According to Quakers, how do they learn God's will?
6. Why were the Quakers unpopular in both England and America?
7. What non-English group of people settled in large numbers in Pennsylvania? Why did many of them come?
8. What colony was originally part of New York? What colony was originally part of Pennsylvania?

▾ Old State House (later called Independence Hall), Philadelphia

2.4 THE SOUTHERN COLONIES

What were the different purposes in the founding of each of the southern colonies?

The southern colonies—Virginia, Maryland, the Carolinas (which was later divided into South Carolina and North Carolina), and Georgia—were settled mainly by the English. Although they were similar in some ways to the middle colonies and New England, the southern colonies developed differently. They had warmer climates, single-crop economies, and slave-labor systems.

Virginia

As mentioned in the previous chapter, the first permanent settlement in Virginia was Jamestown. This settlement did not quickly meet the high expectations of its stockholders. However, the colonists did learn from the Indians how to grow tobacco. That product had become increasingly popular in Europe since the Spanish had first imported it in the mid-1500s. As the demand for it increased, tobacco became the major crop of the Virginia colonists. It was eventually so valuable that it sometimes served as money for payment of taxes and wages.

By the 1620s Virginia was a prospering colony. However, King James I was displeased with the management of the London Company, especially its relations with the Indians. Therefore, he revoked the company's charter and made Virginia a royal colony. He then appointed a colonial governor and council. But he allowed the House of Burgesses to continue meeting.

Throughout the seventeenth century (1600s), settlers branched out from the original Jamestown settlement. Heading inland, they built new towns and plantations along the rivers.

Virginia became the center of Anglicanism in the New World. The Anglicans fined anyone who worshiped apart from the established church. But they had trouble meeting the people's spiritual needs because there were few ministers and because settlements were sometimes far apart.

When fire destroyed much of Jamestown in 1698, the colony's capital was moved to nearby Williamsburg. This colonial city became a leading center of government and culture in the thirteen colonies.

▾ Williamsburg, Virginia, with horse carriage (2020)

GUIDING QUESTIONS

- How did the settlement of the colony of Virginia occur?
- What were the reasons for Maryland's establishment of the Act of Toleration?
- How were the Carolinas settled?
- What were the purposes for the establishment of Georgia?

the "NOXIOUS WEED"

During colonial times, most people were unconcerned about the dangers of tobacco. But in 1604, King James I wrote a pamphlet titled *A Counterblaste to Tobacco*, attacking what he called a "noxious [harmful] weed." He wrote that smoking was "a custom loathsome to the eye, hateful to the nose, harmful to the brain, dangerous to the lungs, and in the black stinking fume thereof, nearest resembling the horrible Stygian [dark, hellish] smoke of the pit that is bottomless."

Maryland

Roman Catholics were unwelcome in England under certain rulers. However, Charles I, the English king between 1625 and 1649, was sympathetic to the Catholics. He gave land in America to his friend George Calvert, who held the title Lord Baltimore. Calvert, a Roman Catholic, wanted a place where Catholics could be free to worship. He also wanted to make money by investing in a colony. The king named the territory Maryland in honor of his wife, Queen Henrietta Maria.

George Calvert died before he could begin his settlement. His son **Cecilius Calvert**, the second Lord Baltimore, founded the colony and sent settlers. In 1634 they established a town called St. Mary's. According to the king's charter, Calvert was the proprietor of Maryland, but all landowners were to have a part in making the laws.

Soon Protestants also settled in the colony. Eventually, they greatly outnumbered the Catholics. The Catholics feared that they might face persecution in their own colony. In 1649, lawmakers passed the **Act of Toleration**, guaranteeing religious freedom to all who believed in the Trinity. This was the first written law of religious freedom in the colonies. William Penn instituted similar laws when he settled Pennsylvania in the 1680s. Earlier, Rhode Island had unofficially allowed religious freedom.

South Carolina and North Carolina

After a period of civil war between the king and Parliament in England, Charles II came to the throne in 1660. He wished to reward those who had been loyal to the royal family during the civil war. In 1663, he granted eight English noblemen a tract of land in America. They named it Carolina in honor of the king (the king's name in Latin was Carolus).

◂ (left) Rice field
◂ (right) Indigo

In 1670, a large group of people settled along the Ashley River at what became known as Charles Town. The settlement later moved to a better site nearby, and the city's name was changed from Charles Town to Charleston. With its fine harbor, the city became an important colonial commercial center. Soon other settlers were attracted to the region. French Huguenots, Scots-Irish, and Englishmen from the Caribbean islands (especially Barbados) moved to the new colony. Although the official church in the region was the Anglican Church, these settlers brought their own religious beliefs with them.

A smaller group had settled on the northern coast of Carolina, near Albemarle Sound, in 1654. This group's settlements grew, and they had little in common with those to the south. In 1712, less than fifty years after receiving its charter, the colony of Carolina was divided into North Carolina and South Carolina.

The Carolinas followed Virginia's example of raising a large cash crop. Tobacco was important in North Carolina, but South Carolina found that its coastal lands and climate were better suited for growing rice. Slaves from Africa's west coast brought rice to the colonies. Indigo, a plant from which a popular blue dye could be made, became a second cash crop for South Carolina.

Georgia

Georgia, the last of the thirteen colonies to be established, had an unusual beginning. The English government was concerned about the nearness of the Spanish forts in Florida. Parliament wanted to use the land south of the Carolinas as a buffer zone, or area of separation, to keep the Spanish at a distance.

Blackbeard

During the early history of the Carolinas, pirates roamed the Atlantic coast, often terrorizing the inhabitants of the coastal towns. An Englishman named Edward Teach was one of the most infamous pirates. With his long, black beard twisted together and tied with ribbons into little "tails," he was soon known as Blackbeard. At one point, he allied with other pirates and blockaded Charles Town's harbor for several days.

In November 1718, a British naval force from Virginia succeeded in killing Blackbeard off the coast of North Carolina. His severed head was prominently displayed on one of the navy's ships.

▲ Debtors being sent from England to the debtor colony of Georgia

▼ James Oglethorpe

While Parliament was considering the idea of such a zone, a wealthy English general named **James Oglethorpe** asked for permission to establish a colony. He was unhappy with the way debtors were treated in England. If a person owed money, he could be thrown in prison until he paid. Oglethorpe thought that debtors should be allowed to work and have a chance to repay their debts rather than be jailed.

King George II gave Oglethorpe and some other trustees title to the new colony of Georgia, which could serve as both a new home for debtors and as the desired buffer for the colonies that lay farther north. Parliament agreed to Oglethorpe's plan and even contributed money for the project. The first settlers arrived in 1733 and founded the city of Savannah under Oglethorpe's direction. Oglethorpe worked hard to ensure the colony's success. He built forts along the coastal islands to protect the colony from Spanish attack. In 1742 a force from Georgia defeated a small Spanish force that came against them. Realizing that the Creek Indians, a powerful tribe in western Georgia, might also be a threat, Oglethorpe sought to keep peace with them.

Only a few debtors actually settled in Georgia, so Oglethorpe's original purpose was defeated. However, other Europeans came to settle the colony.

SECTION REVIEW 2.4

1. What city became the new capital of Virginia when much of Jamestown was destroyed by a fire?
2. Who founded the colony of Maryland? What was his title?
3. What religious group authored the Act of Toleration in Maryland? Why?
4. Who are the Carolinas named for?
5. What cash crop was most important in North Carolina? in South Carolina?
6. What infamous pirate literally "lost his head" for terrorizing the Atlantic coast?
7. What nation's forts to the south of the English colonies were considered a threat?
8. What alternative consequences might be beneficial for debtors instead of being placed into debtors' prison?

CHAPTER 2 REVIEW

Making Connections

1. List the four New England colonies.
2. List the four middle colonies.
3. List the five southern colonies.

Match each person to the correct colony.

4. Cecilius Calvert	a. Plymouth
5. James Oglethorpe	b. Massachusetts
6. William Bradford	c. Rhode Island
7. Roger Williams	d. Connecticut
8. John Winthrop	e. Maryland
9. Thomas Hooker	f. Georgia

10. Why did some oppose the Anglican Church and decide to leave England?
11. How were the Dutch and English different in their reasons for colonization?
12. For each of the following, what group or person was seeking religious freedom?
    a. Plymouth
    b. Massachusetts Bay
    c. Rhode Island
    d. Pennsylvania
    e. Maryland
13. Why was the colony of Georgia established?

Thinking Critically

14. Write a brief paragraph called The _____ [insert your last name] Compact. Include a brief description of how you would organize government upon arriving in an unexplored new land.
15. List the three different types of colonial organization. Discuss the advantages and disadvantages of each type.

Living as a Christian Citizen

16. Compare and contrast Quaker beliefs with Bible teaching.
17. Should religious freedom be granted to religious groups with which you disagree? Why or why not?

Terms to Remember

joint-stock companies
charter colonies
proprietary colonies
royal colonies
Anglican Church
Separatists
Puritans
Pilgrims
Mayflower Compact
Plymouth
Squanto
William Bradford
Massachusetts Bay Company
John Winthrop
Roger Williams
Thomas Hooker
Fundamental Orders of Connecticut
Henry Hudson
New Netherland
mercantilism
Quakers
William Penn
Cecilius Calvert
Act of Toleration
James Oglethorpe

CHAPTER 3 Expansion and Establishment

By 1700 the population of the English colonies was approximately 250,000. In 1760 it reached 1.5 million. America was an attractive place with its growing economy, abundant land, and promises of freedom. Many Europeans who valued these things settled in the new land. As the colonies expanded, patterns of life were established. Despite some uncomfortable and uncertain times, by the mid-1700s the colonies were growing and becoming more stable.

In addition to growth, individualism also characterized the colonies during this period. While colonists enjoyed community and government, they still emphasized citizens' right to vote and their duty to work. Self-reliance was an important part of colonial culture.

GUIDING QUESTIONS

- Why did different people groups come to America and where did they settle?
- What was slavery like in the early colonies?
- How was the frontier settled?

3.1 COLONIAL DIVERSITY

How did the colonies expand?

Although the English colonies were ruled by England, immigrants from several nations populated them. The immigrants increased America's diversity. Each region soon developed a distinct culture because of the background of its inhabitants.

The Colonies Grow in Population

In the early years of colonization, the largest groups of settlers came from Europe. Historians call this wave of immigrants the **Great Migration**. As mentioned in the last chapter, more than fifteen thousand people settled in the Massachusetts Bay Colony during its first ten years alone. After the first waves, immigration slowed until the early 1700s, but the colonies kept growing. Where there were more men than women, as in the southern colonies, the population grew very slowly. Where more families settled in America, especially New England, the population grew faster. This type of growth, called natural increase, had a greater impact on the colonies than immigration. However, the mother country (country from which the immigrants had moved) was still an important influence on the culture that developed in each region.

The English

Most of the Europeans that came to America in the 1600s were from England. English customs, the English language, and the English style of government eventually influenced all the colonies. People from various regions in England settled in different places in the colonies. The Puritans, almost all of whom settled in New England, came from an area in the eastern part of England. The Englishmen in the southern colonies had been aristocrats in southern England. The Quakers were from the Midlands of England. They settled in Pennsylvania, Delaware, and New Jersey. Some Englishmen from northern England (near Scotland) lived in the West, around the Appalachian Mountains.

The influence of the English can still be seen today by America's use of the English system, while the remainder of the world uses the metric system. This tape measure shows both systems of measurement.

Frontiersman holding rifle

Did you know?

The 1700s were the eighteenth century. The 1900s comprised the twentieth century. Even though we live in the 2000s, we live in the twenty-first century.

Confused? Remember that the first century AD began in what we would now label as AD 1. This means the second century AD began in AD 101. Therefore, the eighteenth century began in AD 1701, the nineteenth century began in AD 1801, the twentieth century began in AD 1901, and our present century began in AD 2001.

The Scots-Irish

The Scots-Irish were the second-largest group of immigrants. They arrived in the early eighteenth century (1700s). They were from northern Ireland but had a Scottish heritage; many of them were strong Presbyterians. Most arrived in Philadelphia but soon migrated south and settled in the Appalachian backcountry of Virginia, the Carolinas, and Georgia.

The Germans

Beginning about 1700 Germans came to the colonies. William Penn encouraged many of them to settle in Pennsylvania. By the late 1700s, Germans composed nearly one-third of Pennsylvania's population. Other Germans headed to the Hudson Valley in New York or to western Virginia, North Carolina, and Maryland. Many of these Germans were Lutherans who came to America for religious freedom.

Smaller Groups

There was a strong Dutch presence in New Netherland, which became New York. Some Dutch settlers also lived in New Jersey. Many Swedes came to nearby Delaware. Several thousand immigrants from France and Switzerland also came to the colonies and helped build towns in Virginia and the Carolinas. The French Huguenots, or Protestants, were particularly strong in coastal South Carolina.

The Africans

Estimates state that between ten and twelve million Africans were enslaved and sent to the New World, mostly during the seventeenth and eighteenth centuries. Probably two million did not survive the voyage. Most slaves were taken to South America or the Caribbean. Only a small portion of those slaves, approximately a half a million, were shipped to the area that became known as the United States. However, by 1730, 30 percent of the population south of Pennsylvania was black, and by 1760 blacks comprised 60 percent of South Carolina's population. Despite their growing numbers, these Africans had no representative voice in society nor did they enjoy the freedoms provided to other immigrants.

As southern planters sought cheap labor, they relied more and more on African slaves. The South based its economy on cash crops. If a farmer had many workers, he increased the amount of land that could be planted and harvested. Greater harvests led to greater profits. In New England and the middle colonies, the cooler weather meant the growing and harvesting seasons were shorter. Consequently, farmers in those areas planted mainly food crops, crops for which slave labor proved less profitable. Thus, northerners used slaves most often as servants in upper-class homes, not as farm workers. However, slave trade developed into a profitable business for New England merchants, shipbuilders, and sea captains as they transported slaves from Africa to the New World.

With people drawn from so many countries, the colonies truly were a cultural "melting pot." The middle colonies, with English, German, Dutch, and Swedish settlers, were the most diverse.

As we have seen, many people came to the colonies for religious freedom while many others came to escape famine or financial problems or to acquire land. Still others arrived as transported convicts or, in the case of the Africans, as slaves. The cultures represented by each of these groups had both positive and negative aspects. All contributed to the formation of a unique society in America.

Advertisement for a slave auction in South Carolina

TO BE SOLD on board the Ship *Bance-Yland*, on tuesday the 6th of *May* next, at *Ashley-Ferry*; a choice cargo of about 250 fine healthy

NEGROES,

just arrived from the Windward & Rice Coast. —The utmost care has already been taken, and shall be continued, to keep them free from the least danger of being infected with the SMALL-POX, no boat having been on board, and all other communication with people from *Charles-Town* prevented.

Austin, Laurens, & Appleby.

N. B. Full one Half of the above Negroes have had the SMALL-POX in their own Country.

The Colonies Grow in Size

Each colony began on or near the Atlantic coast. The increase in population brought the need to increase the number of settlements; thus, colonists moved slowly inland. Even so, all three colonial regions always had a **frontier** (an undeveloped area at the edge of the settled areas). As settlers moved west, the frontier also moved westward. Easterners often called the frontier the backcountry. For more than a hundred years, the Appalachian Mountains formed a western boundary for the British colonies.

Settlers usually followed rivers inland. The rivers made it easier for them to move and then send their crops back to the markets. The Susquehanna and Allegheny Rivers opened paths into western Pennsylvania. The Hudson River helped settlers move north and inland in New York. Along the Delaware River, Philadelphia grew from a few thousand people in 1690 to more than forty thousand by 1776.

Many settlers also began following wilderness trails southward along the Appalachian Mountains. The main north–south pathway came to be known as the Great Wagon Road. It stretched seven hundred miles from Philadelphia, Pennsylvania, to Augusta, Georgia. The travelers on the wilderness trails often used **Conestoga wagons** to carry their belongings. The bottom was curved to keep its con-

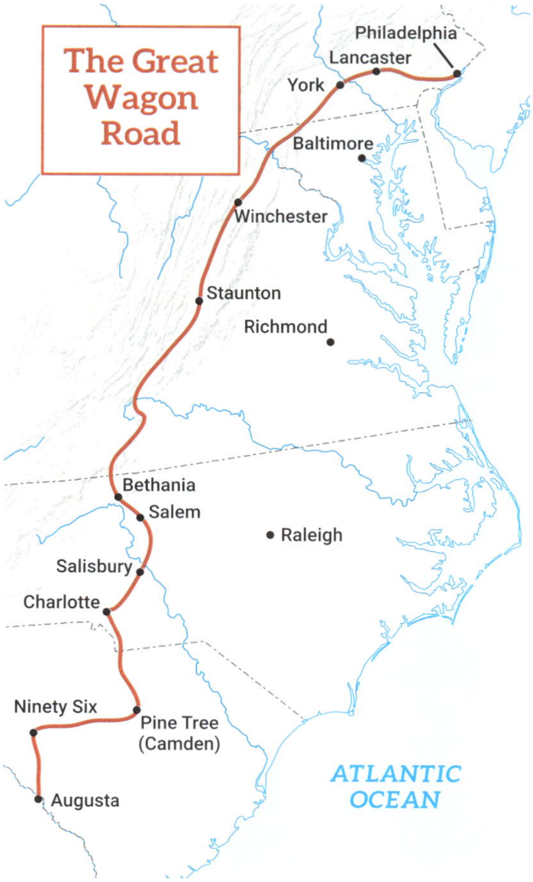

tents from rolling outside the wagon, and the cover protected the wagon's interior from weather. At night, settlers typically slept near their wagon or underneath it. These wagons became popular and were used to haul people and freight until railroads became a more efficient transportation system in the mid-1800s.

Danger and violence sometimes characterized life on the frontier. The settlers claimed land almost anywhere they wished, and those claims often led to skirmishes with the Indians. Settlers included ordinary people, debtors, and escaped convicts from a variety of ethnic groups. The mix of Scots-Irish, German, and English migrants sometimes led to violence as the diverse cultures clashed.

Despite the frontier's many dangers, thousands continued to move westward. Large numbers of settlers who moved into present-day Tennessee, Kentucky, and Ohio came through a natural passage in the Appalachian Mountains known as the Cumberland Gap. In 1775 explorer Daniel Boone led the clearing of a trail through the gap. This route, which became known as the Wilderness Road, helped people cross the mountains more easily.

Thomas Walker and the Cumberland Gap

Thomas Walker was a wealthy doctor and a member of the House of Burgesses in Virginia. One of his patients was Thomas Jefferson's father, a farmer and explorer. Walker soon also learned to love exploring. He became an agent of the Loyal Land Company in western Virginia.

Walker headed into Tennessee in 1743; then, in 1750 he was the first colonist to explore the Cumberland Gap. This proved to be his greatest achievement because it led to migration and settlement in the West. He built the first cabin in Kentucky, and, later in life, he surveyed the line that became the border between Kentucky and Tennessee.

SECTION REVIEW 3.1

1. In what two ways did the population of the colonies increase?
2. Most of the Europeans who came to America were from what three groups?
3. How was the migration of Africans into the Americas different from the migration of other groups?
4. Why did slave labor become more prominent in the southern colonies than in the others?
5. Which colonial region included the most diverse nationalities?
6. On what two types of routes did settlers move west?
7. What are some benefits and drawbacks of multiple nationalities and ethnic groups with diverse religions living in the same areas?

3.2 COLONIAL ECONOMIES

What were the economic structures of the early colonies?

With the increase in the colonies' population came economic growth. Most farmers were originally **subsistence farmers**, people who could raise just enough crops and livestock to provide for their families. But as life became more stable, the colonists could focus on producing not only food but also extra goods that they could sell in America or in Europe. Each region usually provided different products, and eventually a trade network developed. In return for colonial goods, this network brought European goods to the colonies.

The climate, geography, and resources of the land were important to the early settlers. They had to depend mainly on what they could make or what would grow on or near their land. This was especially true for the farmers, who comprised 90 percent of the population. Even colonists who were not farmers depended on locally grown food. Many also used local resources for their work. For example, shipbuilders and carpenters used trees harvested from nearby forests, and blacksmiths often used metals mined from nearby deposits.

The New England Colonies

The geography of New England is rough compared to that of other regions in America. The landscape bulges with hills and low mountains. The region lacks not only flat farmland but also fertile and abundant soil. Its thin, rocky cover of soil makes farming difficult. In addition, New England has a short growing season and long, cold, snowy winters.

Because New England's land is not good for farming, there was little profit in it. Most farmers harvested only enough to survive. Many New Englanders looked to the ocean for their livelihood. New England's harbors became important centers of settlement and trade. Fishing along the coast and off the Grand Banks of Newfoundland became a valuable industry. Colonists caught, salted, and exported fish—especially cod—to the middle colonies, the Caribbean, and Europe. Whaling also developed in New England. Because whales were processed for their oil and bone in New Bedford and Nantucket, Massachusetts, those towns became busy whaling ports.

At first, fishermen and whalers sailed on ships made in England, but soon the Americans began building their own ships. As New England had plenty of timber for a shipbuilding industry, they also

GUIDING QUESTIONS

- How did the economies vary in the New England, middle, and southern colonies?
- What was life like for a settler on the frontier?
- What is an appropriate biblical response to the problems of triangular trade?

▲ Subsistence farming

▼ Whaling expedition

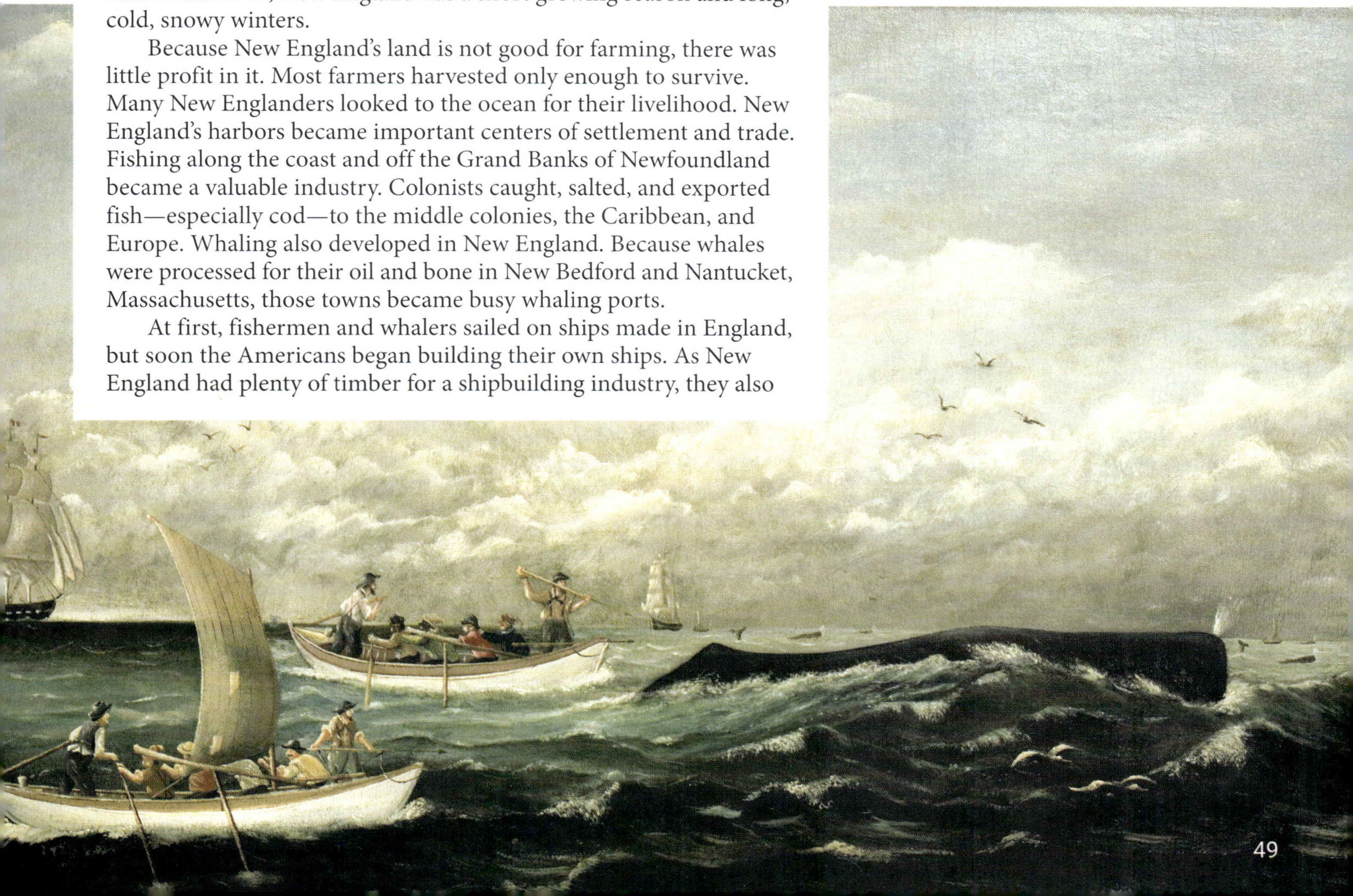

COLONIAL SHIPBUILDING

Building a ship required the skill and labor of many colonial tradesmen. Before construction began, a shipwright would make a small model of the ship. From this model he would devise full-size patterns of ship pieces using thin pieces of wood. When workers cut trees for lumber, they needed these patterns to ensure that the wood was the proper size and shape.

After the ship was constructed and launched into the water, its masts were set in place. Special tradesmen produced the different ropes and sails needed for the ship while ironworkers provided the axles, bands, and the anchor. Clearly, a completed ship was a tribute to hard work and skill.

began supplying many ships for England. By 1776 the colonists were making nearly one-third of Britain's trading ships. Unfortunately, they were also providing ships and captains for the profitable slave trade.

British ships mostly carried raw materials from America or manufactured goods from England. New Englanders made some products at home during the winter, but for many years it was only enough for their own use. Later the colonies did export many manufactured products.

The Middle Colonies

The middle colonies had many navigable rivers. They served as water highways to inland settlements and farms, providing transportation routes for trade. The middle colonies also had rich, thick soil. Although the region had plenty of hills and mountains, it also had fertile coastal plains. As a result, settlers could grow cereal grains, such as corn, oats, barley, and wheat. For this reason, the middle colonies were known as the bread colonies.

Farming became the major activity in the middle colonies. Some farmers were able to sell extra produce for profit. And because the rich soil provided good pasture for cattle and horses, colonists began exporting livestock. Other industries arose to meet farmers' needs. Skilled workers used lumber from the forests to produce barrels and wagons. Merchants in the towns bought farmers' produce and sold them needed supplies.

Settlers in the western parts of the middle colonies, where fewer people lived, trapped animals for their fur. Europeans used fur to make clothing and hats. The frontiersmen also traded with the Indians for additional furs. They then traded in the towns and made large profits. Albany, New York, became an early fur-trade center. Located just south of the junction of the Hudson and Mohawk Rivers, Albany was close to the Iroquois tribes.

Did you know?

Today a dollar is commonly referred to as a "buck." This term may have originated when the skin of a buck, a male deer, was used as currency in frontier areas. After the dollar became the official American currency in the late 1700s, buck became synonymous with our dollar bill.

▾ Fur trapper

The Southern Colonies

Agriculture became the primary activity in the South because of the region's rich soil and long growing season. Besides growing some basic food crops, colonists focused on more profitable cash crops. They grew and exported tobacco, rice, and indigo as these were in demand in Europe. Because the colonists could make greater profits if those crops were raised in large fields, large farms called **plantations** became a major part of southern culture. Port cities and river towns grew to meet the transportation and trading needs of these plantations and other farms. Few industries developed because planters chose to invest in land and slaves instead.

As noted earlier, planters relied heavily on slave labor to perform the difficult tasks in growing cash crops. The slaves were required to spend long hours in terrible working conditions and received no pay. Many died early deaths because of the hardships of their jobs or from the treatment of their masters.

▲ Middleton Plantation, Charleston, South Carolina

▼ A now-abandoned rice field at Brookgreen Plantation in South Carolina

The geography of the southern colonies suited plantation agriculture. The South's wide coastal plain, called the **tidewater** (low land along coastal rivers and inlets), gave these colonies plenty of flat farmland. Cash crops thrived in the warm climate. The plantations of wealthy planters resembled the large country estates back in England. However, the vast majority of the southern colonists were not wealthy plantation owners; instead, they lived on small farms and were subsistence farmers.

Tobacco became the first important cash crop in the South. Although the English recognized that it contains an addictive substance, the desire for profit made it a popular trading item. It was the leading cash crop in Maryland, Virginia, and North Carolina.

Rice was raised in the tidewater, especially in Georgia and the Carolinas. The tides could be used to raise and lower water levels in rice fields. At high tide, farmers opened floodgates to cover the fields with water. Later, as the tide ebbed, the floodgates were opened again to drain the fields.

Indigo also proved to be a good cash crop because it grows at a different time of year than rice and tobacco. The indigo plant produces a dye of rich blue color. It became an especially important crop in South Carolina.

Though many crops were grown throughout America, the most common food crop in all the colonies was corn. It can grow almost anywhere, is easy to hoe and weed, grows quickly, and has many uses. For settlers, in addition to the corn being eaten, cornstalks could be used to stuff mattresses, make children's toys, or feed livestock. Dried husks and cobs could be used to kindle fires. Almost every part of the plant was put to practical use.

The Frontier

On the frontier, settlers lived almost independently of outside influences. They claimed whatever land was available. Since the land had to be cleared, few farms there exceeded two hundred acres. A farmer might grow a patch of corn and perhaps some peas, potatoes, and wheat. At first, most grew only enough food to feed their families. But as was true in other areas, eventually many produced extra wheat, tobacco, indigo, and other products to sell for a profit.

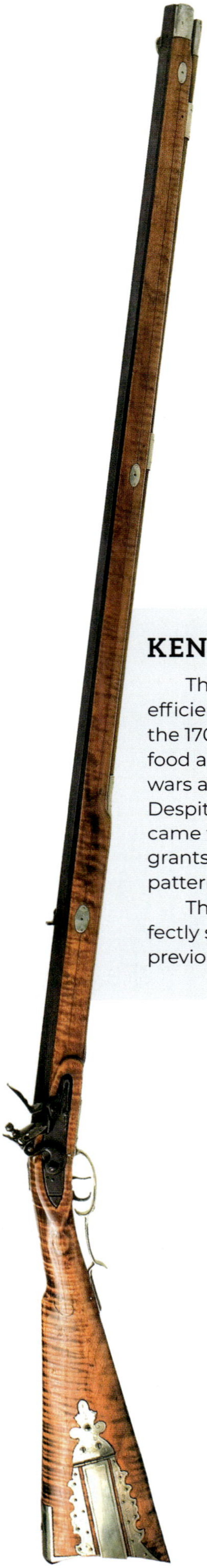

KENTUCKY RIFLES

The Kentucky rifle was an accurate and efficient weapon used by frontier settlers in the 1700s. It helped them hunt animals for food and fur trading, and they used it in their wars against the Indians and colonial powers. Despite its name, the Kentucky rifle actually came from Pennsylvania. German immigrants to that colony devised the longrifle by patterning it after the German Jaeger rifle.

The features of the Kentucky rifle perfectly suited frontier settlers' needs. Unlike previous firearms, it required less gunpowder, a precious commodity for those far away from supplies. It also conserved lead because it fired smaller bullets. To increase the Kentucky rifle's accuracy, gunsmiths added spiral grooves inside the barrel. This caused bullets to spin and fly straighter once they left the barrel. Consequently, a Kentucky rifle could reliably hit a target 200 yards away. By comparison, the barrels of muskets in this period had smooth interiors. As a result, bullets wobbled when fired and accuracy was limited to under 100 yards.

The Triangular Trade

As the colonists began to produce extra goods beyond what they needed for their own use, a trade network developed. It was called the **triangular trade** because the trade routes formed a triangle on a map. Basically, this trade network carried slaves, cash crops, and manufactured goods between west Africa, the Caribbean or American colonies, and Europe.

Boston (and later Providence, Rhode Island) became one of the most prominent shipping centers in this trading system. New England merchants began importing African slaves into the Caribbean in exchange for sugar from that region. They shipped the sugar to New England, where it was made into rum (an alcoholic drink made from fermented sugar). The rum and other products—such as whale oil, lumber, furs, rice, indigo, tobacco, and fish—were then shipped to England.

The American products passed through England to other nations on the European continent. In return, England sent manufactured goods—including tools, clothing, and luxuries that only the

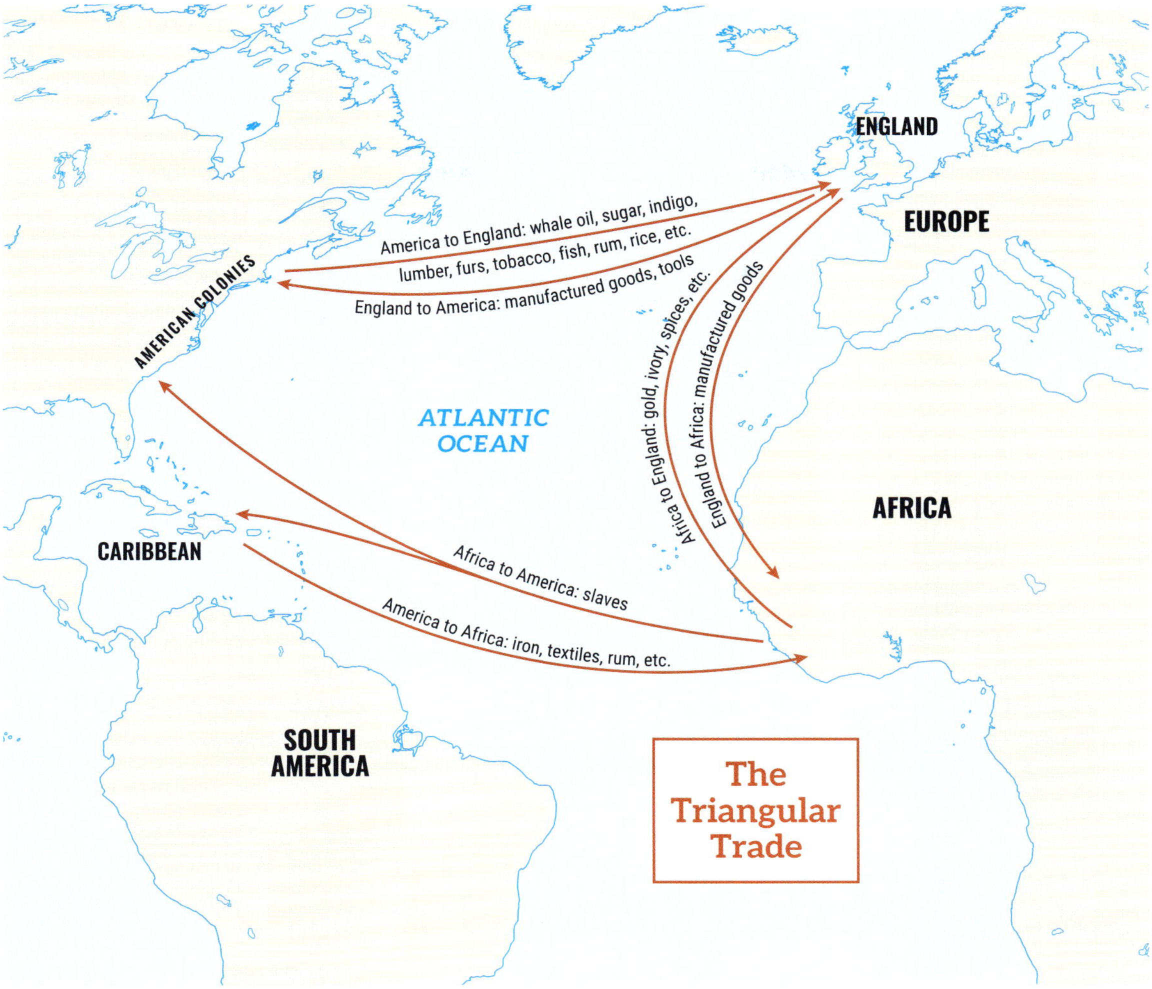

wealthy could afford—to the colonies. England and America also sent manufactured goods to Africa. In Africa, traders bought slaves to work on plantations in the Caribbean and in England's American colonies. These traders sold the slaves for tobacco, sugar, and other products.

The triangular trade allowed some colonists to become very wealthy, especially merchants who owned ships. Some merchants in Rhode Island and Massachusetts depended on the slave trade for their wealth and fought against abolition and any limits to the slave trade. Even though the slave trade was outlawed in New England by the mid-1780s, many ship owners there continued to reap profits from the slaves they sold in other colonies.

During this period, lifestyles improved for almost all European colonists. As America's economy became more established, the colonists began to feel that they played a very important role in the British Empire.

The increased wealth in the colonies caused some spiritual anxiety. Christian leaders in the North, such as Jonathan Edwards, were concerned that the move from farming to trading would result in a tendency to consider possessions and personal comforts more important than spiritual values. Edwards was bothered that many people were using their leisure time for personal enjoyment rather than in ways to glorify God. Meanwhile, in the South the growth of plantations led to more slavery.

SECTION REVIEW 3.2

1. In all the colonies, what was the main occupation necessary for survival?
2. What three factors influenced the economies of the early settlers?
3. Compare the geography of the New England, middle, and southern colonies.
4. What main types of products were exported from each of the colonial regions?
5. What was the most common food crop in all America?
6. What geographic regions were the three main points on the trading triangle?
7. What were some benefits and problems of the triangular trade?

GUIDING QUESTIONS

- Did the mission work among the Indians follow biblical patterns?
- Why did major conflicts occur between the Indians and the colonists?

3.3 COLONIAL CHALLENGES

What challenges did the colonists and the Indians face?

Although the period before the late 1700s was generally a time of growth, the colonists continued to face many challenges. A major one was their relationship with the Indians.

As the colonies expanded, settlers often lived on lands that the Indians had inhabited for many years. Indians, unlike Europeans, shared land among their tribes. Europeans believed that landowners did not have to share their land and that ownership was permanent. Although some colonists paid the Indians for the lands on which they settled, most did not. Even when the colonists did provide compensation, the Indians were generally pushed aside and had less access to sources of food, such as deer or fish.

In addition to dealing with greater numbers of settlers, Indians soon realized that the colonists had much more powerful weapons. Furthermore, as Indians became increasingly dependent on trade with the colonists, some Indian leaders thought that they were losing power over their own people. At times, both the colonists and the Indians captured, held for ransom, or killed members of the other group.

Missions to the Indians

Although the relationship between the Indians and the Europeans was strained, not all colonists saw the Indians as enemies. Many colonists hoped to convert the Indians to Christianity. As early as the 1500s, Europeans justified colonization by promising to send missionaries to the Indians.

The colonists had several reasons for wanting to convert the Indians. The most important was a genuine concern for the Indians' souls. But often, the colonists had other motives as well. Most Europeans believed that Indians were inferior and uncivilized. They wanted Indians to become settled farmers. Thus, a second common reason for evangelizing the Indians was so that they would become more like the Europeans. As a result, the Indians could be controlled and America would be a safer place to live. Those colonists became frustrated when the Indians did not see the need to embrace the lifestyle and customs of Europeans.

Both Protestants and Catholics sent missionaries to the colonies. The French sent missionaries to the regions they controlled in the North and the West, especially to the areas around the Great Lakes and the St. Lawrence River in Canada. In the British colonies, the Puritans were the most active participants in Indian missions. Roger Williams, the founder of Rhode Island, spent much of his time ministering to the Indians. One Puritan minister named **John Eliot** learned the language of the Algonquin Indians in Massachusetts. He devoted himself to translating the Bible into their language. In 1661, he printed the New Testament in Algonquin. Two years later, he printed the entire Bible. It was the first Bible, in any language, to be printed in America. Eliot also established several "**praying towns**." Indians who became Christians lived in praying towns to learn about the Bible and European law, manners, and town life. These towns thrived until later wars between the Indians and the settlers destroyed them.

John Eliot

John Eliot was born in England in 1604. He traveled to Boston in 1631 and soon became pastor of a church in the nearby town of Roxbury. He served that church for nearly six decades, until his death in 1690. In addition, with the support of his congregation and other ministers, he was actively involved in mission work with the Indians.

When Indians fought with settlers, captured Indians were sometimes sold into slavery. In 1675 Eliot appealed to the Massachusetts governor and other officials to abandon this practice. He said, "The design of Christ . . . is not to extirpate [destroy, eliminate] nations, but to gospelize them. . . . To sell souls for money seemeth to me a dangerous merchandise. . . . The country is large enough . . . for them [the Indians] and us too." Unfortunately, in spite of Eliot's concerns, enslavement in such circumstances continued.

Other colonists organized schools and colleges for the Indians, including Dartmouth College in New Hampshire and Brafferton Academy, which was part of the College of William and Mary in Virginia. Overall, however, the colonists saw few converts from their efforts, partly because evangelizing was not a major emphasis for most colonists. In addition, many of them believed that civilizing and converting the Indians went hand in hand. But it was difficult for the Indians to accept a different culture, language, and a new religion while facing war and disease. And some colonists who claimed to be Christians were bad role models for the Indians because they quarreled, cheated Indians in trade, and sold Indian land for profit. In most areas, a good relationship with the Indians was difficult to maintain.

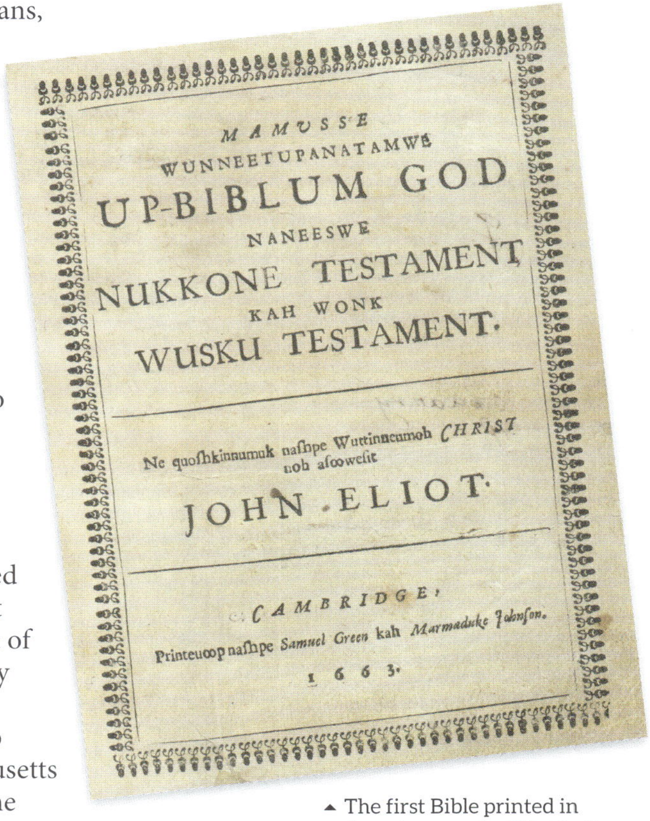
MAMUSSE
WUNNEETUPANATAMWE
UP-BIBLUM GOD
NANEESWE
NUKKONE TESTAMENT
KAH WONK
WUSKU TESTAMENT.

Ne quoshkinnumuk nashpe Wuttinneumoh CHRIST
noh asoowesit
JOHN ELIOT.

CAMBRIDGE:
Printeuoop nashpe Samuel Green kah Marmaduke Johnson.
1663.

▲ The first Bible printed in America was the Eliot Indian Bible in 1663. It was written in the Algonquin language.

Indian Wars

Although some Indians adopted English ways, many more resented the loss of land and power. Sometimes violence erupted between the colonists and the Indians, and Indian tribes fought each other as well. In 1622, fifteen years after the establishment of Jamestown, a quarter of its population was killed in an attack by the Powhatan Indians.

Shortly after the Puritans arrived in New England, they too were at war with Indians. At first, the Indians around Massachusetts Bay welcomed the colonists. But soon they felt threatened by the growing number of settlers. The Pequots were one of the most powerful tribes in the area. After a number of conflicts, some Englishmen were murdered in the 1630s. The colonists blamed the Pequots. Although the details of the event were unclear, soldiers sent from the Massachusetts Bay Colony burned Pequot villages and farm fields. The Indians responded by attacking an English fort.

▼ Attack on a Pequot's fortified village, 1637

By 1637 the **Pequot War** was underway and it continued for almost a year. It involved thousands of Indians and settlers. During the worst battle the colonists ambushed an Indian fort and killed many Indians. The remaining Indians were captured and sold as slaves in New England and the Caribbean. Though some Puritans objected to allowing the practice of slavery, others embraced it.

After the Pequot War, New England remained peaceful for nearly forty years. However, the conflict between the Indians and the colonists was far from resolved. By 1675 one of Massasoit's sons ruled the Indians who lived near the colonists. (Massasoit was the Indian leader who helped the first colonists in Plymouth.) Metacomet, or King Philip, as the new leader was called by the Europeans, disliked the English. He opposed English efforts to convert Indians to Christianity, and he was upset that his brother had died

▲ Attack on Brookfield, Massachusetts, during King Philip's War, 1675

▼ Burning of Jamestown during Bacon's Rebellion

shortly after being released from arrest by the English. Numerous other conflicts hastened the outbreak of what became known as **King Philip's War**.

Eventually, the English, with a force of more than a thousand, began burning Indian villages and attacking their forts. The Indians fought back by burning towns, taking livestock and crops, and killing or capturing hundreds of colonists. The war spread throughout Massachusetts, Rhode Island, Connecticut, New Hampshire, and Maine. During the three-year conflict (1675–78), at least six hundred colonists and more than two thousand Indians were killed. Metacomet was killed and his head was placed atop a pole for twenty years at Plymouth. Deaths from war and disease, along with the flight of many Indians, cut the region's Indian population by half. Meanwhile, colonists continued to move farther west.

In the southern colonies, one of the worst incidents involving Indians and settlers was called **Bacon's Rebellion**. That conflict, which lasted from 1676 to 1677, began with the Indians and ended with violence among the colonists. At the time, Virginia was suffering from financial problems and bad weather. When Indians attacked, the colonists retaliated. Unfortunately, the settlers attacked the wrong group of Indians. Matters worsened.

Virginia's governor, William Berkeley, tried to keep peace with the Indians. But other colonists, including Nathaniel Bacon, did not think the governor was doing enough to protect those who lived on the frontier. Settlers also objected to the governor's high taxes. Despite the governor's wishes, Bacon led a group of colonists to attack the Indians. Berkeley then declared Bacon a rebel.

Bacon and his followers later gained control of Jamestown, the capital at the time, and the governor fled. Bacon burned the town in September 1676. By the time Berkeley returned, Bacon had died of disease.

During the many wars, both the Indians and the colonists made terrible mistakes and misjudgments. Each side misunderstood the other. The colonists, many of whom knew God's Word, failed to love their neighbors as themselves (Matt. 22:39). As a result, the colonies, and later the United States, often treated the Indians unjustly. Although there was sufficient land for both the settlers and the Indians, many colonists preferred taking additional land over spreading the gospel to the Native Americans.

SECTION REVIEW 3.3

1. How did colonists' and Indians' view of land ownership differ?
2. List two reasons for mission work among the Indians.
3. What printed work was completed by John Eliot? Why was it significant?
4. What war in New England ended with the capture and slavery of many Indians?
5. How did King Philip's War affect the Indians?
6. After attacking Indians in Virginia, Bacon next took control of what city, later burning it?
7. Could the colonists have dealt with the Indian threat to their way of life without going to war? Defend your answer.

3.4 COLONIAL GOVERNMENT

How were the early governments in the colonies structured?

GUIDING QUESTIONS

- What were the differences between the three types of colonial governments?
- How did the colonial justice system operate?
- What was the primary tax that financed colonial governments?
- How did local government in the colonies operate?

God ordained government to rule over mankind. A central obligation of government is to ensure justice by rewarding righteousness and punishing unrighteousness.

The early colonists recognized their need for government. They established their own governments to provide local leadership, knowing that Europe was too far away to offer much immediate control. The principles to which they adhered, along with their ideas regarding their rights as Englishmen, became a pattern for the government of the United States.

Governors and Legislatures

Each of the three types of colonies licensed by the Crown (king or queen)—royal, proprietary, and charter—had different types of local government. Some governments were more powerful than others. The charter colonies—Massachusetts, Connecticut, and Rhode Island—elected their leaders (governors, judges, and legislators). They had the least interference from Britain. In proprietary colonies, such as Pennsylvania and the Carolinas, the proprietor or his heirs named the governor. In royal colonies, the king chose the governor.

Sometimes, the governor stayed in England and sent a deputy governor to rule for him. On occasion, colonists tried to persuade officials to give them a new governor or to force the old one to be more cooperative.

In proprietary and royal colonies, the governor was initially quite powerful. He could typically veto laws, regulate land grants, and command the local army, called the **militia**. But the legislature, or elected assembly, had the "**power of the purse**" since it paid the governor's salary and financed government activities. If the governor failed to do what the legislature wanted him to do, it could refuse to pay for his programs or even his salary.

Did you know?

Almost every able-bodied male was expected to participate in the militia. Some colonies assembled the militia for drills as often as once a week, usually on Sunday. Men would carry their rifles or muskets to church and would drill afterward.

▾ Governor's Palace, Williamsburg, Virginia. In 1698, the capital of Virginia moved from Jamestown to Williamsburg.

◂ (top) Colonial capitol building, Williamsburg, Virginia

◂ (below) Colonial courthouse, Williamsburg

The Crown allowed each colony to choose its own legislature. Free adult white male property owners (**freeholders**, or freemen) could vote for representatives. Early in colonial times, parts of New England established church membership as an additional voting requirement. Thus a republican form of government became an early feature of American life.

The Courts

Most ideas for the colonial court systems came from England, but they were changed to meet local needs. Governors appointed local magistrates, or judges, often called **justices of the peace**. These officials held trials for people accused of crimes and settled disputes between citizens. They also collected taxes, granted licenses, recorded property deeds, and served other public needs. Sometimes the justices even conducted elections. This system usually worked well because these officials knew the people in their communities. Many communities still have a justice of the peace today.

Taxes

The colonists financed their governments by paying taxes. The primary tax was a property tax. Anyone who owned land or other valuable property paid a certain amount to the colony in which he lived. The more property owned, the higher the tax. Some colonies had poll taxes that citizens had to pay before they could vote. The New York poll tax in 1702 was a graduated tax—that is, wealthy people had to pay more than poor people. For example, those who wore wigs, a common fashion for the rich in colonial times, paid more. Other forms of taxes were tried, but property taxes eventually became the main source of income for colonial governments.

▴ Wealthy men wearing curly wigs of human hair tied with silk paid more taxes than poor people.

◂ British coins used in the colonies

Local Governments

Most of the colonies were divided into counties. Those counties, along with the towns that developed in them, were run by specially designed agencies. Although the British government sometimes exerted control, the colonists usually operated their own towns and counties.

In New England the **township** was the basic unit of government. At announced times, all the freeholders could attend town meetings. The town meeting was the purest form of democracy, or direct government, in America. A freeholder could have his say in a town meeting. He did not have to rely on an elected representative to speak for him. Some towns still use this system today.

At a town meeting, important issues were settled by majority vote. Less critical matters were also handled. For example, the citizens often appointed night watchmen to protect the town. All able-bodied men over sixteen were expected to take turns serving on night watch.

ELECTION DAY *in the* COLONIES

As mentioned earlier, the rights to vote and hold office were usually given only to free adult white males who owned property (usually fifty acres or fifty British pounds' worth of personal property). If a colonist met these qualifications, he could participate in elections.

Voting in a colonial election was very different from going to the polls, or voting places, today. The sheriff or the justice of the peace often opened the polls on Election Day by standing in front of the door of the polling place and reading the official notice of election. If a candidate had no opposition, he might be elected simply by voters raising their hands to support him. When there was more than one candidate, each voter entered, his name was called, and the official cried, "How vote ye?" The voter then answered aloud, and the town clerk recorded the vote. This type of voting was called *teller voting* because voters "told" their votes aloud.

Sometimes the candidates stayed at the polls. When someone voted for a candidate, that candidate might stand, bow, and thank the voter. When the sheriff or the justice thought sufficient time had passed, he went to the door and called out, "Gentlemen, freeholders, come into the court and give your vote, or the poll will be closed."

Election Day was often a day of celebration. Many people had to travel some distance to vote, so they often handled other business in town as well. They stayed part of the day to visit friends, gather news, and perhaps celebrate the results of the election.

▲ Town meeting in early New England

Wealthy people who did not want to serve paid others to serve for them. Besides patrolling the streets, watchmen called out the time of night and weather conditions.

At town meetings, citizens also considered ways to help the poor. The simplest type of relief was to send a poor person "round the town" to live several weeks with each family. In some instances, a single family provided food and shelter and received money from the town for doing so.

Larger towns, throughout the colonies, sometimes built almshouses for the needy. Most people considered poverty a shame and individuals usually had to be very desperate in order to ask help. Towns wasted little sympathy on the lazy or beggars. Such individuals were often jailed, or even whipped and expelled from town. Many American colonists believed that it was important to take individual responsibility for one's well-being.

In the southern colonies, there were fewer towns. The population lived mostly in rural areas (places outside cities and towns). Local government was often organized by counties. When elections were held for local officials, prominent plantation owners were usually the winners. The middle colonies formed local governments similar to those in both New England and the South.

SECTION REVIEW 3.4

1. Who chose the leaders in charter, proprietary, and royal colonies?
2. Who could vote in the colonies?
3. What types of things might the justice of the peace have done?
4. What type of tax became the main source of income for the colonies?
5. Contrast New England's local government with that of the southern colonies.
6. If government is instituted by God, why might different types be formed?

CHAPTER 3 REVIEW

Making Connections

1. What is a "mother country"?
2. In what centuries were the years AD 190, 1400, and 2020? (Remember that centuries start with year 01 and end with year 00.)
3. What percentage of the approximately ten million Africans sent to the New World arrived in the future United States?
4. How was frontier life more dangerous than life in the more populated areas of the colonies?
5. Why were so many colonists farmers?
6. Compare and contrast farming in the three colonial regions.
7. How did the colonists' expansion affect Indian lands?
8. How did the King Philip's War in New England affect both the colonists and the Indians?
9. What power did the legislature have over the governor? What effect could this have on the governor?
10. How did the basic unit of government in New England function?

Thinking Critically

11. Use a globe or map to determine the geographical relationship between the mother countries of the two most populous groups that came to the early colonies. What do you notice?
12. Economic growth can be seen as both good and bad. How does the triangular trade illustrate this?
13. Who do you think should have been allowed to vote in the colonies? Why?

Living as a Christian Citizen

14. Should cultures in a nation merge together in a "melting pot" or retain their own distinct ways of life in more of a "salad bowl"? Write a brief paragraph of your opinion.
15. How does the mission work among the Indians in colonial times show both biblical and unbiblical motivations in presenting the gospel?

▾ Stocks for punishing offenders

Terms to Remember

Great Migration
frontier
Conestoga wagons
subsistence farmers
plantations
tidewater
triangular trade
John Eliot
praying towns
Pequot War
King Philip's War
Bacon's Rebellion
militia
"power of the purse"
freeholders
justices of the peace
township

CHAPTER 4 Daily Life in the Colonies

Life in the colonies was quite unlike life in America today. If you traveled back in time, your world would seem much smaller. In colonial America, most people were familiar with only the town or county in which they lived. They walked or journeyed by horseback nearly everywhere they went. Their friendships were usually limited to their own social class. The food they ate and the clothes they wore were different from today. They might have spoken with an accent that you would not recognize. Most modern Americans would be uncomfortable in that almost foreign world.

Despite the significant changes that have occurred since colonial times, the people in that period were much like us. Though the majority embraced the values of equality, individualism, growth, and freedom, they often viewed these values differently than we do today. Most cared for their families, believed hard work was essential, and thought that churches were important.

GUIDING QUESTION

- What were the characteristics of the upper, middle, and lower classes?

▾ Silver creamer

4.1 SOCIAL CLASS

What were the typical lifestyles of the colonial social classes?

Individuals in colonial times were generally more concerned about a person's social class than people are today. Class often determined where people sat in church, which occupation a person could follow, educational opportunities, and voting rights. Even so, most people who worked hard could move into a higher class.

The Upper Class

All three colonial regions had an upper class. Its members were also called aristocrats. In New England, the upper class generally included merchants, traders, and some members of the clergy. In the middle and southern colonies, the upper class included those who owned large pieces of land. A few gained their positions by holding high offices or by marrying wealthy people. The upper class in the South consisted primarily of plantation owners.

In all three regions, upper-class families enjoyed more comforts and luxuries than the middle and lower classes. Usually, those in the upper class imported much of their fabric, clothing, furniture, and other goods from Europe. Their sons received good educations. Their servants helped perform the household chores.

Many in the upper class viewed themselves as protectors of culture. They did not want the music, plays, architecture, fashion, and customs of Europe to be forgotten in America.

▾ Portrait of John Copley, a famous colonial artist, and his family

◂ George Whitefield preaching in London

▾ Blacksmith using a colonial forge

COLONIAL TRADESMEN

A variety of tradesmen worked in each colonial town. Some of their tasks are familiar to us while others are less common today.

Apothecary: prepared medicines and visited the sick
Baker: baked breads and pastries
Blacksmith: prepared horseshoes and metal tools
Bookbinder: assembled books and pamphlets
Cabinetmaker: built furniture
Carpenter: built houses
Chandler: made candles
Cooper: made barrels and buckets
Dressmaker: made women's clothing
Gunsmith: made guns
Midwife: served at the birthing of babies
Miller: ground grain
Milliner: sewed hats
Pewterer: made spoons, dishes, and cups from an alloy of tin and lead
Printer: printed newspapers and pamphlets
Shoemaker: made and repaired shoes
Tailor: made and altered clothing
Tanner: treated hides to make leather
Weaver: made fabrics
Wheelwright: built wheels
Wigmaker: prepared fashionable wigs and dressed hair

The Middle Class

The middle class included colonists who were neither wealthy nor poor. Unlike Europe, America had plenty of land, and the land was available to almost everyone. A good effort at farming would usually feed and clothe a family. Many in the middle class gradually moved up the social ladder in the New World. They generally owned some land and had reasonably comfortable homes. But they lacked the servants and the luxuries that the aristocrats could afford. The middle class included the more prosperous small farmers, shopkeepers, ship captains, tradesmen, and less prominent members of the clergy. These people formed the core of colonial society.

The Lower Class

Though many subsistence farmers (see Chapter 3) and unskilled laborers were in the lowest class, the poorest were usually servants and slaves. Servants owned no land and had few material possessions. At the bottom of the social scale was the growing number of slaves.

Servants

The lowest rungs on the social ladder in white society were occupied by servants. Many of these were **indentured servants**, individuals who had gained their passage to America in return for four to seven years' labor upon arrival in the colonies. They were usually single men who were eighteen to thirty years old, though a few women also came. An indentured servant could not marry without his master's consent. Few masters consented because they would have to pay the cost of rearing children that might result from the marriage. Indentured servants who ran away from their masters and were caught usually paid for their action with additional years of service. Though some servants lived in relative comfort, others lived difficult lives.

When his service was completed, an indentured servant received his "freedom dues"—perhaps a new suit, some tools (such as an ax and a hoe), and sometimes even cash. Some received land. Many former indentured servants moved quickly into the middle class, and some became quite successful. For example, in 1629 seven members of the Virginia House of Burgesses were former indentured servants.

Slaves

As mentioned in Chapter 1, the first Africans in the English colonies arrived in Jamestown in 1619. Though these individuals appeared to have been treated as indentured servants, most future Africans who arrived were slaves, brought to America because the white colonists wanted a cheap and lasting source of labor for their plantations.

Slaves lacked many privileges that white colonists enjoyed. Although people in other classes could move up the social ladder, those enslaved could not. Freed blacks in the South had to carry papers to prove that they were free. Laws in southern colonies placed limitations on their rights to own land, vote, get an education, carry weapons, testify in court, or choose their jobs and religion.

Most slaves worked five and a half days a week, usually fifteen to sixteen hours a day in the summer and fourteen hours a day during the remainder of the year. Many free workers in those days kept similar hours—even the masters. However, there were dramatic differences. Free workers and masters were working for pay, they were able to spend their money and leisure time as they wished, and they were not the personal property of another individual.

During the colonial period, some leading colonists questioned slavery. Many religious leaders criticized the kidnapping of Africans for the slave trade and emphasized the Bible's teaching that all people are equal. These views led to the earliest antislavery movements. Thus, years before the War for Independence, tensions over slavery were already mounting. Slavery is one of the most horrible aspects of American history. For years, both during its existence and long after it was abolished, it produced devastating consequences.

opposing SLAVERY

A number of early colonists voiced opposition to slavery. In 1700 the Puritan leader Samuel Sewall wrote *The Selling of Joseph*. It was the first antislavery pamphlet published in the colonies. A Quaker leader named Francis Daniel Pastorius helped write the "1688 Germantown Quaker Petition Against Slavery." John Woolman—a Quaker merchant, journalist, and preacher—traveled throughout the frontier regions condemning slavery. Sadly, the inhumane practice grew in America because of its profitability.

SECTION REVIEW 4.1

1. What three groups of people belonged to the upper classes in New England? in the middle and southern colonies?
2. How was the upper class different from the middle or lower classes in colonial America?
3. What was abundant in America that allowed colonists to become members of the middle class more easily than those who lived in most European countries?
4. Identify at least three groups of people in the middle class.
5. Compare and contrast the two poorest groups in the lower class.
6. How do social classes benefit society? How can they create problems?

▾ Cutting sugar cane on a southern plantation

COLONIAL HOMES

Colonial Americans lived in a very exciting era. The colonies were constantly growing and changing. During this time, styles for houses and furniture were becoming more refined, and Americans began to develop their own fashions.

Many early colonial homes had two rooms on each floor and a central chimney. Often the structures had wood siding. Log cabins proved to be practical on the frontier because they did not require nails, an expensive item in that day. Brick was used where clay was abundant, especially in areas where fire had devastated earlier dwellings. Boston had a disastrous fire in 1679 and was rebuilt mostly with red brick.

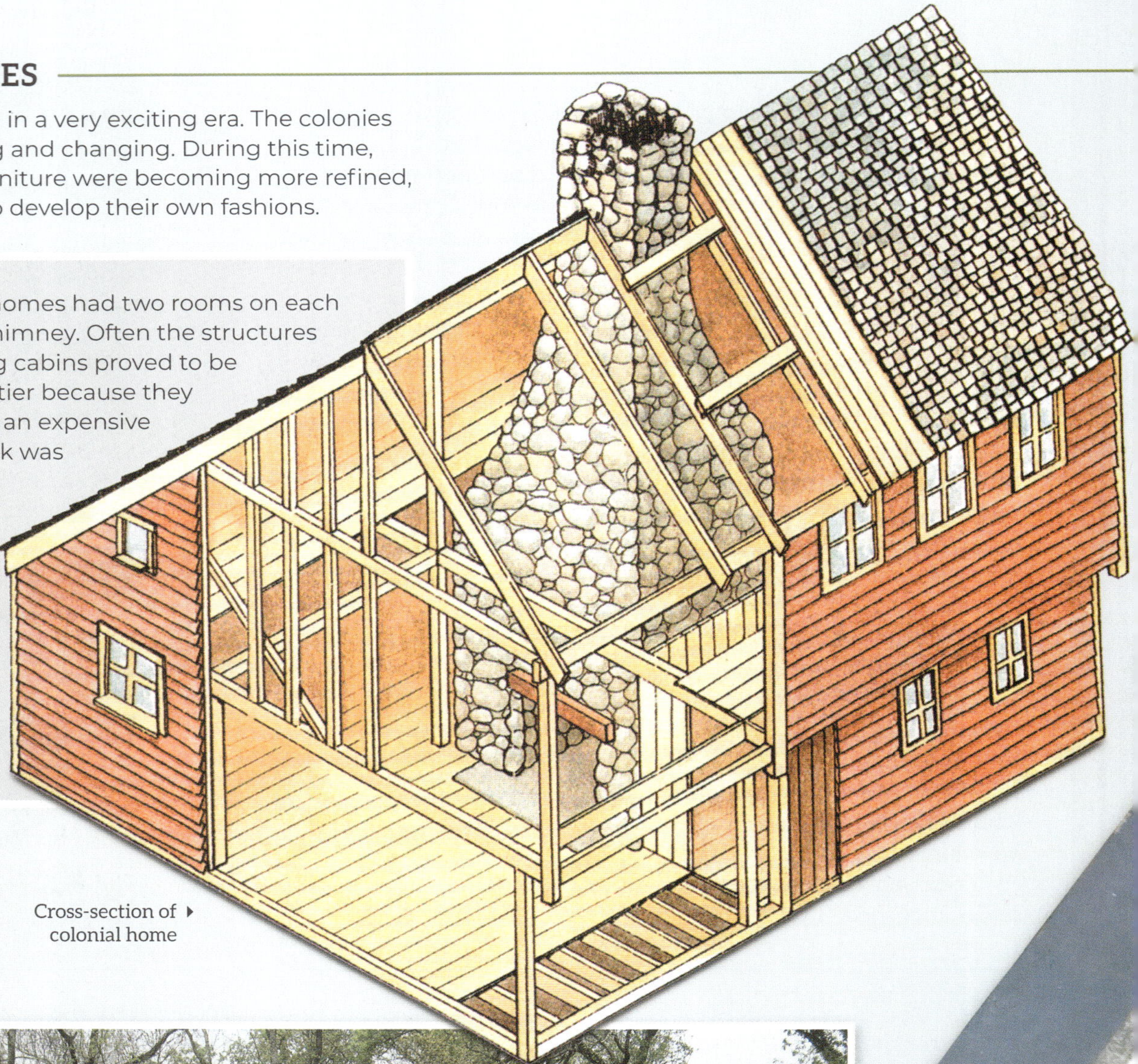

Cross-section of colonial home

Slave cabin

Draw knife for smoothing wood

By the 1700s, houses, especially those in cities, began to acquire a tidy appearance. While the outsides stayed the same, the interiors became more elaborate. Walls might be finished with fancy moldings and paneling. And for the first time, some walls were painted. Wealthy colonists began to use wallpaper, which was printed by hand. Rugs were arranged on the floors.

(Top right) Dining room of a wealthy colonist

Colonial home with Georgian architecture, New York

At first, most settlers made their own furniture. They usually did so in winter, when they could not work in the fields. They made cabinets, chests, tables, chairs, and other needed items. These pieces typically had little decoration. By the late seventeenth century, furniture craftsmen became established. Although they often used other local woods, they reserved walnut and mahogany to craft the finest furniture. Furniture also became more comfortable. For example, wingbacked armchairs were padded and upholstered. To provide more privacy and to keep the area warmer, curtains were sometimes placed around beds.

Wingback armchair

Mahogany dressing table

GUIDING QUESTIONS

- What were household responsibilities of family members in colonial times?
- How were length of life and marriage standards different from today?
- How did slaves deal with the hardships they faced?

4.2 FAMILY LIFE

What were the roles of family members in colonial society?

Household Roles

As the colonies changed, so did the colonial family. Though the first families arriving in the colonies struggled to survive, families brought stability and order to society. Despite the uniqueness of each region and colony, most colonists had similar ideas about the family and the role of each member. (We will see later that slave families, however, were vastly different from free families.)

Throughout the colonies, the family was the center of life. In the typical family, the father was the head. Among the Puritans, the family was considered to be a reflection of God, who delights in order. God intends the family to be the foundation on which society is built. The Puritans believed that if the family did not function properly, neither the church nor the government would function properly.

The southern colonists were not as concerned about the religious reasons for an orderly family. But they still believed that families led by the father were an essential part of society. On the plantations, families became wealthy and powerful. Fathers passed their wealth to their sons. Many families remained powerful for generations.

▾ Colonial medical supplies

▴ *The Artist and His Family* by James Peale

Throughout the colonies, the family was tasked with many responsibilities. Like parents today, colonial parents had to feed and clothe their children. In addition, they had to be doctors and nurses to their sick of all ages because there were almost no hospitals. With a limited number of schools, most education began and ended at home. Parents were expected to raise moral and disciplined children. Devout Christians taught their children about the Bible and the need for salvation.

In addition to serving as a hospital and school, the home was the center of economic activity. Farmers, of course, worked the land near their homes. And in the days before factories, nearly everyone else worked from home as well. Tradesmen often had their shops in the same building where they lived. Each member of a tradesman's family was expected to help make or sell the product. If the tradesman hired servants or apprentices to help with his work, they were often treated as family members.

The home was also the center of social activity. Colonial journals show that friends and neighbors visited at nearly all hours of the day. In wealthy homes, families spent leisure time together reading, dancing, and talking about the issues of the day. Parents normally took an active part in their children's social lives, most importantly by choosing whom they courted and married.

Men in Colonial Times

Within the colonial household, each member had certain rights and duties. Husbands and fathers were expected to provide financially for their families; and in many areas, including those controlled by Puritans, they could be punished for not doing so.

Men spent their days working on their farms or at their trades. Sometimes they had to spend time away from home on business or other work-related matters. They were not heavily involved in the day-to-day operation of the house. Free adult white men who owned property had the right to vote and hold government positions.

Women in Colonial Times

Colonial women played vital roles in society and had great power in their areas of responsibility and influence. They were normally expected to submit to their husbands, and Christians noted that Scripture taught them to do so.

One of the main daily tasks for women was preparing family meals. Unlike modern kitchens, which have stoves and refrigerators, the colonial kitchen had a fireplace and no running water. Feeding a family was a demanding job. Women also had to feed the animals, milk the cows, bake bread, and harvest and preserve food. If they were far from a weaver's shop, they had to spin and weave fibers into fabric before they could sew clothing. Even the wealthiest women on southern plantations often worked long hours to oversee the household chores.

In addition, women supervised their children all day. Most colonial families were quite large, with perhaps six or more children living at home. If a family was wealthy, the wife would also manage the servants.

Women were also vital in their husbands' work. Many wives worked alongside their husbands in the fields or in the shops. When her husband was away, a wife was in charge of all business. Some women also earned money on their own by selling produce or homemade goods and performing services for their neighbors. Women helped one another sew, teach children, and deliver babies.

Although colonial women performed many important tasks, they did not have the same legal rights as men. It was extremely rare for women to have the right to vote. Married women could not hold property. A single woman could own land or a business, but if she married, her property was placed under her husband's control.

Did you know?

A few women were allowed to vote in colonial times. For example, until 1777, women who owned property and whose husbands had died were allowed to vote in New York. Women who met certain requirements were allowed to vote in Massachusetts until 1780 and in New Hampshire until 1784.

In 1776 New Jersey gave voting rights to adults who possessed property or a significant amount of cash. However, women could vote only if they were single because married women could not legally own property. In 1807 the state restricted voting to males.

Carding, spinning, and weaving wool in a colonial home

Colonial kitchen

COLONIAL *games*

Colonial children did not have a wide variety of toys. Most were constructed from the materials which colonists had available. For example, they made dolls from rags, cornhusks, corncobs, and sticks. They played with hoops from barrels and made rackets in order to play a game similar to badminton. Though toys were simple, they were valued highly because there were few of them.

Children also played with marbles and enjoyed ninepins, a game similar to bowling. Hopscotch, whoop-and-hide (hide-and-seek), and shuffleboard were also favorites of the time. In addition to games, swimming and fishing were popular in the summer. In colder climates, ice skating and sleigh rides were common.

Playing at hoops ▲

▲ The Cadwalader family portrait shows family love and tenderness.

Children in Colonial Times

Colonial children learned early how to be helpful around the home and were expected to work diligently. Girls learned how to complete household chores, and most boys had chosen an occupation by age fourteen.

Life Expectancy and Marriage

In the earliest years of the colonies, death often interrupted normal family life. The colonists were much more familiar with death than we are today. Life expectancy was remarkably low compared to modern times. Parents could expect to outlive nearly half of their children, although many women died in childbirth. When one parent died, the other parent frequently remarried. This was often because assistance was needed with work and raising a family. Because life was short and death was all around them, many colonists recognized their daily need to be right with God.

People in this time did not usually marry because they had fallen in love. Nevertheless, once they were married, great emphasis was placed on the love that husbands and wives showed each other. This was certainly true of Puritans and other groups who believed that companionship and raising a godly family were the primary purposes of marriage. Devout Christians from all denominations taught their children to love and honor God and to obey their parents.

Hardships Facing the Slave Family

Although there were some free black families, most Africans were slaves and had to build families under the whites' control. In Africa, the Africans were part of extensive clans and families that gave them a sense of pride. When they were brought to America and separated from their relatives, their social networks collapsed. Many Africans in America could not even speak to one another because they were from different tribes that had different languages.

Diseases, required adjustments to a new environment, harsh treatment, and a variety of other factors meant that the earliest slaves struggled to survive in America. Eventually, slaves lived longer, and large groups were gathered on the plantations. Although slave marriage was not recognized by law, men and women often married and had families. Tragically, slave families could be torn apart when owners sold slaves to new masters.

▲ A slave couple preparing to "jump the broom," an African wedding tradition

Slave families bore little resemblance to free families. Instead of depending on fathers and husbands, slave families depended on their owners for everything. Many families were not allowed to live together. If family members were owned by different masters, they lived on separate plantations and were allowed to visit one another only at night or over the weekend if the master gave permission and they lived close enough. House slaves usually lived in or near the house, rather than in the slave quarters. Unlike mothers of white families, who ran the household and trained the children, slave mothers were away from home working in the fields or in the house all day. Young children were left in the care of elderly slave women. By age ten, the children were required to work.

Protecting and nourishing slave families was not a priority among colonists. In fact, this failure was one of the greatest injustices in this unjust system. Nevertheless, the fragile family structure was still one of the most important institutions that helped the slaves endure terrible hardships. Family members depended on each other through sickness, suffering on the plantations, and the death or removal of loved ones. The desire to improve the lives of their families led some slaves, who were allowed to do so, to raise their own crops or work elsewhere to earn a little extra money. Families were able to spend some free time together, particularly on Sundays.

SECTION REVIEW 4.2

1. What were the typical roles in colonial households for each of the following?
   a. Men
   b. Women
   c. Girls
   d. Boys
2. Create a chart with column headings "colonial times" and "modern times." Row headings should be "life expectancy," and "love before and after marriage." Complete the chart.
3. How were slave families different from free families?

GUIDING QUESTIONS

- How were schools organized in the colonies?
- Why were colleges started in the colonies?
- What was an apprenticeship?

4.3 EDUCATION

What was education like in colonial times?

In seventeenth- and eighteenth-century Europe, few people were educated except the wealthy. Common people rarely had access to schools or books. They worked from the time they were children to the time they died, without having time or money to formally learn about the world around them.

Most Americans valued educating their children. This was particularly true in New England where Puritans wanted their children to be able to read the Scriptures.

▾ New England dame school

Schools in New England

In the earliest colonial days, education took place at home. Parents were responsible for teaching their children to read and write. In 1642 the Massachusetts General Court passed a law ordering parents to teach their children about religion and the laws of the colony. If a child did not learn to read, the parents could be fined. Parents sometimes delegated the authority to educate their children to widows or single women who established small schools in their homes. Because the teachers were usually females, these schools were called **dame schools** (*dame* was a title for a woman at this time). These schools taught reading, writing, and math and emphasized moral and religious subjects. They typically provided the first instruction for boys and often the only schooling for girls.

Some villages organized **grammar schools** and hired teachers to manage their children's education. These schools provided more in-depth education than dame schools but were normally limited to males. Older students learned Greek and Latin. Subjects such as math, rhetoric (using speaking and writing to persuade), and philosophy were difficult to master, but the colonists believed that they were important and so they were taught at these schools. The upper class believed that correct grammar and accent, fluency in Greek and Latin, and knowledge of ancient literature set wealthy families apart from average people. Grammar school studies typically provided several years of education. In colonial days, graduation exercises usually involved graduates giving memorized speeches in Latin or Greek. Debates, using all the knowledge gained in grammar school, also occurred. If a student did well and had financial support, he might be able to enter college while still in his early teens.

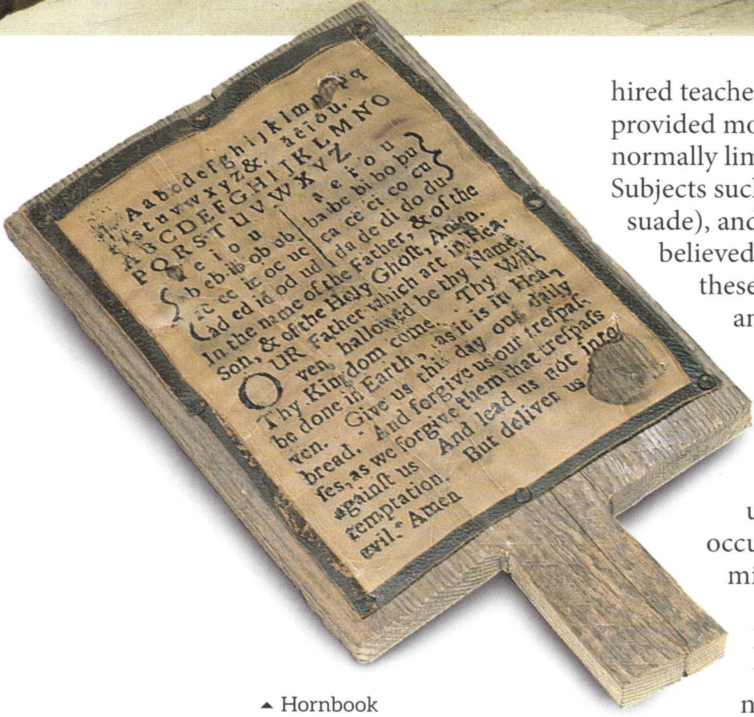

▴ Hornbook

Most colonial children first learned to read from a **hornbook**, a board that looked much like a paddle and was covered with a printed sheet. The board received its name because it had a thin, transparent sheet of animal horn that protected the printed portion. Hornbooks always had the alphabet listed on them. Sometimes they also included a list of vowels, some syllables to sound out, or the Lord's Prayer. Children from the upper class sometimes had fancy hornbooks that were made of brass or pewter. As students learned from their hornbooks, they often practiced forming their letters by tracing them in the sand that was put in front of fireplaces to catch sparks and prevent fires.

A child usually graduated from using the hornbook to using a primer, or textbook, for more thorough reading training. *The New England Primer,* the most popular textbook of the colonial period, provided basic grammar and vocabulary instruction along with moral lessons.

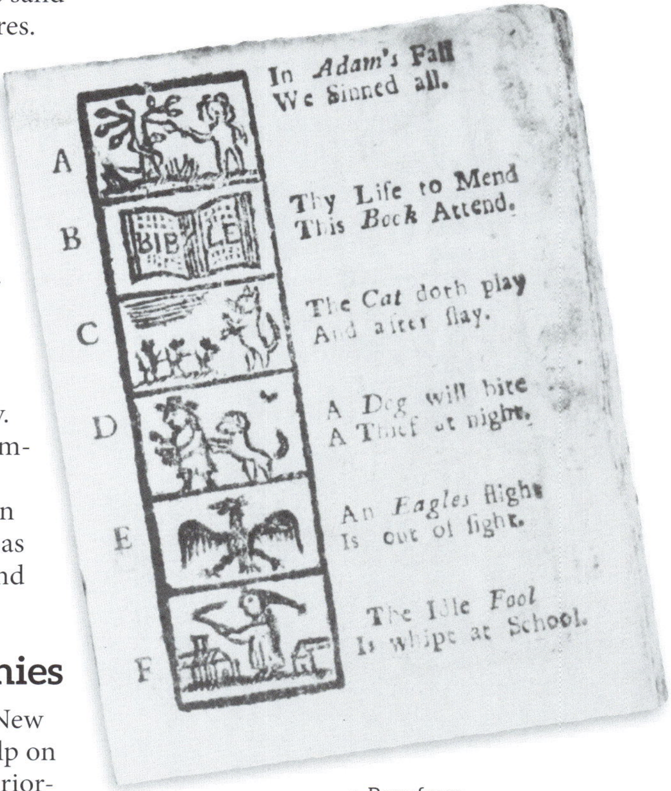

▲ Page from *The New England Primer*

In 1647 there were only eleven grammar schools in New England. In that year, the General Court of Massachusetts passed the **Old Deluder Satan Act** to prevent that "Old Deluder [deceiver], Satan" from keeping people "from the knowledge of the Scripture." The act required all towns of fifty or more families to appoint a schoolmaster to teach the children to read and write. The schoolmaster was to be paid from the public treasury. Most other New England colonies followed Massachusetts's example and established town schools.

By 1750 academies sometimes replaced grammar schools. In addition to Latin and Greek, these schools taught subjects such as English composition and literature, math, modern languages, and natural science.

Schools in the Middle and Southern Colonies

The middle and southern colonies had fewer schools than New England. Because long growing seasons required children to help on farms for much of the year, time for schooling was often not a priority. In addition, distances between farms made establishing schools difficult.

Some of the middle colonies established grammar schools, but churches organized most of them. For example, the Quakers established seventy schools in Pennsylvania and admitted students from all social classes.

Sometimes wealthy planters and farmers united to hire a schoolmaster, but this was rare. More often, children stayed at home and learned the basics from their parents. The wealthiest southerners sent their children to boarding schools in the colonies or in England. Others, in order to keep their children at home, hired private tutors. The tutors lived with the students' families and became like family members. Only the children of the upper class could receive such an education.

Colonial schoolroom ▸

Did you know?

College in the colonies was not always a time of serious study. Rebellions and vandalism occurred numerous times at Harvard College and other institutions during the 1700s and 1800s.

Documented events include food fights (sometimes with the use of utensils and dishes), cannonballs rolled down stairs, loud scraping of chairs across the floor during chapel, and gunpowder placed into firewood (with explosive results). Occasionally, whole classes were fined or even expelled for their disorderly conduct.

Colleges

Most early colleges in the colonies were established to train ministers. The first institution of higher learning in America was **Harvard College** in Cambridge, Massachusetts. The Puritans founded it in 1636 "to advance learning and perpetuate [preserve] it to posterity [future generations]; dreading to leave an illiterate ministry to the churches, when our present ministers shall lie in the dust." The college was named after John Harvard, a young minister in nearby Charlestown who died of tuberculosis. He left his library of four hundred books and half his estate to the school. The money from the sale of the estate was used to purchase additional books. Yale College, in Connecticut, was founded in 1701 because Puritans believed that Harvard had drifted from some of its earlier strong religious teachings.

The College of William and Mary was established in 1693 in Virginia. It was the only college in the southern colonies for many years. Its law school was the first in America.

Many aristocratic families that could afford to do so continued to send their sons across the Atlantic for college. This practice helped keep Americans interested in the current scientific discoveries, fashions, and thinking in Europe.

▾ Harvard College

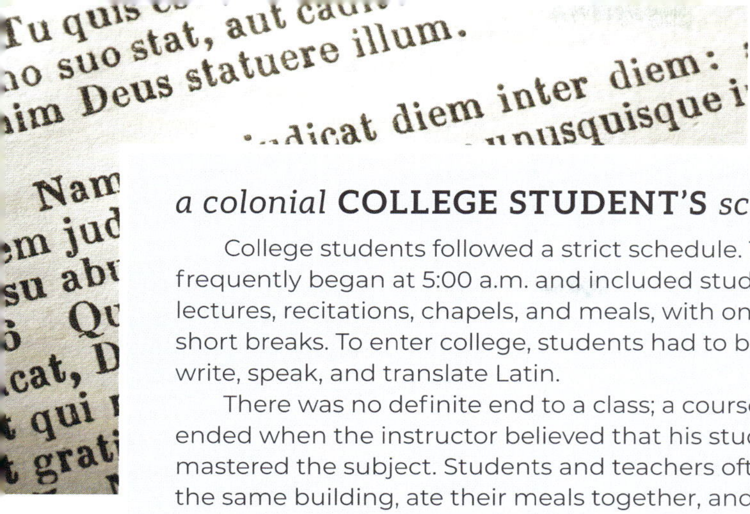

a colonial COLLEGE STUDENT'S schedule

College students followed a strict schedule. Their days frequently began at 5:00 a.m. and included study, prayers, lectures, recitations, chapels, and meals, with only two short breaks. To enter college, students had to be able to write, speak, and translate Latin.

There was no definite end to a class; a course of study ended when the instructor believed that his students had mastered the subject. Students and teachers often lived in the same building, ate their meals together, and studied and worshiped together.

▲ A tailor teaching his apprentice

Trades and Apprenticeships

Not all colonial children completed formal schooling. For many children, particularly those outside the upper class, education was limited to what they needed to make a living. The **apprenticeship** system was used to teach trades. Young boys left home and lived with someone who was skilled at performing their chosen trade. An apprenticeship usually lasted seven years or until the apprentice turned twenty-one.

Benjamin Rush, a doctor and a signer of the Declaration of Independence, was once apprenticed to a Philadelphia doctor. Rush wrote that when he was an apprentice, he had little free time. During his five-and-a-half-year apprenticeship, he was absent from work only eleven days and away from the home of the doctor who was training him on only three evenings.

Apprenticeships sometimes led to wealth, and men who completed them could reach positions of high esteem. Like Rush, several other signers of the Declaration of Independence were once apprentices. Roger Sherman began as a shoemaker's apprentice, George Taylor served as an iron maker in Pennsylvania, and Benjamin Franklin was apprenticed to his brother, a printer.

▼ Case holding letters for a printing press

SECTION REVIEW 4.3

1. Identify two types of schools in colonial New England. What did each type teach?
2. What Massachusetts law required all towns of fifty or more families to hire a schoolmaster? Why was it given this name?
3. How was education in the southern and middle colonies different from that in New England?
4. Public education in the colonies began for religious reasons. What was the original reason for public schools? How has that changed over time?
5. Why was Harvard founded?
6. Explain the system used in the colonies to teach trades.

GUIDING QUESTION

- What religious groups were common in the colonies?

4.4 RELIGIOUS BACKGROUND

How much religious diversity and religious freedom existed in the colonies?

America has always been a place of religious diversity. With people from so many different backgrounds, the colonies were home to many religious groups, most of which lived together fairly peacefully.

New England

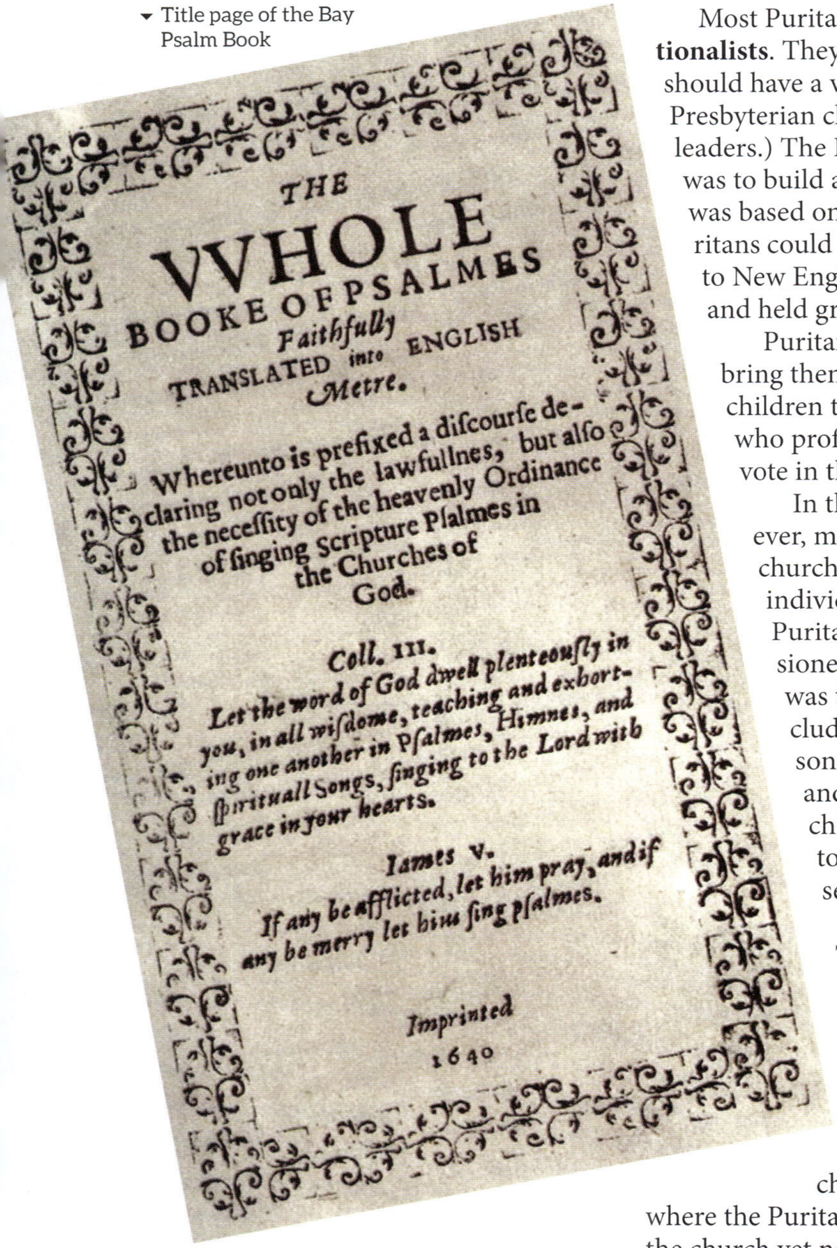

THE
VVHOLE
BOOKE OF PSALMES
Faithfully
TRANSLATED into ENGLISH
Metre.

Whereunto is prefixed a diſcourſe declaring not only the lawfullnes, but alſo the neceſſity of the heavenly Ordinance of ſinging Scripture Pſalmes in the Churches of God.

Coll. III.
Let the word of God dwell plenteouſly in you, in all wiſdome, teaching and exhorting one another in Pſalmes, Himnes, and ſpirituall Songs, ſinging to the Lord with grace in your hearts.

Iames V.
If any be afflicted, let him pray, and if any be merry let him ſing pſalmes.

Imprinted
1640

Title page of the Bay Psalm Book

Most Puritans in New England became known as **Congregationalists**. They believed that the members of church congregations should have a voice in how the church operated. (Anglican and Presbyterian churches were governed by bishops, elders, or other leaders.) The Puritans believed that one of their responsibilities was to build a Christian society, one in which every aspect of life was based on biblical teaching. As a minority in England, the Puritans could not accomplish this goal there. But when they came to New England, they comprised the majority of the population and held great influence in society.

Puritans baptized their children as infants in order to bring them into their Christian society. They expected the children to profess salvation when they grew older. Adults who professed salvation could become full church members, vote in the church, and participate in the Lord's Supper.

In the second generation of American Puritans, however, many people failed to profess salvation and join the church. This caused Puritan pastors great concern. If these individuals and their children were not part of the church, Puritans could not build the Christian society they envisioned. What would preserve their vision? Their solution was the **Half-Way Covenant** (1662). This measure excluded those who had been baptized yet did not personally profess salvation from taking the Lord's Supper and from voting in church matters, but it allowed their children to be baptized into the church. The goal was to keep everyone in the community attending church services where they would hear biblical teaching.

A few pastors opposed the Half-Way Covenant. They believed that allowing the children of people who did not personally profess salvation to be baptized was wrong. Those leaders worried that it might be the beginning of the weakening and corrupting of the standards in the Puritan church. They were unable to stop the measure, and some of their concerns proved true. After additional changes by the early 1700s, many people in the areas where the Puritans had settled, including some pastors, were part of the church yet needed to be converted.

Puritan influence in Massachusetts declined further when the colony lost its charter. The new one, issued by the English king in 1691, allowed non-Puritans to vote in colonial elections. This was a significant change from how the colony had been governed.

the Salem WITCH TRIALS

In January 1692 in Salem Village, Massachusetts, a group of young girls began having hysterical fits. They threw objects, screamed, made bizarre sounds, and bent their bodies into strange shapes. They claimed that witches were afflicting them and began to name certain people in the village as witches. Over 150 people were accused of witchcraft in the next few months. The resulting trials were known as the **Salem witch trials**.

Oddly, only those who maintained their innocence were executed; those who confessed to witchcraft were imprisoned. Realizing this fact, some of the accused confessed to save themselves. Still, nineteen people were hanged. A seventy-one-year-old man was pressed to death with heavy weights, and several people died in prison.

As the trials continued, some Puritan ministers in Massachusetts recommended that officials use caution and restraint. For example, Boston pastor Increase Mather said, "It were better that ten suspected witches should escape than that one innocent person should be condemned." By late October 1692, after months of frenzy, the governor of the colony prohibited further arrests and released many of the accused witches. By May 1693 he pardoned all those in prison that had been charged with witchcraft.

Within five years the citizens of Massachusetts held a day of prayer and fasting to implore God's pardon for their actions. One of the judges in the trials, Samuel Sewall (the author of the antislavery pamphlet, *The Selling of Joseph,* mentioned earlier in the chapter) was overcome with guilt. He publicly asked forgiveness for his actions in the Salem witch trials. Ann Putnam, one of the hysterical girls, stood before the church congregation in Salem Village and apologized for being "an instrument for the accusing of several persons of a grievous crime, whereby their lives were taken away from them, whom now I have just grounds and good reason to believe they were innocent persons."

How can the events of Salem Village be explained? The causes have been debated for centuries. It is certain, however, that innocent people died because of fear and hysteria and that the reputation of the Massachusetts Puritans was blemished. Regrettably, the worthy contributions of early American Puritanism have been overshadowed by the wild, fanatical actions of a few.

▲ Gemeinhaus, or "congregation house," a Moravian church in North Carolina

▼ Bruton Parish Church, the original Anglican church in Williamsburg, Virginia, still functions today.

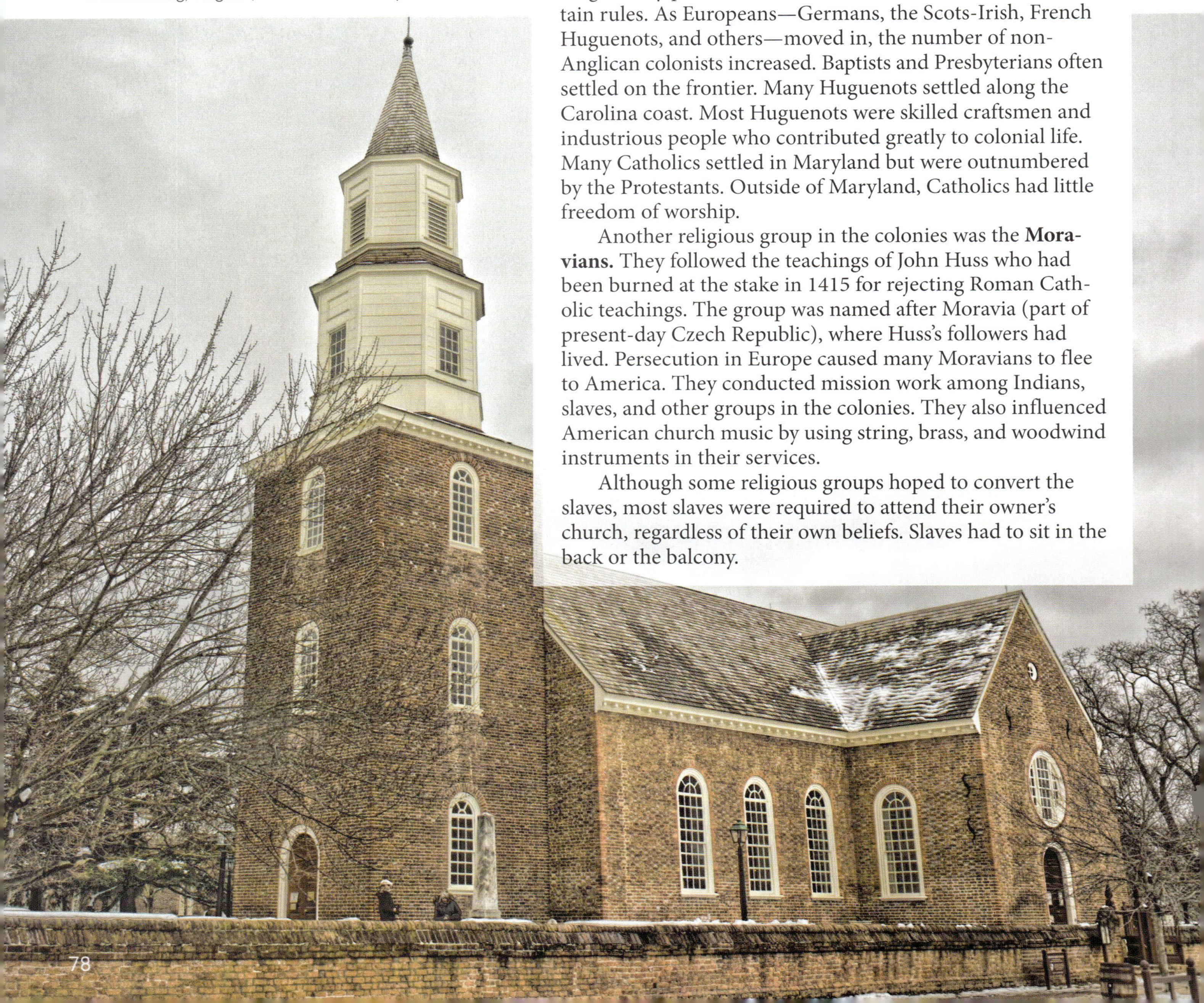

The Southern Colonies

The Church of England, or the Anglican Church, was the official church in every southern colony. The bishop of London was in charge of the Anglican congregations in America. Although he never visited the colonies, he appointed people to report conditions to him and to advise American pastors.

The Anglican Church was strongest in the cities. Often there were not enough ministers to serve in the rural areas. Each church served a neighborhood or an area called a parish. Each Anglican rector, or pastor, received a house and sometimes a small farm. He also earned a small salary from taxes (usually on tobacco), as well as wedding and funeral fees. The Anglican Church was not as zealous in seeking new converts as many other groups. It was, however, popular with members of the upper class.

Other religious groups were permitted in the South as long as they paid taxes to the state church and followed certain rules. As Europeans—Germans, the Scots-Irish, French Huguenots, and others—moved in, the number of non-Anglican colonists increased. Baptists and Presbyterians often settled on the frontier. Many Huguenots settled along the Carolina coast. Most Huguenots were skilled craftsmen and industrious people who contributed greatly to colonial life. Many Catholics settled in Maryland but were outnumbered by the Protestants. Outside of Maryland, Catholics had little freedom of worship.

Another religious group in the colonies was the **Moravians.** They followed the teachings of John Huss who had been burned at the stake in 1415 for rejecting Roman Catholic teachings. The group was named after Moravia (part of present-day Czech Republic), where Huss's followers had lived. Persecution in Europe caused many Moravians to flee to America. They conducted mission work among Indians, slaves, and other groups in the colonies. They also influenced American church music by using string, brass, and woodwind instruments in their services.

Although some religious groups hoped to convert the slaves, most slaves were required to attend their owner's church, regardless of their own beliefs. Slaves had to sit in the back or the balcony.

The Middle Colonies

The middle colonies had the greatest religious diversity. Members of many denominations, such as Anglicans, Baptists, Lutherans, Dutch Reformed, Presbyterians, and Quakers, settled there.

Jews also moved to the middle colonies, as well as to other regions in America. Because most Jews do not believe that Jesus is the Son of God, many Protestants throughout the colonies tried to limit their influence and freedoms. For example, although the Jews could trade and buy land, they were normally not allowed to be shopkeepers or tradesmen. In many places they were not allowed to construct synagogues.

Pennsylvania, a Quaker colony, was more tolerant than any other middle colony. A small number of Catholics settled in Pennsylvania, building the first public Catholic church in America in 1733. Many Amish and Mennonites settled in Lancaster County. The Dunkers, a German group whose name was derived from their method of baptism, established a settlement nearby in 1745. Christopher Sauer, a German printer and Dunker leader, printed America's first German Bible in 1743. He also edited and printed the first German newspaper in America. In the 1740s, Moravians established the cities of Nazareth and Bethlehem in Pennsylvania.

▼ As part of their communion service, Dunker Brethren share a love feast after a ritual foot washing.

Did you know?

Puritans in Massachusetts did not celebrate Christmas for several reasons. First, they knew that it is unclear when Jesus was actually born since no specific date is mentioned in the Scriptures. Second, they were unhappy that Christmas was observed near the time Romans had celebrated festivals associated with their religion. Third, Christmas in Europe sometimes included heavy drinking, crude behavior, and little reference to the birth of Christ. For these reasons and others, Puritans did not observe the holiday.

Anglicans, however, celebrated the Twelve Days of Christmas from December 25 through January 6 with feasts and decorations, including mistletoe, but exchanged few gifts.

▲ Mistletoe with Christmas ribbon

SECTION REVIEW 4.4

1. Why were the Puritans often called Congregationalists?
2. What were the good and bad effects of the Half-Way Covenant?
3. Do you agree with the Half-Way Covenant? Why or why not?
4. Where did the witch trials begin? How many people died?
5. What was the official church in the southern colonies?
6. What religious group followed the teachings of John Huss? Why did this group come to America?
7. What colonial region had the greatest religious diversity?

GUIDING QUESTIONS

- Who were the key leaders in the Great Awakening?
- What was the impact of the Great Awakening?
- What other religious influences existed during the Great Awakening?

4.5 THE GREAT AWAKENING

What was the Great Awakening and how did it affect colonial culture?

By the 1720s, several factors had led to a declining interest in spiritual matters among colonists. Increasing prosperity from trade caused some to turn to materialism. Puritan churches had lost much of their spiritual strength. Fewer churches in the southern and middle colonies preached the gospel. Some ministers were unconverted. Many colleges that were formed to prepare men for the ministry now focused students on other careers. The colonies needed a revival. One began in the 1720s and was so powerful that historians call it the **Great Awakening**.

Log College ▲

Leaders of the Great Awakening

The revival began in New Jersey in Dutch Reformed churches and quickly spread. Presbyterian minister William Tennent trained a number of young men, including his sons, in a log cabin (nicknamed "the Log College"). Log College graduates helped spread the revival throughout the middle colonies, especially New Jersey and Pennsylvania, and to the South where William Robinson and Samuel Blair preached. Another Presbyterian, Samuel Doak, ministered in frontier Tennessee. In Virginia, the most important figure of the Great Awakening was probably Samuel Davies.

Jonathan Edwards in New England

Jonathan Edwards also played a key role in the Great Awakening. Edwards, who was from Massachusetts, entered Yale at age thirteen. After college, he became associate pastor of his grandfather's Congregational church in Northampton, Massachusetts. Two years later, he became the senior pastor. He earned a reputation as one of the most brilliant philosophers and theologians in the colonies.

In 1737 Edwards began preaching sermons that led to the conversions of both young and old. Within two years, more than three hundred were saved. A high point in the New England revival occurred in July 1741 when Edwards preached one of the best-known sermons of all time, "Sinners in the Hands of an Angry God." As he preached on the judgment of God, conviction of sin was so great that Edwards had to stop several times when the cries of the people made it nearly impossible to hear the sermon. Many listeners were overcome with guilt and their need for repentance. The resulting hatred for sin brought genuine repentance and godly living.

After leaving his church in Northampton, Edwards served as a missionary to Indians. In 1757 he became president of the College of New Jersey (later renamed Princeton University). But after only a few months at the college, he died from complications after receiving a smallpox vaccination.

George Whitefield from England

God also mightily used an English preacher during the Great Awakening. **George Whitefield** attended the University of Oxford in England where he became a close friend of the Wesleys. John Wesley later became a famous preacher, and his brother Charles wrote thousands of hymns. Whitefield was a gifted speaker and an outstanding evangelist. He traveled to America seven times in his thirty-four-year ministry to conduct preaching tours. He preached at least eighteen thousand times during his ministry (an average of once every seventeen hours).

Some ministers opposed his bluntness while others believed his preaching was too emotional. As a result, he often had to preach in open fields because churches refused to let him use their pulpits. But his voice reached greater crowds outdoors than could have gathered in even the largest church buildings. When Benjamin Franklin heard Whitefield preach in Philadelphia, he calculated that thirty thousand people could hear the minister's powerful voice.

Whitefield was instrumental in the Great Awakening throughout the colonies, but his influence was felt especially in the South. He was concerned for all people, but he had a particular burden for children. In 1740 he established an orphanage near Savannah, Georgia. He also preached to slaves, wrote a gospel tract for Indians, and had an indirect influence in starting several colleges. Whitefield died during a preaching tour in New England and is buried beneath the pulpit of a church in Newburyport, Massachusetts.

Samuel Davies in the South

Samuel Davies was a major leader of the Great Awakening in the South and a great speaker. He was born in Delaware on November 3, 1723. He was licensed as a Presbyterian preacher in 1746, and the following year he began serving as an evangelist in Hanover County, Virginia.

For more than eleven years, Davies led services in seven churches in five different counties. He traveled by horseback over the whole state of Virginia, organizing revival meetings. He gave young preachers practical training and distributed books to frontier homes and slave dwellings. He visited plantations to preach to slaves and organized his church members to teach slaves how to read so they could study the Scriptures. Davies also worked for more freedom of religion in Virginia, where the Anglican Church was the established church.

As a pastor, Davies was careful to challenge his congregations by setting a good example. He preached to meet people's needs because he believed that preaching should help individuals solve the problems of life and prepare to face death.

Shortly after Jonathan Edwards died in 1758, Samuel Davies was named his replacement as the president of the College of New Jersey (Princeton University). Davies held that position until his death in 1761.

David Brainerd ▸

Effects of the Great Awakening

The Great Awakening achieved widespread results. It has been said that the revival knew no boundaries—political, social, ethnic, or geographic. Seven effects are clearly evident.

CONVERTS

First, the most obvious result was the number of converts. Between 1740 and 1742, thousands became Christians in New England alone (whose total population was only three hundred thousand).

CHURCH AND GOVERNMENT

Second, the Great Awakening increased the distinction between church and government. Roger Williams and others had already established the principle of separation between church and state. During the revival, many church members began to organize worship on their own. They realized that their churches could exist without the government's support. Many now believed that a church's official status in the colony mattered little.

MISSIONS

Third, the emphasis on missions substantially increased, particularly of the need to evangelize African Americans and Native Americans. Under Whitefield, many black people came to Christ, some of whom were allowed to form their own churches. The best-known missionary to the Indians during this period was David Brainerd, who worked in New York, New Jersey, Pennsylvania, and Massachusetts. He died of tuberculosis at the age of twenty-nine, but his diaries continue to inspire others to devote their lives to missionary work. Another missionary, Samuel Kirkland, began his work in 1764 with the Iroquois tribes in New York. Simon Horton, a Presbyterian, reached the Indians on Long Island, New York. Moravians worked among Indian tribes throughout the colonial era.

HUTS *of* PEACE, HUTS *of* GRACE

David Zeisberger was born in Moravia in 1721. In 1738, he traveled to America and settled in the colony of Georgia. Later, he moved near Bethlehem, Pennsylvania, and worked as a Moravian missionary to various Native American tribes in that colony and in New York.

The English forced the Delaware Indians, with whom Zeisberger worked, to move further west in the Pennsylvania territory. The Moravians and some of their Indian followers established a town called Gnadenhutten ("huts of grace") and another known as Friedenhutten ("huts of peace").

Soon many political difficulties disrupted these Christian communities. Both the English and the French wanted to control the region and were in frequent conflict with each other. An Indian tribe allied with the French attacked and burned Gnadenhutten in November 1755. The community was rebuilt; however, conflict between whites who wanted to expand westward and neighboring Indian tribes who opposed them caused frequent problems.

Later, some of the Delawares established another Gnadenhutten, this one in Ohio. Zeisberger continued his missionary work in that town and the surrounding region. Unfortunately, that community was also attacked in 1782. This time, the assault was by militiamen from Pennsylvania. In what became known as the Gnadenhutten massacre, or the Moravian massacre, almost a hundred Indians were brutally killed. Most were women and children.

After the 1782 massacre, Zeisberger's missionary efforts continued and even extended into present-day Michigan. He spoke several Indian languages fluently and worked diligently to produce materials that aided Christian Indians. These included hymns, Bible translations, and educational materials. In 1808, he died in Ohio at age eighty-seven. With the exception of a few short intervals, he had spent more than six decades as a missionary among the Indians. His tireless work and commitment to spreading the gospel continue to be an inspiration.

BLACK *churches and* PREACHERS

Throughout the colonial period, many slave preachers held meetings on plantations. Some of these men could read, but most could not. There were also some free black preachers. Unfortunately, many whites viewed black preachers, free or slave, with suspicion. They were worried that preachers would use speaking opportunities to create discontent among slaves.

After the revival, blacks were drawn to Baptist and Methodist churches. The first black churches in America appear to have started in the 1770s. George Liele and David George, both former slaves, were important pastors of early black congregations.

HIGHER EDUCATION

Fourth, the revival affected higher education. Many Christians acknowledged that early colleges had departed from biblical teachings and emphasis, so they built new schools to train pastors and missionaries. The College of New Jersey—where Jonathan Edwards and Samuel Davies later served as presidents—was founded by Presbyterians in 1746. King's College (now Columbia University) was founded by Anglicans in 1754. The College of Rhode Island (now Brown University) was founded by Baptists in 1764, and Queen's College (now Rutgers University) was founded by the Dutch Reformed in 1766. Dartmouth College, established in New Hampshire in 1769, was originally opened by Congregationalists to teach Indians about Christianity and the English way of life.

▾ King's College, now Columbia University

DIVISION WITHIN CHURCHES

Fifth, the Great Awakening brought unexpected results within churches. It caused some division. For example, nearly every denomination had disagreements between those who favored the revival and those who opposed it. In addition, the revival weakened the Anglican Church in the South. As mentioned earlier, it was the official church in every southern colony. However, more of its ministers opposed the Great Awakening than those in any other denomination. Because many people in the region supported the revival, other denominations increased in popularity, while support for the Anglican Church diminished.

EQUALITY

Sixth, the revival brought a greater emphasis on equality. For example, classes within society became less important. Revivalists like Edwards noted that class distinctions did not determine spiritual growth—a member of the upper class could have little concern about spiritual matters while someone in the lower class might be a devoted follower of Christ. Furthermore, the Great Awakening stressed the equality of all people. Respect declined for clergy who opposed the movement or whose life showed no evidence of true conversion.

POLITICAL FREEDOM

Seventh, the Great Awakening influenced thinking about colonists' political freedom. As colonists began to question their spiritual authorities, they used the terms *liberty* and *rights* regarding the church. They also used these terms in politics. They called for a change in political leadership, just as they called for a change in church leadership. The Great Awakening was the first unifying event for the colonies. As all three regions of the colonies became united by spiritual ties, they began to think more about their status in the British Empire. Some historians believe that these thoughts helped prepare the way for the War for Independence.

Other Influences during the Great Awakening

The Great Awakening changed the religious thinking of many Americans, but it was not the only influence on eighteenth-century minds. Many colonists, especially those who were educated in Europe, were affected by the **Enlightenment**. This was a philosophical movement that emphasized science and reason above all else. Some of its followers viewed human reasoning as the source for all truth and discarded any religious teaching that they could not understand or explain. Some exalted man's abilities above the truths God reveals in Scripture.

▲ Old Ship Church in Hingham, Massachusetts, is the oldest continuously used church in North America. Originally a Puritan church, today it is a Unitarian Universalist church.

Deism

The Enlightenment produced an influential but flawed philosophy known as **deism**. Deists thought that the Bible had to be tested by human reason. They were willing to ignore the parts that disagreed with that reasoning. They believed that their own analysis showed them all they needed to know about God and their moral duties.

Deists generally believed that God created a perfect and balanced universe, but they said He then allowed the world to function under certain laws of nature and rarely, if ever, intervened in human affairs. They rejected many traditional Christian teachings such as miracles and the virgin birth of Jesus.

Deism was a diverse movement. Few colonists embraced its most extreme forms. However, some famous men—including Benjamin Franklin and Thomas Jefferson—accepted some aspects of deism, though they rejected other deistic beliefs. For example, Franklin strongly believed in prayer and in asking for divine intervention, but he denied key Christian doctrines such as the atonement for sins by Christ on the cross.

Unitarianism

A related influential philosophy was Unitarianism. This movement denied the doctrine of the Trinity (the belief that the one God is God the Father, God the Son, and God the Holy Spirit). Unitarians believed that God is simply one being, that He did not exist in three persons.

Unitarians also denied that Jesus was divine, insisting that He was only a great man. Although they claimed to believe the Bible, they did not think that people needed salvation through the blood of Christ. According to Unitarianism, people need only to live moral lives. The influence of Unitarianism continued to grow even after the War for Independence. Unitarianism became especially strong among some intellectuals and influenced American writers for decades.

SECTION REVIEW 4.5

1. When did the Great Awakening begin?
2. What New England preacher played a key role in the Great Awakening? What was the title of his famous sermon?
3. What evangelist from England was instrumental in America's Great Awakening? What neglected groups of people did he minister to?
4. What southern leader of the Great Awakening traveled throughout the state of Virginia preaching revival meetings?
5. Choose the two effects of the Great Awakening you consider most important. Explain each choice.
6. What did deists believe about the Bible? What are some parts they did not believe?
7. What key doctrine of Christianity do Unitarians deny? Explain this doctrine.

false TEACHINGS

False teachings have always been part of history. Studying such teachings can remind us of our need to test all new ideas to see whether they are consistent with God's Word. The apostle Paul cautioned believers not to be led astray by philosophy and tradition (Col. 2:8).

CHAPTER 4 REVIEW

Making Connections

1. Classify the following professions as upper, middle, or lower class: indentured servants, New England merchants, bakers, plantation owners, slaves, and blacksmiths.
2. What other functions did homes in colonial times serve besides normal household duties such as providing food and clothing?
3. Why was it difficult for students to attend school in the middle and southern colonies?
4. Name three non-Anglican religious groups in the southern colonies.
5. Name six religious groups that settled in the middle colonies.
6. What were the seven effects of the Great Awakening?
7. How did the Great Awakening lead some colonists to begin thinking more about their political liberty?

Thinking Critically

8. How are social classes in current American society different from those in colonial society?
9. How do the roles of men, women, and children today differ from those roles in colonial times?
10. Has teaching the general public to read stopped the "Old Deluder Satan"? How does he deceive the world today?
11. What philosophical ideas from the Enlightenment are still common today?

Living as a Christian Citizen

12. Should Christians desire a society in which all people are socially equal? Defend your answer.
13. Schools arose to meet the needs of the times. What would be the ideal type of school today? What and how would it teach?

Benjamin Franklin

Thomas Jefferson

Terms to Remember

indentured servants
dame schools
grammar schools
hornbook
Old Deluder Satan Act
Harvard College
apprenticeship
Congregationalists
Half-Way Covenant
Salem witch trials
Moravians
Great Awakening
Jonathan Edwards
George Whitefield
Enlightenment
deism

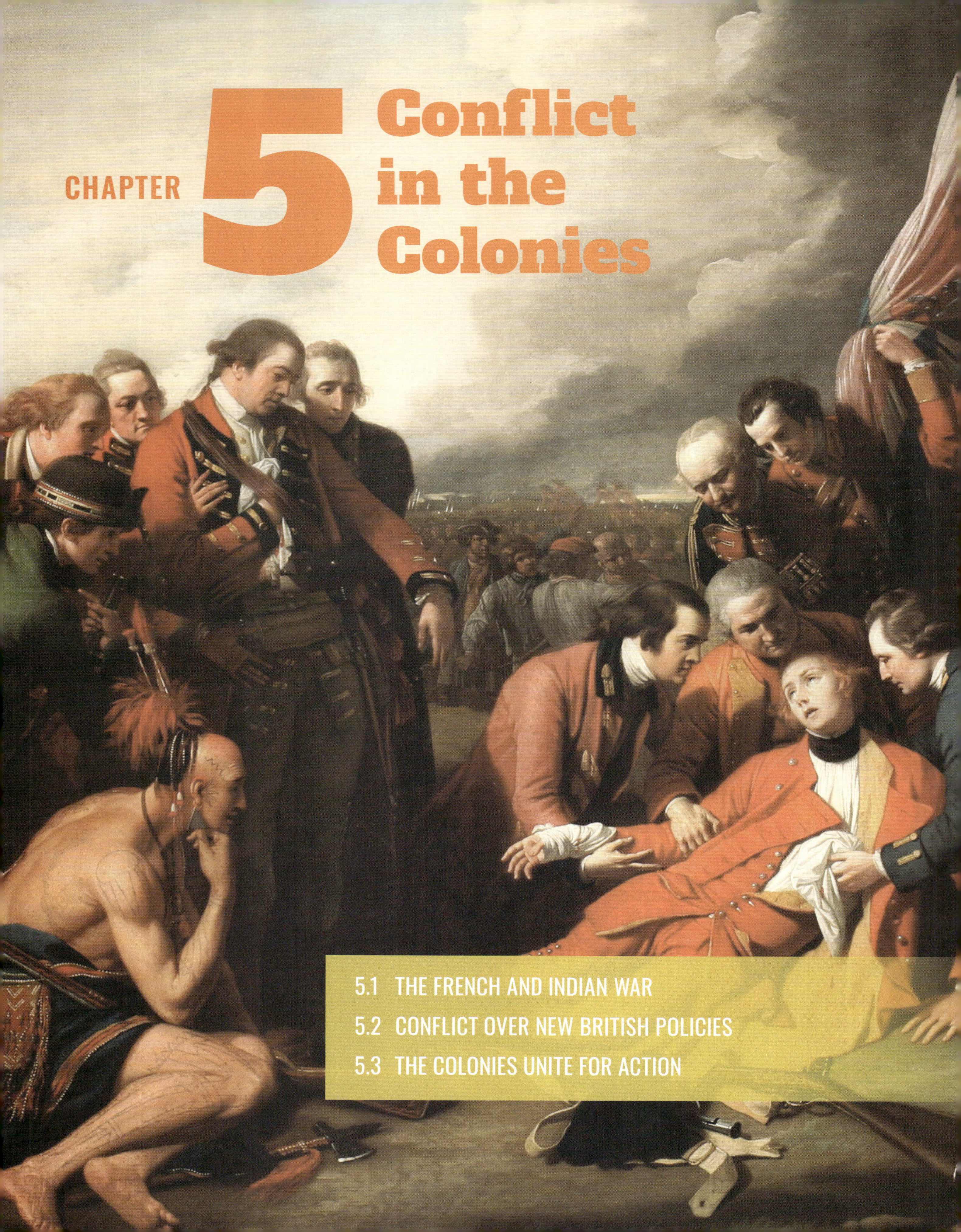

CHAPTER 5 Conflict in the Colonies

5.1 THE FRENCH AND INDIAN WAR

How did the French and Indian War progress?

GUIDING QUESTION

- What happened during the French and Indian War?

At the outset of the 1700s, France and Britain were the two leading European powers. Both nations were actively involved in expanding their territories and building overseas empires. By establishing new colonies, they hoped to increase their wealth and power. The intense rivalry between the two led to a series of wars.

The Background of the Struggle

North America was important to both the French and the British. The British settled along the Atlantic coast and the French along the St. Lawrence River in the Great Lakes region. The French also settled near the Mississippi River. Both groups, however, claimed the whole continent. Both wanted control of the fur trade in the vast, open area west of the Appalachian Mountains. They also sought to control the rich fishing region off the coast of Newfoundland, Canada. Soon, their rival interests led to open conflict.

French Strengths and Weaknesses

The French had many advantages in their struggle against the British. The French colonial government was strong and unified. The French built forts at strategic points along the inland waterways. They also had a well-trained army and the support of many Native American tribes, especially the Algonquins, who hated the British.

Despite these advantages, the French had a major weakness. New France was a vast territory with widely scattered and sparsely populated French settlements. Defending such a large region was difficult.

British Strengths and Weaknesses

The British colonies had a few advantages as well. They had nearly fifteen times the population of New France. In addition, they had the support of the **Iroquois**, the strongest confederation of Indian tribes in America. Furthermore, the English navy was the strongest in the world.

Perhaps Britain's greatest weakness was a lack of unity among its colonies. There was no central organization in and little cooperation among the thirteen colonies. There was also little cooperation between the colonies and the British government. Each colony protected its own interests rather than the interests of the colonies as a whole. When faced with Indian attacks and French expansion, many colonists, unless they were personally threatened, did not want to help other colonies. They were willing to take action only to defend their own homes, families, and livelihoods.

French and British Claims in North America (ca. 1750)

◂ General James Wolfe, British commander at the Battle of Quebec, dying on the battlefield

WARS *between the* FRENCH *and* BRITISH

1689–97	King William's War
1702–13	Queen Anne's War
1744–48	King George's War
1756–63	Seven Years' War (known as the French and Indian War in America, 1754–63)

▲ Site of Fort Duquesne, later renamed Fort Pitt, in present-day Pittsburgh

Wars between the French and British

Between 1689 and 1763, the rivalry between France and Britain led to four wars. The first three began in Europe and spread to America. The results of these three wars were indecisive. Neither side could gain an upper hand. The fourth war, however, decided who would control the North American continent. In this last war, unlike the earlier three, fighting began in America. Europeans named it the Seven Years' War (1756–63). In America, where it began in 1754, it was called the **French and Indian War** because the French and some Indians joined forces against the British and the colonists.

The Outbreak of the French and Indian War

Struggle for control of the Ohio Valley was the immediate cause of the French and Indian War. The British hoped to open the region to settlement. This plan alarmed the French, who feared that British settlers would disrupt the French fur trade. The French wanted to gain control, stop further British expansion, and keep the British colonists restricted to the area along the Atlantic coast.

The key to the Ohio Valley was the point where the Allegheny and Monongahela Rivers joined to form the Ohio River, at the present site of Pittsburgh, Pennsylvania. In 1754 the governor of Virginia sent a force under the leadership of Lieutenant Colonel **George Washington** to construct a fort there. He soon learned that the French had already completed one and had named it **Fort Duquesne** in honor of the new governor of Canada (an area the French controlled). Fighting erupted between Washington and the French. Realizing he was outnumbered, he hastily built a small defensive structure forty miles away and named it Fort Necessity.

On July 3, 1754, a large force of Frenchmen and their Native American allies attacked George Washington. After a day-long battle, Washington was forced to surrender. About 100 of his 300 men were dead or wounded. The French allowed Washington and his men to return to Virginia, but the French and Indian War soon followed.

▼ A reconstruction of Fort Necessity stands where George Washington (at left) built the original fort.

The Course of the French and Indian War

During the early years of the war, the French successfully drove the British from the Ohio Valley. Native American tribes that allied with the French used a style of fighting that was very effective in the wilderness. They hid behind trees and brush, ready to ambush the British. This approach was later called **guerrilla warfare**. In contrast, the British used the European style of fighting. They marched into battle dressed in full uniform. The rows of colorfully dressed soldiers made easy targets for Indians hiding in the forests.

Benjamin Franklin published this early political cartoon to promote unity among the colonies.

The Albany Plan of Union

Even before war began, the British and colonial governments had concerns. First, they wanted to make sure that the Iroquois would continue to support them rather than join the many other Indian tribes that were siding with the French. Second, they wanted to bring greater unity to the colonies in case of another war with the French. In June 1754 delegates from several American colonies met at Albany, New York, to address these issues. Iroquois chiefs were also present. The Albany Congress, as it was called, was still in session when the battle at Fort Necessity occurred in July.

The delegates at the congress adopted a proposal. It was primarily the work of **Benjamin Franklin**. The **Albany Plan of Union** called for the creation of a grand council consisting of representatives from all the colonies. The assembly would have power to raise an army, build forts, and govern Indian affairs. It also recommended that the British king appoint one person to serve as president for the colonies. But both Britain and the colonies rejected the ideas. Britain feared that such a union would threaten its control of the colonies, while the colonies feared that they might lose some of their freedom. Even so, the plan was significant because it was the first attempt to unite the American colonies.

General Edward Braddock was fatally wounded before he reached Fort Duquesne.

Braddock's Defeat

The first major British action in the war was an attempt to capture Fort Duquesne. British general **Edward Braddock** took about 1,500 British soldiers and 1,000 Virginia militiamen and marched from Virginia to the fort. Braddock moved his men slowly, having them clear a roadway and build bridges as they marched. George Washington, an aide to Braddock on the mission, tried in vain to warn Braddock that the French and their Indian allies would not fight in the open, organized fashion that the general knew in Europe. Indeed, Braddock's forces were ambushed six miles from the fort on July 9, 1755. The French and Indians won a great victory. Washington had two horses shot from under him and later found four bullet holes in his coat. Braddock was critically wounded and died a few days afterward.

▲ William Pitt

William Pitt's System

In 1756 the war expanded into a worldwide conflict. The British and the French battled on three continents: North America, Europe, and Asia. To meet the new challenges, the struggling British placed the war effort in the hands of **William Pitt**. Though he did not hold the title, he was essentially prime minister (the most important nonroyal official in the country). His energetic leadership brought a dramatic change in the war. He commented, "I know that I can save this country, and that no one else can."

Pitt turned Britain's weak defensive tactics in America into aggressive action. He replaced older generals with younger, more energetic ones. He also agreed that the British would pay to outfit colonial soldiers to aid British troops. Now backed with the full support of the British government, British troops teamed with American colonials and began their assault on French strongholds in America.

One by one, French posts began falling to the British. Late in 1758, a British force ousted the French from Fort Duquesne. The British rebuilt the badly damaged fort and renamed it Fort Pitt. The following year, they began preparations to capture Quebec. Pitt hoped its capture would be the crucial blow that would defeat the French.

Fun Fact

During the war some upper-class military leaders attempted to remain polite. For example, in 1758 a British commander sent pineapples to the French commander's wife and apologized for the chaos to her home. She sent a gift in return.

The Battle of Quebec

Quebec was the strongest city of New France. Perched high above the St. Lawrence River and protected by steep cliffs, it was a seemingly invincible fortress. Nevertheless, the British, under the command of General **James Wolfe**, besieged the city. But the French were content to stay within their stronghold and wait.

After several failed attempts to take the city, General Wolfe devised a daring plan. Under cover of night, British troops crossed the river downstream from the fort. By morning on September 13, 1759, more than 4,000 British troops had silently scaled the cliffs protecting Quebec. They took battle positions on a field known as the Plains of Abraham, which was a short distance from the fortress. When the surprised French commander, the **Marquis de Montcalm**, learned what the British had done, he ordered an immediate attack. He hoped to defeat the British before they could become entrenched. In the brief—but deadly—battle, the British won a great victory. The French surrendered Quebec. The opposing generals, Wolfe and Montcalm, were both critically wounded. Wolfe died during the battle and Montcalm lived until the next morning.

Plains of Abraham ▼ and nearby cliffs

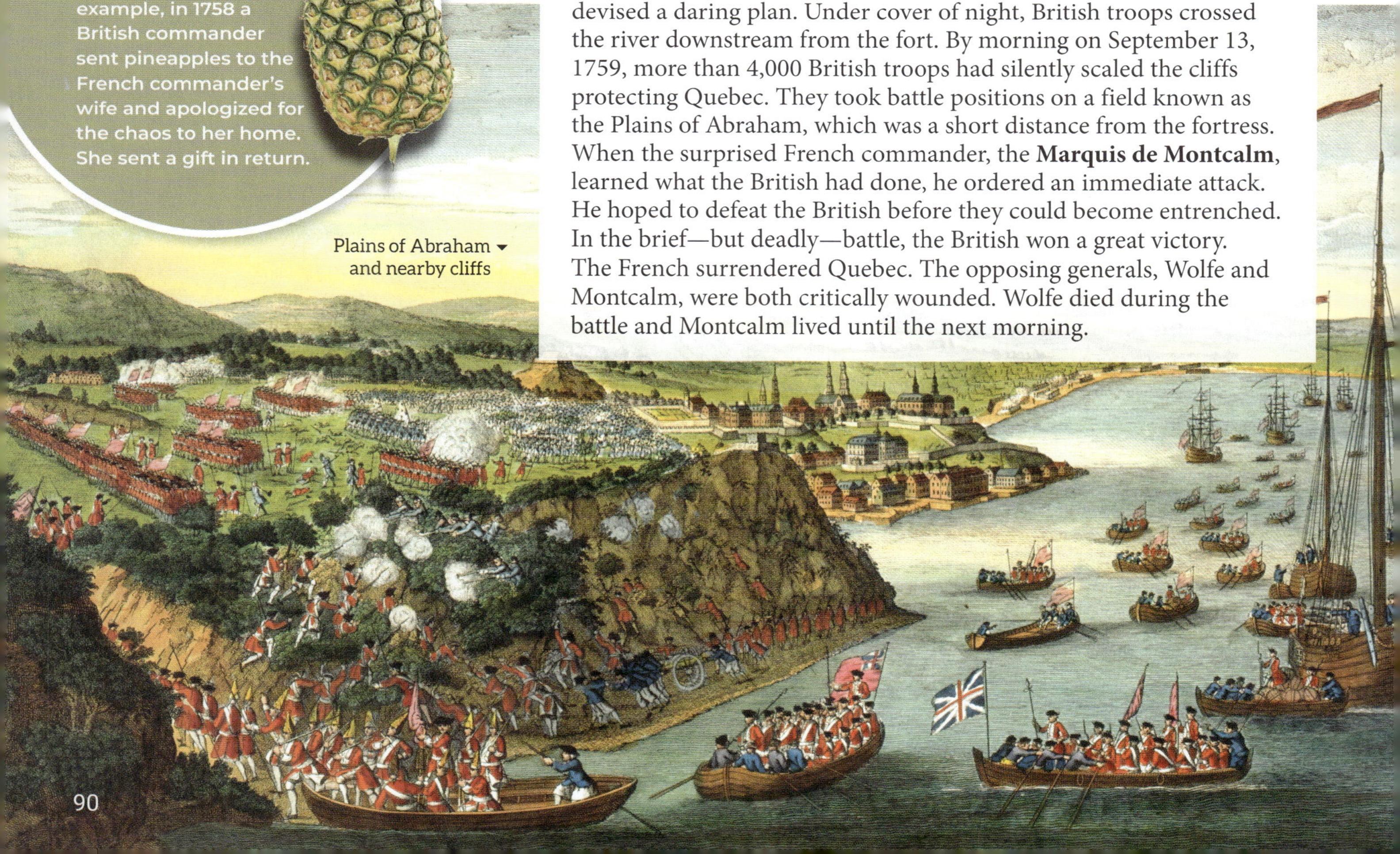

Benjamin Franklin

Historians sometimes refer to Benjamin Franklin as "the First American." As a writer, printer, philosopher, scientist, inventor, and politician, he was widely known. He devoted much of his life to serving his country and trying to improve the lives of others.

Franklin was born in Boston in 1706. He was the fifteenth of seventeen children born to Josiah Franklin, a soap and candlemaker. At age twelve, Franklin was apprenticed to his much-older brother James, who was a printer.

Franklin submitted several letters to his brother's newspaper, the *New England Courant*, but they were rejected. Afterward, he wrote letters using an assumed name—Mrs. Silence Dogood. Fourteen of those witty letters were published and were popular with readers. However, when James discovered that they had actually been written by his younger brother, rather than a middle-aged widow, he grew angry. This conflict resulted in seventeen-year-old Franklin leaving his apprenticeship in Boston without permission. He soon settled in Philadelphia.

Franklin established himself as a printer. He published the *Pennsylvania Gazette* and *Poor Richard's Almanack*, which was known for its wise sayings and advice.

Franklin, heavily influenced by the Enlightenment, hoped to improve himself and the world around him. In 1727 he and a group of friends organized the Junto, a club that discussed important issues and sought to advance society. In their meetings they formulated proposals for the creation of the first lending library, a volunteer militia, Philadelphia's first volunteer fire department, and the city's first public hospital. Their ideas also led to the creation of the University of Pennsylvania and the establishment of the American Philosophical Society, which was devoted to scientific and academic pursuits.

Franklin earned fame in Europe and America for his scientific experiments. He was especially famous for his work with electricity. He determined that thunderclouds carry electricity and that lightning is like a giant spark. While experimenting with electricity, he invented the lightning rod to protect buildings from lightning strikes. His other inventions include bifocals, the Franklin stove, and an odometer to be used in carriages.

Franklin was also known for his work in politics. In 1754 he drafted the Albany Plan of Union. Between 1757 and 1775 he represented the colonies in England. In the colonies in 1776 he was one of the five members of the committee that wrote the Declaration of Independence. Later that year, he was sent to Paris to seek military aid for the colonies. He remained in France throughout the War for Independence and helped negotiate the Treaty of Paris, which ended the conflict in 1783. At the Constitutional Convention in 1787, he was the oldest delegate.

Although Franklin supported morality and integrity, he often did not follow his own advice. He fathered a child out of wedlock, William. That son served as colonial governor of New Jersey from 1763 to 1776. (During the War for Independence, William supported Britain rather than independence for the colonies and moved to Britain near the end of the war.) Benjamin Franklin was well aware of his own shortcomings. Commenting on his attempts to become humble, he stated, "Even if I could conceive that I had completely overcome [pride], I should probably be proud of my humility."

From a religious standpoint, Franklin was sometimes difficult to understand. Though he was born into a devout Puritan family, he described himself as "a thorough deist" in his early life. But later, he rejected that description and even called deism irrational. At age eighty-one at the Constitutional Convention, he said, "I have lived, sir, a long time; and the longer I live, the more convincing proofs I see of this truth, that God governs in the affairs of men!" Nevertheless, Franklin rejected some core Christian beliefs, such as the deity of Christ.

Franklin knew the gospel. He was friends with the evangelist George Whitefield. He printed Whitefield's sermons and gave money to support an orphanage operated by Whitefield. But in a letter to Franklin in 1752, Whitefield wrote, "As you have made a pretty considerable progress in the mysteries of electricity, I should now humbly recommend to your diligent unprejudiced study, the mystery of the new birth." His youngest sister, a devoted Christian, wrote letters urging him to return to the faith of his childhood. Sadly there is no evidence that Franklin was ever converted.

Did you know?

There were actually dozens of treaties written in Paris, France, and most were called the "Treaty of Paris." Two of the most famous dealt with major events in American history. The 1763 Treaty of Paris ended the French and Indian War and the 1783 Treaty of Paris ended the American War for Independence.

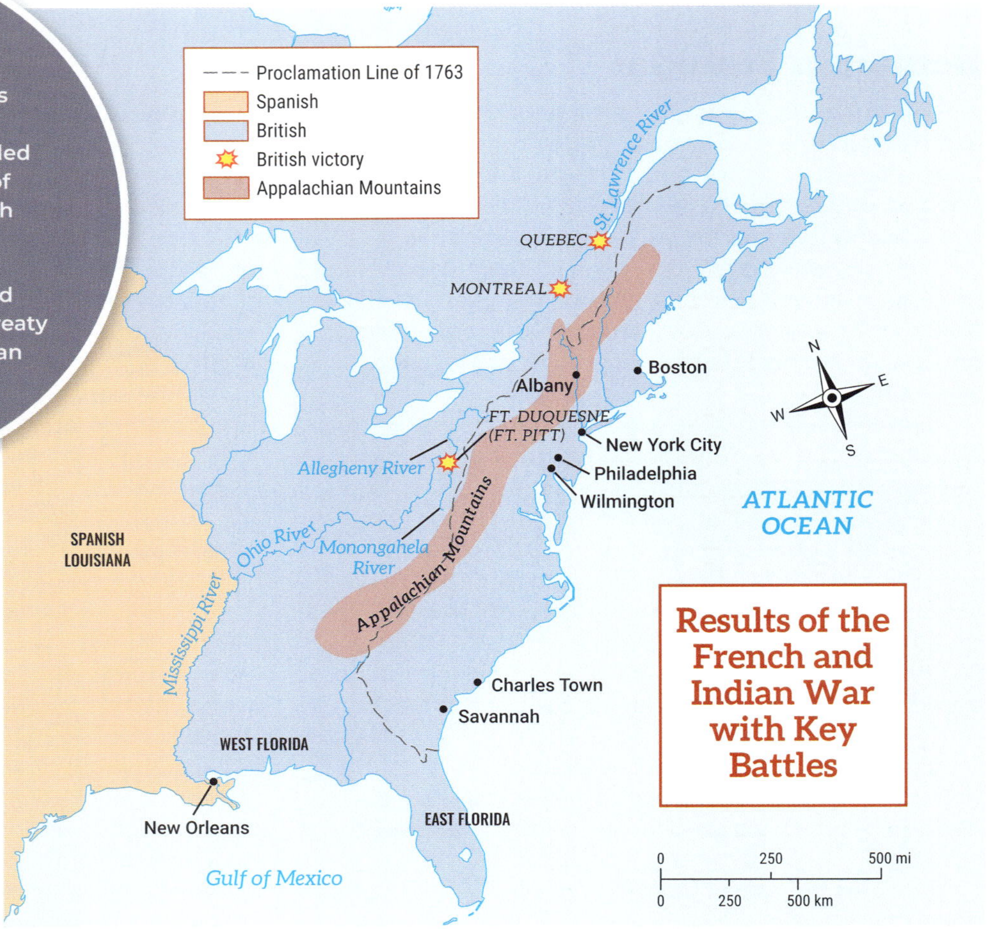

Results of the War

In 1760 the British captured Montreal, another important city in Canada. The struggle for North America was over; however, the war in Europe continued until 1763, when the Treaty of Paris was negotiated. In that agreement, France surrendered its claim to all territory east of the Mississippi River, including the port city of New Orleans. In addition, Britain gained control of Canada and received Florida from Spain, which had been a French ally. To compensate Spain for the loss of Florida, France gave Spain a large area west of the Mississippi River that was known as the Louisiana Territory.

▲ The French surrendering the city of Montreal

SECTION REVIEW 5.1

1. What were the strengths and weaknesses of the French and British in the early 1700s?
2. How might the colonists' lack of unity have hurt the British war effort?
3. What was the name for the war that settled the question of who would control North America? What was this war called in Europe?
4. How was Native American and French fighting different from that of the English?
5. What were the two primary reasons for the meeting that produced the Albany Plan of Union? Was it accepted?
6. What British general was defeated and critically wounded while advancing to Fort Duquesne?
7. What new leader turned the tide of the war in favor of the British? What methods did he use?

5.2 CONFLICT OVER NEW BRITISH POLICIES

Why was there conflict in the colonies over British policies?

GUIDING QUESTIONS

- Why did Britain tighten its control of the colonies and close western lands?
- What important acts were passed by Parliament, and how did the colonists respond to them?
- What were the British and American viewpoints regarding the Boston Massacre?
- How did the colonists react to British policies?
- What were the Intolerable Acts?

Britain at the End of the French and Indian War

Britain emerged from the war as the world's strongest nation. It controlled India, some islands in the Pacific, territory in Australia, the land acquired in North America as a result of the war, and the thirteen colonies.

Many British leaders believed that the American colonies had only halfheartedly helped in the war effort. Some accused colonial merchants of trading with Britain's enemies during the war. In addition, some members of Parliament believed that the colonies had been allowed too much freedom. As a result of these views and because Britain now had an even larger empire to manage, the British government enacted policies to bring the colonies under tighter British control. Action came in many forms—the closing of western lands to further settlement, additional trade regulations, new taxes, and other acts. Many in Parliament failed to realize that they had encouraged the colonists' attitude of independence by allowing them to handle their own local affairs for so long. The changes implemented increased tensions between Britain and its American colonies.

The Closing of Western Lands

After the war, colonists wanted to continue their expansion into the western frontier by allowing additional trappers and settlers to move there. **Pontiac**, an Ottawa Indian chief, strongly opposed such action. He objected because the English were more numerous than the French and were not as friendly toward the Native Americans as the French had been. He formed alliances with other tribes from Canada to the lower Mississippi. The Indians then captured British forts and attacked settlers along the frontier.

The hostilities with Pontiac eventually ended when he negotiated a settlement with the British. In the meantime, George III, who had become Britain's king in 1760, issued the **Proclamation of 1763**. It prohibited colonists from settling beyond the Appalachian Mountains. Trappers and traders were allowed into the region, but only if they had official licenses. The British issued this decree in order to reduce conflict with the Indians. However, it outraged many colonists. During the war, they had fought to open the frontier to expansion. They viewed Britain's restrictions as a violation of colonial charters that gave the colonies the land from the Atlantic to the Pacific. They resented the fact that for the first time American territorial expansion was controlled by royal officials.

▾ Pontiac and his men surround Fort Detroit, located in present-day Michigan, in 1763.

Acts and Opposition

The Navigation and Trade Acts

The **Navigation and Trade Acts**, passed between 1651 and 1733, were part of Britain's mercantile policies (see "Mercantilism" on p. 35). These acts controlled the colonies' trade. They stated that certain products could be shipped only to England or to other English colonies and that their sale to Britain's rival nations was prohibited. Such rules were intended to help British manufacturers and raise revenue for the British treasury. Acts passed before the French and Indian War were not effective, and they quickly became outdated. Furthermore, the British did not strictly enforce them. Some colonial merchants took advantage of Britain's leniency and smuggled goods into the colonies from other countries.

This illegal trade helped Britain's enemies during the French and Indian War. It also deprived Britain of badly needed income. After the war, British officials began strictly administering the trade laws. They gave customs officials **writs of assistance** (general search warrants) to search for smuggled goods anywhere—even in homes. Several colonial leaders protested these writs because they gave British officials unlimited authority to search private property and thus violated the rights of Englishmen.

▲ The Sugar Act taxed items like molasses (above), while playing cards (below) were among items taxed by the Stamp Act.

The Sugar Act

In April 1764 Parliament passed the **Sugar Act**, placing duties (taxes on imported goods) on such items as sugar, molasses, and coffee. The American colonies imported these products from the West Indies in the Caribbean. Colonists were accustomed to paying taxes to their colonial and local governments for local needs. They had also paid some taxes that Parliament had passed that were designed to regulate trade. However, the money from this new tax was to be used to help pay for the cost of defending the colonies from Native Americans and foreign countries. This, along with the fact that Parliament had no representatives from the colonies, concerned many Americans.

The Stamp Act

To raise additional income for the defense of the colonies, Parliament proposed another tax—a stamp tax. This tax differed from the duties on imported goods because it taxed an activity that occurred only in the colonies (as opposed to trade, which affected both England and the colonies). The **Stamp Act** of 1765 required colonial businessmen and lawyers to purchase special stamps and place them on items that were taxed, thus increasing the price that colonists paid. Among the items taxed were legal documents, newspapers, calendars, and playing cards. Without a stamp, such items were considered illegal. Because these were common items, the tax affected virtually every person in the colonies.

The Quartering Act

After the French and Indian War, Britain had thousands of troops in America. This force could be used to protect the colonies or to enforce British policies if the colonists refused to obey. Many colonists saw the British troops as a greater threat to their liberty than the Native Americans or foreign countries.

Protests grew after Parliament passed the **Quartering Act of 1765**. The act required colonies to house British troops in barracks, stables, taverns, and empty buildings and to provide them with some supplies. Colonial governments were unhappy because of the extra expenses this act required them to pay.

▲ British troops in Boston enforced British policies (above). Below, residents of the city protest against the Stamp Act. They have hung an effigy (crude likeness of a hated person) of a tax official.

Colonial Opposition

A storm of controversy erupted in the colonies over the Stamp Act. The tax particularly affected lawyers and printers, individuals who were among the most vocal colonists. They quickly spread their objections of the new legislation.

Colonial protests were not primarily about the amount of the tax; the new tax was only a small sum per colonist. The outcry centered on whether Parliament had the right to tax the colonies at all. Many colonists argued, as they had done with the Sugar Act, that since the thirteen colonies had no representatives in Parliament, it could not tax them. "**No taxation without representation**" became a colonial rallying cry. By taxing the unrepresented colonists, they asserted, England was failing to treat them as the political equals of other English citizens.

British leaders had an entirely different view of the new taxes. They faced huge debts from the recent wars and the large expense of maintaining an army to support an expanding empire. British leaders thought it only fair that the thirteen colonies assume some of the financial burden for protecting the Americans from Indians and foreign governments. Furthermore, they insisted that every member of Parliament represented everyone who resided in the British empire. In addition, people in Britain paid substantially higher taxes, more than twenty or thirty times as much, than the people in the colonies.

Throughout the colonies, groups called the **Sons of Liberty** organized and held rallies to protest the Stamp Act. These groups sometimes used violence to obtain their ends; however, many colonists believed that violence was not a proper response, even to actions they considered unjust.

King George III

America's last king, George III, came to the throne in 1760 at the age of twenty-two. The following year, he wed Sophia Charlotte, a German princess. Early in the marriage, George purchased Buckingham House, now part of Buckingham Palace, for her. There, the couple reared their fifteen children.

As king, he desired to bring the American colonies under tighter control. His determination to do so was one of the reasons the War for Independence occurred. The defeat of his armies and the independence of the American colonies were a great embarrassment to him.

In 1788 George endured several months of violent mental illness. For a time, he was restrained in a straitjacket. Though he recovered the next year, afterward he suffered periodic bouts of insanity. A major episode occurred in 1804. Again he recovered, but by 1810 he was permanently insane. The next year, his eldest son—whom George despised, partly because of his poor moral character—assumed the responsibilities of ruling. George was technically the king until he died in 1820 at age eighty-one.

▲ Samuel Adams

Peaceful protests arose from an assembly commonly known as the **Stamp Act Congress**. This colonial congress met at the urging of Massachusetts's **Samuel Adams**, who was perhaps the most famous leader of colonial opposition and a prominent member of the Sons of Liberty. In October 1765, delegates from nine colonies gathered in New York. They sent a petition to **King George III** and affirmed their loyalty to him. They also insisted on their right as Englishmen to be taxed only by their own representatives.

Parliament finally revoked the Stamp Act in March 1766. The repeal brought rejoicing in the colonies. However, at the same time, Parliament passed the Declaratory Act. It stated that Parliament had the right to tax the colonies and any other part of the British empire.

The Townshend Acts

An uneasy calm followed the repeal of the Stamp Act. But soon there were renewed efforts to tax the colonies. Parliament passed the **Townshend Acts** in 1767, placing new taxes on such items as glass, paper, lead, paint, and tea. In reaction, colonists organized **boycotts** (refusals to buy) of British goods. Many colonial merchants would not unload goods from British ships. Boycotts had real impact on British trade. Their merchants made less money, their factories needed fewer workers, and some workers lost their jobs.

To replace the boycotted goods, some colonial merchants smuggled goods past British customs agents. The British, in turn, increased their efforts to stop this illegal activity by widening the use of writs of assistance. Resentment mounted between merchants and British agents. Samuel Adams and the Massachusetts legislature condemned the Townshend Acts as a financial burden and a violation of the colonists' right to representation. Adams wrote a letter urging united colonial action. He sent the letter to all the colonial legislatures. The British placed troops in several port cities to maintain order. Their presence only deepened colonial anger.

Tea, held in canisters like this, ▶ was one of the items taxed by the Townshend Acts.

The Boston Massacre

Distrust between the colonists and British soldiers was especially evident in Boston. Many colonists resented the two regiments of British soldiers now stationed there to calm a hotbed of colonial resistance. Some showed their resentment by booing as the troops marched in the streets. Some threw rotten eggs and seashells at the soldiers.

▲ Colonists and British soldiers clash during the Boston Massacre.

The situation came to a climax on the night of March 5, 1770. A crowd of men and boys began taunting several soldiers by throwing snowballs and stones at them. After one soldier was knocked down, the troops fired into the mob, killing five people and wounding several others. It is still uncertain who gave the command to fire.

The troops' leader, Captain Thomas Preston, and eight other soldiers were charged with murder. Attorney John Adams, cousin of Samuel Adams, defended them. All were acquitted of murder, but two were found guilty of manslaughter. As punishment, their thumbs were branded and then they were released.

News of the incident quickly spread to the other colonies. Most accounts of what happened, however, were exaggerated by those who hoped to rouse public sentiment against the British. These people labeled the incident "the **Boston Massacre**" and praised the victims as "martyrs."

Reaction

In April 1770, faced with renewed criticism, Parliament repealed the taxes from the Townshend Acts, except for the tax on tea. The British hoped that the repeal would restore peace in the colonies. But it only divided the colonists. Some thought that Britain had conceded enough. Others again raised the cry of "no taxation without representation."

The Committees of Correspondence

In late 1772 Samuel Adams urged Boston to form a **Committee of Correspondence**. The group provided written information about British threats to liberty in the form of letters that were sent to other parts of the colony. Soon eighty other Massachusetts towns followed Boston's example of organizing such a committee. The following year, the Virginia House of Burgesses established such a committee and soon committees were created throughout the colonies. The chief goal of the committees was to spread word of British threats on liberty. It was also an important step toward establishing a united response to British actions.

Fun Fact

Two million dollars in $100 dollar bills would weigh about 44 pounds and fit in two oversized suitcases.

The Boston Tea Party

The British East India Tea Company was one of the most important businesses in Britain, but the company faced a crisis—its warehouses were filled with millions of pounds of tea. It turned to its powerful friends in Parliament for help. With the urging of the prime minister, that body passed the Tea Act of 1773. The act basically granted the British East India Company a monopoly, or exclusive control, on the shipment and sale of tea in America.

Colonists viewed this law as interference with their trade and resented it for two main reasons. First, since the British tea was cheaper than smuggled Dutch tea, many American merchants could not compete with such low prices. Second, if Parliament could grant a monopoly on tea, it might approve other such arrangements in the future. Protests, fueled by the work of the Committees of Correspondence, spread through the colonies.

When British tea ships arrived in Boston, the colonists asked the governor to have the tea returned to England. The governor refused. On the night of December 16, a group of more than one hundred men dressed like Indians (to disguise their identities) boarded the ships and threw the tea overboard. A crowd along the shore watched this "**Boston Tea Party**" in silence. After the "Indians" tossed all 342 chests of tea, they cleaned the ships' decks and left the ships without damaging them.

Though many colonists applauded what occurred at the Boston Tea Party, others were unhappy. For example, Benjamin Franklin denounced the destruction of private property and said the British East India Company should be compensated for its loss. He was in London at the time and wrote to colonial leaders to say that the action would harm the American cause, not help it. In today's money, the tea was worth almost $2 million.

The Intolerable Acts

News of the Boston Tea Party angered the British. They viewed the incident as an act of defiance and were outraged at the theft and destruction of property. They believed that the colonists had gone too far, so they called for swift retaliation. That action came in 1774 in the form of several parliamentary acts designed to punish Massachusetts. In Britain, they were called the Coercive Acts; colonists called them the **Intolerable Acts**.

Did you know?
Coerce means to force someone to do something. *Intolerable* means unbearable.

The Intolerable Acts

1 One act closed the port of Boston, effective June 1, 1774, until the cost of the destroyed tea was repaid.	2 Another act allowed royal officials charged with crimes to be tried in London or in another colony.
3 A third act changed Massachusetts's charter and gave British officials more control. The colonists lost their right to elect representatives, name judges, and select juries. And they could not conduct town meetings without the royal governor's consent.	4 A fourth act was the new Quartering Act of 1774. It gave governors power to demand supplies or buildings that were needed for British troops in the colonies.

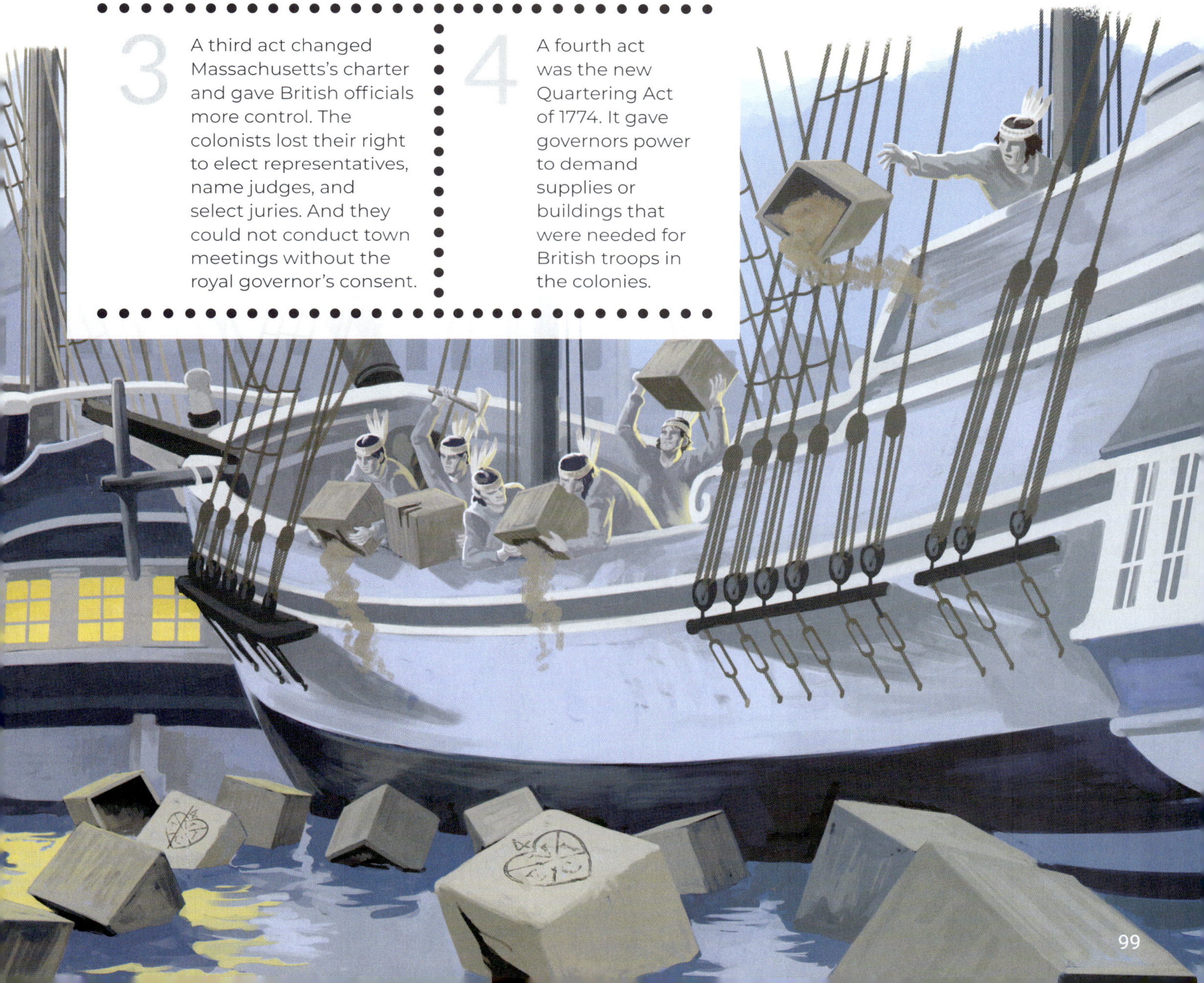

In 1774 Parliament also passed the **Quebec Act**. The act dealt with the newly acquired territory in Canada and was not meant to punish the colonists. However, the timing could not have been worse. Many colonists viewed the act as another example of Parliament's unwanted interference with life in North America. First, it allowed French law to be used in some court cases in Quebec. Second, it extended Quebec's borders south to the Ohio River. The colonists feared this extension as an additional obstacle to their westward expansion. Third, Parliament recognized Roman Catholicism as the leading religion in Quebec. Colonists, who were overwhelmingly Protestant, vigorously objected to this part of the law.

SECTION REVIEW 5.2

1. Why did Britain tighten its control over the American colonies?
2. What conflict caused Britain to issue the Proclamation of 1763?
3. Why did the British allow "writs of assistance"?
4. What were the first two acts Parliament passed in order to raise money to help protect the colonies?
5. Do you agree with the colonial rallying cry, "No taxation without representation"? Why?
6. Samuel Adams was a member of what two groups organized to protest the Stamp Act?
7. How did colonists react to the Townshend Acts?
8. What happened on the night of March 5, 1770, that resulted in British troops firing into the crowd and killing five people?
9. How did Samuel Adams work to spread information to other parts of Massachusetts?
10. What two things were the participants of the Boston Tea Party protesting?
11. Why were the same acts called "Coercive Acts" by the British and "Intolerable Acts" by the colonists?
12. Why did colonists object to the Quebec Act?

▾ British warships in Boston Harbor in 1774

5.3 THE COLONIES UNITE FOR ACTION

How did the colonists unite to resist the British?

GUIDING QUESTIONS

- What were the purposes and actions of the First Continental Congress?
- What happened at Lexington and Concord?

The discontent concerning the Coercive, or Intolerable, Acts spread beyond the port of Boston. Other colonies became concerned that their liberties would also be taken away.

The Virginia House of Burgesses declared a day of fasting and prayer when the port of Boston was closed. Angered by this show of sympathy for the "rebels" in Massachusetts, the royal governor of Virginia dissolved the House of Burgesses. Its members then gathered at the nearby Raleigh Tavern in Williamsburg. There they called for a general colonial congress to address the complaints of the colonies.

The First Continental Congress

On September 5, 1774, more than fifty delegates gathered at Carpenters' Hall in Philadelphia. Men from every colony except Georgia attended. The delegates were united in their opposition to the Intolerable Acts. But they were divided in deciding what action to take against the British. Those who wanted to retain the benefits of British protection and trade urged peace. Others, however, believed that to yield would be to lose their right of self-government.

Sessions of the **First Continental Congress** lasted for more than seven weeks. The delegates adopted a formal statement of protest, the Declaration of Rights and Grievances. This declaration voiced their objections to the recent acts of Parliament. The delegates called the acts "unjust, and cruel, as well as unconstitutional, and most dangerous and destructive of American rights."

The delegates also organized the Continental Association. That group recommended that every community form local association committees to enforce a boycott of all imported British goods. That boycott was scheduled to begin December 1, 1774. It also stated that exporting any goods to Britain would end on September 10, 1775.

▲ Prayer in the First Continental Congress

John Locke and the Right of Rebellion

As the conflicts and disagreements between the colonists and the British government grew in the 1760s and 1770s, some in America embraced the ideas of John Locke. This English philosopher, who lived from 1632 to 1704, recognized the danger that rebellions posed to a society. However, he also believed that citizens had the right to overthrow tyrants, or unjust leaders.

Locke argued that leaders had a contract between themselves and those they ruled. Leaders should be allowed to rule as long as they protected the rights and liberties of those they governed. When leaders failed to protect such rights, he believed they were tyrants and that the people had a right to overthrow them.

How could one identify a tyrant? Locke said that a ruler who makes an error or who occasionally oppresses the people is not a tyrant. He said that tyrants are those who commit a series of abuses. Eventually, many colonial leaders would argue that King George III's actions demonstrated that he had reached that point.

PRIMARY SOURCE: LIBERTY OR DEATH

It was March 23, 1775. One hundred twenty delegates from across Virginia had gathered at St. John's Church in Richmond to discuss how Virginia should react to the controversy with Britain. Among the delegates were George Washington, who had distinguished himself as a military leader in the French and Indian War, and a young Thomas Jefferson. But these men were not the center of attention on this day.

A tall gentleman in the third pew rose to his feet. He viewed the events of recent months with great alarm and wanted to motivate the convention to action. With a commanding voice and bold gestures, **Patrick Henry** addressed the convention.

"They tell us . . . that we are weak—unable to cope with so formidable an adversary. . . . Three millions of people armed in the holy cause of liberty, and in such a country as that which we possess, are invincible by any force which our enemy can send against us. . . . There is no retreat but in[to] submission and slavery! . . . The war is inevitable—and let it come! I repeat it, sir, let it come! . . . Gentlemen may cry peace, peace—but there is no peace. The war is actually begun! The next gale that sweeps from the north will bring to our ears the clash of resounding arms! Our brethren are already in the field! Why stand we here idle? What is it that gentlemen wish? What would they have? Is life so dear, or peace so sweet, as to be purchased at the price of chains and slavery? Forbid it, Almighty God! I know not what course others may take; but as for me, give me liberty, or give me death!"

Patrick Henry took his seat. The closing line of his speech had a great impact on those present and on many others who later read it.

The delegates at the First Continental Congress declared, "We do solemnly bind ourselves . . . to adhere to this association, until such parts of the several acts of parliament passed since the close of the last war [the French and Indian War] . . . are repealed."

Throughout their meetings, the delegates declared their loyalty to the king. They sent him their petitions, hoping he would correct the injustices of Parliament's actions. They also called for a second meeting the following year if the pleas went unheeded.

TARRING *and* FEATHERING

Colonial resistance to British policies sometimes turned violent. One of the most popular means of threatening British agents was tarring and feathering. It involved stripping a person's upper body of clothing, pouring hot tar over the skin, and throwing feathers on the tar. Often, the tar caused burns and blisters. It could be difficult to remove for days.

The primary purpose of tarring and feathering was to humiliate the victim. Colonists hoped that the mere threat of such action would cause British officials to leave town or stop enforcing unpopular regulations.

Seven thousand people across the colonies served on committees of the Colonial Association. Those who refused to support the boycott faced intimidation and harassment. Others were tarred and feathered at the hands of mobs supported by these committees.

Many colonists fully expected Britain to repeal the Intolerable Acts. After all, Britain had responded to earlier colonial protests by repealing the Stamp Act and the Townshend Acts (except for the tax on tea). But the king and many members of Parliament were outraged by the colonists' actions.

"The British Are Coming!"

In rural towns surrounding Boston, the colonists began storing arms, or weapons, and ammunition in case armed resistance against the British took place. They also prepared their local militias. The most determined militiamen became **minutemen**. These men were to be ready to fight at a moment's notice.

The British commander, General Thomas Gage, learned of a stockpile of weapons in nearby Concord. He ordered a detachment of over seven hundred British soldiers to destroy it. It appears Gage also wanted to arrest two men who had been leading opposition to the British in nearby Lexington: Samuel Adams and John Hancock, who had left Boston seeking safety.

On the night of April 18, 1775, British troops left Boston and began their march toward Lexington and Concord. They hoped to surprise the colonists, but their departure did not go unnoticed. Samuel Prescott, William Dawes, and **Paul Revere** rode through the countryside, warning the colonists, "The British are coming!" As the soldiers marched, the alarm was spread—bells rang and guns fired. Early the next morning, the soldiers reached **Lexington**. In the middle of the town square, they encountered about seventy colonial minutemen. No one knows who fired first, but shots rang out. In the end, eight colonials lay dead; ten more were wounded. The remainder of the militiamen scattered.

▾ Paul Revere warned the colonists of the British approach.

▲ The "shot heard round the world" was fired at the Old North Bridge in Concord.

The British continued to **Concord**, where they destroyed what military supplies they could find. More minutemen gathered, and another brief skirmish occurred at the North Bridge. Later, the poet Ralph Waldo Emerson would describe the first shot fired by colonists there as "the shot heard round the world." The British advanced no farther but began a retreat to Boston. All along the way, colonial minutemen from other towns harassed them, firing at them from behind trees, buildings, and stone fences.

The skirmishes at Lexington and Concord marked the beginning of the War for Independence. The British force suffered more than 300 **casualties** (killed, wounded, captured, or missing), nearly three times the number of colonial casualties. Word of the conflict spread quickly throughout the colonies. Colonial militiamen from other colonies rallied to Massachusetts's aid. The first shots had been fired, and a war that neither side really wanted nor was prepared to fight had begun.

This growing conflict in America illustrates an important point about values. Values should hold a civilization together. But arguments about values may tear a civilization apart. Both the Americans and the British respected similar values, such as freedom and equality. Yet, war occurred because of disagreements regarding how government should address those values.

SECTION REVIEW 5.3

1. Why were the other colonies concerned about the Intolerable Acts although they directly affected only Massachusetts?
2. What formal protest statement did the First Continental Congress adopt? What did it object to?
3. What was the purpose of Continental Association committees?
4. Who said, "Give me liberty or give me death"? Do you agree with such a statement? Why?
5. Why were some of the colonial militiamen called minutemen?
6. For what reason did the British send soldiers to Lexington and Concord?
7. Who were the three people who warned colonists of the approaching British force?

CHAPTER 5 REVIEW

Making Connections

1. Which Indian confederation supported the British in the French and Indian War?
2. The French built Fort _____ at the site of modern-day Pittsburgh, Pennsylvania, and George Washington built Fort _____ forty miles away.
3. List an accomplishment of Benjamin Franklin in each of the following categories: writer, printer, philosopher, scientist, inventor, politician.
4. What American lands did Britain receive as a result of the Treaty of Paris?
5. How did some colonists ignore the Navigation and Trade Acts?
6. In what years were the two Quartering Acts passed?
7. How might the British justify the Boston Massacre? How did the colonists view it?
8. Explain why the colonists protested the Tea Act of 1773, even though the price of tea fell.
9. How did the British react after the Boston Tea Party?
10. What were the four parts of the Intolerable Acts?
11. Which colony did not send delegates to the First Continental Congress?
12. What was significant about the battles of Lexington and Concord?

Thinking Critically

13. Were the British-imposed taxes after the French and Indian War reasonable? Why or why not?
14. How might a boycott be an effective way to peacefully protest?

Living as a Christian Citizen

15. If you were a pastor in Boston in the 1760–70s, what would you have told your congregation about John Locke's theory of the right of rebellion? Use 1 Samuel 24:5–7; 26:9–11; Acts 4:19–20; 5:29; Romans 13:1–7; and 1 Peter 2:13–14.
16. If you were elected by your colony to serve in the First Continental Congress, would it be acceptable for you to serve? Explain your reasons.

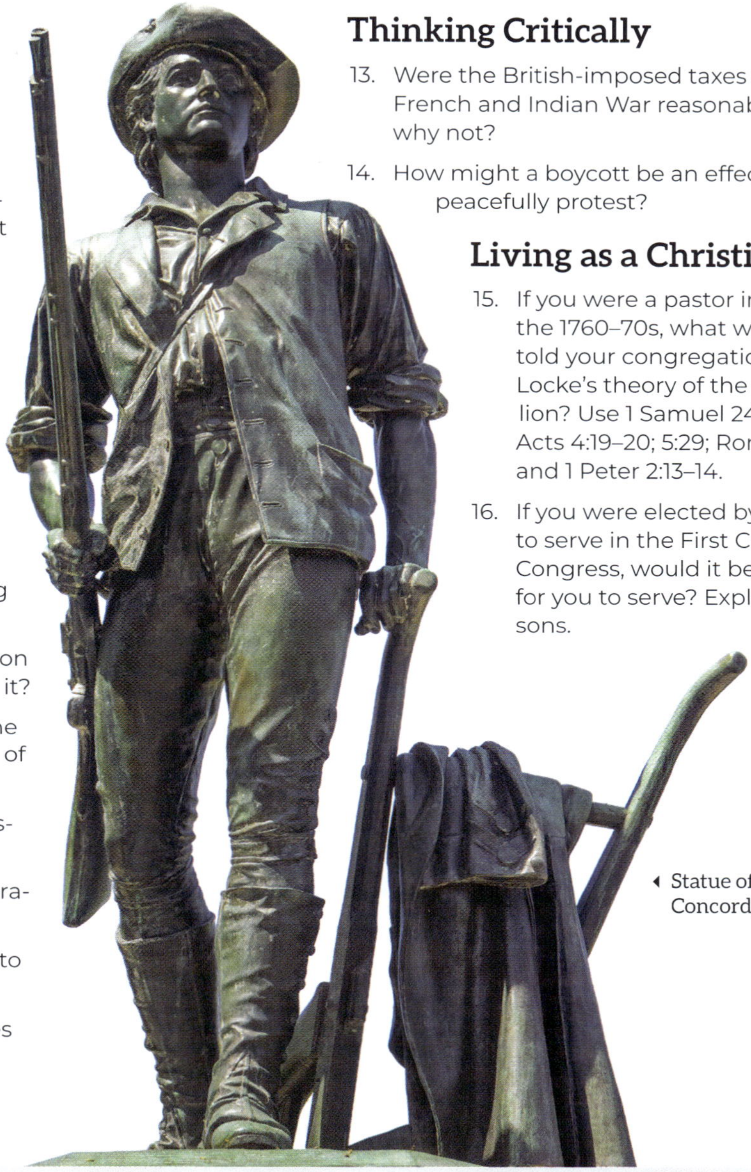

Statue of a minuteman in Concord, Massachusetts

Terms to Remember

Iroquois
French and Indian War
George Washington
Fort Duquesne
guerrilla warfare
Benjamin Franklin
Albany Plan of Union
Edward Braddock
William Pitt
James Wolfe
Marquis de Montcalm
Pontiac
Proclamation of 1763
Navigation and Trade Acts
writs of assistance
Sugar Act
Stamp Act
Quartering Act of 1765
"no taxation without representation"
Sons of Liberty
Stamp Act Congress
Samuel Adams
King George III
Townshend Acts
boycotts
Boston Massacre
Committee of Correspondence
Boston Tea Party
Intolerable Acts
Quebec Act
First Continental Congress
Patrick Henry
minutemen
Paul Revere
Lexington
Concord
casualties

UNIT

2 Establishing a Country

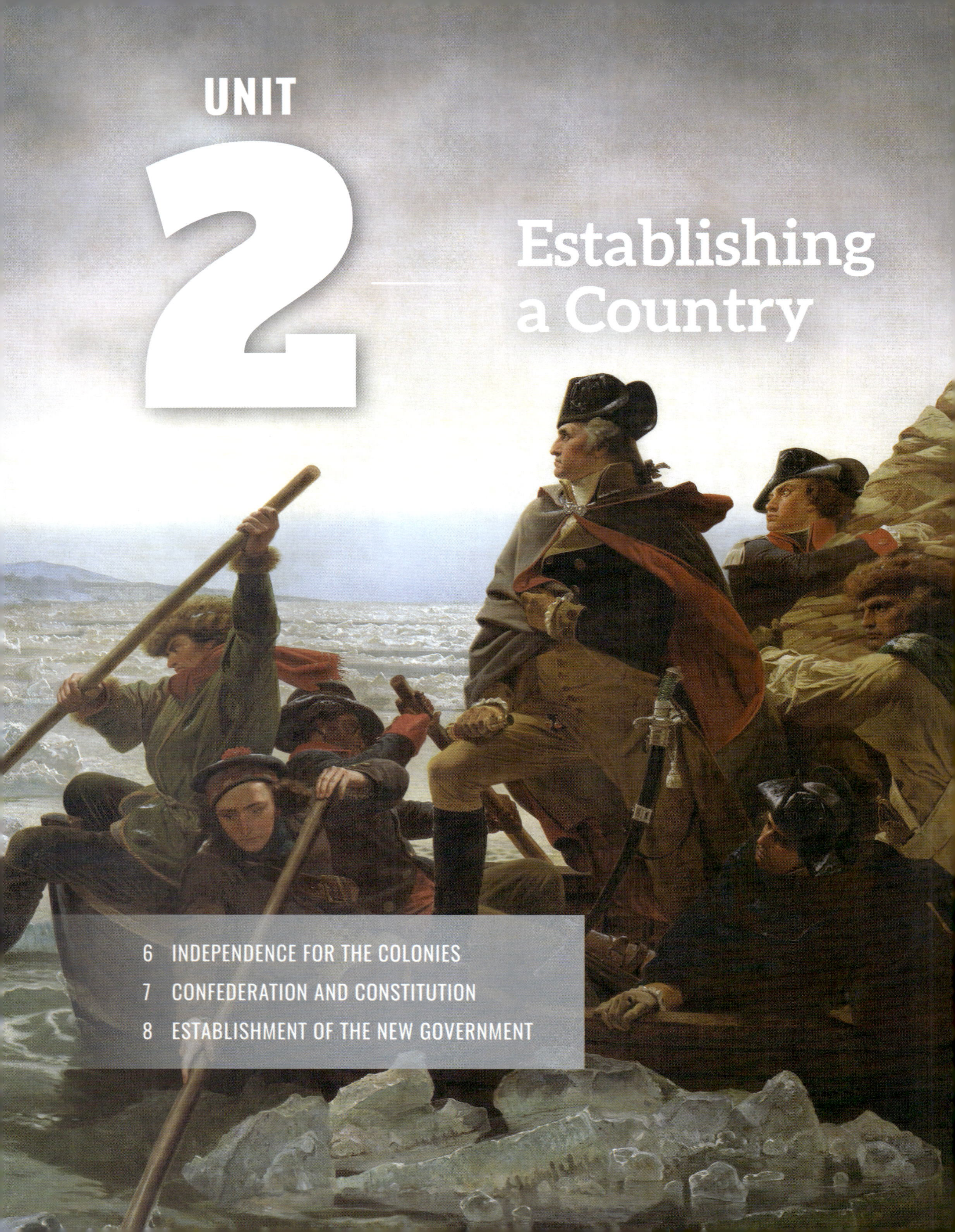

Washington Crossing the Delaware, by Emanuel Leutze

- **1775** — Second Continental Congress assembled
- **1776** — *Common Sense*; Declaration of Independence
- **1777** — Battle of Saratoga; American winter encampment at Valley Forge 1777–78
- **1780** — Battle of Kings Mountain
- **1781** — Articles of Confederation adopted; British surrender at Yorktown
- **1783** — Treaty of Paris
- **1786** — Shays's Rebellion 1786–87
- **1787** — Constitutional Convention in Philadelphia; Northwest Ordinance
- **1789** — Inauguration of George Washington, the first president
- **1791** — Bill of Rights adopted; Whiskey Rebellion 1791–94
- **1793** — Proclamation of Neutrality
- **1798** — XYZ Affair; Alien and Sedition Acts

CHAPTER 6

Independence for the Colonies

After the fighting at Lexington and Concord, the British under General Thomas Gage returned to Boston. Events in those two towns upset many colonists. Soon, thousands of angry Americans gathered near Boston. They were ready to stop any further British actions.

GUIDING QUESTIONS

- What did the Second Continental Congress do?
- What were the early battles in the War for Independence?

6.1 MOVING TOWARD INDEPENDENCE

What were the colonists' early moves toward independence?

Although many colonists were determined to resist the British, there was not yet a unanimous call for independence. Most still hoped to convince the king and Parliament that the colonies were loyal to the British Empire. However, more and more colonists felt they were not receiving rights they deserved. Soon events occurred that led many Americans to call for separating from Britain.

The Second Continental Congress

On May 10, 1775, the **Second Continental Congress** assembled in Philadelphia, Pennsylvania. It took control of the army at Boston and asked the colonies for war supplies and troops. Congress called the troops the **Continental army** and named George Washington the army's commander in June.

In July the delegates sent a letter to the king, asking him to preserve their rights. The petition conveyed a desire for peace and, since the olive branch is a symbol of peace, became known as the **Olive Branch Petition**. But the day after the petition was adopted, Congress approved a document entitled Declaration of the Causes and Necessity of Taking Up Arms, which outlined why they were fighting the British.

The king refused to even read the Olive Branch Petition. Instead, he called the colonists "enemies." He saw their gathering of an army and clashes with his soldiers as armed rebellion and ordered his army to suppress it. He asserted that peace could be restored only when the colonies were willing to submit to British rule. It was becoming clear that colonists would have to choose between submitting and fighting for independence. Americans differed about which choice was best.

◂ Colonists fighting the British at Lexington, Massachusetts (left)

To the Kings most excellent Majesty

Most gracious Sovereign,

We your Majesty's faithful subjects of the colonies of New-Hampshire, ...busetts bay, Rhode island and Providence ...ticut, New-York, New Jersey, ... New Castle Kent & ... Virginia, ...

▾ Olive Branch Petition

▲ Fort Ticonderoga

Early Military Action

Even before Congress met, the events in Boston and the disagreements with the king and Parliament upset many colonists. Some were ready to take up arms.

Fort Ticonderoga

The news of Lexington and Concord quickly traveled to western New England. There, **Ethan Allen**, the leader of a force called the Green Mountain Boys, decided to capture **Fort Ticonderoga**. It was located in New York along Lake Champlain. Capturing it would prevent the British from moving down the Hudson River and dividing New England from New York and the remainder of the colonies. Allen's forces were joined by soldiers led by Benedict Arnold.

In May 1775, the colonists launched a late-night surprise attack. The commander of the poorly guarded fort surrendered it without any shots being fired. In addition to gaining a strategic location, they seized the artillery and ammunition there. The following day, the same forces captured Crown Point, another nearby British fort.

The Battle of Bunker Hill

The conflict continued to escalate. While the Second Continental Congress debated the issues, back in Boston, the **Patriots** (the name for individuals who favored fighting the British) took possession of Bunker Hill and Breed's Hill, just across the bay from the city. American colonel William Prescott then ordered his men to build trenches in case of attack.

In June 1775, General Gage wanted to force the Americans from these hilltop positions. Reinforced by General William Howe and his three thousand men, Gage ordered Howe to attack. The fighting became known as the Battle of **Bunker Hill**, though it actually occurred on Breed's Hill. The first two British assaults were driven back. On the

▼ *The Battle of Bunker Hill* by Howard Pyle actually shows the British marching up Breed's Hill.

third attempt, the colonists ran out of ammunition and were forced to retreat. Howe won, but his casualties were heavy. That day, more than a thousand British soldiers were killed or wounded compared to just over four hundred of the Patriot forces.

The British were determined to stop colonial resistance. They quickly increased their military action. In addition, to prevent any trade of weapons and supplies between colonies, the British ordered a blockade (keeping ships from entering or leaving ports) of New England. They also hired several thousand troops to help them. These hired soldiers, or mercenaries, were called **Hessians**, because most were from the German province of Hesse-Cassel.

▲ Henry Knox and his men moving captured British cannons from Fort Ticonderoga to Boston

Freeing Boston

During the winter of 1775–76, the Americans concentrated on getting the British out of Boston. Colonel Henry Knox, a twenty-five-year-old Boston bookseller-turned-soldier, performed one of the most amazing feats of the war. Knox and his men hauled fifty-nine pieces of artillery, weighing sixty tons, from Fort Ticonderoga to Boston. They used forty-two sleds pulled by eighty teams of oxen. They hauled the artillery over mountains, snow, and ice, covering a distance of about three hundred miles in fifty-six days. The Americans placed the cannons on Dorchester Heights, overlooking Boston, on the night of March 4, 1776.

When the British saw the cannons looming over them, they left the city on March 17. About a thousand **Loyalists** (colonists who opposed fighting the British) also left Boston.

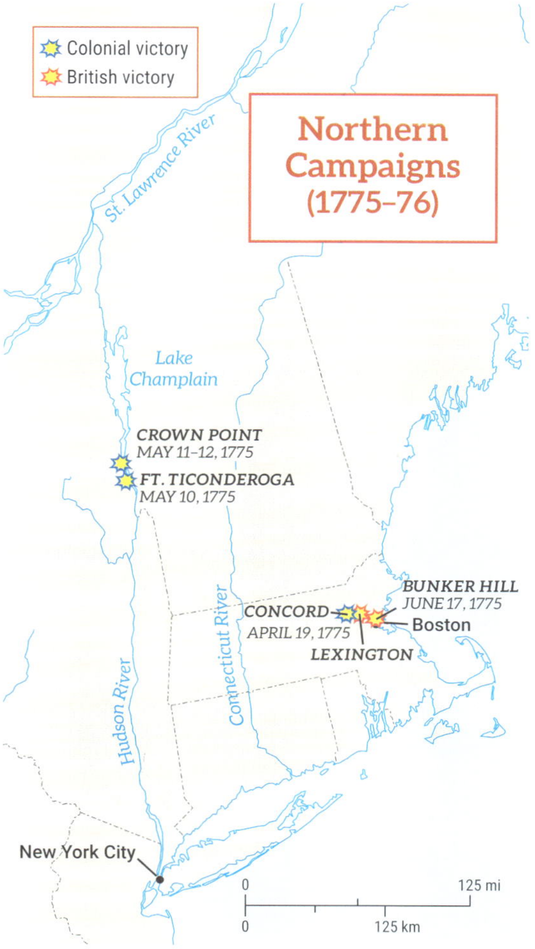

SECTION REVIEW 6.1

1. What new leadership position was given to George Washington?
2. Compare the Olive Branch Petition with the declaration approved the following day.
3. Would you have responded to the Olive Branch Petition in the same manner as the king? Why?
4. Who led the Green Mountain Boys of New England in capturing Fort Ticonderoga? What did they hope to accomplish with the capture of the fort?
5. What name was given to those who favored fighting the British?
6. How might the battle of Bunker Hill be considered an unsuccessful victory for the British?
7. Why were the mercenaries hired by the British forces called Hessians?
8. What name was given to those who opposed fighting the British?

GUIDING QUESTIONS

- What three positions did the colonists take regarding the War for Independence?
- How did Thomas Paine's writings affect the colonists?
- What steps were taken to declare independence?

6.2 DEBATING INDEPENDENCE

How did colonists' opinions differ regarding independence?

As months passed, more people realized that they would have to choose to either submit to the British or fight against them. Many factors influenced the decisions that colonists finally made. There were good people on both sides. Unfortunately, the debate over independence often divided friends and families. Not all colonists wanted to support the British, but not all believed in independence either.

Taking Sides

It is difficult to determine the number of people that were Loyalists or Patriots during the war. One reason is that the numbers changed during the course of the conflict. Though estimates vary, it appears that between one-fifth and one-third were Loyalists, while one-third to one-half were Patriots. The remainder were neutral.

Loyalists

Some colonists remained loyal to England for political, religious, and economic reasons. Patriots sometimes called them Tories, after the British political party that was strongly loyal to the Crown. Although most Loyalists saw the Intolerable Acts as abuses, some feared that a fight for independence would lead to a civil war that would devastate the colonies. Some feared that after achieving independence, mob rule and chaos might result. Some saw the king as God's authority over them, and they believed that it was wrong to rebel. For them, Romans 13:2 settled the matter: "Whosoever . . . resisteth the power, resisteth the ordinance of God: and they that resist shall receive to themselves damnation." Some also feared that cutting ties with Britain would remove the colonies from profitable trade relations in the British Empire. Others remained loyal to Britain because of family connections.

Some Loyalists fled to England, Canada, or the British West Indies. But most Loyalists stayed in the colonies. Many did so because they were born and raised in America. Others did not want to risk losing their property. To avoid trouble, they often kept their opinions to themselves. Some Loyalists fought for Britain, especially when Britain seemed to be winning. These colonists also aided the British by selling them food and other supplies. Unfortunately, thousands of Loyalists were assaulted, imprisoned without trial, or had their property confiscated because of their political beliefs.

Eventually, some British officers offered freedom to slaves if they would fight on Britain's side. Of the half-million slaves in the colonies, it appears that as many as twenty thousand became Loyalists. Likewise, several Native American tribes supported the British. Many resented the decades of mistreatment by American colonists.

British private

Patriots

The Patriots also had political, religious, and economic reasons for their cause. They believed that their political right to representative government was at stake. For many years, the American colonies had enjoyed a government free from domination by England. As mentioned in Chapter 1, the earliest English settlement at Jamestown had a representative assembly, the House of Burgesses. The colonists were accustomed to representing themselves locally by creating many of their own laws and taxes. They believed that they were following an English tradition of liberty. When faraway Parliament began to place additional taxes on the colonies, many Americans saw this as a loss of their liberty.

Religious beliefs also greatly influenced the Patriots. In fact, the war might not have been as popular without the influence of preachers, many of whom called for independence. Most colonists saw themselves as Christians in the Puritan tradition. Baptists also played an important role in the war by showing nearly unanimous support of the Patriot cause. Patriots such as Samuel Adams reminded Americans that their forefathers left England to escape persecution and gain religious freedom. They argued that if Parliament continued to expand its control over the colonies, then the colonists' religious liberties might be threatened and the Anglican Church might be established as the state church in all the colonies.

Religious colonists wrestled with the decision of which authority they should submit to. For more than a century, the colonists had established their own governments. Patriots had no problems with these authorities; their conflict was with Parliament and the king, whom colonists believed were determined to take away some of their rights. Patriots believed they should submit to local governments. Some pastors even suggested that it would be wrong not to defend God-given rights.

Some colonists became Patriots for economic reasons. Parliament's tax and trade policies hurt many prosperous American merchants. They thought that they should be allowed to trade with whomever they wanted, and they resented Parliament's interference with trade.

Patriot soldier

Neutral Colonists

The remaining colonists joined neither side. Some were neutral for business reasons, fearing that they would suffer financial loss if they chose sides. Others lived in remote areas, where they were less affected by the new laws and new taxes. They were not greatly concerned about the conflict unless it came near their homes. Still others, such as the Quakers and Moravians, were pacifists (individuals who oppose war).

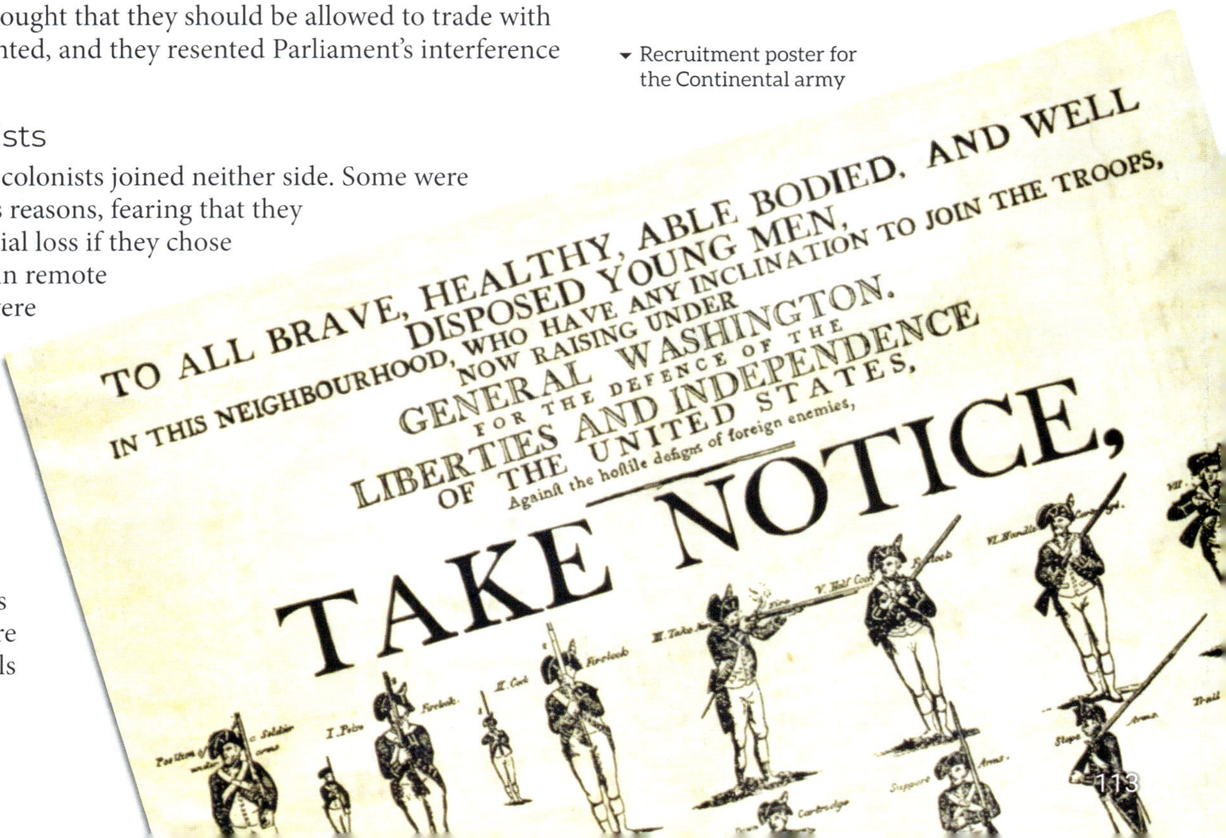

▾ Recruitment poster for the Continental army

PRIMARY SOURCE: *THE AMERICAN CRISIS*

In *The American Crisis* (December 1776), Paine wrote:

THESE are the times that try men's souls. The summer-soldier and the sun-shine patriot will, in this crisis, shrink from the service of their country; but he that stands it now, deserves the thanks of man and woman. Tyranny, like hell, is not easily conquered: yet we have this consolation with us, that the harder the conflict, the more glorious the triumph. What we obtain too cheaply, we esteem too lightly: it is dearness only that gives every thing its value. Heaven knows how to set a proper price upon its goods; and it would be strange indeed, if so celestial [divine] an article as freedom should not be highly rated.

▲ Benjamin Franklin, John Adams, and Thomas Jefferson (left to right) writing the Declaration of Independence

Thomas Paine's Writings

▲ Thomas Paine

Another factor that influenced colonists' thinking was a pamphlet entitled ***Common Sense***, written by Englishman **Thomas Paine**. Paine was an advocate of deism and Enlightenment ideals. Although he had been in America for less than two years, he quickly embraced the Patriot cause. He saw America as a land that had greater opportunity and less poverty than England.

In *Common Sense*, Paine built a case for American separation from Britain. He argued that though government is a "necessary evil" in a world that had much wickedness, a monarchy (king or queen) is an unscriptural form of government that should be opposed because God created all men equal. He identified actions of the king and Parliament that he thought led to the "common sense" conclusion that the colonies should separate from Britain.

COMMON SENSE;
ADDRESSED TO THE
INHABITANTS
OF
AMERICA,
On the following interesting
SUBJECTS.
I. Of the Origin and Design of Government in general, with concise Remarks on the English Constitution.
II. Of Monarchy and Hereditary Succession.
III. Thoughts on the present State of American Affairs.
IV. Of the present Ability of America, with some miscellaneous Reflections.

Man knows no Master save creating Heaven,
Or those whom choice and common good ordain.
THOMSON.

PHILADELPHIA;
Printed, and Sold, by R. BELL, in Third-Street.
MDCCLXXVI.

One of the most influential political tracts in history, *Common Sense* was immensely popular when it was published in January 1776. Over 150,000 copies were circulating in the colonies within three months, and during the war more than a half-million copies were printed. More than any other document, *Common Sense* turned colonists toward independence. Within six months of its publication, the colonies declared independence.

Beginning in late 1776, a few months after the colonies declared independence, Paine published a series of pamphlets entitled *The American Crisis*. George Washington ordered officers to read the first pamphlet to Patriot troops in December 1776. The pamphlets rallied the men amid their hardships to complete or even stay beyond their enlistments. They proved that they were not the mere "summer-soldiers" or "sunshine-patriots" that the pamphlet scorned.

Declaring Independence

During the fall of 1775 and the winter of 1776, the Second Continental Congress took steps toward the colonies becoming a separate nation. It created an American navy, purchased more war supplies, and welcomed some unofficial French aid. By the spring of 1776, most of the colonies favored declaring independence.

On June 7, 1776, Richard Henry Lee of Virginia introduced a resolution that stated, "These United Colonies are, and of right ought to be, free and independent states." Congress appointed five men to write a declaration of independence—John Adams of Massachusetts, Benjamin Franklin of Pennsylvania, Roger Sherman of Connecticut, Robert Livingstone of New York, and **Thomas Jefferson** of Virginia. Jefferson wrote the vast majority of the document.

▲ Declaration of Independence being presented to the Second Continental Congress

On July 2, after weeks of debate, the Continental Congress approved breaking away from Britain. Two days later, on **July 4, 1776**, it unanimously approved the **Declaration of Independence**. In writing this document, Jefferson relied heavily on the work of the English philosopher, John Locke. Locke wrote extensively about a contract between the people and their rulers. He stated that if rulers failed to protect the rights of citizens, they were violating their part of the contract and should lose the right to govern. Jefferson included those ideas in explaining why independence was being declared. The Declaration of Independence emphasized two important values on which the American government would be built—liberty and equality.

SECTION REVIEW 6.2

1. What three "sides" could colonists choose during the War for Independence? Explain why each might be chosen.
2. Who was the author of *Common Sense*? What action did he say was "common sense"?
3. What influence did *Common Sense* have?
4. What do each of the following phrases from *The American Crisis* mean?
   a. "These are the times that try men's souls."
   b. "The summer-soldier and the sun-shine patriot . . ."
   c. "What we obtain too cheaply, we esteem too lightly . . ."
5. Who was the primary author of the Declaration of Independence? On what date was it finally approved?
6. Answer the following questions according to the Declaration of Independence:
   a. What entitled the people to a "separate and equal station"?
   b. What two truths were "self-evident"?
   c. What are the three "unalienable rights"?
   d. What gave the people the right to "alter or abolish" government?
   e. What did the people pledge to each other in support of this declaration?

PRIMARY SOURCE: THE DECLARATION OF INDEPENDENCE

In Congress, July 4, 1776.

The unanimous Declaration of the thirteen united States of America,

When in the Course of human events, it becomes necessary for one people to dissolve the political bands which have connected them with another, and to assume among the powers of the earth, the separate and equal station to which the Laws of Nature and of Nature's God entitle them, a decent respect to the opinions of mankind requires that they should declare the causes which impel them to the separation.

We hold these truths to be self-evident, that all men are created equal, that they are endowed by their Creator with certain unalienable [natural, fundamental] Rights, that among these are Life, Liberty and the pursuit of Happiness.—That to secure these rights, Governments are instituted among Men, deriving their just powers from the consent of the governed,—That whenever any Form of Government becomes destructive of these ends, it is the Right of the People to alter or to abolish it, and to institute new Government. . . . Prudence [wisdom, caution], indeed, will dictate that Governments long established should not be changed for light and transient causes [minor reasons]. . . . But when a long train of abuses [occurs]. . . it is their right, it is their duty, to throw off such Government. . . .

We, therefore, the Representatives of the united States of America, in General Congress, Assembled, appealing to the Supreme Judge of the world . . . do in the Name, and by Authority of the good People of these Colonies, solemnly publish and declare, That these United Colonies are, and of Right ought to be Free and Independent States; that they are Absolved from all Allegiance to the British Crown, and that all political connection between them and the State of Great Britain, is and ought to be totally dissolved. . . . And for the support of this Declaration, with a firm reliance on the protection of divine Providence, we mutually pledge to each other our Lives, our Fortunes and our sacred Honor.

GUIDING QUESTIONS

- What military actions did Washington lead in New York and New Jersey?
- What was the significance of the Battle of Saratoga?
- What difficulties did the Continental army face?
- What happened in the war in the West and at sea?

6.3 BATTLING FOR INDEPENDENCE

What were some important aspects in the colonists' fight for independence?

Washington's Action

The British army evacuated Boston in March 1776. Later, Washington moved his army south to New York City. But because of its sea access, islands, and rivers, New York proved very difficult for the Patriots to defend.

Trouble in New York

During July, seven hundred British ships brought an army of 34,000 to the New York City area. General William Howe was in command. From the summer of 1776 to late fall, the British won a series of easy victories in the area. Several factors contributed to the Patriot losses. Washington's forces were outnumbered four to one. Washington's inexperience as a commanding general, the superiority of the British navy, and the inexperience of American troops worsened matters.

In late August after a humiliating defeat on Long Island, Washington's army appeared to be trapped by the British. On a rainy night, every possible fishing boat, rowboat, and sailing ship was used to evacuate the Patriots to Manhattan Island. As dawn approached, with the retreat still in progress, a heavy fog concealed Washington's actions from the British. Amazingly, Patriots were able to complete the withdrawal of 9,000 soldiers without any loss of life.

Within a few weeks, after a defeat on Manhattan Island, Washington began moving his troops out of New York City. Most were moved across the Hudson River to relative safety in New Jersey and then to Pennsylvania. By November 1776, New York was in British hands.

Nathan Hale: The Teacher Who Gave His Life

In New York, Washington had desperate need for information about British plans and troops on Long Island. When American officers were asked to volunteer for the dangerous task of spying on the British, only one person was willing to do so—a twenty-one-year-old schoolteacher from Connecticut, named Nathan Hale.

Hale, a graduate of Yale College, had no special training for the mission. Unfortunately, the British captured him on September 21, 1776, and hanged him the following day in New York City.

Later, stories circulated that Hale's last words were, "I only regret that I have but one life to lose for my country." It is uncertain whether he actually made that statement. The only record of his last remarks is from Captain Frederick MacKenzie's diary entry. MacKenzie, a British officer present at the execution, wrote, "He behaved with great composure and resolution, saying he thought it the duty of every good officer, to obey any orders given him by his commander-in-chief; and desired the spectators to be at all times prepared to meet death in whatever shape it might appear."

Washington Attacks Trenton and Princeton

Howe settled down in New York for the winter. He sent Hessian soldiers to **Trenton**, New Jersey, to keep an eye on Washington's army. The Patriots were located across the Delaware River in Pennsylvania.

The Americans had been forced out of New York and had not won a major battle in seven months. Their morale was low, and the troop enlistments would expire on December 31, 1776. If men left when their enlistments expired, Washington would have only 1,400 men—unless, of course, he gained some new recruits. He needed a victory to attract more men to the cause.

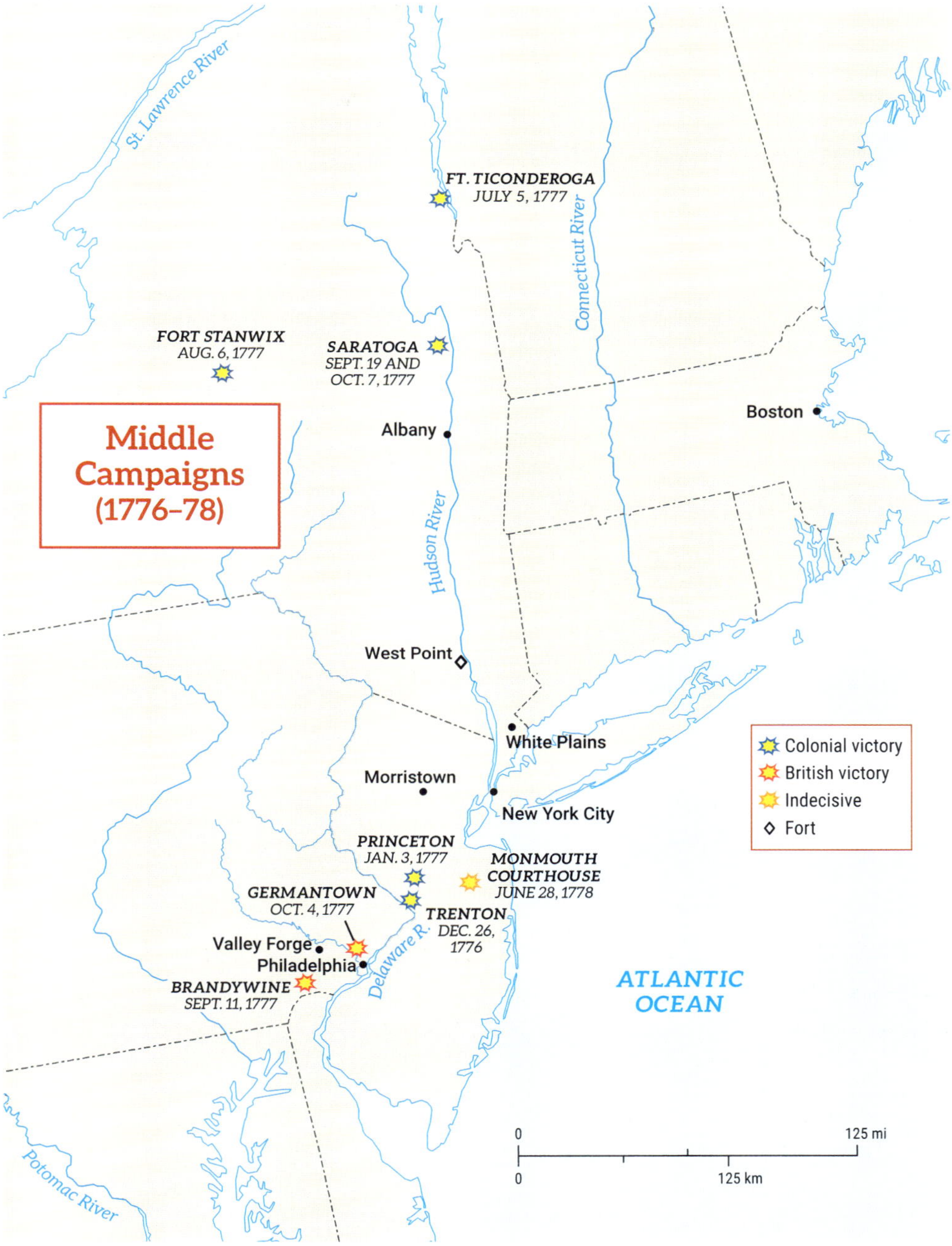

Responding to the challenge, Washington and his army of 2,400 men crossed the icy Delaware River on Christmas night. Snow and freezing rain pelted them as they then marched to Trenton. The next morning, they surprised the Hessians, who were sleeping after their Christmas merry-making. Of the 1,500 Hessians present, more than a hundred men were killed or wounded, about 900 were captured, and the remainder fled. Though two of Washington's men had died because of the cold, none were killed in the actual fighting.

After the Trenton victory, Washington and his men returned to Pennsylvania. About a week later, he left a small group of American soldiers with orders to keep the campfires burning and make noise. Meanwhile, the remainder of his army slipped away, marched north to Princeton, New Jersey, and defeated the British troops there.

Trenton and Princeton were minor events militarily, more like raids than battles. However, the effect on American morale was dramatic. After earlier disasters, any victory would have been welcome. Washington's daring, unconventional moves had freed most of New Jersey from British occupation and gave new hope to the Americans. After these victories, Washington then turned toward Morristown, New Jersey. This was the location he had selected for his winter headquarters.

Victory at Saratoga

General
William Howe

General
John Burgoyne

In 1777 the British developed a strategy that they thought would quickly end the war. They planned a three-pronged assault on New York. First, General William Howe would move north up the Hudson River from New York City. General Barry St. Leger would go down the St. Lawrence River from Canada then cut east through the Mohawk River valley. A third British general, General **John Burgoyne**, would lead a British army south from Canada to New York.

The three generals were to meet at Albany, New York. Their purpose was to isolate New England and upper New York, centers of colonial resistance, from the remainder of the colonies.

In trying to execute their plan, the British made disastrous mistakes. Instead of moving up the Hudson River, Howe decided to subdue Philadelphia. He defeated Washington at Brandywine (west of Philadelphia) and at Germantown in September and October 1777. Howe then decided to spend the winter in the city of Philadelphia, which he had captured, rather than moving northward to Albany. The Second Continental Congress had fled Philadelphia.

St. Leger made some initial progress. But his forces were stopped by American soldiers at Fort Stanwix, New York, and he retreated to Canada in late August. Though he later resumed his march toward Albany, he never reached his destination.

Meanwhile, Burgoyne was marching toward Albany. He easily recaptured Fort Ticonderoga on July 5. From that point on, however, his progress was slowed. First, Patriot troops felled trees and dammed streams to block him. Soon Burgoyne ran short of supplies. In August, he sent 700 men east to Bennington, Vermont, where he had heard there was a stockpile of American military supplies. The Patriots defeated this force. Then, in two separate battles (September 19 and October 7, 1777) south of Saratoga, New York, Americans dealt heavy blows to the British. The British attempted to retreat to Canada. However, the Patriots overtook and surrounded them. On October 17, Burgoyne was forced to surrender.

▲ Surrender of General Burgoyne at Saratoga

The Battle of **Saratoga** was a significant Patriot victory and is considered a major turning point of the war. A British army of more than six thousand had been killed or captured. It forced Britain to abandon any hope of taking the northern colonies. Even more importantly, it brought greater assistance from France. The French were eager to see the colonies win their independence because this would weaken France's greatest rival, Great Britain. France had been providing supplies and loans to America. After the surprising victory at Saratoga, France officially recognized the United States as a separate nation and entered the war against its old enemy, Britain. America now had a powerful ally in its struggle for independence.

Facing Difficulties

News about the alliance with France did not reach America until the spring of 1778. Meanwhile, Washington's army endured a very difficult period. With the British controlling the former capital of Philadelphia, Washington and his men made their headquarters for the winter of 1777–78 some twenty-five miles away at **Valley Forge**, Pennsylvania.

▲ Cabins for Patriot soldiers at Valley Forge, Pennsylvania

The camp they built consisted of wooden barracks and huts where hungry and ill-clothed soldiers lived. Though the weather was brutal, few men had whole uniforms and even fewer had shoes. Many had no blankets. Many horses froze or starved. It is estimated that two thousand or more soldiers died from disease. Others deserted. The Continental army seemed to be crumbling.

Washington could do little to relieve their suffering. Congress had no power to tax. Though they issued paper money, its value rose or plunged depending on the outcome of battles. Thus, nearby farmers and merchants found it far more profitable to sell their goods to the British in Philadelphia, who paid in gold and silver, than to provide items for the Patriot soldiers. Supplies sent by the states rarely reached the men because of poor transportation or theft. Some food that did arrive was spoiled and therefore unusable.

Fun Fact

Baron von Steuben was born September 17, 1730. His full name was Friedrich Wilhelm Ludolf Gerhard Augustin von Steuben.

In February 1778, Baron von Steuben, from Prussia, arrived at Valley Forge to provide military training to those who were healthy. Though he did not know English, he knew how to train men and how to instill pride and discipline. By memorizing a few English phrases, the German was able to teach soldiers to march properly and to maneuver in battle. He transformed the disorganized group into a reasonably efficient fighting force.

After the winter ended, morale improved when the Continental Congress promised extra pay and bonuses at the war's end. The news that France had entered the war to help the Americans also raised spirits.

In June 1778, Sir Henry Clinton, who replaced Howe in the North, moved from Philadelphia. He hoped to use the New York City harbor as a base for sea raids. Washington followed him and attacked at Monmouth Courthouse in New Jersey. Although the battle was a draw, it showed how much Washington's army had improved. Washington and his men spent the winter of 1778–79 at White Plains, New York, some thirty miles away from the British troops.

George Washington (standing right) ▸ with the Marquis de Lafayette at Valley Forge. Lafayette was a Frenchman who became a general in the Continental army.

Did you know?

Henry Hamilton was the Lieutenant Governor of Canada and the British commander of Fort Detroit during much of the War for Independence. He encouraged Indians who were allied with the British to attack American settlements in the Ohio Valley. He was nicknamed "Hair Buyer" or "Hair-buyer General" because he supposedly paid Indians when prisoners or scalps were brought to him.

The War in the West and at Sea

The British, Loyalists, and Indians were also active in the West. In 1778 settlers in the Wyoming Valley of Pennsylvania and Cherry Valley of New York were attacked, with many killed. In response, Americans drove the Loyalists back to their base at Fort Niagara, though they were unable to gain the fort itself.

The British also raided settlements in the Ohio Valley. **George Rogers Clark**, a Patriot general, organized a force of 175 men to go into the region. Braving forests, swamps, and icy rivers, as well as the threat of Indians and Loyalists, Clark captured two frontier outposts—Kaskaskia in Illinois and Vincennes in Indiana.

Clark's victories were not as numerous as those in the East, but they had great strategic importance. Clark's expedition reduced Indian attacks, and the captured outposts allowed the United States to later lay claim to territory bordering the Mississippi River and north of the Ohio River.

Throughout the war, America was involved in fighting at sea. At first, it did not have a navy. When one was created, it consisted mostly of merchant ships that had been modified to serve as fighting vessels. They were called privateers.

George Rogers Clark leading his soldiers

Benedict Arnold: American Traitor

The war record of General **Benedict Arnold** was one of the finest in the Continental army. In May 1775, along with Ethan Allen, he led Patriot forces in capturing Fort Ticonderoga in New York. It was one of the earliest American triumphs of the war. In an otherwise ill-fated attack on Canada that same year, Arnold conducted a brilliant march across the winter wilderness of Maine, and he was wounded in a night attack on Quebec during a howling winter storm. At Saratoga, Arnold had injured his leg leading a charge that broke the British lines and turned the tide of battle.

But Arnold was dissatisfied. He was often passed over for promotion by a Continental Congress that seemed more interested in rewarding an officer's political connections than his bravery. George Washington gave him command of Philadelphia after the British retreated. But politicians and jealous fellow officers criticized Arnold and sought to undermine his authority. Arnold became bitter.

Soon Arnold began to look for ways to increase his wealth and satisfy his ego. In 1780, Washington named Arnold as the commander at West Point, an important fort on the Hudson River (now the site of the United States Military Academy). Arnold plotted with the British to surrender the fort to them in exchange for a large sum of money. However, Americans captured his British contact, Major John André. He possessed papers that revealed the plot. André was hanged as a spy.

Meanwhile, Arnold escaped and became a British general and spent the remainder of the war leading raids for the British in Virginia and Connecticut. After the war, he fled to Britain. Although financially comfortable because of a reward and a pension for his treason, Arnold was shunned by British society. Unhappy, he died in London in 1801. Many still regard him as the most despicable traitor in American history.

Since Great Britain had a strong navy, Americans faced an almost impossible task on the seas. When persuading France to enter the war, the Americans hoped that French sea power would come to their aid. America used French ports as bases of operation and even used French ships to attack the British.

The most famous American naval officer of the war was **John Paul Jones**. A native of Scotland, he moved to the colonies shortly before the War for Independence began. Jones gained his greatest fame by defeating the British ship *Serapis* in the North Sea, off the coast of Britain, on September 23, 1779. Jones was commanding the *Bonhomme Richard*, named in honor of Benjamin Franklin and his *Poor Richard's Almanack*. During the intense four-hour battle between the ships, Jones refused to surrender. He supposedly cried out, "I have not yet begun to fight!" In the end, Jones won the battle and provided America with its first great victory at sea.

SECTION REVIEW 6.3

1. What factors led to Patriot losses in New York?
2. What two victories in New Jersey gave new hope to Washington's men?
3. What mistakes did the British make in their attempt to isolate New England and upper New York from the rest of the colonies?
4. What American victory forced the British to abandon hope of taking the northern colonies?
5. What would you have done to make it through the winter camp at Valley Forge?
6. What Patriot general captured western outposts that later helped the United States claim western lands?
7. What types of ships were used by the American navy in the war?
8. Who won America's first great victory at sea? What did he supposedly say during the battle?

▾ American sailors from the *Bonhomme Richard* taking control of the *Serapis*

Joseph Brant: Mohawk Loyalist

Joseph Brant, a Mohawk Indian chieftain, first gained recognition during the French and Indian War. He fought under Sir William Johnson, a British Indian agent, against the French. After the war, Johnson sent Brant to Eleazar Wheelock's Indian school in Lebanon, Connecticut, where Brant became a devout Christian. During Pontiac's Rebellion, Brant again fought on the British side. Meanwhile, he was a missionary to his people.

When the War for Independence began, Brant sided with the Loyalists. He thought that the colonies were wrong to rebel against the king. His influence brought many other Indians to the Loyalist cause as well. He served as a captain in the British army and led several raids on American settlements in Cherry Valley, New York. The colonists soon feared his men.

After the war, the British gave his people money and land in Ontario, Canada. Brant returned to his missionary work and translated the Gospel of Mark into the Mohawk language. As an Indian statesman, he negotiated treaties with other tribes and traveled in the American West in an effort to form an Indian confederacy.

Brant died at age sixty-four in 1807.

WOMEN *at war for* INDEPENDENCE

Many women contributed to the Patriot cause during the war. Some helped in a moment of crisis; others fought throughout the struggle. From the frontlines to the frontier, these women took the call to arms seriously. They were not afraid to fight for the cause in which their families and friends believed—no matter the cost.

Margaret Corbin

Margaret Corbin went to war with her husband. She cooked, washed clothes, and nursed wounded soldiers. She also assisted her husband as he served on an artillery crew. During the British attack on Fort Washington, New York, her husband was killed, and Margaret took his position and continued firing until she was shot. Though she lived more than twenty additional years, the severity of her wounds caused her to suffer the remainder of her life. She received a pension from Congress for her military service.

Mary Hays

Historians have debated whether the story of Mary Hays is true. Accounts say that she earned the nickname "Molly Pitcher" by serving as a water carrier to her husband and other Patriot soldiers during the Battle of Monmouth, New Jersey. After her husband had been wounded on that hot June day, Mary supposedly took charge of his cannon and fired the weapon for him.

Statue of Mary Hays (also painting above) ▸ at her grave in Pennsylvania

Anne Bailey

Anne "Mad Anne" Bailey was an adventurous woman who was a scout and messenger for the Patriots on the western frontier of present-day Ohio, Virginia, and West Virginia. It appears she was given her nickname by Indians who thought she either had special protection from the Great Spirit or was insane. She had a reputation for daring acts of bravery. Once, when chased by Indians, she hid in a hollow log. When the Indians could not find her, they took her horse. After the Indians left, she trailed them to their camp and, that night, retrieved her horse.

▴ Nancy Hart

Nancy Hart

Nancy Hart also helped the Patriots. Her fearlessness led Indians in Georgia to call her the War Woman. According to local legend, several Loyalists approached her home and demanded that she prepare a meal for them. While doing so, she sent her daughter for help. Then, while the Loyalists were eating, she took their muskets. She demanded the men stay still. When two failed to do so, she killed both. She held the others at gunpoint until her husband and neighbors arrived. The surviving men were later hanged. Because there have been several versions of the story, some have questioned its accuracy. In 1912 crews working on a railroad about a mile from where Nancy Hart lived made an interesting discovery. They found several skeletons buried neatly in a row. A few of the skeletons' necks appeared to be broken, which indicated that they may have been hanged. They were estimated to have been buried for at least a century. Some believe this helps validate the story.

6.4 WINNING INDEPENDENCE

How did the War for Independence end, and what were the results?

GUIDING QUESTIONS

- What were the major battles in the South, including Yorktown?
- What were the results of the War for Independence?

By late 1778 British strategy had changed. They would now focus on the South, where the population was more scattered and where there were more Loyalists. Meanwhile, they would continue the naval blockade and coastal raids in the North.

Fighting in the South

In December 1778, the British took control of Savannah—the capital, chief port, and most populated city in Georgia. From March to May 1780, the British besieged, or surrounded, Charleston. Also known as Charles Town, it was South Carolina's most important city. After six weeks, the American general surrendered the city and his army of approximately five thousand on May 12. It was one of the worst defeats of the war.

▲ Nathanael Greene, Patriot general

▲ Charles Cornwallis, British general

With the fall of Charleston, the Carolinas lay open to British General **Charles Cornwallis** and his troops. In August 1780 they dealt the Patriots a crushing defeat at Camden, South Carolina. Two months later, Washington appointed General **Nathanael Greene** as the new Patriot commander in the South. British Lieutenant Colonel Banastre Tarleton used his forces to harass the southern soldiers as they tried to regroup. The situation seemed bleak for the Patriots.

In September 1780, British Major Patrick Ferguson commanded an army that consisted almost entirely of Loyalists. He issued a decree to the frontiersmen of the Carolina foothills. It stated that if those who supported the Patriot cause did not lay down their weapons, he would "lay waste the countryside with fire and sword." Many colonists who had tried to be neutral in the war were now furious. The Patriots crossed the mountains in search of Ferguson and his Loyalist forces. They found them at **Kings Mountain**, South Carolina. On October 7, 1780, the Patriot frontiersmen, known as "over-mountain men," met Ferguson's challenge by killing, wounding, or capturing almost his entire force of 1,000 men. Ferguson himself was killed and buried on the battlefield.

The "over-mountain" men defeat Loyalist forces at the Battle of Kings Mountain. ▶

Nathanael Greene divided his outnumbered army and sent a detachment south under General Daniel Morgan. Morgan, with six hundred Continentals, hoped that Cornwallis would also divide his force and pursue him. Indeed, Cornwallis sent Lieutenant Colonel Tarleton and his Loyalist soldiers to catch the Continentals. On January 17, 1781, at Cowpens, South Carolina, Morgan and his men won a great victory. Morgan suffered just over one hundred casualties while Tarleton's force suffered over nine hundred.

After the unsettling losses at Kings Mountain and Cowpens, Cornwallis was determined to crush Greene. In mid-March 1781, the American army faced Cornwallis at a crossroads in North Carolina called Guilford Courthouse. The British won a victory, but Cornwallis lost one-fourth of his men.

Did you know?

During the War for Independence more battles were fought in South Carolina than in any other colony. Though statistics vary, at least 130 battles took place there.

SONGS *of the* WAR

During the 1700s, both the British and the Americans wrote poems about themselves and their enemies and set them to popular tunes. Sometimes the Americans changed the words of British songs. "Yankee Doodle," the most famous song of the War for Independence, was originally a British song that made fun of the colonists.

Yankee Doodle came to town,
For to buy a firelock,
We will tar and feather him,
And so we will John Hancock.

Yankee Doodle went to town,
A-riding on a pony,
Stuck a feather in his hat
And called it macaroni.

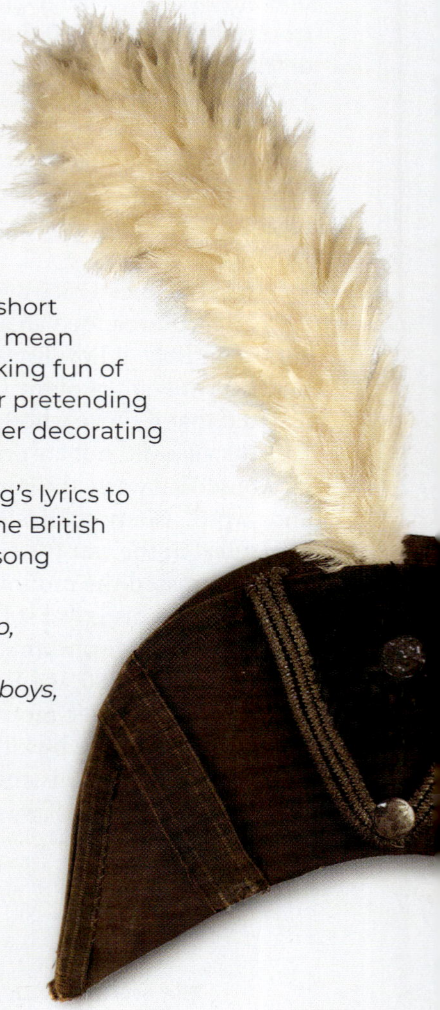

Macaroni was a term used for a short time by the European upper class to mean "sophisticated." The British were making fun of an American "doodle" (simpleton) for pretending that a common item, such as a feather decorating a hat, was "macaroni."

The Americans changed the song's lyrics to the familiar words we know today. The British probably disliked the fact that their song was used to insult them instead.

Father and I went down to camp,
Along with Captain Gooding.
And there we saw the men and boys,
As thick as hasty pudding.

There was Captain Washington
Upon a slapping stallion,
A-giving orders to his men;
I guess there was a million.

Yankee Doodle, keep it up,
Yankee Doodle dandy,
Mind the music and the step,
And with the girls be handy.

British Surrender at Yorktown, Virginia

As Cornwallis chased Greene across the Carolinas, his supply lines lengthened. Guerrilla fighters—such as Francis Marion (the Swamp Fox), Thomas Sumter, and Andrew Pickens—attacked those lines and harassed British troops at every turn. Frustrated, Cornwallis left the Carolinas and headed for coastal Virginia. There, he reasoned, the British navy could keep him supplied, and he could devise a new strategy. He believed that he could subdue Virginia, the main source of Patriot supplies, and resume his attacks in the South.

The only threat to Cornwallis seemed to be a twenty-three-year-old French volunteer, the **Marquis de Lafayette**, whom Washington had sent to Virginia with troops. Cornwallis met little resistance from Americans as he headed for **Yorktown**, where he planned to build a well-fortified base.

▲ Francis Marion, "the Swamp Fox," harassing British forces in South Carolina

Fun Fact

In 2002, the Marquis de Lafayette was awarded honorary US citizenship for his help in the war. He is one of only eight individuals to receive this award.

Marquis de Lafayette

The Marquis de Lafayette was born into a French family of nobles in 1757. The men in his family had long been active in the military, and he joined the army at age fourteen. At the outbreak of war in America, Lafayette was attracted to the American cause. He arrived in the colonies when he was only nineteen, and the Continental Congress made him a major general. He distinguished himself at the Battles of Brandywine and Yorktown.

During the war, Lafayette developed a close friendship with George Washington. The two remained friends for many years. Lafayette returned to France after the war. In 1824 as America was approaching the fiftieth anniversary of the war, he made another trip to the United States. He stayed for more than a year and was warmly greeted by crowds throughout his visit. He died in France in 1834 at age seventy-six. At his request, soil from Bunker Hill was sprinkled on his grave in Paris.

The Patriots had pleaded repeatedly for French naval help. At the end of August 1781, Admiral de Grasse, who had been in the West Indies, was ready to help with his twenty-eight ships. The British did not expect this show of strength. They thought that when a French attack came it would be at New York City, rather than at Yorktown.

Washington slipped out of New York City with most of his forces to help trap Cornwallis in Virginia. De Grasse's French troops arrived to reinforce the Patriot troops and to help prevent Cornwallis's escape. Eight more French warships prevented any of the remaining British ships from fleeing to New York. Now Cornwallis was trapped at Yorktown without the hope of support from the British navy. Outnumbered by more than two to one, Cornwallis offered only brief resistance. On October 19, 1781, he surrendered.

Although the British formally surrendered one army, they still occupied some American territory. They were especially active in the Northwest and controlled some forts there. The conflict between Loyalists and Patriots continued for some time. However, in early 1782 Parliament voted to not continue the war in America.

▲ Surrender of the British at Yorktown, Virginia

Results of the War

Because France had been America's major ally, the peace talks were held in Paris. Discussions continued for months. The American negotiators included Benjamin Franklin, John Jay, and John Adams. The **Treaty of Paris**, signed on September 3, 1783, ended the eight-year war with Britain. It formally granted the American colonies their independence and gave the new nation all lands east of the Mississippi River, with the exception of Florida (which returned to Spanish control). The fighting between the United States and Britain had stopped in April 1783. The last British troops left New York City on November 25, 1783. The war was officially over.

Washington returned to his home at Mount Vernon and his farming activities. He ignored those who urged him to use the army to seize power and become a dictator. Washington believed that the army had done its job in securing the nation's independence.

Obviously, the primary result of the war was America's independence from Britain, but many other changes occurred in American life in the years that followed. After the war, America's population continued to grow rapidly. A number of Loyalists who left during the war returned to claim their property. Many were unable to regain what they had owned earlier. Americans pushed even farther westward, encouraged by the new lands gained from the war. This movement brought conflict with the Indians. The Americans also grew wealthier as they expanded their trade and had more time to concentrate on their professions.

The war brought changes to traditional ways of life. In the family, for example, there was an increased equality among family members. When the men had gone to war, the women had performed extra duties. After the war, women gained more legal rights, although they still could not vote. Historian Gordon Wood argues that traditional life changed in other ways as authorities lost influence. He points to less respect toward the aged, an increase in the number of divorces, more children being born out of wedlock, and a lessening of other moral standards.

More Americans began to view slavery differently. They wondered how slavery could be consistent with the ideals of liberty and equality for which they had fought. Some northern states began abolishing slavery during the war. Though slavery continued in Pennsylvania until 1847, further importation of slaves was prohibited. A law was also passed that provided for the eventual freedom of future slaves born in the state. These ideas gained increasing acceptance in the nineteenth century.

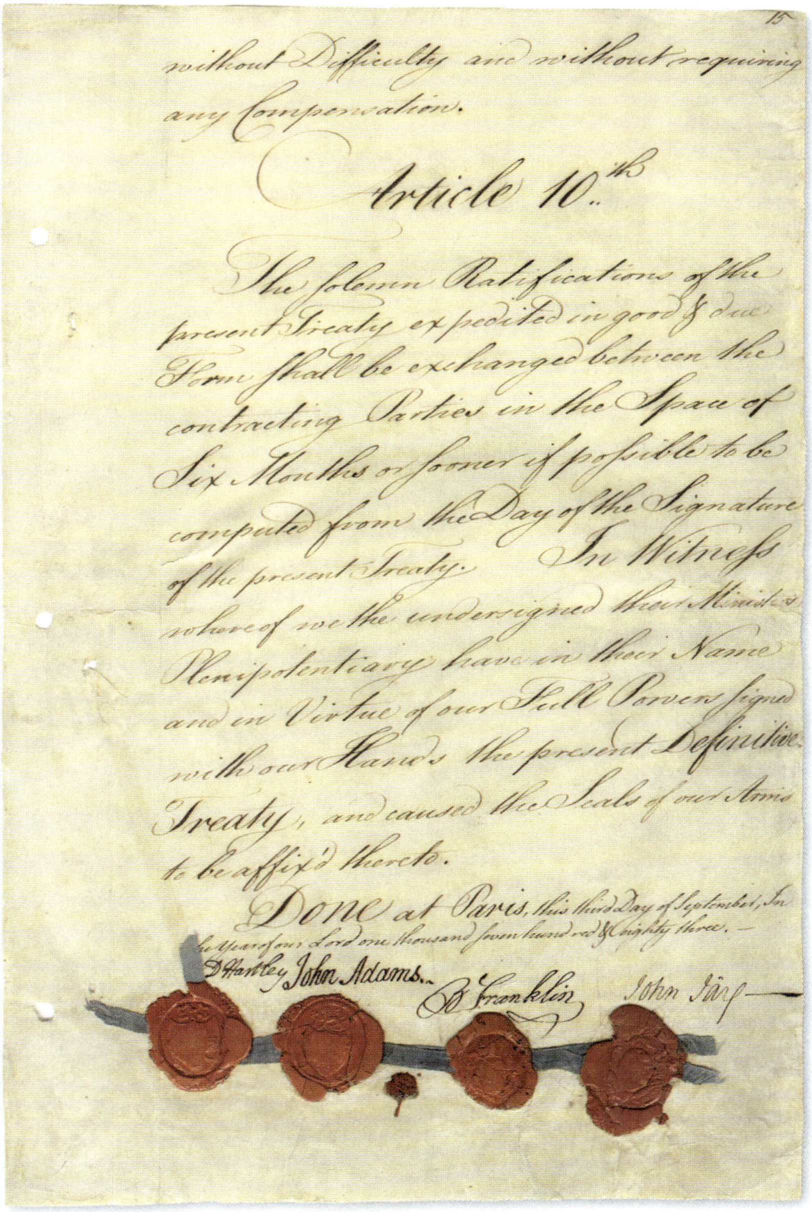

15

without Difficulty and without requiring any Compensation.

Article 10th.

The solemn Ratifications of the present Treaty expedited in good & due Form shall be exchanged between the contracting Parties in the Space of Six Months or sooner if possible to be computed from the Day of the Signature of the present Treaty. In Witness whereof we the undersigned their Ministers Plenipotentiary have in their Name and in Virtue of our Full Powers signed with our Hands the present Definitive Treaty, and caused the Seals of our Arms to be affix'd thereto.

Done at Paris, this third Day of September, In the Year of our Lord one thousand seven hundred & Eighty three.

D Hartley John Adams. B Franklin John Jay

▾ The Treaty of Paris officially ended the war.

The War for Independence impacted American religion. Although some states still had officially recognized churches, Americans began to question state-supported religious authorities. Congregational churches, which were powerful in New England and did not allow religious dissent, became less popular. New groups, such as Baptists and Methodists, zealously spread the gospel and grew much larger. Those two groups, unlike other denominations, allowed unpaid laymen (non-ministers) to pastor churches. This practice helped end the shortage of ministers. Sadly, as the variety and size of denominations grew, people who taught false doctrines or who had strange interpretations of the Scriptures also increased.

With these changes in religion came a greater emphasis on education and reform. Most Americans believed that children who were given a moral education would prevent any future rise of tyranny. But as an independent nation, the United States still faced huge problems. Independence brought change—and many new challenges.

SECTION REVIEW 6.4

1. At what southern port city did one of the worst defeats of the war occur?
2. Who was the primary British general in the South? Who was the primary American general?
3. What motivated many of the "over-mountain men" to fight the battle of Kings Mountain?
4. How were the colonists able to defeat Cornwallis?
5. What treaty officially ended the war with Britain? In what year was it signed?
6. List three results of the War for Independence.
7. Which result in America do you feel was the most important? Why? Can you see evidences of this same change today?

▾ George Washington's home, Mount Vernon, on the Potomac River

CHAPTER 6 REVIEW

Making Connections

1. Earlier battles of the war were mostly fought in the (North/South), while later battles were mostly fought in the (North/South).
2. What feat did Henry Knox accomplish that led to the British leaving the city of Boston?
3. Who were the five men responsible for writing the Declaration of Independence? How many days passed between the Continental Congress approving separation from Britain and approving the Declaration?
4. How many years ago was the Declaration of Independence written?
5. In what order did Washington's troops move through the following locations?
   a. Valley Forge, Pennsylvania
   b. Princeton, New Jersey
   c. Morristown, New Jersey
   d. Trenton, New Jersey
   e. Long Island, New York
   f. Manhattan, New York
6. Why did Washington need a victory at Trenton? How did he gain that victory?
7. Describe housing conditions, the clothing situation, and other difficulties at Valley Forge during the winter of 1777–78.
8. What two foreign volunteers, one German and one French, helped train and lead the Continental army?
9. How did the French help America at the end of the war?
10. Who were the three American negotiators of the Treaty of Paris?

Thinking Critically

11. Why is the War for Independence often referred to as the Revolutionary War? Define the term *revolution* in your answer.
12. Thomas Paine's *Common Sense* influenced many Americans in just a brief amount of time. Describe a time when you have seen many people influenced strongly in a short amount of time. What was the result?
13. What might the result have been if the three British generals had met at Albany as planned?

Living as a Christian Citizen

14. If you were a Christian living during the War for Independence, would you have chosen to be a Loyalist or a Patriot? Why?
15. If you were a Christian in this time period, how would you respond to Thomas Paine's argument that submission to kings is wrong since God made people equal and the Bible speaks against monarchy?

Cannon used during the War for Independence

Terms to Remember

Second Continental Congress
Continental army
Olive Branch Petition
Ethan Allen
Fort Ticonderoga
Patriots
Bunker Hill
Hessians
Loyalists
Common Sense
Thomas Paine
Thomas Jefferson
July 4, 1776
Declaration of Independence
Trenton
John Burgoyne
Saratoga
Valley Forge
George Rogers Clark
Benedict Arnold
John Paul Jones
Charles Cornwallis
Nathanael Greene
Kings Mountain
Marquis de Lafayette
Yorktown
Treaty of Paris

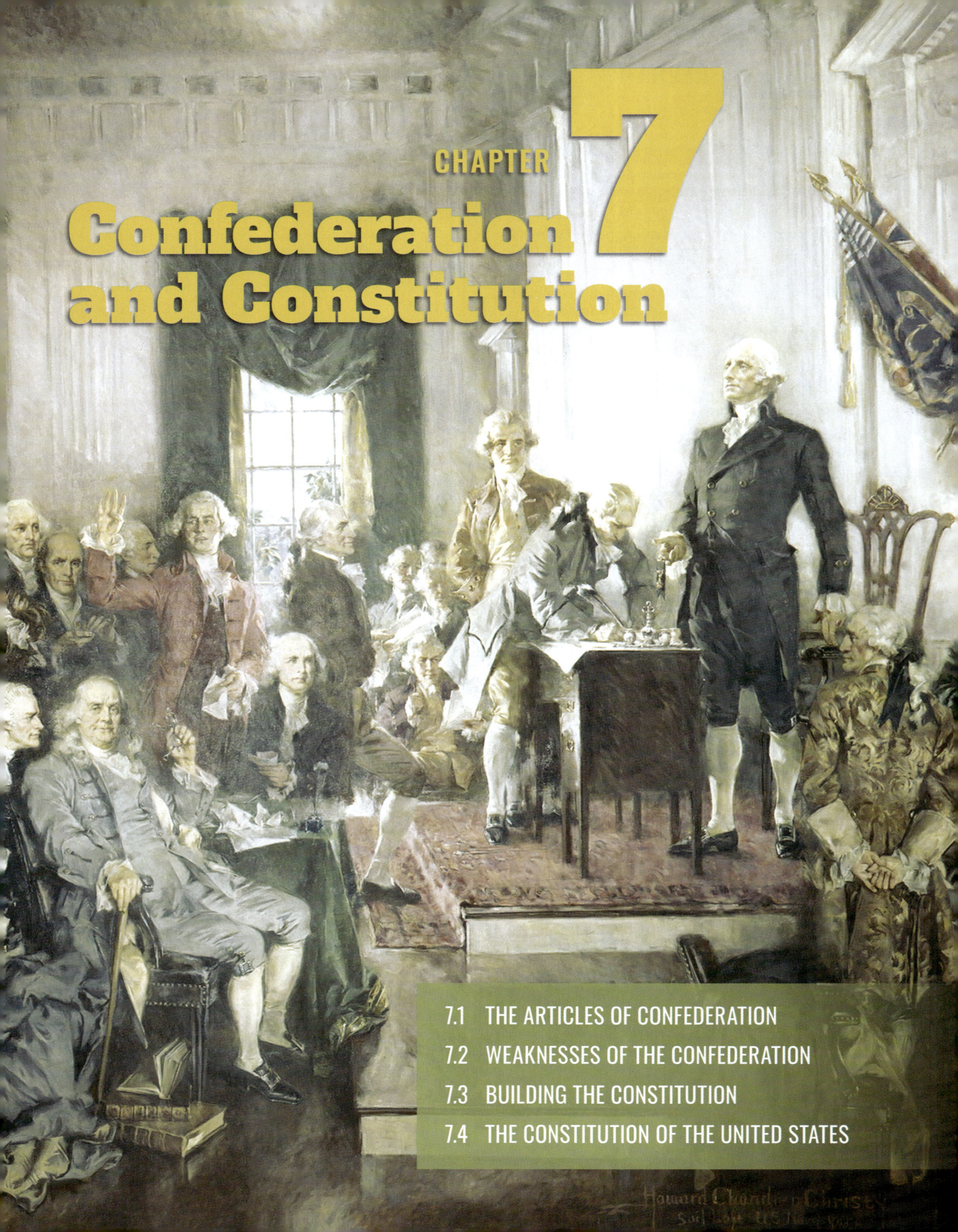

CHAPTER 7

Confederation and Constitution

As the colonists broke ties with England, they tried to govern themselves. During most of the War for Independence, the Second Continental Congress and state assemblies were primarily responsible for governing. Although the people were reluctant to have a powerful government that might threaten their liberty and individualism, the Patriot leaders knew that they needed something more permanent. As a result, in June 1776 the Congress appointed a committee to propose a plan for an improved system of government. The committee suggested a **confederation**—a loose association or league of states.

GUIDING QUESTIONS

- How were the Articles of Confederation ratified and what powers did they have?
- What did the government achieve under the Articles of Confederation?

7.1 THE ARTICLES OF CONFEDERATION

What was the government like under the Articles of Confederation?

Approval

The **Articles of Confederation** were presented to Congress in July 1776. After more than a year of debate and revision, they were finally adopted in November 1777. Under this plan, the government had one governing body, a congress, whose members were to be elected yearly. Because of the colonies' experience with the British monarchy, Americans tended to fear a strong central government. Instead, they placed their hopes in strong state governments. In fact, at the time many Americans were more loyal to their states than to the "United States."

Before the Articles could become law, all thirteen states had to **ratify** (formally approve) them. It was almost four years after the Continental Congress adopted the document before the ratification process was complete. One reason for the long delay was the dispute regarding western lands, the area between the Appalachian Mountains and the Mississippi River. Several states had long claimed parts of that huge tract of land. Others had no such claims and feared the power of those states if they succeeded in controlling that territory. Maryland refused to ratify the Articles until other states abandoned their claims. By early 1781 all of those states had dropped their claims, Maryland adopted the Articles, and the Confederation Congress was organized to govern the country.

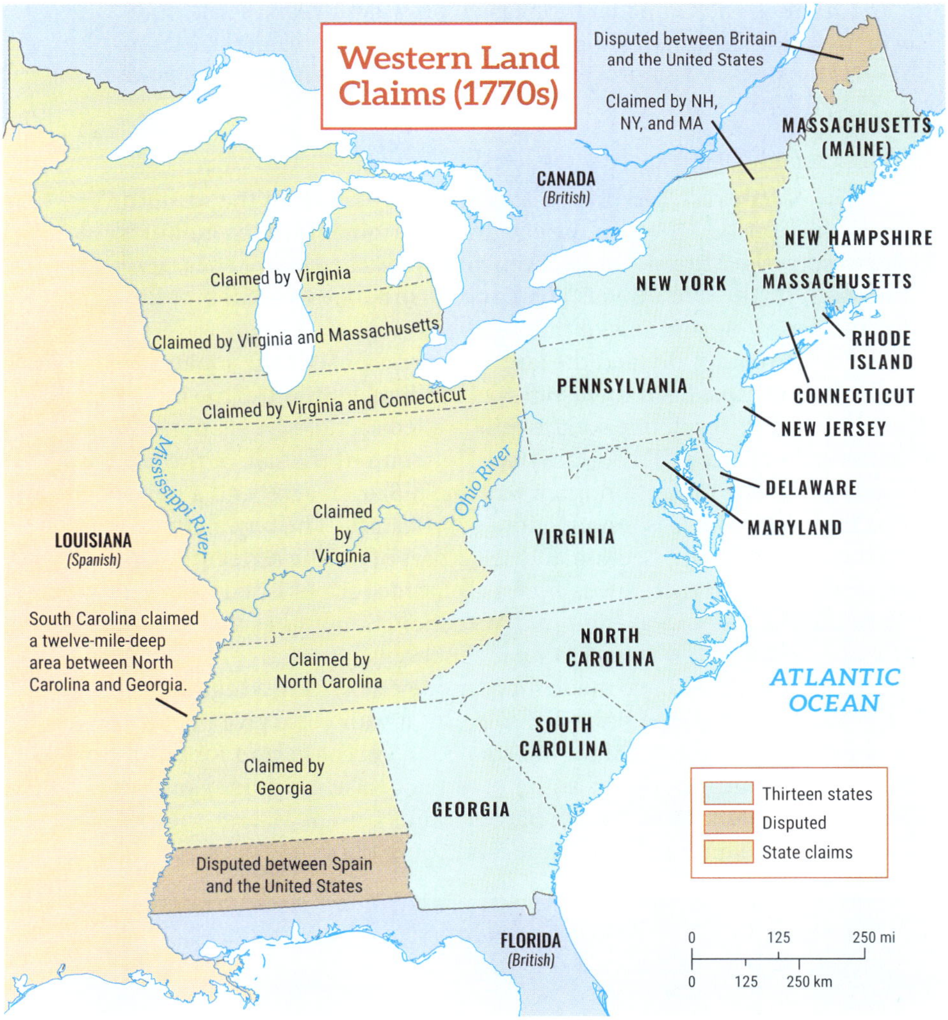

◂ Signing of the US Constitution

Political Power

Under the Confederation, the new Congress had more power than the Continental Congresses; however, its power still had significant limitations. For example, Congress had no power to tax. It could not raise and maintain a national army or navy. Congress could declare war, make treaties with foreign countries, manage Indian affairs, establish and run a postal system, appoint foreign ambassadors, and borrow and coin money. But some of these powers were not held exclusively by Congress. The states could also coin their own monies, deal directly with foreign governments, and even declare war.

Certain powers were held only by the states. For instance, states controlled both domestic and foreign trade. They also had the right to act in economic matters involving debts, contracts, and family affairs. And the states alone had the right to tax citizens.

Under the Articles, laws could be passed only when nine of the thirteen states approved them. The Articles themselves, however, could be changed only with the approval of all states.

The states did cooperate in some matters. For example, they agreed to recognize many legal actions completed in other states, such as marriages and wills. In addition, the states agreed to return criminals and runaway slaves who crossed state lines.

Important Achievements

Although the Confederation lasted only eight years, some noteworthy accomplishments were made. The most important legislation passed by the new Congress was two laws dealing with western lands: the Land Ordinance of 1785 and the Northwest Ordinance of 1787.

The Land Ordinance of 1785

The **Northwest Territory** referred to the portion of the western lands that was bounded on the east by the original thirteen colonies, the west by the Mississippi River, the north by the Great Lakes, and the south by the Ohio River. The **Land Ordinance of 1785** provided for the surveying and sale of that region.

The ordinance divided the land into areas of six-mile squares called **townships**. Each township was subdivided into thirty-six smaller parcels (each one square mile) called sections. A section contained 640 acres. The ordinance also required the sale of the land at auctions. The minimum price was one dollar an acre, and a buyer had to purchase at least one section, or 640 acres. The buyer could further subdivide the section and sell a part of it. The sixteenth section of land in each township was set aside for public education. Sometimes a school was built in that section. Sometimes that section, or a part of it, was sold to finance schools.

Congress could have made more money by setting a higher price or by using a different method of sale. But it wanted to give people of average, or even low, incomes the chance to purchase land for family farms. Many did, but others either could not raise the money or saw no need to purchase such large parcels. Thus Congress, ever short of cash, sold the land to several large land companies.

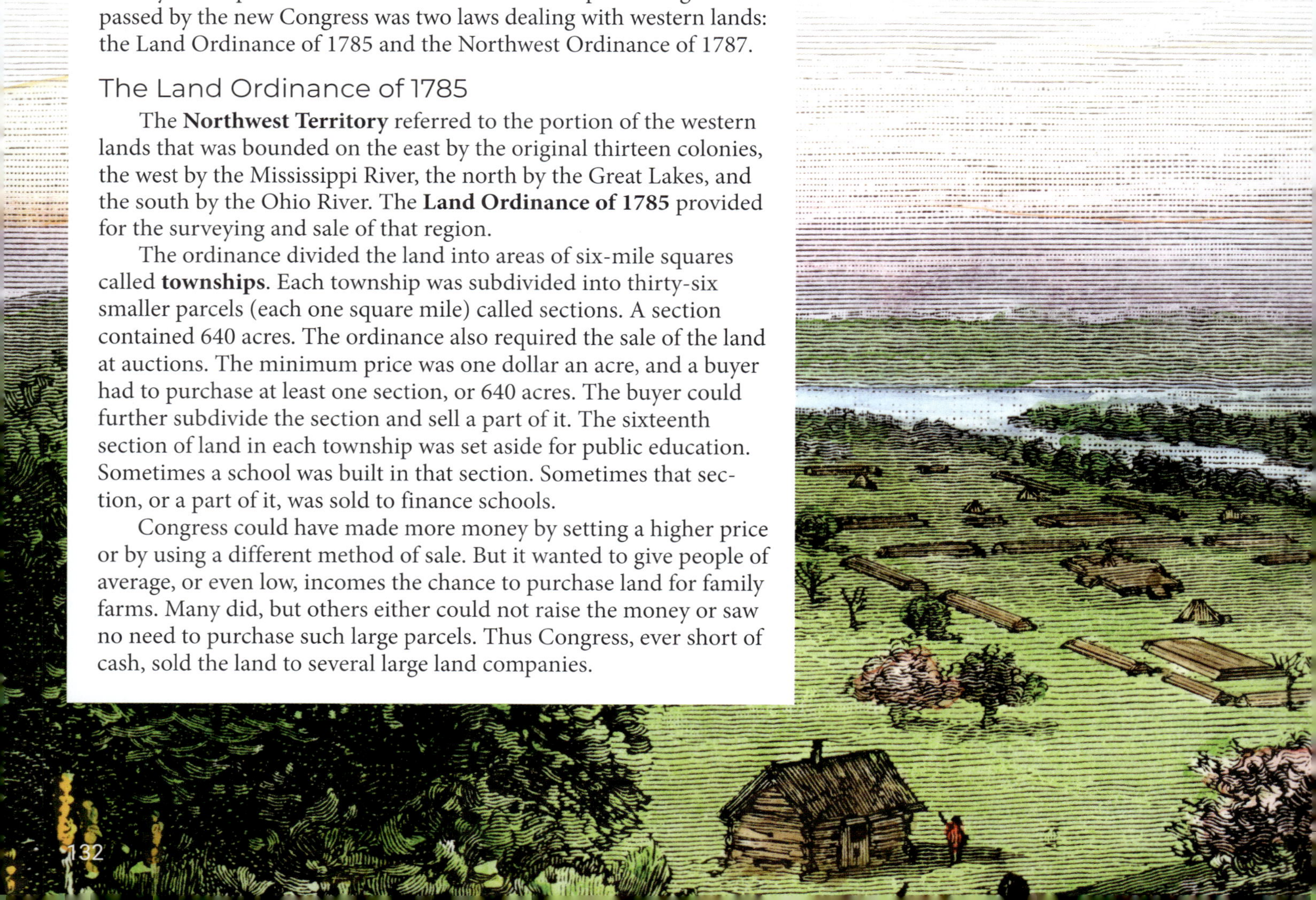

▾ Marietta, Ohio, part of the Northwest Territory, was settled in 1788.

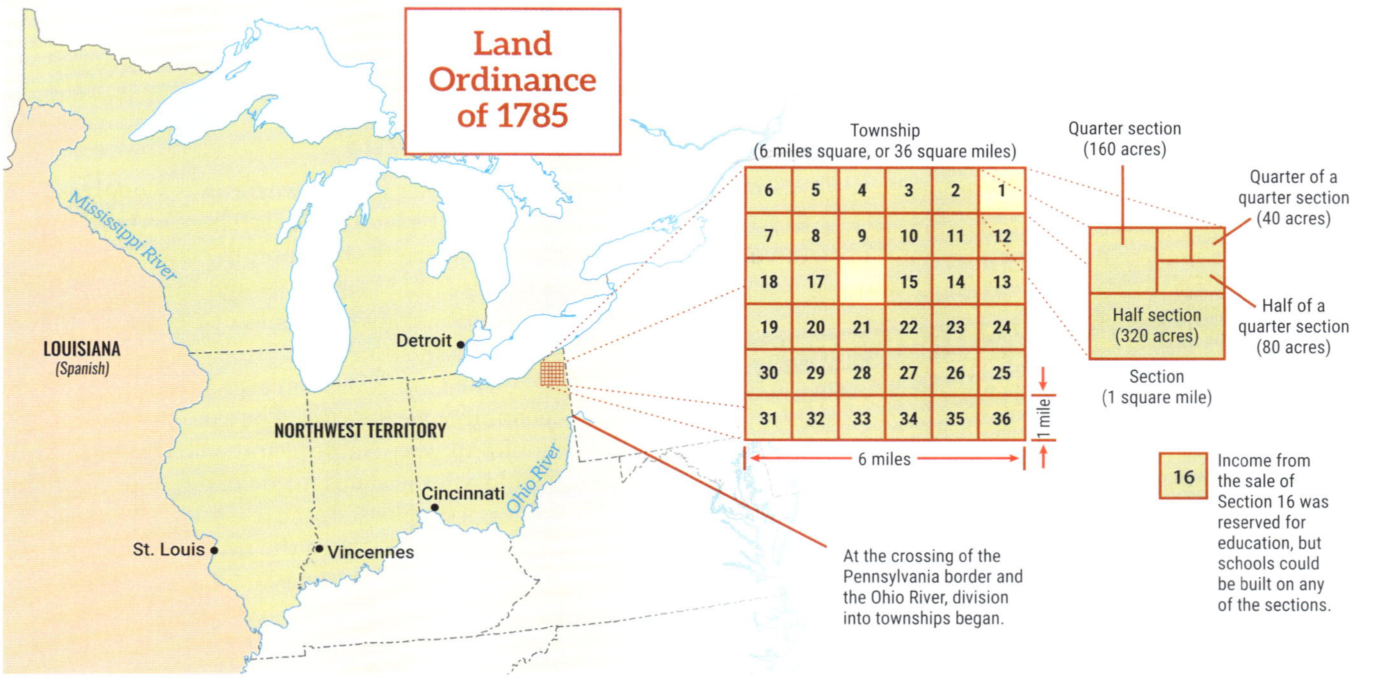

The ordinance established a system of surveying land that has had a lasting effect on America. Most new territories and states, even those outside the Northwest Territory, were surveyed according to the ordinance's specifications. In addition, many farms and roads were then constructed in straight lines and at right angles. This layout is still visible today, especially in the Midwest and the Plains states.

The Northwest Ordinance of 1787

A second piece of legislation, called the **Northwest Ordinance of 1787**, required the area be divided into at least three but no more than five territories. There were three required stages through which each territory must proceed to become a state. In the first, each territory would be under the control of a governor and judges appointed by Congress. When the area reached five thousand free, adult, male inhabitants, it entered the second stage. Settlers could then write a temporary constitution and elect their own legislature. The third stage occurred when the population in a territory grew to sixty thousand free inhabitants. Settlers could then devise a permanent constitution and apply for statehood. When Congress granted that status, each new state would have the same powers and rights as the original states.

Eventually, five states were created from the Northwest Territory—Ohio, Indiana, Illinois, Michigan, and Wisconsin. The Northwest Ordinance prohibited slavery throughout the region. Thus, the Ohio River became the dividing line between the slave and the free states.

SECTION REVIEW 7.1

1. What groups were primarily responsible for governing the colonies during the War for Independence?
2. How long did it take for the Articles of Confederation to be ratified? Why did it take this much time?
3. List three things that both Congress and the states could do under the Articles of Confederation.
4. What were two important achievements under the Articles of Confederation?
5. Draw a township as planned under the Land Ordinance of 1785. Mark the appropriate section for education. How much did each acre cost? How much did each section cost?
6. How many territories did the Northwest Ordinance of 1787 require?
7. How many free inhabitants needed to live in a territory before it could apply for statehood?
8. What states were eventually created out of the Northwest Territory?
9. What is an advantage and a disadvantage of requiring all states to ratify a governing document such as the Articles of Confederation?

GUIDING QUESTIONS

- What problems were created by the Articles of Confederation?
- Which key leaders helped change the government?

7.2 WEAKNESSES OF THE CONFEDERATION

What were the weaknesses of the Articles of Confederation?

Administrative Problems

One of the primary weaknesses of the Articles was Congress's lack of authority to implement the laws it made. There were no executive or judicial branches to enforce or interpret the laws. States and citizens could—and did—ignore or disobey the national government's decrees with little risk of punishment.

The Confederation also had serious economic weaknesses. For example, Congress could not levy (impose and collect) taxes. It would ask the states for help, but the states seldom complied. Because Congress lacked the power to tax, it lacked the necessary funds to operate the government and pay war debts. This meant that money owed to soldiers, foreign nations, and those who had bought war bonds went unpaid. (War bonds were purchased by individuals. The money was then used by the government to pay for war supplies. The purchaser was promised repayment, with interest. These were similar to modern savings bonds.)

Congress also lacked the power to regulate trade, either domestic or foreign. States argued over whether they should tax one another's imports.

In addition, Congress did not have the sole authority to coin money or set its value. Gold and silver, needed to make coins and to back the paper money in circulation, were scarce. As a result, states printed paper money with so little backing that it was almost worthless. When creditors rejected this money, people who owed debts could not repay them.

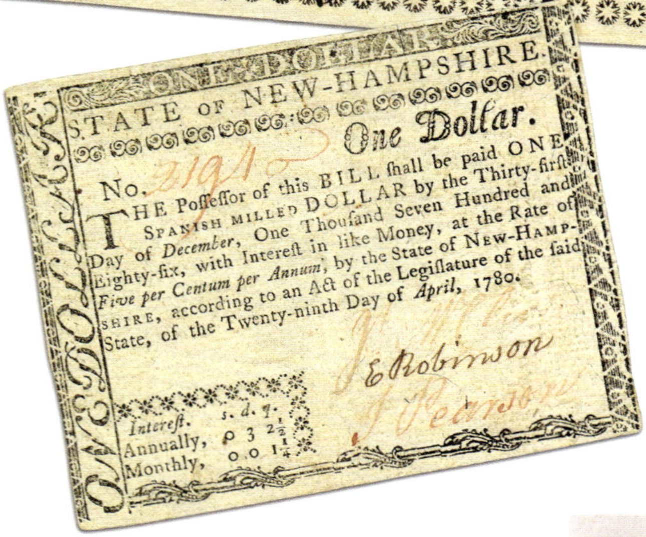

▲ Before there was a national currency, each colony (and later state) printed its own money.

▼ New Orleans in 1803

Poor Foreign Relations

The United States was so young and its government was so weak that Congress had trouble dealing with foreign countries. It lacked the political power needed to gain respect overseas.

Problems with Britain

Although the Treaty of Paris called for the removal of all British troops in the colonies, they kept the western forts that they had held before the war. The British defended this action by saying the United States was not fulfilling all its requirements in the treaty. For example, some Americans, particularly merchants and large farmers, still owed money to British banks and British citizens. Though repayment had been promised in the treaty, American courts were interfering with the collection of those debts. Since the Americans did not send an army to remove the British troops, Britain saw no need to call the troops home.

Also in the Treaty of Paris, the United States agreed that Loyalists would be treated fairly after the war. Many Americans, however, were still bitter toward those who had supported Britain. They sometimes confiscated the Loyalists' property and even killed a number of them. Loyalists who had fled America and returned were often unable to regain land and possessions that had been taken from them. The British government was justifiably angered.

Americans had to contend with Britain on the seas. The British navy stopped American ships that were using old British trading routes. The American navy was small and unable to protect those ships; as a result, Americans had to find new trade routes.

▾ Flatboat on the Mississippi River

Problems with Spain

Although Spain fought against Britain in the war, it was not a close American ally. The Spanish still held land in North America and wanted to discourage further American settlement. They warned the local Indians, especially in the Southeast, that the Americans would deprive them of their lands and urged them to raid American frontier settlements.

American flatboats regularly transported goods to New Orleans, a port city controlled by Spain at the mouth of the Mississippi River. Americans needed the **right of deposit** (the freedom to stockpile goods until ships came to transport them overseas). However, there was frequent conflict between Spain and the United States concerning that issue. At times, Spain denied that right and at other times it required Americans to pay a tax on goods brought to New Orleans.

The boundary between Spanish-controlled Florida and the United States was another matter of dispute that continued for many years before the two nations finally signed a treaty in 1795.

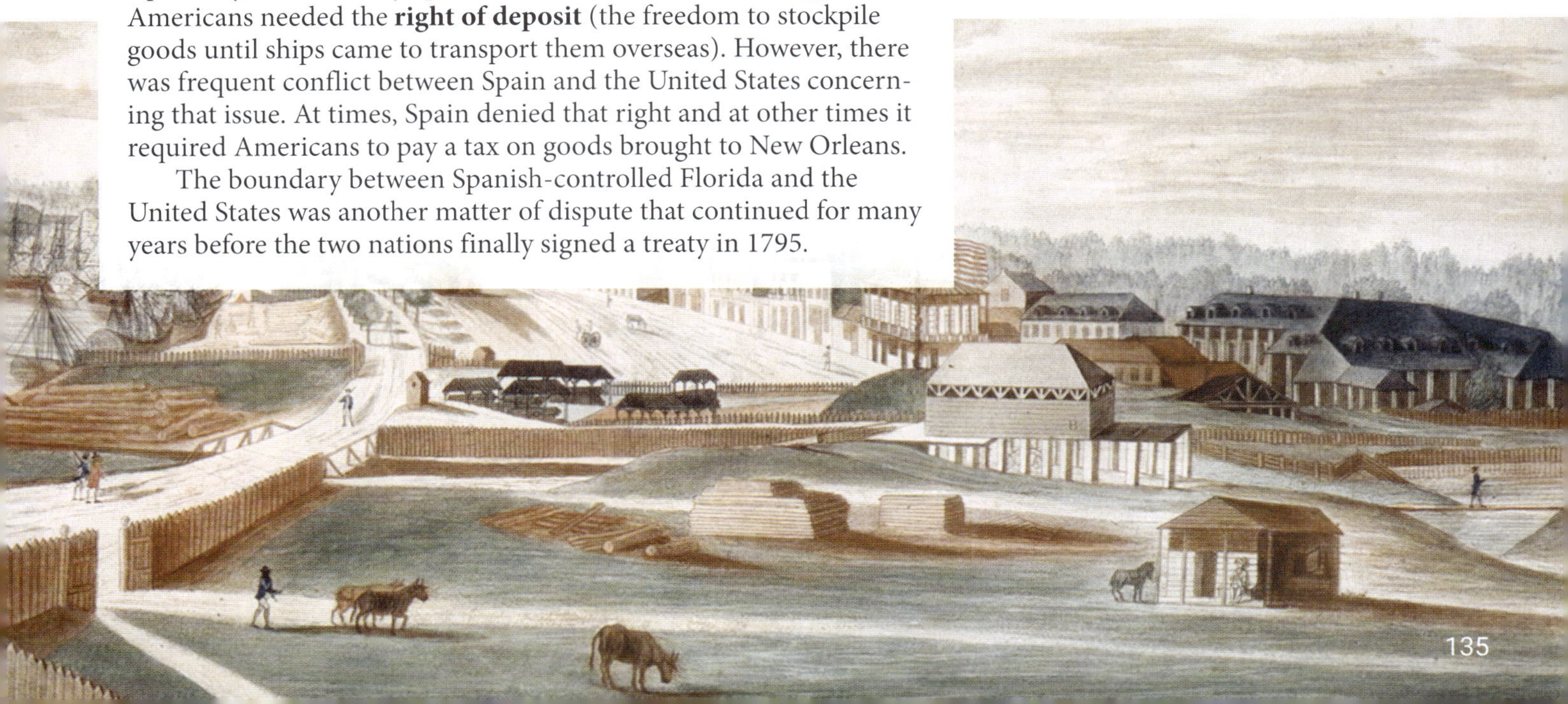

Problems with Other Nations

Since France had been an ally during the war, the United States wanted its continued friendship. But the United States could not pay even the interest owed on the loans it had obtained from France to help fight the war. When the United States asked France for more loans, France refused.

The United States also owed the Netherlands for its financial aid to the war effort. Although the Dutch pursued claims with less vigor than France, they still wanted to be paid.

American ships faced difficulties with pirates. This was especially true in the Mediterranean Sea off the coast of North Africa, where raiders from a region known as the Barbary States frequently interfered with US trade.

▲ Shays's Rebellion seizing control of a courthouse

Discontent at Home

After the War for Independence, more men were given the right to vote and some of these men were elected to state legislatures. Once in office, some of them were more interested in helping themselves and their friends than in doing what was best for those they governed. Some wrote bills that benefited their home districts rather than the whole state. Though corruption among government officials, even well-educated ones, had occurred earlier, some Americans argued that it was now becoming more widespread. They worried that some who were governing were not really qualified to do so.

Other turmoil further heightened people's concerns. Many state governments had imposed high taxes to obtain funds to pay war debts. When economic trouble made it difficult for farmers to sell their products, they lacked money to pay their taxes and other debts. As a result, courts approved confiscating their property. In September 1786 several hundred men, led by a Continental army veteran named **Daniel Shays**, forced some courts in Massachusetts to close. This action prohibited the seizure of additional farmland. In January 1787 Shays led a mob of 1,200 men through the snow, toward Springfield, Massachusetts. They wanted to capture guns and ammunition stored there. The state militia stopped Shays's men, killing four farmers in the process. Though Shays and his men fled and the rebellion ended, many Americans were fearful that additional instances of unrest and violence might occur.

Independence Hall in Philadelphia ▸

Recognition of Weaknesses

Shays's Rebellion magnified the weaknesses of the Confederation. Most of America's leaders recognized the need to strengthen the national government. Some thought that minor changes could be made to the Articles of Confederation. These changes would give Congress the power to tax and to regulate interstate commerce. However, other leaders saw the need for much greater reform.

Preparation for Change

Leaders from several states called for a national meeting to be held in Annapolis, Maryland, to discuss interstate trade. The **Annapolis Convention** met in September 1786. Because only five states sent representatives, little was accomplished. Delegates did agree to ask the Confederation Congress to schedule a convention of all the states to discuss revising the Articles of Confederation. That meeting was scheduled to begin on May 14, 1787, in Philadelphia. The Philadelphia Convention was later called the **Constitutional Convention**.

Because the delegates were slow in arriving, the Convention did not formally begin its work until May 25. Fifty-five delegates from twelve states attended. Fearing that the work of the Convention might lead to a strong central government, Rhode Island did not send representatives. The Convention was held in Independence Hall, the same building where the Declaration of Independence had been signed.

Attendees decided to keep their discussions secret. This provided them the freedom to speak and change their minds without fear of public criticism or pressure. Also, since they knew there were many disagreements to address, they did not want to release their work until it was completely finished.

Did you know?

Not only were the debates heated during the Constitutional Convention, but the summer of 1787 was quite hot. With no air conditioning, meeting together in a crowded room with closed windows (to prevent eavesdropping), and wearing all the fashionable gentlemanly clothes of the era could be stifling—even smelly.

▲ James Madison

Fun Fact

It was generally agreed that Madison's diary of the proceedings of the Constitutional Convention would not be made public until the death of the last signer, which was, interestingly, Madison himself.

People Who Brought Change

George Washington, a delegate from Virginia, was elected to serve as the Convention chairman. One of the most influential members of the Convention was another Virginian, **James Madison**. He was a lawyer and keen student of government. The diary, or journal, he kept provides us the most accurate information about the Convention's proceedings. His work at the Convention and his role in supporting its ratification later earned him the nickname "the Father of the Constitution." Another Virginia delegate, George Mason, had written Virginia's Declaration of Rights and much of the state's constitution. Adopted in June 1776, Virginia's declaration influenced a number of later documents, including the US Declaration of Independence.

Philosopher-scientist Benjamin Franklin was one of the Pennsylvania delegates. At age eighty-two, he was the oldest person present. His sense of humor helped relieve tension. One of Franklin's Pennsylvania colleagues was James Wilson. Wilson's broad knowledge of history and government made him a great asset to the Convention. Gouverneur Morris was a third noteworthy Pennsylvanian. He was a captivating speaker, persuasive debater, and gifted writer.

Did you know?

Gouverneur was Mr. Morris's first name. It should not be confused with the political position of governor.

Alexander Hamilton, one of the New York delegates, favored a strong central government. He would later be an important leader in advocating for the adoption of the new Constitution.

Some of the men who were key leaders during the War for Independence were absent from the Convention. Thomas Jefferson was serving as minister (ambassador) to France, and John Adams was minister to Great Britain. Thomas Paine was also in Europe. Well-known Patriot leaders Samuel Adams, John Hancock, and Patrick Henry did not join their states' delegations. Henry declined the offer to serve as a delegate to the Convention. He feared that changes to the Articles might lead to a national government that had too much power and state governments that did not have enough.

▼ Alexander Hamilton

SECTION REVIEW 7.2

1. What was one of the primary weaknesses that caused most of the failures of the Confederation Congress?
2. Why was it difficult for the national government to raise money under the Articles of Confederation? What happened because Congress had insufficient income?
3. What were two issues the new American government had with foreign nations?
4. What uprising of 1786–87 protested a heavy tax burden in Massachusetts?
5. Do you think Shays was justified in his rebellion? Explain.
6. What did the members of the Annapolis Convention agree to do?
7. When did the Philadelphia Convention formally begin its work? In what building was it held? Who was the chairman?
8. Why did the Convention decide to keep its discussions secret?

7.3 BUILDING THE CONSTITUTION

How did the process of writing the Constitution lead to its success?

The delegates in Philadelphia soon realized that the Articles of Confederation could not be changed to make an effective government. Instead, they decided to devise a completely new plan of government and began writing a **constitution**, a document that describes how a government is to work.

Points of Agreement

As they prepared to write the constitution, the delegates agreed on several points. They agreed that the United States needed a more effective central government. And they reasoned that the national, or central, government should have the power to handle certain matters that affected all the states. The delegates thought that the state and local governments could solve problems affecting only their citizens. Thus there would be a division of powers limiting the national government.

The delegates agreed that the new system should be a **republic**, a government in which elected representatives govern the people. The power of these representatives, as well as other parts of the government, is limited by law.

In addition, the delegates wanted to create a government with multiple branches, each with different powers. They agreed that no one branch should become too powerful. They also wanted to preserve the rights and properties of individuals, just as the Declaration of Independence had stated.

Concerns and Compromises

Although the delegates agreed on many points, they raised many valid concerns during the writing of the Constitution. For instance, they disagreed about the central government. Many delegates feared that it would be too powerful, while others worried that it would not be powerful enough. Some worried that certain states would become more powerful than others. Other disagreements arose between the northern and southern states regarding the issues of slavery and commerce, or trade.

The delegates realized that they would have to compromise in order to appeal to all the states during the ratification process. In the end, they adopted so many compromises that the Constitution was called "a bundle of compromises."

◂ The Constitution was signed in Independence Hall in September 1787.

GUIDING QUESTIONS

- What foundational issues were agreed upon at the Constitutional Convention?
- What compromises were made at the Constitutional Convention?
- What important principles were included in the Constitution?
- What issues were debated concerning the ratification of the Constitution?
- What were the reasons for the Constitution's success?

why a REPUBLIC?

Why did the leaders at the Constitutional Convention choose to form a republic? They believed that a system where the people elect representatives to make laws would best ensure the freedoms of Americans. They placed limits on the representatives' power and established two additional branches of the government, each with specific powers.

What did the leaders want to avoid? They did not want a government which gave too much power to the people. They knew that if all decisions were made by majority vote of the citizens that sometimes the rights of smaller groups, or the minority of the people, could be ignored. They feared that majority rule or a pure democracy could lead to mob rule. They knew from studying history that people's desires can change and that some people can be easily manipulated.

Our republic is sometimes called a representative democracy, or indirect democracy, because people elect representatives. It is very different from a pure, or true, democracy. In that system, voters make all the decisions.

The men at the convention wrote a constitution that contains many protections for Americans, and they deliberately made it difficult to change. It has served as a model for the governments of many nations.

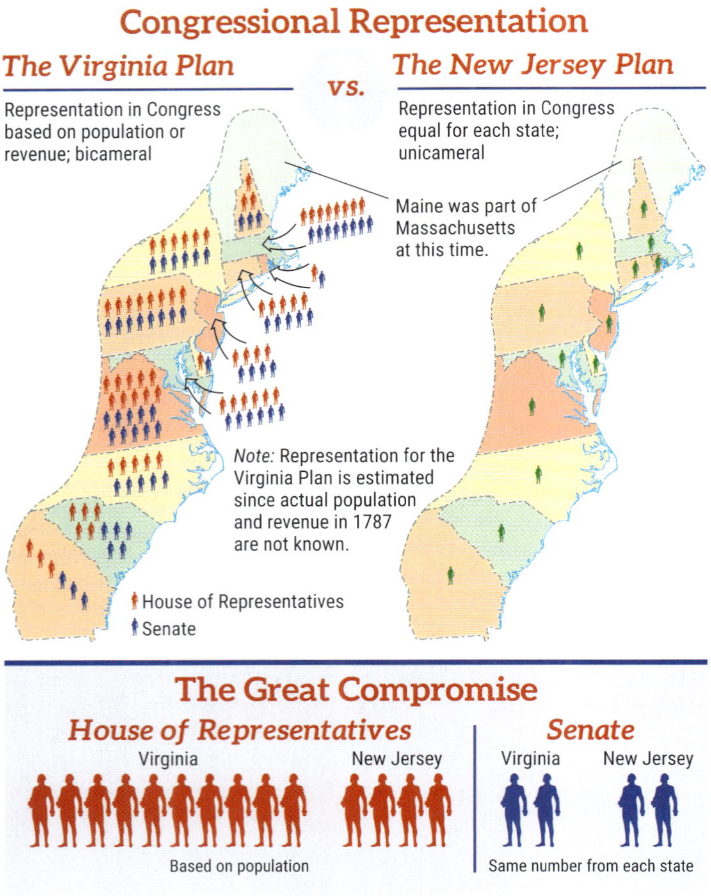

The Great Compromise

One of the primary disputes at Philadelphia arose between the large states and the small states concerning the number of votes each state should have in the lawmaking body. Edmund Randolph proposed the **Virginia Plan**, which had been written largely by James Madison. It proposed that the new government have a **bicameral system**, or two legislative houses. Since membership in both would be based on each state's population, the large states supported this plan.

Meanwhile, the small state of New Jersey proposed a plan written by William Paterson. It became known as the **New Jersey Plan**. It called for a **unicameral system**, or one legislative house, in which all the states would have one vote.

During the debate, Roger Sherman of Connecticut proposed the **Great Compromise**, or the Connecticut Compromise. His plan provided for a bicameral system. In the upper house, called the **Senate**, all states would be equally represented by two senators per state. In this way, the power of the small states would be preserved. In the lower house, called the **House of Representatives**, population would determine representation. The larger the population of a state, the more representatives it would receive. This part of the compromise favored the large states. Every ten years, the national government would determine the population of the states by taking a **census**, or a count of the population. That information would be used to determine if changes should be made in the number of representatives each state received in the lower house. The people would elect the members of the House of Representatives while the state legislatures would elect members of the Senate.

Fun Fact
The 2020 census was the first one to be conducted online.

Roger Sherman: Big Man from a Small State

Roger Sherman of Connecticut was a tall, lean, brown-eyed man with an outstanding reputation. John Adams spoke of him as "an old Puritan, honest as an angel." Thomas Jefferson described him as "a man who never said a foolish thing in his life."

Born in Massachusetts, Sherman was an apprentice to his father, a shoemaker and farmer. Although his formal education was limited, Sherman loved books. Customers at his shoe shop said there was always a book lying on the cobbler's bench. Sherman showed special interest in mathematics, law, and politics, but his most enduring love was the Bible. Sherman was active in church work and served many years as a deacon.

Sherman's religious views affected his political decisions. He opposed giving the public office to men who attacked Christianity. Sherman said his experience had shown him that people who boasted of their unbelief were often untrustworthy.

After his father's death, Sherman left Massachusetts and moved to New Milford, Connecticut. He joined his brother in operating a country store. Sherman also studied law and was admitted to practice in 1754. He held several local government offices and was elected to the state legislature. He represented Connecticut in the Continental Congresses. He was on the committee of five that drafted the Declaration of Independence.

In 1787 Sherman served as a delegate to the Constitutional Convention. There he introduced the famous Connecticut Compromise. Later, he signed the Constitution, just as he had signed the other two

The Three-Fifths Compromise

The delegates also differed over how to count slaves for taxation and representation. If the government taxed states by population, the South's tax burden would be heavier if slaves were counted. But if slaves were counted, the South (where almost one-third of the people were enslaved African Americans) would have significantly more votes in the House of Representatives.

The Convention settled the matter by passing the **Three-Fifths Compromise**. As a result, the Constitution stated that, for representation and taxation, every five enslaved people would count as three people in the state's population total. That total would be used to determine representation in Congress and would be used for taxation purposes.

Sadly, the delegates at the Convention never considered abolishing slavery. Certainly there were those present who strongly denounced the practice as immoral, but the issue so deeply divided the country that no agreement could have been reached about ending it.

The Compromise Concerning Commerce

One of the reasons for the Philadelphia Convention was the Confederation's inability to deal with interstate and international trade. Most delegates agreed that Congress needed a role in commerce (trade) but they disagreed about the extent of that role. The South feared that the new Constitution might eliminate the slave trade and try to raise money by placing taxes on exports. The southern economy depended heavily on the export of raw goods, such as cotton, timber, and indigo; thus, the South opposed any tax on such items.

A compromise settled the issue. The agreement gave Congress control over foreign and interstate commerce. However, that body was prohibited from interfering with the slave trade for at least twenty years (until 1808) or from imposing any export taxes.

Three-Fifths Compromise: Representatives from Virginia
US Congress, 1793

Based on the 1790 census and 1 representative per 33,000 people as established by the Apportionment Act of 1792

Roger Sherman (highlighted) ▸ with fellow delegates at the Constitutional Convention

great documents of America's early history: the Declaration of Independence (1776) and the Articles of Confederation (1777). When he returned to Connecticut, Sherman led the campaign to ratify the Constitution. In the new government, he served first in the House of Representatives and then in the Senate.

Sherman died on July 23, 1793. To him, honest devotion to God was more important than any material gain. The words on his tomb describe him as "a man of approved integrity, a cool discerning judge, [a] prudent, sagacious [wise] politician, a true faithful and firm Patriot."

Principles in the Constitution

The delegates included several vital principles in the Constitution.These principles affect the nature and operation of the US government, even today.

Written Law

Under the Constitution, leaders rule by written law. Government leaders cannot change their own powers according to their desires. The Constitution limits those powers, establishing what government may and may not do. Only an amendment can change the written law of the Constitution. Because amendments are somewhat difficult to enact, major changes in constitutional law are rare.

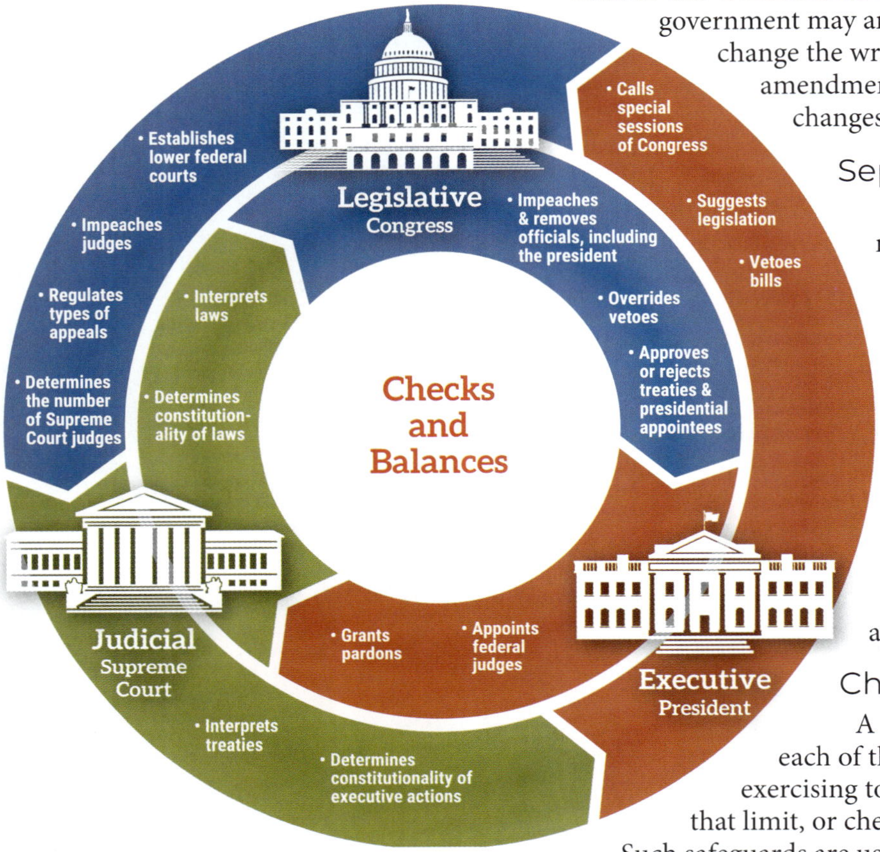

Separation of Powers

The Constitution divides the government's powers among three branches: the legislative, executive, and judicial branches. The delegates relied heavily on the ideas of the French philosopher Montesquieu in developing the idea of the **separation of powers**. This principle ensures that no branch has too much power. Congress, which is the legislative branch, makes the laws. The executive branch, led by the president, enforces the laws. And the courts of the judicial branch interpret the laws as they apply to specific cases.

Checks and Balances

A system of **checks and balances** keeps each of the three branches of government from exercising too much power. Each branch has powers that limit, or check, the powers of the other two branches. Such safeguards are useful because government leaders might be tempted to take additional powers. Checks keep the powers of each branch balanced with those of the other branches.

A Federal System

Under the Articles of Confederation, the states acted almost as independent nations. They reserved, or kept, most powers for themselves; Congress had only limited ones. At the Constitutional Convention, the delegates sought to strengthen the national government's power, but they did not intend to take all powers from the states. To accomplish this, the delegates established a **federal system** that divides the government's powers between the national government and the states.

The Constitution assigns duties and powers to the level of government best equipped to handle them. Neither level has total power. Under the Constitution, the national government has power over issues that are important to the whole nation, such as common defense. Many other powers, such as those relating to health, safety, elections, and punishment for crimes, are shared by the national and state governments.

a BROADER USE *of the term* FEDERAL

Though the term *federal* refers to dividing the powers of the country's government between the national government and the state governments, it can be used in a broader way. For example, we often call the national government in Washington, DC, the *federal government*. And we describe things that are related to the national government as "federal," such as federal employees, federal regulations, and federal agencies.

Ratification

Instead of amending the Articles of Confederation, the delegates at the Constitutional Convention had devised an entirely new plan for the United States. It was impossible to know how the states would respond.

On September 17, 1787, the delegates gathered for their last session and signed the Constitution. Three of the delegates—George Mason, Edmund Randolph, and Elbridge Gerry—refused to sign because they wanted a bill of rights to be added. (A bill of rights would guarantee personal rights and freedoms to citizens.) Those who did place their signatures on the document returned to their states with a big job: promoting the new Constitution so that the states would ratify it.

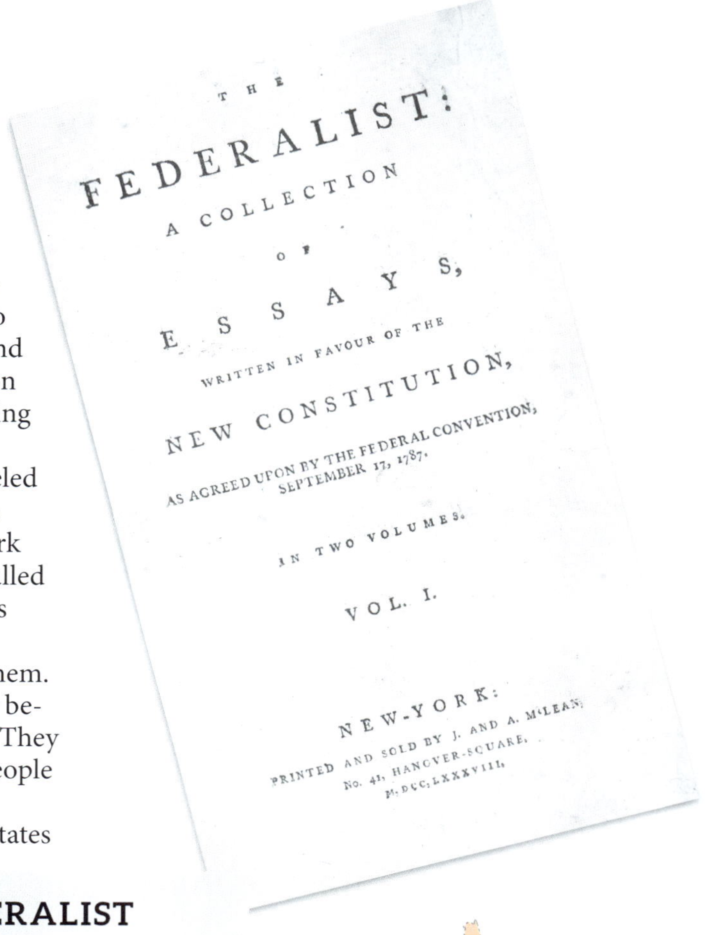
THE FEDERALIST: A COLLECTION OF ESSAYS, WRITTEN IN FAVOUR OF THE NEW CONSTITUTION, AS AGREED UPON BY THE FEDERAL CONVENTION, SEPTEMBER 17, 1787.

IN TWO VOLUMES.

VOL. I.

NEW-YORK: PRINTED AND SOLD BY J. AND A. M'LEAN, No. 41, HANOVER-SQUARE, M,DCC,LXXXVIII.

Those who favored the adoption of the Constitution labeled themselves **Federalists**. Some of the leading members of this group wrote a series of essays that were published in New York newspapers in 1787 and 1788. The essays were collectively called the ***Federalist Papers***. Written by Alexander Hamilton, James Madison, and John Jay, the articles stated the most common objections to the Constitution and then carefully answered them.

Some Americans opposed the Constitution because they believed that it gave the national government too much power. They believed that state governments should be supreme. These people fought ratification and were called **Anti-Federalists**.

According to the Articles of Confederation, all thirteen states had to accept any changes to the document. However, the Constitution stated that it would take effect when nine states approved it. Any state that did not ratify the Constitution would not be part of the United States. The debate over ratification was intense in some states. Eventually, some states agreed to ratify only after being assured that a bill of rights would be added later.

the ANTI-FEDERALIST PAPERS

The Anti-Federalists wrote their own set of papers. Some famous individuals, such as Patrick Henry, were part of this group. Many of the Ati-Federalists' concerns were later addressed by the Bill of Rights.

In June 1788 New Hampshire became the ninth state to ratify the Constitution. The two largest states, New York and Virginia, approved it later that summer. The last two states to ratify were North Carolina (in 1789) and Rhode Island (in 1790).

In late 1788 and early 1789, the eleven states that had ratified the Constitution held elections for the new Congress. In April 1789 the votes from the **Electoral College**, the body established by the Constitution to elect the president, were counted. George Washington was elected president by unanimous vote, and John Adams received enough votes to become vice president. They took office later that month.

In September 1789 Congress passed twelve amendments to the Constitution and submitted them to the states for approval. Over the next two years, ten were ratified by enough states to become part of the Constitution. The **Bill of Rights**, the name for those first ten amendments, took effect on December 15, 1791.

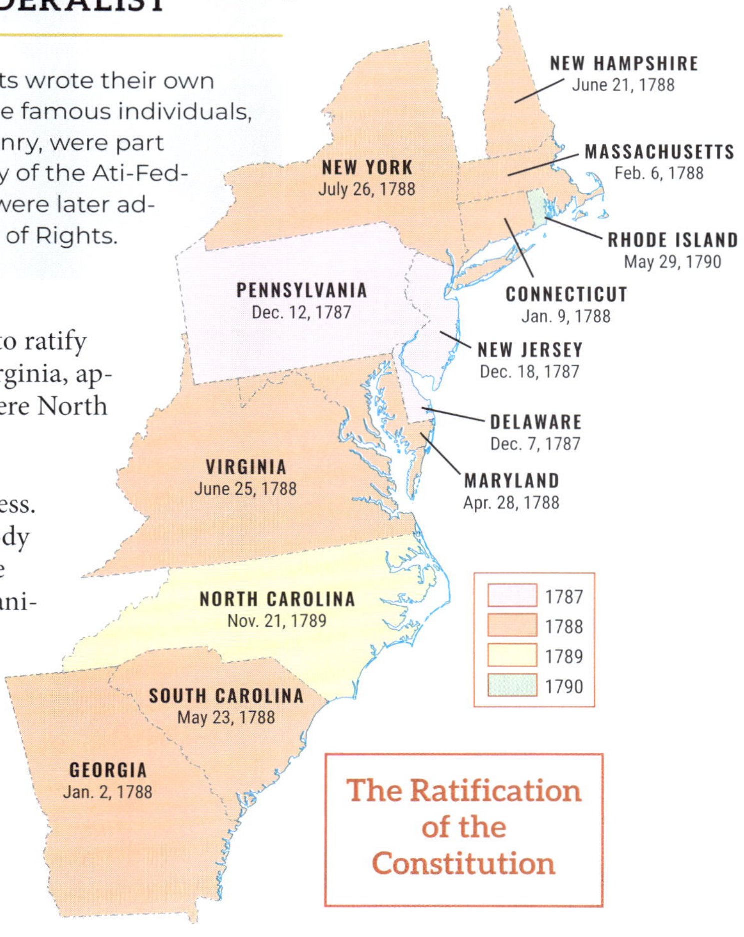

The Ratification of the Constitution

The Constitution's Success

America's Constitution is now over 235 years old. It is the oldest in existence that is still in use. Nearly all the national constitutions in the world have been written or significantly revised in the past 50 years. Only about a dozen were written before World War II. Because many nations have modeled their own governing document after ours, some have referred to the Constitution as America's most important export. It is an extraordinary work, not simply because it has lasted, but because it has worked so well with so few changes.

One reason for the Constitution's success is that Americans have expended much effort to make it work. When certain parts have not functioned as planned, because they were flawed or outdated, it has been changed through a formal amendment process. In some nations, disagreements regarding the governing document have led to its being completely discarded (as was true of the Articles of Confederation)—some have even resulted in revolution.

A second reason for the Constitution's success is closely associated with the first reason. It is a flexible document. The wording is detailed enough to provide the structure needed for the government, but not so comprehensive that it is impossible to adapt to changing circumstances. It established foundational principles—such as separation of powers, checks and balances, federalism, and limited government—that have worked extraordinarily well. Surprisingly, after the Bill of Rights was adopted in 1791, only seventeen more amendments have been ratified.

A third reason for the success of the document is that the founders recognized the shortcomings of all people. They knew that power should be limited and divided to prevent corruption and abuse. Some of the political thinking at the time was certainly influenced by biblical principles. Although there is no evidence that the Constitution's writers intentionally looked to the Scriptures while writing, some understood the biblical teaching regarding human sinfulness.

▾ Both the Constitution and the Declaration of Independence are displayed at the National Archives in Washington, DC.

Though the Constitution was viewed as exceptional by many, it was not without critics. As mentioned earlier, some criticized it because they felt it would create a central government that was too powerful. Others were unhappy with it for different reasons. For example, some noted that though references to God, or the Creator, were made in the Declaration of Independence and in several state constitutions, none are contained in the US Constitution.

No structure of government is perfect. The American founders understood this. They knew that a republic needs honest, principled citizens and rulers in order to succeed. They believed people of character were essential to the survival of the nation. Fortunately, most Americans at the time held moral principles and strong religious beliefs. Most were keenly aware of the importance of taking responsibility for their actions and the necessity of obeying laws.

SECTION REVIEW 7.3

1. Why did the founders create a republic rather than a pure democracy?
2. What is an advantage and disadvantage of a republic?
3. What was the Virginia Plan? What was the New Jersey Plan?
4. Who wrote the Great Compromise? How did it merge the Virginia and New Jersey plans?
5. Explain the Three-Fifths Compromise.
6. What compromises concerning commerce resulted from the fears of the southern colonies?
7. Define checks and balances.
8. Define the federal system of government.
9. What series of persuasive newspaper essays was published by the Federalists to support the ratification of the Constitution?
10. Why did some Americans become Anti-Federalists?
11. What are three reasons for the success of the Constitution?
12. What does a republic need to succeed?

e **PLURIBUS** *unum*

In 1776 the Second Continental Congress appointed a committee to design a seal for the United States. Committee members suggested placing on it the motto E Pluribus Unum, "Out of Many, One." The Confederation Congress officially approved the seal in 1782.

Throughout the Constitutional Convention, those present worked diligently to implement the nation's motto. Though the states had many differences and did not want to lose their distinct characters, they recognized their need to unify under a single central government. Through debates and compromises, each state agreed to sacrifice something it valued in order to achieve unity. In the end, the Constitution produced by the delegates preserved many of the states' values and formed the foundation of a unified nation.

7.4 THE CONSTITUTION OF THE UNITED STATES

What are the major parts of the Constitution?

[*Note*: The numbers preceding each clause were added to separate individual clauses under each section; they are not in the original document.]

GUIDING QUESTIONS

- What are the three branches of government and their major functions?
- What does the Constitution say about the relationship between states?
- How can the Constitution be amended?
- What are the amendments to the Constitution?

Preamble

The **Preamble** introduces the Constitution. It states the source of government's power and the six purposes of government.

We the People of the United States, in order to form a more perfect union, establish justice, insure domestic tranquility, provide for the common defense, promote the general welfare, and secure the blessings of liberty to ourselves and our posterity, do ordain and establish this Constitution for the United States of America.

Article I: The Legislative Branch

Art. I The legislative branch of the government. This branch's primary function is to make laws. This power belongs to Congress, which has two houses. A two-house legislative system is called a bicameral system.

Section 1

All legislative powers herein granted shall be vested in a Congress of the United States, which shall consist of a Senate and House of Representatives.

Section 2

I.2.1 Members of the House of Representatives serve two-year terms.

I.2.2 House members must (1) be at least twenty-five years old, (2) have been US citizens for at least seven years, and (3) be residents of the state they represent.

I.2.3 The number of representatives a state receives is determined by the state's population. Also, any direct federal taxation of the states must be distributed according to population. Today, the House membership is set at 435. A census is taken every ten years to determine how many representatives each state will receive.

I.2.5 The head of the House, the Speaker of the House, is elected by the House members. The House has "the sole power of impeachment"—the power to bring charges against a major federal official.

1. The House of Representatives shall be composed of members chosen every second year by the people of the several states, and the electors in each state shall have the qualifications requisite for electors of the most numerous branch of the state legislature.
2. No person shall be a representative who shall not have attained to the age of twenty-five years, and been seven years a citizen of the United States, and who shall not, when elected, be an inhabitant of that state in which he shall be chosen.
3. Representatives and direct taxes shall be apportioned among the several states which may be included within this Union, according to their respective numbers, which shall be determined by adding to the whole number of free persons, including those bound to service for a term of years, and excluding Indians not taxed, three-fifths of all other persons. The actual enumeration shall be made within three years after the first meeting of the Congress of the United States, and within every subsequent term of ten years, in such manner as they shall by law direct. The number of representatives shall not exceed one for every thirty thousand, but each state shall have at least one representative; and until such enumeration shall be made, the state of New Hampshire shall be entitled to choose three, Massachusetts eight, Rhode Island and Providence Plantations one, Connecticut five, New York six, New Jersey four, Pennsylvania eight, Delaware one, Maryland six, Virginia ten, North Carolina five, South Carolina five, and Georgia three.
4. When vacancies happen in the representation from any state, the executive authority thereof shall issue writs of election to fill such vacancies.
5. The House of Representatives shall choose their speaker and other officers; and shall have the sole power of impeachment.

Section 3

1. The Senate of the United States shall be composed of two senators from each state, chosen by the legislature thereof, for six years; and each senator shall have one vote.
2. Immediately after they shall be assembled in consequence of the first election, they shall be divided as equally as may be into three classes. The seats of the senators of the first class shall be vacated at the expiration of the second year, of the second class at the expiration of the fourth year, and of the third class at the expiration of the sixth year, so that one-third may be chosen every second year; and if vacancies happen by resignation, or otherwise, during the recess of the legislature of any state, the executive thereof may make temporary appointments until the next meeting of the legislature, which shall then fill such vacancies.
3. No person shall be a senator who shall not have attained to the age of thirty years, and been nine years a citizen of the United States, and who shall not, when elected, be an inhabitant of that state for which he shall be chosen.
4. The vice president of the United States shall be president of the Senate, but shall have no vote, unless they be equally divided.
5. The Senate shall choose their other officers, and also a president pro tempore, in the absence of the vice president, or when he shall exercise the office of president of the United States.
6. The Senate shall have the sole power to try all impeachments. When sitting for that purpose, they shall be on oath or affirmation. When the president of the United States is tried, the chief justice shall preside: and no person shall be convicted without the concurrence of two-thirds of the members present.
7. Judgment in cases of impeachment shall not extend further than to removal from office, and disqualification to hold and enjoy any office of honor, trust or profit under the United States: but the party convicted shall nevertheless be liable and subject to indictment, trial, judgment and punishment, according to law.

I.3.1 Each state has two senators who serve six-year terms. Originally, state legislatures elected senators.

I.3.2 One-third of the senators are elected every two years. This system ensures that there are always experienced people in the Senate.

I.3.3 Senators must (1) be at least thirty years old, (2) have been US citizens for at least nine years, and (3) be residents of the states they represent.

I.3.4 The president of the Senate is the vice president of the United States. He only votes in case of a tie.

I.3.5 The Senate also elects a president pro tempore who serves as leader of the Senate when the vice president is absent. Today, this official is third in line to the presidency (after the vice president and the Speaker of the House).

I.3.6 The Senate acts as a trial court for impeachment cases. Two-thirds of the senators must vote for conviction in order to remove an official from office.

▾ Congress meets in the US Capitol in Washington, DC.

Section 4

1. The times, places and manner of holding elections for senators and representatives, shall be prescribed in each state by the legislature thereof; but the Congress may at any time by law make or alter such regulations, except as to the places of choosing senators.
2. The Congress shall assemble at least once in every year, and such meeting shall be on the first Monday in December, unless they shall by law appoint a different day.

I.4.1 State legislatures have the right to administer congressional elections in their states, but they must follow any regulations established by Congress.

I.4.2 Congress is to meet at least once a year.

Section 5

1. Each house shall be the judge of the elections, returns and qualifications of its own members, and a majority of each shall constitute a quorum to do business; but a smaller number may adjourn from day to day, and may be authorized to compel the attendance of absent members, in such manner, and under such penalties as each house may provide.
2. Each house may determine the rules of its proceedings, punish its members for disorderly behavior, and, with the concurrence of two-thirds, expel a member.
3. Each house shall keep a journal of its proceedings, and from time to time publish the same, excepting such parts as may in their judgment require secrecy; and the yeas and nays of the members of either house on any question shall, at the desire of one-fifth of those present, be entered on the journal.
4. Neither house, during the session of Congress, shall, without the consent of the other, adjourn for more than three days, nor to any other place than that in which the two houses shall be sitting.

I.5.1 Each house judges its own elections. A quorum is the minimum number needed to transact business. A simple majority (half the members plus one) is the quorum required.

I.5.3 Each house keeps a journal, or record, of what it does each day. Today this journal is called the *Congressional Record*.

I.5.4 Since the two houses work together to pass legislation, one house cannot adjourn (go out of official session) for more than three days without the other's permission.

Section 6

1. The senators and representatives shall receive a compensation for their services, to be ascertained by law, and paid out of the treasury of the United States. They shall in all cases, except treason, felony and breach of the peace, be privileged from arrest during their attendance at the session of their respective houses, and in going to and returning from the same; and for any speech or debate in either house, they shall not be questioned in any other place.
2. No senator or representative shall, during the time for which he was elected, be appointed to any civil office under the authority of the United States, which shall have been created, or the emoluments whereof shall have been increased during such time; and no person holding any office under the United States, shall be a member of either house during his continuance in office.

I.6.1 Senators and representatives are public employees who are paid salaries by the US Treasury. They cannot be arrested for what they say in Congress nor as they are going to or from Congress (except for the offenses listed in this clause).

I.6.2 A congressman must resign any other federal offices (positions) held in order to become a congressman. He cannot take any federal office created by his house of Congress until his term ends. And until his term expires, he cannot take an office that Congress has increased the pay for during his term. This rule prevents congressmen from giving themselves offices with larger salaries.

Section 7

1. All bills for raising revenue shall originate in the House of Representatives; but the Senate may propose or concur with amendments as on other bills.
2. Every bill which shall have passed the House of Representatives and the Senate, shall, before it becomes a law, be presented to the president of the United States; if he approve, he shall sign it, but if not he shall return it, with his objections to that house in which it shall have originated, who shall enter the objections at large on their journal, and proceed to reconsider it. If after such reconsideration two-thirds of that house shall agree to pass the bill, it shall be sent, together with the objections, to the other house, by which it shall likewise be reconsidered, and if approved by two-thirds of that house, it shall become a law. But in all such cases the votes of both houses shall be determined by yeas and nays, and the names of the persons voting for and against the bill shall be entered on the journal of each house respectively. If any bill shall not be returned by the president within ten days (Sundays excepted) after it shall have been presented to him, the same shall be a law, in like manner as if he had signed it, unless the Congress by their adjournment prevent its return, in which case it shall not be a law.
3. Every order, resolution, or vote to which the concurrence of the Senate and House of Representatives may be necessary (except on a question of adjournment) shall be presented to the president of the United States; and before the same shall take effect, shall be approved by him, or being disapproved by him, shall be repassed by two-thirds of the Senate and House of Representatives, according to the rules and limitations prescribed in the case of a bill.

I.7.1 Bills dealing with raising revenue (money) must begin in the House, but the Senate may make changes if it desires.

I.7.2 For a bill to become a law, it must be passed by both houses and signed by the president. This process is part of the system of checks and balances. If the president opposes the bill, he may return it to the body where it started, stating his objections. This is a **veto**. Congress may override the president's veto with a two-thirds vote of both houses. If it does so, the bill becomes law.

I.7.3 All other acts requiring approval of both houses of Congress (except the decision to adjourn Congress) must be approved by the president. If the president vetoes the acts, Congress may override his veto by a two-thirds vote of both houses.

I.8.1–18 Congress has specific, stated powers which include the power to:

1. tax;
2. borrow money;
3. regulate commerce [trade] with foreign nations, within the country, and with the Indians;
4. regulate naturalization and bankruptcy laws. Naturalization is the process by which a foreign-born person gains citizenship. Bankruptcy is the way a debtor is declared unable to pay his creditors;
5. control the nation's currency and standard weights and measurements;
6. punish those who illegally interfere in the currency system;
7. provide needed offices and roads for the Postal Service;
8. issue copyrights and patents;
9. establish federal courts other than the Supreme Court;
10. determine what acts committed at sea are crimes and to commit offenders to courts for trial;
11. declare war;
12. create an army, but not set aside money to support the army more than two years ahead of time;
13. create a navy and vote for money to support it;
14. make the rules for the armed services;
15. call the state militias (now the National Guard) into service for the national government;
16. organize, arm, and discipline the militias, but the states appoint officers and train the militias;
17. make laws for the District of Columbia and for all federal properties, such as military installations or bases;
18. do what it believes is "necessary and proper" to carry out any listed power. Clause 18 is sometimes called the "elastic clause" because it can be used to extend or stretch the power of Congress.

Section 8

1. The Congress shall have power to lay and collect taxes, duties, imposts and excises, to pay the debts and provide for the common defense and general welfare of the United States; but all duties, imposts and excises shall be uniform throughout the United States;
2. To borrow money on the credit of the United States;
3. To regulate commerce with foreign nations, and among the several states, and with the Indian tribes;
4. To establish a uniform rule of naturalization, and uniform laws on the subject of bankruptcies throughout the United States;
5. To coin money, regulate the value thereof, and of foreign coin, and fix the standard of weights and measures;
6. To provide for the punishment of counterfeiting the securities and current coin of the United States;
7. To establish post offices and post roads;
8. To promote the progress of science and useful arts, by securing for limited times to authors and inventors the exclusive right to their respective writings and discoveries;
9. To constitute tribunals inferior to the Supreme Court;
10. To define and punish piracies and felonies committed on the high seas, and offenses against the law of nations;
11. To declare war, grant letters of marque and reprisal, and make rules concerning captures on land and water;
12. To raise and support armies, but no appropriation of money to that use shall be for a longer term than two years;
13. To provide and maintain a navy;
14. To make rules for the government and regulation of the land and naval forces;
15. To provide for calling forth the militia to execute the laws of the Union, suppress insurrections and repel invasions;
16. To provide for organizing, arming, and disciplining, the militia, and for governing such part of them as may be employed in the service of the United States, reserving to the states respectively, the appointment of the officers, and the authority of training the militia according to the discipline prescribed by Congress;
17. To exercise exclusive legislation in all cases whatsoever, over such district (not exceeding ten miles square) as may, by cession of particular states, and the acceptance of Congress, become the seat of the government of the United States, and to exercise like authority over all places purchased by the consent of the legislature of the state in which the same shall be, for the erection of forts, magazines, arsenals, dockyards, and other needful buildings;—and
18. To make all laws which shall be necessary and proper for carrying into execution the foregoing powers, and all other powers vested by this Constitution in the government of the United States, or in any department or officer thereof.

Section 9

1. The migration or importation of such persons as any of the states now existing shall think proper to admit, shall not be prohibited by the Congress prior to the year [1808], but a tax or duty may be imposed on such importation, not exceeding ten dollars for each person.
2. The privilege of the writ of habeas corpus shall not be suspended, unless when in cases of rebellion or invasion the public safety may require it.
3. No bill of attainder or ex post facto law shall be passed.
4. No capitation, or other direct tax shall be laid, unless in proportion to the census or enumeration herein before directed to be taken.
5. No tax or duty shall be laid on articles exported from any state.
6. No preference shall be given by any regulation of commerce or revenue to the ports of one state over those of another: nor shall vessels bound to, or from, one state, be obliged to enter, clear, or pay duties in another.
7. No money shall be drawn from the treasury, but in consequence of appropriations made by law; and a regular statement and account of the receipts and expenditures of all public money shall be published from time to time.
8. No title of nobility shall be granted by the United States: and no person holding any office of profit or trust under them, shall, without the consent of the Congress, accept of any present, emolument, office, or title, of any kind whatever, from any king, prince, or foreign state.

Section 10

1. No state shall enter into any treaty, alliance, or confederation; grant letters of marque and reprisal; coin money; emit bills of credit; make any thing but gold and silver coin a tender in payment of debts; pass any bill of attainder, ex post facto law, or law impairing the obligation of contracts, or grant any title of nobility.
2. No state shall, without the consent of the Congress, lay any imposts or duties on imports or exports, except what may be absolutely necessary for executing its inspection laws: and the net produce of all duties and imposts, laid by any state on imports or exports, shall be for the use of the treasury of the United States; and all such laws shall be subject to the revision and control of the Congress.
3. No state shall, without the consent of Congress, lay any duty of tonnage, keep troops, or ships of war in time of peace, enter into any agreement or compact with another state, or with a foreign power, or engage in war, unless actually invaded, or in such imminent danger as will not admit of delay.

I.9.1–8 The following powers are forbidden to the federal government:

1. Congress could not interfere with the slave trade until 1808.
2. Congress may not take away a person's right of habeas corpus except in times of extreme danger. A writ of habeas corpus forces authorities to charge a person with a crime if he is held in jail.
3. Congress cannot pass a bill of attainder, which permits punishment without a trial, or an ex post facto law, which makes an action that was legal at the time it occurred illegal.
4. Congress cannot levy an unequal direct tax.
5. Congress cannot tax the states' exports.
6. Congress cannot give preference to any port or state through its laws, and it cannot tax trade between states.
7. Money from the Treasury can be spent only if Congress approves, and a record of income and expenditures must be published.
8. The United States cannot grant titles of nobility (duke, earl, baron, etc.), nor can its officials accept titles or other honors from foreign countries without Congress's permission.

I.10.1–3 States are forbidden to do many things that the national government does. Both the states and the national government are forbidden to do certain things. By limiting state powers, the Constitution makes the central government stronger and more united. According to Section 10, states are forbidden to keep ships or troops (except a state militia), make alliances with foreign powers, or declare war. However, states may respond to attacks if invaded.

Art. II The executive branch of government. This branch's primary function is to enforce the nation's laws. Both the president and the vice president serve four-year terms.

▲ The White House is the home of the president, the head of the executive branch.

II.1.3 The president is still elected by the Electoral College. But the original process was modified by the Twelfth Amendment in 1804.

II.1.5 The president must (1) be a natural-born citizen, (2) be at least thirty-five years of age, and (3) have been a resident of the United States for at least fourteen years.

II.1.6 In 1948, Congress established the current line of presidential succession: (1) the vice president (as stated in the Constitution), (2) the Speaker of the House of Representatives, (3) the president pro tempore of the Senate, and (4) the members of the president's cabinet in order of the creation of their departments. The State and Treasury Departments are the oldest.

Article II: The Executive Branch

Section 1

1. The executive power shall be vested in a president of the United States of America. He shall hold his office during the term of four years, and, together with the vice president, chosen for the same term, be elected, as follows:
2. Each state shall appoint, in such manner as the legislature thereof may direct, a number of electors, equal to the whole number of senators and representatives to which the state may be entitled in the Congress: but no senator or representative, or person holding an office of trust or profit under the United States, shall be appointed an elector.
3. The electors shall meet in their respective states, and vote by ballot for two persons, of whom one at least shall not be an inhabitant of the same state with themselves. And they shall make a list of all the persons voted for, and of the number of votes for each; which list they shall sign and certify, and transmit sealed to the seat of the government of the United States, directed to the president of the Senate. The president of the Senate shall, in the presence of the Senate and House of Representatives, open all the certificates, and the votes shall then be counted. The person having the greatest number of votes shall be the president, if such number be a majority of the whole number of electors appointed; and if there be more than one who have such majority, and have an equal number of votes, then the House of Representatives shall immediately choose by ballot one of them for president; and if no person have a majority, then from the five highest on the list the said House shall in like manner choose the president. But in choosing the president, the votes shall be taken by states, the representation from each state having one vote; a quorum for this purpose shall consist of a member or members from two-thirds of the states, and a majority of all the states shall be necessary to a choice. In every case, after the choice of the president, the person having the greatest number of votes of the electors shall be the vice president. But if there should remain two or more who have equal votes, the Senate shall choose from them by ballot the vice president.
4. The Congress may determine the time of choosing the electors, and the day on which they shall give their votes; which day shall be the same throughout the United States.
5. No person except a natural born citizen, or a citizen of the United States, at the time of the adoption of this Constitution, shall be eligible to the office of president; neither shall any person be eligible to that office who shall not have attained to the age of thirty-five years, and been fourteen years a resident within the United States.
6. In case of the removal of the president from office, or of his death, resignation, or inability to discharge the powers and duties of the said office, the same shall devolve on the vice president, and the Congress may by law provide for the case of removal, death, resignation or inability, both of the president and vice president, declaring what officer shall then act as president, and such officer shall act accordingly, until the disability be removed, or a president shall be elected.

7. The president shall, at stated times, receive for his services, a compensation, which shall neither be increased nor diminished during the period for which he shall have been elected, and he shall not receive within that period any other emolument from the United States, or any of them.
8. Before he enter on the execution of his office, he shall take the following oath or affirmation:—"I do solemnly swear (or affirm) that I will faithfully execute the office of president of the United States, and will to the best of my ability, preserve, protect and defend the Constitution of the United States."

II.1.7 The president's salary stays the same throughout his term.

II.1.8 The Constitution dictates the president's oath of office.

Section 2

1. The president shall be commander in chief of the army and navy of the United States, and of the militia of the several states, when called into the actual service of the United States; he may require the opinion, in writing, of the principal officer in each of the executive departments, upon any subject relating to the duties of their respective offices, and he shall have power to grant reprieves and pardons for offenses against the United States, except in cases of impeachment.
2. He shall have power, by and with the advice and consent of the Senate, to make treaties, provided two-thirds of the senators present concur; and he shall nominate, and by and with the advice and consent of the Senate, shall appoint ambassadors, other public ministers and consuls, judges of the Supreme Court, and all other officers of the United States, whose appointments are not herein otherwise provided for, and which shall be established by law: but the Congress may by law vest the appointment of such inferior officers, as they think proper, in the president alone, in the courts of law, or in the heads of departments.
3. The president shall have power to fill up all vacancies that may happen during the recess of the Senate, by granting commissions which shall expire at the end of their next session.

II.2.1 The president is the commander in chief of the armed forces. He may call for the opinion of his cabinet. He may also grant reprieves (temporary delays in punishment) and pardons (complete forgiveness of crimes and their punishments).

II.2.2 Treaties must be approved by a two-thirds majority of the Senate. The president appoints ambassadors, ministers, consuls, federal judges, and other officers as allowed by the Constitution with the Senate's approval.

II.2.3 The president can fill vacancies in offices without Senate approval if the Senate is out of session.

Section 3

He shall from time to time give to the Congress information of the state of the Union, and recommend to their consideration such measures as he shall judge necessary and expedient; he may, on extraordinary occasions, convene both houses, or either of them, and in case of disagreement between them, with respect to the time of adjournment, he may adjourn them to such time as he shall think proper; he shall receive ambassadors and other public ministers; he shall take care that the laws be faithfully executed, and shall commission all the officers of the United States.

II.3 The president has many duties:

1. He informs Congress about the nation's condition (state of the Union).
2. He can suggest that Congress pass certain legislation.
3. He can convene (call into official session) both houses of Congress. This power, to call a special session, has been used to deal with national emergencies.
4. If the House and the Senate cannot agree on adjournment, he can intervene.
5. He receives foreign ambassadors and public ministers of foreign powers.
6. He grants military officers their commissions.

Section 4

The president, vice president and all civil officers of the United States, shall be removed from office on impeachment for, and conviction of, treason, bribery, or other high crimes and misdemeanors.

II.4 The president, vice president, and all civil officers of the government can be impeached for aiding an enemy; illegally giving or accepting money, gifts, or other favors; committing serious crimes; or showing other bad behavior.

Article III: The Judicial Branch

Art. III The judicial branch of government. Traditionally, the function of the judicial branch has been to interpret the law. This function is not listed in the Constitution; it was established through the court case of *Marbury v. Madison*.

Section 1

III.1 The nation's highest court is the Supreme Court. Inferior, or lower, federal courts may be and have been created by Congress. They include circuit courts of appeal and federal district courts, as well as tax, claim, and military courts. Federal judges do not have terms of office and may serve as long as they serve responsibly.

The judicial power of the United States, shall be vested in one Supreme Court, and in such inferior courts as the Congress may from time to time ordain and establish. The judges, both of the Supreme and inferior courts, shall hold their offices during good behavior, and shall, at stated times, receive for their services, a compensation, which shall not be diminished during their continuance in office.

▲ The Supreme Court building is located across the street from the US Capitol.

Section 2

III.2.1 Section 2 lists the cases that the federal courts must decide. No other courts can have jurisdiction in these cases.

III.2.2 Original jurisdiction means that a court has the first opportunity to hear and decide a case. When a case that has already been brought to trial at least once is sent from a lower court, a higher court hears the case on appeal; this is appellate jurisdiction.

III.2.3 A trial for a crime occurs in the judicial district where the crime was committed, unless the defendant cannot get a fair trial there.

1. The judicial power shall extend to all cases, in law and equity, arising under this Constitution, the laws of the United States, and treaties made, or which shall be made, under their authority;—to all cases affecting ambassadors, other public ministers and consuls;—to all cases of admiralty and maritime jurisdiction;—to controversies to which the United States shall be a party;—to controversies between two or more states;—between a state and citizens of another state,—between citizens of different states,—between citizens of the same state claiming lands under grants of different states, and between a state, or the citizens thereof, and foreign states, citizens or subjects.
2. In all cases affecting ambassadors, other public ministers and consuls, and those in which a state shall be party, the Supreme Court shall have original jurisdiction. In all the other cases before mentioned, the Supreme Court shall have appellate jurisdiction, both as to law and fact, with such exceptions, and under such regulations as the Congress shall make.
3. The trial of all crimes, except in cases of impeachment, shall be by jury; and such trial shall be held in the state where the said crimes shall have been committed; but when not committed within any state, the trial shall be at such place or places as the Congress may by law have directed.

Section 3

1. Treason against the United States, shall consist only in levying war against them, or in adhering to their enemies, giving them aid and comfort. No person shall be convicted of treason unless on the testimony of two witnesses to the same overt act, or on confession in open court.
2. The Congress shall have power to declare the punishment of treason, but no attainder of treason shall work corruption of blood, or forfeiture except during the life of the person attained.

III.3.1 To be convicted of treason, the accused must either confess that he committed treason, or two people who saw the accused commit treason must testify in an open court.

III.3.2 The punishment for treason extends only to the life of the accused, not to his family.

Article IV: Interstate Relations

Section 1

Full faith and credit shall be given in each state to the public acts, records, and judicial proceedings of every other state. And the Congress may by general laws prescribe the manner in which such acts, records and proceedings shall be proved, and the effect thereof.

IV.1 Each state is to respect the public civil acts of other states. Thus items like marriage licenses, wills, and contracts are respected among the states. Today, states can control their own long-term licensing for such occupations as barbers, beauticians, lawyers, teachers, and doctors.

Section 2

1. The citizens of each state shall be entitled to all privileges and immunities of citizens in the several states.
2. A person charged in any state with treason, felony, or other crime, who shall flee from justice, and be found in another state, shall on demand of the executive authority of the state from which he fled, be delivered up, to be removed to the state having jurisdiction of the crime.
3. No person held to service or labor in one state, under the laws thereof, escaping into another, shall, in consequence of any law or regulation therein, be discharged from such service or labor, but shall be delivered up on claim of the party to whom such service or labor may be due.

IV.2.1 If a person passes through another state or moves there, he still has his rights as an American citizen.

IV.2.2 A governor can request that a criminal who flees to another state be returned to the state where the crime was committed to stand trial. The process of returning the criminal is called extradition.

IV.2.3 Runaway slaves were to be returned to their owners on demand. This clause explains why the Underground Railroad existed in Northern states. To avoid being returned, some fugitive slaves escaped to Canada with the help of abolitionists, individuals who wanted to eliminate slavery.

Section 3

1. New states may be admitted by the Congress into this Union; but no new state shall be formed or erected within the jurisdiction of any other state; nor any state be formed by the junction of two or more states, or parts of states, without the consent of the legislatures of the states concerned as well as of the Congress.
2. The Congress shall have power to dispose of and make all needful rules and regulations respecting the territory or other property belonging to the United States; and nothing in this Constitution shall be so construed as to prejudice any claims of the United States, or of any particular state.

IV.3.1 Congress admits new states to the Union. If a state is formed out of another state or by the combination of states or parts of states, the legislatures of the states involved must approve.

IV.3.2 Congress regulates the territories.

Section 4

The United States shall guarantee to every state in this Union a republican form of government, and shall protect each of them against invasion; and on application of the legislature, or of the executive (when the legislature cannot be convened) against domestic violence.

Article V: Amending the Constitution

Art. V There are two ways to propose amendments—two-thirds of both houses of Congress may pass an amendment or two-thirds of the states may call a convention to propose amendments. Ratification, approval to put an amendment into effect, requires approval by three-fourths of the state legislatures or three-fourths of the states in their own conventions.

The Congress, whenever two-thirds of both houses shall deem it necessary, shall propose amendments to this Constitution, or, on the application of the legislatures of two-thirds of the several states, shall call a convention for proposing amendments, which, in either case, shall be valid to all intents and purposes, as part of this Constitution when ratified by the legislatures of three-fourths of the several states, or by conventions in three-fourths thereof, as the one or the other mode of ratification may be proposed by the Congress; provided that no amendment which may be made prior to the year [1808] shall in any manner affect the first and fourth clauses in the ninth section of the first article; and that no state, without its consent, shall be deprived of its equal suffrage in the Senate.

Article VI: Constitutional and National Supremacy

VI.2 The supreme law of the land in the United States is the Constitution (as interpreted by the Supreme Court), the laws of the nation, and treaties.

VI.3 All national and state officers promise to support the Constitution. Holding specific religious beliefs is not a requirement for holding public office.

1. All debts contracted and engagements entered into, before the adoption of this Constitution, shall be as valid against the United States under this Constitution, as under the Confederation.
2. This Constitution, and the laws of the United States which shall be made in pursuance thereof; and all treaties made, or which shall be made, under the authority of the United States, shall be the supreme law of the land; and the judges in every state shall be bound thereby, any thing in the constitution or laws of any state to the contrary notwithstanding.
3. The senators and representatives before mentioned, and the members of the several state legislatures, and all executive and judicial officers, both of the United States and of the several states, shall be bound by oath or affirmation, to support this Constitution; but no religious test shall ever be required as a qualification to any office or public trust under the United States.

Article VII: Ratifying the Constitution

Art. VII Nine of the thirteen original states had to ratify the Constitution to begin the new form of government.

The ratification of the conventions of nine states, shall be sufficient for the establishment of this Constitution between the states so ratifying the same. . . .

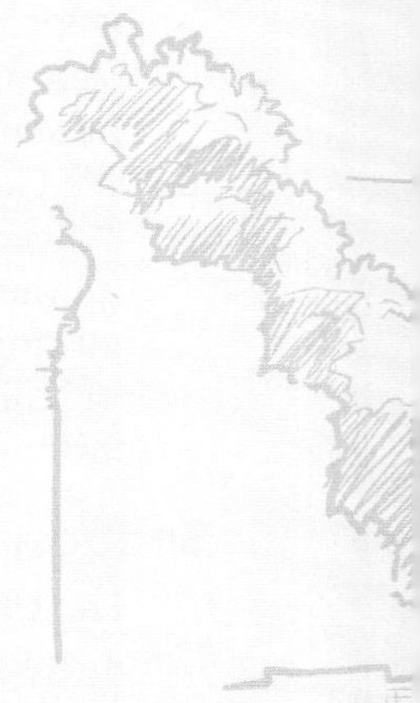

Done in convention by the unanimous consent of the states present the seventeenth day of September in the year of our Lord [1787], and of the independence of the United States of America the twelfth. In witness whereof we have hereunto subscribed our names,

George Washington, president and deputy from Virginia

Delaware
George Read
Gunning Bedford Jr.
John Dickinson
Richard Bassett
Jacob Broom

Maryland
James McHenry
Daniel of St. Thomas Jenifer
Daniel Carroll

Virginia
John Blair
James Madison Jr.

North Carolina
William Blount
Richard Dobbs Spaight
Hugh Williamson

South Carolina
John Rutledge
Charles Cotesworth Pinckney
Charles Pinckney
Pierce Butler

Georgia
William Few
Abraham Baldwin

New Hampshire
John Langdon
Nicholas Gilman

Massachusetts
Nathaniel Gorham
Rufus King

Connecticut
William Samuel Johnson
Roger Sherman

New York
Alexander Hamilton

New Jersey
William Livingston
David Brearley
William Paterson
Jonathan Dayton

Pennsylvania
Benjamin Franklin
Thomas Mifflin
Robert Morris
George Clymer
Thomas FitzSimons
Jared Ingersoll
James Wilson
Gouverneur Morris

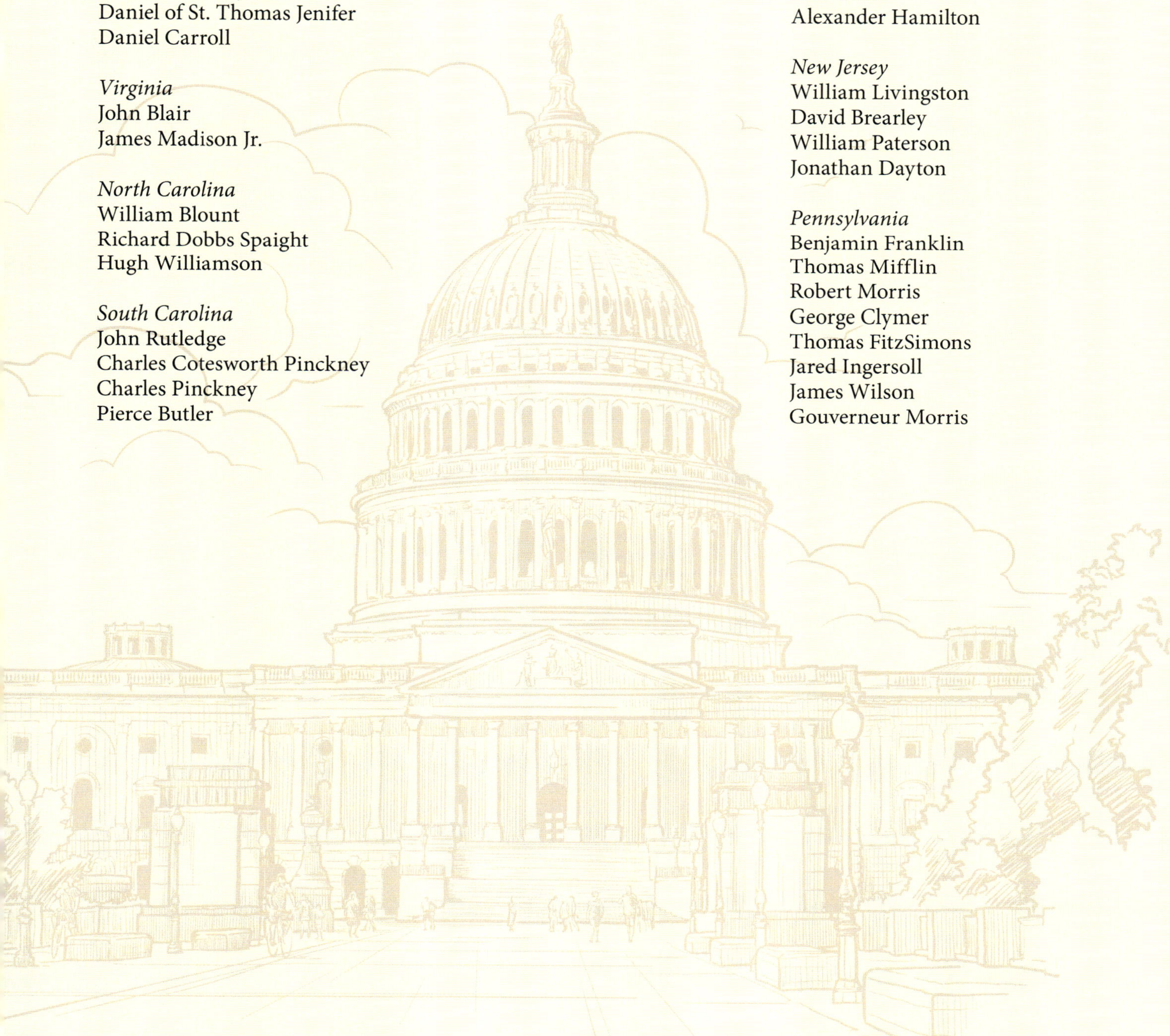

the BILL *of* RIGHTS

The first ten amendments, known as the Bill of Rights, had been introduced by House member James Madison. Two years and five months later, on December 15, 1791, they were ratified and took effect. The freedoms listed in the Bill of Rights already existed, but the amendments ensured that they would remain. The amendments illustrate the principles of limited government. At first, the limitations in the Bill of Rights applied only to the central government, not to the states. But by the twentieth century, the courts began using the "due process" rule in Amendment XIV to apply them to the states.

The First Amendment protects five freedoms: religion, speech, press, assembly, and petition. The First Amendment also contains other guarantees. Congress cannot establish any church or denomination as a state-sponsored church. People are free to practice their religions as they choose. Freedom of speech is also important to our political system because it permits citizens to criticize or petition those in power. But freedom of speech is not unlimited. Slander (defaming a person verbally) and libel (defaming a person in writing) are not protected. Without the right of assembly, there could be no clubs, churches, or other private organizations except those approved by the government. People could not unite to change the government by legal means.

The Second Amendment forbids Congress to infringe on citizens' right to keep weapons.

The Third Amendment protects the people from military intrusion into their homes.

Amendments to the Constitution

Amendment I: Five Freedoms

Congress shall make no law respecting an establishment of religion, or prohibiting the free exercise thereof; or abridging the freedom of speech, or of the press; or the right of the people peaceably to assemble, and to petition the government for a redress of grievances.

Amendment II: The Right to Bear Arms

A well regulated militia, being necessary to the security of a free state, the right of the people to keep and bear arms, shall not be infringed.

Amendment III: No Quartering of Troops

No soldier shall, in time of peace be quartered in any house, without the consent of the owner, nor in time of war, but in a manner to be prescribed by law.

Amendment IV: No Unreasonable Searches and Seizures

The right of the people to be secure in their persons, houses, papers, and effects, against unreasonable searches and seizures, shall not be violated, and no warrants shall issue, but upon probable cause, supported by oath or affirmation, and particularly describing the place to be searched, and the persons or things to be seized.

Amendment V: Rights of the Accused

No person shall be held to answer for a capital, or otherwise infamous crime, unless on a presentment or indictment of a grand jury, except in cases arising in the land or naval forces, or in the militia, when in actual service in time of war or public danger; nor shall any person be subject for the same offense to be twice put in jeopardy of life or limb; nor shall be compelled in any criminal case to be a witness against himself, nor be deprived of life, liberty, or property, without due process of law; nor shall private property be taken for public use, without just compensation.

Amendment VI: Rights of the Accused in Criminal Trials

In all criminal prosecutions, the accused shall enjoy the right to a speedy and public trial, by an impartial jury of the state and district wherein the crime shall have been committed, which district shall have been previously ascertained by law, and to be informed of the nature and cause of the accusation; to be confronted with the witnesses against him; to have compulsory process for obtaining witnesses in his favor, and to have the assistance of counsel for his defense.

Amendment VII: Rights in Civil Trials

In suits at common law, where the value in controversy shall exceed twenty dollars, the right of trial by jury shall be preserved, and no fact tried by a jury, shall be otherwise re-examined in any court of the United States, than according to the rules of the common law.

Amendment VIII: Cruel, Unusual, and Unjust Punishments

Excessive bail shall not be required, nor excessive fines imposed, nor cruel and unusual punishments inflicted.

Amendment IX: Unlisted Rights

The enumeration in the Constitution, of certain rights, shall not be construed to deny or disparage others retained by the people.

Amendment X: Reserved Rights of the States and the People

The powers not delegated to the United States by the Constitution, nor prohibited by it to the states, are reserved to the states respectively, or to the people.

The Fourth Amendment guarantees the privacy of homes from illegal searches. It does not keep authorities from conducting legal searches or seizures with search warrants.

The Fifth Amendment ensures that no citizen can be forced to give evidence against himself. A grand jury determines whether there is enough evidence against a person to warrant a jury trial for guilt or innocence. This amendment protects citizens from being tortured or brainwashed to obtain information. No person can be tried twice for the same crime. In addition, a person cannot be imprisoned, have his property taken away, or be sentenced to death without a fair and proper trial.

The Sixth Amendment guarantees the right to a speedy, public trial. An accused person has the right to see and face his accuser and his witnesses. The court calls a witness to appear by serving a subpoena. A counsel for the defense (a lawyer) is provided, even at public expense.

The Seventh Amendment allows a trial by jury for any court case involving money or property of more than twenty dollars' value.

The Eighth Amendment prevents excessive bail or fines and cruel, unjust, and unusual punishments. The courts decide when bail and fines are excessive and when punishments are cruel, unjust, and unusual.

The Ninth Amendment states that even if the Constitution does not list a specific right, this does not mean that the right does not exist.

The Tenth Amendment gives the states or the people any powers that the Constitution does not forbid them to have or does not specifically mention. The federal government cannot take such rights away from them.

The Eleventh Amendment states that a citizen of a state (or of a foreign country) may not sue another state in a federal court without that state's consent. Suits must be pursued in a state's own courts.

The Twelfth Amendment says that electors are to vote separately for the president and the vice president. Thus the possibility of a tie between the president and the vice president is eliminated.

Amendment XI: Suing States (1795)

The judicial power of the United States shall not be construed to extend to any suit in law or equity, commenced or prosecuted against one of the United States by citizens of another state, or by citizens or subjects of any foreign state.

Amendment XII: Separate Ballots for President and Vice President (1804)

The electors shall meet in their respective states and vote by ballot for president and vice-president, one of whom, at least, shall not be an inhabitant of the same state with themselves; they shall name in their ballots the person voted for as president, and in distinct ballots the person voted for as vice-president, and they shall make distinct lists of all persons voted for as president, and of all persons voted for as vice-president, and of the number of votes for each, which lists they shall sign and certify, and transmit sealed to the seat of the government of the United States, directed to the president of the Senate;—the president of the Senate shall, in the presence of the Senate and House of Representatives, open all the certificates, and the votes shall then be counted;—the person having the greatest number of votes for president, shall be the president, if such number be a majority of the whole number of electors appointed; and if no person have such majority, then from the persons having the highest numbers not exceeding three on the list of those voted for as president, the House of Representatives shall choose immediately, by ballot, the president. But in choosing the president, the votes shall be taken by states, the representation from each state having one vote; a quorum for this purpose shall consist of a member or members from two-thirds of the states, and a majority of all the states shall be necessary to a choice. And if the House of Representatives shall not choose a president whenever the right of choice shall devolve upon them, before the fourth day of March next following, then the vice-president shall act as president, as in case of the death or other constitutional disability of the president.—The person having the greatest number of votes as vice-president shall be the vice-president, if such number be a majority of the whole number of electors appointed, and if no person have a majority, then from the two highest numbers on the list, the Senate shall choose the vice-president; a quorum for the purpose shall consist of two-thirds of the whole number of senators, and a majority of the whole number shall be necessary to a choice. But no person constitutionally ineligible to the office of president shall be eligible to that of vice-president of the United States.

The Thirteenth, Fourteenth, and Fifteenth Amendments are sometimes called the Civil War Amendments because they were all ratified just after that war.

The Thirteenth Amendment abolished slavery.

Amendment XIII: Slavery Abolished (1865)

Section 1. Neither slavery nor involuntary servitude, except as a punishment for crime whereof the party shall have been duly convicted, shall exist within the United States, or any place subject to their jurisdiction.

Section 2. Congress shall have power to enforce this article by appropriate legislation.

Amendment XIV: Citizenship (1868)

Section 1. All persons born or naturalized in the United States, and subject to the jurisdiction thereof, are citizens of the United States and of the state wherein they reside. No state shall make or enforce any law which shall abridge the privileges or immunities of citizens of the United States; nor shall any state deprive any person of life, liberty, or property, without due process of law; nor deny to any person within its jurisdiction the equal protection of the law.

Section 2. Representatives shall be apportioned among the several states according to their respective numbers, counting the whole number of persons in each state, excluding Indians not taxed. But when the right to vote at any election for the choice of electors for president and vice-president of the United States, representatives in Congress, the executive and judicial officers of a state, or the members of the legislature thereof, is denied to any of the male inhabitants of such state, being twenty-one years of age, and citizens of the United States, or in any way abridged, except for participation in rebellion, or other crime, the basis of representation therein shall be reduced in the proportion which the number of such male citizens shall bear to the whole number of male citizens twenty-one years of age in such state.

Section 3. No person shall be a senator or representative in Congress, or elector of president and vice-president, or hold any office, civil or military, under the United States, or under any state, who, having previously taken an oath, as a member of Congress, or as an officer of the United States, or as a member of any state legislature, or as an executive or judicial officer of any state, to support the Constitution of the United States, shall have engaged in insurrection or rebellion against the same, or given aid or comfort to the enemies thereof. But Congress may by a vote of two-thirds of each House, remove such disability.

Section 4. The validity of the public debt of the United States, authorized by law, including debts incurred for payment of pensions and bounties for services in suppressing insurrection or rebellion, shall not be questioned. But neither the United States nor any state shall assume or pay any debt or obligation incurred in aid of insurrection or rebellion against the United States, or any claim for the loss or emancipation of any slave; but all such debts, obligations and claims shall be held illegal and void.

Section 5. The Congress shall have power to enforce, by appropriate legislation, the provisions of this article.

> The Fourteenth Amendment says that all persons, regardless of ethnicity or status as former slave or free, born in the United States or naturalized, are both American citizens and citizens of the state in which they live. A state cannot deprive any person of life, liberty, or property without due process. States that deny voting rights can be denied representation in Congress, but this has never occurred.
>
> Sections 2, 3, and 4 of the Fourteenth Amendment deal with restrictions and provisions made for the states that were in the Confederacy during the Civil War.

Amendment XV: Voting Rights for Black Americans (1870)

Section 1. The right of the citizens of the United States to vote shall not be denied or abridged by the United States or by any state on account of race, color, or previous condition of servitude—

Section 2. The Congress shall have the power to enforce this article by appropriate legislation.

> The Fifteenth Amendment says that "race, color, or previous condition of servitude" cannot prevent any US citizen from voting.

The Sixteenth through Nineteenth Amendments are sometimes called the Progressive Amendments because they were passed at the height of the Progressive Era.

In the Sixteenth Amendment, Congress was given the power to tax incomes rather than basing taxes on population.

The Seventeenth Amendment gave the people, rather than the state legislatures, the right to elect their senators. Anyone who is qualified to vote in a state legislative election is also qualified to vote in a US Senate election. Senate vacancies may be filled by special election or by the state governor, depending on state law.

The Eighteenth Amendment is called the Prohibition Amendment and prohibited the manufacture, sale, or transportation of liquor. In 1919, Congress passed the Volstead Act to define "intoxicating liquors" and to enforce Amendment XVIII. Amendment XXI repealed this amendment in 1933.

Amendment XVI: Income Tax (1913)

The Congress shall have power to lay and collect taxes on incomes, from whatever source derived, without apportionment among the several states, and without regard to any census or enumeration.

Amendment XVII: Direct Election of Senators (1913)

The Senate of the United States shall be composed of two senators from each state, elected by the people thereof, for six years; and each senator shall have one vote. The electors in each state shall have the qualifications requisite for electors of the most numerous branch of the state legislatures.

When vacancies happen in the representation of any state in the Senate, the executive authority of such state shall issue writs of election to fill such vacancies: provided, that the legislature of any state may empower the executive thereof to make temporary appointments until the people fill the vacancies by election as the legislature may direct.

This amendment shall not be so construed as to affect the election or term of any senator chosen before it becomes valid as part of the Constitution.

Amendment XVIII: Prohibition (1919)

Section 1. After one year from the ratification of this article the manufacture, sale, or transportation of intoxicating liquors within, the importation thereof into, or the exportation thereof from the United States and all territory subject to the jurisdiction thereof for beverage purposes is hereby prohibited.

Section 2. The Congress and the several states shall have concurrent power to enforce this article by appropriate legislation.

Section 3. This article shall be inoperative unless it shall have been ratified as an amendment to the Constitution by the legislatures of the several states, as provided in the Constitution, within seven years from the date of submission hereof to the states by the Congress.

The Nineteenth Amendment gave women the right to vote. The right to vote is also called ***suffrage***.

Amendment XIX: Women's Suffrage (1920)

The right of citizens of the United States to vote shall not be denied or abridged by the United States or by any state on account of sex.

The Congress shall have power to enforce this article by appropriate legislation.

▾ Women's suffrage march in New York City in 1913

Amendment XX: Lame-Duck Amendment (1933)

Section 1. The terms of the president and the vice president shall end at noon on the 20th day of January, and the terms of senators and representatives at noon on the 3rd day of January, of the years in which such terms would have ended if this article had not been ratified; and the terms of their successors shall then begin.

Section 2. The Congress shall assemble at least once in every year, and such meeting shall begin at noon on the 3rd day of January, unless they shall by law appoint a different day.

Section 3. If, at the time fixed for the beginning of the term of the president, the president elect shall have died, the vice president elect shall become president. If a president shall not have been chosen before the time fixed for the beginning of his term, or if the president elect shall have failed to qualify, then the vice president elect shall act as president until a president shall have qualified; and the Congress may by law provide for the case wherein neither a president elect nor a vice president elect shall have qualified, declaring who shall then act as president, or the manner in which one who is to act shall be selected, and such person shall act accordingly until a president or vice president shall have qualified.

Section 4. The Congress may by law provide for the case of the death of any of the persons from whom the House of Representatives may choose a president whenever the right of choice shall have devolved upon them, and for the case of the death of any of the persons from whom the Senate may choose a vice president whenever the right of choice shall have devolved upon them.

Section 5. Sections 1 and 2 shall take effect on the 15th day of October following the ratification of this article.

Section 6. This article shall be inoperative unless it shall have been ratified as an amendment to the Constitution by the legislatures of three-fourths of the several states within seven years from the date of its submission.

Amendment XXI: Repeal of Prohibition (1933)

Section 1. The Eighteenth Article of amendment to the Constitution of the United States is hereby repealed.

Section 2. The transportation or importation into any state, territory, or possession of the United States for delivery or use therein of intoxicating liquors, in violation of the laws thereof, is hereby prohibited.

Section 3. This article shall be inoperative unless it shall have been ratified as an amendment to the Constitution by conventions in the several states, as provided in the Constitution, within seven years from the date of the submission hereof to the states by the Congress.

The Twentieth Amendment changed the starting dates for the terms of the president, senators, and representatives. Presidential terms begin on January 20 of every fourth year. Terms for senators and representatives begin on January 3 and last for six and two years, respectively. Amendment XX shortened the length of time between the November elections and the taking of office. If the president-elect dies before taking office, the vice president-elect takes his place.

The Twenty-First Amendment repealed Prohibition, but states and territories could prohibit the sale of alcohol within their borders.

Destruction of illegal alcohol during Prohibition

The Twenty-Second Amendment states that presidents can be elected for only two terms in their own right. If elevated from the vice-presidency during the second half of a previous president's term, a vice president who becomes president can serve a maximum of ten years.

Amendment XXII: Presidential Terms Limit (1951)

Section 1. No person shall be elected to the office of the president more than twice, and no person who has held the office of president, or acted as president, for more than two years of a term to which some other person was elected president shall be elected to the office of the president more than once. But this article shall not apply to any person holding the office of president when this article was proposed by the Congress, and shall not prevent any person who may be holding the office of president, or acting as president, during the term within which this article becomes operative from holding the office of president or acting as president during the remainder of such term.

Section 2. This article shall be inoperative unless it shall have been ratified as an amendment to the Constitution by the legislatures of three-fourths of the several states within seven years from the date of its submission to the states by the Congress.

The Twenty-Third Amendment gives residents of the District of Columbia the right to vote in presidential elections, and the district has three electoral votes.

Amendment XXIII: Voting Rights for Washington, DC (1961)

Section 1. The District constituting the seat of government of the United States shall appoint in such manner as the Congress may direct:

A number of electors of president and vice president equal to the whole number of senators and representatives in Congress to which the District would be entitled if it were a state, but in no event more than the least populous state; they shall be in addition to those appointed by the states, but they shall be considered, for the purposes of the election of president and vice president, to be electors appointed by a State; and they shall meet in the District and perform such duties as provided by the twelfth article of amendment.

Section 2. The Congress shall have power to enforce this article by appropriate legislation.

The Twenty-Fourth Amendment prohibits the payment of a poll tax to a state in any federal election. A poll tax was a tax that some states charged people before letting them vote.

Amendment XXIV: No Poll Tax (1964)

Section 1. The right of citizens of the United States to vote in any primary or other election for president or vice president, for electors for president or vice president, or for senator or representative in Congress, shall not be denied or abridged by the United States or any state by reason of failure to pay any poll tax or other tax.

Section 2. The Congress shall have power to enforce this article by appropriate legislation.

Amendment XXV: Presidential Succession and Disability (1967)

Section 1. In case of the removal of the president from office or of his death or resignation, the vice president shall become president.

Section 2. Whenever there is a vacancy in the office of the vice president, the president shall nominate a vice president who shall take office upon confirmation by a majority vote of both houses of Congress.

Section 3. Whenever the president transmits to the president pro tempore of the Senate and the Speaker of the House of Representatives his written declaration that he is unable to discharge the powers and duties of his office, and until he transmits to them a written declaration to the contrary, such powers and duties shall be discharged by the vice president as acting president.

Section 4. Whenever the vice president and a majority of either the principal officers of the executive departments or of such other body as Congress may by law provide, transmit to the president pro tempore of the Senate and the Speaker of the House of Representatives their written declaration that the president is unable to discharge the powers and duties of his office, the vice president shall immediately assume the powers and duties of the office as acting president.

Thereafter, when the president transmits to the president pro tempore of the Senate and the Speaker of the House of Representatives his written declaration that no inability exists, he shall resume the powers and duties of his office unless the vice president and a majority of either the principal officers of the executive department or of such other body as Congress may by law provide, transmit within four days to the president pro tempore of the Senate and the Speaker of the House of Representatives their written declaration that the president is unable to discharge the powers and duties of his office. Thereupon Congress shall decide the issue, assembling within forty-eight hours for that purpose if not in session. If the Congress, within twenty-one days after receipt of the latter written declaration, or, if Congress is not in session, within twenty-one days after Congress is required to assemble, determines by two-thirds vote of both houses that the president is unable to discharge the powers and duties of his office, the vice president shall continue to discharge the same as acting president; otherwise, the president shall resume the powers and duties of his office.

The Twenty-Fifth Amendment talks about presidential succession.

Section 1 states that the vice president becomes president if the president dies, resigns, or is removed from office.

Section 2 states that if the vice-presidency becomes vacant, the president can appoint a new vice president with the approval of both the House and the Senate.

Section 3 states that the president can transfer his duties to the vice president when he is unable to perform them. The president may do this, for example, when he is undergoing surgery and therefore unable to make decisions.

The Twenty-Sixth Amendment gave eighteen-year-olds the right to vote. Previously, the voting age was twenty-one (unless an individual state approved voting at a lower age).

The Twenty-Seventh Amendment states that any vote for a pay increase for senators and representatives cannot take effect until after the next election.

Amendment XXVI: Eighteen-Year-Old Vote (1971)

Section 1. The right of citizens of the United States, who are eighteen years of age or older, to vote shall not be denied or abridged by the United States or by any state on account of age.

Section 2. The Congress shall have power to enforce this article by appropriate legislation.

Amendment XXVII: Congressional Pay Raises (1992)

No law, varying the compensation for the services of the senators and representatives, shall take effect, until an election of representatives shall have intervened.

▲ Supporters of the Twenty-Sixth Amendment (left) and a nineteen-year-old voting in Chicago after the amendment's adoption (right)

CHAPTER 7 REVIEW

Making Connections

1. What is a confederation?
2. How many years after the Declaration of Independence were the Articles of Confederation ratified?
3. What were the three stages to becoming a state?
4. Why could the Confederation Congress not pay its debts?
5. In what Spanish-controlled city did America want a right of deposit?
6. To what three countries did Americans have difficulty repaying debts?
7. What violent occurrence led to fear and the recognition that the government needed to be strengthened?
8. Why was a meeting in Annapolis called? How many states sent representatives?
9. What two important founding fathers were away during the Constitutional Convention? Where were they?
10. The debate concerning representation was solved with the _____ Compromise.
11. The debate concerning population and taxation was solved with the _____ Compromise.
12. The debate concerning slave trade and exportation was solved with the compromise concerning _____.
13. Summarize the four important principles used in the Constitution.
14. Who were the authors of the *Federalist Papers*?
15. What are the primary functions of the legislative, executive, and judicial branches?
16. What are the first ten amendments called?

Thinking Critically

17. If you were creating a new government for a nation, would you choose a pure democracy or a republic? Why?
18. What do you think will be necessary for the continued success of the United States Constitution?

Living as a Christian Citizen

19. If you were at the Constitutional Convention, would you have accepted the Three-Fifths Compromise? Explain your answer.
20. The Bible affirms that all Christians are equal in Christ (Gal. 3:28; Col. 3:11), yet it limits church leadership to those who meet certain qualifications (1 Tim. 3:1–12; Titus 1:5–9). If you had the chance to apply this principle to those who hold political office, what qualifications would you require these leaders to have?

Terms to Remember

confederation
Articles of Confederation
ratify
Northwest Territory
Land Ordinance of 1785
townships
Northwest Ordinance of 1787
right of deposit
Daniel Shays
Shays's Rebellion
Annapolis Convention
Constitutional Convention
James Madison
Alexander Hamilton
constitution
republic
Virginia Plan
bicameral system
New Jersey Plan
unicameral system
Great Compromise
Senate
House of Representatives
census
Three-Fifths Compromise
separation of powers
checks and balances
federal system
Federalists
Federalist Papers
Anti-Federalists
Electoral College
Bill of Rights
Preamble
veto
suffrage

CHAPTER 8

Establishment of the New Government

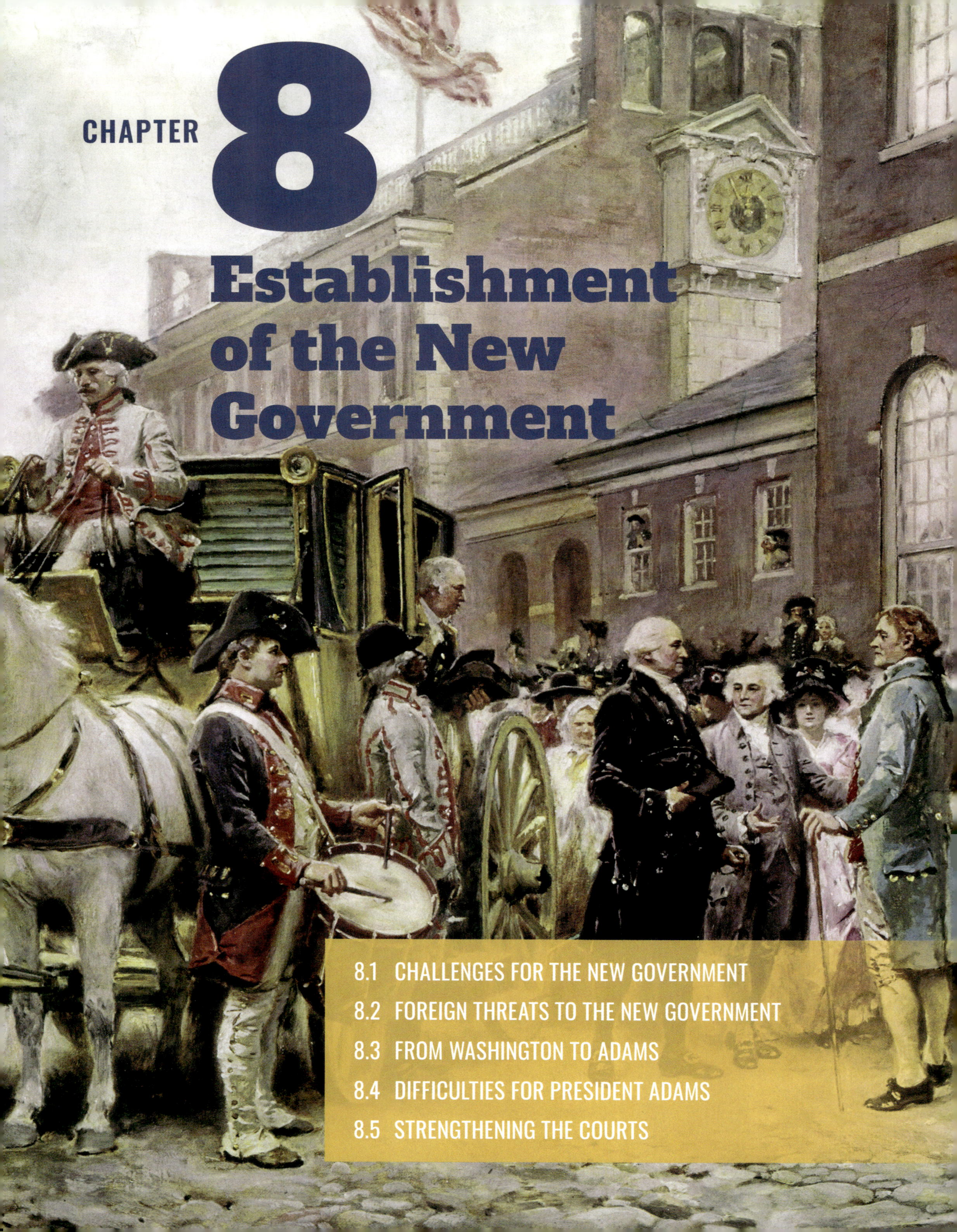

On April 16, 1789, George Washington left Mount Vernon, his home in Virginia. A week later he arrived in the nation's capital, New York City.

8.1 CHALLENGES FOR THE NEW GOVERNMENT

What challenges did the new government face?

Washington Takes Office

On April 30, a solemn Washington stepped out on the balcony of Federal Hall on the corner of Wall and Broad Streets. His **inauguration**, the formal ceremony starting a president's term, began at noon. Washington placed his left hand on a Bible and raised his right hand to take the oath of office. He then repeated the thirty-five words required by the Constitution.

> I do solemnly swear that I will faithfully execute the office of president of the United States, and will to the best of my ability, preserve, protect and defend the Constitution of the United States.

After taking his oath, he entered the Senate chamber to deliver his inaugural address to both houses of Congress. Washington had good reason to be solemn. At that time, the United States had slightly fewer than four million people, about seven hundred thousand of whom were slaves. Other nations were unfriendly to the United States and its new form of government. The country had no money in its treasury, and it lacked a strong army and navy.

The Constitution outlined a framework for the new government but lacked many exact details. The government that Washington would lead was completely new. No other country had a working republic to serve as an example for Washington and the other leaders. Washington began to build an administration that could help him meet the problems to come. His first challenge was to establish a **cabinet**, or a group of advisors, to assist with his responsibilities.

GUIDING QUESTIONS

- Who were the four members in the first cabinet?
- How did Alexander Hamilton and Thomas Jefferson each view issues facing the new country?
- Why did the Whiskey Rebellion occur?
- What federal court system did Congress establish?
- Why did Americans fight Indians on the frontier?

PRIMARY SOURCE: WASHINGTON'S FIRST INAUGURAL ADDRESS

It would be peculiarly improper to omit in this first official act my fervent supplications [sincere appeals] to that Almighty Being who rules over the universe, who presides in the councils of nations. . . that His benediction [approval] may consecrate to the liberties and happiness of the people of the United States a government instituted by themselves. . . . No people can be bound to acknowledge and adore the Invisible Hand which conducts the affairs of men more than those of the United States. Every step by which they have advanced to the character of an independent nation seems to have been distinguished by some token of providential agency [divine involvement].

Washington's first inauguration occurred in April 1789 in New York City (this page).

(Opposite page) Washington is shown arriving for his second inauguration. It was held in Philadelphia in March 1793.

George Washington

Born	February 22, 1732	1
Died	December 14, 1799	
Home state	Virginia	
Wife	Martha Custis	
Home	Mount Vernon	
Church	Anglican	
Occupations	surveyor, military aide, soldier, planter	
Party	none (but Federalist leaning)	
Years served as president	1789–97	
Terms	2	
Vice president	John Adams	

MR. PRESIDENT

It was surprisingly difficult for the members of the first Congress to determine a title for the president of the United States. The Constitution prohibited the government from granting titles of nobility. The American people, who had recently won their independence, wanted to stay far away from royal titles as well.

John Adams thought that the simple title "President" was too plain. For such a high office, he suggested "His Excellency," "His Highness," "His Elective Majesty," "His Majesty," or even "His Highness, the President of the United States of America and the Protector of their Liberties."

But these titles had no popular support. In the end, Congress decided on simply "President of the United States." Today, when people speak to the president, they address him as "Mr. President."

Washington Establishes a Cabinet

Although the Constitution provides for executive departments to give advice to the president, it says nothing about how to select the leaders of these departments or how to organize them. Washington established four departments and placed men he trusted at their heads. The State Department was headed by Thomas Jefferson, the Treasury by Alexander Hamilton, the War Department by Henry Knox, and what became known as the Justice Department by Attorney General Edmund Randolph. These leaders became Washington's **cabinet**, advising him on policies and problems.

Two cabinet members, Jefferson and Hamilton, had very different visions for America. Jefferson wanted the states to have more power than the national government. His vision for America was agricultural and primarily rural, or focused on people living in the countryside. Hamilton believed that the central government should be limited but strong. He wanted America to be an industrial country with a diverse economy and a collection of cities and towns, or urban areas. These different visions for the nation shaped the decisions that Jefferson and Hamilton made regarding many issues facing the new government.

Thomas Jefferson

Alexander Hamilton

Henry Knox

Edmond Randolph

Dealing with Financial Issues

One of the biggest problems facing the new administration was a lack of funds. Not only was money needed to operate the newly formed government, but the nation owed a large debt. Much of that money had been borrowed in order to fight the War for Independence. In order to maintain the respect of Americans and of other nations, the government would have to meet its obligations.

Hamilton's Plan

Secretary of the Treasury Hamilton designed a financial program to help the new nation pay its debts and fund the government. First, the government would levy (impose and collect) taxes to obtain revenue. A **tariff** (a tax on imported goods) on merchandise from foreign countries would be charged. An **excise tax** (a tax paid on the manufacture or sale of certain goods and services within a country) on whiskey would also be imposed.

Second, the government would repay the money borrowed during the War for Independence. To settle this debt, the government had to repay Americans who owned bonds that had been purchased to finance the war. The Continental Congress had not been able to pay this debt, and most of the bond owners doubted that they would ever be repaid. Thinking the bonds were worthless, many sold their bonds to speculators for a fraction of their value. When Hamilton's financial plan became law in 1790, it arranged for the government to repay the bonds at their printed value plus interest. Those who had sold bonds for small sums were angry. Nonetheless, the act helped the government stand by its promises.

Third, Hamilton wanted the government to take the responsibility of paying the states' debts. He hoped the payment would increase state loyalty to the national government. This idea resulted in the Assumption Act of 1790, so named for the national government assuming, or taking the responsibility for, the states' debts.

Fourth, Hamilton wanted to establish a **national bank**. The bank would hold tax revenue in one place, and the nation's financial dealings could be handled through the bank. Congress established the Bank of the United States in 1791.

Hamilton's Plan

1 Raise money through taxes	2 Repay war debts
3 Pay the states' debts	4 Establish a national bank

First Bank of the United States in Philadelphia (the first national bank)

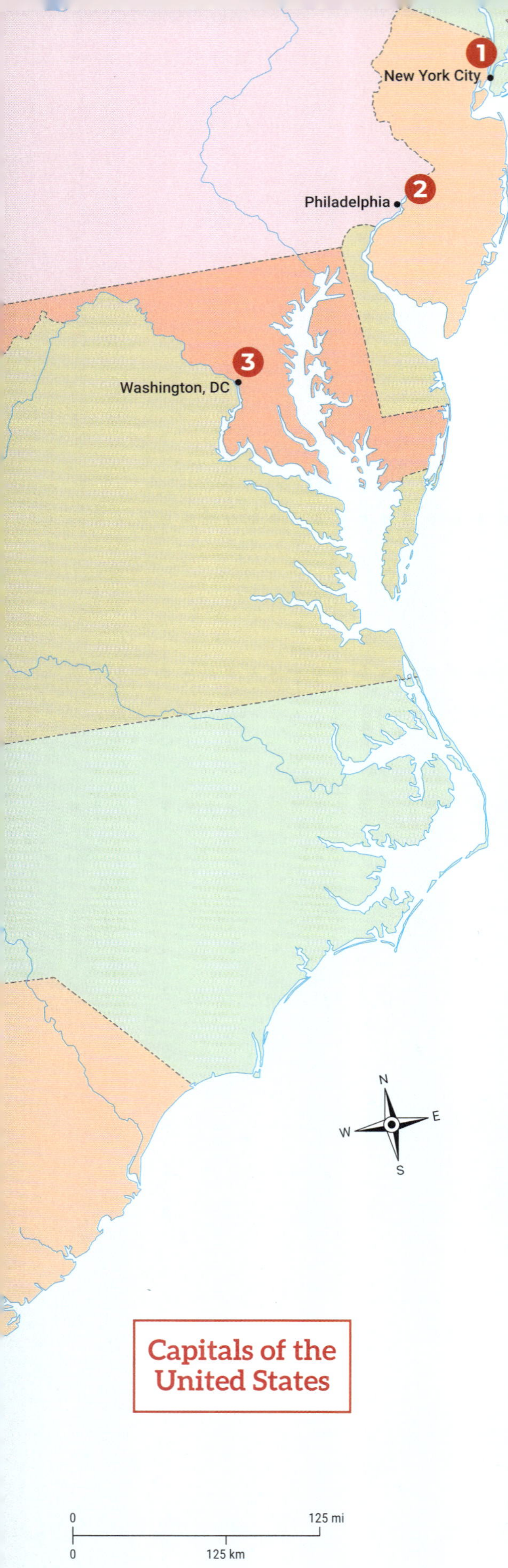

Jefferson's Views

Several of Hamilton's ideas brought widespread disagreement. In particular, there was opposition to the assumption of state debts and to federal involvement in banking. A group that was opposed to both ideas emerged, led by Jefferson. Jefferson and many other southerners opposed assumption because the southern states had already paid most of their debts. These states did not want to help pay the debts of the northern states. Furthermore, Jefferson opposed the national bank because it would help northern industries but not southern agriculture. He also believed the Constitution did not give Congress the power to create a national bank.

In 1791 Hamilton's program was adopted, but only after a compromise was reached. In return for Jefferson's and the South's support of the debt assumption, the national capital would permanently move to the South. Maryland and Virginia donated land along the Potomac River for a federal district that was later named in honor of Christopher Columbus and George Washington. The new capital—Washington, District of Columbia (DC)—was built on the land from Maryland, and the government moved there in late 1800. The other land was later returned to Virginia. (New York City served as the capital from 1789–90, and Philadelphia was the capital from 1790–1800.) Despite the criticisms, Hamilton's program worked, and the nation's credit and status improved.

▲ A statue of Washington is located in New York City at the site of his first inauguration.

Washington had hoped that there would be no factions, or political parties. But the groups that formed around Hamilton and Jefferson eventually became the basis of America's two-party political system. Hamilton's party was called the **Federalist Party**. Jefferson's party was called the **Democratic-Republican Party**; its members were often merely called "Republicans." (This group should not be confused with the modern Republican Party, which was not established until 1854.)

The Whiskey Rebellion

Washington and his troops during the Whiskey Rebellion

The excise tax on whiskey, passed by Congress in 1791, led to a problem that tested Washington and the new government. On the western frontier, corn was used not only as food for people and animals but also to make whiskey. Because of the shortage of money and the desire for whiskey, some people even used whiskey as a form of money. Therefore, westerners resented the excise tax because it affected many of their purchases. If a man exchanged a gallon of whiskey for an item, he still had to pay the tax on the whiskey. If he refused to pay the tax and was arrested, he had to go to a federal court for trial. The federal courts were sometimes miles away in coastal cities.

In western Pennsylvania during the summer of 1794, angry farmers attacked a federal marshal who tried to arrest an individual for not paying the tax. The mob also burned the home of a tax inspector and tarred and feathered other officials. President Washington wanted Pennsylvania to handle the problem, but the state's governor refused. Washington offered the rebels a group pardon (amnesty) if they would agree to abide by the law, but they refused his offer. The president then summoned about 13,000 militiamen to serve as a federal force. He commanded the rebels to disperse by September 1. Otherwise, the militia would move in.

After Washington's order went unheeded, he moved to forcefully quell the protesters. He told the troops to "combat and subdue all who [were] found in arms in opposition to the national will and authority." When the army arrived at the scene, the rebellion collapsed. Of the few rebels who were arrested and tried, two were condemned to death, but Washington pardoned them.

Washington's response to this **Whiskey Rebellion** proved his commitment to the rule of law. Americans realized that they could not allow their newfound freedoms to produce lawlessness. Many nations, such as France, experienced a period of violence after revolutions that had intended to secure liberty. America's future was still uncertain, and Washington wanted to ensure that similar problems did not occur in America.

Did you know?

To increase the image of the federal power and to show his willingness to deal decisively with the rebellion, Washington himself led the front units of the troops for some miles. Although the Constitution states that the president is the commander in chief of the nation's military, this is the only instance in which a president personally led troops while serving in the nation's highest office.

Establishing the Federal Court System

In the Judiciary Act of 1789, Congress created a working court system. The law stated that the Supreme Court would have five associate justices and one chief justice. Washington appointed **John Jay**, who had helped negotiate the Treaty of Paris in 1783 and was one of the authors of the *Federalist Papers*, as the first chief justice.

Although the Constitution established only one court—the Supreme Court—it gave Congress the power to establish lower federal courts. So Congress established thirteen federal district courts, one per state. Most cases involving violations of federal laws could be tried in those courts. Congress also set up three circuit courts to hear cases appealed from the district courts and state supreme courts. Today's federal court system follows a similar pattern but has been expanded in scope to meet the needs of a growing population.

John Jay

Fighting Indians on the Frontier

Americans, desiring to expand, wanted to move into the lands of the Northwest Territory. Much of this land still belonged to the Indians, and the United States had made treaties with many of the tribes concerning the protection of this land.

Washington and Congress hoped for a slow and orderly movement westward, in which the government would sell plots of land to new communities on the edges of American civilization. But the national government found it impossible to regulate the flow of people into the western territories. A growing number of Americans saw the western lands as uncultivated agriculturally and theirs for the taking. Tragically, the settlers ignored treaties with the Indians and seized valuable Indian territory.

Many tribes responded to this invasion by fighting for their lands. The British in the Northwest region urged the Indians to attack Americans. Sometimes the British openly promised to help the Indians if they would halt the spread of American settlements. The US government made several vain attempts to stop the Indian attacks. Finally, in 1794 Anthony Wayne, a hero during the War for Independence, and his well-trained force entered what is now northwestern Ohio. They defeated a band of Indians and their allies at the Battle of **Fallen Timbers**, near modern-day Toledo. The defeated Indians attended a peace conference at Fort Greenville in 1795. They surrendered their claim to about half of Ohio in return for gifts and annual payments.

During the 1790s, three new states joined the Union: Vermont (1791), Kentucky (1792), and Tennessee (1796). In 1803 Ohio was admitted to the Union as the first state from the Northwest Territory. Despite harsh conditions and the continuing threat of Indian attack, more pioneers went west.

SECTION REVIEW 8.1

1. What were the four original cabinet departments and who headed each?
2. How did Hamilton's and Jefferson's visions for the new nation differ concerning the role of the national government?
3. How did Hamilton and Jefferson disagree on financial issues?
4. What were the first political parties in the United States? Who was the leader of each?
5. Why did two important Founding Fathers such as Hamilton and Jefferson differ so greatly in their views regarding American values?
6. What did Washington's response to the Whiskey Rebellion prove? Why was this important?
7. Who was allowed to establish other courts besides the Supreme Court? How many total justices were permitted in the Judiciary Act of 1789? How many federal district courts did it establish? How many circuit courts?
8. Why did fighting occur between the settlers moving west and the Indians? What did each side see as the problem?

▾ Battle of Fallen Timbers

8.2 FOREIGN THREATS TO THE NEW GOVERNMENT

What foreign threats did the new government face?

GUIDING QUESTIONS

- What were various American viewpoints regarding the French Revolution?
- What were America's issues with France, Great Britain, and Spain?

Although the United States had established its independence with its victory against Britain, other nations were unsure of the new nation's strength. Some European powers doubted that the United States could protect its rights and believed the young country could be harassed and intimidated.

America and the French Revolution

By late summer in 1789, the Americans learned that the French had rebelled against King Louis XVI. At first, most Americans approved of those actions. They cheered, celebrating the French phrase "Liberty, Equality, Fraternity." The Marquis de Lafayette sent George Washington the key to the Bastille, a French prison. The fall of the prison symbolized the start of the French Revolution. Lafayette saw many similarities between the revolution in France and the American War for Independence.

But by 1793 an increasing number of Americans were horrified by what was occurring in France. The new French government, although a republic in name, was highly unstable and citizens lived in terror. Thousands were killed in the violence that spread through the nation. The new French leaders campaigned against religion and tried to remove all traces of it from public life. Also in 1793, France declared war on Britain.

Did you know?

Today the Bastille key hangs in the main hallway of George Washington's home, Mount Vernon.

▼ The Bastille was captured by a French mob on July 14, 1789.

America's Position of Neutrality

In 1778 during the War for Independence, America and France became allies upon signing the Treaty of Alliance. The help the French provided, as a result of that treaty, was crucial to the United States winning its fight for independence.

The Federalists, led by Alexander Hamilton, urged President Washington to terminate this agreement. They argued that the treaty had been made with a government and king that the French Revolution had destroyed; therefore, the United States was under no obligation to support France in its war with Britain. Thomas Jefferson, an early supporter of the French Revolution, and his fellow Republicans believed that America should honor the treaty by helping France.

On April 22, 1793, Washington issued the **Proclamation of Neutrality**. He declared the United States would pursue a policy of friendliness toward both France and Britain and would not involve itself in their conflict. He urged Americans to be "impartial" toward all foreign foes and to cease actions that would involve the United States in foreign wars.

▾ Edmond-Charles Genêt (right) met with President Washington (center) and Secretary of State Thomas Jefferson (left).

Citizen Genêt

The new French ambassador was **Edmond-Charles Genêt**. He rejected titles of nobility and referred to himself simply as Citizen Genêt. His arrival in Charleston, South Carolina, in April 1793 complicated the relationship between his country and the United States. Before he traveled to Philadelphia, the capital, he met with many pro-French supporters. He attempted to raise an army to fight Britain's ally Spain in Florida, and he managed to convince a number of private American ship captains to attack British cargo shipping.

When the ambassador met with George Washington in May, the president gave him a courteous, but cold, reception. By that time, the Proclamation of Neutrality had been issued, and the president made it clear that America would remain neutral in the conflict between France and Britain. Nevertheless, Genêt continued to encourage Americans to support his country. Washington later asked France to replace Genêt as their ambassador. Just as France agreed to do so, leadership in the French government shifted. When it was clear that the new French government would likely execute Genêt, Washington kindly allowed him to remain in the country.

Citizen Genêt moved to New York where he married the daughter of the state's governor, George Clinton. He became an American citizen and lived in the country until his death is 1834.

Trouble with the British

The Proclamation of Neutrality and the end of the Genêt affair may have calmed England's fears of an American alliance with France, but the threat of another war between America and Britain continued.

Neutral Rights at Sea

The nations disagreed over what rights neutral countries (specifically the United States) should have at sea. The United States had opened trade with the French West Indies and France, Britain's enemies. To retaliate, Britain seized American ships that were sailing to French ports or that carried French goods. By early 1794, hundreds of US ships in the West Indies, along with their cargoes and crews, had been confiscated.

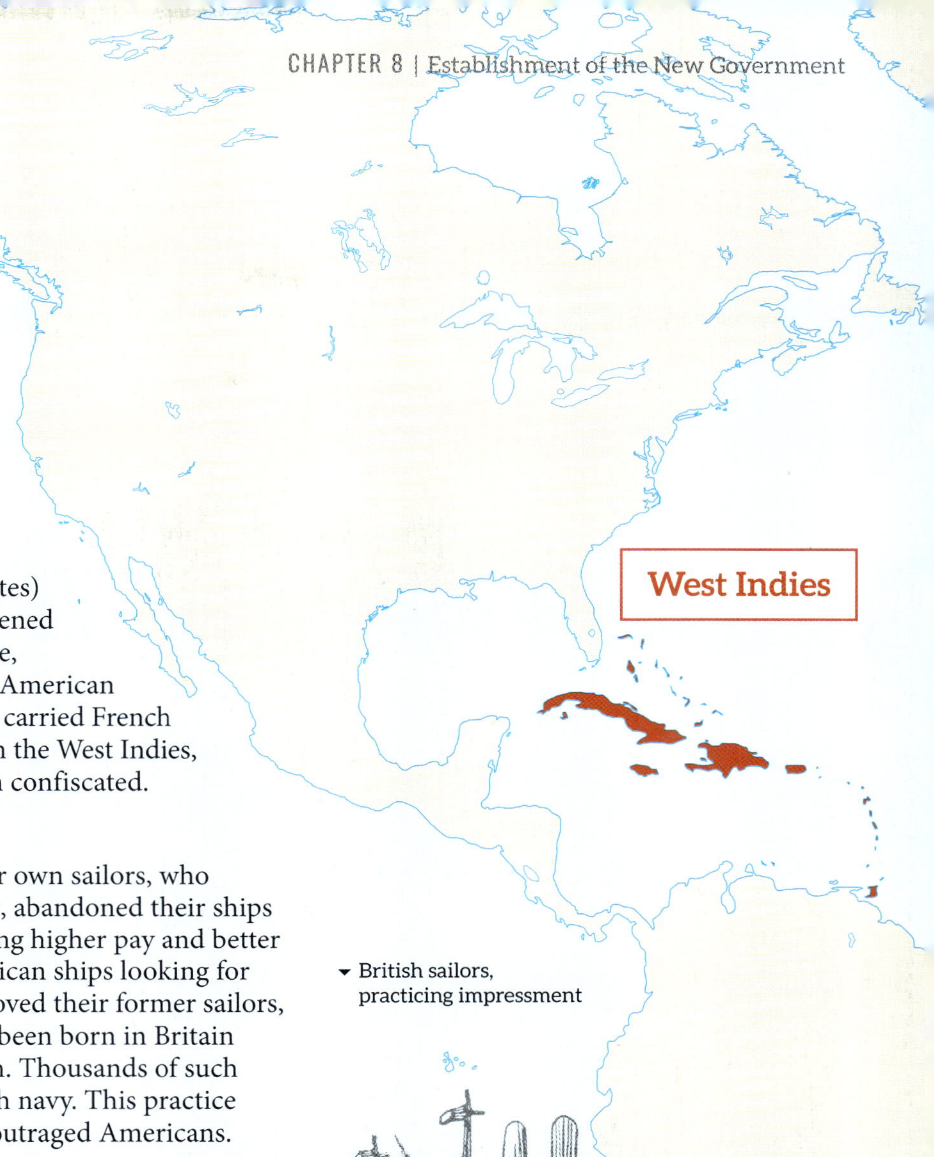

Impressment

The British were also angered when their own sailors, who complained of bad food and harsh discipline, abandoned their ships and joined American ships. They were seeking higher pay and better treatment. The British began stopping American ships looking for these deserters. But the British not only removed their former sailors, but also often captured Americans who had been born in Britain or even those who looked or sounded British. Thousands of such individuals were forced to serve in the British navy. This practice was known as **impressment**. These actions outraged Americans.

▾ British sailors, practicing impressment

Did you know?

In many towns, residents constructed an effigy (a model of a person) of John Jay and set it ablaze to show their displeasure with the Jay Treaty. He remarked that he could have found his way across America at night by using the light from the many burning effigies.

The Jay Treaty

To avoid war, Washington sent John Jay, the chief justice of the Supreme Court, to lead a peace mission to Britain. Because Britain was a strong world power and the United States was a small, new republic, Jay faced a difficult task. The United States agreed to limit trade with France, Britain's enemy, and to arrange payment of debts that were still owed to British banks and citizens from before the War for Independence. In return, Britain agreed to abandon its forts in the Northwest, pay the United States for ships seized, and open some ports in the British West Indies to American trade.

The **Jay Treaty** (1794) did not fully settle the issues of the British encouraging Indians in the Northwest to attack settlers there nor the matter of neutral rights at sea. Thus, many Americans felt the treaty gave too much to the British and gained too little for the United States. They were angry at both Jay and his treaty. Others believed the agreement was better than another option—war with Britain.

After intense debate, the treaty barely received the two-thirds vote required in the Senate. Nevertheless, many of Jay's opponents compared him to Benedict Arnold, the general who betrayed the United States during the War for Independence.

Disputes with Spain

Spain still controlled Florida and the Louisiana Territory (the land west of the Mississippi River), including the port city of New Orleans. Tension between Spain and the United States had existed for years. Washington sent Thomas Pinckney of South Carolina to Spain to settle some of those disagreements.

In the Pinckney Treaty, signed in 1795, Spain gave the United States the right of deposit at New Orleans, and the two nations settled the longstanding dispute regarding the boundary between the United States and Florida. This agreement, unlike the Jay Treaty, was popular with Americans.

SECTION REVIEW 8.2

1. What did Federalists and Republicans believe about America's treaty with France? What solution did George Washington provide?
2. Which French ambassador caused problems for America by attempting to raise armies and funds to fight Britain?
3. Why did Britain seize American ships? Why did Britain impress American sailors?
4. What was impressment? Was this policy fair?
5. What unsettled issues contributed to the Jay Treaty's unpopularity?
6. What results made the Pinckney Treaty popular?

8.3 FROM WASHINGTON TO ADAMS

How did the government transfer from President Washington to President Adams?

Washington's presidency was a time of great trials for the new government, but the young nation survived. The time soon came for a new administration to take charge of the government and continue what Washington had begun.

Washington's Farewell

Unlike revolutionary leaders in other nations, George Washington chose not to extend his power and often refused new opportunities to exercise additional control. His restraint proved to be one of his most important contributions to the nation.

In September 1796, six months before he left office, Washington released his Farewell Address to a newspaper. It was soon reprinted throughout the nation. Although some people thought that he should seek the presidency an additional time, he stated that serving two four-year terms was enough.

In his Farewell Address, Washington also provided advice for the future. Washington warned against disputes that would divide Americans into factions, or political parties. He encouraged commercial, or trading, ties with foreign countries; however, he cautioned against permanent political alliances with other nations. Washington urged the nation to avoid accumulating debt.

Washington was sixty-five years old when he retired to his beloved home, Mount Vernon. After eight years of the pressures of the presidency, the Washingtons welcomed the change. But they had only a little more than two years to enjoy his retirement.

▾ Martha Custis (left) married George Washington in 1759. Their Virginia home (below) was known as Mount Vernon.

GUIDING QUESTIONS

- What was Washington's advice in his Farewell Address?
- What happened in the election of 1796?
- What challenges did John Adams face as president?

establishing PRESIDENTIAL *traditions*

Washington's actions established many traditions that have continued since his time in office. For example, all presidents have continued, and sometimes expanded, the cabinet system he established. Furthermore, like Washington, other presidents have traveled throughout the country and given many Americans the opportunity to see them.

The way Washington took office also became a tradition. He placed his hand on the Bible while being sworn into office and is credited with adding the words "So help me God" upon completing the oath. Afterward, he gave a speech. None of those were constitutional requirements, yet all have been widely followed.

Washington served as the US president for two four-year terms. No other president served for more than two terms until Franklin Roosevelt broke that tradition in 1940, almost 150 years later. He was elected four times. Within a few years after Roosevelt's presidency, the Twenty-Second Amendment to the Constitution was ratified. It permanently set the two-term limit for president.

▲ Statue of George Washington in Philadelphia

John Adams

Born	October 30, 1735	2
Died	July 4, 1826	
Home state	Massachusetts	
Wife	Abigail Smith	
Home	Peacefield	
Church	Unitarian	
Occupation	lawyer	
Party	Federalist	
Years served as president	1797–1801	
Terms	1	
Vice president	Thomas Jefferson	

On Thursday, December 12, 1799, Washington rode on horseback in the snow and sleet to inspect his farm. Despite a sore throat, he did so again the following day. Saturday, his throat was inflamed and he had difficulty breathing. Doctors drew blood from his body, a common medical practice of the time. Late that evening, he died. The country mourned his death and sought to honor his memory. Washington is the only American for which a state is named. Hundreds of cities, towns, counties, and parks bear his name. Monuments and memorials honoring him exist throughout the country. No other American has been celebrated so widely. In addition, his image appears on currency, postage stamps, and other national symbols. Upon Washington's passing, fellow Virginian Henry Lee wrote that he was, "first in war, first in peace, and first in the hearts of his countrymen."

The Election of 1796

Washington had not faced opposing parties or needed to campaign for office in his elections. But the presidential election of 1796 was completely different. This time there were political parties. The party leaders met and chose their candidates. Everyone expected the Republicans to choose Thomas Jefferson, and they did. **Aaron Burr**, a US senator from New York, was the vice-presidential candidate. The Federalists chose **John Adams**, who had served as Washington's vice president for eight years, as their presidential candidate. Thomas Pinckney, known for the treaty he had negotiated with Spain, was their vice-presidential choice.

Until the adoption of the Twelfth Amendment in 1804, each elector in the Electoral College cast two votes. The person who received the most votes became president while the runner up became vice president. In the 1796 election, Adams received the most votes while Thomas Jefferson received the second highest number. As a result, the president and the vice president were from different parties. This situation made it difficult to create a unified administration.

The election of 1796 was notable because a peaceful transfer of power occurred. Although two parties with different viewpoints were involved, the losing party did not respond with violence or rebellion. Nonviolent transitions have continued throughout the country's history.

In Washington's Shadow

Few presidents have entered office as qualified as John Adams. He began a law career in his early twenties. Two decades later, he served in both of the Continental Congresses. He gained valuable experience, over nearly a decade, in foreign affairs by representing the United States in France, the Netherlands, and Britain. He then held the nation's second highest office from 1789 to 1797.

Following Washington as president, however, was no easy matter. On Inauguration Day in Philadelphia when Adams took office, the cheers for the departing president were louder than those for Adams. Tears of sadness streamed from people's eyes for the great man who was leaving office, but there was little praise for the man who succeeded him. And on what was probably the greatest day of Adams's public life, his devoted wife, Abigail, was not there to share it. She was home in Massachusetts caring for her husband's dying mother.

the creation of a NEW CAPITAL

Leaders of the young United States called for a permanent capital that would be an entirely new city. Most people assumed that the new capital would be located in the North since the first two capitals, New York City and Philadelphia, were there. But Southerners wanted the capital in their region. In 1790, Congress compromised, ordering that the city be located along the Potomac River on land donated by Virginia and Maryland (as noted earlier, the Virginia land was later returned to the state).

Andrew Ellicott surveyed the area, assisted by a free black man, Benjamin Banneker. President Washington appointed Pierre Charles L'Enfant to design the city under the supervision of three commissioners. L'Enfant's plan called for wide streets and grand avenues with the Capitol on a high point on the land. Because of conflicts with the commissioners, Washington dismissed L'Enfant, and Ellicott revised the original plans.

The government officially moved to Washington, DC, in 1800 during the last months that John Adams, the second president, was in office. Most of the area was still a wilderness of swamps and forests. Members of Congress reached the President's House, later called the White House, by using a muddy trail through woods. There were no paved streets or street signs.

Adams decided to retain Washington's cabinet rather than naming his own. A number of historians believe this was one of his biggest mistakes. The cabinet consulted with Alexander Hamilton, who was no longer in office. Though he was also a Federalist, Hamilton often opposed Adams's ideas. Several times, the cabinet made decisions that violated the new president's wishes. This opposition hindered some of Adams's policies. Furthermore, criticisms from his political opponents throughout his term of office turned many Americans against him. Adams would never be as popular as George Washington.

This postage stamp, released in the 1950s, honored Washington.

SECTION REVIEW 8.3

1. What three things did Washington warn against in his Farewell Address?
2. Why was the election of 1796 unusual?
3. Why do you think it was important that the election of 1796 was peaceful?
4. Why was it hard for John Adams to follow George Washington as president?
5. What two states donated land to make a national capital? Which state eventually had its land returned?

GUIDING QUESTIONS

- What was the XYZ Affair?
- Why were the Alien and Sedition Acts controversial?
- How was the election of 1800 decided?

8.4 DIFFICULTIES FOR PRESIDENT ADAMS

What difficulties did John Adams face as president?

To people outside his own family, Adams often seemed reserved and distant. But he had a strong sense that it was his duty to serve others, regardless of the personal cost. He kept this in mind as he faced not only internal problems with his cabinet and vice president but also outside conflict with other nations.

The XYZ Affair

The British were still seizing American ships when Adams took office. But the greatest problem came from America's recent ally, France. A new French government, angered by the Jay Treaty with Britain, became hostile. The French ordered their navy to seize American ships that carried cargo to Britain. Hundreds of American ships were captured. To add to the insult, the French refused to meet with the American minister to France, Charles Cotesworth Pinckney (brother of Thomas Pinckney, who had negotiated the Pinckney Treaty).

Did you know?

In modern currency, the bribe demanded in the XYZ Affair would equal over $5 million and the loan $200 million.

American Representatives Meet French Agents

Although some Federalists believed that Adams should break with France and perhaps even declare war, he first chose to negotiate. He sent two additional representatives to assist Pinckney. The trio sought a meeting with Talleyrand, the French minister of foreign affairs. But nine months after seeking the hearing, they had yet to see the man. However, they did meet his three agents. The agents demanded a $250,000 bribe and the promise of a $10 million loan for France.

Adams, still a lawyer at heart, went to Congress to expose this insult to the United States. In March 1798 he presented the evidence, but substituted the letters *X*, *Y*, and *Z* for the names of the French agents. Soon the whole episode was known as **the XYZ Affair**.

Abigail Adams

Abigail Smith Adams loved her husband, John, for more than fifty years of marriage. He was often gloomy and uncompromising, but his wife's charm cheered him and soothed his impatience. John always delighted in her wit and opinions. Her many letters addressed him as "my dearest friend" and "my best friend."

Although Abigail never had a formal education, she was an extraordinarily intelligent woman. She took every opportunity to learn, whether from her father's library or by studying the sails on a ship.

She was fifteen years old when she met John, who was twenty-four, in 1759. Her parents disliked him because of the age difference, the fact that he was born into a lower-class family, and because he was a lawyer. Though her father considered law a dishonest and unworthy profession, after a three-year courtship, in 1764 he agreed to allow John and Abigail to marry.

The first of the couple's several separations came in 1774, when John left their home in the Boston area to represent his state in the Continental Congress at Philadelphia. Abigail's numerous letters were sources of encouragement when John became disheartened and lonely during the time he was absent.

Abigail's many letters reveal much about her wide scope of interests. She discussed politics as well as life on the farm. Writing as often as three times a day, she kept John up-to-date on the military and political situations at home during the War for Independence. Abigail was a keen observer and understood the historical importance of the times. She advised him to support independence from Britain.

Abigail did not permit hardships at home to depress her. She operated the family farm and cared for needy American soldiers during the War for Independence. Despite outbreaks of smallpox in the area and her own health issues, she took great care in rearing her children. She prodded her talented son John Quincy to make the most of himself. To teach him Latin, Abigail learned the language herself.

John Adams returned home briefly in 1778, but he was soon sent to France as an ambassador. Abigail consented to him taking along the ten-year-old John Quincy, believing that the boy would profit from the experience. For six years, except for a short leave in 1779, the couple was separated. When she joined him in France in 1784, they sent John Quincy back home to attend Harvard. Abigail kept in constant contact, showering him with motherly advice.

In 1785 John traveled to London as the first ambassador from the former American colonies, and he took his wife with him. In 1788, he resigned, and Abigail rejoiced when they returned to Massachusetts. But in nine short months, national duty called her husband away to New York to be vice president under George Washington. John presided over the Senate and shared all the news with Abigail. When he was away, which was often, he said that her letters kept him going.

After serving eight years as vice president, John became president in 1797. Abigail became the First Lady, a role for which she was extremely well suited. She had traveled to Europe and had been active in politics from the beginning of John's career. Experienced with running a large estate, she knew how to spend money wisely. She kept the family budget, directed thirty servants, read, wrote, planned entertainments, received visitors, and made public appearances.

Four months before John was to leave office, the family moved into the Executive Mansion (later called the White House) in the new capital, Washington, DC. Only six rooms were completed, the stairs were unfinished, the walls were unplastered, and Abigail had to yell for her servants because the bells had not yet arrived. Every day, thirteen fires were kept burning in an attempt to dry the walls. Abigail even had to use the audience chamber—today's East Room—to wash and hang the family laundry.

At the end of Adams's presidency, the couple left Washington and politics to spend the next seventeen years together at their Massachusetts home. The year Abigail died, in 1818, her son John Quincy was appointed secretary of state. The future president wrote of his mother, "She had been fifty-four years the delight of my father's heart, the sweetener of all his toils, the comforter of all his sorrows, the sharer and heightener of all his joys."

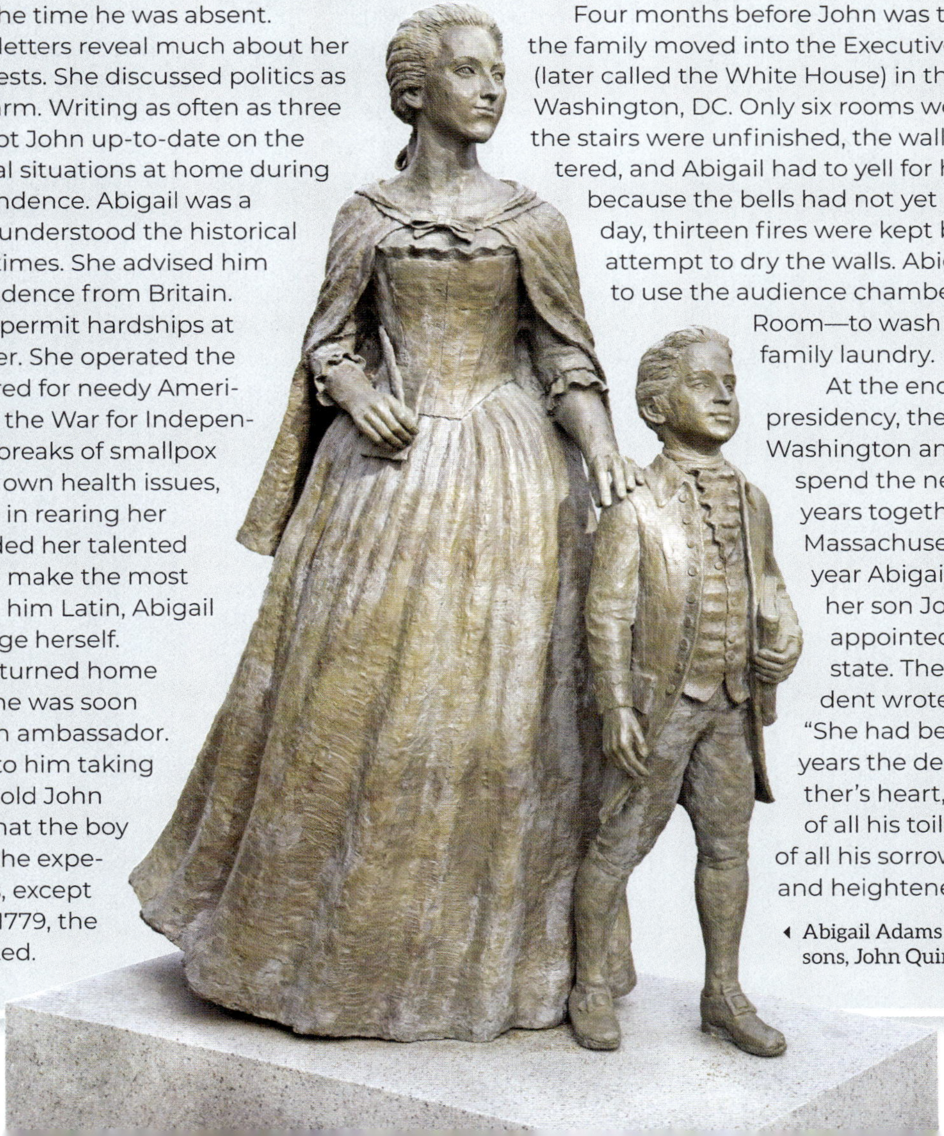

Abigail Adams with one of her sons, John Quincy Adams

A Call to Arms

France's actions angered Congress, which soon took measures to arm the country for action. Adams called for a stronger navy, and Congress voted, over Republican opposition, to make the navy a separate department and begin constructing ships.

Congress also vastly increased the size of the army. Adams asked Washington to leave his retirement in 1798 to serve as the commander. He agreed—with the condition that Alexander Hamilton be appointed his second in command. Congress also discarded the Treaty of Alliance (1778) that had been signed with France.

Although Congress never actually declared war, the Americans captured numerous French vessels by the fall of 1800. Because some fighting did occur, this conflict is sometimes called the "Quasi War" (a conflict resembling war in nearly every way, except no official declaration of war is issued). The public cheered the victories, and many pressured for real war. But Adams was hesitant. He believed that a full-scale war was unwise and that the United States was not prepared to fight one.

War Avoided

Meanwhile, France faced yet another change. General Napoleon Bonaparte seized control of the government in 1799. He was willing to discuss peace arrangements with the United States. Adams wanted Napoleon to pay the damages for France's actions against America, but Adams settled for an agreement in which Napoleon accepted the cancellation of the Treaty of Alliance and promised to leave American ships alone. In exchange, the United States agreed not to seek repayment for the shipping damages it suffered in the Quasi War. Many Republicans, as well as displeased Federalists, denounced the agreement. Nevertheless, with Adams's strong support, it was later ratified by the Senate. He was happy that all-out war had been avoided.

▾ During the many battles in the Quasi War, the USS *Constellation* defeated the French ships *La Vengeance* and *L'Insurgente*. The medal (above) and the painting (below) commemorate these events.

The Alien and Sedition Acts

While Adams was contending with foreign affairs, he faced numerous struggles within the nation. With the possibility of a war with France and increasing criticism from their political opponents, the Federalist-controlled Congress had passed four laws in 1798 called the **Alien and Sedition Acts**. Federalists said the laws would help protect the country during the threat of war. But they also intended the acts to harm the Democratic-Republican Party and keep it from gaining power. President Adams had not asked for these acts.

The first of the laws, the Naturalization Act, extended the time that an immigrant had to live in America before he could gain American citizenship. The requirement was changed from five to fourteen years. Since most immigrants joined the Republican Party, which they saw as the party of the common man, this act would keep foreigners from voting so soon. The delay would allow the Federalists more years in power. However, the states controlled their own elections, and as the Republicans had control in many states, the law was not really enforced and thus had little effect.

The Alien Enemies Act and the Alien Act allowed the president to imprison or expel any "dangerous" foreigners. The first act gave the president this power during times of war or invasion, and the second allowed him to deport any aliens thought to be dangerous, even if war had not been declared. The laws were purposely vague. The terms *peace*, *safety*, and *war* were not defined. These two laws were not actually enforced.

But the government did enforce the fourth law, the Sedition Act. This act declared that any person who said, wrote, or published anything false or malicious against the government or its officials could be fined and imprisoned. The Republicans saw this act as an attempt to stop both their mouths and their pens. They protested the law as a violation of their freedoms of speech and the press, which were guaranteed by the First Amendment to the Constitution. Many people were arrested under this law, and more than twenty were brought to trial. Ten of those were convicted. Though both Democratic-Republican and Federalist journalists had indeed published lies and misrepresentations, all those arrested had embraced the ideas of the Republican Party.

The Republicans and even a few Federalists worked hard to overrule the Alien and Sedition Acts. In November 1798 Thomas Jefferson wrote the Kentucky Resolutions. They were approved by that state's legislature. The following month fellow Republican James Madison wrote the Virginia Resolutions, which later received approval of the state legislature. The **Virginia and Kentucky Resolutions** claimed that the states, as a group, had the right to decide whether the national government exceeded its powers. Jefferson and Madison held that the union of states had been built on an agreement in which the states freely gave up some of their rights to a central government. But they said that the states still held powers of their own. Jefferson and Madison believed that the states should be allowed to decide whether actions of the federal government are constitutional. (The Kentucky Resolution used the term ***nullification*** to describe the states' act of declaring void any federal law.) Supporters of this idea based their thinking on the Tenth Amendment of the Constitution, which reserves powers not given to the federal government for the states.

Did you know?

The word *alien* does not necessarily mean a being from outer space. It is also used to refer to foreigners.

The Alien and Sedition Acts

1 Naturalization Act	2 Alien Enemies Act
3 Alien Act	4 Sedition Act

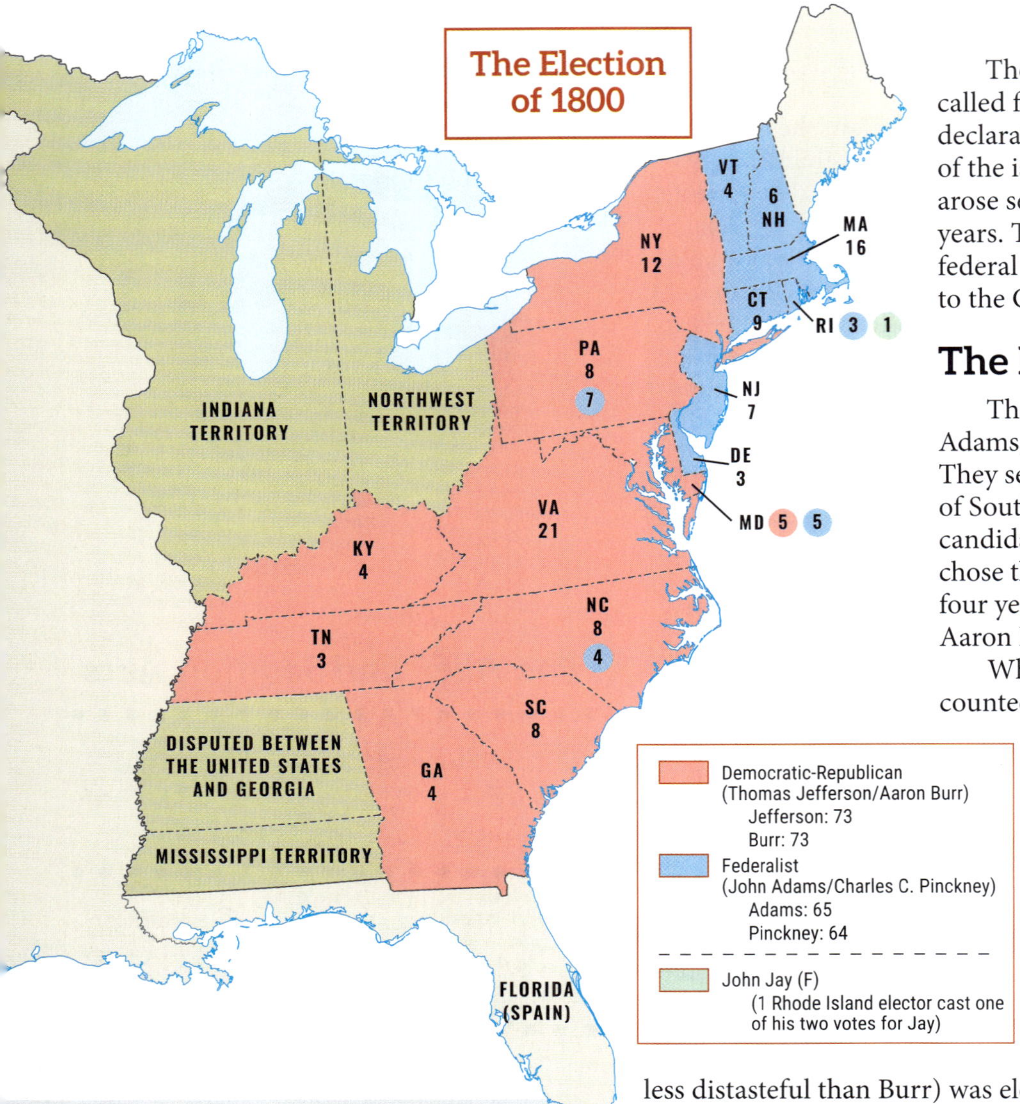

Though each of the two resolutions called for other states to adopt similar declarations, none did so. However, some of the issues discussed in the resolutions arose several times over the next sixty years. The conflict between states and the federal government eventually contributed to the Civil War.

The Election of 1800

Though many Federalists disliked Adams, they chose him to run for reelection. They selected Charles Cotesworth Pinckney of South Carolina as their vice-presidential candidate. The Democratic-Republicans chose the same candidates they had selected four years earlier, Thomas Jefferson and Aaron Burr.

When the Electoral College votes were counted, Jefferson and Burr both received equal numbers of votes, more than Adams or Pinckney. The Constitution stated that in the event of a tie, the House of Representatives would select the president. The Federalist-controlled House was left to choose between the two Democratic-Republican candidates. After a deadlock that lasted several days, Jefferson (whom Federalists considered less distasteful than Burr) was elected president on the thirty-sixth ballot. Burr became vice president.

Prior to the next election, the Twelfth Amendment to the Constitution was adopted. It called for electors to cast separate ballots for president and vice president. This prevented a recurrence of the complications that occurred in the 1796 and 1800 elections.

SECTION REVIEW 8.4

1. Describe France's reaction to Jay's treaty with England.
2. Who were *X*, *Y*, and *Z*? What did they demand?
3. Why was the fighting with the French considered a "quasi war"?
4. Which new French leader was willing to discuss peace arrangements with the United States?
5. What law extended the time immigrants had to live in America before they could become citizens?
6. Were the Alien Enemies Act and the Alien Act enforced?
7. Why did the Democratic-Republicans think the Sedition Act was unfair? Do you agree? Why or why not?
8. What powers did the Virginia and Kentucky Resolutions say that the states have?
9. How was the election of 1800 decided?

PARTY NEWSPAPERS

As soon as political parties began to play a role in the United States, they were aided by a variety of newspapers. The *Gazette of the United States* and the *National Gazette* were the most powerful papers. The *Gazette of the United States* supported the Federalists and their administrations. The *National Gazette* offered Democratic-Republican criticisms of the Federalist administrations.

These newspapers participated in a violent war of words during the first administrations of the government. Federalists passed the Sedition Act with their most outspoken critics in mind. One of the newspaper publishers arrested under the act was Benjamin Bache, Benjamin Franklin's grandson. Federalists considered his paper, the *Philadelphia Aurora*, dangerous to the country.

8.5 STRENGTHENING THE COURTS

Why were early changes to the judicial system important?

One of John Adams's most important acts was appointing a new chief justice to the Supreme Court. This appointment had far-reaching effects on the power of the Court.

GUIDING QUESTIONS

- What events led to the judicial branch becoming stronger?
- What is *judicial review*?

The Appointment of John Marshall

The Federalists lost control of both the executive and legislative branches in the election of 1800. Before leaving office, Adams took steps to strengthen Federalist control of the judicial branch. Oliver Ellsworth, the third chief justice of the Supreme Court, resigned because of health issues shortly before Adams's term expired. In January 1801 **John Marshall**, President Adams's nominee, was confirmed by the Senate as the new chief justice. Marshall, who would serve in that position for thirty-four years, delivered some of the court's most important decisions. His appointment proved to be one of Adams's most significant actions.

Democratic-Republicans tended to distrust the judicial branch because it was the least democratic of the branches. Some were unhappy that federal judges were appointed rather than elected and could serve for the remainder of their lives. But Federalists thought that having a strong judiciary was necessary to check the more democratic legislative branch.

John Marshall agreed with Alexander Hamilton, who called the judicial branch "the weakest of the three departments of power." Marshall looked for ways to increase the Supreme Court's influence. He unified the Court by having the justices hold private conferences to discuss cases and by having them issue one opinion, now called the majority opinion, to support each ruling. If some justices disagreed with the decision, they could write dissenting opinions. Before this time, every judge had written his own opinion.

Marshall also kept the justices out of political campaigns. Previously, they had participated in party politics. As more Republicans were appointed to the Court, Marshall worked to build consensus, or unity, with them regarding court decisions.

John Marshall

Fun Fact

In 1918 a $500 bill was printed that had John Marshall's picture on the front. The bill includes a blue seal and an image of Hernando de Soto discovering the Mississippi River on the back. Later $500 bills featured other individuals. Since 1945, the largest bill printed has been the $100 bill.

William Marbury

The Judiciary Act and the Midnight Judges

Less than a month before John Adams left office, Congress passed the Judiciary Act of 1801. It increased the number of federal judges, federal attorneys, clerks, and marshals. Adams filled the majority of those appointments with Federalists.

Because Adams appointed dozens of judges to full-time positions late in the night before he left office, these judges have often been called the "**midnight judges**." The Republicans later repealed the act. But Adams was within the law in naming the judges.

One of Adams's midnight judges was Federalist William Marbury. Though he had actually been appointed two days before Adams left office, his official commission (the document indicating his appointment) was not delivered prior to Jefferson becoming president. James Madison, the new secretary of state, refused to release the commission. Marbury sued for his job. He believed that Madison could not block him from receiving it.

The Supreme Court decided the case of ***Marbury v. Madison***. Chief Justice John Marshall realized that if he ordered Madison to deliver the document, Madison would probably ignore the order. This action would further weaken the image of the Supreme Court.

In 1803 Marshall cleverly wrote, with the approval of the other justices, a ruling that preserved—and even expanded—the authority of the Supreme Court. Although Marshall believed that Marbury should receive the commission, Marshall said the power to issue an order that it be given to Marbury was not one of the powers that the Constitution gave to the Supreme Court. Marshall ruled that the federal law permitting the Court to issue such orders was unconstitutional and therefore invalid. Thus in *Marbury v. Madison*, the Supreme Court established the principle of **judicial review**, the right of the Court to declare a law passed by Congress as unconstitutional.

Though *Marbury v. Madison* never granted William Marbury his appointment, it established the Supreme Court as the final judge of constitutional interpretation. Since this decision, the Court has ruled that over 150 laws passed by Congress are not constitutional. In addition, more than 1,100 acts of state legislatures have been overturned by the Court because they violated the Constitution.

SECTION REVIEW 8.5

1. What are the benefits of having judges who are appointed for life? What are the dangers?
2. What things did Marshall do to help unify the Supreme Court?
3. Who were the "midnight judges"? Why might they have been a problem for Jefferson's presidency?
4. What is judicial review? What court case established this principle?

CHAPTER 8 REVIEW

Making Connections

1. Why do you think Washington created each of the four cabinet positions?
2. What is the difference between tariffs and excise taxes?
3. What were the four parts of Hamilton's financial plan for the new nation?
4. Why did political parties form?
5. Identify the two political parties that emerged during Washington's presidency and the leader of each.
6. Which of the following was not an accomplishment of John Jay?
   a. helped negotiate the Treaty of Paris that ended the War for Independence
   b. was an author of the *Federalist Papers*
   c. negotiated an unpopular treaty with Britain
   d. negotiated a popular treaty with Spain
   e. was the first chief justice of the United States
7. What major political event was occurring in France during both Washington's and Adams's presidencies?
8. How did the British respond to the Proclamation of Neutrality?
9. How did the French respond to the Jay Treaty?
10. What two states passed resolutions against the Alien and Sedition Acts?
11. What amendment was passed because of the unexpected results of the elections of 1796 and 1800?
12. John Marshall served as chief justice for thirty-four years. Under which presidents did he serve? You may need to consult outside resources.

Thinking Critically

13. How were the beginnings of the War for Independence and the Whiskey Rebellion similar?
14. Why did many Americans feel little or no guilt about breaking treaties with the Indians? What should they have done?
15. Why is George Washington considered such a distinguished and respected leader in American history?
16. Should Adams have gone to war with France over the XYZ Affair? Why or why not?

Living as a Christian Citizen

17. The Founding Fathers looked to Proverbs 28:2 and Exodus 18:21 to establish leadership qualifications. Based on these passages, what does the Bible view as important leadership qualifications?
18. Concerning the judicial branch, the Federalists wanted broad laws that judges could apply to specific situations, and the Democratic-Republicans favored specific laws requiring judges to simply determine whether a law had been broken. If you had to support one of these groups, which would you choose? Why?

Terms to Remember

inauguration
cabinet
tariff
excise tax
national bank
Federalist Party
Democratic-Republican Party
Whiskey Rebellion
John Jay
Fallen Timbers
Proclamation of Neutrality
Edmond-Charles Genêt
impressment
Jay Treaty
Aaron Burr
John Adams
the XYZ Affair
Alien and Sedition Acts
Virginia and Kentucky Resolutions
nullification
John Marshall
midnight judges
Marbury v. Madison
judicial review

UNIT 3

Spanning a Continent

Settlers from Connecticut entering Northwest Territory after the American Revolution

- Second Great Awakening ca.1800–ca.1825
- **1803** Louisiana Purchase
- **1804**–**1806** Lewis and Clark Expedition 1804–6
- **1811** Battle of Tippecanoe
- **1812**–**1815** War of 1812 1812–15
- **1817** Construction of the Erie Canal begins
- **1820** Missouri Compromise
- **1823** Monroe Doctrine
- **1828** Tariff of Abominations
- **1830** Indian Removal Act
- **1836** Siege of the Alamo
- **1846**–**1848** Mexican War 1846–48
- **1848** Gold discovered in California
- **1850** Compromise of 1850
- **1854** Gadsden Purchase

CHAPTER

9 Growth of a Nation

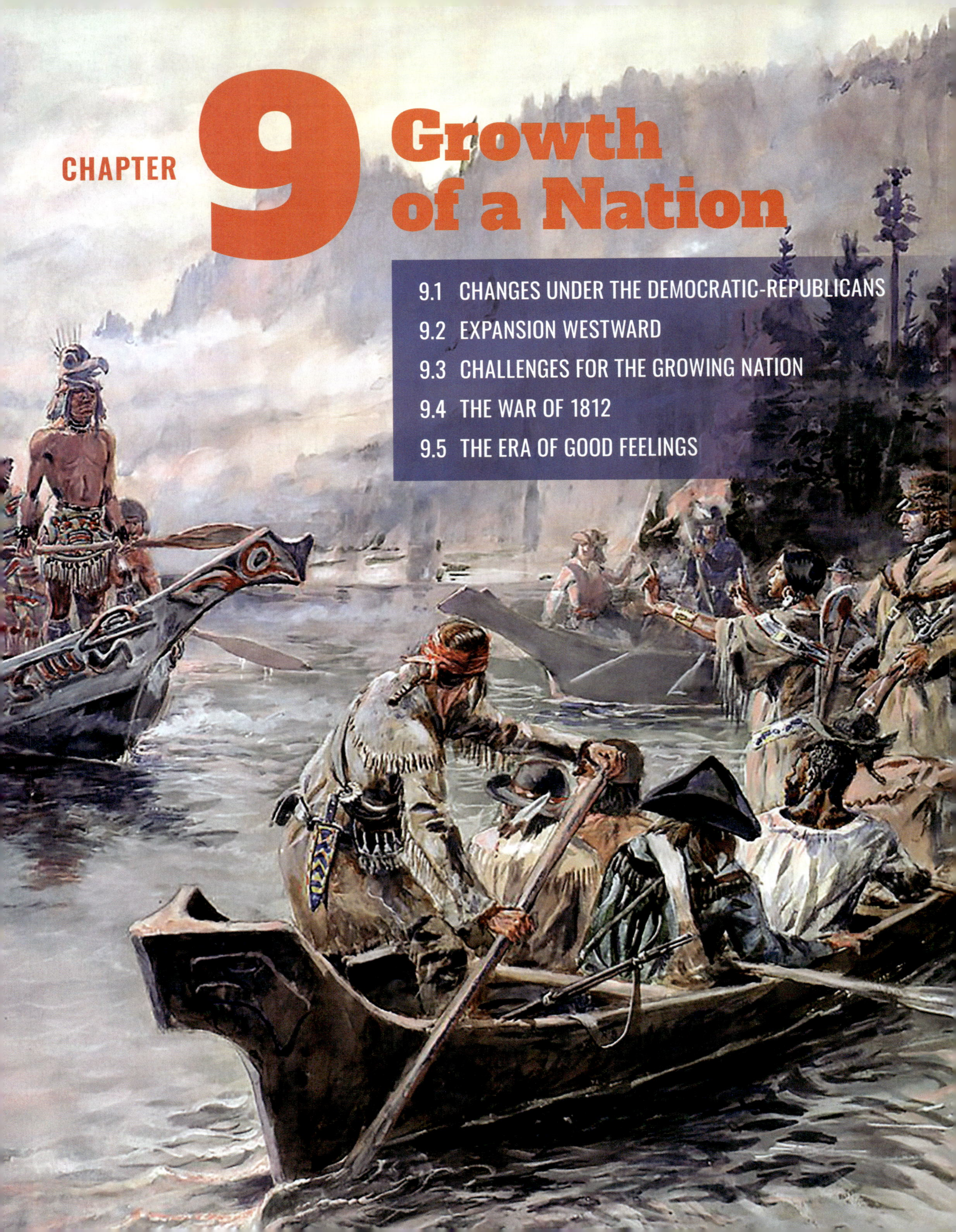

When Thomas Jefferson became the nation's third president on March 4, 1801, Canada was a British possession. Spain owned Florida and Mexico. A year earlier, control of the area known as Louisiana, west of the Mississippi River, had shifted from Spain to France. The new president faced the continuing challenges of dealing with foreign countries, both on this continent and abroad, as well as the demands of handling difficulties within the nation.

GUIDING QUESTIONS

- How did Jefferson's Democratic-Republicans differ from the Federalists?
- How were the Barbary pirates defeated?

9.1 CHANGES UNDER THE DEMOCRATIC-REPUBLICANS

What were the changes made by the Democratic-Republicans?

The election of 1800 brought the Democratic-Republicans, also called Republicans, into power. Their leader, Jefferson, was the first president to be inaugurated in Washington, DC, the nation's new but still-unfinished capital.

Federalists and Republicans differed in many ways. The Federalists, led by Alexander Hamilton, emphasized business. They believed that a strong merchant and manufacturing base was necessary for the nation to be free from outside interference. On the other hand, Jefferson's party wanted the United States to be a nation primarily of independent farmers.

The Federalists did not think that all citizens were equally good or equally able to participate in government. They argued that government should be managed by those with wealth and education. Most Federalists believed average Americans did not have the necessary knowledge and understanding to make governmental decisions. By contrast, Jefferson—an intelligent, cultured, and accomplished individual—defended the right of the common man to govern. His party believed people were naturally good and that ordinary people could exercise good judgment and make sound decisions regarding matters of government.

The Federalists, having seen the weaknesses under the Articles of Confederation, preferred a strong national government to advance the nation. The Republicans supported the principle that less government was better. They advocated a limited central government and believed that state governments could best handle many matters.

Both parties wanted leaders who would govern with the common good in mind, rather than personal gain; but they differed on where those leaders should be found. With the best of intentions, the Federalists overestimated the goodness of the upper class, and the Republicans overestimated the goodness of the common man.

Some have written that Jefferson's election was a "Jeffersonian revolution." Though the election of 1800 was indeed a change, it was no revolution. The Democratic-Republicans did not destroy all that the Federalists had done during the early years of the republic, but they did alter some of the practices they disliked. Control by the Democratic-Republican Party did signal a movement toward greater democracy. That change would bring both benefits and problems.

Thomas Jefferson 3

Born	April 13, 1743
Died	July 4, 1826
Home state	Virginia
Wife	Martha Skelton
Home	Monticello
Church	Unitarian
Occupations	lawyer, architect, inventor
Party	Democratic-Republican
Years served as president	1801–09
Terms	2
Vice presidents	1st—Aaron Burr 2nd—George Clinton

◂ (Opposite) Members of the Lewis and Clark expedition meet with Native Americans in October 1805.

▲ Monticello, Jefferson's home, located near Charlottesville, Virginia

Jefferson and Federalist Policies

During his first term, Jefferson grew in popularity. When he had an opportunity, he replaced Federalists whom he believed had abused their powers, including those who had enforced the Sedition Act. He pardoned people convicted under that act. Congress repealed the Naturalization Act and restored the five-year residence condition for citizenship. The Alien and Sedition Acts were allowed to expire.

Jefferson chose Albert Gallatin as secretary of the treasury. Gallatin and the president decreased the national debt by one-half. Republicans opposed a standing army and navy. Jefferson wanted instead to rely on state militias, which were cheaper to maintain because they served only part-time. Though not eliminated, the size of the nation's army and navy was significantly reduced. Federalists objected to this change. Jefferson used some of the savings obtained by cutting expenses to abolish the whiskey tax.

At Jefferson's request, Congress repealed the Judiciary Act of 1801. As a result, many of the positions created by that legislation and filled largely with Federalists were eliminated. Some Republicans then advocated using the impeachment process to remove additional Federalist judges. According to the Constitution, federal judges hold their offices "during good behavior." This means they normally serve until retirement or death. However, they can be impeached for "treason, bribery, or other high crimes and misdemeanors." Attempts to remove Federalists for political reasons failed. Only one federal judge was removed after he was found mentally unstable and an alcoholic.

Jefferson realized the wisdom of leaving some Federalist policies alone. For example, although he had opposed the founding of a national bank, he left the bank intact because it was working well. He also kept the Federalist plan for repaying war debts.

Although he had often denounced the growth of federal power under George Washington and John Adams, Jefferson began to believe that such power was not necessarily bad. As his presidency progressed, he increasingly used his presidential authority. He soon extended his reach further than the first two presidents.

Jefferson's RELIGIOUS VIEWS

As an Enlightenment thinker, Jefferson believed that human reason, not divine revelation, is the basis for knowledge. He rejected virtually anything that did not align with his view of reason. Those views affected his beliefs about Christianity.

Jefferson did believe that the universe was created by a supreme, intelligent being and that God was active in maintaining it. He believed in God's divine intervention in the lives of both men and nations. He also thought that there would be life after death.

Regarding Jesus, Jefferson wrote, "Of all the systems of morality, ancient or modern, which have come under my observation, none appears to me so pure as that of Jesus." Although he embraced the moral and ethical teachings of Jesus, he did not believe that He is the Son of God. This erroneous view of Jesus led Jefferson to assemble his own version of the four Gospels (Matthew, Mark, Luke, and John). Using a razor and glue, he cut and pasted various verses from these books, taking care to omit miracles and most mentions of the supernatural. He included only what he thought Jesus actually did and said, rather than what others in Scripture said about Him. He never published this edition; it was only for his personal use.

Many Americans have followed Jefferson's approach to Scripture. Jefferson wanted to live by evidence rather than by faith. But all humans are forced to live by faith. The Christian puts faith in God and the Bible. Those who follow the thinking of the Enlightenment place their faith in human reason. The main problem with Enlightenment faith is that it repeats the sin of the Garden of Eden: it rejects God's Word—the only completely reliable testimony in the world.

Defeating the Barbary Pirates

The small Muslim countries in North Africa known as the **Barbary States** demanded tribute (a fee or tax) from ships that sailed on the Mediterranean Sea. If ships refused to pay, Muslim sailors took the ships' goods and enslaved the crews. For years, the United States paid the tribute because it was cheaper than fighting a war with the pirates. Some nations could not afford the tribute, so they simply avoided trading in the region. Britain and France paid tribute and then tolerated the pirates because their piracy meant the British and French had fewer trading rivals in the Mediterranean.

When the Barbary States increased their charges in 1801, Jefferson refused to pay. The ruler of Tripoli then declared war. Jefferson sent Commodore Stephen Decatur to the region. In February 1804, Decatur boldly sailed into Tripoli's harbor and seized the American ship *Philadelphia*, which had run aground and been captured. Rather than let Tripoli keep the ship, he burned it. The war with Tripoli ended in June 1805 with the signing of a peace treaty. The United States agreed to pay $60,000 for the release of American prisoners, and Tripoli agreed to stop demanding tribute.

Although the United States no longer paid tribute to Tripoli, it continued paying other Barbary States. In 1815, the United States fought the Barbary States again. After winning the conflict, America ended all payments along the Barbary Coast.

▲ Burning of the USS *Philadelphia*

SECTION REVIEW 9.1

1. Draw a table with three columns and five rows. Title the second column *Federalists* and the third column *Democratic-Republicans*. Label the second row *Leader*, the third row *Beliefs about business and farming*, the fourth row *Beliefs about government leaders*, and the fifth row *Beliefs about the government*. Complete the information in each block.
2. Looking at the table you created in #1, which group's philosophy do you think is better, the Federalists or the Democratic-Republicans? Explain your choice.
3. List three changes Jefferson made to Federalist policies.
4. What two Federalist policies did Jefferson keep?
5. Why did the United States pay tribute to the Barbary States? Why did it stop paying? What was the result? How did tribute payments finally end?

9.2 EXPANSION WESTWARD

How did America expand westward?

GUIDING QUESTIONS

- Why did the United States purchase the Louisiana Territory?
- What were the dangers and benefits of exploring the West?

The Louisiana Purchase

The city of New Orleans was vital to Americans west of the Appalachians. Nearly half of American trade passed through this port in Spanish-owned Louisiana. In 1800 Spain gave Louisiana back to France, which had controlled the area before the French and Indian War ended in 1763. Though France had been an American ally that helped the United States win its independence, Napoleon Bonaparte now ruled France as a dictator. Jefferson suspected that Napoleon was planning to extend his empire to the Americas. Napoleon already had many troops in the French colony of Haiti. That position was an easy launching point for an invasion of North America.

In 1801 Jefferson told Robert Livingston, the American ambassador to France, to try to buy the New Orleans area. Although the French originally rejected the American offer, a series of events forced Napoleon to reconsider the sale. First, a yellow-fever epidemic occurred in Haiti and then a slave rebellion took place there. Napoleon decided to abandon Haiti and his plan for a North American empire. Thus, he now wanted to sell Louisiana to raise funds for his continuing conflict with Britain.

In May 1803, months after the Americans' first offer, the French asked Livingston whether he wanted to buy the entire Louisiana Territory. After negotiating, a price of $15 million was reached. Americans later discovered that the territory contained nearly 530 million acres, so the cost was only 2.8 cents per acre. Livingston nervously wrote Jefferson to inform him of the offer. James Madison called it "a truly noble acquisition." But the Federalists opposed the purchase. They worried that the inhabitants of New Orleans, with their different government, culture, and religion, would be difficult to add to America. They also worried about the spread of slavery in the new territory. The Democratic-Republicans, however, supported the purchase, partly because it provided land for American farmers.

Jefferson had mixed feelings about the **Louisiana Purchase**. Though he believed gaining the land was a splendid opportunity, he worried that the Constitution did not grant the national government the right to buy this vast area. Jefferson considered asking Congress to pass a constitutional amendment to make such a land purchase legal. The amendment would ensure the bargain and make the treaty explicitly constitutional. But Jefferson's cabinet warned him that the treaty had to be signed soon to be valid and that there was not time to pass an amendment. In addition, the American representatives to France worried that the restless Napoleon might change his mind about the offer.

Republican leaders in Congress told Jefferson that they thought the right to purchase land was implied in the constitutional authority to make treaties. Jefferson was forced to choose between two things he valued: strictly following the Constitution and helping America grow. In the end, he chose growth. At Jefferson's urging, the Senate approved the purchase and rushed the money to France. On December 20, 1803, the American flag was raised over the Louisiana Territory.

The Western Expeditions

The Lewis and Clark Expedition

Even before America purchased the Louisiana Territory, Jefferson wanted to learn more about the western part of North America. Jefferson asked his secretary, **Meriwether Lewis**, to lead an expedition to explore the region. Lewis chose as his co-leader **William Clark**. Clark had been one of Lewis's commanding officers during the War for Independence, and Clark's brother, George Rogers Clark, had served as a general in the Continental army. Although William Clark lacked a formal education, his wilderness experience and interests made him a good surveyor, mapmaker, and naturalist.

After the Louisiana Purchase, the project became even more necessary. Jefferson ordered Lewis to carefully study the geology, botany, and zoology of the territory. Lewis was also to gather information on any natives the expedition met, search for the source of the Missouri River, and report on any commercial possibilities. In addition, Jefferson wanted him to seek evidence of British soldiers or forts in the vast area.

Lewis hurried to Philadelphia, where he took quick classes from five leading scientists. He learned about geology, medicine, and how to use the stars to navigate. He even learned to perform emergency surgery. Congress originally approved approximately $2,500 for the expedition. In the end, the trip cost about $39,000.

Most of the party left St. Louis on May 14, 1804, five months after the United States had officially taken possession of the Louisiana Territory. The group of more than forty men included carpenters, scouts, soldiers, sailors, a cook, and two interpreters. York, an enslaved African American owned by William Clark, proved to be a key member of the expedition. Most Native Americans had never seen a black person and were drawn to him.

▲ Meriwether Lewis (top) and William Clark (above)

Dugout canoes were carved from a single, large tree trunk. A dugout with a seven-foot hull could weigh up to 2,400 lb.

One of the boats Lewis and Clark used was a fifty-five-foot keelboat (right). It could be sailed, rowed, or poled like a raft.

Hauling a dugout canoe overland was extremely difficult because of its weight and the terrain near rivers.

▲ Sacagawea (left)

The men followed the Missouri, Snake, and Columbia Rivers for most of their journey. They built Fort Mandan, in what is now North Dakota, and spent the winter of 1804–5 there. At that time, a French fur trapper named Charbonneau joined the expedition. His wife, **Sacagawea**, also came along. She was a Shoshone Indian who had been stolen from her tribe as a child. She served as an interpreter and occasionally as a guide.

When the explorers had no transportation and desperately needed horses, they met a group of Shoshones, including Sacagawea's brother, who was now a chief. They obtained much-needed horses from the Shoshones.

The expedition typically covered ten to twenty miles daily. The scenery was breathtaking but dangerous. Clark nearly lost his life when he encountered a bear that was more than seven feet tall. The men named it the "grizzly" bear. Near the end of the trip, someone mistook Lewis for an elk and shot him in the thigh; fortunately, he was able to continue the journey.

They built Fort Clatsop, near present-day Astoria, Oregon, on the Pacific coast, where they spent the winter of 1805–6. On their return trip, the group split to explore the two branches of the Missouri River. Lewis's group navigated the upper Missouri while Clark's group followed the Yellowstone River. The groups met on the Missouri near Fort Mandan. They completed the trip back to St. Louis on September 23, 1806. They had covered more than eight thousand miles in twenty-eight months. Only one man had died on the trip. His passing in August 1804 appears to have been caused by a ruptured appendix.

Lewis and Clark were celebrities in their day. They were famous, just as early aviators and astronauts were in the twentieth century. In its explorations, the team had discovered nearly two hundred plants

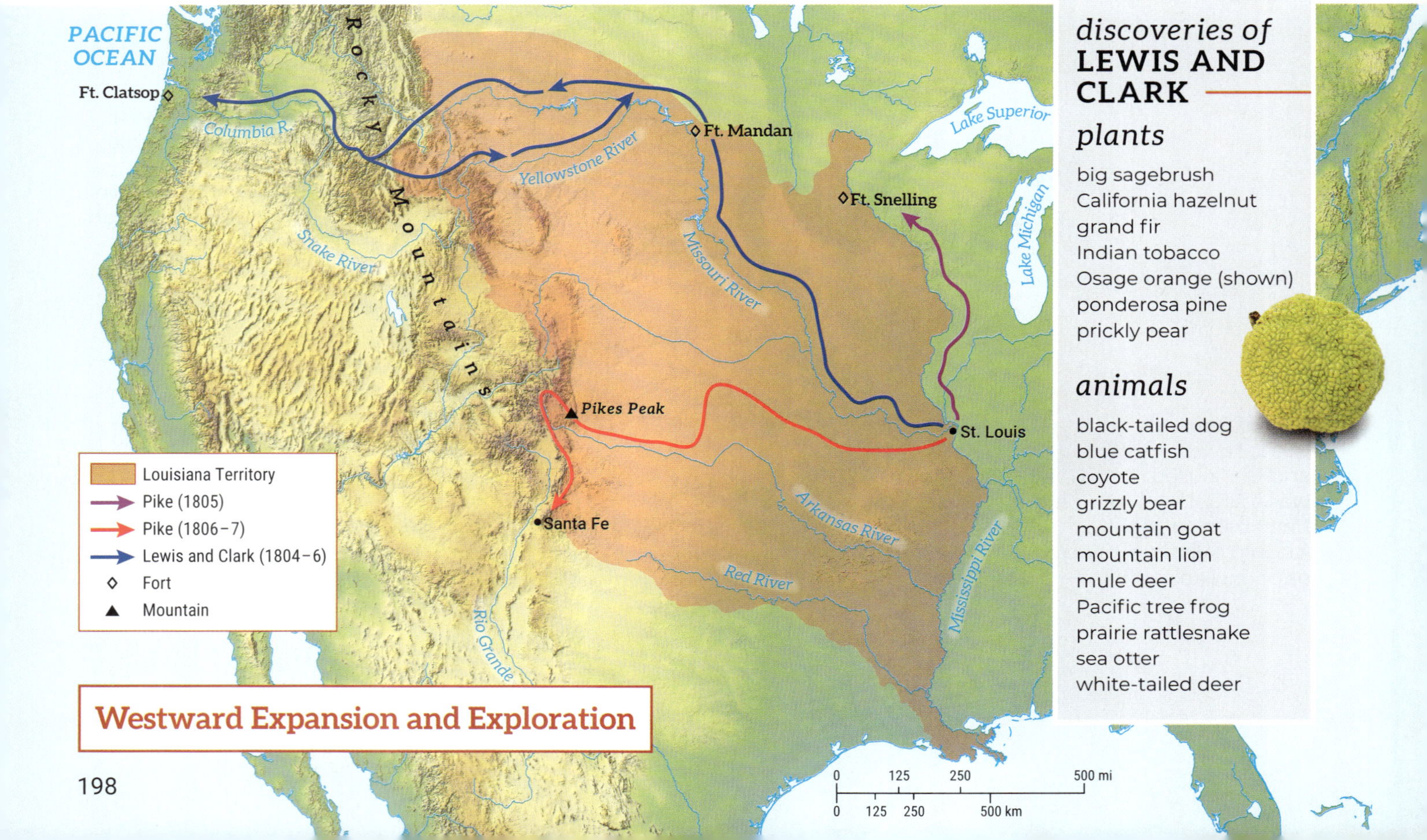

Westward Expansion and Exploration

discoveries of
LEWIS AND CLARK

plants

big sagebrush
California hazelnut
grand fir
Indian tobacco
Osage orange (shown)
ponderosa pine
prickly pear

animals

black-tailed dog
blue catfish
coyote
grizzly bear
mountain goat
mountain lion
mule deer
Pacific tree frog
prairie rattlesnake
sea otter
white-tailed deer

and more than one hundred animals. Clark used his artistic talent to draw the plants, animals, and Native Americans he saw on the trip. The men's journals stirred interest in western settlement. Lewis and Clark were among the last white men to contact western Indians who were still unaffected by the American way of life. They found most of the Indians to be friendly and curious. For good reasons, the western Native Americans would soon learn to be suspicious of American settlers.

The Pike Expeditions

Zebulon Pike led two expeditions westward. On the first, in 1805, Pike followed the Mississippi River in search of its source. He also let the British know that the Americans now owned the Louisiana Territory. However, he did not have enough military force to oust the British from their forts in that region.

During his second trip, in 1806–7, Pike traveled up the Arkansas River into Spanish-held territories. He explored the Rockies of Colorado, where he sighted the peak that today bears his name—Pikes Peak. He planned to use the Rio Grande for his return trip, but the Spanish captured him and some of his group. They were later released. Other explorers also visited the region in preparation for the settlement of its mountainous lands.

SECTION REVIEW 9.2

1. Why was New Orleans important to Americans living west of the Appalachian Mountains?
2. Why did Napoleon sell Louisiana to America? Do you think it was a wise purchase? Why or why not?
3. What did Jefferson order Lewis and Clark to do during their expedition in the Louisiana Territory?
4. Who served as an interpreter and occasional guide for Lewis and Clark? From what tribe had she been kidnapped?
5. What was Zebulon Pike looking for on his first expedition? What did he explore on his second expedition?

"AMERICA *the* BEAUTIFUL"

Katharine Lee Bates, an English professor from Massachusetts, visited Colorado in 1893 to teach a college summer session. On her train trip, she was inspired by numerous sites. After enjoying the view from the summit of Pikes Peak, she wrote a poem that would become one of America's favorite patriotic songs, "America the Beautiful."

▾ Zebulon Pike, accompanied by three other men, views Pikes Peak from a distance.

GUIDING QUESTIONS

- What challenges did America face at sea with the British and French?
- What difficulties did President James Madison face?

Did you know?

In 1801 Alexander Hamilton's nineteen-year-old son, Philip, died after being shot in a duel. It took place on the same spot where the Burr-Hamilton duel later occurred in 1804.

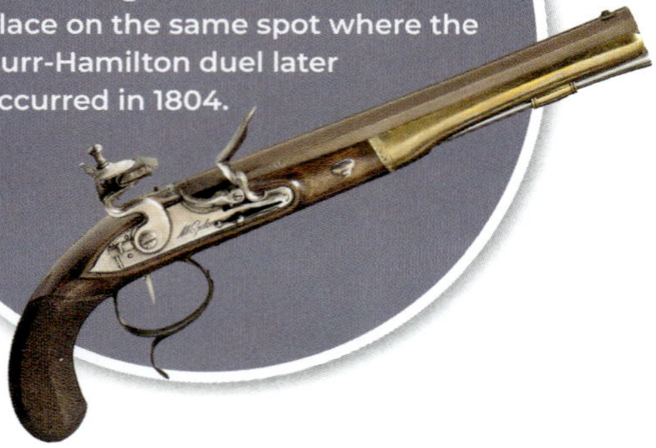

9.3 CHALLENGES FOR THE GROWING NATION

What troubles did America face at sea and with Native Americans?

As Jefferson was preparing to seek reelection in 1804, it became clear that he did not want Vice President Aaron Burr to be his running mate again. Burr decided to seek the governorship of New York. He lost the 1804 election there, partly due to Alexander Hamilton's opposition. After exchanging some tense letters, Burr challenged Hamilton to a duel. On July 11, 1804, Burr shot Hamilton in the **Burr-Hamilton duel.** Hamilton died the following day.

Jefferson was reelected as president. His new running mate, New Yorker George Clinton, became vice president. Jefferson won every state except Connecticut and Delaware but soon faced several new challenges.

Trouble at Sea

The first challenge involved the defense of neutral rights at sea. France and Britain were again at war, but Americans traded with both warring powers. Although Britain remained supreme at sea, Napoleon's armies controlled much of Europe. By 1807, the war was a stalemate. Both countries now tried to destroy each other's economy by destroying each other's trade. The United States was caught between the two great powers.

The British blockaded all French-controlled ports. In 1807, they declared it illegal for neutral nations to trade in European ports unless they first stopped at a British port for inspection. Meanwhile, France ordered a blockade of British ports. Napoleon announced that neutral ships trading with Britain or obeying Britain's requirement to proceed to a British port for inspection could be seized. The potential profits of trading were so high, however, that Americans risked defying both powers.

Both Britain and France seized American ships and their cargoes. In addition the British stopped American ships, as they had done in the 1790s, looking for British sailors who had deserted. Again, they not only seized deserters but also forced thousands of American sailors to serve in the British navy. The renewal of impressment outraged Americans.

The British learned there were deserters serving on the USS *Chesapeake*. When the *Chesapeake* left a

▾ Battle between the HMS *Leopard*, a British ship, and the USS *Chesapeake* in June 1807

Virginia harbor on June 1, 1807, the British were watching for it. The British *Leopard* fired on the ship when the American captain refused to allow it to be boarded. Three Americans were killed, eighteen were wounded, and the USS *Chesapeake* surrendered. The British forcibly removed four men who were indeed deserters.

The Chesapeake affair stirred a desire for war among many Americans; however, Jefferson took a more moderate course. Since he had substantially reduced the navy and the army to reduce his budget, he had few options. He chose an economic strategy. He believed that the United States should close its ports to all trade. He thought this action would make Britain and France beg for American goods.

Jefferson asked Congress for an **embargo**—an end to all exports from the United States. Congress agreed and passed the Embargo Act in December 1807, also forbidding American ships to import goods from Europe. Domestic coastal trade, however, was still allowed. Though some shippers turned to smuggling, most American trade stopped. The embargo was a disaster. It angered Americans more than impressment and the seizure of ships. Farmers, merchants, and others who depended on trade suffered. Resentment of the legislation was especially common in Federalist New England, the area most affected. The embargo hurt America more than it hurt Britain or France.

Both Republicans and Federalists attacked the embargo, and it was repealed shortly before Jefferson left office in March 1809. A new law was enacted that allowed trade with foreign nations except France and Britain. That new law was neither popular or successful.

Difficulties for James Madison

Thomas Jefferson did not seek a third term as president. His secretary of state, James Madison, became the Democratic-Republican candidate in the 1808 election. He defeated Federalist Charles Cotesworth Pinckney. Madison served two terms. During his eight years in office, the country continued to endure conflicts with Britain and France.

Like Jefferson and Adams, Madison hoped to avoid war. In 1810, Congress passed a new trade law. It permitted trade with both France and Britain. But, it also stated that if either Britain or France would repeal its anti-trade regulations, the United States would continue trade with that side and refuse to trade with the other nation. Napoleon responded by removing his restrictions in 1810. Thus, the United States resumed its embargo with Britain. Nevertheless, France continued to seize American ships. America was again upset with both Britain and France.

Native American Stirrings

In 1810 frequent Indian attacks occurred in the western Indiana Territory. Settlers blamed the English and Canadians for encouraging the raids. Though that was sometimes true, a much larger problem was the unfair treaties that Native Americans had been forced or persuaded to accept. Often one tribe agreed to give land to settlers that actually belonged to numerous tribes. Furthermore, a number of treaties were later broken by the white settlers. As a result, Native Americans lost millions of acres of their land.

Did you know?

John Adams and Thomas Jefferson died on the same day in 1826. Both deaths occurred on July 4, the fiftieth anniversary of the adoption of the Declaration of Independence. Adams was age ninety and Jefferson was eighty-three. Adams's last words were, "Thomas Jefferson survives." But Adams was wrong—Jefferson had died about five hours earlier, hundreds of miles away.

James Madison

4

Born	March 16, 1751
Died	June 28, 1836
Home state	Virginia
Wife	Dolley Todd
Home	Montpelier
Church	Episcopalian
Occupation	lawyer
Party	Democratic-Republican
Years served as president	1809–17
Terms	2
Vice presidents	1st—George Clinton 2nd—Elbridge Gerry

▲ Tecumseh

As a chief of the Shawnee Indians, **Tecumseh** saw the necessity of unifying the various tribes. He knew that individually the tribes could never stand against the United States. He traveled from Canada to the Gulf of Mexico in an attempt to organize tribes into an Indian confederation. His goal was to stop the westward expansion of the white settlers. His strong personality and persuasive speeches wooed many Native Americans to his cause.

Tecumseh's brother, Tenskwatawa, became a religious leader among Indians. Though he was once an alcoholic, he began urging the Native Americans to stop drinking alcohol, as he had done, and revive their traditional way of life. He warned that the Great Spirit was angry because many tribes had rejected their ancient customs. He became known as the Prophet. Tecumseh and his brother gained a large following and established a settlement called Prophetstown on the Tippecanoe River in the Indiana Territory. British troops and supplies aided the brothers in their efforts.

The governor of the Indiana Territory, **William Henry Harrison**, was alarmed by the growing influence and power of Tecumseh and the Prophet. Harrison met with Tecumseh on two occasions, but no agreement was reached. In November 1811, Harrison led a force of a thousand soldiers to the Prophetstown area while Tecumseh was away continuing to expand his confederacy. A battle erupted between the Native Americans and Harrison's forces. Harrison won the Battle of Tippecanoe, burned the town, and destroyed the supplies there.

Later, Tecumseh and the Prophet moved to Canada. Tecumseh joined with British forces in the region but was killed during the War of 1812 at the Battle of the Thames (October 1813). The Prophet eventually returned to the United States, living until 1836.

▼ Battle of Tippecanoe

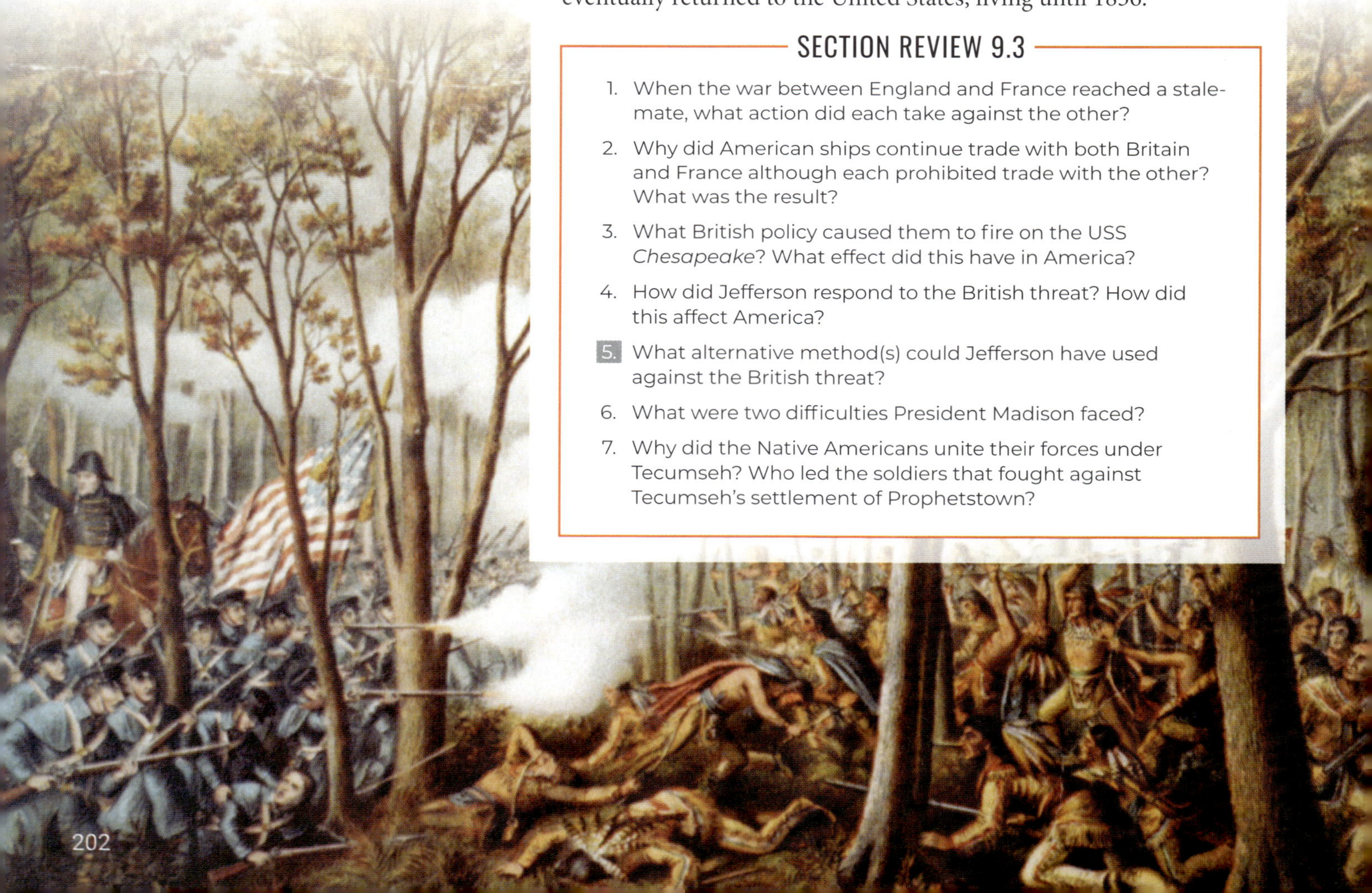

SECTION REVIEW 9.3

1. When the war between England and France reached a stalemate, what action did each take against the other?
2. Why did American ships continue trade with both Britain and France although each prohibited trade with the other? What was the result?
3. What British policy caused them to fire on the USS *Chesapeake*? What effect did this have in America?
4. How did Jefferson respond to the British threat? How did this affect America?
5. What alternative method(s) could Jefferson have used against the British threat?
6. What were two difficulties President Madison faced?
7. Why did the Native Americans unite their forces under Tecumseh? Who led the soldiers that fought against Tecumseh's settlement of Prophetstown?

9.4 THE WAR OF 1812

What were the causes, events, and results of the War of 1812?

War Again

Tensions between Britain and the United States continued to mount. The Battle of Tippecanoe had somewhat eased the fears of the westerners; but many did not believe that they could really be safe until the British were out of Canada.

The War Hawks

In the US House of Representatives, a group of western and southern members formed a coalition under the leadership of Kentucky's **Henry Clay**. They were united by their strong desire to expand America's borders and power. Called the **War Hawks**, these representatives supported war with Britain. They resented that nation's trade restrictions because they hurt Southern planters and western farmers, who earned much of their income by shipping goods overseas. Some wanted to seize Canada and thereby eliminate the British from further assisting Native Americans. Clay was elected Speaker of the House in 1811 and placed many of his supporters on important congressional committees. While holding these influential positions, the War Hawks denounced Britain and pushed for a stronger military.

War Declared

As relations with Great Britain worsened, President Madison asked Congress for a declaration of war against Britain on June 1, 1812. Among the reasons he gave for doing so were (1) Britain's continued impressment of American sailors, (2) its interference with American trade (including continued seizure of American ships), and (3) its encouragement of Indians to fight against Americans.

Debate about the declaration of war was intense. Federalists, New Englanders, and easterners generally opposed it. Many of them depended on the sea for their livelihood, and they feared a war would only disrupt trade more. Some Republicans also opposed war because they feared it might strengthen the national government and increase the country's debt.

Congress declared war on Britain on June 18. The House voted 79–49 and the Senate 19–13 to support the action. The conflict lasted two-and-a-half years and became known as the **War of 1812**. On June 16 Britain had actually decided to end their policy of searching and seizing American ships. But since there were no quick means of communicating across the Atlantic, word did not reach the United States until after war had been declared.

American Handicaps

The United States was unprepared for the War of 1812. As a result, the first year of fighting was a disaster. The Democratic-Republicans had largely followed a policy of small government and low taxes and had opposed having a large army and navy. As a result, the army had fewer than 5,000 men. There were an additional 50,000 to 100,000 poorly trained soldiers in state militias, but some states, especially those in New England where Federalists dominated,

GUIDING QUESTIONS

- What events led to the War of 1812?
- What handicapped America during the War of 1812?
- Where were the major areas of fighting in the War of 1812?
- What were the results of the War of 1812?

the ORIGIN *of* "UNCLE SAM"

The figure Uncle Sam is well-known to Americans. The origin of the term seems to date to the War of 1812. During the conflict, troops received meat from a supplier in New York named Samuel Wilson, whose nickname was "Uncle Sam." Each package of meat was stamped "US" to indicate it was government property. The troops joked that the meat was from Uncle Sam. That identification supposedly led to the widespread use of the nickname Uncle Sam for the United States.

Eventually, the picture of Uncle Sam was created. It became more and more popular with time. Today, Uncle Sam is usually seen dressed in red, white, and blue stars and stripes.

refused to commit their troops. The British army, though scattered throughout the world, had nearly 250,000 men. Furthermore, America's generals hurt the war effort. Most were older men who had not fought actively since the War for Independence.

The navy had only sixteen vessels. Britain, on the other hand, had hundreds of frigates, or warships, that usually contained twice the number of mounted guns on each vessel as American ships.

Financing was a problem too. The treasury had little money to pay for war supplies, and reduced trade had cut the income from tariffs. Many citizens, divided over the war, refused to buy war bonds to support it.

Communications was yet another problem. The West had few roads. With the coast blockaded and the West isolated, it was hard to move men and supplies to where they were needed. Sometimes the president had little idea where his troops were actually located.

Fighting the War

In the North (1812)

America's plan was to attack British-controlled Canada, intending to accomplish two things—eliminate British influence among the Indians in America and provide a new area for land-hungry Americans. Because there were nearly 8 million Americans and only 300,000 Canadians, many believed that victory in Canada would be easy. In addition, since some Canadians were French and were not particularly loyal to the British, Americans believed that Canadians might help them fight the British.

In August an American army on its way to attack the British in the Ontario region of Canada surrendered in disgrace to the British at Detroit. General William Henry Harrison's attempt to regain Detroit also failed. Also, Fort Dearborn (located in what would become Chicago) fell to the British. The United States had lost control of much of the Northwest.

In the first year of the war, America succeeded only at sea. American ships won two notable victories over British vessels. First, the American frigate USS *Constitution* defeated the HMS *Guerriere* in August, and then in October the USS *United States* victoriously battled the HMS *Macedonian*. Meanwhile, Madison was elected to a second term in the presidential election of 1812.

In the Great Lakes (1813)

General Harrison soon realized the necessity of taking control of Lake Erie, one of the Great Lakes, from the British. US Commodore **Oliver Hazard Perry** was given this task.

Perry oversaw construction of a fleet and met the British in battle on September 10, 1813. In the difficult fight, Perry and his ships defeated the British naval force. Perry wrote General Harrison, saying, "We have met the enemy and they are ours." As a result of the victory, the British abandoned Fort Detroit.

A month after Perry's victory, Harrison invaded Canada and won a great victory at the Battle of the Thames. As noted earlier, Tecumseh was killed during the fighting there.

After the victories by Perry and Harrison, the British decided to focus their attention elsewhere. They launched a three-pronged attack—on the Northeast, the Chesapeake Bay, and the Mississippi Valley.

the USS CONSTITUTION

In 1797 the USS *Constitution* was completed. It would become one of the nation's most famous naval warships. After a century of use, it was retired from active service in 1881. It became a museum ship in 1907 and is visited by thousands each year at its home in Boston harbor.

The ship received a nickname as a result of its battle with the British *Guerriere* during the War of 1812. It destroyed the British vessel, but sustained little damage itself. During the battle, some of the British cannonballs bounced harmlessly off the American ship. Though its sides were actually made of oak, it was soon called "Old Ironsides."

In the East (1814)

When the War of 1812 began, the British were fighting the French. By April 1814, Napoleon had been defeated and forced to give up his throne. At that point, the British were able to devote more time and resources to defeating the United States.

In the first prong of the three-pronged attack, the British moved south from Montreal, Canada. They wanted to conquer New York City and separate New England from the rest of the country. However, the British were defeated at Plattsburgh, New York.

In the second prong, the British sailed into the Chesapeake Bay, off the coast of Virginia and Maryland, to launch an attack on Washington, DC. They easily pushed back an inexperienced militia at Bladensburg, Maryland, on August 24, 1814. This victory left the capital open to attack. Madison, who had been present at the battle, fled to avoid capture by the British.

That same evening, the British marched into Washington, just a few miles from Bladensburg, unopposed. Madison's wife, Dolley, helped save important items from the Executive Mansion, the home of the president, before fleeing. British officers dined there on a meal that had been prepared for the Madisons and other government officials. Soldiers set fire to the Capitol, the president's home, and several other important government buildings. A heavy downpour later that night extinguished the flames and prevented heavier damage to the buildings. The Capitol and the president's house could be rebuilt because the outside walls were in good condition. Prior to the war, the president's home was sometimes called the White House because of the whitewash on its sandstone exterior; that name was officially adopted in 1901.

The War of 1812

British troops burning the White House

DOLLEY MADISON *in the* WAR *of* 1812

When the British neared Washington, President Madison told his wife, Dolley, to leave the city. She crammed two trunks with her husband's and cabinet members' papers and packed much of the silver. These things were sent to Virginia in the only wagon she could find.

The last thing Dolley took was a full-length portrait of George Washington painted by Gilbert Stuart. The portrait's frame was screwed to the wall, and the servants were unable to get it down. At Dolley's insistence, the portrait was then cut from the frame and rolled up. That portrait hangs today in the East Room of the White House.

"OUR FLAG *was* STILL THERE"

In "The Star-Spangled Banner," Francis Scott Key writes that as dawn was breaking over Fort McHenry, "our flag was still there." Mary Young Pickersgill, a widow, had sewn that flag the previous year. It was gigantic. She used three hundred yards of cloth to make the thirty-by-forty-two-foot flag. Each of its fifteen stars is twenty-four inches across; each of the flag's fifteen stripes is two feet wide.

The commander of Fort McHenry, Major George Armistead, had requested a flag so large that the British would be able to see it from a great distance. Indeed, on a clear day it was visible from several miles away. After the thrilling victory, Armistead clipped part of the flag to give away. More than a century ago the flag was donated to the Smithsonian Museum in Washington, DC. Millions of dollars have been spent to preserve the flag from further deterioration. It is protected from temperature and humidity changes and is viewed annually by tourists from around the world.

Did you know?

Two days before the United States declared war, Britain decided to end its policy of searching and seizing American ships. And two weeks before the Battle of New Orleans occurred, the Treaty of Ghent was signed. Better communication might have radically changed the events of this period.

The British next launched a joint land-sea attack on Baltimore, Maryland, the nation's third-largest city. The city was protected by **Fort McHenry**. The British navy began bombarding the fort on September 13, 1814, and continued bombing for 25 hours.

From aboard a nearby ship, **Francis Scott Key** watched during the night as bombs burst in the air over the fort. As the pounding continued, he anxiously strained to see what was occurring. As dawn broke, he saw the American flag flying proudly above the fort, signaling that the attack had failed. Key began writing on the back of an envelope the first verse of a poem. What he called "The Defense of Fort McHenry" is now known as "The Star-Spangled Banner." He wrote other verses after returning to shore. Having failed to capture Fort McHenry, the British abandoned the plan to capture Baltimore.

The third prong of the British attack came at New Orleans, the nation's second busiest port, on January 8, 1815. General **Andrew Jackson** from Tennessee rushed south to save the city. At the battle, Jackson's men hid behind thick cotton bales and other barricades they had erected. As the British marched forward, they were easy targets for the American soldiers, while many British bullets were absorbed by the cotton bales or stopped by the other barriers. The British suffered more than 2,000 casualties, while the Americans had fewer than 100.

The **Battle of New Orleans** was the biggest American victory of the war, and Andrew Jackson became the war's greatest American hero. Although neither side knew it at the time, the battle was fought after the War of 1812 had officially ended.

Battle of New Orleans ▸

Signing of the Treaty of Ghent ▸

The Treaty of Ghent

In February 1815, more than a month after the Battle of New Orleans, Americans learned that a treaty had been signed in Ghent, Belgium, that ended the War of 1812. Slow communications from Europe delayed news that the **Treaty of Ghent** had been signed on December 24.

John Quincy Adams, son of former president John Adams, headed the American delegation that concluded the agreement. The treaty failed to settle some key issues over which the war had been fought—seizure of American ships by the British and impressment. Nothing in the treaty addressed either. Basically, Britain and the United States simply agreed to stop fighting. Neither side was victorious. However, they did decide that officials would meet in the future to address disputes between the two nations.

Results of the War

The War of 1812 did have some important results. First, the United States received increased respect from other nations. These countries now realized that the United States had the ability to fight for what it believed was right, such as freedom of the seas, and to protect its own interests.

Second, the war inspired a greater sense of national pride or patriotism within America. Many Americans developed a stronger love for their country, and national confidence grew significantly.

Third, new heroes emerged from the fields of battle. The fame Andrew Jackson and William Henry Harrison received helped them later win election to the presidency.

Fourth, the American people developed more industries before and during the war. Because they could not obtain goods from England and France, they focused on making more of their own. After the war, their dependence on foreign countries diminished greatly.

Fifth, Napoleon's defeat in Europe and Britain's stalemate in North America ended the long struggle between France and Britain for colonies in North America and for supremacy in Europe. The war brought America nearly a century of freedom from European conflicts. This freedom enabled Americans to focus on their own affairs. Instead of fighting wars with European nations, they concentrated on expanding westward.

Sixth, the War of 1812 affected both American political parties. The Federalist Party, already in decline, lost the respect of many because it opposed the war. Meanwhile, the Democratic-Republican Party changed its stand slightly on some issues. Before the war, it opposed efforts to strengthen the national government. But after the war, some Republicans wanted America to maintain a stronger army, build roads and canals to improve transportation, and re-create a national bank (the first one had ceased to exist in 1811).

Results of the War of 1812

1. Increased *respect* from other nations
2. Greater sense of national *pride*
3. New *heroes*
4. More *industries*
5. *Freedom* from European conflicts
6. Effect on *political parties*

SECTION REVIEW 9.4

1. What sections of the country did the War Hawks represent? Who was their leader in Congress?
2. For what reasons did Madison ask Congress for a declaration of war against Britain? Do you think he was right to do so? Why or why not?
3. In what ways was the United States unprepared for war with Britain?
4. What was the only area of American success during the first year of the war?
5. List the three regions the British planned to invade in 1814. Where were they defeated in each area?
6. How did the White House get its name?
7. What treaty ended the war? What was unusual about the Battle of New Orleans?

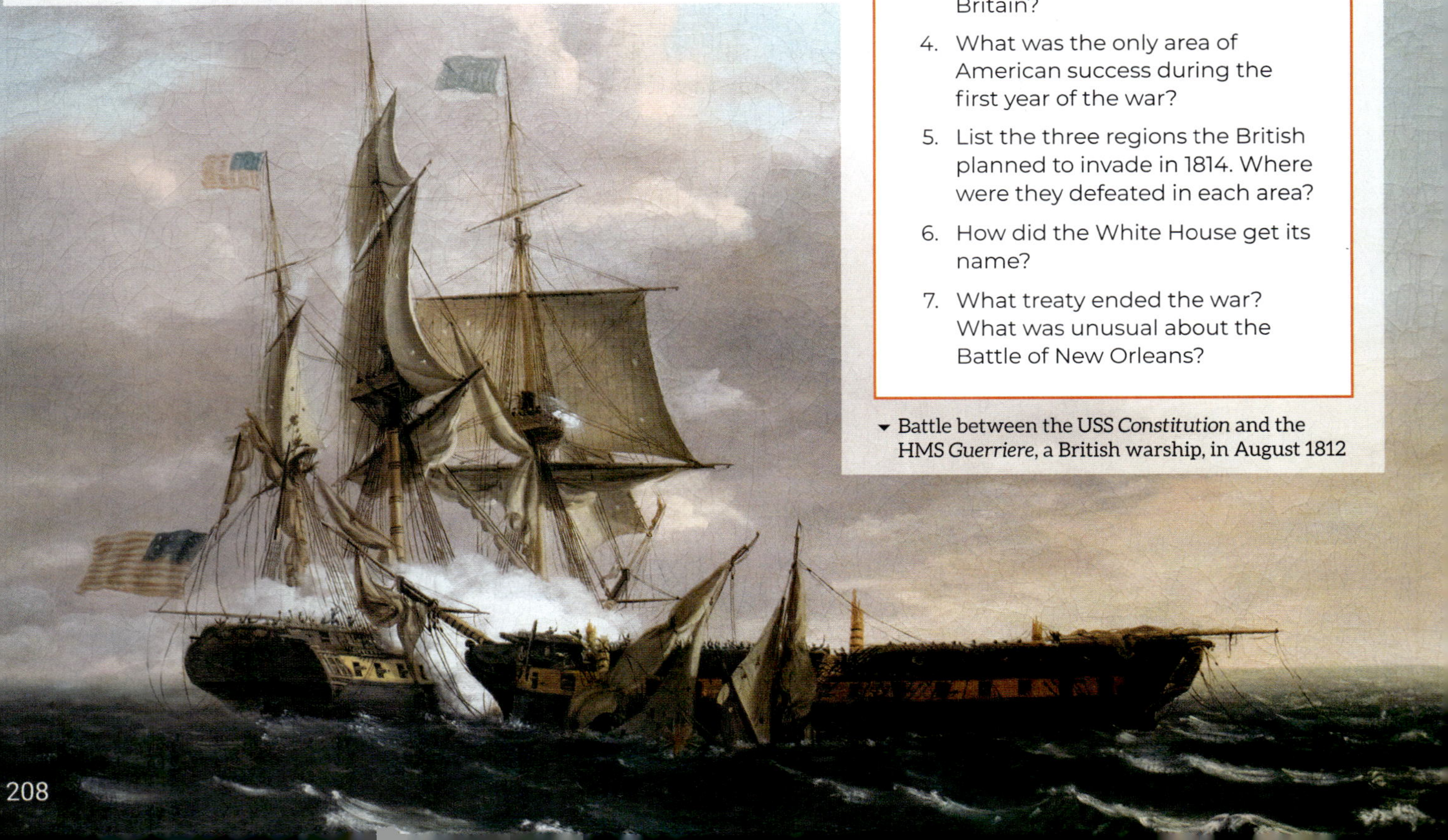

▾ Battle between the USS *Constitution* and the HMS *Guerriere*, a British warship, in August 1812

9.5 THE ERA OF GOOD FEELINGS

What was the Era of Good Feelings?

After the War of 1812, the United States experienced a brief period of harmony. No major international conflicts appeared to be approaching. Political rivalries at home were rarely intense. Sectional differences between the North, the South, and the West remained calm. Americans eagerly awaited their country's fiftieth anniversary. This was the state of America when the new president, **James Monroe,** came to office. A Boston newspaper called the time period of his presidency the "**Era of Good Feelings**." Although the good feelings would not last, America continued to grow.

The Election of James Monroe

James Monroe had served in Congress, as US ambassador to both France and Britain, and as governor of Virginia before becoming Madison's secretary of state in 1811. In 1816 he defeated the Federalist candidate, Rufus King, to become president. Monroe was the fourth Virginian to become president (of the first five presidents, only John Adams was not from Virginia).

One reason for the Era of Good Feelings was the collapse of the Federalist Party. Throughout the War of 1812, the Federalists protested against the war. In late 1814, during the darkest days of the conflict, representatives from the New England states—most of them Federalists—met in Hartford, Connecticut. The **Hartford Convention** opposed the war, and some of the more radical Federalists present hinted that New England might secede, or withdraw, from the United States. There was widespread disapproval of this meeting. News of the Treaty of Ghent and the Battle of New Orleans soon followed the Hartford Convention and removed much of the reason for its existence. The Federalist Party, which had been dying before the war, collapsed within a few years.

The 1816 election was the last one in which the Federalists had a presidential candidate. In 1820, James Monroe had no official opponent for reelection and received all electoral votes except one.

Monroe supported the Democratic-Republican ideals, but he also agreed with some ideas of the dying Federalist Party, such as recreating a national bank and supporting a tariff. He wanted the most capable men in the country to work with him. He chose John Quincy Adams to be secretary of state and South Carolina's John C. Calhoun to be secretary of war.

Foreign Concerns

Some of Monroe's accomplishments resulted from championing American interests abroad. With the war over, the United States faced a variety of difficulties in foreign affairs.

Florida

Florida brought the first challenge. Spain's power in North America had weakened. In 1810, Americans in West Florida (the part of Florida extending to the Mississippi River, also known as the Panhandle) had revolted against Spanish rule. They asked to become part of the United States. The US government argued that West

GUIDING QUESTIONS

- What foreign challenges did Monroe face?
- What was happening in America during the Era of Good Feelings?

James Monroe 5

Born	April 28, 1758
Died	July 4, 1831
Home state	Virginia
Wife	Elizabeth Kortright
Home	Ash Lawn
Church	Episcopalian
Occupation	lawyer
Party	Democratic-Republican
Years served as president	1817–25
Terms	2
Vice president	Daniel D. Tompkins

Fun Fact

In 1820 William Plumer of New Hampshire was the only person in the Electoral College who did not vote for James Monroe. Some accounts say that he did so to ensure that Washington would remain the only president to have been unanimously elected by electors. Other accounts say that it was because Plumer disliked Monroe. He voted for future president John Quincy Adams, the son of John Adams.

Florida was actually a part of the Louisiana Purchase and over the next few years took control of sections of the region. Spain objected but took no action. Some members of Congress, especially the War Hawks, had hoped that the War of 1812 would result in America obtaining control of all Florida.

In 1817 trouble developed in East Florida and the small part of West Florida still under Spanish rule. Florida had become a haven for smugglers. In addition, runaway slaves fled to the area by the hundreds. Some joined the Seminole Indians; others started their own farms, plantations, or ranches. Native Americans, and sometimes runaway slaves and smugglers, often crossed the border into Georgia and attacked American settlements. Then they retreated to Florida.

Secretary of State John Quincy Adams complained to Spanish leaders. He warned them that if they could not control their own territory, the United States would take action. When the Spanish did nothing, Secretary of War Calhoun gave General Andrew Jackson command of the Tennessee and Georgia militias. He ordered Jackson to go to the Florida border and stop any invasions. Jackson interpreted his order loosely and invaded Florida. He fought the Seminole Indians and the other groups that had attacked settlers in Georgia. Jackson captured towns and Spanish forts, and even overthrew Spanish officials.

Spain soon demanded money for damages and asked that Jackson be punished. Monroe refused. Lacking funds and troops, Spain decided that it would be better to sell Florida. In 1819 the United States made a treaty with Spain, purchasing East Florida for five million dollars. The United States kept ownership of the lands it had already taken in West Florida. The **Adams-Onís Treaty** also defined the Spanish boundary west of the Mississippi. Spain kept Texas and its other western lands.

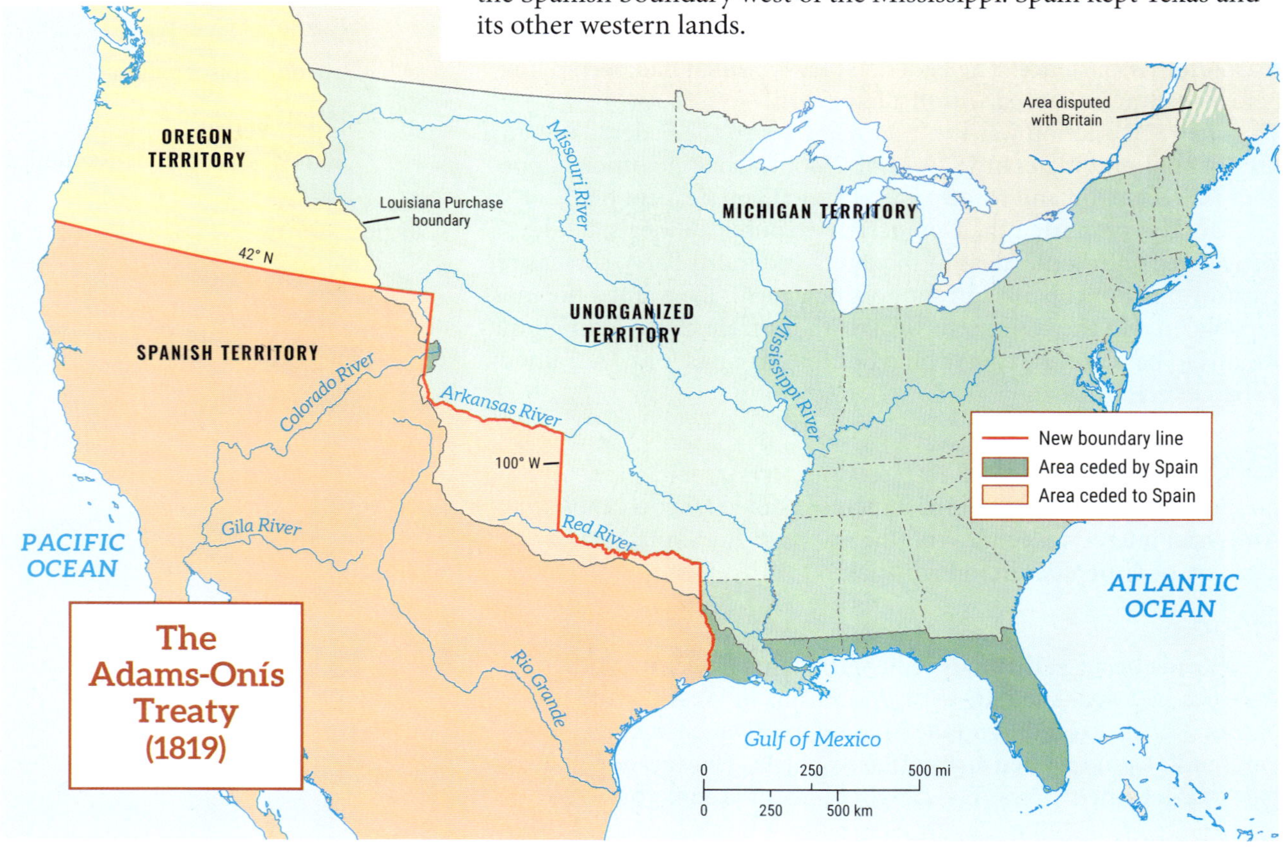

The Adams-Onís Treaty (1819)

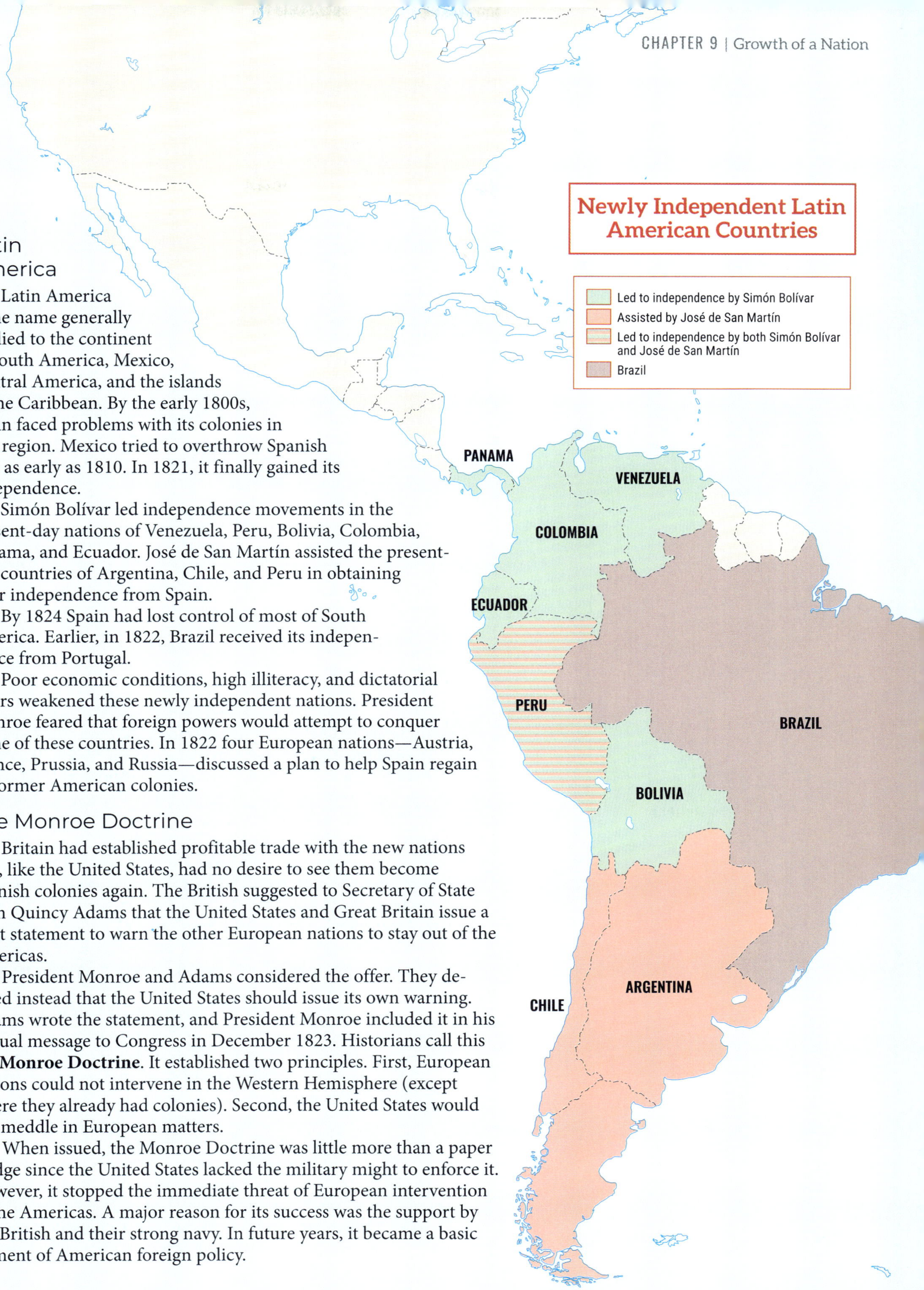

Latin America

Latin America is the name generally applied to the continent of South America, Mexico, Central America, and the islands in the Caribbean. By the early 1800s, Spain faced problems with its colonies in this region. Mexico tried to overthrow Spanish rule as early as 1810. In 1821, it finally gained its independence.

Simón Bolívar led independence movements in the present-day nations of Venezuela, Peru, Bolivia, Colombia, Panama, and Ecuador. José de San Martín assisted the present-day countries of Argentina, Chile, and Peru in obtaining their independence from Spain.

By 1824 Spain had lost control of most of South America. Earlier, in 1822, Brazil received its independence from Portugal.

Poor economic conditions, high illiteracy, and dictatorial rulers weakened these newly independent nations. President Monroe feared that foreign powers would attempt to conquer some of these countries. In 1822 four European nations—Austria, France, Prussia, and Russia—discussed a plan to help Spain regain its former American colonies.

The Monroe Doctrine

Britain had established profitable trade with the new nations and, like the United States, had no desire to see them become Spanish colonies again. The British suggested to Secretary of State John Quincy Adams that the United States and Great Britain issue a joint statement to warn the other European nations to stay out of the Americas.

President Monroe and Adams considered the offer. They decided instead that the United States should issue its own warning. Adams wrote the statement, and President Monroe included it in his annual message to Congress in December 1823. Historians call this the **Monroe Doctrine**. It established two principles. First, European nations could not intervene in the Western Hemisphere (except where they already had colonies). Second, the United States would not meddle in European matters.

When issued, the Monroe Doctrine was little more than a paper pledge since the United States lacked the military might to enforce it. However, it stopped the immediate threat of European intervention in the Americas. A major reason for its success was the support by the British and their strong navy. In future years, it became a basic element of American foreign policy.

Domestic Affairs

Although the United States avoided major foreign problems during the Era of Good Feelings, there were difficulties within the country that had to be addressed.

The Economy

Because of limited trade with Europe before and during the War of 1812, there was a greater demand for raw materials and farm products produced within the United States. The economic boom that resulted continued after the war. As farmers earned higher prices for their crops, more people went west and bought farmland. At the same time, other nations were expanding their production of agricultural and industrial materials. Soon, there was a surplus of crops and factory-produced items in America. The prices of farm products and other items began to drop.

Decreased prices kept many farmers from making a profit when selling their goods, leaving them unable to repay their loans. Land speculators (people who purchase land with the intent to sell later at a higher price) were unable to sell all their land and could not repay their loans. With these loans unpaid, people who had deposited their savings in banks lost much or all of that money (banks used the deposits from saving accounts to provide loans and normally made money from charging interest on such loans). These factors, along with others even more complex, led to a collapse of the economy in 1819. The economic crisis, or panic, became known as the **Panic of 1819**. Many people lost their homes, businesses, land, and savings. Many banks closed. The collapse was especially hard on southern and western farmers.

Did you know?

The American Colonization Society was a controversial group that helped freed American slaves move to the west African colony, and eventual nation, of Liberia. Its capital city, Monrovia, is named in honor of President Monroe in recognition of his support for that organization.

Slavery and the Missouri Compromise

One of the largest looming crises for the nation was the issue of slavery. By 1819 there were twenty-two states in the Union. An equal number were slave and free states—eleven each. Some free states had completely eliminated slavery; in the others there was a limited number of slaves, but slavery was on its way to extinction in those states. Slavery continued to flourish in the South.

As the nation expanded westward, Congress debated the future of slavery in the new lands. In 1819 Missouri asked to join the Union as a slave state. At the time the North had 105 members in the House of Representatives and the South had 81. Since each state has two senators, the slave and free states each had 22 members. If Missouri entered as a slave state, it would upset the balance between slave and free states.

Representative James Tallmadge of New York added an amendment to Missouri's statehood bill that prohibited the arrival of more slaves in Missouri. In addition, all enslaved children born there after Missouri received statehood would obtain freedom at age twenty-five. It did not free any slaves already in the state. Tallmadge delivered a passionate speech denouncing slavery as immoral and supporting his amendment. His remarks were republished and widely circulated. The amendment narrowly passed the House of Representatives but was rejected by the US Senate.

Coin commemorating the Missouri Compromise

The possibility of a compromise arose in late 1819 when Maine, which was then a part of Massachusetts, applied for statehood. If Maine was admitted as a free state and Missouri entered as a slave state, the balance would be maintained. Though some saw this as an acceptable solution, it left many questions unanswered. For example, would Congress permit slavery in the remainder of the Louisiana Purchase? If Florida grew in population and applied for statehood, would it be a slave state? Could the Supreme Court abolish slavery? The debates over these and other related questions were long and heated.

23rd state
March 15, 1820

Speaker of the House Henry Clay of Kentucky, a state on the border of the North and South, finally proposed the **Missouri Compromise**. According to the proposal, Maine would be admitted as a free state and Missouri would become a slave state. With the exception of Missouri, slavery would be prohibited north of the 36°30′ line of latitude, Missouri's southern boundary. It would be permitted south of that line. Congress adopted the compromise in 1820.

Emotions on the Missouri issue ran deep. Many leaders predicted that this was just the beginning of a greater crisis. John Quincy Adams wrote, "I take it for granted that the present question is a mere preamble [introduction]—a title-page to a great tragic volume." Jefferson said, "This momentous question, like a fire-bell [alarm] in the night, awakened and filled me with terror. I considered it at once as the knell [signal of disaster] of the Union. It is hushed, indeed, for the moment. But this is a reprieve only, not a final sentence."

24th state
August 10, 1821

The Missouri Compromise

The Supreme Court

The National Bank's charter had expired in 1811, and Congress allowed the bank to close. In 1816 Congress issued a new charter and created a second national bank. The number of state and private banks had grown during this time. Unfortunately, they were issuing their own paper money, even when they lacked silver and gold to back it.

▲ Money issued by the state of Vermont

Many states disliked the national bank, and some began to tax its branches within their states. They hoped that increasing the operational cost of the national bank would discourage people from using it. When Maryland tried to tax the Baltimore branch of the National Bank, a court case resulted that eventually reached the US Supreme Court. In ***McCulloch v. Maryland*** (1819), the Court ruled that a state cannot tax the federal government because the "power to tax involves the power to destroy." In the decision, Chief Justice John Marshall also noted that although the Constitution did not specifically give Congress the right to create the National Bank, it did provide Congress the power, according to the "necessary and proper clause" (in Article I, Section 8), to pass legislation to perform its duties. Thus, Marshall said, the National Bank was constitutional.

In other cases, Marshall declared some state laws unconstitutional. For example, the Court ruled in *Gibbons v. Ogden* (1824) that a state cannot forbid ships to operate in state waters if the ships are licensed by the national government. The case upheld Congress's power to regulate **interstate commerce** (the sale and transport of goods and services from one state to another).

SECTION REVIEW 9.5

1. Was "The Era of Good Feelings" an appropriate name for this time period? Why or why not?
2. Why did the Federalist Party collapse?
3. What treaty determined the southern border of the United States? Describe the treaty.
4. Why did Monroe issue his famous doctrine?
5. What two principles did the Monroe Doctrine establish?
6. Is it appropriate for a nation to issue a policy such as the Monroe Doctrine? Why or why not?
7. Why did the Panic of 1819 occur?
8. Can a state tax the federal government? What court case provides the answer?
9. Describe the terms of the Missouri Compromise.

CHAPTER 9 REVIEW

Making Connections

1. Why did Jefferson have mixed feelings about the Louisiana Purchase? What did he have to choose between?
2. What types of people did Lewis and Clark take on their expedition? How did York help the group?
3. What had happened during Sacagawea's childhood? What exciting event occurred later for her?
4. How many months did the Lewis and Clark Expedition last?
5. Why did Jefferson respond to the *Chesapeake* affair the way he did?
6. How did the embargo hurt America more than it hurt Britain or France?
7. What political position did Madison hold before becoming president?
8. Why did Tecumseh fight for the British during the War of 1812?
9. What did the War Hawks want?
10. Who opposed the War of 1812?
11. What were six results of the War of 1812?
12. What two future presidents were military heroes?
13. Which state was the home of four of the first five presidents?
14. In what election did the Federalists last have a presidential candidate?
15. Why was Florida considered foreign until the presidency of James Monroe? What future portions of America did Spain keep according to the Adams-Onís Treaty?
16. What Latin American nations won independence from Spain?
17. How did the support of Great Britain ensure the success of the Monroe Doctrine?
18. Why do you think John Quincy Adams and Thomas Jefferson were concerned about the Missouri Compromise?

Thinking Critically

19. Should the United States have stopped trading with Britain and France because of those countries' orders during their conflict with each other? Why or why not?
20. Why do you think America declared war against Britain but not France?
21. Do you agree with the statement from *McCulloch v. Maryland* that the "power to tax involves the power to destroy"? Why or why not?
22. What do you consider the two most significant events during the Era of Good Feelings? Why did you choose these two?

Living as a Christian Citizen

23. What were the provisions of the Tallmadge amendment to Missouri's statehood bill? If it had passed, would it have been just or unjust? Why? What does it reveal about the country at the time that this amendment could not pass the Senate?

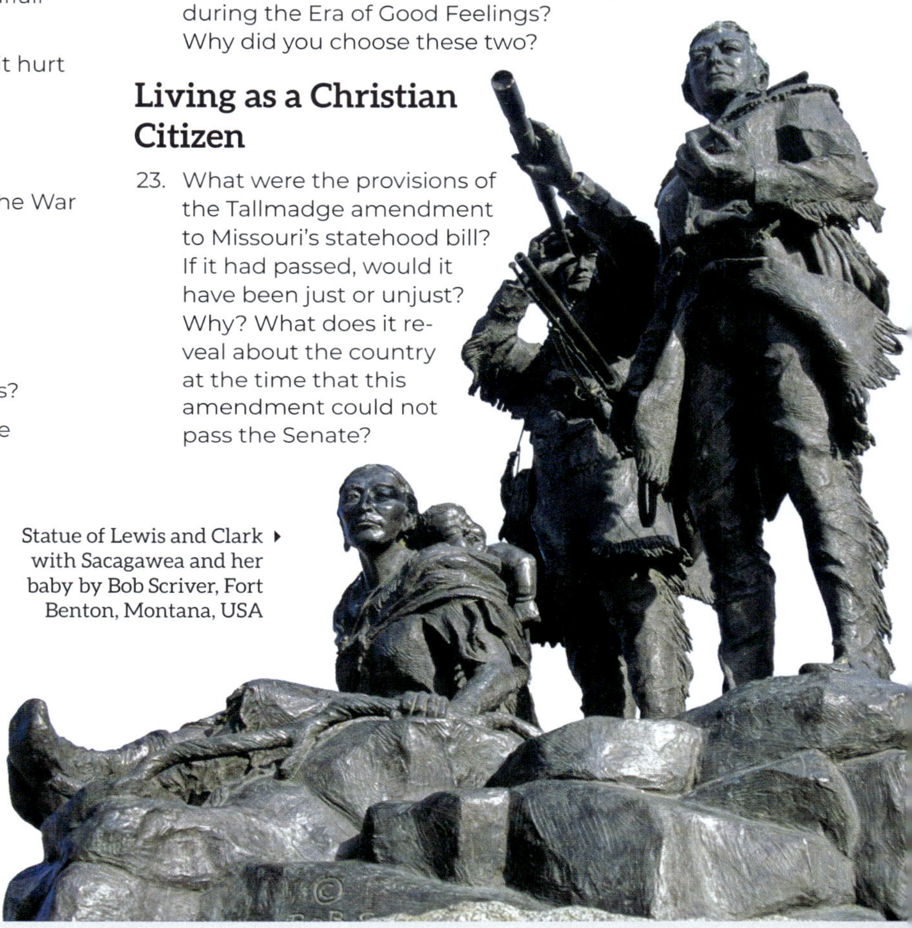

Statue of Lewis and Clark with Sacagawea and her baby by Bob Scriver, Fort Benton, Montana, USA

Terms to Remember

Barbary States
Louisiana Purchase
Meriwether Lewis
William Clark
Sacagawea
Zebulon Pike
Burr-Hamilton duel
embargo
Tecumseh
William Henry Harrison
Henry Clay
War Hawks
War of 1812
Oliver Hazard Perry
Fort McHenry
Francis Scott Key
Andrew Jackson
Battle of New Orleans
Treaty of Ghent
James Monroe
Era of Good Feelings
Hartford Convention
Adams-Onís Treaty
Monroe Doctrine
Panic of 1819
Missouri Compromise
McCulloch v. Maryland
interstate commerce

CHAPTER 10

Jacksonian America

10.1 AN END TO GOOD FEELINGS

What was unique about the election and presidency of John Quincy Adams?

Good feelings, whether between individuals or nations, are often hard to maintain. James Monroe and his successor, John Quincy Adams, soon saw national harmony turn to discord, ending the Era of Good Feelings. The problems of national government loomed again as the sections of the United States dealt with increasing political differences.

GUIDING QUESTIONS

- What was unique about the election of 1824?
- What difficulties did John Quincy Adams face as president?

William H. Crawford

John Quincy Adams

Henry Clay

Andrew Jackson

The Election of 1824

Candidates

From 1796 to 1820, the process of each party selecting a presidential and vice-presidential candidate was largely conducted by a **caucus**, a closed meeting of each party's members of Congress and other party leaders. With the collapse of the Federalists, selection of candidates began to change. As the 1824 presidential election approached, the Democratic-Republicans were the only political party. They were far from united. Though their caucus selected a candidate, other individuals entered the race as well.

William H. Crawford of Georgia, Monroe's secretary of the treasury, was the choice of the party caucus for president. He thought much like Thomas Jefferson. He disliked tariffs (taxes on goods imported from another country). He opposed federal support of internal improvements, such as roads and canals, because he said they would increase taxes for everyone but benefit people only in specific regions. He wanted to guard against the national government gaining too much power. His candidacy was hampered by the fact that he was still suffering from the effects of a stroke that had occurred in 1823. Some worried that his health problems would make it difficult for him to handle the rigors of office.

A second candidate, **John Quincy Adams** of Massachusetts, was a career diplomat who had served as Monroe's secretary of state for eight years. Kentuckian Henry Clay, the third candidate, was the Speaker of the House. Clay was a strong proponent of what he called the **American System**. The plan supported the National Bank, a high tariff, and nationwide internal improvements paid by the national government. Adams also supported the American System, though he was less enthusiastic about the tariff than Clay. Both Clay and Adams believed that internal improvement projects would help the nation grow and would also benefit their sections of the country—New England and the West.

The fourth major candidate was Andrew Jackson of Tennessee. During the 1824 campaign, he avoided taking a stand on specific issues. Jackson had been a lawyer and US senator. But he had won his fame fighting Indians in Spanish Florida, and he was the hero of the Battle of New Orleans. Because of his perseverance and determination, some of his soldiers stated that he was as tough as a hickory tree; thus, he received the nickname "Old Hickory." One of Jackson's slogans was "Old Hickory, the Nation's Hero, and the People's Friend." His humble background appealed to many Americans. However, some people distrusted Jackson. His harsh treatment of the Creeks

◂ Jackson's first inauguration, March 4, 1829

and Cherokees during the War of 1812 and his efforts to deprive them of huge sections of their land concerned a number of Americans. Others believed that Jackson had exceeded his orders when he was sent to fight in Florida (1817–18).

The House of Representatives Decides

In the election, Jackson received the highest number of popular votes, ballots cast by individual Americans, and the most votes in the Electoral College. He surprised many people with his level of national support, carrying some states from each section of the country. Adams received the second highest number of popular and electoral votes. Crawford placed third in the Electoral College, while Clay was last. But none of the four candidates won a majority of the electoral vote. In such cases, according to the Twelfth Amendment, the House of Representatives selects the president from the three candidates who received the most electoral votes. Each state, regardless of population, receives one vote during this process.

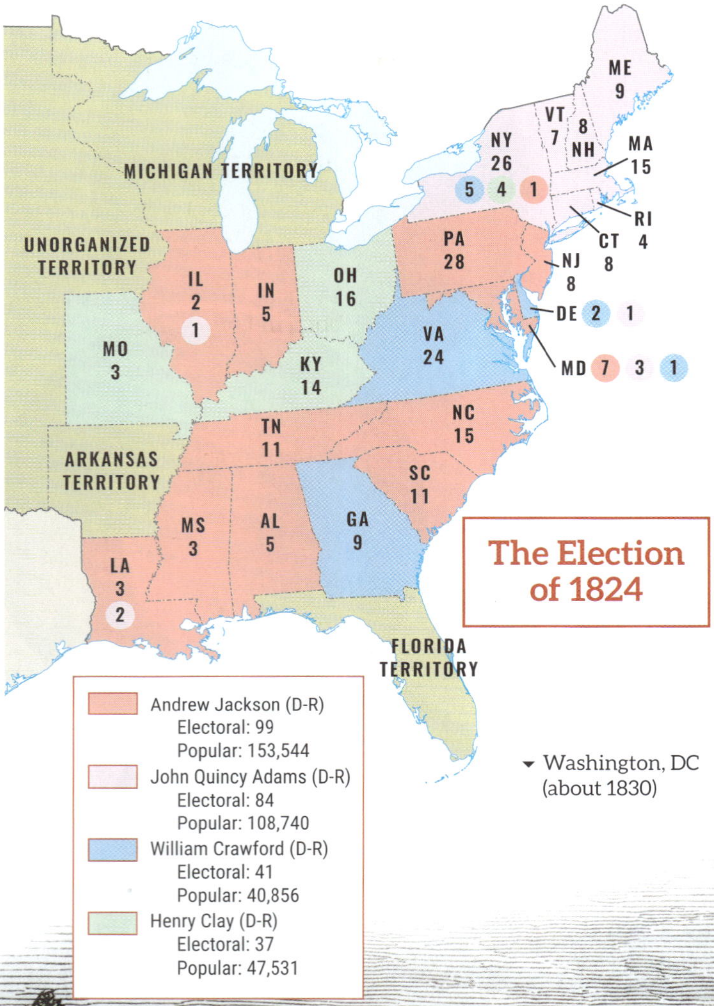

Since Jackson received the most popular and electoral votes, his followers insisted that the House had a moral responsibility to select him. However, the Constitution simply stated that the election would be determined by the House.

Henry Clay was placed in a unique position. Though he could not win the election, he could help decide who would. Clay's views were most closely aligned with those of Adams and he considered Jackson unqualified; consequently, he supported Adams. The House then selected Adams as president on the first ballot.

Jackson and his supporters were outraged. Their anger increased when Adams later named Clay as his secretary of state. Since four of the first six presidents had held that position (Jefferson, Madison, Monroe, and John Q. Adams), many believed that office was a steppingstone to the presidency. Jackson's followers

▾ Washington, DC (about 1830)

bitterly charged that Adams and Clay had made a "**corrupt bargain**." They claimed that Adams and Clay had made a deal in which Clay would support Adams for president in return for a high political appointment. Adams insisted that no such deal had been made and that he had chosen Clay because of his qualifications and experience. An infuriated Andrew Jackson later resigned his Senate seat and returned to his home in Tennessee. Almost immediately after the 1824 election, his supporters launched a campaign to elect him president in 1828.

John Quincy Adams

6

Born	July 11, 1767
Died	February 23, 1848
Home state	Massachusetts
Wife	Louisa Catherine Johnson, born in London
Church	Congregationalist
Occupation	lawyer
Party	Federalist, Democratic-Republican, National Republican
Years served as president	1825–29
Terms	1
Vice president	John C. Calhoun

Difficulties for John Quincy Adams

John Quincy Adams had been involved in public service for more than three decades before becoming president. His positions included serving as US ambassador to the Netherlands, Portugal, Prussia, and Russia. He was also a US Senator from Massachusetts and President Monroe's secretary of state. He was one of the best-educated men of his day and had a distinguished political record. But he seemed cold, aloof, and unexciting. He avoided distributing government jobs as rewards, even though other politicians did so.

As president, Adams called for the use of public funds to build roads and canals to aid the communication "between distant regions and multitudes of men." He also wanted lighthouses along the coast to aid shipping. In addition, he called for the construction of harbors, bridges, and the creation of a national university to improve the minds of Americans. He wanted to build an observatory for viewing and studying the skies as well. Many opposed his idea of spending government money for these projects, and others were more interested in their own sections of the country than in the nation as a whole. Some of Adams's critics made fun of his suggestion that Congress should promote art, literature, and science. Consequently, many of his ideas were rejected.

Shortly after Adams became president, he signed a treaty that forced Creek Indians to sell their lands to the state of Georgia and move west of the Mississippi River. After Creek leaders met with him and presented information indicating the treaty had been unfairly negotiated, Adams ordered the treaty to be rewritten. This action hurt Adams politically because of the large number of people who wanted Indians moved westward as quickly as possible.

One of Adams's goals was to expand American trade with foreign countries. He was able to reach numerous trade agreements with other nations that advanced this cause.

A Foreign-Born First Lady

Louisa Catherine Johnson was born in London in 1775. Her father was a Maryland businessman who lived in Britain, and her mother was an Englishwoman. She and John Quincy Adams fell in love when he was in Europe serving as a US diplomat. They married in 1797.

When Adams became president in 1825, Louisa became the first foreign-born First Lady. The second was Melania Trump. She was born in 1970 in Yugoslavia (her birthplace is now part of the nation of Slovenia). Though Mrs. Adams was a US citizen at birth (because her father was a US citizen), Mrs. Trump did not become a citizen until 2006 when she was in her mid-thirties.

The President Who Never Retired

John Quincy Adams's career continued after he left the White House in March 1829. The following year, he was elected to the House of Representatives from his home district in Massachusetts.

Adams was highly respected in Congress, was a skillful speaker, and was soon nicknamed "Old Man Eloquent." A lifelong foe of slavery, he forced the House to repeal a rule that had forbidden antislavery petitions from being submitted to the House. In 1839 he proposed a constitutional amendment stating that every child born in the United States after July 4, 1842, would be free. It failed to pass. As the slavery debate continued in America, he predicted correctly that a war would be fought if the country did not settle the issue.

Adams was involved in an eleven-year campaign that led to the establishment of a national museum in 1846. That institution, the Smithsonian, is named in honor of James Smithson, a British chemist, who had left $1.5 million to the United States for the purpose of expanding knowledge.

In Adams's last term in Congress, he served with a newly elected Whig congressman from Illinois, Abraham Lincoln. On February 21, 1848, Adams collapsed from a stroke on the floor of the House of Representatives. He was carried to a room nearby. Too sick to be moved, he died there two days later at age eighty.

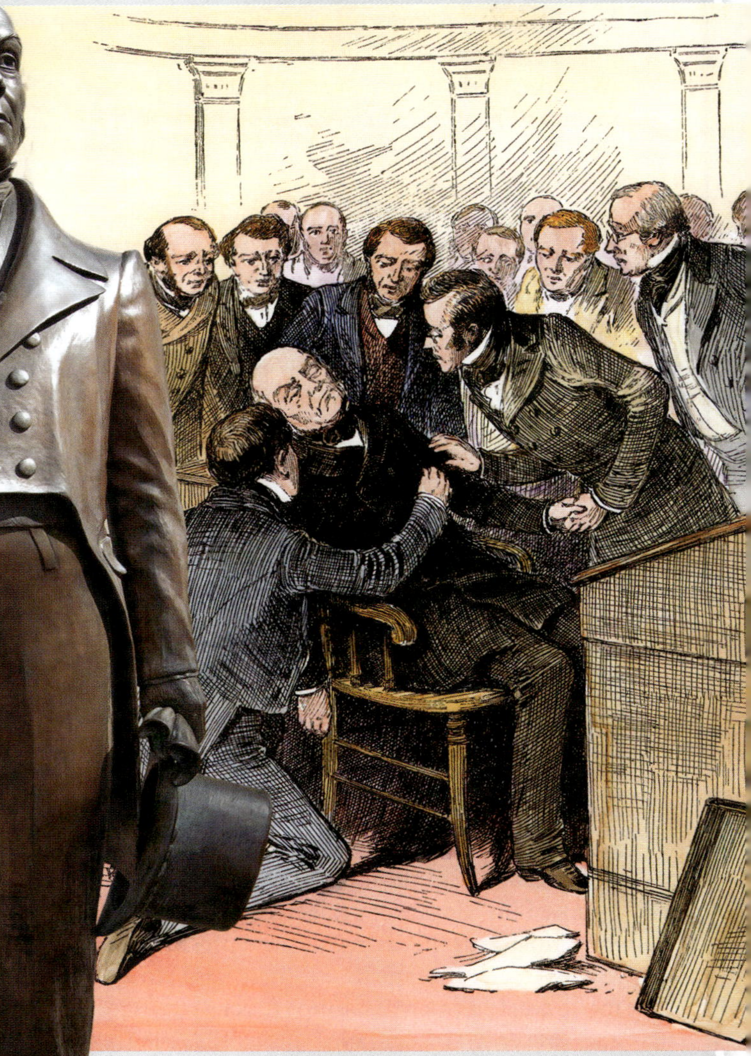

SECTION REVIEW 10.1

1. Why did Andrew Jackson lose the election of 1824 even though he had the largest number of both popular and Electoral College votes?
2. How did Jackson's supporters interpret John Quincy Adams's choice of Henry Clay as secretary of state? Why did Adams say Clay had been chosen?
3. What types of improvements did Adams want to make using public funds? Why were many of his ideas rejected?
4. How did Adams's reaction to the unfair treaty with the Creek Indians prioritize justice over democracy? Why should justice be prioritized over democracy?

10.2 THE PEOPLE'S PRESIDENT

What were the strengths and weaknesses of Andrew Jackson's presidency?

GUIDING QUESTIONS

- What methods did political parties use during the election of 1828?
- What is the spoils system?
- How did Andrew Jackson treat the Indians?

The Election of 1828

By 1828 the Democratic-Republican Party was split. Jackson's supporters retained the name, but later called themselves the **Democratic Party** (the same party as modern Democrats). Those who wanted Adams reelected formed the National Republican Party (different from the current Republican Party).

During the election campaign of 1828, many new techniques of campaigning were introduced. Parties used posters, banners, newspaper editorials, and testimonials to present their points of view. They also held barbecues, banquets, rallies, and torchlight parades to win voter support. The expansion of suffrage—the right to vote—was occurring as many states lowered or eliminated property ownership as a voting requirement. Largely because of the expansion of suffrage and the increasing population of the country, the number of voters more than tripled between 1824 and 1828. Whereas approximately 350,000 people voted in the 1824 presidential election, more than 1.1 million voted in 1828. By the 1840 election, the number of voters exceeded 2 million.

The election of 1828 was one of the most vicious political campaigns in American history. **Mudslinging**, or the process of spreading negative information about opponents, became popular. The Democrats claimed that Adams was snobbish and displayed fancy foreign manners. They reminded Americans of his "corrupt bargain" with Clay. Adams had installed a billiard, or pool, table in the White House. Since the game of billiards was sometimes associated with gambling, it was illegal in some states. Adams's opponents used this as opportunity to accuse Adams of both wasteful government spending and gambling.

Adams's followers claimed that Jackson was a murderer because he had killed at least one man in a duel and had sentenced others to death while in the military. They also accused him of adultery. Jackson had married Rachel Donelson Robards. He and his wife later stated that they thought a divorce from her previous husband had been granted. When it was clear that the divorce had not been finalized at the time of their marriage in 1791, they were subsequently married a second time in 1794.

Jackson won the election with 178 electoral votes. He was victorious in every southern state except Maryland (where he narrowly lost), every western state, and in Pennsylvania and New York. His appeal to the common man was successful. Adams received 83 electoral votes.

Unfortunately, Rachel died on December 22. Jackson loved his wife dearly; when he took office several weeks later, and for the remainder of his life, he blamed the National Republicans for causing her death. Although the candidates were not directly involved in the election mudslinging, they did not use their influence to try to stop it.

Andrew Jackson

7

Born	March 15, 1767
Died	June 8, 1845
Home state	South Carolina/North Carolina border (He claimed South Carolina); from Tennessee at the time of presidency
Wife	Rachel Donelson Robards
Home	The Hermitage
Church	Presbyterian
Occupations	lawyer, planter, soldier
Party	Democrat
Years served as president	1829–37
Terms	2
Vice presidents	1st—John C. Calhoun 2nd—Martin Van Buren

Rachel Jackson

Andrew Jackson presented himself as the champion of the common man. He placed great trust in popular opinion, and he made changes that he believed the people wanted. These changes represented a shift toward democracy. Not all leaders agreed that more democracy was good. Many worried that some voters would be easily influenced by politicians who made promises merely to win elections rather than by focusing on what was best for the country.

Jackson used the powers of the presidency more than anyone else before him. He made friends—and enemies—easily. He turned his thoughts into actions so swiftly that he sometimes seemed reckless and unthinking. His short temper, which had been evident throughout his life, continued when he occupied the White House.

Andrew Jackson

Andrew Jackson's mansion outside of Nashville, Tennessee, is very different from the home in which he was born. Jackson's rise from a log cabin to his stately home, the Hermitage, represents the many hopes and dreams that Americans of his day had for the future. Like Jackson, they wanted the opportunity to improve themselves and their country. Many readily supported him, partly because of his humble background.

Jackson was born in a log cabin on the border of North and South Carolina in 1767. His parents had moved to America from Ireland two years earlier. His father died three weeks before Andrew's birth. As a child, Jackson was scarred by the violence in the South that occurred in the War for Independence. One of his brothers died during the war. Later in the war, another brother died from smallpox contracted as a prisoner of war, and his mother died from cholera, an intestinal disease, after nursing sick soldiers. At fourteen years old, Jackson was entirely on his own.

Embittered by the experiences of his early years, Jackson lived a wild life for a time. Eventually, however, he studied law and moved to Tennessee. There he became an attorney, judge, land speculator, politician, Indian fighter, and planter. He won national fame as the commander at the Battle of New Orleans during the War of 1812.

Jackson was the first president from a state west of the original thirteen states and the first president from a poor family. But he was not the crude frontiersman that his political enemies claimed. He owned much land and was one of the richest planters in Tennessee, yet he championed the causes of the common people.

▾ A small portion of the crowd attending Jackson's first inauguration

Jackson soon became a symbol of the age. He embodied many American values. First, he was a determined individualist. His persistence and boldness were evident throughout his life. Second, he believed that liberty was necessary for growth and prosperity. Sadly, liberty for white Americans often came at the expense of American Indians and African Americans. Several times, Jackson made or supported unjust and illegal treaties that sought to remove Indians from their lands. He also owned more than a hundred slaves. Third, Jackson's rise from poverty demonstrated that powerful leaders can overcome difficult conditions.

Although Jackson exemplified American values, he often showed a less admirable side. To expand the prospects of some Americans, he took advantage of others. Jackson's presidency proved to be good for the nation in many ways but harmful in a number of others.

Jackson and the Spoils System

At the beginning of his administration, Jackson replaced hundreds of government workers with his followers. The act of distributing government jobs to loyal followers is known as the **spoils system**. The spoils system was not new. Earlier officials had often replaced workers who retired or died with supporters (though John Quincy Adams was known for placing a strong emphasis on choosing workers based on their merits). Jackson, however, took the step of removing some government workers from their positions and replacing them with his supporters.

In effect, the spoils system was a way to eliminate officials who might not support the new president. Jackson and his followers defended the system, claiming that loyal workers would do a better job than uncaring ones. Jackson also believed that giving new people jobs gave the government fresh vigor and provided more people a chance to see how government really functioned. This knowledge, he argued, would make them more useful citizens. In reality, the spoils system gave the party in power more political strength.

Despite Jackson's arguments, the spoils system had several disadvantages. It did not encourage efficiency or ensure that only highly qualified workers were hired. It sometimes caused corruption as some people paid bribes to get well-paying jobs. It also aided the growth of **political machines**, organized groups of politicians who sought to control the government. These political machines used their power to keep their members in office and to gain profits from public funds. The politicians in these machines often joined parties not to give but to get.

▲ In this cartoon, Andrew Jackson is shown riding a pig. The statue is entitled "To the Victors Belong the Spoils," meaning that those who won elections could distribute government jobs to supporters.

The effects of the spoils system were mixed. Most of the government jobs in the Jacksonian era did not require special skills or a high level of training. Many of the common people to whom Jackson gave offices had the qualities of good frontiersmen: determination, honesty, hard work, and common sense. Unfortunately, several of Jackson's appointees brought scandal to his presidency by their weak morals and character. Though Jackson replaced only nine percent of government officials in his first year in office and twenty percent in his entire first term, some say he set an unwise precedent, or example. Other presidents extended the system. In 1883 Congress sought to reform the process of filling government positions by adopting new laws.

Jackson also appointed cabinet members based on their party loyalty. Although Jackson had a formally appointed cabinet, he rarely consulted it as a group. Instead, he worked informally with another group of men who were his close friends. These men became known as Jackson's "**Kitchen Cabinet**" because they supposedly slipped into the White House through the kitchen.

▼ This cartoon of Jackson's Kitchen Cabinet implies that the group had frequent disagreements.

Sequoyah: Cherokee Scholar

One of the most remarkable Indians of this period was not a tribal chieftain. Though he fought in the US Army in the War of 1812, this individual is not remembered for his service as a warrior. Instead, he is remembered as a scholar.

As a silversmith, Sequoyah had regular contact with settlers as well as his Cherokee tribesmen. He was impressed by the English system of writing. Since the Cherokees had no written language, he decided to develop a Cherokee alphabet. Between 1809 and 1821, he created a system of 86 characters or letters. Using his alphabet, Sequoyah taught many Cherokees to read and write.

Sequoyah has been memorialized in many ways. Schools in various states bear his name. In 1980 the United States Postal Service issued a stamp to recognize his contributions. The giant sequoias, massive trees in California, appear to be named in his honor (Sequoia is the Latin feminine form of Sequoyah).

Jackson and the Indians

As American settlers continued their movement westward from the original thirteen states, many Indian tribes were still located east of the Mississippi River. Many of those settlers wanted to remove the Indians from those lands. Jackson agreed with this view and acted on it—with tragic results.

Relations with the Cherokees

In the late 1820s, the Creeks, Chickasaws, Choctaws, Seminoles, and **Cherokees** still owned significant portions of land in the eastern United States. The Creeks lived in parts of Alabama and Georgia. The lands of the Chickasaws and Choctaws covered much of the state of Mississippi. The Seminoles were located in Florida. The Cherokees' land covered parts of North Carolina, South Carolina, Tennessee, Georgia, and Alabama.

Two primary opinions existed among Americans about what should be done with the Indians. Many believed that the Indians should be moved west of the Mississippi to lands set aside for them, where they could preserve their unity and their way of life. Supporters of this view said it was dangerous for the United States to allow the Indians to live among Americans. They feared that if the United States were attacked, the Indians might side with America's enemies. This was the view supported by Andrew Jackson. Other Americans held a different opinion. They thought the Indians should be educated and taught to live like white Americans so that someday they could become US citizens. They believed only Indians who voluntarily agreed to do so should move west of the Mississippi River. James Monroe and John Quincy Adams generally supported this view.

The Cherokee were not a military threat to the United States. In fact, after the Americans won independence from Britain, the Cherokee made a peace treaty with the United States. They also helped Andrew Jackson defeat the Red Stick Creeks in the War of 1812.

The Cherokee also adopted many American customs. In the early 1820s one of their tribesmen, Sequoyah, developed a writing system for them. This system enabled them to print a newspaper. In 1827 they wrote a constitution for their nation that was modeled on the US Constitution. In addition, the Cherokee built towns and farms and developed trading relationships with Americans. Cherokees were also interested in Christian teachings. Many of them converted to Christianity and established churches in their towns.

Nevertheless, in 1828 the Georgia legislature passed a law placing Cherokee lands under the state's laws. This new law violated federal treaties that the United States had made with the Cherokee. When Jackson became president, he supported the law because he believed that the Indians were "subjects of the United States." Yet the United States signed almost one hundred treaties with Indian tribes during Jackson's presidency, showing that the government viewed the Indian tribes as foreign nations.

In 1829, gold was discovered on Cherokee land in Georgia, and prospectors quickly moved to the area. Jackson withdrew federal troops assigned to protect Cherokee borders, asserting that the only way to protect the Cherokees was to move them west. In 1830 Congress narrowly passed and Jackson signed the **Indian Removal Act**. The bill said that Indians who left their lands east of the Mississippi would be given lands west of the river. It also stated that the national government would pay the costs of moving and the costs of the first year of settlement. The bill did not force the Indians to move, but Jackson said that the United States would no longer honor treaties that promised the Indians protection from trespassers.

The military succeeded in removing most of the tribes by 1833. The Creeks, Choctaws, and Chickasaws moved to lands west of the Mississippi River. But the Cherokees refused to surrender their lands. Christian missionaries to the Indians were their strongest defenders. The American Board of Commissioners for Foreign Missions supported many of these missionaries. One of the board's leaders petitioned Congress and wrote many newspaper articles in support of the Cherokees' rights.

In response, the Georgia legislature passed a law targeting missionaries. It prohibited them from living among the Cherokee unless they affirmed the supremacy of Georgia's laws over the Cherokee and obtained a state license to live there. Several missionaries were arrested for continuing their ministry among the Cherokee. All were convicted and sentenced to four years of hard labor at the state prison. Two of those convicted, Samuel Worcester and Elizur Butler, appealed to the US Supreme Court, and the Court ruled in favor of the missionaries in 1832. In *Worcester v. Georgia*, Chief Justice John Marshall stated that Georgia had no right to interfere with the Cherokee, that they should be treated as an independent nation, and that they were not subject to Georgia laws. But Georgia and President Jackson ignored the Court. Jackson reportedly said, "John Marshall has made his decision. Now let him enforce it."

▲ Cherokee leaders regularly met at the Council House in their capital city in North Georgia. This is a replica of that building.

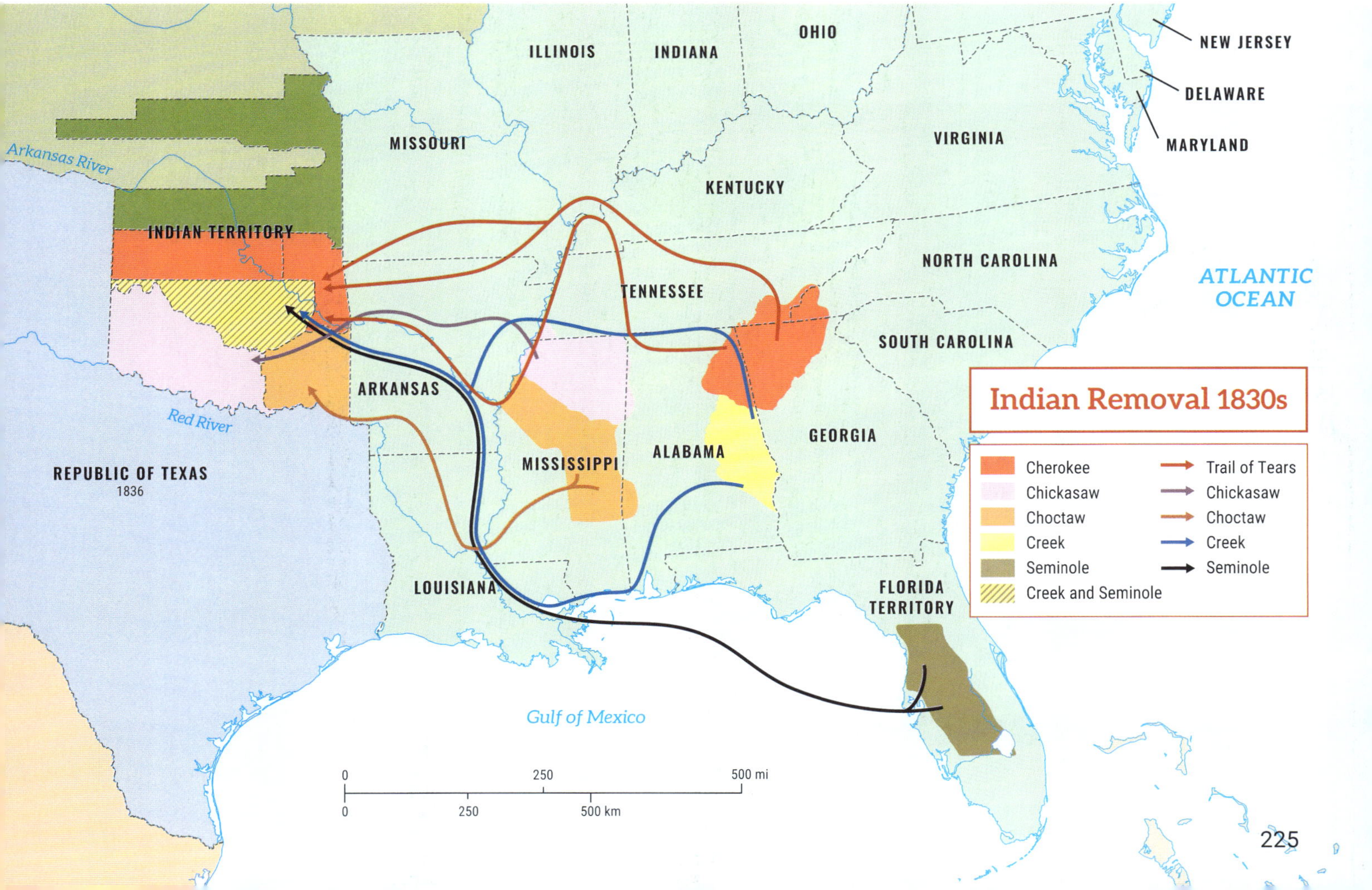

ADAMS on INDIAN REMOVAL

When John Quincy Adams became president, he was troubled about how to handle Indian matters. During his four years as president, more than thirty treaties were concluded with Indian nations. In many of them, Indians surrendered control of their land. By the third year of his presidency, Adams expressed in his personal writings a deep disillusion with Indian policy.

After he left the White House, he served in the US House of Representatives from 1831 until his death in 1848. In 1837 Adams condemned the United States' actions toward the Indians. He said, "We have done more harm to the Indians since our Revolution than had ever been done to them by the French and English nations before. . . . These are crying sins for which we are answerable before a higher jurisdiction [divine judgment]."

In 1841 he was offered the chairmanship of the House Indian Affairs Committee, but he declined the position, calling federal Indian policy fraudulent and brutal. "It is among the heinous [outrageous, shocking] sins of this nation," Adams wrote in his diary in June 1841. "I turned my eyes away from this sickening mass of putrefaction [rottenness], and asked to be excused from serving as chairman of the committee."

John Ross

The Cherokee were divided concerning their next actions. By 1835 the national government convinced a small number of the tribe to sign a treaty agreeing to surrender all their land and move to **reservations** (tracts of land set aside for Indians) located in present-day Oklahoma by 1838. The chief of the Cherokee, John Ross, protested to Congress that the treaty represented only 500 of the 17,000 Cherokees in the region. Nevertheless, the US Senate narrowly approved the treaty in 1836.

By 1838 only about 2,000 Cherokees had moved westward. Jackson's presidency had ended a year earlier. The next president, Martin Van Buren, sent 7,000 soldiers to forcibly move the Cherokees. US soldiers dragged many Cherokees from their homes—sometimes at gunpoint—and placed them in detention camps until the marches west began.

These forced marches west began in the summer, and sickness and drought killed many of the travelers. Several groups waited until fall, but heavy rains became a problem. Travel was difficult, and food was scarce. As winter set in, frigid weather and bad water caused more disease. About 4,000 Cherokees died en route to the Indian Territory. The tragedy became known as the **Trail of Tears**.

▾ Trail of Tears

The Black Hawk War

Black Hawk, an Indian leader of the Sauk and Fox tribes of northern Illinois, tried to stop the advance of white settlers. He had fought alongside the British in the War of 1812 and was a friend of Tecumseh.

By 1830 the US government had forced him and other Indians in the region to move to Iowa Territory to settle on land designated for them. There, Black Hawk and his followers found themselves facing starvation. In 1832 he led about a thousand Indians across the Mississippi River. They returned to their original land in search of food and with the intention of resettling in the region.

The settlers in the area panicked, viewing his actions as an act of war. They called for assistance from the army and militiamen. Black Hawk and his men did well in a number of battles and skirmishes but were eventually forced to flee into the swamps of Wisconsin. The army and militia pursued and located them. In the attack, almost all of Black Hawk's followers were killed. Black Hawk escaped the Bad Axe Massacre in August 1832, as this battle was called, but he later surrendered. Black Hawk was placed in captivity until the following year. Afterward, he lived the remaining five years of his life in Iowa.

▲ Black Hawk

SECTION REVIEW 10.2

1. For what two reasons did the number of voters triple between 1824 and 1828? How does greater democracy both help and hurt the election process?
2. What accusations against each candidate were part of the mudslinging in the election of 1828?
3. What did Jackson claim were the advantages of the spoils system? What were the disadvantages?
4. What Cherokee scholar created an alphabet for his people?
5. What bill removed protection for the Indians in Georgia?
6. Describe the ruling of the Supreme Court in *Worcester v. Georgia*. How did Jackson respond to it?
7. Why was the forced removal of the Cherokees to Indian Territory known as the Trail of Tears? What was the outcome of the march?
8. What Indian leader lost most of his followers at the Bad Axe Massacre?

▼ Bad Axe Massacre

GUIDING QUESTIONS

- How did the ideas of tariffs and states' rights relate to each other?
- What were the controversies concerning the National Bank and "pet" banks?

10.3 DOMESTIC CONTROVERSIES

What controversies occurred while Jackson was president?

Two additional issues caused much controversy during the Jackson presidency. One concerned the states and their rights in relation to the power of the national government. The states' rights issue played a prominent role as Congress considered the use of tariffs. The second contentious issue was whether or not the National Bank should exist.

The Tariff and States' Rights

The idea of a tariff was not new. Congress had passed a **revenue tariff** (a tariff designed to raise money) during Washington's presidency. But by Jackson's time, different sections of the country disagreed sharply on the value and purpose of tariffs.

Reasons for Tariffs

This disagreement stemmed in part from the change in the purpose of tariffs. Initially, the nation used revenue tariffs to obtain money for the national government. Later, it began using tariffs to limit the importation of foreign goods and to protect American industries from foreign competition. But this latter type of tariff, called a **protective tariff**, also raised the price of foreign goods.

American industries had developed rapidly in the years just before the War of 1812. The Embargo Act of 1807 and

Example of How a Tariff Works

Before a Tariff

Because Britain was more industrialized, a British hat might cost $3.00, while an American hat might cost $3.50.

British hat	American hat
$3.00	$3.50

The Effects of a Revenue Tariff

A British hat with an 8 percent revenue tariff costs $3.24, while an American hat still costs $3.50.

Revenue tariffs add money to the US federal Treasury. A British hat maker can still undersell his American competitor. The American hat maker, however, will have trouble competing (from a price perspective) unless he uses more efficient methods or new technology to reduce the price of his product.

In this example, the British manufacturer, US federal Treasury, and American consumer (the people purchasing hats) benefit the most. The American manufacturer is at a disadvantage.

British hat	American hat
$3.24	$3.50

The Effects of a Protective Tariff

A British hat with a 28 percent protective tariff costs $3.84, while an American hat still costs $3.50.

The British manufacturer will have trouble competing (from a price perspective). He will sell fewer hats in America. The American hat maker will sell significantly more. The US federal Treasury will collect less money. The American manufacturer might become less competitive and less open to making improvements.

In this example, the American manufacturer benefits the most. The American consumer and the British manufacturer are at a disadvantage.

British hat	American hat
$3.84	$3.50

other acts that limited trade from Europe meant that generally only American goods were available for purchase. The British blockades during the War of 1812 caused Americans to build more factories to make needed products. Most of these factories were in New England, New York, Pennsylvania, and New Jersey. These areas had the waterpower and capital (money) that were necessary to operate factories. They also had plenty of people to work in the factories. The South, on the other hand, attracted fewer factories because many southerners had already invested their money in agricultural pursuits, often by purchasing slaves.

Although the northern industries had grown rapidly and were doing well, they wanted to protect themselves from foreign competition. They wanted to keep Americans from buying foreign goods so they fought to keep the protective tariff.

The Tariff of Abominations

After the War of 1812, British goods flooded the United States. Because British factories were often more advanced than American ones, they were producing items that were of better quality and less expensive than those made in America.

In 1816 Congress responded to the pleas from American manufacturers and levied a higher tariff. Congress increased the tariff again in 1818 and in 1824. Many Americans protested the increasing tariff rates. Southerners were particularly upset. Because the South remained primarily agricultural, it needed to buy most of its manufactured goods from either the North or foreign countries. The Southerners depended on the profits they made from their crops to pay for those goods. The high tariffs increased their costs and thus decreased their profits.

In 1828 Congress increased the tariff yet again. This new tariff drew even wider protests. Southerners called it the "**tariff of abominations**." Besides increasing the cost of products Southerners purchased, they feared that foreign nations would be so angered by ever higher tariffs that they would buy fewer American products. The Southern economy depended heavily on selling cotton and other items to foreign nations. Some Southern politicians even threatened to secede, or withdraw, from the Union because of the tariff of abominations.

▾ A South Carolina rice field. The vast majority of factories were located in the North. The South was primarily agricultural and increasingly relied on slave labor.

Nullification and States' Rights

Economic problems, particularly the controversy about the tariff, and worry over the continued existence of slavery increased political tensions within the nation. They also brought a stronger defense of states' rights.

John C. Calhoun, Jackson's vice president, became the leading defender of **states' rights**. This view asserted that each state, as a largely independent body, had voluntarily joined the Union (United States) and that each state had the right to control its most important affairs. Calhoun also promoted the nullification theory, the belief that a state had a right to **nullify**, or refuse to accept, a federal law that it considered to be unconstitutional.

The Webster-Hayne Debate

Calhoun's nullification theory was attacked when tariff reform was debated in a series of Senate speeches in January 1830. Those exchanges were between Senator **Robert Y. Hayne** of South Carolina and Senator **Daniel Webster** of Massachusetts.

Hayne was a strong supporter of nullification and states' rights. He emphasized that since the Tenth Amendment made it clear the states or the people kept all powers not given to the national government, the national government is limited in its actions. He argued that the Constitution does not give the national government power to pass laws that hurt one group of people or region of the country while helping another. Since he believed that such laws were unconstitutional, Hayne said that the states had the right to nullify them.

Webster attacked nullification point by point, carefully defending his view of the Constitution and the federal Union. Webster argued that the people, rather than the states, had established the Union. Thus, he said, the Constitution and the Union were superior to state governments. He believed that nullification would lead to the end of the Union and stated that no state had the right to disobey federal law. He closed one of his speeches by contending, "Liberty *and* Union, now and for ever, one and inseparable!"

Calhoun and Jackson Clash

President Jackson had not yet taken sides in the Senate debate. He had a deep respect for states' rights and believed that the South was justified in its complaint about the tariff. But to Jackson, nullification was out of the question.

On April 13, 1830, the Democrats gathered for a dinner in honor of their party's founder, Thomas Jefferson. A series of toasts (short statements honoring someone) was a regular part of such gatherings. When President Jackson rose to make his toast, he looked squarely at John C. Calhoun and said, "Our Federal Union: it must and shall be preserved!" Calhoun responded, "The Union! Next to our liberty, most dear!" This incident was but one of many in a growing rift between Jackson and Calhoun.

Eventually, Calhoun resigned the vice-presidency. The South Carolina legislature had elected him to the Senate, where he led the fight for states' rights.

A Time of Crisis

The issue of states' rights simmered dangerously for another two years. It boiled over when Congress passed a new tariff in 1832. This tariff gained some support in the South and West because it was lower than the 1828 tariff; however, it was still high. When Jackson signed the tariff, nullification supporters were enraged.

South Carolina legislators called a state convention late in November and declared that the tariffs of 1828 and 1832 were "null, void, and no law, nor binding upon [the] State, its officers or citizens." The declaration, called the Ordinance of Nullification, prohibited state and federal officers to collect tariffs in South Carolina after February 1, 1833. If the federal government tried to force the tariff on South Carolina, the state would issue an order of **secession**—it would leave the Union.

▲ John C. Calhoun served as vice president to both John Quincy Adams and Andrew Jackson.

Jackson met the crisis head-on. He made it clear that he viewed nullification as an act of treason, and he privately threatened to hang John C. Calhoun as a traitor. He sent armed forces to Charleston, South Carolina. Nullifiers mobilized the state militia. Jackson said that he understood the South Carolinians' plight but that nullifying a federal law defied the Constitution. He told South Carolinians that their state could not leave the Union. Congress supported Jackson by passing the Force Bill, which allowed him to use the army and the navy to enforce the laws.

▲ Charleston harbor, South Carolina

The Compromise of 1833

Although Jackson opposed nullification, he wanted to lower the tariff. He also wanted to avoid violence. Henry Clay, who had been Speaker of the House at the time of the Missouri Compromise, was now one of Kentucky's US senators. Clay, who was skillful at settling disputes, worked with Calhoun to promote a compromise tariff. The new tariff lowered duties gradually, so that by 1842 no tariff was to be more than 20 percent. This plan gave the industries in the North time to grow stronger before they lost their protection. Congress adopted this **Compromise of 1833**.

Two weeks later, South Carolina withdrew its nullification of the tariff. But it declared the Force Bill to be null and void. Jackson, however, ignored this action. Although Jackson and Clay had managed to keep the Union together, the question of states' rights remained unsettled. Many Southerners still believed that they could leave the Union if they desired to do so.

▲ Nicholas Biddle

The National Bank

As the election of 1832 approached, the most important campaign issue was the future of the Bank of the United States, also known as the National Bank.

The first National Bank existed from 1791 until 1811, when its twenty-year charter expired. The second one, which also had a twenty year charter, was not created until 1816. Thus the Bank would cease to exist after 1836 unless Congress renewed its charter and the president endorsed the action.

Jackson's Conflict with Biddle

Nicholas Biddle, a talented, wealthy Philadelphian, was the president of the Bank of the United States in 1832. He had handled the Bank skillfully. Its twenty-nine branches had efficiently regulated the nation's finances. Because it controlled one-fifth of all bank deposits in the nation, it was a powerful institution. Private individuals, most of whom were rich easterners, held four-fifths of the Bank's stock, so it was largely accountable to them. Most of the Bank's profits went to these private owners.

Jackson had little understanding of banking practices and had a distaste for all banks. Furthermore, he believed the national government had too much power, and he saw the National Bank as yet another example of that problem. Many westerners and southerners agreed with Jackson's view. He also thought the Bank was unconstitutional. Though the Supreme Court had ruled otherwise in *McCulloch v. Maryland*, Jackson ignored that decision. Jackson had the support of state bankers in his campaign against the National Bank. He led them to believe that Biddle would eventually destroy state banks.

The Election of 1832

In the summer of 1832, Biddle submitted the Bank's charter for a twenty-year renewal to Congress, even though the current charter did not expire until 1836. Jackson soon learned that Henry Clay had instigated the early renewal request, hoping it would help him be elected president that year. Clay knew that the recharter bill would likely pass Congress but be vetoed by Jackson. Clay thought his support for the bill would prove to be a winning campaign issue.

Congress approved the new charter, which even received support from many members of Jackson's party. Jackson was sick in bed when the bill was brought to him. He angrily vetoed it and responded, "The bank is trying to kill me, but I will kill it."

▼ This cartoon depicts Jackson's victory in getting rid of the Bank of the United States.

The National Republican Party, which had nominated John Quincy Adams in 1828, did choose Henry Clay as their presidential candidate. The Democrats, as the Democratic-Republicans were now being called, renominated Jackson. His actions against the bank did not harm his campaign, and he won 219 electoral votes to Clay's 49.

Jackson and the "Pet Banks"

Jackson's veto meant that the National Bank would dissolve after 1836. But that was not enough for Jackson. He was determined to wage war on the Bank and on Biddle as head of the Bank. Jackson instructed the secretary of the treasury to begin removing money from the Bank and placing it into new accounts in dozens of state banks, which were soon known as Jackson's "**pet banks**." Whether the president had the legal authority to do this became a matter of dispute. When the secretary opposed Jackson's orders, Jackson removed him and appointed a new secretary of the treasury. When that secretary also refused to follow Jackson's decree, Jackson fired him. Jackson appointed a third secretary. The new official found a way around legal restrictions by depositing new revenues, from taxes and land sales, in pet banks and paying government bills with money from the National Bank.

In March 1834 the US Senate, by a vote of 26–20, passed a resolution censuring, or condemning, Jackson's actions regarding the Bank. It stated that Jackson had abused his power as president and had assumed authority that the Constitution and laws did not provide him. In January 1837, after Jackson's supporters regained control of the Senate, the senators voted to withdraw the earlier resolution.

After Jackson stopped placing new funds into the National Bank, the amount of money in the Bank dropped dramatically. Lacking funds and hoping to show the dangers of Jackson's actions, Biddle ordered state banks to repay the loans they owed to the National Bank as quickly as possible. He also stopped the Bank from making additional loans. Unfortunately, that action caused hundreds of state banks to fail and wiped out the savings of thousands of Americans. What Jackson had feared—financial chaos—was now a reality, and he was partly to blame for it.

Did you know?

The first six presidents vetoed a total of ten bills. Presidents John Adams, Thomas Jefferson, and John Quincy Adams did not veto any bills. Early presidents were reluctant to use that power. But in Jackson's two terms of office, he used his veto power on twelve occasions.

▾ In this cartoon, the National Bank watches as Jackson feeds his pet banks.

▾ Jackson's home, the Hermitage

PRIMARY SOURCE: JACKSON'S PROFESSION OF FAITH

Jackson's faults are numerous and well-documented. He rebelled against authority on a number of occasions; he vigorously promoted unjust treatment of American Indians; and his hatred for those who opposed him was frequently evident.

During much of his life, he attended church infrequently. Yet his wife, Rachel, became a dedicated Christian, and Jackson himself joined the Presbyterian Church after her death and his presidency. On his deathbed, he gave the following testimony of his Christian faith: "I am in the hands of a merciful God. I have full confidence in his goodness and mercy. . . . The Bible is true. . . . I have tried to conform to its spirit as near as possible. Upon that sacred volume I rest my hope for eternal salvation, through the merits and blood of our blessed Lord and Saviour, Jesus Christ."

Later, when asked about the pain that he was experiencing, Jackson replied, "When I have suffered sufficiently, the Lord will then take me to Himself—but what are all my suffering compared to those of the blessed Savior, who died upon that cursed tree for me? Mine are nothing."

(Jackson's words quoted from Robert V. Remini, *The Course of American Democracy, 1833–1845*, Vol. 3, *Andrew Jackson* [New York: Harper and Row, 1984], 519, 521.)

Angry bankers and other businessmen pleaded with Jackson for help. He replied, "Go to Nicholas Biddle." Responding to pressure, Biddle began making additional loans. Problems mounted. Jackson blamed Biddle, while Biddle insisted the fault lay with Jackson.

Across the nation, hundreds of new state banks were started. Banks were allowed to print their own paper money with the assumption that they would keep sufficient gold and silver in the bank so that if individuals wanted to redeem paper money for those precious metals, they would be able to do so. Many banks ignored this policy.

Fun Fact

"Paper" money in the United States today is not made of paper. It is 75 percent cotton and 25 percent linen.

The Specie Circular

As a result of the banking practices and other economic problems, inflation occurred. **Inflation** is an increase in the prices for goods and services that is often caused by an increase in the money supply. This alarmed Jackson. He reacted by asking the Treasury Department to issue the Specie Circular, which required anyone who bought government lands to pay for them in **specie** (gold or silver coins) rather than in paper money.

Soon, people did not trust paper money at all. More banks failed. Without enough banks from which to borrow money, businesses failed. The economic crisis worsened. Shortly after Jackson's handpicked successor took office, the nation faced an economic depression.

SECTION REVIEW 10.3

1. What was the purpose of each of the two basic types of tariffs?
2. What region of the country was most interested in fighting for the protective tariff? Why?
3. What did Southerners call the tariff of 1828? Why?
4. What is nullification? Who was the leading defender of a state's right to nullify a law? Who spoke against it?
5. How did President Jackson respond to South Carolina's threat of secession? What did the Force Bill allow him to do?
6. How did the Compromise of 1833 temporarily quiet the issue of nullification?
7. Should a state be able to nullify a federal law with which it does not agree? Why or why not?
8. What were three reasons that Jackson did not favor a national bank?
9. What problems occurred when "pet banks" were created and funds in the National Bank declined?

10.4 THE JACKSONIAN LEGACY

How effective were the presidents who followed Andrew Jackson?

GUIDING QUESTIONS

- What happened during the election of 1836?
- What issues did Martin Van Buren face as president?
- How did the Whigs campaign during the election of 1840?
- What happened during President Tyler's administration?

Although Jackson's term ended in 1837, he left a deep imprint. He had greatly increased the powers of the executive branch. When challenged about the tariff by advocates of states' rights, he had staunchly defended the Union. But when Indian policy was the issue, he supported actions the states favored and removed Native Americans. He believed in free enterprise, yet his resentment for those who controlled the National Bank was enormous. Despite these inconsistencies, the next few presidents, no matter their party, reflected Jackson's influence.

The Election of 1836

A new political party appeared in the 1830s. The **Whigs** united several diverse groups into one party. The central element uniting those groups was their opposition to Jackson.

Whigs derived their name from the British party that traditionally opposed Britain's royalty. Jackson's intimidating methods and the manner in which he dictated his policy to Congress and his cabinet seemed to his opponents to have the appearance of monarchy. The Whigs dubbed the so-called people's president, "King Andrew the First."

The Democrats and Whigs had differing views. The Whigs supported the American System (a national bank, a high tariff, and nationwide internal improvements funded by the national government). They believed Congress should have more power than the president. They thought strong industries and businesses were essential to a stable economy. Most Democrats opposed the American System and insisted that parts of it were unconstitutional. Most were content with the strong presidency that had developed during the Jackson administration. They favored an economy dominated by agriculture.

Many northern Whigs saw slavery as sinful, but most southern Whigs supported slavery. Most Whigs opposed the United States expanding its territory westward. Conservative Protestant groups, such as Presbyterians, Baptists, and Congregationalists tended to favor the Whig Party. Democrats generally supported slavery and favored westward expansion. Though many Democrats were Protestants, the party also attracted many Catholics, particularly among Irish immigrants.

The Democrats continued to emphasize that they were the party of the common man. Many in the Whig Party, which often attracted the more educated citizenry, were sometimes skeptical about how much the common man really understood about government and politics.

In the presidential election of 1836, **Martin Van Buren** was the choice of Andrew Jackson and the Democrats. Van Buren had served as Jackson's vice president during his second term. The Whigs, on the other hand, chose several candidates. They included Senator Hugh L. White of Tennessee, famed Indian fighter General William Henry Harrison of Ohio, and the great orator from Massachusetts, Senator Daniel Webster. The Whigs' strategy was to prevent Van Buren from

▲ Cartoon showing Andrew Jackson as a king; his opponents believed he had too much power.

Did you know?

Martin Van Buren was born in Kinderhook, New York. He was later nicknamed "Old Kinderhook." During the 1840 election, his supporters organized O.K. Clubs and referred to him as O.K.

The term "O.K." may actually have originated and obtained its present meaning even before 1840. However, it appears the election made it a popularly accepted term.

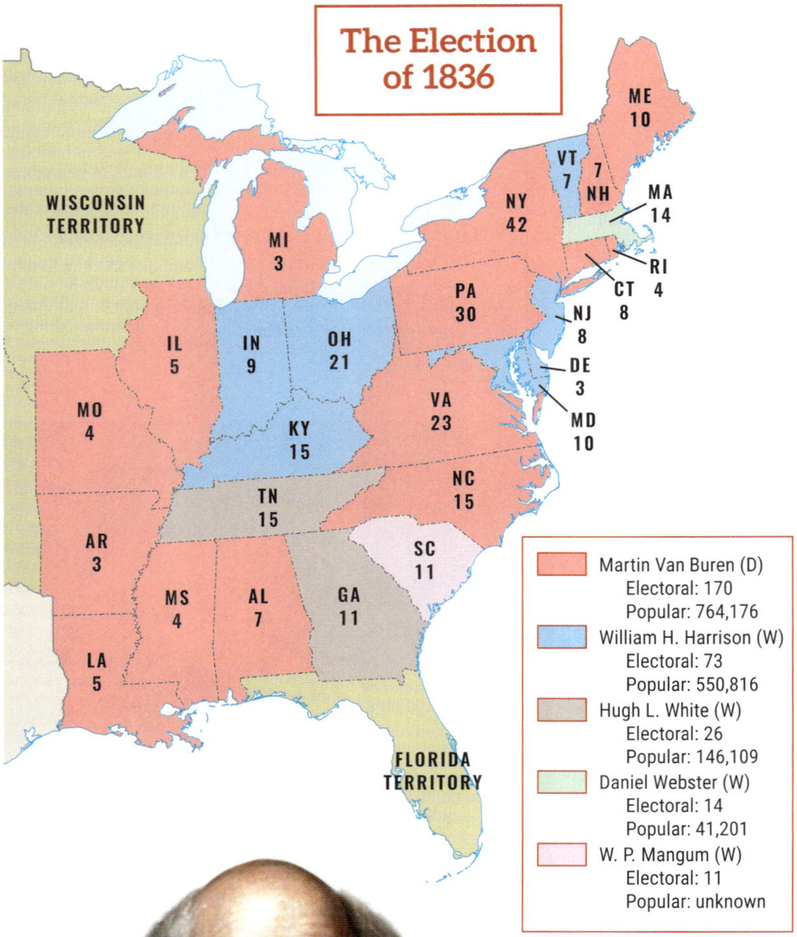

Martin Van Buren

Born	December 5, 1782	8
Died	July 24, 1862	
Home state	New York	
Wife	Hannah Hoes	
Home	Lindenwald	
Church	Dutch Reformed	
Occupation	lawyer	
Party	Democrat	
Years served as president	1837–41	
Terms	1	
Vice president	Richard M. Johnson	

receiving a majority in the Electoral College by running strong sectional candidates. Since the House would then choose the president, they hoped one of their candidates would win there. The Whig strategy failed. Van Buren received 51 percent of the popular vote, as well as a majority of the electoral vote.

The Van Buren Years

Van Buren was born in 1782 after the United States declared independence. Thus, he was the first president who was not born a British subject. His family was Dutch American and had never been prominent in society. He had limited formal education but had mastered the practical: he learned how to unite people, motives, and issues into a plan of action. He proved to be a skilled politician.

Shortly after Van Buren's inauguration, the Panic of 1837 began. It led to a depression (a severe economic downturn). Banks closed, businesses collapsed, and many farmers lost their land. By the fall of 1837, one-third of workers had lost their jobs. Many still employed faced huge reductions in their salary. Many people could not afford food or a place to live. Trade with other countries dropped sharply. Cotton prices plummeted, bringing disastrous effects to the South's economy. Though the president called a special session, or meeting, of Congress in 1837 to address the chaos, little changed. The depression lasted for five years.

In 1840 Congress approved Van Buren's plan for an independent treasury system. It would consist of several federal vaults where the Treasury would store its funds rather than banks. Gold and silver, rather than paper money, would be used for all federal business.

Both Jackson and Van Buren had significant impact on the Supreme Court. When Chief Justice John Marshall died in 1835, Jackson appointed Roger B. Taney, of Maryland, to the position. Jackson also appointed five new associate justices during his term. Changes continued in 1837 when Van Buren was able to appoint two justices because a new law had increased the number of justices from seven to nine. All but two of the eight members selected by Jackson and Van Buren were from southern states. The Whigs were panic-stricken. Whigs admired Marshall, who had been a Federalist before the collapse of that party, and strongly supported his views. They feared that the Democrat-dominated Court would reverse all of Marshall's decisions. That did not happen, and few dramatic changes occurred.

The Election of 1840

In the presidential election of 1840, the Democrats again chose Van Buren as their candidate. Convinced that Clay would not attract eastern voters, the Whigs turned to **William Henry Harrison**, a man

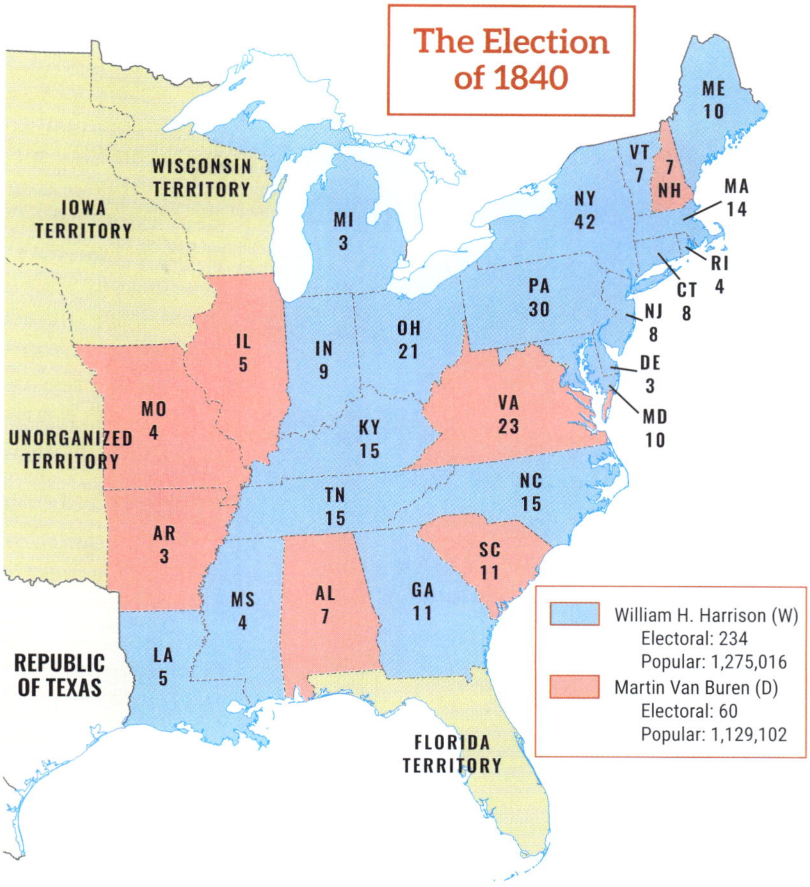

not closely linked with either party. Harrison had been born in Virginia and could attract Democratic votes in the South. He was also a military hero, known for his victory at Tippecanoe and his efforts in the War of 1812. He served as governor of the Indiana Territory and as a US senator from Ohio. Since his political views were largely unknown, they would not hurt him in the campaign.

The Whigs portrayed Harrison as a humble backwoodsman, symbolized by a log cabin. In contrast, they described Van Buren as a snobbish aristocrat. In reality, Harrison was born in a mansion belonging to his prominent political family. His father, a Virginia plantation owner, was a signer of the Declaration of Independence and later governor of the state. Van Buren, who was the son of a New York tavern keeper, hardly had a luxurious upbringing. But facts were thrown aside during the campaign.

The Whigs campaigned with gusto. Dressing up as Indians, they emphasized Harrison's victory over Tecumseh's forces at the Battle of Tippecanoe. They served gallons of cider to voters and staged parades complete with bands, banners, and flags. Voter turnout exceeded two million. As noted earlier, this was double the number who had voted in 1828 and six times as many as had cast ballots in 1824.

Harrison and his running mate, **John Tyler**, won nineteen of the twenty-six states and 53 percent of the popular vote. With campaign slogans such as "Tippecanoe and Tyler Too!"; "Van, Van, is a used-up man!"; and "To guide the ship, we'll try old Tip!" the Whigs put Van Buren out of office.

At age sixty-eight on March 4, 1841, Harrison was older than any previous president when taking office (a record that was later broken by Ronald Reagan, Donald Trump, and Joseph Biden). His inaugural address, almost two hours in length, is still the longest in American history. On that cold day, he wore no overcoat or hat. He later developed a cold that turned into pneumonia. Harrison died exactly a month after taking office.

William Henry Harrison

9

Born	February 9, 1773
Died	April 4, 1841
Home state	Ohio
Wife	Anna Tuthill Symmes
Home	Grouseland (Vincennes, IN)
Church	Episcopalian
Occupations	soldier, planter
Party	Whig
Years served as president	1841
Terms	partial term (one month)
Vice president	John Tyler

John Tyler

Harrison was the first president to die in office, and John Tyler was the first vice president to become president after the death of his predecessor. Tyler was a Whig in name only. He had disagreed with Jackson on nullification and the removal of bank deposits; however, he also disagreed with most of the Whig policies. He soon clashed with members of his own cabinet and party. Henry Clay said that since Tyler had not been elected president, he should let a congressional committee of Whigs make crucial decisions. Clay, of course, intended to head the committee. Tyler refused. He stated that according to the Constitution, he was the rightful president.

John Tyler

Born	March 29, 1790	10
Died	January 14, 1862	
Home state	Virginia	
Wives	1st—Letitia Christian 2nd—Julia Gardiner	
Home	Sherwood Forest	
Church	Episcopalian	
Occupation	lawyer	
Party	Whig	
Years served as president	1841–45	
Terms	1 (minus one month)	
Vice president	none	

The Man without a Party

Meanwhile, Clay took charge of Whig legislation in Congress as one of Kentucky's senators. Under his leadership, Congress abolished the independent treasury system, and Tyler supported the change. But when Clay submitted a bill establishing a new national bank, Tyler vetoed it as unconstitutional. Clay was outraged. At Clay's urging, all of Tyler's cabinet resigned in September 1841, except Secretary of State Daniel Webster. (Webster remained until he could complete negotiations with the British over a border dispute.) The Whigs, who called Tyler "his accidency" because of how he had gained office, expelled him from the party. Tyler became "a man without a party."

The depression continued, and the national debt increased during Tyler's early presidency. In 1842 Tyler felt forced to sign a bill that raised the tariff back to its 1832 level.

The Webster-Ashburton Treaty

The Tyler administration faced problems with Britain, primarily from the vaguely drawn northeastern border with Canada. The main point of contention was the northern border of Maine.

Daniel Webster and Lord Ashburton, a British diplomat, met to resolve these matters. The resulting Webster-Ashburton Treaty of 1842, was a compromise. It gave the United States a little more than half of the disputed area, and the British received the remainder.

Webster later resigned from the cabinet. He joined other Whig leaders in their protest against President Tyler.

The End of Tyler's Term

One of Tyler's goals was to add Texas to the Union (Texas will be discussed in greater detail in Chapter 12). He sought this goal partly because he believed that Texas would aid his reelection. But his early efforts failed. Texas remained outside the Union, and Democrat **James K. Polk** won the election of 1844.

During Tyler's **lame-duck period** (the time between the election and his leaving office), he kept promoting the admission of Texas. When the Senate refused to ratify a treaty to annex Texas by the required two-thirds vote, Tyler proposed that Texas be admitted by a joint resolution. The resolution, which required only a simple majority vote, passed, and Tyler signed it just days before leaving office.

The Webster-Ashburton Treaty (1842)

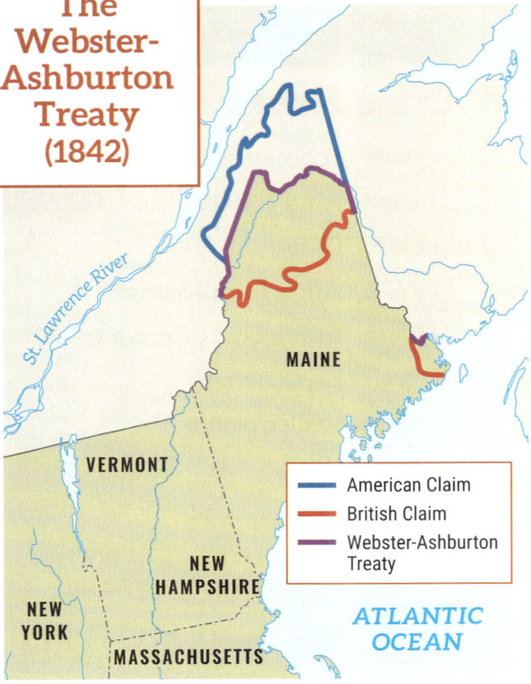

SECTION REVIEW 10.4

1. What central element unified the new Whig party?
2. What was the Whig strategy in the election of 1836? How did it fail?
3. What was Van Buren's plan to replace the banking system instituted by Andrew Jackson?
4. How did the Whigs campaign during the election of 1840? Was it successful?
5. How did John Tyler become president?
6. Why was President Tyler expelled from the Whig party?
7. What treaty divided the disputed lands in Maine and Canada between America and Britain?
8. Should Tyler have allowed Henry Clay and his congressional committee to make crucial decisions? Why or why not?

CHAPTER 10 REVIEW

Making Connections

1. Who were the four candidates in the election of 1824? What state was each candidate from?
2. What public service experience did John Quincy Adams have before entering the presidency?
3. Which of Adams's goals as president was he able to accomplish relatively successfully?
4. What political position did John Quincy Adams fill after his presidency? For how long?
5. How many people voted in the presidential election of 1824? 1828? 1840?
6. What was Jackson's "Kitchen Cabinet"? How did it earn this nickname?
7. What tribes were encouraged or forced to move west of the Mississippi River? List the states each was from.
8. What types of publications were the Cherokees able to produce using Sequoyah's alphabet?
9. What reason did Jackson give for the Indians to move west when he signed the Indian Removal Act? Who were some of the strongest defenders of the Indians?
10. What other part of the country besides the southeast was also dealing with conflict between settlers and Native Americans?
11. What issues led to the clash between Jackson and Calhoun?
12. What state nullified laws in November 1832? What laws did it nullify?
13. What was the problem with banks printing their own money?
14. Label each description *W* if supported by Whigs or *D* if supported by Democrats.
    A. The American system
    B. Congress should have more power than the president
    C. Strong industry and business
    D. Dominant agricultural economy
    E. Expansion westward
    F. Conservative Protestants tended to favor
    G. Catholics tended to favor

Thinking Critically

15. Who do you think was the rightful winner of the 1824 election? Why?
16. Is the spoils system an acceptable way to give government jobs? Why or why not?
17. What did Jackson mean after the *Worcester v. Georgia* Supreme Court decision when he reportedly said, "John Marshall has made his decision. Now let him enforce it"?
18. What might be a wise situation in which to institute a revenue tariff? a protective tariff?

Living as a Christian Citizen

19. Why do you think the US government removed Native Americans from their lands? How does this show the twisting of the value of growth? What lesson can you learn from this for today?
20. Does mudslinging work? Use biblical principles to show why it is wrong.

Terms to Remember

caucus
John Quincy Adams
American System
corrupt bargain
Democratic Party
mudslinging
spoils system
political machines
Kitchen Cabinet
Cherokees
Indian Removal Act
reservations
Trail of Tears
Black Hawk
revenue tariff
protective tariff
tariff of abominations
John C. Calhoun
states' rights
nullify
Robert Y. Hayne
Daniel Webster
secession
Compromise of 1833
Nicholas Biddle
pet banks
inflation
specie
Whigs
Martin Van Buren
William Henry Harrison
John Tyler
James K. Polk
lame-duck period

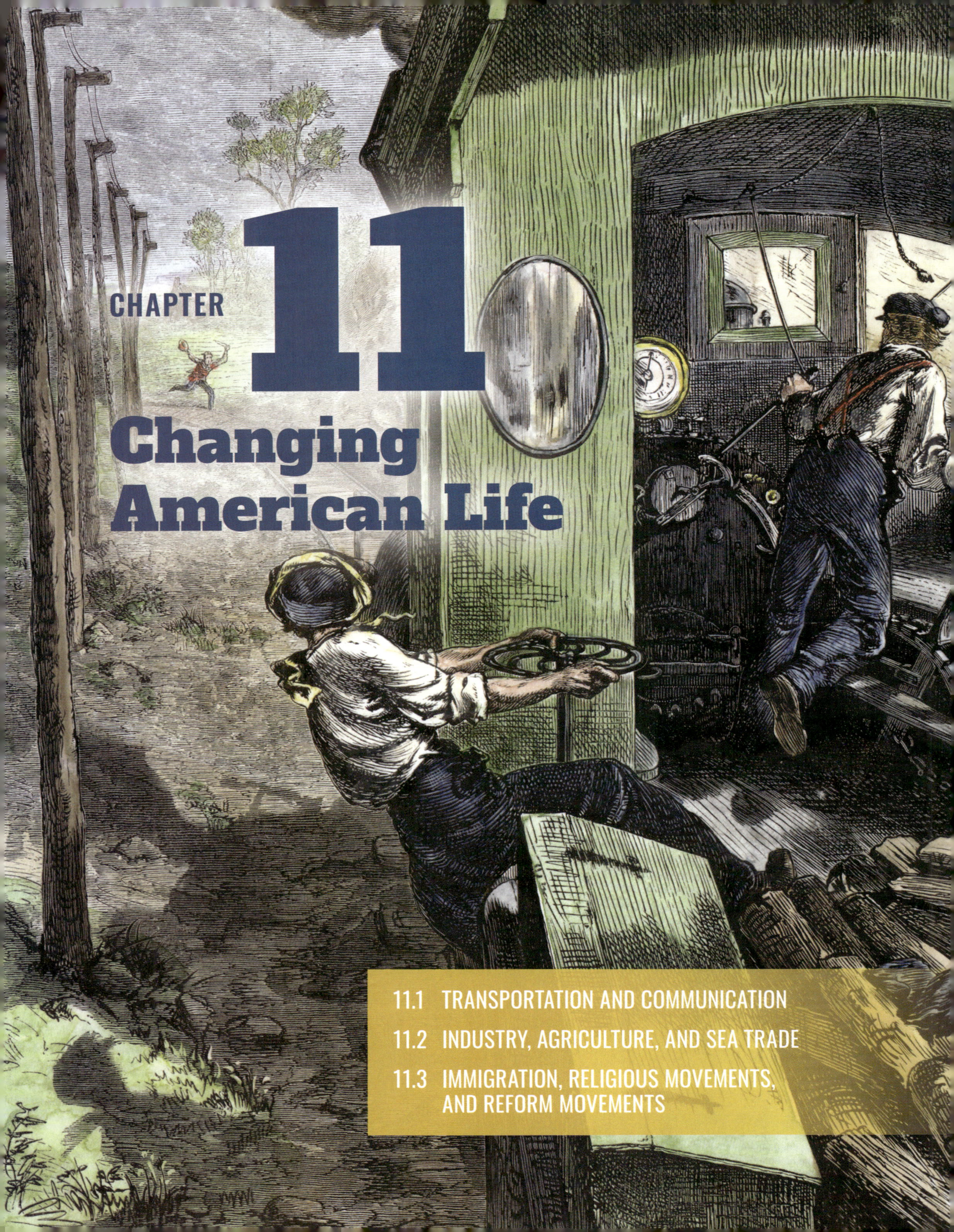

CHAPTER

11 Changing American Life

The Jacksonian era was a time of growth and innovation in all areas of life. Americans tried to improve society not only in technical areas such as transportation, communication, agriculture, industry, and trade but also through reform movements and religion. This era offered many people a chance to make their mark on the history of America, just as the Founding Fathers had done fifty years earlier.

But Americans soon learned that they needed to shape and guide their innovations with moral values. Without moral guidance, Americans could pursue any growth imaginable without considering its value or goodness. A result of such unguided growth could twist the blessings of growth and technology into a heavy burden or evil.

GUIDING QUESTION

- What was the impact of advancements in transportation and communication during this period?

11.1 TRANSPORTATION AND COMMUNICATION

What changes occurred in transportation and communication during the early 1800s?

Transportation

America's early settlements were located along the coast because water made transportation easy. Over the years, however, the nation acquired vast areas of new land. Explorers and traders told of the value of these western lands, and many Americans wanted to settle there. But the distances were great, and there were no good roads to the West.

Early Roads

Most colonial roads were merely dirt paths or muddy ruts. Many of them had been animal paths or Indian trails. Settlers later cut away brush and trees to widen the roads.

A few roads linked major cities. For example, the Boston Post Road connected Boston and New York City. A road also connected New York City and Philadelphia, though it took three days for a covered wagon to travel that distance. By 1766, stagecoaches cut the time by a day (when the weather was good). Because the South had a fairly good water-transportation system, settlers there spent little time building roads.

Three major roads—the Great Wagon Road, the Wilderness Road, and the National Road—provided transportation routes for thousands of courageous early Americans and their livestock and supplies that were moving to the frontier. These roads stretched into the frontier to help open new areas of settlement.

The Great Wagon Road

Native Americans had traveled through the Appalachian Mountains long before the arrival of white men. They used a series of trails called the Great Warrior's Path, which ran north and south along the eastern slope of the mountains. Thousands of German and Scots-Irish farmers from Pennsylvania followed the road, which was widened and then called the **Great Wagon Road**, southward to settle less-crowded lands. Many left from Philadelphia, eventually crossing the Potomac River into Virginia and settling across the Carolinas as far south as Augusta, Georgia.

◂ A flagman warns a railroad crew of danger ahead on the tracks.

ROAD CONSTRUCTION: *how* ROADS WERE BUILT

In rainy or snowy weather, early roads were nearly impassable. Even packed-dirt roads quickly developed deep ruts. To improve travel on roads, people developed several construction techniques.

In cities, cobblestones or bricks were used to build roads. From 1845 to 1855, plank roads became popular outside of cities. Workers laid two parallel rows of stringers, or log pieces. The space between the rows was covered with earth. The builders then nailed an eight-to-twelve-foot-wide plank floor to the stringers. This type of road was a great improvement; however, the toll companies found that, at an average cost of $2,000 a mile, the plank roads were expensive to build and maintain.

In other areas, logs were laid side by side to form a rough road surface. Such "corduroy roads" provided a bumpy ride, but they could be hastily constructed to help travelers avoid being stuck in mud holes. They were also used in swampy areas.

From England came the idea of macadamized roads (named after engineer John McAdam). To make them, workers placed crushed stone in predug roadbeds. Such roads multiplied when in 1858 American Eli Whitney Blake invented a stone crusher.

The Wilderness Road

In 1775 Richard Henderson, a land speculator, purchased millions of acres in Kentucky and western Virginia from the Cherokee Indians. Henderson asked woodsman **Daniel Boone** to cut a road into Kentucky. This road would be an extension of the Great Wagon Road. Boone and thirty other men started the work in March 1775. Their route took them through the **Cumberland Gap**, a natural passage through the Cumberland Mountains. Thomas Walker had discovered the gap in 1750. The **Wilderness Road** stretched to Boonesborough in east central Kentucky—more than two hundred miles from the road's starting point. It was later lengthened to reach Louisville, Kentucky.

▾ Daniel Boone escorting pioneers through the Cumberland Gap into Kentucky

The National Road

Despite reluctance to use government funds, Congress approved the first federally funded road in 1806. Construction began in 1811 at Cumberland, Maryland. The first section, which reached Wheeling (now in West Virginia), opened in August 1818. The original **National Road** (or Cumberland Road, as it was sometimes called) cost $1.7 million, or about $13,000 a mile—an enormous sum for that time period.

INTERNAL *improvements* and POLITICS

Using government money to pay, or help pay, for transportation projects was the main part of the Whigs' plan for internal improvements. It was also part of the American System. Jacksonian Democrats generally opposed such spending; they argued that these projects benefited one region at the expense of all other regions and were, therefore, unconstitutional. Whigs believed that advancements in transportation would benefit all Americans.

Turnpikes

Private companies built **turnpikes**. They hoped to make a profit by charging a toll, or fee, for use of these roads. The name *turnpike* came from the sharp sticks guarding the entrance to the roads. Upon payment of the toll, the sticks were turned to allow access.

One early turnpike was the Philadelphia and Lancaster Turnpike. It was built during the 1790s using stone. It stretched more than sixty miles and connected the two Pennsylvania cities in its name.

Early Use of Waterways

Although colonial America had developed a valuable coastal trade and American ships now sailed to Europe, there had been little development of inland waterways.

Early river craft included flatboats, barges, and canoes of all sizes. Moving downstream with these vessels was relatively easy because they could float with the current. Moving upstream against the current, however, required extra effort. Wind power was unreliable. Some small boats could be moved upstream by using poles, provided the water was not too deep and the current not too strong. Animals could also tow boats with a rope. But with the difficulties and expenses involved, many boats never returned upstream. Instead, the owners dismantled them and used them for lumber or firewood.

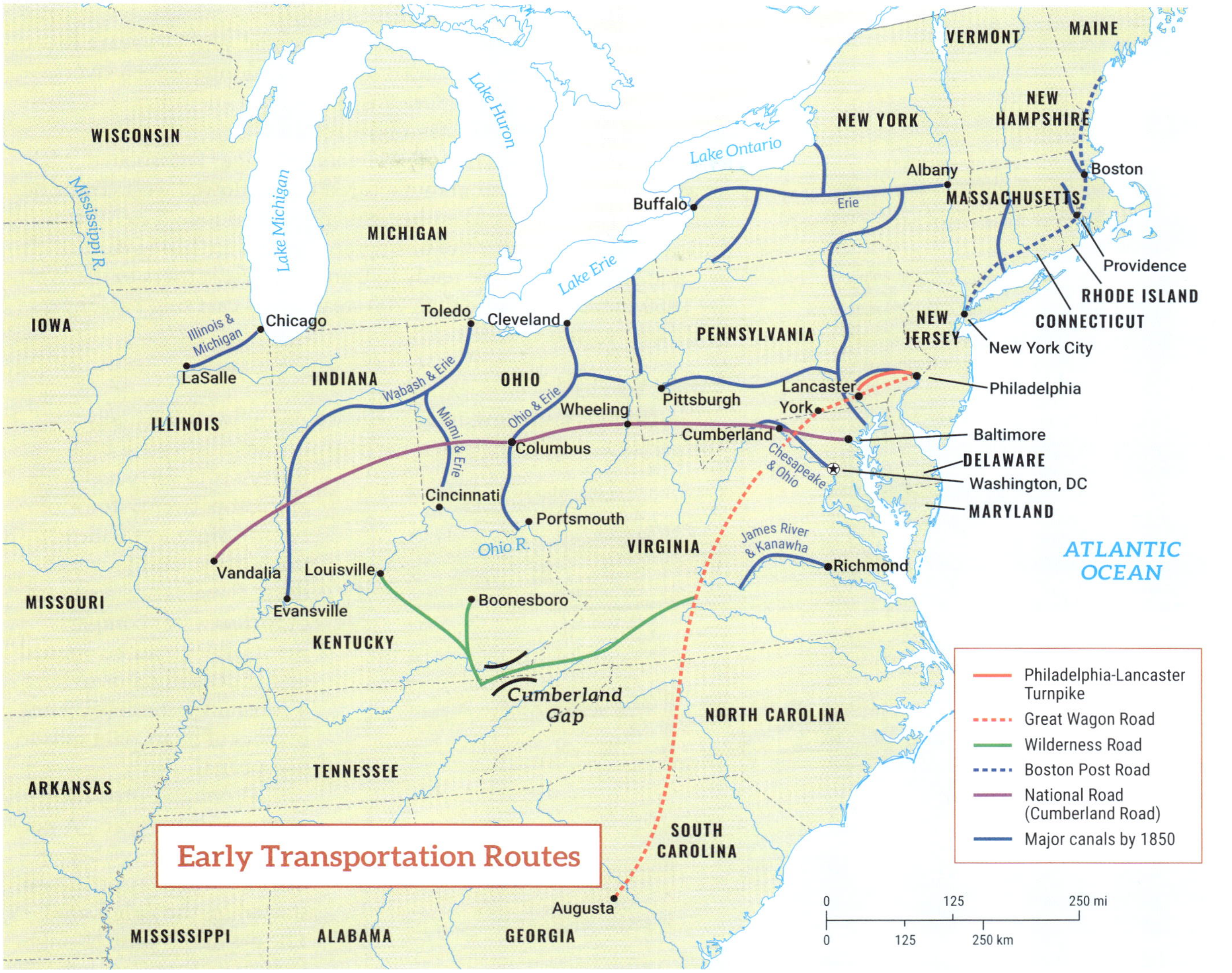

▲ Robert Fulton's *Clermont* helped make steamboat travel popular.

By 1790 inventors built and operated **steamboats**, vessels powered by a steam engine. But those efforts received little attention until **Robert Fulton** launched his vessel, the *Clermont*, in 1807. It traveled the distance from New York City to Albany, some 150 miles, in thirty-two hours. Making that trip using sails would have required four days. The 133-foot-long ship allowed passengers to walk on the deck or enjoy the sleeping accommodations below deck. It provided a smooth, though noisy, ride. Fulton was soon hailed as a national hero.

Steamboats quickly became a vital part of America's transportation system. They made the Hudson, Potomac, and Delaware Rivers busy waterways. They also aided settlement along western rivers. Major cities—such as New Orleans, St. Louis, Cincinnati, and Pittsburgh—grew along these steamboat routes.

Settlers within reach of steamboats no longer felt isolated. Mail, newspapers, books, and manufactured goods flowed west. Trade between the East and the West became more profitable. The West was full of opportunities for the immigrants who were filling eastern cities, and steamboats were ready to transport new settlers to the West. By 1850 there were more than 700 steamboats carrying passengers and cargo within the United States.

The pictures below show a boat passing through a canal lock.

1. The boat approaches the lock.
2. The lock gate opens and the boat enters.
3. The gate is closed and the water level is raised until it is even with the upstream water.
4. The upstream lock gate is opened and the boat continues its journey.

Early Canals

A **canal** is a shallow, man-made water highway. It usually connects two bodies of water. Early American canals were typically thirty-six to forty feet wide at the top, twenty-four to twenty-eight feet wide at the bottom, and four feet deep. Canals used a system of **locks** (water compartments that could be opened and shut) and dams to keep a constant water level. The owners of boats paid tolls to use a canal.

Although Europe had used canals for years, America's great canal age began in 1817, when construction started on the **Erie Canal**. The era lasted until about 1840. The Erie Canal, the most famous canal in the country, was completed in 1825. It connected Lake Erie (at Buffalo, New York) with the Hudson River (at Albany, New York). It was 363 miles long. Boats could also travel from Albany to New York City along the Hudson River. Thus, the canal could be used to efficiently transport goods between the Atlantic Ocean and the Great Lakes.

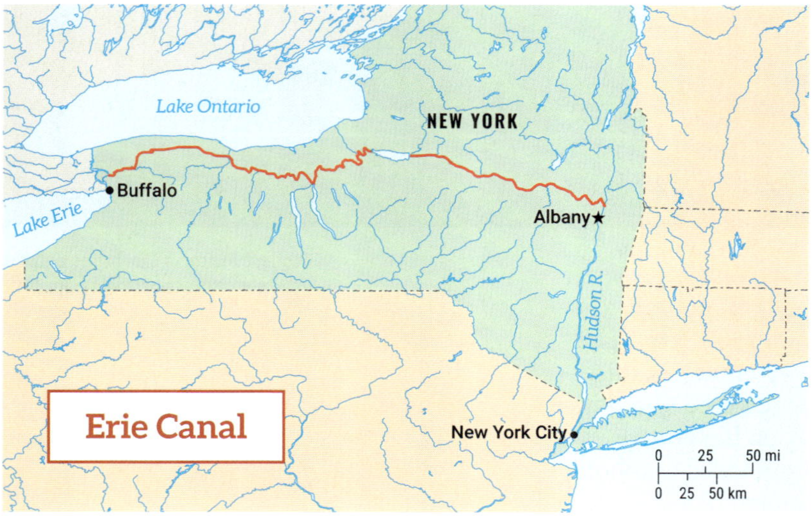

Other states, quick to follow New York's example, built their own canals. At its height in the 1840s, the canal craze produced a water-highway network of 3,326 miles. But canals were expensive to build and maintain. They also froze over in the winter. The greatest problem for canals, however, was competition from the new railroads. The canal era soon drew to a close, but even after the canals' decline, a few continued to provide service.

At the grand opening of the Erie Canal, New York's governor poured water from Lake Erie into the Atlantic Ocean at New York City.

the ERIE CANAL: "CLINTON'S BIG DITCH"

"You must have heard of it," Herman Melville wrote in *Moby Dick* in 1851, referring to the Erie Canal. The Erie Canal was so famous that it became a tourist attraction. It was called "the eighth wonder of the world."

New York's governor, DeWitt Clinton, convinced the state legislature to approve paying for the canal that would link New York City with the Great Lakes. He believed it would make New York City the nation's leading port by diverting traffic from New Orleans, which was more prosperous. The canal would also give New York City an advantage over Philadelphia and Baltimore in the race for trade.

The canal was dug through all types of terrain: river valleys, mosquito-infested marshes, and solid rock. Sometimes rock had to be blasted with gunpowder. The cost of the canal was $7 million. It had dozens of locks that were used to raise and lower the water level. Each lock was just long enough to hold a canal boat. Giant gates at both ends of each lock opened and closed to let the water in or out.

Travel along the canal was slow, from one and a half to three miles an hour. Mules or horses walking on narrow paths beside the canal pulled freight barges or passenger canal boats. The fare for a canal boat was much cheaper than the fare for a stagecoach.

The canal's completion on October 25, 1825, was marked by huge celebrations. The canal paid for itself through tolls within seven years, and the cost of shipping a ton of freight dropped by 95 percent—from one hundred dollars a ton to about five dollars. New York City, where boats bound for the canal entered the Hudson River, soon became the nation's busiest port and most prosperous city.

Early Railroads

The earliest railroads in the United States consisted of horses pulling trains along tracks. The first steam-powered passenger locomotive in the country, called the *Tom Thumb*, was designed by Peter Cooper in 1830. Over the next twenty years, railroads added a new dimension to American travel.

Travel was faster and cheaper on railroads than on canals. Moreover, railroads were not affected much by weather. Winter ice, spring floods, and summer droughts did not hinder railroads as much as they hindered canals. Since railroads were not dependent on waterways, they could be built in areas where canal construction would have been impractical.

Northeasterners were quick to see the potential value of railroads for moving their manufactured goods and raw materials. In the New England states, there were five times as many railroads in 1850 as there had been a decade earlier. Also, better technology made locomotives safer and more powerful.

"Railroad fever" swept the nation. Private investors financed many railroads by buying stocks and bonds from railroad companies. State governments and local communities also furnished money or gave tax breaks to attract the companies. The federal government bought stock in the railroads and gave the companies grants of land.

More than two-thirds of the total track mileage was in the North and the West. This situation tended to unite the economic interests of those regions—a factor that would be of great importance when the nation was later fighting a civil war. Fewer railroads were built in the agricultural-focused South. In 1840 the United States had about 3,000 miles of railroad track. By 1860 it had increased to about 31,000 miles.

Fun Fact

The wedge-shaped piece on the front of a locomotive is called a "cowcatcher." It was used to push obstacles off the track so the train would not have a collision.

the LITTLE ENGINE THAT COULDN'T

Peter Cooper's steam-powered locomotive, the first in the United States, was called the *Tom Thumb* because of its small size (Tom Thumb was a character in an English fairy tale who was no larger than his father's thumb). Some referred to the locomotive as "a tea kettle on a track." Cooper demonstrated it on railroad track that existed between Baltimore and Ellicott Mills, Maryland, a distance of about 13 miles. During that trip the train reached the unheard-of speed of 18 miles per hour.

Fun Fact

Peter Cooper also patented a gelatin powder, well-known today as Jell-O.

On the return to Baltimore, stories indicate that the *Tom Thumb* was involved in a race with a horse-drawn railway car on a parallel track. The locomotive was said to have an early lead, but a belt slipped off a pulley, causing the engine to lose power. Cooper cut his hands trying to tug the pulley back on, but the horse-drawn railway car won. Nevertheless, railway travel was soon common. In 1833 Andrew Jackson became the first president to ride a train.

Communication

In early colonial times, news generally spread by word of mouth. People often gathered in local businesses to hear the latest news from travelers. Sometimes special messengers took important news to someone, but only the wealthy could afford that type of communication. News published in the few newspapers, particularly if it related to events faraway, was often old by the time it reached readers.

The Postal Service

Ships arriving in America often carried letters from people in Europe or various American ports. Generally, those letters had to be delivered by friends and neighbors. There was no regular postal service. However, as early as 1639, the Massachusetts Bay Colony gave Richard Fairbanks permission to use his home in Boston as a post office. He received the incoming mail from the ships and distributed it. People could also leave letters with him to be sent by ship to other places. Similar arrangements developed in other colonial areas, but service was slow, irregular, and unreliable. The king authorized a colonial postal system in 1692, but it was unpopular with colonists. The system charged a high postage rate, and letters could be opened if the authorities suspected disloyalty to the king.

In 1775 Benjamin Franklin was appointed the first postmaster general of the United States by the Second Continental Congress. He helped organize a working postal service for the new nation.

Samuel Osgood was appointed postmaster general by President Washington. The young country had fewer than seventy-five post offices at that time, but the postal system grew. Some roads were built or improved as "post roads" (roads used for the delivery of the mail). Ships, stagecoaches, and later trains carried the mail. As settlement spread westward, the postal service expanded with it.

Perhaps the most exciting event involving mail delivery was the creation of the **Pony Express**. Beginning on April 3, 1860, riders carried mail on horseback from St. Joseph, Missouri, to Sacramento, California. The trip took eight to ten days. Young riders rode about seventy-five miles before turning the mail over to other riders. They changed horses at relay stations every ten to fifteen miles along the route. Although the Pony Express was quite successful in delivering the mail, it ended on October 24, 1861—only a year and a half after service began. The reason for its collapse was the success of another innovation in communication—the telegraph.

Fun Fact

Throughout US history, a number of unusual items have been sent through the Postal Service. Many live items were banned after some package contents, such as ladybugs, got loose from their containers. In 1914, the parents of four-year-old May Pierstorff mailed their daughter to her grandparents, who lived about seventy-three miles away. The unpackaged girl arrived via train. Within a short time, the practice of mailing children was banned.

▾ Pony Express relay station

▲ Samuel F.B. Morse and his telegraph machine

The Telegraph

The telegraph was developed partly in response to a serious problem facing railroads. Lack of communication presented a difficulty in operating. Early railroads did not have two sets of tracks to allow trains to go in opposite directions at the same time. There were sidings, or pull-offs, at specific spots for trains to stop to let others pass, but head-on collisions were always a danger. Railroads needed a dependable way for the train stations to communicate with one another and keep track of the moving trains.

An American artist, Samuel F. B. Morse, solved this problem by developing a telegraph. His device sent messages using electrical impulses through a wire over long distances in just a few seconds. In 1838 Morse applied for government funds to develop his idea, but Congress did not grant the money until 1843. Morse was down to $0.37 when he heard that he had received the grant. The grant—$30,000—was for a telegraph line from Washington, DC, to Baltimore, Maryland. In fourteen hectic months, workers strung about forty miles of copper wire between trees and poles.

On May 24, 1844, Morse was at a telegraph key in the Supreme Courtroom of the Capitol. A crowd of judges, senators, and congressmen stood by. Morse's first message was "What hath God wrought!" (Num. 23:23). A few days later, news of James K. Polk's nomination for president arrived from the Democratic convention in Baltimore by telegraph.

Soon, telegraph poles ran alongside railroad tracks. Cities and towns were linked by a giant network of telegraph communication. By 1852 more than 23,000 miles of telegraph cable crisscrossed the nation. Railroad stations relayed information that kept the trains operating more safely and on schedule.

By 1861 telegraph wires reached across the continent to California. Because that state could now receive communications almost instantly by wire, there was little need for the Pony Express. Telegraphy also transformed the newspaper industry. Because news could now travel quickly, newspapers made recording the most current news a priority.

▲ Telegraph poles shown along the first railroad that crossed the continent

SECTION REVIEW 11.1

1. What three major roads provided transportation routes to the frontier?
2. What was the name of Robert Fulton's steamboat? Why did it become famous?
3. What canal was the most famous in the country? What two points did it connect?
4. What three advantages did railroads have over canals?
5. How did the growth of roads, canals, and railroads impact America?
6. What mail delivery service could take mail from St. Joseph, Missouri, to Sacramento, California, in ten days? Why did it last for only a year and a half?
7. How did the invention of the telegraph aid the railroad industry?
8. For the first time in human history, people were able to communicate instantly over long distances. What good effects did this create? What bad effects did it allow to develop?

11.2 INDUSTRY, AGRICULTURE, AND SEA TRADE

How did industry, agriculture, and sea trade advance?

GUIDING QUESTIONS

- How did the rise of factories impact the nation?
- How did new inventions impact agriculture?
- How did sea trade expand?

Industry

The innovations in transportation and communication helped bring many other transformations to American life. New ideas and products spread quickly as businessmen saw opportunities to make a profit from these advances. The nation was experiencing the Industrial Revolution, a period of social and economic change that was occurring as machines and other new inventions replaced hand tools.

An iron works factory in New York City

In 1800 most Americans were still subsistence farmers who owned and worked their own lands with their family's help. By using simple tools and working hard, the farmer raised enough food for his own family. He sold or traded any surplus for items that he could not grow or make at home.

Most manufactured items were made by artisans, or specialized laborers, who worked in or near their homes. They usually made one type of item, such as barrels, shoes, pottery, metalwork, or silverware. They hired apprentices to assist them and traded primarily with people in their own area.

With the expansion of transportation, goods could be sent across the country. Settlers in the West and the South could purchase goods made in New England. People with large amounts of money to invest began gathering many workers in one place. They quickly produced large quantities of goods and made a profit as they shipped those goods across the nation.

The Industrial Revolution had less impact in the South than in the North. One reason for this was that the South had fewer fast-flowing rivers to turn the water wheels that powered machinery. An even more important factor for the South's lack of industrialization was its reliance on agriculture. Most southerners invested their money, or capital, in land and slaves. A few southerners tried to reduce the South's dependence on the North by building textile mills and ironworks. But widespread industrialization did not come to the South until the latter half of the 1800s.

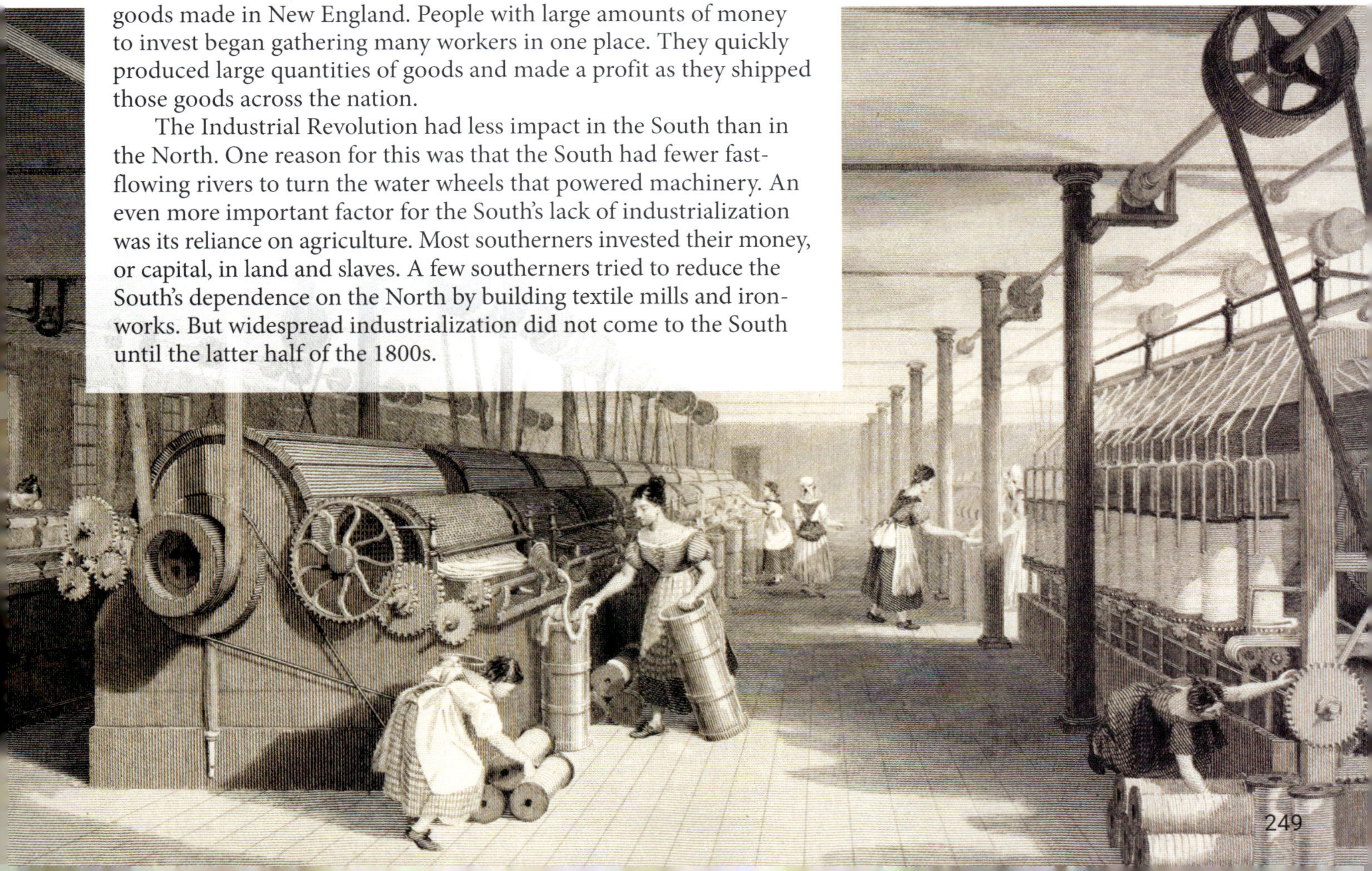
▾ In textile mills, cotton was turned into thread, yarn, and cloth.

▲ Slater Mill Historic Site in Rhode Island

The Factory System

The factory system was a major part of the Industrial Revolution. Factories employed workers to produce many similar items in one day. Schedules rarely varied, and the workers did not enter and leave as they wished. In most factories, there was a division of labor among the workers: each worker performed only one part of a multistep process. One person, a group of individuals, or numerous investors owned the building, the machinery, and the tools. The workers received a fixed wage, and the owners received the profits. But the owners also paid all the costs and took all the financial risks.

The factory system began in England, where the Industrial Revolution originated. In the late 1700s the few American factories that existed were largely unsuccessful. Their machinery was inferior, and most Americans still preferred British imports. Some states were so eager for better factories that they offered rewards to people who would start them. They even advertised in British newspapers, asking men to start factories in America. But the British feared losing their industrial advantage to the United States. To protect the British textile industry, the British government prohibited the export of British machinery and the emigration of men who could build and operate it.

An Englishman named **Samuel Slater** learned how to use and repair every machine in his employer's mill. He also memorized the design of the machines. He secretly left England in 1789. Once in the United States, Slater learned of Moses Brown, a famous Quaker merchant who had just built a textile mill in Rhode Island and needed someone to manage it. Brown hired Slater for the position.

Upon arrival at his new job, Slater examined the machines. He was disheartened and wrote, "These will not do; they are good for nothing in their present condition." Slater then built a whole series of machines from memory.

Slater operated the factory by hiring children as young as seven years old, as was done in English factories. However, he appears to have treated them more humanely than children were treated in England. Since American children on farms went to work when they were very young, using such young laborers did not seem improper to many people of that time. Some Americans noted that farm labor and factory work were different; for example, on farms children were usually supervised by family members, were able to breathe fresh air, and were less likely to be injured by the equipment used.

▼ Pittsburgh, Pennsylvania, became one of the nation's major industrial centers during the nineteenth century. Below is a panoramic view of the city.

Slater's factory, with its simple machines, was ideally suited to a young country with a shortage of skilled labor. Yet the workplace was dangerous, and work in the factory limited educational opportunities for children. As these problems became more obvious, some people questioned the use of child labor. At the same time, supporters noted that the system provided employment that helped feed and clothe people and enabled them to purchase items they had not been able to afford earlier.

▲ Textile mill museum in Lowell, Massachusetts

The factory system grew quickly in New England, where fast-moving streams turned the water wheels that made machines work. When steam power replaced waterpower, the vast forests of New England provided fuel for steam engines. Since New England soil was too poor for most heavy agriculture and because the colder climate limited the growing season, New Englanders willingly tried other ways to earn a living.

New England was an ideal place for factories because a labor force was readily available there. Although families and single men sometimes went west or to other regions to seek better opportunities, many stayed, and young women often chose employment in factories. Francis Cabot Lowell, a New England cloth maker, organized a mill town for girls in Waltham, Massachusetts, in the early 1800s. His town's factory provided their room and board and strict supervision.

▼ Early sewing machine

By the early 1800s other developments of machinery and methods of production helped boost American industries. For example, **Eli Whitney** showed how the use of **interchangeable parts** (parts of a device that could be replaced by identical parts) could dramatically decrease the amount of time required to produce an item. He and other men assembled products, guns in particular, by producing large numbers of each part. In the past, skilled craftsmen made specific parts and assembled each gun individually. But Whitney made molds that could form large numbers of each part. Workers could then assemble more guns faster with the interchangeable parts; this led to the **mass production** (production in large quantities) of products.

The invention of the sewing machine further aided the growth of the factory system. The sewing machine allowed seamstresses, who previously hand-stitched material, to drastically reduce the time they needed to sew garments and other products. Factories with hundreds of sewing machines soon sprang up.

Although Elias Howe was not the first person to develop a sewing machine, he received a patent for his model in 1846. Isaac Singer, another inventor, patented his version of the sewing machine in 1851. Differing from Howe's, Singer's machine used a foot pedal rather than a hand crank so that the operator's hands were free.

UNDERSTANDING *why people accepted their* WAGES

In 1818, $1 was the equivalent of about $20 in 2022. Although wages in the 1800s might seem small to us today, they were enticing to people at the time. In fact, some farm workers left the land and moved to towns and cities because higher wages were available in many factories.

Many people were able to gain the knowledge and experience needed to move into higher-paying jobs. Some were able to save more than they spent and thereby improve the quality of their lives over time. They showed initiative and good stewardship. Others, because of illness, the loss of a job, an injury at work, inability to obtain jobs that paid more, or other issues, struggled to survive.

This 1835 leaflet called for reducing the number of work hours from 12 to 10.

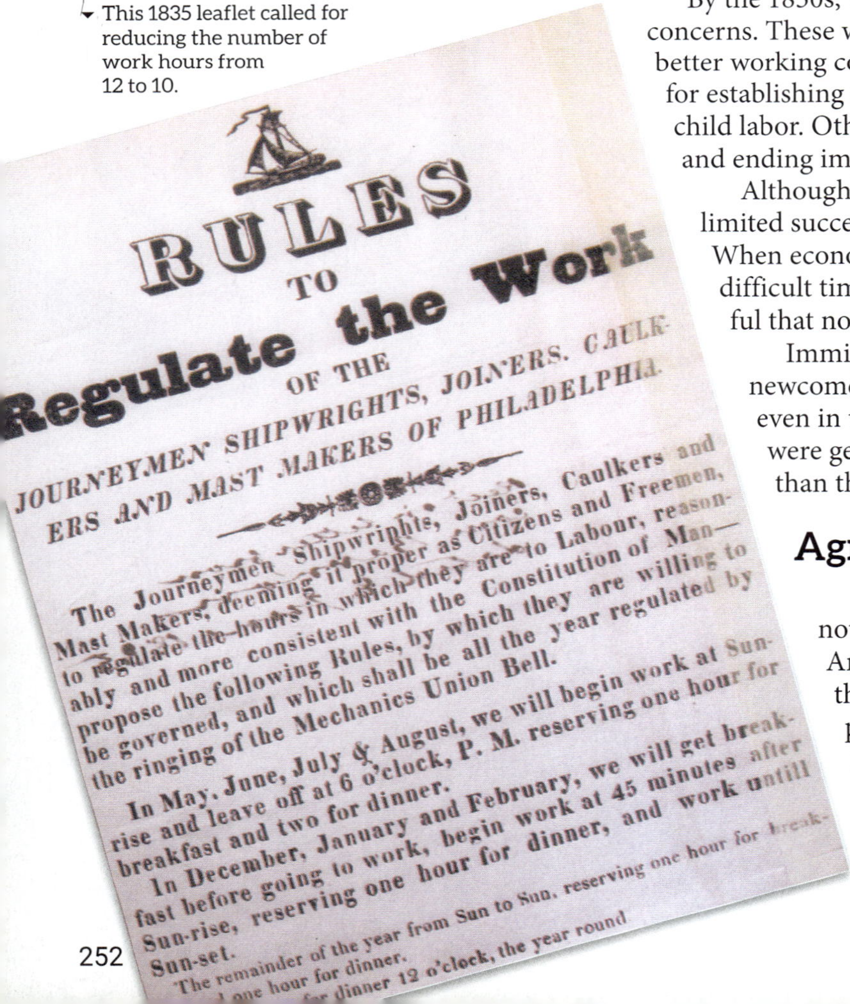
RULES
TO
Regulate the Work
OF THE
JOURNEYMEN SHIPWRIGHTS, JOINERS, CAULKERS AND MAST MAKERS OF PHILADELPHIA.

The Journeymen Shipwrights, Joiners, Caulkers and Mast Makers, deeming it proper as Citizens and Freemen, to regulate the hours in which they are to Labour, reasonably and more consistent with the Constitution of Man—propose the following Rules, by which they are willing to be governed, and which shall be all the year regulated by the ringing of the Mechanics Union Bell.

In May, June, July & August, we will begin work at Sun-rise and leave off at 6 o'clock, P. M. reserving one hour for breakfast and two for dinner.

In December, January and February, we will get breakfast before going to work, begin work at 45 minutes after Sun-rise, reserving one hour for dinner, and work untill Sun-set.

The remainder of the year from Sun to Sun, reserving one hour for breakfast and one hour for dinner.

... for dinner 12 o'clock, the year round

Results of the Rise of Industry

Industrialization influenced the lives of nearly all Americans. New inventions made work easier. Many people moved from farms to cities for new jobs. Money earned in factories enabled some to enjoy a higher living standard. Factories were near sources of waterpower, and towns and cities grew up around these sites. The factories also gave many immigrants the opportunity for a new life in America.

Although the factory system contributed much that was positive, there were many negative aspects. For example, workers typically labored six days a week for a total of more than seventy hours. Wages were low. As a result, several people in a family, including children, had to work to provide enough income for survival. In 1818 a factory in Paterson, New Jersey, reported the following weekly wages: men earned $5.00, women earned $2.37, and children earned $1.37. By the early 1850s, pay for some common laborers and factory workers reached a new high of $6.00 a week.

Factories were stuffy, cramped, and noisy. Machines did not have safety devices, so they caused many injuries. In addition, workers feared losing their jobs with the arrival of new machines. And factory towns were usually crowded and drab. Working families often squeezed into one-room apartments as the urban population more than doubled between 1820 and 1860. Because many children worked, few could attend school. By the 1860s, many factory owners had sacrificed the good of their workers for the sake of growth and technology. Although most Americans believed that growth was beneficial to society, many worried that the cost of obtaining it was becoming too great.

By the 1830s, workers organized **labor unions** to address their concerns. These were groups of workers who wanted to obtain better working conditions and better pay. Many such groups called for establishing a ten-hour workday and reducing or eliminating child labor. Others supported establishing free public education and ending imprisonment for failure to pay debts.

Although some improvements were made, the unions had limited success. When the nation prospered, so did unions. When economic downturns came, the unions floundered. In difficult times, workers were willing to accept wage cuts, fearful that not doing so would cause them to lose their jobs.

Immigration hindered the success of the unions. Most newcomers to the nation were eager to work and knew that even in the worst conditions in the United States, they were generally living and working in better conditions than those they had endured in their native country.

Agriculture

The Industrial Revolution profoundly affected not only the American factory worker but also the American farmer. New farm machinery enabled the farmer to improve his methods, increase his production, lower his costs, and thereby increase his profits. Since fewer farmers were needed to produce more food, some farmers joined the growing urban work force in factories, shipyards, and other businesses.

Agricultural Advances

Early American farmers used tools similar to those used centuries before. But new farm machines that were developed during the Industrial Revolution made it easier for farmers to plow, plant, and harvest more acres, more quickly and efficiently. In addition, new machines made some farm products easier to process. As a result, America's farm production increased rapidly. Farmers could meet the needs of their own families and make a profit by selling the extra they produced. American grain became an important export to Europe after crop failures and political disputes created food shortages there. Three particular inventors and inventions played important roles as America expanded its agricultural production.

John Deere's Plow

By 1838 a young blacksmith named **John Deere** realized that he could improve the common iron plow. A major problem with that plow was soil sticking to the blade, making it necessary to clean the blade frequently. Deere developed a superior plow using a steel blade. Soon, his product was in great demand. Later, he built a factory that produced hundreds, then thousands, of plows yearly. Eventually, almost every wagon going west carried a John Deere plow. The steel plow was important because it helped farmers cultivate the prairies of the West.

▾ Plow designed by John Deere

Cyrus McCormick's Reaper

Planting grain could be profitable, particularly if a farmer could harvest crops quickly; however, that was difficult because only hand-held cutting tools existed for completing the task. In the 1820s **Cyrus McCormick**, the son of a Virginia blacksmith, developed a reaper, a machine for cutting and harvesting grain.

▾ Cyrus McCormick's mechanical reaper

Cotton (at top) was placed into the cotton gin (right) to remove seeds.

Eli Whitney's Cotton Gin

Tobacco had been a profitable crop for the South since colonial days, but it had a limited appeal. The English were using new machines to make cloth; thus, selling them raw cotton, which grew well in the South, was an appealing idea. However, cotton had little profitability because it was extremely time consuming to remove the seeds from it. If a workman cleaned seeds for an entire day, his yield would be just one pound of cleaned cotton. In 1793 Eli Whitney developed the **cotton gin** to remove the seeds quickly and efficiently. With his hand-cranked device, one person could clean fifty pounds of cotton a day. Later, when operated by water power, it could clean many times that amount.

Cotton production in America surged from about 1.5 million pounds in 1790 to 89 million pounds by 1810. By 1850 more than 1 billion pounds were produced in the nation and by 1860, almost 2 billion pounds. By 1850 cotton accounted for more than half the value of all American exports. It was little wonder that Southerners proclaimed that "Cotton is King."

Southern Agriculture and Slavery

Plantations in the South produced tobacco, cotton, and other products in large quantities. Groups of unskilled laborers could complete the tiring, but simple, tasks. Though for a number of years many Americans thought that slavery would gradually disappear, the invention of the cotton gin made growing cotton more profitable than ever. Tragically, cotton production continued to depend heavily on the use of slaves.

Rather than disappearing, the number of slaves in the South increased. In 1790 there were nearly 700,000 slaves in the South; in 1810 there were about 1.2 million; and by 1860 the number had reached almost 4 million.

Most southerners were not slaveowners. During the first half of the nineteenth century, about one-fourth of all southern families owned slaves. Most slave-owning families owned fewer than ten slaves, and probably only about five thousand planters in the entire South had fifty or more slaves. Nevertheless, the vast majority of Southerners believed slavery was important and necessary because cotton and other crops produced on plantations by slave labor were an essential part of the South's economy. Lacking industries, the South depended more and more on the money earned from its cotton exports. Furthermore, as the number of New England textile mills and their output of cotton cloth increased, so did the demand for raw cotton. Factory owners in the North recognized their dependence on slave-grown cotton, so many of them opposed ending slavery.

Cotton and Slavery (1790–1860)

Year	Number of pounds	Number of slaves in the South
1790	about 1.5 million	nearly 700,000
1810	89 million	about 1.2 million
1850	more than 1 billion	about 3.2 million
1860	almost 2 billion	almost 4 million

The number of bales of cotton produced increased from 4,000 in 1792 to 3,841,416 in 1860.

Sea Trade

While Americans enjoyed wider markets for their manufactured goods at home, new markets overseas also opened. Trade with European countries expanded—France, Prussia, the Netherlands, and countries with Baltic and Mediterranean ports all traded with the United States. Americans traded their surplus goods—such as cotton, tobacco, and lumber—for items that were unavailable or scarce in America, such as hemp, raisins, olive oil, and iron.

Fishing and Whaling

From America's earliest years, fishing had been an important way of making a living. Cod were abundant off Newfoundland's Grand Banks, and herring and lobster were caught off the Atlantic coast. Whaling ships regularly sailed to the Bering Sea. Though the trips were long and treacherous, they attracted adventurers. Profits came from selling whale oil, which was burned to give light. Sailors spent the long hours aboard ship carving whalebone or whale ivory, producing a new and exquisite art called scrimshaw.

Over the years, the United States developed a highly productive shipbuilding industry. In the 1840s shipbuilders developed the **clipper**, a new type of sailing vessel designed for increased speeds. In contrast to earlier oceangoing vessels, the clipper had a much sharper point on its bow (front) that could "clip" into the waves rather than plow into them. Some clippers had as many as thirty-five sails. Before the invention of the clipper, it usually took 21 to 28 days to travel from New York City to Britain. A clipper could usually make the trip in half that time.

Clippers reached their heyday after 1848, when gold was discovered in California. They carried many gold seekers west who preferred a sea route rather than an overland one. The clipper-ship era lasted only about fifteen years. It ended by the mid-1850s, when new advances, such as railroads and steamships, outdated the clipper ships.

the AGE OF INVENTION

The nineteenth century was an age of invention. Until that time, information had traveled at the speed of a fast horse. But in the 1840s, people could send messages between cities in the eastern United States instantly through the telegraph. In 1861 the telegraph could send messages across the entire continent.

Human inventiveness comes through the image of God in people, and it is used to exercise dominion over the earth as God intended (Gen. 1:26–28). Christians can and should enjoy the many benefits that new devices bring to human life.

However, the explosion of inventions in the nineteenth century led to problems. Some people thought that if a thing could be done, it should be done. Progress, for these people, was not evaluated by biblical principles. Christians should not reject technological advances, but they should understand that not all change is good. Though new items may provide tremendous advantages, they must be used cautiously to avoid negative consequences.

The challenge of properly using new resources continues today. The Bible provides guidance for discerning between right and wrong and for the wise use of innovations.

◂ A clipper

▲ This 1953 stamp celebrated the 100th anniversary of Matthew Perry's trip to Japan.

New Asian Markets

Americans had heard of Europeans gaining riches by trade in China and wanted to take advantage of opportunities there. In 1784 New York merchants refitted a ship, the *Empress of China*, for a trading expedition. The *Empress* sailed across the Atlantic to Africa, around the coast of South Africa, and across the Indian Ocean to China. The Chinese welcomed the Americans, and the *Empress* later brought home tea, spices, silk, chinaware, and stories of its profitable trip. By 1786 America had opened its first trading company in that nation.

Although America profited by trading with China, it wanted to expand into other Asian markets as well. For two centuries, Japan had rejected almost all contact with the outside world. However, in 1853 **Commodore Matthew Perry** took several warships to that nation with the goal of securing a trade treaty. He refused to obey Japanese orders to leave Tokyo Bay and demanded that the Japanese accept a letter he brought from US President Millard Fillmore asking that the two nations begin trade. Perry attempted to intimidate the Japanese by firing blank shots from the 73 cannons aboard his ships. Perry then delivered the letter. The implication was clear—the Japanese should willingly agree to begin trade with the United States or be forced to do so by a superior navy.

Perry then sailed to China to give the Japanese government time to consider his demand. The Japanese realized they could not defend themselves against America's power and its insistence that Japan open trade. Thus, when Perry returned to Japan in 1854, the two nations signed a treaty agreeing to begin trade.

▼ Chinese goods (such as the punch bowl and tea shown below), became popular products in America.

SECTION REVIEW 11.2

1. What name is given to the time period of social and economic change as machines and inventions replaced hand tools?
2. What were two reasons for the slow development of the South's textile industry?
3. Who rebuilt the machines in a textile mill in Rhode Island? How did he rebuild them?
4. Why was it considered appropriate to hire children to work in the factories? Would you support this today? Why or why not?
5. What section of the country was ideal for building factories? Why?
6. What were some positive and negative effects of the Industrial Revolution?
7. What were two reforms many labor organizations called for?
8. What were the inventions of John Deere, Cyrus McCormick, and Eli Whitney? How did each impact agriculture?
9. How did America open trade with China? Japan?

◂ This quilt was made from both Chinese and European fabric.

11.3 IMMIGRATION, RELIGIOUS MOVEMENTS, AND REFORM MOVEMENTS

What changes occurred in society in the early 1800s?

America experienced many changes in the daily operation of its farms, businesses, and transportation systems during the early 1800s. In addition, millions of immigrants entered the country. And as part of the innovative spirit of the era, reformers tried to change the hearts and minds of Americans.

Immigration

During the first few decades after America won its independence, immigration slowed to nearly a standstill. But after 1815, conditions in Europe prompted millions to move to America. Between 1820 and 1860 more than five million people entered the country.

The largest groups of immigrants came from Ireland and Germany. In the 1840s a fungus on potatoes (Ireland's main crop) led to a famine, or food shortage, in that nation. Many Irish starved, and many others died from diseases made worse by malnutrition. Hunger and the promise of rich farmland drew many Irish to America. Almost 1.5 million arrived in the United States between 1845 and 1860. Sadly, most of the Irish were so poor that they could not afford to leave the cities along the East Coast of America. They overwhelmed northern cities, where they accepted the new industrial jobs. Because they had so little money, they were willing to take the worst jobs and live in the worst neighborhoods. Americans soon became prejudiced against them, partly because the Irish were Catholics while most Americans were Protestant.

The German immigrants had a different experience in America. Like the Irish, most Germans left Europe for new farmland. The Industrial Revolution in Europe had changed traditional German life,

▾ This memorial in Philadelphia honors the Irish who came to America during the famine in their country.

GUIDING QUESTIONS

- How did immigration impact America in the early 1800s?
- How did religious movements affect America during the early 1800s?
- How did ideas about education, slavery, and women's rights change during the early 1800s?

Levi Strauss: Immigrant

Levi Strauss, born Loeb Strauss, moved to New York City from Germany with his mother and sisters in 1847. His two older brothers had already moved to New York and had started a dry-goods business, which Strauss joined. But he soon moved west to California after gold was discovered.

He decided to make his fortune by supplying miners with clothing and other goods. His business, named Levi Strauss & Co., grew rapidly, and he became famous in San Francisco. In the 1870s a tailor friend of Strauss's told him of the new pants that he was making, which had rivets to strengthen the seams. Strauss and his friend entered business together, received a patent for the pants, and began to produce the now world-famous Levi Strauss blue jeans. Strauss was generous with his fortune. He donated funds to many charities and Jewish organizations.

causing many Germans to lose their shops and farms. Others left after political revolutions in Germany. Unlike the Irish, many Germans had enough money to move from the cities. A sizable number settled in the Midwest. Americans generally welcomed the Germans because they tended to be educated Protestants and efficient producers. A number of German Jews also came to America. Many of them remained in the cities and became successful in business.

Regardless of their country of origin, the immigrants made a lasting impact on the character of America. They brought traditions from Europe that still exist today, such as the Christmas tree, which came from Germany. Many descendants of these immigrants still cluster in their ancestors' areas of settlement. For example, the Scandinavians tended to settle in Minnesota, and there are still many people of Scandinavian ancestry there.

POPULAR CULTURE *in the* 1800S

The early 1800s was a time of great change in popular culture and in nearly every other aspect of American life. The changes came as the nation advanced in industry and became more urban. Before this period, public entertainment, such as theater and opera, was more refined and was open mainly to the wealthy. But now entertainers appealed to a wide audience. Popular culture became lighthearted and, at times, wild.

Before the 1830s newspapers were generally expensive and appeared only once a week. They discussed trade and politics. But with new inventions, such as the rotary press, papers could easily be printed daily and for a much cheaper price. Some began emphasizing sensational topics, such as murders and scandals, and spread rumors and hoaxes. By the 1840s more balanced newspapers appeared that resembled the newspapers of today.

Americans also began to read magazines and inexpensive novels called "dime novels." The working classes enjoyed these stories of crime and adventure. The upper classes enjoyed more "respectable" sentimental novels. Most of these popular books are not considered serious literature today.

By far, the most popular form of entertainment of the time was the theater. Actors performed in comedies and magic shows. Minstrel shows also popularized new music and dances. Stephen Foster wrote new songs that were sung in these shows, such as "Camptown Races" and "Oh! Susanna." The minstrel shows also featured blackface actors (actors who painted themselves to look like blacks). Sadly, these actors made fun of blacks and sometimes joked about slavery. Some theaters served alcohol, which often made for a rowdy show.

This era was also a time of sensationalism. People enjoyed watching events such as dogfights, cockfights, and boxing. P. T. Barnum, "the Great Showman," took advantage of interest in the "freakish." He traveled the country, displaying a supposedly 161-year-old woman whom he claimed had been a slave of George Washington. Soon he opened Barnum's American Museum in New York City. His exhibits included Tom Thumb, a very short man (referred to as a dwarf at the time), and the Siamese, or conjoined, twins Chang and Eng. In his later years, Barnum started the traveling circus and museum called "the Greatest Show on Earth."

Preachers and reformers tried to stop some of the sensationalism and the drunkenness of the period. The alcohol served in theaters inspired the formation of many temperance societies, groups dedicated to stopping the consumption of alcohol. But these societies met with little success. Many Americans drank alcohol everywhere, from barn raisings to political events.

Poster advertising a circus in 1897 ▸

Religious Movements

With the changes and growth of the early nineteenth century, some Americans wanted to change Christianity. In a world filled with railroads and telegraphs, the biblical miracles and statements of human sinfulness seemed old-fashioned and out of place to some. In an age of factories, machines, and modern inventions, some thought dependence on God was unnecessary.

Unitarianism and Transcendentalism

After the War for Independence, many American churches entered a period of spiritual apathy. New England's traditional Congregational and Presbyterian Churches suffered the most. True Christianity in these churches was replaced by Unitarianism, which denies the doctrine of the Trinity. The movement became much stronger in the 1800s after Harvard became closely associated with it.

The Unitarians were usually intellectuals, and many of them were political and educational leaders. William Ellery Channing, a persuasive preacher and writer in Boston, was the most famous Unitarian of this time.

▲ William Channing

Transcendentalism, a philosophical movement that believed that people were basically good but had been corrupted by society, became popular during this period. It also promoted the idea that people could find truth on their own—they did not need to accept the authority of the Scriptures. Its followers also embraced romanticism, which placed a great emphasis on emotion and nature. Ralph Waldo Emerson and Henry David Thoreau were two of the best-known transcendentalists.

The Second Great Awakening

At this low point in America's spiritual life, God sent a sweeping revival to the young nation. In this **Second Great Awakening** thousands came to Christ who had never before demonstrated any interest in religion.

The revivals in the East began in colleges, the battlegrounds between Unitarianism and traditional Christian teachings by men such as Jonathan Edwards. At Yale, the students debated the truth of Christianity. In 1795 Jonathan Edwards's grandson **Timothy Dwight** became the new president of Yale. Dwight dealt directly with the students' unbelief. He debated students on questions such as "Is the Bible the Word of God?" and he clearly argued that it is. Dwight also preached a series of sermons on true Bible doctrine. After seven years of his lecturing and preaching, Yale experienced a revival in which one-third of the students professed faith in Christ. This was the first of several revivals at Yale. Other colleges experienced similar revivals.

▲ Asahel Nettleton

Churches in the East also stirred to new life through the preaching of faithful men, such as Connecticut evangelist Asahel Nettleton. Fearful of the extreme emotionalism of some earlier revivals, Nettleton always insisted on calm, orderly services. He wanted to be sure that converts knew what they were professing and were not just submitting to emotional pressure.

The revival took a different form on the frontier. The West, which at that time included states such as Kentucky and Tennessee, was mostly Baptist and Methodist. Revivals there usually occurred at **camp meetings**. Hundreds of people gathered in a central location

▲ Methodist camp meeting

and pitched their tents for days or weeks. They came to listen to preachers and to sing camp-meeting songs. These camp meetings were sometimes very emotional and sensational. They were also social events because most of the attendees had little other social interaction on the frontier. The most famous camp meeting took place in 1801 at Cane Ridge, Kentucky, not far from the city of Lexington. That gathering numbered at least ten thousand people.

Some preachers and theologians believed that simply using the right techniques would produce revivals. The most famous revivalist to advocate this idea was **Charles Finney**, who worked primarily in New York State. He reached large crowds through new publicity measures and by adapting his style to the cities where he preached. Just as Andrew Jackson brought democracy to politics, so Finney brought democracy to religion, involving people from all walks of life in his revivals. However, he and others like him departed from some essential doctrines in order to win converts. Finney placed more emphasis on his special techniques than on the power of the Holy Spirit.

▲ Charles Finney

During these years, many people were truly converted under the ministries of faithful preachers like Nettleton. Others responded with great emotion to evangelists like Finney; but without a true supernatural work by the Spirit of God, emotional responses did not last. In fact, some have argued that people actually became uninterested in hearing preaching in some areas where Finney had spent a great amount of time.

The revivals also affected American political and moral life. While they strengthened the trend toward democratization, they also placed a check on some of the negative aspects of increased democracy—such as the belief, by some, that if the majority of people approve of a behavior, it is fine to participate in it. The revivals stirred Americans to examine their behavior and to press for moral reforms in the nation.

Reform Movements

Many revivalists believed that their converts' duty was to promote reform. Societies for improvement emerged throughout the country. Americans joined forces to raise money for causes and to influence people to change. Organizations were formed for nearly every interest group. Some supported missionaries and Bible distribution; others focused on studying morality and literature. Societies often did charity work or supported labor or ethnic groups. Christian groups tried to stop common social ills, such as smoking, drinking, and immorality. Many reform movements focused on three major areas of American life—education, slavery, and women's rights.

Education

Most colonial children learned to read and write at home and in small schools. After America gained its independence, many people believed that one of the focal points of education should be training children how to be good citizens. This was necessary, they believed, for future generations to govern successfully.

As industrialization spread, the number of children working in factories and receiving no education troubled many. Laborers wanted their children to have a free education. In addition, most Americans believed that the children of immigrants would benefit from receiving an education that would "Americanize" them, or make them aware of the nation's heritage and culture.

▲ Horace Mann

The reformers believed that the best way for children to learn was through tax-supported public schools. **Horace Mann**, of Massachusetts, was the most influential of these reformers. He led the drive for statewide public schools in his state and in 1837 became the first secretary of the Massachusetts Board of Education.

Many states began to require children to attend schools for most of the year. Students were divided into grades for the first time. Educational reforms allowed many poor children to have the same opportunities as children of the wealthy.

Many school reformers were Unitarian. They supported Bible reading, generic prayers, and the teaching of morality in schools. However, some did not want specific Christian teachings to be taught in the public schools.

Abolition

Slavery was the issue that stirred reformers more than any other. In 1808 the United States became the last major Western nation to ban the foreign slave trade (see Article I, Section 9, of the Constitution). Some slave smuggling continued, but most new slaves were born to existing slaves already in America.

▲ An abolitionist speaking about the need to outlaw slavery

Reformers, strengthened by the revivals, viewed slavery as a grave sin. In the 1740s Jonathan Edwards, though a slave owner himself, had condemned the slave trade. In the 1770s men whom Edwards had trained, including preacher Samuel Hopkins, began to preach against slavery itself. Those who wanted to abolish slavery called themselves **abolitionists**. Opposition to slavery became a major issue for many ministers in the Northeast. In the 1800s the Quakers expanded efforts to end slavery. Some abolitionists at this time thought the slaves should be gradually emancipated, or freed, and moved to Africa to establish colonies. Other abolitionists argued later that freedmen should be allowed to live in the United States.

Although there were some antislavery societies in the South, Northern abolitionists were much more numerous and led the movement. They used public lectures and newspapers to gain support and affect politics.

By the 1830s the debate over slavery became more widespread and heated as some people tried extending slavery to newly settled territories. The debate was not limited to groups of Quakers and abolitionists. Many Americans grew to realize that slavery was not just another system of labor. The morality of slavery remained the central issue. Those who depended on slavery defended the institution. Some people justified slavery on religious grounds. They said that bringing the "uncivilized" slave to America helped to

"Christianize" him. Other people praised slavery because slaves were provided a job, shelter, food, and clothing. They argued it was better than "wage slavery" in the northern factories, where workers had dangerous jobs and terrible living conditions.

Opposition to slavery increased as its wrongs were exposed. Samuel Hopkins argued that Christ commanded Christians to go to the nations to preach the gospel—not to enslave the nations. He noted that enslaving people led them to resist the gospel. Opponents to slavery did not deny the need to reform northern factories. But they argued that slaves' living conditions were often much worse than the defenders of slavery would admit.

Women's Rights

Women became heavily involved in reform movements, especially the antislavery societies. While aiding the abolitionists, women began to think more about their own position in society. In the early 1800s, women were not allowed to vote. Very few were allowed to attend college. Married women could not own property. Some of them began to compare their position to that of the slaves in the South.

Three of the most famous female abolitionists, **Lucretia Mott**, **Elizabeth Cady Stanton**, and Susan B. Anthony, decided to call for women's rights, just as they had called for an end to slavery. Mott and Stanton helped organize the **Seneca Falls Convention** in July 1848 at Seneca Falls, New York. Over three hundred attendees discussed women's rights and proposed changes to the law, such as allowing women to vote. The movement started slowly. But later groups, inspired by Stanton and her successors, triumphantly gained the vote for women with ratification of the Nineteenth Amendment in 1920.

The movement's initial lack of success was partly due to the antagonistic attitude of leaders such as Stanton to the institution of marriage and the inspiration of Scripture. Stanton eventually claimed that marriage submits women to bondage and that the Bible was written by men to oppress women. These claims offended many Americans. Others resisted the movement by saying women should be moral leaders of the home, while men should lead outside the home. This view taught that women could best reform society by teaching their children.

▲ Elizabeth Cady Stanton

Dorothea Dix

Dorothea Dix (1802–87) spent her early career as a teacher in Massachusetts. Later, in 1841, she visited a jail in East Cambridge, Massachusetts. Among the prisoners were those termed "insane." The jails of that time mistreated such individuals in various ways. Some were locked in underground cells, left unclothed, and even chained to the walls. What she saw spurred her career as a reformer. During the next two years, Dix traveled and examined the condition of the insane throughout the region. Other leaders in Massachusetts, such as William Ellery Channing and Horace Mann, supported her efforts.

In 1843 Dix submitted a report to the Massachusetts state legislature with her findings. She repeated this process in other states. Her efforts led legislators in fifteen states to establish state asylums, or facilities, for the mentally ill. Her work was also influential in Canada, Europe, and even Japan.

SECTION REVIEW 11.3

1. What two nationalities were the largest groups of immigrants that arrived in America in the early 1800s? Why did each come? Where did they tend to settle?
2. What Christian doctrine does Unitarianism deny? What did Transcendentalists believe about man? What does the Bible say about these ideas?
3. How did the Second Great Awakening affect eastern colleges?
4. What were revivals on the frontier like?
5. How did Charles Finney bring democracy to religion?
6. What did education reformers want?
7. How was being a slave different from being a northern factory "wage slave"?
8. What were most women not allowed to do in the early 1800s that led to the call for increased women's rights?

CHAPTER 11 REVIEW

Making Connections

1. How were turnpikes different from other roads?
2. What major cities developed along the steamboat routes?
3. How do canals keep a constant water level between two bodies of water with differing elevations?
4. Which two sections of the country built the most railroad track? Why?
5. Who was the first postmaster general of the United States?
6. How did the Pony Express work?
7. What two cities did the first telegraph lines connect?
8. Which of Eli Whitney's ideas increased the speed and efficiency of making products? What did this lead to?
9. Why could clothing be produced much more rapidly during the Industrial Revolution?
10. Why were unions not very successful during the early 1800s?
11. How did Eli Whitney's cotton gin affect slavery in the South?
12. Why were many northern factory owners opposed to ending slavery?
13. How did the development of the clipper allow traders to reach farther ports of trade?
14. Why were the Irish and German immigrants treated differently by those already living in America?
15. Both the first steam-powered locomotive in the United States and one of P. T. Barnum's popular attractions were named "Tom Thumb." What did they have in common?
16. What did Timothy Dwight do to influence his students for Christ?
17. What Connecticut evangelist insisted on calm, orderly services?
18. In what areas of society were reformers active besides the major movements of education, slavery, and women's rights?
19. What group wanted to abolish slavery? What were two differing ideas about how to treat freed slaves?
20. How long after the Seneca Falls Convention did it take to ratify the Nineteenth Amendment granting women the right to vote?

Thinking Critically

21. How was factory life better than farm life? How was it worse?
22. In what manner should employers pay their employees? Use Leviticus 19:13 and Deuteronomy 24:14–15 to defend your answer. What would this look like today?

Living as a Christian Citizen

23. Choose a technological device that you use daily. How does it help you as you seek to live for the glory of God? How does it hinder you as you seek to live for the glory of God? How should you change the way you use this device based on your observations?
24. Why might you be tempted to act unjustly toward coworkers or those you have hired? What biblical truths would you need to anchor yourself as a Christian businessperson?

Terms to Remember

Great Wagon Road
Daniel Boone
Cumberland Gap
Wilderness Road
National Road
turnpikes
steamboats
Robert Fulton
canal
locks
Erie Canal
Pony Express
Samuel F. B. Morse
Industrial Revolution
Samuel Slater
Eli Whitney
interchangeable parts
mass production
labor unions
John Deere
Cyrus McCormick
cotton gin
clipper
Commodore Matthew Perry
Second Great Awakening
Timothy Dwight
camp meetings
Charles Finney
Horace Mann
abolitionists
Lucretia Mott
Elizabeth Cady Stanton
Seneca Falls Convention
Dorothea Dix

CHAPTER 12

Westward Expansion

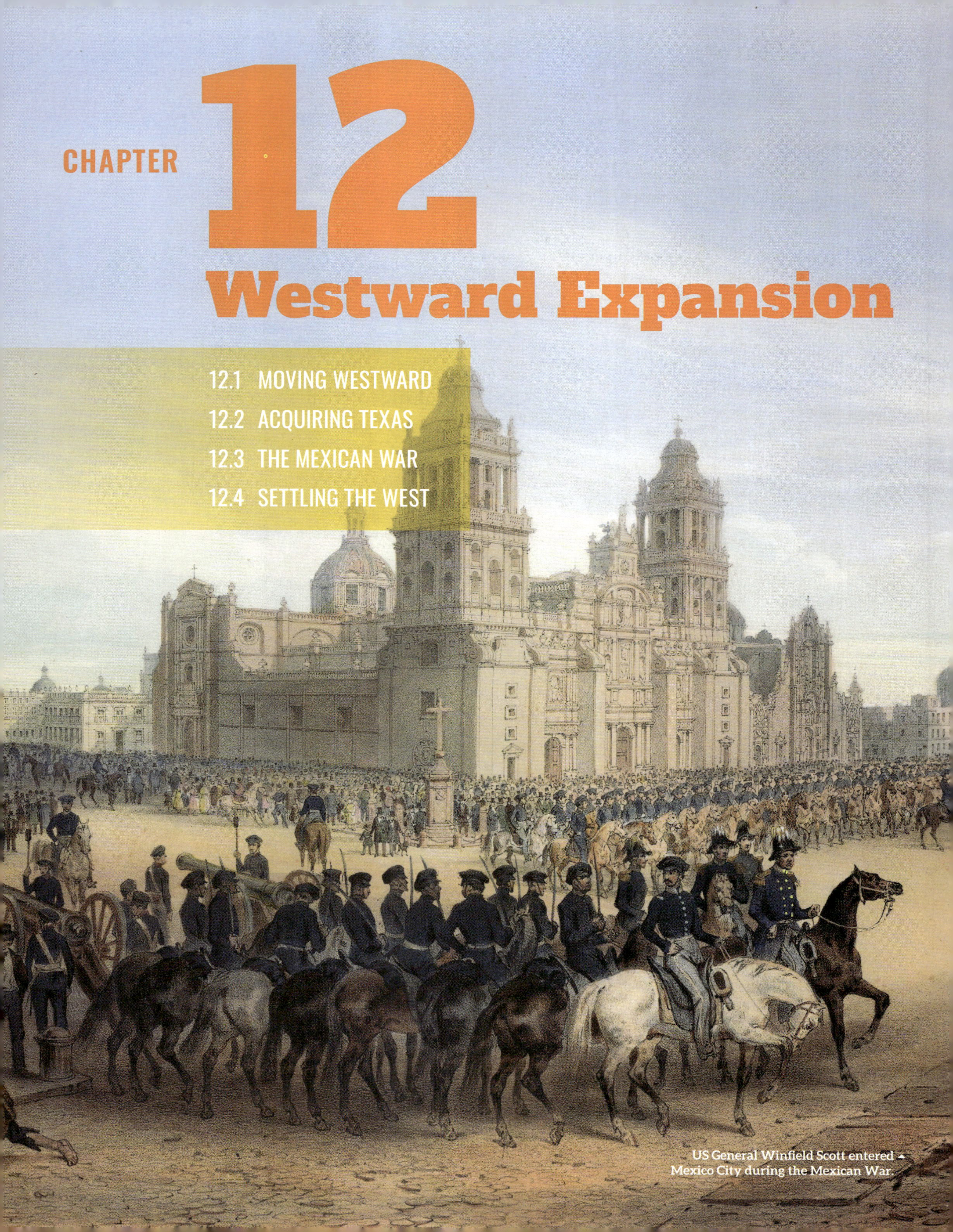

US General Winfield Scott entered Mexico City during the Mexican War.

When George Washington became president in 1789, 4 million people lived in the young nation, and most of them were in the East. By 1830 the total population had grown to 12.8 million, 4 million of whom lived west of the Appalachians. By 1850 the population was 23.2 million, and half lived west of the Appalachians. Settlers felt the constant desire to move west.

GUIDING QUESTIONS

- Why did the settlers go west in the early 1800s?
- What did trailblazers do?
- Why did Americans and Indians fight during the westward expansion?

12.1 MOVING WESTWARD

Why did settlers move west?

Over the mountains into Kentucky, Tennessee, and the old Northwest Territory, and on past the Mississippi River, Americans moved westward. The nation's expansion from sea to sea was not at all guaranteed in the early 1800s. But over time many Americans had come to believe it was the country's fate, or destiny, to have all the western lands to the Pacific Ocean. Others believed that God intended for this to occur. Newspaperman John L. O'Sullivan called this belief America's "**Manifest Destiny**." Other Americans disagreed. They argued that the United States should promote trade with, send missionaries to, and model a democratic government for the Mexicans and Native Americans who lived in the West. They did not think the United States had a divine or God-given right to conquer this land. Thus, while many Americans believed that westward expansion was ordained by God, some Christian leaders were concerned that God's name was sometimes being used to violate biblical teaching.

The general mood of the nation encouraged people to go west. This was a time of great optimism. Americans believed they could make their country greater. They also believed that the West was theirs to claim. Many saw neighbors and relatives pack up and head west. It was easy to catch the excitement and dreams of others. Many leaders of the day, especially President James K. Polk, who was elected in 1844, encouraged expansion. Many people willingly followed.

Reasons to Go West

Americans had many reasons for moving westward, and the areas there had much to offer. First, the West had a nearly irresistible attraction for American farmers who were seeking good, inexpensive land. Eastern planters with worn-out soils felt certain that the rich land near the Mississippi River could restore their prosperity. For some in the North, moving west simply meant moving across the Mississippi to land in Minnesota and Iowa. Poor southern farmers who could not compete with large-plantation owners but could afford the cheap new western lands thought they also could improve their lives by moving west. These settlers first moved to Missouri and Arkansas and then headed even farther west.

Second, western land also became a refuge for thousands of immigrants seeking to escape the troubles of other countries. Political problems, low wages, high taxes, lack of new jobs, religious persecution, and famine drew immigrants from such places as Ireland, Germany, and later Scandinavia to the American West.

▾ Settlers carried items they needed to begin a new life in the West.

Reasons to Go West

1 Good land for farming	2 Refuge
3 Riches	4 Adventure
5 New start in life	6 Spreading the gospel

A third reason for moving west was to seek riches. With the discovery of gold in California and silver in Colorado and Nevada, many men went west seeking their fortunes. A few did become rich by mining, but others sought wealth in land. Land speculators took the risk of buying land from the government. They hoped that they could then develop settlements and resell the lands at a profit. Some lost money, others broke even, and a few became prosperous. Many people who invested in western railroads and supply companies also made large profits.

Another reason Americans moved west was to seek adventure. The challenges were numerous—taming the land, dealing with Native Americans, and starting new local and state governments.

A fifth reason some traveled west was to seek a new start in life. Some left their debts or criminal records behind. A few even abandoned their wives and children.

A sixth reason some easterners journeyed west was a desire to spread the gospel among both Native Americans and new settlers. In 1833 the *Christian Advocate and Journal* printed a letter about four Native Americans who went to St. Louis seeking the "white man's Book of Heaven." A few Methodist and Presbyterian groups read about the request and responded to the challenge. Missionaries were grieved when many Native Americans rejected Christianity, while others witnessed the conversion of many Native Americans. Some Native Americans who were converted became missionaries to their own people.

Trailblazers

Trappers and traders, known as **mountain men**, were usually the first whites to arrive in a new western area. In the early 1800s, a few hundred of these individuals lived in the Rockies and trapped animals or bought animal pelts (skins) from the Native Americans. Each summer, many mountain men, Native Americans, and fur-company agents gathered in one place. They usually met near Fort Laramie in Wyoming. There the trappers traded their furs for goods and learned about the year's events. The rendezvous, or meeting, brought out the worst in some mountain men: gambling, drinking, and fighting.

▾ Fort Laramie, Wyoming

Nevertheless, mountain men did provide valuable services. They marked the best routes, explored rivers, and found passes across mountains. **Jedediah Smith**, known for his Christian beliefs, located the most useful pass—South Pass (located in present-day Wyoming). It was used by western caravans of settlers, and it enabled missionaries to take the gospel to the West. Often, once the mountain men trapped most of the animals in a given area, some served as guides for wagon trains. Joe Meek, who led missionaries Marcus and Narcissa Whitman, and Kit Carson were two of the most notable guides.

For many years, American pioneers moving west of the Mississippi wanted to bypass the vast Great Plains region. Its dry climate and the presence of Native Americans discouraged settlement. The riches of western trade, California gold, and Oregon farms tempted many to make longer journeys to reach their western goals. Following the trails that the mountain men had blazed, pioneers eventually developed several major westward routes.

Settlers and Native Americans

After the amount of game and the number of furbearing animals decreased, the mountain men moved to new hunting grounds. Pioneers then followed the trails blazed by those trappers and traders.

Settlers brought a degree of civilization to the wilderness. They built homes; established local governments; started stores, mills, and other businesses; and built churches. Until stores were established, many goods came from peddlers, individuals who traveled from place to place selling goods. Such businessmen carried pots, pans, tools, cloth, thread, and other goods to meet the needs of pioneer families.

Like earlier Americans before them, the settlers were often insensitive to the Native Americans' claims to the land. At first, the Indians usually left the settlers along the trails alone, but conflict quickly arose as more and more people poured in to mine or farm the land. Some tribes nearly disappeared after continual warfare with the settlers. Others stopped fighting, surrendered their lands, and moved onto small reservations. The Native Americans of the Great Plains fought the hardest to keep their land, and the Indian conflict continued to grow as pioneers increasingly populated the region. Eventually, the Plains Indians also agreed, or were forced to agree, to live within certain boundaries.

Those who supported the concept of Manifest Destiny claimed that God intended the United States to extend across the western lands to the Pacific. But many of these advocates paid little attention to the God-given rights of the people already living in those lands. They disregarded God's commands against coveting and stealing.

SECTION REVIEW 12.1

1. What was the idea of Manifest Destiny? What did those who opposed it believe Americans should do instead?
2. What were six reasons Americans wanted to move west?
3. Who were the first pioneers to normally arrive in new western areas? What services did they provide for those who followed?
4. What are the positive and negative aspects of growth as shown in westward expansion?

▲ Smith crossed the Mojave Desert on his 1826 journey to California.

Jedidiah Smith

Jedidiah Smith was the first known white man to travel by land to California. He was also the first to cross the mountains called the Sierra Nevada from the west and the first to cross the arid Great Basin. He was among the greatest explorers of the American West.

He fearlessly explored lands unknown to white men and faced numerous obstacles. Once, he was almost killed by a grizzly bear. The bear bit him on the head. After the attack, as Smith lay on the ground bleeding, he calmly supervised a friend who sewed up his wounds.

His life as a mountain man is a stark contrast to the common image of others in his profession. He was a man of faith who did not drink, smoke, or curse. Along with his trapper's gear, he carried his Bible. Fellow trapper William Waldo testified, "No one who knew [Smith] well doubted the sincerity of his piety [devotion to God]." In a December 1829 letter to his brother, Smith asked for prayer to "bear me up before a Throne of Grace." Despite the hostile environment of the mountains and the ungodly influences of other mountain men, Smith maintained his commitment to Christian principles.

Smith died in 1831 at the age of thirty-two. While scouting for a group of pioneers, he was killed in a skirmish with Comanches. However, the testimony of his Christian character lives on today.

GUIDING QUESTIONS

- How did Texas become an independent country and then a state?
- Were the Texans right to fight against the Mexican government?

12.2 ACQUIRING TEXAS

How did Texas become a state?

The Spanish had explored Texas and the Southwest in the 1500s and 1600s. Spain tried to advance its claim on the area by establishing Catholic missions in the region. Because of conflicts with Native Americans, this system did not work well in Texas. One result was that by 1800 there were only three prominent Spanish settlements in Texas: San Antonio, Goliad, and Nacogdoches. After 1810, unrest in Spanish Mexico spread into Texas. When Mexico gained its freedom from Spain in 1821, Texas and the Southwest came under Mexican control.

▲ Stephen Austin led the first American settlers into Texas.

Americans Settle in Texas

Spain, and later Mexico, allowed a number of Americans to enter Texas. In 1821 a Missourian named Moses Austin obtained permission to relocate three hundred American families to Texas. He died before any families moved, but his son **Stephen Austin** continued the project. Each American family received hundreds of acres of land at low cost for farming or ranching. Each was also free from paying taxes to the Mexican government for several years. The settlers were required to pledge allegiance to Mexico and become Roman Catholics. The Mexicans wanted the newcomers to accept the Mexican culture. However, most settlers kept their American identity and expected to have the same rights Americans enjoyed.

Mexico frowned on slavery and in 1823 prohibited the sale or purchase of slaves and declared that the children of slaves be freed when they reached age fourteen. Nevertheless, many Americans who moved to the area brought slaves with them. In 1830 Mexico officially abolished slavery in Texas. However, because Mexico allowed indentured servitude, settlers circumvented the slavery law by converting their slaves to indentured servants for life.

By 1830 Texas's population had grown to over ten thousand US immigrants, while the native Mexicans numbered about four thousand. That year, Mexico outlawed additional Americans from entering Texas, yet many continued to arrive. Stephen Austin traveled to Mexico City in 1833 to ask that officials allow the American-settled area to become a separate Mexican state. Austin opposed revolt and tried to advance the interests of Texans, or Texians as they were also called, through legal means. But the Mexicans discovered a letter that Austin had written, advising the Texans to form their own state even if his mission failed. As a result, the Mexicans arrested him for treason. He spent the next year in jail.

▲ Antonio López de Santa Anna

Texas Battles for Independence

Antonio López de Santa Anna was elected president of Mexico in 1833. The following year he dissolved the national congress, discarded the Mexican constitution of 1824, and made himself a dictator.

In 1835 Texans prepared to fight for reinstating the discarded constitution which guaranteed them a degree of self-government within Mexico. However, when Santa Anna approached Texas with thousands of troops, the Texans changed their demands to outright independence from Mexico.

Although the United States sent no official aid to Texas, an influx of volunteers arrived, particularly from the southern states. Texans easily took Goliad, which was a Mexican supply base, and then took control of San Antonio. The commander of the Texan forces, Sam Houston, believed that his men stood a chance of winning if they fought in the field. They knew the terrain, and American rifles were more accurate than Mexican muskets. The last place Houston wanted to fight a battle was at San Antonio's abandoned mission, **the Alamo**. Since the Alamo was not a fort, it would be difficult to defend. Houston ordered the Texans to abandon the mission before the Mexicans arrived.

Davy Crockett (shown below with his rifle above his head) was killed at the Alamo (above).

"Remember the Alamo!"

Occupants of the Alamo, commanded by **William Travis**, decided to remain there. **Jim Bowie** and **Davy Crockett**, both well-known frontiersmen and the latter a former congressman from Tennessee, were among the nearly 190 individuals present. Although their resources were limited, they secured the three-acre mission as well as possible with wood and earthen barricades and positioned cannons for their defense.

Santa Anna soon marched his army toward San Antonio. Once there, he demanded unconditional surrender. He said that every man in the mission would be "put to the sword in case of refusal." The defenders answered with a cannon shot, and on February 23, 1836, approximately 5,000 Mexican troops began the attack.

Over the next thirteen days, Santa Anna launched several assaults on the mission. On March 6th his gun batteries opened two holes in the walls, and his men placed ladders at other points. In the hand-to-hand fighting that followed, Santa Anna's forces prevailed.

About a half dozen defenders of the Alamo survived and were captured. Santa Anna ordered the men executed. A few women, children, and slaves were allowed to leave afterward. They carried the news of defeat to the Texan forces. Enraged upon hearing of the events, most Texans wanted revenge.

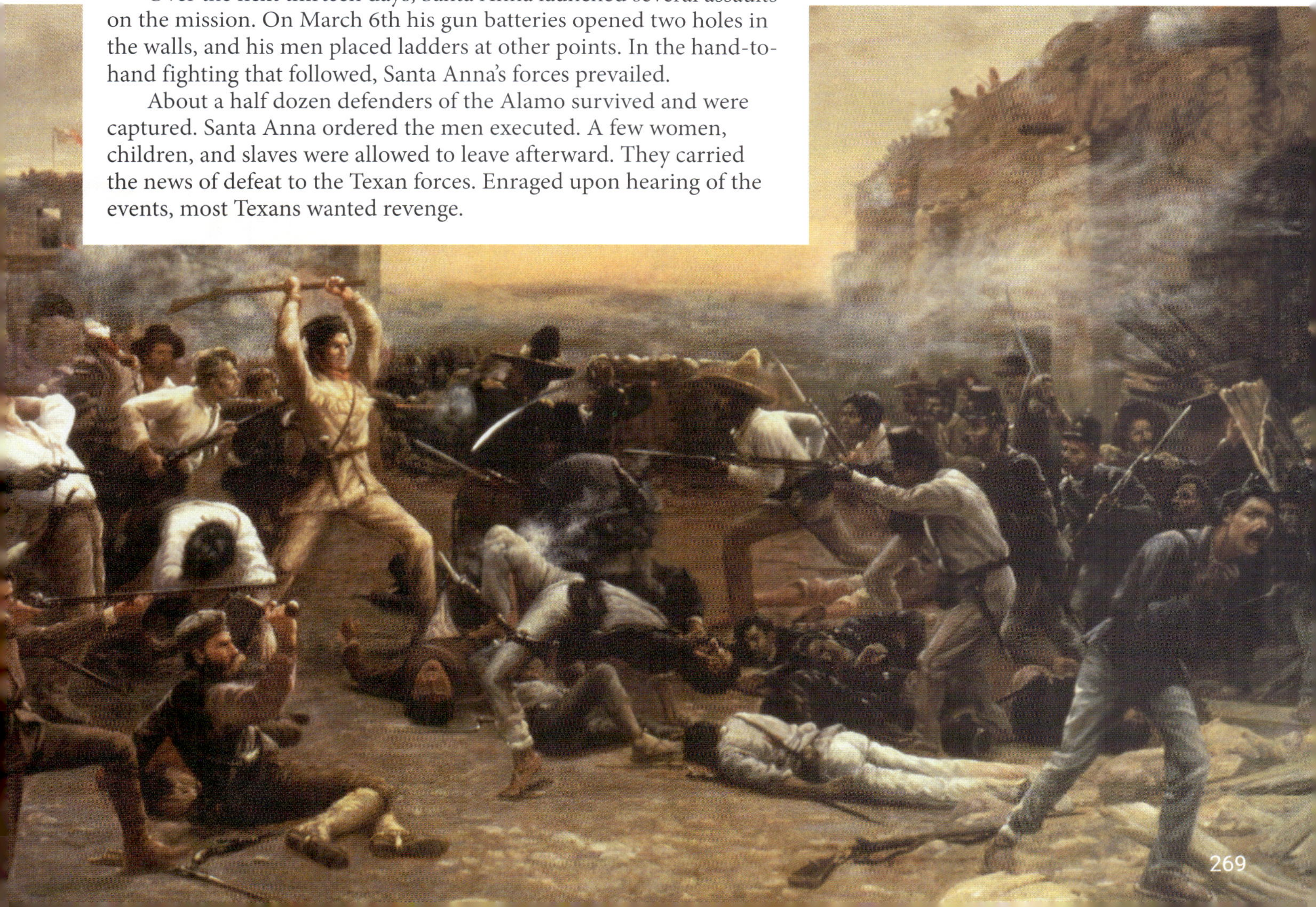

▲ Originally from Virginia, Sam Houston served as Tennessee's governor and represented that state in Congress before moving to Texas.

San Jacinto

Sam Houston, a former member of Congress from Tennessee and a former governor of that state, had moved to Texas in 1832. He became commander of the Texan forces in 1835. After hearing of the defeat at the Alamo, he planned carefully for a battle at San Jacinto, near the present-day city that bears his name.

On April 21, 1836, Houston's army of about 900 men launched a surprise attack on Santa Anna yelling, "Remember the Alamo!" as they charged. The **Battle of San Jacinto** ended in eighteen minutes. In this brief battle, the Texans either killed or captured almost the entire Mexican army of 1,400 men. The next day Santa Anna was captured. Houston kept the Texans from killing him, choosing rather to hold him hostage. In exchange for his release, the Mexican dictator signed a treaty recognizing the independence of Texas. Shortly afterwards, Mexico's Congress overthrew Santa Anna and renounced the treaty.

The Lone Star Republic

During the fighting at the Alamo, delegates from across Texas were meeting in a convention. They issued a declaration of independence and began writing a constitution for the new nation, called the Republic of Texas.

Yet most Texans preferred joining the United States, so Texas applied for admission to the Union in 1836. President Andrew Jackson realized that accepting Texas might spark a war with Mexico. He also knew that antislavery forces in the United States opposed Texan annexation (the formal process of adding new land) because Texas would almost certainly enter as a slave state. Thus, Jackson recognized the independence of Texas but did not support it becoming a part of the United States.

For almost a decade, the Republic of Texas, better known as the **Lone Star Republic,** existed. Sam Houston served as its first president.

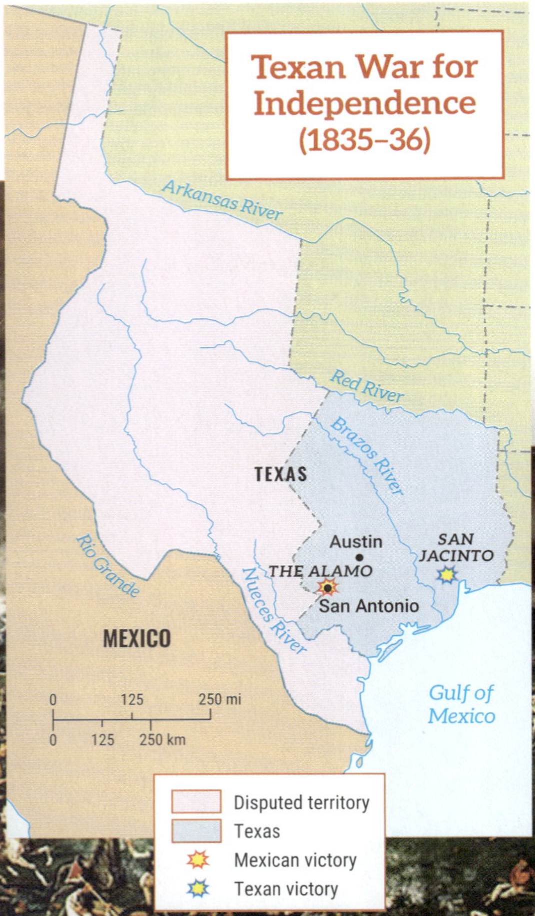

▼ Battle of San Jacinto

Texas Gains Statehood

By 1844 (a presidential election year) many Americans were calling for the Oregon Territory to be brought into the Union as a free state. At the same time, some people wanted Texas to join the Union as a slave state.

The Whig candidate, Henry Clay, opposed Texas entering the Union, as did former president Martin Van Buren, whom many thought would be the Democratic candidate.

Keeping Texas out but allowing Oregon to enter would give the northern states more power in the government. Former president Andrew Jackson astutely read public opinion. He said that his fellow Tennessean "Young Hickory," **James K. Polk**, could win both the nomination and the presidency by promising "All of Oregon, All of Texas." This pledge lured both northerners and southerners into the Democrats' fold. Polk, the Democratic dark horse (little-known candidate), won the presidency. Shortly before Polk became president, outgoing president John Tyler convinced Congress to pass a resolution authorizing Texas to become a part of the United States (see Chapter 10). Texas officially became a state in December 1845.

SECTION REVIEW 12.2

1. What requirements did Mexico have for American families settling in Texas? Were these requirements generally followed?
2. How did Texans bypass the Mexican government's prohibition of slavery?
3. Were the Texans right to fight against the new Mexican government under Santa Anna? Why or why not?
4. What were the disadvantages of the Texans at the Battle of the Alamo?
5. At what short battle in 1836 did the Texans defeat the Mexicans and secure Texan independence? Who led the Texans in that battle?
6. What did James K. Polk promise that helped him win the presidential election?

James K. Polk

11

Born	November 2, 1795
Died	July 15, 1849
Home state	Tennessee
Wife	Sarah Childress
Church	Presbyterian
Occupation	lawyer
Party	Democratic
Years served as president	1845–49
Terms	1
Vice president	George M. Dallas

Did you know?

Henry Clay was a candidate for president three times, each time representing a different party. In 1824 he campaigned as a Democratic-Republican. In 1832 he was the National Republican nominee against Andrew Jackson. In 1844 he was the Whig candidate. Although he was a career politician known for his ability to negotiate compromises, he was never successful in his bids for the presidency.

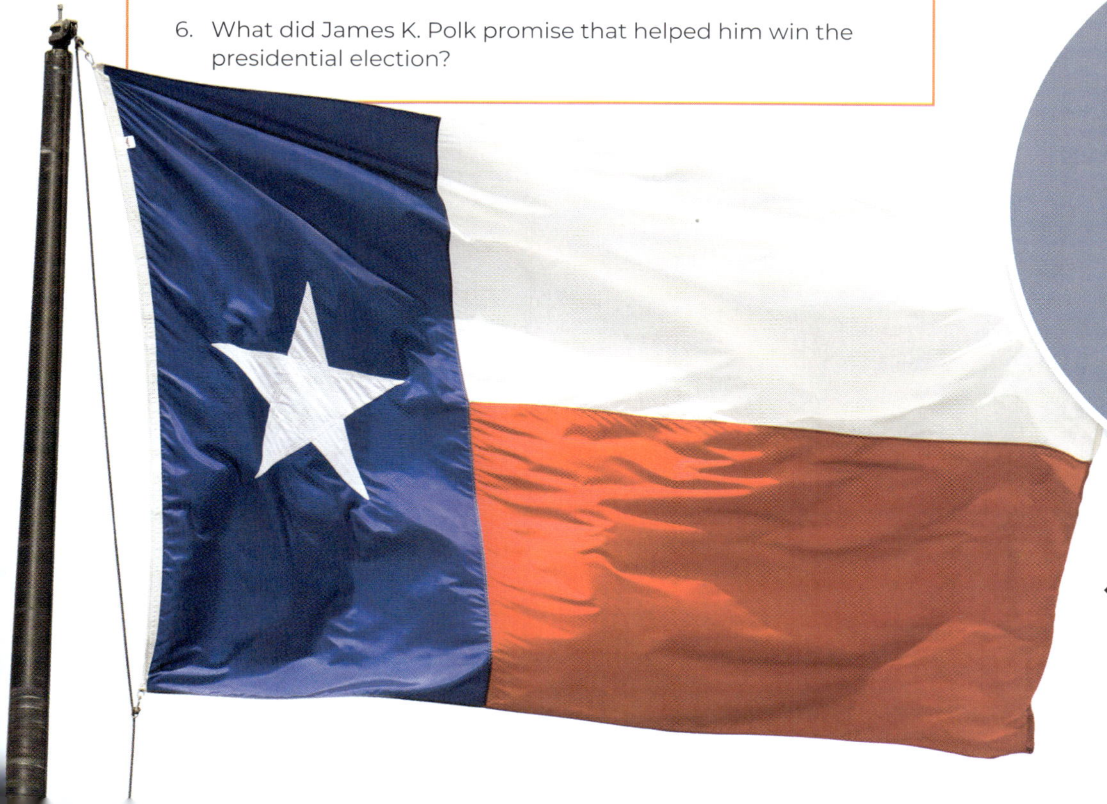

◂ The Lone Star Flag has been both a national and a state flag. It represented the Lone Star Republic from 1839 to 1845 and the Lone Star State from 1845 to the present.

GUIDING QUESTIONS

- What happened during the Mexican War?
- What lands did America gain as a result of the Mexican War and the Gadsden Purchase?

12.3 THE MEXICAN WAR

What happened during the war with Mexico?

Mexico objected to the addition of Texas to the United States. Nevertheless, the Mexican president invited Americans to send a representative to discuss the Texas matter. In November 1845 Polk sent John Slidell with instructions to offer $5 million to settle the disputes about Texas and up to $25 million to purchase California and New Mexico, areas to which many Americans were moving. The Mexican government considered the proposal an insult to their national honor and feared that even discussing the ideas might lead to a revolution within the country.

▲ Rio Grande

A major point of disagreement between Mexico and Texas was the location of the boundary line. Mexico insisted that it was the Nueces River; however, officials in Texas and President Polk said it was the Rio Grande, a river well over a hundred miles south of the Nueces. Furthermore, many in Mexico still wanted their country to regain Texas.

In March 1846 President Polk ordered General **Zachary Taylor** to move his 4,000 men from Corpus Christi, Texas, to the Rio Grande. Taylor insisted the troops were still on American soil. But since that area was south of the Nueces, Mexico viewed Taylor's action as an invasion of its country and continued to insist the United States had no legitimate claim to land as far south as the Rio Grande.

In April and May, Mexico attacked Taylor's forces. Both American and Mexican soldiers were killed. On May 11 Polk told Congress that Mexicans "invaded our territory and shed the blood of our fellow-citizens on our own soil." Two days later, at the president's request, Congress declared war on Mexico.

▼ General Zachary Taylor's army camp at Corpus Christi, Texas

Fighting the War

Many Americans celebrated news of war. They believed it was necessary to defend American territory against the Mexican attacks while others saw it as an opportunity to expand the nation's borders by obtaining additional land from Mexico. Many Americans enthusiastically volunteered to fight.

However, many Americans opposed the conflict. One American officer present said, "We have not one particle of right to be here. . . . It looks as if the [US] government sent a small force on purpose to bring on a war, so as to have a pretext [excuse] for taking California and as much of this country [Mexico] as it chooses."

Future president Abraham Lincoln was elected to the US House of Representatives a few months after war began. He later authored the Spot Resolutions, which questioned whether the Mexicans had actually shed American blood on American soil. He called upon Polk to provide Congress with the exact spot, or location, that blood was shed. Some politicians criticized Lincoln for this action, calling him "Spotty Lincoln."

Some New Englanders believed the war was a well-planned attempt by Southerners for more land to create new slave states. Some southern Democrats, notably John C. Calhoun, also opposed the war. Calhoun thought it was unjust and dangerous. While some Christians promoted the war as a way to advance Christianity, others worried God would judge the nation for provoking an unnecessary war. James W. Alexander, a pastor and later professor at Princeton Seminary, wrote about the Mexican War. "It is a war of pretexts. None of the alleged causes [for the war] existed. . . . Never have I so much feared the judgments of God on us as a nation."

Santa Fe and California

In the **Mexican War**, Polk saw an opportunity to fulfill the dream of Manifest Destiny. The Mexican provinces of California and New Mexico were tempting prizes that soon became war objectives. Polk made plans to seize both territories, and many Americans already in those areas were ready to support the US government.

General Stephen Kearny led an army toward San Diego, California, from Fort Leavenworth in Kansas. His first objective was to take New Mexico; therefore, the first part of his trek took him to Santa Fe. When he arrived in August 1846, the Mexicans in Santa Fe fled their positions. Kearny took the town without firing a shot. After securing New Mexico, he seized a portion of northern Mexico and then marched on to California.

When Kearny arrived in California in December, he found the United States had already taken it in July. Captain **John C. Frémont** (called "the Pathfinder" for his western explorations) had headed to California with 60 soldiers in 1845, claiming to be on a geographic survey. But Frémont secretly planned to take control of California and become a hero. In June 1846 he led his band and some American settlers in seizing control of the area and declaring it an independent country called the "**Bear Flag Republic**." Over the Sonoma town square, they raised a flag with an image of a grizzly bear.

About the same time, Commodore John Sloat landed in California with several US warships to take the area for the United States. He proclaimed California to be American territory, and the Bear Flag Republic ceased to exist, less than a month after its creation.

Fun Fact

Santa Anna brought "chicle" to the United States in the 1850s. Indians had used this tree gum as a chewable snack. Santa Anna hoped it might be a substitute for rubber. When that failed, it was developed into modern chewing gum.

The Bear Flag Republic, which existed for less than a month, was represented by this flag.

General Zachary Taylor began his military career almost four decades before the Mexican War.

Old Rough and Ready

After the fall of California and New Mexico, Zachary Taylor's task was to subdue the opposition in the remainder of Mexico. Although Taylor was not a brilliant strategist, he was a brave soldier. He had no love for military formalities; his field uniform included a wide-brimmed straw hat, a soiled white linen jacket, and baggy trousers. His nickname, earned while fighting Native Americans in Florida during the Second Seminole War, was "Old Rough and Ready." He was popular with his men.

By September 1846 Taylor had marched into Mexico toward Monterrey. Mexican resistance in Monterrey was stronger than expected, but the Americans captured the city by house-to-house fighting.

After a period of inactivity, Taylor's forces fought the Mexicans at the Battle of Buena Vista in February 1847. Despite nearly being defeated, Taylor was able to win an important victory over General Santa Anna, who was once again commanding Mexican forces.

General Winfield Scott was nicknamed "Old Fuss and Feathers."

The Battles of Veracruz and Mexico City

President Polk, a Democrat, grew concerned over Taylor's growing popularity after his victories at Monterrey and Buena Vista. He believed that Taylor might become a presidential candidate for the Whig Party. To take the focus off Taylor, Polk appointed General **Winfield Scott** commander of the Veracruz operation, the campaign to take Mexico City. Scott was just about everything Zachary Taylor was not. Scott was a handsome six-foot-four-inch man who had a taste for dress uniforms and expected his men and others to adhere to military regulations. His liking for discipline and formality had won him the nickname "Old Fuss and Feathers," but he was a skilled soldier. Scott and his troops landed, by ship, south of the Mexican port of Veracruz. After a siege lasting about three weeks, the Americans captured the city in March 1847.

Despite his losses at Buena Vista and Veracruz, Santa Anna would not concede defeat. Scott's forces marched almost three hundred miles to Mexico City, the capital. Along the way, he fought and won several battles against the Mexican army. In September 1847, Scott's forces were able to capture Mexico City.

Fighting at Buena Vista

The Treaty of Guadalupe Hidalgo

Opponents of the war asked how a war begun to defend American borders ended with the occupation of Mexico City. Undeterred by the question, Polk sought not only his original goals but also much of northern Mexico. However, Nicholas Trist, the American negotiator, believed these demands were unreasonable. He negotiated with Mexico for the minimum territorial gains that Polk would accept. On February 2, 1848, the **Treaty of Guadalupe Hidalgo** officially ended the war. It made the Rio Grande the boundary of Texas and added the **Mexican Cession** (the future states of California, Nevada, and Utah and parts of Wyoming, Colorado, Arizona, and New Mexico) to the United States. In return, the United States paid Mexico $15 million for the land and paid Americans to whom Mexico owed debts $3.25 million.

Nicholas Trist

Nicholas Trist was the US representative who negotiated the treaty that ended the Mexican War. As the treaty was about to be signed, one of the Mexicans, Don Bernardo Couto, remarked to him, "This must be a proud moment for you; no less proud for you than it is humiliating for us." To this Trist replied, "We are making peace, let that be our only thought."

Later Trist wrote to his wife, "Could those Mexicans have seen into my heart at that moment, they would have known that my feeling of shame as an American was far stronger than theirs could be as Mexicans. For though it would not have done for me to say so there, that was a thing for every right minded American to be ashamed of, and I was ashamed of it, most cordially and intensely ashamed of it."

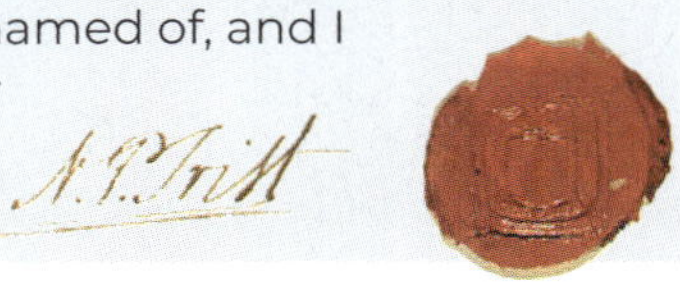

▾ San Francisco, California, in 1847

Results of the Mexican War

The Mexican War made the expansionists' dream of Manifest Destiny a reality. It also made a hero of Zachary Taylor, helping propel him into the White House in the next election. In addition, the war reopened the old controversy over slavery. Would the new lands of the Mexican Cession be slave or free? The North wanted them to be free, while the South wanted them open to slavery. "The United States will conquer Mexico," author Ralph Waldo Emerson wrote, "but it will be as the man [who] swallows the arsenic, which brings him down in turn. Mexico will poison us."

The Mexican War served as a training ground for the Civil War, which came just thirteen years later. Many of the men who became famous leaders in that conflict gained valuable experience during the Mexican War. Jefferson Davis, Robert E. Lee, Ulysses S. Grant, Thomas "Stonewall" Jackson, George McClellan, and George G. Meade, were among the many army officers who fought in Mexico.

The lands gained in the Mexican War proved valuable. By 1849 California applied for statehood. Realizing the value of California's fine harbors and rich gold mines, the United States was eager to annex it. In later years, settlers also found major sources of silver and uranium in the land gained from the war. Through irrigation, some of the region became useful for farming. As we will see later in this chapter, the annexation of California was delayed until the Compromise of 1850 was adopted.

The Gadsden Purchase

In 1853, just five years after the war's end, the United States wanted another section of Mexican land on the border of New Mexico and Arizona. The United States thought that this narrow strip of land could be a possible southern railroad route. Mexico agreed to sell the land, and diplomat James Gadsden arranged the American purchase for $10 million. The **Gadsden Purchase** completed the territory that comprises the continental United States.

SECTION REVIEW 12.3

1. What sparked war between Mexico and the United States?
2. Identify two well-known politicians who opposed the war in Mexico.
3. What two additional Mexican territories did President Polk want to obtain? Which military officers conquered each for America?
4. What was the name of California as an independent country? How long did the country last?
5. What were the two main battles during Zachary Taylor's campaign to subdue Mexico?
6. Who did Polk send to lessen the fame of Zachary Taylor? What were the two main battles of his campaign?
7. What treaty ended the Mexican War?
8. How did the Mexican War contribute to the fulfillment of the dream of Manifest Destiny?
9. What purchase completed the land of the continental United States?

12.4 SETTLING THE WEST

How did America continue to expand westward?

Even before the Mexican War began in 1846, a great rush of settlers and miners moved to Oregon, Utah, and California. The Santa Fe Trail, the Oregon Trail, the Mormon Trail, and the California Trail were the most common routes westward.

The Santa Fe Trail

The **Santa Fe Trail**, the first American route west of the Missouri River, was primarily a trade route. Traders knew that goods—such as cotton, wool, tools, and needles—could bring much profit when transported on the ten- to twelve-week journey on the Santa Fe Trail.

To ensure safety on the trail and to discourage Indian attacks, the traders often gathered at one spot, usually Independence, Missouri, and formed a caravan. The men usually chose a captain to lead them. Other positions included wagon boss, pack-train boss, chief scout, lieutenants for divisions, and wranglers for the loose livestock the caravan took along. The heavily laden wagons formed a circle at night. Horses and mules were placed in the middle since one of the Native Americans' favorite and most deadly strategies was to stampede the animals and scatter them. Without water (which was often miles away) or animals for travel, the traders could not last long.

In 1827 with the establishment of Fort Leavenworth in Kansas, the military began patrolling first the Santa Fe Trail and then the Oregon Trail. With the start of the Mexican War in 1846, the Santa Fe Trail became even more important. Troops and supplies moved over it to Mexico and California. But later, as parts of the Atchison, Topeka and Santa Fe Railroad opened up, the trail shrank in both length and importance.

GUIDING QUESTIONS

- What trails did people use to travel west?
- Why did the Mormons settle in Utah?
- What factors influenced the settlement of California?
- What was the Compromise of 1850?
- How did politics change during the 1850s?

▲ Bent's Fort

The Bents

William and Charles Bent were brothers who established a trading outpost on the Santa Fe Trail. Bent's Fort, as it was known, was in the southeastern part of present-day Colorado.

The fort had walls fifteen feet high and four feet thick that were constructed over a period of four years. It included several cannons. The Indians were familiar with musket and rifle fire and had little fear of either. However, cannon fire was another matter, usually causing them to scatter.

The fort was in operation from 1833 to 1849. More than a century later it was reconstructed and is now a National Historic Site that attracts thousands of visitors annually.

◀ Covered wagons are shown entering Sante Fe, the end of the Santa Fe Trail.

Did you know?

Hudson's Bay Company currently owns Saks Fifth Avenue and owned Lord and Taylor until 2019.

Oregon

Furs first lured people to the Oregon Territory. That region included the present-day states of Oregon, Washington, and Idaho, as well as parts of Wyoming, Montana, and Canada.

After trapping on the Pacific coast, traders turned eastward to the Rocky Mountains. Later, various fur-trading companies went to the area, joining the Hudson's Bay Company (a British business active in the frontier since its founding in 1670 and still in existence today).

John Jacob Astor, a German immigrant, established the American Fur Company in 1808. The Rocky Mountain Fur Company—which employed such trappers as James Bridger and Jedediah Smith—was also active in the region.

Great Britain and the United States both claimed the Oregon area. In 1818 they had agreed to a joint occupation of the area. This meant individuals from both countries were allowed there.

Settlers traveling to Oregon from the eastern part of the United States followed the route called the **Oregon Trail**. Early fur trappers had established a trail from Missouri to Astoria, Oregon, by way of the South Pass in 1812–13. But Americans forgot about the trail until 1824, when Jedediah Smith rediscovered it. The Oregon Trail became the most important route for settlers and missionaries going west.

Each spring, settlers wanting to follow the trail's two-thousand-mile route gathered at the trail's starting points. Time and weather were always concerns. If the settlers' wagons did not reach Independence Rock (in what is now Wyoming) by July 4, the settlers risked running into early snow in the mountains. The Great Migration of 1843 included nearly one thousand people. Leaving Kansas on May 22, they arrived at Oregon City on October 27, more than five months later. This group made a number of trail improvements along the way that made the route faster and more passable for future pioneers.

▾ Fort Astoria (top) was built in Oregon 1811. Pioneers who later traveled the Oregon Trail passed such landmarks as Chimney Rock in Nebraska (center) and Independence Rock in Wyoming (bottom).

Wagon wheel ruts are still visible along what was once the Oregon Trail.

As every new wagon with American settlers started for Oregon, British efforts to hold Oregon became less certain. In 1844 alone, 1,500 emigrants made the trip. The next year, about 2,500 people used the trail. By 1847 emigration had swelled to 4,000.

The Oregon Territory stretched from 42° latitude in the south to 54°40′ latitude in the north. Many Americans clamored for the United States to take the whole region, even if it meant a war with Britain. During the 1844 presidential election, one of James Polk's campaign slogans was "54°40′ or Fight."

Though Polk supported taking control of all Oregon, he was willing to compromise on the matter. After his election, the United States and Britain negotiated an agreement. Since the furs in the Columbia River valley seemed depleted, the British were less interested in the southern part of the territory. Also, there were now more Americans than British in the region. The British moved their base north to Vancouver Island. In 1846 the two nations set the boundary line between the United States and Canada, which was British controlled, at the forty-ninth parallel. That remains the boundary today.

LIFE *on the* TRAIL

Settlers on the trails westward faced many hardships. Missionary Narcissa Whitman rejoiced at being able to wash clothes near Parma, Idaho. It was only the third time she had been able to do so in fifteen hundred miles of travel. Diaries tell of travelers with cracked lips and dry noses in the arid lands.

Along the westward trip, the turf changed to bunch grasses, and the colors shifted from greens to browns and tans. New animals emerged. Bison (buffalo), jack rabbits, prairie dogs, and horned lizards surprised the travelers. Rattlesnakes struck at both livestock and humans. Their venom was fatal to animals although it did not always kill humans. Bolts of lightning zigzagged across the sky and touched the earth as late-afternoon thundershowers struck. Sleepy children fell off wagons. Almost every mile on the trail held stories of hard work, determination, courage, and answered prayers.

The Whitmans: Missionaries in Oregon

Marcus and Narcissa Whitman were the most famous missionaries in the Oregon region. Along with other missionaries, they built a compound near the site of modern Walla Walla, Washington, and tried to reach the fiercely independent Cayuse Indians. Although the mission featured a thriving farm, the area proved less fertile for the gospel. The Cayuse distrusted the settlers. The missionaries did not help matters by suggesting that the Native Americans could better please God by abandoning hunting and fishing and becoming farmers like the settlers.

Sadly, the Whitmans proved more successful at recruiting settlers than reaching Native Americans. They sent messages eastward not only calling for more workers but also providing exciting descriptions of the rich, unsettled lands. Marcus Whitman even served as a scout for some parties of settlers traveling to Oregon.

The increasing number of white settlers angered the Cayuse and caused them to worry that the white man was more interested in taking Native American land than in saving their souls. Marcus Whitman wrote optimistically in a letter in 1844, "The Indians are anxious [concerned] about the consequences of settlers among them, but I hope there will be no acts of violence on either hand." Whitman's hopes proved vain. A measles epidemic, apparently carried into Oregon by settlers, wiped out nearly half the tribe despite Whitman's efforts to treat the ill. Afterward, in 1847, a party of Cayuse attacked the mission compound, murdering Marcus, Narcissa, and twelve other settlers.

This statue of Marcus Whitman (left) is in the state capitol in Olympia, Washington. His wife was Narcissa (right).

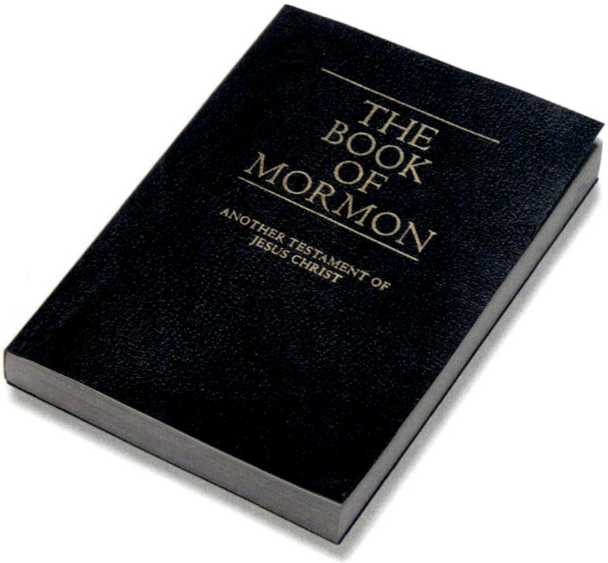

The Mormons and Utah

Many Americans disagreed with the teachings and practices of a religious group known as the **Mormons**, also called the Church of Jesus Christ of Latter-Day Saints. To escape mistreatment, Mormons moved west and built their own settlements where no one else lived. They were the first American settlers in the Utah Territory.

Joseph Smith and the Book of Mormon

Joseph Smith, a young man from New York, developed the system of Mormon beliefs in the 1820s. He said that an angel appeared to him and led him to tablets covered with divine writing. Smith stated that he translated the tablets into English, and in 1830 he published the writings as the Book of Mormon. He quickly gathered a group of followers.

Smith and his followers had trouble finding a suitable place to live because many objected to their teachings. For example, most people did not believe an angel had actually appeared to Smith nor did they accept the Book of Mormon. The Mormons started in New York but moved to Ohio, then Missouri, and then Illinois. Their town in Illinois, called Nauvoo, became quite prosperous. But as had happened in the previous towns, the non-Mormon citizens became suspicious of Mormon ideas, and tensions quickly arose. Smith and his male followers began teaching that men could have more than one wife at a time, a practice known as polygamy. The non-Mormon citizens became alarmed. In 1844 a mob killed Smith. Rather than ending Mormonism, his followers viewed him as a martyr, and his death increased their determination to continue his teachings.

▲ Brigham Young was sometimes called the "American Moses" because he led Mormons on the long journey to Utah.

The Mormon Trail and Salt Lake City

After Smith's death, the Mormons decided to move yet again. Their new leader, **Brigham Young**, led them to the Great Salt Lake. Though now part of the state of Utah, it was in Mexican territory at the time. In 1846 twelve thousand Mormons left Illinois and headed west.

The Mormons' trek to the Great Salt Lake, along what became known as the **Mormon Trail**, was successful because of Young's planning. A smaller group always traveled ahead of the main group of settlers. They built cabins and planted food crops to be used by the main group as it passed through the area. The Mormons rose each morning for worship before resuming their journey and completing their twenty-miles-a-day goal. They arrived at the Great Salt Lake in July 1847.

The region where the Mormons chose to live was dry and desert-like. It had little food and few trees for lumber. Young organized an irrigation system and divided the land into farming plots according to the needs of each family. The new settlement, Salt Lake City, was not democratically controlled. Instead, Young used his forceful leadership to keep his followers unified and help them survive.

Over the next decade, thousands of converts to Mormonism traveled to Utah. Some of the new arrivals planted other cities around existing ones. Young directed settlers to build southward and westward. These new settlers built mills and factories. By the mid-1850s, more than twenty thousand Mormons lived in the area they called "Deseret."

▼ A drawing of Salt Lake City, Utah, during its early days

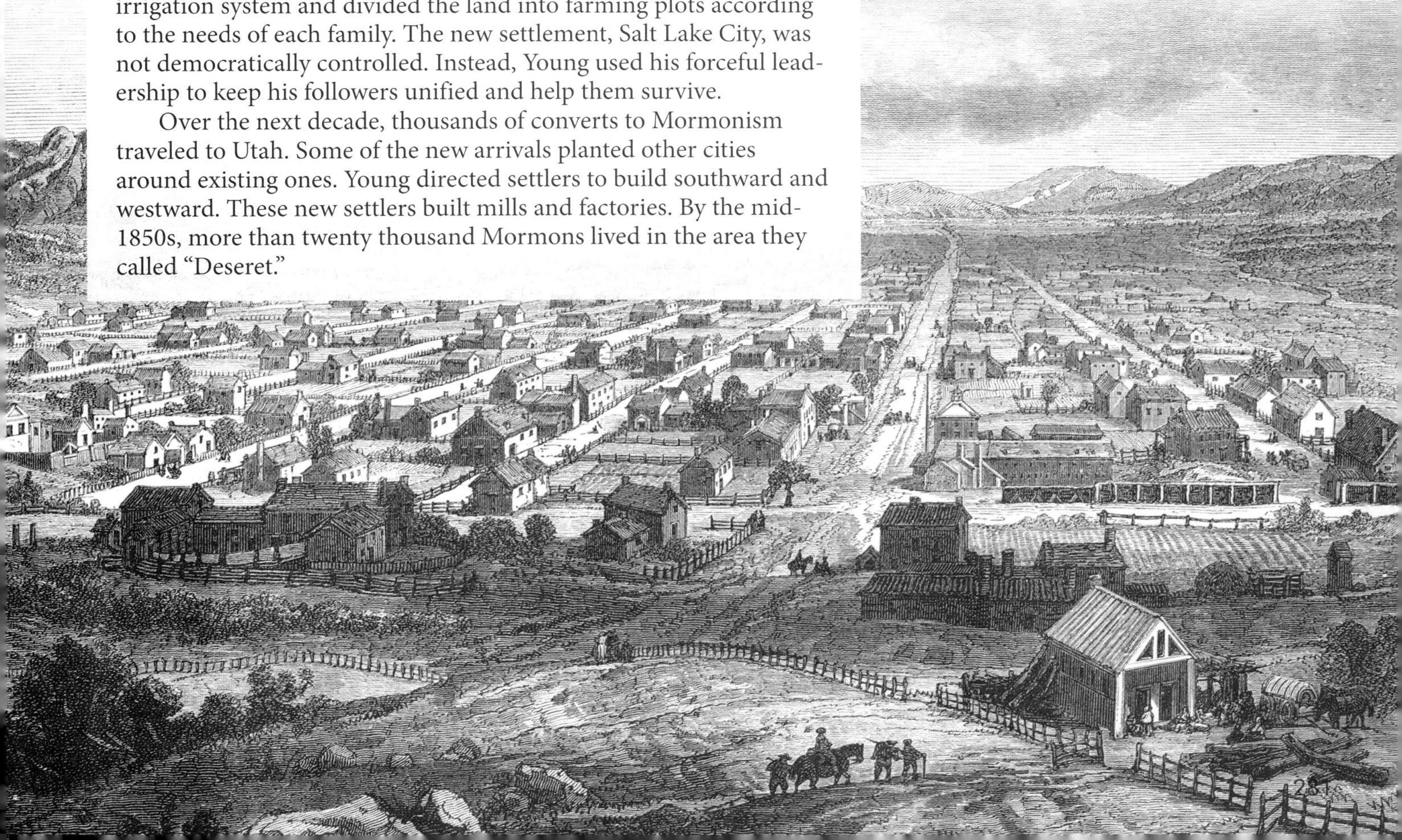

California and Gold

When the Spanish explorer Juan Rodríguez Cabrillo claimed California in 1540, the Spanish shared it with the Native Americans. After 1769, when the British and the Russians threatened to move into the area, the Spanish began to settle more of the area. They established a settlement at Monterey in 1770 and established missions in San Diego, San Francisco, and Los Angeles. These missions prospered by farming and raising cattle. After Mexico declared its independence from Spain in 1821, Californians declared allegiance to Mexico.

The California Trail

As in Oregon, traders and trappers were the first Americans to explore Spanish California. Jedediah Smith discovered the first overland path to California. Other routes were developed over time, but the most popular was the **California Trail**.

The California Trail followed the Oregon Trail for twelve hundred miles before turning southwest. It left the Oregon Trail at Fort Hall, which was located in what is now southeastern Idaho. Few travelers had any idea what lay ahead over the next eight hundred miles. They faced the challenge of the rugged Rockies; weeks of struggling through loose, warm desert sand; and days of drinking only the water that they could carry in barrels on the wagons. A four-hundred-mile stretch along the Humboldt River provided the wagon trains with the grass and water they needed before they entered the forty-mile desert or began the dangerous ascent through the Sierra Nevada. Despite the difficulties of the trail, almost 200,000 people risked their lives journeying to California in the 1840s and 1850s.

▾ Settlers traveling to California

▾ John Sutter's mill

The Discovery of Gold

At first, American pioneers traveled to California because they had heard of its rich farmland. Shortly before California became an American territory, however, something happened that drastically shaped its history. **John Sutter**, a Swiss immigrant, had secured a fifty-thousand-acre grant from the Mexicans in 1839. He built his own community called Sutter's Fort and hired James W. Marshall to build and operate a sawmill. The mill was located on the American River, forty miles upstream from the fort, to provide lumber for Sutter's extensive ranch.

While making his daily inspection of the area in January 1848, Marshall saw a sparkling object in the sand. Using a tin plate, he sifted the dirt and found yellow particles of metal. He found more metal the next morning. Since no one was sure whether it was real gold, Marshall performed several tests. He returned to Sutter's Fort to share the news with his employer. Sutter also tested the metal and was convinced that it was gold. Though the two men tried, it was impossible to keep the news secret. News soon leaked about the discovery, and the **California gold rush** began.

Fun Fact

John Sutter gave land to his son John Sutter Jr. The son built the city of Sacramento, the present capital of California, on a portion of it.

The Forty-Niners

The gold seekers were generally hard-working men who set out for California full of hope and energy. In 1849 alone, more than eighty thousand men went to California. Because the first wave occurred that year, all gold hunters who journeyed there became known as "**forty-niners**." Thirty-nine thousand went by sea on the four- to five-month trip around South America. Others sailed to Panama, crossed the narrow bridge of land there on foot or horseback, boarded a ship on the other side, and sailed up the Pacific coast. More than forty thousand others made the trip by land, using trails on which pioneers journeyed.

Advertisement for ▸ a lecture regarding California gold mines

Miners used pans to sort gold from rocks and dirt. They also used water-filled troughs to help separate these items.

Zachary Taylor

Born	November 24, 1784	12
Died	July 9, 1850	
Home state	Louisiana (born in Virginia)	
Wife	Margaret Mackall Smith	
Home	Cypress Grove Plantation	
Church	Episcopalian	
Occupations	soldier, planter	
Party	Whig	
Years served as president	1849–50	
Terms	partial	
Vice president	Millard Fillmore	

Hard physical labor in the goldfields was the key to wealth. Mining camps emerged wherever miners spotted gold. They used pans and troughs to separate gold from dirt. Crime became rampant in many of the camps. Claim disputes, robberies, and murders were common. Few struck it rich. About half of the would-be miners chose to make a living another way. They became farmers, ranchers, and storekeepers who provided the miners with the goods and services they all needed.

Long before miners struck gold in California, the United States wanted to control that area. Jackson was the first president to show interest in the region. He thought that the San Francisco Bay would be valuable to the nation. Presidents Tyler and Polk tried to bargain with the Mexicans, offering to purchase the land for a high price. But Mexico had no desire to sell California. However, that land was part of the Mexican Cession that the United States gained in 1848 at the end of the Mexican War.

Increasing Sectional Rivalry

In 1846 during the Mexican War, Representative David Wilmot from Pennsylvania proposed that the United States ban slavery in any territory it gained from the war. Southerners were outraged, and southern senators made sure Congress rejected his **Wilmot Proviso**.

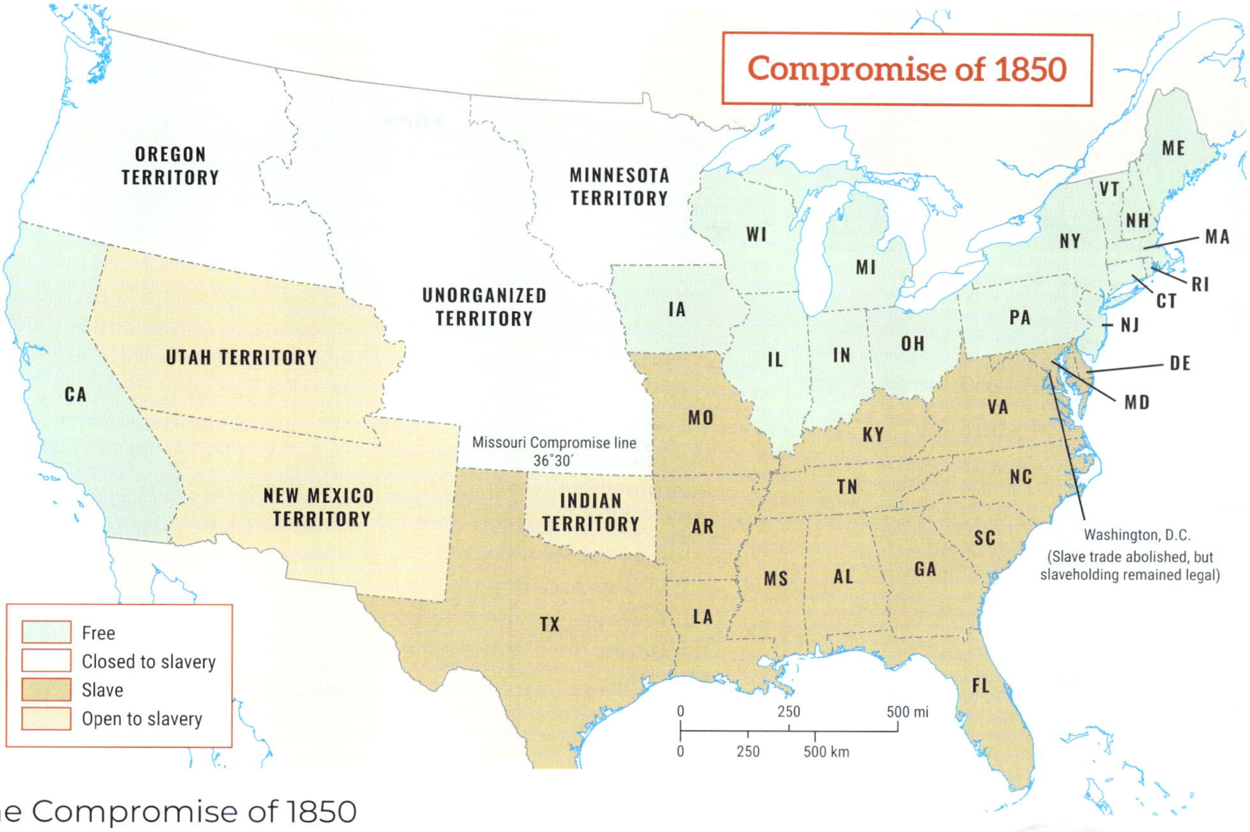

The Compromise of 1850

In 1848 Americans elected Zachary Taylor, the hero of the Mexican War and the Whig candidate, as president. He was a Southerner and a slave owner who had taken little interest in politics before 1848. In fact, he had never voted in a presidential election.

Many Northerners had supported his candidacy because he was not a strong supporter of extending slavery to new territories. In fact, later Taylor angered Southerners by encouraging California to apply for statehood as a free state. By 1849 California wrote a state constitution that banned slavery.

At the time there was an equal number of slave and free states. Southerners opposed the admission of California because it would give the free states control of the US Senate. To settle the issue, Henry Clay and other leaders in Congress proposed the **Compromise of 1850**. This plan called for California to be admitted as a free state and for the remainder of the Mexican Cession to be divided into the New Mexico and Utah Territories. In both territories, the citizens would decide whether they wanted to permit slavery. The process of allowing citizens to make this decision became known as **popular sovereignty**. In addition, the Compromise of 1850 passed a stricter national fugitive slave law that required federal government officials to help return runaway slaves or face fines. The law would also outlaw the slave trade, though not slavery, in the District of Columbia.

While the compromise was intensely debated in Congress, President Taylor announced his opposition to the measure. However, after only sixteen months in office, Taylor died on July 9, 1850. He had been ill for a few days and had suffered severe stomach pains. It appears that some sort of intestinal illness caused his death. Taylor's vice president, **Millard Fillmore**, became president. After Congress passed the legislation, Fillmore signed the provisions of the compromise into law.

Millard Fillmore

13

Born	January 7, 1800
Died	March 8, 1874
Home state	New York
Wives	1st—Abigail Powers 2nd—Caroline Carmichael McIntosh
Church	Unitarian
Occupation	lawyer
Party	Whig
Years served as president	1850–53
Terms	partial
Vice president	none

Franklin Pierce

Born	November 23, 1804
Died	October 18, 1869
Home state	New Hampshire
Wife	Jane Means Appleton
Home	Pierce Homestead
Church	Episcopalian
Occupation	lawyer
Party	Democrat
Years served as president	1853–57
Terms	1
Vice president	William Rufus King (died one month after inauguration)

14

▲ In 1848 the Free Soil Party nominated former president Martin Van Buren for the presidency. Charles Adams, son of John Quincy Adams, was their vice-presidential candidate.

Political Changes

The face of Congress and the nation was changing. Men who had been prominent political leaders for years—Henry Clay, John C. Calhoun, and Daniel Webster—were passing from the scene.

New leaders were now emerging. In Congress, Charles Sumner (Massachusetts), William H. Seward (New York), Thaddeus Stevens (Pennsylvania), and Salmon P. Chase (Ohio) bitterly opposed slavery. Meanwhile southerners still fought to protect it.

Stephen Douglas, one of the US senators from Illinois, and a number of northern Democrats were willing to compromise on the slavery issue. They did not oppose the proslavery position but rather sympathized with southern congressmen. They wanted to concentrate on other political issues and let the South handle its own affairs.

The Free Soil Party was formed in 1848. This new political party opposed the extension of slavery into western territories. Its slogan was "free soil, free speech, free labor, and free men." It remained small during the few years that it existed.

The Whigs nominated war hero Winfield Scott for president in 1852. But because he attracted few northern Free-Soilers and southern Democrats, he lost the election to the Democratic candidate, **Franklin Pierce**.

SECTION REVIEW 12.4

1. What were the four most common westward routes?
2. What two countries jointly occupied Oregon? What line became the boundary between them in 1846?
3. Why was the Mormon Trail created? Where did it end?
4. The California Trail was part of what other trail for 1,200 miles before turning southwest?
5. If you were a pioneer going west, which territory would you head for: Oregon, Utah, or California? Why?
6. At whose sawmill was gold found in 1848?
7. What did the Compromise of 1850 propose concerning slavery in California? New Mexico and Utah? What new laws did it implement about slavery?
8. How did Millard Fillmore become president?

CHAPTER 12 REVIEW

Making Connections

1. What happened to many Native American tribes during the time of westward expansion?
2. What actions did Santa Anna take the year after being elected president of Mexico? What was the reaction from the Texas settlers?
3. How long did it take Santa Anna's army to defeat the Alamo? What was the response among Texans?
4. How long did the Battle of San Jacinto last? Who won?
5. Use outside sources to answer the following: What is the capital of Texas today? What city in Texas is the largest? What historical connection do you see in the names of the cities?
6. Why was Texas its own country for almost ten years? What was it called?
7. What is a "dark horse"?
8. What river did Mexico claim was the boundary between Texas and Mexico? What river did the United States claim as the boundary? Approximately how far apart were the rivers?
9. What general moved his troops from Corpus Christi to the Rio Grande?
10. In what order did the three American military leaders attempting to control California arrive? Which one was ultimately successful in controlling it for America?
11. Contrast Zachary Taylor and Winfield Scott by explaining their nicknames.
12. What future states or parts of states were included in the Mexican Cession gained from the Mexican War?
13. What future Civil War military leaders participated in the Mexican War?
14. Why did the first mountain men travel to Oregon? How long was the Oregon Trail?
15. How did the Mormons make a desert-like land livable?
16. Why were the forty-niners given that nickname?
17. Which military commander in the conquest of Mexico became president?

Thinking Critically

18. Which of the reasons for westward expansion would have drawn you to travel west? Explain.
19. How did the culture in which the American settlers originally lived differ from the culture in Mexican Texas?
20. Based on the freedom of religion clause in the First Amendment, should polygamy be allowed? Explain.
21. How did issues such as the Wilmot Proviso push the United States further toward disunion?
22. Was popular sovereignty a good compromise concerning slavery? Why or why not?

Living as a Christian Citizen

23. If you were in Congress during the Mexican War, what would your position have been regarding the war? Why?
24. Congress needs to compromise on many issues in order to function. If you were to become a member of Congress, what principles should guide when or when not to make compromises? Refer to Proverbs 8:12–16 in your answer.

Terms to Remember

Manifest Destiny
mountain men
Jedediah Smith
Stephen Austin
Antonio López de Santa Anna
the Alamo
William Travis
Jim Bowie
Davy Crockett
Sam Houston
Battle of San Jacinto
Lone Star Republic
James K. Polk
Zachary Taylor
Mexican War
John C. Frémont
Bear Flag Republic
Winfield Scott
Treaty of Guadalupe Hidalgo
Mexican Cession
Gadsden Purchase
Santa Fe Trail
Oregon Trail
Marcus and Narcissa Whitman
Mormons
Joseph Smith
Brigham Young
Mormon Trail
California Trail
John Sutter
California gold rush
forty-niners
Wilmot Proviso
Compromise of 1850
popular sovereignty
Millard Fillmore
Franklin Pierce

UNIT 4

Facing a Crisis

The USS *Monitor* and the CSS *Virginia* (which had earlier been called USS *Merrimack*) fought each other in March 1862. This Civil War battle was the first between ironclad naval vessels.

- **1850** Compromise of 1850
- **1852** *Uncle Tom's Cabin* published
- **1854** Republican Party founded; Kansas-Nebraska Act
- **1857** *Dred Scott* decision
- **1859** John Brown's raid on Harpers Ferry
- **1860** Election of Abraham Lincoln; Secession of South Carolina
- **1861** Firing on Fort Sumter
- **1863** Emancipation Proclamation; Battle of Gettysburg
- **1865** Robert E. Lee's surrender at Appomattox; Thirteenth Amendment ratified; Assassination of Abraham Lincoln
- Civil War 1861-1865
- **1867** Reconstruction Act of 1867
- **1868** Impeachment of Andrew Johnson; Fourteenth Amendment ratified
- **1870** Fifteenth Amendment ratified
- **1877** Withdrawal of Union troops from the South

CHAPTER

13 Storm Clouds over the Nation

A slave family flees the South hoping to obtain freedom.

The 1850s was a time of unusual growth and prosperity for the nation. The population rose rapidly, and food production and manufacturing set records. However, differences between the North and the South were swiftly leading to a crisis that would threaten the survival of the United States. Previous compromises that had delayed the resolution of these differences would soon prove insufficient to stop the march toward war.

GUIDING QUESTION

- How were the North and South different before the Civil War?

13.1 DIFFERENCES BETWEEN THE NORTH AND THE SOUTH

What were the differences between the North and the South during the antebellum period?

Differing Views regarding Values

Though great problems existed during the **antebellum** ("before the war," in America used mainly with the Civil War) period, Americans still dearly held the same values—freedom, equality, individualism, and growth. But they did not always agree about how to define these values, particularly as they related to the matter of slavery.

Both North and South talked about freedom. Many Northerners thought that individuals should be free from bondage. However, when Southerners spoke of freedom, it was often about keeping states free from the national government's control, including regarding the matter of slavery.

Both sides also talked about equality. The South asserted the equality of the states: the right of each state to make its own decisions in most matters. Many Northerners, however, thought that a culture of slavery could not be a culture of equality.

Both North and South valued individualism. Some in the North believed that slavery was evil because it kept people from choosing their own course in life. But Southerners argued that many in the North wanted to prevent individual whites in the South from living as they had a right to live.

In addition, both North and South valued the growth of their own ways of life. Many Northerners feared that if slavery spread to new states, Southern culture would become dominant. Likewise, Southerners were concerned that forbidding the expansion of slavery would cause Northern culture to become dominant.

▲ Charleston, South Carolina, was one of the South's most important cities.

Economic and Lifestyle Differences

The South was primarily agricultural. It had fewer large towns and villages than the North. It had even fewer cities. Even the largest Southern cities were relatively small. Most cities had fewer than 40,000 people. In 1860, only New Orleans (pop. 168,675) was comparable to Northern cities in size and diversity. Instead of factories, the South had plantations and small farms. It grew cotton, sugar cane, rice, tobacco, indigo, hemp, and other crops. It also raised horses, cattle, and hogs. Much Southern business involved agriculture in some way.

In the South, the upper class included planters who owned large plantations operated by many slaves. This group led the region politically, socially, and economically. Because of their wealth and

▲ A busy intersection in New York City

success, the planters had an influence on Southern society that was greater than their numbers. Only one-fourth of families in the South owned slaves, and most of those owned fewer than ten slaves. Probably about five thousand planters in the entire South had fifty or more slaves.

Most Southerners believed that slavery was vital to a stable society. Sadly, during this period most white people—even in the North—did not believe that black people had the ability or understanding to participate alongside whites in society. Therefore many people believed that setting slaves free would place them in a worse condition. Others contended that suddenly freeing slaves would lead to crime and class warfare.

The North was much more industrialized than the South, and virtually all African Americans who lived there were free. There were many large cities and towns. Some towns grew so quickly that they struggled to accommodate their growth. New York City's population soared to more than 800,000 by 1860. Chicago, which had only 4,470 people in 1840, had a population of 112,172 by 1860.

About five million immigrants entered the United States between 1820 and 1860. Almost 90 percent of them settled in the North or the West. At first, many of them lived in filth and misery in the cities. They labored long hours for low wages. The working and living conditions of some Northern workers were so poor that some Southerners called them "wage slaves," meaning that their need for a salary required them to work in deplorable conditions. But most immigrants soon adopted American ways and were able to raise their standard of living.

The Northern population was largely merchants, factory workers, and owners of small farms. Though 80 percent of the nation's factories were in the North, most people were still farmers. With the use of new machines, farms provided food for nearby towns. Railroads carried food from farms to the cities. By 1860 the North had about 22,000 miles of railroad track, while the South had only about 9,000 miles. Many owners of factories, railroads, and other industries became wealthy and influential in Northern society.

Differences between the North and South (1860)

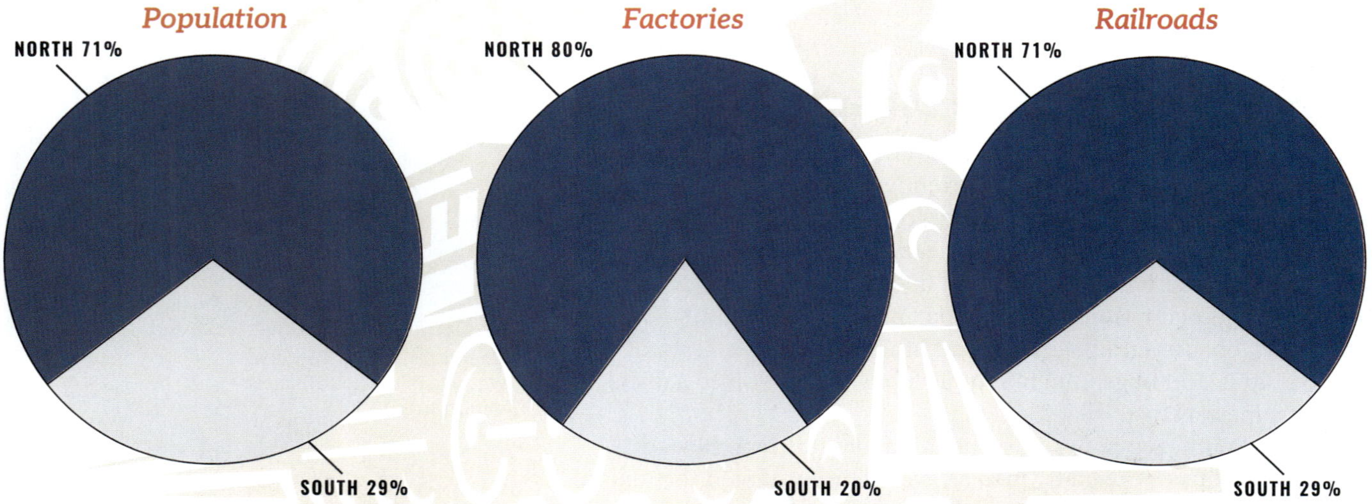

Political Differences

The regions also differed in their political views. Most Northern leaders favored a strong national government. They thought the national government had the powers given to it by the Constitution along with powers that were "necessary and proper" for using the powers that the Constitution specified. They thought that the states kept all other powers. Although some Northerners did worry that, as the United States gained more territory, the national government might become too powerful, they knew that the Constitution was designed to provide protection from excessive government. Therefore, they believed that the Constitution and federal law would overrule any conflicting state and local laws. Northerners based their views on Article VI, Section 2 of the Constitution.

> This Constitution, and the laws of the United States . . . and all treaties made . . . under the authority of the United States, shall be the supreme law of the land; and the judges in every state shall be bound thereby, any thing in the constitution or laws of any state to the contrary notwithstanding.

Most Southerners believed that the local and state governments should be stronger than the federal government. They argued that the national government was the creation of the states. The states had contracted together to form a union. Therefore, they said that the national government could not overrule the rights of the states. They believed that the Constitution granted only limited powers to the national government. Some believed that states had the right to nullify national laws or leave the Union if the national government exceeded its powers. Thus, they said that the states' sovereignty (authority) prevailed over national sovereignty. Southerners based their views on the contract theory of government that John Locke embraced. They also emphasized Amendment X of the Constitution.

> The powers not delegated to the United States by the Constitution, nor prohibited by it to the states, are reserved to the states respectively, or to the people.

These different views of government led to different ideas of what the government should do. Illinois lawyer Abraham Lincoln expressed the common Northern view when he said government should "do for a community of people, whatever they need to have done, but can not do, at all, or can not, so well do, for themselves—in their separate, and individual capacities." This view meant that Northerners traditionally supported government funding of internal improvements. They reasoned that farmers could not build roads and canals themselves. But if the government built the roads and canals, the farmers would benefit.

Many Southerners argued that the national government lacked the constitutional authority to fund internal improvements. They also objected to collecting funds from the whole nation to benefit only those who lived where a road or canal was being built. They said that this practice was unfair because it tended to benefit only the North.

The tariff was another issue of disagreement. It was an effective source of income for the US government, and the North favored a high tariff as a major means of providing money to fund internal improvements. Many in the North also argued that the tariff protected American manufacturers by allowing them to produce goods and hire American workers. The tariff was also preferred over taxing the people directly.

The South opposed a high tariff for two reasons. First, because the South had little industry, foreign imports and trade supported its economy. A high tariff hurt trade and made foreign countries less likely to buy the South's crops. Southerners believed that they were, in effect, being forced to pay the tariff to support Northern industry. Second, the South believed that the tariff should be used only for generating revenue rather than protecting industries.

The issue of slavery played a role in many of these differences. As the country was expanding, the South strongly favored the expansion of slavery into newly settled lands. The North opposed such expansion. Both sides knew that the addition of more free states or slave states would shift the balance of power in Congress.

SECTION REVIEW 13.1

1. How did the North and South differ in their interpretation of values such as freedom, equality, individualism, and growth?
2. How did the economies of the South and North differ?
3. What groups of people were most influential in the South and the North?
4. How did Northerners and Southerners differ in their interpretation of the Constitution and the Bill of Rights? Which viewpoint do you think was more valid? Why?
5. What were two economic issues besides slavery that the North and the South did not agree on?

▾ Cotton bales at the Charleston, South Carolina, harbor

13.2 SLAVERY IN ANTEBELLUM AMERICA

What was slavery like in antebellum America?

GUIDING QUESTION

- What was the life of a slave like in the South?
- How were Northern and Southern views regarding slavery different?
- How was the Bible used in the slavery debate?

Although slavery was an ancient practice, slavery in antebellum America was different from other times in history in three ways:

1. It involved only those of African descent.
2. It became a permanent condition for most slaves.
3. It was the result of buying stolen Africans and selling them.

To ensure Southern support for the Constitution, the Founding Fathers had delayed finding a permanent solution to slavery. They included three-fifths of each state's total slave population in the count of each state's population to determine representation in Congress. They also guaranteed that Congress would not prohibit the importing of slaves before 1808. In that year, the United States became the last major nation in the Western hemisphere to ban foreign slave trade. (See Article I, Section 9, of the Constitution.) Some slave smuggling did continue, but most new slaves after this time were the children of slaves already living in the United States. The American slave trade was now confined within the borders of the United States.

By the 1830s, the question of whether slavery was morally right had become the subject of intense debate. Some praised it as good when they compared it with conditions in factories at this time. But opposition to slavery increased as abolitionists emphasized its great injustice.

▲ Five generations of slaves are pictured on a South Carolina plantation.

Slave Life in the South

The condition of slave life in the South depended on the masters, the amount of property they owned, and the type of system they employed to manage the slaves. Some masters were unquestionably cruel. Others treated slaves much more humanely. But slavery, even under a kind master, was still unjust. Slaves longed to be free.

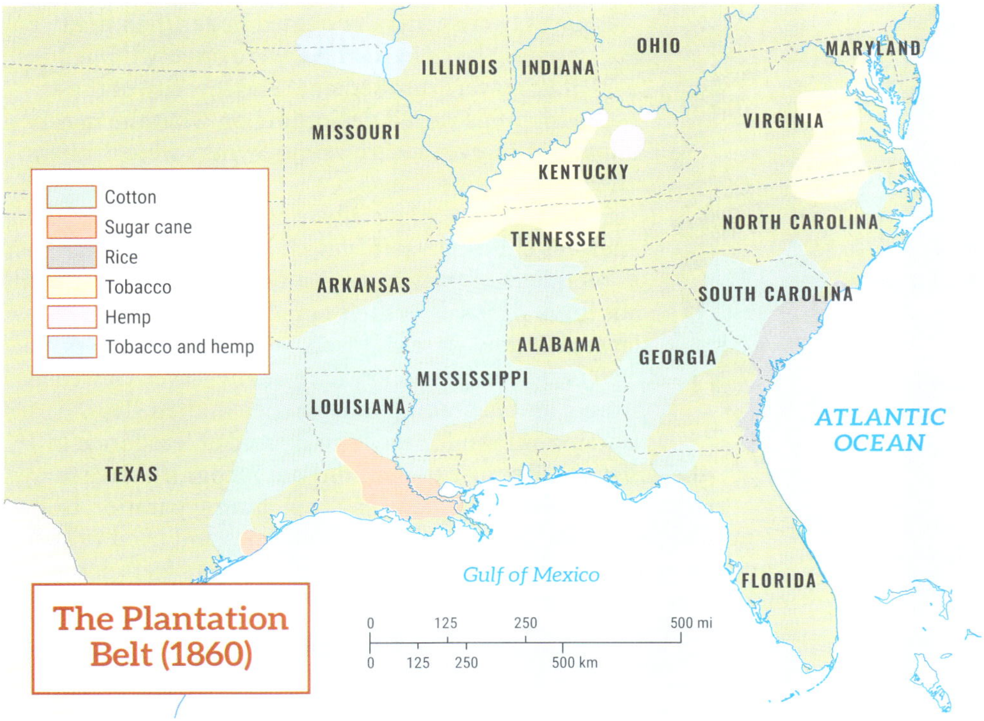

The Plantation Belt (1860)

Did you know?

Members of some Native American tribes (such as the Cherokees, Chickasaws, and Choctaws) owned African American slaves. This usually occurred because of the intermarriage between slave holders and Native Americans. The children born as a result of those marriages inherited both tribal rights and slaves.

Life on a Southern Plantation

Life on a plantation centered on the work of the master, the overseer, and the slaves. The master instructed the **overseer** who distributed the work among the slaves and ensured that they did as expected. Usually he was a hired white man. After it became difficult to find reliable overseers who would work for little pay, some slave owners simply used a trusted slave as an overseer.

The slaves' work varied with the types of crops grown and the season of the year. Jobs in the fields included clearing land, planting seeds, weeding, cultivating, harvesting, cutting wood, and digging ditches. Other jobs included caring for animals; repairing fences, dikes, buildings, or other structures; cooking; and caring for the master's children.

Slave labor varied by the type of working arrangement used. Some masters used the **gang system**. The slaves worked in large groups for a set amount of time each day—usually from sunup to sundown or longer. Other masters used the **task system**, which most slaves preferred. Under the task system, the overseer gave the slaves specific tasks. When the slaves completed their tasks, they could use what remained of the day to do other things, such as working for themselves.

▾ At slave auctions such as this one in Richmond, Virginia, individuals were sold like cattle to the highest bidder.

Slaves had no legal rights; thus, if masters mistreated them, there was little that could be done. Slaves had no basic rights other than what their masters granted. Their marriages were not recognized. Children born to them belonged to the master. Some masters even insisted on personally naming slave children.

Masters often kept slaves fit and healthy. Unfortunately, the motivation was not typically out of concern for their well-being but because slaves were an economic investment. It was the same reason a farmer would give for keeping his animals healthy.

Slaves who worked in the master's house, house slaves, were generally treated better than field slaves. Slaves in the field were often whipped if they were disobedient. The severity of these whippings varied depending on what the master allowed; however, clearly some owners were brutal in their treatment of slaves.

Some slaves, especially those who cared for the master's children, were viewed by their owners almost as members of the family. But the owners certainly did not think of slaves as their equals. Most treated adult slaves as if they were children. What some masters believed to be compassionate care, many slaves viewed as continual and degrading interference in their lives.

It was common for slaves to be sold at least once in their lifetime. Because the law did not recognize slave marriages, many sales meant a heart-wrenching separation from family. Some slave owners tried to avoid sales and tried to keep families together, but even well-intentioned owners were sometimes forced to sell slaves to pay debts. Slaves particularly feared being sold "down the river" to sugar plantations in the lower Mississippi River valley. Cutting and processing sugar cane was especially brutal work.

Responses to Plantation Conditions

Thousands of slaves ran away. This was a constant problem for many masters. Masters offered large rewards for a slave's return. Slaves who followed the **Underground Railroad** could reach northern states and thereby gain their freedom. This "railroad" was actually a network of people who aided runaway slaves. People called "conductors" hid the slaves by day. At night, they directed them to the next safe location, or "station." Conductors at the next station did the same. In this way, runaway slaves slowly made their way to freedom. When the Fugitive Slave Act of 1850 required Northern states to return runaways, the Underground Railroad extended its route farther north. Ontario, Canada, became the final destination for many slaves. However, some slaves actually went south. They developed isolated settlements hidden in the swamps of Georgia and northern Florida.

$100 REWARD!
RANAWAY
From the undersigned, living on Current River, about twelve miles above Doniphan, in Ripley County, Mo., on 2nd of March, 1860, A NE-GRO MAN, about 30 years old, weighs about 160 pounds; high forehead, with a scar on it; had on brown pants and coat very much worn, and an old black wool hat; shoes size No. 11.
The above reward will be given to any person who may apprehend thi[s] said negro out of the State; and fifty dollars if apprehended in this State outside of Ripley county, or $25 if taken in Ripley county.
APOS TUCKER.

Although slave rebellions seldom occurred, whites still feared them because by 1860 slaves made up one-third of the Southern population. With that many slaves, a well-organized revolt could become a revolution. Some revolts were led by slaves such as "Cato" in South Carolina (1739), Denmark Vesey in South Carolina (1822), and Nat Turner in Virginia (1831). All such uprisings failed, however. The blacks involved were hanged. The hangings made other slaves reluctant to rebel. But the revolts panicked the whites. They slept with guns. They passed even stricter laws relating to slavery that became known as slave codes. Several states made it illegal to teach slaves to read and write. They feared that ideas of revolt would spread if blacks had those skills. These laws bothered many Christians who recognized that the ability to read the Bible is important to Christian growth.

▲ *The Underground Railroad* by Charles Webber

Several African Americans became famous for their work opposing slavery in the troubled years before the Civil War. **Frederick Douglass**, a leading black abolitionist, escaped from slavery in 1838. He was a talented speaker who lectured in the North against slavery. He used much of the money earned from his lectures to help other escaped slaves. He also wrote an influential autobiography, *The Narrative of the Life of Frederick Douglass*. Douglass risked his freedom by naming his former master in the book. To escape possible capture, he fled to Britain. Douglass addressed large crowds during the two years he spent there. (The British Empire had abolished slavery by 1833, largely due to the untiring influence of abolitionist William Wilberforce.) Supporters purchased Douglass's freedom, and he returned to the United States in 1847. He began publishing an anti-slavery newspaper, the *North Star*. He also supported women's rights.

Frederick Douglass ▸

Harriet Tubman ▾

After enduring much abuse as a slave, **Harriet Tubman** escaped from slavery in 1849. With the help of Quaker friends, she returned to slave territory nearly twenty times to help other slaves escape, leading about three hundred people along the Underground Railroad. She even helped her own parents escape in 1857. Because she helped to free slaves, she became known as the Moses of her people.

Charles Hodge

Charles Hodge, a professor at Princeton Theological Seminary and a leading theologian of the nineteenth century, opposed both slavery and immediate abolition. Instead, he favored gradual emancipation.

He argued that the Bible requires Christians to work within their system of government to bring about justice. He believed that pushing for a revolution to remedy injustice will only bring about greater injustices, as the French Revolution had demonstrated.

AFRICAN AMERICANS, *the Church, and* SLAVERY

Influenced by years of preaching, African Americans tended to have a very high view of Scripture. They did not believe the Bible supported slavery. African Americans noted that slavery in America was racist. The South enslaved only blacks.

Religion played a major role in the slave community. Slaves often attended the same churches as their masters. In some churches, blacks and whites worshiped together. In other churches, the blacks sat in the balcony, and the whites sat on the main floor. Some blacks, however, formed their own churches. Some of these churches were independent, but most were supervised by whites. Masters sometimes feared that the slaves might use their church services to plan revolts. If whites thought that black churches were a potential threat, they would order them to disband.

Opposing Views of Slavery

Most Northerners were not abolitionists, and not all those in the South supported slavery. Nevertheless, by the middle of the nineteenth century, clear differences about slavery existed between the two sections of the nation.

Northern Responses to Slavery

Northerners held a wide variety of views about slavery. Abolitionists objected to slavery for moral reasons. Two of the leading white abolitionists were **William Lloyd Garrison** and **Horace Greeley**. Both published newspapers that opposed slavery and called for its immediate elimination. Christian abolitionists called upon fellow Christians to denounce slavery and to work diligently to end it.

Other Northerners also thought that slavery was a great evil. But they believed that freeing all slaves at once would be harmful to everyone. They wanted slaves to be educated, trained for freedom, and freed at a certain age. This concept was called gradual emancipation. Some Northerners wanted the government to pay slave owners whose slaves were freed. This plan was called compensated emancipation.

Still other Northerners were concerned about slavery only as an economic and political issue. For example, some objected to it because it was undemocratic. Others opposed its spread to the territories because it gave the South greater power in Congress. But some Northerners did not favor abolition because of the economic impact it would have on the nation.

Opposition to slavery did not always mean opposition to racism. Though some Northern states allowed black Americans to vote and benefit from public education, many Northern states not only denied black Americans political rights but also enforced segregation (separation of the races) in public. Sadly, most white Americans were not willing to accept African Americans as their equals when they were freed. Opponents of slavery often suggested that black Americans should be sent to Africa to establish their own colonies.

▲ William Lloyd Garrison (left) and Horace Greeley (right) were two leading abolitionists.

Southern Responses to Abolitionism

The more abolitionists opposed slavery, the more Southerners—even those who were not slaveholders—defended it. The economic success of the South seemed to depend on slavery. Many Southern businesses relied on cotton produced by slave labor. Some Southerners opposed slavery but saw it as a necessary evil. As time passed, more Southerners said that slavery was actually good. They argued that it provided educated Southerners the time necessary for moral and mental growth. They said that a slave society thus promoted the virtues of honor, courage, duty, and dignity—virtues they thought were lacking in the North. They also considered slavery good for the slaves themselves. They argued that slaves had better living and working conditions than many factory workers in the North. In addition, many thought that black Americans were "morally inferior." Since whites considered themselves morally upright, they contended it was good that they ruled those "beneath" them.

Many Southern Christians defended slavery and opposed abolition, but they warned their fellow Southerners to end the abuses of slavery. They especially urged that the law recognize slave marriages and forbid breaking families apart. They also appealed to slave owners to stop resisting others' attempts to evangelize, disciple, and educate slaves.

Many people in the South defended slavery on constitutional grounds. They believed that the Constitution recognized slavery. They said that the Constitution gave the states, not the national government, primary authority over slavery.

Other Southerners saw slavery as an issue of economics. If the North could force the South to use paid labor, the North would gain an advantage over the Southern economy. A high tariff also hurt the Southern economy and favored Northern industry.

Not everyone in the South favored slavery. Small farmers in the Appalachian Mountains of the South generally opposed slavery because it gave owners of large plantations greater influence over state governments. Many people from the Appalachia area would later join the North in the coming war.

Slaves themselves, of course, opposed the practice of slavery. This is clear because tens of thousands of them tried to escape. They often revealed how they felt about their condition with songs that came to be known as "**spirituals**." Songs such as "Nobody Knows the Trouble I Seen" and "Sometimes I Feel like a Motherless Child" expressed the suffering they endured as slaves. Spirituals such as "Steal Away to Jesus" and "Go Down, Moses" expressed their desire for freedom. Many spirituals dealt with various biblical subjects.

John Jasper

John Jasper was born in Virginia in 1812. His parents were slaves, and he worked first on a plantation and then in a tobacco factory. In his mid-twenties, he was converted. He convinced a fellow slave to teach him to read and write and began studying to become a minister. Jasper could preach only with his master's permission, yet he gained a following by preaching at slave funerals and by speaking regularly at a church in Petersburg, Virginia.

After being a slave for a half century, he gained his freedom because of the Civil War. He then established the Sixth Mount Zion Baptist Church in Richmond, Virginia, and the congregation grew to over two thousand members.

Jasper rose to prominence as a preacher and spoke throughout the Eastern United States. His electrifying preaching style attracted both blacks and whites. His sermon on Joshua 10, entitled "The Sun Do Move," became his most requested sermon. He delivered his last message just days before his death in 1901 at age eighty-eight.

African American slaves singing on a southern plantation

The Bible's Role in the Slavery Debate

Most Americans during this period respected the Bible. This meant that the question of slavery was not just a political question but also a biblical one. However, neither side of the slavery debate could agree on what the Bible taught.

The slavery issue also split the major religious groups. The Methodists split in early 1844. In the South, they formed the Southern Methodist Church. In the same year, the Baptists split over whether slaveholders could be appointed to mission boards or serve as missionaries. The Southern Baptist Convention was formed in May 1845. The Presbyterians also split because of disagreements about slavery.

The Second Great Awakening sparked many reform movements. Not all Christians were reformers, and not all reformers were Christians. But Christians played a major role in many of the reforms, especially the antislavery movement. Lyman Beecher and Nathaniel Taylor in New England and Charles Finney in New York were among the preachers who sparked the movement. They influenced many future antislavery leaders.

▲ Lyman Beecher served as a Presbyterian minister for more than a half century.

The Bible and Slavery

Christians who opposed slavery appealed to biblical principles. African Americans and other Christian leaders argued that the practice of slavery contradicted the Bible's teachings. They emphasized that people were created in the image of God and that Christians are to treat one another as brothers, regardless of differences in ethnicity or economic condition (Gal. 3:28; John 13:34).

Those who appealed to the Bible to defend the system of slavery failed to recognize several facts. For example, in the Old Testament God prohibited kidnapping people and enslaving them. The punishment for doing so was death (Exod. 21:16). The American system had been founded on manstealing. Furthermore, Israelite slavery typically involved a person working six years to pay debts. However, in America, people were slaves for their whole lives, and their children were enslaved as well. In New Testament times, slavery was so embedded in the Roman Empire that a minority group, like Christianity, could not end it or separate itself from it.

In addition, proponents of slavery usually ignored the fact that although the apostle Paul sent the slave Onesimus back to his master, Philemon, as required by Roman law, he pointedly sent him back "not . . . as a [slave]" but as Paul's "son" and Philemon's "brother beloved" (Philem. 1:10, 16). Paul also forbade masters from even threatening slaves, much less beating them, reminding them that slaves were their equals and commanding them to treat slaves fairly (Eph. 6:9; Col. 4:1).

A Biblical Crisis

The debate over slavery brought American culture into crisis. Americans on both sides of the issue tried to use Scripture to resolve this problem, sometimes by attempting to make the Bible fit what they wanted it to say rather than looking at the meaning of the passage and the Bible as a whole. The disagreement regarding what the Bible taught intensified, and finding a resolution became increasingly difficult. The split within the nation worsened and deepened.

SECTION REVIEW 13.2

1. How was slavery in pre-Civil War America different from other times in history?
2. What were the two types of systems masters used for slave labor?
3. What normal aspects of family life did Southern culture not allow for slaves? What could happen as a result?
4. How were slaves sometimes treated like a farmer would treat an animal?
5. What were two ways that blacks responded to conditions on the plantations?
6. Why did some Southern states make it illegal to teach slaves to read and write? Why did many Christians object to this?
7. What three plans for freeing slaves did abolitionists propose?
8. Why was slavery neither just, free, nor equal?

13.3 THE SLAVERY ISSUE INTENSIFIES

What caused the slavery controversy to intensify?

GUIDING QUESTIONS

- How did new events heighten the slavery debate?

The nation had tried to deal with the spread of slavery through compromise. But neither the Missouri Compromise in 1820 nor the Compromise of 1850 solved the problem. They only postponed its resolution. The slavery issue was like a covered pot of water sitting on a hot stove. Several incidents brought the issue to a boil.

Fugitive Slave Act of 1850

One such incident was the passage of the Fugitive Slave Act of 1850. The Constitution stated that if slaves fled to another state, they must be returned when they were claimed by their masters (Article IV, Section 2, clause 3). Increasing numbers of slaves were escaping through the Underground Railroad, and Southerners said the free-state governments were hindering their ability to recapture them. As a result, Southern states wanted a law that provided for better enforcement of the constitutional provision. Thus, as a part of the Compromise of 1850, the Fugitive Slave Act was passed.

These two runaway slaves were captured in Boston and then returned to South Carolina in the 1850s.

The Fugitive Slave Act essentially took the power of settling fugitive-slave cases from state courts and gave it to US court commissioners. It stated that alleged fugitives were not entitled to a trial by jury nor could they testify in their own behalf. A statement by a slave owner was all that was required for a slave to be returned. A US commissioner was paid ten dollars if he ruled in favor of the alleged owner of the accused. The commissioner was paid five dollars if he ruled that the alleged fugitive was wrongly accused. The higher payment was supposedly because ruling against an alleged fugitive required more paperwork, but opponents of slavery argued that the higher payment was really a bribe to influence the decision of officials. Furthermore, the act stated that anyone convicted of helping a fugitive slave was subject to a fine of $1,000, imprisonment for six months, or both.

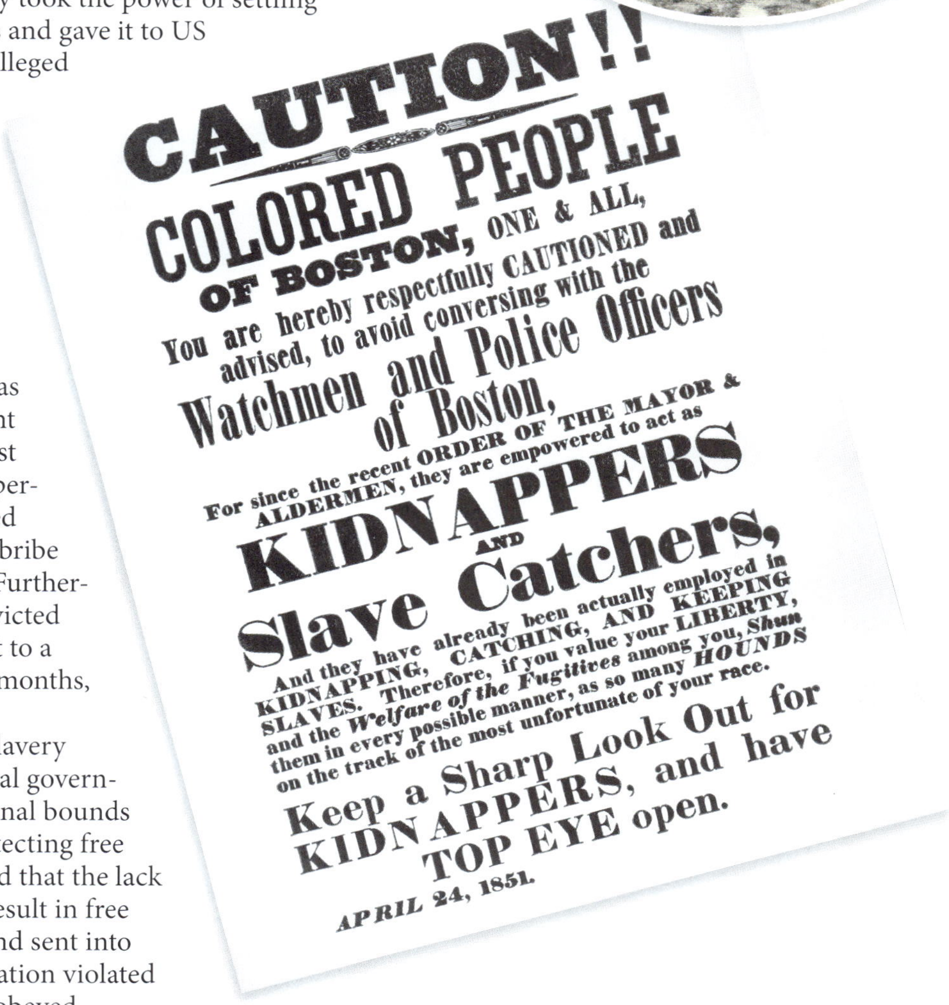

The law provoked a strong antislavery reaction. Some argued that the federal government had overstepped its constitutional bounds by prohibiting state courts from protecting free black men and women. Others feared that the lack of safeguards in the new law could result in free black Americans being kidnapped and sent into slavery. Some asserted that the legislation violated God's higher law and should not be obeyed.

Uncle Tom's Cabin

Another decisive event was the publication of an innocent-sounding novel—***Uncle Tom's Cabin***. The book's author was **Harriet Beecher Stowe**, a Connecticut preacher's daughter who lost a young son to cholera in 1849. She believed that her loss helped her understand how slave mothers felt when their children were sold and taken from them. She vowed to bring the plight of slave families and runaways to public attention.

The Stowes had lived for a while in Cincinnati, Ohio, across the Ohio River from the slave state of Kentucky. There, Stowe had seen the conditions of fugitive slaves. Using that experience and what she read in abolitionist papers, she wrote the novel. It was first published in installments by the *National Era*, an antislavery paper, from 1851 to 1852 and later released in book form. Within a year, three hundred thousand copies of the book had sold.

Stowe tried to capture the wide variety of American experience with slavery. She showed both well-intentioned slave owners caught in an unjust system as well as cruel masters. Northern abolitionists and Northern racists both appeared in the book. Black Christians appeared alongside unsaved blacks. But the point was consistent: the system of slavery was inescapably unjust. The book stirred opposition to slavery. But it angered Southerners. Some accused Stowe of lying about the conditions of slaves. In response, she wrote *A Key to "Uncle Tom's Cabin"* to defend the accuracy of her novel.

▾ Harriet Beecher Stowe

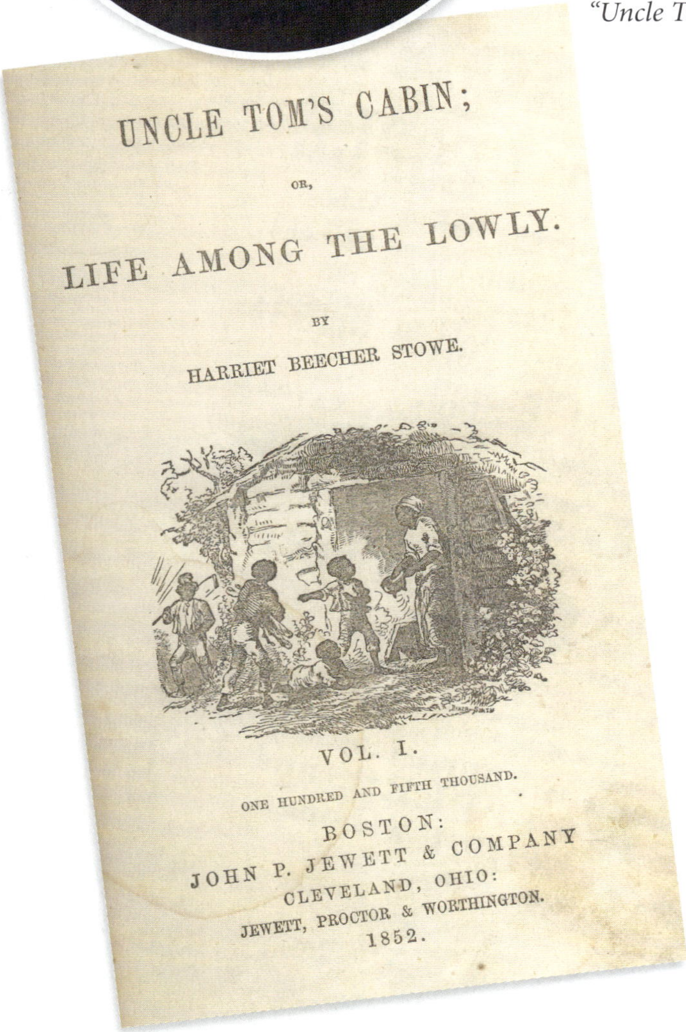

UNCLE TOM'S CABIN;

OR,

LIFE AMONG THE LOWLY.

BY

HARRIET BEECHER STOWE.

VOL. I.

ONE HUNDRED AND FIFTH THOUSAND.

BOSTON:

JOHN P. JEWETT & COMPANY

CLEVELAND, OHIO:

JEWETT, PROCTOR & WORTHINGTON.

1852.

▴ Harriet Beecher Stowe (far right) was the daughter of Lyman Beecher, seated.

Fun Fact

Harriet Beecher Stowe and Mark Twain, the author of *Tom Sawyer* and *Huckleberry Finn*, were neighbors in Connecticut between 1874 and 1891.

Kansas-Nebraska Act

In 1854 **Stephen Douglas**, a Democratic Senator from Illinois, proposed the **Kansas-Nebraska Act**. It called for organizing two territories—Kansas, just west of Missouri, and Nebraska, just west of Iowa. To settle the slavery issue, Douglas returned to the idea of popular sovereignty; each territory would decide the status of slavery for itself. To make popular sovereignty work, the act would repeal the provision of the Missouri Compromise that banned slavery north of 36°30′ line of latitude. Congress passed the measure in May 1854.

Abraham Lincoln denounced popular sovereignty and the Kansas-Nebraska Act in a speech a few months later. He stated,

> When the white man governs himself that is self-government; but when he governs himself, and also governs another man, that is more than self-government—that is despotism [tyranny]. If the negro is a man, why then my ancient faith teaches me that "all men are created equal;" and that there can be no moral right in connection with one man's making a slave of another.

Both proslavery and antislavery groups urged their supporters to move west to influence the voting in Kansas and Nebraska. Conflict was inevitable. The two sides clashed, especially in Kansas, which suffered such bitter warfare that it got the nickname "Bleeding Kansas." The conflict there was a foretaste of what would happen nationally.

On May 21, 1856, a group of men attacked Lawrence, Kansas, which was settled by abolitionists. Since the citizens did not fight back, the attackers did not kill them. Instead, the attackers looted and burned the town. This violence worsened the hatred and determination of the two groups.

▲ Pro-slavery forces (shown here) and antislavery groups moved to Kansas during this period.

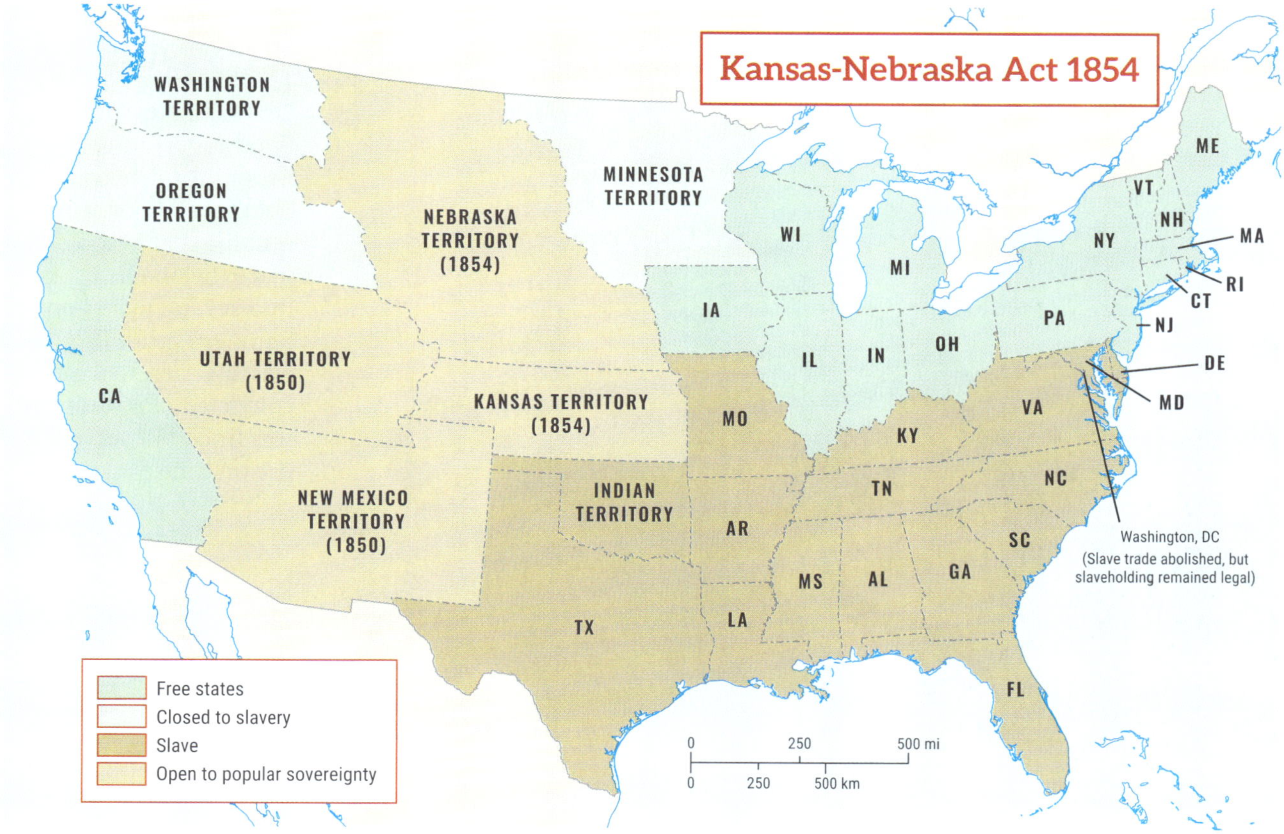

James Buchanan

15

Born	April 23, 1791
Died	June 1, 1868
Home state	Pennsylvania
Wife	not married
Church	Presbyterian
Occupation	lawyer
Party	Democrat
Years served as president	1857–61
Terms	1
Vice president	John C. Breckinridge

Creation of the Republican Party

By 1852 the Whigs had split into two factions over slavery: the Cotton Whigs and the Conscience Whigs. After the Kansas-Nebraska Act passed, the Cotton Whigs, the smaller of the factions, joined the Southern Democrats in supporting slavery. But the Kansas-Nebraska Act angered Conscience Whigs and Northern Democrats. Those two groups, along with the Free Soil Party, opposed the spread of slavery.

In 1854 the antislavery groups formed a new political party: the **Republican Party**. It grew with startling speed. In the party's first year of existence, the Republicans elected congressmen. Two years later, in the election of 1856, they ran their first candidate for president, John C. Frémont. He had become famous as an explorer, a military leader, and later as a US senator from California. Though Democrat **James Buchanan** defeated him, Republicans gained national attention and laid the groundwork for the next presidential campaign in 1860.

Sumner-Brooks Episode

Symbolic of the tensions that were building throughout the country was an incident in Congress in May 1856. Senator **Charles Sumner** of Massachusetts delivered an angry speech about the fighting in Kansas. For two days, he verbally attacked his colleagues who supported slavery. He made particularly abusive comments about Andrew Butler, a South Carolina senator, who was not present to respond.

A few days later, South Carolina representative **Preston Brooks**, Butler's cousin, strode into a nearly empty Senate chamber. He proceeded to Sumner's desk and began to beat Sumner with a walking cane. Several senators stood idly by or kept others from interfering. Later, two representatives intervened. Sumner was so badly injured that he did not return to the Senate for more than two years. Some Northerners claimed that the episode proved that Southerners were violent brutes. But Southerners praised Brooks for defending Southern honor. They sent him canes to replace the one he broke into several pieces on Sumner's head. Brooks was later arrested and convicted of assault. He was fined but served no prison time.

Preston Brooks's caning of Charles Sumner in the Senate was only a foretaste of future violence.

Dred Scott Decision

Two days after Buchanan became president in March 1857, the Supreme Court made one of its most historic rulings. It involved the case of an elderly black man, **Dred Scott**.

Scott was born into slavery. He was the slave of an army doctor, John Emerson of Missouri. When the army transferred Emerson to military posts in the free state of Illinois and the free territory of Wisconsin, he took Scott with him. In 1838 Emerson returned to Missouri, again taking Scott with him. When Emerson died, lawyers in Missouri helped Scott sue Emerson's heirs for his freedom. The Missouri Supreme Court had ruled in 1824 that if a slave owner moved to free territory and lived there, his slaves would be free.

Because of this precedent, Scott's lawyers said that Scott should be a free man. Although Scott won in a lower court, he lost the appeals that followed. The case eventually reached the Supreme Court as *Dred Scott v. Sandford*. **Roger B. Taney**, a Southerner, was the chief justice.

Seven of the nine justices ruled against Scott. In the decision, Taney wrote that Scott was black and thus not a citizen. Therefore, said Taney, Scott did not have the right to sue in the nation's courts. Taney also said that in the past, black people were viewed as "so far inferior, that they had no rights which the white man was bound to respect." Furthermore, Taney ruled, Scott was not free simply because he had lived in areas that were free. Taney reasoned that the Fifth Amendment forbade the government to deprive a person of "life, liberty, or property, without due process of law." So he ruled that the Missouri Compromise and popular sovereignty were unconstitutional because they deprived citizens of property (slaves).

The results of the Dred Scott decision were serious. Briefly, the South rejoiced that the Court had upheld slavery and that Congress could not prevent slavery's expansion into new territories. But politically, the case wrecked any chance of a compromise. The Republicans had suffered a setback, but the antislavery forces would not be silenced.

Three of the nation's ablest negotiators—Henry Clay, John C. Calhoun, and Daniel Webster—had all died a few years earlier. They were replaced by men who displayed less ability in dealing with difficult matters. Presidents Fillmore, Pierce, and Buchanan all proved to be weak leaders at the time the nation needed extraordinary wisdom. Furthermore, many leaders on both sides of the slavery debate believed it would be wrong to compromise their beliefs. Events were leading the nation closer and closer to even greater crises.

dissenting OPINION

Two of the nine justices disagreed with the Supreme Court's ruling in the *Dred Scott* case. One of them noted that at the time of the Constitution's ratification in the late 1780s, free black men could vote in five of the thirteen states; thus, they were recognized as citizens.

Roger Taney (left) and Dred Scott (center and alongside his wife) were involved in one of the most important court cases of the nineteenth century.

▲ Abraham Lincoln (standing) debated Stephen Douglas (seated front left) seven times in 1858.

▲ Photo of present-day Harpers Ferry, Virginia

Lincoln-Douglas Debates

In the mid-1850s, Abraham Lincoln left the Whig Party and joined the recently formed Republican Party. In 1858 he became the Republican candidate for the US Senate in Illinois. At that time he delivered what became known as the "House Divided" speech. In it he argued,

> "A house divided against itself cannot stand." I believe this government cannot endure, permanently half slave and half free. I do not expect the Union to be dissolved—I do not expect the house to fall—but I do expect it will cease to be divided. It will become all one thing or all the other. Either the opponents of slavery, will arrest [stop] the further spread of it, and place it where the public mind shall rest in the belief that it is in [on] course of ultimate extinction; or its advocates will push it forward, till it shall become alike lawful in all the States, old as well as new—North as well as South.

Lincoln's opponent in the race was the incumbent (current officeholder), Democrat Stephen Douglas. Lincoln challenged Douglas to a series of debates. Douglas accepted, and the two debated in seven locations throughout Illinois. Thousands of spectators attended, and the events were widely covered in newspapers.

The primary subject in the debates was slavery. Douglas continued to promote the idea that the people in territories had the right to decide whether slavery should be allowed. Lincoln opposed slavery existing in any territories. The state legislature, which elected the senators from each state, reelected Douglas in a close vote. However, Lincoln's reputation spread throughout the country.

John Brown's Attacks on Slavery

John Brown was an abolitionist who traveled to Kansas to fight for its becoming a free territory. While most abolitionists were advocating a peaceful end to slavery, Brown said that violence was the only solution. He quoted part of Hebrews 9:22—"Without shedding of blood is no remission"—to show the price that slaveholders would pay for their support of slavery. His message convinced many people.

Responding to the violence in Lawrence, Kansas, and the attack on Charles Sumner in the Senate, Brown made his first strike against slavery in Pottawatomie, Kansas, in 1856. He and four of his seven sons murdered five proslavery men one night by hacking them with razor-sharp swords. After escaping prosecution for the Pottawatomie Massacre, Brown began to develop a strategy so radical that many abolitionists withdrew their support of him. In the summer of 1859, Brown armed twenty-one men, including some of his sons and five African Americans, and planned his attack in earnest.

On October 16, 1859, Brown and his little army rode into Harpers Ferry, Virginia (now West Virginia). They took several well-known slaveholders as hostages and seized the federal arsenal (building for storage of weapons). Brown hoped that this action would stir local slaves to rebel and that thousands of other slaves would rally to him as word of his deed spread. But no such revolt occurred.

Local militia blocked all of Brown's escape routes. Federal troops led by Colonel Robert E. Lee and a young officer named J. E. B. Stuart arrived the next day and demanded that Brown and his men surrender. Brown refused, so the troops stormed the building. Two of Brown's sons and more than a dozen others were killed in the fighting. Brown, who was wounded, was placed on trial less than two weeks later. During the trial, he won many admirers, but none of them were on the jury, which convicted him of murder. He was hanged.

Brown's revolt failed, but his actions had a profound effect on the nation. Southerners feared a slave revolt more than ever. And Brown's death made him a martyr for the abolitionist cause. Some Northern soldiers later marched to war singing, "John Brown's body lies a-mouldering in the grave, but his soul goes marching on." Julia Ward Howe, an abolitionist, used the melody of this song with her own lyrics to create "The Battle Hymn of the Republic."

Troops recapturing the building (below) which John Brown (above) had seized at Harpers Ferry

SECTION REVIEW 13.3

1. Why might a court commissioner have been tempted to rule in favor of the alleged owner of a runaway slave?
2. Why was *Uncle Tom's Cabin* so important? Who wrote it? What was the main point of the book?
3. What two territories were opened to popular sovereignty, causing the slavery issue to intensify? What nickname did Kansas receive?
4. What groups joined together to form the Republican Party? What was their foundational belief?
5. Who were the two members of Congress involved in an incident in which one was beaten severely? Which state did each represent?
6. What might have been the result if the *Dred Scott* case had been decided with an opposite ruling?
7. How did most Southerners respond to John Brown's failed raid on Harpers Ferry? How did many abolitionists respond?
8. What was wrong with the way John Brown attempted to solve the slavery issue?

GUIDING QUESTIONS

- What happened during the election of 1860?
- Why did some Southern states secede?

13.4 THE ELECTION OF 1860 AND SECESSION

How did the election of 1860 lead to the secession of some Southern states?

The tensions that grew during the late 1850s erupted in the election of 1860. The Democratic Party split. New alliances and regional bonds formed. These events influenced the nation for decades.

The 1860 presidential candidates (top to bottom): Stephen Douglas, John C. Breckinridge, Abraham Lincoln, John Bell

Election of 1860

The South was worried about the election of 1860. Southern extremists were called fire-eaters, a reference to their hotheadedness. They threatened **secession** (the act of leaving the Union) if the Republicans won. Many Southerners wanted the national government to press for the repeal of state laws that complicated the return of fugitive slaves. They also wanted a national slave code that would protect slavery in all the territories and perhaps a constitutional amendment to guarantee the preservation of slavery.

The Democrats thought their best chance to capture the White House was to choose a moderate candidate in their convention, someone who appealed to both the North and the South. Stephen Douglas seemed to be that candidate. But fire-eaters considered him their enemy and would not accept him as a compromise candidate. The fire-eaters had great influence among Southern Democrats. Rather than unite behind Douglas, the fire-eaters walked out of the convention. Douglas was then selected as the nominee of the Northern Democrats. During the election, he continued to insist that slavery in the territories should be handled by popular sovereignty.

Southern Democrats then held their own convention. They selected **John C. Breckinridge** of Kentucky as their candidate. They also adopted a platform (a statement of political positions) based on the *Dred Scott* decision, calling for a federal slave code to protect slavery in all the territories.

With the Democrats divided, the Republicans had real hopes for victory. In an effort to keep the Union intact, they chose a man who would campaign as a moderate rather than as an abolitionist or a Free-Soiler. Their choice was **Abraham Lincoln**. Lincoln had declared slavery a moral evil. He argued that the Declaration of Independence's words "All men are created equal" applied to black men as well as white. Nonetheless, Lincoln promised he would not attempt to interfere with slavery where it already existed. He did pledge to oppose the spread of slavery.

A number of former Whigs and other voters—mostly in the border states of Delaware, Maryland, Virginia, Tennessee, and Kentucky—joined together as the Constitutional Union Party and chose **John Bell** of Tennessee as their candidate. Their platform was vague, but they hoped Bell could keep the country from splitting.

As the election neared, more Southerners began to fear a Republican victory. If that happened, many said, the Southern states should secede and form their own government. They based that proposal on the view that the states had voluntarily joined the Union and could therefore voluntarily leave it.

When the votes were tallied, it was clear that Lincoln had carried the Northern and western states, gaining more popular votes than

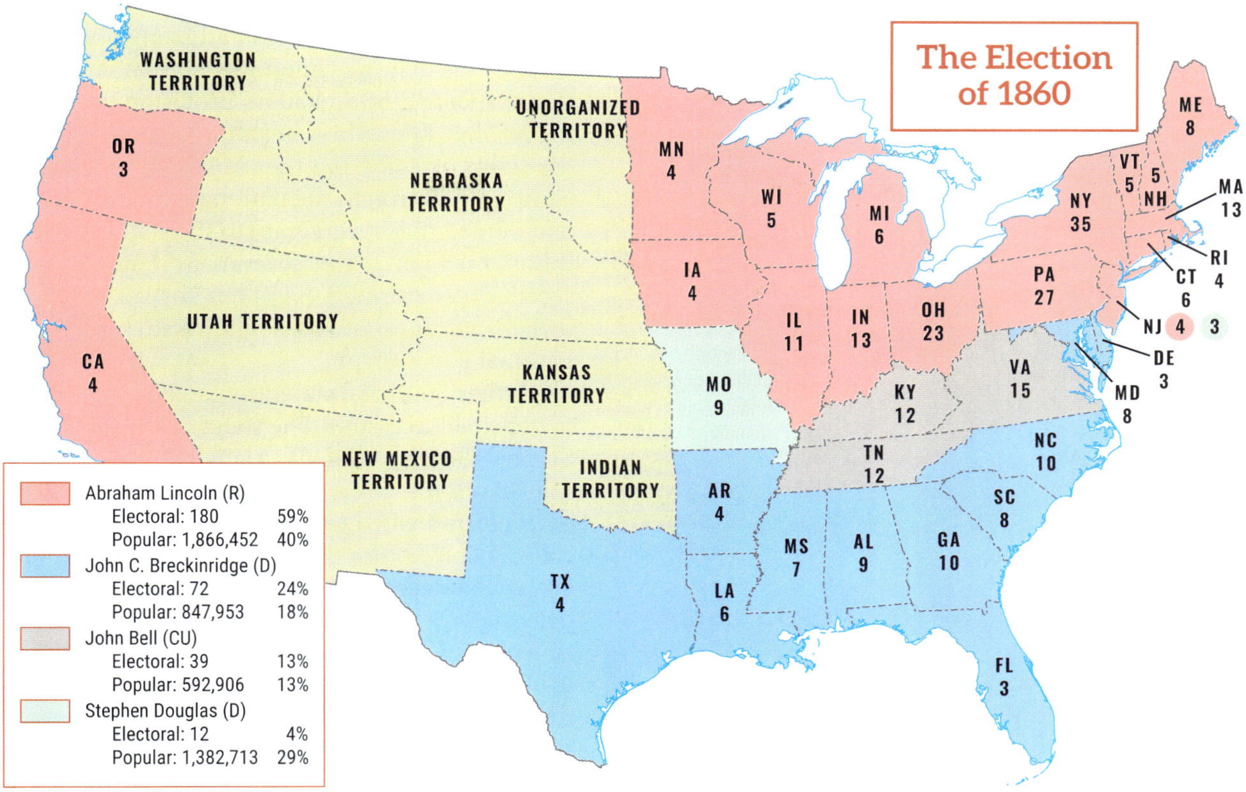

each of the other candidates. Douglas was second in the popular vote, followed by Breckinridge and then Bell. Lincoln's victory, however, was far from overwhelming. More than 60 percent of the voters had voted for someone other than Lincoln. Lincoln was not on the ballot in any Southern state and failed to carry a single border state.

Secession of Southern States

The South believed that states were sovereign (self-governing) authorities that had voluntarily joined the Union. They had done so based on the contract theory of government. Southerners believed that as long as the national government kept its part of the contract, which was to protect the rights of the states, the states were bound to support it. But if the national government failed to protect the rights of states, then states had the right to withdraw (secede) from the Union just as they had entered it—as sovereign states.

With Lincoln elected, South Carolina feared that its right to slavery might no longer be safe. It feared that Republican judges might not return fugitive slaves. Also, South Carolina knew that if future states could not be slave states, one day the free states would have the power to abolish slavery throughout the nation. On December 20, it voted to secede. A few days later, the state government issued the "Declaration of the Immediate Causes Which Induce and Justify the Secession of South Carolina from the Federal Union." The document stated that the federal government was interfering with states' rights and described "an increasing hostility on the part of the non-slaveholding states to the institution of slavery."

The nation awaited Buchanan's response. Although Buchanan, now a lame-duck president, believed that secession was illegal, he did not believe the federal government had the right to prevent states from seceding. Thus, instead of taking action, he did nothing. He left the problem for Lincoln to solve.

Abraham Lincoln

16

Born	February 12, 1809
Died	April 15, 1865
Home state	Illinois (born in Kentucky)
Wife	Mary Todd
Church	no formal affiliation
Occupation	lawyer
Party	Republican
Years served as president	1861–65
Terms	1 and partial (assassinated 1 month into 2nd term)
Vice presidents	1st—Hannibal Hamlin 2nd—Andrew Johnson

The position of Lincoln and many other leaders was that the Union was permanent and that the Constitution had no provision for ending it. They knew the Constitution recognized the rights of states, but they said it gave sovereignty, or control, to the national government and denied that sovereignty to the states. In addition, they noted how several of the states that seceded were formed out of territory originally owned, and in some cases purchased, by the national government.

Other Southern states called conventions to consider secession. The states of the Deep South—Georgia, Florida, Alabama, Mississippi, Louisiana, and Texas—followed South Carolina's example and voted to secede. South Carolina called a convention of those states in Montgomery, Alabama, on February 1, 1861. There the delegates voted to form the **Confederate States of America**. They wrote their own constitution, using the US Constitution as a pattern. However, their constitution differed in a number of ways. It recognized the "sovereign and independent character" of the states and guaranteed states' rights. It also promised that no law against slavery could ever be passed, allowed cabinet members to take part in legislative debates, and gave the president a single six-year term.

▲ At the Alabama State Capitol (above), Jefferson Davis (below) was inaugurated as the Confederate president. Alexander Stephens (bottom) was his vice president.

Secession was driven by radicals, but in choosing its leaders, the Confederacy preferred moderates. The Confederates hoped to win the support of Southerners who were still unsure about seceding. They elected **Jefferson Davis** of Mississippi—a US senator, a hero in the Mexican War, and former secretary of war—as president. They chose **Alexander Stephens**, a Georgian who had earlier opposed secession, as vice president.

Next, the Confederacy sent commissioners to the Southern states that had not yet seceded. The commissioners hoped to convince them to join the Confederacy. Those states, all Upper South and border states, were taking a "wait-and-see" position on secession. They were not convinced that the election of Lincoln alone was enough to make secession right.

The next episode in the chain of continuing events would move many of them to action.

SECTION REVIEW 13.4

1. Who were the four presidential candidates in the 1860 election, and what political party did each represent?
2. What state was the first to secede? What did it say was one of the causes of its secession?
3. What six other states joined the first to create the Confederate States of America? Was it wise to form a new union so soon? Why or why not?
4. Who were elected president and vice president of the Confederacy?

13.5 FORT SUMTER AND THE BEGINNING OF WAR

What circumstances existed in the North and the South when Fort Sumter was fired upon?

GUIDING QUESTIONS

- What event led to the outbreak of war?
- What were the advantages of the North and the South?

On March 4, 1861, Lincoln took the oath of office. In his inaugural address, he appealed to the people of the South, "In your hands, my dissatisfied fellow-countrymen, and not in mine, is the momentous issue of civil war." He hoped to reconcile the sections, but he would fight, if necessary, to preserve the Union. He would use the power of government "to hold, occupy, and possess the property and places belonging to the government."

By "property," Lincoln meant the two federal forts in the South where the Stars and Stripes still flew: Fort Pickens at Pensacola, Florida, and **Fort Sumter** in South Carolina's Charleston Harbor. During the last weeks of Buchanan's presidency, the Confederacy had seized all other federal properties within its borders. Lincoln had been reluctant to suggest the recapture of those seized properties. But the Northern states saw the forts as Lincoln's first test as a president. To control Fort Sumter and Fort Pickens, Lincoln would have to send supplies to them. How would the South react to such an attempt?

Did you know?

Fort Pickens remained under Union control for the entire Civil War.

▲ Fort Pickens

Firing on Fort Sumter

Neither Lincoln nor Jefferson Davis sought war. Lincoln hoped the Union could be preserved without fighting. Davis hoped that Lincoln would see that the South was determined to create a new nation and would allow it to do so. Fort Sumter would test the two sides' willingness to engage in battle.

In January 1861, before Lincoln's inauguration, Confederate cannons around Charleston Harbor pushed back a Union merchant ship that approached Fort Sumter with supplies. The Union troops at Fort Sumter held their fire. From South Carolinians' view, Fort Sumter was a garrison of foreign soldiers in their territory. To allow the Federal troops to remain supplied would be a threat to the South's independence. From Lincoln's view, withdrawing Federal troops from Federal forts would mean allowing a rebellion against the United States to succeed. Therefore, although most of Lincoln's cabinet and General Winfield Scott advised against resupplying the fort, Lincoln decided to send a small, unarmed fleet with food, but no military supplies, to Fort Sumter in April 1861.

▼ Fort Sumter

▲ Bombardment of Fort Sumter in April 1861

Lincoln then sent a note to the governor of South Carolina, saying that ships would be arriving at the fort. The governor relayed the note to Jefferson Davis, and Davis replied that under no circumstances was the fort to be resupplied.

Confederate General P. G. T. Beauregard, who was in command of Charleston, sent several aides to Fort Sumter on April 11. They told the fort's commander, Major Robert Anderson, that he must surrender. He refused. The following morning at four-thirty, Confederates opened fire. After forty hours of constant bombardment, Anderson surrendered the fort.

Neither side wanted to be seen as the aggressor. Even after the attack on Fort Sumter, both sides resisted issuing declarations of war. Lincoln, however, did view the attack as a revolt and issued a call for troops to suppress the uprising.

Choosing Sides

Lincoln called for 75,000 volunteer soldiers. The eight slave states that had not joined the seven seceded slave states were forced to decide: would they supply troops to fight their fellow Southerners? Or would they join the Confederacy? First Virginia, then Arkansas and North Carolina voted to secede and join the Confederacy. Finally, on June 8, the people of Tennessee did the same.

Parts of two Upper South states opposed secession. Fifty counties of western Virginia had long disagreed with the eastern counties. Also, the western counties had the fewest slaves in the state. The people there saw the secession crisis as their chance to free themselves from domination by the eastern part of the state. They established their own state government and applied to Congress for statehood. In June 1863 **West Virginia** entered the Union.

Most of the people in the hills and mountains of East Tennessee opposed secession. The slave population there was small (about 10 percent of the region's population). East Tennesseans also resented the greater influence of Middle and West Tennessee in state politics. The Unionists in the eastern counties held a convention and voted to petition the state legislature to let them secede from the state. Their request was refused, and troops were sent to East Tennessee to ensure that the eastern counties would not revolt.

With eleven states joining the Confederacy, there were still four slave states remaining in the Union. Because of their location, these four—Missouri, Kentucky, Maryland, and Delaware—were called border states. People within those states were sharply divided on the issue of secession. Lincoln moved quickly to ensure that they stayed in the Union.

Did you know?

No one was killed while Fort Sumter was being attacked. However, two Union soldiers died from an accidental cannon explosion during the 100-gun salute that was being fired as Union soldiers prepared to evacuate the fort.

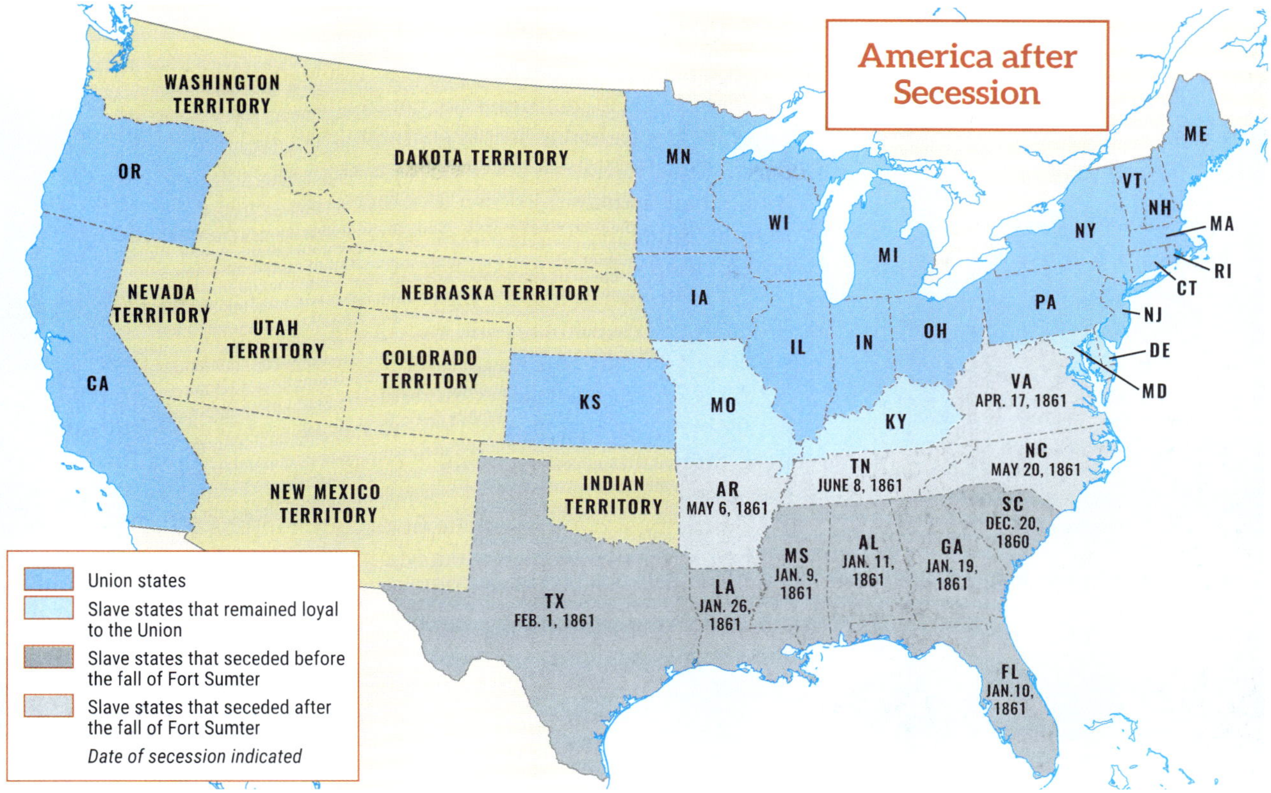

Of the four border states, Maryland concerned Lincoln most. If Maryland seceded, the Union capital, Washington, DC, would be surrounded by Confederate territory. Lincoln sent Union troops to the state to close bridges, and he declared martial law in the state. That meant the military controlled Maryland. In addition, Lincoln suspended the right of habeas corpus. These actions were some of the most controversial of Lincoln's presidency. The Constitution says that habeas corpus (the requirement that a person cannot be jailed without being charged with a crime) can be suspended "in cases of rebellion," but some argued that only Congress could suspend it. Lincoln contended that "the Constitution itself is silent as to which, or who, is to exercise the power; and . . . the provision was plainly made for a dangerous emergency." His actions kept Maryland in the Union.

Northern Advantages

Looking at the resources available to the North and the South, it is obvious that the North had a number of advantages. One of the most important was its industrial output. As the war began, almost 90 percent of the nation's goods were produced there. Consequently, the South had to buy foreign goods to supplement what it could not produce at home. But only at the outset of the war would it have the money and the freedom to do this. The South's lack of sea power to maintain its trade routes would soon greatly hinder its war effort.

Another decisive advantage for the North was its population. Its army would be drawn from the 22 million people that lived in the Union. The states that seceded had only 9 million people, which included 3.5 million enslaved African Americans. In addition, the North was adding approximately 300,000 immigrants a year to its population.

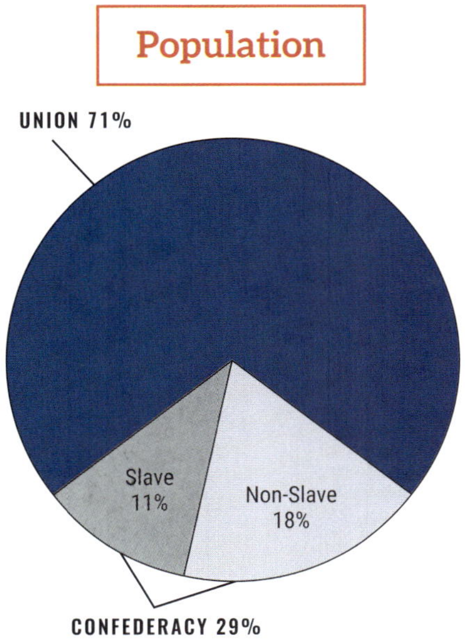

Southern Advantages

If the North had the greatest overall advantage, why did the Confederate leaders think they could succeed as a separate country? First, the South had a simple goal: establish and defend an independent nation. It did not need to defeat the Union armies decisively. It only had to defend its own territory and outlast the North's will to fight. Since the South was so large, Union armies would have to protect long supply lines in order to attack and occupy it.

Second, in a defensive war, Southerners would fight intensely to protect their own homes and way of life.

Third, because the South was the source for most of Great Britain's cotton, Confederate leaders thought they would obtain foreign help.

Fourth, the coastline of the South was long. The North would need thousands of ships to block commerce and keep military supplies away from the South.

Fifth, most of the Confederacy's commanding officers were well trained and battle experienced. Many of them were West Point graduates. During the war, the Southern armies would be commanded by a number of outstanding generals.

Southern Advantages

1. Defend, not defeat
2. Intense protection of homeland
3. Expected foreign aid
4. Long coastline
5. Experienced officers

War Comes

As mentioned at the beginning of this chapter, Americans in the North and South shared many of the same values: freedom, equality, individualism, and growth. However, they viewed these values differently. Lincoln argued that the words "All men are created equal" included black Americans, but many did not accept his belief. Many Northerners wanted freedom for the slaves while Southerners argued for freedom from Northern interference in the South's way of life.

Regarding growth, both sides wanted states with their values to be established from the western territories. Eventually, many Southerners concluded they could no longer remain in the Union. Ideally, this clash over values could have been resolved by Scripture. The disagreements would instead be decided by war.

SECTION REVIEW 13.5

1. How did South Carolinians view Fort Sumter? How did Abraham Lincoln view it?
2. What new Union state was carved out of a Confederate state?
3. What were the four key border states? Which of those states concerned Lincoln the most? Why?
4. What were the Union's two decisive advantages?
5. What five factors gave the South a fighting chance despite the North's advantages?
6. Which side began the war, the North or the South? Defend your answer.

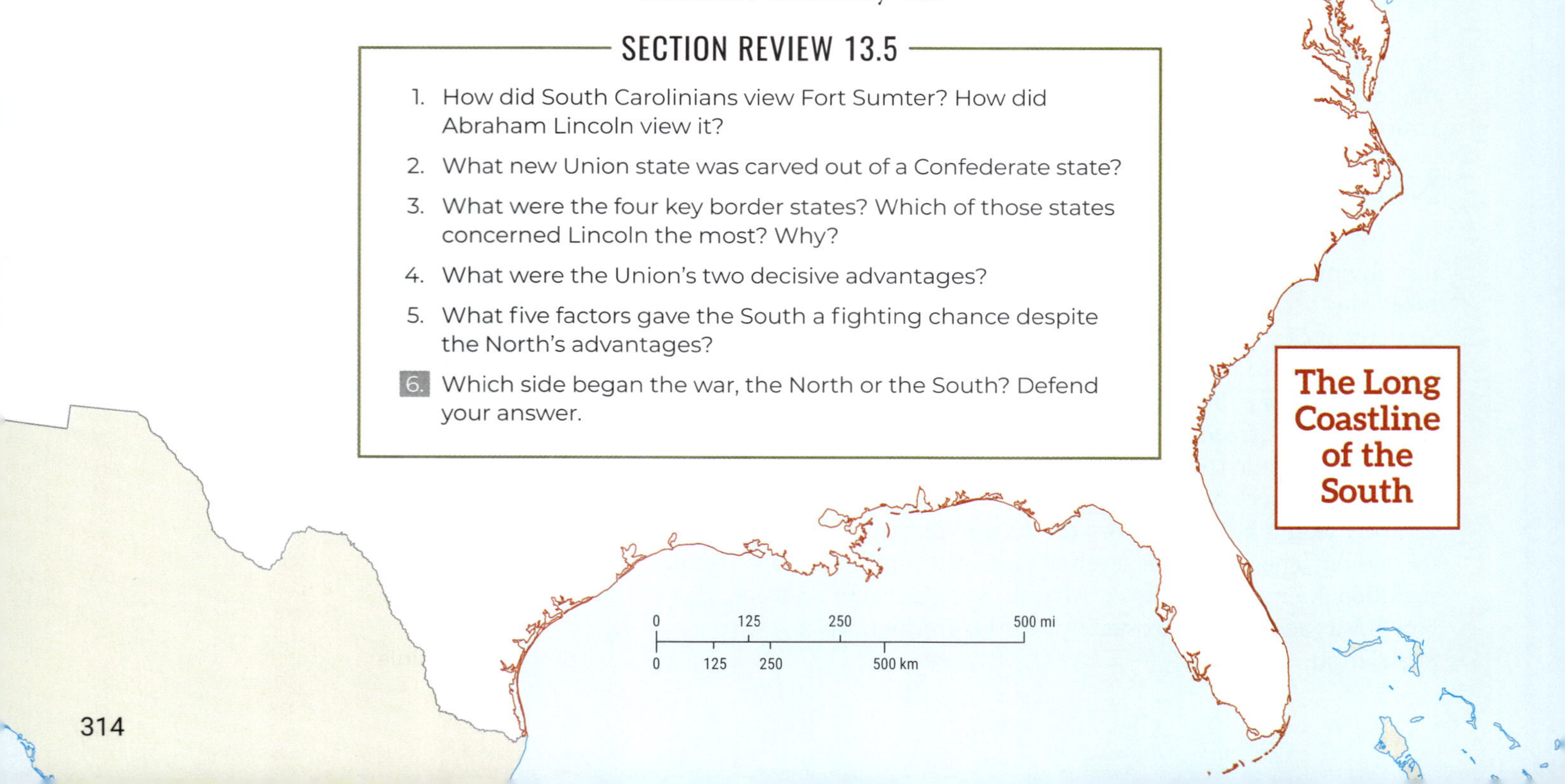

CHAPTER 13 REVIEW

Making Connections

1. Why did Southerners call some Northern workers "wage slaves"?
2. How many miles of railroad track did the North have by 1860? How many miles did the South have?
3. On which part of the Constitution did Northerners base their views regarding the national government? Which part did Southerners emphasize?
4. Why did the South oppose government funding of internal improvements and high tariffs?
5. What parts of the Underground Railroad were the railroad, conductors, and stations?
6. Why was Harriet Tubman called the Moses of her people?
7. Which Southerners generally opposed slavery? Why?
8. How did the slavery question lead to a crisis in American religion?
9. What effect did the Kansas-Nebraska Act have on the Missouri Compromise?
10. How many years after the creation of the Republican Party was one of its candidates elected president?
11. What were three reasons listed by Chief Justice Taney in his decision against Dred Scott?
12. How did Lincoln and Douglas differ in their ideas of slavery?
13. Use the map on p. 309 to answer the following questions: How many popular votes did Lincoln receive in 1860? How many did the other three candidates receive in total? How many electoral votes did Lincoln receive? How many total electoral votes did the other three candidates receive?
14. How did the constitution of the Confederate States of America differ significantly from that of the United States?
15. What states joined the Confederacy after the firing on Fort Sumter?
16. What is the relationship between the number of people in the North and South and their respective miles of railroad track?

Thinking Critically

17. Why were Frederick Douglass's speeches and writings more influential than those of most other abolitionists?
18. How was racism still evident in states that did not allow slavery?
19. How did John Brown take Hebrews 9:22 out of context? Why is taking Scripture out of context a problem?
20. Do you think states have the right to secede? Defend your answer.
21. Which of the following statements by Alexander Stephens best describes the reason for secession and the Civil War? Defend your answer.
    a. "[Slavery] was the immediate cause of the late rupture and present revolution."
    b. "[The Civil War] arose from different and opposing ideas as to the nature of what is known as the General Government."

Living as a Christian Citizen

22. If you had to prepare a speech about what Paul says in the Bible about slaves and masters, what points would you develop?
23. Imagine that you are a Christian US senator in the 1850s and are voting against the Fugitive Slave Act. What reasons would you give for voting against it?

Terms to Remember

antebellum
overseer
gang system
task system
Underground Railroad
Frederick Douglass
Harriet Tubman
William Lloyd Garrison
Horace Greeley
spirituals
Uncle Tom's Cabin
Harriet Beecher Stowe
Stephen Douglas
Kansas-Nebraska Act
Republican Party
James Buchanan
Charles Sumner
Preston Brooks
Dred Scott
Roger B. Taney
John Brown
secession
John C. Breckinridge
Abraham Lincoln
John Bell
Confederate States of America
Jefferson Davis
Alexander Stephens
Fort Sumter
West Virginia

CHAPTER

14 The Civil War

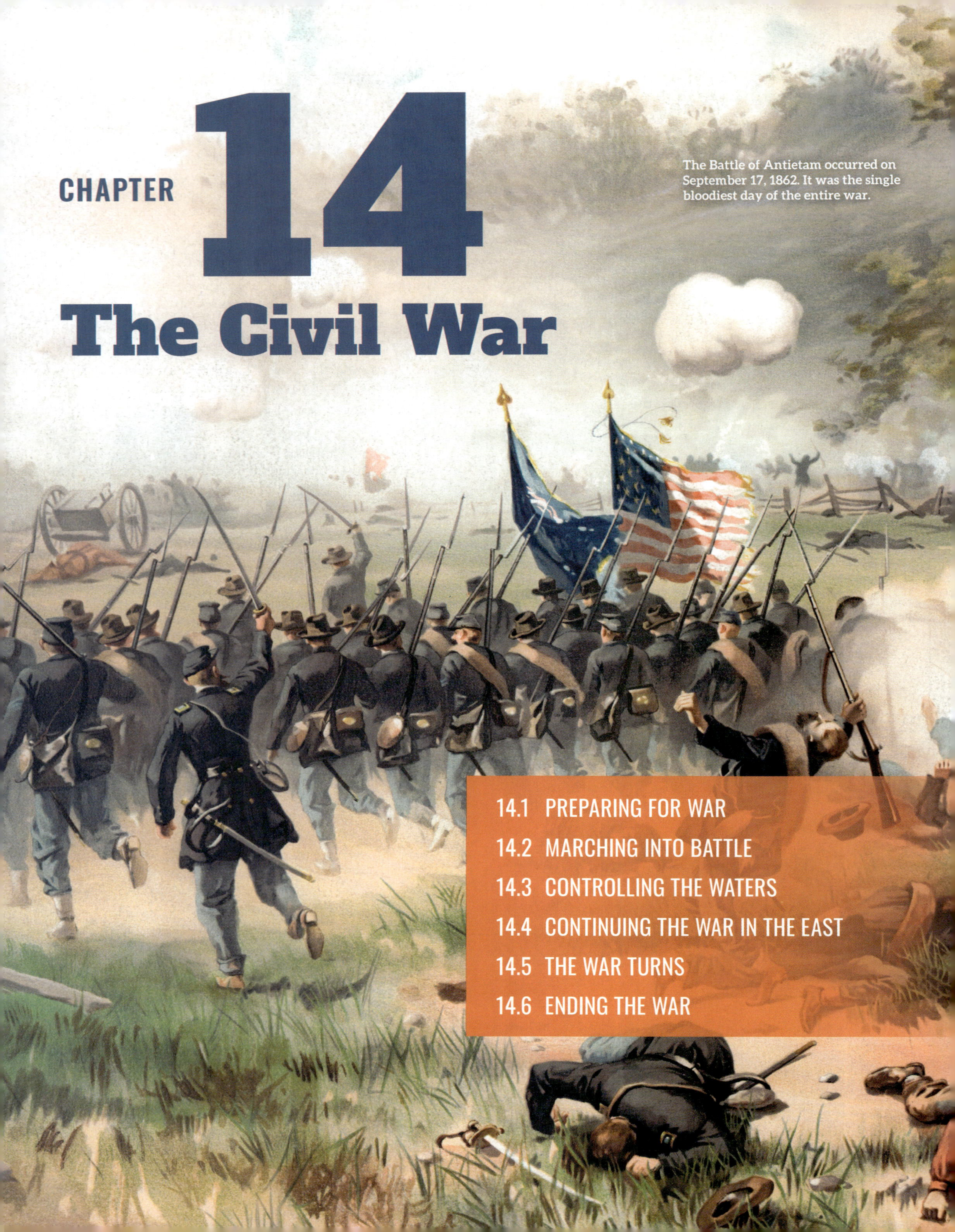

The Battle of Antietam occurred on September 17, 1862. It was the single bloodiest day of the entire war.

After the election of Lincoln but before the firing on Fort Sumter, Kentucky senator John Crittenden introduced a proposal that he hoped would avoid war. There were numerous problems with his plan, and it failed to pass the Senate. The defeat proved to be doubly disappointing for Crittenden because his own family was divided over secession. One son, George, became a general in the Confederate army; another son, Thomas, became a Union general.

Throughout the country, families divided. Brother fought against brother, and father fought against son in the four years of bloody conflict. Even Abraham Lincoln's wife, Mary Todd Lincoln, had relatives who fought for the South.

Devout Christians were on both sides in the war. Each side said that God would bless its efforts. By the end of the war, many people in the North and South were confused by the workings of **providence** (God's control over all events). This confusion led to a crisis of faith for some people. For other people, especially soldiers in the two armies, the war led to revival.

GUIDING QUESTIONS

- How were soldiers in the North and South recruited?
- What civilian preparations had to be made for the war?
- What military improvements and plans were used during the Civil War?

NAMING *the* WAR

The war between the North and the South has been called many different names. The two most common are the Civil War and the War Between the States.

Northerners also called it the War of the Rebellion, the War Against Slavery, the War for Abolition, and the War for the Union. Southerners used such names as the War for Southern Independence, the War of Secession, the War for Southern Rights, the War Against Northern Aggression, and (after the war was over) the Lost Cause. Numerous other names have also been used.

14.1 PREPARING FOR WAR

How did the North and South prepare for war?

After the fall of Fort Sumter, the nation was torn by a bitter four-year war that involved over 10,000 military skirmishes and battles. About half of them occurred in Virginia and Tennessee. Over 620,000 soldiers died. Civilians, individuals who were not part of the military, also suffered hardships, death, and destruction.

Turning Men into Soldiers

Stirred by patriotism, thousands of young men joined the armies. At first, both sides relied completely on volunteers, and they thought that the war would be short. But as the war continued, volunteers became so scarce that both sides resorted to drafting men.

Life in the camps was far from exciting. A soldier typically spent 65 percent of his time in camp, 30 percent marching or camping in the open air, and only 5 percent fighting. Though some soldiers fought in multiple battles, others were assigned to duty in forts and never fired a shot at the enemy.

▾ Union soldiers

▾ Early in the war, blue was adopted as the color for uniforms in the Union army.

Raising Northern Forces

Prior to the Civil War, the US military consisted of about 16,000 troops. About one-fourth of them resigned to join the Confederate army. During the war, the total number of soldiers, including both sides, was nearly 3 million.

When Lincoln called for 75,000 volunteers just after the conflict at Fort Sumter in April 1861, he asked them to serve for three months. In July, Lincoln called for 500,000 additional volunteers, this time to enlist for three years. Later, additional volunteers were recruited. Most of the states paid a large bonus, called a **bounty**, to those who joined.

Because the number of volunteers was insufficient by March 1863, Congress passed a **conscription** (or *draft*, a requirement by the government to serve in the military) law to raise a national army. Typically men between the ages of twenty and forty-five were subject to regular army service. The law exempted, or excused, certain officeholders and those who were physically or mentally unfit. A draftee could hire a substitute or pay $300 for an exemption. Recent immigrants were not subject to the draft, but many often served as substitutes to earn money. In the 1860s, $300 was basically the equivalent of a year's salary. Some immigrants joined to prove their allegiance to their new country.

Raising an army for the Union caused many problems. At first, the number of men who hired substitutes was quite high. Then, many soldiers deserted. Furthermore, the draft law caused much controversy. Believing that the law was unfair, many poor whites—especially Irish Americans—rioted for four days in New York City during July 1863. They were already suffering from runaway wartime inflation, and the mob blamed African Americans for causing the war. They resented that they were being drafted to free slaves while black people were exempt from fighting in the military. They were also upset that blacks were competing with them for unskilled jobs in the city. Most of the hundreds who were killed or injured during the rioting were African Americans.

▾ The Spencer rifle was used by many Union soldiers during the war.

Raising Southern Forces

Some of the best graduates of West Point Military Academy became Confederate commanders. Many had gained valuable combat experience in the Mexican War. They provided able leadership during the new war.

At first, the South had no problem getting enough men to fight. In fact, it had more volunteers than it could train and equip. Such enthusiasm, however, was short-lived. When the first one-year enlistments expired and no special benefits were offered, the number of recruits declined. In April 1862, the South resorted to drafting all men aged eighteen to thirty-five. Later, the upper limit was extended to fifty, and men up to sixty-five could be placed in a home guard (a unit that protected the area around their own community).

As was true in the North, the South's system for filling the army had problems. Men had so many ways of avoiding service that a War Department clerk joked, "Our Bureau of Conscription ought to be called the Bureau of Exemptions." The most disputed exemption law stated that for every twenty slaves on a plantation, one white person there would be exempt from military service. Its supporters claimed that those planters and overseers were needed at home to supervise and control the slaves. But poor Southerners who were drafted resented that exception granted to the rich. It reinforced the idea that the war was "a rich man's war but a poor man's fight." Understandably, when the war began to go badly for the South, the Confederacy struggled even harder to find recruits.

▲ Gray uniforms were typical in the Confederate army.

the UNITED STATES CHRISTIAN COMMISSION

One of the volunteer groups that sought to provide for the spiritual and physical needs of Union soldiers was the United States Christian Commission (USCC). It was founded in 1861, and its work continued throughout the war.

USCC records show that it had 4,859 workers during its existence. During the war, these volunteers preached 58,308 sermons and conducted 77,744 prayer meetings. They also wrote 92,321 letters for soldiers—the sick, the wounded, and the illiterate. Because soldiers craved reading material, the USCC distributed large numbers of Bibles, tracts, hymnals, books, magazines, and newspapers. And since soldiers had a difficult time surviving solely on army rations, the USCC also prepared many meals.

Preparing Civilians for War

The Civil War affected almost everyone, both those in the military and civilians. Virtually no one escaped having to sacrifice in some manner. To fight effectively, both sides needed to mobilize their populations.

In the North

Before the war, the North had begun to widen its industrial base. Many women entered the workforce. Many of the eight hundred thousand immigrants who came to America between 1861 and 1865 worked in Northern factories. When war erupted, Northern factories produced war materials including uniforms, blankets, tents, weapons, ammunition, wagons, canned foods, lumber, shovels, steamships, and surgical instruments.

The war also affected farm production. Although thousands of men left their farms to fight, farm production in the North did not decline. Instead, as the demand for food products increased, farmers began to use machines even more. This allowed them to produce more food with fewer workers and thus freed more men to fight. Northern farms fed not only the Union army but also Europeans. Forty percent of England's wheat and flour came from the North.

The war also strengthened private volunteer groups. Those groups, sometimes called commissions, helped purchase medicines and provide Bibles and other reading material for soldiers. Commissions also sent money home to soldiers' families. And they found food, shelter, and clothing for slaves who had fled the South.

In the South

The war affected the South in many of the same ways that it impacted the North. The South, however, did not have as many factories as the North. Although many Southerners received government contracts to make weapons, ammunition, and other war materials, they could not produce as much as Northern factories. Furthermore, the South did not have a good transportation system for moving those goods from the factories to the war fronts.

Agriculture in the South was severely affected by the war. Large numbers of farmers and plantation owners enlisted or were drafted into the army. Later in the war, draft laws required even more of them to enter the army. On many farms, women were left to do the work. In the South, as in the North, volunteer organizations helped soldiers and their families. In both regions, churches offered spiritual help, while local women's groups made bandages, socks, and other items. Even after the war, women remained active in caring for wounded veterans and honoring the memory of deceased soldiers.

▲ Supply kit used for amputation

Innovations in Warfare

The Civil War was in many ways the first modern war. Industry and technology improved weapons and forced changes in tactics and strategy.

For the first time, armies used railroads to move soldiers and equipment quickly. Manned balloons, which could rise high above surrounding trees or other natural obstructions, allowed observers to report the enemy's movements. Both armies also used mines (explosive devices), trench warfare, wire barricades, and other new ideas and devices.

Both governments used the telegraph to communicate with their commanders. For example, almost every evening before he went to bed, Lincoln walked to the War Department to read the dispatches telegraphed from the front lines. The telegraph allowed him to stay in close contact with his generals and to know what was occurring. Since both armies used the telegraph, they continually tried to destroy each other's telegraph lines.

Recall from Chapter 3 that an important weapon innovation was making small spiral grooves inside the barrel of guns and cannons. This is called rifling and causes a bullet or shell to spin as it leaves the barrel. That spin makes the bullet or shell travel in a straighter line, ensuring greater accuracy. The Civil War was the first conflict where many units from both sides were equipped with rifled weapons.

Clockwise from top: soldiers cutting telegram wires; a Civil War bullet; a mortar (a type of artillery)

▲ The *Monitor* battling the *Virginia*

In addition, ironclad (iron-plated) warships proved their superiority over wooden vessels. The *Monitor*, a Union ship, and the *Virginia* (which had earlier been called the *Merrimack*), a Confederate ship, met in the first battle between ironclad naval vessels. The March 1862 clash ended in a tie, but it marked the beginning of modern naval warfare. Both sides also constructed submarines.

Another historic innovation was photography. Photographs from the Civil War era allow us to see the terrible destruction of the war. Photography was developed twenty years before the war, but its use was limited. By 1861, however, photography was more affordable and less complicated. Many soldiers had their pictures taken for loved ones. Mathew Brady and a team of photographers followed troops and photographed them. His photographs of corpses on the battlefield shocked Americans. It was the first time that most people had seen war deaths. His photographs continue to give new generations revealing glimpses of the war.

▼ Diagrams of the interior of the *Hunley* (below)

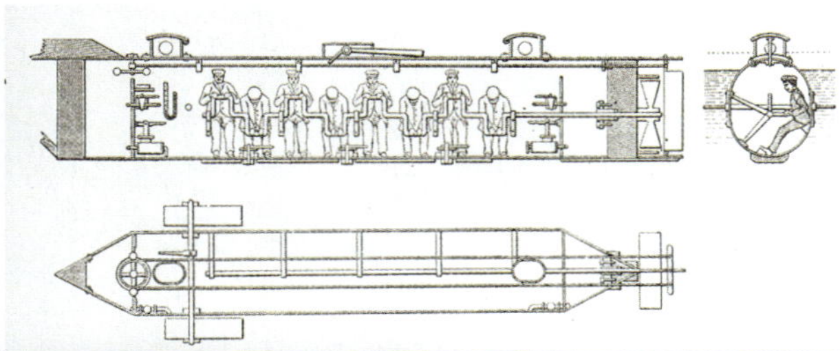

the HUNLEY

The *H. L. Hunley* was an experimental underwater craft developed by the Confederacy. On February 17, 1864, it became the first submarine to sink an enemy warship when it sank the Union warship *Housatonic*. (The submarine *Turtle* had been used in the War for Independence but had not sunk any ships.)

The *Hunley* mysteriously sank shortly after the attack, killing all eight of its crew. Its wreckage was located in 1995 and was raised in 2000. It is on display in Charleston, South Carolina.

Replica of a Civil War camera ▶

▼ A photo by Mathew Brady

War Strategies

Each side established a strategy for winning the war. As mentioned earlier, the Confederate plan was largely defensive. The South had only to protect its territory and outlast the North's will to fight. Though defending the homefront strengthened the will to fight, if the strategy was unsuccessful, the South could be devastated by the attacking Union forces.

The Northern strategy was to invade the South. General Winfield Scott, commander of the Union army at the beginning of the war, devised a plan. First, he proposed a blockade of Southern ports to make it difficult for the South to obtain necessary supplies. Second, he called for control of the Mississippi River. This would split the Confederacy and hamper its ability to move men and supplies from west to east and its trade with the world through New Orleans.

Unlike most of his subordinates, Scott believed that a quick military victory over the South was unlikely. Thus, his plan involved slowly eliminating the Confederacy's ability to wage war. The Northern press, reflecting the popular view that the war would last only a few weeks, mockingly called Scott's strategy the **Anaconda Plan**, after the large South American snake that slowly crushes its prey within its coils. Scott's ideas, though, would eventually prove both realistic and successful. Later the strategy was modified to include two additional goals: capture Richmond, Virginia, the Confederate capital, and divide and conquer the Southern heartland (this was eventually achieved by capturing Chattanooga, Tennessee, and Atlanta, Georgia, and marching to the Atlantic coast).

Union War Strategies

1. Impose a naval blockade to shut off the South's trade
2. Control the Mississippi River to split the Confederacy
3. Capture the Confederate capital of Richmond, Virginia
4. Divide and conquer the Southern heartland

SECTION REVIEW 14.1

1. How did each side raise troops when the war first began? As the war progressed, how was each side forced to obtain needed soldiers?
2. Contrast the North's and the South's efforts to prepare for war.
3. What were five innovations in warfare during the Civil War? Which do you think was most important? Why?
4. What were the first two goals of the Anaconda Plan?

GUIDING QUESTION

- What were the results of the Battles of Bull Run?

Did you know?

Lincoln asked Robert E. Lee to lead the Union armies, but Lee declined because he felt that he could not fight against his native state of Virginia. Lee was later the leading general for the Confederate forces.

14.2 MARCHING INTO BATTLE

What was the significance of the Battles of Bull Run?

After the fall of Fort Sumter, Northerners were eager to take action. But the Union army, led by its seventy-five-year-old general Winfield Scott, consisted mostly of inexperienced recruits. Since many Northerners believed that they could win the war and be home before harvest, the pressure to attack Richmond, Virginia, grew greater. Richmond was only about one hundred miles from Washington, DC. Newspapers cried, "On to Richmond!" So loud and frequent was the call for action that Congress soon joined the chorus.

The First Battle of Bull Run

Prodded by such pressure, General Irvin McDowell, commander of the Federal (or Union) troops in northeastern Virginia, moved south toward Richmond in July 1861. The Confederate army was at Bull Run Creek near Manassas Junction, Virginia, about twenty miles south of Washington. McDowell planned to attack the army there. Northern journalists, congressmen, and the congressmen's wives followed McDowell's forces. They wanted to admire "the greatest army in the world" and enjoy watching it smash the Rebels, as the southern troops were called, while they had picnics.

Confederate General Stonewall Jackson (inset and below)

The Confederates learned of McDowell's advance. Jefferson Davis ordered General Joseph E. Johnston to leave the Shenandoah Valley and join General P. G. T. Beauregard's troops at Manassas Junction. On Sunday, July 21, the combined Confederate armies clashed with the Federal troops. At first, Union troops fought well. The Confederate army lost ground and seemed to be in disarray. But then Confederate General Bernard Bee rallied his troops by pointing to General Thomas Jackson nearby. "Look!" Bee shouted to his men. "There is Jackson . . . standing like a stone wall." Inspired by Jackson's example, the Southerners turned and drove the enemy back. Jackson's brigade saved the day, and he earned a nickname: **Stonewall Jackson**.

Northern troops panicked and retreated. Many abandoned their weapons and equipment and ran for Washington, DC. Dazed spectators joined the stampede. The chaos left Washington unprotected. Some Confederate officers wanted to push forward to capture the Union capital. But the Confederate troops were tired and almost as disorganized as their enemies and did not take advantage of the victory to march northward.

▲ First Battle of Bull Run

Results of the First Battle of Bull Run

The **First Battle of Bull Run** (also called the First Battle of Manassas) affected both sides. The North realized that its troops were not yet ready to fight and that the South would not be easily defeated. Shortly after the battle, Lincoln ordered General **George McClellan** to take command of all Union troops protecting Washington and to lead a new army in the East. McClellan soon turned the army into a well-drilled machine. He was popular with his troops and some nicknamed him "Young Napoleon." In November 1861, when Winfield Scott retired, McClellan was placed in charge of all Union troops.

The South had won its first major battle so easily that some Southerners became overconfident. They thought that the war would soon be over. But they failed to act upon their victory, even after they were refreshed and reorganized. Because the Confederate strategy was to fight a defensive war, some Southern commanders did not view the capture of Washington, DC, as a major goal.

Did you know?

Because of McClellan's consistent reluctance to attack Lee's army, Lincoln reportedly said, "If General McClellan does not want to use the army, I would like to borrow it for a time!"

Hesitation and Loss for the North

The North's goal of taking Richmond proved difficult to achieve. Lincoln and Congress grew frustrated by McClellan's failure to attack. McClellan claimed that he needed more men and more time. He overestimated the strength of the Confederate army. That made McClellan unnecessarily cautious. Lincoln finally had enough of delay, and in early 1862 he ordered McClellan to move toward Richmond.

McClellan moved his army down the Potomac River and around the Virginia peninsula. The army landed between the James and York Rivers. Since the Confederates had not spent much time fortifying that area, McClellan thought that it would be the best place to attack them. The attack caught General Johnston by surprise. McClellan should have used that surprise to his advantage, but he delayed, believing that he needed more men to win.

This was only the beginning of McClellan's troubles. When Johnston was wounded in battle, his replacement as commander of the Army of Northern Virginia was General **Robert E. Lee**. Although Lee's troops were outnumbered, Lee knew his men, his resources, and the area.

On June 25, McClellan was only nine miles from Richmond. But in a span of seven days, Lee attacked McClellan in six different places and drove the Union army back.

Union General ▼
George McClellan

◀ Confederate General
Robert E. Lee

▲ Confederate General J. E. B. Stuart

The Second Battle of Bull Run

Lincoln appointed General John Pope to command a newly formed army in Virginia. Lee decided that the Confederacy could beat Pope before he gained strength.

Lee left half his army in Richmond. He sent the other half north to keep Pope busy. Meanwhile, General **J. E. B. Stuart**, Lee's cavalry commander, raided Pope's headquarters while Pope was absent. Stuart, seeking revenge for losing his favorite hat to Federal troops in a skirmish several days earlier, captured mules, horses, money, and Pope's dispatch book that detailed where Union forces would be going. This gave Lee the advantage he needed.

The Union and Confederate armies met on August 29, 1862, for the second time at the Bull Run battlefield. The two-day fight, called the **Second Battle of Bull Run** (Second Battle of Manassas), again ended with the Union troops retreating to Washington. After Lee's victory, Lincoln relieved Pope of his command and merged his army with McClellan's forces.

Did you know?

Union armies usually named battles for natural features such as a creek or river. Confederate armies normally named the same battle for the nearest town or landmark.

Naming Battles

Union	Confederate
Bull Run	Manassas
Pittsburgh Landing	Shiloh
Antietam	Sharpsburg

▲ Bridge across Antietam Creek near Sharpsburg, Maryland

SECTION REVIEW 14.2

1. What key city did the Union army try to capture? Why?
2. What did each side realize after the First Battle of Bull Run?
3. What proved to be a major flaw in McClellan's leadership? How might he have corrected this issue?
4. What was the result of the Second Battle of Bull Run?

14.3 CONTROLLING THE WATERS

How did the North seek to control the waters?

As outlined in the Anaconda Plan, the Union's strategy for closing the South's major links to water transportation involved two goals. The first was to blockade Southern ports. The purpose of a **blockade** is to prevent entry or exit of passengers and products. The second was to capture and control the Mississippi River.

Blockading the South

On April 19, 1861, only a few days after the fall of Fort Sumter, Lincoln ordered a naval blockade of the coast from South Carolina to the Mexican border. Later, he extended the blockade northward to the Potomac River. Because of the shortage of ships, however, it was difficult for the Union to maintain a successful blockade. The secretary of the navy began a giant ship-buying program and leased or bought virtually any vessel big enough to be armed. The North concentrated its blockade on ten major Southern ports, each of which had inland connections by rail or river.

The South tried to overcome the blockade with **blockade-runners**. These fast ships were long and narrow and could dart into shallow inlets to hide. Since the Union ships needed deeper water to operate, they could not follow the blockade-runners. Blockade-runners were usually painted dull gray, which made them difficult to spot on the seas. Most were steam powered. Some of the steamers could travel at eighteen knots (about twenty-one miles per hour), enabling them to outrun Union sailing vessels. Some blockade-runners burned hard coal that produced less noticeable smoke and made them even harder to see on the horizon.

The best ports from which blockade-runners operated, such as Wilmington, North Carolina, had more than one outlet. From such ports, blockade-runners, loaded with cotton and other goods, usually traveled south to British-held islands. (Bermuda and the Bahama Islands were only about a three-day journey away.) The ships then transferred the goods to vessels that flew the flags of neutral countries. On return voyages, the blockade-runners brought weapons and other necessities to the South.

Blockade-running was a dangerous activity and often unsuccessful. Eventually, the blockade resulted in the South's foreign trade declining by two-thirds. This was a major economic blow to the Confederacy. Though the war effort was concentrated on the battlefield, the Union navy's blockade caused significant damage to the South's ability to conduct the war.

GUIDING QUESTIONS

- How successful was the North's blockade of the South?
- How did the North gain control of the West and the Mississippi River?

BLOCKADE-RUNNING

For many, the potential wealth to be gained from blockade-running made it worth the risks. In 1861 slipping through the blockade was relatively easy. Nine of every ten Southern ships succeeded. During the four years of the war, it is estimated that Confederates dodged the blockade more than 8,500 times.

But as the months passed, the Union blockade became tougher to evade. As port cities in the South fell to Union armies, the North had more land bases to make the blockade even more effective. In the closing months of the war, only about 50 percent of incoming ships were able to bypass the blockade. This meant that millions of dollars worth of food and supplies never reached the South.

Blockade-runner ▸

Aerial view of the Mississippi River

War in the West

The western front in the war involved all conflict that occurred west of the Appalachian Mountains. A major goal of the North's "War in the West" was to gain control of the Mississippi River. One Union general referred to the river as the "spinal column of America." If the Union controlled it, the Union could separate Texas, Arkansas, and Louisiana from the remainder of the Confederacy. It could prevent those states from sending cattle and other supplies to the armies in the East. Furthermore, the South would be unable to use the river to transport men and supplies. The Union armies, however, could use the river to their advantage.

Gaining the Upper Mississippi

A major factor in the capture of the Mississippi was the leadership of Union General **Ulysses S. Grant**, sometimes called U. S. Grant. He had retired from the army in 1854. After struggling in both farming and business ventures, he rejoined the army when the Civil War erupted. Grant believed that the key to success in the West was control of the Tennessee and Cumberland Rivers. These rivers empty into the Ohio River, which in turn flows to the Mississippi. Leaving Cairo, Illinois, he and his troops moved to Tennessee and captured Fort Henry on the Tennessee River. They captured Fort Donelson on the Cumberland ten days later. The fall of these forts in February 1862—followed by victory at the Battle of Shiloh (in Tennessee) in April and the capture of Corinth, Mississippi—gave the Union control of the upper Mississippi and access to points in the South. Grant became a hero. He also gained a nickname. When he demanded that a Confederate general surrender his troops, the officer asked what terms Grant would offer. "No terms except an unconditional and immediate surrender," Grant replied. Soon U. S. Grant became known as Unconditional Surrender Grant.

Ulysses S. Grant eventually became the most well-known of the Union generals.

Clara Barton

Clara Barton (1821–1912) is one of the most famous American nurses. Born in Massachusetts, she began her career as a schoolteacher. Barton excelled in her job, demanding and receiving wages equal to those of male teachers, which was unusual at the time. She later worked at the US Patent Office in Washington, DC.

When the war began, Barton volunteered her services for the North. She gained permission to visit the front lines and was dismayed at what she found. She spent the rest of the war helping soldiers and became known as the "angel of the battlefield." President Lincoln asked her to begin a government department to look for missing troops after the war. Barton did this while traveling the country lecturing about her experiences. She also spoke in support of women's suffrage (right to vote).

In 1869 Barton traveled to Europe, where she became associated with the International Red Cross, which had been established a few years earlier. In 1870, while she was working with the Red Cross, she helped soldiers in the Franco-Prussian War.

Upon her return home in 1873, she was determined to create a division of the Red Cross in the United States. Working with influential individuals, including Frederick Douglass, she established the American Red Cross in 1881. She served as president of that organization for more than two decades.

Besides aiding wounded soldiers, she expanded the group's work to provide aid to victims of peacetime emergencies, such as floods, hurricanes, earthquakes, and epidemics. In 1898 during the Spanish-American War, Barton, by then in her late seventies, traveled to Cuba and managed nursing efforts there.

Though Barton is best remembered for her role as a wartime nurse, her contributions span many other areas and make her a hero for many causes.

▲ Union soldiers fought for weeks before they were able to capture Vicksburg, Mississippi.

Gaining the Lower Mississippi

◀ Admiral David Farragut led the Union navy up the Mississippi River, helping gain control of the Confederacy's western waterways.

Next, the Union army moved to gain control of the lower Mississippi. Admiral **David Farragut** of the Union navy devised a plan that, with the aid of a land force, helped him capture New Orleans. In April 1862 Farragut's gunboats slipped past Forts Jackson and St. Philip below New Orleans despite heavy fire from the Confederates. Then Farragut scattered and disabled the Confederate fleet. New Orleans was captured two days later.

The Union navy moved steadily up the Mississippi River, capturing first Baton Rouge, Louisiana, and then Natchez, Mississippi. By July 1863 the Union controlled the whole Mississippi River except for **Vicksburg**, Mississippi.

Vicksburg sat on high bluffs overlooking the river. The Union army attacked the town six times. Each time Southern troops repelled the army, inflicting heavy casualties.

Grant then sought a new strategy. He moved his soldiers down the west bank of the Mississippi and crossed the river south of Vicksburg. He ordered his troops to carry some rations but to obtain the rest of what they needed from the countryside. Grant then moved east to cut Confederate rail access to Vicksburg. This deprived the city of desperately needed food and supplies.

For six weeks, the Union forces shelled Vicksburg around the clock. Food became so scarce in the town that the people ate mules, rats, and even their family pets. Finally, with no more food and no hope of relief, the Confederate troops surrendered Vicksburg on July 4, 1863. Grant had captured the Mississippi.

SECTION REVIEW 14.3

1. How was the South sometimes able to evade the Northern blockade?
2. Was blockade-running worth the risk? Explain your answer.
3. Who were the leading Union general and admiral in the war in the West?
4. Why was Vicksburg difficult for the Union to capture? How was it finally captured?

GUIDING QUESTION

- Why were the Battles of Antietam, Fredericksburg, Chancellorsville, and Gettysburg significant?

14.4 CONTINUING THE WAR IN THE EAST

How did the battles in the East impact the war?

While Grant was fighting for control of the Mississippi River, Lee was taking the offensive in the east. In September 1862 he invaded the border state of Maryland. Many Marylanders were Southern sympathizers. Lee hoped that a Confederate victory there would cause Marylanders to rebel and free the state from Union control. The grain-rich state could then help provide much-needed supplies for his troops. He also hoped a Southern victory in Maryland might convince Britain to officially acknowledge the Confederacy as an independent nation, the first step toward offering their assistance.

Antietam

Although McClellan was aware that Lee's troops were in Maryland, he had no idea where Lee planned to attack. But Union soldiers made an amazing discovery. When the Union army was crossing an area through which the Confederates had recently marched, Union soldiers found a bundle of three cigars wrapped in a paper beside the road. That paper had been lost by a Confederate messenger. It held orders to Lee's commanders and revealed both Lee's location and the fact that he had divided his army. With this information, McClellan moved to force Lee into a battle before Jackson could return to help Lee.

When Lee learned of the lost orders, he had to change his plans. He pulled back his forces across the Potomac River into Virginia. But on September 17, before Lee could escape, McClellan launched a massive attack against him near Sharpsburg, Maryland, along **Antietam** Creek. At first, Lee's embattled troops held the line. If McClellan had attacked once more, he might have defeated Lee, but he hesitated. At the end of the day, the Confederates still controlled the battlefield. Under cover of darkness, Lee retreated and returned to the safety of Northern Virginia. McClellan failed to pursue Lee's army.

Approximately 24,000 soldiers were killed or wounded in the Battle of Antietam. It was the bloodiest one-day battle in American history. The battle was technically a tie, though the Union claimed victory because the Confederates had withdrawn from the state. Several weeks after the battle, Lincoln replaced McClellan for his failure to win the battle and for not pursuing Lee's army after it had ended.

Since the South did not win the battle, Britain did not recognize the independence of the Confederacy. Because the Union did not lose, Lincoln used the event to issue the Emancipation Proclamation. It stated that slaves in Confederate-held areas would be freed.

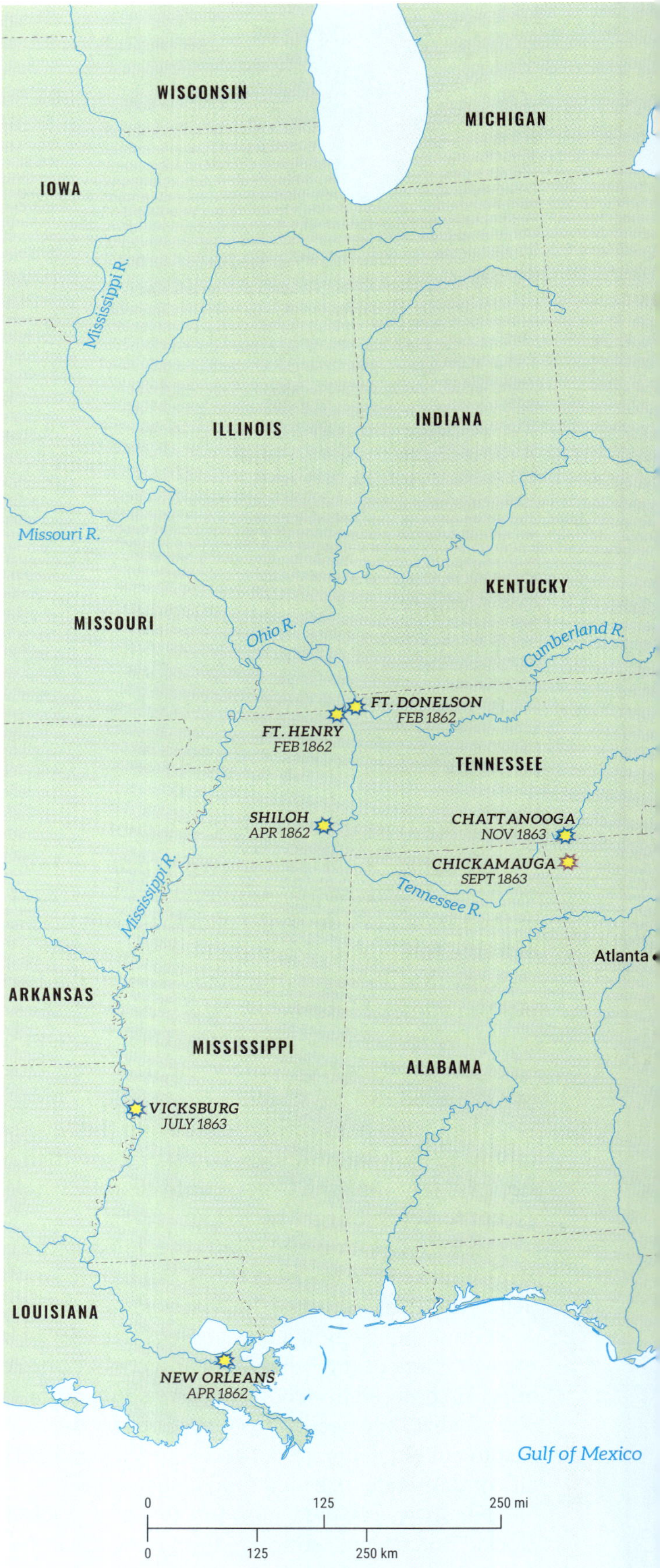

Fredericksburg

▲ Union General Ambrose Burnside's whiskers eventually became known as sideburns.

Ambrose Burnside, McClellan's replacement, had no better success than McClellan. On December 13, 1862, Burnside's troops attacked Confederates, led by General Lee, at **Fredericksburg**. Wave after wave of Union soldiers tried to dislodge the Confederate forces. But Union soldiers fell without success. That day, the Union army suffered about 13,000 casualties while the Confederate army had about 4,500.

Union morale dipped to its lowest point of the war. In twenty months, the North had organized a grand army in the East, but no Union general seemed able to win with it. Lincoln appointed yet another general, replacing Burnside with Joseph Hooker—known as Fighting Joe. The year had been very bloody for both sides.

Chancellorsville

Hooker's goal was to capture Richmond. During the first two years of the war, four major previous attempts by Union generals had failed. In April 1863, Hooker had 130,000 soldiers compared to Lee's 60,000. The Union forces also had an overwhelming advantage in supplies. The first phase of Hooker's plan was to attack Lee by going west to **Chancellorsville**, Virginia. He boasted confidently, "May God have mercy on General Lee, for I will have none."

Lee disregarded traditional military wisdom by dividing his army even though he was vastly outnumbered. His risky move caught the Federal troops by surprise. Though fighting raged for several days, the battle was a major Confederate victory. Many military historians consider it Lee's greatest success.

However, the victory proved costly to the South. During the battle, Stonewall Jackson was fatally wounded. Jackson and his staff had been out scouting. In the darkness of the woods, Confederate soldiers mistook the group for enemy troops and fired on them, hitting Jackson. He was carried from the battlefield, and his arm had to be amputated. When Lee learned of Jackson's wounds, he sent word: "Tell [Jackson] to make haste and get well, and come back to me as soon as he can. He has lost his left arm, but I have lost my right." However, Jackson contracted pneumonia and died eight days after being wounded. Lee and the Confederacy felt the loss keenly. Jackson's skill on the battlefield would be sorely missed.

Fun Fact

Stonewall Jackson's arm was buried in Chancellorsville, where it was amputated. Jackson was buried a hundred miles away in Lexington, Virginia.

▲ Little Round Top

▲ Union soldiers killed at Gettysburg

▼ Pickett's Charge

Gettysburg

After his victory at Chancellorsville, Lee decided to make a bold advance into Pennsylvania. He believed that if the citizens of the North could feel firsthand the effects of war on their own soil, their support for the conflict would decline. He also thought that this strategy would force Lincoln to pull some troops out of the campaign along the Mississippi River and reduce pressure there. In addition, Lee hoped that his hungry army could resupply itself as it passed through lush Pennsylvania farmlands.

Lee's Hopeful Advance

In early June 1863, Lee started north through the Shenandoah Valley. He crossed the Potomac, entered western Maryland, and moved into Pennsylvania. Hooker, even with 90,000 men, did not try to stop Lee. On June 28, Lincoln replaced Hooker and gave the Army of the Potomac (the Union army in the East) its fifth commander in two years: George Meade. Meade was shy and scholarly but well qualified as a general.

On July 1, a few of Lee's troops entered a small town called **Gettysburg**. There they unexpectedly met a Union scouting party. Both armies quickly moved to two ridges and prepared to fight. The Confederates were on Seminary Ridge; the Union forces stood on Cemetery Ridge, about a mile away. At the southern end of Cemetery Ridge were two rocky points called Round Top and Little Round Top. In front of Little Round Top was a field of huge boulders called Devil's Den. Neither side had chosen Gettysburg as the site for a major battle. The two armies had stumbled on each other.

On the first day of the three-day battle, Lee's troops forced the Union lines back. The next day, July 2, Lee ordered General James Longstreet to attack the Union left, which was on the Round Tops. Longstreet delayed his attack. After he finally pushed his men through a peach orchard, a wheat field, and Devil's Den toward the Round Tops, he was beaten back. Lee then planned an assault on the Union center. Several of his officers, including Longstreet, advised him to instead attack the Union left again. But Lee overruled them.

Pickett's Charge

Lee's attack on July 3 began late. But it launched with the heaviest bombardment the South had delivered in the war. Nearly 140 cannons opened fire on Union troops. Then, early in the afternoon, 15,000 Confederate troops under General George Pickett marched

in formation across a mile-wide cornfield toward the Union lines. Protected behind a low stone wall, the Union soldiers fired into the advancing Confederates, killing hundreds. The casualties were especially severe whenever they slowed their march to cross fences and re-form. The Union cannons, shooting at point-blank range like giant shotguns, mowed down Confederate ranks. As they approached the stone wall that the Federal troops were firing from, the Southerners turned toward a group of trees in the center of the Union line. They shouted the "Rebel yell" and charged straight into the Union line. Reaching the wall, they fought hand to hand against the Northern troops (also known as Yankees during the war). The slaughter was horrific.

After intense fighting, Pickett's men retreated and straggled back across the cornfield. **Pickett's Charge** lasted less than an hour, but the casualties were shocking. It is estimated that the number killed or wounded on the Union side was 1,500 while Confederate casualties exceeded 6,000. Pickett lost all 15 of his regimental commanders, including 2 brigadier generals and 6 colonels. When Pickett returned to the Confederate lines, Lee ordered him to regroup his division for the expected Union counterattack. Pickett replied, "General Lee, I have no division now."

The counterattack never came. Meade did not know that the Confederates were nearly out of ammunition. The next day, in a downpour, Lee's tattered army withdrew into Virginia. The Confederate army was stretched over seventeen miles but returned with little harassment from the Union army. Meade missed the opportunity to deal Lee's army a decisive blow and possibly even bring an end to the war.

SECTION REVIEW 14.4

1. What battle proved to be the bloodiest one day of the war?
2. What discovery was made by Union soldiers prior to the Battle of Antietam? What information did it provide?
3. How was the Battle of Chancellorsville a mixed blessing for the Confederates? Which result was more important?
4. For what three reasons did Lee invade the North?
5. Why was Pickett's Charge doomed to failure?

PRIMARY SOURCE: THE GETTYSBURG ADDRESS

Four months after the Battle of Gettysburg, a cemetery was dedicated there. Present were more than 15,000 spectators, including governors and members of the Cabinet. The first speaker, noted orator Edward Everett, spoke for two hours. President Lincoln delivered ten eloquent sentences, lasting only two minutes, in what became known as the **Gettysburg Address**.

November 19, 1863

"Four score and seven years ago our fathers brought forth on this continent a new nation, conceived in liberty, and dedicated to the proposition that all men are created equal.

Now we are engaged in a great civil war, testing whether that nation, or any nation so conceived and so dedicated, can long endure. We are met on a great battlefield of that war. We have come to dedicate a portion of that field, as a final resting place for those who here gave their lives that that nation might live. It is altogether fitting and proper that we should do this.

But, in a larger sense, we can not dedicate—we can not consecrate—we can not hallow—this ground. The brave men, living and dead, who struggled here, have consecrated it, far above our poor power to add or detract. The world will little note, nor long remember what we say here, but it can never forget what they did here. It is for us the living, rather, to be dedicated here to the unfinished work which they who fought here have thus far so nobly advanced. It is rather for us to be here dedicated to the great task remaining before us—that from these honored dead we take increased devotion to that cause for which they gave the last full measure of devotion—that we here highly resolve that these dead shall not have died in vain—that this nation, under God, shall have a new birth of freedom—and that government of the people, by the people, for the people, shall not perish from the earth."

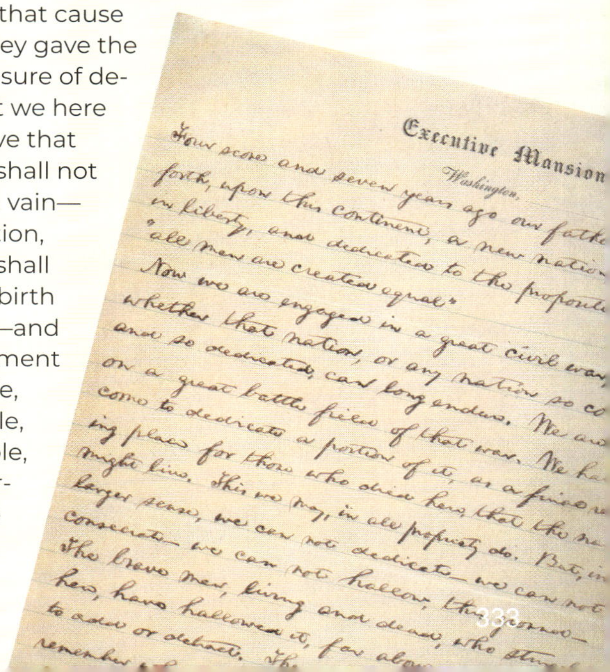

GUIDING QUESTIONS

- What did the Emancipation Proclamation do?
- How did the North destroy much of the South?
- What happened in the election of 1864?

Did you know?

During the war, prices in Richmond skyrocketed. The price for a pound of bacon rose from $1.25 per pound in 1860 to $10.00 in February 1863. In that same time period, the price of flour more than doubled; sugar was fifteen times more expensive; and coffee prices rose forty-fold.

AFRICAN AMERICANS *in the* ARMIES

Black soldiers served in the Confederate armies in noncombatant (nonfighting) positions. They worked as cooks, wagon drivers, laborers, and personal servants to officers. During the war, the Confederate Congress ignored advice from some generals who said that blacks should fight in the Southern armies.

However, as the war neared its end, the South experienced a severe manpower shortage. In March 1865, the Confederate Congress passed a bill allowing blacks to fight in the army. It appears that none were ever involved in actual combat for the Confederacy because the war ended just a few weeks afterward.

About 180,000 black soldiers served in the Union army, and another 20,000 served in the Union navy. During the war, 25 black Union soldiers won the Congressional Medal of Honor, the nation's highest award for bravery when fighting the enemy.

14.5 THE WAR TURNS

How did the North turn the tide of the war?

As the Civil War progressed, both sides were growing weary of the fighting. Despite early Confederate successes at Fort Sumter and Bull Run, conditions in the wartime South quickly deteriorated. The Union blockade created severe shortages. Confederate money lost its value. This drop in value resulted in outrageously high prices. Many Northerners were also tired of the war and wanted to negotiate peace.

The Emancipation Proclamation

When the Civil War began, Lincoln indicated that the fighting was to preserve the Union, not a battle against slavery. But he continued to speak of his "personal wish that all men every where could be free." As the war progressed and casualties increased, Lincoln concluded that his duty to save the Union and his desire to free the slaves could both be accomplished. He believed that his emergency war powers enabled him to end some slavery.

In September 1862, shortly after the Battle of Antietam, Lincoln issued the **Emancipation Proclamation**. As of January 1, 1863, it declared all slaves in Confederate-controlled territory would be free. It excluded slaves in the border states for two reasons. First, Lincoln believed his emergency war powers did not give him the authority to free slaves in those states. Second, Lincoln feared that attempting to free slaves there might risk losing the loyalty of those state governments, perhaps even pushing some to secede from the Union.

Since the Confederacy did not recognize Lincoln as its leader, the Emancipation Proclamation technically did not free *any* slaves. However, as the Union army continued to advance, slaves in captured areas were freed.

▾ African American soldiers celebrating the Emancipation Proclamation

Sergeant William Carney

The Fifty-Fourth Massachusetts was the first all-black regiment in the Union army. Sergeant William Carney, who was in the regiment, received the Congressional Medal of Honor for his actions during the attack on Fort Wagner in Charleston, South Carolina. He was the first black soldier to receive the medal. The following is an account of his heroism.

After an exhausting march, and without the troops having had time for food, the bombardment began. The line of battle was formed with the Fifty-Fourth Massachusetts assigned to the post of honor and danger, in front of the attacking column.

Suddenly such a terrific fire was opened on the regiment when ascending the wall of the fort with full ranks that, using the words of Sergeant Carney, "they melted away almost instantly" before the enemy's fire.

During the attack, Colonel Robert G. Shaw, commanding the brigade, was killed. So disastrous was the fire that the brigade was compelled to retire [fall back]; but Sergeant Carney, who was with the battalion in the lead of the storming column, and who, with the regimental colors [flag of the United States and flag of the regiment], had pressed forward near the colonel leading the men over the ditch, planted the flag upon the parapet [embankment], and, lying down in order to get as much shelter as possible, for half an hour, until the second brigade came up, kept the colors up all the time. He received a severe wound in the head. When this brigade retired, he, creeping on his knees, having by this time received a wound in the thigh also, followed them, but still holding up the flag. Thus he held the flag over the wall of Fort Wagner during the conflict of two brigades, and received two wounds.

When he entered the field hospital where his wounded comrades were, they cheered him and the colors. Nearly exhausted from the loss of blood, he exclaimed: "Boys, the old flag never touched the ground!"

Booker T. Washington, "Heroes in Black Skins," *Century Illustrated Monthly Magazine*, September 1903, 724–25.

Regardless of its limitations, the Emancipation Proclamation was an important step toward eliminating slavery. By its existence, it transformed the conflict from a war to save the nation into a war of liberation. "We shout for joy that we live to record this righteous decree," rejoiced Frederick Douglass.

The proclamation hurt the South's war efforts. Thousands of slaves left their masters. The document's release ended all Southern hopes of recognition from Britain, or any military assistance from that nation, since most of the British opposed slavery. Moreover, the proclamation paved the way for public acceptance of the formal end of slavery with the Thirteenth Amendment in December 1865.

African American soldiers had asked to fight for the Union since the beginning of the war, but prejudice had kept them from being accepted into the army. After the Emancipation Proclamation was issued, black regiments began to form. Unfortunately, these soldiers were not treated the same as white Union soldiers. Until 1864, black soldiers were paid less and received medical care far below normal. As a result, the death toll for blacks in the army was about 35 percent higher than that for Northern whites. Also, they were often assigned the lowliest routine tasks.

If a black soldier were captured wearing a Union uniform, he would likely be enslaved or killed. Nevertheless, tens of thousands of African Americans fought for the Union. Their performance in battle demonstrated that their courage was second to none.

This memorial to the Fifty-Fourth Massachusetts regiment is in Boston, Massachusetts

Fighting on Missionary Ridge ▸ in Chattanooga, Tennessee

▾ Part of the Shenandoah Valley

The Destruction in the South

By 1863 some Northern commanders believed that winning the war would require waging **total war**. Total war involves fighting not just the enemy's military and government but also the civilian population (since civilians produce the food and weapons that the military needs). Such war focuses on destroying the enemy's ability and willingness to fight. Thus, when Union armies began invading the very heart of the Confederacy, many used the policy of total war.

Some condemned the idea of total war. For example, in January 1863, Northern theologian Charles Hodge warned, "Better let the rebels succeed, than offend God, by reverting to the cruel and wicked usages of former ages." He argued that Christians should treat prisoners of war with humanity. He also said that noncombatants should not be harassed or penalized. For instance, he said, if the military needed civilians' provisions or horses, it should compensate the civilians lest God's commandment against stealing be violated. He said that houses and cities should not be burned except in the natural course of fighting. Hodge's warnings went unheeded.

The Shenandoah Valley

Lee was aware of the North's war weariness. Hoping to capitalize on it, he sent some of his cavalry north. Lee did not expect them to win any major battles, but he wanted to create anxiety in the North. From their base in the Shenandoah Valley of Virginia, those troops raided Maryland farms for supplies and livestock. In July 1864 they rode to the outskirts of Washington, DC. The threat they posed kept some Union troops near the city and out of the fight against Lee.

In response, General Grant recommended that Union troops be sent into the Shenandoah Valley to ruin "Virginia clear and clean … so that crows flying over it for the balance of the season will have to carry their provender [food] with them." General Philip Sheridan was chosen to complete that task. He followed his orders with grim efficiency. His army not only defeated Southern troops three times but also devastated the valley that had fed Lee's army for three years. Soldiers killed livestock; burned barns, houses, and crops; and caused terror in the valley. The Shenandoah, called the "breadbasket of the South," was left desolate. Lee's armies had even more trouble finding food, and civilians suffered greatly.

Tennessee and North Georgia

After the Union victories at Gettysburg and Vicksburg, fighting occurred in the area around Chattanooga, Tennessee. The city was an important railroad center. In early September, 1863, Union General William Rosecrans forced Confederate General Braxton Bragg's troops to evacuate Chattanooga. Rosecrans's forces then marched south of Chattanooga into Georgia.

On September 19, 1863, the Confederates attacked Rosecrans and in two days shattered his army at Chickamauga. Complete disaster for the Union was avoided only through the courage of General George Thomas. He held firm against repeated Confederate attacks. He protected the retreating forces and then slowly withdrew. His determined stand saved much of the Union army and won him a nickname: the Rock of Chickamauga. The Battle of Chickamauga was one of the bloodiest battles during the war. The Union suffered over 16,000 casualties, and the South, though victorious, suffered more than 18,000.

Union forces retreated to **Chattanooga**, where they were soon surrounded by enemy troops. Bragg positioned his Confederate forces on the high ground of Lookout Mountain and Missionary Ridge and besieged the city, hoping to starve the Union soldiers into surrendering. Within a month, additional troops commanded by Generals Grant and William T. Sherman provided reinforcements for the Union. Grant took command of all Union troops in the city.

On November 23, Grant ordered his Union troops to break out from Chattanooga. They attacked Confederate positions on Missionary Ridge and Lookout Mountain (fighting on the mountain became known as the "battle above the clouds"). The Union army dislodged the Confederates and sent them retreating into Georgia. Bragg had earned a reputation for angering easily, refusing to listen to suggestions, and failing to act decisively. Confederate president Jefferson Davis removed Bragg as leader of the Confederate troops in the region.

Meanwhile, in early 1864, Lincoln appointed Grant commander of all Union forces in the war. In Grant, Lincoln found a general who was willing not just to fight but to do whatever it took to win.

Sherman's March to the Sea

After the Union victory in Chattanooga, Grant placed General **William Sherman** in charge of all troops in the West. Sherman's two-part task was to destroy the Southern army led by General Joseph E. Johnston, Bragg's replacement, and to capture Atlanta, Georgia. Grant had ordered Sherman to chase the Confederate army and "to break it up and to get into the interior of the enemy's country as far as [he could], inflicting all the damage [he could]." Sherman followed this decree without hesitation.

General Johnston tried to stop Sherman's advancing troops. Each time he set his forces to make a stand, Sherman was able to outmaneuver him. Consequently, Johnston continued to retreat toward Atlanta. Jefferson Davis replaced Johnston with General John Bell Hood, who promptly lost a costly battle to Sherman in Atlanta. By September 1, 1864, Hood realized that he could save his army only by abandoning Atlanta. The loss of Atlanta, one of the South's most important remaining railroad and manufacturing centers, was devastating to the South.

The Union was determined to break the Confederacy's desire to fight. Thus, in November 1864, Sherman burned much of the city of Atlanta. He then divided his army into four columns and sent each column by a different road toward Savannah on the Atlantic coast. His commanders carried maps that marked every village and plantation along the 60-mile-wide, 250-mile-long band between Atlanta and Savannah. Sherman ordered his commanders to "forage [obtain supplies and food] liberally on the country during the march," keeping a ten-day supply on hand at all times. Everything they did not need, they were to destroy. Sherman wrote to Grant, outlining his plan and promising that he would "make Georgia howl."

▾ When Confederate General John Bell Hood abandoned Atlanta, he destroyed materials he was unable to evacuate. He wanted to prevent the Union army from using them.

Sherman's written orders to his commanders said that Union soldiers were not to enter private dwellings or "commit any trespass" unless local citizens attacked them. Since citizens almost always resisted, wholesale destruction resulted.

In addition to the devastation caused by regular Union soldiers, "Sherman's bummers" robbed, destroyed, and burned the countryside. This was a shabby collection of men, some still in the army and some who were deserters. Sherman made little attempt to stop them. As a result, his **March to the Sea** caused a great deal of bitterness among the people of the South, especially those in Georgia.

By December 10, Sherman's army had reached the coastal town of Savannah. Eleven days later, the city fell easily. Sherman telegraphed Lincoln to present Savannah to him as a Christmas gift. Sherman then turned north to march across the Carolinas and join Grant in Virginia. His policy of total war devastated the Carolinas as well, leaving behind even more resentment and hatred.

The Election of 1864

Northerners were weary of war. They wanted peace. Horace Greeley, editor of the *New York Tribune*, one of the North's leading newspapers, wrote that nine-tenths of all Americans were "anxious for peace—peace on almost any terms." Some members of Lincoln's own party did not think he was waging the war effectively. They also wanted to see greater action to secure the emancipation and civil rights of all black Americans. Northern Democrats criticized Lincoln at every turn. They believed some of Lincoln's actions were unconstitutional. For instance, they noted that he had restricted both freedom of speech and freedom of the press, had instituted a draft, had broadly used his war powers to stop those who opposed him, and had no authority to issue the Emancipation Proclamation. Many wanted to preserve the Union through negotiation rather than war.

Lincoln faced opposition in his bid for reelection. Former Union general George McClellan was the nominee of the Democratic Party. Lincoln at one point even told his own cabinet that he did not think he would be reelected.

But Lincoln had political skills. He selected former senator **Andrew Johnson**, a Democrat from Tennessee, to be his running mate. He believed that Johnson could help him bring the Southern states back into the Union more easily after the war was over. During the election, the Republicans temporarily renamed themselves the National Union Party.

During the autumn of 1864, military victories, such as the capture of Atlanta, increased Lincoln's popularity. In addition, Lincoln had ensured that the Union army in the field could vote by absentee ballot. Those factors contributed to his victory over McClellan and winning reelection.

▲ Campaign poster of Abraham Lincoln and his running mate, Andrew Johnson

SECTION REVIEW 14.5

1. Which slaves did the Emancipation Proclamation declare free? Which slaves were not declared free by its provisions?
2. What type of war did Northern commanders believe was necessary? What did this require? Do you agree with this strategy? Why or why not?
3. What food-supplying area of the South did Sheridan devastate?
4. What was another name for the Battle of Lookout Mountain?
5. Between which two major cities in Georgia did Sherman destroy much that was in his path?
6. Why did Lincoln choose Democrat Andrew Johnson to be his running mate in 1864?

GUIDING QUESTIONS

- How did the Civil War end?
- What impact did the Civil War have on the nation?

14.6 ENDING THE WAR

How did the war end?

The Road to Surrender

Pushing to Richmond

By May 1864 Grant was ready to open a new military campaign in Virginia. His army moved into a heavily wooded area west of Fredericksburg called "the Wilderness." There Grant hurled a force of about 120,000 men against Lee's scant 60,000. Grant's casualties numbered about 18,000, while Lee's forces suffered about 10,000. Though Grant's losses were heavier, he knew that he could more easily replace the men he lost because of the size of the Union army. He knew that Lee could not do so.

Northern newspapers and even Union soldiers complained that Grant seemed unconcerned about the number of his soldiers who were killed, calling him "Lincoln's butcher." But Grant believed that if he continued to attack Lee's army, he could gradually erode Lee's ability to fight and force his surrender.

Grant next moved east, then south. Between May 5 and May 12, Grant lost more than 26,000 who were killed or wounded. Later at the Battle of Cold Harbor, the Union dead covered five acres. Although "Butcher Grant" had lost more than 50,000 men in one month, he continued to press forward. He said, "I propose to fight it out on this line if it takes all summer." Lincoln supported Grant. Earlier in the war, the president had reportedly said, "I cannot spare this man. He fights."

In June 1864 Grant crossed the James River and moved toward Richmond. To get there, he had to take Petersburg. Lee rushed to protect the city, and Grant was able to hold him there and bombard the city with cannon fire. Grant was being continually resupplied and reinforced, but Lee's force was getting smaller and weaker every day. The standoff would last until April 1865.

Lee realized he could resist no longer. His army had often been hungry during the war, but now it faced starvation. On the night of April 2, 1865, he evacuated Petersburg. Union troops outnumbered his army more than two to one; Lee soon realized that continuing to fight was hopeless.

▾ Battle of the Wilderness in May 1864

PRIMARY SOURCE: EXCERPT FROM LINCOLN'S SECOND INAUGURAL ADDRESS

On March 4, 1865, with the war nearing its end, Lincoln took the presidential oath again. As he concluded his inaugural speech, he previewed his ideas for healing a divided nation.

"With malice toward none, with charity for all, with firmness in the right as God gives us to see the right, let us strive on to finish the work we are in, to bind up the nation's wounds, to care for him who shall have borne the battle and for his widow and his orphan, to do all which may achieve and cherish a just and lasting peace among ourselves and with all nations."

▲ Robert E. Lee (right) surrendering to Ulysses S. Grant (left)

Appomattox Court House

As Lee saw it, his last hope was to link with Johnston's army in upper North Carolina and make one last stand. Perhaps then he could deal Grant a decisive blow. But Union troops commanded by Sheridan blocked Lee's retreat to the Blue Ridge Mountains. On April 7, Grant offered to discuss terms of surrender with Lee. Both commanders knew that further resistance was hopeless. On April 9, Lee and Grant met in a farmhouse in the village of **Appomattox Court House** to sign the surrender papers.

Grant was generous in his treatment of the vanquished army, allowing the officers to keep their side arms (pistols, knives, and swords) and their horses. Lee asked that the common soldiers also be allowed to keep their horses, which had been supplied to the military and would be needed to work the farms. Grant agreed. Throughout the surrender process, Grant showed deep respect for the feelings of his former enemies. He did not ask Lee to surrender his sword, as was typical during such ceremonies. Grant required the Confederate soldiers to sign pledges that they would not fight again. Then he issued them provisions for their journey home.

After Lee's surrender of the South's main army, it was only a matter of time before the other scattered units surrendered. On April 18, Johnston surrendered to Sherman in Durham, North Carolina. Jefferson Davis, who had fled Richmond with part of his cabinet, was captured in Georgia on May 10. Though for all practical purposes the war had ended with Lee's surrender, the final army of the Confederacy did not surrender until May 26 in Texas.

The Woes of Wilmer McLean

Wilmer McLean lived on a farm in Manassas and suffered the effects of both battles of Bull Run. Tired of seeing his property destroyed and his family's lives and income threatened by war, he moved over 150 miles away to Appomattox Court House.

His new home was chosen as the meeting place where Generals Grant and Lee would negotiate the South's surrender on April 9, 1865. Later, McLean reportedly said that the war "began in [his] front yard and ended in [his] front parlor." Soldiers took many of McLean's belongings as souvenirs of the historic surrender site.

Costs of the War		
	Union	Confederacy
Total expenditures	$6,190,000,000	$2,099,808,707
Inflation at worst	$1 in gold = $2.59 in paper money	$1 in gold = $60–$70 in paper money
Combat deaths	110,100	94,000
Wounded	277,401	194,026
Deaths from disease	224,580	164,000

▲ John Wilkes Booth shot Abraham Lincoln in Ford's Theater just five days after Confederate troops had surrendered at Appomattox Court House.

Results of the War

Costs

The Civil War was the most destructive war in American history. More than 620,000 died, more than the number of Americans who died in World War I and World War II combined.

Almost one-fourth of those in the military died during the conflict. One of every thirteen who survived lost one or more limbs. Much personal property and industrial capacity had been destroyed, mostly in the South. Noncombatants lost homes, farms, and businesses. Roads and farmlands were ruined. Perhaps as important as the human and material loss was the deep bitterness that remained long after the war was over. Many were upset by the ruin from the North's total war policy. Others saw Southerners as traitors who started an unnecessary war. Distrust and even hatred lingered between the North and the South for decades.

Lincoln's Assassination

The war would claim one additional casualty that affected both sides. On Good Friday, April 14, 1865, President Lincoln and his wife went to Ford's Theatre in Washington to attend a play. **John Wilkes Booth**, an actor and Confederate sympathizer, entered Lincoln's private box and shot the president in the back of the head. Lincoln died the next morning. Booth was later tracked to a barn in Virginia. The barn was burned, and Booth either took his own life or was shot and killed by one of his pursuers.

Lincoln was buried in his hometown of Springfield, Illinois. The country then turned to deal with problems that it had never before faced. Those problems would plague the nation for the next century.

Understanding Providence

During the war, people struggled to understand God's role or God's will in the conflict. Early in the war, Northerners were puzzled at their military failures. If their cause was right, why was God not giving them victory? Later in the war, Southerners were distraught at their defeats. How could God ignore the prayers of devoted Christians such as Robert E. Lee and Stonewall Jackson? Some people on both sides lost faith in God.

Lincoln's view was different. In the middle of the war, Lincoln reasoned that God's ways are not always people's ways. He said,

> In great contests each party claims to act in accordance with the will of God. Both may be, and one must be, wrong. God can not be for and against the same thing at the same time. In the present civil war it is quite possible that God's purpose is something different from the purpose of either party.

SECTION REVIEW 14.6

1. Why did Grant continue pursuing Lee despite the heavy losses the Union army was suffering?
2. On what date and in what town did Lee surrender his army?
3. How did the South feel about the North for decades after the war? Why?
4. Who assassinated Lincoln?
5. Why do you think Grant was so generous to the Confederates during their surrender when he had previously ordered a total war?

CHAPTER 14 REVIEW

Making Connections

1. Based on the percentages given, what was the amount of time a soldier spent fighting during an average week?
2. How were people able to avoid conscription in both the North and the South?
3. How did many women help with the war effort in the North? in the South?
4. What was the South's strategy for winning the war?
5. How was the North's plan like an anaconda?
6. How did the First Battle of Bull Run reveal the people's misconception of war? How did each side finish the battle?
7. How far did the Union blockade of the South extend? Why was it difficult at the beginning for the Union to maintain the blockade?
8. What did Ulysses S. Grant see as the key to success in the West? What four places did he capture to gain control of the upper Mississippi River region?
9. What branch of the US military assisted in capturing the lower Mississippi River? Who led this force?
10. Which Union general commanded each of the following battles?
    a. Antietam
    b. Fredericksburg
    c. Chancellorsville
    d. Gettysburg
11. Who was the commanding Confederate general in each of the four battles listed in the previous question?
12. How did the outcome of the Battle of Antietam affect the North and the South?
13. In what battle did Union morale reach its lowest point in the war?
14. What did the Emancipation Proclamation achieve?
15. What was the main state where each of the following areas of fighting occurred?
    a. the Shenandoah Valley
    b. Chattanooga
    c. Sherman's March to the Sea

Thinking Critically

16. How might the Emancipation Proclamation have been seen as a justification for total war? What strategy might the North have used to avoid total war?

Living as a Christian Citizen

17. Why did both sides think that God was on their side? How should Christians react when a cause for which they struggled does not result in victory?
18. Rephrase Lincoln's quote at the end of the chapter in your own words.

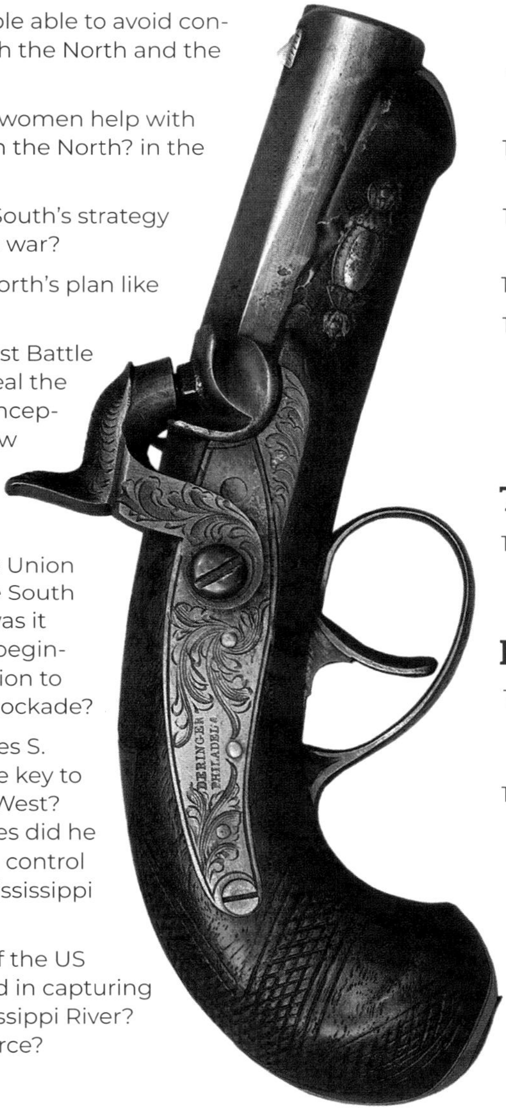

◂ Booth used this pistol (shown actual size) to assassinate President Lincoln.

Terms to Remember

providence
bounty
conscription
Anaconda Plan
Stonewall Jackson
First Battle of Bull Run
George McClellan
Robert E. Lee
J. E. B. Stuart
Second Battle of Bull Run
blockade
blockade-runners
Ulysses S. Grant
Clara Barton
David Farragut
Vicksburg
Antietam
Fredericksburg
Chancellorsville
Gettysburg
Pickett's Charge
Gettysburg Address
Emancipation Proclamation
total war
Chattanooga
William Sherman
March to the Sea
Andrew Johnson
Appomattox Court House
John Wilkes Booth

CHAPTER 15

Reconstruction

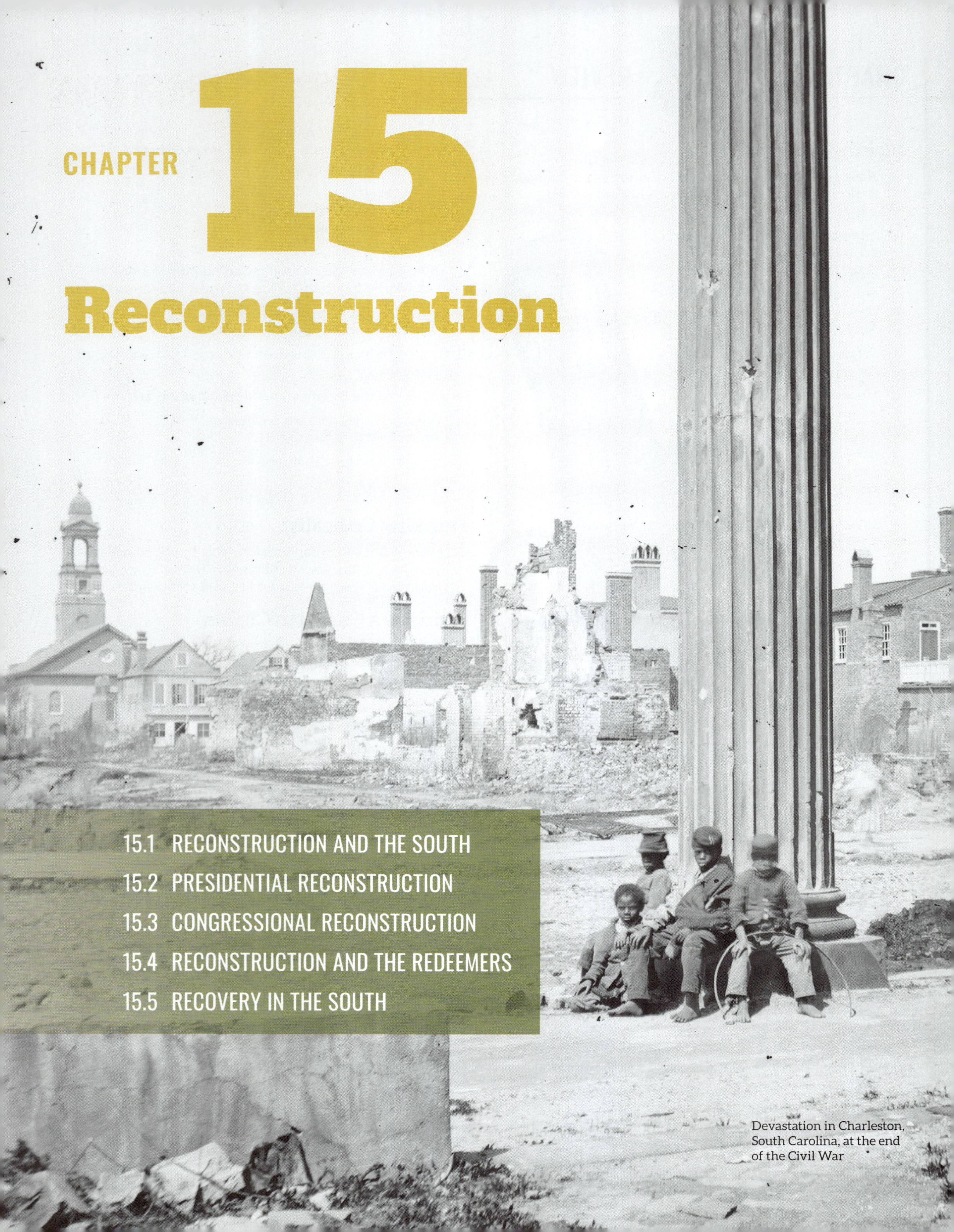

Devastation in Charleston, South Carolina, at the end of the Civil War

Reconstruction, the period from the end of the Civil War to 1877, proved to be a time of testing for American values. The Civil War had secured liberty for black Americans. Some Americans, including many leading Republicans, were determined to also give former slaves, or **freedmen**, equality and the opportunity to prosper as individuals. After the war, Union troops remained in the South. Many Republicans in Congress wanted to keep the Southern states under military occupation, partly because they wanted to make sure freedmen received fair treatment.

Growth in this period meant rebuilding shattered lives. The destruction of Southern cities and plantations that occurred during the war made life very difficult for Southerners of all races.

During Reconstruction, there were many struggles over what the American values of freedom, individualism, equality, and growth meant and over who should enjoy these benefits. It was a difficult time reuniting the nation and trying to solve its postwar problems.

GUIDING QUESTIONS

- What challenges confronted the South during Reconstruction?
- What were the three phases of Reconstruction?

15.1 RECONSTRUCTION AND THE SOUTH

Why was Reconstruction needed in the South?

The Need for Reconstruction

For Northerners, life after the war was not much different from life before the war. Though the North had lost thousands of men, and it felt that wound deeply, industry had progressed. In addition, little Northern property had been damaged in the war, so soldiers could return to their farms or jobs with little hindrance. Immigration continued to add to the Northern population.

The situation in the South, however, was different. The South had lost many of its young men and slavery no longer existed; therefore, its labor force was entirely disrupted.

The South had also suffered severe property damage. The war had left many Southern cities—including Atlanta, Columbia, and Richmond—in ruins. The South's fields were stripped bare in many areas. Its livestock had been taken or destroyed. Homes, businesses, and railroads were demolished. After the war, little remained with which the South could rebuild.

Most Southerners were bewildered, despondent, and bitter. The South's plantation system was dead. Many formerly wealthy Southerners found themselves in poverty. Confederate paper money was worthless. The South was bankrupt, and its economy was destroyed.

White Southerners generally believed that their liberties were being trampled by troops within their states. Many did not believe that black Americans should be treated as the equals of white Americans. They insisted that the desire for equal treatment was part of a Northern attempt to destroy Southern culture.

▾ Confederate money had no value at the war's end. Savings deposited in Southern banks were now worthless.

▲ Like many other Southern cities, much of Richmond, Virginia, was destroyed during the war.

Black Southerners, numbering about four million, were now free; however, they faced enormous challenges integrating into Southern society. Former slaves soon found that freedom from slavery did not necessarily mean freedom in other areas. For example, most freedmen did not wish to continue the type of work they had done as slaves, even if their former owners had money to pay them. Instead, most preferred to secure land so that they could build their own independent farms. Unfortunately, they had no money, and it was nearly impossible to obtain credit because they were black. Furthermore, a number of laws limited the kind of work they could pursue. They also sought political and social equality, but they often faced violence for not continuing to act like slaves.

Moreover, the South had to reestablish its state governments. The Union victory had removed the Confederate governments that were in control during the war. New governments had to be formed to deal with the problems in the South.

All these difficulties were major concerns of the national government. The central question was who—the president, Congress, or the states—would control the methods for solving the problems of Reconstruction.

Phases of Reconstruction

Officially, Reconstruction covered the twelve years from 1865 to 1877 during which the federal government directly supervised the rebuilding of the South. The period can be divided into two phases—Presidential Reconstruction and Congressional Reconstruction.

SECTION REVIEW 15.1

1. What was the period in America from the end of the Civil War to 1877 called?
2. Why did many Republicans in Congress want to keep Union troops in the South after the war? Was this reason justified? Explain.
3. How were the North and South different after the war, regarding work and property?
4. What struggles did newly freed black Southerners face?
5. What were the two phases of Reconstruction?

15.2 PRESIDENTIAL RECONSTRUCTION

What were the presidents' plans to reconstruct the South?

Under Lincoln

The period during which Presidents Abraham Lincoln and Andrew Johnson directed the Reconstruction process was known as **Presidential Reconstruction**. Even before the Civil War ended, Lincoln developed a plan for returning the seceded states to the Union. When Andrew Johnson became the nation's leader after the assassination of Lincoln, he took charge of Reconstruction and developed his own plan.

Lincoln believed that the Southern states, by seceding, had committed an act of rebellion. He believed that his duty as commander in chief was to crush their insurrection. Once this was completed, he had the power under the Constitution to pardon any wrongdoing. Lincoln made the terms of Reconstruction lenient in order to encourage the Southern states to stop fighting and return to the Union.

Lincoln's Plan

In December 1863, Lincoln formulated his **Ten Percent Plan** for restoring the South. As the Union army advanced through the South, Lincoln appointed a military governor for each captured state. Each governor was to reestablish a civilian government as soon as a number equal to 10 percent of those who had voted in the 1860 election took an oath of allegiance to the Union. Once a state government had formed under these conditions, states could send representatives to Congress. The plan offered pardons to most former Confederates who would swear to support the Constitution and the Union.

Radical Republicans Object

Lincoln's plan met resistance, however, from a group known as **Radical Republicans**. Though they were a minority within the Republican Party, they were highly influential.

Radical Republicans believed Southerners who had led the Confederacy should not be allowed to return to power. They knew that since freed black Southerners would now count as full persons for representation, the South would receive more votes in Congress than before the war. They worried that if Democrats continued to dominate Southern politics, they could align with Northern Democrats and gain control of the national government. Another priority of the Radicals was to secure political and civil rights for black Americans, including the right to vote.

Earlier in the war, the Radicals had also opposed the increase of presidential powers. Lincoln had made many decisions without consulting Congress. When Congress met in 1861, it approved Lincoln's actions and wrote legislation to support some of his policies. But the Radicals opposed these measures and asserted that Lincoln had exceeded his powers. They wanted to shift the balance of power back in favor of Congress.

In 1864 Congress had developed its own Reconstruction plan: the **Wade-Davis Bill**. Under this plan, a state could reenter the Union only when more than 50 percent of white male citizens took an oath of allegiance to the Union. Further, the states had to abolish slavery and

GUIDING QUESTIONS

- How did Congress react to the presidential plans for Reconstruction?
- What were black codes?
- What did President Johnson achieve in foreign affairs?

Long Abraham Lincoln a Little Longer.

This illustration of President Lincoln was published in one of the nation's best known magazines, *Harper's Weekly*.

abandon claims on the federal government to repay their war debts. They had to agree that former Confederate military and political leaders would not be allowed to vote or hold political office. In addition, people who wanted to help write the new state constitutions had to swear that they had never voluntarily supported the Confederacy.

The Wade-Davis Bill passed both houses of Congress. Congress was clearly asserting its intention to control readmitting states and to determine the selection procedures for the South's members of Congress. Lincoln, however, objected to the bill. He stated that a constitutional amendment would be necessary to abolish slavery and that he believed some aspects of the Wade-Davis Bill were too harsh. As a result, he vetoed it.

The conflict between Congress and Lincoln had not yet been resolved when Lincoln was killed in April 1865. The new president was left to battle with Congress for control of Reconstruction.

Andrew Johnson

Born	December 29, 1808	17
Died	July 31, 1875	
Home state	Tennessee (born in North Carolina)	
Wife	Eliza McCardle	
Church	no formal affiliation	
Occupation	tailor	
Party	Democrat (or Unionist Party)	
Years served as president	1865–69	
Terms	1 (minus 1 month)	
Vice president	none	

Under Johnson

Vice President Andrew Johnson had been born in poverty in North Carolina. He worked for a cruel tailor and later ran away to Tennessee. There he met and married his wife, who was a teacher. While Johnson worked in his tailor shop in Greeneville, Tennessee, his wife taught him to read and write. His business was also where local townsmen often discussed politics. Johnson became a staunch Democrat. He was elected first to local offices, then to the US House of Representatives, and eventually to the US Senate.

Johnson opposed Tennessee's vote to secede in 1861. He was the only Southern senator not to resign his Senate seat. When Nashville, the capital of Tennessee, was captured by Union troops, Lincoln named Johnson military governor of the state. Later, in a shrewd political move, Lincoln chose Johnson to be his running mate. Johnson's public statements won him the support of Radical Republicans. He once said that Jefferson Davis and other leading Confederates should be hanged. He told people that "treason must be made odious [disgusting]."

When Johnson became president, Congress was not in session. Until Congress reconvened in December 1865, he was able to state his ideals and implement them without congressional interference.

Johnson's Plan

Johnson's plan was to first offer **amnesty** (a group pardon) to Southerners who would swear loyalty to the Union. But Johnson excluded those whose taxable property was worth more than $20,000. Those people—which included former large-plantation owners, bankers, and merchants—had to apply to him personally for a pardon. Unpardoned Southerners could not vote, hold office, or reclaim property seized by the government.

Next, he planned to appoint provisional (temporary) state governors to hold state conventions. Those conventions would draft new state constitutions that would refuse to pay Confederate debts and would adopt the **Thirteenth Amendment**, which abolished slavery.

By December 1865, almost all the former Confederate states had organized their new governments and had elected members to Congress based on Johnson's plan. The president approved thousands of individual pardons.

Thirteenth Amendment

Neither slavery nor involuntary servitude, except as a punishment for crime whereof the party shall have been duly convicted, shall exist within the United States, or any place subject to their jurisdiction.

Black Codes

▲ In 1867 a freedman (standing on the steps) was unable to pay a fine he owed. As a result, his services were auctioned to the highest bidder. The proceeds were used to pay the money he owed. This system was frequently abused. For example, sometimes freedmen were arrested for minor crimes or on false charges and then forced to work for those who could pay their fines.

While following Johnson's plan, no Southern states gave voting rights to blacks. Furthermore, in late 1865 and 1866, they began instituting **black codes**. These were very restrictive laws that placed African Americans in an inferior position to white people. They kept them in a condition similar to slavery.

In some states, for example, black codes allowed blacks to work only as servants for white families or as farmers. Some codes prohibited black people from living in towns or cities, while others restricted many blacks to the same fieldwork they had done as slaves. Black people who wanted to practice trades or do anything besides farming had to obtain training from whites and often had to pay for costly licenses. Since few blacks had money, these regulations vastly limited their opportunities.

Many black codes said that blacks who were not employed could be arrested. Those who could not pay fines were forced to work for any whites who paid the fines for them. Some black codes prohibited black people from carrying weapons, and other codes told them where they could own property. Only a few states allowed blacks to serve on juries. These injustices convinced moderate Republicans that Reconstruction had to include rights for black Americans, leading many to join the Radical Republicans.

Radical Republicans React

Republicans believed Johnson's plan was flawed. They insisted it did not address all the issues and noted its numerous shortcomings.

First, the Radical Republicans had long believed that black Americans should be not only freed from slavery but also given the full rights of citizenship. If those rights were not secured by the national government during Reconstruction, they might never be secured.

Second, as was true with Lincoln's plan, Southern states would now have more power in the national government than they had before the war. Because former slaves were now counted as full persons in the census, the South would gain representatives in Congress and the Electoral College.

Third, when Southern states held their elections in late 1865, most of them elected former Confederates. Georgia, for instance, elected the Confederacy's vice president to the Senate. Newly elected members of Congress also included four former Confederate generals, eight former colonels, and six former cabinet members. Radical Republicans thought it was wrong for the leaders of a rebellion against the government to obtain important positions in that government.

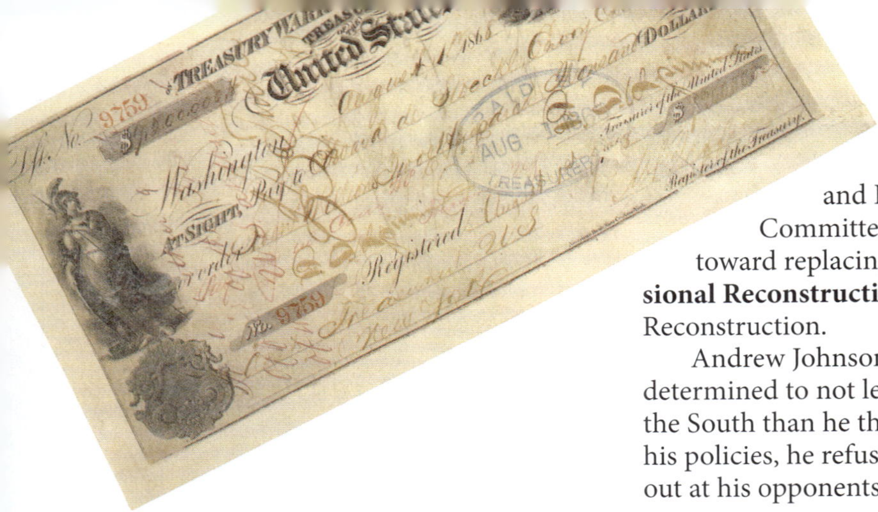

Congress refused to seat the newly elected Southern representatives. Instead, moderate and Radical Republicans formed their own Joint Committee on Reconstruction. This was the first move toward replacing Presidential Reconstruction with **Congressional Reconstruction**, the period during which Congress controlled Reconstruction.

Andrew Johnson was firm in his views on Reconstruction and determined to not let the Radicals make reunification any harder on the South than he thought it needed to be. When Congress defied his policies, he refused to change. Unfortunately, he also lashed out at his opponents. Though he had worked hard to overcome his poverty and lack of formal education, he did not display the skill and tactfulness that the nation needed in its leaders during this difficult period. His inflexibility often disheartened moderates, driving more of them into the Radical camp. With most of Congress united against Johnson, the days of Presidential Reconstruction were numbered.

▲ The check for the purchase of Alaska is shown at top. At bottom is a cartoon showing an American politician trying to find voters in sparsely populated Alaska.

Johnson and Foreign Affairs

Though Congress blocked most of Johnson's policies at home, his administration achieved some accomplishments in foreign affairs. The most significant involved Alaska. In 1867 **William Seward**, who served as Lincoln and Johnson's secretary of state, secretly negotiated a treaty with Russia to purchase Alaska. The price was $7.2 million, just two cents per acre. When Johnson sought Senate approval of the purchase, the press ridiculed Alaska as "Seward's Folly," "Seward's Icebox," and "Johnson's Polar Bear Garden." But the deal sailed through the Senate quickly with a 37–2 vote. In time, the purchase proved to be a great bargain for the United States. Seward also signed a treaty of friendship and commerce with China in 1868.

SECTION REVIEW 15.2

1. Why did Lincoln purposely make his Reconstruction plan lenient on the South?
2. For what reasons did the Radicals in Congress not like Lincoln's Ten Percent Plan?
3. What were the requirements of the Wade-Davis Bill?
4. What was unique about Andrew Johnson's time as a senator? To what position did Lincoln appoint him during the war?
5. What flaws did the Radicals in Congress see in Johnson's Reconstruction ideas?
6. Which path would you choose if you had lived during Reconstruction: Lincoln's and Johnson's plans to allow easy reentry for Southern states or Radical Republican plans to make reentry more difficult? Why?
7. What significant land purchase occurred during the Johnson administration?

15.3 CONGRESSIONAL RECONSTRUCTION

How did Radical Republicans in Congress control Reconstruction?

Thaddeus Stevens of Pennsylvania led the Radical Republicans in the House of Representatives while the Radical leader in the Senate was **Charles Sumner** of Massachusetts. After refusing to seat Southerners, the Radicals enacted bills stating that Congress, not the president, would control Reconstruction.

Johnson vetoed their bills. But by February 1866, the Radicals and their moderate supporters had achieved a two-thirds majority in both houses. This allowed them to override Johnson's vetoes.

GUIDING QUESTIONS

- What laws did Republicans pass during Congressional Reconstruction?
- Who were carpetbaggers and scalawags?
- Why was President Andrew Johnson impeached?
- What events occurred when Ulysses S. Grant was president?

Republican Legislation

The Freedmen's Bureau

In March 1865 Congress had passed laws to establish a short-term agency called the **Freedmen's Bureau**. Its primary purpose was to assist former slaves. It issued surplus army food and clothing to them and also to poor whites. The bureau tried to locate jobs for the freedmen and prevent employers from taking advantage of them. It sent agents into the South to establish schools and hospitals for blacks of all ages.

Original legislation had intended for the organization to exist for just a year after the war's end. However, in 1866 Congress extended its time (it would exist until 1872) and gave the bureau power to deal with abuses created by the black codes. For example, it could assist black people in negotiating fair work contracts that specified the pay for workers and the number of hours they were required to work. The bureau could also establish special courts to settle disagreements between workers and their employers, and it could intervene when courts issued unjust judgments or when blacks' rights were violated. Johnson also vetoed this bill, but Congress overrode the veto.

Though the Freedmen's Bureau faced opposition from some southern whites, it accomplished much. One of its most significant contributions was helping to educate blacks. The agency provided buildings for schools, paid teachers, and helped establish colleges to train African American teachers.

▾ Many former slaves attended schools operated by the Freedmen's Bureau. This one was located in North Carolina.

▲ The cartoon above portrays President Johnson as being too small to handle the US Constitution and then being crushed by it. Below he (with raised right arm) is campaigning against Radical Republicans.

The Fourteenth Amendment

Next, in the Civil Rights Act of 1866, Congress granted full citizenship to black people. Because Johnson believed that the Constitution gave the states, not the national government, power over citizenship, he vetoed the act. Again, Congress overrode his veto. But Congress feared that the act would be declared unconstitutional or repealed by a future Congress. In June 1866, Congress sought to solve the problem by proposing the **Fourteenth Amendment**.

Fourteenth Amendment

1. All Americans are citizens of both the nation and the states where they reside. Every state is prohibited from depriving a person of life, liberty, or property without due process of law (proper legal procedures and trial). A state cannot deny equal protection of its laws to any person under its jurisdiction.

2. A state's representation in Congress would be based on its whole population. All black people, not just three-fifths, were to be counted to determine the state's representation. But if states denied voting rights to blacks, the number of representatives in Congress from those states would be reduced.

3. Those who had sworn an oath to support the Constitution (such as members of Congress, state legislatures, and judges) and had broken that oath by supporting the Confederacy were barred from holding government offices. But Congress, not the president, could pardon them by a two-thirds vote to remove this restriction.

4. Congress would not pay any Confederate debts and would not accept claims for any costs of freeing the slaves.

When ratified, the amendment would cancel not only black codes in the South but also laws against blacks in some midwestern states. Johnson urged Southern states to vote against it.

Johnson realized that he was powerless as long as the Radicals and their moderate supporters had a two-thirds majority. So he campaigned against Radical candidates in the 1866 congressional races. He traveled to the North and the Midwest, speaking against the Radicals. But his efforts backfired. His audiences heckled him. Instead of ignoring them, Johnson lost his temper and responded harshly. Most candidates Johnson opposed won reelection.

When Congress convened in 1867, Reconstruction was more firmly in Radical hands. Congressional Reconstruction was now actually **Radical Reconstruction**. Radicals exercised even greater influence, putting their program into effect speedily and with little resistance. When the president vetoed their legislation, Congress quickly overrode his vetoes.

The Reconstruction Act of 1867

The **Reconstruction Act of 1867** ordered the army to ensure that the South followed the laws Congress enacted. First, the act divided the South into five military districts, each ruled by a Union general and a provisional governor. Second, Southern states wanting to reenter the Union had to hold state conventions that included both black and white voting delegates. (Those who had previously taken an oath to uphold the Constitution and then supported the Confederacy were excluded from participation.) These conventions would write new state constitutions, using guidelines given by Congress. Third, new state constitutions had to guarantee that adult black males had the right to vote. Fourth, former Confederate states had to submit their new constitutions to Congress for approval. Fifth, the states had to ratify the Fourteenth Amendment.

When a state met all the act's requirements, troops stationed there would be withdrawn. Tennessee had already adopted the Fourteenth Amendment and, as a result, was the only one of the eleven former Confederate states exempt from this law.

The black delegates to the state conventions tended to be well educated. They were pastors, teachers, and skilled workers. Some of them had spent their lives before the war in the North, and some already had political experience. Because most Southern leaders had served in the Confederacy, few were eligible to hold public office. Their exclusion opened the way for Northerners, black Americans, and Southern Unionists (Southerners who had supported the Union during the Civil War) to hold office.

Black delegates and legislators typically opposed efforts by some Southern Unionists to restrict the voting and officeholding rights of former Confederates. Black politicians wanted political rights to be extended to black Americans, not denied to others. Sadly, their views were not shared by many whites. Many white Southerners, both in the Democratic and Republican parties, wanted black political involvement to be limited.

▲ Though a slave, Robert Smalls became a steamboat pilot. He obtained freedom during the Civil War by hijacking the boat he was piloting and surrendering to the Union. During Reconstruction, he served in both the South Carolina state legislature and the US House of Representatives.

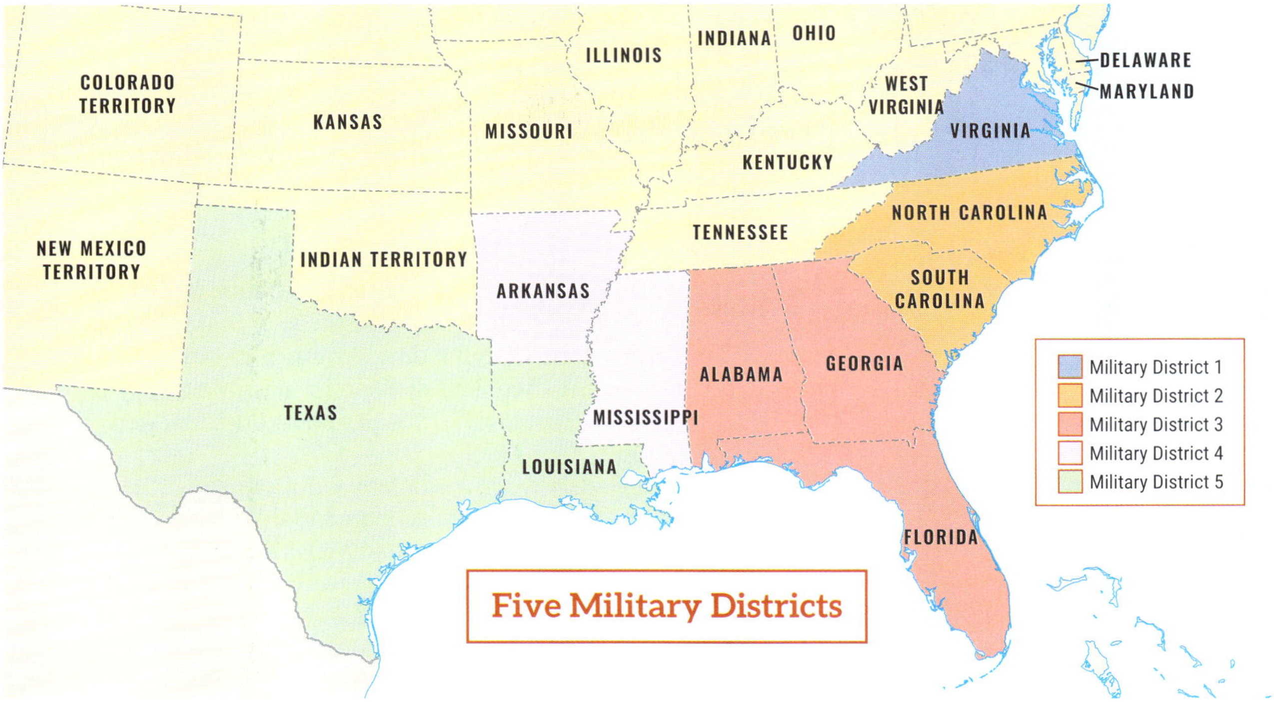

Carpetbaggers and Scalawags

Quite a few Northerners moved to the South after the war. They did so for many reasons. Some wanted to be involved in rebuilding the South, while others wanted to help the freedmen build schools and other institutions. Many, though not a majority, wanted to take advantage of the South's difficulties for personal profit.

In some places, Northerners took control of Southern politics for a while. Some Northerners brought with them the money necessary to build businesses, factories, and railroads. These business activities contributed to the South's recovery.

But many Southerners resented the Northerners' presence in the South. They called these Northerners **carpetbaggers**, after the Northerners' suitcases that were made of pieces of carpet. Many Southerners viewed the carpetbaggers as individuals who merely sought their own gain at the expense of the South. This was true of some carpetbaggers, and their wrong actions were used to discredit many others.

▲ A typical carpetbag

A white Southerner who supported Reconstruction was called a **scalawag**. This term basically meant "scoundrel" or "worthless person." Some scalawags had been Southern Unionists, and their behavior was consistent with their political beliefs. Others endorsed Radical Reconstruction because they believed that it was in the South's best interest. However, other scalawags deserved their bad name. They saw the postwar situation as a chance to seek personal gain—with the help of Radical Republican support and military protection. Most Southerners viewed scalawags as traitors.

Did you know?

Andrew Johnson was the first of three presidents to be impeached. Bill Clinton and Donald Trump, who was impeached twice, were the other two. As with Johnson, the Senate did not convict those presidents during their trials. Another president, Richard Nixon, resigned when it became apparent that he would be impeached.

The Impeachment of Johnson

Although Congress passed its Radical Republican agenda over Johnson's vetoes, Johnson still enforced the laws that were passed because it was his constitutional duty. As much as Radicals despised Johnson for opposing them and disliked his personal behavior, they knew that he was both a loyal Unionist and a consistent defender of the Constitution.

But the Radicals were still unhappy with Johnson. They sought ways to limit his powers. They also feared that he would remove officials who were sympathetic to their views and replace them with his supporters. As a result, Radicals passed the **Tenure of Office Act** in 1867, making it illegal for the president to remove any appointee who had been approved by the Senate unless the Senate also approved the dismissal.

Johnson tested the law by firing **Edwin Stanton**, the secretary of war whom Lincoln had appointed. Stanton had often disagreed with Johnson and was now openly siding with the Radicals. Stanton ignored the dismissal and barricaded himself in his office. He accepted food through the windows and cooked for himself. He even slept in his office.

Because of Stanton's firing, many in Congress believed they had grounds to remove Johnson from office. The Constitution provides a two-step process for removal. First, the House of Representatives, by majority vote, can bring charges against the president. This is called **impeachment**. If the vote passes, the president must face trial in the Senate. Two-thirds of the Senate must declare the president guilty of the charges in order to remove him from office.

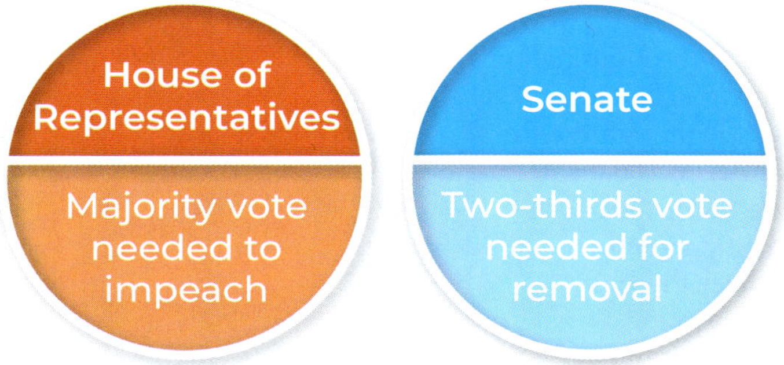

The Constitution states that the basis for removal is "conviction of . . . treason, bribery, or other high crimes and misdemeanors" (Article II, Section 4, of the Constitution). On February 24, 1868, the House voted 126–47 to impeach Johnson on eleven charges. The president's trial began on March 13 and lasted until May 26. As stipulated in the Constitution, Chief Justice Salmon P. Chase presided. Johnson never attended the trial. He believed that he had done nothing wrong and that his attendance would only lend credibility to his accusers.

Senators could not agree. Was the Tenure of Office Act constitutional? Even if it was, did it apply in Stanton's case? Stanton was, after all, Lincoln's appointee before the Tenure of Office Act was passed. The real issue was that Radicals were trying to get rid of the president because they disagreed with him politically. He had committed no crime, nor had he violated the Constitution. Removing a president for political reasons would set a dangerous precedent. Some senators, including some who disliked Johnson, realized that danger.

If Johnson were removed, Benjamin Wade would become president. Wade was the president pro tempore of the Senate and one of the most extreme Radicals. (Johnson had no vice president, so according to the law at the time, the president pro tempore of the Senate was next in line. In 1947 the law was changed to make the Speaker of the House the next in line after the vice president.)

When the final vote was taken, thirty-five senators voted to convict Johnson. Nineteen voted to acquit him. The Radicals were one vote short of the two-thirds needed to remove Johnson. His presidency was preserved, but his reputation was never the same. Years later, the Supreme Court declared the Tenure of Office Act unconstitutional.

▲ The Senate's sergeant at arms (at left) presents Andrew Johnson with notification of the president's forthcoming impeachment trial.

Johnson after the Presidency

After finishing his term of office in March 1869, Johnson returned to Tennessee. In 1875, he was elected to the US Senate. He is the only former president to serve in that body after leaving the White House.

He took the oath for his new position in March 1875. In late July, he suffered a stroke and died a few days later. He is buried in Greeneville, Tennessee.

Ulysses S. Grant

18

Born	April 27, 1822
Died	July 23, 1885
Home state	Illinois (born in Ohio)
Wife	Julia Boggs Dent
Church	Methodist
Occupations	soldier, farmer, clerk
Party	Republican
Years served as president	1869–77
Terms	2
Vice presidents	1st—Schuyler Colfax 2nd—Henry Wilson

President Ulysses S. Grant

By 1868 Andrew Johnson had lost almost all his influence with Republicans. That year, the party chose war hero Ulysses S. Grant as their presidential candidate. The Democrats were still hampered by both their ties to Civil War issues and the fact that Radical Republicans were in control of Reconstruction.

Grant was victorious over the Democrats' candidate, New York governor Horatio Seymour. Almost six million popular votes were cast, and Grant won by 300,000. A half-million black voters cast ballots for the first time for a president, and they overwhelmingly supported the former general.

The Fifteenth Amendment

The Radical Republicans had long sought to secure voting rights for black Northerners. However, as late as 1868, only about half of the Northern states had legalized black suffrage. Although the Reconstruction Act of 1867 stated that new state constitutions in the South must guarantee adult black males the right to vote, Radicals knew those constitutions could later be changed. Many moderate Republicans wished to avoid the controversial issue of black voting rights. But when it became clear that Grant would not have won the election without black voters, Radicals were able to convince moderates to support the **Fifteenth Amendment**. That amendment kept states from denying the vote to any citizen "on account of race, color, or previous condition of servitude." It was approved by Congress in 1869 and received approval from enough states to take effect the next year.

▲ Former slaves voting

Scandals

Grant lacked political experience and soon learned that leading a nation is quite different from leading an army. Nevertheless, Grant was elected to a second term in 1872.

During his eight years in office, numerous scandals occurred. Most were the result of greed and involved a number of his friends and appointees. Those individuals took advantage of his position to personally enrich themselves. There is no evidence that Grant himself personally profited from any of the fraud or that he was involved in any of the illegal activities. However, his poor choice of friends and associates as well as his lack of good judgment were evident and resulted in widespread criticism. For example, he was often reluctant

Fun Fact

Ulysses S. Grant's memoirs were published by Mark Twain and became a bestseller.

One of the scandals during the Grant Administration involved whiskey manufacturers. They bribed government officials to avoid paying millions in taxes. The scandal became known as the Whiskey Ring.

to dismiss ineffective officials. And when corruption among office-holders was uncovered, the president often avoided prosecuting the guilty. Rather, he allowed them to resign. He believed that prosecution would only further divide the nation. Unfortunately, the Grant administration was one of the most scandal-ridden of any American president.

Successes

For many years, historians ranked Grant as one of the worst American presidents. Recently, however, some scholars have re-examined his actions and argued that his successes have often been overlooked.

Indeed, Grant did defend the political rights of African Americans. In his second inaugural address, he mentioned that freedmen still were not being given the rights of citizenship that were lawfully theirs. He signed legislation to combat the Ku Klux Klan, a group that used violence against blacks.

Though some of Grant's appointees were poor choices, others proved very capable in their positions. For example, his first secretary of the treasury, who served from 1869 to 1873, improved tax collection procedures and made other reforms that led to reducing the country's debt by more than $12 million (worth twenty times that amount today). Benjamin Bristow, who served as secretary of the treasury from 1874 to 1876, dismissed hundreds of incompetent people during his first eleven months in office. He also successfully had prosecuted more than two hundred people involved with the theft of millions of dollars in tax money. One of Grant's attorneys general vigorously fought corruption in New York City.

President Grant sympathized with the problems facing Indian tribes and took some steps to improve treatment of Native Americans. While some have praised those efforts, others have noted they fell far short of what was needed.

SECTION REVIEW 15.3

1. How were the Radicals in Congress able to pass legislation over the president's veto?
2. What agency did Congress create to assist former slaves in locating jobs and to establish schools and hospitals for them?
3. State in your own words what the Fourteenth Amendment said regarding citizenship, representation in Congress, those who had supported the Confederacy, and Confederate debts.
4. Into how many military districts did the Reconstruction Act of 1867 divide the South?
5. Why do you think many black leaders did not want to restrict voting and holding office from former Confederates?
6. How were carpetbaggers and scalawags different? How were they similar?
7. What was the real reason Radicals impeached President Johnson? Why was this a problem?
8. What amendment prohibited denying the vote to any citizen "on account of race, color, or previous condition of servitude"?
9. Why is Grant's administration often viewed negatively?

GUIDING QUESTIONS

- What was the goal of the Redeemers?
- How did Rutherford B. Hayes become president?

◂ Joseph Rainey

Hiram R. Revels ▸

Rutherford B. Hayes

Born	October 4, 1822	19
Died	January 17, 1893	
Home state	Ohio	
Wife	Lucy Ware Webb	
Church	none	
Occupation	lawyer	
Party	Republican	
Years served as president	1877–81	
Terms	1	
Vice president	William A. Wheeler	

15.4 RECONSTRUCTION AND THE REDEEMERS

How did the Redeemers impact Reconstruction?

The Redeemers

Attitudes toward Reconstruction were changing. By the 1870s many Northerners had lost interest in the fate of African Americans in the South. They were more concerned about the return to economic prosperity. Others were more interested in the West—in its opportunities for expansion and the Indian wars taking place there. Many Northerners thought that it would be better to abandon black people than to lose the whole country to the turmoil created by some of the Radical Republicans. They believed that peace in the South would be better for business. The country was tired of scandal and controversy. Meanwhile, Congress passed the Amnesty Act of 1872. It pardoned all but a few hundred former Confederate leaders and thus allowed those individuals to hold government offices.

Until this time, a number of blacks, often from the North, participated in Southern politics. By the mid-1870s, six hundred blacks served as state legislators; hundreds more held local offices, including working as judges; and more than a dozen were elected to Congress. Joseph Rainey of South Carolina was the first black man elected to the US House of Representatives. Hiram R. Revels of Mississippi was the first black man elected to the US Senate.

Although African Americans had gained some rights, most white Southerners did not wish to accept blacks as their social or legal equals. Black Republicans were able to maintain political offices for a while, but in some parts of the South they were still beaten, expelled from towns, or even killed by angry white Southerners.

The growing disinterest of many Northerners in Reconstruction and the passage of the Amnesty Act paved the way for the emergence of a group of Southern whites who became known as "**Redeemers**." They wanted to redeem, or save, the South and its culture by overthrowing blacks and other Republicans who held offices.

Republicans soon found they could not match the organization and experience of the Redeemers. Furthermore, Redeemers and their followers sometimes used violence and intimidation to gain support. Consequently, Southern voters began electing white Democrats to replace black officials and other Republicans. Only in areas still occupied by federal troops were Radical Republican governments able to retain power. But even President Grant was growing more reluctant to use troops to quell violence and keep Republicans in power.

The Disputed Election of 1876

While Grant's administration suffered from scandals at the national level, state and local corruption also existed. As a result, both major political parties chose reformers as their candidates in the 1876 presidential election. Democrat **Samuel J. Tilden**, former governor of New York, won the popular vote. The Electoral College vote was 184 for Tilden and 165 for his Republican opponent, **Rutherford B. Hayes**, who had served as governor of Ohio. But the results

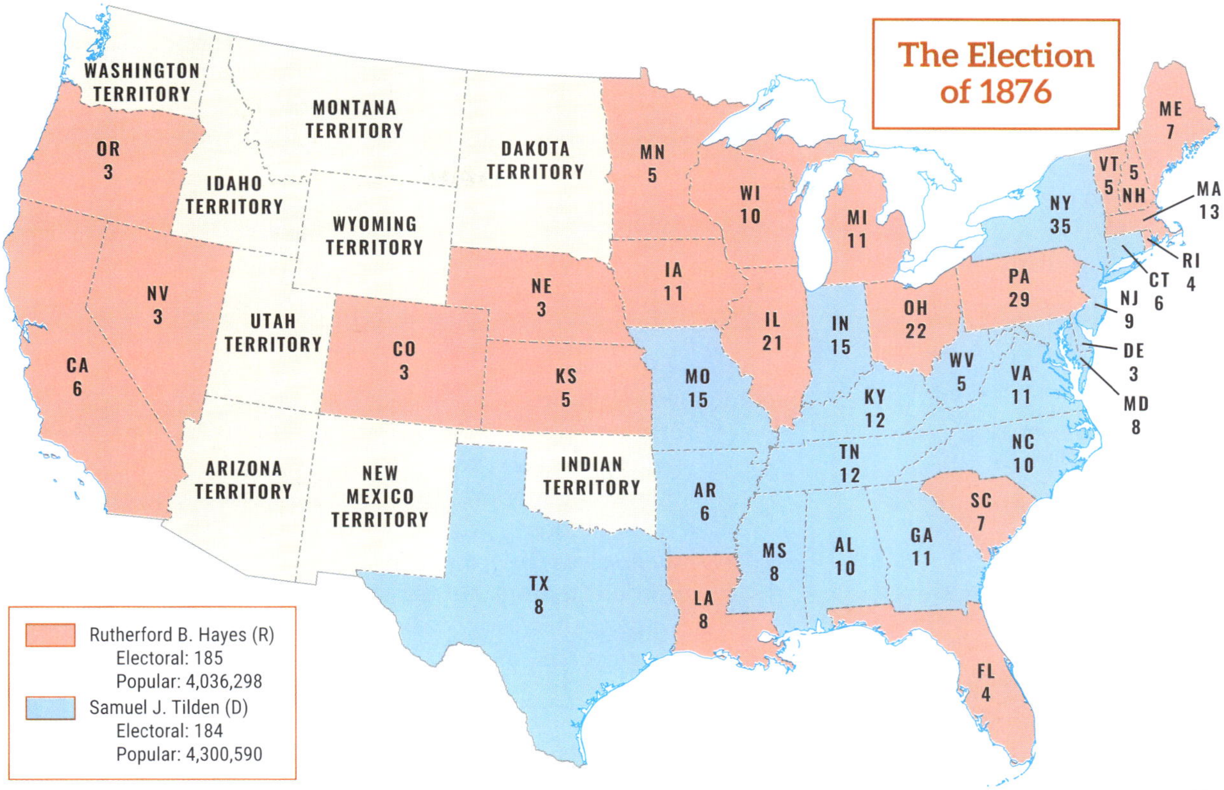

in three Southern states—Florida, Louisiana, and South Carolina—each occupied by federal troops, were disputed. Both sides claimed victory in those states, and accusations of election fraud were made. Republicans knew that if Hayes could win the disputed states, he would then win the Electoral College by one vote, 185 to 184.

To resolve the dispute, Congress named a fifteen-member special commission: five senators, five representatives, and five Supreme Court justices. Eight commissioners were Republican and seven were Democrat. Each commission member sided with his political party in settling the dispute. Thus, by a vote of eight to seven, all disputed electoral votes were awarded to Hayes, and the Electoral College vote was 185 for Hayes and 184 for Tilden. It is difficult to determine which candidate deserved to be elected. Voting corruption by both parties had occurred.

As expected, the Democrats contested the commission's decision. They threatened to prevent the official counting of the electoral votes in Congress so that Hayes could not take office. The deadlock was broken, however, when a group of Southern Democrats secretly met with Republicans to make a deal. They agreed that Republicans would withdraw the last federal troops from the South, and the Democrats would accept the election of Hayes and the Reconstruction amendments (the Thirteenth, Fourteenth, and Fifteenth Amendments) to the Constitution.

Although the Republicans won the presidency in 1876, the election was the final blow to Radical Reconstruction. In April 1877, the month after Hayes took office, he withdrew the last troops from the South. Troops were no longer present to monitor elections. The Democrats soon replaced Republicans who were in power. With the military gone and white Southern Democrats back in control in the South, Reconstruction effectively ended.

Samuel J. Tilden ▸

SECTION REVIEW 15.4

1. What were the Redeemers trying to save? How did they want to do this?
2. What deal did Republicans make with Democrats to accept the election of Rutherford B. Hayes as president?
3. What effect did the removal of Union troops have on the South?
4. Contrast the term *redeem* as used in the Bible and as used by Southern Democrats. Was the term used appropriately in the South? Why or why not?

GUIDING QUESTIONS

- How did the Southern economy change during Reconstruction?
- What effect did the Ku Klux Klan and civil rights legislation have on the South during Reconstruction?
- How effective was Reconstruction?

15.5 RECOVERY IN THE SOUTH

How did the South recover after the Civil War?

The problems of the South during Reconstruction and efforts to solve them molded Southern life, affecting the South's economy, political organization, and people.

The Southern Economy during Reconstruction

Because the war had destroyed the South's plantation system, the freedmen were without jobs. Some freedmen hoped that the government would seize the old plantations and from those lands give every freed slave "forty acres and a mule." Some politicians supported such a plan, but it was not passed. Without jobs, many former slaves were unable to support themselves. To grow crops in the South, farm owners needed laborers, but they had no money to pay workers. To meet the needs of Southern agriculture, many people began sharecropping.

▾ African Americans working in a Georgia cotton field

Sharecropping

Blacks, as well as poor whites, became involved in this new economic system. **Sharecroppers** farmed small plots owned by planters and gave a portion, or share, of the crop to the planter. This rental payment was for use of the land. Since sharecroppers had little money, especially at the beginning of the season, they borrowed money for seed and provisions. Often, the landlord was their creditor. Landlords sometimes also owned local stores. At harvest, each sharecropper "squared up," or settled his

account, with the creditor. If the sharecropper broke even, he was fortunate. But he often started the next season in debt since interest rates could be extremely high.

The average sharecropper rarely showed a profit. As a result, he was locked into a cycle of debt and poverty. He had little chance of breaking free from the cycle. For many freedmen, sharecropping seemed to be merely another form of slavery. Under such conditions, the right to vote provided little comfort. Most sharecroppers struggled just to put food on their tables.

Industry

Near the end of Reconstruction, the Industrial Revolution began to have a greater impact on the South. Southerners had little money for investing, but many Northerners had money and an eagerness to invest in railroads, steel production, and textile industries that were expanding in the South. The industries needed workers. In what became known as the "**New South**," many Southerners moved from rural areas to factory towns and cities for industrial jobs. The South's economy boomed. Southerners hoped the New South would rival the North as an economic force.

One new feature of Southern industry was the **mill town**. Mill towns had some of the same features as plantations. The owners or investors built the workers' housing, usually rows of identical houses, near the factories or mills. In addition, they often built churches, schools, and doctors' offices in these company towns. They also built company stores, where workers could buy such necessities as food and clothing. Generally, employers in the textile industry hired whole families. If parents wanted to be hired, they had to agree that their children would also work in the mill. Loom makers lowered the heights of their looms so that children could operate them. Similar towns for such industries as coal mining developed in both the North and South.

During the Civil War, one of the Confederacy's major manufacturing centers was Columbus, Georgia. Located about 100 miles south of Atlanta, parts of the city were destroyed during the fighting. During Reconstruction, many of its factories were rebuilt and new ones constructed. It is shown below in the late 1860s.

Political Trends during Reconstruction

The prosperity of the nation during Reconstruction helped the Republicans retain control of the presidency and usually Congress. Republicans sometimes used a technique called "waving the bloody shirt." It was an attempt to appeal to voters by blaming the Civil War on Democrats and thereby urging them to vote for Republicans. However, most white Southerners blamed the war, the hardships of Reconstruction, and black political participation on Republicans, so they generally supported Democrats.

Reforms in the South

Before the war, the South collected few taxes for public purposes. During Radical Reconstruction, however, both taxes and spending increased. Many people criticized the high spending by Southern state governments. Others believed the spending was justified. They noted that, for the first time, Southern states began providing free public education. They also pointed to the improved prison systems, care for people with mental and physical disabilities, and the abolition of imprisonment for debt. But many states went deeply into debt from such spending, and some of the tax money was wasted or stolen by corrupt politicians.

Members of the Ku Klux Klan wrapped themselves in sheets to disguise themselves as ghosts. They threatened and terrorized African Americans as well as white Southerners who did not support the Klan's views.

The Ku Klux Klan

In 1866 some former Confederate soldiers formed a secret organization called the **Ku Klux Klan** (**KKK**). Many of them were determined to place black people firmly under white control. They targeted successful black businessmen and landowners. They also intimidated white people who did business with black businesses. Sometimes simply dressing well was enough to make a black person the target of a beating. Often black schools and churches were burned to prohibit gatherings of black people and to prevent them from gaining the education needed to become self-sufficient. Sometimes, African American landowners were driven from their land.

The Klan also targeted black officeholders and white Republican leaders. Black men who participated in state constitutional conventions or were elected to office were sometimes beaten or killed. The violence disrupted or destroyed the Republican Party in parts of the South. Party leaders occasionally had to flee for their safety. In other parts of the South, the bloodshed made it impossible for Republicans, white or black, to run for office or even vote.

Many Southerners, both those who approved of and those who disapproved of Klan violence, wanted to "redeem" the South from black and Northern rule. When the Redeemers came to power, the Republican Party declined quickly in the South. For a century, most Southerners voted solidly for Democratic candidates, earning the region the nickname "Solid South."

The KKK included many prominent citizens, and this fact added to the Klan's power. Many white citizens who disliked the violence of the Klan did not voice their concerns publicly. Testifying against Klan members in court would make the witness a target for Klan violence. While fear was one motivation for silence, other whites secretly approved of the KKK's goals and thus chose not to denounce their intimidating and brutal methods.

Hundreds of freedmen were lynched (executed, often by hanging, without a legal trial). Many of them were dragged from their homes at night and killed in the presence of their families. Because local law enforcement could not or would not deal with the Klan, Congress acted. It passed the Enforcement Act in 1870, the Ku Klux Klan Act in 1871, and other laws that outlawed using force to prevent people from voting. These measures also gave President Grant the power to place federal troops at polling places to ensure everyone's voting rights.

Eventually, hundreds of Klansmen were arrested for their actions. Though the Klan's power was greatly diminished, it was not destroyed. In addition, small groups or individuals continued violent activities, though on a smaller scale. The Klan later reemerged in the twentieth century.

Civil Rights

As mentioned earlier in the chapter, Congress passed the Civil Rights Act of 1866. It provided full citizenship for blacks and all the privileges of citizenship, or civil rights. These rights were guaranteed regardless of local laws. A second act, the Civil Rights Act of 1875, guaranteed equal treatment for African Americans in public transportation and in public places, such as inns and theaters. It also said that blacks could serve on juries. But the bill did not provide a means to enforce the law. The Supreme Court further weakened the legislation in 1883 when it declared that some provisions of the bill were unconstitutional.

The years passed, and concern for the rights of black people continued to decline. As Redeemers gained control, they made it difficult for blacks to vote by requiring special voting fees called *poll taxes*. Literacy tests, often unfairly administered, were also designed to disqualify black voters. Furthermore, laws similar to the black codes were introduced, and the civil rights acts were no longer enforced. African Americans found little political equality.

a TRAGIC FACT

Over two thousand black people were lynched during the Reconstruction years.

▾ In the cartoon, a white Southerner threatens to use a whip against an African American.

▲ In late April 1877, federal troops who had monitored Reconstruction were withdrawn from Louisiana (above). These were the last such troops located in the South. With this action, Reconstruction officially ended.

Results of Reconstruction

Reconstruction was a difficult period in American history. Black Americans were struggling to overcome black codes and violence and take their place as free and equal citizens. Many white Southerners were embittered by the changes thrust upon them and struggled to rebuild a devastated region while being treated as a conquered nation. Many Northerners were unhappy with or unconcerned about Reconstruction.

Many of the social advances during Reconstruction were soon discarded. Though steps were taken toward providing civil rights for black Americans, they did not become permanent. As we have seen, when white Southerners regained control of state governments, many of the blacks' civil rights were eliminated. But, even in the North, few white people were willing to give black citizens significant social and political power.

Another result of the Civil War and Reconstruction was the development of a stronger, more centralized federal government. Though many in the South objected to this expansion of power, it occurred largely because local and state governments in the former Confederacy failed to prevent the unjust treatment of black Americans and Southern Unionists. Remember that one of the primary biblical purposes of government is to ensure justice.

Historian Richard M. Weaver favored this description of Reconstruction, written by black newspaper editor Richard Harvey Cain of Charleston, South Carolina: "When the smoke and fighting is over, the Negroes have nothing gained, the whites have nothing left, while the jackals [scavengers] have all the booty [plunder]."

SECTION REVIEW 15.5

1. What new system arose because freedmen had no land to farm and white farm owners had no money to pay workers? How did this system work?
2. Why did this new system sometimes seem like another form of slavery?
3. In what kind of community did Southern factory workers sometimes live? What did the owners provide? Who was usually hired?
4. What was "waving the bloody shirt"?
5. How did the activities of the Ku Klux Klan affect the civil rights of blacks? How did Congress respond?
6. How did the positive effects of Reconstruction soon dwindle?

CHAPTER 15 REVIEW

Making Connections

1. What three groups wanted to control Reconstruction efforts?
2. How long did Reconstruction technically last?
3. Under what two presidents did Presidential Reconstruction occur?
4. Why did Lincoln veto the Wade-Davis Bill?
5. How many Southern states gave voting rights to blacks under Johnson's plan?
6. How did the black codes lead moderate Republicans to join the Radical Republicans?
7. What were some of the mocking names the press gave Alaska?
8. Who led the Radical Republicans in the House of Representatives? Who led in the Senate?
9. What were two of the powers granted to the Freedmen's Bureau after a year of existence?
10. Congressional Reconstruction was often called _____ Reconstruction after Congress reconvened in 1867.
11. What were the five parts of the Reconstruction Act of 1867?
12. Why did some Northerners go south during Reconstruction?
13. Why did senators disagree about whether the firing of Edwin Stanton should lead to Johnson's removal from office?
14. How many senators were needed to remove Johnson from office in his impeachment trial? How many voted against him?
15. What Civil War hero became president after Johnson?
16. Why did Grant often not prosecute those involved in scandals? How did he work to help African Americans?
17. Why were Democrats willing to accept that Rutherford B. Hayes won the election of 1876?

Thinking Critically

18. Is Reconstruction a good name for the time after the Civil War? Why or why not?
19. Do you agree with Radical Republicans who believed that it was wrong for the leaders of the rebellion against the government to be allowed to return to power? Why or why not?
20. Why do you think those whose taxable property was worth more than $20,000 were excluded from group amnesty?

Living as a Christian Citizen

21. Black codes were harsh, restrictive laws that placed African Americans in an inferior position and kept them in a condition similar to slavery. Imagine that you lived at this time; write a letter seeking to persuade a legislator to take a biblical approach to these laws (Acts 10:34; Gen. 1:26–28; James 3:9; Matt. 22:36–40; Gal. 3:26–28).
22. Create a table (like the one shown here) to evaluate the two phases of Reconstruction and the Redeemers in each box.

	Justice	Freedom	Equality
Presidential Reconstruction			
Congressional Reconstruction			
Redeemers			

Terms to Remember

- Reconstruction
- freedmen
- Presidential Reconstruction
- Ten Percent Plan
- Radical Republicans
- Wade-Davis Bill
- amnesty
- Thirteenth Amendment
- black codes
- Congressional Reconstruction
- William Seward
- Thaddeus Stevens
- Charles Sumner
- Freedmen's Bureau
- Fourteenth Amendment
- Radical Reconstruction
- Reconstruction Act of 1867
- carpetbaggers
- scalawag
- Tenure of Office Act
- Edwin Stanton
- impeachment
- Fifteenth Amendment
- Redeemers
- Samuel J. Tilden
- Rutherford B. Hayes
- sharecroppers
- New South
- mill town
- Ku Klux Klan (KKK)

UNIT

5 Expanding the Nation

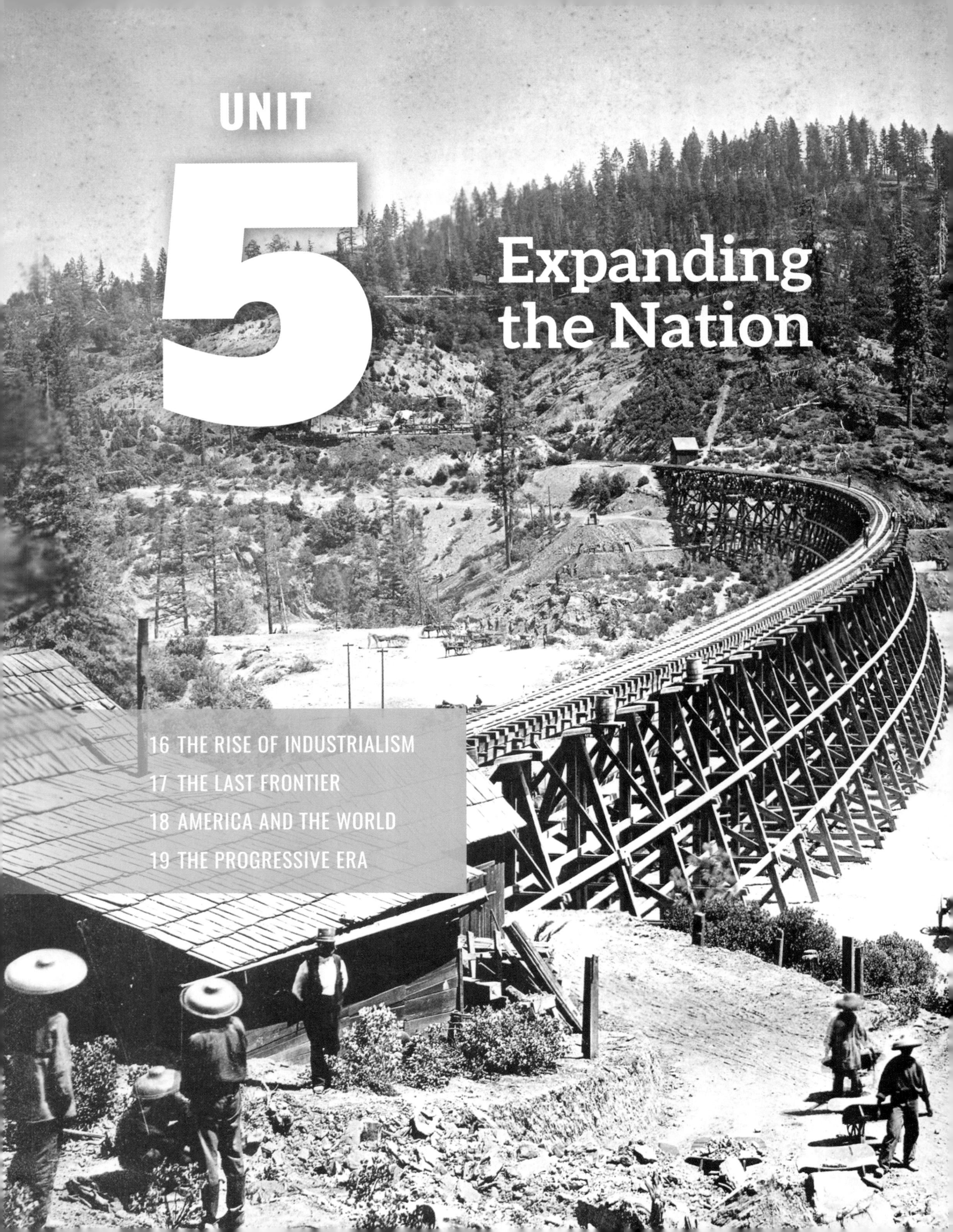

Homestead Act — 1862

1869 — Transcontinental railroad completed

Invention of the telephone — 1876

1887 — Dawes Act; Interstate Commerce Act

Oklahoma Land Rush — 1889

1890 — Sherman Antitrust Act

Spanish-American War; Acquisition of Hawaii — 1898

1903 — Wright brothers' first flight

Opening of the Panama Canal — 1914

United States enters World War I — 1917

World War I
1914-1918

1920 — Prohibition begins

This trestle bridge was built by the Central Pacific Railroad in California during the 1860s.

CHAPTER 16

The Rise of Industrialism

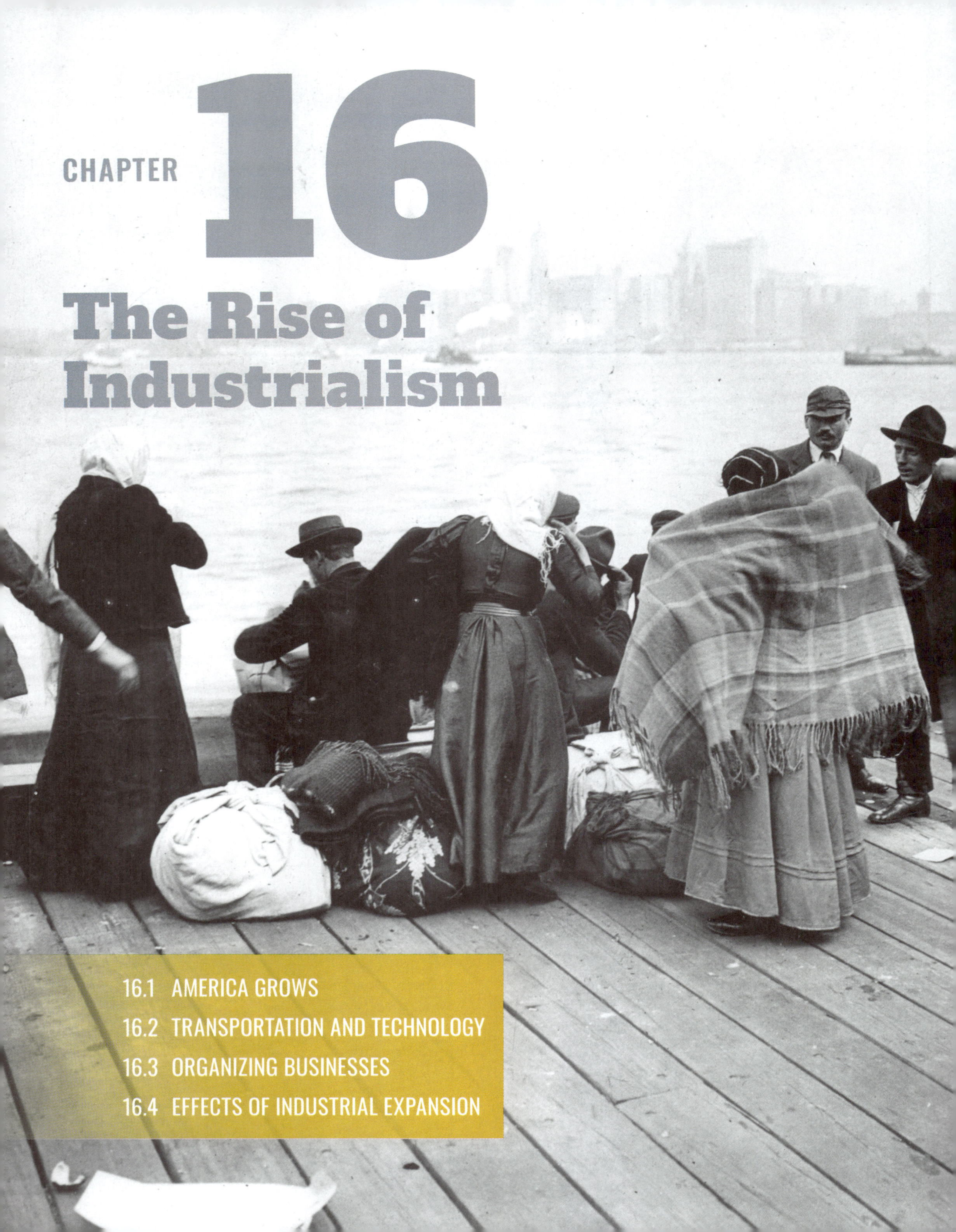

16.1 AMERICA GROWS

How did natural resources and immigration influence America?

GUIDING QUESTIONS

- What presidents were in office during the expansion of industrialization?
- How did the abundance of natural resources help America grow economically?
- Why did immigrants come to America?

As the nineteenth century began, America was a quiet land. It consisted of family farms, small villages, and some cities near the Atlantic coast. Only four cities had more than 25,000 residents—New York City (with approximately 60,000) was the largest, followed by Philadelphia, Baltimore, and Boston.

After the Civil War, the industrial strength of the North set the pattern for the expansion to come. By the end of the century, crowded cities, busy factories, and mechanized farms spanned the country. As technology and industry developed, the percentage of Americans living in rural areas declined. Although most people still lived in rural areas, the number living in urban areas was steadily increasing.

America's population swelled. In 1800 it had been less than 5.5 million. The 1870 census showed the population was almost 40 million. By 1910 it had reached 92 million. The birthrate was high, but a major reason for the population growth was immigration.

The land area of the United States was also growing. In 1800 the country consisted of only sixteen states. After the purchase of Alaska in 1867, little geographic growth occurred. Hawaii, Puerto Rico, and a few other small areas were added in the last years of the nineteenth century. But by 1900, there were forty-five states.

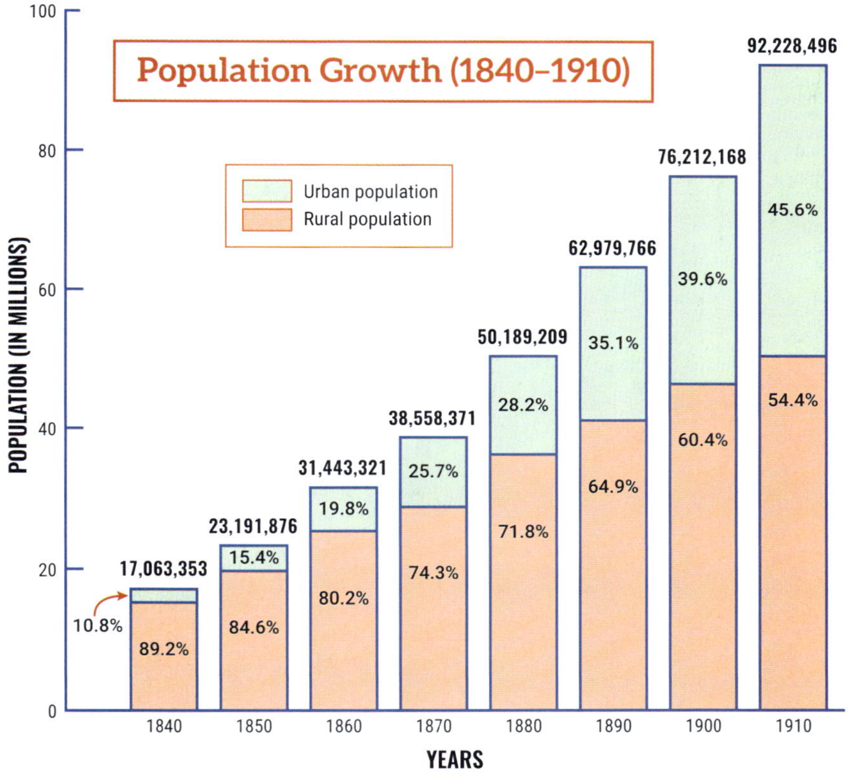

The country and its people were uniquely suited for large-scale industrial projects. The United States was on its way to becoming the world's greatest industrial power. The values cherished by Americans made this growth possible. The United States' free economy gave businesses opportunities to succeed, and its individualism helped ingenious people develop new industrial techniques.

But the nation's industrial growth also led to conflicts about values. The period from the 1870s to about 1900 is often called the **Gilded Age** ("gilded" refers to something covered with a thin layer of gold). The term, based on Mark Twain's novel of that name, describes a period in which all appeared well but beneath the surface lay serious problems. For example, while success in industry allowed a few to become extremely wealthy, many people remained poor.

The power of large businesses became controversial during the Gilded Age. Previous generations defended freedom by limiting the power of government. Now some thought the government needed to protect freedom by limiting powerful businesses. Whether business or government was the bigger threat to freedom became a matter of intense controversy.

◂ Immigrants arriving in New York City

James Garfield

Born	November 19, 1831	20
Died	September 19, 1881	
Home state	Ohio	
Wife	Lucretia Rudolph	
Church	Disciples of Christ	
Occupations	carpenter, teacher, lay preacher	
Party	Republican	
Years served as president	1881	
Terms	partial (assassinated)	
Vice president	Chester A. Arthur	

Chester A. Arthur

Born	October 5, 1829	21
Died	November 18, 1886	
Home state	New York (born in Vermont)	
Wife	Ellen Lewis Herndon	
Church	Episcopalian	
Occupations	teacher, lawyer	
Party	Republican	
Years served as president	1881–85	
Terms	partial (almost 1 full term)	
Vice president	none	

▲ Garfield was the second president to be assassinated.

Presidents of the Growing Nation

Garfield and Arthur

In 1880 the Republican candidate, **James Garfield**, was elected president. Unfortunately, Garfield's time in office would be shorter than any president except William Henry Harrison.

Four months after taking office, Garfield was leaving the White House to vacation on the New Jersey seashore. On July 2, 1881, he walked through the railway station in Washington, DC, to board his train. Charles Guiteau, an unsuccessful applicant for a government job, fired two shots from a revolver before being wrestled to the ground. One bullet grazed the president's shoulder. The other struck him in the back. The first doctors examined the wound in the president's back with their fingers and a metal probe. They could not find the bullet but assumed that it was somewhere in his abdomen. Garfield, in great pain, complained of numbness in his legs and feet.

Garfield was moved to the White House, and other doctors were consulted. Over a dozen examined him, most of them exploring the wound repeatedly with either their fingers or unsterilized instruments. By the time Garfield died on September 19, the doctors had turned what was initially a three-inch-deep wound into a twenty-inch-long infected gash as they repeatedly searched for the bullet. After his death, the bullet was finally located. It had narrowly missed his spinal column and come to rest behind his pancreas. Garfield had lived seventy-nine days after the shooting and had been in office a total of two hundred days.

Fun Fact

Because of his strange behavior, doctors removed Guiteau's brain (after his death) in order to study it. Parts of it are preserved in a jar at a Philadelphia museum.

Guiteau, the assassin, had a history of mental problems. He had a very minor role on the Garfield presidential campaign, but the president would not appoint him as a representative to France, a position Guiteau thought he deserved. At his trial, he claimed that the president's doctors, not he, were responsible for the president's death. Nevertheless, the jury found him guilty of murder, and he was hanged on June 30, 1882.

The death of Garfield made clear what many had been arguing—the civil service (government employee) system needed reform. **Chester A. Arthur**, Garfield's vice president, called upon Congress to make needed changes when he became the nation's leader.

In January 1883 Arthur signed the Pendleton Act. It provided for the elimination of much of the spoils system, where political offices were awarded based on loyalty to a political party or politician. Instead, appointment to many federal government jobs would now be given to those who passed civil service examinations. The **Civil Service Commission** would oversee this new system. Within a few years, about 12 percent of the federal offices were filled using these new procedures, and that number steadily continued to increase.

Cleveland, Harrison, and Cleveland Again

In the 1884 presidential election, Republicans bypassed Arthur and nominated James G. Blaine of Maine. Blaine's candidacy was hurt by allegations that he had been involved in scandals. Democrats nominated New York's former governor **Grover Cleveland**, noted for his honesty and for fighting corruption.

The 1884 election was a spirited, hard-fought event better remembered for its mudslinging than for any issues that were debated. Cleveland won a narrow victory. Had Blaine won the extremely close race in New York—he lost there by only a thousand votes of more than a million cast—he would have won the election. Cleveland's election was the first Democratic presidential victory in twenty-eight years.

The Democrats renominated the popular Cleveland in 1888. The Republicans nominated Indiana's **Benjamin Harrison**. He was the grandson of President William Henry Harrison, a fact the Republicans loudly proclaimed. Cleveland won more popular votes, but Harrison won more electoral votes and hence the presidential election.

The next presidential election, in 1892, was a rematch between Benjamin Harrison and Grover Cleveland. Former president Cleveland made a former president of Harrison by recapturing the White House with a clear victory. Cleveland is the only president to serve two nonconsecutive terms. He had been the twenty-second president, and in 1893 he became the twenty-fourth president.

Did you know?

Because Grover Cleveland was both the 22nd and 24th presidents, there is some confusion today. For example, although Ronald Reagan is listed as the 40th president, he was the 39th person to occupy the position.

Grover Cleveland

22 | 24

Born	March 18, 1837
Died	June 24, 1908
Home state	New York (born in New Jersey)
Wife	Frances Folsom
Church	Presbyterian
Occupation	lawyer
Party	Democrat
Years served as president	1885–89 and 1893–97
Terms	2 nonconsecutive
Vice presidents	1st—Thomas A. Hendricks 2nd—Adlai E. Stevenson

Benjamin Harrison

23

Born	August 20, 1833
Died	March 13, 1901
Home state	Indiana (born in Ohio)
Wives	1st—Caroline Scott 2nd—Mary Dimmick
Church	Presbyterian
Occupation	lawyer
Party	Republican
Years served as president	1889–93
Terms	1
Vice president	Levi P. Morton

▲ Logging became a big business. A sled of logs is shown in Michigan in 1899.

Natural Resources

The United States was able to achieve rapid industrial growth in the nineteenth century for several reasons. Two of the most important were the abundance of natural resources and a strong labor force.

America's republican form of government, strong religious and moral foundation for decisions and actions, and free-enterprise system were ideal for developing those natural resources (raw materials). New minerals were discovered, and regions that had been inaccessible before were opened by new means of transportation. Great lodes (deposits) of gold, silver, and copper were found in the Rocky Mountains, the Far West, and Alaska. The rich iron-ore deposits of northern Minnesota provided raw materials for the growing iron and steel industries. Additional petroleum and coal deposits were discovered and used to fuel expanding industries.

Waterpower proved helpful in producing electricity. And the vast forests covering the Northwest and other areas of the country supplied timber for lumber, pulp, and other uses.

Immigration

A nation's greatest resource is its people. In the second half of the nineteenth century, developing industries needed workers. Most of the American population was hard at work, but to expand its industrial production, the country needed even more laborers. The growing tide of immigrants met that need.

Getting to America

▼ Immigrants could bring with them only what they could wear, carry, or afford to ship.

For the majority of the nineteenth century, most of the immigrants came from northwestern European countries, such as Britain, Ireland, Germany, and the nations of Scandinavia. They crossed the Atlantic by the shortest and cheapest routes. Many traveled first to Liverpool, England, or to Bremen or Hamburg, Germany, where the major steamship companies were located. Those companies often used freighters, or cargo-carrying vessels, to transport passengers to the United States. When returning to Europe, the freighters carried raw materials or manufactured goods. Those who did travel on passenger ships normally purchased the cheapest tickets. Their accommodations were located in the noisiest, most-crowded part of the ships, located below deck near the engine and the rudder. Passengers brought their food with them in their bundles. Seasickness or disease often made voyages miserable experiences, and some immigrants lost their lives. People from different countries and walks of life, who spoke different languages, were thrown together under strange conditions.

Some immigrants had been recruited in their homelands by agents of various American companies that needed laborers. These companies made contracts with the immigrants. The companies agreed to pay the immigrants' fares if the immigrants would work a specified length of time for the companies. Other immigrants used most of their life savings to come to America, while others had tickets that had been purchased by relatives who had come to America earlier.

Because recent immigrants were usually happy just to have a job, they were generally willing to work for lower wages than other Americans received. They saw their jobs as a way of advancing, which was often impossible in their home countries. Immigrants who complained about hours or conditions risked losing their jobs because there were always newcomers waiting to be hired. Employers also liked to hire immigrants because most of them worked hard and were reluctant to join labor unions.

Did you know?

Prior to the 1890s, the official immigration center and main point of entry into New York City was Castle Garden. It had been an old fort and was later the site of the New York City Aquarium for 45 years.

Ellis Island and Ports of Entry

The largest number of European immigrants entered America through **Ellis Island** in New York Harbor to undergo admission procedures. Those who appeared healthy enough to hold a job and who could prove that they had the means to reach distant destinations usually took a ferry from the island to New Jersey and rode a train inland. Others traveled by ferry to New York City. Public Health Service doctors assisted the immigrants who were ill. If these immigrants could be cured, they were treated and sent on their way as soon as possible.

The immigration center at Ellis Island operated from 1892 to 1954 and handled the entry of more than 12 million immigrants. The one-day record for immigrants processed occurred on April 17, 1907, when 11,747 went through the system.

Most immigrants stayed at Ellis Island for an average of only three to five hours. About 20 percent of them had problems or questions that required them to stay overnight in dormitory-like facilities until their cases could be resolved. Immigrants often feared being denied entry into the country, but of the millions who came, more than 98 percent were admitted.

Some immigrants landed in Montreal; others, especially the Irish, entered at Boston. Baltimore and Philadelphia were also major arrival ports. New Orleans was a port of entry for many immigrants who planned to go to the Midwest or the Far West.

Immigrants often settled in neighborhoods where others of their nationality lived. Some of those neighborhoods came to be known by such names as Chinatown or Little Italy. In later years, after immigrants had learned English and saved enough money, many of them moved to other areas of their city or the suburbs, leaving inner cities to be occupied by newer immigrants.

▾ Millions of immigrants were processed at Ellis Island.

WELCOME to AMERICA

After 1886, as ships of immigrants entered New York City's harbor, one of the first sights they saw was the Statue of Liberty. At the base of the monument is a plaque engraved with the poem "The New Colossus" by Emma Lazarus, which includes these famous lines:

"Give me your tired, your poor,
Your huddled masses yearning to breathe free,
The wretched refuse of your teeming shore.
Send these, the homeless, tempest-tost to me,
I lift my lamp beside the golden door!"

Nationalities

Irish

A large number of the immigrants in the middle to late 1800s were Irish. In the 1840s, a potato fungus had spread across Europe. The plant disease devastated Ireland, where the potato was the major farm crop and food. About one-eighth of Ireland's population died of starvation or from diseases caused by malnutrition. Approximately one-fourth, or two million, left the country. Many of them came to the United States, settling primarily in Boston and New York City.

The Irish played important roles in the construction of America's transportation systems. An early group of Irish immigrants helped build the Erie Canal, which opened in 1825. Later, crews of Irishmen were responsible for laying the tracks for western railroads. The Irish took these jobs despite a high risk of injury because they saw the jobs as a means to escape poverty. Other Irish Americans sought altogether different work as police officers or firefighters. Some Irish women became teachers or domestic servants.

▲ Irish immigrants

Germans and Scandinavians

In addition to the Irish, other northern Europeans came to America. Political and religious unrest swept the German states during the 1840s. As a result, many Germans fled Europe. Some had been landowners there, so they had enough money to buy land in the United States when they arrived. They often settled in the farming areas of America's heartland, such as Indiana, Ohio, and Wisconsin. Others worked as lumberjacks in the northern woods, saved money, and then bought farmland.

Scandinavians—Norwegians, Swedes, Danes, and Finns—who came to America tended to settle whole towns or counties in Minnesota, Iowa, Wisconsin, and the Dakotas. They had their own newspapers and started their own colleges. Most were Lutheran. Some had come to America to protest the policies of the state-sponsored church back home. Some Scandinavians worked in logging camps; others worked in the iron mines of northern Minnesota or the copper mines of Michigan.

German (left) and Chinese (below) immigrants

Chinese

Many Chinese people also immigrated to America. American ships trading with China spread news of the 1848 discovery of gold in California. Because parts of China were overpopulated and frequently faced floods and famines, many were attracted to America. Opportunities in the California goldfields brought them to America in great numbers. Instead of mining for gold themselves, the Chinese often established service businesses, such as restaurants and laundries. Later, Chinese workers were hired to construct western sections of the first transcontinental railroad.

Chinese immigrants continued to come to the United States. As long as jobs were available, Americans did not object very much. But when the nation's economic growth slowed, many became hostile. Californians claimed that the Chinese, who were willing to work for lower wages, were getting the jobs that white people deserved. In 1882 Congress passed the **Chinese Exclusion Act**. It prohibited Chinese workers, with a few exceptions, from entering the United States for ten years. It was extended in 1892 and again in 1902. The regulation, though not always enforced, continued until 1943.

Influence on American Religion

Protestantism dominated American life before the mid-1800s. In the 1840s, the influx of Irish, who were overwhelmingly Roman Catholic, began. Change continued after 1880 when a greater proportion of immigrants came from eastern and southern Europe and from northern Russia. Only a few immigrants from these countries were Protestant. Many were Catholic, Jewish, or Eastern Orthodox.

The two largest religious groups, Protestants and Catholics, had concerns about each other. While Protestants worried about the increasing influence of the Catholic Church, some Catholics feared their children would be taught Protestant beliefs in public schools. Some within each group formed their own parochial (church-run) schools. This educational issue highlighted the difficulty of including religion in the public life of a nation that had multiple religions.

America's increasing religious pluralism (the variety of religious beliefs accepted by a society) brought problems. Such diversity of beliefs actually contributed to making the nation more secular, or less religious. Since many Americans could not agree on religious teachings, they often avoided using God's Word to settle public-policy issues. They felt pressure to ignore the Bible when dealing with matters of law and government.

SECTION REVIEW 16.1

1. Who did Charles Guiteau claim had killed the president? Who do you think was to blame? Why?
2. How did the Civil Service Commission change the spoils system?
3. What is unique about Grover Cleveland's presidency?
4. The grandson of which president served as president between Cleveland's two terms?
5. What natural resources were mined or used as fuel or power during this time?
6. At what port did most immigrants enter? What other ports also admitted large numbers of people?
7. Beginning in the 1840s, with which religions were most immigrants associated?
8. How did the rise of religious pluralism move the United States toward secularism?

GUIDING QUESTIONS

- How did the new railroads affect American industry?
- Who were important inventors during the late 1800s?

16.2 TRANSPORTATION AND TECHNOLOGY

How did transportation and technology impact industry?

Two additional factors had major impacts on the expansion of American industry—improvements in transportation and technology. Promoting the development of these features became an important national goal.

Railroads

While steamships improved transportation for trade with foreign countries and within parts of the nation, railroads enabled Americans to travel rapidly across the country's immense territory. Railroads also moved America's raw materials to distant factories and distributed manufactured goods to ready markets.

Statue of Cornelius Vanderbilt at Grand Central Station in New York City

In 1860 most railroad tracks in the United States were in the East. There were still no railroad bridges across the Hudson, Ohio, or Mississippi Rivers. Not all railroads were built with the same gauge (width between rails), so trains could not travel on all tracks. Some railroads used a narrow gauge, while others used a wider one. To get goods from one area to another required transferring them from one train to another. Such problems made it difficult to travel by rail or to send freight long distances. For example, though Chicago and New York City had rails between them, passengers and cargo had to change trains six times when traveling from one to the other. The Civil War highlighted these problems and spurred the building of more track. Perhaps the most significant change was the eventual acceptance of a standard gauge—4 feet 8 ½ inches.

Consolidation of the Railroads

One factor contributing to the development of more efficient and economical railroads was consolidation—combining small railroads with larger ones. Usually, this was done when one company purchased another one. Several men sought to develop large railroad networks. **Cornelius Vanderbilt**, who already had a steamship line on several of the Great Lakes, dreamed of connecting the Great Lakes states to New York City by rail. He convinced, sometimes by exerting great pressure, all his competitors to sell their railroads to him. Thus, he assembled a railroad empire.

Vanderbilt's success encouraged other men to build railroad empires and make their fortunes. J. Edgar Thomson quietly purchased small railroad companies in Pennsylvania and Ohio. Then, he cut his rates below his competitors' rates, putting them out of business. Then he raised his rates. Some denounced such tactics because they hurt small railroad companies; others noted that the process helped the nation acquire an efficient railroad transportation network.

Building Railroads

A second factor leading to the development of a better railroad system was government policy. As mentioned in Chapter 12, the Gadsden Purchase, negotiated with Mexico in 1853, provided some of the land needed for building a transcontinental railroad that would follow a southern route. However, during the Civil War, Congress decided that the first railroad across the continent would follow a route much farther north.

In the 1860s railroad companies began approaching Congress for the right to build the first transcontinental railroad. They also wanted the government to provide much of the money to build the tracks as well as the land on which they would build. Congress approved the **Union Pacific** and **Central Pacific** Railroads to begin construction. The Union Pacific laid track westward, starting from Omaha, Nebraska, using many Irish workers and Civil War veterans. The Central Pacific laid track eastward from Sacramento, California, primarily using Chinese laborers.

▲ Workers for the Central Pacific Railroad are shown laying track in Nevada (top). Their tracks would join with those of the Union Pacific at Promontory Point, Utah, on May 10, 1869, to complete the nation's first transcontinental railroad (bottom).

The challenges for the two companies laying a combined total of more than 1,700 miles of track were enormous. The Central Pacific faced the trial of crossing the steep Sierra Nevada. The Union Pacific had problems too. Because of the lack of wood on the prairie, most of the Union Pacific's railroad ties had to be shipped long distances. A lack of water and the danger of attacks from Plains Indian tribes also hindered the work. Nevertheless, the official "wedding of the rails" took place at Promontory Point near Ogden, Utah, on May 10, 1869. The railroad was completed with the driving of the final spike, made of gold, on that day.

The railroads received government money for each mile of track laid. In addition, the government gave each railroad company large strips of land on alternating sides of the tracks. Therefore, the companies were highly motivated to lay as much track as possible. The railroads held on to some of the lands next to their tracks. More often, however, they sold these lands to eager settlers or individuals who later resold the land.

The national government retained much land near the railroad and later sold it at low prices or made it available for free under the Homestead Act of 1862 (discussed in Chapter 17). Thus, even more settlers moved into railroad-connected regions.

Unfortunately, the immense amounts of government money for railroads invited corruption. Scandals occurred that were not discovered until years later. In their haste, the railroads often used inferior materials and did not take time to build the tracks well. Some tracks washed away, other tracks shifted out of alignment, and ties rotted or broke. These problems had to be corrected at great expense.

Because some of the people who invested in railroads accumulated enormous wealth, more companies soon sought government land grants for railroads. In 1864 Congress approved generous land grants to the Northern Pacific Railroad. In 1883 that railroad finished a line that joined Duluth, Minnesota, to the states of Washington and Oregon.

A government grant to the Atchison, Topeka, and Santa Fe Railroad provided some of the funds for a more southerly transcontinental route. Another grant allowed the Texas and Pacific Railroad to build yet another southern route across Texas, linking to the Southern Pacific Railroad's line (which passed through the Gadsden Purchase) at El Paso. When that transcontinental route was finished, New Orleans was linked by rail with Los Angeles and San Francisco. By 1900 the United States had several transcontinental railroads.

The early large railroad companies relied heavily on grants from the national government. But **James J. Hill** proved that a large high-quality railroad could be built using only private funds. He bought several railroads and created a company called the Great Northern Railroad.

Hill not only refused to ask for government funds to build the railroad but also used a radical approach to build and operate it. Rather than climbing over or boring through mountains, his line went around them. This route allowed Hill to operate longer trains carrying heavier loads. He also kept costs low. The Great Northern became the most successful transcontinental railroad and the only one not eventually forced into bankruptcy.

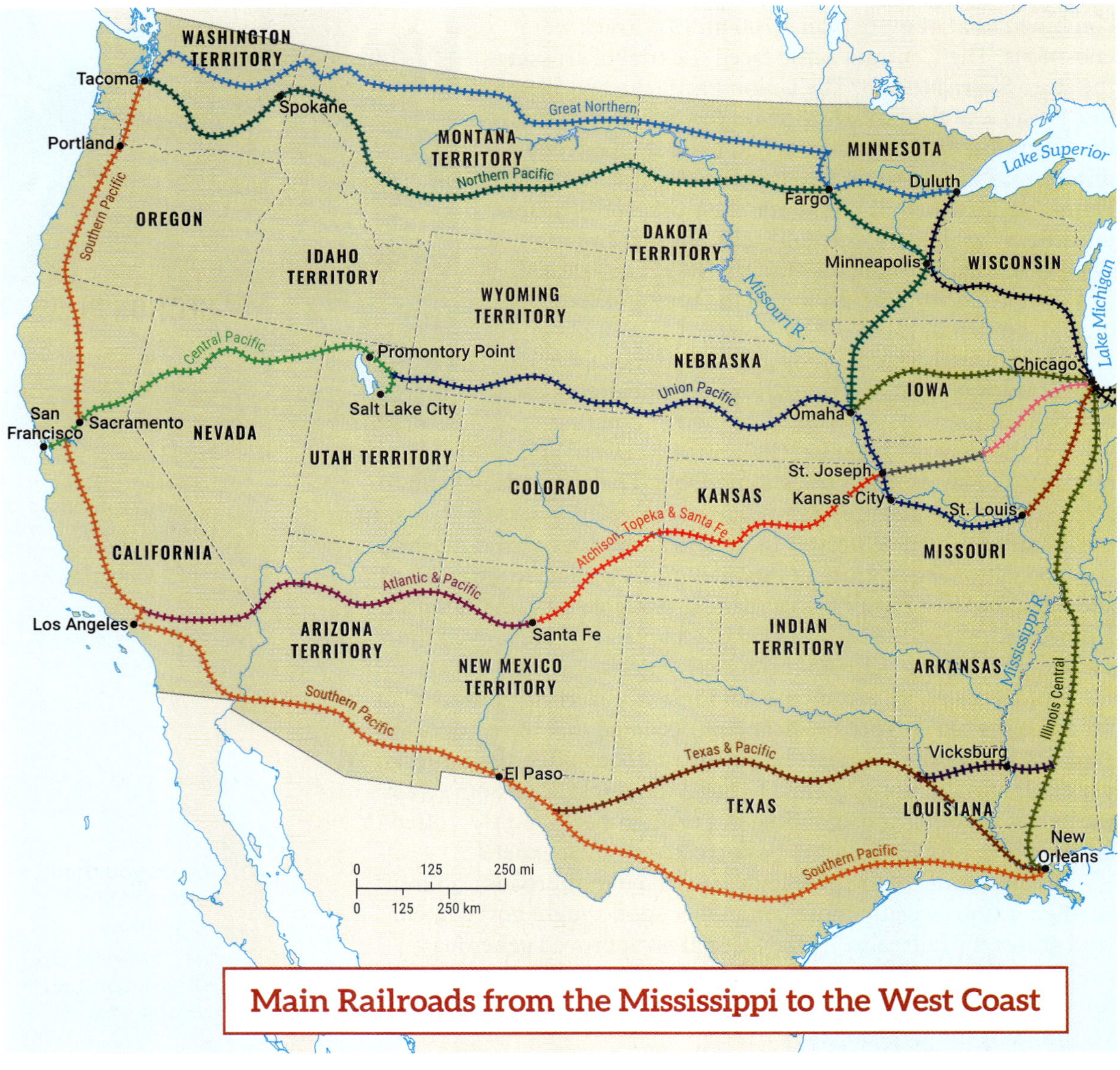

Main Railroads from the Mississippi to the West Coast

Inventions

Another critical ingredient in the development of American industry was technology—scientific inventions and improved methods of doing things. A strong work ethic, determination, and the absence of extensive government restrictions resulted in Americans' remarkable ability to innovate. Americans, often without intending to, fulfilled God's command in Genesis to "subdue" the earth and "have dominion over" it. Innovations improved the lives of an increasing number of people. Hundreds of inventors made important contributions to American industry.

George Pullman made long train trips more comfortable by inventing the Pullman car, which contained sleeping compartments.

Inventions, such as **Alexander Graham Bell**'s telephone in 1876, led to new industries and major changes in American life. The increased use of electricity was especially beneficial to the advancement of both industry and technology.

Fun Fact

Edison stated, "Genius is 1 percent inspiration and 99 percent perspiration."

Thomas Edison promoted generating electricity for practical uses. The harnessing of electricity led him to invent numerous electrical appliances. His incandescent light bulb was among the most important of his 1,093 patented inventions. Edison once commented, "There is no substitute for hard work."

For the railroad industry, no invention was more important than George Westinghouse's air brake for trains. That 1869 invention saved many lives and prevented the loss of thousands of dollars' worth of property.

Overall, advances in technology improved most Americans' standard of living. Nonetheless, success led to certain dangers. A growing number of people put financial wealth above love for God. Some businesses gave more attention to profits than safe working conditions and just wages. In addition, some Americans came to believe that technology could solve most, if not all, problems. They looked to inventors and scientists rather than to God and His Word for answers. When scientists disagreed with Scripture, the Bible was sometimes rejected in favor of scientific theories.

SECTION REVIEW 16.2

1. What factors contributed to a better, more efficient railroad system?
2. What major areas did Cornelius Vanderbilt want to connect by rail?
3. From what city did the Union Pacific railroad company build westward? From what city did the Central Pacific railroad company build eastward?
4. What difficulties did the railroad companies that built the first transcontinental railroad face?
5. Who showed that a high-quality railroad could be built using only private funds? Which railroad did he create?
6. Who invented each of the following? Which do you think was most important? Why?
   a. telephone
   b. incandescent light bulb
   c. sleeper compartments for trains
   d. air brake for trains

GUIDING QUESTION

- What were three ways businesses could be organized?

16.3 ORGANIZING BUSINESSES

What were new ways of organizing business?

Expanding industries were constantly looking for ways to improve their production, but such improvements required investment money, or **capital**. As a result, businesses began to find new ways to obtain and organize capital.

Sole Proprietorships and Partnerships

In America's early years, most businesses were either **sole proprietorships**, businesses that were owned by one person, or **partnerships**, businesses that were owned by two or more people. Both types worked well for small-scale operations.

Sole proprietorships had the advantage of meeting individual needs. The owner of a proprietorship received all the profit; however, he also absorbed all the losses and often lacked the funds to expand his business.

Partnerships had the advantages of increasing capital in businesses and of sharing the losses of those businesses. However, the latter meant that the failures or faults of one partner could lead to financial hardship, or even ruin, of the other partners.

Andrew Carnegie (1835–1919)

Andrew Carnegie was born in Scotland. His family struggled to make a living and immigrated to America when he was twelve to seek a better life. He soon began a job earning $1.20 per week in a textile mill. Over the next several decades, Carnegie accumulated a fortune of more than $400 million and became one of the richest men in the United States. Though he was involved in a variety of business ventures, most of his financial success was in the steel industry.

Carnegie had a gift for hiring people with exceptional ability. They provided him with expertise in areas about which he knew little. He suggested that his tombstone should read, "Here lies a man who knew how to get around him a great many men who were much cleverer than he was himself." Even as he gained great wealth, he also gave much of it away; he was well-known as a **philanthropist** (wealthy person who generously donates money to worthy causes).

In 1889 he wrote an article entitled "The Gospel of Wealth" about his goals of philanthropy.

> This, then, is . . . the duty of the man of Wealth: First, to set an example of modest, unostentatious [not showy] living, shunning display or extravagance [excessive spending]; to provide moderately for the legitimate [valid] wants of those dependent upon him; and after doing so to consider all surplus revenues [moneys] which come to him simply as trust funds [money held for another], which he is called upon to administer . . . in the manner which, in his judgment, is best calculated to produce the most beneficial results for the community—the man of wealth thus becoming the mere agent and trustee for his poorer brethren, bringing to their service his superior wisdom, experience, and ability to administer, doing for them better than they would or could do for themselves.

Corporations

Incorporation, a new way to organize business, became very popular in the late 1800s. A **corporation** was formed when a business gained a legal charter and sold stock to many individual investors. Although the stockholders were essentially the owners of the business, they could lose only the amount they invested in the stock if the corporation failed. If the corporation made a profit, the stockholders received dividends from that profit.

A corporation was legally considered a "person" and could conduct legal dealings without all of its stockholders being present. Also, its existence was not ended by the death of a manager or a single stockholder.

Because of such advantages—especially the opportunity to raise large sums of capital quickly—more executives sought to incorporate in the years after the Civil War. Steel, petroleum, and chemical manufacturers were a few of the many industries that used the corporate form of business.

There are some disadvantages of a corporation. For example, as the organizational structure is usually more complicated than a sole proprietorship or partnership, it is more difficult to make important decisions in a timely manner.

In addition to individuals purchasing stock, the nation's banking system helped provide businesses with capital. As more Americans entered the work force and the number of businesses grew, the number of bank deposits increased. Banks invested that money in corporations to make even more money. Furthermore, banks also offered credit to corporations to cover the expansion of industry. As corporations grew larger, they needed better internal organization.

John D. Rockefeller was the most famous and prosperous businessman in the oil industry. In 1882 his company, Standard Oil, combined with other companies to form the first **trust**. A trust combines several separate companies into one supersized corporation. The executives of the trust organize and manage all the combined companies as they wish. Other industries followed Rockefeller's example and established trusts of their own in the 1880s.

▲ Some viewed John D. Rockefeller as an uncaring, money-loving, selfish individual. Others admired him for hard work, determination, and skill as a businessman.

SECTION REVIEW 16.3

1. Complete the table:

	Sole Proprietorship	Partnership	Corporation
number of owners			
advantage(s)			
disadvantage(s)			

2. What is a *trust*?

3. Using Proverbs 30:8; 21:13; and Galatians 6:10, how does Andrew Carnegie's "The Gospel of Wealth" compare to scriptural references to money?

GUIDING QUESTIONS

- How did industrial expansion change American life?
- What is *capitalism*?
- What laws did the government pass to regulate business?
- How did labor unions develop?

16.4 EFFECTS OF INDUSTRIAL EXPANSION

How did industrial expansion affect America?

The growth of industry increased Americans' standard of living, reduced poverty, and brought many other changes to America.

Changes in American Life

URBAN POPULATION GROWTH

First, the population in urban areas increased tremendously. Immigrants swelled the size of cities. As farms used more inventions and improvements to equipment, production increased and fewer farm workers were needed. Farmers—or at least several of their children—often moved to towns and cities, where other types of jobs were available.

INCREASED TRADE

Second, America's trade increased greatly. Products from the farms and the factories found their way to distant parts of the world. This trade also made many more products available to Americans.

MORE LEISURE TIME

Third, industrialism meant that many Americans had more leisure time. Some machines freed people from certain types of work. Other machines were laborsaving devices that made work easier. Americans soon found ways to use their extra time. Some played sports. Others watched. New spectator sports like basketball, boxing, and baseball captured the public's interest. Bicycling and tennis also became popular.

URBAN PROBLEMS

Fourth, industrialization magnified urban problems. Air and water pollution, overcrowding, and crime became serious issues.

SHIFTING FAMILY LIFE

Fifth, industrialism affected American family life. Because inventions made housekeeping easier and less time consuming, women started finding other jobs. Some women had worked outside the home during the Civil War, and a few had continued doing so afterward. Others now worked in new or expanding industries. The number of women in the work force continued to grow, changing the lifestyles of more and more families.

INCREASED WEALTH

Sixth, industrialism brought an increase in wealth, both national and individual. It is estimated that there were fifty millionaires in America in 1850 and that the number grew to five thousand by 1900. The buying power of the average worker had increased by over 50 percent during that period. Most people, regardless of their social class, were living better than they had before.

Some of those who gained wealth became philanthropists. Doubtless, some believed that philanthropy would help them gain merit with both God and people. Others genuinely wanted to help people. Christian philanthropists often invested in building churches, contributing to missions, and caring for the sick and needy.

Sadly, in the industrial era, many Americans were not satisfied despite increasing their wealth. They wanted and sought more. Some of the rich competed with one another in boasting of and displaying their wealth. **Materialism**, placing great emphasis on money and possessions, became a significant American problem. Many valued what they owned more than their relationship with God.

A Focus on Capitalism

America's rapid rise in industrialization was possible because of its capitalistic economy. **Capitalism** is an economic system in which businesses and property are privately owned and privately operated. People are free to invest and seek profits. Anyone can go into business and compete with others. That competition usually causes a business to sell good products or services so that it can grow. Poor products or services drive customers away.

The freedom of the capitalistic system enabled people to use labor and investments to help both the nation and its citizens. It brought a higher standard of living to most Americans. However, some used that same freedom to treat others unjustly. For example, some industrialists were ruthless when dealing with their competitors. Some focused on amassing huge fortunes while employees labored long hours at dangerous work for low pay. They ignored the biblical rule that "the labourer is worthy of his hire" (Luke 10:7). But others displayed genuine interest in both their workers and their working conditions.

Consequently, the success of capitalism led to new challenges about how to use both money and power. Americans in this period wrestled with how to keep the great benefits of the capitalistic system while avoiding the evils that could accompany it.

Mulberry Street in New York City

a SCRIPTURAL *view of* WEALTH

God's Word does not denounce wealth or money. God promised material blessing to Israel if its people would keep the covenant He made with them (Deut. 8:6–10). But God also warned the people that their prosperity could cause them to forget Him. The love of money is the source of all sorts of evil (greed and envy, for example—see 1 Tim. 6:10).

Jesus warned people against making the treasures they collect on this earth their god. He said, "Ye cannot serve God and mammon [riches]" (Matt. 6:24). Wealth is a tool to be used in ways that please God. The first portion of one's income should be given to God's work (Prov. 3:9). Scripture also encourages people to work hard so they can meet their families' needs and have extra with which to help others (Eph. 4:28).

social DARWINISM

During this period, a philosophy that justified harsh actions became popular. People used Charles Darwin's theory of evolution to defend the idea that people can accumulate wealth by any means they want. Darwin's theory said that there is a constant struggle in nature and that only the fittest members of the species survive. Applied socially, this thinking was called **social Darwinism**. Social Darwinists showed little mercy. In industry, they argued that driving weaker competitors out of business was just a part of the struggle for survival. Making a profit, according to their philosophy, could be accomplished by any means, even if others were hurt.

This idea ignored the fact that humans are precious beings made in God's own image (Gen. 1:26–27). Therefore, it is wrong for them to harm one another (Eph. 4:32; Luke 6:31). People should work hard to make their business endeavors successful, but they should be motivated by a desire to honor God and to help their fellow humans.

Government Regulation of Business

Most Americans embraced the idea of **laissez faire**, a French phrase meaning "let it alone," regarding government involvement in businesses. In other words, they believed the best way for a capitalist economy to develop was to operate without government interference. Supporters of laissez faire policies argued that government regulation would disturb the balance between supply of products and the public's demand for those products. They said that the economy might be ruined by regulation.

However, many Americans came to believe some government regulation was necessary. They thought the problems—some viewed them as injustices—that had emerged in how companies conducted business required government intervention. Some even worried that large corporations, rather than elected representatives, might control the nation. As a result, a number of Americans called for the federal government to regulate some business practices. But this led to controversy as Americans disagreed about how to balance the values of freedom and equality that often seemed to conflict.

Interstate Commerce Act of 1887

Many western farmers and smaller companies objected to the rates charged by railroads. They argued that rates were unfairly set. For example, railroads often established rates based on whether there were competing railroad companies in the area. Thus, in an area that had only one railroad company operating, the rate might be much higher to transport goods a short distance than the rate (in an area where there was competition) for transporting goods a much greater distance. In addition, larger companies were given much cheaper rates for shipping.

In 1887 Congress addressed this issue by passing the **Interstate Commerce Act**. It directed railroads to set "reasonable and just" rates. It also created the Interstate Commerce Commission (ICC) to examine complaints and, when necessary, take offenders to court. But when the offenders came to court, judges usually decided in favor of the railroads. The ICC lost nearly every case filed from 1887 to 1906. Yet the ICC still had an impact since some companies changed their policies to avoid investigations and costly court cases. The ICC set a precedent for the government to organize other independent regulatory agencies. The power of the ICC and other agencies became a matter of public debate. Some praised their actions and others denounced them.

▲ Freight yard for two major railroads in New York City in the 1890s

Sherman Antitrust Act of 1890

Many Americans were suspicious of trusts. They believed that trusts' size and power gave them an unfair edge that harmed free enterprise. They were upset that large trusts, such as John D. Rockefeller's Standard Oil Company, had driven small companies out of business.

▲ This 1881 political cartoon depicts monopolies (businesses with complete or nearly complete control of a product) as a snake that threatens Americans' liberty. Antitrust laws were designed to regulate monopolies.

By 1880 both political parties promised to regulate trusts, and in 1890 Congress passed the **Sherman Antitrust Act**. Its aim was to control trusts. Its vague language was confusing and the legislation at first had little effect; but, in the early twentieth century, it was eventually used to "break up," or dismantle, some large companies.

Labor Unions

As mentioned in Chapter 11, labor unions developed by the early 1830s; however, they had limited success at the time. The rapid increase of industries in the second half of the nineteenth century brought the growth of labor unions. Abuses in some factories opened the door to organized protests by the workers in which they demanded better wages and working conditions. Unions fared less well when there were more workers than available jobs or when there were economic depressions.

The Knights of Labor

The **Knights of Labor** was formed in 1869. Its goal was to form one big union for all workers—skilled and unskilled, men and women. It sought equal pay for men and women, an eight-hour workday for workers, safety measures, and compensation (payment for loss) for injuries occurring on the job.

The union's membership rose from 9,000 in 1879 to 115,000 by 1884. By 1886 membership reached 700,000 workers.

But 1886 was a difficult year for unions. In Chicago, thousands of workers, many from the Knights of Labor, went on strike to demand that the workday be restricted to eight hours without a pay cut. (A **strike** occurs when employees refuse to work in protest of an employer's actions.) On May 3, violence erupted and several workers were killed or injured by policemen who were attempting to end the disturbance.

▼ Striking workers in the late 1800s

▲ The Haymarket Riot in Chicago resulted in the deaths of seven policemen and several protesters.

The following day, a protest rally was staged at Chicago's Haymarket Square. A number of anarchists (people who oppose government and promote political disorder and confusion) were involved in the event. The police moved in to break up the meeting. Then someone threw a bomb at policemen. Police opened fire and chaos erupted. Seven police officers and several protesters were killed.

The **Haymarket Riot**, sometimes called the Haymarket Affair, hurt the reputation of the unions because people then linked them with violence. Membership in the Knights dropped to just 100,000 in four years.

The American Federation of Labor

A second union, the **American Federation of Labor** (AFL), was established in 1886. Its first president was a British-born cigar maker, **Samuel Gompers**. Unlike the Knights, the AFL consisted only of skilled workers.

The AFL pushed for an eight-hour day and **collective bargaining** (the right of unions to represent workers in negotiations with owners and managers). In addition, it wanted companies to hire only union members. The AFL also used the threat of strikes. And when strikes occurred, it used its membership dues to support workers who were on strike and not earning wages. But a violent strike over a wage cut at Andrew Carnegie's steel plant in Homestead, Pennsylvania, in 1892 hurt the AFL's efforts to recruit more members.

▲ Samuel Gompers

Reaction to Unions

Employers often opposed unions and their demands. They wanted the right to bargain with workers individually, largely because they knew that it was easier to reject the concerns of individuals than those of a group that represented large numbers. Employers hated strikes because they hurt production.

Courts often sided with the employers and sometimes issued **injunctions**, official court orders, to stop strikes. Local newspapers usually sided with employers, partly because most of their income was derived from local businesses that purchased advertisements.

SECTION REVIEW 16.4

1. What six changes in American life were due to the growth of industry?
2. How can increased wealth be both good and bad (see Matt. 6:24 and 1 Tim. 6:10)?
3. What is *capitalism*?
4. What industry did the Interstate Commerce Act of 1887 regulate?
5. What legislation sought to break up large trusts?
6. What goals did the Knights of Labor have?
7. Why did the Haymarket Riot hurt the reputation of unions?

CHAPTER 16 REVIEW

Making Connections

1. How many states were part of the United States in 1800? in 1900?
2. How did some neighborhoods receive such names as Chinatown or Little Italy?
3. From what four areas did many of the immigrants come during the middle and late 1800s?
4. Where did the majority of each immigrant group from the previous question settle?
5. Why was the Chinese Exclusion Act passed? How many total years did it last, although not always enforced?
6. What size was eventually agreed upon as the standard railroad gauge?
7. Besides money, what did the government grant to the railroad companies building tracks?
8. What type of business near you is owned by a sole proprietor? partners? a corporation?
9. What sports became popular because of an increase in leisure time?
10. What is the base word of *capitalism*? Why do you think it is used?
11. Why is social Darwinism wrong?
12. What was the main difference between the Knights of Labor and the American Federation of Labor?

Thinking Critically

13. Why might a civil service examination be a better way to fill government jobs than the spoils system?
14. What does Thomas Edison's quote, "Genius is 1 percent inspiration and 99 percent perspiration" mean?
15. Should government place controls on industry? Why or why not?

Living as a Christian Citizen

16. Can Christians be wealthy without being materialistic? Can they be materialistic without being wealthy? Explain your answers.
17. If you owned your own company, what policies might you introduce to ensure that you ran your business in light of the two greatest commandments (see Matt. 22:35–40)?

Unexploded bomb from the 1886 Haymarket Riot

Terms to Remember

Gilded Age
James Garfield
Chester A. Arthur
Civil Service Commission
Grover Cleveland
Benjamin Harrison
Ellis Island
Chinese Exclusion Act
Cornelius Vanderbilt
Union Pacific
Central Pacific
James J. Hill
Alexander Graham Bell
Thomas Edison
capital
sole proprietorships
partnerships
Andrew Carnegie
philanthropist
corporation
John D. Rockefeller
trust
materialism
capitalism
social Darwinism
laissez faire
Interstate Commerce Act
Sherman Antitrust Act
Knights of Labor
strike
Haymarket Riot
American Federation of Labor
Samuel Gompers
collective bargaining
injunctions

CHAPTER 17 The Last Frontier

An American cowboy in 1888

As we have mentioned, the term *frontier* refers to an undeveloped area at the edge of settled areas. During the nation's history, the frontier had gradually moved west. First, Americans moved across the Appalachians. Then they moved on to the Mississippi River. The next frontier was the distant West. The discovery of gold and rich lands on the West Coast lured settlers who bypassed much of the land from the Mississippi River to the Rocky Mountains. That region, known as the **Great Plains**, remained largely unsettled until after the Civil War.

GUIDING QUESTIONS

- How did mining impact westward migration?
- What was the controversy regarding silver in the late 1800s?

17.1 MOVING WESTWARD

How did mining affect the American West?

As Americans migrated west in increasing numbers, they encountered a variety of Native American tribes with a total population that may have exceeded three hundred thousand. In the Southwest, tribes such as the Hopis, Navajos, and Pueblos practiced agriculture. Native American tribes to the north, such as the Chinooks and Yuroks, hunted deer, elk, and moose. The Yakamas and other tribes harvested large quantities of salmon from the rivers. Along the Pacific coast, the Tlingits hunted and gathered food from the abundant coastal resources. The removal of these native populations should have and could have been avoided. Tragically, the Native American way of life suffered greatly because of American migration.

The Great Plains, or simply the Plains, presented many hindrances to settlement. Explorers and settlers in wagon trains crossing the region believed that the hard soil was not fertile. Also, the climate seemed unsuitable. The winters were very cold; the summers were very hot. Rainfall was scarce: many areas received less than twenty inches of it a year. Good water supplies were rare. Furthermore, the Plains lacked trees for the settlers to use in building the log cabins and other wooden structures that had been common in the East.

Despite these many discouragements and the presence of Native American tribes, Americans were determined to settle the West. Going west appealed to people's rugged individualism and desire for growth. In the West, a person could largely determine his own future. Free from the constraints of eastern society, people were more able to work hard and enjoy the fruits of their own labor and ingenuity.

Technological advances, especially the transcontinental railroads, sped the move westward. The railroads made it possible for people and agricultural products to move easily across the grasslands.

As railroad crews laid tracks across the prairies, crew members shot buffalo to prevent them from damaging the tracks. They also shot them for food and sport. Sometimes trains stopped so passengers could shoot buffalo. Over the years, the vast herds of buffalo, on which Native Americans depended, nearly disappeared. Experts estimate that when Europeans first arrived in North America, thirty million or more buffalo existed. By 1900 there were only about five hundred.

Did you know?

The American buffalo really should be called "bison." Though the terms are often used interchangeably, there are differences between the two animals. Buffalo are native to Africa and Asia, and bison are found in North America and Europe.

Passengers and crew shooting buffalo from one of the transcontinental railroads in the 1870s

People of many different nations settled the West. Most of the settlers were of European descent. The Germans, Irish, and Scandinavians settled in remote areas such as the Dakotas. Asians, especially the Chinese, worked on the railroads. More than two hundred thousand Chinese arrived in the West between 1876 and 1890. By 1880 as many as twenty-six thousand blacks had migrated from the South to Kansas. Called "Exodusters" (a reference to the Old Testament Israelites who left Egypt in the Exodus), they were fleeing discrimination in the South and trying to start a new life in the West. Hundreds of thousands of African Americans lived west of the Mississippi River by 1880.

New inventions and flexibility aided Plains settlers in their quest to thrive on the prairie. Although writers had predicted that it would take seventy-five to a hundred years to settle the remaining western lands, by 1890 the frontier had largely ceased to exist. The large open spaces of the West became symbolic of American growth and optimism. But sadly, some people's desire for growth was spurred by greed. Their quest for more land, gold, or silver led them to deny others, especially Native Americans, equality and justice.

▲ "Exodusters" board a riverboat.

The Miners

When gold was discovered in California in 1848, large numbers of settlers flooded areas where Native Americans lived. Later, as the gold diminished, prospectors turned to other jobs or moved elsewhere. Some wandered into largely unexplored mountainous areas of the West. Many of those people were not disappointed by what they found. For about a generation, the region yielded new riches.

Riches in the West

Several new gold and silver strikes, or discoveries, brought more miners to the West. After the California gold rush, the next big strike occurred in 1859 near Pikes Peak in Colorado. Many prospectors raced across the prairie with "**Pikes Peak or Bust!**" written on their wagons. Though that strike made some people rich, other fortune seekers returned home with a new message on their wagons: "Busted!" But the discovery did bring attention to the region.

Farther west, one of the largest and richest mines was the **Comstock Lode** in Nevada. The **lode** (rich deposit of ore) was named for Henry Comstock, an early prospector there. Miners eagerly dug gold from the ground, but they were disappointed to find that it was contaminated by some other metal and therefore sold for less. Upon closer examination, the "other metal" was determined to be silver. In fact, more than half of the ore eventually mined from the Comstock Lode was silver; the remainder was gold. Miners extracted some $400 million worth of gold and silver from the Comstock Lode between 1859 and 1900.

▲ Miners work in a Colorado gold mine.

To the north, the Fraser and Columbia River valleys also yielded rich finds. And strikes in Idaho and Montana along the Bitterroot and Salmon Rivers attracted thousands of miners. In 1864 prospectors discovered gold in Helena and Butte, Montana. In the 1880s copper mines were developed in Butte as well.

In the mid-1870s gold was discovered in the Black Hills of South Dakota, an area that belonged to the Sioux Indians. Fortune seekers ignored the Native Americans' ownership and invaded the area. Although the army was present to keep miners out, it did not do so.

When the government tried to buy back the land from the Sioux—land it had given them in 1868—the Sioux refused to sell. War with the Sioux followed, and the miners retained control of the area. The Homestake Mine near Deadwood, South Dakota, became one of the world's richest gold mines.

Mining Camps and Towns

Some miners went west alone. But for safety and economy in buying supplies, mining guidebooks suggested four-man companies. Miners gathered in makeshift mining camps, where they lived in tents or in hastily constructed small structures.

They staked their claim (claimed land) quickly. The mining claims were not really official because the miners did not own the land; however, certain rules were usually followed. For example, to keep a claim, a miner typically had to work on it one day in three. If a miner was absent for ten days, someone else could take the claim.

As more people went west, businesses developed around them. Supply stores and saloons were usually the first businesses to arrive in an area. Soon after their arrival, a

▾ Main Street in Deadwood, South Dakota, during the gold rush in the Black Hills in 1876

▲ Towns that had thrived during the gold or silver booms turned into ghost towns when the mines were depleted.

meeting would usually be called to plan a town. Streets were drawn out, and a town name was chosen. Lots were drawn for home sites. A church, a school, processing mills for ore, and other buildings soon filled the town. Where competition was lacking, enterprising people could often set their own fees. For example, one woman supposedly earned $18,000 in one year just by baking pies for the miners.

A few people made fortunes in mining. Many more made only enough to survive. If the ore in an area was depleted or prices dropped, the mines closed. Often, miners, storekeepers, hotel owners, and their families then left. If everyone in a town left, the empty buildings deteriorated, and the town became known as a ghost town. Ghost towns also resulted when railroads were rerouted, lumber mills closed, or when farms could no longer produce crops.

Silver and the Currency System

Before the Civil War, the government minted both gold and silver coins. During the war, Congress issued paper money called "**greenbacks**" (so called because they were printed with green ink) to help pay for the war. Unlike earlier currencies, however, the greenbacks were not backed by gold or silver, but simply by the government's promise to honor them. As a result, most Americans viewed greenbacks as less valuable than "hard money" (gold and silver).

After the war, many bankers and other financial leaders wanted to get rid of the greenbacks and base money entirely on gold. As a result, in 1873 the government stopped buying silver to make coins. Consequently, the price of silver plunged sharply. Miners and many other westerners were upset.

Later, in 1878, Congress passed the Bland-Allison Act. It required the secretary of the treasury to buy $2–$4 million a month in silver. That silver was then used to make a limited number of dollar coins that were still backed by gold in the Treasury's vaults.

Farmers, silver miners, and mine owners were not satisfied. They supported "free silver"—the unlimited use of silver for coins—and the use of both gold and silver for currency. When six new states that had agricultural and mining interests entered the Union, support for both "free silver" and using gold and silver coins grew. By 1896 the Democratic party supported those ideas.

▲ Greenbacks from the Civil War

SECTION REVIEW 17.1

1. What discoveries lured many to the West?
2. What hindrances prevented people from settling the Great Plains before the Civil War?
3. In what states were large lodes of precious metals such as gold, silver, and copper found?
4. What situations created a "ghost town"?
5. How were greenbacks different from previous currency? How were they viewed? Would you have preferred to use greenbacks or coins? Why?
6. Why did the price of silver decrease?

17.2 THE COWBOYS

What was it like to be a cowboy?

GUIDING QUESTIONS

- What were cowboys, cattle trails, and cattle drives like?
- How did the meatpacking industry develop?
- Why did the open range end?

Cowboys also played an important role in the development of the American West. They tamed more of the new frontier than the miners or the farmers. Their role during this period has fascinated people around the world for well over a century.

Cattle had roamed the Southwest since the Spanish explorers first brought them to America in the 1500s. By the 1800s, a huge number of cattle grazed the **open range** (unfenced lands). After the Civil War, the cattle industry boomed. This was the era of the cowboy, and it was brief—its peak came in the 1880s. By the early 1890s, the cowboys' way of life had largely passed into legend, leaving only the cowboys' outfit and songs to be copied and idealized by modern Americans. In the twenty-five years that the cattle drives flourished, about forty thousand men drove an estimated ten million head of cattle over a network of trails. Most of these trails led north from Texas. Almost one-fourth of the cowboys on the cattle drives were African Americans, and a significant number were Mexicans.

The term *cowboy* was fitting. Photographs of the era and artwork by cowboy artists show the faces of young men. Arrest records from cowboy towns show that most people who were jailed were under age twenty. Young cowboys spent a few years riding the range or trail and then usually married, settling down as farmers or ranchers.

cattle BRANDS

With so many cattle grazing freely on the Plains, it was often difficult to tell who owned which animal. Ranchers had to develop a way to determine what belonged to them. Their solution was branding. They heated specially designed iron rods red hot and applied them to cows' sides. Branding made permanent marks on the cows' hides. When cattle were rounded up before a drive to market, ranchers separated cattle according to brands.

Ranchers tried to develop unique and interesting brand designs that could not be easily altered by thieves, known as rustlers. Some examples of brand designs are shown here.

▾ Branding irons enabled ranchers to identify the cattle that belonged to them.

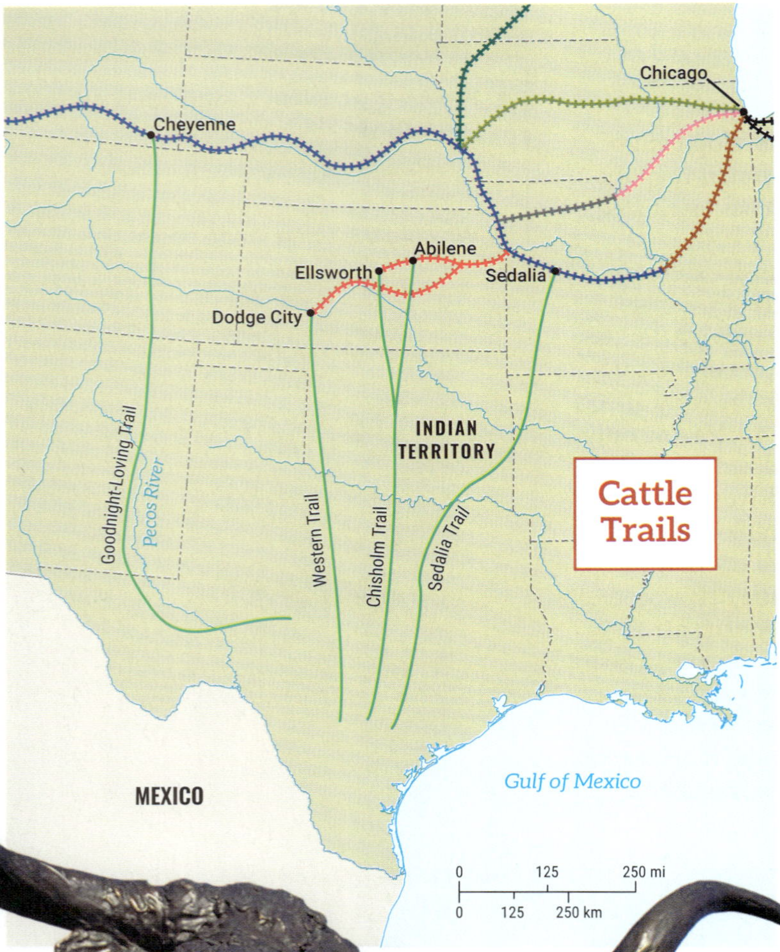

A Wealth of Cattle

After the Civil War, Texans realized that the growing herds of longhorn cattle on their lands would bring high prices at market. People in the rapidly growing eastern cities were hungry for beef, and they had the money to buy it. But because no railroads reached to Texas yet, the only way to get cattle to market was to move them to the rail lines.

The Cattle Trails

With the large supply of cattle in Texas, each sold for only $3 or $4 there. But in cities in the North and East, cattle sold for $25 to $40 per head. To take advantage of such profits, cattlemen began to move herds in 1866. The closest railroad at that time was at Sedalia, Missouri. Cowboys drove cattle hundreds of miles north along the Sedalia Trail to that city. Sedalia and other cities where cattle were loaded into railway cars were called cow towns. The long cattle drive included many challenges. First, cattle were difficult to drive through the forests and brush of eastern Oklahoma and southern Missouri. Second, cattle ticks clung to Texas longhorns for hundreds of miles. The ticks then attached themselves to cattle in Oklahoma and Missouri. Since those cattle lacked the immunity of the longhorns, many animals died from outbreaks of Texas fever transmitted by the ticks. Third, laws were passed to prohibit the passage of Texas herds through land along the route. Some farmers shot cattle being herded by cowboys who violated those laws.

In 1867, Joseph G. McCoy, a shrewd cattle broker from Illinois, built large corrals in Abilene, Kansas. He also constructed a bank, hotel, office building, and barn. Using the railroad, which had just reached that city, he shipped cattle to the Chicago stockyards. Cowboys now used the **Chisholm Trail** to reach Abilene, thereby reducing the distance of the long drive and freeing cattlemen from the dangers of armed farmers farther east. The Chisholm Trail became the busiest trail north. Although cattle drives were common on the trail, they continued to meet difficulties. The trail ran through the **Indian Territory** (now Oklahoma). Native Americans began levying a grazing tax on all the cattle driven through the area. Also, farmers near the trail erected fences to keep cattle out. The fences meant less open range and fewer watering holes for

◂ Statue of longhorns in Fort Worth, Texas

the moving livestock. So the cowboys began to swing farther west before they headed north. They connected with newly extended railroad lines at Ellsworth and Dodge City, Kansas. The route to Ellsworth was a cutoff from the Chisholm Trail. The trail to Dodge City was named the Western Trail.

Two ranchers in New Mexico looked for a route that would allow them to drive their cattle to the Pecos River and then up the Pecos to the markets in Colorado. Many people thought such a trail was impossible because of one eighty-mile stretch that had no water. But in 1866 Charles Goodnight and Oliver Loving hired eighteen well-armed men, rounded up two thousand head of cattle, and set out for the Pecos. On the first trip, they lost nearly four hundred cattle. On their second trip, they lost no cattle at all. The **Goodnight-Loving Trail**, as it was known, later extended to Cheyenne, Wyoming.

The Cattle Drive

The heart of the cattle industry and the most important part of a cowboy's job was the cattle drive. Getting ready for a drive took careful planning. A rancher or cattle buyer would begin gathering a herd in the early spring. Herds would range between 2,000 and 5,000 head of cattle.

The **trail boss** was in charge of the men, equipment, and animals. His responsibility was to get the herd to market safely. A minimum of eight cowboys were hired to work a typical herd. Two were "point men," who rode in the lead. Two were "swing men," and two were "flank men"; these four men rode beside the herd and kept the stock from wandering off. Two were "drag men," who rode in the rear. Despite choking dust, they had to keep any weak and tired stragglers moving along. A wrangler also joined them; he was usually the youngest of the men and was paid the least. He took care of the horses and the riding equipment. The outfit was accompanied by a cook. He rode the chuckwagon, filled with food and cooking equipment, a mile or two ahead of the herd. At the end of the day, he stopped to cook a hot meal for a tired crew. The cook's day could start as early as 3:00 a.m. and sometimes lasted until midnight.

A drive would start at daylight and go until dusk—or even later if the trail boss could not find good grass and water. After dinner, a cowboy's work was still not done. Each was required to serve a two-hour shift of guard duty. Two riders circled the herd in opposite directions, on guard for any signs of trouble. Cowboys hated night duty not only for its loneliness but also for its dangers. Most stampedes, the most frightening and dreaded experience cowboys faced, started at night. The snap of a twig, a strange smell, the flight of a nervous jack rabbit, or a bolt of lightning could set off a stampede. If they could not stop a stampede quickly, the cowboys faced several days of gathering a scattered herd. Even worse, a cowboy could be trampled to death by the herd if his horse stumbled.

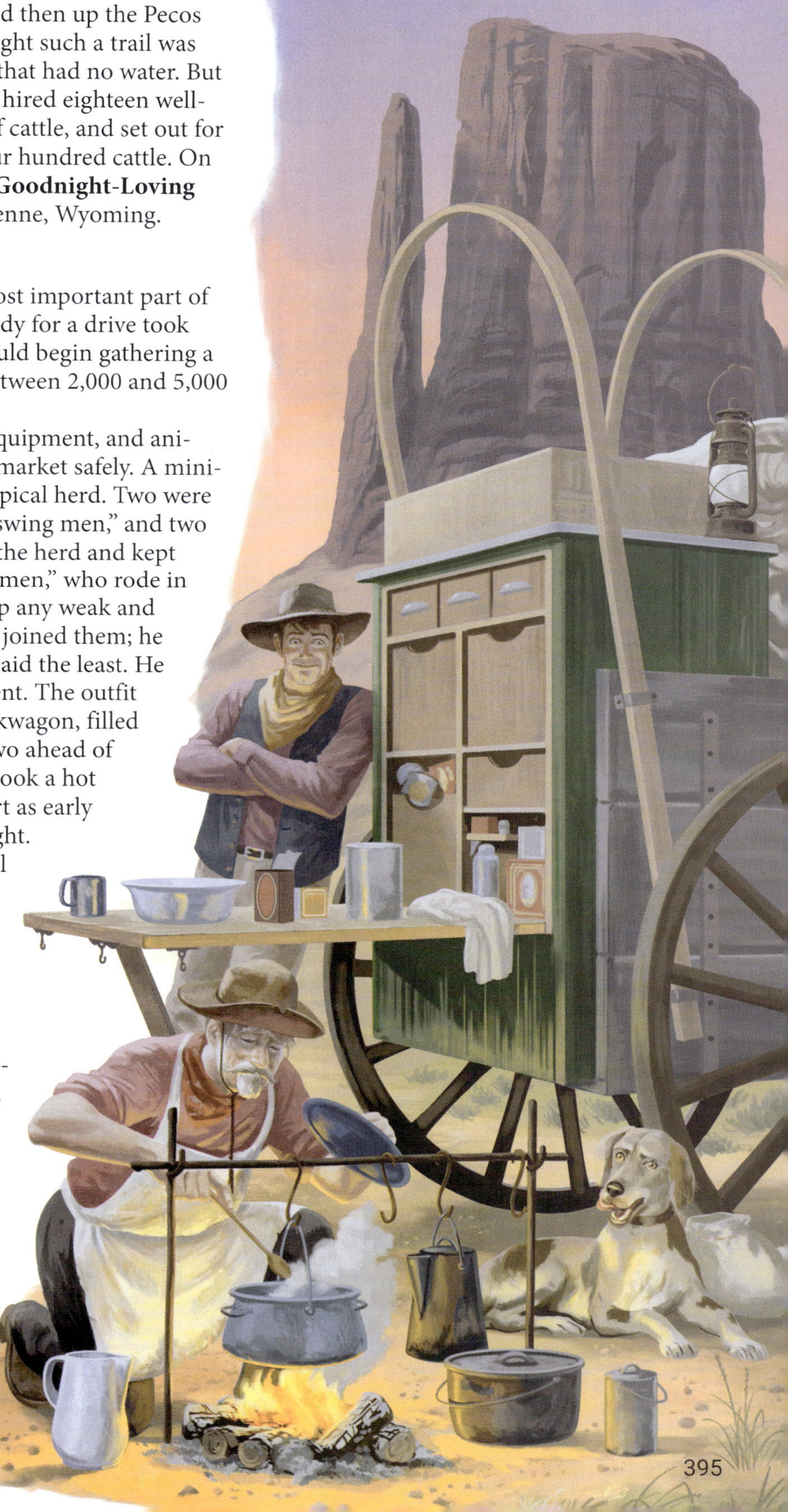

A cowboy watches as the cook prepares a meal at the chuckwagon.

▲ An advertisement from Philip Armour's company

The Meatpacking Industry

The continued success of the open-range cattle industry was ensured for a time by the development of a new industry: meatpacking. Philip Armour and Gustavus Swift led the way in making that industry successful. They were willing to try new ideas and methods of doing things.

Before and during the Civil War, meat was usually slaughtered locally and only limited amounts could be preserved for transport (a process called meatpacking) by salting, drying, canning, or pickling. After the war, Armour developed meatpacking into a successful large-scale business. He realized that there would be a huge market for meat in eastern cities if he could ship it in massive amounts. Cattle drives helped supply the cattle he needed, and he used the railroads to ship the meat to the packing plants. Because the cattle were shipped quickly and slaughtered almost immediately upon arrival at the meatpacking plant, they lost little weight and yielded hefty amounts of beef.

In 1875 Armour moved to Chicago and opened a packing plant. In addition to processing meat, Armour saw the potential value of by-products—bones, hides, and other parts that were not generally used for food. Since his company handled many thousands of animals daily, selling such by-products would further increase his profits rather than discarding by-products as waste. He hired chemists to find ways of turning the large volume of by-products from his plants into sellable items. They used fat to make soap; bones to make glue, buttons, and fertilizer; and hides to make shoes and gloves. Someone commented that meatpackers used "every part of a pig but the squeal."

Gustavus Swift also believed that there was a market for fresh meat. In 1875 he too established a meatpacking company in Chicago and began shipping fresh meat across the country. The meatpackers knew that chilled meat, whether frozen in winter or chilled with ice in summer, stayed fresh for as long as a month. They put beef on ice in railroad cars and shipped it to Boston. But since the meat had lain directly on the ice, it became discolored. Later, specially designed refrigerator cars with separate ice bins came into common use. Their ability to carry fresh meat long distances from meatpacking plants boosted the industry.

▼ Gustavus Swift's use of refrigerator railroad cars in the 1870s made it possible for meat to be transported to eastern cities and arrive fresh.

The End of the Open Range

By the 1890s, the open-range cattle industry was declining. The last long drive was completed in 1896. Many factors combined to cause this decline. One problem was a drop in meat prices. With the efficiency of production and the greater amount of meat processed, meat prices plummeted. It became less profitable to raise huge herds. But the drop in meat prices also had positive results. For example, more people were able to add more and better cuts of meat to their diets.

Overgrazing was also a problem for the industry. As more people participated in the cattle industry, the number of cattle grazing increased, causing the grasses to be shorter and scarcer. Each year as the season wore on, the problem became more acute, particularly when there was little rain. Dry ranges with short grasses left herds in poor condition. Along with overgrazing, formerly pure, clear springs became stinking mud holes. Harmful weeds replaced lush prairie grasses. Erosion turned cattle trails into ravines.

Even water could be a danger to the cattle. Sometimes when thirsty steers ran for water holes or rivers, they charged atop one another, drowning some. In addition, some cattle died while crossing rain-swollen rivers. Deadly flash floods were frequent; the sun-baked prairie ground could not absorb all the drainage from sudden thunderstorms.

Droughts and blizzards also threatened cattle. When water could not be found, cowboys and cattle alike suffered terribly. Lack of water made the cattle unmanageable; some even went blind. Winter's cold could kill the livestock if they were stranded in a blizzard without food or shelter.

The summer of 1884 brought severe drought that was followed by a severe winter in which thousands of cattle starved or froze. The cycle of drought and blizzards repeated in 1886–87 when temperatures dropped to 40 degrees below zero. Thousands more cattle died, and many cattlemen went bankrupt.

Horse thieves and cattle rustlers hid along the trails. Cattlemen tried to rid the Plains of such thieves by hanging or shooting them. Indians often demanded that cattlemen pay a toll in beef or horses. If the cowboys refused, the Indians caused stampedes.

Another problem that cattlemen faced was sheepherders. The vast, vacant grasslands of the Plains were as attractive to sheepherders as they were to cattlemen. Cattlemen had reached the grasslands first. They were angered to see sheepherders invading the area with their "woollybacks," as cowboys called sheep. To cowboys, sheep on the already overgrazed ranges meant disaster. Cattlemen said that sheep ate grass down to the roots and then trampled what little grass was left. The sheep stripped the ground so that no new growth appeared until the next spring's rain. They fouled water holes, leaving a smell that made cattle refuse to drink.

▾ The introduction of sheep to the grasslands of the West was a threat to the cattlemen's way of life.

One of the homes used by sheepherders

the CANDLISH MOVABLE HOME *on the range*

Until the late 1800s, sheepherders slept on the ground on blankets. The ground was very bumpy and cold. But in 1884 James Candlish, a Wyoming blacksmith, provided an alternative. He converted an old wagon into a home on wheels, a forerunner of the mobile home. Open in the front, the wagon had a canvas flap to block the wind. Later, a hardware company built an improved model that had a window, a stove with an oven, and Dutch doors (a door divided into two parts horizontally, allowing one half to be shut and the other open) among its many "conveniences." Soon, many sheepherders, especially those on the northern Plains, owned their own home on wheels.

Some sheepherders objected to the invention. But for many sheepherders, "home, home on the range" came with wheels.

As grass ran out and tempers grew short, the cowboys resorted to bullying, intimidating, and even attacking the outnumbered sheepmen and their flocks. Clubbing, shooting, torching, stampeding, and rim-rocking (driving sheep over cliffs) were all effective means of destroying herds. The murder of sheepherders was common.

Several events eased disputes. The winter of 1886–87 reduced the number of cattle that needed to graze. Fences divided rangelands. Some cattlemen found that it was possible for sheep and cattle to share some of the same rangelands.

SECTION REVIEW 17.2

1. About how many years was the cowboy era?
2. Why were cattle owners willing to drive their cattle hundreds of miles to the nearest railroad line?
3. What was the greatest danger during a cattle drive?
4. What does the phrase "every part of the pig but the squeal" mean in the meatpacking industry? What types of products did they make besides meat?
5. List at least three reasons for the end of the open range. Which do you think contributed the most?

17.3 SETTLING THE WEST

What was it like to be a homesteader?

Homesteading

The **Homestead Act** of 1862 gave 160 acres of land to an individual who paid a $10 filing fee. To maintain ownership of the land, the person was required to live on it for five years and to make improvements to it. Additional land could be purchased from the government or the railroads. A dwelling and its land was called a homestead.

By making western lands available, officials sought to achieve several goals. First, an increased population would lead to greater stability for the nation and the eventual creation of additional states. Second, development of the Plains would result in expanded economic opportunity for settlers. Third, more markets would be available for goods made in the East.

The Morrill Land-Grant Act of 1862 gave existing states 30,000 acres of federal land for every representative and senator they had. The land or the proceeds from its sale was to be used to establish colleges (or fund existing ones) that specialized in agricultural and mechanical education.

As more farmers went west to stake claims on public lands, the space left for open-range grazing decreased. Because the homesteaders did not want their crops overrun by livestock, they erected fences.

For a time, cattlemen fought the homesteaders by destroying the fences and threatening the farmers. But cattlemen eventually changed their tactics. Instead of grazing their cattle on public lands, they began ranching on their own land or on land that they leased from the government or other owners.

GUIDING QUESTIONS

- How did the homesteaders acquire land?
- How was Oklahoma settled?
- What inventions helped settlers overcome prairie hardships?

Fun Fact

Texas A&M, one of the largest colleges in the nation, opened in 1876 as the Agricultural and Mechanical College of Texas using funds provided by the Morrill Land-Grant Act.

▾ Homesteaders went westward seeking a better life and greater opportunities.

▲ Thousands of settlers rushed into Oklahoma hoping to gain the best available land.

The Oklahoma Land Rush

In the 1830s, the national government had moved the Cherokee and other southeastern tribes west to Indian Territory (Oklahoma). It later moved five southwestern tribes, all farming tribes, there. By the 1880s, most of the desirable farmland in the West had been claimed. Many new settlers looked greedily at the Indian Territory. It was reserved for Native Americans, but some of the land was unused. Railroad owners, land speculators, and land-hungry settlers saw an opportunity and pressured the federal government to open Oklahoma to settlers.

In 1885 the government bought lands in the Indian Territory. President Benjamin Harrison announced that some of the lands would be opened to settlers at noon on April 22, 1889. The US Army was there to keep settlers out until the stated hour. Thousands of pioneers were poised on the border that day. At the sound of cannons, they raced across the border to claim their land. Those who participated in that land boom were called Boomers. Some settlers had illegally staked their claim ahead of time, leading to many legal disputes. They were called **Sooners** (source of the state's nickname today). Settlers claimed about 1.9 million acres in only a few hours.

In the 1890s, government officials opened additional Oklahoma land to setters. In 1907 the area became the forty-sixth state.

▼ Because trees and lumber were so scarce on the prairie, settlers usually built sod houses for themselves.

Overcoming Obstacles

As farmers settled on the Plains in the late 1800s, they faced some of the same difficulties that cowboys and ranchers encountered. But they were also confronted with additional ones. The ways that they overcame those problems demonstrated their perseverance and inventiveness.

Lack of Resources

Because trees were rare on the Plains, wood had to be brought from other places. As a result, log cabins were both expensive and impractical. Some settlers first lived in dugouts braced by a few purchased boards. These dreary homes were little more than ditches dug into hillsides and covered with roofs of sod (grass and soil).

Sod houses, or "soddies," on the other hand, were a little more pleasant and became the classic dwellings on the prairie, especially where there were no hillsides for dugouts. A sod house was drier, sturdier, and more comfortable than a dugout. The sod strips used to build a soddie were cut from the hard ground. Strips were staggered like bricks, grass side down, to form the thick walls of the house. Soddies were warm in the winter and cool in the summer. Usually, a settler would weave a lattice of willow branches and cover it with clay from a nearby creek bed to form the base of the roof. Then he would lay sod shingles over the base. In heavy rains, such roofs leaked like soaked sponges. Debris often fell from the roofs, but pioneer wives hung cloth below the rafters to catch mud and bugs. The inside walls of soddies were whitewashed with a mixture of lime and sand. Tight construction was crucial, not just to keep out the cold but also to deter snakes and field mice. A few sod houses were built with some lumber and were two stories high.

The lack of wood on the Plains gave farmers (called "sodbusters") two other obstacles to overcome. One was scarcity of fuel for fires. Until the railroads brought coal to heat prairie homes, pioneers used corncobs, hay, and even manure ("buffalo chips") as fuel. Another problem was that the lack of wood kept farmers from building the split-rail fences used back east. Although prairie farmers were generally glad that their lands were not rocky, they had no stones to use for building purposes. They had no practical material to build fences with until barbed wire was invented (discussed later in this chapter).

Water was also scarce on the Plains, but a sodbuster had to have an adequate water supply. Some settlers used rain barrels or dug ditches to collect rain. Others settled near creeks. Most found water by digging wells, but wells had to be exceptionally deep to reach water in many areas of the dry Plains. Even with wells, the farmers could not pump enough water by hand to provide for their livestock and to irrigate their cropland. Windmills, however, allowed them to harness the energy of the strong breezes of the region to pump water. Farmers found other ways to deal with the lack of water. Some began raising crops that required less water. Some farmers used mulch to protect what little moisture was in the ground.

▾ Windmill-powered pumps brought water to the surface for people and crops.

Hardships of the Prairie

Besides lacking some needed resources, homesteaders had to deal with many hazards of prairie life. One such problem arose as more western lands were plowed. Especially in dry years, the wind blew tons of exposed topsoil across the dry ground. Keeping a house clean was nearly impossible in those conditions; dust settled everywhere. Outside, the dust was blinding. But the blowing dust was more than an inconvenience. The erosion of precious topsoil left much land infertile. The cultivation of more land led to more erosion and moisture loss.

Another danger for sodbusters was prairie fires. What little rain fell came in the spring and early summer. As the grasses became dry, the smallest spark from a campfire, chimney, or bolt of lightning could turn the prairie into an inferno. Settlers used several methods to extinguish such fires. Sometimes they used damp clothing and blankets to beat out small fires. At other times, farmers used the carcasses of slaughtered livestock, dragging them over the flaming grass to smother the flames. When flames were fanned by winds, the settlers were powerless to stop the spreading fire. The heavy sod of the houses and wet sheets over openings might protect people, but they could not prevent the crops from burning.

Hailstorms and tornadoes sometimes did as much damage as fires. Hailstorms flattened crops, leaving little for harvest. Tornadoes often destroyed everything in their paths. So many tornadoes occurred on the Plains that the region was called "tornado alley." Sodbusters often sought protection in the cellars that they had dug for storing food.

Large swarms of locusts and grasshoppers were another challenge of the Plains. Swarming across the prairies in the 1870s, they devoured anything that grew. Some accounts reported that locusts covered the ground in a wiggling layer up to six inches deep. The locusts ate crops, grasses, leaves, tree bark, leather boots, harness straps, and even fence posts and door frames. No one knew what caused the swarms to drop from the skies or what caused them to leave, but everyone feared them. Their arrival usually meant a two-year crop loss because the locusts laid eggs that hatched the next year.

Hardships

1. Wind
2. Prairie fires
3. Hailstorms and tornadoes
4. Swarms of locusts
5. Loneliness

Homesteaders fighting a prairie fire

Homesteads were often miles from a settlement. Because neighbors were few and the distances between homesteads great, loneliness was a problem. Many homesteaders combated loneliness by making great efforts to attend church, even if they had to travel long distances to churches built in towns.

Mail provided another link to the outside world. Mail-order catalog companies began with Montgomery Ward and Company, in Chicago in 1872. Twenty years later, Sears, Roebuck and Company also started. Catalogs offered Americans a wide range of products that they could order. Many of the products could be delivered to a customer's door while others were shipped to the nearest town for pickup.

Farmers also dealt with loneliness by forming their own social groups. The **Grange**, founded in 1867, began as a social and educational organization in New York. Later, it became involved in political issues to promote the interests of farmers. Its members pressured state legislatures to regulate the rates charged by railroads and warehouses. It worked to increase prices for selling farm products and to lower costs for needed supplies. By the mid-1870s, membership had reached approximately one million.

▲ Sears, Roebuck and Company catalog from 1894

Easing Prairie Farming

The late 1800s brought many new and helpful developments for western settlers. One was the use of barbed wire. As mentioned earlier, without wood and rocks, fences could not be built in the Great Plains. As long as cattle grazed contentedly in a farmer's corn and wheat, the farmer could not hope to prosper. Farmers tried to build plain wire fences, but they failed to hold when herds pressed on them. Some farmers started thorn hedges, but it often took years for the hedges to become tall enough to do any good. In 1874 Joseph Glidden, an Illinois farmer, designed the first practical **barbed wire**. He used part of a coffee grinder to cut and coil small lengths of wire and then strung the barbs (short, sharp spikes) by hand. Soon a machine was invented to do the work. Within a decade, millions of pounds of barbed wire were being sold per year.

Another development was a greatly improved windmill invented by Daniel Halladay, a Connecticut mechanic. It was built to take advantage of the high prairie winds. It included a wind-operated pump that helped farmers obtain water.

Railroads helped ease some of the transportation problems on the vast Plains. Many railroads built spurs (extensions) to the scattered towns to deliver goods and obtain farmers' harvests in order to transport them to markets. The railways also made it easier to travel to other cities or regions.

Inventors designed heavier steel plows to cut through the matted sod and mechanical grain drills to plant seeds at the proper depth. They also improved the reaper, the device that cut and harvested grain. After 1850, steam engines provided power for larger inventions. Crews that had specialized equipment often traveled through various areas to assist farmers. During the 1890s, the steam-driven tractor proved to be a valuable invention.

SECTION REVIEW 17.3

1. What were the requirements to obtain and keep a homestead?
2. What was the difference between Boomers and Sooners?
3. What three problems were caused on the Plains by the lack of wood?
4. What other natural resource did settlers often lack?
5. What were three hardships faced by Plains settlers? What do you think might have been the worst?
6. How did Joseph Glidden's invention improve prairie farming? How did Daniel Halladay's invention do so?

GUIDING QUESTION

- Who were famous outlaws and lawmen of the Old West?

17.4 OUTLAWS AND LAWMEN

Who were famous outlaws and lawmen in the Old West?

Settlement of the West occurred quickly. As a result, local governments there had difficulty organizing fast enough to enforce the law. Without that enforcement, human sinfulness showed itself more frequently. Outlaws manifested the American values of individualism and growth in twisted ways. To control and punish lawbreakers, the national government appointed US marshals. Later, towns and communities hired local lawmen called sheriffs. Sometimes these individuals had been lawbreakers themselves. They decided to use their gunfighting skills to bring order to some of the chaos. Many outlaws and lawmen of this time became legends.

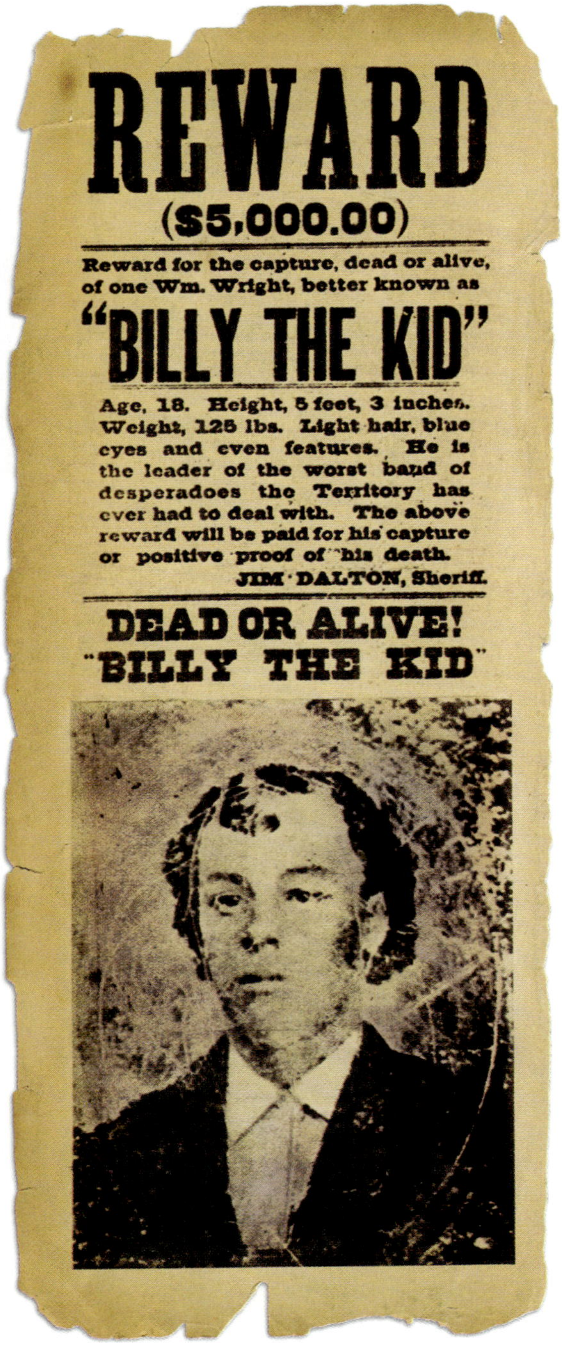

Outlaws

Jesse and Frank James

Jesse and Frank James were brothers who had fought in the Civil War as part of Quantrill's Raiders, a Confederate group led by William Quantrill that employed brutal guerrilla warfare tactics. After the war, Jesse and Frank formed a gang and began robbing banks, trains, and stagecoaches in Missouri and other nearby states.

▲ Jesse James

The James brothers claimed that misdeeds by Northerners during the war had driven them to a life of crime. They were sometimes portrayed as "Robin Hoods" because they were said to have robbed the rich and given money to the poor. That appears to be a myth; though allegedly, they would steal the money in safes when robbing trains but not take money from passengers.

Jesse died in 1882, shot in the back by a "friend" who wanted the reward for killing or capturing him. Jesse was thirty-four. Frank surrendered five months later, was placed on trial, and was acquitted of all charges. Afterward, he worked a variety of jobs and lived a crime-free life until his death in 1915.

▲ Frank James

Billy the Kid

Billy the Kid was also known as William Bonney and Henry McCarty. In his early teens, he began a career of theft and lawlessness. By the time he was eighteen, he was accused of having committed at least a dozen murders.

In late 1880, he was captured by Sheriff Pat Garrett in Lincoln County, New Mexico. A few months later, he was convicted of murder and sentenced to hang. However, he killed two guards and escaped. Garrett tracked him down and killed him in July 1881. Billy was only twenty-one years old.

Black Bart

Black Bart, whose real name appears to have been Charles Bolton or Charles Boles, was another Civil War veteran who turned to crime. "Black" evidently referred to the color of his beard or hair.

He allegedly committed almost thirty stagecoach robberies between 1875 and 1883. He was called "the gentleman bandit" because of his reputation for style and sophistication and for reportedly treating everyone with the best of manners. On a couple of occasions, he even left a poem at the scene of his crime. Although he carried a shotgun, he was never known to have fired it at anyone. Bart was captured in 1883 when a handkerchief dropped at a robbery was traced to him.

▲ Black Bart

The Dalton Gang

A group of outlaws known as the Dalton Gang committed most of its crimes over an eighteen-month period. Four of the Daltons were brothers. Three of them were present, along with two other gang members, when they attempted to rob two banks in Coffeyville, Kansas, in October 1892. All the bank robbers were killed except Emmett Dalton, who suffered multiple wounds. After spending fourteen years in prison, Emmett moved to Los Angeles. He was a respectable businessman in the city until his death in 1937.

the importance of GOVERNMENT *and* LOCAL CHURCHES

The conflict between outlaws and lawmen highlights the importance of government. Government is an institution ordained by God to punish evil and praise good (Rom. 13:3). In the early western towns, people had immense freedom, but it became dangerous when people used it to do wrong.

The lawlessness in western towns also shows the importance of local churches. Christianity was initially absent in these towns. The values of individualism, freedom, equality, and growth can benefit a society when directed by Christian teachings and exercised within the boundaries of law. But when they are not bound by either God's law or human law, they can produce great evils.

Did you know?

Emmett survived twenty-three gunshot wounds during the robbery in which two of his brothers died.

Lawmen

Wyatt Earp

Besides serving as a lawman, Wyatt Earp was a businessman with interests in a variety of activities including mining, gambling, operating a saloon, and horse racing. He is probably best known for his participation in the 1881 gunfight near the OK Corral in Tombstone, Arizona. Earp, two of his brothers (one serving as the town's marshal), and Doc Holliday, a friend, engaged in a shootout with outlaws. Three of the outlaws were killed.

In addition to Tombstone, Earp served as a lawman in a variety of places—particularly the Kansas towns of Wichita and Dodge City. His work as a lawman became legendary, though some of his exploits have proven greatly exaggerated. He died in 1929 at the age of eighty.

▾ Bat Masterson (below) and Wyatt Earp (at right) were close friends.

Bat Masterson

Like his good friend Wyatt Earp, Bat Masterson was a gambler, saloonkeeper, and lawman in the West. Later, he worked as a newspaper writer in New York City. He became a friend of President Theodore Roosevelt and was a frequent guest at the White House. In 1905 Roosevelt appointed him as a deputy US marshal.

Allan Pinkerton

Allan Pinkerton worked as a deputy sheriff and eventually established the Pinkerton National Detective Agency. This private company, formed in 1850, provided security for railroads and other businesses. Its detectives were frequently hired to guard factories during labor disputes and often clashed with striking workers. The firm also solved a number of train robberies, pursued outlaws, and transported money and valuables.

▾ This paper, distributed by the Pinkerton Agency, describes some of the outlaws its detectives were seeking to locate.

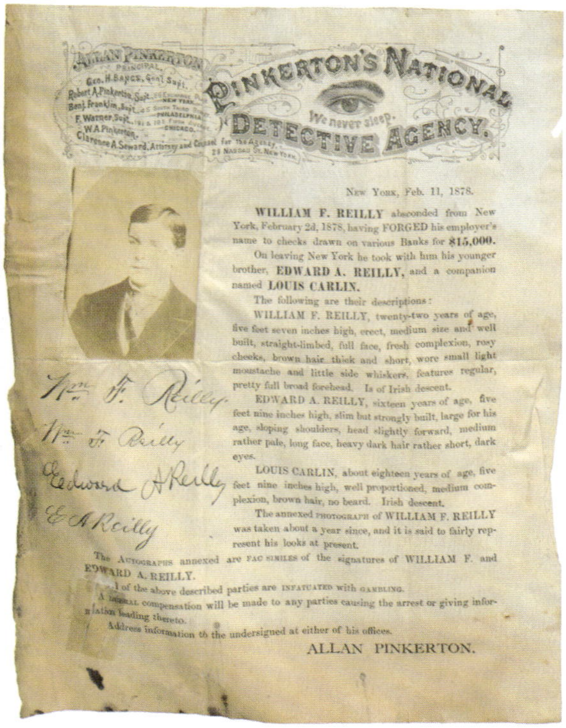

ALLAN PINKERTON, PRINCIPAL,
Geo. H. Bangs, Gen'l Supt.
Robert A. Pinkerton, Supt. New York.
Benj. Franklin, Supt. Philadelphia.
F. Warner, Supt. Chicago.
W. A. Pinkerton.
Clarence A. Seward, Attorney and Counsel for the Agency, 29 Nassau St. New York.

PINKERTON'S NATIONAL DETECTIVE AGENCY.
We never sleep.

New York, Feb. 11, 1878.

WILLIAM F. REILLY absconded from New York, February 2d, 1878, having FORGED his employer's name to checks drawn on various Banks for **$15,000.**

On leaving New York he took with him his younger brother, **EDWARD A. REILLY,** and a companion named **LOUIS CARLIN.**

The following are their descriptions:

WILLIAM F. REILLY, twenty-two years of age, five feet seven inches high, erect, medium size and well built, straight-limbed, full face, fresh complexion, rosy cheeks, brown hair thick and short, wore small light moustache and little side whiskers, features regular, pretty full broad forehead. Is of Irish descent.

EDWARD A. REILLY, sixteen years of age, five feet nine inches high, slim but strongly built, large for his age, sloping shoulders, head slightly forward, medium rather pale, long face, heavy dark hair rather short, dark eyes.

LOUIS CARLIN, about eighteen years of age, five feet nine inches high, well proportioned, medium complexion, brown hair, no beard. Irish descent.

The annexed PHOTOGRAPH of WILLIAM F. REILLY was taken about a year since, and it is said to fairly represent his looks at present.

The AUTOGRAPHS annexed are FAC SIMILES of the signatures of WILLIAM F. and EDWARD A. REILLY.

[illegible] of the above described parties are INFATUATED with GAMBLING.

A [illegible] compensation will be made to any parties causing the arrest or giving information leading thereto.

Address information to the undersigned at either of his offices.

ALLAN PINKERTON.

SECTION REVIEW 17.4

1. How did individualism with few governmental constraints lead to injustice in the West?
2. Which brother outlaws had been part of a Confederate band of raiders?
3. Which outlaw was accused of twelve murders by the time he was eighteen?
4. Explain why Black Bart was known as "the gentleman bandit."
5. How many Dalton brothers were killed when they attempted to rob two banks in Coffeyville, Kansas? Which brother survived multiple wounds during the robbery?
6. What is Wyatt Earp's best-known gunfight? Where was it?
7. What lawman was a good friend of Wyatt Earp and a frequent guest of President Theodore Roosevelt?
8. What agency provided security for railroads, guarded factories, and pursued outlaws?

17.5 CONFLICTS BETWEEN SETTLERS AND NATIVE AMERICANS

What were relations with the Indians like?

GUIDING QUESTIONS

- Why did Americans fight the Indians in the West?
- What were the results of the Dawes Act?

When many Americans moved to the Great Plains, they were entering land that had been occupied by Native Americans for centuries. But most Americans believed they were merely settling the American wilderness. They ignored the needs and desires of thousands of people whose ancestors had occupied the land before any Europeans arrived.

War and Surrender

When Native Americans tried to remove trespassers, the US government made new treaties. These treaties promised the Native Americans peace if they would remain in certain restricted areas of the West. However, illegal prospecting by whites often led to the discovery of gold or silver in those same areas. Repeated violations by prospectors and settlers made the treaties worthless, and the failed promises led to war.

Native Americans were skilled fighters, and the US Army was not accustomed to fighting an unconventional enemy. The army often responded to Indian attacks by waging total war, destroying Native American villages and crops and sometimes killing Native American women and children.

As mentioned earlier, gold was discovered on Sioux land in the Black Hills of South Dakota. The Sioux refused to sell their land, and war erupted. Probably the most famous battle of the Indian wars occurred in June 1876 near the Little Bighorn River in Montana Territory. The fame of this battle lies partly in the personalities involved: Lieutenant Colonel **George Armstrong Custer** of the US Army and Native American leaders Sitting Bull and Crazy Horse.

Custer was a rash, dashing, self-centered Indian fighter. He misjudged the strength and determination of a group of Sioux warriors and their allies. With about two hundred men, Custer launched what he thought would be a surprise attack. Instead, the Native Americans surprised Custer by fighting him with overwhelming numbers—perhaps two thousand warriors. At the **Battle of the Little Bighorn**, also known as "Custer's Last Stand," the Sioux were led by one of their chiefs, **Crazy Horse**. Another chieftain, **Sitting Bull**, was not at the battle but had been involved in the preparation for it. Custer and his men were killed in less than an hour.

▲ Lieutenant Colonel George Custer is shown standing and firing two pistols at the Battle of the Little Bighorn. Custer and all of his soldiers were killed during the fighting.

▲ Chief Joseph

▲ Geronimo

Shocked and sobered by the defeat, the US government quickly sent more men and supplies west to defeat the Sioux. Within months of Custer's defeat, the army had forced them to accept peace on the government's terms. Most Sioux were sent to the reservations.

Native American resistance ended as much from the destruction of buffalo herds as from defeat in war. The frontiersmen had little sympathy for Native Americans. But some easterners said that mistreatment of Native Americans was inexcusable. In 1877 President Rutherford B. Hayes admitted in a national address, "Many, if not most, of our Indian wars have had their origin in broken promises and acts of injustice upon our part."

Sadly, recognition of the problem did little to change the Native Americans' plight. In the same year that President Hayes made his speech, the peaceful Nez Perce tribe in Idaho, led by **Chief Joseph**, made a desperate attempt to avoid captivity by fleeing to Canada. He and his followers retreated almost 1,700 miles over a period of about three months. But the US Army stopped the tribe forty miles from the border. Cold, hungry, and outnumbered, the Native Americans had little choice but to surrender. A young army officer present wrote that the chieftain said, "I am tired of fighting. . . . It is cold, and we have no blankets. The little children are freezing to death. . . . My heart is sick and sad. From where the sun now stands, I will fight no more forever." Chief Joseph was taken prisoner and transported to Kansas where he stayed for several months. He then lived on reservations in Oklahoma and Washington State. He died in 1904.

By 1885 all but a few scattered groups of Native Americans had been forced onto reservations. Those that resisted included Apache leader **Geronimo**. For several years he and a small band of Native Americans frustrated the army's attempts to keep them on a reservation. Finally, in 1886 he surrendered. He was held prisoner until his death in 1909.

In 1890 some Sioux gathered for a ceremony called the Ghost Dance. The ritual celebrated a future envisioned by the tribe. They believed that one day the earth would die and be reborn. The white men would go to another world. The buffalo would return, and Native Americans would then have their lands restored. As tensions between Native Americans and settlers increased, the Ghost Dance became more popular. Some who participated claimed that they received special powers to kill whites, and some claimed that the ghost shirts worn at the dance could stop bullets.

On December 29, 1890, near Wounded Knee Creek in South Dakota, the US Army tried to disarm and capture a band of Sioux who had left the reservation. In the process, someone fired a shot. It is still unclear who did so, as versions of the story vary. Fighting quickly

▾ Burial of Indians who died at the Wounded Knee massacre

started. When it was over, 25 soldiers and more than 150 Native Americans (half of them women and children) were dead. The **Wounded Knee massacre** was a tragic conclusion to the Indian Wars.

Missionaries often offered help for the Native Americans, meeting their physical needs while presenting them with the gospel. But tragically, Americans had given the Native Americans little reason to embrace "the white man's God."

Reform Attempts

In 1881 author Helen Hunt Jackson published ***A Century of Dishonor***. It portrayed the government's ruthless and often deceitful dealings with Native Americans. Her book, combined with the decreasing threat of the Plains Indians, inspired some overdue sympathy for Native Americans.

In 1887 Congress tried to undo some of the damage by passing the **Dawes Act**. It assumed that the Native American way of life no longer worked. It said that the government would help Americanize the Native Americans, or absorb them into mainstream American life. Under the Dawes Act, tribal unions were weakened. Individual Native Americans were to receive lands and become self-supporting. Each head of a household was assigned 160 acres.

But the reformers, who were mostly easterners, did not understand the Native Americans' needs. First, most western tribes who were given lands had been hunters and traders, not farmers. Second, the lands the Native Americans had been allotted were very dry. The government had given them to the Indians because they were undesired by settlers. Such plots of land could not sustain a family. Third, some Native Americans were

Sitting Bull

In 1877 Sitting Bull fled to Canada. In 1881 he returned to the United States and lived on reservations in North and South Dakota. For a few months, in 1885, he was allowed to tour with Buffalo Bill's Wild West, a traveling show operated by famed cowboy William "Buffalo Bill" Cody. Upon returning to the reservation, he continued to criticize US policies against Indians and opposed the planned sale of tribal lands.

In 1890 officials accused him of encouraging Native Americans to rebel. They also feared that he would support the Ghost Dance movement. The US Indian agent, a government official in the area, ordered Indian reservation police to arrest him. In doing so, a fight occurred. More than a dozen policemen and tribesmen were killed. Sitting Bull was among them.

how were NATIVE AMERICANS TREATED?

In 1869 the Board of Indian Commissioners, a US government agency, presented a stunning report about the mistreatment of Native Americans. Though it noted that some settlers dealt fairly with Native Americans, it stated that the American government and many whites were brutal in their dealings. Sadly, the government did little to handle the problems noted in the report. The following are excerpts:

> The history of the government connections with the Indians is a shameful record of broken treaties and unfulfilled promises.
>
> The history of [some of the] white man's connection with the Indians is a sickening record of murder, outrage, robbery, and wrongs committed by the former [whites] as the rule, and occasional savage outbreaks and unspeakably barbarous deeds of retaliation by the latter [Indians] as the exception.
>
> [There are] men on the frontier who . . . are just and honorable . . . and . . . have been powerless to prevent these wrongs. . . . There are many good men on the border . . . some of the most earnest remonstrants [protesters, objectors] against the evils [Indians have suffered]. . . .
>
> The testimony of some of the highest military officers of the United States is on record to the effect that, in our Indian wars, almost without exception, the first aggressions have been made by the white man. . . . There is a large class of professedly reputable men who use every means in their power to bring on Indian wars, for the sake of the profit to be realized from the presence of troops and the expenditure of government funds in their midst. They proclaim death to the Indians at all times, in words and publications. . . . Every crime committed by a white man against an Indian is concealed. . . ; every offense committed by an Indian against a white man is borne on the wings of the post [letter written and mailed] or the telegraph to the remotest corner of the land.

not accustomed to the idea of private ownership of land, so land deeds meant little to them. Fourth, the Native Americans' basic social structures were the tribe and the extended family (several generations, including grandparents, aunts, uncles, and cousins). When these two units weakened, the Native American way of life suffered even more.

Eager to make money, some settlers offered to buy Native American lands. Since Native Americans now owned the land personally, they had the option to sell it, and they often did. Because they had limited understanding of a money economy, however, they were frequently cheated. When oil was found on Native American lands, speculators bought even more of their land.

In later years, the US government made additional attempts to remedy some of the wrongs done to Native Americans. In 1924 Congress gave Native Americans full citizenship. In 1934 the Indian Reorganization Act gave reservations limited self-government. Congress also made it easier for Native Americans to seek damages for past violations of treaties and other agreements. However, these acts failed to address all the injustices they had suffered.

SECTION REVIEW 17.5

1. How did the US Army often respond to Native Americans?
2. What is probably the most famous Indian battle? What was the outcome of that battle?
3. How did the Dawes Act fail to meet the needs of the Indians?
4. According to the Board of Indian Commissioners, how were the Indians mistreated? Why is this treatment unjustified in the name of American freedom and growth?

CHAPTER 17 REVIEW

Making Connections

1. What major technological advance enabled more people to move west?
2. Who were the "Exodusters"? Why were they given this name?
3. What would be built in mining towns to serve the miners?
4. To what city did each of the following trails lead?
   a. Sedalia Trail
   b. Chisholm Trail
   c. Western Trail
   d. Goodnight-Loving Trail
5. What were the seven jobs a cowboy could have on a cattle drive?
6. How did future meat shippers solve the problem of ice causing discolored meat?
7. How did cattlemen deal with the loss of open range because of land given to homesteaders?
8. What two companies began selling their items through mail-order catalogs?
9. Why do you think the old West was often referred to as the Wild West?
10. With what tribe is each of the following chiefs associated?
    a. Crazy Horse
    b. Sitting Bull
    c. Chief Joseph
    d. Geronimo

Thinking Critically

11. Design a brand for your herd of cattle. Explain how you determined the design.
12. Why might homesteaders, rather than miners or cowboys, be given more credit for actually settling the frontier?
13. How could the Indians have been treated differently during the settlement of the West?

Living as a Christian Citizen

14. Even today, good local churches are less numerous in the West than in the East. What actions could you take now and in the future to help develop churches in the American West?
15. Imagine that you are a citizen in a newly built western mining town. What challenges will you face in working with others to build a local government? What will motivate you to overcome those challenges?

Sioux chieftains ▸

Terms to Remember

Great Plains
Pikes Peak or Bust!
Comstock Lode
lode
greenbacks
open range
Chisholm Trail
Indian Territory
Goodnight-Loving Trail
trail boss
Homestead Act
Sooners
sod houses
Grange
barbed wire
George Armstrong Custer
Battle of the Little Bighorn
Crazy Horse
Sitting Bull
Chief Joseph
Geronimo
Wounded Knee massacre
A Century of Dishonor
Dawes Act

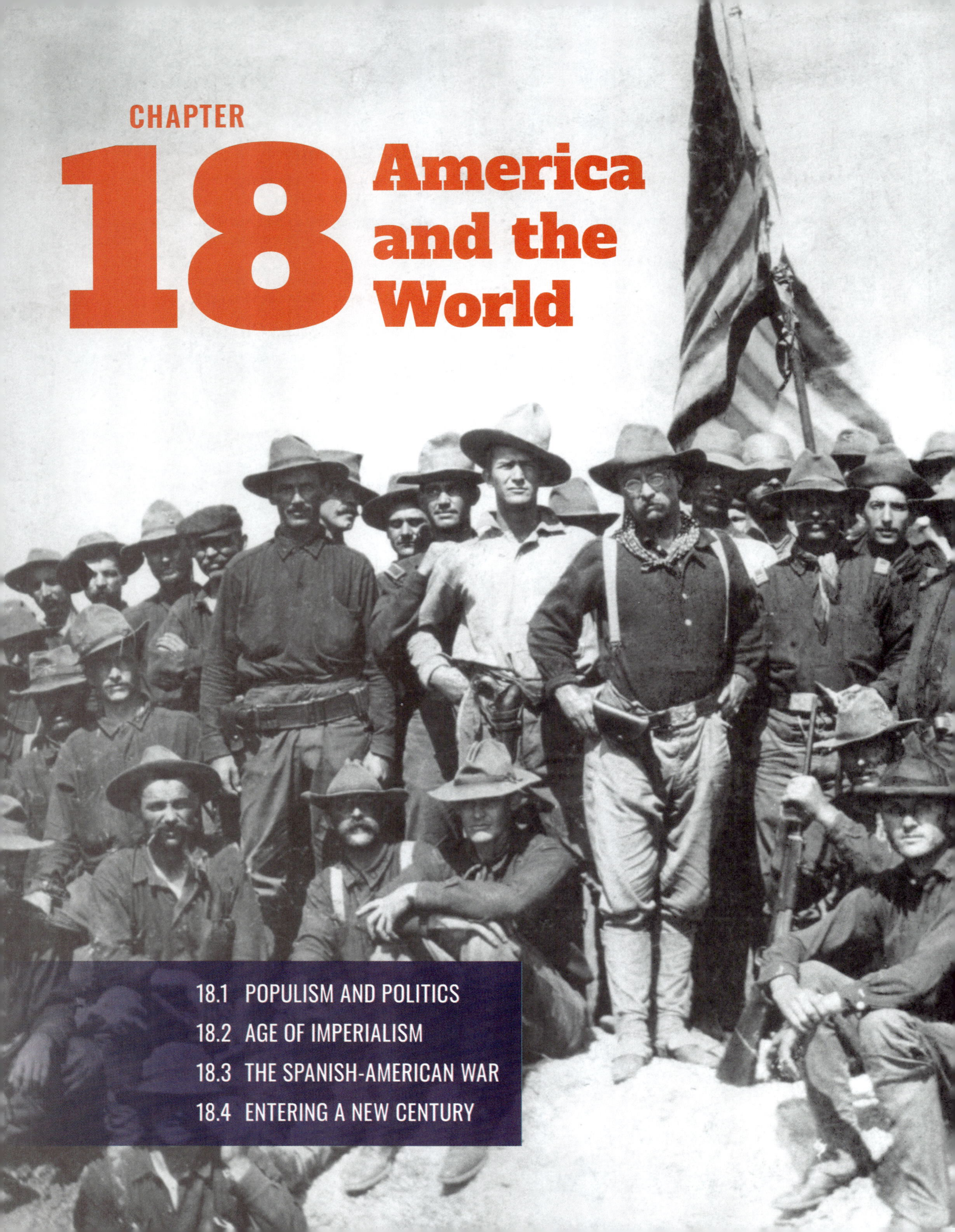

CHAPTER

18 America and the World

18.1 POPULISM AND POLITICS

18.2 AGE OF IMPERIALISM

18.3 THE SPANISH-AMERICAN WAR

18.4 ENTERING A NEW CENTURY

Throughout the nineteenth century, America increased its population, built its industries, and expanded its settlement across the continent. As it grew, the nation became stronger and extended its influence. Having spread their culture from the East Coast to the West Coast, some Americans now wanted to spread it to more distant lands. However, seeking such growth posed challenges to other values. In their desire for the growth of America they might disregard the equality, freedom, and individualism of other peoples.

GUIDING QUESTION

- How did the development of the Populist Party impact the election of 1896?

18.1 POPULISM AND POLITICS

What led to the rise of the Populist Party?

The Populist Party

By the late 1880s, farmers were increasingly unhappy with both the Democratic and Republican parties. They believed neither adequately addressed their concerns. As a result, in 1891 farmers formed the People's Party. It was also known as the **Populist Party** because its goals were based on populism (appealing to the common people). They urged members of labor unions to join their group. In the 1892 election, their presidential candidate, James B. Weaver, received more than a million votes (8.5 percent of the votes cast).

Populists supported a long list of reforms. These included limiting the president and vice president to serving only one term; having US senators elected by the people rather than the state legislatures; transferring ownership of all railroads and telegraphs to the government; limiting the workday to eight hours for factory workers; and establishing government loans for farmers. They also supported "free silver"—the unlimited use of silver for coins—and the use of both gold and silver for currency (see Chapter 17).

The Election of 1896

As the next presidential election approached, Democrat Grover Cleveland was completing his second term. When his party gathered to nominate their candidate for 1896, **William Jennings Bryan** delivered an electrifying speech in support of free silver. Bryan, a congressman from Nebraska, was only thirty-six. Yet he was named the Democratic candidate for president. Bryan received the nickname "the Great Commoner" because of his sympathy for the common man. He was also a passionate Christian. His understanding of the problems that farmers faced and his support for many of the Populist ideas led the Populist Party to also support him in the election.

At the 1896 Democratic convention, William Jennings Bryan delivered an electrifying speech (later called the "Cross of Gold" speech). It led to his nomination as his party's candidate for president. In that election, the top of this campaign poster showed Bryan, his family, and quotes from that speech. The full text was at the bottom.

Future president Theodore Roosevelt (center, with spectacles) shown with his fellow Rough Riders during the Spanish-American War

◂ McKinley delivered speeches at his home.

▾ Bryan spoke from the back of a train.

Republicans nominated **William McKinley** as their candidate. He had served in Congress for fourteen years and as Ohio's governor for four. He received the support of most business leaders in the country.

The 1896 campaign was a study in contrasts. Bryan conducted a whirlwind tour of the country. He made hundreds of stops along an 18,000-mile trek and was heard by audiences totaling nearly five million. He delivered dynamic speeches. McKinley, however, stayed home. In a carefully organized effort, McKinley ran a "front porch campaign" from his home in Canton, Ohio. Trainloads of people were given all-expense-paid trips to Canton to hear McKinley read a prepared script. Meanwhile, hundreds of speakers traveled throughout the country to promote him. Republicans spent about twenty times as much money on the campaign as the Democrats.

Bryan received six and a half million votes, but McKinley received more than seven million. McKinley won the Electoral College by a margin of 271 to 176.

William McKinley

25

Born	January 29, 1843
Died	September 14, 1901
Home state	Ohio
Wife	Ida Saxton
Church	Methodist
Occupations	teacher, clerk, lawyer
Party	Republican
Years served as president	1897–1901
Terms	1 and partial (assassinated)
Vice presidents	1st—Garret Hobart 2nd—Theodore Roosevelt

SECTION REVIEW 18.1

1. What reforms did Populists support?
2. Which specific Populist reform did William Jennings Bryan emphasize in his 1896 speech at the Democratic convention?

18.2 AGE OF IMPERIALISM

What were the effects of American imperialism in the late nineteenth century?

During much of the nineteenth century, America focused on itself. The country had little concern for foreign affairs that did not affect it directly. When a country largely stays out of all world politics, it is taking a position called **isolationism**.

During the late 1800s, a number of Western European nations—including Britain, France, and Germany—were building large empires by gaining economic and political control over weaker nations that usually became colonies of the stronger country. The United States watched as this process, called **imperialism**, brought greater wealth and power to those nations. Would the United States join those imperialist powers by building its own overseas empire?

GUIDING QUESTIONS

- Why do countries become imperialistic?
- How did Americans view imperialism?
- What territories did America gain during this period?

Reasons for Imperialism

PRESTIGE AND PRIDE

First, a large empire gave a country prestige and became a source of national pride.

POWER

Second, nations were motivated by the desire to increase their power. Because taking control of foreign lands often required military force, an imperialist power increased its military strength. A large and well-trained army and navy were needed to govern the empire and defend against enemies. Thus, the military established important bases (both naval and army) around the world on lands the nation controlled. Those bases further increased the nation's power.

ACCUMULATION OF WEALTH

Third, imperialism enabled the accumulation of wealth. Imperialist countries, or mother countries, controlled their colonies' trade and development of natural resources. Mother countries sent their own citizens to oversee the colonies' industries. These individuals hired local peoples for low wages and sent profits to the mother countries, which benefited from mine and plantation production. Mother countries held every economic advantage over their colonies. For instance, they ensured that the colonies bought all their imports from the mother countries. Sometimes the mother countries took advantage of the poverty and ignorance of native peoples to keep them working for the benefit of the mother countries. Such practices are called **exploitation**.

CIVILIZATION

Fourth, some people in imperialist countries thought that they needed to "civilize" other nations of the world. The British writer Rudyard Kipling wrote about "the white man's burden." He said it was the duty of whites to help other nations. He and many Europeans viewed their societies as superior to the "backward" civilizations of Asia and Africa. They thought it was their responsibility to share the fruit of their culture—education, medical care, better farming methods, industry, and technology. Thus, they launched efforts to improve education, abolish slavery, and stamp out disease and famine in other parts of the world. Although many native peoples profited from such assistance, or **humanitarian aid**, they understandably objected to the superior attitude of most Europeans. They were also unhappy that they often lost control of their governments and their valuable resources.

THE SPREAD OF CHRISTIANITY

Fifth, imperialism allowed for the spread of Christianity. Missionaries sincerely wanted to help foreign nations by preaching the gospel and teaching the truths of Christianity. Many opposed attempts by some imperialists to exploit the people to whom the missionaries were ministering. These missionaries educated both men and women so that they could read the Bible. Because they cared about others, they also engaged in humanitarian aid; however, this was not normally the primary focus of their work.

Dwight L. Moody

Missions work expanded rapidly during the age of imperialism. In the second half of the 1800s, **Dwight L. Moody**, one of the most famous American preachers of the period, promoted missions as he spoke in the United States and Great Britain. Through his efforts, the Student Volunteer Movement for Foreign Missions (SVMFM) was established in 1886. Its members sought to evangelize the world in their generation. New advances in transportation and communication made this goal seem possible to achieve. But sadly, within a few decades many in this group replaced the biblical gospel (the teaching that Jesus died for the sins of mankind, was resurrected, and offers salvation to all who repent and believe) with the social gospel. The social gospel movement, discussed more in Chapter 19, made humanitarian aid its predominant goal.

the STUDENT VOLUNTEER MOVEMENT *for* FOREIGN MISSIONS

The Student Volunteer Movement for Foreign Missions (SVMFM) was an outgrowth of the Young Men's Christian Association (YMCA). The motto of the SVMFM was "the evangelization of the world in this generation." The group flourished through the leadership of several college students.

Doctrinally, the organization tried to make room for both conservatives and liberals (those who denied clear biblical teachings, such as the deity of Jesus Christ). That position contributed to the organization's decline after World War I. Until then, it thrived. By the time the SVMFM ended in 1966, it had encouraged thousands of college students to preach the gospel throughout the world.

Differing Views about Imperialism

Americans saw the economic benefits and other advantages of empire building. By 1880 they were producing far more food than they could sell at home. The nation also wanted new markets for the goods it manufactured. Americans were also looking for new sources of raw materials. In addition, some wanted a stronger army and navy. To transport its raw materials and manufactured goods, the nation needed refueling stations in the Pacific. Consequently, some Americans began to view imperialism favorably. Some even believed that the United States would become a second-rate nation if it did not build an empire.

But some Americans opposed expansion. They argued that the United States was large and lacked few natural resources. They said the nation did not need to dominate foreign countries; it could simply purchase any necessary materials from them. Opponents of imperialism argued that it contradicted American ideals. After all, Americans had fought for their own liberty. Would they now take away the liberty of others?

WELL, I HARDLY KNOW WHICH TO TAKE FIRST!

"Well, I hardly know which to take first," says Uncle Sam to "waiter" William McKinley as he views a menu listing various parts of the world.

New American Territories

Alaska

Even before the United States involved itself in imperialism, it had begun acquiring foreign land. As mentioned in Chapter 15, it had purchased Alaska from Russia in 1867. Unlike all the land the United States had acquired before that time, Alaska was not connected to the other land areas of the United States. It was a "distant land" bought for America's benefit.

Alaska proved to be very beneficial. The discovery of gold there in 1896 brought a flood of miners to the area around the Yukon River. The gold rush boosted the economy of the United States. Later, prospectors found silver, copper, and oil in Alaska. Their discoveries further increased the nation's resources. Fishing also became important to Alaska's economy. In 1959 Alaska became the forty-ninth state.

The Midway Islands

In 1859 American sailors discovered and claimed some uninhabited islands approximately halfway between North America and Asia. Because of the location, they became known as the Midway Islands. In 1867 the United States annexed the area. Midway's strategic importance was emphasized during World War II when a major battle for control of the Pacific occurred there.

Hawaii

The United States made its first imperialistic move in early 1898. That year, Congress annexed the islands of Hawaii. American missionaries and businessmen had gone to the islands in the early 1800s. Sadly, some of their sons became businessmen who took advantage of Hawaiian workers to build sugarcane plantations. Americans also gained influence in Hawaii's government. In 1893 they forced Hawaii's queen, Liliuokalani, from power. They were assisted by a US official who ordered US Marines and sailors to land in Honolulu.

The businessmen asked the United States to annex the islands. President Grover Cleveland refused because the queen had been removed from power illegally. After William McKinley became president, Congress approved annexing Hawaii. Decades later, in 1959, it became the fiftieth state.

SECTION REVIEW 18.2

1. What were five reasons for imperialism?
2. What is exploitation?
3. How was humanitarian aid both good and bad?
4. What was the goal of the Studenwt Volunteer Movement for Foreign Missions? How can you continue working toward this goal today?
5. What territory did America acquire from Russia in 1867? What resources did it provide?
6. What territory was America's first purposeful imperialistic acquisition? Why did President Cleveland refuse to annex the area?

GUIDING QUESTIONS

- What caused the Spanish-American War?
- What happened during the Spanish-American War?
- What were the results of the Spanish-American War?

18.3 THE SPANISH-AMERICAN WAR

What happened during the Spanish-American War?

In 1898 America entered a war with Spain that greatly expanded its overseas empire. Although it was a short and inexpensive war (compared with other wars), the Spanish-American War had huge consequences for American imperialism.

Cuba, located less than one hundred miles from the southern coast of Florida, was the cause of a quarrel with Spain. Cuba had been ruled by Spain for four hundred years. By the end of the 1800s, more and more Cubans were calling for independence from Spain.

Causes of the War

One reason the United States eventually entered the war was that many Americans were upset by the unjust treatment Cubans were receiving from the Spanish. They believed Spain was exploiting its colony and allowing its officials to govern it poorly. Cubans had long been dissatisfied with conditions in their country. Many suffered from poverty and cruel treatment. The United States and other nations tried to help the Cubans and encouraged Spain to improve the situation, but little change occurred. Americans watched as conditions for their Cuban neighbors worsened.

In 1895 revolution erupted in Cuba. The revolutionaries had three goals, which they hoped would lead to eventual independence:

1. To terrorize Cuba
2. To destroy its main industry, sugar processing
3. To draw the United States into the conflict

The intent of the first two goals was to frustrate the Spanish government to the point they gave independence to Cuba. The revolutionary forces in Cuba had agents in the United States who assisted with the third goal. Those supporters raised money for the revolution and provided the American press with exaggerated reports about various incidents, all of which they blamed on Spain. They hoped the stories would make Americans angry enough to declare war on Spain.

▲ Joseph Pulitzer (left) and William Randolph Hearst (right)

A second reason for the war was the impact of the information presented by American newspapers. Many of these newspapers fiercely competed with each other to sell subscriptions. One method increased sales by providing sensational descriptions of events. Reporters often twisted news stories, trying to make each more exciting than the previous one. That practice is called **yellow journalism**, or the yellow press. Two powerful newspapermen were involved in this struggle: **William Randolph Hearst**, owner of the *New York Journal*, and **Joseph Pulitzer**, owner of the *New York World*. Some of what they printed was either inaccurate or greatly exaggerated. They knew that by encouraging reporters to write such stories they could provoke great interest in the growing conflict. Their news reports stirred the sympathies of readers and made them want to help the Cubans. They wanted Cubans to have the freedoms and advantages that Americans enjoyed and to be free of Spanish mistreatment.

the PRESS, PUBLIC OPINION, *and* COMIC STRIPS TOO

In 1864, as a teenager, Joseph Pulitzer emigrated from Hungary to the United States. After fighting in the Civil War, he eventually moved to St. Louis. There he worked for a number of newspapers including the *St. Louis Post-Dispatch*. In 1883 he purchased the *New York World*. Alert reporting, sensational stunts, and vivid pictures helped the *World* become a thriving newspaper. Pulitzer was a crusader. No matter what the cause, he could arouse excitement and inspiration among readers.

Editors across the country studied and imitated Pulitzer's methods. His most successful imitator, William Randolph Hearst, copied him so well that Hearst quickly became Pulitzer's chief competitor. Hearst had been given the *San Francisco Examiner* by his father. Hearst later inherited his father's enormous wealth, and in 1895 he purchased the *New York Journal*. He soon convinced a number of Pulitzer's writers to work for him. When news was lacking, Hearst made his own news. He turned reporters into detectives to pursue criminals and made crime columns more exciting.

Hearst and Pulitzer fiercely battled each other for subscribers. In 1897, artist-reporter Frederic Remington was ready to leave Cuba, where he had been stationed, believing there was nothing significant to report. Hearst allegedly cabled a message to him: "Please remain. You furnish the pictures, and I'll furnish the war."

As editors of smaller papers imitated Hearst and Pulitzer, thoughtful citizens were troubled as they realized that newspapers' journalists were not just reporting public opinion but creating and controlling it. After all, the issue that was involved—entering a war—was deadly serious. This was not the first time the American press had *created* rather than *reflected* opinion, but it had never done so on such a wide scale.

After the war, Pulitzer focused on providing more accurate reporting. When he died in 1911, he left money for the establishment of a school of journalism at Columbia University.

Meanwhile, Hearst established or acquired newspapers throughout the country. He also owned several magazines. Trying to capture working-class families as newspaper readers, Hearst added an eight-page Sunday supplement, in color, to the *New York Journal* in 1896. The *Journal* published such cartoons as the *Katzenjammer Kids*, *Mutt and Jeff*, *The Yellow Kid*, and *Krazy Kat*. Editors found that the comics, or funnies, were the first part of the paper that most people read. The funnies became a kind of American folk art, expressing what some Americans thought or felt or at least what amused them.

▾ This selection from the popular comic strip, *The Yellow Kid*, was published in January 1898.

▾ The USS *Maine* exploded in the Havana, Cuba, harbor on February 15, 1898 (top). The ship is shown arriving in Havana the previous month (below).

As tensions rose over the Cuban situation, a third reason for war occurred. In February 1898, the *New York Journal* published a letter written by Enrique Dupuy de Lôme, the Spanish ambassador to the United States, to one of his personal friends. It was never meant for publication, but Cuban rebels stole it and gave it to the Hearst newspaper. The **de Lôme letter** described McKinley as "weak and a bidder for the admiration of the crowd besides being a would-be politician." Most Americans considered this foreign criticism of the president to be a national insult. The yellow press demanded that Spain be punished. De Lôme resigned and Spain apologized for the incident; however, the uproar did not diminish.

A fourth reason for war was the sinking of the **USS *Maine***. Since January 1898 the American battleship had been docked in Havana, Cuba. At 9:40 p.m. on the evening of February 15, the *Maine*

mysteriously exploded. About 260 American sailors died. This event occurred less than a week after the publication of the de Lôme letter. The yellow press concluded that Spain was responsible. Other explanations were possible, but many Americans wanted to blame Spain. They demanded action. The battle cry became "Remember the *Maine*!"

In mid-April, Congress issued a resolution that approved the use of force in Cuba to establish a stable government. It declared "that the people of Cuba are, and of right ought to be, free and independent . . . demanding the government of Spain to relinquish its authority." The resolution included the **Teller Amendment**, which said that the United States had no intention of adding Cuba to its empire and that the United States desired only Cuba's independence. The amendment gave Americans confidence that further action would only help the Cubans and not promote American imperialism.

The Spanish did not agree to the US demands, and on April 24, 1898, they declared war on the United States. The following day, the United States issued a declaration of war against Spain. The **Spanish-American War** had begun.

Most Americans wanted the Cubans to have a better life and thought that the United States could help them achieve progress. But such interest in Cuba opened the way for expansion of American power and influence, and expansion included the problems that accompany empire building.

WHAT REALLY HAPPENED *to the* USS *MAINE*?

In spite of several attempts to determine the cause, no one knows precisely why the USS *Maine* exploded in 1898. A study by US naval investigators in 1976 concluded that the explosion resulted from an accident inside the ship, where coal for the engine was stored.

Yet, a 1998 analysis stated a mine might have caused the explosion. If this was true, who planted the mine? The Spanish? If so, why? Some have argued that Cuban revolutionaries may have planted it, hoping that the United States would blame Spain and issue a declaration of war. It is unlikely that the complete story about the explosion will ever be known.

863,956 WORLDS CIRCULATED YESTERDAY

The World.

"Circulation Books Open to All."

NEW YORK, THURSDAY, FEBRUARY 17, 1898.

863,956 WORLDS CIRCULATED YESTERDAY

MAINE EXPLOSION CAUSED BY BOMB OR TORPEDO?

Capt. Sigsbee and Consul-General Lee Are in Doubt---The World Has Sent a Special Tug, With Submarine Divers, to Havana to Find Out---Lee Asks for an Immediate Court of Inquiry---Capt. Sigsbee's Suspicions.

CAPT. SIGSBEE, IN A SUPPRESSED DESPATCH TO THE STATE DEPARTMENT, SAYS THE ACCIDENT WAS MADE POSSIBLE BY AN ENEMY.

Dr. E. C. Pendleton, Just Arrived from Havana, Says He Overheard Talk There of a Plot to Blow Up the Ship---Capt Zalinski, the Dynamite Expert, and Other Experts Report to The World that the Wreck Was Not Accidental---Washington Officials Ready for Vigorous Action if Spanish Responsibility Can Be Shown---Divers to Be Sent Down to Make Careful Examinations.

WAS US INVOLVEMENT JUSTIFIED?

For more than a century, people have debated whether the United States should have been involved in the Spanish-American War. Making judgments about historical events is difficult. People alive today often do not fully understand the worldviews and concerns that motivated people in the past. Some have been quick to criticize earlier generations based on current worldviews.

While Christians should consider past events in light of their time, Christians should also evaluate all matters according to God's Word. Using biblical principles, many Christians argue that the United States was wrong to fight a war with Spain in 1898. They note that the inaccurate and dishonest reporting in leading newspapers and the failure to investigate the explosion aboard the *Maine* helped propel the nation into a war that it could have avoided. They contend that the biblical teachings regarding honesty, diligence, and wisdom were lacking in the decision-making process.

Fighting the War

The United States was not really ready for a full-scale war, but the Spanish government and army were weak. As a result, the United States won every battle it fought in the Spanish-American War. The war was over in 114 days.

By late spring of 1898, the American troops had gathered at a military base in Tampa, Florida. Many soldiers had been issued wool uniforms, which proved to be excessively hot in the subtropical area where the war was fought. Also, some cavalry troops lacked horses. Nevertheless, the invasion force sailed on June 14.

The US Army fought bravely. Several regiments gained special fame. But the navy played the most important role in the war. During the Cleveland presidency, the United States had developed a program to build a fleet of steel ships. Those ships proved critical during the war. The navy's success showed that the United States had become a major world power.

Long before war was declared, Assistant Secretary of the Navy **Theodore Roosevelt** had sent secret orders to Commodore George Dewey, who was in Hong Kong with the American Pacific fleet. Roosevelt ordered Dewey to prepare for an attack on the Spanish fleet in the Philippines, a Spanish colony, in case war erupted with Spain. On April 30 the American force arrived in Manila, Philippines. It met the Spanish Pacific fleet the next morning. By noon, the **Battle of Manila Bay** was over. The Americans wrecked the outdated Spanish fleet, sank eight ships, and killed or wounded almost 400. American losses were slight—one warship damaged, one sailor dead, and nine others wounded.

In June, an American fleet trapped a Spanish fleet in the harbor of Santiago, the capital of Cuba at that time. American troops landed near Santiago and stormed the city. They pushed the Spanish back to defenses on **San Juan Hill**. Earlier, Theodore Roosevelt had resigned his office in the Navy Department to help command an all-volunteer cavalry unit called the **Rough Riders**. They included cowboys, miners, college students, and adventurers from the West. Ironically, Roosevelt was the only Rough Rider with a horse. The others fought on foot because most of the horses were still in Florida. The unit launched a famous charge up San Juan Hill and helped defeat the Spanish. Two days later, the Spanish fleet attempted to escape the harbor at Santiago but lost all its ships in a sea battle. On July 17 the Spanish in Santiago officially surrendered. Later, the American army also captured Puerto Rico, another Spanish possession.

▾ Rough Riders charging up San Juan Hill

Roosevelt as an Author

Theodore Roosevelt's writing reveals his wide-ranging interests. Topics on which he wrote ranged from history and politics to biography and outdoor sports. The following is a list, arranged by subject, of some of his books:

History

The Naval Operations of the War between Great Britain and the United States, 1812–1815

New York

The Winning of the West

The Rough Riders

Politics

Essays on Practical Politics

Biography and Autobiography

Thomas Hart Benton

Gouverneur Morris

Oliver Cromwell

Theodore Roosevelt: An Autobiography

Outdoor Life

Hunting Trips of a Ranchman

American Big-Game Hunting

The Wilderness Hunter

The Strenuous Life

Fun Fact

The Rough Riders were commanded by Colonel Leonard Wood, who was assisted by Theodore Roosevelt. Because no one had horses except Roosevelt, they were also called "Wood's Weary Walkers."

Statue of Theodore (Teddy) Roosevelt in San Antonio, Texas

By the time the war was officially over in August, fewer than 400 American soldiers had died in combat or from combat wounds. But diseases killed thirteen times as many Americans as combat. More than 5,000 soldiers died of typhoid, malaria, yellow fever, or other disease. Over 60,000 Spanish soldiers died of disease or wounds.

Spain signed a truce on August 12, 1898. Spanish and American diplomats met in Paris on October 1. By December 10, they had produced the Treaty of Paris. In it, Spain agreed to give up Cuba. Puerto Rico in the Caribbean and Guam in the Pacific became US possessions. In addition, the United States gave Spain $20 million for the Philippines.

A debate erupted about the treaty. Influential anti-imperialists (including Andrew Carnegie, former president Grover Cleveland, and author Mark Twain) voiced their opposition to it. They said that it violated an important American principle—that people should be self-governing rather than subjects of another nation. However, William Jennings Bryan, a leading Democrat, supported the treaty by arguing that American control of the Philippines would open the door for its future independence. Eventually, the US Senate did ratify the treaty. It narrowly received the required two-thirds vote.

American Deaths

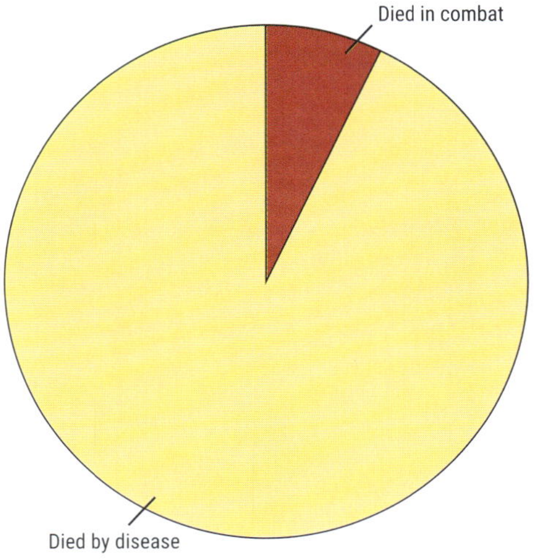

Impact of the War

Whether Americans approved or not, the United States now had an empire—and all the problems that it entailed.

Did you know?

In recent years "Gitmo," as the Guantánamo Bay base is sometimes called, has been used to imprison terrorists. The first such terrorists were taken there a few months after the September 11, 2001, attack on the World Trade Center and Pentagon.

Cuba

The Teller Amendment promised Cuba its independence. But because the United States felt that Cuba was not ready for full independence, it became a US **protectorate** (a country that is technically independent but has to submit to some control by another nation). In 1901 Congress passed the **Platt Amendment** that contained strict regulations for Cuba's new government. It prohibited Cuba from making alliances with countries other than the United States, allowed American oversight of Cuba's financial affairs, and authorized the United States to send forces to Cuba to keep order, if needed. The Platt Amendment remained in effect until the United States and Cuba signed a new treaty in 1934.

Cuba allowed the United States to establish and keep a naval base on the island. The US Navy still uses that base, located at **Guantánamo Bay**.

Despite its reluctance to give complete independence to Cuba after the war, the United States did much to help the island. For example, the United States helped combat yellow fever. A Cuban physician, Dr. Carlos Finlay, believed that the disease was carried by mosquitoes. A US Army doctor, **Walter Reed**, proved that Finlay was correct. As a result, Major William Gorgas and a crew of army engineers drained swamps and other low-lying areas in Cuba and succeeded in eliminating much of the water where the mosquitoes bred. The United States also provided food and clothing for the poor and built roads, schools, railroads, and hospitals in Cuba.

Puerto Rico

The United States gave Cuba and Puerto Rico similar aid. In 1917 the Jones-Shafroth Act made Puerto Rico a US territory with a governor appointed by the president. It also established a two-house legislative assembly and granted citizenship to all Puerto Ricans.

The Philippines

Not all Americans supported US control of the Philippines. The Philippines consists of more than seven thousand islands over a wide area, a challenge for any government. Since the Filipinos had almost no

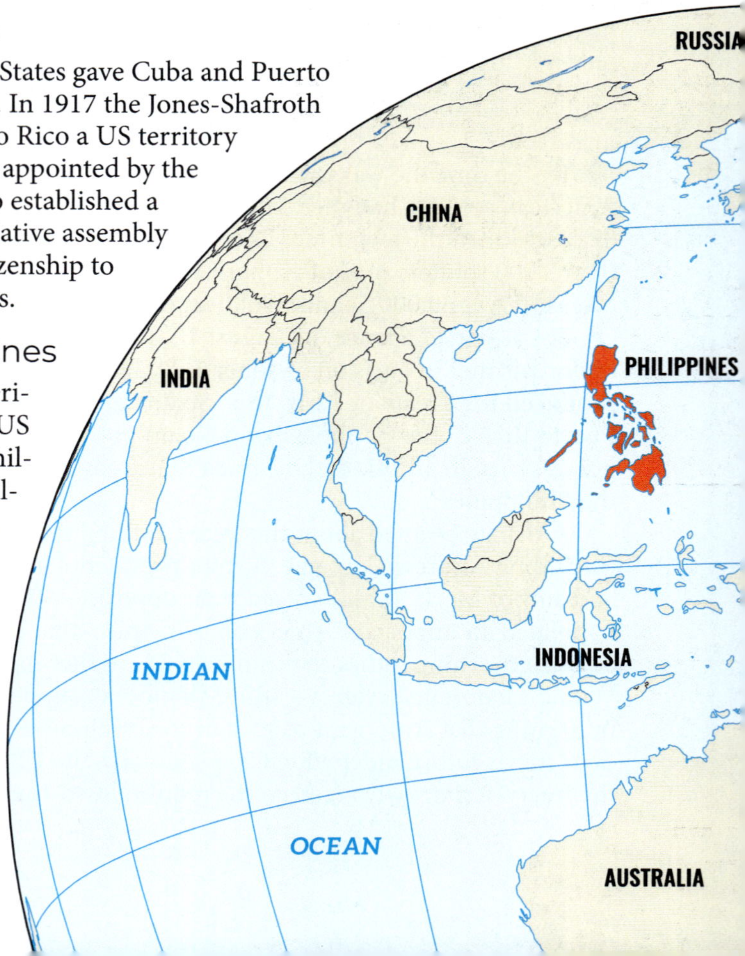

experience in self-government, the United States would have trouble helping them establish a republic. Also, opponents of US control believed that annexation of the Philippines would violate the American ideal of liberty and might even be unconstitutional. Some believed that a US presence in the Philippines might lead to a needless war.

But President McKinley believed that if left alone, the Philippines might fall into chaos and disorder or be conquered by another country. He also believed that the land would make a good base for trade with China. In addition, he thought American missionaries could go to help the Filipinos. McKinley's view prevailed, and Congress agreed to control the islands.

▲ Emilio Aguinaldo

Under Emilio Aguinaldo's leadership, the Philippines had long fought against Spanish rule. When the United States won the Spanish-American War, Aguinaldo and his followers expected the United States to grant the Philippines independence. The Filipinos were angry when they learned that the Americans would replace their Spanish rulers. Aguinaldo and his followers decided to fight the American occupying force. The fighting lasted for two and a half years. Suppressing the uprising cost the United States more time, money, and casualties than it had lost in the entire Spanish-American War.

The United States worked to prepare the Philippines for independence by establishing a public school system to teach Filipinos about citizenship. The United States also built hospitals, railroads, and power plants. It greatly improved communication systems. It banned individual Americans from acquiring large tracts of land in the Philippines. Filipinos were granted almost all the rights held by individuals living in America. American governors ruled the islands for more than thirty-five years. In 1934, the United States granted the islands more self-governing rights. World War II delayed the Filipinos' independence, but they finally received it on July 4, 1946.

PRIMARY SOURCE: MCKINLEY ON AMERICA'S ACQUISITION OF THE PHILIPPINES

"When next I realized that the Philippines had dropped into our laps I confess I did not know what to do with them. . . . I walked the floor of the White House night after night until midnight; and I am not ashamed to tell you, gentlemen, that I went down on my knees and prayed Almighty God for light and guidance more than one night. And one night late it came to me . . . (1) That we could not give them back to Spain—that would be cowardly and dishonorable; (2) that we could not turn them over to France or Germany—our commercial rivals in the Orient—that would be bad business and discreditable; (3) that we could not leave them to themselves—they were unfit for self-government—and they would soon have anarchy [disorder and lawlessness due to lack of government] and misrule over there worse than Spain's was; and (4) that there was nothing left for us to do but to take them all, and to educate the Filipinos, and uplift and civilize and Christianize them, and by God's grace do the very best we could by them, as our fellow-men for whom Christ also died. And then I went to bed, and went to sleep and slept soundly."

SECTION REVIEW 18.3

1. What were four causes of the Spanish-American War?
2. Where did the Rough Riders earn fame by pushing back Spanish defenses?
3. How did America help the island of Cuba after the war?
4. In addition to exercising some control over Cuba, what lands did the United States control as a result of the Spanish-American War?
5. What four conclusions influenced President McKinley to finally "sleep soundly" concerning the annexation of the Philippines? Choose one of these conclusions and explain why it might not be justifiable.

GUIDING QUESTIONS

- Why did America become involved in Latin America and Asia?

18.4 ENTERING A NEW CENTURY

What was American foreign policy during this time?

As America approached a new century, its foreign policy was changing. The government no longer avoided disputes between foreign countries, particularly when it was in America's interest to become involved. If American trade and power could be advanced or if other countries could be protected from tyranny, the United States became involved, especially in Latin America and eastern Asia. This policy had both advantages and disadvantages.

Fun Fact

Although Theodore (Teddy) Roosevelt was an avid hunter, he once refused to shoot a captured bear. Because of this incident, toy makers began selling stuffed bears which quickly became known as "teddy" bears.

Election of 1900

In the 1900 presidential election, the Democrats again nominated William Jennings Bryan. Republicans renominated President McKinley and named "rough-riding" Theodore Roosevelt as their vice-presidential candidate. When Roosevelt was the governor of New York, many Republican politicians there discovered that they could not control him. As a result, they helped nominate him for the vice-presidency. At that time, the position was considered a political graveyard. They thought making him vice president would keep him out of the public spotlight.

During the campaign, one of the major issues was American imperialism. Bryan opposed it while Republicans overwhelmingly supported it. McKinley won the election by a comfortable margin.

On September 6, 1901, President William McKinley hosted a public reception at the Pan-American Exposition in Buffalo, New York. The president stood in a receiving line greeting the well-wishers who filed past him. One tall, thin, young man in the line wore what looked like a white bandage on his right hand. McKinley reached toward the man's unbandaged hand. The young man, however, pushed the president's outstretched hand aside, and from the "bandage" came the sharp bang of a pistol. Two shots struck the astonished president.

One bullet grazed the president while the other penetrated his abdomen. Doctors were unable to locate the bullet. Eight days later, after infection set in, McKinley died.

For the third time, the nation's president had been assassinated. Vice President Theodore Roosevelt took office as the nation's twenty-sixth president. The change was more than a simple switch in personnel. Two presidents of the same party could hardly have been more different. McKinley was quiet, reserved, and sedate; Roosevelt was energetic, active, and outgoing. At forty-two, he was the youngest person ever to become US president. Furthermore, McKinley was a political conservative, a cautious man who favored the long-accepted Republican policy of supporting "big business" and advocating "little government." Roosevelt advocated aggressive actions and favored a vigorous, active government.

▾ President McKinley lived for eight days after being shot in Buffalo, New York.

Latin America

Since the proclamation of the Monroe Doctrine in 1823, the United States had carefully watched its Latin American neighbors. It helped drive French forces out of Mexico in 1867. It also helped solve a boundary dispute between Venezuela and British Guiana (now Guyana) in 1895. By 1900 the United States had become the leader of the Western Hemisphere.

Theodore Roosevelt and the Big Stick

President Theodore Roosevelt applied his foreign policy with the same zest he showed in his charge up San Juan Hill. He followed one of his favorite proverbs: "Speak softly and carry a big stick; you will go far." Roosevelt believed that the United States was the most important nation in the Western Hemisphere. Some noted that he treated the Caribbean Sea as though it was an American lake. His foreign policy relied on America's military strength to persuade foreign nations to act properly. His philosophy became known as the "**big stick**" **policy**.

In 1902, Britain, Germany, and Italy sent warships to blockade Venezuelan ports. The forces were there to collect unpaid loans. Venezuela asked the United States to intervene. Great Britain asked Roosevelt to mediate. He eagerly obliged, but he saw the incident as a warning that European interests in Latin America were growing. He viewed the European presence as a violation of the Monroe Doctrine. To eliminate any misunderstanding, he issued a corollary (an explanation or addition) to the Monroe Doctrine. The **Roosevelt Corollary** stated that the United States had the right to be an "international police power" in the Western Hemisphere. As such, he said, the United States reserved the right to intervene in order to maintain stability.

During the next sixty years, the United States sent forces to Cuba, Venezuela, the Dominican Republic, Nicaragua, Guatemala, Haiti, and Mexico. Although Roosevelt's policy protected American interests, many Latin Americans began to view America as an unwelcome, powerful neighbor—"the colossus [giant] of the North."

Theodore Roosevelt

26

Born	October 27, 1858
Died	January 6, 1919
Home state	New York
Wives	1st—Alice Hathaway Lee 2nd—Edith Kermit Carow
Home	Sagamore Hill
Church	Dutch Reformed
Occupations	historian, rancher
Party	Republican (later Progressive, or Bull Moose)
Years served as president	1901–9
Terms	1 partial and 1 full
Vice presidents	1st—none 2nd—Charles Fairbanks

This cartoon shows Roosevelt enforcing his corollary to the Monroe Doctrine with the help of his "big stick" and the US Navy.

The Panama Canal

A major US goal in Latin America was to build a canal across Central America. American naval officers supported this project. They knew a canal would enable the American fleet to defend both the Atlantic and Pacific coasts more easily because it would allow ships to move quickly between the two oceans. The Spanish-American War helped prove that America needed such speed. During the war, it took two months to sail a warship from Puget Sound, along the coast of Washington state, to the East Coast (by sailing around South America). In addition, a canal would improve trade by greatly reducing the amount of time and money required to ship goods between the Atlantic and Pacific.

At first, the United States thought that Nicaragua might be a good place to build a canal, but later it decided Panama was a better location. In the early 1900s, Panama was part of Colombia, so the United States offered Colombia $10 million for the right to build the canal in Panama and an annual rental fee of $250,000. Colombia rejected the agreement, believing the price was too low.

Many leaders in Panama wanted independence. America realized that if the Panamanians revolted against Colombia and gained independence, the new Panamanian government would gladly sell the rights for a canal to the United States. The politicians wasted no time. Several American warships moved into positions off the Panama coast on November 2, 1903. The next day, Panamanians rioted and declared their independence from Colombia. When Colombia tried to send troops to quell the violence, American ships blocked the harbors. The rebels overcame the Colombian opposition within Panama and won their independence.

On November 18 the United States signed the Hay-Bunau-Varilla Treaty with Panama. Secretary of State John Hay and Panama's new foreign minister, Philippe-Jean Bunau-Varilla, had negotiated the terms. The United States received use of a ten-mile-wide strip of land in perpetuity (forever). The United States would control and defend that "canal zone." It would build a canal that would be open to all nations equally through the payment of tolls. Panama would receive the same payment for the canal that the United States had offered Colombia.

▾ A ship approaches one of the Panama Canal locks.

Eleven years later, in 1914, the **Panama Canal** opened. In 1977 the United States signed a new treaty with Panama that gave Panama ownership of the canal on December 31, 1999. That agreement was highly controversial and barely received the two-thirds vote required in the US Senate.

building the PANAMA CANAL

Between 1859 and 1869, a French company built the Suez Canal in Egypt. It connected the Red and Mediterranean Seas. Frenchman Ferdinand de Lesseps was the mastermind behind the construction. In 1881, again supervised by de Lesseps, Frenchmen began building a canal across Panama. The effort was abandoned in 1889 because of financial problems—the unfinished project had already cost nearly $300 million—and the deaths of more than 20,000 workers from malaria and yellow fever.

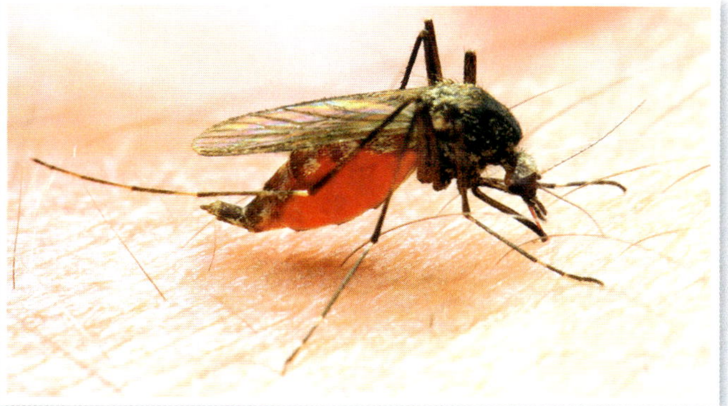

With the United States interested in building a canal in Central America, some Americans wanted to take over and complete the French project in Panama. Others proposed cutting through Nicaragua to the north. Senator Mark Hanna of Ohio, the chief proponent of a canal in Panama, spoke convincingly in favor of that route. He used detailed maps, charts, engineering plans, and endorsements by esteemed engineers. Other Americans continued to favor the route through Nicaragua. In 1902, as US senators debated the location, a massive volcanic eruption occurred in the Caribbean. Though more than 1,500 miles away from Nicaragua, it created concerns about possible volcanic activity in that country. Nicaraguans denied that their nation had any volcanoes. But Hanna discovered a Nicaraguan postage stamp that showed an erupting volcano, Momotombo. He mailed one of the stamps to each of the senators shortly before they voted. The final tally was 42–34 in favor of the Panama route.

◂ This Nicaraguan postage stamp was sent to all senators.

Recognizing Hanna's influence over the decision, some began calling the project the "Hannama Canal."

Theodore Roosevelt had become president in 1901. He knew the problem of disease had to be resolved before the canal could be completed. He named William Gorgas, a Christian and an authority on tropical diseases, to head the effort. Gorgas continued the type of work he had done in Cuba—draining ponds and swamps, fumigating (spraying chemicals to kill mosquitoes), and using mosquito netting.

Construction began in 1904. Two years later, while still president, Roosevelt decided to visit Panama. He timed his trip for November, the peak of the rainy season, so he could see the project under the worst conditions. During his two-week tour, he inspected every conceivable activity and praised the work of the men. Roosevelt's most famous moment on his trip was jumping from his train in the rain and climbing aboard a steam shovel. A photographer snapped his picture, and it appeared in newspapers across America.

The project required sixty-one million pounds of dynamite. The most productive month was March 1909 when sixty-eight steam shovels removed more than two million cubic yards of soil. More than 75,000 people, from ninety-seven different countries, worked on the ten-year-long project (1904–14).

Roosevelt posing on a steam shovel ▸ during his 1906 trip to Panama

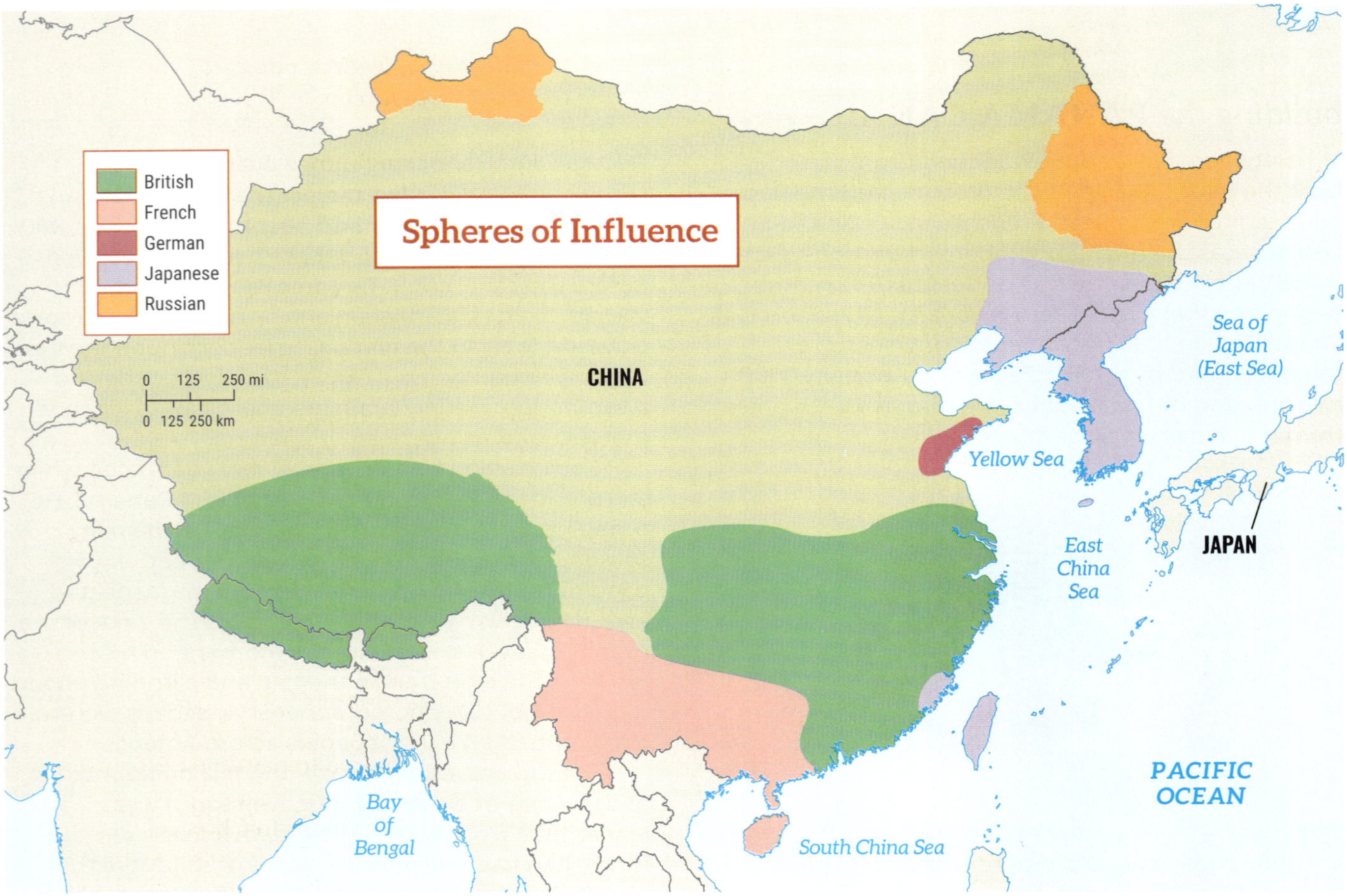

▲ A helpless Chinese official looks on as Britain, Germany, Russia, France, and Japan carve apart his country.

Asia

By the late 1800s, China had become one of the most profitable trading spots in the world. Britain, France, Germany, Russia, and Japan divided China into **spheres of influence**. Each of those countries controlled all trading operations within its sphere, or division, of the country. The United States was not part of that arrangement but was eager for trading opportunities of its own.

China and the Open Door Policy

Some of the foreign powers in China wanted more than control of trade—they wanted land. Japan and some European nations began to seize Chinese territory and establish colonies. The United States objected to such efforts, wanting China open to everyone for trade.

In 1899 Secretary of State John Hay sent a series of letters to the countries involved in China. His memos formally stated an **Open Door policy**. No longer would any nation have its own sphere. All of China would be open to all nations equally. Other nations interested in Chinese trade accepted Hay's proposal.

China's regions were not united, and no army existed to protect them. China had no choice but to tolerate the foreign trade invasion. But some Chinese people aligned themselves with a secret group called the Society of Righteous and Harmonious Fists that had been formed many years earlier. Foreigners called this group the **Boxers** because one of its rituals was a form of Chinese boxing. At first, the Boxers

▲ Chinese Christians sought safety in various locations after thousands were killed during the Boxer Rebellion.

▼ American, British, and Japanese troops are shown fighting in Peking during the rebellion.

focused on opposing Chinese leaders, but later they concentrated on demanding that all foreigners leave China. They started an uprising called the **Boxer Rebellion**. It began in rural areas and moved to Peking (now known as Beijing), the capital. The Boxers surrounded and terrorized sections of the city where foreigners lived, murdering some. Boxers also attacked and killed many Chinese Christians. The foreigners and Chinese Christians took refuge together and tried to survive until help could arrive.

In August 1900 about 20,000 soldiers arrived from Britain, France, Germany, Japan, the United States, and other nations. After weeks of fighting, they were able to free the hostages and end the uprising. Altogether, at least 30,000 Chinese Catholics, Protestants, and Russian Orthodox had been killed. More than 200 missionaries and their family members also had died.

Some countries thought that they should receive land to compensate for their expenses and losses caused by the Boxer Rebellion. But under the agreement signed on September 7, 1901, none of them received territory. However, several Chinese officials responsible for supporting the rebellion were executed, and numerous Chinese forts were destroyed. China was required to pay damages of about $333 million over the next forty years. That sum was divided among the nations that had sent troops to China.

The United States placed most of its share of the money into a fund to educate Chinese students in America. Some of the money was also used to build schools and colleges in China. American churches and mission boards sent workers and money to China. Because of such efforts, the Chinese were friendlier to the United States than to the other imperialist powers. The United States and China remained friends until Communists took control of China in 1949.

Imperialism in Japan

After Commodore Matthew Perry and the US Navy opened Japan to trade with the outside world in 1853, Japan quickly shifted away from its isolationist policy. In less than forty years, it transformed itself into a modern industrial and military power.

It is a short step from an emphasis on military might to imperialism. Japan began to demand a sphere of influence from China. In the first Sino-Japanese War (1894–95), Japan easily defeated the Chinese and took the land it wanted. As mentioned, Japan joined the international force that defeated the Boxers. Then in 1904–5 Japan fought Russia in the Russo-Japanese War.

John Hay and President Roosevelt tried to use American influence in Asia to maintain a **balance of power** (preventing any one nation from gaining enough power to dominate other nations). Roosevelt foresaw the threat that an imperialistic Japan could become. He believed that US power could offset Japan's power and that the United States should command the respect of the world. In 1905 he persuaded representatives from Russia and Japan to meet him on a ship anchored off Portsmouth, New Hampshire. There Roosevelt helped negotiate a treaty that officially ended the Russo-Japanese War and attempted to maintain the desired balance of power. For those efforts, he won the Nobel Peace Prize. He was the first American president given this honor.

In 1907 Roosevelt made a dramatic show of American military strength. He sent the entire US battle fleet on a world cruise that lasted fourteen months. Although Congress protested the expense, the sixteen battleships sailed. Called the Great White Fleet because of the ships' color, a major reason for the expedition was to make other nations aware of America's naval might. Roosevelt hoped this would also encourage the Japanese to curb their imperialistic ambitions and avoid conflict with America.

▾ The Great White Fleet began its voyage in December 1907 when it departed Virginia. Below it is shown leaving San Francisco in July 1908. Its next destination was Hawaii.

SECTION REVIEW 18.4

1. How did Theodore Roosevelt become president?
2. What did Theodore Roosevelt's "big stick" policy mean?
3. For what two reasons did the United States want a canal across Central America?
4. What treaty purchased the rights to build a canal across Panama? How much would the treaty cost the United States?
5. How was the Open Door policy different from spheres of influence? Which policy do you think was better? Why?
6. What were the goals of the Boxers?
7. What two countries did imperialist Japan fight between 1894 and 1905?

CHAPTER 18 REVIEW

Making Connections

1. Which two parties supported William Jennings Bryan in the 1896 election?
2. How were the campaigns of William Jennings Bryan and William McKinley different?
3. What strategically located, uninhabited islands in the Pacific claimed by the United States were the site of a major battle in World War II?
4. Which two newspaper owners competed to sell subscriptions? How did their yellow journalism contribute to the outbreak of the Spanish-American War?
5. During what battle was the Spanish fleet in the Pacific destroyed? Where was another Spanish fleet defeated?
6. What did the Teller Amendment state? How was it modified by the Platt Amendment?
7. What did the Jones-Shafroth Act state concerning Puerto Rico?
8. Who led the fight against Spanish, and later American, control of the Philippines? When was independence granted to the Philippines?
9. The Monroe Doctrine stated that European nations should no longer seek to colonize the Western Hemisphere. What did the Roosevelt Corollary add to the Monroe Doctrine?
10. Why did Roosevelt send the US battle fleet on a world cruise? What was the fleet called?

Thinking Critically

11. Why do you think many factory workers and farmers felt the need to join the Populist Party?
12. Does the news media still use yellow journalism? Defend your answer.

Living as a Christian Citizen

13. You are a newspaper owner during the time of imperialism. Write an editorial (an article stating one's opinion or position) about America's involvement in the annexation of Hawaii or the Philippines. Make sure to include a title and applicable biblical principles.
14. You are responsible for creating a policy that lends humanitarian aid to a foreign people without exploiting them. What will your policy include?

▾ Wreckage of the USS *Maine*

Terms to Remember

Populist Party
William Jennings Bryan
William McKinley
isolationism
imperialism
exploitation
humanitarian aid
Dwight L. Moody
yellow journalism
William Randolph Hearst
Joseph Pulitzer
de Lôme letter
USS *Maine*
Teller Amendment
Spanish-American War
Theodore Roosevelt
Battle of Manila Bay
San Juan Hill
Rough Riders
protectorate
Platt Amendment
Guantánamo Bay
Walter Reed
"big stick" policy
Roosevelt Corollary
Panama Canal
spheres of influence
Open Door policy
Boxers
Boxer Rebellion
balance of power

CHAPTER

19 The Progressive Era

Theodore Roosevelt campaigning for the presidency in 1912

The turn of the century was an exciting time. There seemed to be a promise that America would grow and prosper as a world power. Cities and industries were expanding. Technology made more conveniences available to the American people. However, the nation also faced challenges—materialism, dishonesty, and immorality were a few that troubled the nation.

Americans valued the growth of their businesses, but they also cherished equality and liberty. When the leaders of some businesses became much wealthier than others in the country, some Americans worried that powerful businesses could threaten the prosperity of ordinary Americans. Other Americans felt government leaders were not responsive to the needs of society. As the twentieth century began, many Americans were embracing a political and social movement called progressivism as a means of addressing some of their concerns. The period from approximately 1890 to 1920 is often called the Progressive Era.

GUIDING QUESTION

- What changes were occurring in American life at the beginning of the 1900s?

19.1 CHANGES IN AMERICAN LIFE

How was American life changing at the turn of the century?

Life was changing in the United States. There were new living and working conditions, new opportunities, new possessions, and new attitudes. There were other changes as well. Some were pleasant; others brought an abundance of problems.

People

The US population at the turn of the century was about seventy-six million. It was growing by more than a million a year, and immigration accounted for a large portion of that growth. Most of the immigrants were absorbed by cities.

By 1900, **urbanization** (the movement of people to cities) had changed America. Many young people who were reared in rural areas moved to cities, seeking greater opportunities. Between 1860 and 1910, the percentage of Americans involved in farming decreased from sixty percent to thirty-one percent. By 1920, more than half of Americans lived in cities and towns. Some urban areas became sprawling giants whose inner cities were often plagued with crime, poverty, poor sanitation, and crowded tenements (apartments).

By the beginning of the twentieth century, Chicago was the nation's second-most populated city. Only New York City had more people.

Almost all immigrants faced difficulties adjusting to their new home. In fact, not all first-generation immigrants became "Americanized." But most of their children did. These children learned English quickly, but the first few months of their early education were difficult. Few schools of the time offered bilingual education. Many immigrants actually opposed bilingualism because they wanted their children to become Americanized as fast as possible. They knew that learning the language of their new country was the key to achieving that goal.

The new immigrant groups contributed much to the building of America. They became the workforce for many of the nation's diverse new industries. But immigrants brought more than their labor; they brought the traditions, foods, music, and literature of their homelands. All of these made America's unique culture more diverse.

▲ Booker T. Washington (top) served as the leader of Tuskegee Institute (below) for more than thirty years.

Education

Americans enjoyed more freedom to improve their lives through education. During much of the 1800s, the only public education available at taxpayers' expense was elementary school. In 1860, there were only a few hundred high schools. Most were not taxpayer funded. But by 1900, thousands of tax-supported high schools existed, and the number was rapidly increasing.

The same trend occurred in higher education. Colleges began to offer more choices of studies, including programs to prepare students for specific professions. Schools that taught agriculture and mechanical arts increased, and graduate schools offered advanced training.

In the middle of the nineteenth century, upper-class white males were about the only people who attended colleges or universities. But by 1900, more people, including some blacks and women, enrolled in college. Black students almost always attended separate schools founded just for them. One of the nation's first black colleges was Ashmun Institute in Pennsylvania. It opened in 1854 and was renamed Lincoln University in 1866. Fisk University in Nashville was established in 1866, and Howard University in Washington, DC, was founded the following year.

One of the most famous black schools is the **Tuskegee Institute** in Alabama, whose first leader was **Booker T. Washington**, a former slave. Tuskegee's philosophy emphasized hard work, self-worth, and self-reliance. Washington stressed the need for African Americans to learn a vocational skill that would prepare them for a job, bringing them economic improvement.

Washington hired a botanist, **George Washington Carver**, to teach at the school. Carver, a devout Christian, boosted the school's reputation and finances not only through his teaching but also through his scientific experiments. He found many uses for clay, pecans, and sweet potatoes, but especially peanuts. He also discovered numerous medical uses for plants of the South. His work helped the South become less dependent on cotton.

The increased availability of education affected American life. In the nation's early years, colleges taught the philosophy (system of thinking) and ancient languages of Western civilization. In the early 1900s, however, there was an increased focus on modern languages, science, and practical studies.

Before this time, theologians and pastors were often the best-educated men in their communities. Many times Americans turned to them for guidance about challenges facing the United States. As the twentieth century began, some considered Christian viewpoints old-fashioned and placed greater faith in scientists or other educated individuals than in clergymen. Christians treasured the opportunities that expanded education brought. They embraced the benefits of modern science and technology. But they were concerned about unbiblical ideas that were sometimes taught. As a result, some Christians worked to preserve or establish distinctly Christian colleges.

Income

Education and opportunities to work and advance in business and industry helped many Americans raise their standard of living. Many people who had been penniless immigrants, poor farmers, or poverty-stricken factory workers found a way to improve their situation. Hard work and some business sense could bring financial gain. The fact that a person was born in poverty did not condemn him to stay poor.

Some people never escaped poverty, but many Americans joined the ranks of the growing middle class. They had more income to spend. They had enough money to enjoy comfortable homes, adequate food, and some of the new consumer goods that were being developed. They also spent some money on leisure activities.

Only a few Americans became millionaires. Some businessmen with wealth helped colleges and universities by providing large sums of money to finance specific programs or salaries. Some businessmen even founded schools. Universities such as Tulane (founded in 1834), Cornell (1865), Drew (1867), Vanderbilt (1873), Johns Hopkins (1876), and Stanford (1885) are named for such philanthropists. Russell Conwell founded Philadelphia's Temple University in 1884 to educate talented young men who wanted to succeed but lacked money. The University of Chicago, established in 1890, received more than $80 million from John D. Rockefeller.

George Washington Carver

George Washington Carver was born into slavery in Missouri during the early 1860s. Shortly after birth, he and his mother were kidnapped by Confederate guerrillas. George's owner, Moses Carver, ransomed him by giving the kidnappers a horse, but George's mother was never found. The Carvers, who were devout Christians, reared George themselves.

He worked his way through college by washing clothes. After earning a master's degree at what is now Iowa State University, he became a teacher at Tuskegee Institute. There, he dedicated himself to serving others through teaching and science. He experimented with all kinds of plants, especially peanut plants. He also developed techniques to improve nutrient-depleted soil caused by repeated planting of cotton.

Carver was popular with his students because of his work ethic, knowledge, and humble attitude. His work benefited a wide range of people, including farmers and housewives. Carver took no money for his discoveries, and he did not charge for the practical advice he provided.

Carver enjoyed recounting how he once asked God to show him the meaning of the universe. He said that God told him that he wanted to know more than his little mind could grasp. God said, "Ask for something your size." So Carver asked to know what people were made for. But God said, "Little one, you are still asking too much. Bring down the extent of your request." Carver then humbly said, "Tell me, . . . Creator, what the peanut was made for." Carver said that God then told him "how to take the peanut apart and put it together again" to make many helpful products.

(The last paragraph is adapted from page 119 of *George Washington Carver: God's Ebony Scientist* by Basil Miller.)

Leisure

In the early 1800s, many people had to work six days a week, and some worked 70 hours or more. Workers complained about such long hours. They were also unhappy with poor working conditions and low wages. By 1910 the average workweek had dropped to about 55 hours. This change gave many Americans more leisure time—time they could use to improve themselves or to enjoy their families.

Interest in both spectator and participatory sports mushroomed. Baseball, basketball, and football were relatively new sports that had developed in the United States. All three were popular, but baseball became the favorite. The first World Series occurred in 1903. Baseball greats such as Walter Johnson, Christy Mathewson, and Shoeless Joe Jackson and the double-play combination of Joe Tinker, Johnny Evers, and Frank Chance became familiar in many households.

In addition to baseball, basketball, and football, other sports were popular. Boxing was the second-most popular sport of the era. Heavyweight fights attracted large crowds. In addition, roller skating and bicycling became new fads. Golf and tennis also gained attention.

America's concert halls, theaters, and amusement parks offered other popular forms of entertainment. Interest in opera and classical music surged, especially in areas where European immigrants settled. Many symphony orchestra members and most conductors in the nation had been born overseas. Immigrants who could afford tickets packed concert halls to hear the music of European composers.

Literature took on new importance in the era. Because more people had the ability to read and because people had more money for books, reading became more popular. Americans were especially fond of new American themes and regional settings in literature. The most popular American writer of the day was Samuel L. Clemens, who used the pen name Mark Twain. He wrote such famous books as *The Adventures of Tom Sawyer*, *Adventures of Huckleberry Finn*, and *A Connecticut Yankee in King Arthur's Court*.

▲ Samuel L. Clemens, better known as Mark Twain

Magazines that appealed to literary types were common but expensive (thirty-five cents per issue). As a result, magazines such as *Harper's* and *Atlantic Monthly* never enjoyed wide circulation. But better printing presses and papermaking methods later reduced prices. For example, publisher Cyrus Curtis sold the *Ladies' Home Journal* for ten cents a copy and the *Saturday Evening Post* for only a nickel.

◂ Football and roller skating were two popular activities.

Discrimination

The situation for African Americans in the South (where the overwhelming majority of blacks lived) was worsening as the nineteenth century ended. Though black Americans held elective or appointive offices during this period (for example, in every session of Congress from 1869 to 1901 except one, there was at least one black member of the House of Representatives), their number was small.

Discrimination grew in the 1890s as states began passing **Jim Crow laws**. (Jim Crow was a black character in a nineteenth-century show who was mocked.) This legislation required the forced **segregation**, or separation, of the races in trains, restaurants, hotels, schools, and other social settings. Segregation was so extensive that whites and blacks even had separate restrooms and drinking fountains.

▾ Segregated water fountains, such as the one shown below, were common during this period.

In addition, southern states began depriving black people of their right to vote by establishing **literacy tests** or requiring a special tax, called a **poll tax**, in order to vote. African Americans were often given a more difficult literacy test, to determine reading and writing ability, than whites. Poor people often could not afford to pay the poll tax. Many times, election officials were far less strict in collecting the poll tax or applying literacy requirements to white men.

Later, many states also passed a **grandfather clause** which typically said a person did not have to pay the poll tax or pass the literacy test if he, his father, or his grandfather had been eligible to vote before 1867. No black citizens met this requirement. As a result of these laws, the number of southern black voters plummeted. For example, the number of registered black voters in Louisiana was 130,000 in 1896 but only about 1,300 in 1904.

Segregation was strengthened when the Supreme Court issued a series of decisions that made the enforcement of Reconstruction civil rights legislation difficult. The most famous was ***Plessy v. Ferguson***, a case in 1896 which decreed that "separate but equal" facilities for blacks and whites (in this case, on trains) were constitutional. These decisions gave state legislatures the legal justification they needed to pass Jim Crow law codes.

One of the most outspoken critics of discrimination was **W. E. B. Du Bois**, the first African American to receive a doctorate from Harvard University. He and his supporters argued that blacks could not truly improve themselves economically until they enjoyed equal participation in the political process as American citizens. In 1909 Du Bois and other like-minded leaders—black and white—formed the **National Association for the Advancement of Colored People (NAACP)**. Their goal was to seek equality for blacks; in order to achieve that objective, they focused on fighting legal battles.

SECTION REVIEW 19.1

1. The urbanization of America occurred when what two groups of people continued to move to American cities?
2. What did Booker T. Washington emphasize to students at the Tuskegee Institute?
3. For what natural items did George Washington Carver find many uses?
4. What were three sports that became popular with new leisure time? What other entertainment options became available?
5. How did discrimination grow during this time?

GUIDING QUESTIONS

- What were challenges to Christianity in the early 1900s?
- What were some Christian responses to changing religious attitudes?

19.2 RELIGIOUS ATTITUDES

How did religious practices change during the Progressive era?

The Pilgrims, the Puritans, and a number of other early settlers in America brought with them the desire to serve and worship God. Although not all newcomers were Christians, most of them respected the Bible as the Word of God and believed in its moral standards. But during the nineteenth century, changes in American society greatly altered the nation's religious attitudes.

▲ Jewish synagogue in Savannah, Georgia

Challenges to Christianity

Between 1860 and 1910, approximately twenty-one million immigrants entered the United States. These individuals were from a variety of religious backgrounds. Some Germans and most Scandinavians were Lutheran. Other Germans and most immigrants from Ireland and Italy were Roman Catholic. Immigrants coming from eastern European countries included Jews, Catholics, Mennonites, and Russian Orthodox.

The arrival of a large number of non-Protestants alarmed many Protestants. They worried that their beliefs would be undermined by these newcomers. Nonetheless, almost all churches increased their memberships during this time, including the well-known mainline denominations, such as the Methodists, Presbyterians, and Baptists. Some people thought that mainline denominations were too formal or were not meeting their needs or did not address issues important to them. These people formed new denominations, such as the Holiness and Pentecostal groups.

During this period, several unorthodox groups (groups that did not follow the foundational beliefs of Christianity) also emerged. For example, Mary Baker Eddy founded Christian Science. She believed that matter, death, sin, pain, and disease are mental illusions. The Watch Tower Society (Jehovah's Witnesses) was founded in 1872 by Charles Taze Russell.

▼ Picture of Charles Darwin in a copy of his most famous book

All these groups were founded by Americans, and each enjoyed the freedom of religion that allowed it the right to exist. American beliefs in individualism made it easy for many to turn from traditional, orthodox Christianity and embrace contrary teachings.

In addition to unorthodox groups, some **agnostics** (those who believe humans cannot know whether there is a God) became vocal during this period. The most famous agnostic, Robert Ingersoll, spoke around the country in the late 1800s. People paid to hear him mock true faith. Though many people attended his lectures more out of curiosity than agreement, agnosticism grew more acceptable to Americans than ever before. This was partly true because of Charles Darwin's 1859 publication, *The Origin of Species*. Darwin proposed the theory of evolution. He said that the variety of species on Earth can be explained by natural selection. Deists had already concluded that the world is a machine with a divine Designer who was no longer needed once the machine was started. Darwin removed the need for the Designer.

Because of the challenges in society, some professing Christians said that Christianity needed to change to survive in the modern world. These people, called liberals, did not want to become agnostics, but they thought that reason and experience were needed to judge what parts of the Bible were true and what parts were false. They thought that miracles and other supernatural events were not rational. Some also denied that the Bible was written by men guided by the Holy Spirit. These liberals treated the Bible as a purely human book.

Liberals did not accept the virgin birth and the deity of Christ. They even denied that Jesus died on the cross for the sins of mankind and rejected the idea that there is eternal punishment in a real hell. Such doctrines, they thought, were unreasonable and unfitting for a loving God. As a result, they believed it was unnecessary to preach the gospel of repentance for sin and of faith in Christ.

Liberals failed to realize that in their efforts to save Christianity from modern challenges, they created an entirely new religion. The teachings of Scripture were abandoned. All that was left were religious experience and the message of Christian ethics—good works.

Responses by Conservative Christians

Conservative Christians responded in various ways to the challenges of liberalism and other belief systems. Conservative Christian scholars, such as Princeton Seminary professor B. B. Warfield, defended the fundamental teachings of Christianity. Warfield wrote many books and articles that defended the accuracy of Scripture, the deity of Jesus, and that salvation comes through redemption purchased by the blood of Christ. Christian scholars knew that the Bible and its teachings would endure far beyond any challenges they faced at the moment.

Many popular preachers and evangelists, such as **Billy Sunday**, attacked both liberalism and social problems while preaching the gospel of personal salvation through the work of Christ. These men attracted large audiences, and their preaching played a significant role in maintaining biblical Christianity in the face of challenges. Many people came to Christ through their preaching, and Christians were encouraged to follow the teachings of the Christian faith.

the SOCIAL-GOSPEL MOVEMENT

In the early twentieth century, a movement known as the social gospel became popular, especially with liberals. It replaced the focus of regeneration, or salvation, of individuals with the regeneration of society through social reform. Supporters emphasized "soup and soap": feeding and cleaning people and society—rather than true salvation (spiritual regeneration).

Advocates of the social gospel spoke of their love for Jesus, and many of their reforms were worthwhile. But some of its leaders denied that man has a fallen nature, as the Bible teaches, and believed instead that man's environment corrupts him. They said that improving a man's environment, therefore, would allow his natural goodness to develop.

However, reforming society without sharing the biblical gospel does not bring salvation—man's greatest need. Instead, it can lead to a false sense of security for those who need to be saved.

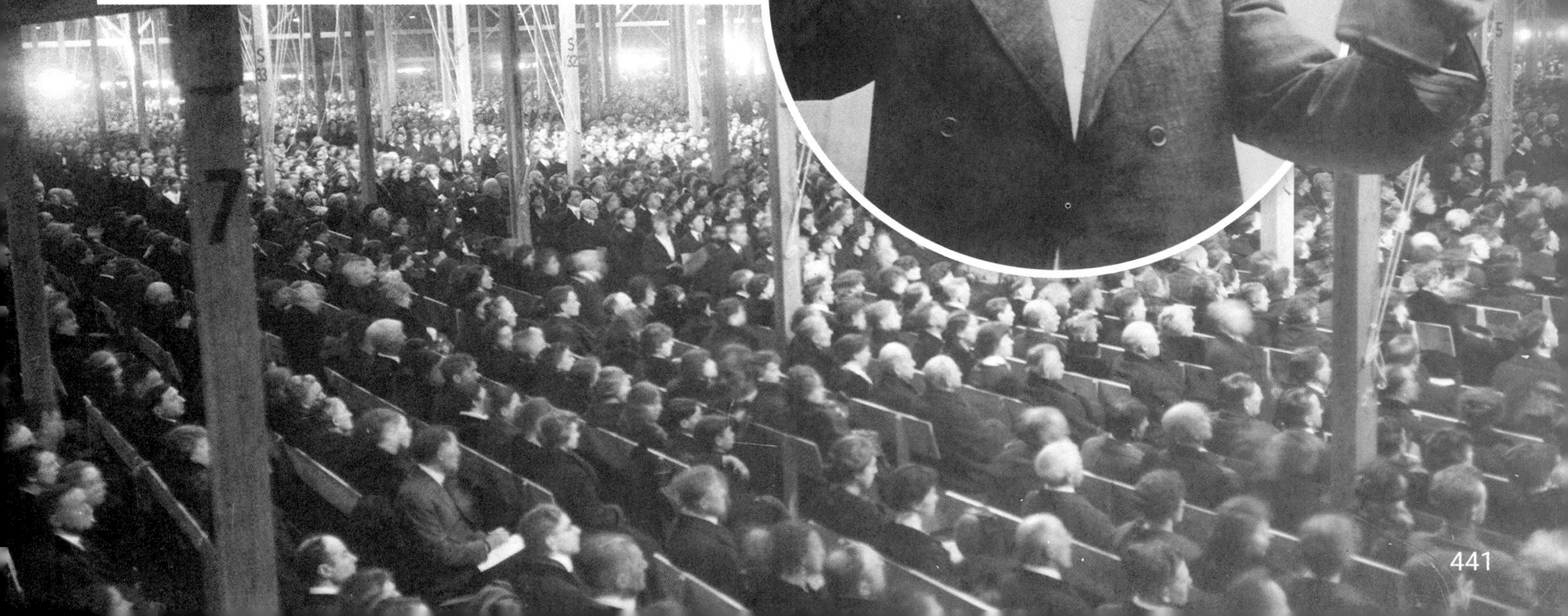

▾ Billy Sunday (right) preached in this Chicago tabernacle in 1918.

▲ Ladies of the temperance movement sing outside a bar.

Reform and Outreach

The coexistence of liberalism and true Christianity in American culture led to a mixture of religious goals in the Progressive Era. Some people sincerely sought to reach souls for Christ. Others tried merely to improve morals or living conditions.

Temperance Movement

The abuse of alcohol had become a huge problem in many areas of the country. Some immigrant groups were particularly heavy drinkers. The behavior of alcoholics was offensive to many, and alcoholism contributed to increased crime, poverty, and violence toward family members.

▼ A New York City YMCA in the early 1900s

Many religious Americans wanted to correct the problem. They formed **temperance societies**, groups dedicated to stopping the consumption of alcohol, to combat the evils of liquor. Most were associated with the Women's Christian Temperance Union (founded in 1874) or the Anti-Saloon League (1893). The efforts of temperance societies, combined with the efforts of evangelists who preached against the sin of drunkenness, led to the prohibition (prohibiting alcohol) movement.

Christian Organizations

British laymen founded the **Young Men's Christian Association (YMCA)** in 1844 to provide wholesome activities and entertainment for young men who lived in the troublesome environments of England's big cities.

RESCUE *the* PERISHING

As American cities grew in the 1800s, so did their problems. Churches tended to move away from the slums and move closer to the homes of more prosperous and "respectable" people, who could support the churches. But some Christians tried to reach the people in the troubled neighborhoods. They held services in rented halls, distributed tracts, and witnessed to people.

One man, Jerry McAuley, wanted to do more. McAuley, who was once jailed for robbery, was converted to Christianity because of the testimony of a former convict. After his release, he was determined to help the "down-and-outers"—the drunks, prostitutes, and others—who lived in the worst parts of New York City. The Water Street Mission, which he started in 1872, is usually considered the first rescue mission in the United States.

Probably the most famous rescue mission was Chicago's Pacific Garden Mission. It was founded in 1877 by Colonel George Clarke and his wife, Sarah Dunn Clarke. It reached thousands of people for Christ. In the mid-1880s, a half-drunk baseball player named Billy Sunday heard a group of mission workers singing on a street corner. After attending services at the mission, he was converted.

Rescue-mission work varied in operation from city to city. Missions were usually open day and night. Services normally consisted of singing gospel songs, testimonies of converted sinners from the slums, and simple salvation sermons. The missions also tried to provide hot meals and a place to stay, at least for a night or two. More ambitious missions tried to provide work for the needy. In those missions, people repaired clothing, made brooms, or did other work to help pay for their room and board.

Evangelist D. L. Moody was a major force in bringing the YMCA from England to the United States. The Y, as it came to be known, emphasized physical, educational, social, and religious growth. It also provided a safe living environment, where young Christian men working in large cities could find room and board. In addition, it sponsored a variety of Christian activities.

Another group of British origin, the **Salvation Army**, became active in the United States. It provided relief for the poor and established **rescue missions** (facilities to provide food, shelter, and spiritual guidance) to help individuals by meeting their physical needs and presenting the gospel. Other groups also began rescue missions to work with such people, many of whom came from immigrant groups.

Missions and Evangelism

Americans were concerned about sharing the gospel overseas. During this period, America sent more missionary workers than any other country. The religious and cultural impact of Christianity was so great by the end of the nineteenth century that some historians have called it the Great Century of Christian Missions.

Throughout the era, the work of evangelists and revivalists was important. They held camp meetings but replaced tents and other temporary shelters with wood-frame tabernacles. Some groups held meetings at modern campgrounds that had cabins for visitors.

SECTION REVIEW 19.2

1. What did each of the following groups believe that presented challenges to Christianity during this time period?
   a. immigrants
   b. unorthodox groups
   c. agnostics
   d. liberals
2. What three issues did B. B. Warfield and other conservative Christians defend as fundamental teachings of Christianity? What do you believe about each of these issues?
3. What was the purpose of temperance groups?
4. What were two Christian organizations established to deal with the physical and spiritual needs of those who lived in the inner cities? Where did these two groups originate?

19.3 GOALS OF PROGRESSIVISM

What were the goals of Progressives?

GUIDING QUESTIONS

- What goals did Progressives hope to accomplish?
- What Progressive reforms were instituted?

Goals

1. Fight corruption
2. Improve quality of life
3. Increase voice in government
4. Increase government efficiency

American society faced many difficulties. Some were caused by powerful businesses or political organizations, others were the result of urbanization. Many people believed that these problems were too big for individuals to solve alone. **Progressivism** was a movement during the late nineteenth and early twentieth centuries that favored achieving political and social reform through education, wider political participation, and direct action by the government.

America's founders sought to limit the power of government to ensure liberty and avoid corruption. However, progressives believed that an enlarged government had become necessary to handle the difficulties the nation faced. Many Christians supported progressives and their ideals, especially when the ideals related to moral issues. But some progressive ideas concerned a number of Christians.

The progressives' first goal was to fight corruption and what they deemed unfair practices in government and industry. They made permanent changes in the way cities, states, and the nation were governed.

Progressives' second goal was to improve quality of life. They wanted government to implement many of these improvements. The biblical responsibilities of government include ensuring justice, providing national defense and public safety, addressing poverty, promoting moral behavior, and providing order. Some areas of progressive reform—such as fighting crime, combating drunkenness, and ending prostitution—addressed these areas. Some argued that progressivism would give government too much power over the lives of individuals.

Progressives believed that people needed a greater voice in governing; this was their third goal. They argued that problems could be solved by making government more democratic. Though many such reforms were good, progressives failed to remember that since all men are imperfect, sometimes voters make poor decisions. Actions are not right simply because the majority of people favor them.

The fourth goal of progressives was to make government more efficient by using qualified technical experts. Thus, they sought to appoint such individuals to important positions within city, state, and national governments. The emphasis on technical specialists started with increased trust of social scientists (people who study societies) to address difficult problems. Yet experts could not provide the answers to all society's problems. Progressives overestimated the ability of specialists to solve problems and underestimated the biases that some experts would display. While relying on specially trained individuals was often beneficial, it could not solve all difficulties.

▾ Tenements in a New York City slum

Fighting Corruption and Industrial Problems

Corruption was widespread in government, business, and industry. Progressives fought that corruption through reform.

In this cartoon, Boss Tweed and his friends blame each other for stealing government funds.

Corruption

Corruption existed at all levels of government. In New York City, local politician **William "Boss" Tweed** and his friends defrauded the city of millions of dollars by using city contracts to make large profits. Tweed and his associates stole between $30 and $200 million before he was sent to prison in 1873. On the state level, officials were bribed to give special favors. On the national level, the many scandals of the Grant administration had disappointed many Americans.

The introduction of the civil-service system in the late 1800s curbed some corruption. It made merit or ability, not party loyalty, the standard by which many jobs were awarded. Yet even civil-service reform could not prevent some political corruption.

Corruption and exploitation of natural and human resources occurred in business and industry. For example, in states where timber was harvested, some lumber companies cut trees from public lands for their own profit.

Labor Problems

Young lady working in a North Carolina textile mill

Some industrialists were unfair and even cruel to their workers. Workers often labored long hours in unsafe conditions, which in some cases led to disasters. Perhaps the worst disaster was a fire at the Triangle Shirtwaist Company in New York City in March 1911. Nearly 150 people, mostly girls and women, died because doors had been locked to keep the workers on the job until the end of the shift. The textile industry had other unsafe conditions. For example, because filtering systems in southern textile mills were rare, textile workers inhaled cotton lint. Some of them contracted what became known as brown lung disease and later died from it.

Long hours and low pay were normal. Employers exchanged lists ("blacklists") of employees who caused trouble or went on strike, so it did little good trying to change jobs. Troublemakers would not be hired. Some companies treated women and children even worse than they treated their male employees. Slowly, child labor laws were enacted that regulated working hours and conditions for children.

▲ Laundry in New York City

▼ Jane Addams with children

Improving Quality of Life

Living conditions were the worst in crowded cities. Rents were high and housing was limited. Entire families sometimes lived in small, even one-room, apartments. Some families allowed non-family members to live with them to help pay the rent. In New York City, hundreds of thousands of residents lived in windowless tenements. Thousands more lived in damp cellar apartments.

In such cramped conditions, epidemics were common. Diphtheria, smallpox, cholera, typhus, scarlet fever, and tuberculosis took many lives. Even such common childhood diseases as measles, mumps, and chicken pox were dangerous under such conditions. Garbage created a terrible stench and was a breeding ground for germs, rodents, and insects. The few sanitation departments could not keep pace with the filth.

Other urban problems included the lack of both a clean water supply and sanitary plumbing. Many tenements did not have running water or indoor bathrooms. People got water from street wells. This water was often impure. Fire hydrants were opened at certain times for bathing or other uses. Where indoor plumbing did exist, it was usually shared by many people and was undependable.

Housing conditions of the poor were bad, but conditions in prisons, mental hospitals, and other institutions were even worse. Filth and cruelty were common there.

Reformers attempted to solve some city problems. They responded to terrible conditions in tenements by founding **settlement houses**. Besides providing food, clothing, medical care, and child-care, settlement houses offered recreation and classes to women in slum areas. America's first settlement house was called the Neighborhood Guild, founded in 1886 in New York City. Probably the most famous settlement house was Chicago's Hull House, which **Jane Addams** founded in 1889. Addams's efforts helped lead to the passage of child-labor laws in several states.

Other citizens and social groups worked to improve prisons and mental institutions and to aid people who lived in poor conditions. The government initially stayed out of most of these social programs, but reformers pressed for government regulation of industries where they felt employees or consumers were being abused.

Increasing Participation in Government

Three government reforms that some local and state governments enacted were initiative, referendum, and recall. An **initiative** allowed voters to propose their own legislation. First, a certain number of voters' signatures had to be collected on a petition for the new law. Next, the proposed law was placed on a ballot, and voters accepted or rejected it. A **referendum** allowed voters to determine by an election whether a law proposed by a governmental body should be enacted or rejected. A **recall** occurred when voters successfully petitioned for a special election to decide whether to remove an elected official from office before his term expired.

Another major government reform was national in scope, the direct election of senators. That reform was enacted in 1913 as the **Seventeenth Amendment**. Previously, senators had been elected by state legislatures. The founders established the House of Representatives to represent the individual citizens of the various states. The president was to represent the entire union of the states. The Senate was designed to represent the individual state governments. In that way, all levels of government were represented in the national government. Progressives charged that senatorial elections had become corrupt auctions in which the wealthy sometimes bribed state legislators to elect them. Direct election, they believed, would end this abuse by giving the decision to the voters of each state. Opponents of the amendment feared that senators elected directly by the people would be more interested in reelection than in making the best decisions for the nation. They also argued that the amendment removed one of the state legislatures' checks on federal power.

Initiative

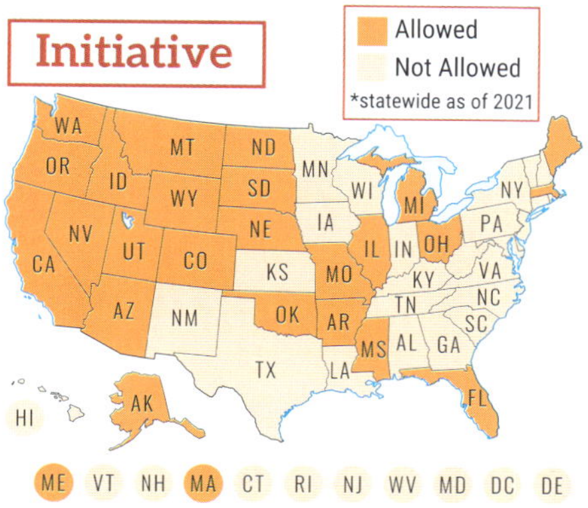

Referendum

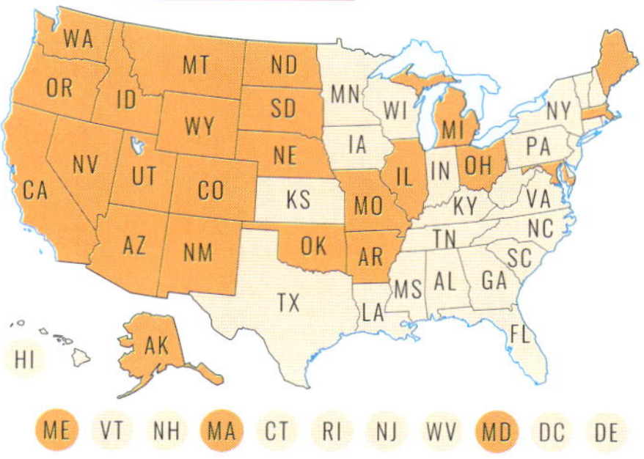

Recall

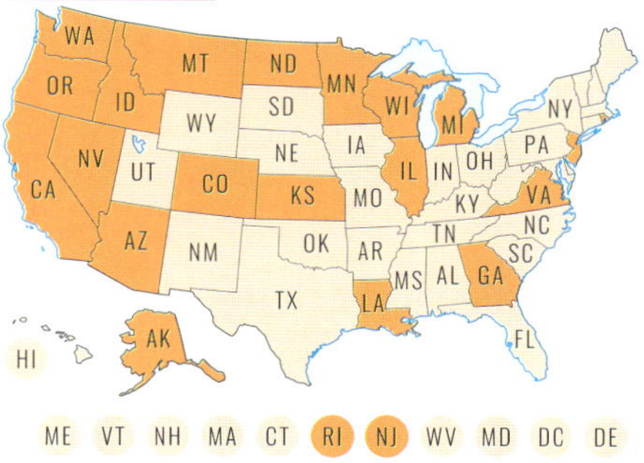

Improving Government Efficiency

During this era, reformers tried new methods of operating city governments. Rather than electing a mayor, some cities hired a trained expert called a city manager. A city manager's position did not depend on his popularity, so reformers believed that such an official would be under less pressure to bow to special-interest groups. Other cities instituted a commission government. In this system, voters elected several commissioners, each in charge of a specific area of government. This system made it much easier to detect corruption. Hiring city managers and electing commissioners allowed cities to select specialists. For example, a city water or street commissioner might be a trained civil engineer.

Were progressive reforms effective? Some were; others were not. Sometimes progressives identified real problems and proposed effective solutions. Other times, their attempts to solve problems failed.

One unfortunate aspect of progressivism was that some of its supporters embraced beliefs rooted in acceptance of discrimination. Some progressives were even openly racist. For example, they believed that people of northern and western European descent were intellectually and culturally superior to other groups such as eastern Europeans and Africans. Such beliefs that encouraged prejudice had long existed. Though progressives focused on governmental and social reforms, they did little to address the injustices that black Americans suffered. Some even supported Jim Crow laws and attempts to prohibit blacks from voting.

SECTION REVIEW 19.3

1. What were the four major goals of progressives?
2. What made ability, rather than party loyalty, the basis for awarding many jobs?
3. What was the goal of settlement houses? What was the most famous one?
4. What four government reforms increased individual participation in government?
5. Would you have supported the Seventeenth Amendment? Why or why not?
6. How did a city manager differ from a mayor?

GUIDING QUESTIONS

- What was the Square Deal?
- What were the primary progressive issues of Roosevelt's administration?

19.4 ROOSEVELT

How did President Roosevelt implement progressivism?

After becoming president upon the death of William McKinley in September 1901, Theodore "Teddy" Roosevelt was elected to his own term in 1904. He and the next two presidents—William Howard Taft and Woodrow Wilson—identified themselves as progressives.

▾ Worker in a coal mine

The Square Deal

Roosevelt believed that the government should regulate big business to promote competition and better working conditions. His efforts in these areas made him very popular with other progressives.

Roosevelt thought many workers were being treated unfairly. In 1902 coal miners in the United Mine Workers' union staged a major strike. Coal was the major source of fuel for steam-operated machinery, including railroad locomotives, and of heat for the nation. The strikers demanded raises, a shorter workday, and more power for their union. The strike dragged on for months as coal mine owners refused to negotiate. As winter drew near and the public grew concerned about a possible coal shortage, Roosevelt warned that he might use troops to operate the coal mines. It was the first time the threat of federal force was used against owners rather than against workers. He also formed a special commission to help settle the dispute. Also for the first time, the federal government worked directly to settle a dispute between workers and owners. Roosevelt later claimed that he wanted to give both sides "a square deal." That phrase became his campaign slogan in the 1904 election.

A compromise reduced the working day for miners to nine hours and raised pay by 10 percent. People still debate today whether such intervention is a proper use of federal executive powers.

Regulation and Conservation

Congress passed the **Pure Food and Drug Act**, and Roosevelt signed it into law. The 1906 law allowed federal inspectors to examine slaughterhouses and meat companies that shipped across state lines. It also forbade the use of harmful additives that concealed bad meat. At that time, medicines were widely advertised and available over the counter or by mail. Although those medicines were often useful, some were addictive (many were derived from opium or a high percentage of alcohol). The Pure Food and Drug Act regulated the use of narcotics and required companies to list the ingredients of medicines on product labels. It also prohibited companies from making unverifiable claims about medicines.

MUCKRAKERS: JOURNALISTS *who* EXPOSED THE WORST

President Roosevelt nicknamed progressive writers who exposed abuse and corruption **muckrakers** (muck means "filth, dirt, or mud"). He compared them to a man in John Bunyan's *Pilgrim's Progress* who ignored everything but filth.

Muckraker Lincoln Steffens revealed many urban problems in his articles for *McClure's Magazine*. The articles were later published in a book titled *The Shame of the Cities*. Steffens accused Philadelphia politicians of using the votes of "dead dogs, children, and non-existent persons" to keep themselves in power.

Ida M. Tarbell, a schoolteacher-turned-author, grew up near Titusville, Pennsylvania, when Standard Oil (established by John D. Rockefeller in 1870) was at its height of power. She wrote a series of articles about the company's allegedly ruthless tactics. In 1903, the articles were published in a two-volume work, *History of the Standard Oil Company*.

John Spargo, another muckraker, wrote of the ills of child labor and of the poverty that sent many children to school hungry each day. His work *The Bitter Cry of the Children* (published in 1906) helped obtain the passage of child-labor laws.

Ray Stannard Baker attacked the lynching of blacks in southern states.

In 1906 **Upton Sinclair** published a novel entitled *The Jungle*. It described how Chicago meatpackers processed diseased cattle and used chemicals and dyes to cover up bad meat. His descriptions of the unsafe and unsanitary conditions helped lead to the adoption of the Pure Food and Drug Act.

▲ Young boy selling newspapers

▲ In this cartoon, a Standard Oil storage tank is portrayed as an octopus. Its tentacles are wrapped around various industries as well as a state capitol and the US Capitol.

As mentioned in Chapter 16, the Sherman Anti-Trust Act, passed in 1890, regulated trusts (several separate companies that had joined together into one super-sized corporation). Roosevelt believed some trusts were good while others were bad. He believed the bad ones were those that used their power to eliminate their competitors and thereby obtain a monopoly over business in an area or industry. The 1890 law had rarely been enforced until Roosevelt's presidency. However, he used its provisions to pursue legal action against trusts he considered harmful. Roosevelt was eventually known as a "trustbuster" for dismantling some trusts.

Did you know?

America's first national park, Yellowstone, had become federal property in 1872. When Roosevelt became president in 1901, there were three more national parks: Sequoia (founded in 1890), Yosemite (1890), and Mount Rainier (1899).

Another issue important to Roosevelt was conservation (the protection of natural resources). He had a lifelong interest in the outdoors and was a devoted hunter. He readily responded to demands that the government protect lands for future generations to enjoy. Roosevelt dramatically increased the amount of land set aside for national parks, national forests, and wildlife preserves. He has been called the first environmental president.

In 1905 Roosevelt convinced Congress to establish the United States Forest Service to oversee the country's forest reserves. He appointed Gifford Pinchot, a close friend and professional forester, to lead the new agency. Pinchot also served as the chairman of the National Conservation Commission, a group Roosevelt appointed in 1908 to make recommendations about preserving the nation's water, timber, land, and mineral natural resources.

In 1902 Congress passed the Newlands Reclamation Act, which permitted the sale of federal lands in arid (extremely dry) areas. The money from those sales was to pay for irrigation projects to make arid lands more usable.

Although Theodore Roosevelt could have run again in 1908, he chose instead to handpick the next Republican presidential candidate. It was the first time since Andrew Jackson that a president in power had enough backing to choose his party's next presidential candidate. Roosevelt chose William Howard Taft, his loyal friend and a diligent public servant.

Did you know?

Teddy Roosevelt was a Harvard graduate. He spoke several languages and was a prolific writer. He authored dozens of books, hundreds of articles, and tens of thousands of letters. His thick glasses and toothy grin were his most prominent features.

SECTION REVIEW 19.4

1. What do you think Roosevelt meant by "square deal"?
2. What act passed during Roosevelt's administration regulated food and medicine production? What novel prompted Congress to pass this act?
3. What law regulating monopolies had been rarely enforced until Roosevelt's administration?

19.5 TAFT

How did President Taft's progressivism differ from President Roosevelt's?

GUIDING QUESTIONS

- What was President Taft's progressivism like?
- Why did the Republican Party split, and how did that affect the election of 1912?

William Howard Taft worked for a number of years as an attorney and then as a federal judge. Roosevelt appointed him governor of the Philippines and later secretary of war. Taft preferred legal work, and his lifelong dream was to be chief justice of the Supreme Court. But on Roosevelt's advice, he set aside that goal to run for president.

William Howard Taft

27

Born	September 5, 1857
Died	March 8, 1930
Home state	Ohio
Wife	Helen Herron
Church	Unitarian
Occupation	lawyer
Party	Republican
Years served as president	1909–13
Terms	1
Vice president	James Sherman

The Taft Administration

Like Roosevelt, Taft thought that government should regulate big business. But when Taft won the 1908 election over Democrat William Jennings Bryan, he took a course that was somewhat different from Roosevelt's. He followed the advice of Republican leaders more readily, and he did not publicly pursue progressive reforms as vigorously as Roosevelt had done. His methods and personality made him seem more casual than Roosevelt. But Taft initiated eighty-nine antitrust suits, whereas Roosevelt had initiated only forty-three. Taft, however, was not as successful at communicating his successes as Roosevelt had been. Many people saw only Taft's mistakes and considered him a failure.

Still, Taft could claim many progressive actions. He helped give the Interstate Commerce Commission more control over railroads. He instituted regulations regarding telegraph and telephone companies. And he backed reforms in the post office, created the Department of Labor to protect workers, and organized the Children's Bureau to assist with the well-being of children and their mothers.

Taft adopted a less confrontational foreign policy than the "speak softly and carry a big stick" approach that Roosevelt had favored. Taft preferred to influence foreign affairs through the investment of American dollars in foreign countries, a policy soon nicknamed "**dollar diplomacy.**" For example, American money enabled Latin American countries to establish industries and helped Latin Americans in other ways. But if Latin American countries did not follow the wishes of the United States, the money could be withdrawn.

During Taft's term, two progressive constitutional amendments were adopted by Congress. The **Sixteenth Amendment** instituted a federal income tax. This additional source of revenue allowed the national government to greatly expand its activities. And the Seventeenth Amendment said that US senators were to be elected directly by the people of their states, rather than by the state legislatures. The Sixteenth Amendment was ratified a month before Taft left office, and the Seventeenth was ratified a month after his term ended.

Fighting within the Republican Party threatened Taft's political future. Disputes over the tariff in 1909 made some Republicans think that Taft had abandoned Roosevelt's ideas. Furthermore, disagreement arose between Gifford Pinchot and one of Taft's cabinet members regarding western forestlands. As a result, Taft fired Pinchot from his position as head of the US Forest Service in January 1910.

Fun Fact

In 1921, eight years after Taft left the presidency, President Warren G. Harding appointed him chief justice of the Supreme Court.

▲ Teddy Roosevelt (center) on his African safari shortly after leaving the presidency

After leaving office, Roosevelt had traveled to Africa for a huge safari and then on to Europe. Though he was absent from the country from March 1909 to June 1910, he heard news about Taft's decisions. Upon returning home, he was increasingly concerned that Taft had compromised progressive principles.

The Election of 1912

Roosevelt had been home for less than two months when he hit the campaign trail. He said that he was trying to persuade voters to elect progressive Republicans to the House and Senate. But his efforts actually widened the rift in the Republican Party and built support for his own nomination at the 1912 Republican convention. By February 1912 Roosevelt, at the urging of other progressive Republicans, announced that he would indeed run for president.

But Taft had the support of most Republican Party leaders. They helped him win the Republican nomination on the first ballot at the convention. Roosevelt declared that Taft had stolen the nomination. So he launched the Progressive Party and became its candidate.

One night during his campaign, Roosevelt was heading to an auditorium in Milwaukee, Wisconsin, to deliver a speech. Suddenly, a gunman came from the crowd and shot him at close range. Against others' advice, Roosevelt still traveled to the auditorium and delivered a "brief" (ninety-minute-long) speech. "It takes more than that to kill a Bull Moose," he declared. As a result, the Progressive Party gained its nickname: the **Bull Moose Party**.

the ATTEMPTED ASSASSINATION *of* TEDDY ROOSEVELT

> Friends, I shall ask you to be as quiet as possible. I don't know whether you fully understand that I have just been shot; but it takes more than that to kill a Bull Moose. But fortunately I had my manuscript, so you see I was going to make a long speech, and there is a bullet—there is where the bullet went through—and it probably saved me from it going into my heart. The bullet is in me now, so that I cannot make a very long speech, but I will try my best.
>
> —Theodore Roosevelt, Address at Milwaukee, Wisconsin, October 14, 1912

Shortly before the former president gave this speech, John F. Schrank shot him. In addition to the fifty-page manuscript of his speech, the bullet was also slowed by his overcoat and a steel-reinforced eyeglass case. Despite his "I cannot make a very long speech" comment above, Roosevelt talked for ninety minutes. But at times, he spoke only in a whisper.

Later in the day, doctors located the bullet lodged against one of Roosevelt's ribs. They determined that attempting to remove it was more dangerous than leaving it in his chest. It remained there until his death in 1919.

Schrank was later declared insane and committed to a mental asylum. He remained there until he died of natural causes in 1943.

▼ The bullet holes in Teddy Roosevelt's eyeglass case and speech

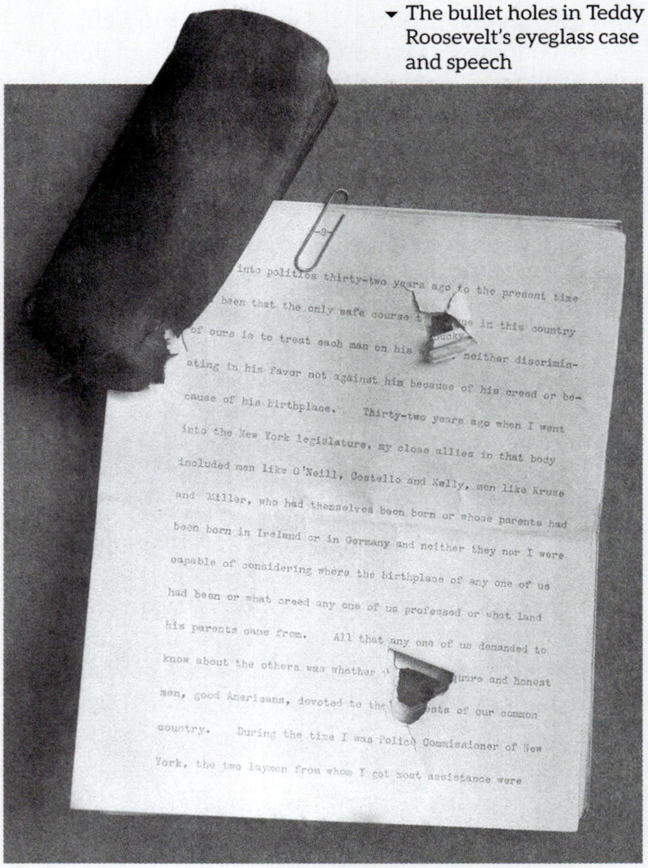

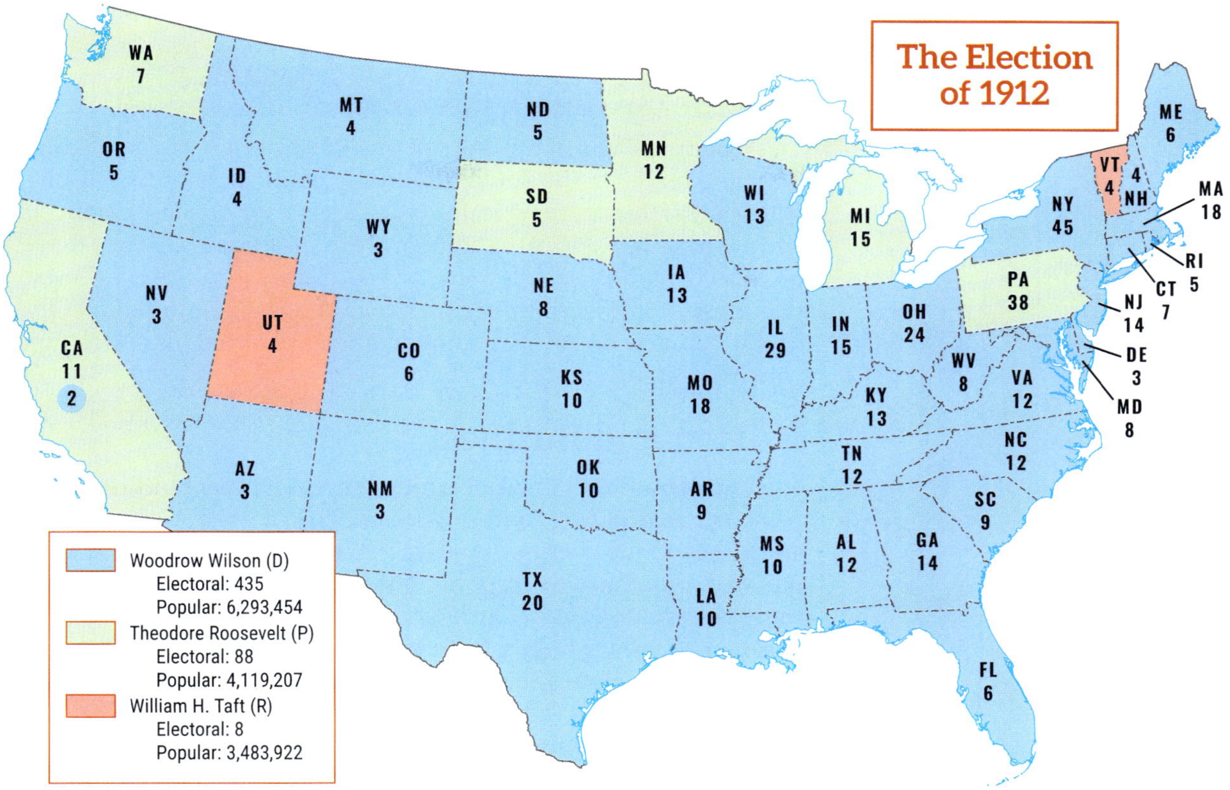

Roosevelt's political program was known as the "New Nationalism." He called for even more federal regulation of businesses and more social reforms. Had he won the presidency, he hoped to extend the federal government's power in a number of areas.

Opposing Roosevelt and Taft was the Democratic nominee, **Woodrow Wilson**. As a historian, professor, and president of Princeton University, Wilson had both studied deeply and written extensively about the American system of government. Elected governor of New Jersey in 1910, Wilson proved to be a zealous progressive. Thus, all three candidates were progressives. Together, Roosevelt and Taft received more votes than Wilson, but the split Republican vote allowed Wilson to win the electoral vote and the presidency.

Another candidate, Eugene V. Debs, received just over 900,000 votes, approximately six percent of those cast. It was the fourth time he had been the candidate for the Socialist Party. In 1920 he made his fifth and final attempt at the presidency. He again received more than 900,000 votes, though he was in prison at the time. He had been convicted in 1918 of violating the Sedition Act, a law later repealed in 1920, that prohibited certain types of speech that were critical of US involvement in World War I.

SECTION REVIEW 19.5

1. What progressive actions occurred during Taft's administration?
2. After serving as president, what other branch of government did Taft head?
3. Why was the Progressive Party created in 1912?
4. Why was Woodrow Wilson, a Democrat, able to win the 1912 presidential election?

GUIDING QUESTION

- What were the main issues during Wilson's administration?

▾ Part of the crowd attending Woodrow Wilson's first inauguration (March 1913)

Woodrow Wilson

Born	December 28, 1856	28
Died	February 3, 1924	
Home state	New Jersey (born in Virginia)	
Wives	1st—Ellen Axson and 2nd—Edith Bolling Galt	
Church	Presbyterian	
Occupations	lawyer, professor, Princeton University president	
Party	Democrat	
Years served as president	1913–21	
Terms	2	
Vice president	Thomas Marshall	

19.6 WILSON

What occurred during Woodrow Wilson's presidency?

Woodrow Wilson was the son of a Presbyterian pastor. He was born and reared in the South. Regarding political matters, Wilson believed that there are typically two sides to every issue—a right side and a wrong side. He clung stubbornly to his ideas and rarely made political compromises. He viewed people idealistically. He believed that most people learn from experience and want to do right. Politically, that view meant Wilson often underestimated his opposition, whether at home or abroad.

Wilson and Business

Two important laws concerning the regulation of business were passed during Wilson's administration. The Clayton Antitrust Act strengthened the Sherman Antitrust Act by expanding the list of practices prohibited to corporations. It defined actions that could cause corporations to be fined or could lead their executives to be jailed. It also legalized practices such as strikes, picketing, and boycotts. Even more sweeping was the establishment of the **Federal Trade Commission (FTC)**, a board of five people authorized to help define and halt unfair business practices. The FTC Act marked a growing tendency for government regulation and enforcement by agencies rather than Congress or the courts. This continued how many progressives viewed government—as the solution to society's problems.

Wilson and Financial Reform

The Democrats had gained majorities in both the House and the Senate during the 1912 election. Wilson's views on the tariff were consistent with the Democrats' historical position; he believed that a high protective tariff would lead to higher prices for consumers. He thought that lowering the tariff would force American businesses to compete with rivals and become more efficient. As a result, he signed the Underwood Tariff of 1913, which enacted the first major tariff reduction since the Civil War. The tariff rate on imports dropped from 40 percent to about 26 percent.

Congress used the recently adopted federal income tax to compensate for the loss of tariff revenue. The income tax was graduated, or progressive. The more individuals earned, the more they had to pay from their income. For married couples, annual incomes under $4,000 were not taxed. This meant nearly all factory workers and farmers were not required to pay an income tax. But annual incomes between $4,000 and $20,000 were taxed at 1 percent. Annual incomes over $500,000, for married couples, were in the top tax bracket at 6 percent. The tax rate for a single individual varied slightly. Eventually, the required percentage of income tax increased, and the higher taxes led to more government spending.

Another financial reform during the Wilson presidency was the establishment, by Congress, of the **Federal Reserve System** in 1913. It divided the nation into twelve banking districts, each served by a regional Federal Reserve Bank, with overall supervision by the Federal Reserve Board. These twelve banks were "bankers' banks."

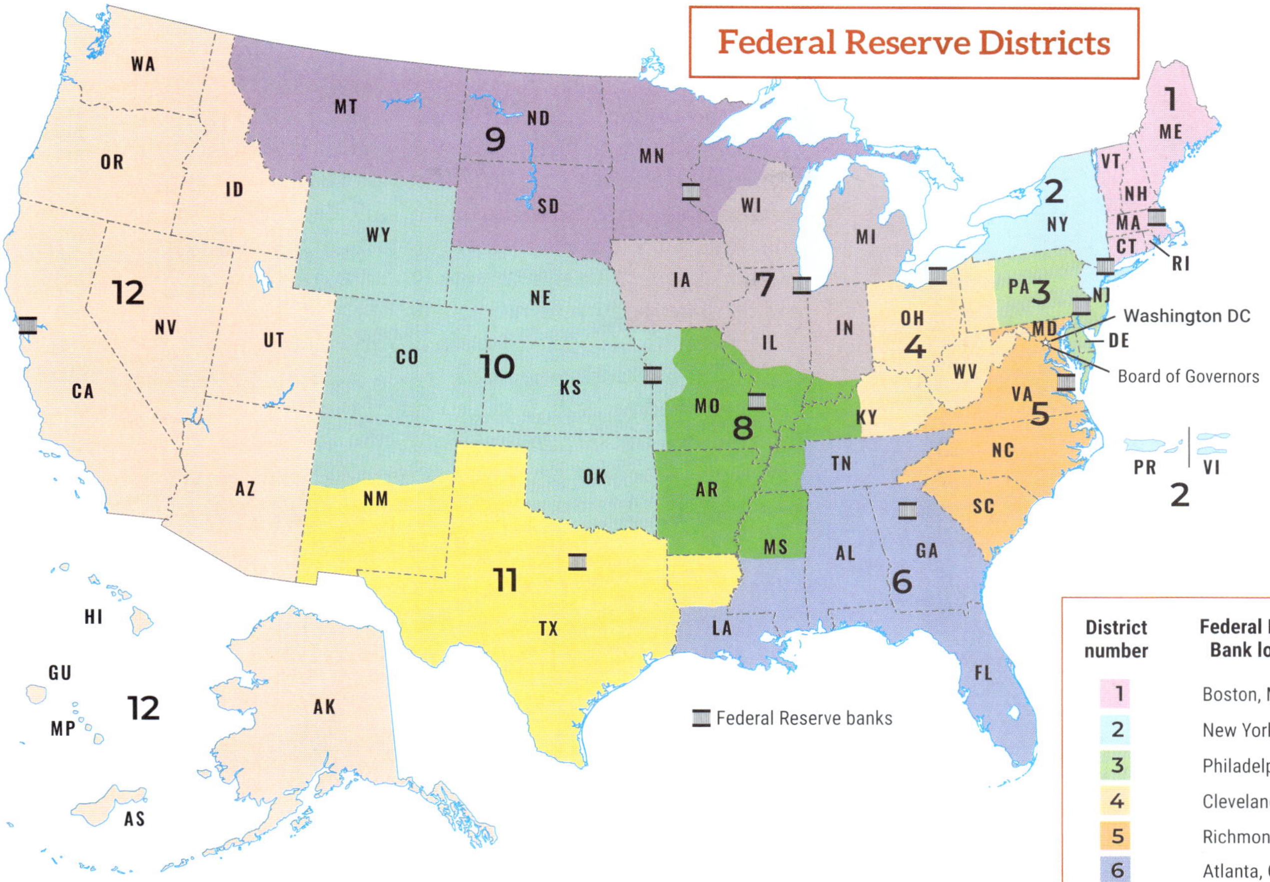

District number	Federal Reserve Bank location
1	Boston, MA
2	New York, NY
3	Philadelphia, PA
4	Cleveland, OH
5	Richmond, VA
6	Atlanta, GA
7	Chicago, IL
8	St. Louis, MO
9	Minneapolis, MN
10	Kansas City, MO
11	Dallas, TX
12	San Francisco, CA

They and the board could increase or decrease the amount of money in circulation, and they exercised control over many banking operations throughout the country. Those powers still exist today.

Wilson's Second Term

As the 1916 election approached, Wilson found himself preoccupied with events involving the war that had erupted in Europe in 1914, eventually known as World War I. His 1916 campaign slogan—"He kept us out of war"—revealed his focus.

When Roosevelt refused to run as the Progressive Party candidate, the Bull Moose Party dissolved. Progressives had to decide whom to follow. Some backed Wilson because of his reforms. Others returned to the Republican party.

The election of 1916 was very close. Wilson's Republican opponent was Charles Evans Hughes, who had served as a New York governor and a Supreme Court justice. The key state in the election was California. Election results from that state arrived late, and the election was in doubt until the following day. After winning the state by fewer than 4,000 votes of the million votes cast, Wilson was reelected president.

Wilson focused on foreign affairs during much of his second term. He believed that all people had the moral right to choose their own government and leaders, as was done in the United States. He continued implementing the "moral diplomacy" that he had started earlier in his presidency. This was a policy of supporting those countries that provided the right to free elections and pressuring those that did not provide that freedom to begin doing so.

Did you know?

Woodrow Wilson is the only president to have an earned doctorate. He had a PhD in political science (the study of government).

In January 1916, the Mexican bandit **Pancho Villa** had stopped a train in northern Mexico, and his men murdered eighteen Americans. Two months later, Villa's men led a raid into New Mexico where they killed seventeen more Americans and burned the border town of Columbus. Wilson sent several thousand soldiers into Mexico to capture Villa. After almost a year of searching fruitlessly for him, the expedition was finally canceled in February 1917. By this time, the European war was nearing its peak. In April 1917, at Wilson's request, Congress voted to enter the war. (Wilson's reasons will be discussed in the next chapter.)

Late in his second term, after World War I ended, two additional constitutional amendments were ratified. The **Eighteenth Amendment**, ratified in 1919, was also called the Prohibition Amendment. It prohibited the sale, manufacture, and transportation of alcoholic beverages. One year later, women won the right to vote when the **Nineteenth Amendment** was ratified.

◂ Pancho Villa

▾ Women's suffrage parade in New York City, May 1913

the NINETEENTH AMENDMENT *and* WOMEN'S RIGHTS

The drive for women's suffrage began before the Civil War. Throughout the late 1800s, "women suffragettes" campaigned unceasingly for the right to vote. Led by women such as Elizabeth Cady Stanton (1815–1902) and Susan B. Anthony (1820–1906), the crusade for women's suffrage was part of an overall campaign for equal rights for women. Many women wanted to control their own property, have custody of their children in divorce cases, and enjoy other privileges. Anthony's campaign for the vote, however, received the most attention. Although Anthony died fourteen years before the Nineteenth Amendment was ratified in 1920, it was often called the "Anthony Amendment" in her honor.

Jeannette Rankin (1880–1973), another promoter of women's rights, was elected to the US House of Representatives in 1916 as a Republican from Montana (a number of states, including Montana, allowed women to vote before the Nineteenth Amendment was adopted). She was the first female member of Congress. As a member of the House from 1917 to 1919 and 1941 to 1943, she voted against US entry into both World War I and World War II. Toward the end of her life, she also opposed US participation in the Vietnam War.

SECTION REVIEW 19.6

1. What was the job of the Federal Trade Commission (FTC)?
2. How did the government compensate for the loss of revenue due to the large tariff reduction?
3. What new reform established district banks to control the country's banking operations? Into how many districts was it divided?
4. What was Wilson's slogan for his 1916 campaign?
5. What nickname was given to the Eighteenth Amendment? Why?

CHAPTER 19 REVIEW

Making Connections

1. What effect did urbanization have on inner cities?
2. How did public education change during the Progressive era?
3. Why did reading become more popular during the Progressive era?
4. What does NAACP stand for?
5. Identify three unorthodox religious groups that became popular at this time.
6. What is agnosticism? What book helped it to grow? Who wrote this book?
7. What four foundational Christian beliefs do liberals not accept?
8. The four major goals of progressivism were to fight _____, improve _____, give people a greater _____ in government, and make government more _____.
9. In how many of the three levels of government (local, state, national) was corruption occurring?
10. What did Roosevelt call his attempt to give both workers and owners fair treatment?
11. What four national parks existed before Roosevelt's presidency?
12. How did the Progressive Party receive the nickname "Bull Moose"?
13. What foreign issue took much of Wilson's time as the 1916 election approached?

14.–27. Complete the chart.

	Theodore Roosevelt	William Howard Taft	Woodrow Wilson
Foreign policy	14. "big _____"	15. "_____ diplomacy"	16. "_____ diplomacy"
Major laws	17. Pure _____ 18. _____ Reclamation Act		19. _____ Antitrust Act 20. _____ Tariff of 1813
Progressive reforms	21. US _____ Service	22. Department of _____	23. Federal _____ Commission 24. Federal _____ System
Party represented during 1912 election	25. _____	26. _____	27. _____

Thinking Critically

28. What was wrong with the *Plessy v. Ferguson* decision approving "separate but equal" facilities for blacks and whites?
29. Why could progressivism, with its goal of changing man's environment to improve society, never be fully successful?

Living as a Christian Citizen

30. What lessons can you learn from B. B. Warfield and Billy Sunday about defending the foundational truths of Christianity?
31. Would it have been appropriate for Christians to support the Progressive reforms of this period? Why or why not?

Terms to Remember

urbanization
Tuskegee Institute
Booker T. Washington
George Washington Carver
Jim Crow laws
segregation
literacy tests
poll tax
grandfather clause
Plessy v. Ferguson
W. E. B. Du Bois
National Association for the Advancement of Colored People (NAACP)
agnostics
Billy Sunday
temperance societies
Young Men's Christian Association (YMCA)
Salvation Army
rescue missions
progressivism
William "Boss" Tweed
settlement houses
Jane Addams
initiative
referendum
recall
Seventeenth Amendment
Pure Food and Drug Act
muckrakers
Ida M. Tarbell
Upton Sinclair
William Howard Taft
dollar diplomacy
Sixteenth Amendment
Bull Moose Party
Woodrow Wilson
Federal Trade Commission (FTC)
Federal Reserve System
Pancho Villa
Eighteenth Amendment
Nineteenth Amendment

UNIT

6

Taking the Lead

1914

World War I
1914–18

1917 — United States enters World War I

1918

Treaty of Versailles signed — **1919** — Eighteenth Amendment ratified

1920 — Nineteenth Amendment ratified

Washington Naval Conference
1921–22

1921

1922

1925 — Scopes trial

Charles Lindbergh's solo flight across the Atlantic Ocean — **1927**

1929 — Stock-market crash

Election of Franklin Roosevelt — **1932**

1933 — Beginning of the New Deal

1939

1941 — Japan's attack on Pearl Harbor; United States enters World War II

World War II
1939–45

1944 — D-day, the Allied invasion of France

1945 — V-E Day, the end of World War II in Europe; V-J Day, the end of World War II

CHAPTER 20

World War I

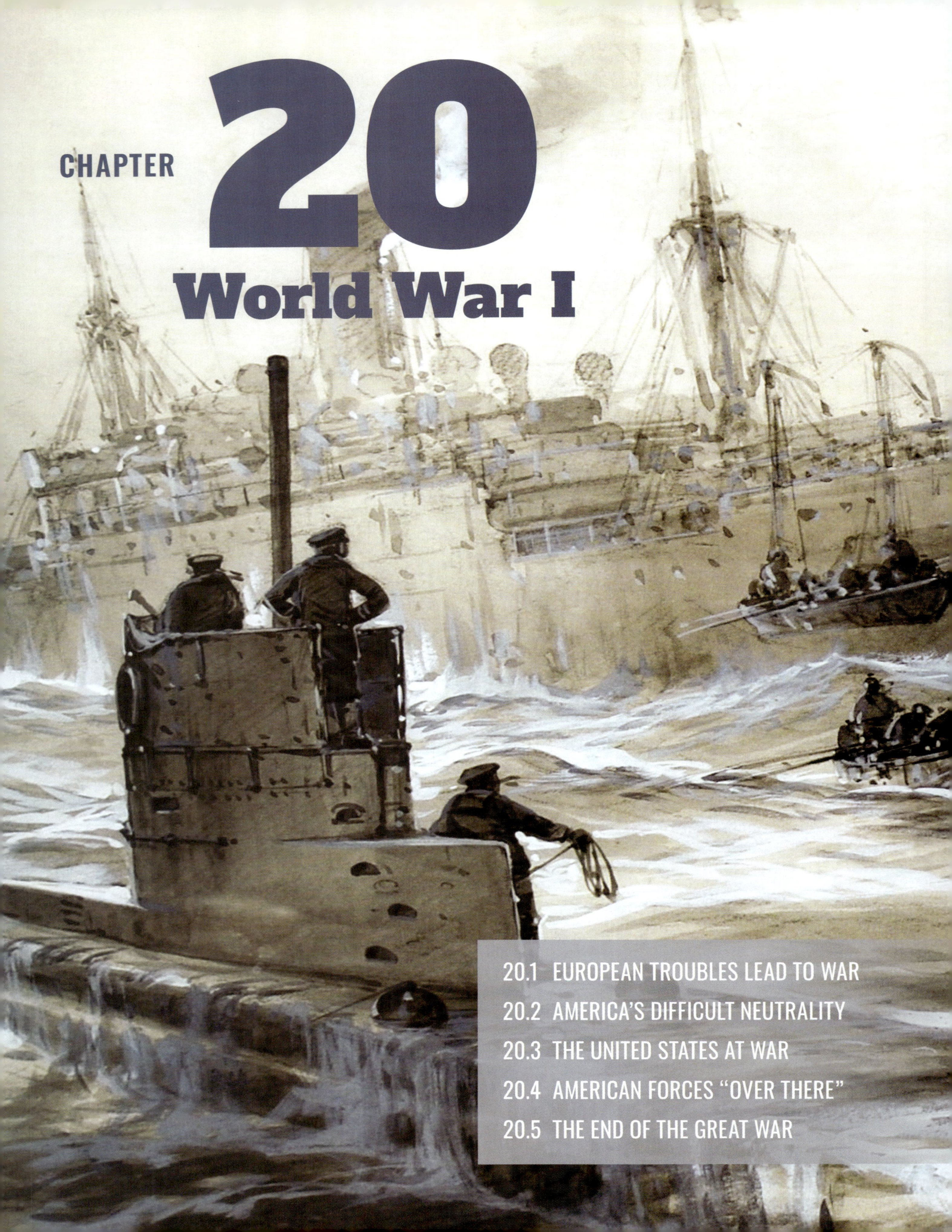

20.1 EUROPEAN TROUBLES LEAD TO WAR

What were the causes of World War I?

War erupted in Europe in July 1914. For three years—from the summer of 1914 until mid-1917—the United States watched the "Great War" devastate Europe. It destroyed more property and life than any previous war in history. But most Americans believed that the war was Europe's affair. They agreed with President Woodrow Wilson when he said that Americans should be neutral in both thought and deed. They hoped that the Atlantic Ocean would shield them from the conflict.

Americans had reelected Wilson in 1916 on the slogan "He kept us out of war." But on April 6, 1917, hopes of staying at peace were dashed when the United States entered World War I.

GUIDING QUESTIONS

- What factors contributed to the outbreak of World War I?
- What happened during the Great War before America's entrance?

Reasons for the War

Europe was in turmoil in the early 1900s. Four major factors created this uneasiness and eventually led to the first world war.

NATIONALISM

First was **nationalism**, the feeling of loyalty or devotion to one's country or cultural group. This led to patriotism within countries, but among cultural groups that did not have their own nation (such as the Czechs, Poles, and Slavs), nationalism created the desire to form one. While nationalism is natural and acceptable, the extreme nationalism sweeping Europe proved dangerous. It created an intense competitiveness and rivalry between countries and cultural groups. Major European nations were determined to increase their power and prestige, and some nationalities sought to create their own countries even if it required violence to do so.

IMPERIALISM

A second reason for rising tensions was imperialism. Several countries either had or wanted large empires. Some were willing to go to war for control of colonies or nearby territories.

Wilhelm II was the *kaiser*, or leader, of Germany from 1888 to 1918.

MILITARISM

Militarism, an increased emphasis on military might, was a third reason for unrest. Several nations had built large armies and expanded their navies to further their imperialistic goals or to protect possessions. Such large and powerful forces threatened weaker neighbors. Furthermore, when one country increased the size of its military, its rivals felt compelled to do the same.

ALLIANCES

The fourth major reason for the eruption of World War I was the system of alliances (agreements to provide mutual military support) created by European nations. Germany, Austria-Hungary, and Italy had formed the **Triple Alliance** in 1882. Britain, France, and Russia created the **Triple Entente** in 1907 (*entente* is French for "agreement or understanding"). Those two opposing alliances involved all the major powers of Europe; thus, once any European country entered a conflict, all the others were likely to be drawn into it.

German submarine sinking a British cargo ship in January 1915

▲ Archduke Francis Ferdinand and his wife leaving city hall in Sarajevo. Minutes later they were both assassinated.

The Spark and Spread of the War

On June 28, 1914, Archduke **Francis (Franz) Ferdinand** and his wife, Sophie, visited the city of Sarajevo in the southwestern part of Austria-Hungary. He was the heir, or next-in-line, to the throne of that country. Seven young men, members of a Slavic terrorist group known as the Black Hand, plotted to murder the archduke. He opposed what they desperately wanted—the creation of a nation for Slavic people who lived in southern Europe. It would include the countries of Serbia and Montenegro as well as a large portion of land in Austria-Hungary where many Slavs lived. The seven young men, all extreme nationalists, positioned themselves along the route where the archduke's motorcade would pass and attempted to launch their coordinated attack. One of the seven hurled a bomb that narrowly missed the archduke's car. It destroyed the vehicle behind him and wounded nearly twenty people.

The motorcade continued to city hall. After a visit there, the motorcade resumed. The archduke's chauffeur took a wrong turn. As he tried to correct his mistake, he stopped within five feet of one of the Slavic assassins, Gavrilo Princip. Princip raised his pistol and fired two quick shots. The world would never be the same. Franz Ferdinand was shot in the neck; Sophie, in the abdomen. Both died soon afterward.

The shooting that day was the "spark" that ignited what became known as the Great War or the World War. The turmoil that had been smoldering in Europe for years meant the spark would result in a huge explosion. About ten million soldiers would die during the next four years and approximately twenty million would be wounded. Millions of civilians also would lose their lives.

After officials in Austria-Hungary learned that the seven terrorists had trained in Serbia, they issued a list of demands to that nation on July 23. One demand was that Serbia allow representatives from Austria-Hungary to enter the country and investigate matters relating to the archduke's death. Serbia did not agree to that demand but indicated it would conduct its own investigation. Austria-Hungary was not satisfied and declared war on Serbia on July 28.

CHOOSING *to* ENGAGE *in* WAR

Although the Bible permits governments to wage war (Rom. 13:3–4), it favors peace over war whenever possible (Rom. 12:18). After Christ returns to rule earth, everyone will be at peace (Isa. 9:6–7).

Many Christians argue that governments must have just reasons for going to war. Defending one's nation or seeking to bring about peace are good reasons for entering a war. Because war results from human depravity and brings death and destruction, most Christians believe that countries should go to war only when other attempts to resolve conflict have failed.

Other countries quickly began the deadly slide into war. Germany had pledged to support its ally, Austria-Hungary. Russia, home to many Slavic people and a friend of Serbia, began mobilizing its troops (assembling of soldiers) on July 30 in case it decided to enter the war on Serbia's side. Germany demanded that Russia stop the mobilization. Russia insisted that it hoped a peaceful solution to the conflict could be found but refused to stop gathering its troops. Consequently, Germany declared war on Russia on August 1.

Four nations were now at war—Austria-Hungary, Serbia, Germany, and Russia. Since Russia and France were allies and were both members of the Triple Entente, Germany demanded to know France's intentions about the war. The French hesitated to give an answer but began mobilizing soldiers. Germany viewed this as an indication the French would join Russia's side. On August 3 Germany declared war on France. That same day Germany invaded Belgium, the quickest route to attack France. Britain had a treaty with Belgium promising to protect the neutrality of that nation, and Germany had previously promised to respect Belgium's neutrality. Thus, the British demanded that Germany withdraw its troops from Belgium. When Germany refused, Britain declared war on Germany on August 4.

In one week's time (July 28 to August 4), seven countries were at war. Others later took sides. Europe found itself in a long and bloody war between the **Central Powers**—Germany, Austria-Hungary, and their later allies, Bulgaria and Turkey (also called the Ottoman Empire)—and the **Allied Powers** (or Allies)—Britain, France, Russia, Italy, numerous smaller nations, and later the United States. (Italy, originally a member of the Triple Alliance, avoided war until it changed sides in 1915.)

▲ Trenches, gas masks, and tanks were important in World War I.

Modern Warfare

At first, the United States was not involved in the European alliances and rivalries, so it had no reason to enter the war. Americans simply watched in horror as soldiers from both sides were slaughtered in the bitter conflict. By the end of 1914, a long, bloody stalemate (or deadlock) had settled at the battlefront in western Europe. Neither the Central Powers nor the Allies made large gains. At the same time, the Russian armies began to attack Germany and Austria-Hungary from the east. They had little success.

The Germans dug trenches (long ditches normally deep enough for a man to stand in) that faced the trenches the British and French had constructed. **Trench warfare** became a major part of the war as the trenches stretched from the English Channel to Switzerland. This system included frontline trenches, support trenches (for men and supplies to assist those on the frontlines), and communication trenches (to assist with moving messages as well as supplies). Beyond the frontline trenches were barbed wire and "no man's land," a neutral zone that varied in size from a few yards to more than a mile. Attacking soldiers faced machine-gun fire, land mines, flamethrowers, and later poison gas. This system of trenches and the weapons defending them made it very difficult for opposing troops to advance.

Both sides introduced new weapons and other equipment that made warfare more efficient, more deadly, and more brutal. For example, the British developed the tank, an armored vehicle with caterpillar tracks that could shoot while moving. It could advance almost continuously over rugged terrain. Soon, the other powers developed their own tanks as well as tactics for attacking with and defending against them.

On April 22, 1915, at the Second Battle of Ypres (in Belgium), the Germans unleashed a deadly new weapon: poison gas. Soon, both sides were hurling shells loaded with chlorine gas or other gases that harmed soldiers' noses, throats, and lungs. Sometimes gas caused short-term or even permanent blindness. It often caused soldiers to die choking. Poisonous gases could temporarily disable whole armies. Mustard gas quickly became the most feared weapon on the battlefield. As a result, the gas mask was developed and became standard equipment in some areas.

There were also innovations in aviation. For a while, Germany used zeppelins, large aircraft similar to blimps, to bomb Britain. But zeppelins moved slowly, so airplanes soon replaced them. Airplanes were first used to spy on the enemy. But they attacked enemy planes and bombed targets as well. Aerial battles between planes were called "dogfights." Pilots fired machine guns at each other. At first, firing forward was risky because they could destroy their own propellers. A new invention, the synchronized machine gun, timed the propeller rotation with the firing of the machine gun.

Fighter pilots who shot down five or more enemy planes became special heroes called "aces." Manfred von Richthofen, nicknamed the Red Baron, was Germany's top ace. He achieved 80 "kills." Other top aces included France's René Fonck (75 kills), Canada's Billy Bishop (72 kills), and Great Britain's Edward "Mick" Mannock (61 kills). When the United States entered the war, Eddie Rickenbacker became the most famous American ace. He finished the war with 26 kills. Rickenbacker, like other American aces, flew in the war three fewer years than pilots from many other countries.

Other modernized equipment was also used in the war. Trucks and automobiles aided in the transportation of military goods and personnel. Improved weapons for more effective fighting included rifles, cannons, grenades, and mines. The German navy made extensive use of submarines, which the Allies called **U-boats** (from *Unterseeboot*, German for "undersea boat," their term for a submarine). Other nations soon began constructing their own submarines.

SECTION REVIEW 20.1

1. What were four major factors leading to the first world war?
2. What event sparked World War I?
3. What countries were part of the Central Powers?
4. What countries were part of the Allied Powers?
5. What three new weapons were first used during World War I?
6. Why do you think the use of poison gas is generally seen as an unacceptable method of warfare?

the LAFAYETTE ESCADRILLE

Early in World War I, a group of American pilots petitioned the French government to create an all-American squadron in the French air force. Permission was granted, and in April 1916 the Escadrille Américaine, consisting of volunteer American pilots, was formed.

Since the United States was neutral at the time and the group's name implied that the United States was helping France, the squadron's name was changed to the Lafayette Escadrille. It honored the Marquis de Lafayette for his assistance to the United States during the War for Independence.

A World War I German airplane (left) and a British one (top right). America's most famous pilot of the war, Eddie Rickenbacker (inset).

GUIDING QUESTION

- What factors led the United States to join the Allied side?

1 American attitudes favored Allies.

2 Majority of trade and loans was to Allies.

3 Allied propaganda influenced Americans.

4 Germany's treatment of other countries harmed relations.

5 German violations resulted in American deaths.

This German poster encouraged young men to join the army. It says, "Your Fatherland is in danger, register!"

20.2 AMERICA'S DIFFICULT NEUTRALITY

Why did America enter World War I?

Although the US government did not initially participate in the war, it was not totally isolated from the warring nations. The war affected transportation, trade, and diplomatic relations with Europe. Americans were involved in all of those areas.

Favoring the Allied Cause

President Wilson had stated that Americans should remain neutral. But maintaining neutrality was difficult for several reasons.

First, American attitudes favored the Allied cause. Although eleven million Americans had some connection to Germany, many more had British ties. Furthermore, America's legal system, much of its form of government, and even its language were English. Also, Americans recalled that France had given military support to America during the War for Independence. In addition, Americans were upset by the German invasion of neutral Belgium.

Second, although American businesses sold goods and loaned money to both the Allied and Central Powers, the vast majority of trade and loans was with Allied countries, especially Britain. As a result, many Americans were more sympathetic to Allied interests because they wanted to protect their own investments. Early in the war, the British and French placed orders with American firms for shipments of grain, cotton, and other supplies. At first, they paid cash for items, which they transported on their own ships. But when their cash ran low, they asked for and received loans. The Germans protested that the loans violated neutrality. They pointed out that American-made shells and guns, bought with money borrowed from Americans, were killing Germans. Wilson, however, chose not to restrict the business deals. He believed that limiting lending would help the Central Powers. By early 1917, the United States had loaned the Allies over $2 billion but only $27 million to Germany.

Third, Americans were influenced by Allied **propaganda** (information spread to advance a cause or damage an opponent's cause). Britain and France controlled the transatlantic cables that brought news to American newspapers. Both nations, but particularly Britain, sent information that portrayed the Allies in the best possible light while presenting only negative information, and even lies, about Germany.

Fourth, Germany's treatment of other countries harmed its relationship with America. As mentioned, when Germany invaded Belgium, it violated one of its treaties. The German government called the treaty "a scrap of paper." Germans executed about five thousand Belgian civilians who resisted them. British propagandists were quick to let Americans know about this action and many others.

The fifth and biggest difficulty in maintaining neutrality was that Britain and Germany were violating America's neutral rights at sea. While both nations were guilty, German actions resulted in American deaths; this was not true of British infractions.

Violations of America's Neutrality Rights

Early in the war, Britain placed mines at the entrances of the North Sea to prevent nations from trading with Germany. As a result, goods intended for Germany were sent by way of such neutral countries as the Netherlands, Denmark, and Sweden. Those nations then sold the items to the Germans. This angered the British, and they began to stop shipping (including American ships) bound for neutral nations. The British were ready to seize anything that could be useful to Germany. Their actions angered Americans because they violated the rights of the United States, a neutral country, to trade freely.

Germany upset the United States when it allowed its submarines to violate America's rights to trade. According to **international law** (rules by which countries agree to abide), warships could not sink a merchant or passenger ship until two conditions were met. First, the presence of war materials aboard those vessels had to be confirmed. Second, the crew and passengers on the ships had to be evacuated. Submarines had difficulty completing these requirements because they would have to surface to do so. Surfacing would make them easy targets for deck guns aboard ships or for ramming by a larger vessel.

In February 1915, Germany announced that it intended to follow **unrestricted submarine warfare**. This meant all ships entering a designated war zone around Britain would be subject to attack without warning. President Wilson reminded the Germans that this was a violation of international law and therefore unacceptable. Nevertheless, Germans implemented their new policy. In late April 1915, the German government placed advertisements in about fifty American newspapers, including the *New York Times*, warning American citizens of the dangers of traveling aboard ships to the war zone.

The British passenger ship ***Lusitania*** left New York City on May 1, 1915. When it entered the war zone near Ireland on May 7, the commander of a German submarine spotted the ship and fired a torpedo. Within eighteen minutes, the large ship sank and 1,198 passengers and crewmen, including 128 Americans, died.

President Wilson was deeply moved by the tragedy. He demanded that the Germans apologize and provide financial compensation for American families affected by the *Lusitania*'s sinking. Many Americans criticized Wilson for not asking Congress to declare war on Germany. Others, like Secretary of State William Jennings Bryan, feared Wilson's words were too harsh. Bryan, a strong believer in keeping America neutral, resigned his position a month after the *Lusitania* disaster.

Germany expressed regret for the loss of life but continued to follow unrestricted submarine warfare. The Germans argued that many passenger and cargo ships were carrying war materials for the Allies. Though the Allies tried to conceal that information, it was true. Germany sank other ships over the next few months, resulting in the deaths of several Americans. After Wilson warned the Germans that another attack on a passenger or merchant ship would likely lead to war, Germany promised in May 1916 that it would abandon unrestricted submarine warfare and resume following international law.

The war dragged on, but the stalemate continued. Determined to win the war, Germany announced on January 31, 1917, that it would resume unrestricted submarine warfare. By this time, the Allies were facing food shortages. Germany hoped its announcement would prevent ships from trying to transport supplies to the Allies. It planned to sink those who disregarded the warning. It was a risky strategy. Germany knew that this action might bring the United States into the war. However, the Germans thought they could win the war before the United States would be able to declare war, draft and train soldiers, and transport an army (whose ships might be sunk by U-boats) to Europe.

▾ This telegram from Arthur Zimmermann, the German foreign minister, outraged Americans. It was one of the reasons the United States entered World War I.

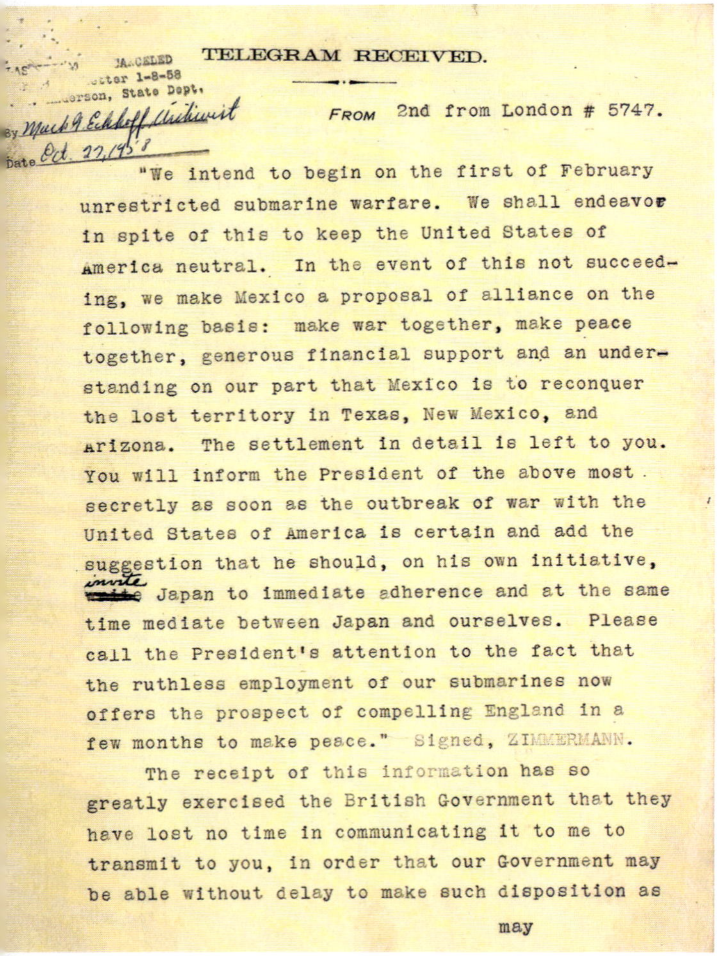

TELEGRAM RECEIVED.

...NCELED
...etter 1-8-58
...derson, State Dept.

By [signature]
Date Oct. 22, 1958

FROM 2nd from London # 5747.

"We intend to begin on the first of February unrestricted submarine warfare. We shall endeavor in spite of this to keep the United States of America neutral. In the event of this not succeeding, we make Mexico a proposal of alliance on the following basis: make war together, make peace together, generous financial support and an understanding on our part that Mexico is to reconquer the lost territory in Texas, New Mexico, and Arizona. The settlement in detail is left to you. You will inform the President of the above most secretly as soon as the outbreak of war with the United States of America is certain and add the suggestion that he should, on his own initiative, ~~invite~~ invite Japan to immediate adherence and at the same time mediate between Japan and ourselves. Please call the President's attention to the fact that the ruthless employment of our submarines now offers the prospect of compelling England in a few months to make peace." Signed, ZIMMERMANN.

The receipt of this information has so greatly exercised the British Government that they have lost no time in communicating it to me to transmit to you, in order that our Government may be able without delay to make such disposition as

may

The Zimmermann Telegram

Wilson began his second term as president on March 4, 1917. Just a week earlier, he had learned of a secret German plot. The German foreign minister, Arthur Zimmermann, sought to gain Mexico's support in case America joined the Allies. He sent a telegram to the Mexican government offering to help it reconquer Texas, New Mexico, and Arizona. Germany hoped that Mexico's involvement would prevent the United States from sending any soldiers to Europe prior to the war ending there.

The British intercepted and decoded the telegram and then enthusiastically forwarded it to the United States. When the details of the **Zimmermann telegram** were first revealed, it seemed so fantastic that some Americans believed it was a British hoax designed to bring them into the war on the Allied side. When the message was verified, however, Americans were outraged.

Also in March, German submarines sank four unarmed American merchant vessels. More than thirty civilians were killed. On April 2, 1917, the president appeared before a joint session of Congress and requested the House and Senate to formally recognize that Germany had "thrust" a state of war upon the United States. Wilson said, "The world must be made safe for democracy. Its peace must be planted upon the tested foundations of political liberty." Within days, the Senate voted 82–6 to declare war on Germany, the leading member of the Central Powers. The House of Representatives agreed by a vote of 373–50. On April 6, the president signed the declaration—America entered World War I, joining the Allies.

SECTION REVIEW 20.2

1. What five reasons made American neutrality difficult to maintain?
2. What is unrestricted submarine warfare? Why is this generally considered an unacceptable method of warfare?
3. The sinking of what ship upset many Americans?
4. What did the Zimmermann telegram offer to Mexico in exchange for its support? What was the result when the United States learned of it?

20.3 THE UNITED STATES AT WAR

How did America prepare for World War I?

GUIDING QUESTION

- What preparations did America make for the war?

By the time the United States entered the war, the Allies were in desperate condition. Thanks to the success of Germany's unrestricted submarine warfare, the British people had only a few weeks' supply of food remaining. To provide supplies for the Allies, Americans had to quickly make major changes. The peacetime economy and production needed to be channeled into a great effort to win what Americans would call "the war to end all wars" and the "war to make the world safe for democracy."

▲ Sign reminding 18- to 45-year-old American males to register for the draft

Preparing the Military

Americans traditionally feared having a strong standing army and during peacetime had purposely kept the country's military force small. When the United States entered the war, its military consisted of about 128,000 full-time soldiers. The United States had limited military equipment and no tanks or aircraft. The United States had to train men, make equipment, and build ships on which to carry everything to Europe.

For the first time since the Civil War, the nation resorted to a draft. Under the Selective Service Act, local draft boards were established under civilian leadership to supply men for military service. In 1917 all men ages 21 to 30 were required to register for the draft, and in 1918 the bracket was expanded to include those 18 to 45 years old. Altogether, 2.8 million men were drafted into the army while hundreds of thousands volunteered to serve. The recruits were trained at thirty-two training camps. The total number of Americans in the military during the conflict exceeded 4 million. About half of those were transported to France to fight.

The United States sent huge shipments of troops and supplies to Europe. To ensure safe arrival, US ships carrying soldiers traveled in groups called convoys. They were protected by naval vessels equipped with antisubmarine weapons, including guns and depth charges. Such protection dramatically reduced the loss of ships. The **convoy system** worked so well that none of the ships carrying American soldiers bound for Europe were sunk.

▼ American ships bound for Europe during the war

Preparing at Home

▾ This poster encouraged Americans to conserve food.

Although American manpower boosted Allied morale, America's biggest contribution was providing supplies for the Allies. Food, clothing, and equipment from the United States poured into Europe. The Central Powers could not match this production and suffered from lack of needed supplies. As America sent its soldiers off to battle, the entire nation had to adjust to the necessities of war. Officials established many programs and agencies to coordinate the war effort. Everything the American forces needed had to be obtained or manufactured and transported quickly. The national emergency and federal involvement reduced the public's resistance to government power and restrictions.

The War Industries Board organized industrial production. Factories were transformed to produce needed war materials—uniforms, guns, ammunition, vehicles, planes, tanks, and medical essentials. The board set standards for thousands of items and established economic priorities for the country.

To ensure that the railroads operated efficiently while carrying extra freight and passengers, the government took control of all railroads. The United States Railroad Administration set rates and schedules and established shipping priorities to ensure that items reached ports for shipment to Europe. Movement of nonessential goods was often delayed to accomplish this.

The Fuel Administration had the job of conserving fuel and directing the nation's use of it. The administration asked civilians to walk more and added "gasless days" to weekly calendars. Auto owners were asked to save gasoline for trucks to carry war goods.

With Allied armies facing starvation, increasing America's food production became a top priority. Herbert Hoover had already gained fame as the head of an international commission that provided food to the war-torn nation of Belgium. (Hoover would later become the US president.) After America declared war, he headed the Food Administration. Rather than force the public to conserve food, the administration instituted a voluntary program. Americans were asked to observe "meatless Tuesdays," "wheatless Wednesdays," and "porkless Saturdays." Many Americans also grew their own vegetables in "Victory Gardens" so that more food would be available for soldiers. These efforts were enormously helpful in providing food for the Allied soldiers and made people feel they were performing their patriotic duty by participating. Just before the war began, the average annual amount of food shipped to Europe was 7 million tons. By 1919, it had reached 18.6 million tons.

▾ Victory Gardens helped increase the country's food supply.

▲ Women shipbuilders in the state of Washington

The war also brought changes in the United States' workforce. The number of people in the military depleted the normal workforce. Because of the urgent need, greater numbers of women began to work outside the home. Some returned home when the war ended, but others continued working outside the home.

Volunteer groups were formed to support the "boys" in France. Memberships in the American Red Cross multiplied as women in local chapters met to roll bandages, knit sweaters or socks, and prepare packages to be sent abroad. Men who could not serve in the military also offered their time to support such efforts.

The labor shortage caused wages to skyrocket, and more jobs became available. Even with high taxes and increased prices for most products, Americans were taking home more money than ever. To keep costs and wages under control, the government created the War Labor Policies Board to regulate workers. Unions were allowed to organize, and they showed significant gains in membership during the war. The board helped the unions settle labor disputes with management. The board also encouraged fair wages and set standards for employing women and children.

The shortage of workers and a drop in immigration provided opportunities for African American laborers. More than half a million blacks moved to northern cities during the war. Their migration permanently changed the ethnic makeup of many northern cities. When the war ended, many of these individuals kept their jobs and remained in the North.

▼ One of the many American recruitment posters

Informing the Public

President Wilson did not want to leave anything to chance. He wanted Americans to believe that their cause was just. To unite them behind the war effort, he founded the Committee on Public Information. Headed by journalist George Creel, 150,000 people became involved in a giant propaganda crusade to "advertise America." Talented artists designed war recruitment posters and ads. An army of lecturers appeared at local assemblies and in silent movies. Called "four-minute men," they gave short talks on any number of patriotic topics and moved crowds to cheers or tears.

Americans' attitude toward the Central Powers, even toward things distantly related to them, became negative. Most Americans soon hated all things German. Although many Germans had been in America for years and had proved their loyalty, some of them were sorely persecuted. Schools stopped teaching German. Orchestras refused to play pieces by German composers, such as Bach and Wagner. Sauerkraut was renamed "liberty cabbage." Hamburgers were called "liberty burgers." Dachshunds were renamed "liberty pups." Mothers whose children caught German measles told the neighbors that the children had "patriotic spots" or "patriotic measles."

Raising Money

The cost of the war was enormous. The United States spent approximately $32 billion. This was an enormous amount of money (the average American worker earned about $750 annually in 1914). About one-fourth of the money came from the new income tax and taxes on businesses. Most of the remainder was raised by selling war bonds, also known as "Liberty Loans."

Four times during the war, the government launched war bond sales. Those who purchased bonds were loaning money to the government. Later, their money would be returned with an interest payment. Individuals went door-to-door, asking people to buy bonds. Workers also bought bonds at their places of employment. Buyers received "liberty buttons" for their lapels. Goals were set, and great celebrations occurred when the drives went "over the top" (a command given to soldiers when they climbed from the trenches to attack the enemy). It was a patriotic venture that raised more than $18 billion.

Children joined the effort to raise money. They sold produce to earn money to purchase thrift stamps each week on "stamp day." They could swap a filled thrift card for a $5 savings stamp; they proudly exchanged ten savings stamps on a card for a $50 bond.

▾ Girl Scouts collecting peach pits. The sign says "You save peach seeds—they will save soldier's lives." The pits were ground up and used as filter material in gas masks.

▴ War bonds were also called Liberty Bonds.

SECTION REVIEW 20.3

1. How many Americans were drafted into the military during World War I?
2. Why were US ships carrying troops to Europe able to arrive safely?
3. On what days of the week were Americans asked to sacrifice the use of some items? List the item and day.
4. What was a result in the workforce as many men shipped overseas?
5. What did the Committee on Public Information do to unite Americans behind the war effort?
6. Was the change in American attitude toward Germans and German culture justified? Why or why not?
7. How did America raise money for the war?

20.4 AMERICAN FORCES "OVER THERE"

How was America's military involved in World War I?

GUIDING QUESTION

- How did American forces help end World War I?

The chief function of the US Navy was to get troops and supplies safely to Europe. Congress provided funds for enlarging the navy even before the country entered the war. Later the navy was significantly expanded to accomplish its major tasks.

Doughboys

In World War I, the American army was called the **American Expeditionary Force (AEF)**. It was commanded by General **John J. Pershing**. Pershing worked closely with Marshal Ferdinand Foch, a Frenchman who served as supreme Allied commander.

After the US declaration of war in April 1917, American troops, often called **doughboys**, began arriving in Europe in late June. At first the numbers were small; for example, the first group numbered fewer than 15,000. More soldiers arrived in the fall. Because of required training (a minimum of three months) and other delays, most American combat troops did not reach Europe until the spring of 1918. About 2 million American soldiers arrived on the continent by the war's end in November 1918.

British and French soldiers were weary and discouraged from three years of war, so the arrival of Americans was a welcome relief. The British and the French wanted to place American doughboys in already existing armies and use them to replace British and French losses, but Pershing refused. Fearing that American morale would suffer, he insisted that the American troops fight as a separate force under the command of American officers. American units were then assigned their own areas of the battlefields to defend.

Did you know?

A 1917 song written by George M. Cohan entitled "Over There" became popular in the United States during the war. Its lyrics included, "Over there, over there . . . the Yanks [used to refer to all Americans] are coming . . . and we won't come back 'til it's over over there."

US soldier teaching two younger ones how to clean a rifle

BLACK AMERICAN SOLDIERS *in* WORLD WAR I

Of the 4 million Americans who served in the war, about 350,000 were African Americans. Military units were segregated, and most blacks were assigned to support roles, such as cooks and laborers. However, some 40,000 were involved in combat.

One of the most distinguished African American units was the 369th Infantry, the "Harlem Hellfighters." The French government honored them with the prestigious Croix de Guerre (the war cross) in recognition of their bravery.

Private Henry Johnson, a member of the Harlem Hellfighters, was one of many who performed heroically in France. When on guard duty during the night of May 14, 1918, he fought Germans who had launched a night attack. He killed four enemy soldiers, wounded an estimated ten to twenty others, and rescued a fellow soldier. In the process, he received 21 wounds in hand-to-hand combat. Though his deeds were reported in the *New York World* and *The Saturday Evening Post* in 1918, it was decades after his 1929 death before he received the honors he deserved.

Johnson was posthumously [after death] awarded the Purple Heart in 1996 and the Distinguished Service Cross in 2002. He eventually received America's highest and most prestigious military award—the Congressional Medal of Honor. President Barack Obama presented it in a ceremony at the White House on June 2, 2015.

African Americans in other units also received awards. For example, Corporal Freddie Stowers of the 371st Infantry received the Congressional Medal of Honor; President George H. W. Bush awarded it posthumously in 1991.

▲ Vladimir Lenin

▼ American soldiers fire machine guns in a battle against the Germans.

Finishing the "War to End All Wars"

The Communist leader **Vladimir Lenin** had been forced to leave Russia years before the war. Lenin was a vocal opponent of Russia's involvement in World War I. He promised Russians peace if he gained power. In March 1917 the Russian leader, Czar Nicholas II, was forced out of power after a revolution in his nation. The following month, Germans helped Lenin return to Russia. In November 1917 a second revolution occurred, and Lenin took control of the country. He ended support for the Allied cause and later signed a peace treaty with Germany. The Germans now had one less nation to fight. They moved their armies from Russia, where they had been fighting, to western Europe, known as the Western Front, to fight France, Britain, and the United States.

The Central Powers launched an all-out attack on the Western Front during the spring of 1918. The Germans hoped to reach the English Channel and to conquer the French capital, Paris. By June 3, 1918, they were approaching the Marne River and were only about fifty miles from Paris.

The combined American and French forces launched a counterattack and pushed the Germans back at a place on the Marne River called Château-Thierry. Next, the American troops moved to Belleau Wood and stopped the Germans from advancing closer to Paris. By the beginning of July Paris was out of danger and the German advance was collapsing.

On July 18 the Allies began their own attack, slowly pushing the Germans back. With more than 250,000 American soldiers arriving monthly, Allied morale climbed. The doughboys won an impressive victory at Saint-Mihiel in mid-September. More than half a million doughboys, assisted by 1,500 planes and 3,200 French and American artillery guns, won the battle in just four days.

The largest American offensive began in the Argonne Forest on September 26. It was one of the costliest military campaigns in American history. American forces faced a maze of barbed wire, steel, and concrete. The region's hills and ridges provided a difficult terrain for fighting. One and a quarter million US troops, concentrated on a twenty-five-mile front, fought for six weeks toward the German rail center at Sedan. The Americans suffered 117,000 casualties, including 26,000 killed in action, but victories there turned the tide of the war.

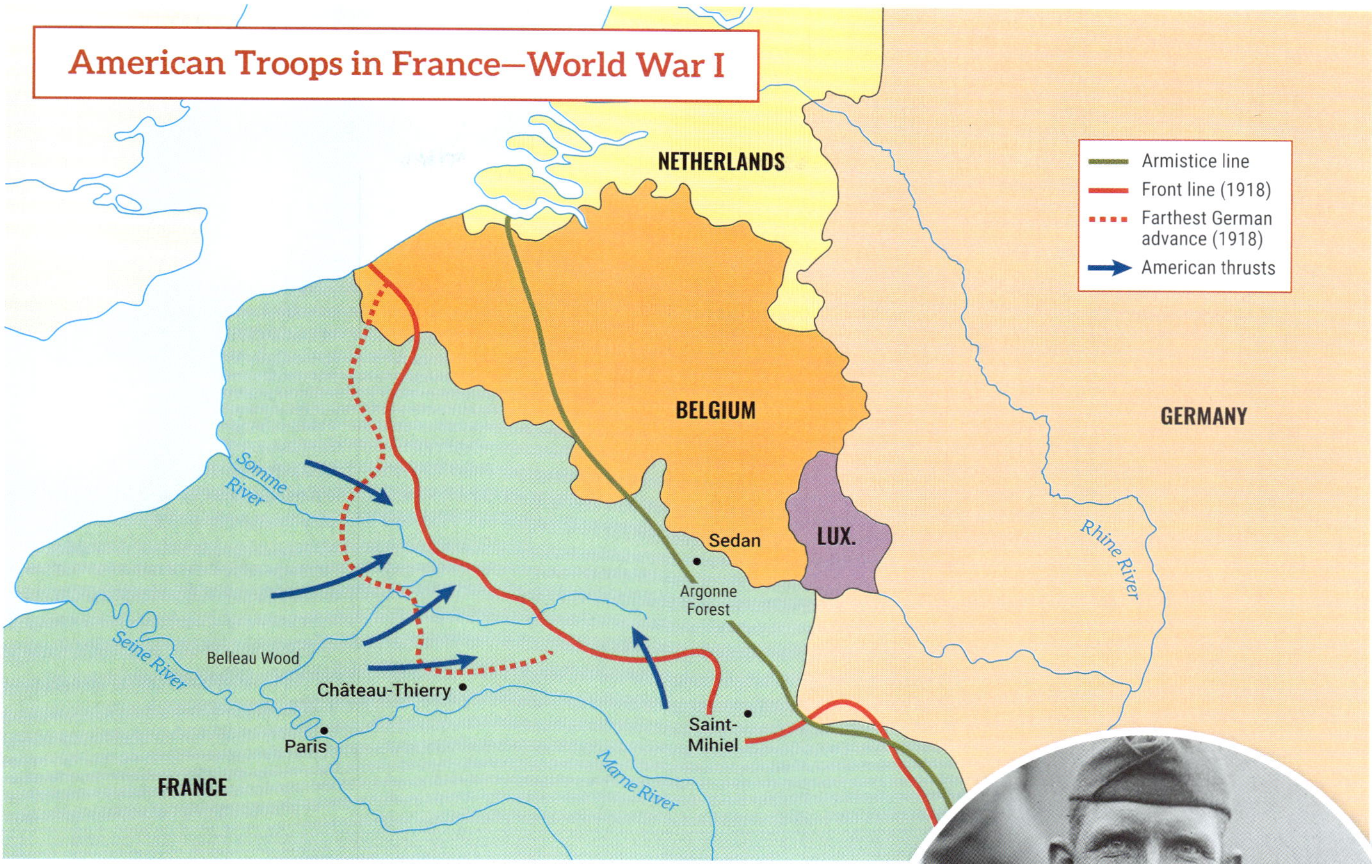

Sergeant York

Alvin C. York, a shy Christian man from the mountains of north central Tennessee, became a hero during the war. He was converted a few years before the United States entered the conflict. His application as a conscientious objector (one who refuses to fight because of religious belief) was denied. When drafted into the army, he faced a crisis; his church taught that killing was always wrong—even in war. He later wrote, "I prayed and prayed. I prayed two whole days and a night out on the mountainside. And I received my assurance that it was all right, that I should go [fight in the war]."

York impressed his superiors with his superior marksmanship (shooting) ability and attained the rank of corporal. On October 8, 1918, his unit was exploring an enemy position in France's Argonne Forest when they found themselves behind enemy lines. They surprised a group of encamped Germans whom they took prisoner. However, other nearby German soldiers opened fire with numerous machine guns. They killed several of York's companions. York took command of the remaining seven American soldiers and began using his shooting skills. One by one, as Germans peered over the embankment to take aim, he shot and killed them. He did this repeatedly until the Germans finally surrendered.

▲ Sergeant Alvin York, of Tennessee, was a devoted Christian who became a hero during the war.

After the battle, York was promoted to sergeant. He received numerous awards for his actions, including the Congressional Medal of Honor, the citation for which states:

> After his platoon had suffered heavy casualties and three other noncommissioned officers had become casualties, [Corporal] York assumed command. Fearlessly leading seven men, he charged with great daring a machine-gun nest which was pouring deadly and incessant fire upon his platoon. In his heroic feat the machine-gun nest was taken, together with four officers and 128 men and several guns.

On returning to his native Tennessee, York married in 1919. He and his wife had eight children. He devoted much of his time to building schools for mountain children in the region. He also established a small, nondenominational Bible college.

▲ The armistice that ended World War I was signed in this railroad car. Posing outside are individuals who signed the agreement.

The German leadership began negotiations to end the war. Their allies were withdrawing from the war. Bulgaria did so on September 29; Turkey withdrew October 30; Austria-Hungary quit the fighting on November 3. On November 9, the German leader, Kaiser Wilhelm II, fled the country. On November 11, 1918—at the eleventh hour of the eleventh day of the eleventh month—an **armistice**, or agreement to stop fighting, took effect. The Great War was over. November 11 became an American national holiday, Armistice Day.

Did you know?

After World War II and the Korean War, Armistice Day was changed to Veterans Day to honor all veterans (former members of the military).

Of the approximately 10 million soldiers who died in World War I, 116,000 were Americans. About 200,000 of the 20 million soldiers wounded were from the United States. Although American casualties were light compared to those of the other major powers, Americans had known the heartache of the war.

LITTLE BIRD *named* ENZA

I had a little bird;
Its name was Enza.
I opened the window,
And in-flu-enza.

In 1918, this poem circulated among America's children. But the "little bird named Enza" was no laughing matter. The deadly virus of influenza struck many American soldiers while they were still in training or after they arrived in Europe.

Warring countries issued few reports about the disease spreading because they feared it would affect the morale of troops. However, in the neutral country of Spain, the newspapers were much more open with their stories. Consequently, the names "Spanish Flu" or "Spanish influenza" were soon used, though there is no evidence that that was where the virus originated.

▼ A few cities jailed people who did not wear masks.

There were four major "waves" of the pandemic from February 1918 to April 1920. Estimates vary widely, but it appears that as many as 500 million were infected (slightly more than one-fourth of the world's population at the time) and 20 to 50 million died. Approximately 675,000 Americans died at a time when about 105 million lived in the country. The deadliest month in the United States was October 1918, the month before World War I ended, when the death total was nearly 200,000.

Most Americans knew little about the Spanish Flu until another pandemic occurred in early 2020. COVID-19, also called the coronavirus, brought a new awareness to the earlier health crisis.

Fun Fact

Before World War I, people shared cups or dippers at public drinking places. The discovery of germs and the global flu pandemic made Health Kups (paper cups) popular. They were later renamed Dixie cups.

SECTION REVIEW 20.4

1. What was the American army called? Who commanded it?
2. What nickname were American troops often called?
3. Why do you think Germany supported Vladimir Lenin in his Communist takeover of Russia?
4. At what time and on what day, month, and year did the war officially end?
5. What pandemic "flew" around the world from 1918–1920?

20.5 THE END OF THE GREAT WAR

What happened at the end of World War I?

GUIDING QUESTIONS

- What agreements did world leaders make at the end of World War I?
- How did America respond to the war and to the Treaty of Versailles?
- How did the war impact Christianity?

The end of the war raised many questions for participants. How would Germany and other members of the Central Powers be treated? Would the victors claim territories and possessions belonging to the defeated nations? Could peace be maintained in Europe?

Wilson's Fourteen Points

Before the war even ended, Woodrow Wilson proposed a set of guidelines to help rebuild European peace. His **Fourteen Points** had been announced in January 1918. Most of his program's points emphasized a just peace and a postwar world in which war would be less likely. The crucial point to Wilson was Point 14, which provided for the **League of Nations**. Wilson was an idealist—he expected people, and countries, to respond unselfishly and properly to difficult situations. He idealistically believed that the League, an organization of cooperating nations, could discuss problems and settle them peacefully, preventing future wars. Other key points in the program were freedom of the seas, an end to secret agreements, and reduction of every nation's military. The Fourteen Points also called for self-determination for the people of Europe. This meant cultural groups could form their own nations if they wished.

President Wilson spoke of having "peace without victory," urging generous terms for the losing countries. He said that the winners should not make territorial gains and that the losers should not be punished.

▾ In this cartoon, Uncle Sam does not like the recipe for peace that President Wilson (at right) is using. Its primary ingredient was the League of Nations. Uncle Sam feared the League might result in the United States becoming too deeply involved with other countries.

▲ The Big Four (left to right): David Lloyd George of Britain, Vittorio Orlando of Italy, Georges Clemenceau of France, and Woodrow Wilson of the United States

The Paris Peace Conference

The Allied leaders met outside Paris at the Palace of Versailles on January 18, 1919, to shape the peace. President Wilson represented the United States. He hoped that his presence would help ensure the victors' acceptance of a just and lasting peace. About two million people welcomed Wilson to Paris, regarding him almost as the savior of Europe. This reception strengthened his resolve to push for a treaty based on his Fourteen Points.

But the representatives from the other major nations were equally determined. **Georges Clemenceau**, the French premier, knew that his country had suffered at German hands in both the Franco-Prussian War (in 1870) and World War I. He wanted to ensure that Germany would never again be strong enough to hurt France. **David Lloyd George** represented Britain. **Vittorio Orlando** represented Italy. Wilson and these three leaders became known as the "**Big Four**."

Five treaties were signed between the Allies and the defeated countries in 1919 and 1920. Bulgaria, the Ottoman Empire, and Germany each signed a separate agreement with the Allied Powers. Austria-Hungary was split into separate nations, Austria and Hungary. Each signed a treaty with the Allies. The defeated nations and Russia were excluded from the peace table, so the treaties made by the Big Four have sometimes been called "a victors' peace."

The Treaty of Versailles, between the winning countries and Germany, was the most important of the five agreements. Because Germans were not permitted to take part in the peace negotiations and because they considered the treaty too harsh, they resented its provisions. But Germany was forced to sign the **Treaty of Versailles** anyway on June 28, 1919. It was very detailed, more than 200 pages long. Against Wilson's wishes, it placed blame for the war entirely on Germany and forced Germany to pay **reparations** (money a defeated country must pay for war damages). Those reparations were later set at more than $30 billion, a huge sum at the time. In addition, the treaty forced Germany to surrender its colonies as well as some of its own land. Although Wilson was disappointed with the treaty, he convinced the other leaders to insert a provision for the formation of the League of Nations. He believed that all the weaknesses of the treaty could be repaired through further negotiations in the League.

American Responses

When Wilson returned to the United States, he faced the task of convincing the Senate to ratify the Treaty of Versailles. Obtaining the required two-thirds vote proved to be an impossible job.

Although most Americans appear to have supported the treaty, many senators were not pleased with it. Wilson had unwisely ignored the Republican leaders in the Senate while he helped formulate the treaty. Now those leaders refused to ratify the treaty without some changes. Wilson stubbornly opposed their ideas.

The president decided to take the issue to the people. In a marathon mission of 8,000 miles in twenty-two days, he delivered forty speeches in favor of the treaty and membership in the League of Nations (if the United States adopted the treaty, it would also be agreeing to join the League). Wilson's crusade, however, nearly killed him. On September 25, 1919, after an enthusiastic rally in Pueblo, Colorado, the president slumped with exhaustion. His aides canceled the remainder of the tour and took Wilson back to Washington, where he suffered a serious stroke that paralyzed him on one side.

Wilson's wife and a few close friends shielded his condition from the public, but his fighting days were over. For seven critical months, Wilson did not meet with his cabinet. Most of his work was performed on his behalf by his wife and closest advisors. In November, the Senate vote on the treaty fell short of ratification.

The US Senate never ratified the Treaty of Versailles, and the country never joined the League of Nations. Not until October 1921, after Wilson's term ended, did the Senate ratify a new agreement with Germany, ending the official state of war between the two nations.

(Bottom) President Wilson standing in the center of the car while visiting San Francisco as part of his 8,000 mile trip in September 1919

(Below) Wilson reviewing papers at his desk as his second wife, Edith, looks on. Edith was sometimes called the "secret president" because of her role in Wilson's presidency during his long illness after a stroke.

The Impact of the War

Before the war, Americans were generally optimistic about the prospects for world peace and the advancement of mankind. But the war was so horrible that it led to despair and disillusionment. To some, the ideas of progressivism and the emphasis of the social gospel now seemed foolish and naïve. Most Americans realized that mankind was getting more brutal and destructive, not better. Many poets, novelists, artists, philosophers, theologians, progressives, and even ordinary Americans became very pessimistic.

Some viewed Christianity with great skepticism. Europe was supposed to be a Christian continent. Yet the great nations there had led their young men to barbaric slaughter. Often, pastors and government leaders had equated fighting for one's country with service to God. Some ministers declared that the conflict was a holy war and that participants were actually helping save Christianity. When a government uses religion for its own purposes, it is promoting a religion called civil religion. After the war, many rejected not only civil religion but also true religion. Some families stopped praying together, church attendance declined, and some rejected the morality taught in Scripture.

Many Americans failed to see that the inhumanity, cruelty, and ruthlessness of World War I was not because of Christianity but the result of rejecting or distorting it. The war had shown that sinful man was capable of committing and defending horrible deeds. The country desperately needed to embrace the Bible and its teachings.

SECTION REVIEW 20.5

1. What was the last and most important of Wilson's Fourteen Points?
2. Why can a treaty or organization never really prevent future wars?
3. Who were the Big Four at the Paris Peace Conference? What country did each represent?
4. What were three provisions of the Treaty of Versailles that Germany resented?
5. What action did the United States take regarding the Treaty of Versailles and the League of Nations?
6. Why did some Americans reject Christianity after the war? Why was this response incorrect?

CHAPTER 20 REVIEW

Making Connections

1. Why did the Black Hand want to murder the archduke of Austria?
2. Most of the member countries of the Triple Alliance became members of which alliance during World War I?
3. All member countries of the Triple Entente became members of which alliance during World War I?
4. Why was trench warfare not a very effective means of fighting?
5. How did propaganda influence Americans to join the Allied side?
6. How did Britain violate America's neutral rights at sea?
7. What percentage of the Senate voted against entering the war? What percentage of the House of Representatives voted against it? (Divide the number of those who voted against entering by the total number of votes.) Round to the nearest whole percentage.
8. What means of transportation did the government take control of, after entering the war?
9. What two groups of people had increased opportunity for employment once America joined the war?
10. What did President Wilson believe the League of Nations would accomplish?

Thinking Critically

11. Who was at fault for World War I? Support your answer.
12. Were the advances in weaponry during World War I beneficial? Why or why not?
13. Should America have joined the League of Nations? Support your answer.

Living as a Christian Citizen

14. If you were a member of Congress in 1917, would you have voted to enter the war? Draft a paragraph that makes use of biblical principles and encourages others to support your view.
15. If you were an advisor to the leader of an Allied nation, would you have advised him to sign the Treaty of Versailles? What biblical principles would support your answer?

▾ The *Lusitania* was sunk on May 7, 1915.

Terms to Remember

nationalism
militarism
Triple Alliance
Triple Entente
Francis (Franz) Ferdinand
Central Powers
Allied Powers
trench warfare
U-boats
propaganda
international law
unrestricted submarine warfare
Lusitania
Zimmermann telegram
convoy system
American Expeditionary Force (AEF)
John J. Pershing
doughboys
Vladimir Lenin
armistice
Fourteen Points
League of Nations
Georges Clemenceau
David Lloyd George
Vittorio Orlando
Big Four
Treaty of Versailles
reparations

CHAPTER

21 The 1920s: A Decade of Change

The expanding availability of automobiles and the prosperity of the 1920s made America a much more mobile society.

With the end of World War I, most Americans looked forward to better times. Some thought that they could return to normal life and to the ideals and ways of earlier days. But the 1920s, sometimes called the "Roaring Twenties," was a decade of startling changes.

How should the nation respond to the difficulties it faced after the war? How would the prosperity that later developed affect the country? An even greater concern soon emerged—how would the social, political, and religious changes impact America?

In prewar years, many Americans sought changes that they believed would bring justice and equality to the nation. Then Americans united with other countries to wage a world war. Freedom in the 1920s, however, departed from the traditional American ideal. Instead of seeking political freedoms, many Americans focused on freeing themselves from moral restraints. For example, in the twenties an increasing number of Americans embraced smoking, drinking, and swearing. As a result, the 1920s were years in which people practiced sin more openly than they had in earlier periods of American history.

GUIDING QUESTIONS

- Why were attempts at isolationism and disarmament ineffective?
- How did Americans respond to communism?
- What caused the economy to weaken after World War I?

21.1 DIFFICULTIES AFTER WORLD WAR I

What were some difficulties in postwar America?

America emerged from the war with some attitudes and problems that set the stage for the decade to come. Troubled by the war, most Americans wanted to avoid getting involved in future foreign conflicts. An economic downturn and a growing fear of communism also affected the nation.

Isolationism and Disarmament

As mentioned in the last chapter, President Woodrow Wilson eagerly sought American approval of the Treaty of Versailles, with its League of Nations. Many members of the Senate and other Americans, however, feared that membership in the League would draw the United States into future wars. This fear and a general lack of concern for foreign affairs brought a return to isolationism.

Americans desired a return to normal business and embraced isolationist ideas. In the presidential election of 1920, the Republican candidate, **Warren G. Harding**, emphasized a "return to normalcy." He handily defeated James Cox, the Democratic candidate.

Disarmament (reduction in the size of a nation's military and its weapons) became popular after the devastation of World War I. Many understood that the emphasis on militarism, which had spurred a race between countries to build strong armies and navies, had helped lead to the war. At the **Washington Naval Conference** of 1921–22, nine nations met (the United States, Japan, China, France, Britain, Italy, and three smaller countries). They agreed to destroy dozens of existing naval vessels and to limit the size of their future navies. But the agreement said nothing about the size of armies.

SINK ALL YOUR SHIPS IN THE OCEAN BLUE and "Sail on the Ship of Love"

Now that everyone is praying for the world's disarmament,
And is seeking for the right above the wrong,
While every eye is turned upon our noted President,
This little song may help the cause along!
Sink all your ships in the Ocean blue,
Throw in your guns and torpedoes too,
Many brave hearts are asleep in the deep,
I hear them praying and while the wild waves keep on saying,
Let's have a good ten year Holiday,
That's what we're all thinking of,
Let us get together soon,
Have a Peace time HoneyMoon,
and Sail on the Ship of Love.

This 1921 song refers to President Harding and some of the agreements reached at the Washington Naval Conference (including a ten-year holiday from building large battleships).

When Harding died in 1923, Vice President **Calvin Coolidge** became president. His secretary of state, Frank B. Kellogg, made another attempt to keep America free from the threat of war by signing the **Kellogg-Briand Pact** in 1928. Eventually, a total of sixty-two nations signed the agreement that outlawed war as a means of settling international disputes. The treaty was virtually worthless. It had no means of enforcement; furthermore, the signing nations stated that war was acceptable if it involved self-defense.

The attempts to preserve peace were admirable. However, World War II (which began in 1939) would demonstrate that, in a fallen world, such approaches are insufficient.

▾ Destruction caused by a bombing outside the New York Stock Exchange in September 1920

The Red Scare

Americans had read how Communists in Russia, also known as the Bolsheviks, staged a revolution in November 1917 and installed Vladimir Lenin as the nation's ruler. Communists based their ideas on the writings of Karl Marx and believed, in theory, that people could share wealth equally and that the need for government would disappear. Fear of the Communists grew when more Americans realized Communists intended to take control of other countries. Russian leaders organized the Third International in 1919. That agency called for worldwide revolution and tried to export communism anywhere by any method. Communists attracted followers in various European countries and also organized a political party in the United States. The term ***Red Scare*** refers to the time when there was increased public concern about communism within America. (*Reds* was a common term for Communists.) The first Red Scare occurred after World War I. A second one occurred after World War II.

One of the Communists' goals was to create a struggle between common workers and the property-owning capitalists. Americans began to worry that any sign of worker discontent, strikes in particular, were part of the Communist plot. In April 1919 bombs were mailed to more than thirty businessmen and government officials, including John D. Rockefeller and Supreme Court Justice Oliver Wendell Holmes Jr. In June a bomb exploded in front of Attorney General A. Mitchell Palmer's home. The following year, in September, more than thirty people were killed and hundreds injured when a bomb exploded in front of the New York Stock Exchange.

Average net paid circulation of THE NEWS, July, 1927. Sunday, 1,317,467 Daily, 1,177,817

DAILY NEWS

NEW YORK'S PICTURE NEWSPAPER

FINAL EDITION

Vol. 9. No. 50. 32 Pages ** New York, Tuesday, August 23, 1927. 2 Cents

DEAD!

SACCO VANZETTI

SACCO AND VANZETTI PAY SUPREME PENALTY!—Nicola Sacco, Massachusetts shoemaker, and Bartolomeo Vanzetti, fishmonger and philosopher, were put to death early today in the electric chair at the Charlestown, Mass., state prison. After seven years of legal delays, during which their cause was taken up by millions of sympathizers and become a matter of international importance, Massachusetts justice exacted its penalty for the South Braintree payroll murders on April 15, 1920. Until the last moment the execution of the sentence remained in doubt. The two men, waiting in their death cells, did not know positively that the governor would not intervene until they were ready to be led to the chair.—Story, p. 3; other pictures, pp. 16 and 17.

▴ Headline from the *New York Daily News* announcing that Sacco and Vanzetti had been executed

Believing that Communists were involved in these attacks, Attorney General Palmer crusaded for increased government investigations. Beginning in late 1919, thousands of people were arrested. Most were later released for lack of evidence. The government deported, or expelled, from the country a few hundred Russians that had been jailed. Later it became clear that Palmer had collected evidence illegally and had overreacted to the crisis.

Fear of communism increased Americans' resentment of immigrants, many of whom were from southern and eastern Europe where radical political ideas were spreading. Ill feeling toward both Communists and immigrants combined in a noted court case in 1921. The case involved two Italian immigrants, Nicola Sacco and Bartolomeo Vanzetti, who were arrested and tried on suspicion of

A farming family marching to the fields to work

murdering two shoe company employees in a payroll robbery. More than a century later, the facts of the case are still disputed. The trial divided the nation. Though both men had been involved in radical activities, the evidence regarding the murders was difficult to interpret. Sadly, the men's trial was also flawed by the biased conduct of the judge. In the end, the defendants were found guilty and sentenced to death. In 1927 they were executed.

Economic Downturn

After the war, the United States experienced a time of economic depression. The high demand for war products had kept industries and farms busy; but when the war was over and demand dropped, businesses, industries, and farms all suffered. Because many war products were no longer needed, factories had to return to producing peacetime materials. That process took time and money. During the war, American farms had sent millions of tons of food to Europe, but soon Europe could feed itself again. As a result, American farmers had little foreign demand for their great surplus of food.

As war industries closed, there were not enough jobs available for soldiers returning home. During the war, the shortage of workers had resulted in African Americans and immigrants holding a substantial number of jobs in cities. Unfortunately, many Americans resented those two groups for holding jobs that returning soldiers now wanted. Partly to remedy this issue, Congress passed new laws that set quotas (fixed numbers) for how many immigrants could enter the United States. Those laws were intended to stop the heavy flow of immigrants, especially those from the Roman Catholic countries of southern and eastern Europe.

American farmers continued to struggle through the 1920s as high production and low prices continued. Representatives of the farming states pressed for government aid and regulation, but Presidents Harding and Coolidge believed that the federal government should avoid involvement in regulating farms or businesses.

SECTION REVIEW 21.1

1. What was one shortfall of the Washington Naval Conference?
2. What limited the effectiveness of the Kellogg-Briand Pact?
3. Why are efforts at disarmament ineffective at ending warfare? When will these efforts finally be effective?
4. To what does the term *Red Scare* refer?
5. Ill feeling toward what two groups led to the notorious Sacco and Vanzetti case?
6. Why was it difficult for returning soldiers to find jobs? Whom did they blame for the lack of jobs?

GUIDING QUESTIONS

- How did cars, airplanes, and electricity change American life?
- How did business grow in the 1920s?

21.2 PROSPERITY AFTER WORLD WAR I

Why was America prosperous in the 1920s?

Within a short time, businesses rebounded. The 1920s soon became a decade of prosperity for many Americans. While the economy was recovering, technological advances emerged. Many of these new devices were timesavers and thus provided Americans with additional leisure time.

The Growth of Technology

Inventions and improved industrial products greatly changed the American way of life in the 1920s. The automobile and electric household appliances revolutionized daily life for many Americans.

Automobiles

The first successful American automobile was built by Charles and Frank Duryea in 1893. Henry Ford began making cars in 1903. The success of these pioneers prompted others to plunge into the business of producing automobiles. Although the number of cars quickly increased, the vast majority of American families were without a "horseless carriage" during the war years. After the war, however, factories geared up to produce cars by the thousands. Families were eager to have their own cars, and the prices of all but the luxury models were becoming more affordable. Even if a family did not have enough money to pay for a car in full, they could buy it on an **installment plan** (a system that allows a person to pay for an item in weekly or monthly payments, often with interest).

The shift to automobile transportation had many direct effects on Americans. For example, the automobile allowed those who lived in rural areas to be less isolated. When traveling to town took several hours on horseback or by horse and wagon, a farmer and his family might venture into town only a few times a year. With a car, however, the whole family could make the same trip in a short time, day or night. Farm families could visit town more often to shop or attend social functions.

▾ In June 1924, the ten-millionth Ford automobile was completed. Henry Ford is standing between it (left) and his first automobile, completed in 1896 (right).

The automobile also changed life for many who worked in the city, making it possible for them to live away from the inner-city area where they worked. They could buy houses in the suburbs at the edge of the city and commute to and from work by car. With this practice came a by-product of the automobile—traffic jams.

Cars made travel easy for common Americans. As people began to drive everywhere, many industries arose to meet drivers' needs. Gas stations, motels, and drive-in restaurants sprang up along busy highways. Department stores, supermarkets, and other businesses were built where they could be easily reached by car and where they could have large parking lots for their customers.

▲ Traffic on New York City's Fifth Avenue in the 1920s

▼ First flight by the Wright brothers (1903)

Airplanes

Although the airplane was not a major form of transportation for most Americans during the 1920s, people admired it for its capabilities. In 1903 Orville and Wilbur Wright had made what is generally accepted as the first successful machine-powered flight. World War I boosted aviation. Soon the government provided airmail service between major cities. Pilots called "barnstormers" performed in air circuses at county fairs and offered short rides for passengers over towns.

The biggest sensation in flight occurred in 1927 when a twenty-five-year-old aviator named **Charles A. Lindbergh** won a prize for making the first nonstop solo flight across the Atlantic Ocean. He flew his specially designed plane, the *Spirit of St. Louis*, from New York City to Paris in thirty-three-and-a-half hours. When Lindbergh landed in Paris, he became an instant hero. Called "Lucky Lindy" and the "Lone Eagle," he came home to a huge parade in New York City and received an invitation to the White House. Wherever he appeared over the next few years, he was mobbed by admiring fans.

Lindbergh's transatlantic flight and the record-setting flights of other pilots did much to encourage air transportation. The first public international passenger carrier was Pan American's "Clipper." Regularly scheduled commercial flights soon connected all the major American cities.

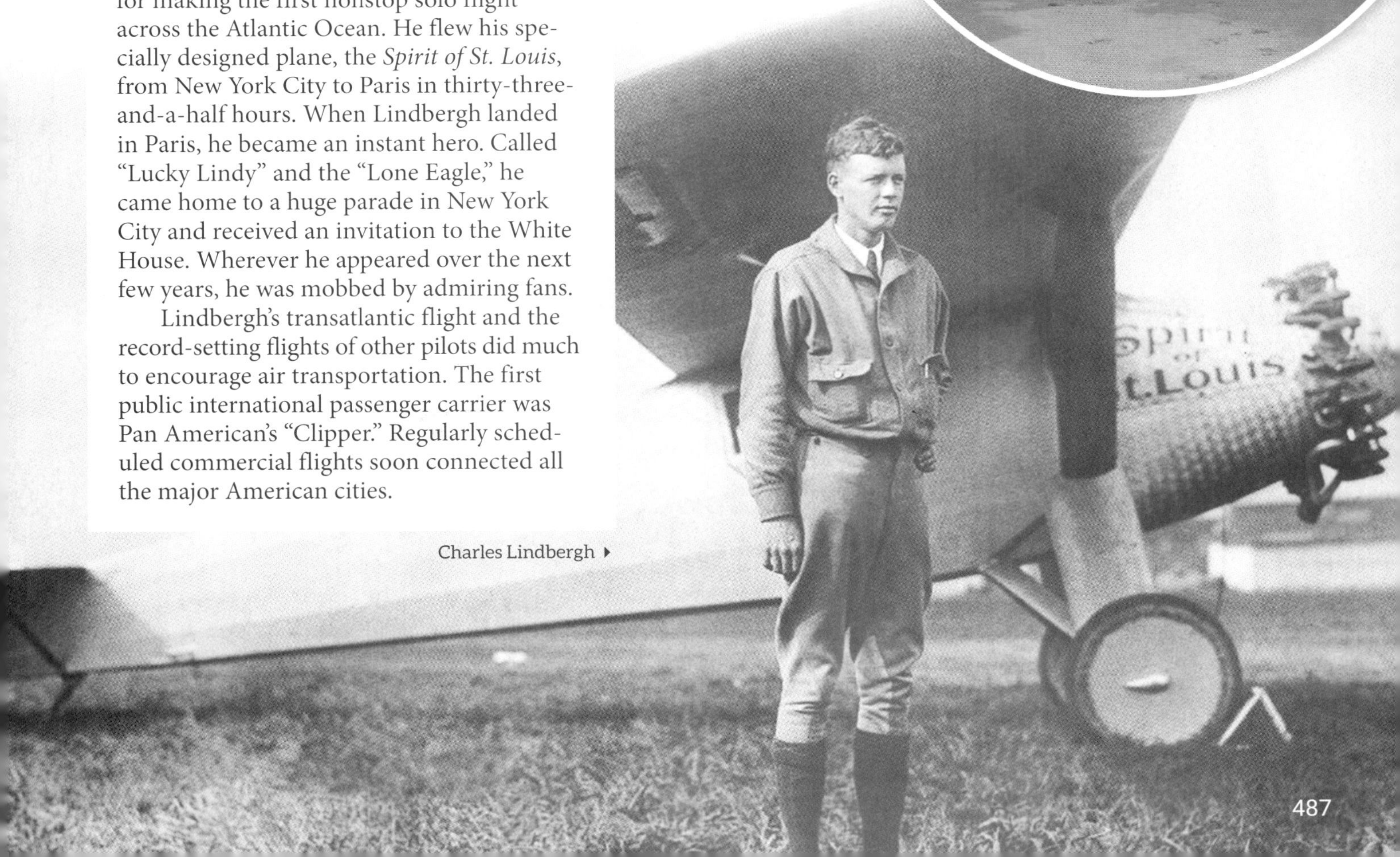

Charles Lindbergh ▶

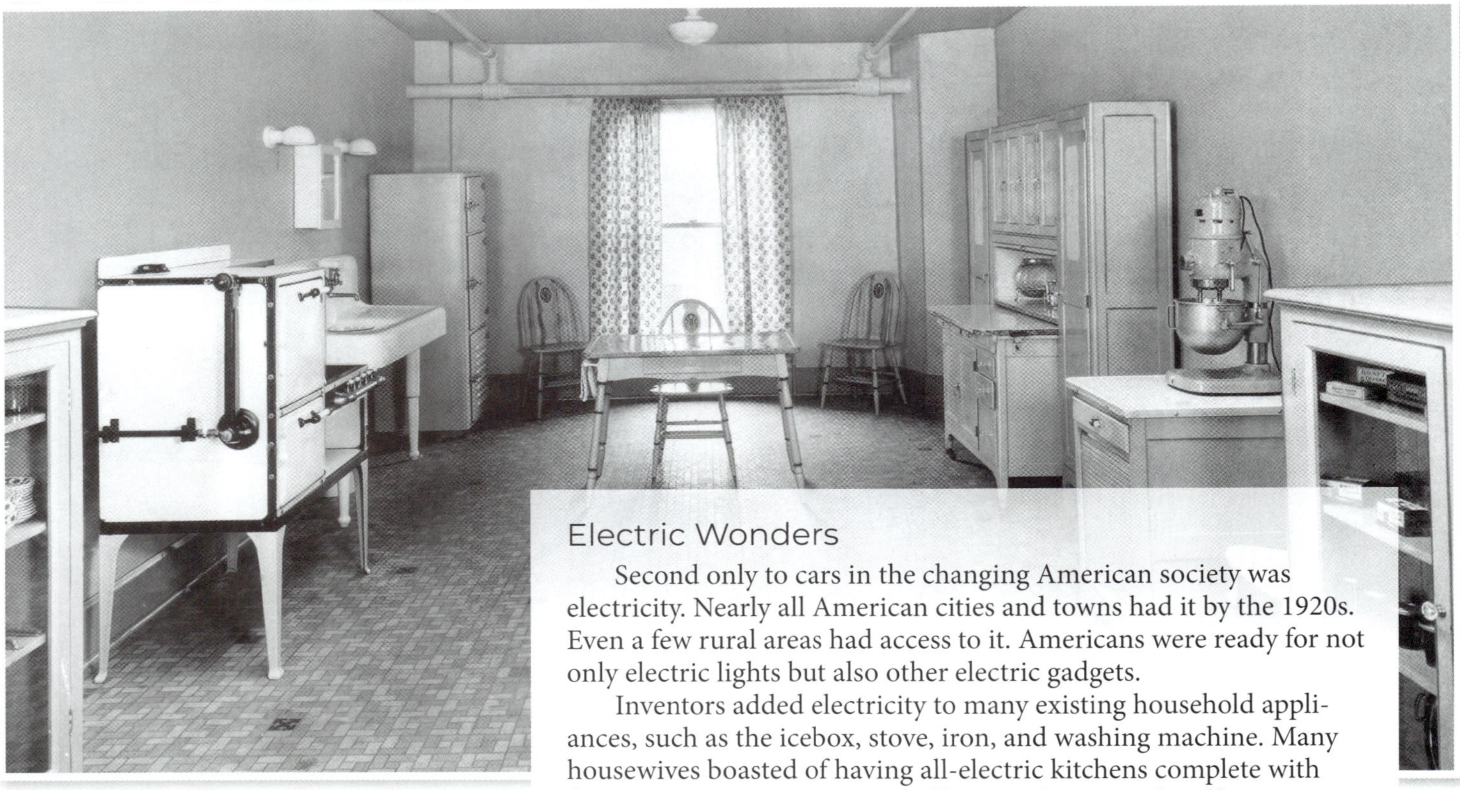

▲ A well-equipped kitchen in the 1920s

Electric Wonders

Second only to cars in the changing American society was electricity. Nearly all American cities and towns had it by the 1920s. Even a few rural areas had access to it. Americans were ready for not only electric lights but also other electric gadgets.

Inventors added electricity to many existing household appliances, such as the icebox, stove, iron, and washing machine. Many housewives boasted of having all-electric kitchens complete with fans, water heaters, toasters, coffee percolators, and waffle irons. Of course, electricity was also used in other ways. It powered large machines in factories.

The electric radio was the greatest mass communication device of the 1920s. The basis for its invention was a sound transmitter created by the Italian Guglielmo Marconi in 1895. This "wireless" could transmit messages without using a telegraph or telephone wires. Soon inventors began using the wireless to transmit the human voice. Station KDKA in Pittsburgh received its broadcasting license six days before the 1920 presidential election. The first commercial broadcast—on November 2, 1920—announced Harding's election to the presidency.

▲ Radios, similar to this one, were popular features in American homes.

Soon, radios provided Americans with hours of news and entertainment and changed the way Americans lived. By 1930 more than twelve million American homes—40 percent of the households in the country—had a radio. Many Americans listened to comedian Jack Benny, singer Rudy Vallee, and comic Will Rogers, who made humorous remarks and did impersonations of Calvin Coolidge. Broadcasts of sports events also gained large popular followings. With Americans from different areas listening to the same programs, some regional differences soon began to fade. The radio drew Americans closer to events and people that affected their lives. They could hear the voices of the president and other leaders, and they could hear broadcasts of events as they happened or shortly after.

The Growth of Business

Soon after the depression that followed the war, the economy recovered and improved. America entered a period in which businesses boomed. Some workers had saved money during the war while wages were high. Others were now earning money in new businesses. Both groups were ready to spend money on automobiles, clothes, entertainment, electric appliances, and other new pleasures of the 1920s. The demand for new goods caused industries to grow. When Americans did not have money, they borrowed it or used the installment plan.

Automobiles being produced on an assembly line at a Ford plant in Michigan

In his automobile manufacturing plants, Henry Ford used mass production techniques. Though Ford did not invent the **assembly line**, he implemented and used it very effectively. In this process, workers were placed beside a moving conveyor belt. Each performed a certain task, such as adding a part to a product. By 1914 the time required for Ford to produce an automobile had dropped from 12.5 hours to 93 minutes. Similar assembly lines soon produced phonographs, vacuum cleaners, and countless other consumer goods. Clever advertising campaigns enticed customers into buying more and more new products.

Some Americans who had extra money after paying for routine expenses invested in the stock market. Their investments were used to create new businesses, build factories, expand existing companies, and create new products. All these business activities required workers, so more people were hired. As stockholders were paid larger dividends, more people purchased stocks. Some even borrowed money to do so.

Others invested in real estate. Property in Florida was especially tempting because shrewd promoters portrayed the state as a future resort paradise. Thousands bought property in the hope of reselling it for much higher prices, even though little development was taking place at the time. Many people borrowed money to pursue such get-rich-quick land schemes.

Prior to the 1920s, many Americans had a negative attitude toward big business. However, by this decade, public opinion and government policies favored big business. Some Americans developed a new respect for business and businessmen that was perhaps too optimistic. Calvin Coolidge declared, "The chief business of the American people is business." To some, business and materialism had become the saviors of the age. Because of the prosperity of the period, business owners typically ignored requests for change from labor unions. Government rarely interfered with the growing business empires of the 1920s.

SECTION REVIEW 21.2

1. How did the automobile change everyday life for Americans?
2. What was Charles A. Lindbergh able to accomplish in 1927?
3. What new communication device allowed news and entertainment to be relayed almost instantaneously?
4. What mass production technique did Henry Ford use effectively? How did it work?
5. What are some problems of reducing Jesus to just a great businessman as presented in *The Man Nobody Knows*?

THE MAN NOBODY KNOWS

The enthusiasm for business during the 1920s even affected religion. Bruce Barton, a preacher's son who had become a famous advertising executive, wrote a book, *The Man Nobody Knows*. In it he portrayed Jesus as a model businessman. According to Barton, Christ was "the founder of modern business" who "picked up twelve men from the bottom ranks of business and forged them into an organization that conquered the world." Barton said that Christ was a "sociable man" and "the most popular dinner guest in Jerusalem." Barton claimed that Jesus practiced "modern salesmanship"—persuading by asking pointed questions and even advertising by using parables. Barton's favorite quotation from the Bible was Christ's reply to His parents in Luke 2:49: "Wist ye not that I must be about my Father's business?"

The Man Nobody Knows enjoyed great success after it was published in 1925. It was on the bestseller list for two years.

In a book entitled *The Christ We Know*, conservative Bible teacher A. C. Gaebelein argued that Barton's sketch of Christ struck at the heart of Christianity by denying that Christ was the Son of God. Gaebelein said, "Can the conception of Christ as a business man, as a leader, or advertiser or sociable man, give our consciences rest and bring us nigh unto God? No! Nothing but the blood of Jesus [can do that]." Gaebelein also expressed great disappointment that Barton's book ended with Christ's death, not his miraculous resurrection.

Fun Fact

Eventually some land in Florida did indeed become a mouse-eared resort paradise—but not until 1971.

GUIDING QUESTIONS

- What changes in morality occurred during the 1920s?
- How did Americans spend their leisure time in the 1920s?
- How did Prohibition affect the country?
- How did Americans respond to the Ku Klux Klan and other forms of racism?
- How did conservative Christians react to the changes in the Roaring Twenties?

21.3 THE ROARING TWENTIES

What cultural changes occurred during the Roaring Twenties?

The decade of the twenties well earned the label "Roaring Twenties." It roared with change—changes of all sorts. Those years witnessed a social transformation in the United States. Technological improvements led many people to live in cities, far away from family and friends. This trend weakened social ties and gave people greater leisure time for new entertainments. In addition, new ideas about Christianity gained influence. Much of the literature of the decade contradicted basic teachings of Christianity.

▲ Many Americans attended movies weekly (top). A group of high-school girls pose in the mid-1920s (bottom).

Moral Decay

Many Americans revolted against traditional morality during the 1920s. This rebellion often began among young people and was most obvious on college campuses. Wild parties, drunkenness, and sexual immorality were common at many schools. The loosening morals of the younger generation were reflected in some of the most popular songs played on the radio.

Open discussion of sex was encouraged by a popular psychologist from Austria named **Sigmund Freud**. In his writings, Freud emphasized the "danger" of repressing one's sexual desires and thoughts. Some Americans came to believe that sexually suggestive comments and behavior as well as immoral conduct were acceptable.

Leisure Activities

This openness was displayed in the major visual medium of the era—the motion picture. The American film industry exploded in the 1920s. In 1922 about forty million Americans attended movies each week. In 1929 the number was ninety million. The romances featured in many of these films glamorized those who violated traditional boundaries of morality. The American public seemed to have an appetite for following the personal lives of the actors and actresses in these films, even if the stars had immoral lifestyles.

Influenced by movies, many young women adopted the dress and lifestyle of "**flappers**." They delighted in shocking their elders by wearing shorter skirts and heavy makeup, using slang, drinking, and smoking. Dancing and jazz music were especially popular with young people.

Though the era was roaring along, the literature of the period revealed the despair and disillusionment that lay beneath the surface. Some writers questioned the emptiness of life and the damage World War I had done to society. T. S. Eliot's poem *The Waste Land* reflected the hopelessness that followed World War I. Ernest Hemingway wrote stories in which characters fail to find meaning in life. Author F. Scott Fitzgerald was himself a symbol of the age. He and his family lived extravagantly, but beneath the glitter lay Fitzgerald's alcoholism and his wife's mental illness. Fitzgerald's novel *The Great Gatsby* tells the story of a man corrupted by the new morals of the era.

Did you know?

In 1928 a bacteriologist in Scotland, Alexander Fleming, accidentally discovered penicillin. This antibiotic has had a huge impact throughout the world.

The growth in leisure time also resulted in a growing interest in sports. More people actively participated in athletic events. Still more attended as spectators or listened to radio broadcasts of sporting events. Women athletes made names for themselves. In 1926, Gertrude Ederle became the first woman to swim the twenty-one miles across the English Channel. Helen Wills achieved fame on the tennis court.

College football drew thousands of fans. Harold "Red" Grange, the "galloping ghost" of the University of Illinois, received the longest ovation in the history of college football when he ran for four touchdowns within twelve minutes. Knute Rockne, a Norwegian immigrant who became head football coach at the University of Notre Dame, unleashed his players' talents to thrill spectators and radio audiences on Saturday afternoons. His running backs, known as the "Four Horsemen of Notre Dame," dazzled fans and gained fame and glory on the gridiron.

Athletes in other sports also gained fame. Boxer Jack Dempsey, who was described as having "a neck like a bull, a granite jaw, and fists like iron," was responsible for attracting the first million-dollar gate (paid attendance) for a sporting event. Other famous names of the era were golfer Bobby Jones and baseball star George Herman "Babe" Ruth. Ruth played for the New York Yankees; he hit more home runs than any other player until Henry "Hank" Aaron broke his record in the 1970s. Horseracing and auto racing also drew crowds. Racecar driver Barney Oldfield not only entered major races but also raced at county fairs. And a horse named Man o'War won twenty of the twenty-one races in which his owners entered him.

▾ Helen Wills in 1929 (top), "Red" Grange in 1925 (center), and auto racing (bottom)

Prohibition

By the 1830s the average American over eighteen drank the equivalent of eighty-eight bottles of whiskey a year. Realizing the serious problems this created, thousands of Americans rallied in temperance societies throughout the 1800s. In the early 1900s, many progressives had made **prohibition** (forbidding the sale, manufacture, and transportation of alcohol) a major reform issue. By 1915, fifteen states had outlawed what many called "demon rum."

During World War I, when the United States was selling all its surplus grain to the Allies for food use, it was considered unpatriotic to make liquor. In December 1917 the Eighteenth Amendment, which called for nationwide prohibition, passed Congress and was sent to the states for ratification. The widespread support for prohibition was evidenced by the states' quick approval of the amendment. All states except New Jersey, Rhode Island, and Connecticut ratified it in less than fifteen months. As noted in the last chapter, in 1919 the Eighteenth Amendment became part of the Constitution. It stipulated that its provisions would take effect one year after ratification. The period during which alcohol was illegal in the country is known as **Prohibition**. It began in 1920 and ended in 1933 when the Eighteenth Amendment was repealed.

In 1919 Congress passed the **Volstead Act** to provide federal implementation of the amendment. It outlawed any beverage that contained more than 0.5% alcohol content. The Bureau of Prohibition was established to enforce this law. Prohibition proved difficult to enforce for multiple reasons. First, although the law was important to many Americans, including the vast majority of Christian denominations, it was not popular among many Americans of foreign ancestry. Irish, German, and eastern European immigrants considered

◂ In this 1921 picture, authorities are pouring confiscated liquor into a city sewer.

alcoholic drink an important part of their cultures. They resented the outlawing of alcohol, and most were unwilling to participate in its enforcement. Second, many influential politicians had little desire to enforce the regulations regarding alcohol. Third, the Bureau of Prohibition lacked the budget and necessary number of employees to complete the task they were assigned. Soon, other problems arose.

Bootlegging, making and selling illegal liquor, became a big business and made many people wealthy. Illegal taverns, or bars, emerged across the nation. They were called "**speakeasies**" because people spoke quietly about them in public and often whispered to obtain entry into one. The border with Canada (where alcohol was legal) stretched for nearly three thousand miles. Officers could not effectively patrol the long border, so liquor flowed across it freely. The Atlantic coast also had its share of rumrunners, those who smuggled alcohol into the country. Because it was legal to have alcohol for medical reasons, some people obtained it by a doctor's prescription. Others brewed their own in stills or mixed "bathtub gin."

This bootlegger hid liquor behind what appeared to be lumber.

Violence often accompanied the criminals involved in bootlegging and operating speakeasies. **Al Capone**, also known as Scarface, led a large crime ring in Chicago. He and other ruthless criminals organized networks to supply those who were willing to pay any price for liquor. With alcohol came other criminal activities, including illegal gambling and prostitution. Gangs controlled such activities in certain areas. If a gang tried to operate in a rival gang's territory, a "war" might erupt between the groups. Innocent people were often killed in such wars. These crimes shocked the public. Although there were periodic crackdowns, putting gangsters behind bars was difficult. Criminals often refused to testify against one another. They threatened honest citizens who were called as witnesses. And they sometimes bribed corrupt judges and officials.

This man knocks at a "speakeasy." Those on the inside could see him by using the door's peephole.

By the late 1920s, more and more Amer-icans called for an end to the ban on alcohol. In 1933 the **Twenty-First Amendment** was ratified. It repealed the Eighteenth Amendment and ended Prohibition. It marked the only time a constitutional amendment has been revoked.

Despite its problems, Prohibition did lead to a decline in alcohol consumption that continued long after its end. In the years just prior to Prohibition, adults consumed an average of more than thirty gallons of wine, beer, and hard liquor each year (mostly beer). Americans did not return to that consumption level until decades later.

Protesters in New York City call for an end to Prohibition.

▲ During the 1920s, membership in the Ku Klux Klan increased dramatically. The Klan often used intimidation and violence against immigrants, Roman Catholics, Jewish people, and African Americans. In this parade, members march in Washington, DC.

Racism and Response

In 1915 the Ku Klux Klan (KKK) reappeared. This secretive, racist group was patterned after the original organization that had been established during Reconstruction. It promoted "100% Americanism" and limited membership to native-born white Protestants. The Klan disliked not only African Americans but also immigrants, Roman Catholics, and people of Jewish descent.

The KKK often resorted to intimidation and violence, including beatings and murders, against those groups they disliked and those that did not support their ideas. Through skillful promotion, it expanded nationally through the early 1920s and even became a strong social and political force in many northern cities, where immigrant and black populations were rising. For example, a large portion of Klan members lived in Michigan, Ohio, Indiana, and Illinois.

Because of the Klan's secretive nature, exact membership statistics do not exist, but it may have reached several million during the 1920s. And it had the sympathy of millions more. In August 1925 more than 50,000 members of the KKK openly paraded through Washington, DC.

Klan members tried to justify their movement by using patriotic and Christian symbols, such as the cross, and by condemning immoral behavior. Tragically, many found it too easy to ignore what was behind the KKK's use of these symbols—racism and attacks on the freedoms of fellow Americans.

During the 1920s many African Americans continued to move north where they found greater employment opportunities. By gathering in northern cities, they also gained some political power. Leaders within the black community differed over how to address the challenges of racism. Marcus Garvey, founder of the Universal Negro Improvement Association (UNIA), claimed that whites were incapable of overcoming their racial prejudices. From this opinion, Garvey argued that black Americans should develop their own cultures that would be entirely separate from those of white Americans. Instead of seeking equality in America, he urged emigration to Africa.

Garvey's ideas did not receive as much support among African Americans as the National Association for the Advancement of Colored People (NAACP) did. The NAACP started a journal, the *Crisis*, to educate Americans about racial problems. It also challenged state laws that violated the Fourteenth and Fifteenth Amendments.

From 1919 to 1925 the NAACP promoted an anti-lynching bill that would punish those who permitted lynching. Law enforcement officers who permitted lynching would be punished with five years in prison or a $5,000 fine or both. Counties that failed to apprehend those who participated in a lynch mob were to be fined $10,000. Those who participated in a lynch mob were to be tried for homicide. Because of opposition from many southern senators, the bill never passed. But the publicity surrounding the legislation brought public attention to lynching and helped reduce its frequency.

▲ This 1925 banner, displayed by the NAACP, reminds New Yorkers that lynching was still occurring.

Fundamentalism

Conservative Christians in the 1920s were concerned about the growth of theological liberalism in the churches. Between 1910 and 1915, concerned pastors and theologians wrote a series of books that contained ninety articles. They were called *The Fundamentals* because they dealt with the "fundamentals" or basic, foundational beliefs of the Christian faith. The articles argued that the Bible is true and divinely inspired. They supported the virgin birth and deity of Jesus, His death on the cross for the sins of mankind, His resurrection, and other major doctrines of Christianity.

Two brothers, both Christian businessmen, funded the distribution of *The Fundamentals* to Bible teachers, Sunday school superintendents, and seminary professors, throughout the English-speaking world. These books gave rise to the name **Fundamentalist** for people who believe in the foundational truths of Christianity.

Fundamentals of the Faith

1. Inspiration of the Bible by God
2. Virgin birth and deity of Jesus
3. Death on the cross for mankind's sins
4. Resurrection of Jesus from the dead

Growth of Fundamentalism

J. Gresham Machen was one of Fundamentalism's most respected scholars in the early twentieth century. He was a professor at Princeton Seminary. During the 1920s he worked hard to prevent the spread of theological liberalism at Princeton and within the Presbyterian Church, also known as the PC(USA). In his book *Christianity and Liberalism*, Machen said that liberalism is not Christianity but is its own religion. He also argued that liberalism should start its own institutions rather than taking control of already existing ones.

Sadly, contrary to what Machen had hoped, formerly conservative institutions were soon controlled by liberals. As a result, Fundamentalists were forced to leave or willingly left many Christian denominations, colleges, and seminaries. However, the Fundamentalist movement grew during this period, and a key to its expansion was a network of Fundamentalist Bible institutes, colleges, and seminaries. Some had been long established, while others were founded during this period. These schools provided the training and resources necessary for the battle against theological liberalism. They published religious newspapers and magazines that linked the Fundamentalist movement together.

The Scopes Trial

While firmly supporting historic doctrines of the Christian faith, early Fundamentalists were initially uncertain how to handle Charles Darwin's theory of evolution. Some articles in *The Fundamentals* rejected the theory while others attempted to harmonize some aspects of evolution with Christianity. By the 1920s, however, a greater understanding of evolution and its impact emerged; as a result, most Fundamentalists rallied to oppose Darwinism.

The Tennessee state legislature had passed a law forbidding public school teachers to teach evolution. Wanting to test such laws, the American Civil Liberties Union (ACLU) said that it would defend any teacher in Tennessee who would challenge that law. George Rappleyea, a Tennessee businessman, convinced a number of lawyers and businessmen of Dayton, Tennessee, that the publicity of a big trial would be good for business in the town. The men then persuaded a high-school teacher, John Scopes, to become the defendant. Scopes had substituted for the science teacher for a few weeks, and though it is unclear if he actually taught evolution, he agreed to be arrested for doing so.

In the summer of 1925, the **Scopes trial**, also called the Monkey Trial, turned into a gigantic media event that lasted for more than a week. Two hundred reporters descended on the small town of Dayton, and for the first time, a trial was covered by radio. Two famous attorneys took opposing sides. William Jennings Bryan, a three-time Democratic presidential nominee and secretary of state to Woodrow Wilson, assisted the prosecution. Clarence Darrow, a famous trial lawyer and agnostic, defended Scopes. A famous journalist and well-known atheist, H. L. Mencken, was present at the trial. His reporting was heavily biased against Bryan, whom he called a "buffoon," and others who opposed evolution.

▲ The summer heat forced the Scopes trial outdoors. Clarence Darrow (shown at top with arms folded and on left at bottom) questioned William Jennings Bryan (seated at top left and at bottom right).

Darrow called Bryan to testify during the trial. Darrow tried to portray fundamentalist Christians as foolish, ignorant, and unscientific. Bryan staunchly defended the Christian faith. But since he was neither a Bible scholar nor a scientist, he was not prepared for all of the questions. After eight days of trial, the jury deliberated for only nine minutes. Scopes was found guilty of teaching evolution and ordered to pay a fine of one hundred dollars.

Bryan remained in Tennessee after the trial, making speeches and writing about the event. He died five days after the trial ended. He was age sixty-five. Later, Scopes's attorneys appealed the case to the Tennessee Supreme Court. That court upheld the law that banned the teaching of evolution but overturned Scopes's conviction based on a technicality.

SECTION REVIEW 21.3

1. What behaviors did flappers embrace that shocked their elders?
2. Which amendment outlawed the sale, manufacture, and transportation of alcohol? Which amendment reversed the ban?
3. Should Prohibition have been reversed? Why or why not?
4. What were two conflicting ideas concerning how to address the problems of racism?
5. What did Fundamentalists do as Christian institutions increasingly became liberal?
6. The teaching of what theory led to the Scopes trial?

21.4 PRESIDENTS DURING THE ROARING TWENTIES

What were some major presidential actions in the 1920s?

GUIDING QUESTION

- What was significant about the presidents of the 1920s?

The Republican presidents of the 1920s reflected the attitudes and goals of their day. They promoted the unhindered growth of business and the general enjoyment of prosperity. However, they failed to address some of the nation's problems. Eventually, the era's materialism and selfishness produced a severe crisis.

Warren G. Harding

Warren G. Harding was a likable, handsome newspaper editor from the small town of Marion, Ohio. He was active in state politics and eventually became a US senator. As mentioned earlier, when he campaigned as the Republican nominee for president in 1920, he promised to get the country back to normal. After the turmoil of World War I, most in the country embraced this idea, and he easily won election to the White House.

Once he was in office, Harding supported most of the popular programs of the day, especially those that promoted big business. Though he appointed several talented people to his cabinet, he also gave important positions to a number of his friends who were lacking in character and qualifications. Some of them used the government to promote their own gain. Although Harding may have been honest, a number of those friends tarnished the reputation of his administration. They were often called the "Ohio Gang," a reference to Harding's home state.

Harding took a vacation to several western states and Alaska in the summer of 1923. While in California, he suffered an apparent heart attack and died on August 2.

The worst example of corruption was uncovered after Harding's death. It involved his secretary of the interior, **Albert B. Fall**. He persuaded Harding and the secretary of the navy to transfer control of government-owned oil reserves from the Navy Department to the Interior Department. Fall then leased the reserves at Teapot Dome in Wyoming and Elk Hills in California to two oil businessmen, who paid him back with several "loans" totaling $400,000. When the **Teapot Dome scandal** was uncovered, Fall went to prison. He was the first cabinet member in US history to be imprisoned for misdeeds in office.

Although Harding was not personally involved in public scandal for financial gain, he did not supervise government officials properly. Instead of providing firm direction, Harding allowed national affairs to simply drift along without guidance. By the summer of 1923, however, Harding knew that something was wrong. Talking to journalist William Allen White, he said, "I have no trouble with my enemies. I can take care of [them] all right. But my . . . friends, . . . they're the ones that keep me walking the floor nights!"

Warren G. Harding

29

Born	November 2, 1865
Died	August 2, 1923
Home state	Ohio
Wife	Florence Kling DeWolfe
Church	Baptist
Occupations	newspaper editor and publisher
Party	Republican
Years served as president	1921–23
Terms	partial
Vice president	Calvin Coolidge

This is a 1924 view of Teapot Dome Rock in Wyoming. Nearby oil fields were named in its honor. Windstorms later altered the appearance of the rock.

Calvin Coolidge

Born	July 4, 1872	30
Died	January 5, 1933	
Home state	Massachusetts (born in Vermont)	
Wife	Grace Goodhue	
Church	Congregationalist	
Occupations	lawyer	
Party	Republican	
Years served as president	1923–29	
Terms	1 and partial	
Vice president	1st—none 2nd—Charles G. Dawes	

Calvin Coolidge

Calvin Coolidge was born in Vermont. He later became an attorney in Massachusetts and entered politics there. He gained a reputation as a "law and order" man when, as governor of Massachusetts, he took a stand during a Boston police strike in 1919. He declared, "There is no right to strike against the public safety by anybody, anywhere, any time." He then forced the police back to work. In a nation that feared disorder and crime, that stand won Coolidge admiration.

Succeeding to the presidency upon Harding's death, Coolidge was in the White House when most of the Harding scandals were revealed. But because Coolidge was not part of the scandals and because he firmly prosecuted the corrupt officials, he was unaffected politically by the wrongdoing.

In the 1924 presidential election, the Democrats chose John W. Davis from West Virginia to oppose Coolidge. Coolidge won the election and continued Harding's policies.

Walter Lippmann, a journalist of the day, said that Coolidge had a "talent for effectively doing nothing" and that "this active inactivity suit[ed] the mood" of the country. Americans credited Coolidge for the nation's prosperity. He was enormously popular. Though he likely would have won reelection easily, he chose not to seek another term. In August 1927 he called a press conference. Reporters gathered eagerly, expecting a major speech from the president. Instead, aides distributed slips of paper that said simply, "I do not choose to run for President in 1928."

Although American business seemed successful, dangerous conditions were developing. Stock prices went higher and higher, well beyond what stocks were actually worth. Buying on credit was so popular that millions of Americans were in serious debt. Farmers were still overproducing and receiving low prices for produce. Those and other features of the American economy would soon lead to catastrophe. Unwise individual economic decisions can sometimes collectively have far-reaching national consequences.

Did you know?

The Star-Spangled Banner, written in 1814, became the official national anthem in 1931 during Hoover's administration.

Herbert Hoover

The United States was still enjoying prosperity when the 1928 election was held. The Republican candidate, **Herbert Hoover**, was swept into office by a nation satisfied with success. Voters expected him to continue the Harding and Coolidge policies of limited government interference. Hoover, who was once a poor, orphaned farm boy, had proven his abilities by becoming a wealthy mining engineer and then devoting his talents to public service. His Democratic opponent, Al Smith, opposed Prohibition and was a Roman Catholic. Because most Americans were Protestant, the nation was not ready to elect a Catholic to the presidency.

Hoover was talented, but he inherited numerous problems when he entered the White House. The excesses of the twenties were about to bear the fruit of disaster. In coming years, he would be forced to deal with the Great Depression.

SECTION REVIEW 21.4

1. What was the Teapot Dome scandal?
2. Looking at Harding's quote about his enemies and friends, what lesson can you learn about friends?
3. How did Calvin Coolidge become president?
4. With what catastrophic time in American history would Herbert Hoover be forced to deal?

CHAPTER 21 REVIEW

Making Connections

1. Why did many Americans not want the country to join the League of Nations?
2. What famous court case was complicated by ill feelings toward immigrants?
3. How were families able to purchase cars if they did not have all the necessary money?
4. What was the famous feat of Charles A. Lindbergh?
5. What was the first radio station? Where was it? When did the first commercial broadcast occur?
6. Whose ideas about open sexuality encouraged some Americans to believe that immoral behavior was acceptable?
7. What were three types of leisure activities that began to fill people's time?
8. What did the literature of the 1920s reflect?
9. What law allowed the federal government to enforce Prohibition?
10. For what three reasons was Prohibition difficult to enforce?
11. What were four ways some people attempted to bypass the Eighteenth Amendment?
12. What famous gangster led a crime ring in Prohibition Chicago?
13. What groups did the revived KKK dislike?
14. Where did the term *Fundamentalist* originate?
15. Who were the three Republican presidents of the Twenties?

Thinking Critically

16. How does the KKK show that sometimes people do evil things while using religious symbols?
17. How is the Scopes trial still relevant today?

Living as a Christian Citizen

18. What benefits and challenges did the growth of technology and business bring to Christians? Formulate a response to the challenges.
19. What are the similarities between the morality of the 1920s and modern American morality? How should your answer shape your entertainment choices?

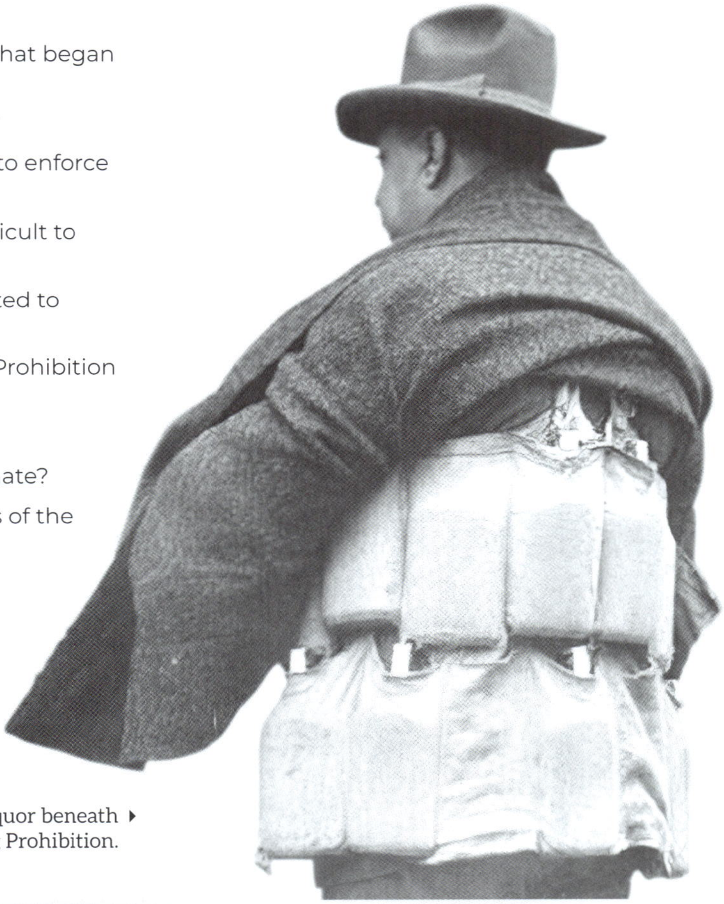

A man hides liquor beneath his coat during Prohibition.

Terms to Remember

Warren G. Harding
disarmament
Washington Naval Conference
Calvin Coolidge
Kellogg-Briand Pact
Red Scare
installment plan
Charles A. Lindbergh
assembly line
Sigmund Freud
flappers
prohibition
Prohibition
Volstead Act
bootlegging
speakeasies
Al Capone
Twenty-First Amendment
Fundamentalist
Scopes trial
Albert B. Fall
Teapot Dome scandal
Herbert Hoover

CHAPTER

22 The Great Depression and the New Deal

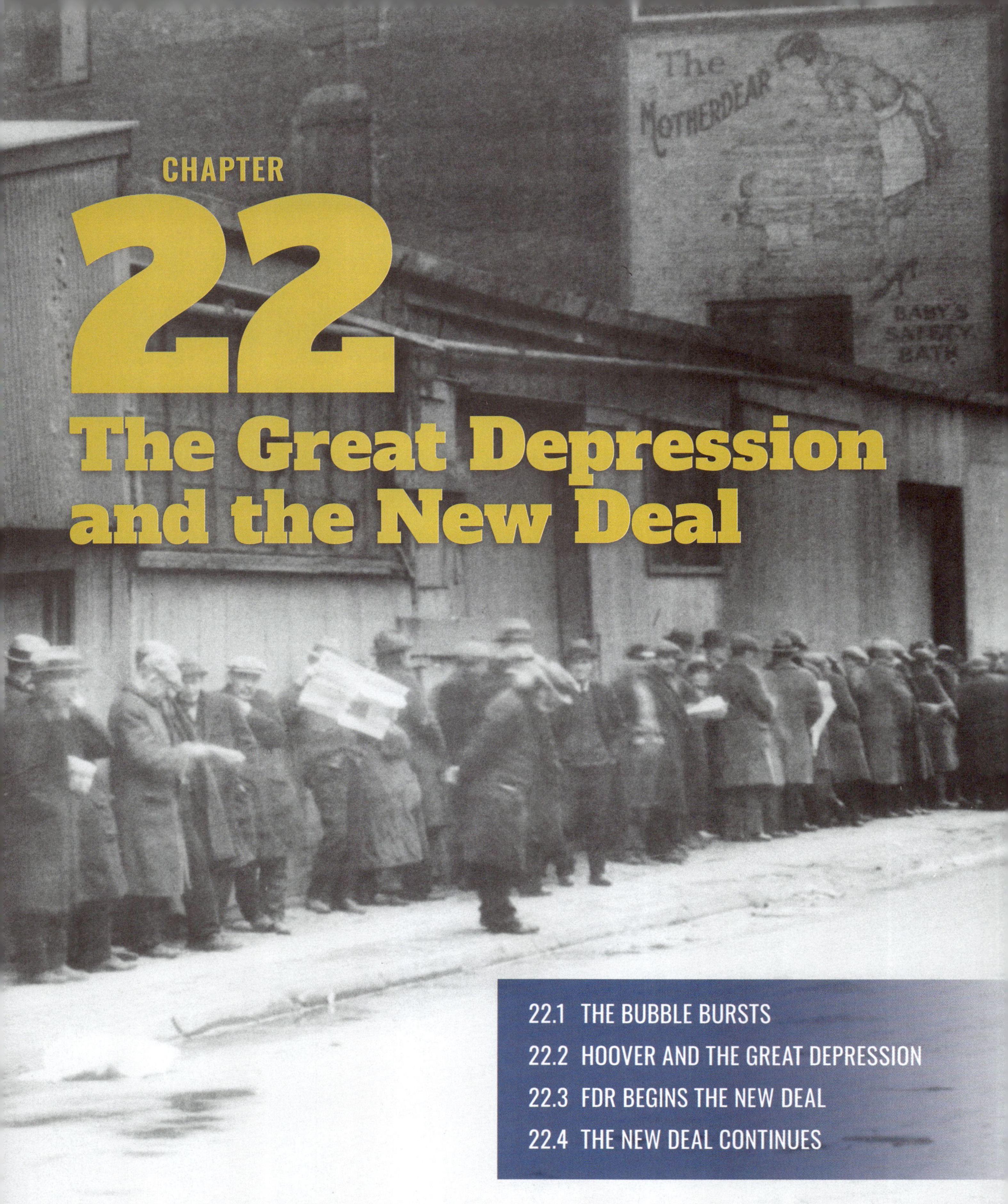

▲ People waiting in line for food in New York City during the Great Depression

Crowds outside the New York Stock Exchange on "Black Thursday" ▸

22.1 THE BUBBLE BURSTS

Why did the Great Depression begin?

American businesses seemed to flourish as stock prices rose ever higher in 1929. The stock market reached a new high in September. However, some investors were worried that prices had become too high, well beyond the actual value of the stocks. Investors who wanted to sell stock began to find fewer buyers and were forced to sell at a reduced price. Prices began to slide. On Thursday, October 24, a record-breaking 13 million shares of stock changed hands as people rushed to sell. Prices dropped so low that investors lost $9 billion on that "Black Thursday." Many investors lost all their money and could not repay stockbrokers the money that they had borrowed to purchase stocks. When the investors could not pay, brokers tried desperately to sell the stock, flooding the market still more.

A few days later, the **stock-market crash** occurred. On October 29, which became known as "Black Tuesday," panic erupted when the Stock Exchange received orders to sell more than 16 million shares. Fortunes that had been made over a period of years vanished in minutes. Prices continued to drop until they finally reached their lowest level on November 13. By that time, investors had lost about $30 billion, an amount equal to what America had spent fighting World War I. The stock-market crash of 1929 signaled the start of the worst economic crisis in American history. Known as the **Great Depression**, the crisis lasted for more than a decade.

During the Depression, many in the United States would face problems that made them question their values. For example, Americans believed that each individual should have an equal opportunity to succeed. But during this period, the loss of jobs and financial savings made many wonder if economic success was even possible. Some were concerned that poor children, whose numbers were increasing, had fewer opportunities than wealthy ones. During the economic uncertainty, many looked to the government for help. Others worried that reliance on the government for assistance would result in the loss of some of their freedoms as government control accompanied government help.

During the 1928 presidential campaign, Herbert Hoover had declared, "We in America today are nearer to the final triumph over poverty than ever before in the history of any land." Instead, the Roaring Twenties ended with a national financial collapse. Soon, millions of Americans were unemployed, homeless, and hungry.

GUIDING QUESTIONS

- Why did the American economy collapse in the late 1920s?
- What was life like during the Great Depression?

Herbert Hoover

31

Born	August 10, 1874
Died	October 20, 1964
Home state	California (born in Iowa)
Wife	Lou Henry
Church	Quaker
Occupations	engineer
Party	Republican
Years served as president	1929–33
Terms	1
Vice president	Charles Curtis

Causes of the Economic Collapse

The widespread desire for wealth and pleasure in the 1920s had much to do with the economic collapse that followed, but a combination of other factors also contributed to the financial disaster.

Economic Slowdown

Despite the general prosperity in the 1920s, many workers had already begun to face economic woes. As noted in the last chapter, American farmers struggled because there was not enough demand for all the items they produced; thus, they were receiving lower prices. Textile workers and coal miners were hurt by layoffs as demand for their products declined. These workers could no longer buy the industrial goods that were filling the market. As the demand for goods declined, industrial output slowed. Laborers worked fewer hours or were laid off. These conditions led to reduced incomes and other hardships. Because industries were often interdependent, when one industry implemented cutbacks, others were forced to do the same. Consumer spending dropped so much that industrial expansion slowed almost to a standstill before the stock market crashed.

Overuse of Credit

The use of credit, especially of the installment plan, had grown steadily in the 1920s, and millions of Americans were in serious debt. They had such high payments for items purchased on credit that they could not afford to buy new merchandise. Auto sales and construction lagged, and workers lost their jobs. Many were then unable to meet their payments. Merchants who had extended loans lost money, and their own businesses began to falter.

Speculation

Speculation, when speaking about financial affairs, refers to a financial transaction that carries a considerable risk of losing value but also holds the possibility of significant financial gain. In the late 1920s, newspapers carried accounts of people involved in speculation who profited greatly. Many bought real estate or stocks at low prices, hoping to sell them quickly for a much higher price.

Land prices increased in the 1920s, especially in urban and suburban areas and in areas near recreational settings. Florida was a big part of the land boom during this period. That state's semitropical climate attracted the enthusiasm of speculators. Those who speculated early and bought good land did make big profits. But some people were swindled into buying undesirable land, such as swamps. In 1926 a massive hurricane devastated southern Florida and helped end people's desire to invest in Florida land. Many who had purchased land on credit found later that they could not make their payments. Bank failures in Florida climbed as loans were not repaid.

▾ During a 1926 hurricane, extensive damage occurred in many parts of Florida. Miami is shown at the height of the storm.

Some Americans engaged in stock speculation. Stock prices had risen steadily since 1927. By September 1929 stock prices were typically 400 percent higher than they had been in 1925. The number of people "playing the market" grew to about 1.5 million in 1929. (This was still a small fraction of the total population, which was a little more than 122 million.) Most of these investors hoped to sell stocks for quick profits when prices rose. Many investors paid little attention to the earnings of the companies in which they invested, even though the earnings could give them an indication of the actual value of stocks. These investors assumed that stock prices would continue to rise.

1929 Prices per Share for Selected Stocks

Company	March 3	September 3	November 13
American Can	77	181 7/8	86
AT&T	179 1/2	304	197 1/4
General Electric	128 3/4	396 1/4	168 1/8
Montgomery Ward	137 7/8	466 1/2	49 1/4
Union Carbide	145	413 5/8	59

The problem was further complicated because stock brokers allowed investors to **buy on margin**. With this practice, an investor paid only part of a stock's purchase price in cash, usually 10 percent, and borrowed the remainder from a broker. The broker then borrowed money from banks and corporations to cover the loan made to his client. If the value of the investor's stock increased, there was no problem. The investor could repay his loan with interest and still gain a profit. But if the stock's value dropped below the value of the loan, the investor's margin (the amount he had borrowed) was due. The investor then had to provide more cash or risk losing both the stock he had purchased and his cash investment. If he could not repay his loan, the broker could take the investor's stock; however, the broker still owed the money borrowed from banks and corporations.

This system satisfied many people and seemed to stimulate the economy. Stock prices climbed. In March 1928, both the volume and the value of traded shares soared. The boom lasted through the summer of 1929, although business profits were falling at the time. Sliding stock prices in the fall of 1929 caused a ripple effect as first investors and then brokers were unable to repay loans in rapidly increasing numbers. The banks and companies that had made the loans were left crippled by debt.

▲ The floor of the New York Stock Exchange in early 1929. For several years the price of many stocks had been increasing dramatically. Though that trend continued through most of the year, in October the prices crashed.

International Economic Problems

After the stock market crashed, international problems made matters worse. In June 1930, the United States passed the **Smoot-Hawley Tariff** to protect American industries from foreign competition. This was the highest tariff ever passed by the US Congress. Other countries retaliated by raising their tariffs on American goods. As a result, not only was it difficult for foreign countries to sell goods in the United States, it was also difficult for America to sell goods abroad.

America had loaned billions to its allies during World War I. After the war, those countries used some of the money received from German reparations (required by the Treaty of Versailles) to repay the United States. Economic problems within Germany caused it to cease paying reparations. With this loss of funds and without profitable trade—largely because of the tariffs—America's allies could not repay their debts. This only deepened the economic crisis.

Conditions during the Great Depression

After the stock-market crash and the deepening economic crisis that followed, prosperity for almost all Americans disappeared. Millions lost their investments, money, jobs, and homes.

Bank Failures

People became increasingly worried that they might lose the money they had deposited in banks. Many withdrew some money to pay their debts; others panicked and withdrew all their funds. In addition, many were unable to repay bank loans because of reduced wages or lost jobs. All these factors meant that banks had a shortage of cash. As a result, many were forced to close their doors, sometimes permanently. Banks that reopened often offered customers only a percentage of their total deposits.

By 1931 a total of more than four thousand banks had closed. Some were small; others were quite large. For example, in December 1930 police had to control a crowd of 20,000–25,000 that had gathered outside a branch of the Bank of the United States, a large private bank in New York City. Thousands of the 440,000 people who had accounts at the bank waited to withdraw their money. Most lost their money when the bank was forced to close from lack of funds. The number of failed banks continued to climb; by the end of the 1930s more than nine thousand had closed.

Unemployment

Millions of Americans lost jobs during the Depression. By 1933 about thirteen million Americans—one out of every four workers—were unemployed. Some workers kept their jobs but worked only a few days a week or a few hours a day; others took wage cuts. Between 1931 and 1933 an average of one hundred thousand people a week became unemployed.

People began to buy less because they had less money. As they bought less, inventories of goods grew. Producers had more than they could sell. Prices fell, but few could buy the cheaper goods. From 1929 to 1932 the country's industrial output fell by another 54 percent. Steel plants were operating at only 12 percent of capacity.

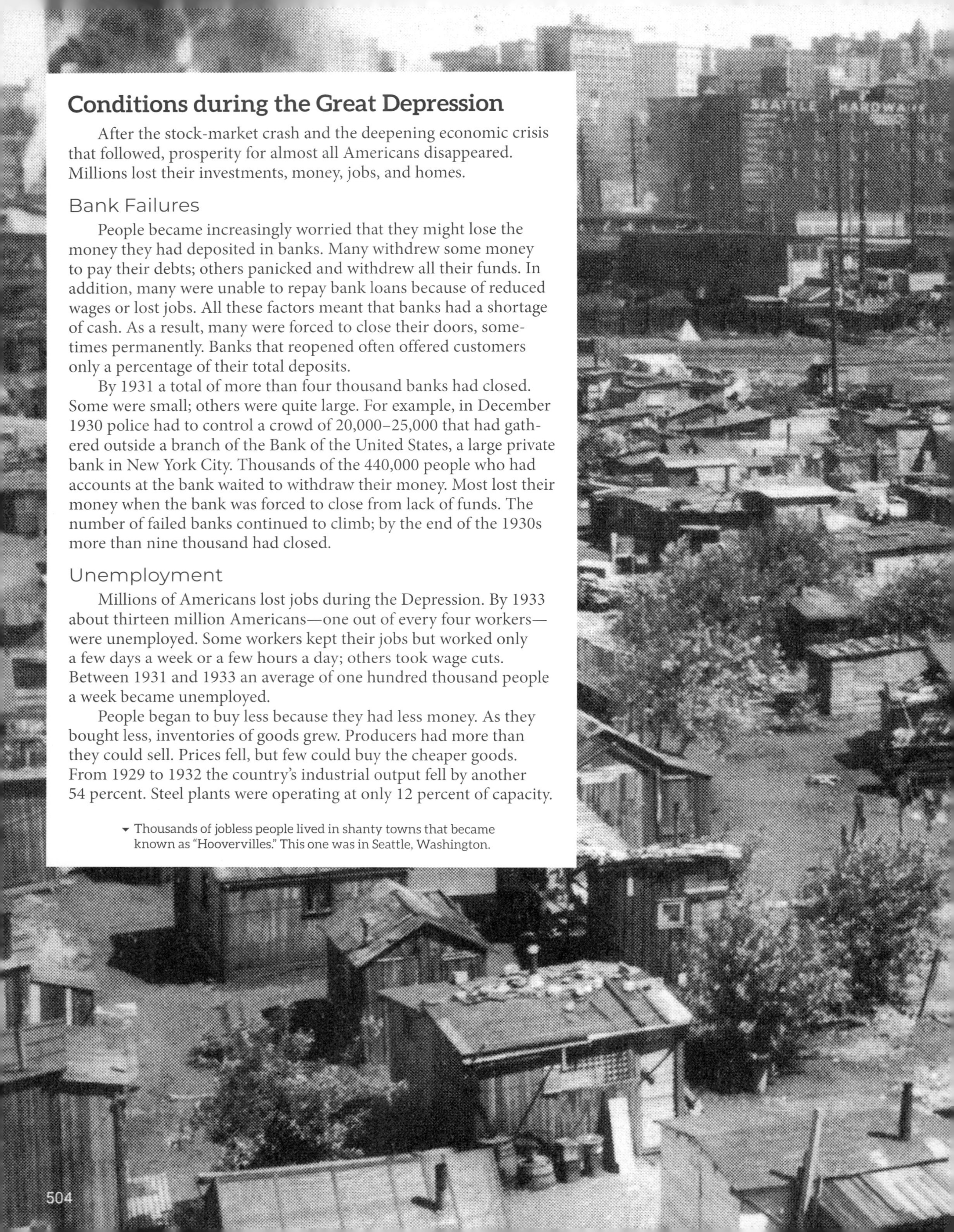

▾ Thousands of jobless people lived in shanty towns that became known as "Hoovervilles." This one was in Seattle, Washington.

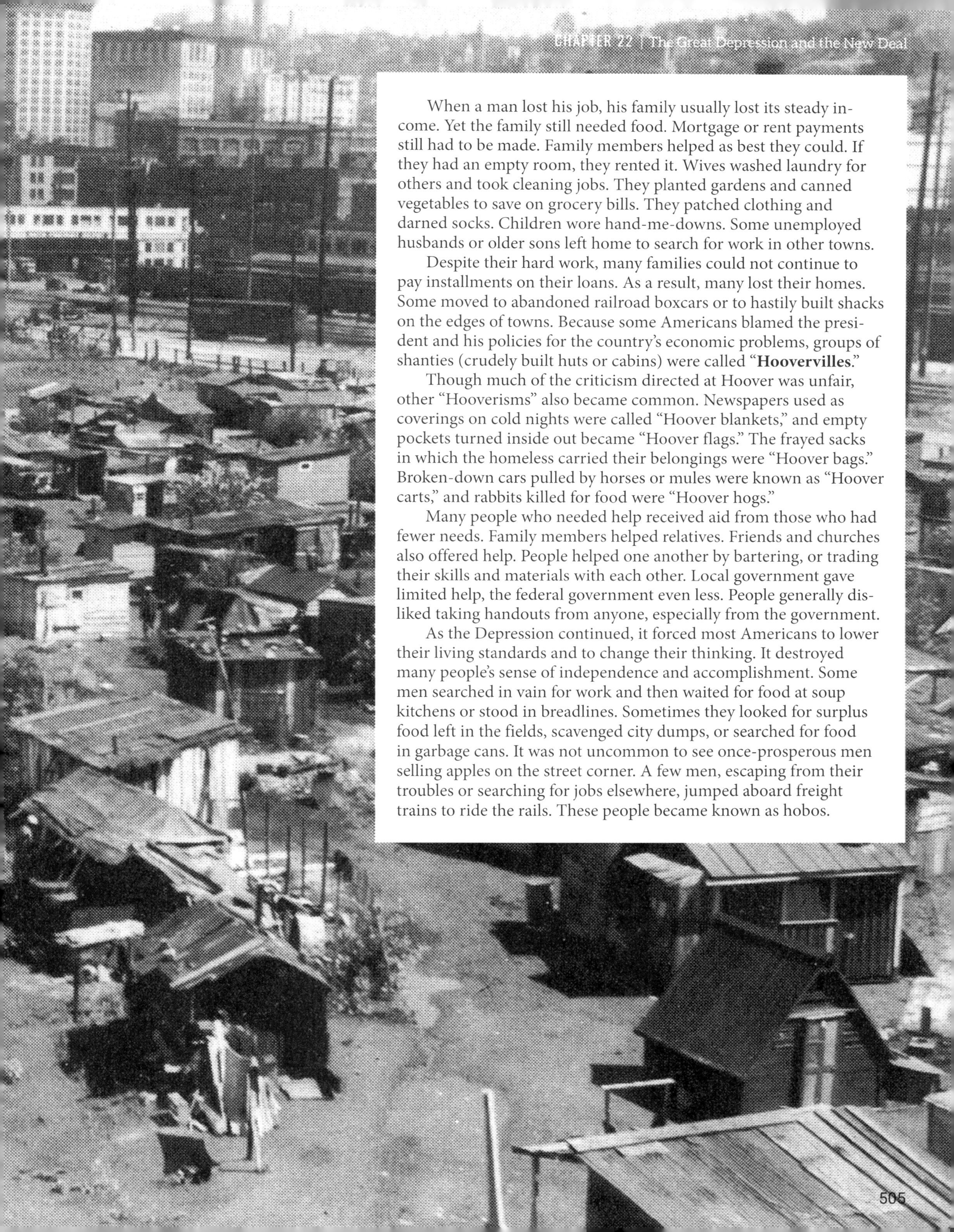

When a man lost his job, his family usually lost its steady income. Yet the family still needed food. Mortgage or rent payments still had to be made. Family members helped as best they could. If they had an empty room, they rented it. Wives washed laundry for others and took cleaning jobs. They planted gardens and canned vegetables to save on grocery bills. They patched clothing and darned socks. Children wore hand-me-downs. Some unemployed husbands or older sons left home to search for work in other towns.

Despite their hard work, many families could not continue to pay installments on their loans. As a result, many lost their homes. Some moved to abandoned railroad boxcars or to hastily built shacks on the edges of towns. Because some Americans blamed the president and his policies for the country's economic problems, groups of shanties (crudely built huts or cabins) were called "**Hoovervilles**."

Though much of the criticism directed at Hoover was unfair, other "Hooverisms" also became common. Newspapers used as coverings on cold nights were called "Hoover blankets," and empty pockets turned inside out became "Hoover flags." The frayed sacks in which the homeless carried their belongings were "Hoover bags." Broken-down cars pulled by horses or mules were known as "Hoover carts," and rabbits killed for food were "Hoover hogs."

Many people who needed help received aid from those who had fewer needs. Family members helped relatives. Friends and churches also offered help. People helped one another by bartering, or trading their skills and materials with each other. Local government gave limited help, the federal government even less. People generally disliked taking handouts from anyone, especially from the government.

As the Depression continued, it forced most Americans to lower their living standards and to change their thinking. It destroyed many people's sense of independence and accomplishment. Some men searched in vain for work and then waited for food at soup kitchens or stood in breadlines. Sometimes they looked for surplus food left in the fields, scavenged city dumps, or searched for food in garbage cans. It was not uncommon to see once-prosperous men selling apples on the street corner. A few men, escaping from their troubles or searching for jobs elsewhere, jumped aboard freight trains to ride the rails. These people became known as hobos.

Farm Problems

Even in the booming 1920s, few farmers had been prosperous. During the Depression, conditions worsened. Farmers produced so much grain, livestock, and other farm products that prices stayed low. Many farmers could not make payments on their mortgaged land or on the trucks, tractors, and other equipment they had purchased on credit. Many farmers were in danger of losing their farms.

Conditions were especially bad for farmers in the Great Plains. Years earlier cattle had overgrazed that area. Then, with the higher demand for food during World War I, the land was plowed more deeply than before. This enabled farmers to produce crops in a dry region, but it caused problems later, when droughts came.

Droughts in the 1930s dried up the crops, and the soil turned to dust. The area became known as the "**Dust Bowl**" and was soon plagued by extreme poverty. From Texas to Canada, winds whipped the topsoil, loosened by deep plowing, off the dry ground. "Black blizzards" of dust blew from west to east, darkening skies as far away as Albany, New York. Soil piled into drifts like snow. Drivers had to use their cars' headlights in the daytime. Families put wet towels under doors to keep out the choking dust. Livestock died of thirst.

Unable to pay taxes or mortgages, farmers sold their farms at a loss. Thousands of families abandoned their homes to go where workers were needed to tend fields and orchards. California was a popular destination. Many Oklahoma farmers migrated in search of jobs, but even California had little work for the people known as "Okies." In his famous novel about farmers fleeing the Dust Bowl, *The Grapes of Wrath*, John Steinbeck tells of a fictional family of Okies, the Joads, and their trek to California searching for farm work.

▾ Dust storms were common in the 1930s.

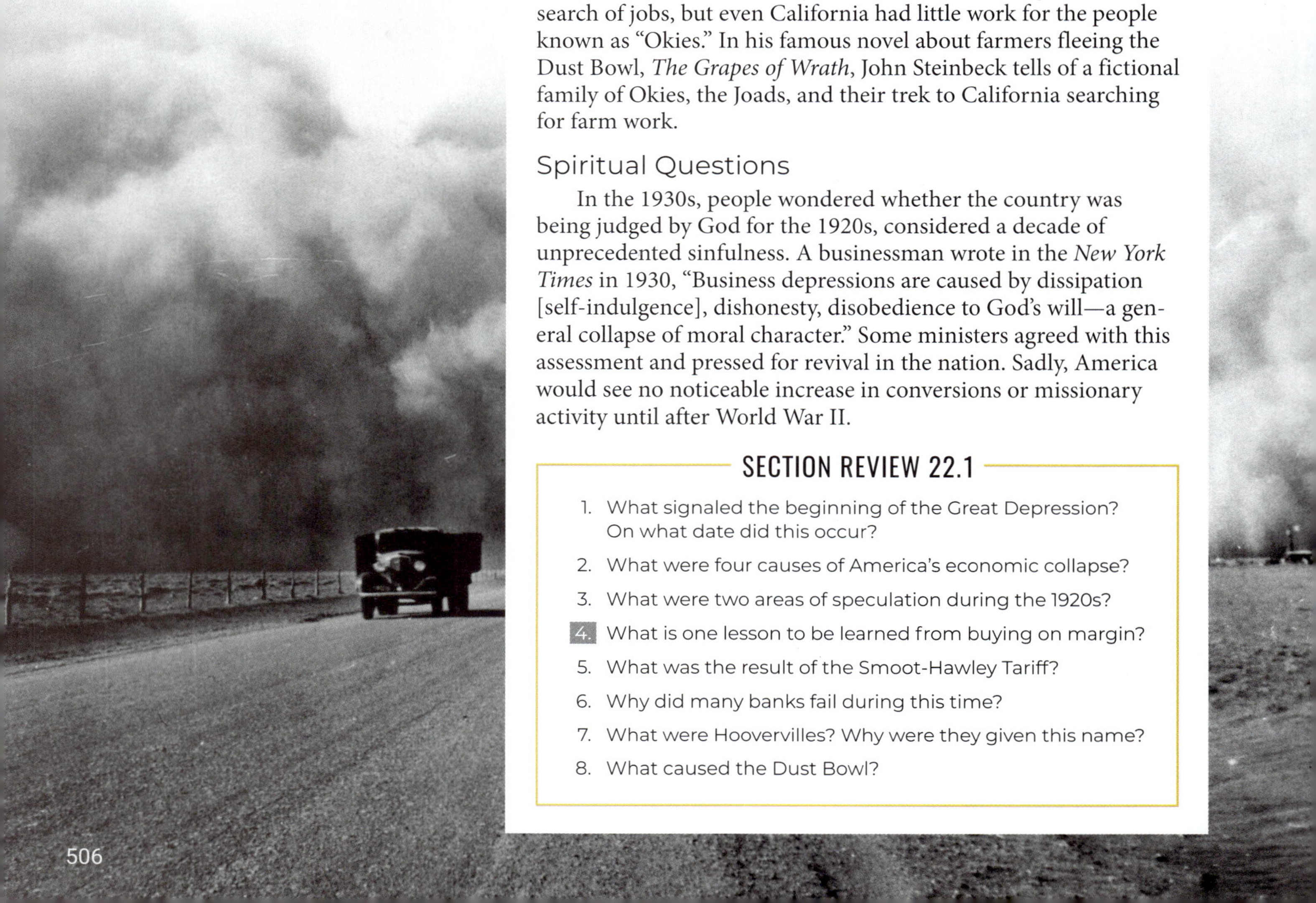

Spiritual Questions

In the 1930s, people wondered whether the country was being judged by God for the 1920s, considered a decade of unprecedented sinfulness. A businessman wrote in the *New York Times* in 1930, "Business depressions are caused by dissipation [self-indulgence], dishonesty, disobedience to God's will—a general collapse of moral character." Some ministers agreed with this assessment and pressed for revival in the nation. Sadly, America would see no noticeable increase in conversions or missionary activity until after World War II.

SECTION REVIEW 22.1

1. What signaled the beginning of the Great Depression? On what date did this occur?
2. What were four causes of America's economic collapse?
3. What were two areas of speculation during the 1920s?
4. What is one lesson to be learned from buying on margin?
5. What was the result of the Smoot-Hawley Tariff?
6. Why did many banks fail during this time?
7. What were Hoovervilles? Why were they given this name?
8. What caused the Dust Bowl?

22.2 HOOVER AND THE GREAT DEPRESSION

How did Hoover handle the Depression?

GUIDING QUESTION

- Were President Hoover's efforts to solve the problems of the Great Depression successful?

Attempts to Solve the Problems

President Herbert Hoover tried to deal with the onset of the Great Depression by being optimistic. The more people panicked, the more damage was done to the economy, so he encouraged Americans to believe that the trials would soon pass and that business would boom again. Few people seemed to listen. Stock prices continued to fall as investors tried to sell. Bank failures continued, and many industries continued to operate at greatly reduced capacity. Because Hoover was the president at the time the crisis began, he received most of the blame for what was going wrong.

Hoover believed that most of the solutions to the nation's problems lay at the local level. He said that "the best hearts and brains in every community" could best "serve their neighbors." He thought that creating government agencies to handle the problems of the unemployed would produce "more red tape [bureaucracy, government regulation] than relief." He wanted federal funds to be used only after all voluntary (that is, private and religious) and local resources were exhausted.

Hoover Dam on the Colorado River

When federal monies were used, Hoover thought that the funds should be carefully managed. He also thought that they should not be given directly to people as a **dole**, or handout. Rather, he said, the monies should fund projects that would benefit many people. For example, if cities and states were given loans to pay for public works projects, they could hire local people who would benefit from the employment. Thus, Hoover did eventually establish government projects that employed thousands of men to do useful work. Those workers constructed public buildings and other structures. In 1931 construction began on what became the Hoover Dam on the Colorado River. The federal government under Hoover also helped pay for the building of thousands of miles of roads.

In January 1932 Congress passed a bill, promoted by Hoover, that created the **Reconstruction Finance Corporation (RFC)**. The corporation loaned billions to industries and businesses, such as banks, to be used in projects that would create jobs. Congress also approved the president's request for twelve Federal Home Loan Banks. Those banks could lend money to loan associations, other banks, and insurance companies. In turn, those institutions could aid homeowners who were having difficulty making mortgage payments.

Despite Hoover's efforts, people continued to criticize him. The steps he took were not dramatic enough to satisfy the many Americans who were still waiting for help. Hoover's actions did result in billions of dollars in **deficit spending** (spending more money than is received in income) by the federal government. The government regularly borrowed money to finance his programs.

Fun Fact

Games such as Scrabble and Monopoly were first sold during the 1930s and became popular during the Depression.

- Veterans march in New York City before leaving for Washington, DC. They sought early payment of the World War I bonus (top).
- Some veterans battle with policemen after refusing to leave the nation's capital (above).

The Bonus Army

In 1924 Congress had passed legislation providing a bonus, averaging about $1,000, to each World War I veteran. Payment would be made in 1945. In the spring and summer of 1932, a large group of unemployed veterans made their way to Washington, DC, to ask for an early payment of that bonus. These veterans called themselves the **Bonus Army**. The House of Representatives approved partial early payment, but the Senate defeated the measure.

Veterans turned to Hoover for help, but he would not meet with them. Most of the 15,000–20,000 veterans returned home. Congress, at Hoover's request, provided money for the protesters' travel. Unwilling to accept defeat, about 2,000 veterans, some with their wives and children, remained in hastily built shanties on the edge of the city. Others occupied some vacant buildings near the Capitol.

On July 28 government agents informed the Bonus Army members that they had to move out of the downtown buildings. They refused. Police with nightsticks in hand were sent to force the illegal occupants from the buildings, but the veterans, reinforced by those who were living in the shanties, met the officers with a volley of bricks. In the clash, some of the policemen began to fire on the veterans, killing two and wounding two others.

Hoover sent troops under General Douglas MacArthur to quell the disorder and destroy the shanties. MacArthur, contrary to Hoover's orders, determined to use all necessary force to drive the veterans completely from the capital city. After an hour's warning, the general's forces marched in with tear gas, tanks, and bayonets. Once the downtown buildings were cleared, MacArthur moved on to the shanties, driving out the veterans who remained and burning their shacks.

Although the action had been much harsher than he intended, Hoover took full responsibility for the affair. In doing so, he seemed more heartless than ever to the needs of struggling Americans.

Fun Fact

A cheap food during the Depression was baked potatoes stuffed with peanut butter.

SECTION REVIEW 22.2

1. What level of government did Hoover believe could solve most of the nation's problems?
2. What massive structure on the Colorado River is an example of a government project created to benefit the public while giving many people work?
3. Explain what the Bonus Army hoped to accomplish by going to Washington, DC.
4. Was Herbert Hoover to blame for the financial problems in the United States during the Depression? Explain your answer.

22.3 FDR BEGINS THE NEW DEAL

What programs did the New Deal establish?

GUIDING QUESTIONS

- Why was Franklin Delano Roosevelt (FDR) elected in 1932?
- What were the major New Deal programs?

Discontent grew. Hoover began to expand government involvement in the economy in ways that no other peacetime president had. However, his actions did not seem to resolve the problems. Voters were drawn to the optimistic promises of **Franklin Delano Roosevelt** (FDR).

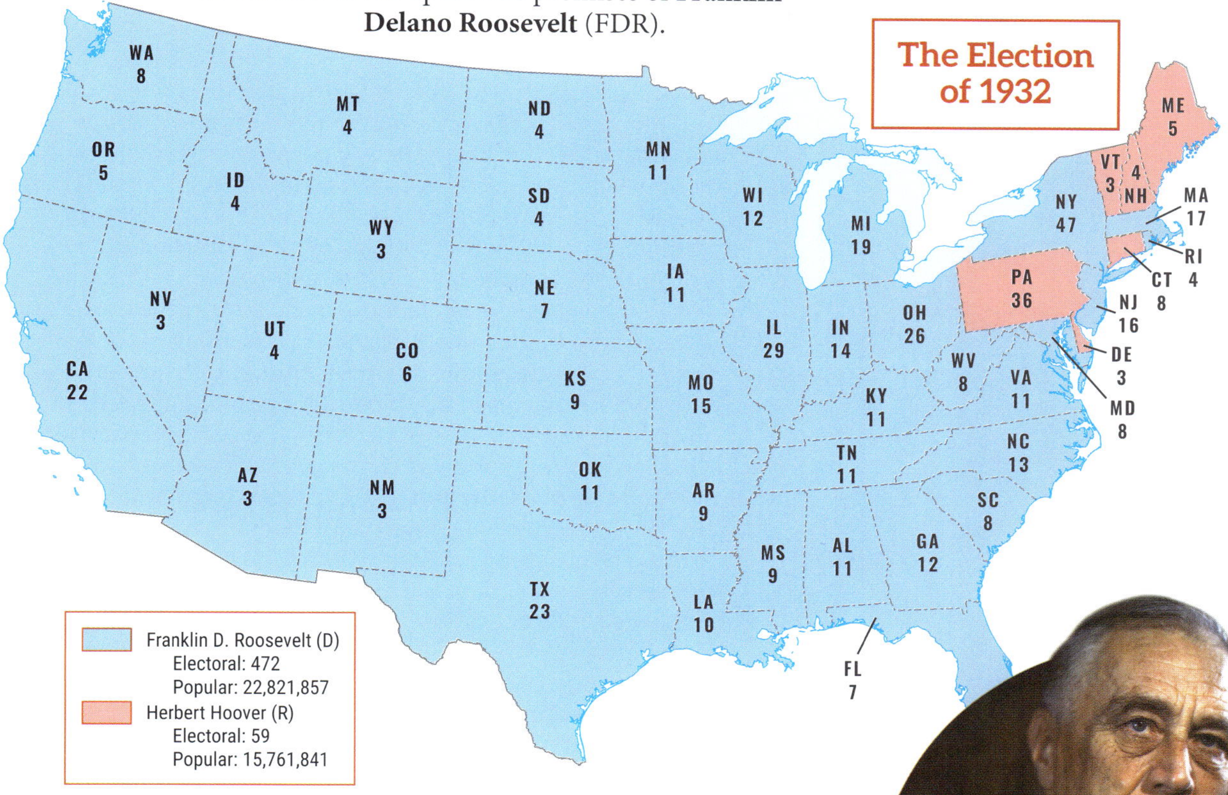

The Election of 1932

The economy was the central issue in the 1932 election, one of the most critical elections in US history. The Republicans renominated Hoover. The Democrats chose FDR, the governor of New York and a distant cousin of Theodore Roosevelt.

When the Democrats nominated Roosevelt at their convention, he broke with tradition and delivered a speech there accepting his nomination. In that address, he stated, "I pledge you, I pledge myself, to a new deal for the American people." That promise of a "**New Deal**" (a name that would soon be permanently attached to his efforts to conquer the Depression) was what many people wanted to hear. Months earlier, he had called on the government to try "bold, persistent experimentation." At this point, no one knew what the experiments might be—not even Roosevelt himself.

Hoover campaigned hard. He praised "rugged individualism" and encouraged industry and labor to take voluntary action to deal with their problems. But knowing that the people were demanding action, he also pledged more government involvement than ever before.

By Election Day, however, millions of voters were convinced that Hoover's way had not worked. Roosevelt carried forty-two of the forty-eight states and was elected president.

Franklin Delano Roosevelt

32

Born	January 30, 1882
Died	April 12, 1945
Home state	New York
Wife	Anna Eleanor Roosevelt (his fifth cousin and Teddy Roosevelt's niece)
Church	Episcopalian
Occupation	lawyer
Party	Democrat
Years served as president	1933–45
Terms	3 plus partial
Vice presidents	1st/2nd—John Nance Garner 3rd—Henry Wallace 4th—Harry Truman

The President's Polio

FDR served as a member of the New York Senate from 1911 to 1913. When Woodrow Wilson was president, he served as assistant secretary of the navy (1913–20). In 1920 the Democrats chose him as their candidate for vice president. The year after the Democrats lost that election, Roosevelt was stricken with polio. At age thirty-nine, he was permanently paralyzed from the hips down. In spite of this personal tragedy, a few years later Roosevelt resumed his political career. In 1928 he was elected governor of the nation's most populated state (at the time), New York.

Every day Roosevelt faced a great struggle. He had to use metal braces just to stand. To minimize his disability's effect on the public, Roosevelt refused to be seen in his wheelchair. He had to be helped to the podium to give his speeches. On one occasion, the podium was not fastened properly, and it and the president went tumbling off the platform and into the orchestra pit. Returning to the podium, Roosevelt simply resumed his speech where he had stopped. For traveling, he had a special wheelchair and a railroad car with a wheelchair lift.

Roosevelt's condition gave him a special tenderness for others with disabilities. He constantly visited hospitals and worked with disabled children or soldiers. He had a car designed that could be operated with hand controls, and he would take particularly discouraged children for a ride and talk. These children often returned with a positive attitude and a desire to persevere. Roosevelt also invested heavily in a treatment center at Warm Springs, Georgia. Because the warm water from natural springs there helped ease the pain from polio, FDR built a small home in the area and regularly visited it. People nicknamed this home the "Little White House." He died there on April 12, 1945.

Roosevelt's battle to overcome polio helped give him optimism and a persevering spirit that would enable him to lead the United States through one of its most challenging periods.

◂ Because of polio, FDR used a wheelchair. The statue at left is displayed at the memorial in his honor in Washington, DC.

Early New Deal Actions

As Roosevelt took office on March 4, 1933, he asserted,

> This great Nation will endure as it has endured, will revive and will prosper. So, first of all, let me assert my firm belief that the only thing we have to fear is fear itself—nameless, unreasoning, unjustified terror which paralyzes needed efforts to convert retreat into advance. . . .
>
> We do not distrust the future of essential democracy. The people of the United States have not failed. In their need they have registered a mandate that they want direct, vigorous action. . . . They have made me the present instrument of their wishes.

▲ FDR delivering one of his famous "fireside chats"

Two days after becoming president, Roosevelt proclaimed a **bank holiday**, closing all banks temporarily. Next, he called Congress into special session. On March 9 Congress passed the Emergency Banking Act. It empowered the Treasury Department to decide which banks were sound enough to reopen. On March 12, the day before the first banks were to reopen, Roosevelt delivered the first of his many radio addresses to the nation. They became know as "**fireside chats**" because he often delivered them from next to his fireplace. It is estimated that sixty million Americans, almost half of the nation's population, listened to the first fireside chat. He urged Americans not to withdraw money from banks and encouraged those that had done so to return their deposits. He said, "I can assure you that it is safer to keep your money in a reopened bank than under the mattress."

Half the banks, which held 90 percent of all banking resources, were back in operation by March 15. Confidence in banks seemed to return as people soon redeposited more than $1 billion.

The Democratic-controlled Congress, realizing that most Americans wanted the action that Roosevelt promised, approved almost anything he proposed. In his first one hundred days in office, fifteen major pieces of New Deal legislation were adopted.

A good public speaker with an understanding of people, Roosevelt radiated warmth, even on the radio. He developed a good relationship with the press by staging numerous press conferences. As his allies, the media could sway public opinion to rally behind his ideas.

Besides his cabinet members, Roosevelt recruited a group of advisors to help him formulate his plans for combating the Depression. This group, called his "**brain trust**," included university professors who offered opinions regarding economic policies and legislation.

▼ This statue displayed at FDR's Washington, DC, memorial portrays one of the millions of Americans who regularly listened to his radio speeches.

Alphabet Soup

New Deal legislation created numerous programs and agencies that came to be known by their initials. Conversations were soon filled with talk of the CCC, the AAA, the NRA, and the TVA. Many referred to them as "alphabet agencies" or "alphabet soup."

In May 1933 Congress approved the creation of the Federal Emergency Relief Administration (FERA). That agency was given $500 million in federal money to distribute to the states to provide food and assistance for needy people.

In June, Congress created the **Federal Deposit Insurance Corporation (FDIC)**, an agency that insured individual bank accounts up to $5,000. (That amount has been raised numerous times. In 2008 the FDIC protection was increased to $250,000.) This protection greatly increased public confidence in the banking system. That same month, the Home Owners' Loan Corporation (HOLC) was established. This agency helped homeowners replace their old loans with new ones that lowered the payment due each month. Over the next two years, it assisted more than a million homeowners. The HOLC applied only to nonfarm homes; however, another agency, the Farm Credit Administration (FCA), provided similar help to farmers.

major ALPHABET SOUP PROGRAMS

AAA	Agricultural Adjustment Act
CCC	Civilian Conservation Corps
FCA	Farm Credit Administration
FERA	Federal Emergency Relief Administration
FDIC	Federal Deposit Insurance Corporation
HOLC	Home Owners' Loan Corporation
NRA	National Recovery Administration
SSA	Social Security Administration
TVA	Tennessee Valley Authority
WPA	Works Progress Administration

▲ An AAA poster

The New Deal also tried to help farmers through the **Agricultural Adjustment Act (AAA)**. The act was intended to quickly increase the prices that farmers received. A reduction in the number of products would raise the prices for food and other items produced. Thus, in 1933 government officials paid farmers to destroy items. One-quarter to one-half of the crops were demolished. Milk was poured into ditches; grain was burned; cattle, sheep, and hogs were killed. Six million pigs were slaughtered and buried. Ten million acres of cotton were plowed under. This destruction made little sense to hungry people. In a nation where thousands of children wore rags and remained undernourished, it brought intense criticism of the entire program.

But many farmers favored the AAA because they were paid to cooperate with it. As the program continued, the AAA paid farmers to plant less and produce less. Farm income improved by about 50 percent over the next three years. Some cotton and wool were stored in warehouses and held off the market until greater need would raise prices.

Despite the AAA's benefits for many farmers, its policies resulted in consumers having to pay more for goods. Many of these individuals were already struggling to pay for food, clothing, and shelter. Moreover, the AAA hindered some farmers. For example, sharecroppers received no benefit from the programs because it was the landowners who received the government payments.

In 1936 the Supreme Court declared the AAA unconstitutional. Nevertheless, a precedent had already been set. Many farmers had become dependent on government payments. Later the AAA was rewritten with adjustments that made it constitutional. Farmers regained those payments. Many conservatives continued to criticize the AAA because its policies required tremendous taxpayer expense and provided much government control of farming.

The **National Recovery Administration (NRA)** was designed to help businesses recover from the effects of the Depression. The agency's goal was to eliminate competition among firms. The NRA wrote more than five hundred codes (government regulations) and gave them to businesses. Under the codes, each company was assigned a share of the national market and given annual production quotas. The codes also set maximum work hours and minimum wages. In addition, the NRA required each company to recognize a union if most of the company's employees wanted to form one. Each firm or business that complied with the NRA codes was allowed to display the NRA's Blue Eagle seal. Many individuals boycotted businesses that did not display the seal.

However, many Americans believed the NRA interfered with the free enterprise system. The agency seemed to favor big businesses over smaller ones and eliminated some competition. The consumer was caught in the middle when prices increased. In 1935 the Supreme Court declared the law that had created the NRA unconstitutional.

Another New Deal law established the **Civilian Conservation Corps (CCC)**. It put young, unmarried men (ages 18 to 25) to work planting trees, building roads, developing parks, and assisting with soil conservation projects under the supervision of the army. About three million young men worked in the CCC. The organization emphasized rigid discipline and team effort. Participants wore uniforms and marched like soldiers, carrying not rifles but shovels, rakes, and hoes.

▲ This seal was displayed by businesses that complied with the codes of the National Recovery Administration (NRA).

CIVILIAN CONSERVATION CORPS (CCC)

They planted more than three billion trees and spent millions of man-hours fighting forest fires. They built more than 420,000 dams, improved old parks and built new ones, constructed or improved miles of trails and roads, and completed more than 46,000 bridges. They earned thirty dollars a month, twenty-five of which was sent home to support their families. The CCC lasted from 1933 until a few months after America entered World War II in late 1941, when most young men were called into the armed forces.

The CCC hired almost three million jobless youths. They were sometimes called the "Tree Army" or "Soil Soldiers." The camps were directed by army officers. Extracurricular activities were mostly oriented toward sports, especially boxing.

Rising time was usually 6:00 a.m., and lights out typically occurred at 10:00 p.m. Camp food had the flavor of army meals and included plenty of potatoes and bologna. For most of its participants, the time spent was rewarding and character building. Hard outdoor work kept them busy.

The CCC's conservation emphasis gave meaning to their efforts. Sending money home to their families gave them added purpose. The Civilian Conservation Corps was perhaps the most popular New Deal program—even Republicans praised it.

▼ Members of the CCC working in Idaho

▲ Workers at a TVA project

In May 1933, Congress established a permanent New Deal agency that had long-range objectives. The **Tennessee Valley Authority (TVA)** involved public projects in seven southeastern states where the Tennessee River and its tributaries were located. The agency eventually built thirty multipurpose dams to produce electricity, control flooding and erosion, and create waterways that could be navigated. It also manufactured fertilizer and established recreation areas. Because the federal government used the TVA to act in areas where it had never been involved before and to compete directly with private companies, the TVA was controversial.

Americans were generally pleased that the new president was taking firm action to deal with the Depression. If one measure did not work, Roosevelt quickly tried another. His actions, however, did not bring a real economic recovery to the nation, and millions of people were still in need. Roosevelt continued experimenting with new programs, hoping they would solve some economic problems. In 1935 he launched the Works Progress Administration (WPA). That agency employed over eight million people between 1935 and 1943. Many worked on construction projects that built hospitals, schools, parks, playgrounds, and airports.

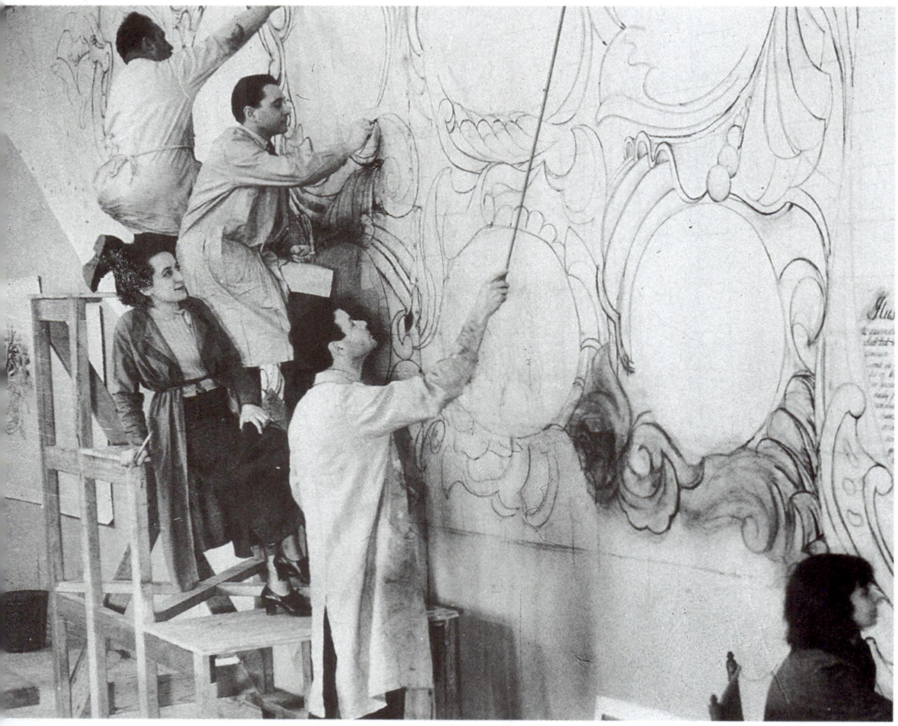

▲ Artists employed by the WPA creating a mural

Later FDR extended the WPA into other areas, including the arts. Actors and directors were hired to perform programs. Authors were hired to write historical and geographic guides for the forty-eight states. Artists were paid to paint murals in public buildings, such as post offices, and to create posters, sculptures, paintings, and other works of art. Some people said the WPA was involved in "made-work"—unnecessary jobs done with mediocre efforts. Critics remarked that the organization's initials actually meant, "We Piddle Around" or "We Poke Along."

SECTION REVIEW 22.3

1. Why was FDR easily elected in 1932?
2. What is the purpose of the FDIC? What is the protected dollar amount as of 2008?
3. How were the HOLC and FCA similar? How did they differ?
4. Do you think the AAA was beneficial? Why or why not?
5. What did the NRA do that made some people believe it interfered with America's free enterprise system?
6. Whom did the CCC employ? What types of work did they accomplish?
7. What agency's goal was to produce electricity along a major river and involved seven states?

22.4 THE NEW DEAL CONTINUES

What were the effects of the New Deal?

GUIDING QUESTIONS

- Who were the leading critics of the New Deal?
- How did President Franklin Roosevelt win the 1936 election?
- Why did the New Deal decline in popularity?
- What were the results of the New Deal?

Critics of the New Deal

Although Roosevelt won the presidency with a large popular vote in 1932, many people opposed him, especially conservatives. Under the New Deal, the government took control of many areas once reserved for private businesses or individuals. Conservatives distrusted such governmental control, fearing the government would intrude into even more areas. The New Deal gave federal officials wide powers over industry and commerce. Conservatives believed that government was assuming too much power and that Roosevelt's agencies were replacing capitalism (private ownership and private operation of businesses and property) with government regulations.

▲ FDR pours billions of dollars into a pump, hoping it will produce a plentiful supply of water. The cartoon implies that the New Deal was not working as intended.

Some liberals who advocated increased government control also opposed FDR. Whereas conservatives believed government was assuming too much control, liberals thought that the New Deal's programs were not doing enough. Some even believed that the government should own certain industries or provide people with a guaranteed income. Some critics suggested radical plans to redistribute wealth (taking wealth from the "haves" and giving it to the "have-nots"). They won many supporters.

One liberal critic was Dr. **Francis Townsend**, a retired doctor from California, who designed a plan to help the elderly. His plan required the government to pay each person over sixty years old a $200-a-month pension. The money for the pensions would come from a national sales tax. To receive pensions, retirees had to agree to hold no job and spend every cent of their pensions each month. Townsend thought such spending would help provide jobs and strengthen the economy.

Dr. Francis Townsend ▸

Did you know?

After shooting Huey Long, Dr. Carl Weiss was immediately shot more than sixty times by Long's bodyguards.

Another opponent of the New Deal was **Huey Long**, a masterful politician (and, according to some people, a virtual dictator) from Louisiana. He called himself the Kingfish. He was easily recognized by his white suits, pastel shirts, flamboyant ties, and popular oratory. When he was governor of Louisiana, Long built thousands of miles of paved roads. He also provided textbooks for children and greatly increased funding for Louisiana State University. Long wanted to confiscate wealth by heavily taxing large incomes. He intended to use this money to provide a minimum annual income of $2,500 for every American family. Long promised to make "every man a king" with his "Share Our Wealth" plan. Originally a supporter of FDR, Long became an outspoken critic after being elected to the US Senate. He was ambitious to be president and had written a book entitled *My First Days in the White House*. Long seemed to be stealing some support from Roosevelt prior to the 1936 election, but the rise of the Louisiana Kingfish ended suddenly with his assassination in September 1935.

A third liberal critic of FDR was Father **Charles Coughlin**, a Roman Catholic priest in Detroit. He turned his weekly radio program of sermons into a national political broadcast. At one point, over thirty million people were listening to his broadcasts. By 1934, he was telling his huge audience that the nation needed to coin large amounts of silver, thereby inflating the money supply. He wanted the government to take over the nation's banks and several important industries, including railroads (which had been returned to private control after World War I). He called for significant increases on taxes on the wealthy.

Huey Long (above) and Father Charles Coughlin (below) were two of the best known critics of the New Deal.

None of FDR's New Deal programs were as radical as those proposed by Townsend, Long, and Coughlin. However, the rise of these critics helped motivate Roosevelt to introduce more government programs. One of Roosevelt's new proposals, passed by Congress in 1935, was the **Social Security Act**. It provided unemployment insurance (temporary pay for people who had lost their jobs) and a monthly pension, or check, for most retired individuals. The plan was funded by a federal tax on wages. Both employers and employees would pay a portion of the required tax.

▾ Social Security card

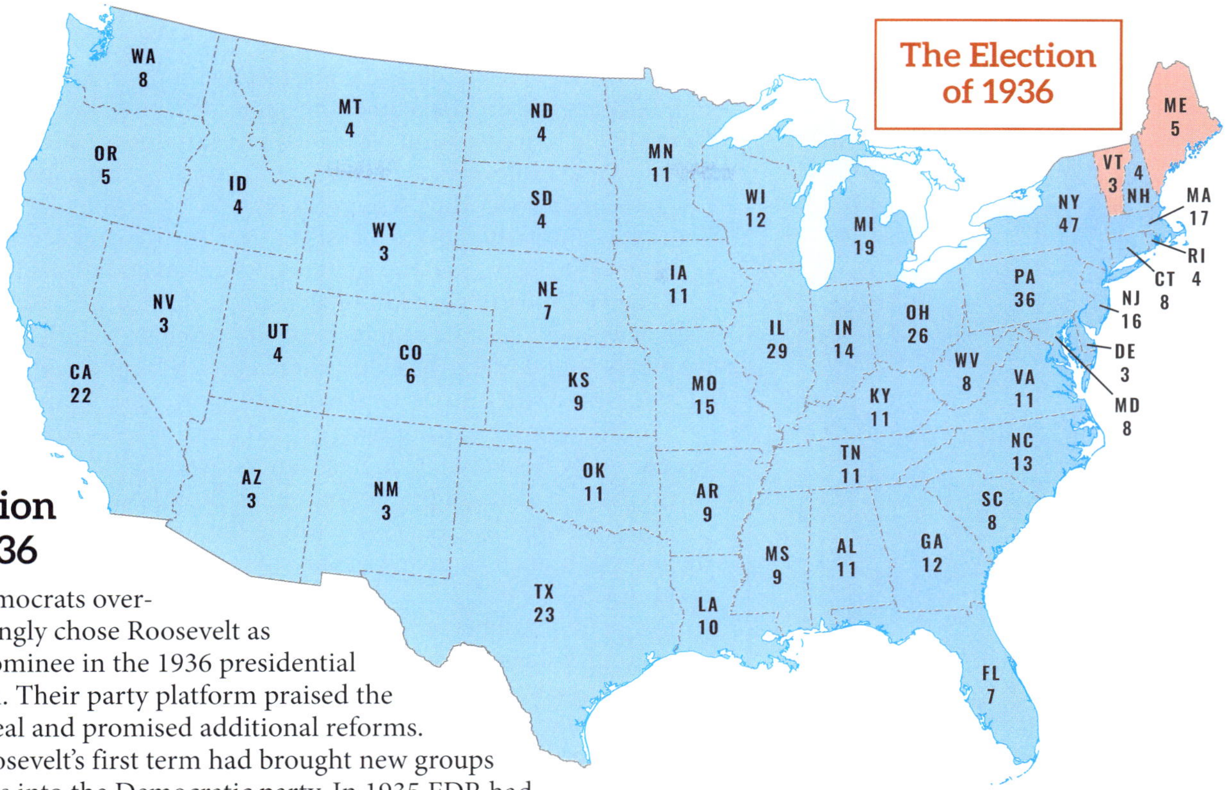

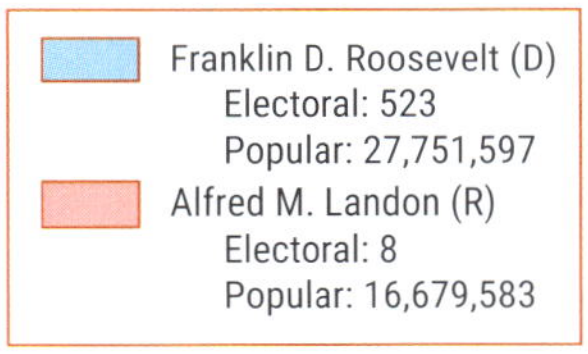

The Election of 1936

Democrats overwhelmingly chose Roosevelt as their nominee in the 1936 presidential election. Their party platform praised the New Deal and promised additional reforms.

Roosevelt's first term had brought new groups of voters into the Democratic party. In 1935 FDR had created the National Labor Relations Board. This group provided government support for labor unions' efforts to bargain, strike, and boycott in order to gain concessions from employers. Roosevelt's endorsement of those measures made the Democratic Party popular with union members. The Depression hit the poor especially hard. Many poor people were very grateful for the New Deal's financial relief and believed Roosevelt's programs had saved them from starvation. As a result, many of these people tended to vote for Democratic candidates for decades.

Also during Roosevelt's presidency, large numbers of African Americans shifted their support from the party of Abraham Lincoln to the Democratic Party. The New Deal was of special importance to black Americans. The program's public works projects offered them jobs with the same wages that white people received. Although black people were not allowed to work with whites and although Roosevelt refused to support civil rights legislation, African Americans believed that the president was moving things in the right direction for them. And they found Eleanor Roosevelt, FDR's wife, an outspoken defender of black rights. In the election of 1936, more than 70 percent of black voters supported Roosevelt. Roughly the same percentage had voted for Hoover in the previous election.

The Republicans had lost heavily in the congressional elections of 1932 and 1934. They lacked a leader and a program to attract voters, so a presidential win in 1936 was unlikely. Their candidate was Alfred M. Landon, who had been a progressive governor in Kansas. Using the phrase "America Is in Peril," Republicans criticized the New Deal for overthrowing traditional ways and betraying its promises to the American people.

Although Landon campaigned hard, he carried only two states, Maine and Vermont. Roosevelt beat him by over eleven million votes. The Congress elected in 1936 was also heavily Democratic.

WHAT NEXT?

▲ In this cartoon, FDR (dressed as a homemaker) watches as the Supreme Court takes away some of his programs. Notice that the AAA and NRA are among those being removed.

The Declining Popularity of the New Deal

Roosevelt's reelection and congressional support encouraged him to challenge the makeup of the Supreme Court. Because the Court had declared several New Deal measures unconstitutional, FDR became more critical of the Court's conservative nature.

In February 1937 he presented a plan to "pack" the nine-member Supreme Court with new justices. For each justice over seventy who did not retire, he wanted the right to appoint an additional justice, up to a maximum of six additional justices. The Court could potentially have a total of fifteen members. Roosevelt argued that the new members would make the Court more efficient. Apparently his real motive was to add justices who would support his programs.

For the first time, Congress rejected a major legislative proposal supported by Roosevelt. Congress saw Roosevelt's plan as a serious threat to the balance of power among the three branches of government. Increasing the Court's size would limit the independence of the judicial branch by giving the president more power to control that branch.

As FDR began his second term in 1937, the nation still faced enormous challenges. In his second inaugural speech, he said, "I see one-third of a nation ill-housed, ill-clad, ill-nourished." Conditions worsened later that year when the nation experienced another sharp economic decline—a depression within the Depression. Many gains that had been made by the New Deal were wiped away. The government was pumping billions of dollars into the economy and plunging the nation deeper into debt, only to find the recovery from the Depression was now facing a major setback. The stock market dropped, unemployment increased, and industrial production declined.

An 18-year-old mother, an Okie who moved to California, is shown with her young child. ▶

CARING *for the* NEEDY

In America, Christians sometimes disagree about the role that government should have in helping the poor. The Mosaic law (the law God gave to Moses to govern the nation of Israel) provides some lessons for us. It stipulated ways that the people of Israel should assist those in need. It required:

- 10 percent tax be stored every three years to provide for the Levites and the poor (Deut. 14:28–29).
- people to leave some food in their fields and vineyards for the poor to harvest (Lev. 19:9–10; Deut. 24:19–21; Ruth 2).
- farmers to leave their fields vacant every seven years and allow poor people to gather whatever grew there naturally (Exod. 23:10–11).
- a way for those in debt to work off their debts within a reasonable timeframe (Deut. 15).

Of course, the modern world is not the same as ancient Israel. Although times have changed, biblical principles, like the following, still apply when deciding the government's role in helping those in need.

First, the Bible recognizes that there is a role for government to help the poor. Mosaic laws were structured so such assistance would encourage, rather than discourage, work.

Second, other God-ordained institutions should provide help. The family is called to care for its own, and the church must assist its truly needy members (1 Tim. 5). Today, many Christian charities and mission organizations also minister to the needy outside the church.

Third, the Bible recognizes that the wealthy, including prosperous employers, sometimes treat the poor unjustly (Prov. 22:16; James 5:4). This is condemned multiple times in the Bible (Prov. 22:22–23; Deut. 24:14). Because one of the chief roles of government is to ensure justice, governments have the responsibility to address injustices through the legal system.

Did the New Deal properly care for those who were needy? What should Christians think of the New Deal? Were the programs beneficial and effective? Were the regulations, laws, and new government agencies an acceptable means of handling the problems of the Great Depression? Or did they begin a pattern of costly government intervention that often made people dependent on the government? Americans have debated the advantages and disadvantages of the New Deal for decades. A Christian analysis should be based on the application of biblical teachings and standards.

▾ Food being distributed outside St. Peter's Mission in New York City

▾ The biblical character, Ruth, gleaning in a field

Results of the New Deal

By 1939, after six years of New Deal programs, the United States had still not recovered from the Depression. Prices for farm products were still low. Overall production and profits by industries lagged far behind 1929 levels. The stock market had not reached pre-Depression levels. Unemployment exceeded 17 percent; more than nine million Americans were still out of work.

Because of its massive spending, the New Deal left the country with record-setting debt. The national debt in 1933 was $22 billion. In 1939 it was $40 billion. The New Deal also brought long-term changes. Under Roosevelt, the size and power of the federal government greatly increased.

▲ In what year was unemployment the highest? In what year was it the lowest?

Was the New Deal a success or failure? Critics argued that it shifted an emphasis from individual responsibility to a reliance on federal government involvement. Although private businesses were still the heart of economic activity, the government had assumed a major role in providing for individual needs. Because farmers and industrial workers had received special help, others would now appeal to the government for aid when new crises occurred. Opponents of the New Deal also expressed great concern about the rapidly increasing national debt.

Supporters of the New Deal pointed to its successes. Business profits and farm prices were higher than they had been in 1933. Unemployment was down from its 1933 high of 25 percent. Annual per capita income had risen from $678 in 1933 to $925 in 1939. Electricity had been extended to many rural areas, and public works projects had improved buildings and parks and encouraged conservation. Many who defended the New Deal argued that its greatest achievement was restoring people's faith and confidence in America. Roosevelt and his programs, they said, offered hope for people who were in crisis.

Though Americans endured enormous challenges during the Great Depression, they continued to enjoy the blessings of living in a free nation and electing their public officials. Many countries around the world were suffering their own depressions at this time. In some nations, dictators used these depressions to overthrow democratic governments. This rise of dictators led to World War II.

SECTION REVIEW 22.4

1. Who were three famous critics of the New Deal who asserted that it did not go far enough?
2. What three groups did Roosevelt's first term bring into the Democratic Party? Why?
3. Why did Congress reject Roosevelt's court-packing plan?
4. What occurred in 1937 that showed pumping millions of dollars into the economy was not as successful as had been hoped?
5. Do you think the New Deal was a success or a failure? Why?

CHAPTER 22 REVIEW

Making Connections

1. What was Black Tuesday?
2. How did German war reparations affect the Depression?
3. What was the percentage of Americans unemployed by 1933?
4. What had happened to the lands of the Great Plains that turned them into the Dust Bowl?
5. The Reconstruction Finance Corporation approved the creation of how many banks?
6. How did General Douglas MacArthur remove the Bonus Army?
7. Why was FDR unable to walk?
8. How many states did FDR win in 1932? in 1936?
9. What legislation paid farmers to destroy crops and livestock?
10. What did Francis Townsend suggest as a solution to the problems of the Depression?
11. How did Huey Long want to "share the wealth"?
12. What did Father Charles Coughlin encourage for economic recovery?
13. Why did FDR want to increase the number of justices on the Supreme Court?
14. How did the New Deal affect the national debt and the federal government?

Thinking Critically

15. Some people believed that the Depression was God's judgment on the loose morals of the 1920s. What do you think?
16. Is the Social Security program, established during the New Deal, a benefit to the nation? Explain your answer.

Living as a Christian Citizen

17. What principles should a Christian use in deciding whether to borrow money (use Prov. 22:7, 26–27; Eccles. 5:5; and Luke 12:15)?
18. Did the new regulations and government agencies of the New Deal effectively care for those who were needy? Pick an agency and evaluate it according to biblical principles of caring for the needy. Suggest improvements if applicable.

▲ This family traveled from place to place in California seeking work harvesting crops. The children sit atop the family's belongings.

Terms to Remember

- stock-market crash
- Great Depression
- speculation
- buy on margin
- Smoot-Hawley Tariff
- Hoovervilles
- Dust Bowl
- dole
- Reconstruction Finance Corporation (RFC)
- deficit spending
- Bonus Army
- Franklin Delano Roosevelt (FDR)
- New Deal
- bank holiday
- fireside chats
- brain trust
- Federal Deposit Insurance Corporation (FDIC)
- Agricultural Adjustment Act (AAA)
- National Recovery Administration (NRA)
- Civilian Conservation Corps (CCC)
- Tennessee Valley Authority (TVA)
- Francis Townsend
- Huey Long
- Charles Coughlin
- Social Security Act

CHAPTER 23

World War II

▾ This picture of American marines raising the flag on the island of Iwo Jima is one of the best-known photos of World War II.

As Americans struggled to overcome the hardships of the Great Depression, they watched troubling events happen overseas. Many Europeans were suffering from economic depressions and great political turmoil. They seemed willing to surrender their freedoms to dictators who promised to solve their problems. In addition, Japan and the United States increasingly disagreed over trade issues. Events in both Europe and Asia soon reached a boiling point. Once again, the world faced a devastating war.

GUIDING QUESTIONS

- How did Italy, Japan, and Germany increase in power?
- How did Americans view foreign issues?

23.1 STORM CLOUDS GATHER

How did the Axis nations increase in power, and how did America respond?

Americans who fought in World War I were told they were fighting a "war to end all wars." But in less than twenty-five years, Americans were back on battlefields in not only Europe but also the Pacific region. Many conditions led to the conflict that began almost before the guns of World War I had cooled.

The peace settlements after World War I satisfied few of the participants. Most countries did not get all they wanted from victory, or they lost too much in defeat. Some of this dissatisfaction led to the rise of three strong, imperialist countries in the 1930s—Italy, Japan, and Germany.

Italian Fascism

Italy was disappointed after World War I. It had joined the Allied side during the war rather than helping its former allies, Germany and Austria-Hungary. Afterward, it did not receive the lands it had anticipated. In addition, postwar Italy suffered many economic and political problems.

In 1922 **Benito Mussolini**, leader of the Fascist Party, seized power. His followers called him Il Duce (the leader). Mussolini advocated **fascism**, a political and economic system that promoted extreme nationalism and placed great emphasis on militarism. Fascism opposed communism and believed that private property should be allowed but heavily regulated. Once in power, Fascists implemented **totalitarianism** (a system of government that regulates every aspect of life).

Mussolini made many changes. He started military groups across Italy. Most notable were his Black Shirts, bullies who ensured that his ideas were enforced. The school system was dedicated to teaching young people their duty to the government. Mussolini maintained popular support by building efficient railroads and major highways, providing houses and lands for thousands of peasants, and making other improvements. Although he denied many freedoms to the people, he promised to restore the pride of a bygone era by establishing a "Second Roman Empire." Such promises initially caused his followers to rank him with Julius Caesar.

Benito Mussolini forced fascism on the people of Italy and tried to revive the glory of the country by establishing an empire.

◂ A chieftain in Ethiopia prepares to lead his villagers to fight Italy's military.

Mussolini began building his foreign empire in 1935. Italian soldiers crossed the Mediterranean and attacked the African country of Ethiopia. Tribesmen with spears and rifles faced Italy's modern military. The world watched in horror. The League of Nations condemned Italy and banned the sale of some materials to that nation, but neither the League nor any individual nation provided military assistance to Ethiopia. That failure made Mussolini bolder. He withdrew Italy from the League, and on April 7, 1939, his forces invaded Albania. Again, the world did nothing.

▴ Japanese soldiers are capturing Chinese land.

Japanese Militarism

Japan's industrial and military power had been growing since the turn of the century. Military leaders steadily gained control of the government. They believed that Japan deserved greater recognition as a world power. They wanted to increase Japanese power in China and throughout East Asia and the Pacific. They convinced the Japanese people that the United States threatened Japan's growth and that Japan should take control of the trade and resources of East Asia.

After World War I, the League of Nations had assigned Japan to govern some of Germany's Pacific islands. In 1931 Japan fortified the islands, then invaded and took control of Manchuria, a northern region of China. The League of Nations condemned the conquest of this resource-rich area but took no other action. Japan merely withdrew from the League. Since no American possessions in the Pacific were yet threatened, the United States reacted by slightly strengthening its defenses in the Philippines. In 1937 the Japanese expanded beyond Manchuria by attacking the remainder of China.

Italian and Japanese Expansion

German Nazism

Germany was the country most upset by the World War I peace agreements. The Treaty of Versailles placed all the blame for the war on Germany and stripped the country of its strong army, some of its land, and its colonial possessions. The treaty also forced Germany to make large payments to the Allies as reparations. Humiliated by those terms and having difficulty paying, Germany struggled through the 1920s. In the midst of the downcast German people arose a man who promised renewed greatness for Germany.

Adolf Hitler denounced the Treaty of Versailles as unjust, blamed the Jews for Germany's problems, and declared the superiority of the German race. Hitler also led the National Socialist German Workers' Party, or the **Nazi Party**. Like Mussolini's Fascist Party, the Nazis promoted fascism. Hitler denounced communism (which Germans greatly feared at that time) and proposed a strong, organized Germany that would become a powerful leader in the world. His book, *Mein Kampf* (*My Struggle*), clearly revealed his racial views and desire to expand Germany's territory; however, few who read the book took it seriously.

▲ Adolf Hitler became the German leader in 1933.

At first, many Germans paid little attention to Hitler. Supporters called him the Führer (the leader) and believed his claim that he would build the Third Reich (empire), which would last for a thousand years. They believed that he would restore Germany to its rightful place in the world. Those Germans enthusiastically accepted the promises Hitler made in his speeches. In addition to these hopes for restored German greatness, Nazi rallies generated great excitement with music, speeches, and elaborate pageantry. Some people continued to mistrust Hitler, but their influence was not strong enough to reverse his power.

As economic depression deepened in the early 1930s, German despair grew. Riding the wave of dissatisfaction, Hitler and the Nazis were swept into power. Hitler became the German chancellor (equivalent of prime minister) in 1933 and was soon given the powers of a dictator. Later that year, he withdrew his country from the League of Nations.

In 1936 Hitler openly violated the Treaty of Versailles by sending troops into the Rhineland near France. He also organized German men and boys into groups for military training. In addition, he ordered German scientists to develop new weapons. Hitler's power and ambition soon threatened world peace.

In October 1936 Mussolini and Hitler signed an agreement that became known as the Rome-Berlin Axis (named for the capitals of their countries), forming the **Axis powers**. Japan joined the Axis powers in a 1940 pact known as the Rome-Berlin-Tokyo Axis. All three nations had totalitarian governments.

Axis Powers

Germany
Italy
Japan

▼ This huge Nazi rally occurred in the city of Nuremberg, Germany, in September 1936.

▲ This poster emphasized a policy that was very different from what Theodore Roosevelt had advocated.

American Foreign Policy

The United States recognized the growing powers of Mussolini, the Japanese military leaders, and Hitler. Some viewed them as threats to world peace. But the isolationism of the 1920s still prevailed in the 1930s. Most Americans were more concerned about domestic problems than foreign affairs. They hoped that the peace pacts signed by major nations and the limits established by naval treaties in the 1920s would discourage war. Though not a member of the League of Nations, the United States hoped the League would help prevent wars. It proved unable to do so.

President Franklin Roosevelt wanted the United States to take a major role in foreign affairs. But he had little popular support as Americans were coping with the Great Depression. Thus, he could do little about the trouble brewing overseas. He made progress, however, in US relationships with the countries of Latin America. Continuing what President Herbert Hoover had initiated, FDR instituted the "**Good Neighbor Policy**." This approach meant that instead of marching into Latin American countries with a big stick when troubles arose, as Theodore Roosevelt had done, the United States let those countries handle their own affairs. Those nations had grown tired and suspicious of US intervention, so the Good Neighbor Policy did much to improve relations with them in the 1930s.

SECTION REVIEW 23.1

1. Who led the Fascist Party in Italy? What countries did he invade in the 1930s?
2. Why do you think the world did nothing as Mussolini began conquering lands?
3. What part of China did Japan conquer?
4. Who led the Nazi Party in Germany? Into what area did he send troops in 1936, violating the Treaty of Versailles?
5. What three countries comprised the Axis powers?
6. What word describes American attitudes on foreign policy during the 1930s?
7. What was FDR's foreign policy toward Latin America? How did it differ from Theodore Roosevelt's "big stick" policy?

23.2 WAR ERUPTS

What occurred in World War II before the United States entered?

In the late 1930s, the world watched as Hitler began his conquest of European territory. His actions eventually made France and Britain realize that they had to take action against him.

GUIDING QUESTIONS

- How did Germany expand in the 1930s?
- What occurred during the early years of World War II in Europe?
- How did Americans react as the war progressed?

Hitler Takes Land

Other nations did not attempt to stop Hitler from violating the Treaty of Versailles, so Hitler continued to disregard it. In 1938 he proposed uniting Austria (a German-speaking land) with Germany. Though the Treaty of Versailles specifically prohibited this action, foreign powers did nothing, and Hitler accomplished his goal without firing a shot.

Hitler next focused on the Sudetenland, an area that bordered Czechoslovakia. That region contained about a million Czechs and three million Germans. Hitler claimed that the Germans there were being mistreated and demanded that the area become part of Germany. He promised that this would be "the last territorial demand [he had] to make in Europe." He secretly ordered his military to invade Czechoslovakia if he did not gain the Sudetenland peacefully by October 1, 1938.

In September 1938 Hitler, Mussolini, Neville Chamberlain (the British prime minister), and Édouard Daladier (the French premier) met in Munich, Germany, to discuss Hitler's demands. At the Munich Conference, both Chamberlain and Daladier continued to follow a policy of **appeasement** (yielding to demands of an aggressor in order to preserve peace). They agreed that Hitler could have the Sudetenland if he promised to leave the remainder of Czechoslovakia alone. Chamberlain returned to Britain proclaiming that this meant "peace for our time." One of the few leaders who protested against the agreement was **Winston Churchill**. As a leading member of Parliament, he warned Chamberlain, "You were given the choice between war and dishonour. You chose dishonour and you will have war." Within two years Churchill replaced Chamberlain as prime minister. By that time, Germany and Britain were at war.

A few months after the Munich Conference, in March 1939, Hitler openly violated his promise and annexed the remainder of Czechoslovakia. Public outrage over Hitler's betrayal forced the British and French leaders to act. Anticipating Hitler's next move, they promised to protect Poland and Romania if those nations were attacked; nevertheless, Hitler soon focused on taking control of Poland. Regarding Britain and France, he said, "Our enemies are little worms, I saw them at Munich."

Hitler did worry that Russia would protest his actions. (In the 1920s Russia had officially become the **Union of Soviet Socialist Republics [USSR]**, also called the Soviet Union.) Hoping to prevent a war with Russia, Hitler and the USSR leader, **Joseph Stalin**, signed a nonaggression pact (an agreement to not attack each other) on August 23, 1939. It was valid for ten years. Since fascism and communism so strongly opposed each other, the agreement was stunning. Secretly, the two nations also agreed that the USSR could

▾ Neville Chamberlain waved the agreement signed at the Munich Conference and proclaimed that there would be peace with Germany.

▴ Winston Churchill denounced Chamberlain's appeasement ideas.

▲ German troops march in Warsaw, the capital of Poland, to celebrate their victory over that country in September 1939.

control the Baltic nations (Lithuania, Latvia, Estonia), a slice of eastern Poland, and parts of Finland and Romania. In exchange, Hitler would invade Poland from the west. The stage was set for World War II to begin.

Blitzkrieg!

On September 1, 1939, Hitler launched a massive attack on Poland. This date is now considered to mark the start of World War II. Sixteen hundred Nazi aircraft bombed military and civilian targets while 1.5 million German soldiers marched across the Polish border. Divisions of panzers (armored vehicles) moved into action. The swift assault was called a **blitzkrieg** (lightning war). Within forty-eight hours, the brave Polish defenders had suffered 100,000 casualties, but they continued to resist for several weeks. During that time, the Soviet Union attacked Poland from the east. The fall of Poland was complete before the month ended.

On September 3 Britain and France declared war on Germany. They became known as the **Allies**, or Allied powers, but they were hesitant and unable to provide much help to Poland. They fought little for the next eight months as they prepared their armies. Americans watched with growing concern yet did nothing. In their minds, it was not their problem. In late November, the Soviet Union invaded Finland.

Then on April 9, 1940, Hitler's forces invaded Denmark and Norway. On May 10 Hitler staged another blitzkrieg, sending his soldiers into Belgium, the Netherlands, and Luxembourg. None of the nations Hitler attacked was able to stand against his military.

Following World War I, France had built the Maginot Line, a series of heavy fortifications with extensive underground bunkers. The Germans bypassed this defensive line by moving into France through the Ardennes Forest. Britain rushed soldiers and equipment to help France, but the Allied army of approximately 400,000 men was forced to retreat to northern France. By late May, the men were trapped near the port of Dunkirk, surrounded by the German army. The German navy moved to block any escape across the English Channel, and the German air force, the Luftwaffe, was given the task of destroying the Allied armies at Dunkirk.

▼ Allied troops evacuating from Dunkirk, a port in northern France

But bad weather kept German planes from bombing the trapped soldiers. The British rushed all available boats to Dunkirk. Approximately 850 vessels—fishing boats, steamers, yachts, even lifeboats—evacuated the Allied troops. Fishermen, dockworkers, merchants, and farmers helped ferry the armies across the channel to safety. They had to leave behind almost all the armies' weapons, vehicles, and equipment. In what some have called the "Miracle of Dunkirk," about 338,000 soldiers were rescued.

On June 10 Mussolini declared war on France and Britain and attacked southern France. On June 14, 1940, German soldiers entered Paris. The next week, France surrendered. The fall of France stunned the world and left Britain on the brink of destruction.

▲ German troops triumphantly entered Paris on June 14, 1940. France surrendered a few days later, on June 22.

The Battle of Britain

After France surrendered, Britain stood alone against two European dictators. Several weeks earlier, Winston Churchill had become the new British prime minister, and the fate of Britain rested on his leadership. Most people expected the Germans to invade and conquer the British Isles. In fact, Hitler planned to do just that. His Operation Sea Lion called first for the Luftwaffe to gain control of the skies by devastating the British Royal Air Force (RAF). Next, the Luftwaffe would bomb port cities and beaches in preparation for the final phase—the landing of troops along the coast.

But the Luftwaffe experienced stiffer opposition than expected from British fighter planes. Hitler ordered devastating bombing raids on English cities, including the capital, London. Many of those attacks targeted civilians and were designed to break the British will to resist. The German bombing began in July 1940 and gained intensity through October. The RAF fought courageously to protect Britain. With the shortage of pilots, RAF pilots sometimes made as many as five flights a day to defend their homeland. Their efforts prevented the fall of Britain.

During the **Battle of Britain**, as the air battle during the summer and fall of 1940 was called, the British destroyed almost twice as many German planes as the RAF lost. Radar, superior aircraft, and brave pilots made this possible. Surprised at the results, in late 1940 Hitler indefinitely postponed his intended invasion of Britain; however, German bombing continued.

▼ RAF pilots rush to their airplanes during the Battle of Britain.

Operation Barbarossa

Hitler was in a stalemate with Great Britain, but he was winning elsewhere. He controlled Hungary and Romania by the end of 1940. Turkey signed a treaty of neutrality with Germany. In 1941 Hitler swept into southeastern Europe. Bulgaria, Yugoslavia, and Greece joined the list of Axis victims.

Hitler then made a decision that would have tremendous consequences. He ordered his armies to attack the Soviet Union. Hitler took this major step partly because he distrusted Stalin and wanted to crush Russia before Russia attacked him. Furthermore, he needed Soviet resources—particularly oil and agricultural products. Hitler ignored warnings from his generals that opening another front, or battleground, in the East was unwise. They knew expanding the war into the Soviet Union late in the summer could be dangerous. But on June 22, 1941, Operation Barbarossa, the blitzkrieg against the Soviet Union, began. Hitler thought this surprise attack would defeat the Soviets in just a few weeks.

At first, the Russian people accepted Hitler's armies as relief from the terrors of Stalin's Communist rule. But they soon learned that the Nazis were not friends. Germans devastated Soviet towns and tortured Russian civilians. In response, the Russians began to practice a "**scorched earth" policy**. Under this strategy, retreating Russians burned their crops and killed their livestock rather than leave them for German soldiers. Supplies that the German army had hoped to capture were gone. The farther the Germans advanced, the longer their supply lines stretched, requiring more time and manpower to provide their armies with food and equipment.

By mid-October, German troops were only forty miles from Moscow. In four months, they had killed, wounded, or captured millions of Russians. The autumn days grew shorter, and temperatures grew colder; yet Hitler refused to stop the offensive and wait until spring for further action. He did not want to give Stalin time to strengthen Russia's defenses. German soldiers marched on with only their summer uniforms and with their vehicles using oil unsuitable for winter. A century before, Napoleon had been in a similar situation and had found the Russian winter far more dangerous than the Russian troops. As the freezing Soviet winter closed in, Soviet troops attacked Hitler's cold and weary forces, breaking through German lines. The Germans were forced into a limited retreat. Though the Russian military and the Russian winter kept Hitler from defeating the Soviet Union in 1941, the invasion was far from over. Intense fighting resumed in the spring of 1942, and German troops would continue combat in Russia for more than two years.

▾ In late 1941, German troops advanced in the snow toward Moscow. Russians used the scorched earth policy, as they had done when Napoleon invaded in 1812.

▲ Young men volunteering to serve in the US Navy

American Sympathies and Fears Grow

After World War I, most Americans desperately wanted to avoid involvement in another war. Congress in the mid-1930s reflected these feelings by passing Neutrality Acts that prohibited selling weapons and making loans to nations at war. After intense debate, Congress made a number of changes with the Neutrality Act of 1939. It provided that warring nations could purchase weaponry from the United States—but only on a cash basis. It further stipulated that buyers must transport the weapons in their own ships. This "cash-and-carry" policy aided England, which had a large navy.

Americans watched events in Europe with increasing alarm. The European dictators had made it clear that they opposed any form of democratic government. Americans generally opposed Hitler and wanted the Allies to win. However, most Americans wanted to avoid direct participation in the war. The America First Committee, which included such prominent members as Charles Lindbergh, and other organizations pleaded for American neutrality.

In 1940 Congress passed a military draft. The draft required young men ages twenty-one to thirty-five to register for possible military service. Some 375,000 men were drafted and started training to be ready for a possible attack. But since the armistice in 1918, America had not been concerned about maintaining a strong armed force. So drafted soldiers had to train with old or substitute equipment until new items were available.

The presidential election of 1940 proved to be historic. For the first and only time in American history, a president was elected for a third term. Roosevelt won reelection partly because he promised to keep Americans out of a foreign war (war not directly involving the United States).

By 1941 Roosevelt decided that Britain desperately needed more help. He sought a way for the Allies to obtain vital war equipment from the United States more easily. Congress complied by approving the **Lend-Lease Act** in March 1941. That act allowed the president to send equipment to any nation in which such equipment might support American defense. Rather than paying for the equipment with money, the recipient countries could pay with services, equipment, or property, such as land. In this way, the United States received land for seven air bases throughout the British Empire in exchange for war supplies sent to Britain. More than $50 billion in supplies was eventually given to Allied countries; over $31 billion was sent to Britain and over $11 billion to the Soviet Union.

▼ Woman in Britain carrying American rifles obtained through the Lend-Lease Act

▲ The Flying Tigers patrolled the skies over China and Burma to combat the Japanese there.

Americans slowly realized that Germany and Italy were not their only causes of concern when Japan joined the Axis powers and began pursuing an empire in Asia. The United States sent China one hundred fighter planes. Claire Chennault, a retired army air force captain, served as an advisor to the Chinese air force. He helped organize a group of volunteer civilian pilots known as the American Volunteer Group (AVG), nicknamed the Flying Tigers. Although always outnumbered, the Flying Tigers became a formidable foe of Japanese pilots, downing almost three hundred Japanese planes in the seven months the group existed. After the United States entered World War II, the AVG became part of the US military. Chennault rejoined the army with the rank of colonel.

Japan's decade-long domination of China expanded in the summer of 1941 when it seized oil fields and rubber plantations in French Indochina (present-day Vietnam, Laos, and Cambodia). Roosevelt responded by stopping the sale of gasoline and other important resources to Japan. He also froze all Japanese accounts in US banks, making it impossible for them to withdraw money. The Japanese, though, had more plans for expansion. With Britain being pounded by the Luftwaffe and the Netherlands under Nazi occupation, the Japanese eyed the resource-rich British and Dutch colonies of the Pacific. First, however, the Japanese would have to deal with the chief naval threat remaining in the Pacific—the United States.

On October 17, 1941, General **Hideki Tojo** became the prime minister of Japan. Though the nation had an emperor, Hirohito, he had little political power. In late November, Japanese diplomats arrived in Washington for negotiations. Meanwhile, Japanese aircraft carriers were sailing across the Pacific.

▼ Hideki Tojo was the Japanese prime minister from October 1941 until July 1944.

SECTION REVIEW 23.2

1. What lands did Hitler claim in the 1930s before the beginning of World War II?
2. Why do you think the British and French leaders chose a policy of appeasement concerning Hitler's demands?
3. With what major power did Hitler make a nonaggression pact? Why did he do this?
4. What is "blitzkrieg"? What countries was Hitler able to conquer in late 1939 and early 1940?
5. How did the RAF defend Britain from German attacks during the Battle of Britain?
6. Why was Germany not able to conquer Russia?
7. How did countries involved in the war "pay" America for equipment under the Lend-Lease Act?

23.3 AMERICA ENTERS THE WAR

Why did the United States enter World War II?

GUIDING QUESTIONS

- What happened at Pearl Harbor and how did America respond?
- How did America prepare for war?

Pearl Harbor

Shortly before 8:00 a.m. on Sunday morning, December 7, 1941, planes from Japanese aircraft carriers in the Pacific bombed US naval and air bases at **Pearl Harbor**, Hawaii. Within two hours, the Japanese sank or damaged eight battleships and thirteen other warships. American air power in Hawaii was crippled as over three hundred aircraft were damaged or destroyed. The two-hour attack took a heavy toll in American lives as well, with 2,403 killed and about 1,200 wounded.

The surprise attack prompted Roosevelt to address Congress the next day, requesting a declaration of war. He described December 7, 1941, as "a date which will live in infamy" [would be remembered as a famous evil event]. Congress declared war on Japan. The Senate's vote was 82–0, and the House's vote was 388–1. (Jeannette Rankin from Montana, who had also voted against World War I, cast the only nay vote.) America was suddenly thrust into World War II. Days later Japan's allies—Germany and Italy—declared war on the United States. No longer neutral, America was directly involved in a fight against all Axis powers.

▾ The USS *Arizona* was among the numerous American ships sunk at Pearl Harbor.

A memorial was later built atop the sunken USS *Arizona*.

Dorie Miller: Hero at Pearl Harbor

Doris "Dorie" Miller worked in the kitchen aboard the USS *West Virginia*, one of the ships attacked at Pearl Harbor. His courageous actions that day led to his becoming the first African American sailor to receive the navy's second-highest award for bravery, the Navy Cross (only the Congressional Medal of Honor is higher).

After a torpedo damaged his ship, he began carrying the wounded to safety. He then manned an antiaircraft gun, for which he had no training, and continued firing until there was no more ammunition. The citation for the award says:

> For distinguished devotion to duty, extraordinary courage and disregard for his own personal safety during the attack on the Fleet in Pearl Harbor. . . . While at the side of his Captain on the bridge, Miller, despite enemy . . . bombing and in the face of a serious fire, assisted in moving his Captain, who had been mortally wounded, to a place of greater safety, and later manned and operated a machine gun directed at enemy Japanese attacking aircraft.

PRIMARY SOURCE: FDR'S REQUEST FOR A DECLARATION OF WAR

Yesterday, December 7, 1941—a date which will live in infamy—the United States of America was suddenly and deliberately attacked by naval and air forces of the Empire of Japan. . . .

Yesterday the Japanese Government also launched an attack against Malaya. Last night Japanese forces attacked Hong Kong. Last night Japanese forces attacked Guam. Last night Japanese forces attacked the Philippine Islands. Last night the Japanese attacked Wake Island. And this morning the Japanese attacked Midway Island [Guam, the Philippines, Wake Island, and Midway Island were all American possessions]. . . .

Hostilities exist. There is no blinking at the fact that our people, our territory, and our interests are in grave danger.

With confidence in our armed forces—with the unbounding determination of our people—we will gain the inevitable triumph—so help us God.

I ask that the Congress declare that since the unprovoked and dastardly [cowardly, despicable] attack by Japan on Sunday, December 7, 1941, a state of war has existed between the United States and the Japanese Empire.

—President Franklin D. Roosevelt
December 8, 1941

America Prepares to Fight

The damage inflicted by the Japanese at Pearl Harbor was severe. Fortunately, the three American aircraft carriers stationed there were at sea the morning of the attack and escaped any damage. The carriers and their warplanes would fight Japan in the coming days. Still, the United States had much to prepare for the long fight ahead.

People to Wage the War

Anger and patriotism swept the nation. Volunteers swarmed recruiting stations to enlist in the military. In all, about sixteen million Americans—more than one in ten—joined the armed forces. Americans who sincerely believed that killing was wrong registered as conscientious objectors and served in the medical corps or other noncombat roles.

In numbers greater than World War I, women joined the civilian work force, taking the places of men who had enlisted or been drafted. Posters featuring "Rosie the Riveter" were used everywhere to recruit women for work. Some women joined the Red Cross. Others worked with the United Service Organizations (USO), entertaining the troops and providing other services.

In addition, women aided the war effort in military jobs. Some served in the Women's Army Corps (WAC). Others joined the Women's Naval Reserve, or the Women Accepted for Volunteer Emergency Service (WAVES). The Women Airforce Service Pilots (WASP) helped fly aircraft from factories to the air bases where they were needed. Women were not assigned combat roles, but they did serve overseas, especially in roles that freed men to fight.

Women Airforce Service Pilots

The need for more workers during the war was a blessing to many Americans who had been struggling during the Great Depression. But at first, it looked as though black Americans would not benefit. Several manufacturing industries declared they would not hire black workers. The African American labor union leader A. Philip Randolph pressured Roosevelt to take action. As a result, FDR signed an executive order that prohibited employers who had contracts with the federal government from excluding workers because of ethnicity. This executive order was a major victory for black Americans. Black leaders also wanted the armed forces to end segregated units. Sadly, this would not happen until after the war.

▲ Women working at a factory in Pennsylvania

Japanese Americans

While African Americans gained some increased opportunities during World War II, Americans of Japanese ancestry—even those born in the United States—were moved to internment, or detention, camps. This forced relocation of 120,000 people was prompted by fear and suspicion that they would betray America. The government had no evidence that these individuals would be disloyal. Yet as a result of the government's policy, most Japanese Americans lost their jobs, homes, and farms; merchants were forced to sell their stores and merchandise at low prices. All were stripped of their rights as American citizens. Most were forced to live at internment camps located in California, Arizona, and Colorado.

But America needed every soldier possible, so beginning on February 1, 1943, Japanese Americans were allowed to enlist for military service. They trained as all-Nisei (American-born Japanese) forces. Because of lingering doubts about their loyalties due to their Japanese ancestry, most Nisei were stationed in Europe. A few Japanese Americans did work in the Pacific where they helped crack Japanese codes. By the end of the war, 33,000 Nisei had served in uniform. Their military units were among the most decorated in the war. Nisei soldiers received twenty-two Medals of Honor along with numerous other awards for their bravery and dedication. Unfortunately because of continued discrimination, many of these were not awarded until long after the war had ended.

▼ Japanese Americans arriving at an internment camp in California

Fun Fact

It appears that the army's general purpose (GP) vehicle was called a "jeep" by soldiers, and the name soon stuck.

War Production and Rations

The United States entered the war without enough materials or preparation, but Americans rose to the challenge. People worked together as teams and sacrificed for the war effort. They quickly converted factories to produce war goods. For example, auto plants produced jeeps and tanks. They doubled production in less than four years. By 1945 American industry had produced more than 300,000 planes, 100,000 tanks and self-propelled guns, and 2.5 million military trucks. It had also cranked out 1.1 million rifles and carbines, 400,000 artillery weapons, and 50 billion rounds of ammunition.

Shipbuilders set to work increasing the United States' naval and merchant marine fleets. They built ships dubbed "liberty ships" at the rate of three every two days. The ships carried war materials to far-flung fronts. Aircraft carriers, destroyers, submarines, and other vessels were also built quickly.

▾ Ration books contained stamps that individuals used to buy restricted products (along with payment for the item).

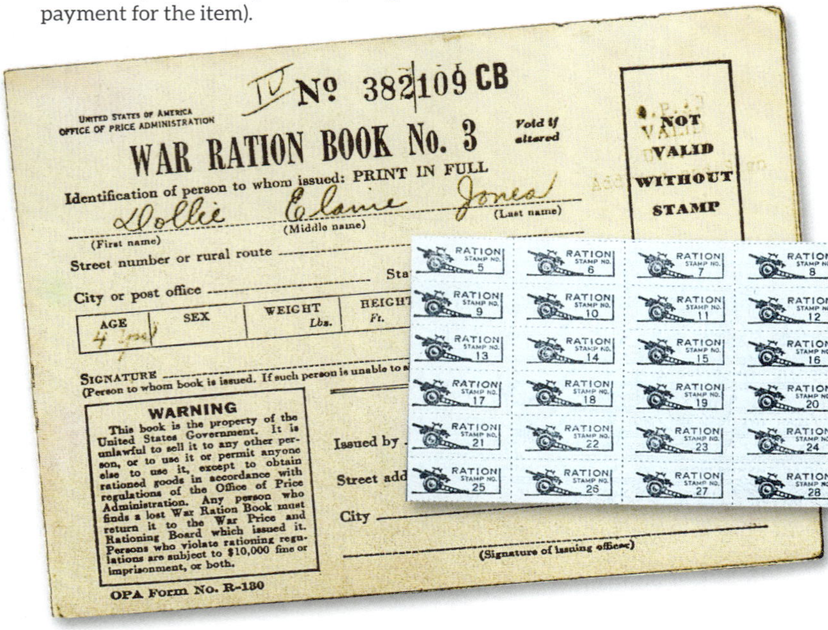

To meet the ever-increasing need for war products, Americans at home had to sacrifice. After 1942 automobiles were no longer made for private sale. With shortages and the need to preserve items for military use, the government began to restrict the use of such items as gasoline, oil, meat, butter, sugar, coffee, shoes, and most canned or frozen goods. Americans received books of ration stamps to purchase these items. **Rations** are fixed allowances of food and other items due to lack of supplies, especially in wartime. People could buy a rationed item only if they had an unused stamp for it. When scarce products were available in stores, there were often long lines to purchase them. Little was thrown away. Drives to collect tin cans, wastepaper, aluminum, and scrap iron to aid the war effort were common.

Did you know?

The then-recently created SPAM was widely used during World War II because it was a transportable meat that did not require refrigeration. It was often called "mystery meat."

Many Americans added to their food supply by planting "Victory Gardens" in backyards, along edges of parking lots, in zoos and parks, and in window boxes. By 1943 these gardens supplied Americans with a third of all their vegetables. Their efforts ensured that more food was available for the men fighting in the war. Americans also bought war bonds to help pay for the fighting.

Supply lines carrying goods to the armed forces stretched around the globe. Besides supplying its own forces, the United States provided other Allied forces with goods. President Roosevelt called the United States "the arsenal of democracy."

▲ Allied leaders meeting in Tehran, Iran (left to right): Joseph Stalin of the Soviet Union, Franklin Roosevelt of the United States, and Winston Churchill of Britain

War Strategy

As commander in chief of all the American armed forces, the president mapped the country's overall war strategy. He sought help from leading military officers, advisors, and international political leaders, including Churchill. FDR and Churchill held their first meeting secretly aboard an American destroyer off the coast of Newfoundland in August 1941, even before the United States joined the war. At later talks the Allied leaders agreed that the first priority would be to defeat Nazi Germany because the Germans were the biggest threat. Once Hitler was defeated, the Allies would focus on defeating Japan.

In other meetings, Allied leaders discussed other military strategies and how to deal with the problems they would face after the war. At Casablanca, Morocco, in January 1943, the Allies decided to invade Europe first through Sicily and Italy.

The Russians had joined the Allies after Hitler's attack. At the Allied leaders' November 1943 meeting in Tehran, Iran, Stalin joined Roosevelt and Churchill. Since Germany had defeated France, most of the fighting was taking place in the east between the Germans and the Soviets. Stalin urged the other leaders to invade northern Europe to take pressure off his troops. They promised Stalin a second European front would be opened in mid-1944 when the Allies invaded western Europe (the first front was Russia fighting the Germans). In return, Stalin promised that the Soviet Union would help defeat Japan once the Allies had defeated Hitler.

Allied Powers

Britain
France
Russia
United States

SECTION REVIEW 23.3

1. What prompted America to finally join the war?
2. Why was Japan's surprise attack on December 7, 1941, not a complete victory?
3. How did women serve in the military during World War II? How did civilian women help the war effort?
4. How did America treat Japanese Americans after the attack on Pearl Harbor? Why was this unjust?
5. How were American factories used during the war?

GUIDING QUESTIONS

- How did the war progress in North Africa and Europe?
- What was the Holocaust?

▾ British military vehicles in the North African desert

23.4 WAR IN NORTH AFRICA AND EUROPE

How did the Allies succeed in North Africa and Europe?

Invading North Africa

Early in the war, Italian forces controlled the deserts of North Africa. The British, however, defeated the Italians in early 1941 and threatened to drive them out of Africa altogether. But the British triumph was short-lived. They had exhausted their resources and soon faced Germany's General Erwin Rommel, whom Hitler had sent to take command of the German forces in North Africa. Rommel organized his soldiers, known as the Afrika Korps, to fight the British.

With a superb military strategy that earned him the nickname Desert Fox, Rommel pushed back the British. By swift and clever maneuvering, he seemed ready to drive all the way into Egypt and capture the Suez Canal. But the British fought back, and battle lines in North Africa shifted across hundreds of miles in 1941 and 1942.

In November 1942 Allied troops landed in northwestern Africa and began to push east toward Libya. This offensive was named Operation Torch and was commanded by General **Dwight D. Eisenhower** (or "Ike," as his men called him). Meanwhile, the British drove west from Egypt. The Allies crushed the Axis forces between them. Some soldiers escaped to Europe, but 240,000 surrendered to the Allies in May 1943. The Axis powers had been defeated in Africa.

Invading Italy

The invasion of Italy began with an attack on the Italian island of Sicily. In Operation Husky, three thousand ships and landing craft carried troops and equipment to Sicily in July 1943. Despite heavy casualties, the Allied forces defeated the Italian army and forced the German army off the island. By the end of the summer, Sicily was an Allied base from which the Allies could invade Italy.

Italy's king had removed Mussolini from power shortly after the Allies attacked Sicily. When Allied soldiers landed on the Italian mainland in September 1943, Italy surrendered and then declared war on Germany. However, the Germans refused to recognize the surrender and fought furiously to stop the Allied advance north. Germany declared that Mussolini was still the Italian leader, and he "ruled" from northern Italy rather than Rome.

The Allied push to capture Rome was slowed by Germans entrenched in the mountains. The Allies finally marched into Rome on June 4, 1944. Most Romans viewed the conquest of their city as a deliverance. Despite the successful capture of Rome, the Italian campaign was far from over. Intense, deadly fighting in northern Italy continued because of tough Nazi resistance. The campaign continued for another eleven months.

▲ American soldiers leave their boats to begin the invasion of Normandy, France, on D-day (top). Over the next few days, US ships brought massive amounts of military equipment and other supplies to Normandy (bottom).

Invading France

As noted earlier, the Allied strategy called for opening a second European front after invading Italy. In England, Eisenhower—as supreme Allied commander, with help from American General Omar Bradley and British General Bernard Montgomery—began planning a huge offensive. The Allies would land in northern France and begin their march toward Germany in what was called Operation Overlord. The Allies assembled men and equipment in southern England while bombing Germany almost continuously, day and night.

In the predawn hours of June 6, 1944, more than 20,000 Allied paratroopers and soldiers in gliders began landing behind German lines in Normandy, France. This was "**D-day**," the beginning of Operation Overlord. At the same time, the largest amphibious (land and sea) invasion force in history moved across the English Channel. Over 150,000 troops headed toward the beaches of Normandy while the Allied air forces provided air protection. Before the attack began, Eisenhower told the Allied soldiers, "You are about to embark upon the Great Crusade, toward which we have striven these many months. The eyes of the world are upon you. The hopes and prayers of liberty-loving people everywhere march with you." The invasion marked the beginning of the end of the war in Europe.

American soldiers landed on beaches code-named Utah and Omaha. The British and Canadians landed on nearby beaches code-named Juno, Gold, and Sword. German defenses were strong and Allied losses heavy, but the Allies began to push inland, yard by yard and mile by mile.

▼ American soldiers man an antiaircraft gun in a snowy churchyard in Belgium in late 1944. Later the Battle of the Bulge occurred in the region.

On August 25, after a grueling, three-month battle, the Allies liberated Paris from German control. Another Allied army landed in southern France, opening new ports and supply bases. Those troops quickly joined the forces in northern France. By the end of 1944, France, the Netherlands, and much of Luxembourg and Belgium had been freed of German control. The three-million-man Allied force was at Germany's border.

But in mid-December, the Germans suddenly launched a major counterattack into Belgium in an attempt to recapture lost territory and divide the Allied forces. The thrust created a "bulge" fifty miles deep into the Allied lines, giving the battle its name—the **Battle of the Bulge**. By Christmas Day, the Germans had captured thousands of troops and surrounded American forces in the city of Bastogne. When the German commander ordered the American commander, General Anthony McAuliffe, to surrender his outnumbered army, the defiant American sent a one-word reply—"Nuts!"

The fighting continued, and the German attack began to falter. Eventually, additional American troops relieved the weary soldiers in Bastogne. By late January 1945, the Allies were once again pushing the German troops back toward Germany.

▲ Jewish women and children, wearing the yellow stars required by Nazis, arrive at a concentration camp.

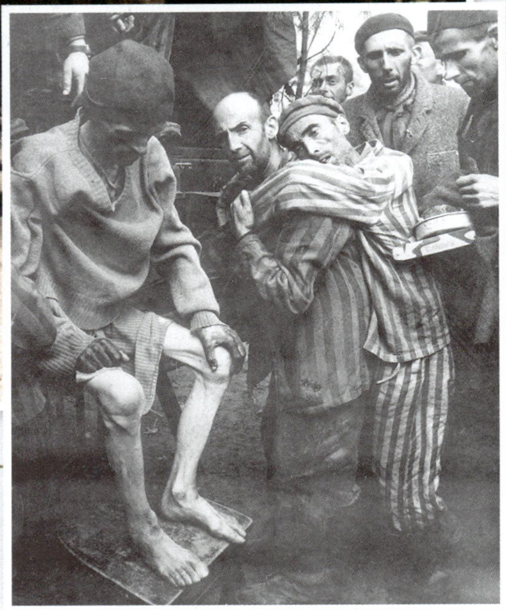

Prisoners at one of the camps being freed in May 1945 ▶

the HOLOCAUST

As Allied forces freed Europe from Nazi rule, they encountered unexpected horrors. They found evidence in Nazi prison camps of mass murder. The astounding massacre of millions of people became known as the **Holocaust**.

Nazis believed in the doctrine of German superiority over all other "lesser" [inferior] peoples. Nazis began to control, isolate, and exterminate "undesirable elements" in Germany and the countries they conquered. Undesirables included political opponents, Jews, Russian prisoners of war, Poles, the Roma (also known as Gypsies), the disabled, religious leaders who disagreed with Hitler, and others. However, Jews had Hitler's special attention.

The first concentration camp opened in Dachau, Germany, in March 1933—less than two months after Hitler became the German leader. Two weeks later, the German parliament began passing laws regarding Jews. Eventually, these laws included forcing Jewish government workers to retire, excluding Jews from the army, revoking citizenship rights for Jews, and requiring Jews to wear yellow triangles or stars of David.

The Nazis encouraged Germans to boycott all Jewish businesses. On November 9, 1938, Nazis vandalized thousands of Jewish businesses, destroyed hundreds of synagogues, and robbed, shamed, and arrested thousands of Jews across Germany. That night is called Kristallnacht (Crystal Night), "the night of broken glass."

In May 1940 the Nazis opened a concentration camp at Auschwitz, Poland, and began transporting thousands of Polish Jews there by train in filthy, unheated, and overcrowded cattle cars. As the war progressed, Hitler ordered the "Final Solution" to be implemented—the mass extermination of all Jews.

Execution in gas chambers was commonly used to implement the Nazi plan. After guards expelled the gas with ventilators, other prisoners removed the bodies and pulled any gold fillings from the teeth before shoving the bodies into ovens for cremation.

Concentration camps and extermination camps existed across Nazi-controlled areas. The most notable ones were in Germany, Poland, and Austria. Auschwitz, Bergen-Belsen, Ravensbrück, Buchenwald, Dachau, Treblinka, Sobibor, Belzec, Chelmno, Mauthausen, and other such camps each revealed their own gruesome secrets. One American soldier related that, as troops neared Dachau, they "could smell the camp from at least five miles away."

An estimated 6 million Jews alone were killed. Combining this number with the number of non-Jews killed, an estimated 11 to 17 million "undesirables" died at the hands of the Nazis.

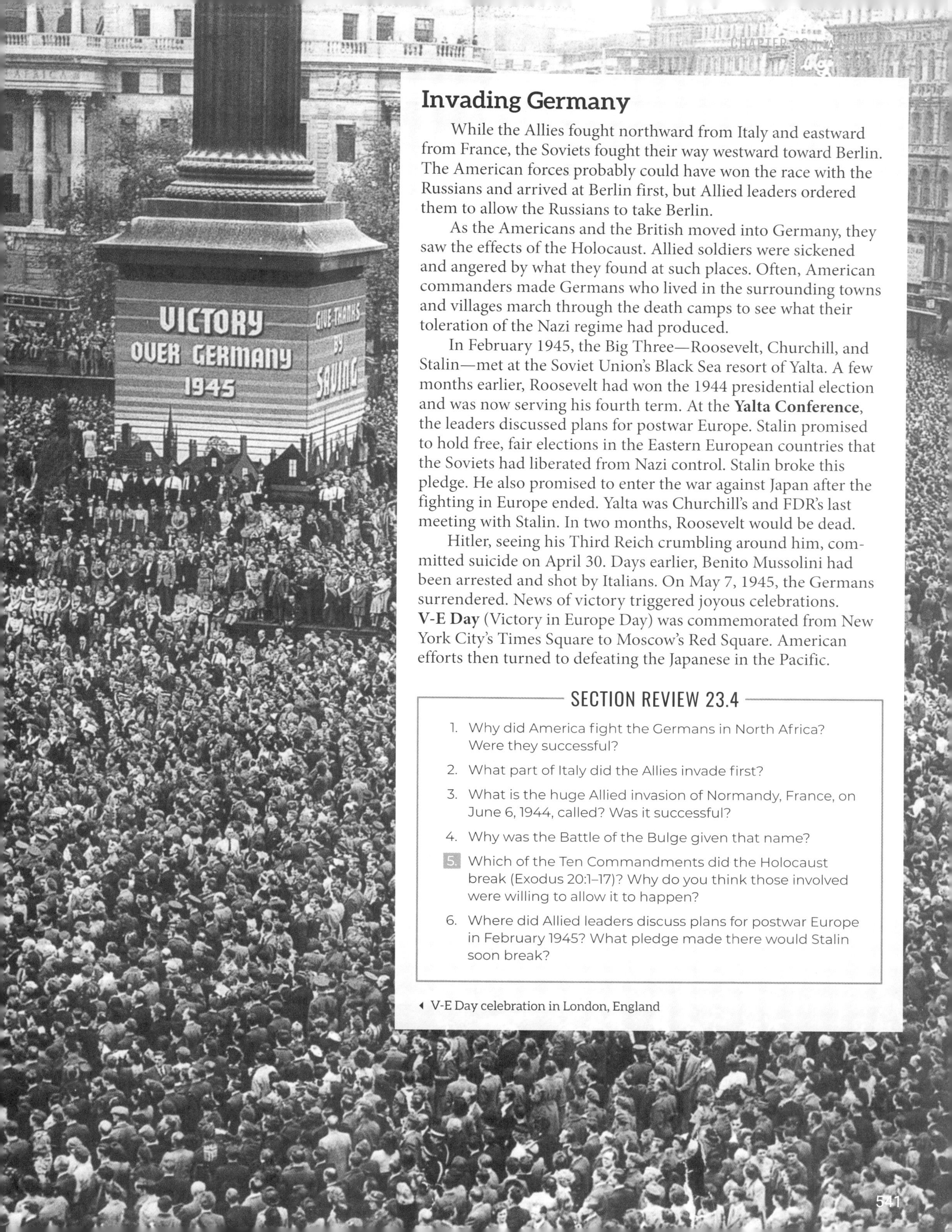

Invading Germany

While the Allies fought northward from Italy and eastward from France, the Soviets fought their way westward toward Berlin. The American forces probably could have won the race with the Russians and arrived at Berlin first, but Allied leaders ordered them to allow the Russians to take Berlin.

As the Americans and the British moved into Germany, they saw the effects of the Holocaust. Allied soldiers were sickened and angered by what they found at such places. Often, American commanders made Germans who lived in the surrounding towns and villages march through the death camps to see what their toleration of the Nazi regime had produced.

In February 1945, the Big Three—Roosevelt, Churchill, and Stalin—met at the Soviet Union's Black Sea resort of Yalta. A few months earlier, Roosevelt had won the 1944 presidential election and was now serving his fourth term. At the **Yalta Conference**, the leaders discussed plans for postwar Europe. Stalin promised to hold free, fair elections in the Eastern European countries that the Soviets had liberated from Nazi control. Stalin broke this pledge. He also promised to enter the war against Japan after the fighting in Europe ended. Yalta was Churchill's and FDR's last meeting with Stalin. In two months, Roosevelt would be dead.

Hitler, seeing his Third Reich crumbling around him, committed suicide on April 30. Days earlier, Benito Mussolini had been arrested and shot by Italians. On May 7, 1945, the Germans surrendered. News of victory triggered joyous celebrations. **V-E Day** (Victory in Europe Day) was commemorated from New York City's Times Square to Moscow's Red Square. American efforts then turned to defeating the Japanese in the Pacific.

SECTION REVIEW 23.4

1. Why did America fight the Germans in North Africa? Were they successful?
2. What part of Italy did the Allies invade first?
3. What is the huge Allied invasion of Normandy, France, on June 6, 1944, called? Was it successful?
4. Why was the Battle of the Bulge given that name?
5. Which of the Ten Commandments did the Holocaust break (Exodus 20:1–17)? Why do you think those involved were willing to allow it to happen?
6. Where did Allied leaders discuss plans for postwar Europe in February 1945? What pledge made there would Stalin soon break?

◂ V-E Day celebration in London, England

GUIDING QUESTIONS

- How did the war progress in the Pacific?
- How was peace achieved in the Pacific?

▲ General Douglas MacArthur

23.5 WAR IN THE PACIFIC

What was war like in the Pacific area?

While the war in Europe was raging, Americans had also been sending men, ships, and planes to the Pacific area. The early results were discouraging. After the Japanese attack on Pearl Harbor, the Japanese military advanced across the Pacific until the Allies found ways to move from the defensive to the offensive.

Japan Advances

As FDR mentioned in his address to Congress, on the same day Pearl Harbor was attacked, Japan attacked four other American possessions in the Pacific—Guam, the Philippines, Wake Island, and the Midway Islands. The largest, the Philippines, had provided an important US base since the end of the Spanish-American War. By January the Japanese controlled Manila, the capital city. The American and Filipino troops, under General **Douglas MacArthur**, held only the Philippine peninsula of Bataan and the small nearby island of Corregidor. When FDR realized that the American forces could not withstand the Japanese assault, he ordered MacArthur to leave. FDR did not want to risk the capture of a valuable general. MacArthur reluctantly escaped to Australia by submarine. As he left, he promised the Filipinos, "I shall return."

With the Japanese controlling the area, American troops who remained in the Philippines lacked supplies and suffered from hunger and disease. They battled to defend Bataan, but their effort was not enough. On April 9, 1942, most of the troops on the Bataan peninsula surrendered to the Japanese. The Japanese forced about 78,000 US and Filipino prisoners of war to march in tropical heat, with little food or water, for sixty-five miles to a prison camp. The Japanese shot or bayoneted those who fell behind, paused for water or rest, or tried to help those who did. Approximately 10,000 prisoners died on the Bataan Death March, as it became known, one of the most brutal episodes of the war in the Pacific.

On May 6, more than 10,000 Americans and Filipino soldiers on Corregidor were forced to surrender. The Japanese now controlled all the Philippines.

Meanwhile, the Japanese captured most of Southeast Asia and many Pacific islands. In June 1942 the Japanese turned northward and captured two of the Aleutian Islands, US possessions located off the tip of southern Alaska. The Japanese seemed to control the entire region of eastern Asia and the western Pacific.

But American shipyards and factories were gradually making progress. In just fifteen months, they were able to construct and commission new aircraft carriers, battleships, and escort vessels. A stream of ships sailed west to stop and then push back the Japanese.

▼ American prisoners during the Bataan Death March in the Philippines

▾ One of the aircraft in the Doolittle raid

The Allies Push Back

In the spring and summer of 1942, the Americans saw a ray of hope in the Pacific war. On April 8 the aircraft carrier *Hornet* secretly sailed within 625 miles of the Japanese mainland. Then sixteen B-25 bombers under the command of Lieutenant Colonel Jimmy Doolittle launched from the ship and shocked the Japanese by dropping bombs on Tokyo and three other Japanese cities. The Japanese had no idea where the planes had originated. Although the **Doolittle raid** did little damage, its success was a tremendous boost to American morale and a great psychological blow to the Japanese.

Since Doolittle's planes did not have enough fuel to return to the *Hornet*, the pilots flew west over China. They hoped to land among friendly Chinese troops and return to American forces. But bad weather and other circumstances foiled the planned landings on the Chinese mainland.

Crews from eleven planes had to parachute out, and four aircraft crash-landed. Of the eighty men involved in the raid, three were killed and eight were captured by the Japanese (four of whom died in captivity). One plane landed in the Soviet Union, where the crew of five was imprisoned for thirteen months. Of the eighty raiders, sixty-four made it to safety with the help of the Chinese.

▴ Merrill's Samurai

MERRILL'S SAMURAI

Members of a special Army Rangers commando unit called Merrill's Marauders served behind Japanese lines in Burma. They were named for the unit's commander, Brigadier General Frank Merrill. Although most Japanese American soldiers fought in Europe, fourteen of them served with Merrill and became known as Merrill's Samurai. All fourteen were born in the United States and volunteered to serve in the US Army. They did everything a typical infantryman did but also translated documents, interrogated prisoners, and tapped enemy telephone lines.

Once when the outnumbered Marauders were about to be attacked, one member of Merrill's Samurai, Master Sergeant Roy Matsumoto, crept under cover of darkness to the enemy camp and listened to the Japanese as they planned their attack on the Americans. He then slipped back to his unit, warned Merrill, and helped devise a trap. When the Japanese attacked, their first wave was slaughtered in an ambush. When the second wave hesitated, Matsumoto stood and yelled in Japanese, "Attack! Attack!" Thinking his voice was that of one of their officers, the Japanese soldiers obeyed, and they too were crushed. The Marauders escaped and continued their work. Roy Matsumoto died in April 2014, a few days short of age 101.

the BROKEN JAPANESE CODE

When American decoders broke the new Japanese code, they learned of a forthcoming attack on a target the Japanese simply called "AF." Naval officers suspected that the target might be the Midway Islands. To test their hunch, they ordered personnel on Midway to send an uncoded message saying that the freshwater distillation plant at Midway was damaged. Then they monitored Japanese transmissions. They soon intercepted a Japanese message that said AF had a shortage of fresh water. Now the Americans knew where the attack was going to occur! That advance warning enabled Americans to surprise and defeat the invasion fleet, saving Midway and stopping the Japanese advance.

▲ At the Battle of Midway, the USS *Yorktown* was sunk.

With the fall of Corregidor in May 1942, the Japanese controlled a huge Pacific empire stretching from Burma to the Bering Sea (near Alaska). Yet this area proved to be the greatest extent of Japanese possessions. That month the United States faced the Japanese at the Battle of the Coral Sea. It was the first sea battle in which all the fighting was done by airplanes; the naval vessels of the opposing sides never saw one another. The American victory there stopped the Japanese advance toward Australia.

Japanese expansion was halted again at the Midway Islands, an American territory west of Hawaii, in June 1942. The **Battle of Midway** was a critical battle—considered by many as the turning point of the war in the Pacific. By breaking Japanese radio codes, the United States could intercept war messages and anticipate Japanese moves. US Admiral **Chester W. Nimitz** skillfully directed carrier forces against the Japanese. The Americans destroyed four Japanese carriers, a cruiser, and about 250 airplanes. More than 3,000 Japanese died. US losses included one aircraft carrier, one destroyer, and about 150 airplanes. Some 300 Americans died. The crucial victory at Midway, combined with the Battle of the Coral Sea, turned the tide of Japanese conquest. However, while these battles stopped the Japanese, they did not take any territory from them. The road to victory would be long and very bloody.

After the Battle of Midway, the United States prepared to take the offensive against Japan. Because it was impossible and impractical to take every island the Japanese controlled, the US commanders—General MacArthur and Admiral Nimitz—implemented a strategy called **island hopping**. It meant they would capture some islands that could be used as air strips and bases but would skip other islands. As they progressed closer to Japan, extensive bombing of the mainland would occur in preparation for an eventual invasion of that country.

MacArthur Moves North

In August 1942, US Marines landed on Guadalcanal, one of the Solomon Islands, located three thousand miles from Tokyo. The Japanese were building an airfield there from which they could bomb Allied ships. Fighting on the jungle island was intense. The Japanese fought furiously and American casualties were heavy. After several sea battles and months of fighting, Japanese troops abandoned the area in February 1943.

▼ American soldiers land at Guadalcanal.

For the next year, American forces slowly reduced the area of Japanese control in the South and Central Pacific. They also retook the western Aleutian Islands that the Japanese had occupied. Early in 1944, US troops captured the Marshall Islands and in April attacked the Japanese in New Guinea.

By October 1944, US forces were ready to retake the Philippines. They landed first on the central island of Leyte. Many liberty-loving Filipino guerrilla fighters who had hidden in the mountains and jungles helped the Americans free the Philippines. When MacArthur waded ashore, he said, "I have returned. By the grace of Almighty God our forces stand again on Philippine soil—soil consecrated in the blood of our two peoples." By March 1945, US forces had moved northward and freed Manila.

Nimitz Moves West

The first target of Admiral Nimitz's Pacific operation was Tarawa, part of the Gilbert Islands. After bombing the island for a whole week and pounding it for hours with heavy naval guns, the Americans did not expect much resistance. But the Japanese were well fortified, and they fought fiercely. American losses soared. The Japanese resisted until only 17 of the 4,500 defenders remained alive.

The battle of Tarawa taught the Americans lessons for future attacks. The Japanese did not surrender easily. It became normal to spend two months bombing before landing troops. Americans knew that their battleships, cruisers, and destroyers would have to hurl thousands of tons of explosives at Japanese defenses.

After successful invasions in the Marshall Islands, Nimitz's forces recaptured Guam. Nimitz's fleet soon moved north toward **Iwo Jima**. US Marines landed there on February 19, 1945. That small island, about 750 miles from Tokyo and consisting of volcanic rock and black sand, became the site of the toughest, costliest battle in the 170-year history of the Marine Corps. On the cave-riddled island, 70,000 marines fought against 21,000 entrenched Japanese defenders. More than 6,800 American soldiers were killed, and 20,000 were wounded before they crushed Japanese resistance. The capture of Iwo Jima allowed emergency landings for American bombers attacking Japan and a takeoff point for shorter-range fighter planes.

As the war came closer to the Japanese homeland, fighting intensified. Allied seamen came to fear a new type of Japanese attack: the **kamikaze**. Kamikazes were pilots who deliberately tried to crash their planes into enemy ships. Such attacks were a product of the Japanese belief that the highest gift one could give the emperor was one's life. In kamikaze warfare, the Japanese would load out-of-date or poorly built planes with explosives and order inexperienced pilots to fly them into ships. Direct hits were devastating. Although American antiaircraft guns stopped most of the fanatical missions, kamikazes sank or damaged over three hundred US ships in the final ten months of the war and inflicted about 10,000 casualties.

the CODE TALKERS

The US military used American Indians, primarily Navajos, to send coded messages on the battlefield during the war. They used Native American languages that the Japanese were never able to decipher. These special troops were known as "code talkers."

The original group that developed the Navajo code consisted of 29 men; more than 400 code talkers served during World War II. The last of the original 29 Navajo code talkers, Chester Nez, died in June 2014 at age ninety-three.

A kamikaze pilot prepares to attack the USS *Missouri*.

Did you know?

The Japanese word *kamikaze* means "divine wind." The term was first used in 1281 to describe a typhoon that had prevented Kublai Khan's huge Mongol navy from invading Japan.

▾ Marines use dynamite to destroy a Japanese cave on the island of Okinawa.

Okinawa was the last obstacle that the Allies faced before reaching the Japanese mainland. The assault on that island began in April 1945 and required almost three months to complete. The Japanese fought fanatically. Kamikazes launched approximately 1,500 attacks, sinking 26 US ships and damaging many others. Thousands of sailors lost their lives. In addition, the Japanese spread rumors among Okinawan civilians, telling them that Americans treated prisoners inhumanely. The Japanese encouraged (some survivors say *ordered*) civilians to commit suicide rather than surrender to the Americans. The Japanese even distributed hand grenades for that purpose. Many civilians followed their advice and blew up their entire families. Others jumped from cliffs onto jagged rocks in the sea.

After gaining control of Okinawa, the Allies were just 350 miles from mainland Japan. They could launch intensive bombing raids on Japan's military, industrial, and population centers.

Japanese Defeat

By the time Germany surrendered in May 1945, more than 400,000 Americans had been killed. Yet Japan was still undefeated. Japan's cities suffered heavily from Allied bombing raids. The American military had learned, however, how hard the Japanese fought. Many experts feared that invading and conquering Japan would cost an additional 350,000 to 800,000 American lives. To avoid that deadly price, American leaders considered using a powerful new weapon that researchers were developing.

German Jewish physics professor Albert Einstein took refuge in the United States after Hitler began persecuting Jewish people. Einstein wrote to Roosevelt in 1939, warning him that the Nazis were trying to develop an atomic bomb. He informed the president of the possibilities and dangers of such a weapon. FDR and his advisors decided to establish a secret program to make the bomb before the Germans. American officials named the top-secret operation the **Manhattan Project**.

The US government bought hundreds of acres in a remote area nestled among the high ridges west of Knoxville, Tennessee. It then built the city of Oak Ridge and gathered thousands of laborers, construction specialists, chemists, and engineers. Inside closely guarded facilities, scientists designed and assembled the secret weapon. Then they shipped it to the desert near Los Alamos, New Mexico. At dawn on July 16, 1945, the first atomic bomb was successfully tested.

Roosevelt had died suddenly from a stroke on April 12, 1945. Vice President **Harry Truman**, who had been in office less than three months, only learned about the Manhattan Project after becoming the new president. He later decided it would be better to end the war quickly by using the new weapon than to waste hundreds of thousands of lives—both American and Japanese—by invading Japan. People have debated the wisdom and morality of Truman's decision, but Truman had no doubts. He wrote in his *Memoirs*, "Let there be no mistake about it. I regarded the bomb as a military weapon and never had any doubt that it should be used."

On July 26 Truman was in Potsdam, Germany, for a conference with the other Allied leaders. Truman and the other powers issued the Potsdam Declaration, demanding that Japan surrender unconditionally or face total destruction.

Although the original military leaders in Japan's war effort were no longer in power, the new prime minister refused to surrender. Eleven days later, on August 6, 1945, at 8:15 a.m., an American B-29 bomber named the *Enola Gay* flew high above the Japanese city of **Hiroshima**. Pilot Paul Tibbets dropped a single atomic bomb nicknamed "Little Boy." The extraordinary weapon destroyed half the city in a single blast. It is estimated that more than 70,000 of 280,000 residents died that day. Tens of thousands later died from injuries and the results of radiation exposure.

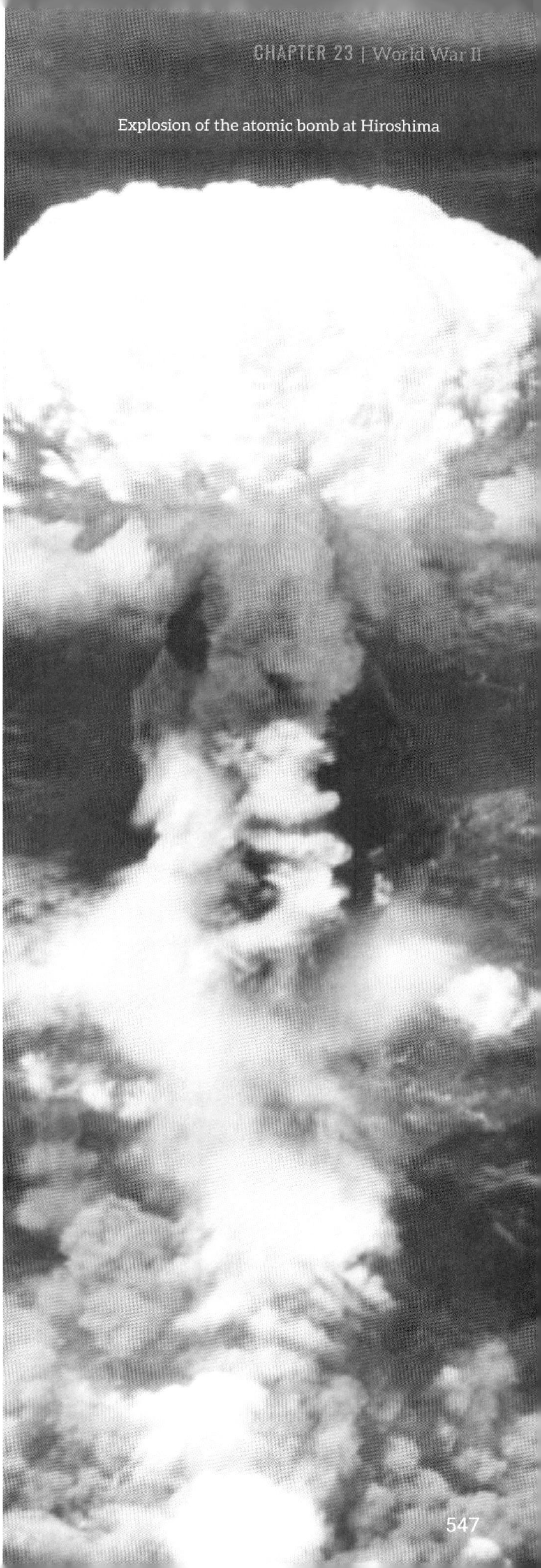
Explosion of the atomic bomb at Hiroshima

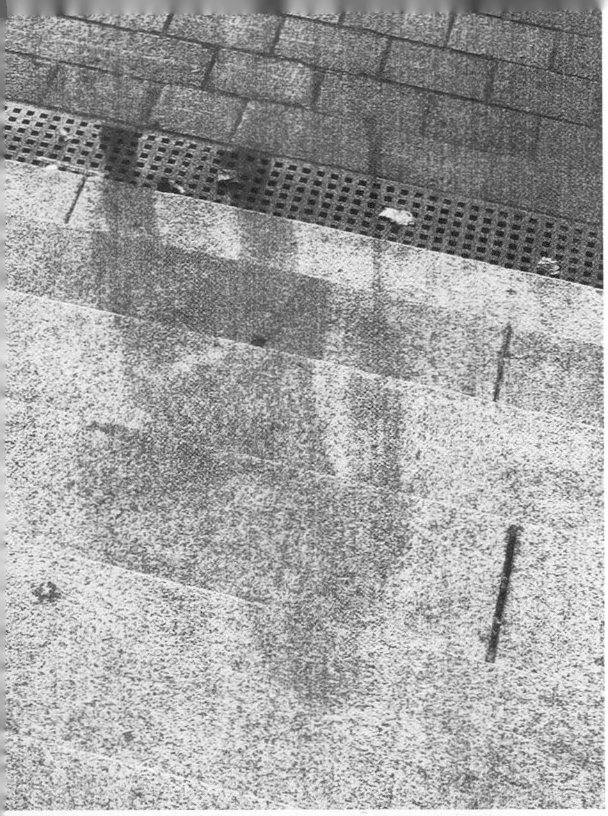

▲ A human shadow was burned into steps in Hiroshima (above). Three days later an atomic bomb was dropped on Nagasaki. The following week, Americans celebrated the announcement of Japan's surrender (bottom).

The Japanese still refused to surrender. Three days later, Charles Sweeney, piloting a B-29 named *Bock's Car*, dropped an atomic bomb nicknamed "Fat Man" on the city of **Nagasaki**. About 40,000 of the 200,000 residents were killed that day. On August 14, the Japanese finally agreed to surrender.

On August 15, for the first time the Japanese people heard the voice of Emperor Hirohito. In a taped radio broadcast, Hirohito told his subjects that the war was over. On September 2, 1945, proclaimed as **V-J Day** (Victory over Japan), the official ceremony took place aboard the USS *Missouri* anchored in Tokyo Bay. General Douglas MacArthur presided while the emperor's representatives signed the formal treaty of surrender.

War Crimes Trials

After the war, the Allies placed many leaders of the Axis powers on trial for war crimes. The leaders were accused of conspiring to commit crimes against peace, planning and waging wars of aggression, and committing war crimes and crimes against humanity.

The trials of major Nazi war criminals were held in Nuremberg, Germany. Some Nazis, such as Hitler, had committed suicide; others had secretly escaped Europe to avoid justice. Of the twenty-four defendants at the **Nuremberg Trials**, three were acquitted and released, twelve were sentenced to death, seven received sentences ranging from ten years in prison to life imprisonment, one committed suicide, and one was released before the trial actually began.

The major Japanese political and military leaders were tried before the International Military Tribunal for the Far East. Of the twenty-eight defendants, Hideki Tojo and six others were condemned to death. Most of the remaining men were imprisoned.

Thousands of additional individuals from the Axis nations who were not categorized as major leaders faced trial in the years after the war. These defendants included brutal prison camp guards and others who had implemented some of the inhumane policies of those countries.

The war was over, and Americans returned to peacetime with great relief. Despite the high price they had paid, they won the war. It then remained for them to take their place in the postwar world.

SECTION REVIEW 23.5

1. What were the conditions like on the Bataan Death March?
2. What was significant about the Doolittle raid?
3. What was the first sea battle fought entirely by airplane?
4. What do many consider the turning point of the war in the Pacific?
5. What was "island hopping"?
6. What islands were taken by MacArthur and Nimitz during this strategy of island hopping?
7. What was a "kamikaze"? Why would a Japanese fighter agree to be one?
8. What was the Manhattan Project?
9. On what two Japanese cities were atomic bombs dropped? Was this an acceptable way to end the war? Why or why not?

CHAPTER 23 REVIEW

Making Connections

1. What three nations made up the Axis Powers? Who led each country?
2. What was the Good Neighbor Policy concerning Latin America?
3. What policy did Britain and France first take in dealing with Hitler's demands? What were the results?
4. What was Russia's new name under its Communist government? What was it also called?
5. The invasion of what country on September 1, 1939, began World War II?
6. From what port were many of the Allied army rescued by many English nonmilitary boats?
7. What is the fighting between Germany and Britain during the summer and fall of 1940 called?
8. What was the German attack on Russia in 1941 called?
9. What act passed by Congress in March 1941 showed that America favored the Allied cause?
10. Who became the prime minister of Japan in 1941?
11. In what American state is Pearl Harbor located? What date was it bombed (day and year)?
12. Why were items rationed in the United States during World War II?
13. Where did American troops launch their first major attack against the Germans? Where did they invade next?
14. Who led the Allied forces in North Africa and then in Europe?
15. What date was D-day, the beginning of Operation Overlord (day and year)?
16. When was V-E Day? V-J Day?
17. How did the Allied forces move steadily closer to the Japanese mainland?

Thinking Critically

18. What should mankind learn about the temptation to appease totalitarian governments?
19. How does the common phrase "the enemy of my enemy is my friend" apply to Russia and its relationship to the other Allied countries during World War II?

Living as a Christian Citizen

20. Rather than complying with Nazi control and actions leading to the Holocaust, how should German Christians have responded (see Acts 5:29)?
21. How should the US government have dealt with Japanese Americans after the attack on Pearl Harbor? What biblical principles support your answer (Exod. 20:16; Prov. 3:30; 18:5)?

The destruction in Hiroshima after the atomic bomb was dropped ▲

Terms to Remember

- Benito Mussolini
- fascism
- totalitarianism
- Adolf Hitler
- Nazi Party
- Axis powers
- Good Neighbor Policy
- appeasement
- Winston Churchill
- Union of Soviet Socialist Republics (USSR)
- Joseph Stalin
- blitzkrieg
- Allies
- Battle of Britain
- scorched earth policy
- Lend-Lease Act
- Hideki Tojo
- Pearl Harbor
- rations
- Dwight D. Eisenhower
- D-day
- Battle of the Bulge
- Holocaust
- Yalta Conference
- V-E Day
- Douglas MacArthur
- Doolittle raid
- Battle of Midway
- Chester W. Nimitz
- island hopping
- Iwo Jima
- kamikaze
- Okinawa
- Manhattan Project
- Harry Truman
- Hiroshima
- Nagasaki
- V-J Day
- Nuremberg Trials

UNIT 7

Facing New Challenges

The presidential helicopter, Marine One, approaches the White House.

NATO founded
1949

1950

Korean War
1950–53

Brown v. Board of Education
1954

1955

Alaska statehood
1959

Hawaii statehood
1959

1960

Assassination of John F. Kennedy
1963

Civil Rights Act
1964

Gulf of Tonkin Resolution
1964

1965

1970

Roe v. Wade
1973

Resignation of Richard Nixon
1974

1975

1980

1985

1990

Persian Gulf War
1991

1995

2000

Terrorist Attacks by al-Qaeda on the United States
2001

2005

Barack Obama, first African American president, inaugurated
2009

2010

2015

Donald Trump inaugurated
2017

2020

Joseph Biden inaugurated
2021

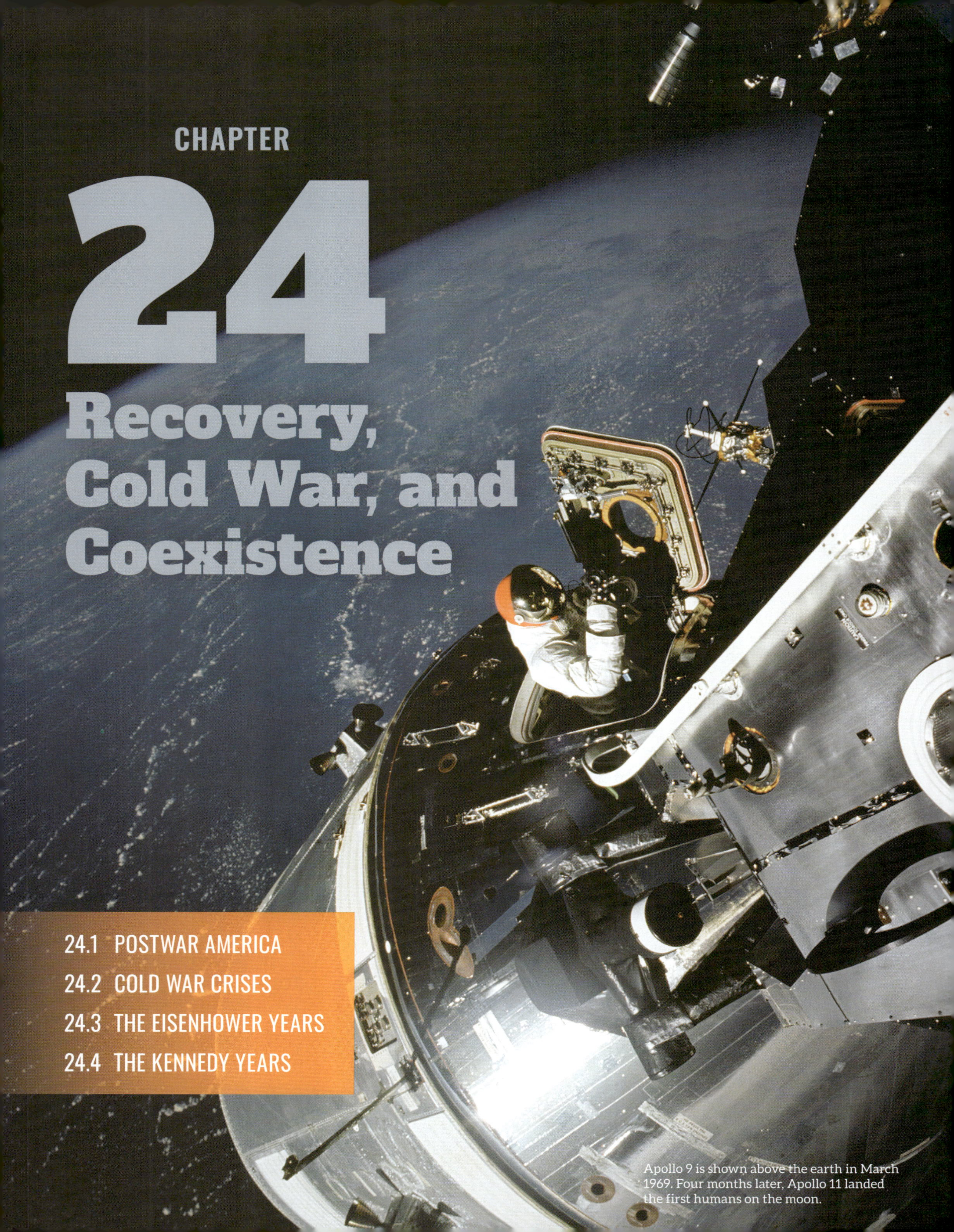

CHAPTER

24 Recovery, Cold War, and Coexistence

Apollo 9 is shown above the earth in March 1969. Four months later, Apollo 11 landed the first humans on the moon.

The years after World War II were a time of economic growth. More Americans became homeowners. This was also a time of scientific and technological advancements. Many Americans had money to buy some of the new, amazing devices being invented. These very successes caused some American thinkers to raise concerns about materialism, but other Americans celebrated the successes as signs of the superiority of American capitalism over Soviet communism.

These years were also a time in which black Americans emphasized that they still did not have the equality they had been seeking for decades. They pressed for equal treatment in schools, on public transit systems, in restaurants, and in all other parts of life. Many advances were made as African Americans began to receive more of their rights guaranteed in the Constitution.

GUIDING QUESTIONS

- What changes occurred in America after World War II?
- How successful was the civil rights movement in the 1940s?
- What was the world like after World War II?

24.1 POSTWAR AMERICA

What was life in America like after World War II?

After the war, millions who had served in the military returned to civilian life. Many Americans feared that a depression would follow the war, as had happened after World War I. Instead, America was poised to experience growth and prosperity.

Home from the War

Jobs were plentiful. Consumers wanted all the things that they had to do without during the war. Americans wanted more labor-saving devices: washing machines, power lawn mowers, cars, and boats. The easy availability of credit encouraged even more spending. Factories could not produce enough to satisfy the public. Waiting lists for high-demand products, such as cars, grew. At first, prices on many goods skyrocketed until the demand was met.

GI Bill

Fearful that soldiers returning from war would be unemployed, Congress passed the **GI Bill**. The bill helped veterans transition to civilian life by giving them many benefits. For example, it helped them find jobs and provided money for education and home purchases. Veterans enrolled in classes to complete high school, vocational school, or college in record numbers. Many attended night classes while working regular jobs.

Baby Boomers

Many young couples who had postponed getting married or having children during the war got married and started families. A "**baby boom**," a massive rise in the birth rate lasting from 1946 until 1964, soon followed. It created even more demands, which changed through the years as the children grew. A demand for housing was followed by a demand for baby-related products. When the children from the baby boom started school, there was an acute shortage of classrooms and teachers. By the mid-1960s, many of those children would be young adults, headed for college or the job market.

Average Births per Woman

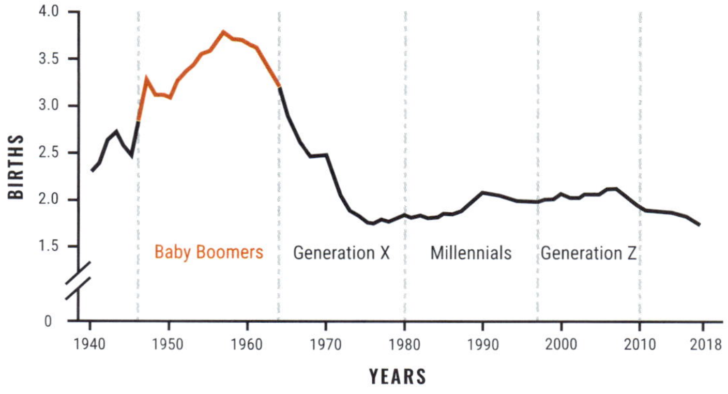

A typical suburb

A scene from *I Love Lucy*

popular **TV SHOWS** *of the* **FIFTIES**

Television of the 1950s offered a variety of programming options, from sports to drama to education. Some of the earliest sporting events featured on television were boxing matches, or "the fights."

One long-popular drama series was *Lassie* (first broadcast in 1954). An early educational series was *You Are There* (1953) in which newsman Walter Cronkite narrated famous historical events as though the viewer were present for them. Early children's programming featured *Howdy Doody* (1947) and *Captain Kangaroo* (1955).

Perhaps the most popular variety program was *The Ed Sullivan Show* (1948), which featured everything from musicians to comedians to acrobats. Westerns were also popular with early TV viewers. The top (and longest-running) westerns included *Gunsmoke* (1955) and *Bonanza* (1959). News and discussion programs included *Meet the Press* (1947) and *Today* (1952).

Undoubtedly, the most popular type of programming for all ages was comedy. Some shows, such as *I Love Lucy* (1951) and *Leave It to Beaver* (1957), are still popular reruns today.

Although some worried whether the world could sustain the increased population growth, technological advances helped make such growth possible. Scientists found other applications for war inventions and materials. They used new medicines and vaccines to treat diseases. They found that synthetic (man-made) fibers, plastics, and other new materials could be used to produce goods.

Better irrigation methods, development of hybrid crops, and improved machinery and fertilizers allowed farmers to grow more crops. Those changes in American agriculture have sometimes been called the "green revolution." The baby boom and the green revolution are examples of how the biblical commands to be fruitful and multiply and to rule over the earth can work in harmony.

Growth of Suburbs

Housing shortages and better transportation made Americans willing to move to residential areas outside cities. Contractors mass-produced homes cheaply and quickly in rows of identical houses. Rolling fields became suburbs in a few weeks or months.

Over 90 percent of those who moved to homes in the suburbs were young whites. Those left in the cities tended to be the poor, the elderly, and ethnic minorities. Cities could not collect heavy taxes from the poor, so some cities began to decay.

The number of cars increased, and with them came more gas stations, parts stores, and other automotive businesses. Shopping centers were built. Cities expanded, producing "urban sprawl." Traffic increased; more roads and highways were built. Americans became more willing to relocate to find better jobs. They were on the move, especially toward the South and the Southwest. This migration was known as the "Sun Belt migration."

Television

Technology affected leisure time. In 1946 only seven thousand television sets were sold. By 1950 millions were sold each year, and almost 20 percent of American homes had one. By 1960, 90 percent of American homes had a television set. Television tended to decrease regional differences. Americans from the North, South, East, and West watched the same programs and the same commercials. Some Americans worried that the new mass culture of television was shallow. They argued that it provided only limited exposure to classical music, art, and great works of literature and philosophy. They feared that since television now occupied so much American leisure time, American society would be affected by what critics believed was the emptiness of many television programs.

Marketers and advertisers seized television as an opportunity to earn profits. For instance, stores sold many Davy Crockett lunch boxes, coonskin caps, and buckskin jackets because of the popularity of a Disney show about Crockett.

▲ A family watching television in the 1950s

Religion

Church attendance grew in both theologically liberal and theologically conservative churches. In 1940 less than half of Americans were church members; by 1960, the number had jumped to 65 percent. Roman Catholicism grew in acceptance. The number of Catholics in America by 1960 was about forty-two million, approximately one-quarter of the population.

While conservative churches grew during this period, many adopted organizational structures based on successful American businesses. Careful teaching of biblical doctrine became less prominent in a number of these churches, even though the gospel was preached.

According to many Americans, belief in God or in religion was a good thing. They thought that this belief set Americans apart from the "godless Communists." In 1954 Congress added the phrase "under God" to the pledge of allegiance. Two years later, Congress mandated that the phrase "In God We Trust" be printed on all paper currency (it had appeared on most coins since the Civil War). The motion picture industry recognized the trend and produced movies with religious themes, such as *The Ten Commandments* (1956) and *Ben-Hur* (1959).

The study of psychology became popular and was reflected in some liberal preaching and writing. For example, Norman Vincent Peale, a prominent liberal minister, wrote about positive self-esteem in his best-selling book *The Power of Positive Thinking* (1952).

In summary, the 1950s and early 1960s were a religious time, but many Americans lacked real understanding of spiritual matters and principles. An emphasis on self and materialism were common.

▼ *The Ten Commandments*, a popular movie, was released in 1956. Actor Charlton Heston, shown on the screen at the drive-in theater below, portrayed Moses.

After the 1948 election, Truman proudly displays the premature headline that said Dewey had won.

The Fair Deal

People wondered whether Harry Truman would continue FDR's New Deal policies. Their wondering ceased when Truman presented Congress with a domestic program that was later called the **Fair Deal**. Through the program, Truman proposed increased aid to science and public education, subsidized medical insurance, and plans for creating jobs and building homes. As was true of the New Deal, it expanded the federal government's role in the lives of American citizens.

Laborers wanted higher wages. Auto, steel, coal, and railroad workers resorted to strikes in their efforts to obtain them. As the number of strikes increased, some people thought that unions had gained too much power.

The Republican-controlled Congress passed the Taft-Hartley Act of 1947 over Truman's veto. The act limited union powers. For example, it outlawed the closed shop, a practice that forced businesses to hire only union members. It also allowed states to prohibit unions from requiring workers to join a union within a certain date of their hiring. It further stated that if a planned strike threatened national health or safety, a court could mandate an eighty-day "cooling off" period. During this time, striking was prohibited, and the workers and management would attempt to settle their dispute through negotiations.

When Truman faced the voters in the 1948 election, prospects for victory looked dim. Though he was the Democratic nominee, the party was split. Many liberal Democrats formed the Progressive Party (different from the one that had nominated Teddy Roosevelt in 1912) and nominated Henry Wallace. Wallace had been FDR's vice president from 1941 to 1945 and afterward was a member of the cabinets of both FDR and Truman. However, he had been very critical of Truman's presidency. Conservative southern Democrats, upset over Truman's support of civil rights for black Americans, formed the States' Rights Party. That group, commonly known as "Dixiecrats," nominated Governor Strom Thurmond of South Carolina. Republicans chose **Thomas Dewey**, the popular governor of New York, as their candidate.

With the Democrats split, pollsters (individuals who take opinion polls) predicted Dewey would be the sure winner. But Truman waged an aggressive campaign, traveling across America and making speeches from the rear of a railroad car. The public apparently admired his fighting spirit. Truman's determination and his idea of giving a "fair deal" to the American people helped him win the election.

Harry S. Truman

33

Born	May 8, 1884
Died	December 26, 1972
Home state	Missouri
Wife	Bess Wallace
Church	Baptist
Occupations	clerk, farmer, soldier
Party	Democrat
Years served as president	1945–53
Terms	2
Vice presidents	1st—none 2nd—Alben Barkley

The Quest for Civil Rights

The term *civil rights* refers to the rights of every citizen to receive equal treatment under the law. The issue of civil rights has stirred debate since the time of the Constitutional Convention. However, despite the guarantees of the Constitution and the brave service of black soldiers in the military, African Americans were still denied many of their civil rights at the time World War II ended. Their struggle for equality became known as the **civil rights movement**.

Congress rejected much of Truman's civil rights legislation, but the president kept trying to reduce discrimination against black Americans through the influence of his position.

Both the North and the South practiced segregation. As mentioned in Chapter 19, Jim Crow laws in the South segregated black people from white people in restaurants, schools, theaters, public transportation, and many other places. Black people and white people usually could not drink from the same water fountains, and typically, black people had access only to inferior accommodations. In the North, although not required by law, black Americans were segregated. In a practice known as redlining, a bank might refuse to offer mortgages for homes located in minority neighborhoods. Some white neighborhoods had rules that prevented black families from living there. Some real-estate agents agreed among themselves to not sell houses in white neighborhoods to black families. This practice effectively segregated school districts as well. Some businesses refused to serve black people, and other businesses avoided locating their shops in black neighborhoods. Whether by law or practice, these forms of discrimination made it very difficult for black Americans to rise to the middle and upper classes, even during a time of great prosperity.

▲ Segregated movie theaters, such as this one for African Americans in Leland, Mississippi, existed throughout the South.

Changes came slowly. As mentioned in the last chapter, during World War II, FDR had ordered the federal government to not contract business with any firms that discriminated against minorities. Truman continued that policy. In 1946 he also formed a committee, the President's Committee on Civil Rights, to investigate instances of alleged discrimination and to propose measures to strengthen and protect civil rights.

Truman risked his reelection in 1948 by supporting efforts to end discrimination against black Americans. First, he called for an investigation of alleged discrimination in the military. Second, he asked Congress to pass laws against lynching and against the poll tax (which was active in some southern states). Third, he called for an end to discrimination by employers and unions alike and an end to discrimination in public transportation. Fourth, he ordered a ban on segregation in the armed forces. Fifth, he was the first president to campaign openly for black votes in Harlem.

Not all of Truman's proposals were adopted. Furthermore, many thought his actions did not go far enough. But his ideas were radical

Jackie Robinson signs autographs.

for the period. On Election Day, Truman's victory was due in part to his receiving two-thirds of the black vote.

In 1949 Truman made civil rights history. He appointed William Hastie to the Third Circuit Court of Appeals. As a result, Hastie held the highest judicial post by a black American up to that time. Truman also appointed blacks to several high-ranking administrative jobs. For example, Edward Dudley was the first black ambassador from the United States when named the ambassador to Liberia.

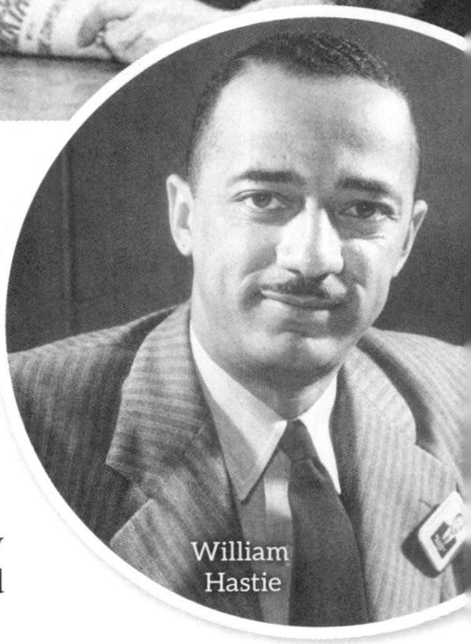
William Hastie

Other changes in society helped continue the end of segregation. In 1947 **Jackie Robinson** became the first African American to play major-league baseball when the Brooklyn Dodgers signed him as their second baseman. Slowly, more colleges began admitting black students. The University of Oklahoma admitted blacks to its graduate school in 1948.

The Postwar World

During World War II, the Big Three—Roosevelt, Churchill, and Stalin—discussed the idea of a postwar peacekeeping body when they met at Tehran and at Yalta. On April 25, 1945, Truman welcomed delegates from fifty nations to San Francisco. The result of the conference was a charter for a new organization, the **United Nations** (UN).

The United Nations

The US Senate ratified the UN charter in 1945 by an overwhelming margin. Eventually, the United Nations established its headquarters in a newly constructed building in New York City.

Jackie Robinson

Professional sports, like most areas of American life before the 1950s, were racially segregated. Baseball was no exception. The best white players joined the major league teams in the National and American Leagues. Black players participated in leagues of all-black teams. However, Jackie Robinson broke the color barrier in 1947 when he signed a contract to play with the Brooklyn Dodgers. Owner Branch Rickey warned Robinson that he would face racial prejudice and even violence. Robinson did, but he controlled his temper and refused to retaliate.

Instead, Robinson let his playing speak for him. That won him the respect of teammates and opponents. In his accomplished ten-year career with Brooklyn, he batted above .300 in six seasons, won the Most Valuable Player award in 1949, and played in six World Series.

Robinson ended his career with a lifetime batting average of .311. In the process, he had opened the door for scores of other talented black players who would follow him and build on his achievements.

The UN has several major organs, or parts. The most important are the General Assembly and the Security Council. The **General Assembly** has one delegate from each nation that is a UN member (193 countries as of 2021). It provides a forum for discussion of world problems. The body has limited power because member nations are not forced to abide by its decisions.

The **Security Council** currently has five permanent members—the United States, Russia, Britain, France, and China—and ten temporary members that are elected by the General Assembly for two-year terms. Permanent members have veto power. This means that if any of those five nations votes against a Security Council resolution, it does not pass. Though the veto was designed to encourage the five permanent members to reach agreements, its use has often prevented the body from taking action.

The highest official in the UN is the Secretary-General. This individual, who serves a five-year term, is nominated by the Security Council and then approved by the General Assembly.

Proponents of the United Nations hoped that the body would provide an avenue for discussion and a means of furthering world peace. Since its founding, its record has seen a mix of both success and failure.

Postwar Europe

The United States emerged from World War II as the most powerful nation in the world, with only one strong rival—the Soviet Union. The differences between the two postwar superpowers led to great tensions. Europe and eastern Asia, lying in ruins after the chaos of war, needed help to rebuild. But American ideas about how that should be done usually conflicted with the demands of the Soviet Union.

The Allies divided Germany into four zones after the war. American, British, and French troops occupied the three western zones. The Soviets occupied the fourth (eastern) zone. The Soviet Union ensured that the East German economy and politics would be Communist. As a result, tensions increased between the Soviet Union and the other three Allied nations.

Postwar Japan

Like Europe, Japan had been destroyed by the war. Cities and harbors lay in ruins. Most of its cargo ships had been sunk. The United States provided billions of dollars to help Japan rebuild. Truman appointed General Douglas MacArthur to head a military government and supervise the recovery efforts. One of MacArthur's first priorities involved religion.

MacArthur called on Americans to send Christian missionaries to Japan. The door to Japan was opened to the gospel. Between 1946 and 1950, more than two thousand missionaries, teachers, and social workers went to Japan to help the country recover both economically and spiritually.

The United States helped the Japanese write a new constitution. The Japanese elected a legislative body and gave rights to all citizens. Women received the right to vote.

Japan quickly rebuilt and eventually became a thriving industrial nation. In 1951 the United States ended its military occupation of the country. The assistance that the United States had provided Japan helped the two nations turn from enemies into strong allies.

Did you know?

The Security Council veto was used 86 times from 1945 to 1969 (80 were cast by the USSR and none by the United States). Since 1970, there have been 170 vetoes. More than 80 were by the United States.

▲ A meeting of the UN General Assembly, in March 2018, at the UN headquarters in New York City.

SECTION REVIEW 24.1

1. How did the government help US soldiers returning from World War II?
2. How did the "green revolution" help provide for the increased population of the "baby boom"?
3. As the suburbs grew, what groups of people typically remained in the cities? How did this affect the cities?
4. What mass media invention greatly changed leisure time?
5. Who were the four presidential candidates in the election of 1948?
6. Did Jackie Robinson achieve equality in playing for the Brooklyn Dodgers? Why or why not?
7. What are the two most important parts of the United Nations? Who makes up each group?
8. How did the United States help Japan recover after the war?

GUIDING QUESTIONS

- What early conflicts emerged in the Cold War?
- How did communism spread after World War II?

▲ Joseph Stalin led the Soviet Union from the mid-1920s until his death in 1953. He was one of history's most brutal leaders.

24.2 COLD WAR CRISES

How did the Cold War begin?

Conflict with the Soviets

The hostility between the United States and its allies and the Soviet Union and its allies became known as the **Cold War**. During this period, the two sides were involved in tense competition. They tried to avoid direct military conflict because they feared that a third world war would erupt. Yet there were occasions in which battles and wars did take place (i.e., a "hot war").

Even when Roosevelt and Stalin had been fighting their common enemy, Hitler, there was much disagreement between their two countries. What really launched the Cold War, however, was the realization that the USSR intended to spread its power throughout the world. The Cold War was waged as the forces of democracy and communism confronted each other in nation after nation.

At Yalta, Joseph Stalin pledged to hold free elections in the countries that the Soviet Union had taken from German control. But even before the war began, the Soviets had organized Communist parties in the countries of Eastern Europe. During and after World War II, Soviet troops occupied Eastern Europe. They placed Communists in power in Bulgaria, Yugoslavia, Albania, Romania, Poland, Hungary, and Czechoslovakia. To ensure that those countries remained Communist, Russia kept pro-Soviet leaders in control despite opposition from the people. Free elections were never held, and these nations became **Russian satellites** (Soviet-dominated countries).

On March 5, 1946, Winston Churchill gave a speech at Westminster College in Fulton, Missouri. He stated that an "**iron curtain**" now separated Communist Eastern Europe from the free

nations of Western Europe. Soon the terms *East* or *Eastern* were used to refer to Communist-controlled areas throughout the world, and *West* or *Western* referred to democratic nations. The term ***Third World*** referred to nations that did not align themselves with either the East or the West. (Today that term refers to underdeveloped, or developing, nations—especially those with widespread poverty.)

Though unhappy with the expansion of communism, Truman feared that trying to force the Communists to withdraw from Eastern Europe might cause another war. Thus, he responded to the Soviet presence in Eastern Europe with the policy of **containment**. Truman declared that communism must be contained within its new boundaries and not allowed to expand.

At the time, Communist-led guerrillas were trying to take control of Greece. In addition, Turkey seemed on the brink of falling to communism. To fund his containment policy, Truman asked Congress for $400 million in military aid to Greece and Turkey. Congress approved, and the funds helped keep those two nations from falling to communism. Giving money or other assistance to support pro-Western, anti-Communist governments was known as the **Truman Doctrine**.

Because of World War II, life seemed hopeless to many Europeans. Their countries were devastated. There were few jobs. The victorious nations were so deeply in debt from their own war efforts that they could do little to help others. Most industries had been destroyed. Cities, railroads, and roads were in ruins. Farmlands did not produce, and near-famine conditions existed in Europe.

The United States helped Europeans recover by shipping tons of food, clothing, and medicine to them. Communists could make easy inroads among discontented and downtrodden people, so the United States showed special concern for such people to keep Communist influence from spreading.

On June 5, 1947, Secretary of State **George C. Marshall** proposed a vast new aid program for Europe. He and Truman asked Congress for huge sums of money to rebuild European countries ravaged by war. The **Marshall Plan** offered aid, even to Eastern European countries already under Soviet control. However, the Soviet Union would not allow its satellites to take advantage of the offer.

Although the Marshall Plan cost about $13 billion, it greatly accelerated European recovery. The Western European countries that received American assistance rebuilt quickly and soon surpassed their prewar production. But the Communist satellites remained in economic despair for decades and never matched the progress of the free nations.

When Germany was divided into four Allied zones at the end of the war, the country's capital, Berlin, was in the middle of the Soviet-controlled portion. Because Berlin was such an important city, the Allies agreed to divide it, just as they had divided the country. Thus, France, Britain, the United States, and the Soviet Union each controlled a part of the city. The French, British, and American zones of Berlin received supplies from the western part of Germany by truck, boat, or train across Soviet-held lands.

The divisions of Germany and Berlin were supposed to be temporary measures that would last for a few years before the nation of Germany would be reunited. In June 1948, the Americans, the British, and the French announced they would consolidate their zones in

Much of Germany was destroyed during World War II. Germans are shown clearing the rubble in the city of Munich.

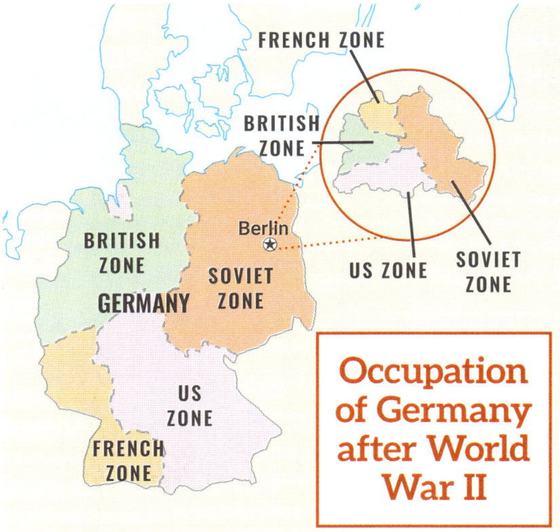

Occupation of Germany after World War II

western Germany and began the process of forming one government. Threatened by the prospect of a unified western Germany, the Soviets blocked highway, water, and rail traffic into the three Berlin zones controlled by the United States, Britain, and France. By blocking all access to that area, Stalin hoped to take over the entire city or force the West to stop the unification of western Germany.

▾ Supplies from US planes are unloaded during the Berlin Airlift.

Did you know?

When celebrating his hundredth birthday in October 2020, Gail Halvorsen received cards, letters, and video messages from many children who had received candy. The majority were then in their eighties.

Stalin's action left the two million residents of western Berlin without food, fuel, and other necessities. Truman responded quickly with a massive airlift of food and supplies. The **Berlin airlift** continued for eleven months. British and American planes departed and landed every few minutes. Some 277,000 flights brought food, fuel, medicine, and other essentials to the city. Nearly 2.5 million tons of supplies were airlifted to western Berlin.

During the airlift, American pilot Lieutenant Gail Halvorsen wanted to do something special for German children. He tied candy bars and gum to handkerchief parachutes and dropped them out of his plane. He received the nickname "Berlin Candy Bomber," and other pilots soon joined him in dropping items. Candy donations began arriving from the United States; eventually, over 250,000 parachutes and a staggering 23 tons of candy were dropped.

In May 1949 the Soviet Union ended the blockade. Afterward, the Federal Republic of Germany (also called West Germany) was created from the American, British, and French zones. The German Democratic Republic (also called East Germany) was created from the Soviet zone. The Communist-controlled zone of Berlin (East Berlin) was part of East Germany, while the remaining three zones (West Berlin) were part of West Germany. Germany would remain divided until 1990.

Reacting to the Soviet military threat, Western nations formed a military alliance. In April 1949, representatives from twelve nations formed the **North Atlantic Treaty Organization (NATO)**.

◂ Children reaching for lollipops dropped by the Candy Bomber

The first members were Great Britain, France, Italy, Portugal, the Netherlands, Denmark, Norway, Belgium, Luxembourg, Canada, Iceland, and the United States. Greece and Turkey joined in 1952 and West Germany joined in 1959. Membership continued to grow during the Cold War. NATO members provided money, troops, and military equipment for mutual protection and pledged to help each other in case of attack. General Dwight D. Eisenhower became the first supreme commander of NATO forces.

In response to NATO, the Soviets created their own military alliance in 1955. Named for the capital of Poland, it was called the **Warsaw Pact**. It included Poland, Albania, East Germany, Bulgaria, Romania, Czechoslovakia, Hungary, and the Soviet Union.

America's memberships in the UN and NATO were a departure from its long-standing policy of isolationism. NATO was the first peacetime defense alliance that the United States had joined.

Communism in China

Meanwhile, the Far East was also experiencing change. China, the most populous nation in the world, was a special concern. Beginning in the 1920s, China endured civil war between the Nationalists led by **Chiang Kai-shek** and the Communists led by **Mao Zedong**. World War II interrupted their fighting as they both battled the Japanese, but after 1945 civil war resumed.

Nationalists supported a free government and a free economy, but corruption and conflicts within their group hurt their efforts. By 1949 the Communists had won the civil war and had won and gained control of mainland China. Chiang Kai-shek fled with his army to Taiwan, an island about a hundred miles off the coast. There he established the Republic of China (also called Nationalist China or Free China). Mainland China, ruled by Mao Zedong, became the People's Republic of China (also called Communist China or Red China).

Communist China presented a new threat when it signed an alliance with the Soviet Union in February 1950. It confirmed American fears that the two Communist nations would work together against the free world.

The United States and the UN continued to recognize the Nationalists in Taiwan as the "real" China. Only in the 1970s did both officially recognize Mao Zedong, on the mainland, as the legitimate leader of China.

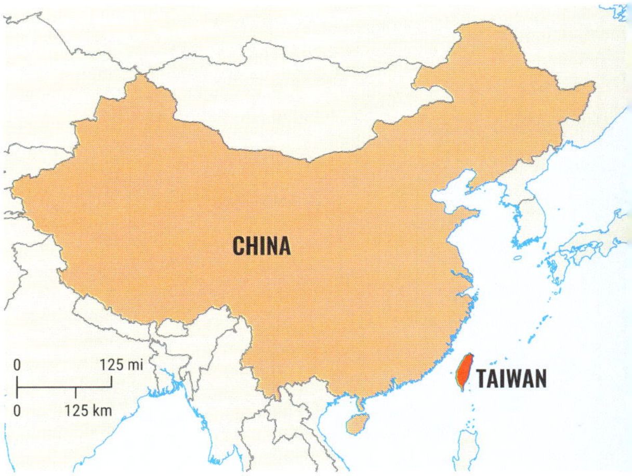

▲ China is 267 times larger than Taiwan.

The Korean Conflict

The Soviet Union had begun to seize part of Korea even before World War II ended. While the United States defeated Japan, the Soviet Union poured troops into Korea. The Allies had agreed that the Soviets could occupy Korea north of the thirty-eighth parallel (latitude 38° N). The Soviets again promised that at the proper time they would hold free elections. Instead, the Communists established their own style of government in North Korea. Below the thirty-eighth parallel, South Korea held its own elections and formed the free Republic of Korea, with Seoul as its capital. Korea, like Germany, was thus divided. The North was Communist; the South was free.

Diplomats held talks, hoping to unify the country, but the talks broke down. Then North Korea launched a surprise attack on South Korea on June 25, 1950. The UN Security Council called an emergency session to deal with the crisis. It discussed a resolution demanding North Korea's immediate withdrawal. The USSR, which could have vetoed the action, was boycotting UN meetings in protest of America's refusal to recognize the government of Communist China. As a result, the resolution passed.

The Security Council suggested that the UN provide military aid to South Korea. Once again, the United States prepared for war. Truman committed American planes and ships to support the South Koreans, and he ordered American troops to move from Japan to Korea. Within a week, the UN voted to send a peacekeeping force to Korea to help end the conflict, which was soon called the **Korean War.** Since 80 percent of the force's soldiers were American, Truman was allowed to name the force's commander. He chose General Douglas MacArthur, the US general who was most experienced in Asian matters.

▲ American soldiers fighting during the Korean War

▼ During the first three months of the Korean War, the North Korean army captured much of South Korea. The tide turned in September 1950 when UN forces invaded Inchon.

▾ American soldiers endured subzero temperatures while fighting at the Chosin Reservoir near the border of Korea and China.

Truman hoped that the UN soldiers could quickly drive the Communist troops out of South Korea. However, a shortage of equipment and America's lack of readiness led to a desperate situation as the North Korean troops, well equipped by the Soviets, continued to push their way south. By the end of August, UN forces held only a tiny southeastern corner of Korea near Pusan. But MacArthur surprised the North Koreans by attacking behind their lines in an amphibious landing at Inchon, near Seoul. In two weeks, the Americans had regained all the lost ground and were pushing the enemy back into North Korea. On October 26, 1950, MacArthur's advancing armies reached the Yalu River, the border between North Korea and China. Suddenly, China sent 260,000 troops across the Yalu River into North Korea to stop the UN forces.

In fierce fighting, the Chinese drove the UN troops back to the thirty-eighth parallel and then into South Korea. MacArthur believed that winning in Korea required a full-scale war. He said that the Chinese bases and the supply lines from China must be bombed—with nuclear weapons if necessary. In making his case, he declared, "There is no substitute for victory."

But Truman and his advisors thought it more acceptable to restore the original boundary with North Korea. Truman decided to wage a limited war that did not involve attacking China. He feared that if UN forces bombed Chinese territory that, based on the alliance Mao and Stalin had signed the previous year, the Soviet Union might enter the war. Matters were complicated by the fact that the Soviet Union had successfully tested its own atomic bomb in 1949.

MacArthur voiced his opposition to Truman's view to the press and to members of Congress. He stated that limited war was a mistake and nothing more than appeasement. Even after Truman warned MacArthur to stop, the general continued to publicly criticize Truman. In early April 1951, Truman fired MacArthur as commander.

In July 1951 cease-fire talks started, but the fighting continued. The talks stalled. Campaigning for the presidency in 1952, Dwight Eisenhower pledged that if elected, he would go to Korea personally to end the war. Upon his election, he did travel to Korea and revive the stalled talks. A cease-fire was signed on July 27, 1953. It established a new boundary between North and South Korea near the thirty-eighth parallel. It also created a demilitarized zone (DMZ, an unfortified "no man's land") between Communist North Korea and free South Korea. The boundary and the DMZ still exist today.

▴ Douglas MacArthur speaking to thousands in Chicago after he returned to the U.S. following his firing by Truman.

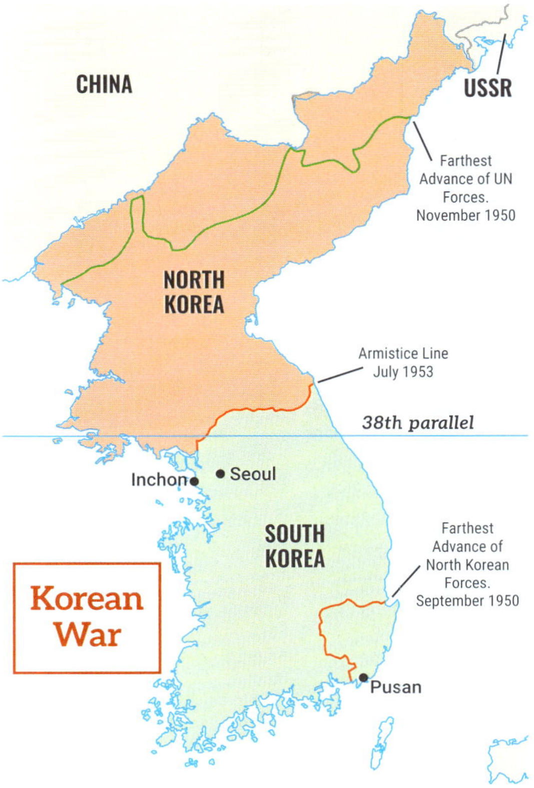

Communism at Home

Communism was also growing within the United States. A second "Red Scare" swept the country. Many Americans suspected that Communists were occupying government positions. They were especially concerned that there might be Communists in the State Department and the military. In response, Truman established a loyalty program in 1947 to investigate government employees and ensure internal security.

In 1948, Whittaker Chambers, a former Communist spy, testified before Congress that Alger Hiss, a State Department official, had passed secret documents to him while Chambers was a spy in the 1930s. Hiss, who denied the allegations, was later convicted of lying under oath.

Two members of a spy ring, Julius and Ethel Rosenberg, were convicted in 1950 of giving atomic secrets to the Soviets. They were executed in 1953.

These incidents prompted congressional investigations, including those of the House Committee on Un-American Activities. Congress passed legislation that made it easier for the government to combat spying and required Communists and their organizations to register with the Justice Department.

In 1951 Senator **Joseph McCarthy** of Wisconsin claimed that more than two hundred Communists were working in the State Department. He conducted hearings on Communists in the government. But by 1954, he was making reckless accusations, and the Senate passed a vote of censure, or formal disapproval, against McCarthy. His opponents coined a new word, McCarthyism, to describe his tactics of attacking someone by distorting facts, casting suspicion, and making outright false accusations. Although many initially supported McCarthy's attempts to uncover any Communists who might have been in the government, McCarthy set back the efforts of legitimate anti-Communists with his reckless statements.

FINAL DAILY NEWS 3¢
NEW YORK'S PICTURE NEWSPAPER
Vol. 32. No. 245 New York 17, Friday, April 6, 1951* 88 Main+4 Manhattan Pages 3 Cents

A-SPY COUPLE DOOMED TO DIE

—Story on Page 3

Use Chiang's Army, Mac Asks

—Story on Page 2

On Way to Chair. Gloved hands folded, Mrs. Ethel Rosenberg, 35, rides in rear of prison van on way to Women's House of Detention. Julius Rosenberg, 32, is separated from his wife by wire screen in van outside U. S. Courthouse. They were sentenced to death for passing A-bomb secrets to Reds, enabling Russia to perfect bomb ahead of schedule. —*Story p. 3*

▲ During numerous Senate hearings, such as the one shown at top, Joseph McCarthy presented allegations regarding American officials who he said were communists. The newspaper headline (above) refers to the death sentence the Rosenbergs (referred to as the "A [atomic] Spy Couple") received after they were convicted of giving secrets to the Soviet Union.

SECTION REVIEW 24.2

1. What was the US policy of containment? How was this demonstrated in the Truman Doctrine?
2. How was Germany divided after World War II? In which section was the capital of Berlin located?
3. How did the United States overcome the blockade of western Berlin by the Soviets? What supplies did it provide?
4. Why was NATO formed? How did the Soviet Union respond to the formation of NATO?
5. Who led Nationalist China? Who led Communist China? Were the Nationalists or Communists victorious in the end?
6. Why was General MacArthur fired from leading the UN forces in Korea? Do you agree with this action? Why or why not?
7. What senator was responsible for reckless accusations against suspected Communists during the Cold War?

24.3 THE EISENHOWER YEARS

What occurred during the presidency of Dwight D. Eisenhower?

GUIDING QUESTION

- What major events occurred during Eisenhower's presidency?

In 1951 the Twenty-Second Amendment to the Constitution was adopted. It declared that no one could be elected president more than twice. Many supported it because they felt that FDR had set a dangerous example by being elected to a third and fourth term. Previously, presidents had followed the tradition set by George Washington of not being elected more than twice.

Elections of 1952 and 1956

Both the Republicans and the Democrats would have been happy to have war hero Dwight D. Eisenhower as their candidate in 1952. But he chose to be a Republican and ran against Democrat Adlai E. Stevenson. The public decided that they "liked Ike" (as Eisenhower was called), and he won the election handily.

When Eisenhower was inaugurated in 1953, the nation was led by a Republican president for the first time in twenty years. In 1956, Ike was easily reelected to a second term.

Dwight D. Eisenhower

34

Born	October 14, 1890
Died	March 28, 1969
Home state	Pennsylvania (born in Texas)
Wife	Mamie Doud
Church	Presbyterian
Occupation	soldier
Party	Republican
Years served as president	1953–61
Terms	2
Vice president	Richard M. Nixon

Domestic Affairs

Civil Rights

The Supreme Court case *Plessy v. Ferguson* (1896) had allowed blacks to be separated from whites as long as their facilities were equal (the decision had established the principle "separate but equal"). For many years, the National Association for the Advancement of Colored People (NAACP) worked to end inequalities. The organization's lawyers challenged segregation in the courts, winning small victories through the decades.

A major victory came in 1954 in ***Brown v. Board of Education***. In that decision, the Supreme Court unanimously declared that separate educational facilities were unequal and ordered an end to segregated schools.

Implementation of the court's decree came slowly, however, because some states resisted. A dramatic incident in 1957 occurred in Little Rock, Arkansas. Governor Orval Faubus used the Arkansas National Guard to block nine black students from entering Central High School, an all-white school with 2,000 students. Later, a court ordered him to withdraw the troops. Violence occurred afterward when the black students tried to attend. President Eisenhower sent more than 1,000 soldiers to protect the black students, to keep order in the school, and to enforce obedience to the *Brown* decision.

A crowd harasses one of the nine African American students who was enrolling at Central High School in Little Rock.

Rosa Parks became a symbol of efforts to secure civil rights for black Americans when she refused to surrender her seat on a Montgomery bus.

In December 1955 **Rosa Parks**, a seamstress and civil rights activist in Montgomery, Alabama, rode a city bus home after a hard day at work. At that time, black passengers were required to sit in the back of all city buses and to give their seats to white customers and stand if the buses became crowded. Parks sat toward the front of the black section. As the seats filled, the bus driver told Parks to give up her seat. She refused and was arrested. To support her, other blacks led by Rev. Martin Luther King Jr. refused to ride city buses for more than a year, depriving the bus company of desperately needed money. This **Montgomery bus boycott** gained national attention as part of the civil rights struggle. In December 1956 the Supreme Court ruled that discrimination in public transportation was unconstitutional. The boycott, which had lasted 381 days, ended with a victory for African Americans.

PRAYER *and* BIBLE READING *in public schools*

In the 1960s, the Supreme Court issued two important rulings regarding public schools. In Engel v. Vitale (1962), the Court prohibited government-sponsored prayers, even if participation was not required and not associated with a specific religious denomination. A year later, the Court stated in *Abington School District v. Schempp* that school-sponsored Bible reading was unconstitutional.

Growth

Three of the most significant domestic events during the Eisenhower era were the completion of the St. Lawrence Seaway, the beginning of the interstate highway system, and the addition of two new states.

In 1954 the United States and Canada undertook a joint project called the St. Lawrence Seaway. The two countries deepened the St. Lawrence River and built canals and locks where necessary. The completed seaway allowed modern oceangoing vessels to sail from the Atlantic Ocean to the Great Lakes and allowed the production of electricity. It benefited the economies of both nations.

To handle the increasing vehicle traffic within the nation, Congress approved, at Eisenhower's recommendation, the construction of an extensive **interstate highway system**. These interstates became the main arteries of highway transportation in the United States and also provided a way to move troops and equipment in case of war. The system was largely funded by the federal government, though the states were required to pay a portion of the cost.

In 1959 Congress admitted two states to the Union: Alaska and Hawaii, the forty-ninth and fiftieth states. These states differ from the others because they are noncontiguous territories (i.e., they are not physically connected to the other forty-eight states). They are also unique because of their populations. About one-fifth of the Alaskan citizens were Alaska Natives (descendants of Yupik, Aleut, or other tribes). Half of Hawaii's citizens were of Asian descent (mainly Japanese, Chinese, Filipino, or Korean). Adding Alaska and Hawaii to the Union gave the United States an even wider cultural heritage.

Fun Fact

Federal highways running east and west are usually even-numbered. Those running north and south are usually odd-numbered.

The Cold War Continues

As president, Eisenhower faced a different kind of tyranny than he had fought during World War II. Communism was expanding in Southeast Asia, Europe, Cuba, and other parts of the world.

Southeast Asia

France had controlled Indochina (present-day Vietnam, Laos, and Cambodia) from the middle of the nineteenth century until Japan captured it during World War II. After the war, France attempted to reclaim its former colony. **Ho Chi Minh**, a Communist, tried to gain independence for Vietnam. He successfully conducted a guerrilla war that climaxed in May 1954 with the defeat of the French at the Battle of Dien Bien Phu.

In July 1954 an international conference in Geneva, Switzerland, recognized Laos and Cambodia as independent nations. It divided Vietnam between the Communist North and the non-Communist South. According to the Geneva agreement, the division would be temporary. It scheduled elections to be held in 1956 that would choose leaders for a united Vietnam. Neither the United States nor South Vietnam signed the agreement.

Later in 1954, Australia, New Zealand, Thailand, Pakistan, the Philippines, Britain, France, and the United States created the Southeast Asia Treaty Organization (SEATO). These nations pledged to contain the spread of communism in Southeast Asia. President Eisenhower sent money and weapons as well as hundreds of military advisors to train the South Vietnamese army. Ike and others believed in the **domino theory**—if one non-Communist nation in Southeast Asia fell to communism, then other nations would fall like a row of dominoes.

Elections did not occur in 1956. Communists in South Vietnam formed a group called the Viet Cong. They tried to overthrow the non-Communist government of South Vietnam and received much assistance from the North Vietnamese. The North Vietnamese and Viet Cong obtained military equipment and supplies from both the Soviet Union and Communist China.

▲ Ho Chi Minh

▲ Many feared that if Communists continued to gain territory in Southeast Asia that, like a row of dominoes, the entire region would fall to communism.

▲ Soviet leader Nikita Khrushchev (left) visited America in 1959. He is shown here with President Eisenhower (right).

The Soviet Union

As the leading nation of the free world, the United States was no longer isolated from international affairs. The more its interests were affected by conditions abroad, the more international problems the United States found itself involved in. Continued Cold War tensions with the Soviet Union were frequently the source.

Joseph Stalin died in 1953. After a power struggle among the Communist party officials, **Nikita Khrushchev** emerged as the new Soviet leader. He seemed to indicate a softening of Stalin's aggressive policies and spoke of "**peaceful coexistence**"—the idea of Communist and democratic nations existing side by side without constant conflict and threat of military action.

Unfortunately, the idea of peacefully coexisting was threatened on numerous occasions as conflict continued between the two superpowers. But there were attempts by the Soviets and Americans to promote goodwill toward each other. For example, in September 1959 Khrushchev became the first Soviet leader to visit the United States.

Europe

People in the Soviet satellites were unhappy under Communist rule. In June 1953 workers in East Berlin began protesting. As discontent spread, more than an estimated million people joined demonstrations throughout East Germany. The uprising in East Berlin was crushed by Soviet troops located in the city; about a hundred Germans were killed. Within days, fear of further Soviet actions led to the end of the protests.

On October 23, 1956, approximately 20,000 protesters gathered in Budapest, Hungary. Soon the crowd swelled to over 200,000. In a short time, thousands of Hungarians were rebelling against Soviet control. Using shortwave radio broadcasts, they pleaded for help from the West, but none came.

▼ In 1953, protesters hurl objects at Soviet tanks that crushed the demonstrations in the eastern part of Berlin, Germany.

▲ Soviet tanks and troops brutally ended the 1956 rebellion in Hungary.

Soviet troops and tanks invaded Hungary and crushed the revolt. Though brave, the Hungarians were armed only with homemade grenades and limited weapons; they could not stop tanks and well-equipped soldiers. They appear to have suffered over 20,000 casualties, including about 2,500 deaths. Thousands more were imprisoned. Almost 200,000 fled the nation. Later the Communist government sealed the borders to prevent others from leaving.

The United Nations condemned the Soviets' invasion of Hungary but took no real action. The Soviets felt secure in ruthlessly crushing the revolution without fear of interference by the free world.

Cuba

Latin America was also a source of Cold War tension. Many there, especially the poor and uneducated, believed the Communists' promises. The growth of communism in that region alarmed Americans because it brought the Soviet threat to the very doorstep of the United States.

In 1959 **Fidel Castro**'s forces defeated those of Fulgencio Batista, the longtime dictator of Cuba. Americans hoped conditions in Cuba might improve under Castro. Instead, they worsened.

Castro became a cruel dictator. He jailed thousands of his political enemies. He seized private property, including that of Americans and American businesses in Cuba. Then he declared openly that he was a Communist. Cuban refugees tried to escape Castro's regime by fleeing to Florida any way they could. Some flew; most floated on flimsy boats. Soviets soon provided aid to Castro. Ninety miles from Florida lay a Communist threat to American freedom.

▲ Fidel Castro

SECTION REVIEW 24.3

1. Why was *Brown v. Board of Education* significant?
2. Whose arrest led to the Montgomery bus boycott? Why was she arrested? Who organized the boycott?
3. For what two reasons was the interstate highway system created?
4. What Southeast Asian leader sought independence for Vietnam?
5. What Soviet leader spoke of a policy of "peaceful coexistence"?
6. Who took over Cuba and turned it into a Communist dictatorship?

GUIDING QUESTIONS

- What major events occurred during Kennedy's presidency?
- What was the Space Race?

John F. Kennedy

Born	May 29, 1917	35
Died	November 22, 1963	
Home state	Massachusetts	
Wife	Jacqueline Bouvier	
Church	Roman Catholic	
Occupations	Navy commander, author, reporter	
Party	Democrat	
Years served as president	1961–63	
Term	partial (assassinated in Dallas, TX, by Lee Harvey Oswald)	
Vice president	Lyndon B. Johnson	

Federal Minimum Wage

Year	Wage
1940	$.30
1950	$.75
1960	$1.00
1970	$1.60
1980	$3.10
1990	$3.80
2000	$5.15
2010	$7.25
2020	$7.25

24.4 THE KENNEDY YEARS

What occurred during the presidency of John F. Kennedy?

The Election of 1960

In 1960 the Republicans selected Richard Nixon as their presidential candidate. He had served as Eisenhower's vice president for eight years. The Democrats selected Massachusetts senator **John F. Kennedy** (JFK). Kennedy's running mate, Texan Lyndon B. Johnson, was the well-known leader of Senate Democrats. With those candidates, the Democratic Party hoped to win the votes of both northerners and southerners.

For the first time in history, the candidates participated in a series of televised debates. JFK entered the debates as an underdog but was handsome, youthful, and charming. In the first debate, Nixon appeared pale and in need of a shave (he had recently been released from the hospital and, unlike Kennedy, had declined studio makeup for the event).

The election was close. Of more than 68 million popular votes cast, Kennedy won by fewer than 120,000—a difference of less than 1 vote per precinct (local voting place). At age forty-three, Kennedy was the youngest person ever elected president. He became the first Catholic to serve as president.

In his inaugural address, Kennedy challenged Americans: "Ask not what your country can do for you—ask what you can do for your country." He also urged America's enemies to join the United States in a quest for lasting peace.

Domestic Affairs

The New Frontier

While campaigning, Kennedy promised a program called the **New Frontier**. Similar to the New Deal, it proposed substantial legislation. It requested economic aid to poor areas, medical insurance for the elderly (later known as Medicare), financial aid for college students, and an ambitious space program.

Kennedy used tax policy to provide needed stimulation for the nation's economy. He pushed Congress to cut taxes. As a result, spending and investing increased and the economy rebounded.

Because Kennedy's victory was so narrow and because conservative southern Democrats often voted with congressional Republicans, Kennedy's New Frontier faced opposition in Congress. But Congress did agree to some of Kennedy's goals. It raised the minimum wage to $1.25 per hour, passed the Trade Expansion Act (which gave the president more authority regarding tariffs), and expanded the Social Security system. But Congress rejected other aspects of the New Frontier.

▾ These scenes from the early 1960s include a demonstration at a lunch counter in Little Rock, Arkansas (above), and two "freedom riders" and a national guardsman aboard a bus (bottom).

Civil Rights

In 1960, while Ike was still president, four black college students sat down at a "whites only" lunch counter at a Woolworth's department store in Greensboro, North Carolina. They refused to leave unless they were served. This sit-in launched similar actions at white lunch counters, churches, and schools throughout the South. Individuals known as "freedom riders" rode on buses from place to place in the South, seeking to integrate public transportation. Civil rights supporters encouraged blacks to register to vote.

Martin Luther King Jr., a Baptist minister, had received national recognition for his part in organizing the Montgomery bus boycott (1955–56). Shortly after it ended, King and his associates organized the Southern Christian Leadership Conference (SCLC). It encouraged nonviolent marches and protests against laws that violated the rights of African Americans. King appealed to middle-class whites through the media and engaged the power and influence of black churches and their ministers.

Almost everywhere civil rights demonstrators went, they faced angry mobs of whites, who sometimes mocked and beat them. In April 1963 King led a nonviolent demonstration to oppose segregation in Birmingham. The protesters were met by police who used tear gas, cattle prods, attack dogs, and high-powered water hoses to breakup their protests. King was arrested on April 12. On April 16, he penned his famous "Letter from Birmingham Jail," which justified his acts of civil disobedience (peaceful refusal to obey unjust laws).

PRIMARY SOURCE: "LETTER FROM BIRMINGHAM JAIL" (EXCERPT)

We have waited for more than 340 years for our constitutional and God given rights. The nations of Asia and Africa are moving with jetlike speed toward gaining political independence, but we still creep at horse and buggy pace toward gaining a cup of coffee at a lunch counter. Perhaps it is easy for those who have never felt the stinging darts of segregation to say, "Wait." But when you have seen vicious mobs lynch your mothers and fathers at will and drown your sisters and brothers at whim; when you have seen hate filled policemen curse, kick and even kill your black brothers and sisters; when you see the vast majority of your twenty million Negro brothers smothering in an airtight cage of poverty in the midst of an affluent society; when you suddenly find your tongue twisted and your speech stammering as you seek to explain to your six year old daughter why she can't go to the public amusement park that has just been advertised on television, and see tears welling up in her eyes when she is told that Funtown [an amusement park in Atlanta, Georgia] is closed to colored children, and see ominous [haunting] clouds of inferiority beginning to form in her little mental sky, and see her beginning to distort her personality by developing an unconscious bitterness toward white people; when you have to concoct an answer for a five year old son who is asking: "Daddy, why do white people treat colored people so mean?"; when you take a cross country drive and find it necessary to sleep night after night in the uncomfortable corners of your automobile because no motel will accept you; when you are humiliated day in and day out by nagging signs reading "white" and "colored"; when your first name becomes "nigger," your middle name becomes "boy" (however old you are) and your last name becomes "John," and your wife and mother are never given the respected title "Mrs."; when you are harried by day and haunted by night by the fact that you are a Negro, living constantly at tiptoe stance, never quite knowing what to expect next, and are plagued with inner fears and outer resentments; when you are forever fighting a degenerating sense of "nobodiness"—then you will understand why we find it difficult to wait. There comes a time when the cup of endurance runs over, and men are no longer willing to be plunged into the abyss [depth] of despair. I hope, sirs, you can understand our legitimate and unavoidable impatience.

▲ In 1963, firemen used hoses to disperse a civil rights demonstration in Birmingham, Alabama.

A number of black Americans were murdered for demanding their civil rights. In June 1963 civil rights activist Medgar Evers was killed in his own driveway in Jackson, Mississippi. Three months later, Ku Klux Klan members placed dynamite at the 16th Street Baptist Church, an African American church in Birmingham, Alabama. The explosion killed four young black girls and wounded more than a dozen other people.

The **Twenty-Third Amendment** gave the residents of the District of Columbia the right to vote in national elections. Because the district's population was heavily black, the amendment was regarded as a step forward in civil rights.

The biggest civil rights event of the sixties occurred in August 1963 when over two hundred thousand people—both black and white—gathered in the nation's capital for a protest known as the **March on Washington**. Martin Luther King Jr. delivered a powerful address on the steps of the Lincoln Memorial. Repeating the phrase "I have a dream," King spoke of an ideal America, where liberty and equality would be a reality for people of all ethnicities.

▾ March on Washington (August 1963)

PRIMARY SOURCE: "I HAVE A DREAM" SPEECH (EXCERPT)

I say to you today, my friends. . . . even though we face the difficulties of today and tomorrow, I still have a dream. It is a dream deeply rooted in the American dream.

I have a dream that one day this nation will rise up and live out the true meaning of its creed: "We hold these truths to be self-evident, that all men are created equal."

I have a dream that one day on the red hills of Georgia, the sons of former slaves and the sons of former slave owners will be able to sit down together at the table of brotherhood.

I have a dream that one day even the state of Mississippi, a state sweltering with the heat of injustice, sweltering with the heat of oppression, will be transformed into an oasis of freedom and justice.

I have a dream that my four little children will one day live in a nation where they will not be judged by the color of their skin but by the content of their character.

I have a *dream* today!

I have a dream that one day, down in Alabama, with its vicious racists, with its governor having his lips dripping with the words of "interposition" and "nullification"—one day right there in Alabama little black boys and black girls will be able to join hands with little white boys and white girls as sisters and brothers.

I have a *dream* today!

I have a dream that one day every valley shall be exalted, and every hill and mountain shall be made low, the rough places will be made plain, and the crooked places will be made straight; "and the glory of the Lord shall be revealed and all flesh shall see it together."

This is our hope, and this is the faith that I go back to the South with.

With this faith, we will be able to hew [carve] out of the mountain of despair a stone of hope. With this faith, we will be able to transform the jangling discords of our nation into a beautiful symphony of brotherhood. With this faith, we will be able to work together, to pray together, to struggle together, to go to jail together, to stand up for freedom together, knowing that we will be free one day.

And this will be the day—this will be the day when all of God's children will be able to sing with new meaning:

My country, 'tis of thee, sweet land of liberty, of thee I sing.
Land where my fathers died, land of the Pilgrim's pride,
From every mountainside, let freedom ring!

And if America is to be a great nation, this must become true.

And so let freedom ring from the prodigious [vast] hilltops of New Hampshire.

Let freedom ring from the mighty mountains of New York.
Let freedom ring from the heightening Alleghenies of Pennsylvania. . . .
Let freedom ring from every hill and molehill of Mississippi.
From every mountainside, let freedom ring. . . .

When we allow freedom ring, when we let it ring from every village and every hamlet, from every state and every city, we will be able to speed up that day when *all* of God's children, black men and white men, Jews and Gentiles, Protestants and Catholics, will be able to join hands and sing in the words of the old Negro spiritual:

Free at last! Free at last!
Thank God Almighty, we are free at last!

▲ Peace Corp workers in India

▼ The two pictures below are of the Berlin Wall. The top one is from 1964. The bottom one shows the celebration in November 1989 when the dismantling of the wall began.

Foreign Affairs

Kennedy entered the presidency with several ideas for helping needy countries and spreading peace.

New Programs

Kennedy introduced the **Peace Corps** in 1961. In this program, the "best and brightest" Americans agreed to volunteer two years of their lives to work in poverty-stricken countries. By 1963 more than five thousand volunteers were improving schools, medical care, and conservation in over 40 countries around the world. The program continues today and has served over 140 nations. It is one of Kennedy's most memorable achievements.

In addition, Kennedy announced a program called the Alliance for Progress to help counter the growth of communism in Latin America. With this program, the United States provided billions of dollars to Latin American nations in the 1960s for housing, schools, and medical facilities. JFK hoped that easing poverty would reduce the unrest that allowed communism to spread.

The Berlin Wall

By 1961, almost three million East Germans had fled communism by crossing into West Berlin. That huge number, more than 15 percent of East Germany's population, clearly showed that Communist boasts of providing a better life for Germans were groundless. Most of those who fled East Germany were under age forty-five. Such a loss of workers dramatically weakened the East German economy.

Britain, France, and the United States still had troops in West Berlin at the time. Khrushchev wanted them withdrawn. President Kennedy, fearing this would merely be the first step in a Communist takeover of the city, refused. The Soviet leader then threatened to restrict access to West Berlin, just as Stalin had done in 1948.

In August 1961 the Communists began erecting the **Berlin Wall** around the free part of the city, West Berlin. It prevented movement between the two parts of the city. Soon, the wall was topped with barbed wire and fortified by guard towers and minefields. Armed guards had orders to shoot anyone who tried to escape to West Berlin. The wall made it virtually impossible for East Germans to flee into West Berlin, but it clearly demonstrated the failure of communism—an immense barrier had to be constructed to keep people from leaving.

In June 1963 Kennedy made a dramatic visit to the Berlin Wall. Thousands of Berliners lit candles to show their support of freedom. Kennedy expressed his support by saying, "Ich bin ein Berliner" (I am a Berliner). With those words, he indicated his support and identification with the struggling people of Berlin. But the wall remained a defiant challenge to freedom until it was opened in November 1989 and later dismantled.

▲ More than one thousand anti-Castro Cubans were captured after the Bay of Pigs invasion failed in April 1961. Some of those prisoners are shown here.

Cuba

Under Fidel Castro, conditions in Cuba continued to worsen. Because his economic policies caused great harm and because of the loss of political freedoms, many Cubans fled to the United States. A large pro-democracy Cuban community developed in Florida. The **Central Intelligence Agency (CIA)** (which gathers and analyzes information regarding foreign affairs, often through the use of spies) had trained about 1,400 Cuban refugees to invade Cuba and overthrow Castro. Soon after JFK took office he allowed the plan, developed while Eisenhower was still president, to proceed. The CIA believed that when Cubans heard about the invasion, they would rise up to overthrow Castro.

The Cuban refugees landed at a place called the **Bay of Pigs** on April 17, 1961. The operation was a disaster. Some of the invading ships ran aground on coral reefs; Kennedy canceled US aircraft that were to support the invading forces; Castro had learned the "secret" attack was coming and had prepared his troops for it; and the anticipated uprising against Castro never occurred. Within two days, almost all the invaders were killed or captured. The incident was a great embarrassment for John Kennedy, who had been president for only three months.

An even more dramatic confrontation over Cuba occurred a little more than a year later. The Soviets, partly because they were upset that America had attempted to overthrow Castro, began secretly installing missiles in Cuba that were capable of carrying nuclear weapons. Such missiles would be able to reach the United States within minutes. On October 22, 1962, after American spy planes confirmed missile sites were under construction, President Kennedy described the situation in a televised speech. He demanded that the Soviets dismantle the sites immediately and established a naval blockade around the island to prevent the arrival of more missiles. Kennedy also stated that any missile attack from Cuba would result in the United States launching a full-scale nuclear attack on the Soviet Union.

▾ This map shows that nuclear missiles fired from Cuba could reach all parts of the continental United States except the Pacific Northwest.

Khrushchev denounced the blockade as illegal and said his ships would not stop for it. For several days, the world faced the possibility of nuclear war during the **Cuban missile crisis**. After intense, secret negotiations, the United States and USSR reached an agreement. Khrushchev agreed to remove the missiles in exchange for Kennedy's public promise not to invade Cuba. In addition, the president privately pledged to remove American nuclear missiles from Turkey, near the Russian border. The crisis ended after two tense weeks.

In the wake of the Cuban missile crisis, the United States and the Soviet Union wanted to ease tensions and make communication easier. A "hot line"—for sending urgent written messages between the two nations—was installed in 1963. A message could now securely be sent to or received from the Soviet Union in a matter of minutes.

The Space Race

On October 4, 1957, the Russians successfully launched a satellite known as ***Sputnik I*** into orbit. Americans were shocked. How could the Communists be the first to develop this technology? It was orbiting the earth at 18,000 miles per hour and circling the globe every 96 minutes. A month after the launch of *Sputnik I*, a second Soviet rocket carried the first living creature to orbit the earth—a dog named Laika. In April 1961 cosmonaut Yuri Gagarin became the first person to orbit the earth.

▴ Laika, the first creature sent into space

In December 1957 America attempted to place a satellite into orbit. The launch was a humiliating failure when the rocket exploded. Nevertheless, the following month an attempt succeeded. Congress established the **National Aeronautics and Space Administration (NASA)** to conduct the space program. Rising to the challenge, NASA scientists overcame many of the complex problems of space travel in a series of projects.

The Mercury project succeeded in sending the first American, Alan Shepard, into space in May 1961. Shortly afterward, President Kennedy announced the goal of landing a man on the moon by the end of the decade. In February 1962 John Glenn, another Mercury astronaut, became the first American to orbit the earth. The Gemini missions tested the technology needed to dock two craft in outer space. The Apollo project blasted astronauts 385,000 miles to the moon and back.

On July 20, 1969, Neil Armstrong, the commander of Apollo 11, stepped from the ladder of the *Eagle* lunar module and became the first person to set foot on the moon. As he did so, he said, "That's one small step for a man, one giant leap for mankind."

Though it received little publicity at the time, the first Communion service was conducted in space during the Apollo 11 moon landing. Buzz Aldrin, an elder in his Presbyterian church in Texas and an Apollo 11 astronaut, quietly opened a kit that his church had provided and partook of the Communion elements while on the moon. Paraphrasing John 15:5, he said, "I am the vine, you are the branches. Whoever remains in me, and I in him, will bear much fruit; for you can do nothing without me."

America's space program did not stop with the moon landing. It continued with other projects such as Skylab, the Space Shuttle, the International Space Station, and the Hubble telescope.

The space program has not been without its tragedies. In 1967 three astronauts were killed during a simulated launch of *Apollo 1*. In 1986 the space shuttle *Challenger* exploded seventy-three seconds after liftoff, killing its seven-person crew. And in 2003 the space shuttle *Columbia* burst into flames upon reentry, killing all seven crew members.

▲ Launch of the Apollo 10 mission on May 18, 1969

◂ Astronaut Buzz Aldrin is shown on the moon's surface during the Apollo 11 mission..

A view of the earth from the moon.

▲ President Kennedy and his wife are shown in the convertible's back seat shortly before he was shot. The governor of Texas and his wife are in the center seat.

Kennedy's Assassination

John Kennedy's presidency came to an abrupt end on Friday, November 22, 1963. On that day, he became the fourth president to die from an assassin's bullet. As the forty-six-year-old leader rode in a convertible through Dallas, Texas, Lee Harvey Oswald fired at him from the sixth floor of a nearby building. Texas governor John Connally, riding in the same car as Kennedy, was also shot but survived. Vice President Lyndon Johnson, in a separate car, was not hurt.

Confusion deepened when millions of Americans watched on television as Jack Ruby, a local nightclub owner, shot and killed Oswald just two days after the president's death. Reasons for the assassination remain unclear, and conspiracy theories abound regarding the possible involvement of other assassins, despite official conclusions that Oswald acted alone.

Like Abraham Lincoln, JFK was viewed as a hero after his death. Congress passed many of Kennedy's New Frontier programs, which had been stalled in that body, partly as a memorial to the late president.

▲ Lee Harvey Oswald (escorted by two police officers) was shot by Jack Ruby (at far right).

SECTION REVIEW 24.4

1. What measures did Kennedy's New Frontier program call for?
2. Why did Martin Luther King Jr. write in "Letter from Birmingham Jail" that he did not want to "wait" for segregation to change? Do you agree? Why or why not?
3. What was the significance of the Twenty-Third Amendment?
4. Why did the Soviets build a wall around West Berlin?
5. What disastrous military operation contributed to the Soviets secretly installing missiles in Cuba?
6. What compromise was reached to end the Cuban missile crisis?
7. What country sent the first satellite into space? the first creature into orbit? the first man into space? the first man on the moon?

CHAPTER 24 REVIEW

Making Connections

1. What was the move to the South and Southwest known as?
2. How did religion change in the 1950s in the following areas: attendance, organizational structure, emphasis?
3. How did the Taft-Hartley Act affect workers in America?
4. How did Truman support efforts to end discrimination against black Americans?
5. Who is the highest official of the United Nations?
6. Into how many districts was Germany divided after World War II? Who occupied them?
7. What countries in Eastern Europe became Russian satellites?
8. What are the two definitions of Third World?
9. What two opposing military alliances were formed by the free world and the Communist world?
10. Where did Nationalist or Free China flee to?
11. At what parallel (line of latitude) was Korea divided after World War II?
12. Which two new states joined the Union in 1959?
13. Who were the main leaders of the following Communist countries during the Cold War: the Soviet Union (list two), China, Vietnam, and Cuba?
14. What tragic event occurred on November 22, 1963?

Thinking Critically

15. How can television both improve and harm leisure time?
16. Should the United States have given money to European countries after World War II to aid in their recovery? Why or why not?

Living as a Christian Citizen

17. If you were a Christian in the 1950s, what practices might you change in the church if you had the benefit of today's hindsight?
18. In what areas of King's "I Have a Dream" speech has progress been made? In what areas is progress still lacking?

Terms to Remember

GI Bill
baby boom
Fair Deal
Thomas Dewey
civil rights movement
Jackie Robinson
United Nations
General Assembly
Security Council
Cold War
Russian satellites
iron curtain
Third World
containment
Truman Doctrine
George C. Marshall
Marshall Plan
Berlin airlift
North Atlantic Treaty Organization (NATO)
Warsaw Pact
Chiang Kai-shek
Mao Zedong
Korean War
Joseph McCarthy
Brown v. Board of Education
Rosa Parks
Montgomery bus boycott
interstate highway system
Ho Chi Minh
domino theory
Nikita Khrushchev
peaceful coexistence
Fidel Castro
John F. Kennedy
New Frontier
Martin Luther King Jr.
Twenty-Third Amendment
March on Washington
Peace Corps
Berlin Wall
Central Intelligence Agency (CIA)
Bay of Pigs
Cuban missile crisis
Sputnik I
National Aeronautics and Space Administration (NASA)

The peace symbol became popular with Vietnam War protesters.

CHAPTER

25 The Turbulent Sixties and Seventies

Americans experienced incredible economic growth in the postwar years, but through the mid-1960s and the 1970s, growth was hindered by controversies—the Vietnam War, expanding social programs, and the continued struggle for civil rights. Disagreements led to dissatisfaction among many Americans. Various groups had different ideas about how the country should move forward. Though these groups appealed to American values such as freedom and individualism, each group viewed them differently.

Some Americans wanted freedom from traditional morality and social norms. They protested the "establishment." Some women argued that they needed freedom from the constraints of marriage and traditional gender roles.

Many Americans during this period were dismayed by growing federal programs and regulations. They wanted freedom to live their lives without constant government oversight. Black Americans continued to press for the same freedoms that white Americans had long enjoyed.

GUIDING QUESTIONS

- What domestic issues were in the forefront during Johnson's presidency?
- What happened during the Vietnam War?
- What were American viewpoints regarding the Vietnam War?

Sarah T. Hughes, a federal judge, is the only woman to have administered the presidential oath. She did so shortly after the assassination of President Kennedy.

25.1 THE JOHNSON ADMINISTRATION

What were the major events during the presidency of Lyndon B. Johnson?

Vice President **Lyndon B. Johnson** (LBJ) took the oath of office on the presidential airplane, Air Force One, just two hours after President Kennedy was shot. The plane then departed Dallas, Texas, for the trip back to Washington, DC.

For twenty-four years, Johnson had served in Congress. He had held the powerful position of Senate majority leader (head of the party that had the most Senate members), and he knew how to navigate the political system to get bills passed.

After entering the White House, Johnson initiated his legislative program, which he called the **Great Society**. It was intended to help America bring an end to poverty and racial injustice.

The Election of 1964

Less than a year after Kennedy was assassinated, President Johnson faced the Republican nominee, **Barry Goldwater**, in the 1964 election. Goldwater, a conservative senator from Arizona, represented a small but growing branch of the Republican Party that openly denounced the expanding power of government. Beginning in the 1960s and continuing into the 1970s, more and more conservatives were identifying with the Republican Party. During the period, an increasing number of Christians, who opposed moral decline and felt that the federal government was undermining traditional values, began supporting Republican candidates.

In 1964 Johnson's campaign ads strongly implied that Goldwater would be dangerous and irresponsible in using nuclear weapons. They also labeled Goldwater an extremist. His supporters said, "In your heart you know he's right—vote for Barry Goldwater." Democrats mocked, "In your guts you know he's nuts—vote for Lyndon Johnson." LBJ won the contest by a landslide, receiving 61 percent of the vote.

Lyndon B. Johnson 36

Born	August 27, 1908
Died	January 22, 1973
Home state	Texas
Wife	Claudia "Lady Bird" Taylor
Church	Disciples of Christ
Occupations	teacher, rancher
Party	Democrat
Years served as president	1963–69
Terms	partial (upon the assassination of JFK) and 1
Vice presidents	1st—none 2nd—Hubert H. Humphrey

Domestic Affairs

Almost forty million Americans, more than one-fifth of the nation's population, were categorized as living in poverty during the early 1960s. Johnson's solution to this problem was to declare a "War on Poverty" with his Great Society programs.

▲ A poor family in Kentucky during the 1960s

The War on Poverty

In waging this war, Johnson created the Job Corps, which was similar to the Peace Corps but focused on needs at home. Other Great Society programs gave aid to people in Appalachia (a region along the Appalachian Mountains long known for its high number of poor people), established a food-stamp program for needy families, and created the Head Start Program for underprivileged children needing preparation before they started regular school. In 1965 Johnson obtained congressional approval for two government health-care programs. Medicare provided health insurance for senior citizens; Medicaid implemented healthcare for low income families.

Johnson also created a new agency—the Department of Housing and Urban Development (HUD). The agency's leader joined the president's cabinet and spearheaded efforts to increase the amount of government-funded housing and to assist cities in providing programs for the needy.

Many hailed the War on Poverty as a success. They pointed to the reduction in the number of poor people. Others noted some of its negative effects. First, it was expensive. The nation had to borrow large sums of money to support it. Second, Americans became more dependent on government programs and benefits. Consequently, some took less personal responsibility in providing for their own needs. Third, the programs gave the government more power over people's lives because of the extensive regulations that usually accompanied government assistance. Fourth, some even alleged that the Great Society was "buying" the votes of those who benefited from it. They argued that if a political party threatened to reduce government spending on programs, the programs' recipients would likely support the party that promised continuation of the spending.

▼ The March on Washington in August 1963 involved more than 200,000 people. As mentioned in the last chapter, Martin Luther King Jr. delivered his "I Have a Dream" speech at this event.

Civil Rights Struggle Continues

Ending injustices faced by black Americans was one of the most significant issues the nation faced at this time. Both parties included those who either supported or opposed civil rights legislation. Sadly, some failed to recognize civil rights as an important moral issue.

After the August 1963 March on Washington and the Kennedy assassination a few months later, Congress passed the **Civil Rights Act of 1964**. That law prohibited segregation in schools and public places, such as restaurants and stores. It also outlawed discrimination based on race, color, religion, sex, or national origin.

In addition, the **Twenty-Fourth Amendment** was ratified in 1964. It forbade the states to levy poll taxes. As noted in earlier chapters, the poll tax required voters to pay a fee before they could vote. Some states used that tax to prevent poor black people, and sometimes poor white people, from voting.

Although the Fifteenth Amendment (1870) prevented states from denying any ethnic group the right to vote, many southern states had devised ways to make such voting difficult. The **Voting Rights Act of 1965** ended many long-standing injustices in federal elections. It prohibited literacy tests. Federal officials were given authority to investigate any complaints of discrimination relating to voter registration or voting. In areas where many black Americans were not registered to vote, the law provided for federal government oversight of the registration process. In places where voter discrimination had been common, it required local and state governments to obtain approval for any changes they wished to enact that affected voting or elections.

The nonviolent protests led by Martin Luther King Jr. were designed to bring political pressure on cities and the nation that would result in changing unjust laws and practices. But some black leaders rejected King's nonviolent views. Among them was **Malcolm X**, a convert to a religious group called the Nation of Islam (also known as the Black Muslims). That group preached black supremacy and the need to create a separate black nation. Malcolm X's views won a large audience, especially in the North. But Malcolm X also had a number of enemies, particularly after he visited Mecca in 1964. After returning, he rejected some of the views of the Nation of Islam and broke with the organization. The following year, rival Black Muslims killed Malcolm X at a rally in New York City.

▲ Malcolm X was a controversial leader in the civil rights movement.

Radical young blacks were also attracted to Stokely Carmichael, who advocated "black power." His emphasis on violence frightened many whites and angered conservative black citizens, who feared that violence would hinder the progress of the civil rights movement.

While the country's attention was drawn to racial injustices in the South, many Americans overlooked the social prejudice that had segregated black communities in the North and on the West Coast. Riots broke out in several cities in those regions. In the summer of 1965, a confrontation between police and black residents in a Los Angeles community known as Watts led to riots lasting six days. Thirty-four people died, and property damage exceeded $35 million. The uprising was finally ended by the National Guard. Over the next two years, more riots occurred. In the summer of 1967, rioters looted and burned parts of Newark, New Jersey. In four days, twenty-six people died and hundreds were injured. A week later, riots in Detroit closed the city for several days. The looting and destruction shocked Americans.

On April 4, 1968, James Earl Ray, a white man, shot and killed Martin Luther King Jr. while King was standing on a hotel balcony in Memphis, Tennessee. King's murder set off a wave of violence in black neighborhoods across America. Despite efforts to improve civil rights, the dream of racial harmony still seemed far away.

▼ Associates of Martin Luther King Jr. were present when he was shot on a hotel balcony. They point in the direction from which the shot was fired.

The Vietnam War

The **Vietnam War**, the conflict between Communists and non-Communists over who would control South Vietnam, was the single biggest issue in foreign affairs in the 1960s. LBJ inherited the conflict that had been brewing in Southeast Asia for nearly a decade. Johnson dramatically increased American involvement in the conflict. This sparked intense disagreement within the United States. By the time the war was over in the mid-1970s, more than 58,000 Americans had been killed. Despite this sacrifice, the war's outcome was a tragic disappointment. While the US government restricted the military to fighting a limited war to contain communism, the Communists fought a total war to achieve total victory. This legacy of the Vietnam War would haunt and hinder US policies for decades.

American soldiers are shown in Vietnam in June 1966 (above). As the war in Vietnam intensified, President Johnson (below holding helmet) felt that the two wars in which he was engaged were pulling him in opposite directions.

Origins of the War

Dwight Eisenhower had pledged that he would not allow South Vietnam to fall to the Communists and had supplied financial aid and military advisors to that country. When Kennedy became president, there were 800 military advisors there. By the time of his death, he had increased the number to 16,000. The advisors were to provide training for the South Vietnamese military rather than to participate directly in combat.

In 1964 Johnson had campaigned on a promise *not* to send "American boys . . . to do what Asian boys ought to be doing for themselves." But he became increasingly concerned that Southeast Asia would be conquered by the Communists, just as China had been in 1949. Like Eisenhower, he believed in the domino theory—that if Vietnam fell to communism, other nations in the area would fall like dominoes.

In August 1964 North Vietnamese patrol boats reportedly attacked two American destroyers (naval vessels) in international waters in the Gulf of Tonkin, off the coast of Vietnam. The president reported this alleged incident to the American people in a televised address. He did not mention that the US destroyers had secretly been assisting the South Vietnamese in spying and conducting raids on North Vietnam. Although the event appeared relatively minor (no Americans were killed), Johnson asked Congress for additional powers. Congress passed the **Gulf of Tonkin Resolution**, authorizing the president "to take all necessary steps, including the use of armed force" against the North Vietnamese. The resolution was not a declaration of war, but it gave the president broad authority to increase American activity in Vietnam.

Later examination of the Gulf of Tonkin incident proved to be quite confusing. Though the president apparently believed an attack had occurred, it was later revealed that one may not have actually taken place at all. Some Americans would later argue that Johnson used the event as an excuse to expand US involvement in Vietnam.

This involvement was hotly debated in the United States. Leaders who favored an increased American presence in Vietnam, or an "escalation" of the war, were called **hawks**. Those who wanted the United States to withdraw completely were called **doves**. Under Johnson, the number of troops in Vietnam escalated rapidly. By 1968 more than half a million Americans were on Vietnamese soil.

▲ Viet Cong navigate a swamp in South Vietnam in preparation for a surprise attack on US troops.

In Vietnam

The United States was committed to protecting the government of South Vietnam. Though the government was non-Communist, some of the leaders were corrupt and unpopular with many Vietnamese. The United States had to fight not only the Communist soldiers from North Vietnam but also Communist fighters in the South, known as the **Viet Cong**. The Viet Cong waged a very effective guerrilla war against American and South Vietnamese troops.

Technically, because Congress had never officially declared war, the United States was engaged in only a "police action." The nation feared that if it declared war, many more countries would join the fight and possibly cause a world war. Yet thousands of Americans were dying in Vietnam for a cause that the nation's politicians were still debating.

Fighting the war posed numerous challenges. Although the United States had modern, high-tech weapons, it could not use them easily in Vietnam. In World War II, the United States had defeated Germany partly by bombing its industrial cities. But North Vietnam had no large industrial plants. Rather, it had thousands of little shops scattered across the land. The jungle terrain also made it difficult for American bombers to identify targets on the **Ho Chi Minh Trail**, the route used by North Vietnamese and Viet Cong forces to move men and goods from North to South Vietnam (through Cambodia and Laos). Even when the Americans identified specific targets, success was not guaranteed. For example, one log bridge was destroyed at least twenty times, but the North Vietnamese kept rebuilding it in only a few days. The North Vietnamese received a steady stream of military supplies from both Communist China and the Soviet Union.

Often, US servicemen could not identify the enemy. The Viet Cong looked just like South Vietnamese civilians. Usually, people in the cities supported the Americans. But in rural areas, Americans did not know whom to trust. The Viet Cong even used children to hurl hand grenades at American soldiers. Guerrilla attacks proved exhausting and demoralizing to American soldiers.

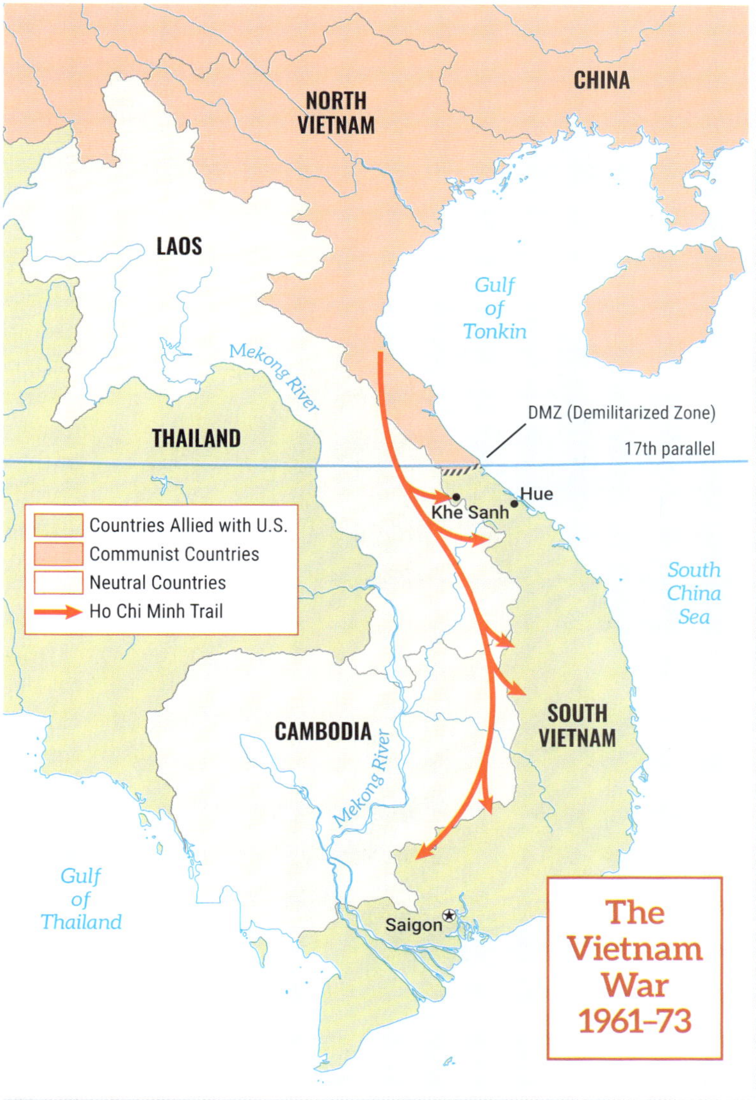

▲ Young men burning their draft cards at a Vietnam War protest

On the Home Front

Americans were shocked to hear reports of a few incidences in which American soldiers purposely killed innocent Vietnamese civilians. Such killings were contrary to moral values. However, most Americans were also infuriated by many of the antiwar protests. Demonstrators often condemned all soldiers fighting in the war, though most were in Vietnam simply because they had been drafted.

As the war continued, a group called the New Left emerged. (In politics, liberals are known as the Left or left wing, while conservatives are called the Right or right wing.) One of the primary concerns for the New Left was the Vietnam War. They questioned why the United States was involved in the conflict. They denounced the deaths, devastation, and chaos that the war had brought to the Vietnamese people. Opponents of this group noted that they said little or nothing about the horrible deeds committed by the Communists in North Vietnam—hundreds of thousands who opposed Communist rule were killed or sent to labor camps. Since members of the New Left burned flags and draft cards and fled the country to avoid the draft, many viewed them as anti-American.

In addition to the war, the New Left expressed other concerns. For example, they actively sought to advance civil rights for black Americans and to reduce poverty.

Cashews ▼

Fun Fact

Vietnam is the world's largest exporter of black pepper and cashew nuts.

The antiwar movement was itself only a part of an overall youth movement in the 1960s and early 1970s known as the **counterculture**. It was a rebellion against the materialism, morals, and values of the previous generation. Proponents of the counterculture believed that the solution to society's problems included self-expression and embracing a philosophy of love and sharing. "Do your own thing" and "All you need is love" were among their simplistic expressions. The counterculture also glorified youth as having the answers to society's problems, illustrated by the popular saying, "Don't trust anyone over thirty."

The "hippie" movement (derived from the slang term *hip*, "approving of current tastes and attitudes") was an important part of the counterculture. Hippies emphasized not conforming to accepted behavior. They rejected the neat clothing and appearance of their parents. Most wore jeans and t-shirts that were dirty, patched, and often oddly colored. They wore beads, and young men grew their hair and beards long as a sign of protest. Rejecting traditional standards, many hippies opposed marriage and advocated unrestricted sexual activity. They embraced rock music with questionable and suggestive lyrics. Hippies were also leaders in the drug culture. They experimented with numerous illegal hallucinogenic drugs, notably LSD. The most popular drug was marijuana.

There was clearly a sharp divide between culture and counterculture. Critics of the counterculture said those who embraced the lifestyle were using it to reject responsibility for their own actions. They argued that the belief that merely expressing "love" as the answer to man's problems was naive and simplistic. Christians noted that the movement's basic philosophy provided an excuse to participate in sinful behavior.

▲ Many in this group identified with the hippie movement of the 1960s and 1970s.

The Tet Offensive

The North Vietnamese, led by Ho Chi Minh, believed that if they could prolong the war, they would win. They said the Americans would give up and pull out.

The United States began Operation Rolling Thunder in March 1965. This campaign dropped massive numbers of bombs on North Vietnamese targets. It continued until October 1968.

By late 1967 Johnson and his advisors were becoming concerned by increasing criticism of US involvement in the war and by decreasing public support for the war. Opinion polls in 1965 showed that 25 percent of Americans believed it was a mistake to send troops to Vietnam, but that percentage had risen to 45 percent by December 1967. Meanwhile, the president assured Americans that the war was going well and that victory would be achieved.

However, the North Vietnamese and the Viet Cong launched multiple surprise attacks on January 31, 1968. It was the beginning of the Vietnamese New Year (Tet). From one end of South Vietnam to the other, they attacked police stations, military bases, government buildings, radio and power stations, and foreign embassies. In what became known as the **Tet Offensive**, more than 85,000 Communist troops attacked every major town and city in South Vietnam and

▼ South Vietnamese soldiers fighting during the Tet Offensive

A news crew interviews American soldiers fighting in Vietnam in 1967.

dozens of others. They captured the ancient capital city, Hue, and the capital city in the South at the time, Saigon. They surrounded the US base at Khe Sanh, hoping to repeat the 1954 victory over the French at the Battle of Dien Bien Phu. It was the largest military operation conducted by either side to that point in the war. The early success of the Communists was stunning.

The American and South Vietnamese forces counterattacked. Within a few weeks, they regained what had been lost. But the cost for both sides was enormous. The combined number of casualties appears to have exceeded 100,000.

After intense fighting, the Tet Offensive ended in crushing defeat for the Communists. Despite this victory, the news media and opponents of the war questioned how an enemy, supposedly near defeat, was able to launch such a huge attack. Many newspapers and magazines ran articles that urged American withdrawal from the war. Walter Cronkite, the respected CBS news anchor, said with dismay during a broadcast, "I thought we were winning the war."

Johnson responded to the antiwar surge by taking several actions. He stopped the bombing of North Vietnam and showed a willingness to negotiate with the Communists in Vietnam. He also slightly increased the number of US troops in the war. He then announced, on March 31, 1968, that he would no longer be a candidate for the Democratic nomination for the presidency that year.

Chappie James: American Hero

In 1975 General Daniel "Chappie" James Jr. became the first black American to attain the rank of four-star general. During World War II, he helped train a group of African American pilots, the Tuskegee Airmen, who became famous for their accomplishments. James also flew combat missions in the Korean and Vietnam Wars. He is buried in Arlington National Cemetery.

SECTION REVIEW 25.1

1. What did Johnson call his legislative program?
2. What was a success of the War on Poverty? What were four negative effects?
3. In what cities did riots occur during this time of civil unrest?
4. What was the Gulf of Tonkin Resolution?
5. What were Communist fighters in South Vietnam called?
6. Describe the New Left.
7. Should Christians have supported the counterculture of the 1960s? Are there areas today in which Christians must not conform to the dominant culture? Give a specific example.
8. On what holiday did the North Vietnamese and Viet Cong conduct multiple surprise attacks?

25.2 THE NIXON ADMINISTRATION

What significant events occurred during the presidency of Richard Nixon?

GUIDING QUESTIONS

- What major events occurred during Nixon's presidency?
- How did the scandals during Nixon's presidency affect the nation?

The Election of 1968

Most Americans were surprised when Johnson abandoned his plans to seek reelection. But the president knew that he faced much opposition within the country. Eugene McCarthy, an antiwar senator from Minnesota, was gaining support for the Democratic nomination as he denounced the country's involvement in Vietnam. Other Americans felt the nation should be in Vietnam in order to contain communism, but they disliked the manner in which Johnson had conducted the war. The president, fearing greater involvement by China and Russia, was fighting a limited war. Some critics believed this was a terrible mistake. Still others disliked Johnson's Great Society programs. Though the programs were popular with many, they were expensive, and some questioned whether they were really working.

▲ Robert Kennedy (shown at the microphones) was assassinated shortly after this photograph was taken.

Shortly before Johnson's withdrawal from the presidential race, **Robert Kennedy** (a Democratic senator from New York and a brother of the late president) announced his candidacy. Soon after Johnson's withdrawal, Johnson's vice president, Hubert Humphrey, also entered the race.

Kennedy was popular with many voters. However, in June 1968, on the night of his victory in the California presidential primary, Kennedy was assassinated at a Los Angeles hotel. Sirhan B. Sirhan, an Arab radical, shot the candidate as he was passing through the hotel kitchen.

Later that summer at their party convention in Chicago, the Democrats nominated Humphrey as their candidate. But the convention was marred by a wave of antiwar riots and demonstrations. Police responded firmly to the protests. Critics of the police said they overreacted. Much of the American public was convinced that the nation was out of control.

The southern states had voted solidly Democratic since the end of Reconstruction. But in the 1960s, the South began to shift away from the Democrats. George C. Wallace, the Democratic governor of Alabama who supported segregation, ran as a third-party candidate in the 1968 election. As the nominee of the American Independent Party, he was victorious in five Deep South states and received forty-six electoral votes. He won more electoral votes than any other third-party candidate since Teddy Roosevelt in the 1912 election.

The Republicans placed former vice president **Richard Nixon** on their ticket with Maryland governor Spiro T. Agnew as their vice-presidential nominee. Nixon attacked the counterculture and Johnson's Great Society. He promised to bring peace in Vietnam but gave few details. In the end, Nixon won the election.

Richard Nixon

37

Born	January 9, 1913
Died	April 22, 1994
Home state	California
Wife	Thelma "Pat" Ryan
Church	Quaker
Occupations	lawyer
Party	Republican
Years served as president	1969–74
Terms	1 and partial (resigned)
Vice presidents	1st—Spiro T. Agnew (resigned) 2nd—Gerald Ford

Fun Fact

One month before Richard Nixon became president, his daughter Julie married David Eisenhower, the grandson of President Eisenhower.

Foreign Affairs

The End of the Vietnam War

Nixon inherited a controversial war, a large national debt, and an economy that was suffering. Johnson's attempt to simultaneously fight a war, run his Great Society programs, and limit inflation had not worked well.

To avoid the failures that had halted Johnson's career, Nixon made ending the Vietnam War his priority. He intended to withdraw the ground troops from Vietnam while waging an intense bombing campaign. Yet he did not want it to seem as though the United States had lost the war.

Vietnamization

Nixon announced his plan to gradually withdraw US troops from the war and transfer responsibility for the fighting to the South Vietnamese. The United States would continue providing supplies, training, and air support. This proposal was known as **Vietnamization.** As it proceeded, many American troops came home. When Nixon took office in January 1969, almost 550,000 US troops were in Vietnam; by December 1971 there were 157,000. In December 1972, as the end of his first term neared, only 24,000 remained.

But as American soldiers left Vietnam, the Communists increased their forces and stockpiled supplies. Between attacks on South Vietnam, the Communists withdrew to bases in Cambodia. Consequently, on March 18, 1969, without Congress's approval, Nixon authorized secret bombing raids over Cambodia. During the next fourteen months, bombers made over 3,500 strikes inside Cambodia.

On April 30, 1970, Nixon publicly announced a temporary expansion of the war into Cambodia. The following year, the United States also attacked North Vietnamese forces and supply convoys along the Ho Chi Minh Trail in Laos.

When the war widened to include Cambodia, demonstrations erupted on college campuses. On May 4, 1970, tragedy occurred at **Kent State University** in Ohio. During several days of student protests, one of the campus buildings had been set ablaze. The state's governor had then sent more than 1,200 National Guardsmen to restore order. On May 4, over 3,000 students gathered for a rally that had been banned by the university. The National Guard ordered the students to disperse. Most of the crowd stayed. Some shouted and threw rocks at the guardsmen, who then fired tear gas and advanced. Later, several guardsmen fired into the crowd. Why they did so has been a matter of intense debate. Four students were killed and nine others were wounded. Two of those killed had been active participants in the demonstration, but the other two were bystanders on their way to class. Student strikes and protests increased after the Kent State shootings. Hundreds of colleges and universities canceled classes to avoid problems.

▾ An antiwar demonstration at Kent State University turned deadly on May 4, 1970. National Guardsmen fired into a crowd of students, killing four. A young lady kneels, distraught, by the body of a student.

America Withdraws

Peace negotiations regarding the Vietnam War began in 1968, while Johnson was still president, but arguments and disagreements caused them to stall. One early source of conflict, which delayed the proceedings for weeks, was whether to use a round table or a rectangular table for talks.

Meanwhile, Nixon was inaugurated in January 1969. Discussions continued for years as the United States implemented Vietnamization. Hoping to pressure the Communists into making a deal, in December 1972 Nixon ordered some of the war's heaviest bombing on North Vietnam. Finally, a cease-fire was signed in late January 1973.

According to the terms of the peace agreement, the United States would withdraw its remaining 24,000 soldiers from Vietnam, and North Vietnam would release nearly 600 American **POWs** (prisoners of war). The United States agreed to continue providing South Vietnam with military supplies.

Though American troop involvement in Vietnam ended, the conflict was not really over. North Vietnam had kept troops in parts of South Vietnam after the war ended. Two years later, North Vietnam launched a major attack on the South. Nixon was no longer in office, and his successor, Gerald Ford, was unable to persuade Congress to help South Vietnam. Within weeks, North Vietnamese soldiers reached Saigon. On April 30, 1975, that city fell to the Communists. Shortly afterward, South Vietnam surrendered. The long war was over, and Vietnam was one nation—controlled by the Communists. Hundreds of thousands of Vietnamese fled the country.

The results of the war at least partially proved the domino theory. After South Vietnam's government collapsed, both Laos and Cambodia soon fell to the Communists.

People in all areas taken by the Communists suffered brutal treatment. The worst example was in Cambodia. Communists there, called the Khmer Rouge, were led by dictator Pol Pot. From 1975 to 1979, the Khmer Rouge slaughtered 1.5 to 2 million Cambodians—nearly one-fourth of the nation's population.

▲ In this March 1973 photo, American POWs are awaiting their release.

▼ South Vietnamese civilians are shown fleeing southward as the Communist forces attacked their region during the Tet Offensive (1968).

the TWENTY-SIXTH AMENDMENT

Prior to 1971, only a few states allowed individuals younger than twenty-one to vote. Though some Americans had supported a younger voting age for decades, the issue received renewed attention during the Vietnam War. Because eighteen-year-olds were eligible to be drafted for military duty and might die in battle, many argued that the voting age should be lowered.

The **Twenty-Sixth Amendment** was passed in 1971. It granted voting rights to citizens age eighteen and older.

The Cost of the War

For the United States, the cost of the Vietnam War was high. As already mentioned, over 58,000 Americans were killed. In addition, 300,000 Americans were wounded and about $150 billion was spent. But the war had cost far more than statistics can show. War veterans came home to a disillusioned country. Few of them were welcomed as heroes; most were ignored. Some were even harassed and ridiculed by war opponents when they returned. Not until 1982 was a national memorial created and dedicated to the members of the military who had served in Vietnam.

Congress reacted to the cost and controversy of the Vietnam War by limiting the president's power to fight such wars in the future. Nixon vetoed the **War Powers Act** (1973), but Congress overrode his veto. The act states that presidents have to inform Congress within 48 hours of sending military forces to an area without a declaration of war. Those troops cannot stay longer than 90 days unless Congress approves. Whether this legislation is constitutional continues to be a matter of debate.

▲ President Nixon (at right) shares a meal with Chinese leader Zhou Enlai, a longtime associate of Mao Zedong, during Nixon's 1972 trip to China.

Communist China and the Soviet Union

As President Nixon was seeking an end to the war in Vietnam, he also sought friendlier relationships with the Communist nations of China and the Soviet Union. He introduced a new era of **détente** (an easing of tensions) between America and those two countries. Nixon relied heavily on Henry Kissinger, a Harvard professor born in Germany, who became his special advisor. In 1973 Kissinger became Nixon's secretary of state.

After Communists had taken control of China in 1949, China became allies with the Soviet Union. But by the 1960s, disagreements emerged between the two nations, and they were soon rivals. Still, Americans worried that because both China and the Soviet Union embraced communism, they might join forces in any conflict with the West. In 1971 Kissinger seized an opportunity to open relations with China and made a secret trip there. While there, Kissinger arranged for a presidential visit to occur the following year. In February 1972, accompanied by American reporters and camera crews, Nixon toured the Great Wall, attended banquets, and met with Chinese leader Mao Zedong. Many historians view this feat as Nixon's greatest achievement. By opening diplomatic relations with the People's Republic of China, Nixon drove a wedge between the world's two largest Communist countries. This wedge helped lead the Soviets to improve their dealings with the United States.

But détente with the People's Republic of China had some negative consequences. As seen in Chapter 24, the United States and the United Nations recognized Taiwan as the "real" China when Chiang Kai-shek fled there in 1949. This meant that Taiwan controlled China's vote in the UN Security Council. As part of his effort to improve relations with Communist China, in 1971 Nixon supported the United Nations in removing Taiwan from the Security Council and giving Taiwan's seat to Communist China. That change gave the Communist country veto power on issues brought to the Security Council.

Just months after Nixon visited China, he continued détente by traveling to the Soviet Union. In May 1972 he met with that nation's leader, Leonid Brezhnev, and discussed the Strategic Arms Limitation Treaty (SALT I). The treaty called for both nations to limit the types and number of their nuclear warheads and missiles. In addition, the leaders discussed trade issues and agreed to cooperate regarding scientific and space projects.

▲ Leonid Brezhnev (left) and President Nixon met three times (1972, 1973, and 1974) during Nixon's years in the White House.

The Middle East

The Middle East was a constant source of problems. In October 1973 Egypt and Syria, armed with modern weapons provided by the Soviet Union, launched a surprise attack against America's ally Israel.

The fighting began on Yom Kippur, the holiest day of the year for Jews. During the first week of the Yom Kippur War, Israel's army was devastated, but the following week, Israel took the offensive. Also, Nixon sent a large supply of weapons to assist Israel. A cease-fire was reached after a few weeks of fighting.

Domestic Affairs

Besides the many issues relating to foreign affairs, President Nixon faced several perplexing domestic problems. One of them, Watergate, would lead to his political downfall.

Economic Problems

During the Vietnam War, the national government spent money for not only the war but also new domestic programs. When Nixon entered office, he had to contend with both a large debt and problems caused by inflation.

Recession

Nixon tried to curb inflation by cutting government spending and increasing taxes. With less money in circulation, the value of the dollar would increase. But such a situation often results in a **recession** (a slowdown in the economy, not as severe as a depression) as it did during Nixon's administration. During a recession, businesses produce fewer products and may have to lay off some workers.

To make the recession less painful to the average American, Nixon increased government spending to create new jobs. But that only increased the national debt.

Nixon tried a number of measures to fight inflation. None worked particularly well. In 1973 the inflation rate was over 6 percent. It nearly doubled the following year.

Energy Crisis

In October 1973 the Organization of Petroleum Exporting Countries (OPEC), which consisted mostly of Arab nations, was angry over American support of Israel. OPEC ordered an embargo (complete ban) of oil shipments to America and other nations that supported Israel. Since America imported a large portion of its oil from Middle Eastern countries, the embargo's impact was enormous.

▲ Long gas lines were common in the energy crisis during the 1970s.

Some gas stations were forced to close. Others limited how much gasoline each customer could purchase. Motorists waited in long lines. Prices for gasoline, fuel oil, plastics, and other petroleum-based products skyrocketed.

Nixon asked Americans to conserve energy. Some people bought smaller cars that got better gas mileage. Many people who lived in big cities started carpooling, and vacationing close to home became popular. Congress lowered the speed limit, even on the nation's interstates, to fifty-five miles per hour. Congress approved a pipeline across Alaska to gain access to oil reserves above the Arctic Circle and began spending money on new programs to develop alternative sources of energy.

OPEC lifted the oil embargo in March 1974, and the energy crisis eased a little. But that organization steadily raised crude oil prices. Some Muslim extremists wanted to destroy America with high oil prices. But moderate Muslims, in nations such as Saudi Arabia, urged caution; they argued that ruining the economies of Western industrialized countries would only hinder the West's ability to buy oil, thereby hurting oil-producing nations.

Abortion

Prior to the 1970s, state laws had long restricted or even prohibited abortion. However, in the landmark case ***Roe v. Wade*** (1973), the Supreme Court ruled that the Constitution protects a woman's right to have an abortion.

After this ruling, the number of abortions rapidly increased. According to National Right to Life, a leading pro-life organization, abortions in the United States exceeded a million each year from 1975 to 2012. In recent

Total Abortions in the U.S. since *Roe v. Wade*

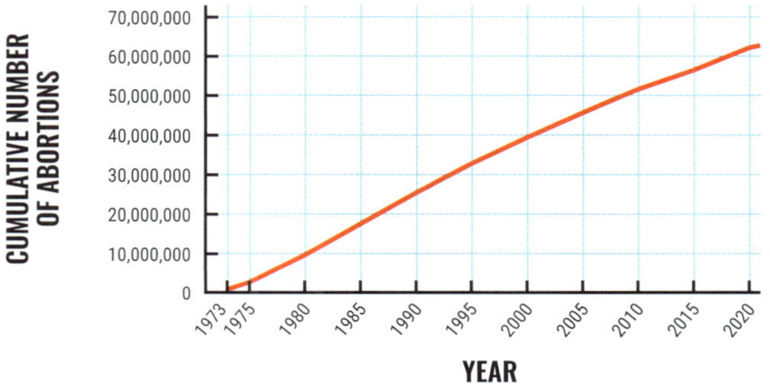

years, several factors—improved technology (such as ultrasounds), more people acknowledging that abortion is the taking of a life, implementation of new laws—have led to a decline in the number of abortions. Yet tragically, more than 800,000 abortions still occur annually in the country. More than 63 million have been performed in the United States since *Roe v. Wade*.

Environment and Gender Issues

In the 1960s a number of issues led activists to start new movements to deal with the abuses of industry and the denial of certain human rights. Sometimes these movements contributed to the unrest of the decade because Americans often disagreed about how to handle these matters.

In 1970 Congress established the Environmental Protection Agency (EPA) to oversee environmental regulations. The Clean Air Act of 1970 (amended in 1977 and 1990) regulated air pollution. The Federal Water Pollution Control Act (1972) and the Clean Water Act (1977) regulated water pollution.

Nixon signed the Endangered Species Act in 1973, granting government agencies the power to decide which species are threatened and how to protect them. Environmentalists complained that the law was too weak. Critics complained that the regulations sometimes did not weigh the costs and benefits before limiting industry and construction, such as logging and dam building. For example, to protect a tiny fish called a snail darter, government officials stopped the construction of a TVA dam on the Little Tennessee River.

Some Christians reacted negatively to the extreme views within the environmental movement. Other Christians noted that the environment should be protected for biblical reasons. They said nature is precious because it is God's creation. They opposed the radical notion of worshiping the earth, which some embraced. A growing number of Christians observed that God has called mankind not to abuse creation but to subdue it and exercise dominion, or control, over it as stewards of God's work (Gen. 1:28). Specifics about how to handle environmental matters caused some disagreement among Christians; however, wise management was recognized as the biblical goal (Gen. 2:15).

▾ During this period, the Florida manatee, the Florida panther, and the Everglade snail kite (all shown below) were categorized as endangered species.

▲ Supporters (top) and opponents (above) of the ERA were active during the 1970s and 1980s. At the time, it was one of the nation's most-debated political issues.

As a group, women had long suffered from various forms of discrimination. For instance, women often received less pay than men working the same job. Widows sometimes discovered after a husband's death that the excellent credit rating they had built together no longer existed; however, a widower's credit rating continued unimpaired. Many states and Congress began to address these injustices through legislation.

In 1972 Congress passed the **Equal Rights Amendment (ERA)**. Supporters of this amendment said that it would guarantee equal rights for women. It stated, "Equality of rights under the law shall not be denied or abridged by the United States or by any state on account of sex." For various reasons, many women opposed the amendment, and they led the successful fight to block its approval in many states.

While ERA proponents argued that it would reinforce the basic rights as citizens that women held under the Constitution, opponents believed that sufficient laws were already being passed to guarantee those rights. Opponents also feared that the amendment would eliminate the traditional protections that women enjoyed, such as exemption from the military draft, and might result in the banning of separate bathrooms for men and women. They were further concerned by how some ERA advocates opposed the scriptural teachings regarding marriage and family roles.

The bitter fight regarding the ERA ended in 1982 when the amendment failed to receive the necessary approval of three-fourths of state legislatures before its ratification deadline expired. It had been approved by thirty-five of the needed thirty-eight state legislatures. However, by 1979 five of those thirty-five had revoked their earlier support, citing concerns voiced by ERA opponents.

Political Scandals

In 1972 Nixon easily won reelection with 61 percent of the popular vote and 520 of the 538 Electoral College votes. He lost only Massachusetts and the District of Columbia to the Democratic nominee, Senator George McGovern of South Dakota. Yet less than two years after his triumph, Nixon would be disgraced and out of office.

The Vice President Quits

Nixon's vice president, **Spiro T. Agnew**, was charged with having accepted bribes from construction companies when he was governor of Maryland. Agnew resigned the vice-presidency on October 10, 1973. He was the second person to resign that office. (John C. Calhoun had resigned for political—not criminal—reasons in 1832.)

For the first time since its ratification in 1967, the Twenty-Fifth Amendment was used to select a new vice president. Following the guidelines in the amendment, Nixon chose Gerald R. Ford, a Michigan congressman. Congress confirmed the nomination by overwhelming margins, and Ford was sworn in on December 6, 1973.

Watergate Scandal

In the early hours of June 17, 1972, during the heat of the presidential campaign, police arrested five burglars, carrying electronic listening devices, who had broken into the headquarters of the Democratic National Committee. That event at the Watergate Office Complex in Washington, DC, initially caused little stir. But the burglary of that office and the attempt to conceal information about it became known as the **Watergate scandal**.

The press learned that the arrested men were members of the Committee to Reelect the President. The trial of the Watergate burglars and two other officials under Nixon began in January 1973. One of the burglars alleged that authorities "higher up" were behind the break-in and were trying to conceal the fact. No evidence linked Nixon directly to the break-in; however, as more details were uncovered, it appeared that he might have tried to hide the involvement of his administration officials in the burglary.

In May, the Senate started its own independent investigation of the scandal. A Senate committee discovered that the White House had secretly tape-recorded all of Nixon's office conversations. By listening to the tapes, the committee would be able to determine whether the president had been involved in an attempt to conceal what had occurred. But Nixon refused to release the tapes. He argued that he had executive privilege (the principle that a president's conversations should remain private) and that turning over the tapes would endanger national security.

His refusal began a long struggle over control of the tapes. Nixon tried to satisfy investigators first by releasing edited transcripts of the tapes and then by releasing just some of the tapes. Meanwhile, he maintained his complete innocence of wrongdoing. But soon the tapes and the investigation exposed a disturbing side of Nixon and his aides—political "dirty tricks," deceit, and outright lies.

Finally, in July 1974 the Supreme Court ruled unanimously that Nixon must release all the tapes. Though the tapes did not indicate that Nixon knew about the Watergate break-in beforehand, they proved that he participated in attempts to cover up the involvement of his White House subordinates.

The House of Representatives discussed bringing impeachment charges against Nixon including obstruction of justice, misuse of presidential powers, and refusal to comply with Congress's requests for evidence. With impeachment by the House a virtual certainty and conviction (and removal from office) by the Senate likely, Nixon resigned on August 9. He is the only president ever to do so.

The American political system successfully exposed and dealt with the Watergate conspiracy rather than pushing it under a rug. It showed that the president is not above the law. The Constitution's system of checks and balances worked. Yet Nixon's corruption seriously damaged the prestige of the presidency and undermined the American people's faith in their political leaders.

Watergate Building

▾ President Nixon is walking to a helicopter to depart the White House after announcing his resignation.

SECTION REVIEW 25.2

1. What was Vietnamization?
2. What tragedy occurred at Kent State University?
3. Why did lowering the voting age receive renewed support during the Vietnam War?
4. What motivated Congress to approve a pipeline across Alaska?
5. What landmark case declared abortion a constitutional right?
6. Should government regulations be passed regarding the environment? Why or why not?
7. Who was Nixon's vice president that had to resign? Why did he do so?
8. What scandal led to the resignation of President Nixon?

GUIDING QUESTION

- What occurred during Ford's presidency?

Gerald Ford

Born	July 14, 1913	38
Died	December 26, 2006	
Home state	Michigan (born in Nebraska)	
Wife	Elizabeth "Betty" Bloomer	
Church	Episcopalian	
Occupations	lawyer	
Party	Republican	
Years served as president	1974–77	
Terms	partial (upon the resignation of Nixon)	
Vice president	Nelson Rockefeller	

25.3 THE FORD ADMINISTRATION

What important events occurred during the presidency of Gerald Ford?

Vice President **Gerald Ford** took the oath of office on the day Nixon left office. He was the first person to serve as president who had never been elected president or vice president in a presidential election. His elevation to the nation's highest office was by an appointment and then a resignation. Ford then appointed, and Congress approved, former New York governor Nelson Rockefeller as vice president. Thus, neither of the nation's top two officials had been elected in a national election.

Ford saw the need to restore the public's confidence in the presidency. He promised "openness and candor" in contrast to Nixon's secrecy and dishonesty. He promised regular news conferences so the public would be informed of his actions. Ford also tried to lower people's expectations. He emphasized that he was only an ordinary man who would try to do his best. "Remember," he told the public, "I'm a Ford, not a Lincoln."

Pardon of Nixon

One month after he became president, Ford ignited a controversy that might have cost him winning the 1976 presidential election. He pardoned Richard Nixon. By pardoning Nixon for any crimes he "may have committed" while in office, Ford angered many of his own supporters. Some Democrats accused him of making a "buddy deal" with the former president in exchange for his nomination as vice president. No evidence of such an agreement was ever found.

President Ford testified at a US House of Representatives committee hearing in October 1974 to explain why he pardoned former president Nixon. He believed that the possible trial of Nixon would worsen the divisions within the nation at a time the country needed to heal. Many Americans strongly disagreed with Ford's actions.

▲ Protesters denounced the pardon of President Nixon.

Ford insisted he issued the pardon because he believed placing the former president on trial would have only prolonged the country's agony from the Watergate scandal. He said that the country needed to heal. Many critics thought it unfair that Nixon should escape punishment while some of his subordinates received prison sentences for their role in Watergate. As a result, Ford's popularity fell dramatically.

Inflation

As noted earlier, Nixon's attempts to control inflation during his last eighteen months in office had not worked. Shortly after Ford became president, the inflation rate reached a stunning 12 percent.

Ford called for a voluntary anti-inflation crusade to help handle the recession he had inherited. Called WIN ("Whip Inflation Now"), Ford's plan urged consumers to stop buying high-priced goods and to save money instead. It also asked workers not to seek wage increases. He urged people to plant gardens to offset rising food costs. But most workers, businesses, and consumers believed that they were the *victims* of inflation rather than the *causes* of it, so they ignored WIN.

With inflation, unemployment climbed. Ford asked Congress for a tax cut and spending cuts. Though taxes were cut, spending was not. The economy continued to suffer. Though inflation eventually declined, it was still above 6 percent in mid-1976.

▲ Ford encouraged his supporters to wear WIN (Whip Inflation Now) buttons.

SECTION REVIEW 25.3

1. What controversial action did Ford take soon after becoming president? Should he have done this? Why or why not?
2. What ongoing economic issue did Ford face? Why did his solution not work?

GUIDING QUESTIONS

- What were important domestic issues during Carter's presidency?
- What were the important international issues during Carter's presidency?

James "Jimmy" Carter

39

Born	October 1, 1924
Died	still living on the date this book was published
Home state	Georgia
Wife	Rosalynn Smith
Church	Baptist
Occupations	naval lieutenant, businessman, peanut farmer
Party	Democrat
Years served as president	1977–81
Terms	1
Vice president	Walter Mondale

25.4 THE CARTER ADMINISTRATION

What major events occurred during the presidency of Jimmy Carter?

The Election of 1976

As the 1976 election approached, the Republican Party was still recovering from Watergate. In addition, Ford's unpopular pardon of Nixon and his inability to handle the economic issues made the Democrats feel confident that they could recapture the White House.

When Republicans gathered at their convention to name their nominee, many opposed selecting Gerald Ford. They supported a former actor and former Democrat, Ronald Reagan. Reagan had joined the Republican party in 1962 and campaigned nationally for Barry Goldwater in the 1964 election. Reagan quickly became a major spokesman for the conservative wing of the party. In 1966 he was elected governor of California and was reelected four years later. At the 1976 convention, Ford narrowly won the party's nomination. Though defeated, Reagan spent the next four years preparing for the 1980 race.

From the many candidates competing for the nomination, the Democrats selected little-known **Jimmy Carter**. He was a successful peanut farmer and the former governor of Georgia. During the campaign, Carter stressed his honesty, his Christianity, and the fact that he was an outsider to Washington politics. He had taken a strong stand on civil rights in Georgia, so he appealed to black voters. Labor unions also supported him.

Carter won the election and entered office with high hopes. Democrats controlled both houses of Congress by large margins. Americans were looking for someone to solve the problems of the day. Carter wanted to bring new faces to Washington and use the same simple, down-home style he had used in Georgia.

But Carter's inexperience in Washington actually hindered his effectiveness in office. He had trouble gaining support in Congress for his ideas. Critics called him a micromanager because of his tendency to get bogged down in the details of governing rather than focusing on his long-term goals. His lack of experience in foreign affairs also proved to be a handicap.

President Carter in one of the peanut fields his family owned in Plains, Georgia

Domestic Affairs

Amnesty

One of President Carter's first acts was to offer amnesty, or a pardon, to those who had fled the country or had failed to register for the draft in order to avoid fighting in Vietnam. This affected hundreds of thousands of individuals. Though some praised Carter's actions, he provoked the wrath of many veterans who had loyally fulfilled their obligation. Family members of those who died in the war also objected. Mercy to "draft dodgers" was not popular with those groups.

▲ In 1977 Carter offered a pardon to individuals who had refused to register for the draft (such as many in this 1969 protest) during the Vietnam War.

Economic Issues

Troubles with the economy continued under Carter. The annual inflation rate once again rose to double digits. By mid-1980 it exceeded 14 percent. Because workers could not afford the higher prices of goods and services, they demanded higher wages. Rising inflation led to interest rates on loans reaching record levels. People were unable to afford home mortgages. Builders found themselves out of work, and construction-related businesses suffered.

From 1973 to 1977, the cost of imported oil skyrocketed from $8 billion to $40 billion a year. Carter wanted to end dependence on foreign oil; in April 1977 he presented his National Energy Plan. It called for nationwide conservation and the development of alternative energy sources. It also created a federal Department of Energy to oversee energy policy.

Carter thought that nuclear power might help solve the energy crisis. But some were deeply concerned about the potential hazards of nuclear waste and nuclear accidents. Support for his program was seriously damaged by an accident at the Three Mile Island nuclear power plant in Pennsylvania in 1979. The accident allowed radioactive steam to be released into the atmosphere.

▼ Three Mile Island nuclear power plant in Pennsylvania

Foreign Affairs

In his inaugural address, Carter had declared that human rights would be central in his foreign policy: "Because we are free, we can never be indifferent to the fate of freedom elsewhere." He believed that all people should be free to own property and make political choices without intimidation or persecution. Such ideas were good, but getting other nations to implement them proved difficult. Critics noted that Carter's human rights policy sometimes actually hurt American interests. For example, Carter condemned the dictatorial government in Nicaragua. That government was later overthrown, but the new government was also a dictatorship. The earlier one had been led by non-Communists while the new one placed Communists in control. At a time when America was trying to contain communism, some said that Carter's policy sometimes made little sense.

The Panama Canal Controversy

As mentioned in Chapter 18, the United States helped Panama win its independence from Colombia in 1903. Afterward, the United States paid Panama for the use of a ten-mile-wide strip of land in perpetuity (forever). The Panama Canal was completed in 1914.

Panamanians had resented American control of the canal for many years. Nixon and Ford had conducted negotiations with Panama to give the canal to that nation. Carter completed the process when he signed the **Panama Canal Treaty** in 1977. The agreement stated that Panama and the United States would operate the canal jointly until December 31, 1999, when Panama would take complete control of it. The United States retained the right to intervene with military force against any threat that might interfere with the canal remaining open to ships of all nations.

The treaty created controversy in the United States. Supporters of the treaty argued that the canal's narrow width and the growth of air power made the canal less important (militarily and economically) to the United States than it had been in earlier years. They noted, for example, that aircraft carriers and oil tankers were too wide to use the canal. Supporters also hoped that the US action would improve relations with Latin American nations, many of which resented US power and dominance in the region.

Opponents of the treaty claimed that the waterway was still vital to American interests and should not be given to a sometimes unstable government. As for its narrowness, it could be widened to accommodate larger ships. (Panama did complete a decade-long widening project in 2016.) They also feared that Panamanians might not have the skill or ability to operate the canal properly. After a heated debate, the Senate narrowly approved the treaty in April 1978.

▾ Aerial view of one set of locks in the Panama Canal

The Camp David Accords

In 1978 President Carter invited Egypt's president, Anwar el-Sadat, and Israel's prime minister, Menachem Begin, to Camp David, a presidential retreat in Maryland. These countries had traditionally been enemies. With Carter as mediator, Begin and Sadat reached a historic accord, or agreement. After nearly two weeks of secret negotiations, Sadat and Begin signed the **Camp David Accords**. Israel agreed to return the Sinai Peninsula to Egypt (which Israel had captured during the Six-Day War in 1967), and Egypt agreed to recognize Israel's right to exist. Egypt was the first Arab nation to recognize that right since the creation of the nation of Israel in 1948.

▲ Egyptian leader Anwar el-Sadat, President Carter, and Prime Minister Menachem Begin (left to right) celebrate the signing of the Camp David Accords.

Cold War Continues

Carter continued détente. As part of that policy, he negotiated another Strategic Arms Limitation Treaty (SALT II) with the Soviets. Like SALT I signed by President Nixon, SALT II sought to further limit the number of nuclear weapons possessed by the United States and the Soviet Union.

SALT II was signed in March 1979. But when Carter submitted the treaty for Senate approval, some senators and Americans opposed parts of the agreement. Opposition grew when the Soviet Union invaded Afghanistan later that year. Eventually, the president withdrew the treaty.

In late December 1979, the Soviets sent more than 30,000 soldiers to invade the neighboring nation of Afghanistan. The Communist government that had taken over Afghanistan was facing much opposition from the Afghan people. The Soviets claimed the Afghan leaders had invited them to enter. Clearly, the USSR was determined to keep Afghanistan a Communist-controlled country.

President Carter denounced the Soviet actions as did other Western leaders. The UN General Assembly overwhelmingly passed a resolution calling for the immediate withdrawal of Soviet troops. Nevertheless, the Soviets refused to remove their soldiers.

To show displeasure, Carter called for a boycott of the 1980 Summer Olympic Games that were being hosted by the Soviets in Moscow. More than sixty nations joined the boycott. Yet the decision to use the Olympics as a means of protest proved controversial. Opponents of the boycott argued that it hurt athletes, who had been training for years, more than it hurt the Soviet Union. President Carter also banned exports of many commodities, such as grain, to the Soviets. American farmers later said that since the Soviets merely purchased these items from other countries, it was really American farmers who suffered.

The Afghans used guerrilla tactics to fight the Communists. The United States sent billions of dollars worth of support and equipment to them. The Soviets continued to occupy the country for a decade, finally withdrawing their forces in 1989.

▼ The 1980 Summer Olympics in Moscow

▲ Muslim extremists in Iran took more than fifty Americans as hostages in November 1979. One hostage is shown blindfolded and cuffed (top). An April 1980 failed rescue attempt ended with the collision of an American helicopter and transport plane (above).

The Iranian Hostage Crisis

During the Cold War, Iran was an ally of the United States. In return, the United States helped the ruler of Iran, known as the shah. In the 1970s many Iranians were unhappy with the shah's harsh and often self-serving rule. Iran was also facing major economic problems, including a high rate of unemployment. In early 1979 a revolution succeeded in overthrowing the shah, Mohammed Reza Pahlavi. He fled the country.

A Muslim extremist, the Ayatollah Khomeini, became the leader of Iran. In October 1979, ignoring warnings from advisors, Carter allowed the shah, who was ill with cancer, to enter the United States for medical treatment. Enraged Muslims stormed the American embassy in Tehran, Iran, on November 4. They took more than fifty Americans hostage, whom they offered in exchange for the shah's return to Iran. They wanted to place him on trial for crimes they said he had committed while ruling the nation. Carter refused to accept their conditions.

The **Iranian hostage crisis** became Carter's foreign policy nightmare. American citizens watched helplessly as, almost daily, television networks broadcast footage of Iranians burning American flags and chanting anti-American slogans. Iranians threatened to kill the hostages or place them on trial as spies.

For months, Carter tried to obtain the release of the hostages. After those efforts failed, Carter ordered a secret military expedition to rescue the hostages. It ended tragically. An American helicopter collided with an American transport plane in the desert of Iran, and eight American soldiers died without ever getting near the hostages.

The crisis continued and became a major issue in the 1980 presidential election. Many Americans voted against Carter for his inability to obtain the hostages' freedom. After 444 days of captivity, their release finally came on January 20, 1981—the day Americans inaugurated a new president, Ronald Reagan.

Did you know?

Two weeks after breaking his pelvis in 2019, Jimmy Carter resumed his long-time tradition of teaching Sunday school. He was ninety-five.

SECTION REVIEW 25.4

1. What did Carter offer to those who had avoided fighting in Vietnam by fleeing the country or by failing to register for the draft?
2. How high did inflation rise during Carter's term of office?
3. What alternative source of energy did Carter support? What event seriously damaged support for his program?
4. What significant event took place at Camp David during the Carter administration? Why was this significant?
5. In what two ways did Carter show his displeasure over the Soviet treatment of Afghanistan?

CHAPTER 25 REVIEW

Making Connections

1. How did Lyndon B. Johnson become president?
2. What groups began identifying more with the Republican party during the 1960s and 1970s?
3. What three pieces of civil rights legislation were passed after the March on Washington and President Kennedy's assassination? What did each do?
4. Contrast the hawks and doves in the Vietnam War.
5. Through what neighboring countries of North and South Vietnam did the Ho Chi Minh Trail also pass?
6. According to polls, how did American opinion of the Vietnam War change from 1965 to 1967?
7. Who were the three Democratic contenders for the presidency in the 1968 election? Who was the American Independent Party candidate? Who ran for the Republicans?
8. What was the result of the Vietnam War, occurring on April 30, 1975, and soon thereafter?
9. How were "peaceful coexistence" (see Chapter 24) and "détente" similar?
10. What was a positive effect of détente with China? What was a negative effect?
11. How did public opinion on the ERA vary? Explain the arguments on both sides.
12. What year was Panama given complete control of the Panama Canal?
13. Why did the Iranian hostage crisis begin? On what day and on what occasion did it end?

Thinking Critically

14. Did Congress have the constitutional authority to create the War Powers Act? Why or why not? You may need to refer to the Constitution in Chapter 7.
15. Thinking about both automobiles and presidents, what does "I'm a Ford, not a Lincoln" mean?

Living as a Christian Citizen

16. How did the Old Testament law deal with poverty (use Lev. 23:22; Lev. 25:35–36; and Deut. 14:28–29)? How could a Christian use these biblical patterns to guide policies toward those in poverty today?
17. What is your personal assessment of the presidency and character of Richard Nixon? Support your answer.

Part of a huge Vietnam War protest at the US Capitol

Terms to Remember

Lyndon B. Johnson
Great Society
Barry Goldwater
Civil Rights Act of 1964
Twenty-Fourth Amendment
Voting Rights Act of 1965
Malcolm X
Vietnam War
Gulf of Tonkin Resolution
hawks
doves
Viet Cong
Ho Chi Minh Trail
counterculture
Tet Offensive
Robert Kennedy
Richard Nixon
Vietnamization
Kent State University
POWs
War Powers Act
détente
Twenty-Sixth Amendment
recession
Roe v. Wade
Equal Rights Amendment (ERA)
Spiro T. Agnew
Watergate scandal
Gerald Ford
Jimmy Carter
Panama Canal Treaty
Camp David Accords
Iranian hostage crisis

▾ Soviet leader Mikhail Gorbachev, President Ronald Reagan, and Vice President George H. W. Bush (left to right) are shown in this December 1988 photograph.

CHAPTER 26

The Political Pendulum

In 1980 many Americans saw the incoming president, Ronald Reagan, as a champion for traditional American values. He was a strong defender of liberty during the time of Communist totalitarianism. He also proposed a program to grow the stagnant economy. Republicans enjoyed wide margins of victory in three consecutive presidential elections beginning in 1980.

During the 1990s, Democrat Bill Clinton captured the White House by promising to improve the economy. He and liberals who supported him had a different view of social values than Republicans. This clash led to culture wars.

GUIDING QUESTIONS

- What major events occurred in America during Reagan's presidency?
- What international issues were important during Reagan's presidency?

26.1 THE REAGAN ADMINISTRATION

What major events occurred during the presidency of Ronald Reagan?

The Election of 1980

President Carter faced a strong opponent, **Ronald Reagan**, in the 1980 election. Many Americans viewed Reagan's speeches as direct, sincere, and stirring. He was optimistic and offered hope. Many were ready to listen to his conservative proposals: strengthening the national defense, cutting the size of the federal bureaucracy, and getting big government "off the backs of the people." He promised to restore American strength and pride.

During the campaign, Reagan referred repeatedly to the "misery index," a combination of the inflation rate and the unemployment rate. He told the voters that if they were better off than they had been when Carter first took office, they should vote for Carter. But, he said, if they were not better off, they should vote for him.

On election night, Reagan carried all but six states and Washington, DC. Riding on his "coattails," Republicans won enough seats to take control of the Senate for the first time since 1954.

On March 30, 1981, just two months after Reagan's inauguration, he was shot and wounded in an assassination attempt. Three others were also wounded in the attack.

Domestic Policies

Determined to "make America great again," Reagan supported smaller government and conservative social values such as the pro-life movement. He offered a new approach to the economy, and he promised to restrain the liberal courts.

Economics

Reagan wanted to lower inflation by decreasing taxes and reducing regulations on businesses and investors. Businesses would then have more money to make products, and individuals would have more money to invest. Reagan called this **supply-side economics**. He argued that tax cuts can actually increase tax revenues. Not everyone agreed. During the 1980 presidential primaries, George H. W. Bush, who later became Reagan's vice president, called the proposed solution "voodoo economics." Others called it "Reaganomics" or "trickle-down economics."

In 1981 Congress passed the first part of Reagan's plan, which cut several types of taxes including corporate taxes. It also made the

Fun Fact

Reagan played football at Eureka College in Illinois.

Ronald Reagan 40

Born	February 6, 1911
Died	June 5, 2004
Home state	California (born in Illinois)
Wives	1st—Jane Wyman 2nd—Nancy Davis
Church	Disciples of Christ
Occupations	actor, broadcaster, lecturer
Party	Republican
Years served as president	1981–89
Terms	2
Vice president	George H. W. Bush

AIR TRAFFIC CONTROL STRIKE

Soon after his inauguration, Reagan showed his firm support of law and order during an illegal strike by the nation's air traffic controllers. When the vast majority refused to return to work, he fired them and had new people trained for the job.

▲ Sandra Day O'Connor (top) takes the oath as the first female Supreme Court justice. Geraldine Ferraro (above) stands with Walter Mondale, the 1984 Democratic presidential nominee, after she became the first female vice-presidential candidate from a major party.

largest income-tax cut Americans had ever received. To help balance the budget (ensure that income equals expenses), the president wanted to reduce the size of government bureaucracy. He also wanted to reduce federal spending increases in most areas except the military, where significantly more money began to be spent. The House of Representatives opposed reducing spending. When Reagan pushed for cuts, he was accused of being hardhearted and wanting to hurt the poor.

The tax cuts boosted the economy, and tax revenues significantly increased. Inflation declined dramatically. Jobs were abundant. However, between defense buildup and spending by Congress, money continued being spent faster than it was received, causing a deficit in the budget; this grew the federal debt to record levels.

The Reagan Court

Reagan worked to appoint conservative judges. His first appointee to the Supreme Court was **Sandra Day O'Connor**, the first female Supreme Court justice. Later, when Chief Justice Warren Burger retired, Reagan named Justice William H. Rehnquist, already on the Court, to be chief justice. Another appointee, Antonin Scalia, helped tilt the Court away from liberalism and toward conservatism. O'Connor and a later appointee, Anthony Kennedy, sided with the more liberal justices on some issues.

The 1984 Election

Former vice president Walter Mondale challenged Reagan in the 1984 presidential election. For a running mate, Mondale chose Geraldine Ferraro—the first female vice-presidential candidate from a major party. The Democrats attacked the high debt, military buildup, and reductions in spending on social programs. On election night, in one of the biggest landslides in American history, Reagan won every state except Mondale's home state of Minnesota.

Religious Right

With the rise of the counterculture in the sixties and seventies, many Christians responded by becoming more politically active. Reagan's opposition to abortion and his conservative views on moral issues appealed to Christians.

Religious conservatives, often known as the **Religious Right** (remember that "the Right" is another term for conservatives, while "the Left" refers to liberals), established organizations that became prominent. These organizations encouraged Christians to become involved in politics since legislation is often written from a moral point of view. They also enabled many Christians to win election to office, and they worked to enact laws on important issues like protecting religious liberty and restricting abortion.

But the Religious Right had some problems. First, sometimes it placed too much faith in the power of politics. Members sometimes forgot that many of society's difficulties are spiritual issues rather than political ones. Second, since the Republican Party was generally more conservative than the Democratic Party, some Christians supported Republican positions as if they were Christian positions. As a result, issues not discussed in Scripture, such as gun rights or tax cuts, were sometimes defended with the same conviction as moral issues directly addressed by Scripture. A third problem was that occasionally the Religious Right's harsh condemnation of its opponents hindered Christian witness.

Foreign Affairs

Reagan believed that previous presidents had taken the wrong approach in dealing with the Cold War. He was not interested in merely containing communism. He intended to defeat the Soviets.

Fun Fact

***Return of the Jedi*, the last movie of the original Star Wars trilogy, was released in 1983—the same year Reagan announced his SDI plan.**

The Soviet Union

Reagan had long been a vocal opponent of communism. During Carter's term, the Soviets had invaded Afghanistan, equipped Cuban soldiers fighting in Africa, and installed long-range nuclear missiles in Eastern Europe. Tensions increased between the United States and USSR when Reagan took office. He boldly referred to the Soviet Union as an "evil empire."

Reagan took a different approach to the Communist threat than some former presidents. Rather than reducing the military, Reagan built it even stronger. He believed in peace through strength. He hoped to dash Communist hopes of defeating the United States. He believed that they would have no choice but to negotiate peace.

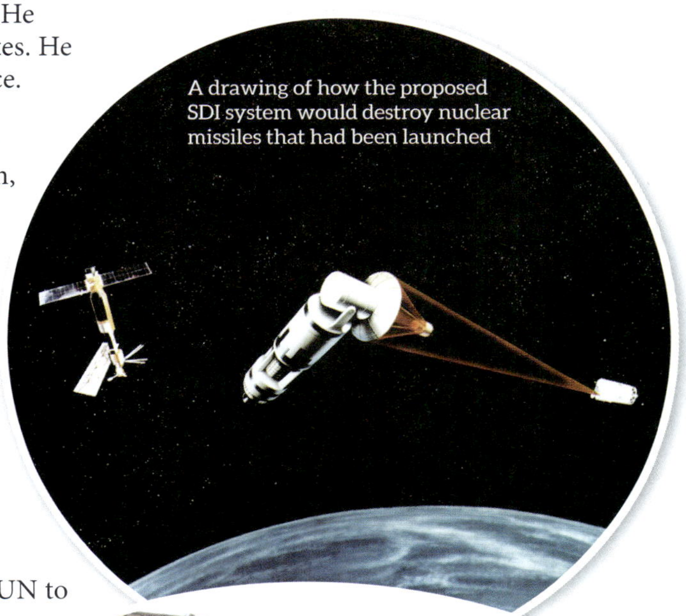
A drawing of how the proposed SDI system would destroy nuclear missiles that had been launched

Reagan also encouraged the development of a defensive system that could destroy enemy nuclear missiles before they could reach their targets. Many mockingly called the program, officially known as the Strategic Defense Initiative (SDI), "**Star Wars**." If the United States could defend itself from a Soviet nuclear attack, the Soviet Union would lose its ability to threaten a nuclear war. As the Cold War came to a close in the early 1990s, the system was never fully developed.

After **Mikhail Gorbachev** became the Soviet leader in 1985, he met with Reagan. In 1987 the two leaders signed the Intermediate Nuclear Forces Treaty (INF), which eliminated most of both nations' medium-range nuclear missiles. It was a first step toward further reductions.

The Middle East

Early in Reagan's first term, civil war in Lebanon led the UN to send in peacekeepers, including US Marines. On October 23, 1983, a truck loaded with explosives slammed into the marine barracks on the outskirts of Beirut, Lebanon. The suicide attack killed more than 200 marines. Within a few months, Reagan withdrew the remaining American forces.

Elsewhere in the Middle East, Islamic terrorists launched a series of attacks on Westerners. Officials in the United States learned that Libya's leader, Muammar al-Qaddafi, was behind some of the terrorism. Reagan responded with a surprise bombing raid on Libya in 1986. The attack got Qaddafi's attention, and the terrorist rampage stopped.

A few months before the suicide attack on the marine barracks in Beirut, Lebanon, a suicide bomber attacked the US embassy in that city. ▸

Latin America

Struggles with poverty, inequality, and dictatorship made Latin American countries ripe for Communist revolutions. In 1983 unrest and riots erupted in the island country of Grenada. Several Caribbean nations asked the United States to intervene. In a surprise attack, American paratroopers joined by forces from five Caribbean nations restored peace to Grenada.

Before Reagan took office, the Sandinistas (a group aided by Communist Cuban and Soviet advisors) had established a government in Nicaragua. Reagan feared Communist revolution would spread to Nicaragua's neighbors. As a result, the CIA began sending aid to the Contras, anti-Communist rebels. At first, Congress supported the plan to help the Contras.

▲ American soldiers in Grenada (top) and Contras in Nicaragua (above)

The Iran-Contra Affair

Reagan's last years as president were tainted by a complicated arrangement known as the **Iran-Contra Affair**. This scandal involved money from the sale of weapons to Iran. In exchange for weapons, Iran helped free Americans who were being held hostage in Lebanon. Some profits from the sale of the weapons went to aid the Contras in Nicaragua.

Congress had ended aid to the Contras before the transactions with Iran because of reported human rights abuses by the Contras. Although members of the president's administration believed that transferring money from the arms sale to the Contras did not violate Congress's ban, opponents argued that it was illegal. Several members of Reagan's administration were convicted of wrongdoing. Some of the convictions were overturned when appealed to a higher court; the next president, George H. W. Bush, issued a pardon to others.

SECTION REVIEW 26.1

1. Why did Reagan believe that lowering taxes and reducing regulations would help the economy?
2. What were three problems of the Religious Right? How should a Christian respond to these problems?
3. What was Reagan's approach to the Communist threat?
4. What was the relationship between arms sales to Iran and the Contras of Latin America?

26.2 THE GEORGE H. W. BUSH ADMINISTRATION

What were important issues during the presidency of George H. W. Bush?

GUIDING QUESTIONS

- How did the Communist governments of East Germany and the Soviet Union collapse?
- What happened during the Persian Gulf War?
- What significant events occurred in America during George H. W. Bush's presidency?

The Election of 1988

As the 1988 presidential election approached, Reagan supported his vice president, **George H. W. Bush**, as the best choice for continuing his vision. Bush could, in effect, give what was termed the "Reagan Revolution" a third term (and possibly even a fourth) by continuing Reagan's policies. In time, Bush expressed his own vision for the nation.

The 1988 election pitted Bush against the Democratic nominee, Massachusetts governor Michael Dukakis. Bush rallied support by returning to popular ideals: American strength at home and abroad. His running mate was Dan Quayle, a young conservative senator. Together they gained a solid win on Election Day.

Bush was a successful Texas businessman and World War II veteran, as well as a former congressman, ambassador, and head of the CIA. He focused mostly on foreign affairs. In domestic matters, he indicated that he would follow Reagan's agenda, but he promised to work with members of the Democratic Party.

George H. W. Bush

41

Born	June 12, 1924
Died	November 30, 2018
Home state	Texas (born in Massachusetts)
Wife	Barbara Pierce
Church	Episcopalian
Occupations	oil businessman
Party	Republican
Years served as president	1989–93
Terms	1
Vice president	Dan Quayle

Foreign Affairs

In foreign affairs, Bush successfully handled several international crises. He cautiously observed and encouraged sweeping changes in the Soviet Union. But his dealings in the Persian Gulf were what defined his presidency.

The Collapse of Communist Governments

During Bush's first year in office, protests mounted in Communist countries. Poland elected a non-Communist prime minister for the first time in over forty years. East Germans began protesting as well. In November 1989 hundreds of thousands gathered at the Berlin Wall. Not knowing how to handle the matter, government leaders and border guards allowed protesters to begin dismantling the wall. For the first time in many years, Germans on both sides of the wall could connect with those on the other. East Germans urged reunification with West Germany. Although many Europeans feared a reunified Germany, Bush supported this movement. He worked with key leaders to bring about a peaceful reunification in 1990.

Similar changes were taking place within the Soviet Union and its European satellites. Bush told Gorbachev and Boris Yeltsin, the new president of Russia, that the United States would support the Soviet Union's democratic movement. On Christmas Day in 1991, Gorbachev announced the end of the Soviet Union. Each of the nation's fifteen republics became a separate country.

Flag of the Soviet Union before that nation broke apart in 1991

US Air Force fighter jets flying over Iraq

The Persian Gulf War

In August 1990 Iraqi dictator **Saddam Hussein** invaded the oil-rich country of Kuwait. He hoped to win glory for himself and easy wealth for his nation. The United Nations told Saddam that he must withdraw from Kuwait by January 15, 1991. It authorized the use of "all necessary means" to liberate Kuwait if Saddam did not comply.

The six-week **Persian Gulf War** (January 16–February 28) began with five weeks of massive, around-the-clock bombing followed by a ground attack. United Nations forces, led by US General Norman Schwarzkopf, encircled the Iraqi army and trapped it in Kuwait. As the Iraqi army attempted to escape northward, US planes attacked it along the "highway of death." Iraqis surrendered in huge groups.

The ground war was finished in one hundred hours. In the wake of this victory, Bush's popularity ratings soared to an unprecedented 89 percent.

Did you know?

In the White House, the Bushes are often referred to by their presidential numbers. George H. W. Bush is often referred to as "41" and his son George W. Bush as "43."

The Persian Gulf War

Domestic Affairs

When Bush took office, he was confronted by a number of domestic challenges demanding immediate attention. A high budget deficit, congressional scandals, and a growing drug-trafficking problem challenged his leadership ability at home. Bush took decisive action, but some of his actions were quite unpopular.

Economic Matters

Bush planned to reduce the deficit by cutting the budget. But this strategy was complicated by a crisis in the savings and loan industry. Savings and loan banks (S&Ls) had begun going bankrupt because of unsound investments. Recognizing that thousands of citizens could lose their savings, Bush worked with Congress to rescue the S&Ls. The price was steep, costing taxpayers around $132 billion.

During the 1988 Republican National Convention, Bush had made a promise—"Read my lips: no new taxes." Two years later, the Democratic-controlled Congress promised to cut spending if Bush would break his "no new taxes" pledge. Bush agreed, but Congress did not cut spending. The resulting major budget deficit and other issues led to a recession. Tax revenues declined, the deficit increased, and Bush received much of the blame.

▲ This cartoon makes reference to President George H. W. Bush's pledge not to raise taxes. Bush's breaking of this promise was one of the reasons he was defeated in the 1992 presidential election.

Congressional Matters

During Bush's presidency, Congress was rocked by several scandals. In 1989 Congress infuriated many taxpayers when it voted to give its members a significant pay raise and automatic annual cost-of-living adjustments. Many states had already approved the proposed **Twenty-Seventh Amendment**, which says that a congressional pay raise cannot take effect until after the next congressional election. With the renewed interest in congressional pay, the amendment received approval by enough additional states to become a part of the Constitution in May 1992.

Earlier in 1992, news had leaked that 247 members of Congress had serious House Bank overdrafts. Overdrawing their checking accounts did not incur any penalty since taxpayers paid the interest.

Investigators found that some members of Congress were abusing their post office privileges (called *franking*), sometimes pocketing money that was supposed to be used for postage. Furthermore, instances were uncovered of employees hired and paid for work never done, while congressional staff was occasionally used for private work.

Because of these issues, support grew for term limits, which restrict how many terms an elected official can stay in office. Several states passed laws limiting members of Congress to a certain number of terms. However, in 1995 the Supreme Court ruled term limits on these federal positions unconstitutional. Later attempts at passing a constitutional amendment for term limits have been unsuccessful.

TWENTY-SEVENTH AMENDMENT

The Twenty-Seventh Amendment was first proposed in June 1789. For almost two centuries (1790s through the 1970s), it was largely ignored. In 1992 renewed interest in the proposed amendment led to its approval by three-fourths of the states.
It says, "No law, varying the compensation for the services of the senators and representatives, shall take effect, until an election of representatives shall have intervened."

Towers and smoke stacks at the port in Los Angeles

Addressing Challenges

Bush supported increasing government power to deal with social issues. For example, he wanted to be known as the "environment president," so he worked with Congress to pass the Clean Air Act Amendments of 1990, which increased federal regulation of businesses in order to improve air quality.

Bush believed that one of his most significant achievements was the **Americans with Disabilities Act** that outlawed discrimination based on certain disabilities. It required governments and businesses to provide better working conditions and access for people with physical limitations.

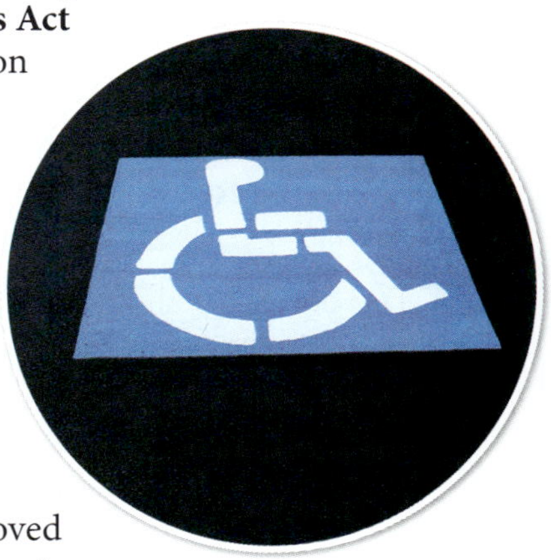

As with Reagan, Bush's Supreme Court nominees yielded conflicting results. His first appointee to the Court was David Souter, a relatively unknown New Hampshire judge. Once on the Court, Souter proved to be liberal. Bush's next Supreme Court nominee was Clarence Thomas, a black conservative. The vast majority of Democrats in the Senate vigorously opposed his appointment, but he was confirmed. He has remained one of the most conservative justices on the Court.

▾ Bush appointed David Souter (left) and Clarence Thomas (right) as Supreme Court justices.

SECTION REVIEW 26.2

1. What two major Communist countries dissolved during the administration of President Bush?
2. What event led to the Persian Gulf War?
3. What action brought renewed attention to the proposed Twenty-Seventh Amendment?
4. Do you think government regulations should be passed regarding people with disabilities? Why or why not?

26.3 THE CLINTON ADMINISTRATION

What major events transpired during the presidency of Bill Clinton?

GUIDING QUESTIONS

- What domestic events occurred when Clinton was president?
- Why was President Clinton impeached?
- What issues led to culture wars during the 1990s?
- What was occurring in the world during Clinton's administration?

The Election of 1992

Republicans placed Bush on the ballot for the election of 1992. The Democrats ran Arkansas governor **Bill Clinton** as a moderate Democrat. A third contender, Ross Perot, entered the race as an independent. He promised drastic measures to eliminate the deficit. Many voters turned to him.

On Election Day, Clinton won by a large margin in the Electoral College (370 to 168). Clinton received about 43 percent of the popular vote; Bush, about 38 percent; and Perot, 19 percent. This was the highest percentage of popular votes for a third-party candidate since Theodore Roosevelt had run for the Progressive (Bull Moose) Party in 1912.

Fun Fact

Ross Perot received nearly 20 percent of the popular vote in the 1992 presidential election.

Domestic Issues

As promised, Clinton brought change, mostly social rather than economic. The day after his inauguration, Clinton began a discussion about lifting the ban on homosexuals in the military. When many people (including military officials) objected, he suggested a compromise called "Don't Ask, Don't Tell." According to this policy, military personnel could not ask whether someone was homosexual. On the other hand, those who told about their homosexuality could be discharged.

Two days later, Clinton eliminated many Reagan-era limitations on the use of government funding for abortions. He appointed Joycelyn Elders to be surgeon general; she had attacked the pro-life movement as a "love affair with the fetus." Clinton also appointed

The Election of 1992

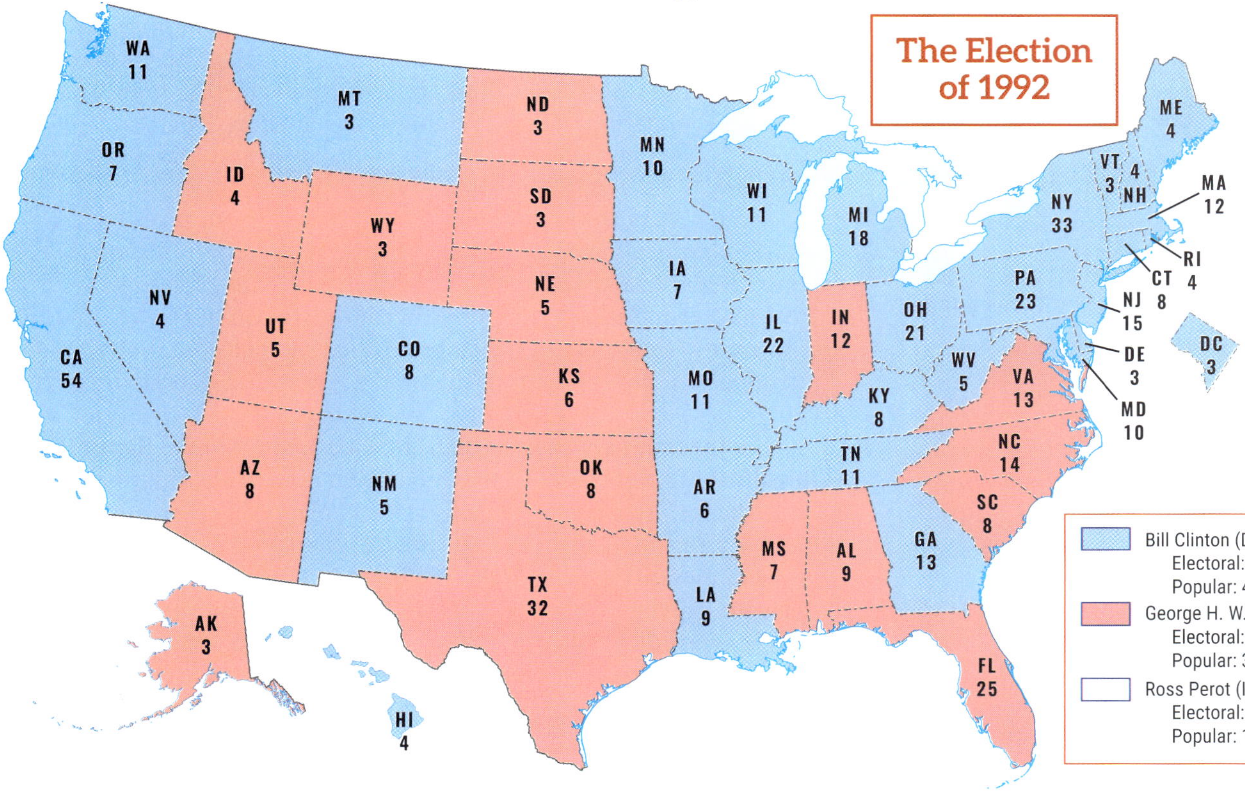

▲ A portion of the Oklahoma City federal building memorial; after the bombing (inset)

Janet Reno, the nation's first female attorney general. With Reno's strong support, Congress passed a law making it a crime to obstruct access to abortion clinics, restricting pro-life protests.

Waco and Oklahoma City

On February 28, 1993, on suspicion of several crimes including illegal weapon stockpiling, the Bureau of Alcohol, Tobacco, and Firearms (ATF) raided the compound of a group known as the Branch Davidians in Waco, Texas. The poorly organized raid failed, and four agents and six Branch Davidians were killed. After a fifty-one-day standoff, Attorney General Reno ordered agents to enter the compound with tear gas and tanks. When they did, the compound erupted in flames, tragically killing over seventy members of the group.

On the second anniversary of the end of the Waco disaster, Timothy McVeigh, angry at the government for the Waco raid and other issues, bombed a federal office building in Oklahoma City, killing 168 people, including 19 children in daycare. The **Oklahoma City bombing** was the deadliest act of domestic terrorism in American history to that point. McVeigh was executed in 2001.

William "Bill" Clinton

42

Born	August 19, 1946
Died	still living on the date this book was published
Home state	Arkansas
Wife	Hillary Rodham
Church	Baptist
Occupations	attorney
Party	Democrat
Years served as president	1993–2001
Terms	2
Vice president	Al Gore

Republican Contract with America

Many voters were upset by Clinton's failure to cut taxes for the middle class. Crime became another major concern. In response, House Republicans under Newt Gingrich devised a plan to win the 1994 midterm elections. Republican candidates united to sign the **Contract with America**, which promised that if elected they would introduce ten popular bills in the first one hundred days of the next Congress.

For the first time in forty years, in what was called the **Republican Revolution**, voters handed control of both houses of Congress to Republicans. Among the ten bills were a balanced budget amendment, a term-limits amendment, and the line-item veto. The balanced budget amendment passed in the House but failed in the Senate by one vote. The term-limits amendment received a majority of votes but not the two-thirds needed to pass. Although the Supreme Court later ruled it unconstitutional, the line-item veto, which gave the president power to cut individual items in approved bills, easily passed the House and the Senate.

Health Care, Budget, and Welfare

The First Lady, Hillary Rodham Clinton, led the president's plan to regulate health care in the nation. This proposal guaranteed health-care coverage for all Americans and legal immigrants (a system known as universal health care). It required businesses to contribute to the program. The plan would have been expensive for taxpayers; it never gained sufficient public support to pass.

Clinton's first budget in 1993 (before the Republican take-over) called for new government programs and higher taxes on almost everyone, with some cuts in spending. His budget received no Republican votes but managed to pass Congress.

Clinton had promised in his campaign to "end welfare as we know it." Prodded by both the public and by congressional Republicans, he signed the **Welfare Reform Act** (officially titled the Personal Responsibility and Work Opportunity Reconciliation Act of 1996). For the first time since the New Deal, the government rolled back financial aid for the poor. The law required welfare recipients to return to work within two years, and it set a lifetime cap of five years for assistance. After the adoption of this legislation, poverty numbers decreased.

Bob Dole was the Republican nominee for president in 1996.

The Election of 1996

Republicans settled on Senate majority leader Bob Dole of Kansas as their 1996 presidential candidate. When the popular votes were counted, Clinton received 49 percent to Dole's 41 percent. Ross Perot, running again as an independent, received 8 percent. The Republicans kept their majority in Congress.

Monica Lewinsky

Scandals and Impeachment

Clinton's administration was rocked by scandals. One involved Clinton's past investment in an Arkansas business called the Whitewater Development Corporation. The Whitewater scandal was a complicated web of questionable relationships that had formed between politicians, law firms, and businessmen when Clinton was governor of Arkansas.

Another scandal led to Clinton's impeachment. In 1994 Paula Jones sued Clinton for previous sexual harassment during her time as an Arkansas government employee. During the investigation, Clinton's inappropriate relationship with White House intern **Monica Lewinsky** came to light.

Kenneth Starr, the lawyer investigating the Whitewater scandal, received court approval to investigate Clinton's relationship with Lewinsky. After months of stalling, Clinton agreed to testify before a grand jury. During his testimony, he eventually admitted to wrongdoing with Lewinsky but insisted that he had done nothing illegal.

After the investigation, Starr sent evidence to the House with a list of Clinton's impeachable offenses. Two articles of impeachment (formal charges or accusations) passed in December 1998. These claimed that the president had committed perjury (lying under oath) in his initial answers about his relationship with Lewinsky and obstruction of justice (hiding evidence from a court). Clinton became the second president to be impeached (Andrew Johnson had been the first). As the Constitution states, the Senate conducted a trial to decide whether the president should be removed from office. The necessary two-thirds majority to convict was again not reached.

At the Clinton impeachment trial, 45 senators voted that the president was guilty of perjury (above). On the charge of obstruction of justice, 50 senators voted guilty.

▲ Pro-life demonstrators (left) and supporters of abortion rights (right)

Culture Wars

In the 1980s and 1990s, economic conservatives banded with religious conservatives to work toward restoring traditional values in America. Economic conservatives saw the government wasting taxpayer money in areas like the funding of abortion and certain environmental regulations, while religious conservatives objected to the lack of morality in some of the liberal agenda. Public education also raised concerns. Religious conservatives noticed a trend in public education of accepting and teaching liberal values. One popular proposal was educational vouchers, which would provide tax money to chosen alternative forms of schooling. The leaders and organizations of the Religious Right believed that the American people should return to Christian principles or at least traditional moral principles. They became a significant force in politics. Because of Clinton's social policies and his aggressive agenda of liberalism, many Christians became active in politics.

A key issue for religious conservatives was abortion. Perhaps the most important proposal passed by Republicans during this time was a ban on partial-birth abortions. Clinton, however, vetoed the bill.

Another key issue for religious conservatives was homosexuality. Liberals said that homosexuals should be allowed to marry. But social conservatives said that homosexual behavior is immoral, even sinful according to the Bible. Congress drafted the **Defense of Marriage Act**, which said the federal government would not recognize any homosexual union as a marriage. Even if a state recognized homosexual marriage, other states were not required to recognize it. The bill moved easily through both houses of Congress, and the president signed it into law.

Foreign Affairs

Clinton's diplomatic policy attempted to reach solutions acceptable to the most countries. He appointed Madeleine Albright as the first woman secretary of state.

Trade

Clinton achieved the passage of the **North American Free Trade Agreement (NAFTA)**. It provided for the elimination of tariffs between the United States, Mexico, and Canada. Congress passed NAFTA in late 1993, and the agreement lasted until it was replaced with a new one in 2020.

The volume of world trade exploded during the 1990s. America was prosperous as Clinton prepared to leave office, and Americans generally liked him despite his personal and political issues.

World Hotspots

In Asia, the isolated country of North Korea appeared to be taking steps to develop a nuclear weapon. Clinton chose a diplomatic route in an attempt to defuse the situation. The United States agreed to help North Korea build two nuclear power plants. In return, North Korea promised to stop developing nuclear weapons; it was an empty promise—in 2006 North Korea tested a nuclear device.

In Africa, the UN decided to disarm warring factions in the country of Somalia in the 1990s, but the most powerful warlord fought back. The UN and the United States tried unsuccessfully to capture him. During a raid by US Army Rangers, the Somalis shot down two helicopters. They dragged the body of a dead soldier through the streets and captured a pilot. The failed raid cost eighteen American lives. Within six months, Clinton ordered the withdrawal of American forces from the country.

▲ A North Korean soldier (top) looks across the border into South Korea. A US Marine patrols a street in Mogadishu, Somalia (above).

In the Caribbean, the military leaders of Haiti overthrew the Haitian president in 1991. Three years later, Clinton ordered an invasion to put an end to the regime and declared the mission a success with the former president reinstated. Yet Haiti remained a violent, poverty-stricken land.

The European country of Yugoslavia, created for Slavic peoples in 1918 after World War I, had become a Communist nation in 1946. With the fall of communism in eastern Europe during the late 1980s and early 1990s, the nation split into multiple countries with competing ethnic groups. Bitter civil wars erupted. The United Nations sent peacekeepers but seemed powerless to stop the bloodshed.

Haiti suffered much violence in the early 1990s. ▸

◂ This British tank was part of the UN peacekeeping force in Bosnia, which had been a part of Yugoslavia.

In 1995 Clinton sent bombers against Serbs engaged in ethnic cleansing (the expelling or killing of members from a certain ethnic group) of Muslims. As a result, the Serbs agreed to negotiations held in Dayton, Ohio. There they signed a peace agreement known as the **Dayton Accords**. But ethnic groups in the area north of Greece, generally referred to as the Balkans, still periodically erupted in warfare and skirmishes.

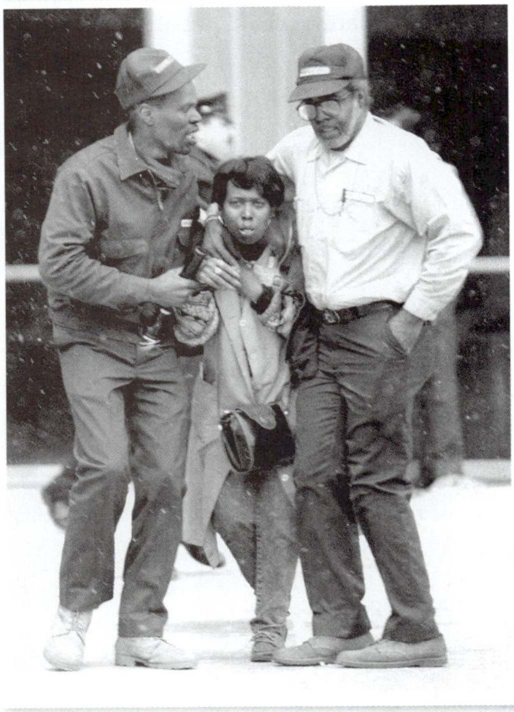

▴ A choking woman is assisted as she leaves the World Trade Center after terrorists placed explosives in the parking garage in 1993 (above).

Islamic Terrorism

In 1993 a car bomb exploded in a parking garage of the World Trade Center in New York City, killing 6 people and injuring more than 1,000 others. Then in 1998 terrorists bombed the US embassies in Tanzania and Kenya, killing 224 people and injuring more than 4,500. On October 12, 2000, terrorists in a small boat approached the destroyer USS *Cole* as it refueled in the country of Yemen. When they drew alongside, a bomb exploded, killing 17 sailors and injuring others.

These attacks were a foretaste of a much larger attack that terrorists would soon make on the United States; each was connected to a new radical Islamic terrorist group known as al-Qaeda.

SECTION REVIEW 26.3

1. What third-party candidate received almost 19 percent of the popular vote in the 1992 election?
2. How are the raid at Waco and the Oklahoma City bombing related?
3. How did Republicans win control of the House of Representatives in 1994? What was this change in leadership known as?
4. How does Clinton's impeachment show that no one is above the law? What were the charges brought against him?
5. What were two key issues that concerned religious conservatives during the culture wars?

A boat tows the USS *Cole* after it was attacked by terrorists in 2000. ▸

CHAPTER 26 REVIEW

Making Connections

1. Who was the first woman appointed to the Supreme Court?
2. Who was the first female vice-presidential candidate from a major party?
3. What nickname was given to the Strategic Defense Initiative?
4. What Soviet leader met with Reagan about a reduction of nuclear missiles?
5. What campaign pledge did Bush make concerning taxes? Why did he break this pledge?
6. What type of banks failed while Bush was president?
7. What was the policy of "Don't Ask, Don't Tell"?
8. Who was the nation's first female attorney general?
9. How did the Welfare Reform Act change welfare as it had been? What was the result?
10. Who was the nation's first female secretary of state?
11. List a country in each of the following world areas that was a hotspot during Clinton's administration. Give a short description of the "hot" issue in each area.
    a. Asia
    b. Africa
    c. Caribbean
    d. Europe

Thinking Critically

12. What do the elections of 1992 and 1996 imply about a strong third-party candidate? How might the outcome of the elections have been different without Perot?
13. What are two of Clinton's ideas that were not acceptable at the time but have become acceptable today? Why do you think public acceptance of these ideas has changed?

Living as a Christian Citizen

14. The legalization of abortion was one of the chief moral issues motivating Christians to get involved in politics in the 1980s and 1990s. Outline the key biblical arguments against abortion (see Gen. 9:6; Exod. 21:22–24; Ps. 139:13–16).
15. How can you defend biblical morals and values without tying them to a particular political party? What steps can Christians take to ensure that their political involvement remains consistent with biblical values?

After dividing Berlin for more than 28 years, the Berlin Wall was dismantled in late 1989. Delighted Germans are shown celebrating.

Terms to Remember

- Ronald Reagan
- supply-side economics
- Sandra Day O'Connor
- Religious Right
- Star Wars
- Mikhail Gorbachev
- Iran-Contra affair
- George H. W. Bush
- Saddam Hussein
- Persian Gulf War
- Twenty-Seventh Amendment
- Americans with Disabilities Act
- Bill Clinton
- Oklahoma City bombing
- Contract with America
- Republican Revolution
- Welfare Reform Act
- Monica Lewinsky
- Defense of Marriage Act
- North American Free Trade Agreement (NAFTA)
- Dayton Accords

CHAPTER 27 The New Millennium

Terrorists attack the World Trade Center in New York City on September 11, 2001.

27.1 THE GEORGE W. BUSH ADMINISTRATION

What events occurred during the presidency of George W. Bush?

GUIDING QUESTIONS

- Why was the 2000 election so unusual?
- How did the events of September 11, 2001, lead to the war on terror?
- What major events occurred during George W. Bush's presidency?

The twenty-first century opened with great promise and great challenges. A controversial presidential election was soon followed by the largest terrorist attack in US history. During the first decade of the new century, the nation was involved in a new style of warfare.

The Election of 2000

The presidential race in 2000 between Bill Clinton's vice president, **Al Gore**, and Texas governor **George W. Bush** was extremely close. Gore surpassed Bush by more than 540,000 popular votes, but the outcome in the electoral college was too close to call. On election night and the following morning, television networks declared that Florida had been won by Gore; then they said it was "too close to call." Then they said that Bush won Florida but later said again that the outcome was too close to call. For weeks, the American people waited through that state's vote recount. Eventually, the US Supreme Court heard arguments regarding disputes about how the recount was being conducted. On December 12, the Court ordered the recount to stop. Bush officially won Florida by a mere 537 votes, and three days later he won the Electoral College vote, 271 to 266. Despite the controversy, the outcome of the election showed that the American democratic system was strong. The people, including Gore, accepted the verdict, although many continued to refer to the "stolen" election.

George W. Bush

43

Born	July 6, 1946
Died	still living on the date this book was published
Home state	Texas
Wife	Laura Welch
Church	Episcopalian/Methodist
Occupation	businessman
Party	Republican
Years served as president	2001–9
Terms	2
Vice president	Dick Cheney

The War on Terror

September 11, 2001

On the morning of **September 11, 2001**, everything suddenly changed for Bush, America, and the world. An airliner, hijacked by terrorists, slammed into the North Tower of the World Trade Center in New York City. Minutes later, a second plane crashed into the South Tower. A third plane hit the Pentagon in Washington, DC. A fourth plane, possibly headed to the White House, crashed in a Pennsylvania field after heroic passengers fought the terrorists for control of the plane. Everyone on board died.

Approximately three thousand people were killed or injured in the attacks on September 11—civilians as well as military personnel, policemen, and firefighters. Many of the victims worked in the "twin towers" of the World Trade Center in New York City. Extensive property damage occurred. The terrorists had targeted symbols of finance and government in New York City and Washington, DC.

Americans responded with both anger and patriotism. They gave generously of their time and money to help the victims and their families. They flew American flags from front porches and car windows. Americans of both political parties joined in public ceremonies across the country to show unity.

One of the many individuals covered in dust and debris after the collapse of the World Trade Center

▲ Osama bin Laden

Bush rallied the nation when he stood at "Ground Zero," the site of the destruction of the World Trade Center, and promised victory over terrorism.

The nineteen terrorists responsible for the attack were connected to the international terrorist network **al-Qaeda**, led by **Osama bin Laden** who was linked to several earlier terrorist attacks against America and its allies. He and other Muslim extremists saw the United States as an obstacle to the spread of Islam. He sought the destruction of Israel, which he believed occupied land that belonged to Palestinian Muslims. He operated from Afghanistan, where the **Taliban** (a Muslim extremist group) controlled the government. The Taliban protected him and aided his global terrorist activities. These terrorist acts were carried out by bin Laden's worldwide band of Muslim extremists, numbering in the thousands, who had trained at al-Qaeda's camps. In addition to receiving religious instruction in radical Islam, recruits learned techniques for killing "infidels" (those who believe in a different religion or even Muslims who do not embrace radical ideas) through bombings and suicide missions.

Confronting Terrorism

Some people in other parts of the world saw Western culture as corrupt. They resisted its intrusion on their own way of life. For radical Muslims, hatred of the West—especially of America—fueled a network of terrorist groups in some sixty countries, mostly in the Middle East, Africa, and Asia. These groups operated in secret, and some were protected by various governments.

After September 11, 2001 (generally referred to as 9/11), America began a war against terrorists both at home and abroad. Bush warned that it would be a long struggle. On October 7, the United States invaded Afghanistan with the assistance of other countries and Afghan citizens who opposed the Taliban. The Taliban government collapsed in two months.

RESCUE *on* 9/11

Immediately after the World Trade Center attack, many people attempted to flee the island of Manhattan. Evacuation was difficult because of the lockdown of all bridges, roads, and tunnels. Subways, buses, and trains had been shut down, some within one minute of the first explosion. People in all types of boats around the island saw the explosions and then the collapse of the towers. They turned toward the island, evacuating over 50,000 people who could not otherwise leave. Covered in dust from the collapsing towers, people ran from the chaos, but they found that escaping the island would not be easy. Some jumped into the water and had to be rescued. Most waited behind guard rails for the next boat. Eventually, over 150 boats came to the rescue, lifting people off the island and delivering them to locations across the Hudson River.

This story sounds remarkably similar to the rescue of Allied soldiers at Dunkirk during World War II, where ordinary people (that time from Britain) saved the day by seeing an urgent need (troops trapped on the shore) and responding.

Smoke rises over the New York City skyline after the September 11 (9/11) attack.

But Muslim extremists could not be restrained by the threat of retaliation. They followed no rules of war. They resorted to suicide bombings and targeted innocent civilians. In response, Bush proposed a policy called the preemptive strike. Rather than wait for another terrorist attack, the military would take action before one could be carried out.

To handle the threat within the United States, Bush created a new agency, the **Department of Homeland Security**, which later became a cabinet department. The office streamlined existing agencies from other departments to fight terrorism at home. Americans accepted delays and long lines for check-in at airports as officials screened for potential terrorists.

At the president's urging, Congress overwhelmingly passed the **Patriot Act** that made it easier to locate and imprison suspected terrorists. One feature of the act allowed the government to listen to phone conversations of people suspected of having terrorist connections. Some Americans viewed this as a practical approach, but others saw it as an invasion of privacy. A few of the Patriot Act's provisions were deemed unconstitutional by the Supreme Court. Key provisions of the Act were renewed in 2012 and again in later years.

The War with Iraq

Since the 1991 Persian Gulf War, Saddam Hussein, the Iraqi dictator, had continued to threaten the Middle East and surrounding regions. He had used chemical weapons against the Kurdish people (a minority ethnic group) in Iraq. UN officials inspected Iraq for these and other **weapons of mass destruction (WMDs)**—specially formulated weapons intended to harm or kill great numbers of people, such as biological, chemical, or nuclear weapons. However, in 1998 Saddam stopped allowing the inspections.

After 9/11, Bush and other world leaders feared that Saddam had links to terrorism. They were also concerned that he was hiding WMDs. In 2003 the United States and other nations joined in a coalition and invaded Iraq. At the time, the action had overwhelming support from both parties in Congress. The coalition defeated Saddam's forces in about a month, and he was removed from power. However, stabilizing Iraq after the war proved difficult. Terrorists continued fighting a guerrilla war. They launched terrorist attacks and encouraged suicide bombings. They set up ambushes and set off improvised explosive devices (IEDs) along roads.

Americans were divided over whether the military should have invaded Iraq. As the war continued, it became increasingly controversial. Opponents argued that it was unnecessary or unwise. Supporters argued that fighting terrorists in Iraq made more sense than fighting them in the United States.

POLITICS *as a* "FAMILY BUSINESS"

George H. W. Bush and George W. Bush were the second father and son who both served as president. The other father-son presidential combination was John Adams and John Quincy Adams. John became president in 1796. Like George H. W. Bush, he failed to win reelection. In 1824 John Quincy was elected in a controversial election, just like George W. Bush in 2000. John Quincy failed to win a majority of the Electoral College vote, and the election went to the House of Representatives, where he won. John Quincy did not win reelection in 1828.

Another political family was the Harrisons. In 1840 America elected William Henry Harrison president. In 1888 voters chose his grandson Benjamin Harrison as president.

▾ American Marines fire an antitank missile in Iraq in May 2003.

Other Foreign Affairs

Bush's administration faced many challenges on the international scene. The British remained a staunch ally, but others in Europe, particularly the French and the Germans, strongly opposed the war in Iraq and disagreed with America's preemptive strategy.

Bush enjoyed some diplomatic successes. He convinced Libya to renounce terrorism, dismantle its WMDs, and seek closer ties with the West. He also obtained a promise from Pakistan, one of the world's most powerful Muslim nations, that it would work closely with him in waging the war on terror.

In Asia, Bush forged closer economic and diplomatic ties with China. However, the pursuit of nuclear weapons by the Communist dictator of North Korea posed a problem. Bush enlisted the help of China, Japan, and South Korea. Iran also seemed eager to acquire nuclear weapons and threatened to destroy Israel.

Domestic Affairs

Bush enlisted faith-based organizations to help administer government social programs that implemented "compassionate conservatism." Such faith-based initiatives became an important part of his domestic program to combat problems in the inner cities.

Both liberals and conservatives supported the No Child Left Behind Act, passed in 2002, which sought to ensure that every child could read and write. This act continued until 2015 when Congress passed a new bill under President Obama.

One of the worst natural disasters in American history occurred in August 2005 when Hurricane Katrina brought flooding to 80 percent of New Orleans, causing many deaths. Television stations showed videos of those who had not evacuated being rescued from their roofs. Gas prices skyrocketed across the country as oil rigs in the nearby Gulf of Mexico were disrupted.

▾ In this aerial view some of the massive flooding in New Orleans, caused by Hurricane Katrina, is visible. The August 2005 storm was one of the worst in the nation's history.

The Election of 2004

Foreign affairs was a major topic in the 2004 election. Senator John Kerry of Massachusetts won the Democratic nomination. Although Kerry had been a soldier during the Vietnam War, he later became an outspoken opponent of the conflict. Many veterans resented his position and would not support his candidacy. He also seemed somewhat indecisive about some issues. For example, after voting for the Iraq War, he later opposed measures that were necessary for fighting it, saying, "I actually did vote for the $87 billion [for the war in Iraq] before I voted against it."

Problems plagued Bush's reelection campaign as well. Daily accounts of violence and mounting casualties in Iraq drove Bush's approval ratings down. The Supreme Court ruled that prisoners of war held at an American base in Guantanamo Bay, Cuba, must be given certain rights that had not been provided to them. Another scandal involved mistreatment of prisoners at the Abu Ghraib prison in Iraq. In the end, most voters believed that Bush was better able to deal with the war on terror. He won reelection by more than three million popular votes, a stark contrast to the disputed 2000 election.

The Supreme Court

The United States had experienced a lengthy time of Supreme Court decisions that undermined traditional values and Christian beliefs. These decisions ranged from barring prayer and Bible reading in public schools to granting women the right to have an abortion. In 2005 and 2006 two justices, who were generally more conservative, were appointed by Bush and confirmed.

Bush nominated John Roberts Jr. to replace retiring Sandra Day O'Connor. Later that year, before the Senate could vote on Roberts, Chief Justice William Rehnquist died. Bush chose Roberts to replace Rehnquist. The Senate confirmed him, and he became the seventeenth chief justice of the United States. To fill O'Connor's spot, Bush picked Samuel Alito Jr., who had served on the US Court of Appeals. The Senate confirmed him in January 2006.

▲ John Roberts (left) became the chief justice of the US Supreme court in 2005. Samuel Alito (right) joined the court in 2006. Both were appointed by President George W. Bush.

Economics

To stimulate the sluggish economy, Bush called for major tax cuts at the same time that federal spending increased—mainly for military and security after 9/11. With both tax cuts and increased spending, the federal budget deficit reached record levels.

The US economy continued to expand throughout the world. Large corporations took advantage of free trade opportunities and spread overseas. With the increased use of the internet, Microsoft and Google became global players. But trade deficits grew as Americans purchased more goods from foreign countries than they sold to those nations. Some complained that free trade was unfair because businesses had to compete with foreign corporations that paid lower wages, causing cheaper goods to flood the American market.

Did you know?

In 2007 Nancy Pelosi became the first female Speaker of the House.

At the beginning of the century, housing prices rose steadily, eventually causing a housing "bubble" (a temporary sharp increase in housing prices). As prices rose, banks provided more and more mortgage loans to allow and even encourage people to buy houses. Banks then sold mortgages to willing investors, since as housing prices rose, so would profits. Banks and other lenders began selling subprime (less than ideal) mortgages for the first time to those who did not meet minimum income requirements or have good credit. Many people who had obtained mortgages were unable to repay them, causing banks to lose money and foreclose on houses. As these foreclosed homes came back on the market, the housing bubble burst, causing the price of houses across the country to drastically fall, investors to lose profits, banks to declare bankruptcy, stores to close, and people to lose their jobs. The **Great Recession** had begun and would last from the end of 2007 into 2009.

▲ One of the many businesses that closed during the Great Recession

SECTION REVIEW 27.1

1. Who were the candidates in the presidential election of 2000? How was the election finally determined?
2. What event changed everything for George W. Bush's presidency?
3. Is it right for a nation to make preemptive strikes against another nation? Why or why not?
4. What diplomatic accomplishments were achieved during the Bush years in Libya, Pakistan, and China?
5. From where did Bush enlist leaders for his "compassionate conservatism" program?
6. Whom did Bush name to be the chief justice of the Supreme Court? Which other justice did Bush nominate during his administration?

27.2 THE OBAMA ADMINISTRATION

What were the significant issues during the presidency of Barack Obama?

The Election of 2008

Leading into the 2008 presidential election, the Democrats gradually narrowed their field of candidates to former First Lady and New York senator Hillary Clinton and **Barack Obama**, an Illinois senator. Clinton was the front-runner for much of the campaign and seemed to be headed for the nomination. But she stumbled in several late primaries, and Obama surged ahead to capture the nomination. He chose Senator Joe Biden of Delaware as his running mate.

John McCain, an Arizona senator and Vietnam War hero, won the Republican nomination. McCain selected Alaska governor Sarah Palin to be his running mate.

Obama was an effective campaign speaker. The fact that he could become the nation's first African American president energized many voters. Although most conservatives opposed Obama for policy reasons, many optimistically noted that within a few decades the nation had moved from prohibiting black and white Americans eating at the same lunch counter to having a black man contending for the highest office in the land. Obama defeated McCain by more than 9.5 million popular votes and easily won in the Electoral College. He was inaugurated on January 20, 2009.

Many Americans looked to the election of the nation's first black president with great hope. Obama had unique opportunities. He provided a positive example as a husband and father. He challenged the black community to not discourage young people from striving for success. He also explained obstacles and prejudices that many black Americans faced.

The Election of 2012

In 2012 President Obama sought a second term. He again chose Joe Biden to be his running mate. The Republicans nominated former Massachusetts governor Mitt Romney, the first Mormon to be a presidential nominee. His running mate was Congressman Paul Ryan of Wisconsin. Although Obama's approval rating was relatively low, he won both the popular and electoral votes by comfortable margins. In his 2013 inaugural speech and in the soon-following State of the Union address, Obama advocated reforms in the areas of climate change, same-sex marriage, health care, early childhood education, immigration, minimum wage, and gun control. When the Republican-dominated Congress would not pass most of his wishes, Obama issued multiple executive orders to produce the desired results. A number of those orders were overturned by the next president.

GUIDING QUESTIONS

- What were the major issues and events in America during the presidency of Barack Obama?
- What was occurring in the world during Obama's presidency?

Barack Obama 44

Born	August 4, 1961
Died	still living on the date this book was published
Home state	Illinois (born in Hawaii)
Wife	Michelle Robinson
Church	Protestant, nondenominational
Occupation	lawyer
Party	Democrat
Years served as president	2009–17
Terms	2
Vice president	Joseph "Joe" Biden

Senator Barack Obama is shown campaigning in Denver, Colorado, shortly before his election to the presidency in November 2008.

— domestic TERRORIST events —

Two of the many domestic terrorist events during this time occurred in Newtown, Connecticut, and Boston, Massachusetts.

On December 14, 2012, a twenty-year-old man shot his way into Sandy Hook Elementary School in Connecticut, killing twenty first-graders and six staff members before shooting himself.

On April 15, 2013, two brothers set off bombs near the finish line of the annual Boston Marathon. Though neither brother was associated with terrorist groups, they were both Muslim extremists. As a result of the bombing, 3 people were killed, 14 required amputations, and 250 others were injured. One brother was killed in a police shootout, and the other was sentenced to death, although the sentence was appealed.

Did you know?

As of 2020, almost all the bailout loans to banks and mortgage, automobile, and insurance companies had been repaid. In addition, the government received $121 billion in profit.

Domestic Issues

The Economy

As unemployment spiked during the Great Recession, Obama worked hard to pass a stimulus package (economic measures meant to help a struggling economy) to help overcome the recession. He used much of a proposal created by the Bush administration. Congress passed the huge and intensely debated stimulus bill. The bill spurred the rise of the Tea Party, a political movement whose goal was to reduce the size and influence of government. The government offered bailout (rescue) loans for large banks, insurance and automobile companies, and major mortgage providers. Although unemployment remained high throughout Obama's first term, it dropped considerably during his second term. The economy slowly recovered. Most of the Bush tax cuts that had been set to expire at the end of 2012 were made permanent. By the end of Obama's presidency, many new jobs had been created, and wages outpaced inflation—although economic growth was still slow.

Health Care

The key legislation of Obama's first term was the passage of the **Patient Protection and Affordable Care Act**, better known as **Obamacare**. Although many Americans received health insurance from their employers, those without jobs or with pre-existing conditions often found health care too expensive or even impossible to obtain. Healthcare costs were rising faster than inflation. Obamacare sought to remedy this situation.

Obamacare would require all Americans to buy health insurance or face a financial penalty. Among other regulations, insurance companies could no longer refuse to pay benefits for people with pre-existing health conditions. Passage of the bill was difficult. After approval, it remained unpopular with many Americans. Contrary to the intentions of the plan, costs of health care soared.

The Supreme Court

When two justices retired, Obama had opportunity to influence the Supreme Court. In 2009 he replaced Justice David Souter with Sonia Sotomayor, the first Hispanic to serve on the Court. The next year Justice John Paul Stevens retired, and Obama named Elena Kagan to replace him. Both the retiring justices and the new appointees usually supported liberal positions.

The Supreme Court handed Obama a victory when Chief Justice John Roberts voted with the more liberal members of the Court in a case concerning the constitutionality of Obamacare. Conservatives had hoped that the Court would find it unconstitutional since Congress is not authorized to impose a penalty for *not* buying something—in this case, health insurance. But Roberts, writing the majority opinion, stated that the penalty portion of the law was a tax and therefore constitutional.

During Obama's second term, the Supreme Court granted marriage rights to same-sex partners in the 2015 ***Obergefell v. Hodges*** case. Afterward, the Obama administration showed its support for the Court's decision by illuminating the exterior of the White House with rainbow colors (a symbol of the homosexual community).

▾ Rainbow colors were projected on the White House after the *Obergefell v. Hodges* decision.

When Justice Antonin Scalia died in February 2016, Republican leaders in the Senate chose to not hold confirmation hearings for Obama's appointee. They said the new president should make the appointment when he took office ten months later.

Foreign Challenges

The Middle East

The Middle East can loosely be defined as countries throughout the Arabian peninsula, other Muslim countries such as Iran and Iraq, parts of North Africa (such as Egypt), and Turkey. Many events connected to the war on terror occurred in this area during Obama's presidency.

Although Obama had earlier opposed the war in Iraq, he kept Bush's secretary of defense. He decreased the number of troops in Iraq by using much of the Bush administration's withdrawal schedule. At the same time, he increased the number of troops in Afghanistan to train that nation's soldiers to successfully defend against the Taliban forces. After this initial surge, the number of troops in Afghanistan declined significantly during the rest of Obama's presidency.

Perhaps the best-known foreign-policy accomplishment of Obama's first term was the killing of Osama bin Laden by Navy SEAL Team Six in May 2011. After locating the compound in Pakistan where the 9/11 mastermind was hiding, the team helicoptered in and shot bin Laden. After removing the body and using DNA samples to confirm bin Laden's identity, American forces buried him at sea.

Libyan rebels, with air support from NATO forces, overthrew dictator Muammar al-Qaddafi. In response, in 2012 on the eleventh anniversary of 9/11, Muslim terrorists attacked a US diplomatic compound in Benghazi, Libya. The American ambassador and three other American officials were killed.

In Egypt, members of various religious groups joined to protest the oppressive Egyptian government. The United States had long supplied aid to Egypt, which in turn provided stability in the Middle East. But the lack of democracy in Egypt made it increasingly difficult for the United States to support leaders whom many Egyptians opposed. Political leaders in the United States pressured the Egyptian president to resign. When he did so, a group known as the Muslim Brotherhood won the presidency. But their abuse of power soon led to more protests, and the Egyptian military removed the president a year later.

A terrorist group known as the **Islamic State of Iraq and Syria** (**ISIS**, also known as ISIL) developed in the Middle East from the remnants of al-Qaeda. This group proved dangerous and ruthless. They kidnapped and beheaded several foreign journalists even after some converted to Islam. ISIS attacked other Muslim groups such as the Iraqi Kurds, and they sought to exterminate Christians in Syria and Iraq.

East Asia and Russia

In East Asia, the United States faced several challenges. North Korea continued to threaten South Korea and Japan by firing missiles at disputed islands. Obama discussed issues such as trade relations and climate change with China. Hong Kong had been leased to Britain for ninety-nine years between 1898 and 1997, but tensions mounted after it was returned to China. The Communist government gradually tried to limit its long-held freedoms. As a result, the people of Hong Kong staged public protests.

Numerous protests have occurred in Hong Kong since it was returned to China's control in 1997. Residents of the city resent the Communist government's limitations on many of that city's freedoms. The march shown here took place in July 2014.

Obama helped Russia join the World Trade Organization. In 2010 the Senate approved a treaty limiting nuclear arms for both countries. But tensions increased after **Vladimir Putin**, who had been Russia's president from 1999 to 2008, returned to that position in 2012. In 2014 Putin annexed the Crimea, claiming to support rebels in that portion of the Ukraine who sought to return the area to Russian control. Putin's actions were a violation of international law.

During the 2016 presidential election in America, Russia interfered with the process. It distributed misinformation, engaged in hacking various internet sites, and attempted to disrupt in a variety of other ways. However, there is no evidence that Russian involvement affected the election outcome in any state.

SECTION REVIEW 27.2

1. Why was the election of Obama significant?
2. Name Obama's first two Supreme Court nominees.
3. Do you agree with the Supreme Court's decision regarding Obamacare? Why or why not?
4. What court case during this time granted marriage rights to same-sex partners?
5. What terrorist group formed from the remains of al-Qaeda?

27.3 THE TRUMP ADMINISTRATION

What were the important events during the presidency of Donald Trump?

GUIDING QUESTIONS

- What domestic events occurred under President Trump?
- Why was President Trump impeached?
- What was occurring in the world during Trump's administration?

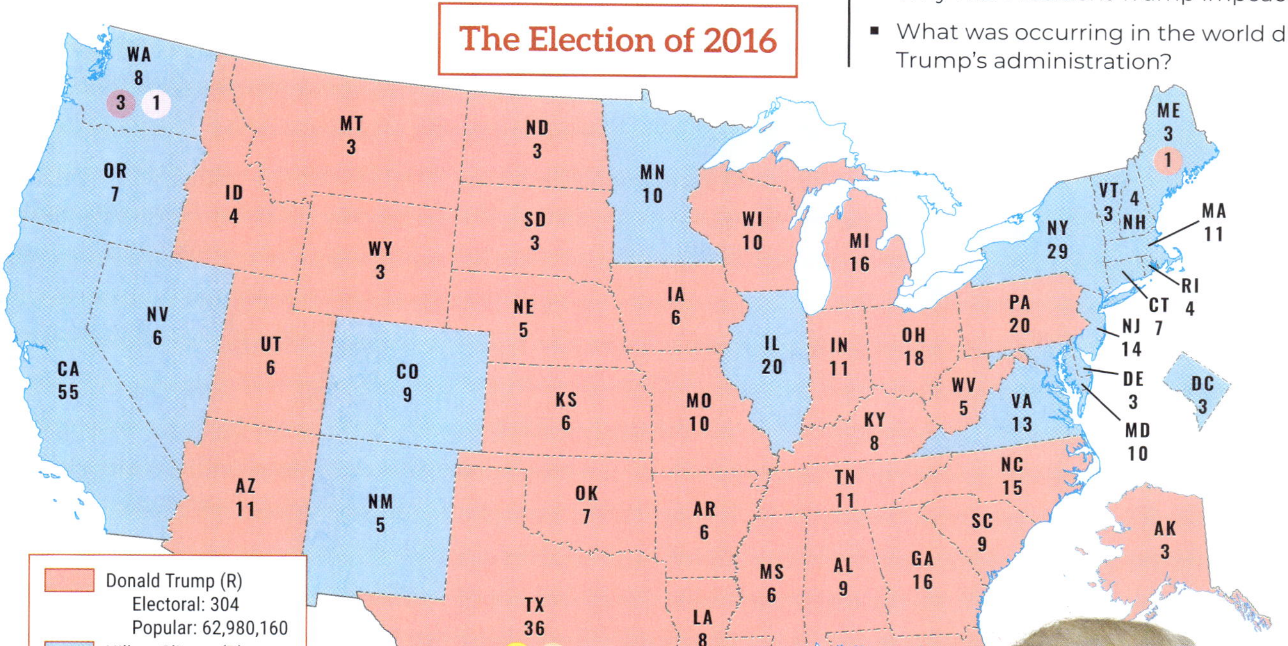

Donald Trump

Born	June 14, 1946	45
Died	still living on the date this book was published	
Home state	New York	
Wives	1st—Ivana Zelnickova 2nd—Marla Maples 3rd—Melania Knauss (First Lady)	
Church	Protestant, nondenominational	
Occupation	businessman	
Party	Republican	
Years served as president	2017–21	
Terms	1	
Vice president	Mike Pence	

Domestic Issues

The Election of 2016

Unlike eight years earlier, **Hillary Clinton**, former First Lady and New York senator, was successful in her attempt to clinch the Democratic nomination for president. She had added to her list of qualifications by serving as secretary of state during Obama's first term. She chose as her running mate Senator Tim Kaine from Virginia.

An unlikely choice from a wide field of candidates received the Republican nomination. **Donald Trump**, billionaire real estate mogul and reality TV show host, had never run for political office or served in the military. His campaign emphasized, among other things, the need for trade agreement changes and for improving and extending a wall along the border with Mexico. His running mate was Mike Pence, governor and a former congressman from Indiana. Pence, who described himself as a born-again, evangelical Catholic, was a popular choice among political and religious conservatives.

Although Clinton won more popular votes across the nation, Trump succeeded in winning the Electoral College, becoming the 45th president of the United States on January 20, 2017.

Economics

One of Trump's major goals was to institute tax cuts for individuals and businesses. During his first year in office, he was able to convince Congress to pass a new tax plan. Afterward, additional money flowed into the economy, and the unemployment rate dipped below the level it had reached during Obama's administration.

Three days after his inauguration, Trump withdrew the United States from the Trans-Pacific Partnership trade deal, an unratified free-trade agreement that had been negotiated the previous year while Obama was president. Not a fan of NAFTA, President Trump pushed for its modification or dismissal. After working with Canada and Mexico for more than a year, the **United States-Mexico-Canada Agreement** (**USMCA**) was passed and signed by each member nation, receiving support from both Republicans and Democrats. It took effect in July 2020.

The Courts

During his four years in office, approximately 230 of the federal judges Trump appointed were approved. By contrast, President Obama had 329 approved during his eight years in the White House. Because federal judges serve for life and thereby have impact for many years, this would prove to be one of Trump's most significant accomplishments. By the time Trump left office, almost 30 percent of the federal judgeships were held by his appointees.

Trump had the opportunity to appoint three justices to the Supreme Court. Within his first two weeks in office, he nominated Neil Gorsuch to take the place of Justice Antonin Scalia. Gorsuch became a member of the court in April 2017.

Trump's July 2018 nomination of Brett Kavanaugh proved controversial. Kavanaugh was chosen to replace retiring justice Anthony Kennedy, for whom he had served as a clerk in earlier years. After intense debate between Democrats and Republicans, the Senate voted to confirm Kavanaugh by a very slim margin.

Then in September 2020, Justice Ruth Bader Ginsburg died. She had been a strong supporter of equal pay and equal opportunity for women but unfortunately also strongly promoted the right to abortion. President Trump was once again able to nominate a justice for the Supreme Court. He chose Amy Coney Barrett, who had clerked for former justice Antonin Scalia. Barrett, a devout Catholic with seven children, was expected to be a conservative voice on the Court. Democrats attempted to block the nomination as Republicans had done to Obama's last Supreme Court nominee four years earlier. But the Republican-led Senate confirmed her nomination in October.

▲ During his term, Trump appointed three justices to the Supeme Court: Neil Gorsuch, Brett Kavanaugh, and Amy Coney Barrett (left to right).

The Mueller Investigation

Evidence emerged that the Russian government had interfered with the 2016 election through social media campaigns and by hacking and releasing embarrassing emails from leading Democrats. The Department of Justice eventually tasked **Robert Mueller**, a former FBI director, to investigate whether links between the Trump campaign and Russian interference in the election existed.

After an investigation lasting almost two years, a report of the Mueller findings was completed in March 2019. It noted, "the investigation did not establish that members of the Trump Campaign conspired or coordinated with the Russian government in its election interference activities." Regarding obstruction of justice, the Mueller report did not reach a conclusion, stating, "while this report does not conclude that the President committed a crime, it also does not exonerate him." Several former advisors to Trump were convicted of making false statements to the FBI or Congress. No one was convicted of collusion with Russia.

Impeachment Proceedings

Near the end of 2019, a government whistleblower (someone who publicly discloses what he believes is illegal or unethical activity) claimed that President Trump had pressured the president of the Ukraine. Eventually, evidence emerged that Trump wanted the Ukrainian leader to launch an investigation into the conduct of Hunter Biden, son of former vice president Joe Biden. Hunter was a board member of a powerful energy corporation in the Ukraine. Trump threatened to withhold military funds Congress had designated for the Ukraine if the Ukrainians failed to investigate. Joe Biden was one of the leading contenders for the 2020 Democratic presidential nomination.

The Democrat-led House of Representatives investigated the matter and soon began impeachment proceedings. The House voted to impeach the president based on two charges—abuse of power and obstruction of justice. No Republican in the House voted for impeachment, but since the majority of House members were Democrats, the measure passed. Trump became the third president to be impeached.

In mid-January 2020, the Senate held a trial, as stipulated in the Constitution, to determine whether the charges should result in the removal of the president from office. Unlike the House, the Senate was controlled by Republicans. Though many acknowledged the president had mishandled the matter, they argued that his actions did not warrant removal from office. All Republican senators voted against the obstruction of justice charge. All Republicans except one voted against the abuse of power charge. As was true in the impeachment trials of Andrew Johnson and Bill Clinton, the Senate failed to reach the two-thirds necessary to convict the president of charges brought by the House.

POPULAR *vs.* ELECTORAL VOTING

There have been five elections in which the candidate who became president did not win the popular vote:

- John Quincy Adams (Democratic-Republican, 1824)—won election in the House of Representatives after Andrew Jackson received more popular and electoral votes, but not a majority of either
- Rutherford B. Hayes (Republican, 1876)—won by only one vote in the Electoral College in an intensely disputed election
- Benjamin Harrison (Republican, 1888)—won the Electoral College 233–168 after losing the popular election by 100,000 votes
- George W. Bush (Republican, 2000)—won the Electoral College 271–266 after losing the popular election by 540,000 votes
- Donald Trump (Republican, 2016)—won the Electoral College 304–227 after losing the popular election by 2.9 million votes

▾ Headline from December 19, 2019

▲ Fires in Australia in 2020

2020: *a* BIZARRE *year*

Many unusual happenings occurred during 2020:

Australian bush fires threatened a large portion of that country.

Giant Asian hornets were found in Washington State. Because of their aggressive attacks and painful stings, they became known, rather inaccurately, as murder hornets.

California and other places in the West suffered an enormous spread of wildfires causing multiple and widespread evacuations.

A gigantic dust storm from the Sahara reached the southeastern part of the United States in June, creating beautiful sunsets but dangerous air-quality levels.

COVID-19: A Global Pandemic

▲ Digital image of the coronavirus

The year 2020 brought a string of challenges, the most critical of which was a global pandemic. A new coronavirus, SARS-CoV-2, arose to which no one had immunity, causing **COVID-19** disease. The first case was reported in Wuhan, China, in December 2019. It soon affected millions across the globe. The death rate (the percentage of those who die after contracting a sickness) varied but remained significantly higher than that of the average yearly flu. At the same time, a large portion of those who contracted the virus had few or no symptoms of infection.

Not since the influenza pandemic that began in 1918 had the nation faced such a health crisis. Much of the economy was crippled as businesses were ordered to close and as many people stayed home to try to stop the spread of the virus. Almost all churches suspended in-person meetings, at least for a time, and used technology to conduct services and fellowship. Court battles between churches and the government occurred in a number of states regarding the First Amendment's guarantee of religious liberty.

Orders to wear masks sparked controversy as some Americans felt their freedom was being limited, while others believed such mandates were necessary to protect the health of citizens. Scientists and doctors did not always agree on health measures. Public debate regarding how to best handle the pandemic was often intense.

Even President Trump contracted the virus in early October 2020 and was hospitalized. After being given an infusion and medicine still in trial stages, he was able to return to the White House three days later. In December the first vaccines received emergency authorization for distribution.

Did you know?

The World Health Organization estimates that one billion people contract a flu virus during a typical year.

A masked student receives a temperature check before entering a high-school building. ▸

Foreign Issues

America First

Between the world wars, an American isolationist movement arose that eventually became known as "America First." President Trump cloned the phrase and used a modified version of its meaning during the 2016 campaign and his time in office. He explained his **America First** policy later with the phrase, "There is no place like home." He meant that he would make decisions based on what he deemed to be in the best interest of the United States and its citizens.

The globalization of the modern world can be seen everywhere, especially when it relates to trade and economics. Tourists can find McDonald's in the Alps of Switzerland and Coca-Cola in the safari parks of South Africa. But in foreign affairs, Trump believed that the United States should reduce its allocation of resources and carefully limit its involvement in issues relating to other countries.

▲ In this 2019 picture, workers are building a larger and more secure wall to replace an outdated section of border wall between the U.S. and Mexico. President Trump believed such measures were necessary to stop the flow of illegal immigrants.

In trade, Trump instituted tariffs that he believed would protect America from job losses due to competition created by lower wages in other parts of the world. In warfare, he sought to end American involvement in the long-running war in Afghanistan by briefly sending more military and then removing most troops by January 2021. He signed an executive order to remove the tax penalty for Americans who could not or would not obtain health insurance as required by Obamacare. He continued building a wall along the Mexican border to reduce access for illegal immigrants. A substantial number of Americans supported this action because they believed illegal immigration drained tax resources, resulted in the loss of jobs for American citizens, and made it easier for criminals, even terrorists, to enter the country.

Asia

Relations with China shifted several times during the Trump administration. While supporting the policy of recognizing only one China (Communist China), the president also reached out to the president of Taiwan. (Remember that many non-Communists had fled from mainland China to Taiwan during China's civil war between Communists and Nationalists after World War II. Taiwan, also known as the Republic of China, considers itself the "real" China and a separate country from the People's Republic of China, also called mainland China). Several visits to America by Chinese officials and to China by American officials occurred.

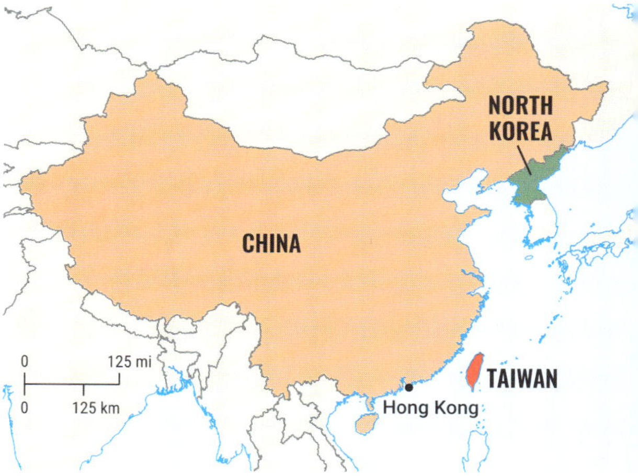

Over the course of his term, Trump drastically raised tariffs with China, even up to a 25 percent rate on certain products. He blamed the previous, mostly free-trade system between the United States and China for serious issues like unfair competition and intellectual property theft (stealing peoples' ideas and inventions). China retaliated by levying their own tariffs. Strained relations resulted.

Another reason for tensions with China was the handling of Hong Kong, the island that had reverted to Chinese control in 1997. For years, people had protested in Hong Kong. In 2020, as protesters had feared, Hong Kong lost much of its remaining autonomy (self-government) to mainland China. Since then, the Chinese government has arrested several members of pro-democratic groups.

In an attempt to reach out to the most notable modern rogue nation (country threatening world peace), President Trump became the first president to visit North Korea while still in office. Beginning in 2018 he held a series of meetings that aimed for an agreement to remove or greatly reduce nuclear weapons in North Korea. Such an agreement was signed, but it is not clear if nuclear weapons have been reduced since North Korea continues to refuse international inspections.

The Middle East

The Middle East has often been at the forefront of many presidents' foreign affairs issues. Soon after his inauguration, Trump withdrew from the Obama-era deal that had sent large amounts of money to Iran in exchange for Iran's promise to limit nuclear weapons. Iran had often been accused of sponsoring terrorism. Trump reimposed economic penalties on the country.

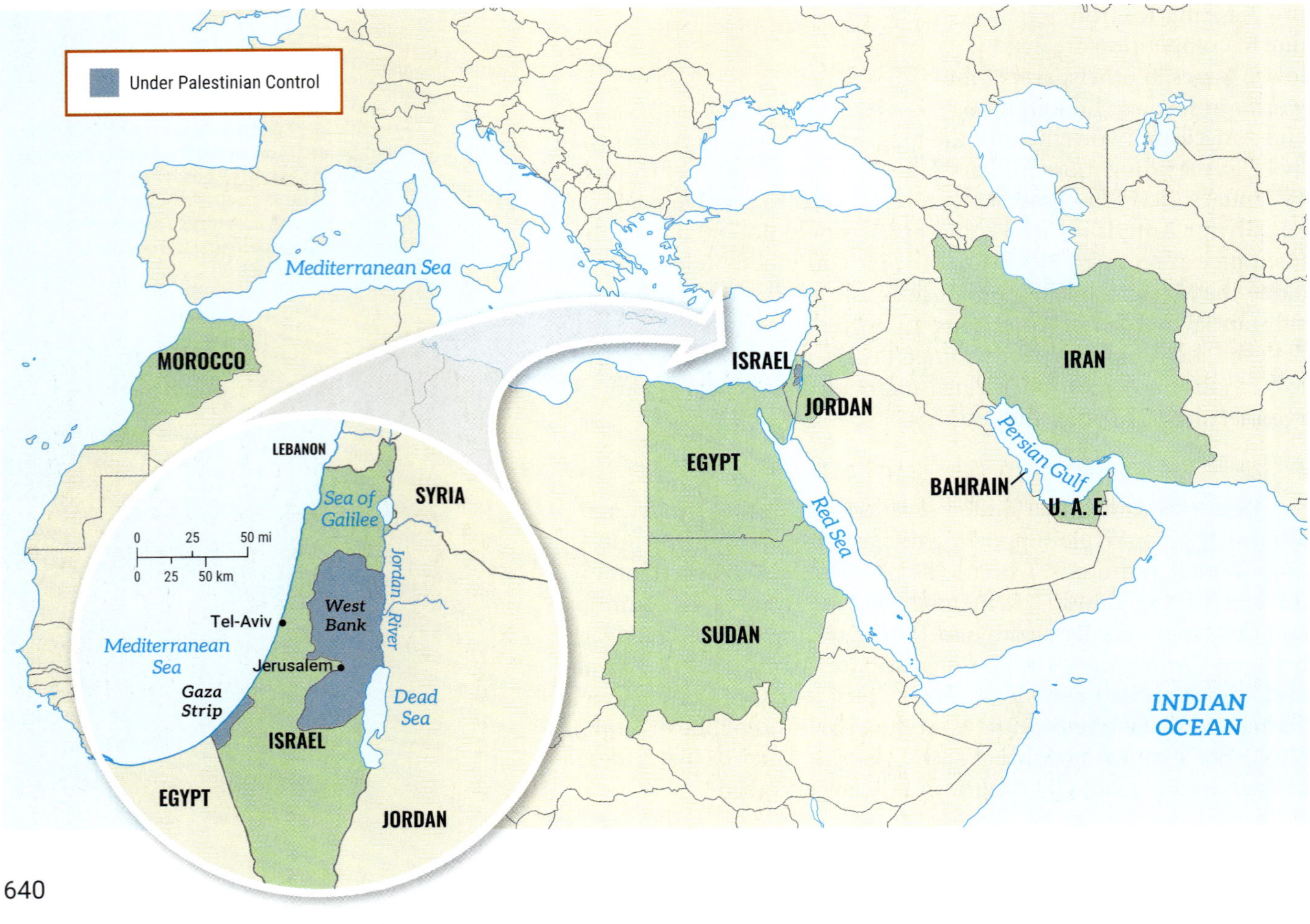

▲ Members of a Muslim terrorist group shown in an Iraqi desert

Trump then decided to honor Israel's wish for Jerusalem to be recognized as its capital. Both Israelis and Palestinians (Arabs who live in self-governing areas within the modern country of Israel) have historically claimed Jerusalem, so most countries of the world have met this difficulty by recognizing the next-largest city, Tel Aviv, as Israel's capital and placing their embassies there. Near the end of 2017, Trump issued a directive for the United States embassy to be moved to Jerusalem, which occurred six months later.

In 2020 Trump used his deal-making abilities to negotiate peace agreements between several Arab nations of the Middle East and Israel. Since the modern nation of Israel was established in May 1948, Egypt (in 1979) and Jordan (in 1994) had been the only Muslim-majority countries to agree to recognize the right of Israel to be a nation. In September 2020 the United Arab Emirates (UAE) signed the Abraham Accords Peace Agreement to open trade and political relations with Israel. Bahrain signed its own peace agreement with Israel the same day. In October, Sudan also voted to open relations with Israel. And then in December, Morocco, which had reacted negatively to the September agreements, joined the others.

Since the downfall of al-Qaeda, ISIS had been the leading international terrorist organization. In 2014 it conquered key cities in Iraq and declared control over a large area. The group continued to plan and execute attacks. But by the end of 2017, ISIS had lost the vast majority of its land, and its major leaders had been killed. Yet the greatly reduced terrorist group continues to be a threat.

The Election of 2020

Campaign and Results

As expected, Republicans nominated incumbent Donald Trump as their presidential candidate. He campaigned on a record of economic success (though the economy had stumbled significantly during the COVID-19 crisis), his America First policy, and his promise to continue combating illegal immigration. Though he was popular with many Americans, many others opposed his policies. Many also viewed his governing style as too confrontational and thought that his remarks regarding those who opposed him were often rude and belittling.

More than two dozen Democratic contenders vied to be their party's presidential candidate. In the end, former vice president **Joe Biden** won the nomination. He chose as his running mate Senator Kamala Harris from California, who had also sought the Democratic nomination. The most important election issue was the handling of the COVID-19 pandemic. Each party claimed to be more competent to handle the continuing crisis.

Partly because of the coronavirus, voting was somewhat untraditional in 2020. There was a dramatic increase in the number of people who voted early, either in person or by mailing their ballots. Though the official election results indicated that Biden had won the popular and electoral vote, disputes continued for weeks regarding the results in states where the election was close. President Trump and many of his supporters believed that a substantial amount of voter fraud had occurred. Approximately fifty legal challenges were made. Citing a variety of reasons, they alleged that fair elections had not occurred in a number of states.

▼ Joe Biden was the Democratic nominee for president in 2020. He chose Kamala Harris as his running mate.

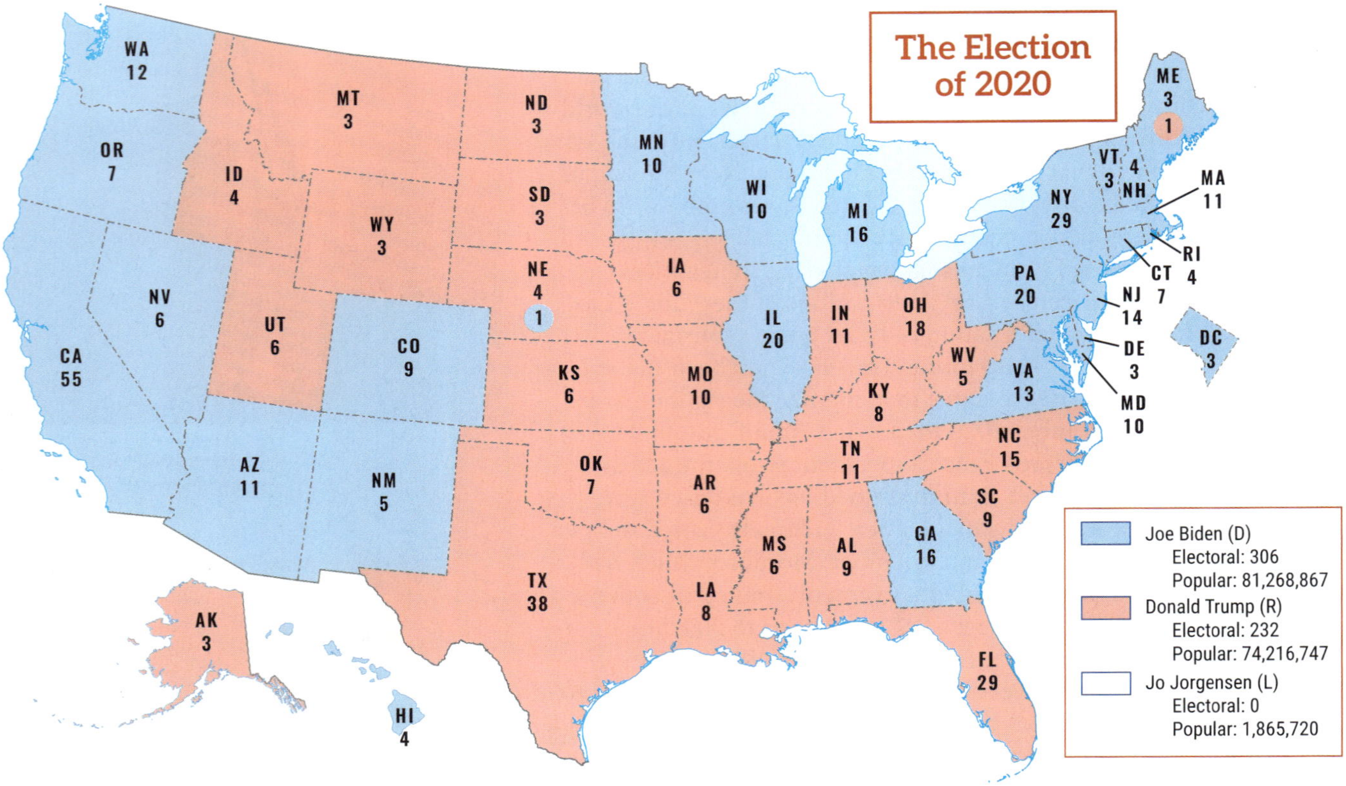

Joseph "Joe" Biden

Born	November 20, 1942	46
Died	still living on the date this book was published	
Home state	Delaware (born in Pennsylvania)	
Wives	1st—Neilia Hunter 2nd—Jill Jacobs	
Church	Roman Catholic	
Occupation	lawyer	
Party	Democrat	
Years served as president	2021–	
Terms	in progress	
Vice president	Kamala Harris	

Judges dismissed most of the cases for insufficient evidence or because the cases were initiated by people or groups that did not have the legal right to present them in the court in which they were filed. In addition, Trump supporters dropped some of the cases; in other instances, judges heard the arguments regarding the case and ruled against Trump. The Trump campaign received a favorable ruling in only one case. When that case was appealed to a higher court, even that victory was overturned. In the end, none of the legal challenges changed the election results of any state.

Aftermath

On December 14 the members of the Electoral College met to cast their ballots. Biden received 306 votes and Trump won 232. After the Electoral College results were announced, President Trump continued to state that the election had been stolen from him. He called for supporters to assemble for a rally in Washington, DC, on January 6, 2021—the day that Congress was scheduled to officially count and certify the Electoral College votes.

Thousands gathered for the rally. Speakers, including Trump, called on Congress to not certify the results, thereby preventing Joe Biden from being declared the winner. The president told supporters to march from the White House to the Capitol to make those views known to Congress.

While the rally was occurring, Congress had already begun discussing the election results. Normally, this would be a routine event that requires little time—a formality in which the electoral vote results forwarded to Congress are merely officially opened and counted. But because of the controversy surrounding the 2020 election, there was much debate about certifying the electoral vote.

Thousands that had gathered for the rally did indeed go to the Capitol grounds, some even before the rally ended. Many swept past barricades and overwhelmed officers. More than a hundred members of the Capitol Police and the city's police department were injured in their attempts to keep back the crowd. Still, hundreds of protesters entered the building, some after smashing windows or breaking through doors.

Rioters roamed the building, making threatening remarks as they sought to locate members of the House and Senate. The congressional proceedings were disrupted as law enforcement officials evacuated Congress members and their staffs to safe locations.

Eventually order was restored and Congress reconvened late in the evening. They stayed in session until the early hours of the next day. They certified the electoral count that had been announced December 14 and declared Joe Biden the winner of the election.

Many members of Congress almost immediately argued that Trump was responsible for the Capitol riot and began calling for his impeachment. On January 13, the House of Representatives, by a vote of 222–197, impeached the president, charging that he had incited the insurrection at the Capitol the previous week. All Democratic members supported the measure, as did ten Republicans. This was the fourth time in the nation's history that a president had been impeached. With just one week left in office, Trump became the only president to be impeached twice.

On January 20, 2021, Joe Biden was inaugurated as the nation's 46th president. He was the second Roman Catholic president. **Kamala Harris** became the first female, the first African American, and the first Asian American to hold the office of vice president. Vice President Pence attended the inauguration, but President Trump refused to do so. It was the first time in more than 150 years that the departing president had not participated.

▲ Hundreds of protesters pushed their way into the US Capitol on January 6, 2021.

▼ President Biden delivered his inauguration speech on January 20, 2021.

▲ Additional fencing and barricades were placed around the Capitol after protesters stormed the building. In this March 2021 picture, some of those barriers are being removed.

The Senate trial did not begin until February 9, almost three weeks after Trump's term ended. Many Republican members of the Senate declared the impeachment trial unconstitutional since Trump was no longer in office; however, they did not have enough votes to stop the trial.

The Constitution states that the chief justice of the Supreme Court should preside at the trial of the president. John Roberts (who had officiated at Trump's first impeachment trial) declined to participate in the second one. He felt no obligation to officiate at the trial because the person charged was no longer president.

The trial lasted five days. Senators who believed the president guilty argued that Trump's repeated claims of election fraud and his speeches (including the one delivered at the January 6 rally) had led the mob to attack the Capitol. Trump supporters noted that he had never called for violence and that his January 6 speech had stated that those gathered in Washington, DC, should "peacefully and patriotically" march to the Capitol. Though fifty-seven senators, including seven Republicans, voted guilty on the charge of inciting an insurrection, the total number fell short of the two-thirds required. If the former president had been convicted, the Senate could have barred him from ever holding public office again.

SECTION REVIEW 27.3

1. Who was the presidential candidate for the Democratic Party in 2016? for the Republican Party?
2. What trade agreement replaced NAFTA?
3. What was the most important issue in both domestic and foreign affairs during 2020?
4. How did Trump change trade with China?
5. What Muslim nations signed agreements with Israel in 2020?
6. Who won the election of 2020? What was significant about his vice president?
7. What were the charges against President Trump in both of his impeachment trials?

27.4 AMERICA TODAY

What is America like today?

GUIDING QUESTIONS

- What are conditions in America like in the twenty-first century?
- What does God's Word say about current religious and moral issues?
- What are the current political issues?

The Modern United States

Demographics

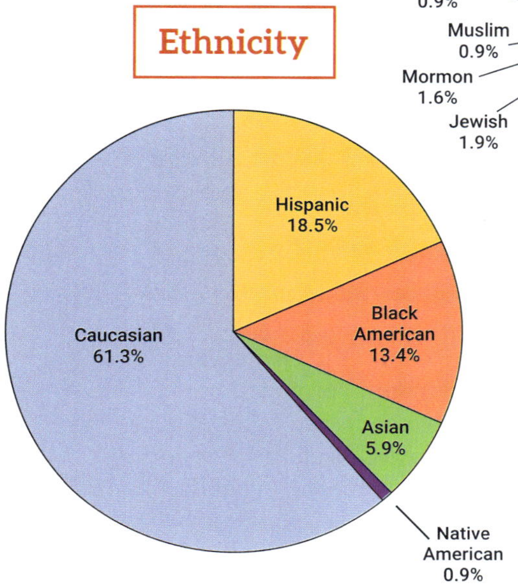

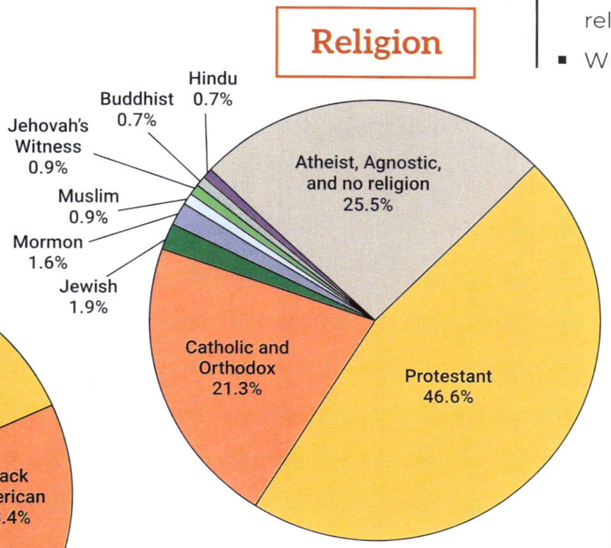

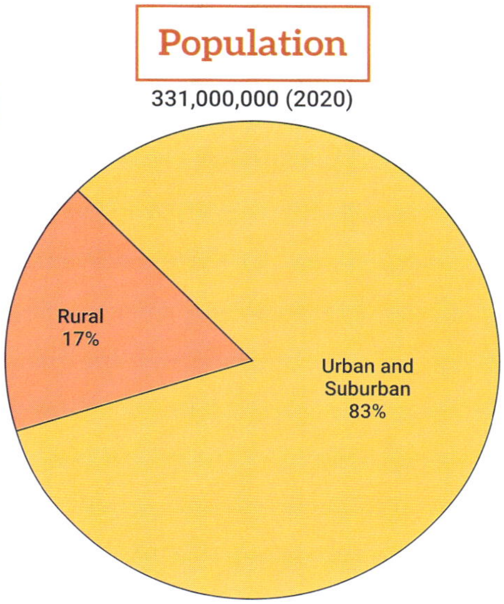

Worldview

A **worldview** is the set of beliefs that a person uses to look at the world and interpret it. Worldviews are used to answer questions like:

Where did everything come from?
Is there a God?
What is good?
What happens to people when they die?

While every person has a worldview, different worldviews frequently produce varying conclusions. People with differing worldviews sometimes have difficulty working together because they may not agree on what is best for society. A person's worldview affects his attitude toward technology, diversity, multiculturalism, religion, and morality.

1975

Personal computers

1977

Atari

Nintendo

1986

PlayStation

1994

Xbox

2001

2004

Facebook

Instagram

2010

Technology

Computers and mobile devices are features of everyday life for most Americans today. But they are much newer than many young people realize. The first modern computers were engineered in the 1960s, but electronic gadgets did not really enter the marketplace until the 1990s. PalmPilots (handheld computers) provided note taking, calendar management, and other applications. BlackBerry followed in 1999, adding features such as text messaging and cameras. In 2000 Apple introduced the iPod, which became the most popular portable media player in the world; later models could hold music, digital photos, and videos.

In 2007 Apple released the iPhone, combining the functions of cellular phones, handheld computers, and iPods. Other companies soon made smartphones, each one containing many times more computing power, speed, and memory than the rocket that sent the first astronauts to the moon in 1969.

Other technological innovations have changed people's everyday lives as well. The internet provides instant access to information. People shop online on eBay, Amazon, and countless other sites. Checks can be deposited and payments can be made through phone apps. Friends can play video games together even while separated by hundreds of miles. A few cars drive themselves. And 3D printers make real items.

Technology and the devices it makes possible are tools. Christians can use these innovations to evangelize. Missionaries previously isolated in distant places can now communicate more easily, even when there is limited electricity, running water, or indoor plumbing.

Because humans are sinful, tools can also be used in wrong ways. Social media can become divisive and can tempt many to write things that they would never say in person. Violations of copyright law and identity theft have become major concerns. The web's ease of access and anonymity has led to the rapid expansion of false information and sometimes sinful material (such as pornography).

Like so many other "good" things, technology threatens to become the master rather than the servant. Time-saving devices increase the pace of life, so it often seems as if people have even less time. Unlimited attention to social media steals time from school, work, family, and friends. Educators complain about shortened attention spans and shallow thinking. Cellphone use often clashes with good manners.

With medical technology, innovations such as cloning and stem cell research have created ethical dilemmas. Cloning raises questions about creating duplicate life forms, whether plant, animal, or even human. And the source of stem cells (often from adult cells, but sometimes from fetal cells of miscarried or aborted babies) can cause moral concerns in some cases. A society not grounded in scriptural absolutes is at a loss to determine right and wrong in these situations.

cellphone MANNERS

1. Speak softly while on a call.
2. Do not interrupt face-to-face conversations to take texts or calls.
3. Put away electronic devices during mealtimes.
4. Turn devices to silent or Do Not Disturb at school, church, or other gatherings.
5. Wait to discuss personal matters until away from others.

In the aftermath of George Floyd's death, demonstrations occurred throughout the nation. A June 2020 Black Lives Matter rally in Pennsylvania is shown above. Many protests turned violent, such as the one shown below in Los Angeles, California.

Diversity and Multiculturalism

A great deal of diversity exists in modern America. How it is viewed has changed over the last several decades. One area that can cause conflict is cultural diversity. Differing cultural groups show the God-given creativity of mankind. These groups can bring glory to God in many different ways, but traditions and values precious to one group may be ignored by others, resulting in occasional clashes.

Another controversial area is ethnic diversity. People often forget that God made everyone from the same parents—both Adam and Eve and Noah and his wife—and they then act in a manner inconsistent with the biblical teaching of humans as image-bearers of God. Pride unfortunately tempts some people to consider themselves better than others.

In 2012 Trayvon Martin, an African American teen, was shot and killed in Florida by a neighborhood watch captain. Though the man was charged with murder, the following year he was acquitted after arguing that he acted in self-defense. The verdict led to protests, some of which turned violent. During this time, the Black Lives Matter (BLM) organization was formed. #BlackLivesMatter is also used by many who do not necessarily identify with that organization. Other groups, such as Blue Lives Matter (showing support for police), rose in response.

In May 2020 George Floyd died after a police officer knelt on his neck for a prolonged time during an arrest. Protests and demonstrations spread throughout the country. While many were peaceful, others turned violent. Riots again ensued in multiple cities across the country as the Black Lives Matter movement resurged. Businesses and homes were vandalized and burned. Property damage was estimated at a record $2 billion. Debate raged about whether the movement aided minorities or added to racial tensions. As a result of these demonstrations, many Americans called for the reevaluation of certain police procedures.

▲ Citizens from a variety of cultural backgrounds wait in line to exercise one of the nation's most cherished freedoms, the right to vote.

Diverse groups live in close proximity within the United States. Many members of multicultural societies believe that different cultures can exist side by side without being dominated by any particular one. Unfortunately, this sometimes leads to the idea that truth is relative to each culture. But all truth must be evaluated by the truth of God's Word.

This intermingling of cultures has both positive and negative aspects. When the apostle Paul first preached the gospel in Europe and Asia, many early Christian churches represented diverse cultures since the gospel did not divide by race, gender, or social status. It was, and still is, for everyone.

Many Americans today believe that **multiculturalism** is a strength to be celebrated; however, some of its supporters attack Western (European) culture. They believe that it has been "poisoned" by Christian ideas and values. They work hard to overcome perceived "restrictions." Many of the terms used to promote this aspect of multiculturalism, such as *tolerance*, sound very promising on the surface but are often applied in an unbalanced or even unbiblical manner.

This emphasis on tolerance is quite popular, especially among those who advocate tolerance for differing viewpoints on controversial moral and biblical issues such as abortion and homosexual rights. But Christians should not accept tolerance of issues the Bible clearly labels as sin. Christians are called to be countercultural in such situations, while at the same time remaining kind and Christlike so that the gospel is not hindered.

Those who promote tolerance of all viewpoints believe they are highlighting the American ideal of freedom. But allowing such freedom for some may bring lack of freedom and even oppression to others. For example, the belief that a woman must be free to choose what to do with her own body means that another American (an unborn baby) must die for the sake of this alleged freedom.

These conflicts demonstrate the difficulty of living together peacefully in a society where the chief goal of each individual is the freedom to pursue his or her own desires. Though not always easy or convenient, people must value what is right above personal freedom.

Religious conservatives sometimes struggle with their role in a multicultural society. Many times the teaching in Titus 3 (to show kindness and courtesy to all people) is ignored—especially with regard to rulers (those in authority). Rude remarks and insults about authorities with whom one does not agree are wrong according to the Bible. On the other hand, when Christians engage in sinful behavior deemed culturally acceptable, it hurts the cause of Christ and allows unbelievers to portray Christians as hypocrites.

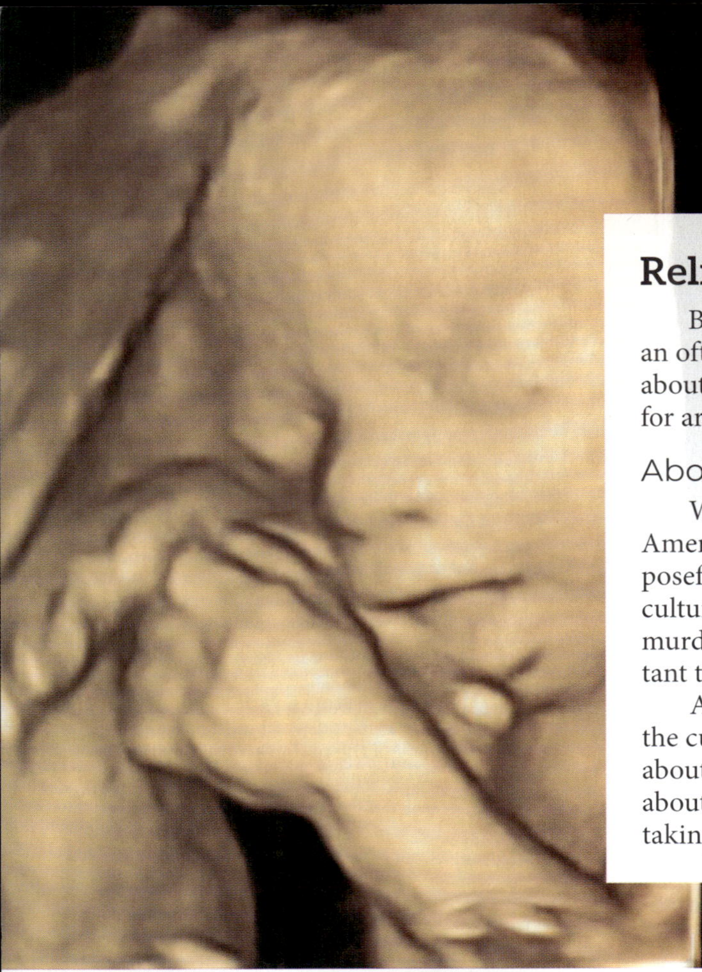

◂ 4-D ultrasound of an unborn baby

Religion and Morality

Because of America's multiculturalism, people view issues from an often-shifting basis of morality. While there are certainly issues about which Christians may freely debate, some issues leave no room for argument since specific biblical principles and commands apply.

Abortion

Why is abortion wrong? The simple answer is that it is murder. Americans do not tolerate child abuse in other forms, yet the purposeful killing of a child inside the womb has somehow become culturally acceptable. The landmark case *Roe v. Wade* allowed this murder to become legal. The mother's "choice" became more important than a child's life.

Abortion is an example of an issue that should not be based on the cultural "norms" of a society. There is clear, biblical teaching about a child being formed by God in the womb (Ps. 139:13–16), about the response of a baby in the womb (Luke 1:44), and against taking away life (Exod. 20:13).

▴ Families are a critical part of God's plan for society.

LGBTQ+ and Marriage

Increasingly, conflicts in American society focus on the meaning of *family*. Like the church and government, the family is a God-created institution (Matt. 19:4–6). God created marriage to be the union of one man and one woman.

In the 1990s and 2000s, there was growing cultural pressure to recognize homosexual behavior and same-sex marriage as normal. Into the 1990s many Americans thought that homosexual behavior should be illegal, and throughout the 2000s most Americans opposed legalizing same-sex marriage. One response to this pressure was an unsuccessful attempt to ratify an amendment to the Constitution that would define *marriage* in the United States as the union of a man and a woman. After several states legalized same-sex marriages, the Defense of Marriage Act (passed when President Clinton was in office) ensured for a time that the federal government and individual states were not forced to recognize other states' acceptance of same-sex marriage.

But in 2015 the Supreme Court decided that, because the Constitution specifically states in Article IV that all states must give "full faith and credit" to the records of other states, it was unconstitutional for states to not recognize marriages legalized by other states. In the wake of the Supreme Court's decision, a number of state bans on same-sex marriage were found to be unconstitutional.

The LGBTQ+ movement has gained many supporters in the last decade and has been increasingly portrayed as normal in the news and in media and entertainment.

Though some Americans have shifted their view of homosexual behavior, the Bible clearly teaches that God created marriage to be between one man and one woman (Matt. 19:4–5). Homosexual behavior and lusts are called an "abomination" by God (Lev. 18:22). Romans 1:26–27 says such behavior is contrary to the creation order and is degrading.

In recent years, transgenderism (understood as a mismatch between a person's biological sex and the gender with which they identify) has become another prevalent social and political issue. Some champion transgenderism as the next civil rights cause. Others see it as psychologically and potentially physically damaging. The Bible teaches that God created humans as male and female (Gen. 1:27; 5:2). God wants people's gender identity to align with their biological sex. Psalm 139:13–16 says that God formed us in our mother's womb, including forming our specific gender. If there is a discrepancy between the way God created persons and the way they think about themselves, the loving course of action is to help them learn to think according to God's reality.

Political Debates

Christians hold varying beliefs about issues not directly addressed in Scripture. Some of these hot-button topics—immigration, gun control, climate change, and the role of government—are frequently debated topics.

Immigration

The United States has always been a nation of immigrants. They have come in several waves since the original European settlers. In the early 1700s, Germans and Scots-Irish flooded into Pennsylvania. During the nineteenth century (1800s), more than thirty million Europeans entered the United States. At first, they came from western Europe, but by the end of the century, most were coming from eastern European countries.

The late 1900s and early 2000s witnessed a large increase in newcomers. Most were from Latin America and Asia. Changes in immigration laws under President Obama removed limits on the number of relatives who could join immigrants in America.

This new wave of immigrants raised an old debate. While some celebrated the nation's cultural diversity since its foundation, others worried about cultural change, higher costs for social programs, and the loss of jobs for Americans already living in the country.

From colonial times to the present, immigration has been a source of both benefits and problems. Today, illegal immigration is a contentious political topic. Donald Trump promised during his 2016 campaign to "build a wall" that would repair, expand, and connect the miles of wall between Mexico and the United States already built or improved during the Bush and Obama administrations.

Concerns over immigration have been, and will likely continue to be, a matter of intense debate.

CIVIL RIGHTS *vs.* HOMOSEXUAL RIGHTS

Defenders of homosexual rights have often compared themselves with those seeking civil rights. However, equating homosexual rights to civil rights is misleading since homosexual conduct is a behavior but ancestry and skin color are not. Homosexual behaviors can be evaluated morally because the Bible teaches that they are sinful. When deciding what to believe about homosexual conduct, the Christian is faced with the choice of submitting to Scripture or to cultural pressure.

It is frequently argued that those who love each other should be able to get married. But this logic is flawed. A woman may not marry a married man, even if they say they love each other. Nor may a man marry two women, despite his claims that he loves both women and they love him. Nor can siblings marry. Marriage is about more than love.

Though debates about homosexual rights are political, the issue is primarily moral. As with all other sins, some believers struggle with same-sex attraction. Christians must minister to people who struggle with these temptations with grace and love. They must avoid hateful speech or actions. When Christians say that homosexual behavior is sinful, however, they are not being hateful. They are simply agreeing with God's Word on the subject.

Gun Control

In colonial times, governments generally required at least one gun be owned by every household for purposes of protection and militia readiness. The right to bear arms (have weapons) was cemented into the Constitution by the Second Amendment, and a federal law in 1792 required every able-bodied male to own and maintain a firearm for battle. Not until 1934 was a federal law created to limit gun ownership as part of FDR's plan to reduce crime by violent gangs.

After President Kennedy, his brother Robert, and Martin Luther King Jr. were assassinated in the 1960s, the Gun Control Act of 1968 was passed, banning certain types of guns. In the 1990s, regulations were instituted requiring background checks for gun purchases.

Renewed attempts to impose greater gun-control measures arose during the 2000s after shootings occurred at Fort Hood in Texas, a shopping center in Arizona (at which Gabby Gifford, a member of the US House of Representatives, was wounded), a theater in Colorado, and multiple schools across the nation. Passionate voices on each side of the gun-control debate continue to be heard.

Climate Change

Another topic of debate in modern America is the climate. Fear of global cooling during the last century has recently switched to fear of global warming. The term *climate change* covers both. The earth shows evidence of cycles of cooling and warming throughout its history.

There are legitimate concerns about how mankind takes care of the earth. While it is wise and biblical to take care of God's earth as its stewards, it is also wise to live in the peace that comes from knowing God is in control (Ps. 46:2–3).

The Role of Government

There is a wide difference in how liberals (the Left) and conservatives (the Right) view the role of government. In general, the Left supports bigger and stronger government with many programs, and the Right supports smaller, less intrusive government that provides defense and basic social programs of limited assistance for those in need.

God instituted government to restrain the sinful nature of humans, and ensuring justice is its primary role (Rom. 13). Just how this is accomplished often leads to debates. How should people be punished for bad behavior? What should be provided by the government rather than by families and churches? When are laws limiting freedom good, and when are they not? These questions and others continue to be intensely debated.

SECTION REVIEW 27.4

1. Why should ethnicity not be a cause of division?
2. How can tolerance be both good and bad?
3. Why is abortion wrong?
4. Why are LGBTQ+ behaviors and lusts sinful?
5. What is another current political issue not mentioned in this chapter? What do those on each side of the issue believe? What do you believe?

CHAPTER 27 REVIEW

Making Connections

1. What terrorist organization was responsible for the attacks on 9/11? Who was its leader?
2. What new department was created to respond to the terrorist threat within the United States?
3. What legislation made it easier to locate suspected terrorists but was seen by some as an invasion of privacy?
4. What caused the Great Recession?
5. What were four countries in the Middle East and Africa that posed challenges during Obama's administration?
6. What were two controversial issues with Russia during Obama's presidency?
7. Which five presidents in American history have become president without winning the popular vote?
8. What did Robert Mueller investigate during Trump's administration? What was the outcome?
9. What three presidents have been impeached?
10. What did Trump mean by his America First policy?
11. What major change did Trump make in America's relationship to Israel?
12. What is a worldview?
13. What is multiculturalism?
14. What biblical principles can be applied to the idea of transgenderism?

Thinking Critically

15. Why do you think that none of the three impeached presidents has been convicted by the Senate?
16. How have technological advances been beneficial in the twenty-first century? How have they been harmful?

Living as a Christian Citizen

17. What would you say to a friend who argued that any two adults should be able to marry as long as they love each other? Use Genesis 2:18–25, Matthew 19:3–6, and Ephesians 5:22–33 in your answer.
18. Some Americans may be tempted to mistreat those of a different culture—especially if they look different, speak differently, or practice a different religion. How would you help a friend who struggles with this issue? Use Exodus 22:21 and Leviticus 19:33–34 in your answer.

Terms to Remember

Al Gore
George W. Bush
September 11, 2001
al-Qaeda
Osama bin Laden
Taliban
Department of Homeland Security
Patriot Act
weapons of mass destruction (WMDs)
Great Recession
Barack Obama
Patient Protection and Affordable Care Act, Obamacare
Obergefell v. Hodges
Islamic State of Iraq and Syria (ISIS)
Vladimir Putin
Hillary Clinton
Donald Trump
United States-Mexico-Canada Agreement (USMCA)
Robert Mueller
COVID-19
America First
Joe Biden
Kamala Harris
worldview
multiculturalism

and on TOWARD ETERNITY

Americans live in a great country. Yes, it has many flaws. But its opportunities for freedom, individuality, equality, and growth are unparalleled. It is, overall, a place of justice where people may worship as they choose. For all these things, American citizens should be grateful.

In our study of the American republic, we have seen sinful people make mistakes that hurt themselves and others. But we have also seen people use the talent and creativity God has given to explore and invent—with wondrous results! We have seen times of prosperity and times of need; times of uncertainty and times of peace. We have seen unwise rulers and those who are wise.

Many Americans vote or volunteer and generally conduct themselves in a peaceful manner, even when they do not agree with others. Yet there are always people and events that cause concern when considering America's free and democratic culture; these can be troubling or even chaotic.

One thing is clear: God is in control. He never wavers. He has made a plan of redemption for mankind, one that is mercifully not based on anything any of us can do on our own behalf. He sent his Son to redeem us because He loves us! The focus of Christians should be to take the gospel to an unbelieving world and to glorify Christ in everything. It is a privilege to do this as a citizen of the United States, but it is a far higher honor to do this for the King of Kings and Lord of Lords.

Appendix A. MAP OF THE UNITED STATES

MINNESOTA
Lake Superior
Saint Paul
WISCONSIN
Madison
Lake Michigan
MICHIGAN
Lansing
Lake Huron
Lake Ontario
Lake Erie
IOWA
Des Moines
ILLINOIS
Springfield
INDIANA
Indianapolis
OHIO
Columbus
Ohio R.
MISSOURI
Missouri R.
Jefferson City
Topeka
WEST VIRGINIA
Charleston
KENTUCKY
Frankfort
ARKANSAS
Little Rock
Mississippi R.
TENNESSEE
Nashville
Great Smoky Mtns.
Appalachian Mtns.
MISSISSIPPI
Jackson
ALABAMA
Montgomery
GEORGIA
Atlanta
LOUISIANA
Baton Rouge
FLORIDA
Tallahassee
Gulf of Mexico
White Mountains
VERMONT
Montpelier
Green Mountains
MAINE
Augusta
Concord
NEW HAMPSHIRE
MASSACHUSETTS
Boston
Albany
NEW YORK
Providence
RHODE ISLAND
Hartford
CONNECTICUT
PENNSYLVANIA
Harrisburg
Trenton
NEW JERSEY
Dover
Annapolis
DELAWARE
Washington, D.C.
MARYLAND
Richmond
VIRGINIA
Raleigh
NORTH CAROLINA
Columbia
SOUTH CAROLINA
ATLANTIC OCEAN
Above 12,000 ft.
9,000–12,000 ft.
6,000–9,000 ft.
3,000–6,000 ft.
0–3,000 ft.
N
W
E
S
0
250
500 mi
0
250
500 km

Appendix B. THE PRESIDENTS OF THE UNITED STATES

George Washington

	1
Years served	1789–97
Terms	2
Party	none (but Federalist leaning)
Vice president	John Adams

John Adams

	2
Years served	1797–1801
Terms	1
Party	Federalist
Vice president	Thomas Jefferson

Thomas Jefferson

	3
Years served	1801–09
Terms	2
Party	Democratic-Republican
Vice presidents	1st—Aaron Burr 2nd—George Clinton

James Madison

	4
Years served	1809–17
Terms	2
Party	Democratic-Republican
Vice president	1st—George Clinton 2nd—Elbridge Gerry

James Monroe

	5
Years served	1817–25
Terms	2
Party	Democratic-Republican
Vice president	Daniel D. Tompkins

John Quincy Adams

	6
Years served	1825–29
Terms	1
Party	Federalist, Democratic-Republican, National Republican
Vice president	John C. Calhoun

Andrew Jackson

	7
Years served	1829–37
Terms	2
Party	Democrat
Vice presidents	1st—John C. Calhoun 2nd—Martin Van Buren

Martin Van Buren

	8
Years served	1837–41
Terms	1
Party	Democrat
Vice president	Richard M. Johnson

William Henry Harrison

	9
Years served	1841
Terms	partial (one month)
Party	Whig
Vice president	John Tyler

John Tyler

10

Years served	1841–45
Terms	1 (minus one month)
Party	Whig
Vice president	none

James K. Polk

11

Years served	1845–49
Terms	1
Party	Democrat
Vice president	George M. Dallas

Zachary Taylor

12

Years served	1849–50
Terms	partial
Party	Whig
Vice president	Millard Fillmore

Millard Fillmore

13

Years served	1850–53
Terms	partial
Party	Whig
Vice president	none

Franklin Pierce

14

Years served	1853–57
Terms	1
Party	Democrat
Vice president	William Rufus King (died one month after inauguration)

James Buchanan

15

Years served	1857–61
Terms	1
Party	Democrat
Vice president	John C. Breckinridge

Abraham Lincoln

16

Years served	1861–65
Terms	1 plus partial (assassinated)
Party	Republican
Vice presidents	1st—Hannibal Hamlin 2nd—Andrew Johnson

Andrew Johnson

17

Years served	1865–69
Terms	1
Party	Democrat (or Unionist Party)
Vice president	none

Ulysses S. Grant

18

Years served	1869–77
Terms	2
Party	Republican
Vice presidents	1st—Schuyler Colfax 2nd—Henry Wilson

Rutherford B. Hayes

19

Years served	October 4, 1822
Terms	1
Party	Republican
Vice president	William A. Wheeler

James Garfield

20

Years served	1881
Terms	partial (assassinated)
Party	Republican
Vice president	Chester A. Arthur

Chester A. Arthur

21

Years served	1881–85
Terms	partial (almost 1 full term)
Party	Republican
Vice president	none

Grover Cleveland

22

24

Years served	1885–89 & 1893–97
Terms	2 nonconsecutive
Party	Democrat
Vice presidents	1st—Thomas A. Hendricks 2nd—Adlai E. Stevenson

Benjamin Harrison

23

Years served	1889–93
Terms	1
Party	Republican
Vice president	Levi P. Morton

William McKinley

25

Years served	1897–1901
Terms	1 plus partial (assassinated)
Party	Republican
Vice presidents	1st—Garret Hobart 2nd—Theodore Roosevelt

Theodore Roosevelt

26

Years served	1901–9
Terms	1 partial and 1 full
Party	Republican (later Progressive, or Bull Moose)
Vice presidents	1st—none 2nd—Charles Fairbanks

William Howard Taft

27

Years served	1909–13
Terms	1
Party	Republican
Vice president	James Sherman

Woodrow Wilson

28

Years served	1913–21
Terms	2
Party	Democrat
Vice president	Thomas Marshall

Warren G. Harding

29

Years served	1921–23
Terms	partial
Party	Republican
Vice president	Calvin Coolidge

Calvin Coolidge

30

Years served	1923–29
Terms	1 and partial
Party	Republican
Vice president	1st—none 2nd—Charles G. Dawes

Herbert Hoover

31

Years served	1929–33
Terms	1
Party	Republican
Vice president	Charles Curtis

Franklin Delano Roosevelt

32

Years served	1933–45
Terms	3 plus partial
Party	Democrat
Vice presidents	1st/2nd—John Nance Garner 3rd—Henry Wallace 4th—Harry Truman

Harry S. Truman

33

Years served	1945–53
Terms	2
Party	Democrat
Vice presidents	1st—none 2nd—Alben Barkley

Dwight D. Eisenhower

34

Years served	1953–61
Terms	2
Party	Republican
Vice president	Richard M. Nixon

John F. Kennedy

35

Years served	1961–63
Terms	partial (assassinated)
Party	Democrat
Vice president	Lyndon B. Johnson

Lyndon B. Johnson

36

Years served	1963–69
Terms	partial plus 1
Party	Democrat
Vice presidents	1st—none 2nd—Hubert H. Humphrey

Richard Nixon

37

Years served	1969–74
Terms	1 and partial (resigned)
Party	Republican
Vice presidents	1st—Spiro T. Agnew (resigned) 2nd—Gerald Ford

Gerald Ford

38

Years served	1974–77
Terms	partial (upon the resignation of Nixon)
Party	Republican
Vice president	Nelson Rockefeller

James "Jimmy" Carter

39

Years served	1977–81
Terms	1
Party	Democrat
Vice president	Walter Mondale

Ronald Reagan

40

Years served	1981–89
Terms	2
Party	Republican
Vice president	George H. W. Bush

George H. W. Bush

41

Years served	1989–93
Terms	1
Party	Republican
Vice president	Dan Quayle

William "Bill" Clinton

42

Years served	1993–2001
Terms	2
Party	Democrat
Vice president	Al Gore

George W. Bush

43

Years served	2001–9
Terms	2
Party	Republican
Vice president	Dick Cheney

Barack Obama

44

Years served	2009–17
Terms	2
Party	Democrat
Vice president	Joseph "Joe" Biden

Donald Trump

45

Years served	2017–21
Terms	1
Party	Republican
Vice president	Mike Pence

Joseph "Joe" Biden

46

Years served	2021–
Terms	in progress
Party	Democrat
Vice president	Kamala Harris

Appendix C.
THE DECLARATION OF INDEPENDENCE OF THE UNITED STATES

IN CONGRESS, JULY 4, 1776.

The unanimous Declaration of the thirteen united States of America,

When in the course of human events, it becomes necessary for one people to dissolve the political bands which have connected them with another, and to assume among the powers of the earth, the separate and equal station to which the laws of nature and of nature's God entitle them, a decent respect to the opinions of mankind requires that they should declare the causes which impel them to the separation.

We hold these truths to be self-evident, that all men are created equal, that they are endowed by their Creator with certain unalienable rights, that among these are life, liberty and the pursuit of happiness.—That to secure these rights, governments are instituted among men, deriving their just powers from the consent of the governed,—That whenever any form of government becomes destructive of these ends, it is the right of the people to alter or to abolish it, and to institute new government, laying its foundation on such principles and organizing its powers in such form, as to them shall seem most likely to effect their safety and happiness. Prudence, indeed, will dictate that governments long established should not be changed for light and transient causes; and accordingly all experience hath shewn, that mankind are more disposed to suffer, while evils are sufferable, than to right themselves by abolishing the forms to which they are accustomed. But when a long train of abuses and usurpations, pursuing invariably the same object evinces a design to reduce them under absolute despotism, it is their right, it is their duty, to throw off such government, and to provide new guards for their future security. — Such has been the patient sufferance of these colonies; and such is now the necessity which constrains them to alter their former systems of government. The history of the present king of Great Britain is a history of repeated injuries and usurpations, all having in direct object the establishment of an absolute tyranny over these states. To prove this, let facts be submitted to a candid world.

He has refused his assent to laws, the most wholesome and necessary for the public good.

He has forbidden his governors to pass laws of immediate and pressing importance, unless suspended in their operation till his assent should be obtained; and when so suspended, he has utterly neglected to attend to them.

He has refused to pass other laws for the accommodation of large districts of people, unless those people would relinquish the right of representation in the legislature, a right inestimable to them and formidable to tyrants only.

He has called together legislative bodies at places unusual, uncomfortable, and distant from the depository of their public records, for the sole purpose of fatiguing them into compliance with his measures.

He has dissolved representative houses repeatedly, for opposing with manly firmness his invasions on the rights of the people.

He has refused for a long time, after such dissolutions, to cause others to be elected; whereby the legislative powers, incapable of annihilation, have returned to the people at large for their exercise; the state remaining in the meantime exposed to all the dangers of invasion from without, and convulsions within.

He has endeavoured to prevent the population of these states; for that purpose obstructing the laws for naturalization of foreigners; refusing to pass others to encourage their migrations hither, and raising the conditions of new appropriations of lands.

He has obstructed the administration of justice, by refusing his assent to laws for establishing judiciary powers.

He has made judges dependent on his will alone, for the tenure of their offices, and the amount and payment of their salaries.

He has erected a multitude of new offices, and sent hither swarms of officers to harass our people, and eat out their substance.

He has kept among us, in times of peace, standing armies without the consent of our legislatures.

He has affected to render the military independent of and superior to the civil power.

He has combined with others to subject us to a jurisdiction foreign to our constitution, and unacknowledged by our laws; giving his assent to their acts of pretended legislation:

For quartering large bodies of armed troops among us:

For protecting them, by a mock trial, from punishment for any murders which they should commit on the inhabitants of these states:

For cutting off our trade with all parts of the world:

For imposing taxes on us without our consent:

For depriving us in many cases, of the benefits of trial by jury:

For transporting us beyond seas to be tried for pretended offences:

For abolishing the free system of English laws in a neighboring province, establishing therein an arbitrary government, and enlarging its boundaries so as to render it at once an example and fit instrument for introducing the same absolute rule into these colonies:

For taking away our charters, abolishing our most valuable laws, and altering fundamentally the forms of our governments:

For suspending our own legislatures, and declaring themselves invested with power to legislate for us in all cases whatsoever.

He has abdicated government here, by declaring us out of his protection and waging war against us.

He has plundered our seas, ravaged our coasts, burnt our towns, and destroyed the lives of our people.

He is at this time transporting large armies of foreign mercenaries to complete the works of death, desolation and tyranny, already begun with circumstances of cruelty and perfidy scarcely paralleled in the most barbarous ages, and totally unworthy the head of a civilized nation.

He has constrained our fellow citizens taken captive on the high seas to bear arms against their country, to become the executioners of their friends and brethren, or to fall themselves by their hands.

He has excited domestic insurrections amongst us, and has endeavored to bring on the inhabitants of our frontiers, the merciless Indian savages, whose known rule of warfare, is an undistinguished destruction of all ages, sexes and conditions.

In every stage of these oppressions, we have petitioned for redress in the most humble terms: our repeated petitions have been answered only by repeated injury. A prince whose character is thus marked by every act which may define a tyrant, is unfit to be the ruler of a free people.

Nor have we been wanting in attentions to our British brethren. We have warned them from time to time of attempts by their legislature to extend an unwarrantable jurisdiction over us. We have reminded them of the circumstances of our emigration and settlement here. We have appealed to their native justice and magnanimity, and we have conjured them by the ties of our common kindred to disavow these usurpations, which, would inevitably interrupt our connections and correspondence. They too have been deaf to the voice of justice and of consanguinity. We must, therefore, acquiesce in the necessity, which denounces our separation, and hold them, as we hold the rest of mankind, enemies in war, in peace friends.

We, therefore, the representatives of the united states of America, in general congress, assembled, appealing to the Supreme Judge of the world for the rectitude of our intentions, do, in the name, and by authority of the good people of these colonies, solemnly publish and declare, that these united colonies are, and of right ought to be free and independent states; that they are absolved from all allegiance to the British Crown, and that all political connection between them and the state of Great Britain, is and ought to be totally dissolved; and that as free and independent states, they have full power to levy war, conclude peace, contract alliances, establish commerce, and to do all other acts and things which independent states may of right do. And for the support of this declaration, with a firm reliance on the protection of divine Providence, we mutually pledge to each other our lives, our fortunes and our sacred honor.

Glossary

A

abolitionists—People who wanted to abolish slavery

Act of Toleration—Guaranteed religious freedom in Maryland to all who believed in the Trinity

Adams-Onís Treaty—Purchased East Florida from Spain for $5 million, also defined the Spanish boundary west of the Mississippi

agnostics—Those who believe humans cannot know whether there is a God

Agricultural Adjustment Act (AAA)—The paying of farmers to destroy farm products in order to raise farm prices quickly and keep farmers in business

Alamo—Abandoned mission in San Antonio where Texans were defeated by Santa Anna in 1836

Albany Plan of Union—The first attempt to unite the American colonies by calling for the creation of a grand council consisting of representatives from all the colonies; primarily written by Benjamin Franklin

Alien and Sedition Acts—Four laws passed by a Federalist-controlled Congress that were designed to protect the country during the threat of war but were used to harm the Democratic-Republican party and keep it from gaining power

Allied Powers—Alliance of Britain, France, Russia, Italy, numerous smaller nations, and (later) the United States during World War I; name also used during World War II for those who opposed the Axis Powers; also called the Allies

Allies—Also known as the Allied Powers; the alliance of Britain and France against Germany in World War II, later joined by the Soviet Union and the United States; name also used in World War I for those who opposed the Central Powers

al-Qaeda—International terrorist network led by Osama bin Laden; responsible for the attack on September 11, 2001, and linked to several earlier terrorist attacks against America and its allies

America First—President Trump's policy of making decisions based on what he deemed to be in the best interest of the country and its citizens

American Expeditionary Force—Name for the American army during World War I

American Federation of Labor—Labor union established in 1886 for skilled workers only

American System—Plan advocated by Henry Clay supporting the National Bank, a high tariff, and nationwide internal improvements paid by the national government

Americans with Disabilities Act—Legislation passed during the George H. W. Bush administration outlawing discrimination based on certain disabilities

amnesty—A group pardon

Anaconda Plan—Name mocking the Union strategy devised by Winfield Scott that called for a blockade of Southern ports and control of the Mississippi River

Anglican Church—The Church of England

animism—Belief that all natural objects, whether living or non-living, have souls

Annapolis Convention—Meeting held in September 1786 in Annapolis, Maryland, to discuss interstate trade; asked the Confederation Congress to schedule a convention of all states to revise the Articles of Confederation

antebellum—"Before [ante] the war [bellum]"; in America used for the time period before the Civil War

Antietam—Creek near Sharpsburg, Maryland; bloodiest one-day battle in American history, resulting in a tie

Anti-Federalists—Those who fought ratification of the Constitution

appeasement—Yielding to demands of an aggressor in order to preserve peace

Appomattox Court House—Village where Lee and Grant met to sign the surrender of the Confederate army; the end of the Civil War

apprenticeship—System used to teach trades to boys who could not go to college; usually lasting about seven years

armistice—Agreement to stop fighting

Articles of Confederation—First plan of government of the United States, in force from 1777 until ratification of the US Constitution in 1789; included one governing body, a Congress; allowed for strong state governments

assembly line—An effective means of production in which workers beside a moving conveyor belt each perform a certain task

Axis Powers—Agreement between Italy, Germany, and Japan, the countries which formed the Rome-Berlin-Tokyo Axis

B

baby boom—Massive rise in the birth rate from 1946 until 1964

Bacon's Rebellion—Conflict in the southern colonies that began with the Indians and ended with violence among the colonists

balance of power—Preventing any one nation from gaining enough power to dominate other nations

bank holiday—The closing of all banks temporarily; specifically at the beginning of Franklin D. Roosevelt's first term of office

Barbary States—The small Muslim countries in North Africa that demanded tribute from ships sailing on the Mediterranean Sea

barbed wire—Practical fencing material for the Great Plains, which lacked wood or rocks; created with short, sharp spikes spaced along strands of wire

Battle of Britain—Air battle between Britain and Germany during the summer and fall of 1940

Battle of the Bulge—German counterattack into Belgium in 1944 that created a fifty-mile-deep bulge into Allied lines

Battle of the Little Bighorn—Also known as Custer's Last Stand (1876); failed attack by Colonel George Armstrong Custer on the Sioux resulting in all US soldiers killed in less than an hour

Battle of Manila Bay—Battle between the American fleet and the Spanish Pacific fleet in the Philippines in 1898, wrecking the Spanish fleet

Battle of Midway—American victory in June 1942 halting Japanese expansion; considered by many the turning point of the war in the Pacific

Battle of New Orleans—Biggest American victory of the War of 1812, resulting in Andrew Jackson becoming the war's greatest hero; fought after the war's official end

Battle of San Jacinto—An 1836 surprise attack to avenge the defeat at the Alamo; led by Sam Houston

Bay of Pigs—Site of disastrous invasion of Cuba in April 1961; led by Cuban refugees who intended to invade Cuba and overthrow Castro

Bear Flag Republic—Name of California while it was an independent country for less than a month under John C. Frémont

Berlin airlift—Massive airlift from June 1948 to May 1949 transporting food and supplies to western Berlin after Stalin blocked access to the area

Berlin Wall—Structure erected around West Berlin to prevent movement between the two parts of Berlin; topped with barbed wire and fortified by guard towers and minefields

bicameral system—Government system consisting of two legislative houses

Big Four—The representatives from the major Allied Powers at the Paris Peace conference after World War I: Georges Clemenceau from France, David Lloyd George from Britain, Vittorio Orlando from Italy, and Woodrow Wilson from the United States

"big stick" policy—Theodore Roosevelt's foreign policy of reliance on America's military strength to persuade foreign nations to act properly

Bill of Rights—Name for the first ten amendments to the Constitution

black codes—Restrictive laws passed in southern states that placed African Americans in an inferior position to white people

blitzkrieg—"Lightning war"; swift assault, the military strategy of Hitler during World War II

blockade—Strategy to prevent the entry or exit by sea of passengers or products; used by the Union against the South during the Civil War

blockade runners—Fast ships that were long and narrow and could dart into shallow inlets to hide

Bonus Army—Nickname for a large group of unemployed veterans who gathered in Washington, DC, in 1932 to ask for early payment of the promised World War I bonus

bootlegging—Making and selling illegal liquor

Boston Massacre—The outbreak of violence between colonists and British troops on March 5, 1770, resulting in the deaths of five people

Boston Tea Party—A protest against the Tea Act of 1773 by colonists disguised as Indians, during which the colonists threw tea from British ships into Boston Harbor

bounty—Bonus given to those who joined the army

Boxer Rebellion—An uprising started by the Boxers who demanded that all foreigners leave China; included attacking and killing many Christians

Boxers—Nickname for the members of the Society of Righteous and Harmonious Fists, a secret group opposing foreigners in China

boycotts—Refusals to buy

brain trust—Group including university professors who offered opinions to Franklin D. Roosevelt regarding economic policies and legislation

Brown v. Board of Education—Supreme Court decision declaring that separate educational facilities were unequal and ordering an end to segregated schools; a major victory in the civil rights movement in 1954

Bull Moose Party—Nickname for the Progressive Party under Theodore Roosevelt

Bunker Hill—Battle on Breed's Hill near Boston in 1775 resulting in a costly British victory

Burr-Hamilton duel—Duel fought between Aaron Burr and Alexander Hamilton in which Burr shot and killed Hamilton

buy on margin—Practice of paying only part of a stock's purchase price in cash and borrowing the remainder from a broker

C

cabinet—A president's group of advisers

California gold rush—Rapid influx of people seeking gold after its discovery in California in 1848

California Trail—Most popular trail to California; split off from the Oregon Trail

Camp David Accords—Agreement mediated by President Carter in 1978 in which Israel agreed to return the Sinai Peninsula to Egypt and Egypt agreed to recognize Israel's right to exist

camp meetings—Revival meetings for hundreds of frontier settlers for days or weeks at a time

canal—A shallow, man-made water highway that usually connects two bodies of water

capital—Investment money

capitalism—An economic system in which businesses and property are privately owned and privately operated

carpetbaggers—Northerners who came South during Reconstruction to take advantage of the post-war situation; named after their suitcase material

casualties—people killed, wounded, captured, or missing during fighting

caucus—A closed meeting of each party's members of Congress and other party leaders

census—A count of the population taken every ten years to determine the number of representatives for each state in the lower house

Central Intelligence Agency (CIA)—Gathers and analyzes information regarding foreign affairs, often through the use of spies

Central Pacific—Railroad company that built the first transcontinental railroad eastward from Sacramento, California; primarily used Chinese laborers

Central Powers—Alliance of Germany, Austria-Hungary, Bulgaria, and Turkey (the Ottoman Empire) during World War I

A Century of Dishonor—Book published by Helen Hunt Jackson portraying the government's ruthless and often deceitful dealings with Native Americans

Chancellorsville—Major Confederate victory; Stonewall Jackson fatally wounded there

charter colonies—Colonies governed by a charter granted by the king to joint-stock companies

Chattanooga—Union victory in Tennessee that resulted in Ulysses S. Grant being appointed commander of all Union forces

checks and balances—System that keeps each branch of government from exercising too much power by limiting, or checking, the powers of the other branches

Chinese Exclusion Act—Law passed in 1882 prohibiting most Chinese workers from entering the United States for ten years; continuously extended until 1943

Chisholm Trail—Trail used by cowboys to reach Abilene, Kansas

Civil Rights Act of 1964—Law prohibiting segregation in schools and public places; outlawed discrimination based on race, color, religion, sex, or national origin

civil rights movement—The struggle for equality by African Americans

Civilian Conservation Corps (CCC)—New Deal agency that put young, unmarried men to work planting trees, building roads, developing parks, and assisting with soil conservation projects under the supervision of the army

Civil Service Commission—Provided for the elimination of the spoils system and appointed many federal government jobs to those who passed civil service examinations

clipper—A type of sailing vessel designed for increased speeds; had a much sharper point on its bow that could "clip" into the waves

Cold War—The hostility between the United States and its allies and the Soviet Union and its allies after World War II; a time of tension and intense competition that tried to avoid direct military conflict

collective bargaining—The right of unions to represent workers in negotiations with owners and managers

Committees of Correspondence—Groups that provided written information in the form of letters about British threats to liberty

Common Sense—Influential pamphlet written by Thomas Paine making a case for separation from Britain

Compromise of 1833—Plan developed by Henry Clay and John C. Calhoun to lower duties gradually, ending the nullification controversy

Compromise of 1850—An attempt to resolve the dispute over slavery by (1) allowing California to be admitted as a free state; (2) dividing the remainder of the Mexican Cession into New Mexico and Utah Territories, where citizens could decide by popular sovereignty whether to permit slavery; (3) implementing a stricter fugitive slave law; and (4) outlawing slave trade in Washington, DC

Comstock Lode—One of the largest and richest mines, yielding both gold and silver; located in Nevada

Concord—Village in which fighting continued shortly after the fighting in Lexington in 1775

Conestoga wagons—Covered mode of transportation that became popular for the wilderness trails

Confederate States of America—Government organized by states that seceded from the Union

confederation—A loose association or league of states

Congregationalists—Believed that the congregation should have a voice in how the church operated; most New England Puritans

Congressional Reconstruction—Period during which Congress controlled Reconstruction

conquistadors—Spanish conquerors of Central and South America

conscription—Also called a draft; requirement by the government to serve in the military

constitution—Document that describes how a government is to work

Constitutional Convention—Originally called the Philadelphia Convention; met for the purpose of revising the Articles of Confederation but instead formulated a new government governed by a constitution

containment—US policy that communism must be contained within its new boundaries and not allowed to expand

Continental army—Troops controlled by the Second Continental Congress and commanded by George Washington

Contract with America—Plan by Republicans in the House of Representatives to win the 1994 midterm elections; plan in which candidates pledged that if elected they would introduce ten popular bills during the first one hundred days of the next Congress

convoy system—Huge shipments of troops and supplies protected by naval vessels equipped with antisubmarine weapons

core values—The guiding ideas and beliefs that create a common culture and bind a people together

corporation—Business that has gained a legal charter and sells stock to many individual investors

corrupt bargain—Idea claimed by followers of Andrew Jackson that John Quincy Adams and Henry Clay had made a deal during the 1824 election in which Clay would support Adams for president in the House of Representatives in return for a high political appointment

cotton gin—Machine developed by Eli Whitney to remove seeds from cotton more quickly and efficiently than by hand

counterculture—Youth movement in the 1960s and early 1970s; rebellion against the materialism, morals, and values of the previous generation

COVID-19—A new illness caused by the SARS-COV-2 virus that started a global pandemic in 2020

Creation Mandate—God's call for humans to exercise authority over His earth

Cuban missile crisis—Time of tension in response to the Soviet installation of nuclear missile sites in Cuba after the failed Bay of Pigs invasion; a period including the US's blockade of Cuba and Russia's agreement to remove the missiles in exchange for the United States agreeing to not invade Cuba and to remove US nuclear missiles from Turkey

Cumberland Gap—A natural passage through the Cumberland Mountains

D

dame schools—Small schools led by women who taught reading, writing, and math with emphasis on moral and religious subjects

Dawes Act—Law passed in 1887 designed to help Native Americans be Americanized; resulted in weakened tribal unions

Dayton Accords—Peace agreement signed between Serbian leaders and persecuted ethnic groups, especially Muslims, living in Serbia

D-day—June 6, 1944, Allied invasion of Normandy, France, that began Operation Overlord

Declaration of Independence—Document adopted on July 4, 1776, declaring the thirteen colonies to be separate from Britain

Defense of Marriage Act—Law passed during the Clinton administration denying federal government recognition of any homosexual union as a marriage

deficit spending—Spending more money than is received in income

deism—Philosophy that believed the Bible needed to be tested by human reason; rejected traditional Christian teachings such as miracles and the virgin birth of Jesus

de Lôme letter—Insulting letter from the Spanish ambassador to a personal friend, published by the *New York Journal*; described President McKinley as "weak"

Democratic Party—The portion of the split Democratic-Republican Party supporting the election of Andrew Jackson in 1828; the same party as modern Democrats

Democratic-Republican Party—Political party led by Thomas Jefferson; believed in stronger state governments

Department of Homeland Security—Newly formed agency created by President George W. Bush following the September 11, 2001, terrorist attacks on the United States; later became a cabinet-level department

détente—An easing of tensions, specifically between America, China, and the Soviet Union during the 1970s

disarmament—Reduction in the size of a nation's military and its weapons

dole—Federal monies given directly to people; a handout

dollar diplomacy—Investment of American dollars in foreign countries in order to influence foreign affairs

domino theory—Idea that if one non-Communist nation in Southeast Asia fell to communism, then other nations would fall, like a row of dominoes

Doolittle raid—Secret attack on April 8, 1942, by American bombers on Tokyo and other cities, causing a boost to US morale and a great psychological blow to the Japanese

doughboys—American troops in World War I

doves—Those who wanted the United States to withdraw completely from Vietnam

Dust Bowl—Nickname for the drought-ridden Great Plains after the land turned to dust, blowing dried topsoil across the country

E

Eighteenth Amendment—Prohibited the sale, manufacture, and transportation of alcoholic beverages; also called the Prohibition Amendment

Electoral College—Body established by the Constitution to elect the president

Ellis Island—New York port of entry that handled the largest number of European immigrants

Emancipation Proclamation—Declaration by Abraham Lincoln that slaves in Confederate-controlled territory would be free on January 1, 1863; excluded slaves in the border states

embargo—An end to all exports; Jefferson's strategy against the British and French because of their disregard of neutral rights at sea

Enlightenment—Philosophical movement that emphasized science and reason above all else

Equal Rights Amendment—Controversial, proposed amendment requiring equal rights for women; passed by Congress in 1972 but not ratified by enough states

Era of Good Feelings—Brief period of harmony after the end of the War of 1812 with no major international conflicts and of rare intense political rivalries at home; James Monroe's presidency

Erie Canal—Most famous canal in early America, connecting Lake Erie (at Buffalo, New York) with the Hudson River (at Albany, New York)

excise tax—Tax paid on the manufacture or sale of certain goods and services within a country

exploitation—Taking advantage of the poverty and ignorance of native peoples to keep them working for the benefit of mother countries

F

Fair Deal—Domestic government program under the Truman administration, intended to increase aid to science and public education, subsidize medical insurance, and encourage job creation and home building

Fallen Timbers—Battle near modern-day Toledo, Ohio, where Anthony Wayne's force defeated a band of Indians who were then forced to abandon their claim to about half of Ohio

fascism—Political and economic system that promoted extreme nationalism and placed great emphasis on militarism

Federal Deposit Insurance Corporation (FDIC)—Agency that insures individual bank accounts (up to $5,000 originally; as of 2008, $250,000 limit)

Federalist Papers—Newspaper essays by Alexander Hamilton, James Madison, and John Jay written to gain support for the Constitution

Federalist Party—Political party led by Alexander Hamilton; believed in a strong central government

Federalists—Those who favored the adoption of the Constitution

Federal Reserve System—Established twelve banking districts, each served by a regional Federal Reserve Bank and all supervised by the Federal Reserve Board; "bankers' banks" having the power to increase or decrease the amount of money in circulation and to exercise control over many banking operations throughout the country

federal system—Division of the government's powers between the national government and the states

Federal Trade Commission—Board of five people authorized to help define and halt unfair business practices

Fifteenth Amendment—Kept states from denying the right to vote to any citizen "on account of race, color, or previous condition of servitude"

fireside chats—Nickname for Franklin D. Roosevelt's radio addresses to America

First Battle of Bull Run—Also called the First Battle of Manassas; first major battle of the Civil War; Confederate victory

First Continental Congress—Sessions that adopted a formal statement of protest (the Declaration of Rights and Grievances)

flappers—Young women of the 1920s who wore shorter skirts and heavy makeup, used slang, drank, smoked, and danced

Fort Duquesne—French fort during the French and Indian War; near present-day Pittsburgh, Pennsylvania

Fort McHenry—Failed British joint land-sea attack on Baltimore, Maryland, during the War of 1812

Fort Sumter—Federal fort in South Carolina's Charleston Harbor; the site of the first shots of the Civil War

Fort Ticonderoga—British fort located in New York; captured in 1775 by Ethan Allen's Green Mountain Boys and other soldiers

forty-niners—People who traveled to California in search of gold beginning in 1849

Fourteen Points—Woodrow Wilson's proposed guidelines to help rebuild European peace after World War I

Fourteenth Amendment—Granted full citizenship to black Americans

Fredericksburg—Battle in Virginia that brought Union morale to its lowest point of the war; Confederate victory

freedmen—Former slaves

Freedmen's Bureau—Short-term agency whose primary purpose was to assist former slaves during Reconstruction

Freeholders—Free adult white male property owners; also called freemen

French and Indian War—War from 1754–63 with Britain and its colonists against France and some Indian tribes; known in Europe as the Seven Years' War (1756–63)

frontier—Undeveloped area at the edge of settled areas

Fundamentalist—Term arising in the 1920s to describe people who believe in the foundational truths of Christianity

Fundamental Orders of Connecticut—The first written constitution in America

G

Gadsden Purchase—Narrow strip of land on the border of New Mexico and Arizona purchased for $10 million in 1853

gang system—Labor system in which slaves worked in large groups for a set amount of time each day

General Assembly—A main part of the United Nations that has one delegate from each member nation

Gettysburg—Union victory near a small town in Pennsylvania

Gettysburg Address—The two-minute speech delivered by President Lincoln dedicating a cemetery at Gettysburg

GI Bill—Legislation helping veterans find jobs and providing money for education and home purchases

Gilded Age—Period from the 1870s to about 1900; the term describing an era in which all appeared well but beneath the surface lay serious problems

Good Neighbor Policy—President Roosevelt's policy of letting Latin American countries handle their own affairs

Goodnight-Loving Trail—Route used by cowboys along the Pecos River to markets in Colorado; extended to Cheyenne, Wyoming

grammar schools—Organized schools with hired teachers, normally limited to males; taught math, rhetoric, and philosophy; Greek and Latin also taught to older students

grandfather clause—Voter law that allowed a person to not pay the poll tax or pass the literacy test if he or his father or grandfather had been eligible to vote before 1867

Grange—Social and political organization for farmers, founded in 1867

Great Awakening—A powerful spiritual revival that swept through the colonies beginning in the 1720s

Great Compromise—Also known as the Connecticut Compromise, written by Roger Sherman; agreement that the US government would have a bicameral Congress consisting of a House of Representatives and a Senate

Great Depression—The worst economic crisis in American history, beginning with the stock market crash of 1929 and lasting for more than a decade

Great Migration—Large wave of immigrants from Europe to America during America's early years

Great Plains—Region from the Mississippi River to the Rocky Mountains

Great Recession—Period from the end of 2007 into 2009; the bursting of the housing "bubble" as more and more homes came back on the market, causing the price of houses to drastically decrease, investors to lose their profits, banks to declare bankruptcy, stores to close, and people to lose jobs

Great Society—Legislative program of Lyndon Johnson which intended to end poverty and racial injustice

Great Wagon Road—Series of Indian trails known as the Great Warrior's Path, which ran north and south along the eastern slope of the Appalachian Mountains; widened and followed by many Germans and Scots Irish

greenbacks—Paper money printed with green ink

Guantánamo Bay—Site of a US naval base in Cuba received as a result of the Spanish-American War

guerrilla warfare—Hiding behind trees and brush in order to ambush the enemy

Gulf of Tonkin Resolution—Act of Congress giving the president authority to take all necessary steps, including the use of armed force, against the North Vietnamese; granted the president broad authority to increase American activity in Vietnam

H

Half-Way Covenant—Puritan measure allowing unbelievers to have their children baptized into the church

Hartford Convention—Meeting of a group of New England Federalists who opposed the War of 1812 and hinted that New England might secede; contributed to the collapse of the Federalist Party

Harvard College—The first institution of higher learning in America; located in Massachusetts

hawks—Leaders who favored an increased American presence in Vietnam or an "escalation" of the war

Haymarket Riot—Also called the Haymarket Affair; a rally that turned violent where police and protesters were killed; hurt the reputation of unions

Hessians—Hired soldiers, or mercenaries, from Germany

Hiroshima—Site of the first atomic bomb, dropped on Japan on August 6, 1945

Ho Chi Minh Trail—Route used by North Vietnamese and Viet Cong forces to move their men and goods from North to South Vietnam through Cambodia and Laos

Holocaust—Massacre of millions of people, especially Jews, political opponents, prisoners of war, Poles, the Roma, and the disabled, at the hands of the Nazis

Homestead Act—An 1862 law giving 160 acres of land to an individual who paid a $10 filing fee, lived on the land for five years, and made improvements to it

Hoovervilles—Nickname for groups of shanties created by those who had lost their homes during the Great Depression

hornbook—Board that looked like a paddle and was covered with a printed sheet including the alphabet; protected by a thin, transparent sheet of animal horn

House of Burgesses—The first representative assembly in America

House of Representatives—The lower house of Congress in which representation is based on population

humanitarian aid—Efforts to improve education, abolish slavery, and stamp out disease and famine

I

impeachment—To bring charges against an elected or appointed official, such as the president

imperialism—Building large empires by gaining economic and political control over weaker nations that usually become colonies of the stronger country

impressment—Act of forcing captured American sailors to serve in the British navy

inauguration—Formal ceremony starting a president's term

indentured servants—Individuals who gained passage to America in return for four to seven years labor upon arrival in the colonies

Indian Removal Act—Law passed by Congress in 1830 declaring that Indians who left their lands east of the Mississippi would be given lands west of the river with costs paid by the national government

Indian Territory—Former name of Oklahoma

Industrial Revolution—Period of social and economic change that was occurring as machines and other new inventions replaced hand tools

inflation—An increase in the prices for goods and services that is often caused by an increase in the money supply

initiative—Allows voters to propose their own legislation by means of obtaining enough signatures on a petition so that the issue is then put on the ballot for voters to accept or reject

injunctions—Official court orders; used to stop strikes

installment plan—System that allows a person to pay for an item in weekly or monthly payments, often with interest

interchangeable parts—Parts of a device that could be replaced by identical parts

international law—Rules by which countries agree to abide

interstate commerce—The sale and transport of goods and services from one state to another

Interstate Commerce Act—Law passed in 1887 directing railroads to set "reasonable and just" rates; created the Interstate Commerce Commission

interstate highway system—System of highways that became the main arteries of transportation in the United States, instituted under Eisenhower; also provided a way to move troops and equipment in case of war

Intolerable Acts—Called the Coercive Acts by the British; closed the port of Boston until the cost of the destroyed tea was paid, allowed royal officials charged with crimes to be tried in London or in another colony, changed Massachusetts' charter and gave British officials more control, and passed a new Quartering Act (of 1774)

Iran-Contra affair—Scandal during Reagan's administration involving money from the sale of weapons to Iran, some profits of which went to aid the Contras in Nicaragua although Congress had banned aid to the Contras

Iranian hostage crisis—Incident in 1979 that developed during unrest in Iran over US support for the exiled shah; incident where Iranian terrorists took more than fifty Americans hostage for 444 days until the day of Reagan's inauguration

iron curtain—Term used to describe the separation of Communist Eastern Europe and the free nations of Western Europe

Iroquois—The strongest confederation of Indian tribes in America; supported Britain in the French and Indian War

Islamic State in Iraq and Syria (ISIS)—Terrorist group developed in the Middle East from the remains of al-Qaeda; also known as ISIL

island hopping—World War II strategy implemented by US commanders of capturing some islands that could be used as air strips and bases but skipping other islands

isolationism—When a country largely stays out of all world politics

Iwo Jima—American World War II victory; battle beginning February 19, 1945; the toughest, costliest battle in Marine Corps history

J

Jamestown—The first permanent English colony in the New World

Jay Treaty—Unpopular treaty by John Jay in which the United States agreed to limit trade with France and to arrange payment of debts still owed to British banks and citizens from before the War for Independence; treaty in which Britain agreed to abandon its forts in the Northwest, pay the United States for ships seized, and open some ports in the British West Indies to American trade

Jim Crow laws—Legislation requiring the forced segregation of the races in trains, restaurants, hotels, schools, and other social settings

joint-stock companies—Corporations where groups of Englishmen pooled money and allowed others to buy shares of stock; businesses in which failure meant the loss of the amount invested and success meant the profits were split according to the number of shares; forerunners of modern corporations

judicial review—The right of the Supreme Court to declare a law passed by Congress as unconstitutional

July 4, 1776—Date of the adoption of the Declaration of Independence

justices of the peace—Local magistrates or judges in the colonies

K

kamikaze—Japanese pilots who deliberately tried to crash their planes into enemy ships during the closing months of World War II

Kansas-Nebraska Act—Proposal by Stephen Douglas calling for the organization of the territories of Kansas and Nebraska; each territory would use popular sovereignty to decide the issue of slavery; repealed the Missouri Compromise

Kellogg-Briand Pact—Pact made in 1928 outlawing war as a means of settling international disputes; signed by many nations

Kent State University—Site of a tragedy in May 1970 when four college students were shot and killed by National Guardsmen during a banned Vietnam War protest rally

King Philip's War—War between Metacomet (King Philip) and New England colonists from 1675–78

Kings Mountain—Patriot frontiersmen victory in battle against Loyalist forces in South Carolina in 1780

Kitchen Cabinet—Informal group of Andrew Jackson's friends whom he consulted about governmental matters

Knights of Labor—Union formed in 1869 whose goal was to form one big union for all workers

Korean War—Conflict from 1950–53 between Communists and non-Communists over who would control South Korea

Ku Klux Klan—Secret organization formed by some former Confederate soldiers in 1866 to place black people firmly under white control through intimidation and violence

L

labor unions—Organized groups of workers who wanted to obtain better working conditions and better pay

laissez faire—French phrase meaning "let it alone"; the idea that a capitalist economy develops best without government interference

lame-duck period—The time between the election of a president and his leaving office

Land Ordinance of 1785—Provided for the surveying and sale of the Northwest Territory

League of Nations—The last of Wilson's Fourteen Points; an organization of cooperating nations that would discuss and solve problems peacefully

Lend-Lease Act—Act of Congress in 1941 allowing the president to send equipment to any nation in which such equipment might support American defense; paid for with services, equipment, or property (such as land) to America

Lexington—Town in Massachusetts where the first shots of the War for Independence were fired

literacy tests—Tests given to determine reading and writing ability as a qualification for voting

locks—Water compartments that could be opened and shut on a canal

lode—Rich deposit of ore

Lone Star Republic—Name for the Republic of Texas between when it won independence from Mexico and when it became a state

Louisiana Purchase—American purchase of the French territory of Louisiana in 1803 for $15 million

Loyalists—Colonists who opposed fighting Britain

Lusitania—British passenger ship that included some American passengers; sunk in 1915 under Germany's unrestricted submarine warfare policy

M

Manhattan Project—Top-secret American operation during World War II to make the first atomic weapon before the Germans

Manifest Destiny—Belief of many that it was the country's fate (or destiny), or that God intended for the country, to have all the western lands to the Pacific Ocean

Marbury v. Madison—Supreme Court ruling establishing the principle of judicial review

March on Washington—The biggest civil rights event of the 1960s; the gathering of more than 200,000 people in the nation's capital to protest civil rights injustices

March to the Sea—General Sherman's sixty-mile-wide band of destruction from Atlanta to Savannah, Georgia

Marshall Plan—US program, proposed by Secretary of State George C. Marshall, providing huge sums of money to rebuild European countries ravaged by World War II

Massachusetts Bay Company—Colony established by Puritans in 1630

mass production—Product production in large quantities

materialism—Placing great emphasis on money and possessions

Mayflower Compact—Agreement the Pilgrims made for establishing the first self-government in the New World

McCulloch v. Maryland—Supreme Court ruling that a state cannot tax the federal government

mercantilism—Economic system that measured wealth by how much gold and silver a nation possessed

Mexican Cession—Land the United States gained from Mexico as a result of the Mexican War: California, Nevada, Utah, and parts of Wyoming, Colorado, Arizona, and New Mexico

Mexican War—The war between the United States and Mexico from 1846–48

Middle Passage—The journey of African slaves in chains across the Atlantic Ocean to the Americas

"midnight judges"—Dozens of judges appointed to office by John Adams the night before he left office

militarism—An increased emphasis on military might

militia—The local army in the colonies

mill town—Towns built by owners or investors for workers near the factories or mills, with housing (usually identical and in rows), churches, schools, doctors' offices, and company stores

minutemen—Colonial militiamen who were ready to fight at a moment's notice

Missouri Compromise—Agreement proposed by Henry Clay whereby Maine would be admitted as a free state and Missouri would become a slave state; slavery would be prohibited north of the 36°30′ line of latitude, Missouri's southern border, with the exception of Missouri

Monroe Doctrine—An 1823 foreign-policy statement by James Monroe that European nations could not intervene in the Western Hemisphere except where they already had colonies and that the United States would not meddle in European matters

Montgomery bus boycott—Boycott of city buses in Montgomery, Alabama, for more than a year in response to the arrest of Rosa Parks for not giving up her seat on the bus; led by Martin Luther King Jr.

Moravians—Followers of the teachings of John Huss; known for their mission work

Mormons—Also called the Church of Jesus Christ of Latter-Day Saints; religion started by Joseph Smith and continued by Brigham Young; settled Salt Lake City, Utah

Mormon Trail—The Mormons' trek to the Great Salt Lake

mountain men—Trappers and traders who were normally the first white people to arrive in western areas

muckrakers—Nickname for progressive writers who exposed abuse and corruption

mudslinging—The spreading of negative information about opponents

multiculturalism—The condition of different cultures existing side by side without being dominated by any particular one

N

Nagasaki—Site of the second atomic bomb, dropped on Japan on August 9, 1945

National Aeronautics and Space Administration (NASA)—Organization established to conduct the American space program

National Association for the Advancement of Colored People (NAACP)—Organization seeking equality for black Americans and focusing on fighting legal battles to achieve that objective

national bank—A place to hold tax revenue and to handle the nation's financial dealings

nationalism—The feeling of loyalty or devotion to one's country or cultural group

National Recovery Administration (NRA)—New Deal agency whose goal was to help businesses recover from the effects of the Depression; attempted to eliminate competition among firms by assigning each company a share of the national market

National Road—First federally funded road; sometimes called the Cumberland Road

Navigation and Trade Acts—Mercantilistic policies passed by Britain between 1651 and 1733 to control colonial trade

Nazi Party—Another name for the fascist National Socialist German Workers' Party led by Hitler

New Deal—Name attached to Franklin D. Roosevelt's efforts to conquer the Great Depression

New Frontier—John F. Kennedy's program that called for economic aid to poor areas, medical insurance for the elderly, financial aid for college students, and an ambitious space program

New Jersey Plan—Proposal that the new US government have a unicameral system in which all states would have one vote; supported by smaller states

New Netherland—The Dutch region that eventually became the colony of New York

New South—Economically revived South in which many Southerners moved from rural areas to factory towns and cities for jobs in industry

Nineteenth Amendment—Provided women the right to vote

nomadic—Constantly on the move in search of game and wild plants

North American Free Trade Agreement (NAFTA)—Agreement passed during the Clinton administration providing for the elimination of tariffs between the United States, Mexico, and Canada; lasted until 2020

North Atlantic Treaty Organization (NATO)—Military alliance formed in reaction to the Soviet military threat to Western nations

Northwest Ordinance of 1787—Required the Northwest Territory to be divided into at least three but no more than five territories, from which the modern states of Ohio, Indiana, Illinois, Michigan, and Wisconsin formed

Northwest Territory—Portion of western lands bound on the east by the original thirteen colonies, the west by the Mississippi River, the north by the Great Lakes, and the south by the Ohio River

"no taxation without representation"—Colonial rallying cry against no representation in Parliament

nullification—State's act of declaring void any federal law

nullify—A state's right to refuse to accept a federal law that the state considered unconstitutional

Nuremberg Trials—Trials of major Nazi criminals held in Nuremberg, Germany, after World War II

O

Obergefell v. Hodges—Supreme Court case in 2015 granting marriage rights to same-sex partners

Okinawa—American assault beginning in April 1945; victory that allowed a base close enough to Japan to launch intensive bombing raids on Japan's military, industrial, and population centers

Oklahoma City bombing—Bombing in 1995 of a federal office building in Oklahoma City by Timothy McVeigh, partly in reaction to the raid on the Branch Davidians two years before in Waco, Texas; deadliest act of domestic terrorism in American history to that point

Old Deluder Satan Act—Law passed by Massachusetts in 1647 requiring all towns of fifty or more families to appoint a schoolmaster who would teach reading and writing so as to prevent the "Old Deluder Satan" from keeping people "from the knowledge of the Scripture"

Olive Branch Petition—Petition for peace sent by the Second Continental Congress to King George III

Open Door policy—Policy proposed by the United States of removing spheres of influence and opening China to all nations equally

open range—Unfenced lands used to graze cattle or other livestock

Oregon Trail—Most important route for settlers and missionaries going west from the eastern part of the United States toward Oregon

overseer—One who distributed work among slaves and ensured they did as expected; usually a hired white man

P

Panama Canal—American-built canal that links the Atlantic and Pacific Oceans through Panama

Panama Canal Treaty—The 1977 treaty stating that the United States and Panama would operate the canal jointly until December 31, 1999, when Panama would take complete control of it

Panic of 1819—An economic crisis leading to the loss of homes, businesses, land, and savings; especially affected southern and western farmers

partnerships—Businesses that were owned by two or more people

Patient Protection and Affordable Care Act, ObamaCare—Key legislation passed during the Obama administration requiring all Americans to buy health insurance or face a financial penalty

Patriot Act—Congressional act making it easier to locate and imprison suspected terrorists and allowing the government to listen to phone conversations of people suspected of having terrorist connections; some provisions were later deemed unconstitutional by the Supreme Court

Patriots—Individuals who favored fighting the British

Peace Corps—Program introduced by President Kennedy in 1961 in which the "best and brightest" Americans would work in poverty-stricken countries for two years

peaceful coexistence—The idea of communist and democratic nations existing side by side without constant conflict and threat of military action

Pearl Harbor—US naval and air base in Hawaii; bombed by the Japanese on December 7, 1941, resulting in a declaration of war by the United States

Pequot War—Indian war started in 1637 between Massachusetts Bay Colony and the Pequot tribe

Persian Gulf War—Six-week war in 1991 successfully ousting the invading country of Iraq (led by Saddam Hussein) from Kuwait

"pet banks"—Dozens of state banks, rather than the National Bank, chosen to receive governmental revenues

philanthropists—Wealthy people who generously donate money to worthy causes

Pickett's charge—Disastrous Confederate attack with staggering casualties led by General George Pickett at the Battle of Gettysburg

Pikes Peak or Bust!—Slogan written on prospectors' wagons referring to the newly discovered gold at Pikes Peak in Colorado

Pilgrims—A group of Separatists that left Europe and went to the New World, establishing Plymouth Colony

plantations—Large farms in the southern colonies

Platt Amendment—Strict regulations for Cuba's new government after the Spanish-American War

Plessy v. Ferguson—Supreme Court case in 1896 declaring "separate but equal" facilities for blacks and whites constitutional

Plymouth—Colony established by the Pilgrims in 1620

political machines—Organized groups of politicians who sought to control the government

poll tax—A special tax required in order to vote

Pony Express—Mail delivery system from St. Joseph, Missouri, to Sacramento, California, taking eight to ten days, with riders traveling about seventy miles each and changing horses every ten to fifteen miles

popular sovereignty—The process of allowing citizens to decide if they wanted to permit slavery

Populist Party—Also called the People's Party; political party formed in the 1890s by farmers with the goal of appealing to the common people

power of the purse—Control of government money

Powhatan Indians—Tribe of Woodland Indians around Jamestown

POWs—Prisoners of war

praying towns—Towns where new Indian converts could come to learn about the Bible, European laws, manners, and town life

Preamble—The introduction to the Constitution

Presidential Reconstruction—Period during which Presidents Abraham Lincoln and Andrew Johnson directed the Reconstruction process

Proclamation of 1763—Prohibited colonists from settling beyond the Appalachian Mountains in order to reduce conflict with the Indians

Proclamation of Neutrality—President Washington's declaration that the United States would pursue a policy of friendliness toward both France and Britain and would not involve itself in their conflict

progressivism—Movement during the late nineteenth and early twentieth centuries that favored achieving political and social reform through education, wider political participation, and direct action by the government

prohibition—Banning the manufacture, sale, and transportation of alcohol

Prohibition—Term for the Eighteenth Amendment; the period from 1920 to 1933 during which alcohol was illegal in the United States

propaganda—Information spread to advance a cause or damage an opponent's cause

proprietary colonies—Colonies given by the king to individuals or groups

protective tariff—A tax designed to limit the importation of foreign goods and to protect American industries from foreign competition

protectorate—A country that is technically independent but has to submit to some control by another nation

providence—God's control over all events

Pure Food and Drug Act—A 1906 law that allowed federal inspectors to examine slaughterhouses and meat companies that shipped across state lines, forbade the use of harmful additives, regulated the use of narcotics, required companies to list the ingredients of medicines on product labels, and prohibited companies from making unverifiable claims about medicines

Puritans—Members of the Anglican Church who hoped to purify it of Roman Catholic practices and ceremonies

Q

Quakers—Known as the Society of Friends; group that separated from the Anglican Church; "tremble[d] at the word of the Lord"; viewed all people as equal; believed that everyone has an "inner light" telling them God's will instead of the Bible

Quartering Act of 1765—Law requiring colonies to house British troops in barracks, stables, taverns, and empty buildings and to provide some supplies

Quebec Act—Allowed French law to be used in some court cases in Quebec, extended Quebec's borders south to the Ohio River, and recognized Roman Catholicism as the leading religion in Quebec

R

Radical Reconstruction—Name for Congressional Reconstruction by 1867

Radical Republicans—Influential minority in the Republican Party that believed those who led the South during the Civil War should not be allowed to return to power

ratify—Formally approve

rations—Fixed allowances of food and other items due to lack of supplies, especially in wartime

recall—Voter petition for a special election to decide whether to remove an elected official from office before his term expires

recession—A slowdown in the economy but not as severe as a depression

Reconstruction—Period from the end of the Civil War to 1877

Reconstruction Act of 1867—Ordered the army to ensure that the South followed these laws Congress enacted: (1) divided the South into five military districts, (2) blacks had to be included with whites in state conventions, (3) new state constitutions had to guarantee that adult black males could vote, (4) Congress had to approve new state constitutions, and (5) states had to ratify the Fourteenth Amendment

Reconstruction Finance Corporation—Hoover's plan to give loans to industries and businesses (such as banks) for use in projects that would create jobs

Redeemers—Group of southern whites that wanted to "save" the South and its culture by overthrowing blacks and other Republicans who held offices

Red Scare—Time of increased public concern about communism in America ("red" was a common term for a Communist)

referendum—Allows voters to determine by an election whether a law proposed by a governmental body should be enacted or rejected

Religious Right—Another name for religious conservatives who established organizations to encourage Christians to be involved in politics

reparations—Money a defeated country must pay for war damages

republic—A government in which elected representatives govern the people

Republican Party—Political party formed in 1854 consisting of anti-slavery groups including Conscience Whigs, Northern Democrats, and the Free Soil Party

Republican Revolution—The result of the 1994 midterm elections, Republicans controlling both houses of Congress for the first time in forty years

rescue missions—Facilities to provide food, shelter, and spiritual guidance

reservations—Tracts of land set aside for Indians

revenue tariff—A tax on imported goods designed to raise money

right of deposit—The freedom to stockpile goods until ships transport them overseas

Roanoke—"The Lost Colony"; disappeared with no trace

Roe v. Wade—1973 Supreme Court decision that the Constitution protects a woman's right to have an abortion

Roosevelt Corollary—An addition to the Monroe Doctrine; stated that the United States had the right to be an international police power in the Western Hemisphere

Rough Riders—All-volunteer cavalry unit famous for its charge up San Juan Hill in 1898

royal colonies—Colonies the king had direct control over

Russian satellites—Soviet-dominated countries

S

Salem witch trials—Trials arising from accusations of witchcraft; held in Salem Village, Massachusetts; sometimes resulting in the execution of those accused

Salvation Army—Group providing relief for the poor; establishes rescue missions to help individuals by meeting their physical needs and presenting the gospel

San Juan Hill—Location in Cuba of famous charge by the Rough Riders, helping defeat the Spanish in 1898

Santa Fe Trail—First American route west of the Missouri River; primarily a trade route

Saratoga—Battle resulting in a significant Patriot victory; a major turning point of the War for Independence

scalawag—A white Southerner supporting Reconstruction; means "scoundrel" or "worthless person"

Scopes trial—Famous trial in Tennessee in 1925 involving the illegal teaching of evolution; also called the Monkey Trial

"scorched earth" policy—Burning crops and killing livestock during retreat rather than leaving them for enemy soldiers; used by Russia in World War II

Sea Dogs—English pirates who disrupted the flow of Spanish wealth from America to Spain

secession—The act of a state leaving the Union

Second Battle of Bull Run—Also called the Second Battle of Manassas; Confederate victory

Second Continental Congress—Colonial government that assembled in Philadelphia, Pennsylvania; took control of the army at Boston and asked the colonies for war supplies and troops

Second Great Awakening—Spiritual revival that swept the nation in the early 1800s

secularism—Belief that religion has no place in government

Security Council—A main part of the United Nations; includes five permanent members (United States, Russia, Britain, France, and China) and ten temporary members elected by the General Assembly for two-year terms

segregation—Separation of races

Senate—The upper house of Congress with each state represented by two senators

Seneca Falls Convention—Meeting in July 1848 of more than three hundred to discuss women's rights and propose changes to the law such as allowing women to vote

separation of powers—Principle attempting to ensure that no branch of the government has too much power

Separatists—Group that chose to separate themselves from the Anglican Church and hold their own worship services

September 11, 2001—Generally referred to as 9/11; the day terrorists hijacked multiple planes, crashing into the two World Trade Center Towers, the Pentagon, and a field in Pennsylvania; attack that left thousands dead and injured

settlement houses—Places providing food, clothing, medical care, childcare, recreation, and classes to women in slum areas

Seventeenth Amendment—Provided for the direct election of senators

sharecroppers—Farmers of small plots of land owned by planters; a portion, or share, of the crop was paid to the planter as rent

Shays's Rebellion—Revolt led by Daniel Shays in Massachusetts to prevent farmers from losing their property; forced some courts to close and attempted to capture guns and ammunition

Sherman Antitrust Act—Law passed in 1890 to control trusts; eventually used to break up, or dismantle, large companies

Sixteenth Amendment—Instituted the federal income tax

Smoot-Hawley Tariff—Passed in June 1930 to protect American industries from foreign competition; the highest tariff ever passed by the US Congress

social Darwinism—Darwin's theory of survival of the fittest applied socially or to business

Social Security Act—Permanent New Deal program that provides unemployment insurance and a monthly pension for most retired individuals

sod houses—Also called "soddies"; prairie houses made of strips of grass and soil cut from the hard ground used as staggered "bricks"

sole proprietorships—Businesses owned by one person

Sons of Liberty—Groups of colonists who organized rallies to protest the Stamp Act

Sooners—Oklahoma settlers who illegally staked their claims ahead of time

Spanish-American War—War between the United States and Spain in 1898; fought mainly in Cuba and the Philippines

speakeasies—Illegal taverns or bars where people would often whisper to obtain entry

specie—Gold or silver coins

speculation—Financial transaction that carries considerable risk of losing value but also holds the possibility of significant gain

spheres of influence—Sphere, or division, of a country in which a single foreign country controls all trading operations

spirituals—Songs sung by slaves revealing how they felt about their condition; dealt with various biblical subjects

spoils system—Distributing government jobs to loyal followers; increased by Andrew Jackson

Sputnik I—The first satellite successfully launched into orbit; built by the Russians

Stamp Act (1765)—Required colonial businessmen and lawyers to purchase special stamps and place them on items such as legal documents, newspapers, calendars, and playing cards

Stamp Act Congress—Colonial assembly in Massachusetts that peacefully protested the Stamp Act; led by Samuel Adams

Star Wars—Nickname for the Strategic Defense Initiative (SDI); the development of a defense system that could destroy enemy nuclear missiles before they reached their targets

states' rights—The view that each state was largely an independent body, voluntarily joined to the Union, and had the right to control its most important affairs

St. Augustine—Oldest permanent city settled by Europeans in the United States; located in Florida

steamboats—Vessels powered by a steam engine

stock-market crash—Beginning of the worst economic crisis in American history on October 29, 1929 (Black Tuesday); panic erupted and fortunes vanished in minutes

strike—Act of refusing to work in protest of an employer's actions

subsistence farmers—Farmers who could raise just enough crops and livestock to provide for their families

suffrage—The right to vote

Sugar Act (1764)—Duties, or taxes, on imported goods such as sugar, molasses, and coffee

supply-side economics—President Reagan's economic policy to lower inflation by decreasing taxes and reducing regulations on businesses and investors

T

Taliban—Muslim extremist group that controlled the government in Afghanistan and protected Osama bin Laden and al-Qaeda terrorists

tariff—A tax on imported goods

tariff of abominations—Nickname for the Tariff of 1828, which increased the cost of goods Southerners needed

task system—Labor system in which overseers gave slaves specific tasks; allowing slaves, upon completion of tasks, to use the remainder of the day to do other things such as working for themselves

Teapot Dome scandal—Scandal during Harding's administration involving the secretary of the interior, Albert B. Fall, who accepted "loans" for leasing oil reserves, resulting in the first imprisonment of a cabinet member for misdeeds in office

Teller Amendment—Resolution stating that the United States had no intention of adding Cuba to its empire and that the United States desired only Cuba's independence

temperance societies—Groups dedicated to stopping the consumption of alcohol

Tennessee Valley Authority (TVA)—Permanent New Deal agency operating public projects in seven southeastern states along the Tennessee River

Ten Percent Plan—Lincoln's plan for restoring the South; the military governor was to reestablish a civilian government as soon as ten percent of those who had voted in the 1860 election took an oath of allegiance to the Union

Tenure of Office Act—Made it illegal for the president to remove any appointee approved by the Senate unless the Senate also approved the dismissal; declared unconstitutional

Tet Offensive—Multiple surprise attacks launched by Communist troops across South Vietnam on January 31, 1968, the Vietnamese New Year (Tet)

Third World—(1) During the Cold War, nations that did not align themselves with the East or the West; (2) today, underdeveloped or developing nations, especially those with widespread poverty

Thirteenth Amendment—Abolished slavery

Three-Fifths Compromise—Agreement reached that, for representation and taxation, every five enslaved people would count as three people in the state's population total

tidewater—Low land along coastal rivers and inlets

totalitarianism—System of government that regulates every aspect of life

total war—Fighting not just the enemy's military and government but also its civilian population; focuses on destroying the enemy's ability and willingness to fight

totem poles—Symbolic poles carved from large trees, crafted by some Native American tribes to depict family history, local legends, and important events

Townshend Acts (1767)—Taxes passed by Parliament on such items as glass, paper, lead, paint, and tea

township—(1) Basic unit of government in New England colonies; (2) divisions of land six miles square, subdivided into thirty-six smaller parcels called sections

trail boss—Cowboy in charge of the men, equipment, and animals on a cattle drive

Trail of Tears—The forced marches west of the Cherokee to the Indian Territory; many died en route

Treaty of Ghent—Treaty ending the War of 1812

Treaty of Guadalupe Hidalgo—Officially ended the Mexican War; made the Rio Grande the southern border of Texas and added the Mexican Cession to the United States

Treaty of Paris—Signed on September 3, 1783, formally granting the American colonies independence

Treaty of Versailles—Peace treaty after World War I; placed the blame for the war entirely on Germany and forced Germany to pay reparations

trench warfare—Major part of World War I, using long ditches normally deep enough for a man to stand in; included frontline trenches, support trenches, and communication trenches

Trenton—Battle against Hessian soldiers in New Jersey after George Washington's crossing of the Delaware River; Patriot victory

triangular trade—Trade network that carried slaves, cash crops, and manufactured goods between west Africa, the Caribbean and American colonies, and Europe

Triple Alliance—Alliance of Germany, Austria-Hungary, and Italy

Triple Entente—Alliance of Britain, France, and Russia

Truman Doctrine—Giving money or other assistance to support pro-Western, anti-Communist governments

trust—Combination of several separate companies into one supersized corporation

turnpikes—Roads built by private companies that charged a toll, or fee, for use of the road

Tuskegee Institute—One of the most famous black schools; founded by Booker T. Washington and located in Alabama

Twenty-First Amendment—Repealed the Eighteenth Amendment and ended Prohibition

Twenty-Fourth Amendment—Prohibits poll taxes

Twenty-Seventh Amendment—Prohibits a congressional pay raise from taking effect until after the next congressional election

Twenty-Sixth Amendment—Grants voting rights to citizens age eighteen and older

Twenty-Third Amendment—Gives the right to vote in national elections to District of Columbia (DC) residents

U

U-boats—Submarines; shortened from the German word *unterseeboot*

Uncle Tom's Cabin—Novel written by Harriet Beecher Stowe; drew public attention to the plight of slave families and runaway slaves

Underground Railroad—Network of people who aided runaway slaves; "conductors" hid escaping slaves by night

unicameral system—Government system consisting of one legislative house

Union of Soviet Socialist Republics (USSR)—Also called the Soviet Union; name for Communist Russia

Union Pacific—Railroad company that built the first transcontinental railroad westward starting from Omaha, Nebraska; used many Irish workers and Civil War veterans

United Nations—International organization formed post-World War II as a peacekeeping body

United States-Mexico-Canada Agreement (USMCA)—Trade agreement passed during the Trump administration, replacing NAFTA in 2020

unrestricted submarine warfare—German policy during World War I whereby all ships entering a designated war zone around Britain would be subject to attack without warning

urbanization—Movement of people to cities

USS *Maine*—American warship sunk in Havana, Cuba; Spain blamed by yellow journalists for the sinking

V

Valley Forge—Washington's army headquarters outside Philadelphia for the winter of 1777–78

V-E Day—Victory in Europe Day; May 7, 1945

veto—President's power to return a bill passed by Congress, stating his objections

Vicksburg—City in Mississippi on high bluffs overlooking the Mississippi River; Union victory that resulted in Union control of the entire Mississippi River

Viet Cong—Communist fighters in South Vietnam who waged guerrilla warfare

Vietnamization—Nixon's plan to gradually withdraw US troops from the Vietnam War and to transfer responsibility for the fighting to the South Vietnamese, while continuing to provide supplies and air support

Vietnam War—Conflict between Communists and non-Communists over who would control South Vietnam

Virginia and Kentucky Resolutions—Response to the Alien and Sedition Acts; resolutions claiming that the states should be allowed to decide whether actions of the federal government are constitutional

Virginia Plan—Proposed that the US government have a bicameral system based on each state's population; supported by larger states

V-J Day—Victory over Japan Day; September 2, 1945

Volstead Act—1919 law providing federal implementation of the Eighteenth Amendment, outlawing any beverage that contained more than 0.5% alcohol content

Voting Rights Act of 1965—Prohibited literacy tests, gave federal officials authority to investigate complaints of discrimination relating to voter registration or voting, provided for federal government oversight of the registration process where many black Americans were not registered to vote, and required local and state governments in places where voter discrimination had been common to receive approval for changes affecting voting or elections

W

Wade-Davis Bill—Congressional plan for Reconstruction requiring more than 50 percent of white male citizens to take an oath of allegiance to the Union before a state would be allowed to reenter; plan requiring states to abandon slavery and any claims on the federal government to repay war debts; states had to agree that former Confederate military and political leaders would not be allowed to vote or hold office

War Hawks—Group of western and southern members of the House of Representatives, led by Henry Clay, that wanted to expand America's borders and power; supported war with Britain

War of 1812—War between the United States and Britain lasting from June 18, 1812, until December 24, 1814

War Powers Act—Congress's attempt in 1973 to limit the president's power to fight wars such as Vietnam in the future; requires presidents to inform Congress within 48 hours of sending military forces to an area without a declaration of war; those troops cannot stay longer than 90 days unless Congress approves

Warsaw Pact—Soviet military alliance formed in response to NATO

Washington Naval Conference—Agreements made in 1921–22 between nine nations to destroy dozens of existing naval vessels and to limit the size of their future navies

Watergate scandal—The burglary of the Watergate Office Complex in Washington, DC, and the attempt to conceal information about it during the election cycle of 1972; led to Nixon's resignation in 1974

weapons of mass destruction (WMDs)—Specially formulated weapons (such as chemical, biological, and nuclear) intended to harm or kill great numbers of people

Welfare Reform Act—Officially titled "The Personal Responsibility and Work Opportunity Reconciliation Act of 1996"; financial aid for the poor rolled back; resulted in a decrease in poverty numbers

West Virginia—Portion of Virginia that opposed secession; separated from Virginia and became a Union state in 1863

Whigs—Political party in the 1830s uniting groups opposed to Andrew Jackson; named after the British party that traditionally opposed royalty

Whiskey Rebellion—Protest against excise taxes on whiskey; quelled by George Washington's forces

Wilderness Road—Road that Daniel Boone cut westward through the Kentucky frontier

Wilmot Proviso—Proposal by Representative David Wilmot to ban slavery in any territory gained from the Mexican War; rejected by Congress

worldview—The set of beliefs that a person uses to look at the world and interpret it

Wounded Knee massacre—Tragic conclusion to the Indian Wars; 150 Native Americans were killed (including women and children) at Wounded Knee Creek, South Dakota, plus the death of 25 soldiers

writs of assistance—General search warrants giving customs officials the right to search for smuggled goods anywhere

X

XYZ Affair—Named for the three French agents who demanded a bribe in order to negotiate with the United States

Y

Yalta Conference—Meeting at Yalta, Soviet Union, of the Big Three (Roosevelt, Churchill, and Stalin) during February 1945 to discuss plans for postwar Europe

yellow journalism—Also called the yellow press; providing sensational descriptions of events, often twisting news stories to make each more exciting than the previous

Yorktown—Formal surrender of British General Cornwallis's army, essentially ending the War for Independence

Young Men's Christian Association (YMCA)—Organization, originating in England, providing wholesome activities and entertainment for young men in the troublesome environment of big cities; emphasized physical, educational, social, and religious growth and provided a safe living environment

Z

Zimmermann telegram—Telegram from the German foreign minister to the Mexican government offering to help Mexico reconquer Texas, New Mexico, and Arizona in return for its support in case America joined the Allies in World War I

Index

C

D

M

N

O

P

T

U

V

W

X

Y

Z

Photo Credits

Key: (t) top; (c) center;
(b) bottom; (l) left; (r) right
(bg) background; (i) inset

Front Matter

iii "Henrik Hudson entering New York Harbor, September 11, 1609" by Edward Moran/Wikimedia Commons/Public Domain; **iv** t "Washington Crossing the Delaware" by Emanuel Leutze/The Metropolitan Museum of Art/Wikimedia Commons/Public Domain; **iv** b North Wind Picture Archives / Alamy Stock Photo; **v** t Archive Images / Alamy Stock Photo; **v** b RBM Vintage Images / Alamy Stock Photo; **vi** Robert Boulware / Alamy Stock Photo; **vii** US Navy Photo / Alamy Stock Photo; **viii** t "Washington Crossing the Delaware" by Emanuel Leutze/The Metropolitan Museum of Art/Wikimedia Commons/Public Domain; **viii** c GL Archive / Alamy Stock Photo; **viii** b incamerastock / Alamy Stock Photo; **ix** t Everett Collection/Shutterstock.com; **ix** c World History Archive / Alamy Stock Photo; **ix** b Malcolm Fairman / Alamy Stock Photo; **x** t John Parrot / Media Bakery; **x** c Paul Thompson/FPG/Archive Photos/Getty Images; **x** b "369th 15th New York"/National Archives /Wikimedia Commons/Public Domain; **xi** t "AS09-20-3064 - Apollo 9 - Apollo 9 Mission image - Scott during EVA"/U.S. National Archives and Records Administration/Wikimedia Commons/Public Domain; **xi** b INTERFOTO / Alamy Stock Photo; **xii** Ariel Skelley/DigitalVision/Getty Images; **xiii** Don Mason/Getty Images; **xiv** Keith Lance/DigitalVision Vectors/Getty Images; **xv** t Ariel Skelley/DigitalVision/Getty Images; **xv** b Sergio Flores/Getty Images News/Getty Images

Unit Openers

xvi–1 "Henrik Hudson entering New York Harbor, September 11, 1609" by Edward Moran/Wikimedia Commons/Public Domain; **106–7** "Washington Crossing the Delaware" by Emanuel Leutze/The Metropolitan Museum of Art/Wikimedia Commons/Public Domain; **190–91** North Wind Picture Archives / Alamy Stock Photo; **288–89** Archive Images / Alamy Stock Photo; **366–67** RBM Vintage Images / Alamy Stock Photo; **458–59** Robert Boulware / Alamy Stock Photo; **550–51** US Navy Photo / Alamy Stock Photo

Chapter 1

2 The History Emporium / Alamy Stock Photo; **3**tl Ignacio Palacios /Stone/Getty Images; **3**tr "Escritura maya" by Juan Carlos Fonseca Mata /Wikimedia Commons/CC By-SA 4.0; **3**b Matteo Colombo/DigitalVision /Getty Images; **5** Jess Kraft/500Px Plus/Getty Images; **6**t Debbie Ann Powell/iStock Editorial/Getty Images Plus/Getty Images; **6**b kjschoen /iStock/Getty Images Plus/Getty Images; **7**t Patrick J. Endres/Corbis Documentary/Getty Images; **7**ct Philip Scalia / Alamy Stock Photo; **7**cb aceshot1/Shutterstock.com; **7**b "Fort Union Trading Post National Historic Site (2bf8ff08-1e4e-44fb-9a14-2943f9d8d613)" by Victoria Stauffenberg/NPS/Wikimedia Commons/Public Domain; **8** snoofek /Bigstock.com; **10** Stocktrek Images/Getty Images; **11** "Christopher Columbus"/Wikimedia Commons/Public Domain; **12**t "La conquista del Colorado" by Augusto Ferrer-Dalmau Nieto/Wikimedia Commons /CC By-SA 4.0; **12**cl, **20**t Album / Alamy Stock Photo; **12**cr 6381380 /iStock Editorial/Getty Images Plus/Getty Images; **12**b The Picture Art Collection / Alamy Stock Photo; **13**l North Wind Picture Archives / Alamy Stock Photo; **13**c "Jacques Cartier 1851-1852" by Théophile Hamel /Wikimedia Commons/CC By-SA 4.0; **13**r Science History Images / Alamy Stock Photo; **14**t GL Archive / Alamy Stock Photo; **14**b, **18**b, **22** incamerastock / Alamy Stock Photo; **16** Richard Cummins / Alamy Stock Photo; **17**t Stock Montage/Archive Photos/Getty Images; **17**b "Antonion Zeno Shindler - Pocahontas - 1985.66.317,435 - Smithsonian American Art Museum" by Antonio Zeno Shindler/Wikimedia Commons /Public Domain; **18**t 4kodiak/iStock/Getty Images Plus/Getty Images; **20**bg–**21**l Jasonfang/E+/Getty Images; **20**b "Dunhuang Star Chart BLX273 OR8210S3326R2 8"/International Dunhuang Project/Wikimedia Commons/CC0 1.0; **21**r Granger, NYC; **23** Carver Mostardi / Alamy Stock Photo

Chapter 2

24 World History Archive / Alamy Stock Photo; **25, 31, 34, 38, 41**b North Wind Picture Archives / Alamy Stock Photo; **26** Public Domain; **27** Michael Sean OLeary/Shutterstock.com; **28** SuperStock / SuperStock; **29** Granger, NYC; **30**tl mrs/Moment/Getty Images; **30**tr DPFishCo /iStock/Getty Images Plus/Getty Images; **30**c GCapture/iStock/Getty Images Plus/Getty Images; **30**b Michael Gordon/Shutterstock.com; **33** Stock Montage/Archive Photos/Getty Images; **36**t "Castelloplan" by John Wolcott Adams and I.N. Phelps Stokes/New-York Historical Society Library, Maps Collection/Wikimedia Commons/Public Domain; **36**b "King James II" by Sir Godfrey Kneller/Wikimedia Commons/ Public Domain; **37**t Private Collection / Look and Learn / Peter Jackson Collection / Bridgeman Images; **37**b Q-Images / Alamy Stock Photo; **39**t alenkadr/iStock/Getty Images Plus/Getty Images; **39**b Khairil Azhar Junos/Shutterstock.com; **41**tl Wesley Hitt/Photographer's Choice RF/Getty Images; **41**tr My-ma-le-wow/Shutterstock.com; **42**t Everett Collection Inc / Alamy Stock Photo; **42**b "James Oglethorpe Statue Augusta GA" by Sir Mildred Pierce/Flickr/Wikimedia Commons/CC By-SA 2.0; **43** PicturePartners/iStock/Getty Images Plus/Getty Images

Chapter 3

44 Pictures Now / Alamy Stock Photo; **45**t sirichai_asawalapsakul /iStock/Getty Images Plus/Getty Images; **45**b davidcrehner/iStock/Getty Images Plus/Getty Images; **47** From The New York Public Library; **48**t, **50**t, b **55**b, **56**t, b North Wind Picture Archives / Alamy Stock Photo; **48**c Olga Popova/Shutterstock.com; **48**b Mary Evans Library - stock.adobe .com; **49**t Michael Ventura / Alamy Stock Photo; **49**b Antony SOUTER / Alamy Stock Photo; **50**c Larry Keller, Lititz Pa./Moment/Getty Images; **51**t Richard Ellis / Alamy Stock Photo; **51**b Eight Arts Photography / Alamy Stock Photo; **52** CreativeHQ/Shutterstock.com; **54** Chronicle / Alamy Stock Photo; **55**t AC6 E£452 663m, Houghton Library, Harvard University/Wikimedia Commons/Public Domain; **57** SeanXu/iStock Editorial/Getty Images Plus/Getty Images; **58**t BDphoto/iStock Unreleased/Getty Images; **58**c David Stuckel / Alamy Stock Photo; **58**bl Michele and Tom Grimm / Alamy Stock Photo; **58**bc, br scottbeard /iStock/Getty Images Plus/Getty Images; **59** *The Colonial Williamsburg Foundation;* **60** FCIT; **61** EntropyWorkshop/iStock/Getty Images Plus /Getty Images

Chapter 4

62, 65b, **71, 73**b, **77, 79**l, **80, 81**t, **83** North Wind Picture Archives / Alamy Stock Photo; **63**t agefotostock / Alamy Stock Photo; **63**b "The Copley Family" by John Singleton Copley/Wikimedia Commons /Public Domain; **64**t Bob Pool/Shutterstock.com; **64**b Dave Fimbres Photography/Moment/Getty Images; **65**t BlackAperture/iStock/Getty Images Plus/Getty Images; **66**l David Forbert / SuperStock; **66**r–**67**cl World History Archive / Alamy Stock Photo; **67**t, **69**b Irene Abdou / Alamy Stock Photo; **67**cr Felix Lipov/Shutterstock.com; **67**bl "Easy chair MET DT275022"/Metropolitan Museum of Art/Wikimedia Commons /Public Domain; **67**br "Dressing Table MET DT3772"/Metropolitan Museum of Art/Wikimedia Commons/Public Domain; **68**t Andrey Zhuravlev/iStock/Getty Images Plus/Getty Images; **68**b "Artist and His Family" by James Peale/Wikimedia Commons/Public Domain; **69**t Granger, NYC; **70**t Emanuel Tanjala / Alamy Stock Photo; **70**b "Portrait of John and Elizabeth Lloyd Cadwalader and their Daughter Anne" /Wikimedia Commons/Public Domain; **72**t Bettmann/Getty Images; **72**b BJU Photo Services; **73**t Library of Congress, LC-USZ62-53676; **74**t HUD 2818.75.45A, olvwork406678. Harvard University Archives.; **74**b Lebrecht Music & Arts / Alamy Stock Photo; **75**t JLGutierrez/iStock/Getty Images Plus/Getty Images; **75**c whitemay/DigitalVision Vectors/Getty Images; **75**b Joshua Moore/iStock/Getty Images Plus/Getty Images; **76** The Picture Art Collection / Alamy Stock Photo; **78**t LEE SNIDER PHOTO IMAGES/Shutterstock.com; **78**b Gene Myers/500px Plus/Getty Images; **79**r CandyBoxImages/iStock/Getty Images Plus/Getty Images; **81**b Gado Images / Alamy Stock Photo; **82** "David Brainerd on horseback" /Wikimedia Commons/Public Domain; **84** KenWiedemann/iStock/Getty Images Plus/Getty Images; **85**l John Parrot / Media Bakery; **85**r John Parrot/Stocktrek Images/Getty Images

Chapter 5

86 World History Archive / Alamy Stock Photo; **88**t Davel5957/E+/Getty Images; **88**b Jeffrey M. Frank/Shutterstock.com; **88**i GL Archive / Alamy Stock Photo; **89**t ruceStanfield/iStock/Getty Images Plus/Getty Images; **89**b, **95**t, b, **97, 100, 102, 103**b North Wind Picture Archives / Alamy Stock Photo; **90**t Archive Images / Alamy Stock Photo; **90**c Zeeking /iStock/Getty Images Plus/Getty Images; **90**b Library and Archives Canada/C-139911; **91** Nick Higham / Alamy Stock Photo; **92, 93** The Picture Art Collection / Alamy Stock Photo;

94–95bg, **103**t Science History Images / Alamy Stock Photo; **94**t mescioglu/iStock/Getty Images Plus/Getty Images; **94**b *The Colonial Williamsburg Foundation. Museum Purchase;* **96**tl "King George III in coronation robes" by Allan Ramsay/Wikimedia Commons/Public Domain; **96**tr IanDagnall Computing / Alamy Stock Photo; **96**bl Picture Partners/Shutterstock.com; **96**br Artokoloro / Alamy Stock Photo; **98** pixs4u/Shutterstock.com; **101**t "Portrait of John Locke" by Godfrey Kneller/Wikimedia Commons/Public Domain; **101**b Granger, NYC; **105** Christian Delbert/Shutterstock.com

Chapter 6

108 The History Emporium / Alamy Stock Photo; **109, 125**r Heritage Image Partnership Ltd / Alamy Stock Photo; **110**t © Bratty1206 | Dreamstime.com; **110**b "Battle of Bunker Hill" by Howard Pyle /Wikimedia Commons/Public Domain; **111** SuperStock / SuperStock; **113, 127** Everett Collection/Shutterstock.com; **114**l Archive Images / Alamy Stock Photo; **114**tr, **123**l The Picture Art Collection / Alamy Stock Photo; **114**br IanDagnall Computing / Alamy Stock Photo; **115** "Declaration of Independence" by John Trumbull/Wikimedia Commons/Public Domain; **116** Everett Collection / SuperStock; **118**t "WilliamHowe1777ColorMezzotint"/Wikimedia Commons/Public Domain; **118**c, **122**tl GL Archive / Alamy Stock Photo; **118**b John Parrot /Stocktrek Images/Getty Images; **119**t aimintang/iStock/Getty Images Plus/Getty Images; **119**b, **120**t, b, **121**b, **122**tr North Wind Picture Archives / Alamy Stock Photo; **121**t "Portrait of the Mohawk Chieftain Thayendanegea, known as Joseph Brant (1742–1807)" by Gilbert Stuart /Wikimedia Commons/Public Domain; **122**b gsheldon/iStock Editorial /Getty Images Plus/Getty Images; **123**r DEA PICTURE LIBRARY /De Agostini/Getty Images; **124–25**l The Metropolitan Museum of Art, New York; Brooklyn Museum Costume Collection at The Metropolitan Museum of Art, Gift of the Brooklyn Museum, 2009; Gift of Celeste H. Chasmer, 1922/CC0 1.0; **126** "Surrender of Lord Cornwallis" by John Trumbull/Wikimedia Commons/Public Domain; **128** Cameron Davidson/Photodisc/Getty Images; **129** Dennis W Donohue/Shutterstock.com

Chapter 7

130, 139, 141b GraphicaArtis/Archive Photos/Getty Images; **132–33, 135**t North Wind Picture Archives / Alamy Stock Photo; **134**t "US -Colonial (NJ-179)-New Jersey-25 Mar 1776 OBV" by Godot13/National Numismatic Collection at the Smithsonian Institution/Wikimedia Commons/CC By-SA 3.0; **134**c "US-Colonial (NH-179)-New Hampshire -29 Apr 1780 OBV" by Godot13/National Numismatic Collection at the Smithsonian Institution/Wikimedia Commons/CC By-SA 3.0; **134**bl "US-Colonial (MD-55)-Maryland-1 Mar 1770 OBV" by Godot13 /National Numismatic Collection at the Smithsonian Institution /Wikimedia Commons/CC By-SA 3.0; **134**br–**35**b The Picture Art Collection / Alamy Stock Photo; **136, 166**r–**67** Bettmann/Getty Images; **137** f11photo/Shutterstock.com; **138**t "James Madison" by John Vanderlyn /Wikimedia Commons/Public Domain; **138**b "Portrait of Alexander Hamilton" by John Trumbull/Wikimedia Commons/Public Domain; **141**t Morphart Creation/Shutterstock.com; **143** Fotosearch/Archive Photos/Getty Images; **144** Library of Congress, LC-DIG-highsm-15714; **145**t nazlisart/iStock/Getty Images Plus/Getty Images; **145**b, **158–59** © iStock.com/CastaldoStudio; **147** © iStockphoto.com/Olga Bogatyrenko; **152** © iStockphoto.com/Cristina Ciochina; **154** Mike Kline (notkalvin) /Moment/Getty Images; **156–57** Anton Tokarev/iStock/Getty Images Plus/Getty Images; **162** Gado Images / Alamy Stock Photo; **163** Everett Collection Inc / Alamy Stock Photo; **166**l Hulton Archive/Getty Images

Chapter 8

168, 169 SuperStock / SuperStock; **170, 656** "George Washington" by Gilbert Stuart/Wikipedia/Public Domain; **171**bg "First national bank US HABS" by Jack Boucher/Library of Congress/Wikimedia Commons /Public Domain; **171** Gary Whitton/Shutterstock.com; **172** © Andreykr | Dreamstime.com; **173**t The Metropolitan Museum of Art, New York; Gift of Edgar William and Bernice Chrysler Garbisch, 1963; **173**b Courtesy National Gallery of Art, Washington; **174, 176, 178, 188** Granger, NYC; **175**t @Painet Inc. / Alamy Stock Photo; **175**b The Picture Art Collection / Alamy Stock Photo; **177** whitemay/DigitalVision Vectors/Getty Images; **179** JacobH/iStock/Getty Images Plus/Getty Images; **179**i National Portrait Gallery, Smithsonian Institution; **180**t gregobagel/iStock/Getty Images Plus/Getty Images; **180**b, **656** John Parrot/Stocktrek Images/Getty Images; **181**t Library of Congress /Geography and Map Division; **181**b microstocker/iStock/Getty Images Plus/Getty Images; **182** Mega Pixel/Shutterstock.com; **183** © Joe Sohm | Dreamstime.com; **184**t Classic Collection 2 / Alamy Stock Photo; **184**b Everett Collection/Shutterstock.com; **187** CNMages / Alamy Stock Photo; **189** Morphart Creation/Shutterstock.com

Chapter 9

192 Pictorial Press Ltd / Alamy Stock Photo; **193, 656** John Parrot /Stocktrek Images/Getty Images; **194** DNY59/iStock Unreleased /Getty Images; **195** "KN-10849" by Photograph Curator/Flickr/Public Domain; **197**t, b Ian Dagnall / Alamy Stock Photo; **198** Pictures Now / Alamy Stock Photo; **198**i Ewa Studio/Shutterstock.com; **199** John Hoffman/Shutterstock.com; **200**t INTERFOTO / Alamy Stock Photo; **200**b The Mariners' Museum and Park, Chesapeake and the Leopard, 1940.0705.000001; **201, 656** "4 James Madison"/GPA Photo Archive /Flickr/Public Domain; **202**t, **205** North Wind Picture Archives / Alamy Stock Photo; **202**b Library of Congress, LC-USZC4-782; **203** Everett Collection/Shutterstock.com; **204** "120824-N-SH953-451" by Kathryn Macdonald/Flickr/Public Domain; **206**t "Fort McHenry flag" by George Henry Preble/Wikipedia/Public Domain; **206**b–**7**b "The Battle of New Orleans" by Edward Percy Moran/Library of Congress/Wikimedia Commons/Public Domain; **207**t Smithsonian American Art Museum /Public Domain; **208** IanDagnall Computing / Alamy Stock Photo; **209, 656** "Portrait of James Monroe" by Samuel Morse/Wikimedia Commons /Public Domain; **212** BJU Photo Services; **213**t Baka Sobaka/Shutterstock .com; **213**b Svetocheck/Shutterstock.com; **214** Kenneth Graff/Shutterstock .com; **215** Tom Bean / Alamy Stock Photo

Chapter 10

216 Everett Collection Inc / Alamy Stock Photo; **217**t SBS Eclectic Images / Alamy Stock Photo; **217**ct "John Quincy Adams" by Gilbert Stuart /Wikimedia Commons/Public Domain; **217**cb, **224, 237, 238, 656, 657** National Portrait Gallery, Smithsonian Institution; **217**b Andia / Alamy Stock Photo; **218, 220**r, **223**t, **227**b, **228**r–**29, 231**b North Wind Picture Archives / Alamy Stock Photo; **219**t, **656** "John Quincy Adams" by George Peter Alexander Healy/Wikimedia Commons/Public Domain; **219**b The History Collection / Alamy Stock Photo; **220**l Mauro Toccaceli / Alamy Stock Photo; **221**t, **656** John Parrot/Stocktrek Images/Getty Images; **221**b The Picture Art Collection / Alamy Stock Photo; **222**t Library of Congress, LC-DIG-ppmsca-50970; **222**b PRISMA ARCHIVO / Alamy Stock Photo; **223**b Granger, NYC; **225** Kenneth S Presley /Shutterstock.com; **226**t, **227**t Glasshouse Images / Alamy Stock Photo; **226**b SuperStock / SuperStock; **228**l Colin Waters / Alamy Stock Photo; **230** Sean Pavone/Shutterstock.com; **231**t "John C. Calhoun" by George Peter Alexander Healy/Wikimedia Commons/Public Domain; **232**t Philadelphia History Museum at the Atwater Kent/Courtesy of Historical Society of Pennsylvania Collection/Bridgeman Images; **232**b Collection of the New-York Historical Society, USA/Bridgeman Images; **234**t Age Fotostock/Walter Bibikow/Media Bakery; **234**bl, br Mark_Kostich /Shutterstock.com; **235** Bettmann/Getty Images; **236, 656** "8 Martin Van Buren"/GPA Photo Archive/Flickr/Public Domain

Chapter 11

240, 248b, **254**b, **261**b North Wind Picture Archives / Alamy Stock Photo; **241** 400tmax/iStock/Getty Images Plus/Getty Images; **242** NMUIM / Alamy Stock Photo; **243, 245**t, **260**t Granger, NYC; **245**b Chronicle / Alamy Stock Photo; **246**t Vintage Images / Alamy Stock Photo; **246**b ATUStudio/iStock/Getty Images Plus/Getty Images; **247** Irina Velikanova/iStock/Getty Images Plus/Getty Images; **248**t Alpha Historica / Alamy Stock Photo; **248**c, **253**t Division of Work and Industry, National Museum of American History, Smithsonian Institution; **249**t The Metropolitan Museum of Art, New York; The Edward W. C. Arnold Collection of New York Prints, Maps and Pictures, Bequest of Edward W. C. Arnold, 1954; **249**b Classic Image / Alamy Stock Photo; **250**t "Slater Mill Historic Site - Pawtucket, Rhode Island" by Doug Kerr/Flickr/CC By-SA 2.0; **250**b–**51**b Library of Congress, LC-DIG -pga-03157; **251**t meinzahn/123RF; **251**c Photos.com/Getty Images Plus /Getty Images; **252** "Ten Hour Day circular 1835"/National Archives /Wikimedia Commons/Public Domain; **253**b The Print Collector / Alamy Stock Photo; **254**t Rafael Goes/iStock/Getty Images Plus/Getty Images; **256**t likxi/iStock/Getty Images Plus/Getty Images;

256ct "Punch Bowl LACMA M.77.41.2 (1 of 2)"/Los Angeles County Museum of Art/Wikimedia Commons/Public Domain; **256**cb FORGEM /iStock/Getty Images Plus/Getty Images; **256**bl The Metropolitan Museum of Art, New York; Rogers Fund and funds from various donors, 1986; **256**br–**57**b R.Babakin/Bigstock.com; **257**i Hatchapong Palurtchaivong /Shutterstock.com; **257**t Nenov/Moment/Getty Images; **258** "Flickr - …trialsanderrors - The realistic jungle menagerie, circus poster for Barnum ^ Bailey, 1897"/Library of Congress/Wikimedia Commons /Public Domain; **259**t Historic Images / Alamy Stock Photo; **259**b "Asahel Nettleton"/Wikimedia Commons/Public Domain; **260**b Zip Lexing / Alamy Stock Photo; **261**t Science History Images / Alamy Stock Photo; **262**t Everett Collection/Shutterstock.com; **262**b National Portrait Gallery, Smithsonian Institution

Chapter 12

264, 274b Heritage Image Partnership Ltd / Alamy Stock Photo; **265, 276**t, **276**b–**77**b North Wind Picture Archives / Alamy Stock Photo; **266** Niday Picture Library / Alamy Stock Photo; **267** The Picture Art Collection / Alamy Stock Photo; **268**t Courtesy of Texas State Library & Archives Commission; **268**b Alpha Stock / Alamy Stock Photo; **269**t © iStockphoto.com/AugustineChang; **269**b, **278**b MPI/Archive Photos /Getty Images; **270**t, **272**b Album / Alamy Stock Photo; **270**b Art Collection 2 / Alamy Stock Photo; **271**t, **284**b, **657** National Portrait Gallery, Smithsonian Institution; **271**b P A Thompson/The Image Bank /Getty Images; **272**t, **279**t zrfphoto/iStock/Getty Images Plus/Getty Images; **273**t DoroO/iStock/Getty Images Plus/Getty Images; **273**b, **286**b Universal Images Group North America LLC / Alamy Stock Photo; **274**t WDC Photos / Alamy Stock Photo; **274**c "Winfield Scott - National Portrait Gallery"/Wikimedia Commons/Public Domain; **275**t "Nicholas Philip Trist"/NYPL/Wikimedia Commons/Public Domain; **275**b "Treaty of Guadalupe Hidalgo, last page"/Library of Congress/Wikimedia Commons/Public Domain; **277**t Zack Frank/Shutterstock.com; **278**t "Fort Astoria"/Clatsop County Historical Society/Flickr; **278**c RobertWaltman/iStock/Getty Images Plus/Getty Images; **279**bl Richard Cummins / Alamy Stock Photo; **279**br "How Marcus Whitman Saved Oregon scan p. 119"/Wikimedia Commons/Public Domain; **280** TimothyOLeary/iStock/Getty Images Plus/Getty Images; **281**t Alpha Historica / Alamy Stock Photo; **281**b Alan King engraving / Alamy Stock Photo; **283**t Historic Collection / Alamy Stock Photo; **283**b Library of Congress, Rare Book and Special Collections Division; **284**t Science History Images / Alamy Stock Photo; **284**c Library of Congress, LC-DIG-ppmsc-02669; **285, 657** "Millard Fillmore-Edit1"/Library of Congress/Wikipedia/Public Domain; **286**t, **657** "Franklin Pierce" by George Peter Alexander Healy/Wikimedia Commons/Public Domain

Chapter 13

290 Niday Picture Library / Alamy Stock Photo; **291, 292**t, **294, 299**b, **301**t, **303** North Wind Picture Archives / Alamy Stock Photo; **292**b sodesignby/Shutterstock.com; **293** aristotoo/iStock/Getty Images Plus /Getty Images; **295** Library of Congress, LC-B8171-152-A; **296** Leemage /Corbis Historical/Getty Images; **297**t, **304**b Bettmann/Getty Images; **297**ct Album / Alamy Stock Photo; **297**cb Pictorial Press Ltd / Alamy Stock Photo; **297**b Alpha Historica / Alamy Stock Photo; **298**l MPI /Archive Photos/Getty Images; **298**r "Horace Greeley"/National Archives /Wikimedia Commons; **299**t From The New York Public Library; **300** Library of Congress, LC-DIG-cwpbh-02529; **301**b Library of Congress; **302**t "Harriet Beecher Stowe" by Alanson Fisher/Wikimedia Commons /Public Domain; **302**bl "UncleTomsCabinCover" by Hammatt Billings /Wikimedia Commons/Public Domain; **302**br Corbis Historical /Getty Images; **304**t, **657** "Portrait of James Buchanan detail" by George Peter Alexander Healy/Wikimedia Commons/Public Domain; **305**l Library of Congress, LC-USZ62-107588; **305**r Dennis MacDonald / Alamy Stock Photo; **305**i The Picture Art Collection / Alamy Stock Photo; **306**t Pictures Now / Alamy Stock Photo; **306**b Matt Anderson /iStock/Getty Images Plus/Getty Images; **307**t Library of Congress, LC-DIG-ppmsca-07773; **307**b Ivy Close Images / Alamy Stock Photo; **308**t "Stephen Arnold Douglas"/Brady-Handy Photograph Collection /Wikimedia Commons/Public Domain; **308**ct "John C Breckinridge -04775-restored"/Brady-Handy Photograph Collection/Wikimedia Commons/Public Domain; **308**cb "Abraham Lincoln O-27 by Hesler, 1860-crop" by Alexander Hessler/Library of Congress/Wikimedia Commons/Public Domain; **308**b Library of Congress, LC-DIG -cwpbh-02532; **309, 657** "Abraham Lincoln" by Alexander Gardner /Wikimedia Commons/Public Domain; **310**t The Color Archives / Alamy Stock Photo; **310**c "President-Jefferson-Davis" by Mathew Brady /Wikimedia Commons/Public Domain; **310**b "AlexanderStephens" by Mathew Brady/Wikimedia Commons/Public Domain; **311**t Library of Congress, LC-USZC2-2353; **311**b PRISMA ARCHIVO / Alamy Stock Photo; **312** Chronicle / Alamy Stock Photo

Chapter 14

316, 325t, **339** John Parrot/Stocktrek Images/Getty Images; **317** The Protected Art Archive / Alamy Stock Photo; **318** (poster), **319** (poster) Provided by BACM; **318–19** (rifle) INTERFOTO / Alamy Stock Photo; **320**t Library of Congress, LC-DIG-ppmsca-31700; **320**b Courtesy of the South Carolina Confederate Museum and Library of Confederate History/BJU Photo Services; **321**t duncan1890/DigitalVision Vectors /Getty Images; **321**b Library of Congress, LC-DIG-ppmsca-08270; **321**i glathrem/Bigstock.com; **322**t Library of Congress, LC-DIG-ppmsca-31277; **322**ct NH 58769 courtesy of the Naval History & Heritage Command; **322**cb Richard Cummins / Alamy Stock Photo; **322**b "Col. Michael Corcoran and staff of nine" by Mathew Brady/National Archives /Wikimedia Commons/Public Domain; **322** (camera) Stan Tess / Alamy Stock Photo; **323** "Scott-anaconda"/Library of Congress/Wikimedia Commons/Public Domain; **324**t National Archives and Records Administration; **324**b Library of Congress, LC-USZC2-1784; **325**c "George B. McClellan - retouched" by Mathew Brady/Wikimedia Commons/Public Domain; **325**b Library of Congress, LC-DIG-cwpb-04402; **326**t Library of Congress, LC-DIG-cwpb-07546; **326**b "Antietam-Bridge -Gardner"/Library of Congress/Wikimedia Commons/Public Domain; **328**t Tracy Burroughs Brown/Shutterstock.com; **328**c "Grant, Lt. Gen. Ulysses S.; three-quarter-length, standing" by Mathew Brady/National Archives/Wikimedia Commons/Public Domain; **328**b Photos.com/Getty Images; **329**t Photo 12 / Alamy Stock Photo; **329**b "Admiral Farragut2" /Library of Congress/Wikimedia Commons/Public Domain; **331**t "Ambrose Everett Burnside" by Mathew Brady/Library of Congress /Public Domain; **331**b Universal Images Group North America LLC / Alamy Stock Photo; **332**t aimintang/iStock/Getty Images Plus/Getty Images; **332**c Library of Congress, LC-DIG-ppmsca-32922; **332**b, **342** Niday Picture Library / Alamy Stock Photo; **333** Library of Congress, Manuscript Division, Abraham Lincoln Papers.; **334** Granger, NYC; **335**t "William Harvey Carney c1864"/Wikimedia Commons/Public Domain; **335**b North Wind Picture Archives / Alamy Stock Photo; **336–37**b eurobanks/iStock/Getty Images Plus/Getty Images; **337**t Keith Lance/DigitalVision Vectors/Getty Images; **338** agefotostock / Alamy Stock Photo; **340** Keith Lance/DigitalVision Vectors/Getty Images; **341**t ClassicStock / Alamy Stock Photo; **341**b Jon Marc Lyttle/Shutterstock .com; **343** Library of Congress, LC-DIG-highsm-04710

Chapter 15

344 Library of Congress, LC-DIG-cwpb-03049; **345** BJU Photo Services; **346** Library of Congress, LC-DIG-cwpb-02888; **347** Historical/Corbis Historical/Getty Images; **348**, 657 Library of Congress, LC-USZ62-13017; **349, 360**t Everett Collection/Shutterstock .com; **350**t "Alaska Purchase (hi-res)"/Wikimedia Commons/Public Domain; **350**b, **351** Granger, NYC; **352**t, c Library of Congress, LC-USZ62-131563; **352**b Pictorial Press Ltd / Alamy Stock Photo; **353** "Robert Smalls - Brady-Handy"/Library of Congress/Wikimedia Commons/Public Domain; **354**t "Carpetbagger" by Thomas Nast /Wikimedia Commons/Public Domain; **354**b Brooklyn Museum Costume Collection at The Metropolitan Museum of Art, Gift of the Brooklyn Museum, 2009; Gift of Mae Schenck, 1963; **355** Library of Congress, LC-USZ62-106849; **356**t, **657** "Ulysses Grant 1870-1880" /Library of Congress/Wikimedia Commons/Public Domain; **356**b Library of Congress, LC-DIG-ppmsca-37947; **357, 363** Bettmann /Getty Images; **358**t "Joseph Rainey - Brady-Handy"/Library of Congress/Wikipedia/Public Domain; **358**c "Hiram Rhodes Revels Brady-Handy2" by Mathew Brady/Library of Congress/Wikimedia Commons/Public Domain; **358**b, **657** "President Rutherford Hayes 1870 - 1880"/Library of Congress/Wikimedia Commons; **359** National Portrait Gallery, Smithsonian Institution; **360**b–**61** "City of Columbus, Georgia (Harper's Weekly Magazine, 1868)" by Raymond Dukes/Flickr /CC By 2.0; **362** North Wind Picture Archives / Alamy Stock Photo; **364** Library of Congress, LC-USZ62-107719

Chapter 16

368 Photo 12 / Alamy Stock Photo; **370**tl, **657** "James Abram Garfield, photo portrait seated"/Library of Congress/Public Domain; **370**tr, **384, 385**b North Wind Picture Archives / Alamy Stock Photo; **370**b, **371**t, **372**t, **379**c, **657, 658** Everett Collection/Shutterstock.com; **371**c, **379**b, **658** World History Archive / Alamy Stock Photo; **371**b Malcolm Fairman / Alamy Stock Photo; **372**b "Immigrant Family in the Baggage Room of Ellis Island" by Lewis W. Hine/The Museum of Fine Arts, Houston /Wikimedia Commons/Public Domain; **373, 375**t Hi-Story / Alamy Stock Photo; **374**t bauhaus1000/DigitalVision Vectors/Getty Images; **374**b Corbis Historical/Getty Images; **375**b CPA Media Pte Ltd / Alamy Stock Photo; **376** Felix Lipov/Shutterstock.com; **377**t Bettmann/Getty Images; **377**b "East west shaking hands by russell" by Andrew J. Russell /Wikimedia Commons/Public Domain; **379**tl Album / Alamy Stock Photo; **379**tr Photos.com/Getty Images; **380** Library of Congress, LC-USZ62-120152; **381** Zuri Swimmer / Alamy Stock Photo; **382** Keith Lance/DigitalVision Vectors/Getty Images; **383** "Mulberry St., New York, N.Y." by Detroit Publishing Co./Library of Congress/Public Domain; **385**t Library of Congress, LC-USZC4-2835; **386**t Stock Montage/Archive Photos/Getty Images; **386**b Imago History Collection / Alamy Stock Photo; **387** Chicago History Museum / Alamy Stock Photo

Chapter 17

388 Science History Images / Alamy Stock Photo; **389, 390**t, **396, 402**b North Wind Picture Archives / Alamy Stock Photo; **390**b, **406**tl Everett Collection/Shutterstock.com; **391, 409**l Everett Collection Inc / Alamy Stock Photo; **392**t Brigitte MERLE/Photononstop/Getty Images; **392**b "US-$5-LT-1862-Fr-61a" by Godot13/Wikimedia Commons/Public Domain; **393** Joseph Sohm-Visions of America/Stockbyte/Getty Images; **393**i CLP Media/Shutterstock.com; **394** John Elk III / Alamy Stock Photo; **397** Allexxandar/iStock/Getty Images Plus/Getty Images; **399** Vintage Images / Alamy Stock Photo; **400**t Victorian Traditions/Shutterstock.com; **400**b "Chrisman sisters" by Solomon Butcher/Wikimedia Commons /Public Domain; **401** © iStockphoto.com/Gary Alvis; **402**t–**3**t nang nang /Shutterstock.com; **403**b Chicago History Museum / Alamy Stock Photo; **404**l PictureLux / The Hollywood Archive / Alamy Stock Photo; **404**tr "Jesse james portrait"/Library of Congress/Wikimedia Commons/Public Domain; **404**br Library of Congress, LC-USZ62-38208; **405**t History and Art Collection / Alamy Stock Photo; **405**b Historic Collection / Alamy Stock Photo; **406**tr IanDagnall Computing / Alamy Stock Photo; **406**b Atomic / Alamy Stock Photo; **407** Bettmann/Getty Images; **408**t Library of Congress/Corbis Historical/Getty Images; **408**b National Archives and Record Administration; **409**r Library of Congress, LC-USZ62-122859; **411** Library of Congress, LC-USZC4-12466

Chapter 18

412 Science History Images / Alamy Stock Photo; **413** History and Art Collection / Alamy Stock Photo; **414**tl McKinley Presidential Library & Museum, Canton, Ohio.; **414**tr Kean Collection/Archive Photos/Getty Images; **414**b, **658** "Mckinley"/Library of Congress/Wikimedia Commons/Public Domain; **416**t Alpha Historica / Alamy Stock Photo; **416**b, **427**b Granger, NYC; **418**l Bettmann/Getty Images; **418**r Hulton Archive/Archive Photos/Getty Images; **419** "Yellow Kid 1898-01-09" by Richard F. Outcault/Wikimedia Commons/Public Domain; **420–21**bg GL Archive / Alamy Stock Photo; **420, 425, 432** Everett Historical /Shutterstock.com; **421** Public Domain; **422** Courtesy Frederic Remington Art Museum, Ogdensburg, New York, Image altered by BJU Press; **423** BILLPERRY/Bigstock.com; **426**t Aleksej Starostin/Shutterstock.com; **426**b PR Archive / Alamy Stock Photo; **427**t, **658** "President Roosevelt - Pach Bros"/Library of Congress/Wikimedia Commons/Public Domain; **428** elmvilla/iStock/Getty Images Plus/Getty Images; **429**t iStockphoto /Thinkstock; **429**bl INTERFOTO / Alamy Stock Photo; **429**br Glasshouse Images / Alamy Stock Photo; **430**t "KCRC China spheres of influence" by Mosr/Wikimedia Commons/CC By-SA 3.0/Map Resources; **430**b Album / Alamy Stock Photo; **431**t Everett Collection Inc / Alamy Stock Photo; **431**b David Monette / Alamy Stock Photo; **433** "Maine unkown" /Wikimedia Commons/Public Domain

Chapter 19

434, 441i Everett Collection/Shutterstock.com; **435** ilbusca/iStock/Getty Images Plus/Getty Images; **436**t "Booker T Washington by Frances B Johnston, c1895"/Library of Congress/Wikimedia Commons/Public Domain; **436**b Jim West / Alamy Stock Photo; **437**t Corbis Historical /Getty Images; **437**b Floortje/E+/Getty Images; **438**t Library of Congress, LC-DIG-ppmsca-19488; **438**b "Mark Twain by AF Bradley"/Wikimedia Commons/Public Domain; **439, 450**b Science History Images / Alamy Stock Photo; **440**t Image Source/Getty Images; **440**b Derek Croucher / Alamy Stock Photo; **441** Chicago History Museum/Archive Photos/Getty Images; **442**t, **449**bl Chronicle / Alamy Stock Photo; **442**b Library of Congress, LC-DIG-det-4a11789; **443, 452**b Bettmann/Getty Images; **444–45**bg, **444** Heritage Image Partnership Ltd / Alamy Stock Photo; **445**t, **449**br North Wind Picture Archives / Alamy Stock Photo; **445**b Library of Congress, LC-USZ62-52642; **446**t Album / Alamy Stock Photo; **446**b George Rinhart/Corbis Historical/Getty Images; **448**t "Coal mining LOC npcc.08267"/National Photo Company Collection/Library of Congress/Wikimedia Commons/Public Domain; **448**b danymages /Shutterstock.com; **449**t "Lewis Hine, Freddie Kafer, 5 or 6 years old, newsboy, Sacramento, California, 1915" by Lewis Hine/Library of Congress/Wikimedia Commons/Public Domain; **450**t Photography by Deb Snelson/Moment/Getty Images; **451, 658** Library of Congress, LC -DIG-hec-15153; **452**t Everett Collection Inc / Alamy Stock Photo; **454**t Library of Congress, LC-DIG-ggbain-11342; **454**b, **658** Archive Pics / Alamy Stock Photo; **456**t "Francisco "Pancho" Villa (restorated)"/Bain News Service/Library of Congress/Wikimedia Commons/Public Domain; **456**b Paul Thompson/Hulton Archive/Getty Images

Chapter 20

460, 464t GL Archive / Alamy Stock Photo; **461, 476**t Chronicle / Alamy Stock Photo; **462** ullstein bild Dtl./Getty Images; **464**c Sabena Jane Blackbird / Alamy Stock Photo; **464**b "Tanks passing dead Germans"/National Library of Scotland/Flickr/No Restrictions; **465** John Parrot / Media Bakery; **466–67**bg, **481** John Parrot/Stocktrek Images/Getty Images; **466** Library of Congress, LC-USZC4-13223; **467** Jay Robert Nash Collection/CRIA.com; **468** National Archives and Records Administration; **469**t, **470**b Science History Images / Alamy Stock Photo; **469**b Library of Congress, LC-DIG-hec-08103; **470**t "Feed a Fighter"/Flickr/No Restrictions; **471**t Everett Collection/Shutterstock .com; **471**b Library of Congress, LC-USZC4-8890; **472**t, **479**t Stock Montage/Archive Photos/Getty Images; **472**b Library of Congress, LC -USZC4-8050; **473**t Paul Thompson/FPG/Archive Photos/Getty Images; **473**b "369th 15th New York"/National Archives/Wikimedia Commons/Public Domain; **474**t Album / Alamy Stock Photo; **474**b "US23rdInfantry37mmGunInActionFrance1918-ARC531005"/National Archives and Records Administration/Wikimedia Commons/Public Domain; **475** Hum Images / Alamy Stock Photo; **476**b Vintage_Space / Alamy Stock Photo; **478** Library of Congress, LC-DIG-ggbain-29038; **479**b Bettmann/Getty Images

Chapter 21

482 Library of Congress; **483** Sheridan Libraries/Levy/Gado/Archive Photos/Getty Images; **484**t, b New York Daily News Archive/New York Daily News/Getty Images; **485, 490**b Kirn Vintage Stock/Corbis Historical/Getty Images; **486** Library of Congress, LC-DIG-det-4a27901; **487**t INTERFOTO / Alamy Stock Photo; **487**c "First flight2" by John T. Daniels/Library of Congress/Wikipedia/Public Domain; **487**b, **493**c, b Science History Images / Alamy Stock Photo; **488**t, **494, 498, 658** Everett Collection/Shutterstock.com; **488**b LockieCurrie/E+/Getty Images; **489** Shawshots / Alamy Stock Photo; **490**t "First-nighters posing for the camera outside the Warners' Theater before the premiere of "Don Juan" with John Barrymore, - NARA - 535750"/Wikimedia Commons /Public Domain; **491**t Trinity Mirror / Mirrorpix / Alamy Stock Photo; **491**b Niday Picture Library / Alamy Stock Photo; **492** GL Archive / Alamy Stock Photo; **493**t Pictorial Press Ltd / Alamy Stock Photo; **495** Granger, NYC; **496**t Library of Congress, LC-USZ62-114986; **496**b, **497**b Bettmann/Getty Images; **497**t, **658** "29 Warren G. Harding"/GPA Photo Archive/Flickr/Public Domain; **499** Vintage_Space / Alamy Stock Photo

Chapter 22

500 Everett Collection Inc / Alamy Stock Photo; **501**t, **504–5, 515**t, **658** World History Archive / Alamy Stock Photo; **501**b, **510**t, **513**t Everett Collection Historical / Alamy Stock Photo; **502** Science History Images / Alamy Stock Photo; **503** Sueddeutsche Zeitung Photo / Alamy Stock Photo; **506** RBM Vintage Images / Alamy Stock Photo; **507**t Tupungato /Shutterstock.com; **507**b Juanmonino/iStock Unreleased/Getty Images; **508**t, b Everett Collection/Shutterstock.com; **509, 658** "FDR 1944 Color Portrait" by Leon A. Perskie/Flickr/Wikimedia Commons/CC By 2.0;

510b D. Hurst / Alamy Stock Photo; **511**t From Original Negative / Alamy Stock Photo; **511**b William S. Kuta / Alamy Stock Photo; **512** Library of Congress/Corbis Historical/Getty Images; **513**b "CCC Camp BR-24 Belle Fourche Project, Homedale, Idaho, Crew placing a lateral drop, Homedale, Idaho - NARA - 293521"/National Archives and Records Administration/Wikimedia Commons/Public Domain; **514**t "1935 - Powerhouse construction worker (9134564317)" by TVA Web Team/Flickr/Wikimedia Commons/CC By 2.0; **514**b New York Times Co./Archive Photos/Getty Images; **515**b Library of Congress, LC-DIG-hec-24268; **516**t Hulton Archive/Archive Photos/Getty Images; **516**bl, **519** Bettmann/Getty Images; **516**br Mega Pixel/Shutterstock.com; **518**t National Archives and Records Administration; **518**b "18-year old mother from Oklahoma now a California migrant - NARA - 195857" /National Archives and Records Administration/Wikimedia Commons /Public Domain; **521** "To harvest the crops of California thousands of families live literally on wheels, San Joaquin Valley" by Dorothea Lange /Library of Congress/Wikimedia Commons/Public Domain

Chapter 23

522 MGPhoto76 / Alamy Stock Photo; **523, 548**t World History Archive / Alamy Stock Photo; **524**t Popperfoto/Getty Images; **524**b AP Photo; **525**bg, **525** Everett Collection/Shutterstock.com; **526** Chronicle / Alamy Stock Photo; **527**t, **528**t, **529**t, **540**t, **548**b Shawshots / Alamy Stock Photo; **527**b GK History Images / Alamy Stock Photo; **528**b Vintage_Space / Alamy Stock Photo; **529**b De Luan / Alamy Stock Photo; **530** The Print Collector / Alamy Stock Photo; **531**t Hulton Archive/Getty Images; **531**b Everett Collection Inc / Alamy Stock Photo; **532** Kyodo News /Getty Images; **533**tl "Naval photograph documenting the Japanese attack on Pearl Harbor, Hawaii which initiated US participation in World... - NARA - 295977"/National Archives and Records Administration/Wikimedia Commons/Public Domain; **533**tr "Doris Miller"/US Navy/Wikimedia Commons/Public Domain; **533**b Ryan Tishken/Shutterstock.com; **534**t, **539**t, **540**b, **545**t, **549** National Archives; **534**b Science History Images / Alamy Stock Photo; **535**t, **537** Corbis Historical/Getty Images; **535**b Eliot Elisofon/The LIFE Picture Collection/Getty Images; **536**t BJU Photo Services/Courtesy of Tim Keesee; **536**b © Adrianadh | Dreamstime.com; **538** Trinity Mirror / Mirrorpix / Alamy Stock Photo; **539**c "NormandySupply edit" /Wikimedia Commons/Public Domain; **539**b US Signal Corps /The LIFE Picture Collection/Getty Images; **541** Pictorial Press Ltd / Alamy Stock Photo; **542**t "General of the Army Douglas MacArthur" /National Archives and Records Administration/Wikimedia Commons /Public Domain; **542**b "American Prisoners Using Improvised Litters"/National Archives and Records Administration/Wikimedia Commons/Public Domain; **543**t "Army B-25 (Doolittle Raid)"/U.S. Navy/Wikimedia Commons/Public Domain; **543**b Bettmann/Getty Images; **544**t "USS Yorktown (CV-5) is hit by a torpedo on 4 June 1942"/National Archives/Wikimedia Commons/Public Domain; **544**b Alpha Stock / Alamy Stock Photo; **545**b Harry S. Truman Library; **546** "OkinawaMarineCaveDemolition"/NARA/Wikimedia Commons/Public Domain; **547** Ewing Galloway / Alamy Stock Photo

Chapter 24

552 "AS09-20-3064 - Apollo 9 - Apollo 9 Mission image - Scott during EVA"/U.S. National Archives and Records Administration/Wikimedia Commons/Public Domain; **554**t, **555**t ClassicStock / Alamy Stock Photo; **554**b CBS Photo Archive/CBS/Getty Images; **555**b J. R. Eyerman/The LIFE Picture Collection/Getty Images; **556**t National Archives; **556**b, **658** "TRUMAN 58-766-06"/National Archives/Wikimedia Commons /Public Domain; **557** Everett Collection/Shutterstock.com; **558**t Science History Images / Alamy Stock Photo; **558**b, **578**t National Archives and Records Administration; **559** a katz/Shutterstock.com; **560, 578**b SPUTNIK / Alamy Stock Photo; **561** dpa picture alliance / Alamy Stock Photo; **562** "C-47s at Tempelhof Airport Berlin 1948"/U.S. Air Force/Wikipedia/Public Domain; **564**t "Fighting with the 2nd Infantry Division north of the Chongchon River, Sergeant First Class Major Cleveland, weapons squad leader, points out Communist-led North Korean position to his machine gun crew."/National Archives /Wikimedia Commons/Public Domain; **564**b "Invasion of Inchon, Korea. Four LST's unload men and equipment on beach. Three of the LST's shown are LST-611... - NARA - 520772"/U.S. National Archives and Records Administration/Wikimedia Commons/Public Domain; **565**t "Chosin" by Corporal Peter McDonald, USMC/Wikimedia Commons /Public Domain; **565**b "Douglas MacArthur speaking at Soldier Field HD-SN-99-03036"/National Archives/Wikimedia Commons/Public Domain; **566**t, **574** Everett Collection Inc / Alamy Stock Photo; **566**b New York Daily News Archive/New York Daily News/Getty Images; **567**t, **658** GL Archive / Alamy Stock Photo; **567**b "Will Counts Collection: Indiana University Archives"; **568**t Underwood Archives /Archive Photos/Getty Images; **568**bl MaxFX/Shutterstock.com; **568**br Joseph Sohm/Shutterstock.com; **569**t CPA Media Pte Ltd / Alamy Stock Photo; **569**b pzAxe/iStock/Getty Images Plus/Getty Images; **570**t Jerry Cooke/Corbis Historical/Getty Images; **570**b mccool / Alamy Stock Photo; **571**t Photo 12/Universal Images Group/Getty Images; **571**b ullstein bild/Getty Images; **572**t, **659** "John F. Kennedy, White House color photo portrait"/National Archives/Wikimedia Common/Public Domain; **572**bl Stephen Plaster/Shutterstock.com; **572**br Fotyma /Shutterstock.com; **573**t, **576**t Bettmann/Getty Images; **573**b Paul Schutzer/The LIFE Picture Collection/Getty Images; **575** Mariano Garcia / Alamy Stock Photo; **576**c Hal Beral/Corbis/Getty Images; **576**b imageBROKER / Alamy Stock Photo; **577** Three Lions/Hulton Archive /Getty Images; **579**t "Apollo 10 Saturn V immediately after lift-off" /NASA/Wikimedia Commons/Public Domain; **579**c "Aldrin Looks Back at Tranquility Base - GPN-2000-001102" by Neil A. Armstrong /NASA/Wikimedia Commons/Public Domain; **579**b "AS11-44-6552" /NASA/Wikimedia Commons/Public Domain; **580**t "John F. Kennedy motorcade, Dallas crop" by Victor Hugo King/Library of Congress/Public Domain; **580**b Shawshots / Alamy Stock Photo

Chapter 25

582 Mira / Alamy Stock Photo; **583**t "Lyndon Baines Johnson takes Presidential Oath of Office. Jay Gildner, Judge Sarah Hughes, Jack Valenti, Congressman... - NARA - 194235"/U.S. National Archives and Records Administration/Wikimedia Commons/Public Domain; **583**b, **594, 659** World History Archive / Alamy Stock Photo; **584**t John Dominis/The LIFE Picture Collection/Getty Images; **584**b, **586** Hulton Archive/Getty Images; **585**t, **588**t, **598**t, b Bettmann/Getty Images; **585**b Joseph Louw /The LIFE Images Collection/Getty Images; **587** Sovfoto/Universal Images Group/Getty Images; **588**b Quang nguyen vinh/Shutterstock .com; **589**t William L. Rukeyser/Hulton Archive/Getty Images; **589**b CPA Media Pte Ltd / Alamy Stock Photo; **590**t tim page/Corbis Historical /Getty Images; **590**b "James DanielChappie"/U.S. Air Force/Wikipedia /Public Domain; **591**t Julian Wasser/The LIFE Images Collection/Getty Images; **591**b, **659** "Richard M. Nixon, ca. 1935 - 1982"/U.S. National Archives and Records Administration/Wikimedia Commons/Public Domain; **592** Howard Ruffner/Archive Photos/Getty Images; **593**t, **605**t David Hume Kennerly/Hulton Archive/Getty Images; **593**b Terry Fincher/Hulton Archive/Getty Images; **595, 607** Wally McNamee/Corbis Historical/Getty Images; **596** ClassicStock / Alamy Stock Photo; **597**t Michael J. Cohen, Photographer/Moment/Getty Images; **597**bl Joe McDonald/The Image Bank/Getty Images; **597**br fotoguy22/iStock /Getty Images Plus/Getty Images; **599**t BrianPIrwin/iStock Editorial /Getty Images Plus/Getty Images; **599**b RBM Vintage Images / Alamy Stock Photo; **600**t, **659** "Gerald Ford presidential portrait (cropped)" by David Hume Kennerly/Wikimedia Commons/Public Domain; **600**b dpa picture alliance / Alamy Stock Photo; **601**t Bill Pierce/The LIFE Images Collection/Getty Images; **601**b "A button from the "Whip Inflation Now" initiative of the 1970's"/Gerald R. Ford Presidential Library and Museum/Wikimedia Commons/Public Domain; **602**t, **659** "JimmyCarterPortrait2" by Department of Defense/Wikimedia Commons/Public Domain; **602**b ZUMA Press, Inc. / Alamy Stock Photo; **603**t David Fenton/Archive Photos/Getty Images; **603**b Grant Heilman Photography / Alamy Stock Photo; **604** Gonzalo Azumendi/Stone/Getty Images; **605**b ITAR-TASS News Agency / Alamy Stock Photo; **606**t MPI /Archive Photos/Getty Images; **606**b AP Photo

Chapter 26

608 "President Ronald Reagan and Vice-President George H. W. Bush meet with Soviet General Secretary Mikhail Gorbachev on Governor's Island New York"/Wikimedia Commons/Public Domain; **609**t Keystone Press / Alamy Stock Photo; **609**b, **659** Library of Congress; **610**t, **616**c MediaPunch Inc / Alamy Stock Photo; **610**b Diana Walker/The LIFE Images Collection/Getty Images; **611**t "Space Laser Satellite Defense System Concept"/U.S. Air Force/Wikimedia Commons/Public Domain; **611**b Francoise De Mulder/Roger Viollet/Getty Images; **612**t Bettmann /Getty Images; **612**b MANOOCHER DEGHATI/AFP/Getty Images;

613t, **659** World History Archive / Alamy Stock Photo; **613**b Vladimir Savin/iStock/Getty Images Plus/Getty Images; **614** Everett Collection /Shutterstock.com; **615** ECONOMIC-POLITICAL CURRENCY, A 1992 Herblock Cartoon, © The Herb Block Foundation; **616**l Hal Bergman /Photodisc/Getty Images; **616**rt DawidMarkiewicz/iStock/Getty Images Plus/Getty Images; **616**rb, **618**c ZUMA Press, Inc. / Alamy Stock Photo; **617** Dennis Brack / Alamy Stock Photo; **618**t Joshua McDonough/iStock Editorial/Getty Images Plus/Getty Images; **618**b, **659** Everett Collection Historical / Alamy Stock Photo; **619**t JOYCE NALTCHAYAN/AFP /Getty Images; **619**c Allstar Picture Library Ltd / Alamy Stock Photo; **619**b AFP/Getty Images; **620**l TIM SLOAN/AFP/Getty Images; **620**r Mark Reinstein/Corbis Historical/Getty Images; **621**t CHOO YOUN-KONG /AFP/Getty Images; **621**c Patrick Robert - Corbis/Sygma/Getty Images; **621**b Steven D Starr/Corbis Historical/Getty Images; **622**t Johnny Saunderson / Alamy Stock Photo; **622**c New York Daily News Archive /New York Daily News/Getty Images; **622**b "USS Cole (DDG-67) Departs" by Sgt. Don L. Maes/U.S. Marine Corps/Wikimedia Commons /Public Domain; **623** INTERFOTO / Alamy Stock Photo

Chapter 27

624 Laperruque / Alamy Stock Photo; **625**t, **659** "George-W-Bush" by Eric Draper/Department of Defense/Wikimedia Commons/Public Domain; **625**b STAN HONDA/AFP/Getty Images; **626**t AFP/Getty Images; **626**b Hiro Oshima/WireImage/Getty Images; **627** "FGM-148 Javelin - ID DM-SD-04-07570" by SGT MAURICIO CAMPINO, USMC /Wikimedia Commons/Public Domain; **628, 636**r REUTERS / Alamy Stock Photo; **629**l, r Rob Crandall/Shutterstock.com; **630** Geraint Lewis / Alamy Stock Photo; **631**t, **643**b, **659** MediaPunch Inc / Alamy Stock Photo; **631**b Beth Schneider / Alamy Stock Photo; **632** dpa picture alliance / Alamy Stock Photo; **634** Lewis Tse Pui Lung/Shutterstock.com; **635, 659** White House Photo / Alamy Stock Photo; **636**l Kristoffer Tripplaar / Alamy Stock Photo; **636**c Patsy Lynch / Alamy Stock Photo; **637** Robert Alexander/Archive Photos/Getty Images; **638**tl PETER PARKS/AFP /Getty Images; **638**tr Radoslav Zilinsky/Moment/Getty Images; **638**b PATRICK T. FALLON /AFP/Getty Images; **639** Contraband Collection / Alamy Stock Photo; **641**t Handout / Alamy Stock Photo; **641**b UPI / Alamy Stock Photo; **642, 659** IanDagnall Computing / Alamy Stock Photo; **643**t Brent Stirton/Getty Images News/Getty Images; **644** Sipa USA / Alamy Stock Photo; **645** Thomas Barwick/DigitalVision/Getty Images; **646** (computer) INTERFOTO / Alamy Stock Photo; **646** (Atari) Chris Willson / Alamy Stock Photo; **646** (Nintendo) robtek/iStock Editorial/Getty Images Plus/Getty Images; **646** (Playstation) JR Moreira /Shutterstock.com; **646** (Xbox) John Muggenborg / Alamy Stock Photo; **646** (Facebook) rvlsoft/Shutterstock.com; **646** (Instagram) tanuha2001 /Shutterstock.com; **648**t Pacific Press/LightRocket/Getty Images; **648**b–**49**b Hayk_Shalunts/Shutterstock.com; **649**t Hill Street Studios /DigitalVision/Getty Images; **650**t whitetherock photo/Shutterstock.com; **650**b PeopleImages/E+/Getty Images; **652**t artphotoclub/Shutterstock.com; **652**b Grant Faint/The Image Bank/Getty Images

All maps from Map Resources